SOUTHERN HISTORY OF THE WAR.

GEN. R. E. LEE.

SOUTHERN HISTORY

OF

THE WAR.

BY

E. A. POLLARD,

EDITOR OF THE "RICHMOND EXAMINER."

TWO VOLUMES IN ONE.

THE FAIRFAX PRESS
NEW YORK

Baltimore. November 5 1865.

C.B. Richardson, Esq
540 Broadway. New York.

Dear Sir,

I have received an instalment of
proof-sheets, and return them corrected
with the greatest possible dispatch. I
thank you for the attention, and request
that you will let me have the remainder
by return mail, or just as soon as
possible. × × × × × ×
I am about leaving for Memphis to take
the editorship of the Memphis <u>Avalanche</u>
If, in connection with this paper, I
can ever serve any of your publishing
enterprises among the people of the
South, I shall be glad to do so. × × × ×
I here desire to declare that you have
carried out your contract, and, on
your part, discharged our business
relations in an upright, honourable
and liberal manner.

Respectfully Yours

Edwd. A Pollard

PUBLISHER'S ANNOUNCEMENT.
1866

In issuing in the convenient form of two volumes the Southern History of the War, by Mr. E. A. Pollard, of Richmond, the actuating motive is the belief that this work is one of permanent historical value.

Of the two classes of historical composition—namely, that which is made contemporaneously with the transactions recorded and that which is made after the interval of years—it must always happen that the former will show errors of fact, errors in the interpretation of facts, and errors in the correlation of facts. These a calm, judicial survey will readily avoid. Yet public appreciation accounts such faults to be fully countervailed by the life-like interest of the narrative, by the revelations of actual motive on the part of the actors and by a tone and color of reality that only portraiture from the life can convey.

The work of Mr. Pollard belongs to the former category. That many things are now known more justly than when the author poured forth, from the warm feeling of the moment, his thoughts, impressions, and aspirations, it is easy to believe. There is also much in the *tone* of the book that now, since the close of the war and the failure of the Secession experiment, might appropriately be changed.

Yet granting all these drawbacks, which are inseparable from contemporaneous composition, the work of Mr. Pollard remains one of marked and peculiar value. Living at the centre of the Confederate power, Mr. Pollard's opportunities for penetrating the real springs of action were excellent. Gifted with a re-markable keenness of observation and analysis, he has expressed with pungent power the judgments of a mind distinguished for its independence. A Secessionist *à l'outrance*, believing with all the strength of his nature in the Confederate cause, he was yet a caustic critic of the Confederate government and of those charged with its administration and the conduct of the war; and he had the talent to express these views in a style of ner-vous and vigorous eloquence.

Such were the circumstances under which this work was composed; and its pre-eminent value arises from the fact that it photographs the events of the war in the circumstances of their actual performance; the motives of action as they really revealed themselves, and the hopes and aspirations of the South as they beat in the breasts of living men. Doubtless some things in this history might be corrected; some made to conform to accomplished facts. But this would be to take away from rather than to add to its essential value, which is that of a *mémoire pour servir*. As such, it must always re-main a valuable contribution to the history of the war; and from the side of the South it is the only complete record of the momentous four years during which Secession was fought for and lost.

CONTENTS.

CHAPTER I.

CHAPTER II.

CONTENTS.

CHAPTER III.

CHAPTER IV.

CHAPTER V.

CHAPTER VI.

CHAPTER VII.

CHAPTER VIII.

CHAPTER IX.

CONTENTS.

CHAPTER X.

CHAPTER XI.

CONTENTS.

CHAPTER XII.

CHAPTER XIII.

CHAPTER XIV.

CHAPTER XV.

CONTENTS.

CHAPTER XVI.

CHAPTER XVII.

CHAPTER XVIII.

CONTENTS.

CHAPTER XIX.

CHAPTER XX.

CONTENTS.

CHAPTER XXI.

CHAPTER XXII.

CHAPTER XXIII.

CHAPTER XXIV.

CONTENTS.

CHAPTER XXV.

CHAPTER XXVI.

REVIEW—POLITICAL IDEAS IN THE NORTH, &C.

SOUTHERN HISTORY OF THE WAR.

THE FIRST YEAR.

CHAPTER I.

THE American people of the present generation were born in the belief that the Union of the States was destined to be perpetual. A few minds rose superior to this natal delusion; the early history of the Union itself was not without premonitions of decay and weakness; and yet it may be said that the belief in its permanency was, in the early part of the present generation, a popular and obstinate delusion, that embraced the masses of the country.

The foundations of this delusion had been deeply laid in the early history of the country, and had been sustained by a false, but ingenious prejudice. It was busily represented, especially by demagogues in the North, that the Union was the fruit of the Revolution of 1776, and had been purchased by the blood of our forefathers. No fallacy could have been more erroneous in fact more insidious in its display, or more effective in addressing the passions of the multitude. The Revolution achieved our national independence, and the Union had n connection with it other than consequence in point of time. It was founded, as any other civil institution, in the exigencies and necessities of a certain condition of society, and had no other claim to popular reverence and attachment, than what might be found in its own virtues.

But it was not only the captivating fallacy that the Union was hallowed by the blood of a revolution, and this false inspiration of reverence for it, that gave the popular idea of its power and permanency. Its political character was misunderstood by a large portion of the American people. The idea predominated in the North, and found toleration in the South, that the Revolution of '76, instead of securing the independence of thirteen States, had resulted in the establishment of a grand consolidated government to be under the absolute control of a numerical majority. The doctrine was successfully inculcated; it had some plausibility, and brought to its support an array of revolutionary names; but it was, nevertheless, in direct opposition to the terms of the Constitution—the bond of the Union—which defined the rights of the States and the limited powers of the General Government.

The first President from the North, John Adams, asserted and essayed to put in practice the supremacy of the "National" power over the States and the citizens thereof. He was sustained in his attempted usurpations by all the New England States and by a powerful public sentiment in each of the Middle States. The "strict constructionists" of the Constitution were not slow in raising the standard of opposition against a pernicious error. With numbers and the most conspicuous talents in the country they soon effected the organization of a party; and, under the leadership of Jefferson and Madison, they rallied their forces and succeeded in overthrowing the Yankee Administration, but only after a tremendous struggle.

From the inauguration of Mr. Jefferson, in 1801, the Federal Government continued uninterruptedly in Southern hands for the space of twenty-four years. A large proportion of the active politicians of the North pretended to give in their adhesion to the State Rights school of politics; but, like all the alliances of Northern politicians with the South—selfish, cunning, extravagant of professions, carefully avoiding trials of its fidelity unhealthy, founded on a sentiment of treachery to its own section, and educated in perfidy—it was a deceitful union, and could not withstand the test of a practical question.

While acting with the South on empty or accidental issues, the "State Rights" men of the North were, for all practical purposes, the faithful allies of the open and avowed consolidationists on the question that most seriously divided the country —that of negro slavery. Their course on the admission of Missouri afforded early and conclusive evidence of the secret disposition of all parties in the North. With very few exceptions, in and out of Congress, the North united in the original demand of the prohibition of slavery in the new State as the indispensable condition of the admission of Missouri into the Union; although the people of Missouri, previous to their application to Congress, had decided to admit within its jurisdiction the domestic institution of the South. The result of the contest was equally unfavorable to the rights of the South and to the doctrine of the constitutional equality of the States in the Union. The only approach that the North was willing to make to this fundamental doctrine was to support a "compromise," by which slavery was to be tolerated in one part of the Missouri Territory and to be forever excluded from the remaining portion. The issue of the controversy was not only important to the slave interest, but afforded a new development of the Northern political ideas of consolidation and the absolutism of numerical majorities. The North had acted on the Missouri matter as though the South had no rights guaranteed in the bond of the Union, and as though the question at issue was one merely of numerical strength, where the defeated party had no alternative but submission. "The majority must govern" was the *decantatum* on the lips of every demagogue, and passed into a favorite phrase of Northern politics.

The results of the acquiescence of the South in the wrong of the Missouri Restriction could not fail to strengthen the idea in the North of the security of the Union, and to embolden its people to the essay of new aggressions. Many of their politicians did not hesitate to believe that the South was prepared to pledge herself to the perpetuity of the Union upon Northern terms. The fact was, that she had made a clear concession of principle for the sake of the Union; and the inference wa plain and logical, that her devotion to it exceeded almost every other political trust, and that she would be likely to prefer any sacrifice rather than the irreverent one of the Union of the States.

The events of succeeding years confirmed the Northern opinion that the Union was to be perpetuated as a consolidated government. It is not to be denied that the consolidationists derived much comfort from the course of President Jackson, in the controversy between the General Government and the State of South Carolina, that ensued during the second term of his administration. But they were hasty and unfair in the interpretation of the speeches of a choleric and immoderate politician. They seized upon a sentiment offered by the President at the Jefferson anniversary dinner, in the second year of his first term—" *The Federal Union—it must be preserved*"— to represent him as a " *coercionist*" in principle; and, indeed, they found reason to contend that their construction of these words was fully sustained in General Jackson's famous proclamation and official course against Nullification.

General Jackson subsequently explained away, in a great measure, the objectionable doctrines of his proclamation; and his emphatic declaration that the Union could *not* be preserved by force was one of the practical testimonies of his wisdom that he left to posterity. But the immediate moral and political effects of his policy in relation to South Carolina were, upon the whole, decidedly unfavorable to the State Rights cause. His approval of the Force Bill gave to the consolidationists the benefit of his great name and influence at a most important juncture. The names of "Jackson and the Union" became inseparable in the public estimation; and the idea was strongly and vividly impressed upon the public mind, that the great Democrat was "a Union man" at all hazards and to the last extremity.

The result of the contest between South Carolina and the General Government is well known. The Palmetto State came out of it with an enviable reputation for spirit and chivalry; but the settlement of the question contributed to the previous popular impressions of the power and perma

nency of the Union. The idea of the Union became what it
continued to be for a quarter of a century thereafter—extravagant and sentimental. The people were unwilling to stop to
analyze an idea after it had once become the subject of enthusiasm; and the mere name of the "Union," illustrating, as it
did, the power of words over the passions of the multitude,
remained for years a signal of the country's glory and of
course the motto of ambitious politicians and the favorite
theme of demagogues. This unnatural tumor was not peculiar to any party or any portion of the country. It was deeply
planted in the Northern mind, but prevailed also, to a considerable extent, in the South. Many of the Southern politicians
came to the conclusion that they could best succeed in their
designs as advocates and eulogists of what was paraphrased as
"the glorious Union;" and for a long time the popular voice
of the South seemed to justify their conclusion.

The settlement of the sectional difficulties of 1850, which
grew out of the admission of the territory acquired by the
Mexican War, was but a repetition of the "Compromise" of
1820, so far as it implied a surrender of the rights of the
South and of the principle of constitutional equality. The
appeals urged in behalf of the Union had the usual effect of
reconciling the South to the sacrifice required of her, and
embarrassed any thing like resistance on the part of her representatives in Congress to the "compromise measures" of
1850. South Carolina was the only one of the Southern
States ready at this time to take the bold and adventurous
initiative of Southern independence. In justice, however, to
the other States of the South, it must be stated, that in agreeing to what was called, in severe irony or in wretched ignorance, the "Compromise" of 1850, they declared that it was
the last concession they would make to the North; that they
took it as a "finality," and that they would resist any further
aggression on their rights, even to the extremity of the rupture
of the Union.

This declaration of spirit was derided by the North. The
anti-slavery sentiment became bolder with success. Stimulated by secret jealousies and qualified for success by the low
and narrow cunning of fanaticism, it had grown up by indirection, and aspired to the complete overthrow of the peculiar

institution that had distinguished the people of the South from those of the North, by a larger happiness, greater ease of life, and a superior tone of character. Hypocrisy, secretiveness, a rapid and unhealthy growth, and at last the unmasked spirit of defiance, were the incidents of the history of the anti-slavery sentiment in the North, from the beginning of its organization to the last and fatal strain of its insolence and power.

Until a comparatively recent period, the Northern majority disavowed all purpose of abolishing or interfering in any way with the institution of slavery in any State, Territory, or District where it existed. On the contrary, they declared their readiness to give their "Southern brethren" the most satisfactory guaranties for the security of their slave property. They cloaked their designs under the disguise of the Right of Petition and other concealments equally demagogical. From the organization of the government, petitions for the abolition of slavery, signed in every instance by but a few persons, and most of them women, had, at intervals, been sent into Congress; but they were of such apparent insignificance that they failed to excite any serious apprehensions on the part of the South. In the year 1836, these petitions were multiplied, and many were sent into both Houses of Congress from all parts of the North. An excitement began. On motion of Mr. H. L. Pinckney, of South Carolina, a resolution was adopted by the House of Representatives, to refer to a select committee all anti-slavery memorials then before that body, or that might thereafter be sent in, with instructions to report against the prayers of the petitioners and the reasons for such conclusion.

On the 18th of May, 1836, the committee made a unanimous report, through Mr. Pinckney, its chairman, concluding with a series of resolutions, the last of which was as follows :

" *Resolved*, That all petitions, memorials, resolutions, propositions, or papers relating, in any way, or to any extent whatever, to the subject of slavery, or the abolition of slavery, shall, without being either printed or referred, be laid upon the table, and that no further action whatever shall be had thereon."

The resolutions were carried by a vote of 117 yeas to 68 nays. A majority of the Northern members voted against the

resolution, alth)ugh there was then scarcely an avowed Abolitionist among them. They professed to be in favor of protecting the slaveholder in his right of property, and yet declared by their votes, as well as by their speeches, that the
right of petition to rob him of his property was too sacred to
be called in question.

The passage of the "Pinckney resolutions," as they were
called, did not silence the anti-slavery agitat.on in the House.
In the month of December, 1837, a remarkable scene was
enacted in that body, during the proceedings on a motion of
Mr. Slade, of Vermont, to refer two memorials praying the
abolition of slavery in the District of Columbia to a select
committee. Mr. Slade, in urging his motion, was violent in
his denunciations of slavery, and he spoke for a considerable
time amid constant interruptions and calls to order. At length,
Mr. Rhett, of South Carolina, called upon the entire delegation from all the slaveholding States to retire from the hall,
and to meet in the room of the Committee on the District of
Columbia. A large number of them did meet for consultation
in the room designated. The meeting, however, resulted in
nothing but an agreement upon the following resolution to be
presented to the House:

" *Resolved*, That all petitions, memorials, and papers touching the abolition
of slavery, or the buying, selling, or transferring of slaves in any State, Dis
trict, or Territory of the United States, be laid on the table without being
debated, printed, read, or referred, and that no further action whatever shall
be had thereon."

This resolution was presented to the House by Mr. Patton,
of Virginia, and was adopted by a vote of 122 to 74.

In the month of January, 1840, the House of Representatives, on motion of Mr. W. Cost Johnson, of Maryland,
adopted what was known as the "Twenty-first Rule," which
prohibited the reception of all Abolition petitions, memorials,
and resolutions.

The Twenty-first Rule was rescinded in December, 1844, on
motion of John Quincy Adams, by a vote of 108 to 80. Several efforts were afterwards made to restore it, but without
success. The Northern people would not relinquish what they
termed a "sacred right"—that of petitioning the government,

through their representatives in Congress, to deprive the Southern people of their property.

During the agitation in Congress upon the right of petition, there was, as before stated, but very few open and avowed Abolitionists in either House, and the declaration was repeatedly made by members that the party was contemptibly small in every free State in the Union. Mr. Pierce, of New Hampshire (afterwards President of the United States), declared, in 1837, in his place in Congress, that there were not two hundred Abolitionists in his State; and Mr. Webster, about the same time, represented their numbers in Massachusetts as quite insignificant. Mr. Calhoun, of South Carolina, with characteristic sagacity, replied to these representations, and predicted that "Mr. Webster and all Northern statesmen would, in a few years, yield to the storm of Abolition fanaticism and be overwhelmed by it." The prophecy was not more remarkable than the searching analysis of Northern "conservatism" with which the great South Carolinian accompanied his prediction. He argued that such a consequence was inevitable from the way in which the professed "conservatives" of the North had invited the aggressions of the Abolitionists, by courteously granting them the right of petition, which was indeed all they asked; that the fanaticism of the North was a disease which required a *remedy*, and that palliatives would not answer, as Mr. Webster and men like him would find to their cost.

In the Thirtieth Congress, that assembled in December, 1849 the professed Abolitionists numbered about a dozen members. They held the balance of power between the Democratic and Whig parties in the House, and delayed its organization for about a month. Both the Whig and Democratic parties then claimed to be conservative, and, of course, the opponents of the anti-slavery agitation.

In the Presidential canvass of 1852, both Pierce and Scott were brought out by professed national parties, and were supported in each section of the Union. John P. Hale, who ran upon what was called the "straight-out" Abolition ticket, did not receive the vote of a single State, and but 175,296 of the popular vote of the Union. The triumphant election of Pierce, who was a favorite of the State Rights Democracy of the South, was hailed by the sanguine friends of the Union as a fair indication of the purpose of the North to abide, in good faith, by the Compromise of 1850. But in this they were deceived, as the sequel demonstrated.

During the first session of the first Congress under Mr Pierce's administration, the bill introduced to establish a territorial government for Nebraska, led to an agitation in Congress and the country, the consequences of which extended to the last period of the existence of the Union. The Committee on Territories in the Senate, of which Mr. Douglas, of Illinois, was chairman, reported the bill, which made two territories—Nebraska and Kansas—instead of one, and which declared that the Missouri Compromise act was superseded by the Compromise measures of 1850, and had thus become inoperative. The phraseology of the clause repealing the Missouri Compromise was drawn up by Mr. Douglas, and was not supposed at the time to be liable to misconstruction. It held, that the Missouri Compromise act, " being inconsistent with the prin ciples of non-intervention by Congress with slavery in the States and Territories, as recognized by the legislation of 1850, commonly called the Compromise Measures, is hereby declared inoperative and void ; it being the true intent and meaning of this act not to legislate slavery into any Territory or State, nor to exclude it therefrom, but to leave the people thereof perfectly free to form and regulate their domestic institutions in their own way, subject only to the Constitution of the United States." The clause here quoted, as drawn up by Mr. Douglas, was incorporated into the Kansas-Nebraska bill in the Senate on the 15th of February, 1854. The bill passed the House at the same session.

The repeal of the Missouri Compromise caused the deepest excitement throughout the North. The Abolitionists were wild with fury. Douglas was hung in effigy at different places, and was threatened with personal violence in case of his persistence in his non-intervention policy. The rapid development of a fanatical feeling in every free State startled many who had but recently indulged dreams of the perpetuity of the Constitutional Union. Abolitionism, in the guise of " *Republicanism*," swept almost every thing before it in the North and Northwest in the elections of 1854 and 1855. But few professed conservatives were returned to the Thirty-first Congress :

not enough to prevent the election of Nathaniel Banks, an objectionable Abolitionist of the Massachusetts school, to the Speakership of the House.

The South had supported the repeal of the Missouri Compromise because it restored her to her rightful position of equality in the Union. It is true, that her representatives in Congress were well aware that, under the operations of the new act, their constituents could expect to obtain but little if any new accessions of slave territory, while the North would necessarily, from the force of circumstances, secure a number of new States in the Northwest, then the present direction of our new settlements. But viewed as an act of proscription against her, the Missouri Compromise was justly offensive to the South; and its abrogation, in this respect, strongly recommended itself to her support.

The ruling party of the North, calling themselves "Republicans," had violently opposed the repeal of the act of 1820, in the same sentiment with which it was fiercely encountered by the Abolitionists. The two parties were practically identical; both shared the same sentiment of hostility to slavery; and they differed only as to the degree of indirection by which their purposes might best be accomplished.

The election of Mr. Buchanan to the Presidency, in 1856, raised, for a time, the spirits of many of the true friends of the Constitutional Union. But there was very little in an analysis of the vote to give hope or encouragement to the patriot. Fremont, who ran as the anti-slavery candidate, received 1,341,812 votes of the people, and it is believed would have been elected by the electoral college, if the anti-Buchanan party in Pennsylvania had united upon him.

The connection of events which we have sought to trace, brings us to the celebrated Kansas controversy, and at once to the threshold of the dissensions which demoralized the only conservative party in the country, and in less than four years culminated in the rupture of the Federal Union. A severe summary of the facts of this controversy introduces us to the contest of 1860, in which the Republican party, swollen with its triumphs in Kansas, and infecting the Democratic leaders in the North with the disposition to pander to the lusts of a growing power, obtained the control of the government, and seized the sceptre of absolute authority.

When Mr. Buchanan came into office, in March, 1857, he flattered himself with the hope that his administration would settle the disputes that had so long agitated and distracted the country ; trusting that such a result might be accomplished by the speedy admission of Kansas into the Union, upon the principles which had governed in his election. Such, at least, were his declarations to his friends. But before the meeting of Congress, in December, he had abundant evidence that his favorite measure would be opposed by a number of Senators and Representatives who had actively supported him in his canvass ; among them the distinguished author of the Kansas Nebraska bill, Mr. Douglas.

In the month of July, 1855, the Legislature of the Territory of Kansas had passed an act to take the sense of the people on the subject of forming a State government, preparatory to admission into the Union. The election took place, and a large majority of the people voted in favor of holding a convention for the purpose of adopting a Constitution. In pursuance of this vote, the Territorial Legislature, on the 19th of February, 1857, passed a law to take a census of the people, for the purpose of making a registry of the voters, and to elect delegates to the Convention. Mr. Geary, then Governor of Kansas, vetoed the bill for calling the Convention, for the reason that it did not require the Constitution, when framed, to be submitted to a vote of the people for adoption or rejection. The bill, however, was reconsidered in each House, and passed by a two-thirds' vote, and thus became a binding law in the Territory, despite the veto of the Governor.

On the 20th of May, 1857, Mr. F. P. Stanton, Secretary and acting Governor of Kansas Territory, published his proclamation, commanding the proper officers to hold an election on the third Monday of June, 1857, as directed by the act referred to.

The election was held on the day appointed, and the Convention assembled, according to law, on the first Monday of September, 1857. They proceeded to form a Constitution, and having finished their work, adjourned on the 7th November

The entire Constitution was not submitted to the popular vote· but the Convention took care to submit to the vote of the people, for ratification or rejection, the clause respecting slavery. The official vote resulted: For the Constitution, with Slavery, 6,226; for the Constitution, without Slavery, 509.

The Abolitionists, or "Free State" men, as they called themselves, did not generally vote in this or any other election held under the regular government of the Territory. They defied the authority of this government and that of the United States, and acted under the direction of Emigrant Aid Societies, organized by the fanatical Abolitionists of the North, to colonize the new territory with voters. The proceedings of this evil and bastard population occasioned the greatest excitement, and speedily inaugurated an era of disorder and rebellion in this distant portion of the Federal territory.

The Free State party assembled at Topeka, in September, 1855, and adopted what they called a "Constitution" for Kansas. This so-called Constitution was submitted to the people, and was ratified, of course, by a large majority of those who voted; scarcely any but Abolitionists going to the polls. Under their Topeka Constitution, the Free State party elected a Governor and Legislature, and organized for the purpose of petitioning Congress for the admission of Kansas into the Union. The memorial of the Topeka insurgents was presented to the Thirty-fourth Congress. It met with a favorable response in the House of Representatives, a majority of that body being anti-slavery men of the New England school; but found but a poor reception in the Senate, where there was still a majority of conservative and law-abiding men.

On the 2d of February, 1858, Mr. Buchanan, at the request of the President of the Lecompton Convention, transmitted to Congress an authentic copy of the Constitution framed by that body, with a view to the admission of Kansas into the Union. The message of the President took strong and urgent position for the admission of Kansas under this Constitution; he defended the action of the Convention in not submitting the entire result of their labors to a vote of the people; he explained that, when he instructed Governor Walker, in general terms, in favor of submitting the Constitution to the people, he had no other object in view beyond the all-absorbing topic .

of slavery; he considered that, under the organic act, the Convention was bound to submit the all-important question of slavery to the people; he added, that it was never his opinion, however, that, independently of this act, the Convention would be bound to submit any portion of the Constitution to a popular vote, in order to give it validity; and he argued the fallacy and unreasonableness of such an opinion, by insisting that it was in opposition to the principle which pervaded our institutions, and which was every day carried into practice, to the effect that the people had the right to delegate to representatives, chosen by themselves, sovereign power to frame Constitutions, enact laws, and perform many other important acts, without the necessity of testing the validity of their work by popular approbation. The Topeka Constitution Mr. Buchanan denounced as the work of treason and insurrection.

It is certain that Mr. Buchanan would have succeeded in effecting the admission of Kansas under the Lecompton Constitution, if he could have secured to the measure the support of all the Northern Democrats who had contributed to his election. These, however, had become disaffected; they opposed and assailed the measure of the Administration, acting under the lead of Mr. Douglas; and the long-continued and bitter discussion which ensued, perfectly accomplished the division of the Democratic party into two great factions, mustered under the names of "Lecompton" and "Anti-Lecompton."

The latter faction founded their opposition to the Administration on the grounds, that the Lecompton Constitution was not the act of the people of Kansas, and did not express their will; that only half of the counties of the Territory were represented in the Convention that framed it, the other half being disfranchised, for no fault of their own, but from failure of the officers to register the voters, and entitle them to vote for delegates; and that the mode of submitting the Constitution to the people for "ratification or rejection" was unfair, embarrassing, and proscriptive.

In reply, the friends of the Administration urged that twenty-one out of the thirty-four organized counties of Kansas were embraced in the apportionment of representation; that, of the thirteen counties not embraced, nine had but a small population, as shown by the fact that, in a succeeding election, to which the Anti-Lecomptonites had referred as an indication of public sentiment in Kansas, they polled but ninety votes in the aggregate; that, in the remaining four counties, the failure to register the voters, and the consequent loss of their representation, were due to the Abolitionists themselves, who refused to recognize all legal authority in the Territory; and that the submission of the Constitution, as provided by the Lecompton Convention, afforded a complete expression of the popular will, as the slavery question was the only one about which there was any controversy in Kansas.

The bill for the admission of Kansas under the Lecompton Constitution, was passed by the Senate. In the House, an amendment, offered by Mr. Montgomery, of Pennsylvania, was adopted, to the effect that, as it was a disputed point whether the Constitution framed at Lecompton was fairly made, or expressed the will of the people of Kansas, her admission into the Union as a State was declared to be upon the fundamental condition precedent, that the said constitutional instrument should first be submitted to a vote of the people of Kansas, and assented to by them, or by a majority of the voters, at an election to be held for the purpose of determining the question of the ratification or rejection of the instrument.

The Senate insisted upon its bill; the House adhered to its amendment; and a committee of conference was appointed. The result of the conference was the report of a bill for the admission of Kansas, which became a law in June, 1858, and substantially secured nearly all that the North had claimed in the controversy.

The bill, as passed, rejected the Land Ordinance contained in the Lecompton Constitution, and proposed a substitute. Kansas was to be admitted into the Union on an equal footing, in all respects, with the original States, but upon the fundamental condition precedent, that the question of admission, along with that of the Land substitute, be submitted to a vote of the people; that, if a majority of the vote should be against the proposition tendered by Congress, it should be concluded that Kansas did not desire admission under the Lecompton Constitution, with the condition attached to it; and that, in such event, the people were authorized to form for themselves a Constitution and State government, and might elect delegates for that purpose, after a census taken to demonstrate the fact, that the population of the Territory equalled or exceeded the ratio of representation for a member of the House of Representatives.

Thus ended the six months' discussion of the Kansas question in Congress in 1858. The substitute to the Land Ordinance was rejected by the voters of the Territory; and Kansas did not come into the Union until nearly three years afterwards— just as the Southern States were going out of it. She came in under an anti-slavery constitution, and Mr. Buchanan signed the bill of admission.

The discussions of the Kansas question, as summed in the preceding pages, had materially weakened the Union. The spirit of those discussions, and the result itself of the controversy, fairly indicated that the South could hardly expect, under any circumstances, the addition of another Slave State to the Union. The Southern mind was awakened; the sentimental reverences of more than half a century were decried; and men began to calculate the precise value of a Union which, by its mere name and the paraphrases of demagogues, had long governed their affections.

Some of these calculations, as they appeared in the newspaper presses of the times, were curious, and soon commenced to interest the Southern people. It was demonstrated to them that their section had been used to contribute the bulk of the revenues of the Government; that the North derived forty to fifty millions of annual revenue from the South, through the operations of the tariff; and that the aggregate of the trade of the South in Northern markets was four hundred millions of dollars a year. It was calculated by a Northern writer, that the harvest of gain reaped by the North from the Union, from unequal taxations and the courses of trade as between the two sections, exceeded two hundred millions of dollars per year.

These calculations of the commercial cost of the "glorious Union" to the South, only presented the question in a single aspect, however striking that was. There were other aspects no less important and no less painful, in which it was to be regarded. The swollen and insolent power of Abolitionism threatened to carry every thing before it; it had already bro-

ken the vital principle of the Constitution—that of the equal
ity of its parts; and to injuries already accomplished, it added
the bitterest threats and the most insufferable insolence.

While the anti-slavery power threatened never to relax its
efforts until, in the language of Mr. Seward, a senator from
New York, the " irrepressible conflict" between slavery and
freedom was accomplished, and the soil of the Carolinas dedi-
cated to the institutions of New England, it affected the insolent impertinence of regarding the Union as a concession on
the part of the North, and of taunting the South with the
disgrace which her association in the Union inflicted upon the
superior and more virtuous people of the Northern States.
The excesses of this conceit are ridiculous, seen in the light of
subsequent events. It was said that the South was an inferior
part of the country; that she was a spotted and degraded section ; that the national fame abroad was compromised by the
association of the South in the Union ; and that a New England traveller in Europe blushed to confess himself an American, because half of the nation of that name were slaveholders. Many of the Abolitionists made a pretence of praying
that the Union might be dissolved, that they might be cleared,
by the separation of North and South, of any implication in
the crime of slavery. Even that portion of the party calling
themselves "Republicans" affected that the Union stood in
the way of the North. Mr. Banks, of Massachusetts, who
had been elected Speaker of the House in the Thirty-first Congress, had declared that the designs of his party were not to be
baffled, and was the author of the coarse jeer—"*Let the Union
slide.*" The New York *Tribune* had complained that the
South " could not be *kicked* out of the Union." Mr. Seward,
the great Republican leader, had spread the evangely of a natural, essential, and irrepressible hostility between the two sections ; and the North prepared to act on a suggestion, the only
practical result of which could be to cleave the Union apart,
and to inaugurate the horrors of civil war.

The raid into Virginia of John Brown, a notorious Aboli
tionist, whose occupations in Kansas had been those of a horse
thief and assassin, and his murder of peaceful and unsuspect
ing citizens at Harper's Ferry in the month of October, 1859
was a practical illustration of the lessons of the Northern Re

publicans, and of their inevitable and, in fact, logical conclusion in civil war. Professed conservatives in the North predicted that this outrage would be productive of real good in their section, in opening the eyes of the people to what were well characterized as "*Black* Republican" doctrines. This prediction was not verified by succeeding events. The Northern elections of the next month showed no diminution in the Black Republican vote. The manifestations of sympathy for John Brown, who had expiated his crime on a gallows in Virginia, were unequivocal in all parts of the North, though comparatively few openly justified the outrage. Bells were tolled in various towns of New England on the day of his execution, with the knowledge of the local authorities, and in some instances, through their co-operation; and not a few preachers from the pulpit alloted him an apotheosis, and consigned his example to emulation, as one not only of public virtue, but of particular service to God.

The attachment of the South to the Union was steadily weakening in the historical succession of events. The nomination in December, 1859, to the Speakership of the House of Representatives of Mr. Sherman, of Ohio, who had made himself especially odious to the South by publicly recommending, in connection with sixty-eight other Republican members, a fanatical document popularly known as "*Helper's Book,*"*

---

* The tone of this book was violent in the extreme. We add a few extracts, which will enable the reader to form a correct opinion of the character and object of the work—

"Slavery is a great moral, social, civil, and political evil, to be got rid of at the earliest practical period."—(*Page* 168.)

"Three-quarters of a century hence, if the South retains slavery, which God forbid! she will be to the North what Poland is to Russia, Cuba to Spain, and Ireland to England."—(*P.* 163.)

"Our own banner is inscribed—No co-operation with slaveholders in politics; no fellowship with them in religion; no affiliation with them in society; no recognition of pro-slavery men, except as ruffians, outlaws, and criminals."—(*P* 156.)

"We believe it is as it ought to be, the desire, the determination, and the destiny of the Republican party to give the death-blow to slavery."—(*P.* 234.)

"In any event, come what will, transpire what may, the institution of slavery must be abolished."—(*P.* 180.)

"We are determined to abolish slavery at all hazards—in defiance of all the opposition, of whatever nature, it is possible for the slaveocrats to bring

from the name of the author, and which openly defended and
sought itself to excite servile insurrections in the South, pro
duced a marked effect in Congress, and was encountered by
the Southern members with a determined spirit of opposition
The entire Southern delegation gave warning that they would
regard the election of Mr. Sherman, or of any man with his
record, as an open declaration of war upon the institutions of
the South ; as much so, some of the members declared, as if
the Brown raid were openly approved by a majority of the
House of Representatives. The Black Republican party defiantly nominated Sherman, and continued to vote for him for
near two months, giving him within four votes of a majority
upon every trial of his strength. Although he was finally
withdrawn, and one of his party, not a subscriber to the
Helper Book, was elected, yet the fact that more than three-
fourths of the entire Northern delegation had adhered to Mr.
Sherman for nearly two months in a factious and fanatical
spirit, produced a deep impression on the minds of Southern
members and of their constituents. The early dissolution of
the Union had come to be a subject freely canvassed among
members of Congress.

With the unveiling of the depth of the designs of the Black
Republican party, another danger was becoming manifest to
the South. It was the demoralization of the Northern Democratic party on the slavery question. This whole party had
been an unhealthy product ; its very foundation was a principle of untruth, and false to its own section, it could not be expected to adhere to friends whom it had made from interest
and who had fallen into adverse circumstances. It had united
with the South for political power. In the depression of that
power, and the rapid growth of the anti-slavery party in the

---

against us. Of this they may take due notice, and govern themselves accordingly."—(*P.* 149.)

"It is our honest conviction that all the pro-slavery slaveholders deserve
at once to be reduced to a parallel with the basest criminals that lie fettered
within the cells of our public prisons."—(*P.* 158.)

"Shall we pat the bloodhounds of slavery ? Shall we fee the curs of
slavery ? Shall we pay the whelps of slavery ? No, never."—(*P.* 329.)

"Our purpose is as firmly fixed as the eternal pillars of heaven ; we have
determined to abolish slavery, and, so help us God ! abolish it we will."—
P. 187.)

North, it had no hesitation in courting and conciliating the ruling element. This disposition was happily accommodated by the controversy which had taken place between Mr. Douglas and the administration of Mr. Buchanan. The anti-slavery sentiment in the North was conciliated by the partisans of the Illinois demagogue, in adopting a new principle for the government of the Territories, which was to allow the people to determine the question of slavery in their territorial capacity, without awaiting their organization as a State, and thus to risk the decision of the rights of the South on the verdict of a few settlers on the public domain. This pander to the anti-slavery sentiment of the North was concealed under the demagogical name of "popular sovereignty," and was imposed upon the minds of not a few of the Southern people by the artfulness of its appeals to the name of a principle, which had none of the substance of justice or equality. The concealment, however, was but imperfectly availing. The doctrine of Mr. Douglas was early denounced by one of the most vigilant statesmen of the South as "a short cut to all the ends of Black Republicanism;" and later in time, while the "Helper Book" controversy was agitating the country, and other questions developing the union of all the anti-slavery elements for war upon the South, a senator from Georgia was found bold enough to denounce, in his place in Congress, the entire Democratic party of the North as unreliable and "*rotten.*"

The State Rights party of the South had co-operated with the Democracy of the North in the Presidential canvass of 1856, upon the principles of the platform adopted by the National Democratic Convention, assembled in Cincinnati, in June of that year. They expressed a willingness to continue this co-operation in the election of 1860, upon the principles of the Cincinnati platform; but demanded, as a condition precedent to this, that the question of the *construction* of this platform should be satisfactorily settled. To this end, the State Rights Democratic party in several of the Southern States defined the conditions upon which their delegates should hold seats in the National Convention, appointed to meet at Charleston on the 23d of April, 1860. The Democracy in Alabama moved first. On the 11th of January, 1860, they met in convention at Montgomery, and adopted a series of resolu tions, from which the following are extracted, as presenting a summary declaration of the rights of the South, a recapitulation of the territorial question, and a definition of those issues on which the contest of 1860 was to be conducted :

Resolved, by the Democracy of the State of Alabama in Convention assem' bled, That holding all issues and principles upon which they have heretofore affiliated and acted with the National Democratic party to be inferior in dignity and importance to the great question of slavery, they content themselves with a general reaffirmance of the Cincinnati platform as to such issues, and also indorse said platform as to slavery, together with the following resolutions :

*   *   *   *   *   *   *   *   *

Resolved, That the Constitution of the United States, is a compact between sovereign and co-equal States, united upon the basis of perfect equality of rights and privileges.

Resolved, further, That the Territories of the United States are common property, in which the States have equal rights, and to which the citizens of any State may rightfully emigrate, with their slaves or other property recognized as such in any of the States of the Union, or by the Constitution of the United States.

Resolved, further, That the Congress of the United States has no power to abolish slavery in the Territories, or to prohibit its introduction into any of them.

Resolved, further, That the Territorial Legislatures, created by the legislation of Congress, have no power to abolish slavery, or to prohibit the introduction of the same, or to impair by unfriendly legislation the security and full enjoyment of the same within the Territories ; and such constitutional power certainly does not belong to the people of the Territories in any capacity, before, in the exercise of a lawful authority, they form a Constitution, preparatory to admission as a State into the Union ; and their action in the exercise of such lawful authority certainly cannot operate or take effect before their actual admission as a State into the Union.

Resolved, further, That the principles enunciated by Chief Justice Taney, in his opinion in the Dred Scott case, deny to the Territorial Legislature the power to destroy or impair, by any legislation whatever, the right of property in slaves, and maintain it to be the duty of the Federal Government, in *all* of its departments, to protect the rights of the owner of such property in the Territories ; and the principles so declared are hereby asserted to be the rights of the South, and the South should maintain them.

Resolved, further, That we hold all of the foregoing propositions to contain " cardinal principles "—true in themselves—and just and proper and necessary for the safety of all that is dear to us ; and we do hereby instruct our delegates to the Charleston Convention to present them for the calm consideration and approval of that body—from whose justice and patriotism we anticipate their adoption.

Resolved, further, That our delegates to the Charleston Convention are hereby expressly instructed to insist that said Convention shall adopt a plat form of principles, recognizing distinctly the rights of the South as asserted in the foregoing resolutions; and if the said National Convention shall refuse to adopt, in substance, the propositions embraced in the preceding resolutions, prior to nominating candidates, our delegates to said Convention are hereby positively instructed to withdraw therefrom.

Under these resolutions the delegates from Alabama received their appointment to the Charleston Convention. The delegates from some of the other Cotton States were appointed under instructions equally binding. Anxious as were the Southern delegates to continue their connection with the Convention, and thus to maintain the nationality of the Democratic party, they agreed to accept, as the substance of the Alabama platform, either of the two following reports which had been submitted to the Charleston Convention by the majority of the Committee on Resolutions—this majority not only representing that of the States of the Union, but the only States at all likely to be carried by the Democratic party in the Presidential election:

I.

Resolved, That the platform at Cincinnati be reaffirmed with the following resolutions:

Resolved, That the Democracy of the United States hold these cardinal principles on the subject of slavery in the Territories: First, that Congress has no power to abolish slavery in the Territories. Second, that the Territorial Legislature has no power to abolish slavery in any Territory, nor to prohibit the introduction of slaves therein, nor any power to exclude slavery therefrom, nor any power to destroy and impair the right of property in slaves by any legislation whatever.

*   *   *   *   *   *   *   *   *

II.

Resolved, That the platform adopted by the Democratic party at Cincinnati be affirmed, with the following explanatory resolutions:

First. That the government of a Territory, organized by an act of Congress, is provisional and temporary; and, during its existence, all citizens of the United States have an equal right to settle with their property in the Territory, without their rights, either of person or property, being destroyed or impaired by congressional or territorial legislation.

Second. That it is the duty of the Federal Government, in all its departments, to protect, when necessary, the rights of persons and property in the Territories and wherever else its constitutional authority extends.

Third. That when the settlers in a Territory having an adequate population form a State Constitution, the right of sovereignty commences, and, being consummated by admission into the Union, they stand on an equal footing with the people of other States; and the State thus organized, ough to be admitted into the Federal Union, whether its Constitution prohibits or recognizes the institution of slavery.

The Convention refused to accept either of the foregoing resolutions, and adopted, by a vote of 165 to 138, the following as its platform on the slavery question:

1. *Resolved*, That we, the Democracy of the Union, in Convention assem bled, hereby declare our affirmance of the resolutions unanimously adopted and declared as a platform of principles by the Democratic Convention at Cincinnati, in the year 1856, believing that Democratic principles are unchangeable in their nature, when applied to the same subject-matters; and we recommend as the only further resolutions the following:

Inasmuch as differences of opinion exist in the Democratic party as to the nature and extent of the powers of a Territorial Legislature, and as to the powers and duties of Congress under the Constitution of the United States, over the institution of slavery within the Territories:

2. *Resolved*, That the Democratic party will abide by the decisions of the Supreme Court of the United States on the questions of constitutional law.

The substitution of these resolutions for those which were satisfactory to the South, occasioned the disruption of the Convention, after a session of more than three weeks, and its adjournment to Baltimore, on the 18th of June. The Cotton States, all, withdrew from the Convention; but the Border Slave States remained in it, with the hope of effecting some ultimate settlement of the difficulty. The breach, however, widened. The reassembling of the Convention at Baltimore resulted in a final and embittered separation of the opposing delegations. The majority exhibited a more uncompromising spirit than ever; and Virginia and all the Border Slave States, with the exception of Missouri, withdrew from the Convention, and united with the representatives of the Cotton States, then assembled in Baltimore, in the nomination of candidates representing the views of the South. Their nominees were John C. Breckinridge of Kentucky for President, and Joseph Lane of Oregon for Vice-President.

The old Convention, or what remained of it, nominated Stephen A. Douglas of Illinois for President, and Benjamin Fitzpatrick of Alabama for Vice-President. The latter declining, Herschel V. Johnson of Georgia was substituted on the ticket.

The Southern Democracy and the Southern people of all parties, with but few exceptions, sustained the platform demanded by the Southern delegates in the Convention, and justified the course they had pursued. They recognized in the platform a legitimate and fair assertion of Southern rights In view, however, of the conservative professions and glozed speeches of a portion of the Northern Democracy, a respectable number of Southern Democrats were induced to support their ticket. Mr. Douglas proclaimed his views to be in favor of non-intervention; he avowed his continued and unalterable opposition to Black Republicanism; his principles were professed to be "held subject to the decisions of the Supreme Court"—the distinction between judicial questions and political questions being purposely clouded; and his friends, with an ingenious sophistry that had imposed upon the South for thirty years with success, insisted that the support of Stephen A. Douglas was a support of the party in the North which had stood by the South amid persecution and defamation. In consequence of these and other protestations, tickets were got up for Mr. Douglas in most of the Southern States. The great majority, however, of the Democracy of the slave-holding States, except Missouri, supported Breckinridge.

A Convention of what is called the "Constitutional Union" party met in Baltimore on the 9th of May, 1860, and nominated for President and Vice-President, John Bell of Tennessee and Edward Everett of Massachusetts. Their platform consisted of a vague and undefined enumeration of their political principles; as, "The Constitution of the Country, the Union of the States, and Enforcement of the Laws."

The National Convention of the Black Republican party was held at Chicago, in the month of June. It adopted a platform declaring freedom to be the "normal condition" of the Territories; but ingeniously complicating its position on the slavery question by a number of vague but plausible articles, such as the maintenance of the principles of the Constitution, and especial attachment to the Union of the States.

The Presidential ticket nominated by the Convention was Abraham Lincoln of Illinois for President, and Hannibal

Hamlin of Maine for Vice-President. Governed by the narrow considerations of party expediency, the Convention had adopted as their candidate for President a man of scanty political record—a Western lawyer, with the characteristics of that profession—acuteness, slang, and a large stock of jokes-and who had peculiar claims to vulgar and demagogical popularity, in the circumstances that he was once a captain of volunteers in one of the Indian wars, and, at some anterior period of his life, had been employed, as report differently said, in splitting rails, or in rowing a flat-boat.

The great majority of the Southern Democracy supported the Breckinridge ticket; it was the leading ticket in all the Slave States, except Missouri; but in the North but a small and feeble minority of the Democratic party gave it their support. In several States, the friends of Douglas, of Breckinridge, and of Bell coalesced, to a certain extent, with a view to the defeat of Lincoln, but without success, except in New Jersey, where they partially succeeded.

The result of the contest was, that Abraham Lincoln received the entire electoral vote of every free State, except New Jersey, and was, of course, elected President of the United States, according to the forms of the Constitution.

The entire popular vote for Lincoln was 1,858,200; that for Douglas, giving him his share of the fusion vote, 1,276,780; that for Breckinridge, giving him his share of the fusion vote, 812,500; and that for Bell, including his proportion of the fusion vote, 735,504. The whole vote against Lincoln was thus 2,824,874, showing a clear aggregate majority against him of nearly a million of votes.

During the canvass, the North had been distinctly warned by the conservative parties of the country, that the election of Lincoln by a strictly sectional vote would be taken as a declaration of war against the South. This position was assumed on the part of the South, not so much on account of the declaration of the anti-slavery principles in the Chicago platform, as from the notorious *animus* of the party supporting Lincoln. The Chicago Convention had attempted to conceal the worst designs of Abolitionism under professions of advancing the cause of freedom in strict accordance with the Constitution and the laws. The South, however, could not be igno rant of the fact, or wanting in appreciation of it, that Lincoln had been supported by the sympathizers of John Brown, the indorsers of the "Helper Book," the founders of the Kansas Emigrant Aid Societies, and their desperate abetters and agents, "Jim" Lane and others, and by the opponents of the Fugitive Slave law. It was known, in a word, that Lincoln owed his election to the worst enemies of the South, and that he would naturally and necessarily select his counsellors from among them, and consult their views in his administration of the government.

Threats of resistance were proclaimed in the South. It is true that a few sanguine persons in that section, indulging narrow and temporizing views of the crisis, derived no little comfort and confidence from the large preponderance of the popular vote in the Presidential contest in favor of the conservative candidates; and viewed it as an augury of the speedy overthrow of the first sectional administration. But those whose observations were larger and comprehended the progress of events, took quite a different view of the matter. They could find no consolation or encouragement from the face of the record. The anti-slavery party had organized in 1840, with about seven thousand voters; and in 1860 had succeeded in electing the President of the United States. The conservative party in the North had been thoroughly corrupted. They were beaten in every Northern State in 1860, with a single exception, by the avowed enemies of the South, who, but a few years ago had been powerless in their midst. The leaders of the Northern Democratic party had in 1856 and in 1860 openly taken the position that freedom would be more certainly secured in the Territories by the rule of non-intervention than by any other policy or expedient. This interpretation of their policy alone saved the Democratic party from entire annihilation. The overwhelming pressure of the anti-slavery sentiment had prevented their acceding to the Southern platform in the Presidential canvass. Nothing in the present or in the future could be looked for from the so-called conservatives of the North; and the South prepared to go out of a Union, which no longer afforded any guaranty for her rights or any permanent sense of security, and which had brought her under the domination of a growing fanaticism in the North, the sentiments of which, if carried into legislation, would destroy her institutions, confiscate the property of her people, and even involve their lives.

The State of South Carolina acted promptly and vigorously, with no delay for argument, and but little for prepara tion. Considering the argument as fully exhausted, she determined, by the exercise of her rights as a sovereign State, to separate herself from the Union. Her Legislature called a Convention immediately after the result of the Presidential election had been ascertained. The Convention met a few weeks thereafter, and on the 20th day of December, 1860, formally dissolved the connection of South Carolina with the Union, by an ordinance of Secession, which was passed by a unanimous vote.

On the same day Major Anderson, who was in command of the Federal forces in Charleston harbor, evacuated Fort Moultrie, spiking the guns and burning the gun-carriages, and occupied Fort Sumter, with a view of strengthening his position. On the 30th of December, John B. Floyd, Secretary of War, resigned his office, because President Buchanan refused to order Major Anderson back to Fort Moultrie—Mr. Floyd alleging that he and the President had pledged the authorities of South Carolina that the existing military *status* of the United States in that State should not be changed during the expiring term of the Democratic administration.

The withdrawal of South Carolina from the Union produced some sensation in the North, but the dominant party treated it lightly. Many of these jeered at it; their leaders derided the "right of secession;" and their newspapers prophesied that the "rebellion" in South Carolina would be reduced to the most ignominious extremity the moment the "paternal government" of the United States should resolve to have recourse from peaceful persuasions to the chastisement of "a spoilt child." The events, however, which rapidly succeeded the withdrawal of South Carolina, produced a deep impression upon all reflecting minds, and startled, to some extent, the masses of the North, who would have been much more alarmed but for their vain and long-continued assurance that the South had no means or resources for making a serious resistance to the Federal authority; and that a rebellion which could at any time be crushed on short notice, might be pleasantly humored or wisely tolerated to any extent short of the actual com mencement of hostilities.

On the 9th day of January, 1861, the State of Mississipp seceded from the Union. Alabama and Florida followed on the 11th day of the same month; Georgia on the 20th; Louisiana on the 26th; and Texas on the 1st of February. Thus, in less than three months after the announcement of Lincoln's election, all the Cotton States, with the exception of Alabama, had seceded from the Union, and had, besides, secured every Federal fort within their limits, except the forts in Charleston harbor, and Fort Pickens, below Pensacola, which were retained by United States troops.

The United States Congress had, at the beginning of its session in December, 1860, appointed committees in both houses to consider the state of the Union. Neither committee was able to agree upon any mode of settlement of the pending issue between the North and the South. The Republican members in both committees rejected propositions acknowledging the right of property in slaves, or recommending the division of the territories between the slaveholding and non-slaveholding States by a geographical line. In the Senate, the propositions, commonly known as Mr. Crittenden's, were voted against by *every Republican senator;* and the House, on a vote of yeas and nays, refused to consider certain propositions, moved by Mr. Etheridge, which were even less favorable to the South than Mr. Crittenden's.

A resolution, giving a pledge to sustain the President in the use of force against seceding States, was adopted in the House of Representatives by a large majority; and, in the Senate, every Republican voted to substitute for Mr. Crittenden's propositions, resolutions offered by Mr. Clarke, of New Hamp shire, declaring that no new concessions, guaranties, or amendments to the Constitution were necessary; that the demands of the South were unreasonable, and that the remedy for the present dangers was simply to enforce the laws—in other words—*coercion and war.*

On the 19th day of January, the Legislature of the State of Virginia had passed resolutions having in view a peaceful settlement of the questions which threatened the Union, and suggesting that a National Peace Conference should be held in Washington on the 4th of February. This suggestion met with a favorable response from the Border Slave States and from professed conservatives in the North. The Conference met on the day designated, and Ex-President Tyler, of Virginia, was called to preside over its deliberations. It remained in session several days, and adjourned without agreeing upon any satisfactory plan of adjustment.

Most of the delegates from the Border Slave States indicated a willingness to accept the few and feeble guaranties contained in the resolutions offered, a short time before, in the Senate by Mr. Crittenden. These guaranties, paltry and ineffectual as they were, would not be conceded by the representatives of the Northern States. The Peace Conference finally adopted what was called the Franklin Substitute in lieu of the propositions offered by Mr. Guthrie, of Kentucky—a settlement less favorable to the South than that proposed by Mr. Crittenden. It is useless to recount the details of these measures. Neither the Crittenden propositions, the Franklin Substitute, nor any plan that pretended to look for the guaranty of Southern rights, received a respectful notice from the Republican majority in Congress.

Shortly after its assemblage in January, the Virginia Legislature had called a Convention of the people to decide upon the course proper to be pursued by the State, with reference to her present relations to the Union and the future exigencies of her situation. The election was held on the 4th of February, and resulted in the choice of a majority of members opposed to unconditional secession. Subsequently, Tennessee and North Carolina decided against calling a Convention—the former by a large, the latter by a very small majority. These events greatly encouraged the enemies of the South, but without cause, as they really indicated nothing more than the purpose of the Border Slave States to await the results of the peace propositions, to which they had committed themselves.

In the mean time, the seceding States were erecting the structure of a government on the foundation of a new Confederation of States. A convention of delegates from the six seceding States assembled in Congress at Montgomery, Alabama, on the 4th of February, 1861, for the purpose of organ-

Jeff. Davis

izing a provisional government. This body adopted a Constitution for the Confederate States on the 8th of February. On the 9th of February, Congress proceeded to the election of a President and Vice-President, and unanimously agreed upon Jefferson Davis, of Mississippi, for President, and Alexander H. Stephens, of Georgia, for Vice-President. Mr. Davis was inaugurated Provisional President on the 18th of February, and delivered an address, explaining the revolution as a change of the constituent parts, but not the system, of the government, and referring to the not unreasonable expectation that, with a Constitution differing only from that of their fathers, in so far as it was explanatory of their well-known intent, freed from sectional conflicts, the States from which they had recently parted might seek to unite their fortunes to those of the new Confederacy.

President Buchanan had, in his message to Congress, denounced Secession as revolutionary, but had hesitated at the logical conclusion of the right of "coercion," on the part of the Federal Government, as not warranted by the text of the Constitution. Timid, secretive, cold, and with no other policy than that of selfish expediency, the remnant of his administration was marked by embarrassment, double-dealing, and weak and contemptible querulousness. He had not hesitated, under the pressure of Northern clamor, to refuse to order Major Anderson back to Fort Moultrie, thus violating the pledge that he had given to the South Carolina authorities, that the military status of the United States in Charleston harbor should not be disturbed during his administration. He added to the infamy of this perfidy by a covert attempt to reinforce Fort Sumter, under the specious plea of provisioning a "starving garrison;" and when the Federal steamship, the Star of the West, which was sent on this mission, was, on the 9th of January, driven off Charleston harbor by the South Carolina batteries on Morris Island, he had the hardihood to affect surprise and indignation at the reception given the Federal reinforcements, and to insist that the expedition had been ordered with the concurrence of his Cabinet, including Mr. Thompson, of Mississippi, then Secretary of the Interior, who repelled the slander, denounced the movement as underhanded, and as a breach not only of good faith towards South Carolina, but of personal confidence between the President and his ad visers, and left the Cabinet in disgust.

On the incoming of the administration of Abraham Lincoln, on the 4th of March, the rival government of the South had perfected its organization; the separation had been widened and envenomed by the ambidexterity and perfidy of President Buchanan; the Southern people, however, still hoped for a peaceful accomplishment of their independence, and deplored war between the two sections, as "a policy detrimental to the civilized world." The revolution in the mean time had rapidly gathered, not only in moral power, but in the means of war and the muniments of defence. Fort Moultrie and Castle Pinckney had been captured by the South Carolina troops; Fort Pulaski, the defence of the Savannah, had been taken; the arsenal at Mount Vernon, Alabama, with 20,000 stand of arms, had been seized by the Alabama troops; Fort Morgan, in Mobile Bay, had been taken; Forts Jackson, St. Philip, and Pike, near New Orleans, had been captured by the Louisiana troops; the Pensacola Navy-Yard and Forts Barrancas and McRae had been taken, and the siege of Fort Pickens commenced; the Baton Rouge Arsenal had been surrendered to the Louisiana troops; the New Orleans Mint and Custom-House had been taken; the Little Rock Arsenal had been seized by the Arkansas troops; and, on the 16th of February, General Twiggs had transferred the public property in Texas to the State authorities. All of these events had been accomplished without bloodshed. Abolitionism and Fanaticism had not yet lapped blood. But reflecting men saw that the peace was deceitful and temporizing; that the temper of the North was impatient and dark; and that, if all history was not a lie, the first incident of bloodshed would be the prelude to a war of monstrous proportions.

CHAPTER II.

Mr. Lincoln's Journey to Washington.—Ceremonies of the Inauguration.—The Inaugural Speech of President Lincoln.—The Spirit of the New Administration.—Its Financial Condition.—Embassy from the Southern Confederacy.—Perfidious Treatment of the Southern Commissioners.—Preparations for War.—The Military Bills of the Confederate Congress.—General Beauregard.—Fortifications of Charleston Harbor.—Naval Preparations of the Federal Government.—Attempted Reinforcement of Fort Sumter.—Perfidy of the Federal Government.—Excitement in Charleston.—Reduction of Fort Sumter by the Confederate Forces.—How the News was received in Washington.—Lincoln's Calculation.—His Proclamation of War.—The "Reaction" in the North.—Displays of Rancor towards the South.—Northern Democrats.—Replies of Southern Governors to Lincoln's Requisition for Troops.—Spirit of the South.—Secession of Virginia.—Maryland.—The Baltimore Riot.—Patriotic Example of Missouri.—Lincoln's Proclamation blockading the Southern Ports.—General Lee.—The Federals evacuate Harper's Ferry.—Burning of the Navy Yard at Norfolk.—The Second Secessionary Movement.—Spirit of Patriotic Devotion in the South.—Supply of Arms in the South.—The Federal Government and the State of Maryland.—The Prospect.

THE circumstances of the advent of Mr. Lincoln to Washington were not calculated to inspire confidence in his courage or wisdom, or in the results of his administration. His party had busily prophesied, and sought to innoculate the North with the conviction, that his assumption of the Presidential office would be the signal of the restoration of peace; that by some mysterious ingenuity he would resolve the existing political complication, restore the Union, and inaugurate a season of unexampled peace, harmony, and prosperity. These weak and fulsome prophecies had a certain effect. In the midst of anxiety and embarrassment, in which no relief had yet been suggested, the inauguration of a new administration of the government was looked to by many persons in the North, outside the Republican party, with a vague sense of hope, which was animated by reports, quite as uncertain, of the vigor, decision, and individuality of the new President. For months since the announcement of his election, Mr. Lincoln's lips had been closed. He had been studiously silent; expectations were raised by what was thought to be an indication of a mysterious wisdom; and the North impatiently waited for the hour when the oracle's lips were to be opened.

These vague expectations were almost ludicrously disappointed. On leaving his home, in Springfield, Illinois, for

Washington, Mr. Lincoln had at last opened his lips. In the speeches with which he entertained the crowd that at different points of the railroad watched his progress to the capital, he amused the whole country, even in the midst of a great public anxiety, with his ignorance, his vulgarity, his flippant conceit, and his Western phraseology. The North discovered that the new President, instead of having nursed a masterly wisdom in the retirement of his home at Springfield, and approaching the capital with dignity, had nothing better to offer to an agonized country than the ignorant conceits of a low Western politician, and the flimsy jests of a harlequin. His railroad speeches were characterized by a Southern paper as illustrating " the delightful combination of a Western county lawyer with a Yankee bar-keeper." In his harangues to the crowds which intercepted him in his journey, at a time when the country was in revolutionary chaos, when commerce and trade were prostrated, and when starving women and idle men were among the very audiences that listened to him, he declared to them in his peculiar phraseology that " *nobody was hurt*," that " *all would come out right*," and that there was " *nothing going wrong.*" Nor was the rhetoric of the new President his only entertainment of the crowds that assembled to honor the progress of his journey to Washington. He amused them by the spectacle of kissing, on a public platform, a lady-admirer, who had suggested to him the cultivation of his whiskers; he measured heights with every tall man he encountered in one of his public receptions, and declared that he was not to be " overtopped ;" and he made public exhibitions of his wife—" the little woman," he called her—whose chubby figure, motherly face, and fondness for finery and colors recommended her to a very limited and very vulgar portion of the society of her sex.

These jests and indecencies of the demagogue who was to take control of what remained of the Government of the United States, belong to history. Whatever their disgrace, it was surpassed, however, by another display of character on the part of the coming statesman. While at Harrisburg, Pennsylvania, and intending to proceed from there to Baltimore, Mr. Lincoln was alarmed by a report, which was either silly or jocose, that a band of assassins were awaiting him in the latter city. Frightened beyond all considerations of dignity and decency the new President of the United States left Harrisburg at night, on a different route than that through Baltimore; and in a motley disguise, composed of a Scotch cap and military cloak stole to the capital of his government. The distinguished fugitive had left his wife and family to pursue the route on which it was threatened that the cars were to be thrown down a precipice by Secessionists, or, if that expedient failed, the work of assassination was to be accomplished in the streets of Baltimore. The city of Washington was taken by surprise by the irregular flight of the President to its shelter and protection. The representatives of his own party there received him with evident signs of disgust at the cowardice which had hurried his arrival in Washington; but as an example of the early prostitution of the press of that parasitical city to the incoming administration that was to feed its venal lusts, the escapade of Mr. Lincoln was, with a shamelessness almost incredible, exploited as an ingenious and brilliant feat, and entitled, in the newspaper extras that announced his arrival, as "*another Fort Moultrie coup de main*"—referring to the fraud by which the government had stolen a march by midnight to the supposed impregnable defences of Fort Sumter.

But Mr. Lincoln's fears for his personal safety evidently did not subside with his attainment of the refuges of Washington. A story was published seriously in a New York paper, that at the moment of his inauguration he was to be shot on the Capitol steps, by an air-gun, in the hands of a Secessionist selected for this desperate and romantic task of assassination. The President, with nerves already shattered by his flight from Harrisburg, was easily put in a new condition of alarm. An armed guard was posted around Willard's hotel, where he had taken temporary quarters. Preparations were busily made to organize a military protection for the ceremony of the inauguration. The city of Washington had already been invested with large military forces, under the immediate command of General Scott, whose vanity and weak love of public sensations had easily induced him to pretend alarm, and to make a military display, more on his own account than for the ridiculous and absurd object of Mr. Lincoln's personal security. For weeks the usually quiet city had been filled with Federal bayonets; the bugle's reveille, the roll of drums, and the tramp of armed guards startled, in every direction, the civilian of Washington, who had been accustomed to nothing more war like than parades at the Navy Yard and rows in Congress: companies of flying artillery daily paraded the streets and thundered over its pavements; and no form of ostentation was omitted by the senile and conceited general in command, to give the Federal metropolis the appearance of a conquered city.

The hour of the inauguration—the morning of the fourth of March—at length arrived. Mr. Lincoln was dressed in a suit of black for the occasion, and, at the instance of his friends, had submitted to the offices of a hair-dresser. He entered the barouche that was to convey him to the Capitol, with a nervous agitation and an awkwardness, that were plainly evident to the crowd. His person attracted the curiosity of the mob. Of unusual height, the effect of his figure was almost ludicrous, from a swinging gait and the stoop of his shoulders; a cadaverous face, whose expression was that of a sort of funereal humor; long, swinging arms, with the general hirsute appearance of the Western countryman, made up the principal features of the new President.

The inauguration ceremony was attended by a most extraordinary military display, under the immediate direction of General Scott; who, to give it an appearance of propriety, and to increase its importance, affected the most uneasy alarms. Previous to inauguration day, the vaults of the Capitol were explored for evidences of a gunpowder plot to hurry Mr. Lincoln and his satellites into eternity. In the procession along Pennsylvania Avenue, the President was hid from public view in a hollow square of cavalry, three or four deep. The tops of the houses along the route were occupied by soldiery watching for signs of tumult or assassination. Artillery and infantry companies were posted in different parts of the city; officers were continually passing to and fro; and as the procession approached the Capitol, Gen. Scott, who was in constant communication with all quarters of the city, was heard to exclaim, in a tone of relief, "every thing is going on peaceably; thank God Almighty for it." The expression of relief was simply ridiculous. The ceremony was disturbed by but a single incident: as the procession neared the portico of the Capitol, a drunken man, who had climbed up one of the trees on the avenue, amused himself by striking with a staff the boughs of the tree and shouting to the crowd. The thought flashed upon the minds of the special police, that he might be the identical assassin with the air-gun; he was instantly seized by a dozen of them, and hurried from the scene of the ceremony with a rapidity and decision that for a moment alarmed, and then amused, the crowd. Mr. Lincoln delivered his inaugural from the East portico of the Capitol, to an audience huddled within the lines of the District militia, and with a row of bayonets glittering at his feet.

The inaugural was intended to be ambiguous; it proposed to cozen the South by a cheap sentimentalism, and, at the same time, to gratify the party that had elevated Mr. Lincoln, by a sufficient expression of the designs of the new administration. These designs were sufficiently apparent. Mr. Lincoln protested that he should take care that the laws of the United States were faithfully executed in all the States; he declared that in doing this, there was no necessity for bloodshed or violence, "*unless* it was forced upon the national authority." He promised that the power confided to him would be used to hold, occupy, and possess the forts and places belonging to the government, "but," continued the ambidexterous speaker, "*beyond what may be necessary* for these objects, there will be no invasion, no using of force against or among any people anywhere."

In the South, the inaugural was generally taken as a premonition of war. There were other manifestations of the spirit of the new administration. Violent Abolitionists and men whose hatred of the South was notorious and unrelenting, were placed in every department of the public service. William H. Seward was made Secretary of State; Salmon P. Chase, Secretary of the Treasury; and Montgomery Blair, Postmastergeneral. Anson Burlingame was sent as representative to Austria; Cassius M. Clay, to Russia; Carl Shurz, to Spain; James E. Harvey, to Portugal; Charles F. Adams, to England; and Joshua R. Giddings, to Canada. In the Senate, which was convened in an extra session to confirm executive appointments and to transact other public business, Charles Sumner was appointed Chairman of Foreign Relations; Wil liam P. Fessenden, of Finance; and Henry Wilson, of Military Affairs. A portion of the time of this extra session was consumed in discussing the policy of the administration. Mr. Douglas, who had represented the Northern Democracy in the Presidential contest, and still claimed to represent it, and who had already courted the new administration of his rival—had held Mr. Lincoln's hat at the inauguration ceremony, and enacted the part of Mrs. Lincoln's cavalier at the inauguration ball—essayed to give to the President's inaugural a peace interpretation, and to soften what had been foreshadowed of his policy. The efforts of the demagogue were ill-timed and paltry. Senators from Delaware, Maryland, Virginia, Kentucky, Arkansas, Missouri, and North Carolina, who still continued in the councils of the government, remained long enough to witness the subversion of all the principles that had before contributed to the prosperity and stability of the American Government; to learn, as far as possible, the course the government would pursue towards the Confederate States; and to return home to prepare their people for the policy of discord, conflict, and civil war which had been inaugurated.

The financial condition of the government at the time of Mr. Lincoln's accession was by no means desperate. There was a balance in the Treasury of six millions, applicable to current expenses; the receipts from customs were estimated at eighty thousand dollars per day; and it was thought that a loan would not be called for for some time, should there be a happy continuation of peace.

The Confederate States government at Montgomery had shown nothing of a desperate or tumultuous spirit; it had not watched events with recklessness as to their conclusion; it was anxious for peace; and it gave a rare evidence of the virtue and conservatism of a new government, which was historically the fruit of a revolution, by the most sedulous efforts to avoid all temptations to violence, and to resist the consequence of war. Soon after the inauguration of Mr. Lincoln, it had deputed an embassy of commissioners to Washington, authorized to negotiate for the removal of the Federal garrisons from Forts Pickens and Sumter, and to provide for the settlement of all claims of public property arising out of the separation of the States from the Union. Two of the commissioners, Martin

Crawford, of Georgia, and John Forsythe, of Alabama, attended in Washington, and addressed a communication to Mr. Seward, which explained the functions of the embassy and its purposes.

Mr. Seward declined for the present to return an official answer to the commissioners, or to recognize in an official light their humane and amicable mission. His government had resolved on a policy of perfidy. The commissioners were amused from week to week with verbal assurances that the government was disposed to recognize them; that to treat with them at the particular juncture might seriously embarrass the administration of Mr. Lincoln; that they should be patient and confident; and that in the mean time the military status of the United States in the South would not be disturbed. Judge Campbell, of the Supreme Court, had consented to be the intermediary of these verbal conferences. When the sequel of the perfidy of the administration was demonstrated, he wrote two notes to Mr. Seward, distinctly charging him with overreaching and equivocation, to which Mr. Seward never attempted a defence or a reply.

The dalliance with the commissioners was not the only deceitful indication of peace. It was given out and confidently reported in the newspapers, that Fort Sumter was to be evacuated by the Federal forces. The delusion was continued for weeks. The Black Republican party, of course, resented this reported policy of the government; but a number of their newspapers endeavored to compose the resentment by the arguments that the evacuation would be ordered solely on the ground of military necessity, as it would be impossible to reinforce the garrison without a very extensive demonstration of force, which the government was not then prepared to make; that the purposes of the administration had not relaxed, and that the evacuation of Sumter was, as one of the organs of the administration expressed it, but "the crouch of the tiger before he leaped."

It was true that the condition of the garrison of Fort Sumter had been a subject of Cabinet consultation; but it was afterwards discovered that all that had been decided by the advisers of the President, among whom General Scott had been admitted, was that military reinforcement of the fort was, under the circumstances, impracticable. There never was an intention to evacuate it. The embarrassment of the government was, to avoid the difficulty of military reinforcements by some artifice that would equally well answer its purposes. That artifice continued for a considerable time to be the subject of secret and sedulous consultation.

While a portion of the public were entertained in watching the surface of events, and were imposed upon by deceitful signs of peace, discerning men saw the inevitable consequence in the significant preparations made on both sides for war. These preparations had gone on unremittingly since the inauguration of the Lincoln government. The troops of the United States were called from the frontiers to the military centres; the Mediterranean squadron and other naval forces were ordered home; and the city of Washington itself was converted into a school where there were daily and ostentatious instructions of the soldier. On the other hand, the government at Montgomery was not idle. Three military bills had been passed by the Confederate Congress. The first authorized the raising of one hundred thousand volunteers when deemed necessary by the President; the second provided for the Provisional Army of the Confederate States, which was to be formed from the regular and volunteer forces of the different States; and the third provided for the organization of a Regular Army, which was to be a permanent establishment. But among the strongest indications of the probability of war, in the estimation of men calculated to judge of the matter, and among the most striking proofs, too, of devotion to the cause of the South, was the number of resignations from the Federal army and navy on the part of officers of Southern birth or association, and their prompt identification with the Confederate service. These resignations had commenced during the close of Mr. Buchanan's administration. On the accession of Mr. Lincoln, Adjutant-general Cooper had immediately resigned; and the distinguished example was followed by an array of names, which had been not a little illustrious in the annals of the Federal service.

While the South was entreating peace, and pursuing its accomplishment by an amicable mission to Washington, a strong outside pressure was being exerted upon the administration of Mr. Lincoln to hurry it to the conclusion of war

He had been visited by a number of governors of the Northern States. They offered him money and men; but it was
understood that nothing would be done in the way of calling
out the State militia and opening special credits, until the
Southern revolutionists should be actually in aggression to the
authority of the Federal government. Another appeal was
still more effectively urged. It was the argument of the partisan. The report of the intended evacuation of Fort Sumter,
and the apparent vacillation of the administration, were producing disaffection in the Black Republican party. This party
had shown a considerable loss of strength in the municipal
elections in St. Louis, Cincinnati, and other parts of the West;
they had lost two congressmen in Connecticut and two in
Rhode Island. The low tariff, too, of the Southern Confederacy,
brought into competition with the high protective tariff which
the Black Republican majority in Congress had adopted, and
which was popularly known as "the Morrill Tariff," was
threatening serious disaster to the interests of New England
and Pennsylvania, and was indicating the necessity of the
repeal of a law which was considered as an indispensable party
measure by the most of Mr. Lincoln's constituents.

For weeks the Cabinet of Mr. Lincoln had been taxed to
devise some artifice for the relief of Fort Sumter, short of
open military reinforcements (decided to be impracticable),
and which would have the effect of inaugurating the war by a
safe indirection and under a plausible and convenient pretence.
The device was at length hit upon. It was accomplished by
the most flagrant perfidy. Mr. Seward had already given
assurances to the Southern commissioners, through the inter-
mediation of Judge Campbell, that the Federal troops would
be removed from Fort Sumter. Referring to the draft of a
letter which Judge Campbell had in his hand, and proposed to
address to President Davis, at Montgomery, he said, "before
that letter reaches its destination, Fort Sumter will have been
evacuated." Some time elapsed, and there was reason to dis
trust the promise. Colonel Lamon, an agent of the Washington
government, was sent to Charleston, and was reported to be
authorized to make arrangements with Governor Pickens, of
South Carolina, for the withdrawal of the Federal troops from
Fort Sumter. He returned without any accomplishment of

his reported mission.   Another confidential agent of Mr. Lincoln, a Mr. Fox, was permitted to visit Fort Sumter, and was discovered to have acted the part of a spy in carrying concealed dispatches to Major Anderson, and collecting information with reference to a plan for the forcible reinforcement of the fort. On the 7th of April, Judge Campbell, uneasy as to the good faith of Mr. Seward's promise of the evacuation of Sumter, addressed him another note on the subject.   To this the emphatic and laconic reply was : " *Faith as to Sumter fully kept—wait and see.*"   Six days thereafter a hostile fleet was menacing Charleston, the Lincoln government threw down the gauntlet of war, and the battle of Sumter was fought.

On the day succeeding the inauguration of Abraham Lincoln, General P. G. Toutant Beauregard* was put in command of the Confederate troops besieging Fort Sumter.   His military record was slight, but gave evidence of genius.   He was the son of a wealthy and influential Louisiana planter.   He had graduated at the military academy at West Point, taking the second honors in his class, and had served in the Mexican war with distinction, being twice brevetted for gallant and meritorious conduct in the field—the first time as captain for the battles of Contreras and Cherubusco, and again as major for the battle of Chapultepec.   He was subsequently placed by the Federal government in charge of the construction of the mint and custom-house at New Orleans.   He had been ordered by Mr. Buchanan to West Point as superintendent of the military academy.   The appointment was revoked within forty-eight hours for a spiteful reason—the family connection of the nominee with Mr. Slidell, of Louisiana; and Major Beauregard, resigning his commission at once, received higher rank in the army of the Southern Confederacy.

---

* Beauregard is forty years of age.   He is small, brown, thin, extremely vigorous, although his features wear a dead expression, and his hair has whitened prematurely.   Face, physiognomy, tongue, accent—every thing about him is French.   He is quick, a little abrupt, but well educated and distinguished in his manners.   He does not care to express the manifestation of an ardent personality which knows its worth.   He is extremely impassioned in the defence of the cause which he serves.   At least he takes less pains to conceal his passion under a calm and cold exterior than do most of his comrades in the army.   The South found in him a man of an uncommon ardor, a ceaseless activity, and an indomitable power of will.

G. T. Beauregard
Gen. Comdg

On taking command of the Confederate forces at Charleston, General Beauregard at once gave the benefit of his eminent skill as a military engineer, which merit had been recognized in him before, and had procured his elevation to the importan and critical command in front of Fort Sumter, to the construction of works for the reduction of the fort, and the defence of the entrances to the harbor. At the time of Major Anderson's removal to Sumter, the approaches to the harbor were only defended by the uninjured guns at Fort Moultrie, and three 24-pounder guns mounted *en barbette* on a hastily constructed and imperfect earthwork on Morris' Island. The injured guns were replaced, and all, amounting to thirty-eight in number, of various calibres, were protected by well-constructed merlons; lines of batteries were constructed on the east and west on Sullivan's Island; at Cummings' Point on Morris' Island, the nearest land to Fort Sumter, batteries of mortars and columbiads were erected, protected by an iron fortification of novel and formidable construction; and another novelty in iron fortifications was perfected by the skilful and practical genius of the commander in a floating battery, constructed of the peculiarly fibrous palmetto timber, sheathed with plate iron, and embrasured for and mounting four guns of heavy calibre.

Notwithstanding the extent and skill of the besiegers' works, Fort Sumter was declared, by a number of military critics, to be impregnable. It certainly had that appearance to the unscientific eye. The fortification, a modern truncated pentagonal fort, rose abruptly out of the water at the mouth of Charleston harbor, three and a half miles from the city. It was built on an artificial island, having for its base a sand and mud bank, which had been made secure by long and weary labors in firmly imbedding in it refuse blocks and chips from the granite quarries of the Northern States. The foundation alone had cost the government half a million of dollars, and had occupied ten years in its construction. At the time of Major Anderson's occupation of the fortification, it was so nearly completed as to admit the introduction of its armament The walls were of solid brick and concrete masonry, sixty feet high and from eight to twelve feet in thickness, and pierced for three tiers of guns on the northern, eastern, and western exterior sides,   They were built close to the edge of the water and without a berme.

The advantages of delay which the Lincoln government had obtained by the pretence of the evacuation of Sumter, and the adroitness of Mr. Seward with the commissioners, had been profitably employed by it in naval and other preparations for its meditated blow on the Southern coasts. Unusual activity was perceptible in all the dock-yards, armories, and military depots throughout the North. The arsenals of Troy and Watertown were constantly occupied, and the creaking of blocks, the clang of hammers, and the hum of midnight labor resounded through every manufactory of arms. Numerous large transports were employed by the government for the conveyance of soldiers and war material, and the signs of the times betokened that the administration was preparing for a long and bloody struggle. Within ten days from the first of April, over eleven thousand men were sent from Fort Hamilton and Governor's Island. The recruiting offices in New York were daily engaged in enrolling men for the Federal service. On the 6th of April, the frigate Powhatan was ready for sea, and, with her armament of ten heavy guns and four hundred men, prepared as convoy to the transports Atlantic, Baltic, and Illinois. On the 8th, the Atlantic sailed with Barry's battery (four guns and ninety-one men), four hundred soldiers and a large store of supplies. The same morning the steam-cutter Harriet Lane, Captain J. Faunce, eight guns and one hundred men, sailed for Charleston harbor. Late at night, the transport Baltic, with twenty surf-boats, stores, and two hundred recruits from Governor's Island, and the transport Illinois, with five hundred cases of muskets, stores, three hundred soldiers, and the steam-tug Freeborn, sailed from New York harbor. On the whole, besides the Powhatan, eleven vessels were ordered to be got in readiness, with an aggregate force of 285 guns and 2400 men. There was now not the slightest doubt that the first blow of the rival forces would be struck at Sumter. The fleet dispatched to Charleston harbor consisted of the sloop-of-war Pawnee, the sloop-of-war Powhatan, and the cutter Harriet Lane, with three steam transports.

No sooner was the hostile fleet of the Federal government safely on its way to the Southern coasts, than the perfidy of

Abraham Lincoln and his advisers was openly and shamelessly consummated. The mask was dropped. The Southern commissioners who had been so long cozened, were distinctly rebuffed; and simultaneously with the appearance of the Federal fleet in the offing of the Charleston harbor, an official message, on the 8th day of April, was conveyed to Governor Pickens, of South Carolina, by Lieutenant Talbot, an authorized agent of the Lincoln government, announcing the determination of that government to send provisions to Fort Sumter, " peaceably if they can, forcibly if they must." The message was telegraphed by General Beauregard to Montgomery, and the instructions of his government asked. He was answered by a telegram from Mr. Walker, the Secretary of War, instructing him to demand the evacuation of the fort, and, if that was refused, to proceed to reduce it. The demand was made; it was refused. Major Anderson replied that he regretted that his sense of honor and of his obligations to his government prevented his compliance with the demand. Nothing was left but to accept the distinct challenge of the Lincoln government to arms.

The most intense excitement prevailed in Charleston. No sooner had the official message of Mr. Lincoln been received, than orders were issued to the entire military force of the city to proceed to their stations. Four regiments of one thousand men each, were telegraphed for from the country. Ambulances for the wounded were prepared; surgeons were ordered to their posts, and every preparation made for a regular battle. Among the portentous signs, the community was thrown into a fever of excitement by the discharge of seven guns from the Capitol Square, the signal for the assembling of all the reserves ten minutes afterwards. Hundreds of men left their beds, hurrying to and fro towards their respective locations. In the absence of sufficient armories, the corners of the streets, the public squares, and other convenient points formed places of meeting. All night long the roll of the drum and the steady tramp of the military and the gallop of the cavalry, reounding through the city, betokened the progress of preparation for the long-expected hostilities. The Home Guard corps of old gentlemen, who occupied the position of military exempts, rode through the city, arousing the soldiers and doing other duty required at the moment. Hundreds of the citizens were up all night. A terrible thunder-storm prevailed until a late hour, but in nowise interfered with the ardor of the soldiers.

On the 12th day of April, at half-past four o'clock in the morning, fire was opened upon Fort Sumter. The firing was deliberate, and was continued, without interruption, for twelve hours. The iron battery at Cumming's Point did the most effective service, perceptibly injuring the walls of the fortifica tion, while the floating battery dismounted two of the parapet guns. The shell batteries were served with skill and effect, shells being thrown into the fort every twenty minutes. The fort had replied steadily during the day. About dark, its fire fell off, while ours was continued at intervals during the night. The contest had been watched during the day by excited and anxious citizens from every available point of observation in Charleston—the battery, the shipping in the harbor, and the steeples of churches—and, as night closed, the illuminations of the shells, as they coursed the air, added a strange sublimity to the scene to men who had never before witnessed the fiery splendors of a bombardment. The next morning, at seven o'clock, the fort resumed its fire, doing no damage of consequence. A short while thereafter, the fort was discovered to be on fire, and through the smoke and glare, its flag was discovered at half mast, as a signal of distress. The Federal fleet, which was off the bar, contrary to all expectations, remained quietly where it was; they did not remove from their anchorage or fire a gun. In the mean time, the conflagration, which had seized upon the officers' quarters and barracks at the fort, continued; it no longer responded to our fire, which was kept up with an anxious look-out for tokens of surrender; its garrison, black and begrimed with smoke, were employed in efforts to extinguish the conflagration, and in some instances had to·keep themselves lying upon their faces to avoid death from suffocation. During the height of the conflagration, a boat was dispatched by General Beauregard to Major Anderson, with offers of assistance in extinguishing the fire. Before it could reach the fort, the long-expected flag of truce had been hoisted; and the welcome event was instantly announced in every part of the city by the ringing of bells, the pealing of cannon, the shouts of couriers dashing through the streets, and by every indication of general rejoicing. Major Anderson agreed to an unconditional surrender, as demanded of him; he received of his enemy in return, the most distinguished marks of lenity and consideration: his sword was returned to him by General Beauregard; himself and garrison allowed to take passage, at their convenience, for New York; and, on leaving the fort, he was permitted to salute his flag with fifty guns, the performance of which was attended with the melancholy occurrence of mortal injuries to four of his men by the bursting of two cannon. There was no other life lost in the whole affair.

Thus ended the bombardment of Sumter. It had continued during two days; it was estimated that two thousand shots had been fired in all; a frowning fortification had been reduced to a blackened mass of ruins; and yet not a life had been lost, or a limb injured in the engagement.

The news of the fall of Fort Sumter, when it was received in Washington, did not disturb President Lincoln. He received it with remarkable calmness. The usual drawing-room entertainment at the White House was not intermitted on the evening of the day of the commencement of civil war. The same evening the President turned to a Western Senator and asked, "Will your State sustain me with military power?" He made no other comment on the news, which was agitating every part of the country to its foundation.

The fact was that the President had long ago calculated the result and the effect, on the country, of the hostile movements which he had directed against the sovereignty of South Carolina. He had procured the battle of Sumter; he had no desire or hope to retain the fort: the circumstances of the battle and the non-participation of his fleet in it, were sufficient evidences, to every honest and reflecting mind, that it was not a contest for victory, and that "the sending provisions to a starving garrison" was an ingenious artifice to commence the war that the Federal Government had fully resolved upon, under the specious but shallow appearance of that government being involved by the force of circumstances, rather than by its own volition, in the terrible consequence of civil war.

On the 14th day of April, Mr. Lincoln published his proc

lamation of war.   He acted to the last in a sinister spirit
He had just assured the commiss_oners from Virginia, who had
been deputed to ascertain the purposes of his government, that
he would modify his inaugural only so far as to "perhaps cause
the United States mails to be withdrawn" from the seceded
States.   The following proclamation was the "modification"
of the inaugural:

"Whereas the laws of the United States have been for some time past, and
now are, opposed, and the execution thereof obstructed in the States of South
Carolina, Georgia, Alabama, Florida, Mississippi, Louisiana, and Texas, by
combinations too powerful to be suppressed by the ordinary course of judicial
proceeding, or by the powers vested in the Marshals by law—

"Now, therefore, I, Abraham Lincoln, President of the United States, in
virtue of the power in me vested by the Constitution and the laws, have
thought fit to call forth, and hereby do call forth the militia of the several
States of the Union, to the aggregate number of seventy-five thousand, in
order to suppress said combinations, and to cause the laws to be duly executed.
The details for this object will be immediately communicated to the State authorities through the War Department.

"I appeal to all loyal citizens to favor, facilitate, and aid this effort to maintain the honor, the integrity, and the existence of our National Union, and
the perpetuity of popular government, and to redress wrongs already long
enough endured.

"I deem it proper to say that the first service assigned to the forces hereby
called forth, will probably be to repossess the forts, places, and property which
have been seized from the Union ; and in every event the utmost care will be
observed, consistently with the objects aforesaid, to avoid any devastation and
destruction of, or interference with property, or any disturbance of peaceful
citizens in any part of the country.   And I hereby command the persons composing the combinations aforesaid, to disperse and retire peaceably to their respective abodes within twenty days from this date.

*   *   *   *   *   *   *   *   *

"ABRAHAM LINCOLN."

The trick of the government, to which we have referred, in
its procurement of the battle of Sumter, is too dishonest and
shallow to account for the immense reaction of sentiment in
the North that ensued.   That reaction is certainly to be attributed to causes more intelligent and permanent than the weak
fallacy that the Lincoln government was not responsible for
the hostilities in Charleston harbor, and that the South itsel
had dragged the government and people of Abraham Lincoln
unwillingly into the inauguration of war.   The problem of
this reaction may be more justly solved.   In fact, it involved

no new fact or principle The Northern people, including all parties, secretly appreciated the value of the Union to themselves; they knew that they would be ruined by a permanent secession of the Southern States; many of them had sought to bring the dissatisfied States back into the Union by the old resource of artful speeches and fine promises; and finding, at last, that the South was in earnest, and was no longer to be seduced by cheap professions, they quickly and sharply determined to coerce what they could not cozen. This is the whole explanation of the wonderful reaction. The North discovered, by the fiery *dénouement* in Charleston harbor, that the South was in earnest, and itself became as instantly in earnest. The sudden display of Northern rancor was no reaction; it was no new fact; it revealed what was already historical, and had been concealed only for purposes of policy—the distinct and sharp antipathy between the two sections, of which war or separation, at some time, was bound to be the logical conclusion.

The crusade against the South involved all parties, and united every interest in the North by the common bond of attachment to the Union. That attachment had its own reasons. The idea of the restoration of the Union was conceived in no historical enthusiasm for restoring past glories; it was animated by no patriotic desires contemplating the good of the whole country ; the South was to be " whipped back into the Union," to gratify either the selfishness of the North, or its worse lusts of revenge and fanaticism. The holiness of the crusade against the South was preached alike from the hustings and the pulpit. The Northern Democratic party, which had so long professed regard for the rights of the Southern States, and even sympathy with the first movements of their secession, rivalled the Abolitionists in their expressions of fury and revenge ; their leaders followed the tide of public opinion : Mr. Edward Everett, of Massachusetts, who some months before had declared in a public speech that if the seceded States were " determined to separate, we had better part in peace," became a rhetorical advocate of the war ; Daniel S. Dickinson, of New York, rivalled the Abolition leaders in his State in inflaming the public mind ; and in the city of New York, where but a few months before it had been said that the Southern

Confederacy would be able to recruit several regiments for its military service, demagogues in the ranks of the "National Democracy," such as John Cochrane, harangued the multitude, advising them to "crush the rebellion," and, if need be, to drown the whole South in one indiscriminate sea of blood. Old contentions and present animosities were forgotten ; Democrats associated with recreants and fanatics in one grand league for one grand purpose ; foreigners from Europe were induced into the belief that they were called upon to fight for the "liberty" for which they had crossed the ocean, or for the "free homesteads" which were to be the rewards of the war ; and all conceivable and reckless artifices were resorted to to swell the tide of numbers against the South.   New England, which had been too conscientious to defend the national honor in the war with Great Britain, poured out almost her whole population to aid in the extermination of a people who had given to the nation all the military glory it had achieved.*

---

* In the war of 1812, the North furnished 58,552 soldiers ; the South, 96,812—making a majority of 37,030 in favor of the South. Of the number furnished by the North—

Massachusetts furnished............................	3,110
New Hampshire "	897
Connecticut "	387
Rhode Island "	637
Vermont "	281

5,162

While the little State of South Carolina furnished 5,696.
In the Mexican war,

Massachusetts furnished............................	1,047
New Hampshire "	1
The other New England States	0,000

1,048

The whole number of troops contributed by the North to the Mexican war was 23,054 ; while the South contributed 43,630, very nearly double, and, in proportion to her population, four times as many soldiers as the North.

When a resolution was introduced into the Legislature of Massachusetts, tendering a vote of thinks to the heroic Lawrence for his capture of the Peacock, that pious State refused to adopt it, and declared—

"That in a war like the present, waged without justifiable cause, and prosecuted in a manner indicating that *conquest* and ambition are its *real motives* it is not becoming a moral and religious people to express any approbation of military and naval exploits not directly connected with the defence of our seacoast and our soil."

The effect of Mr. Lincoln's proclamation at the South was no less decisive than at the North. It remains a problem, which facts were never permitted to decide, but the solution of which may at least be approached by the logical considerations of history, to what extent the Border Slave States might have been secured to the Union by the policy of peace, and the simple energy of patience on the part of the government at Washington. As it was, the proclamation presented a new issue; it superseded that of the simple policy of secession; and it inaugurated the *second secessionary movement* of the Southern States on a basis infinitely higher and firmer, in all its moral and constitutional aspects, than that of the first movement of the Cotton States.

The proclamation was received at Montgomery with derisive laughter; the newspapers were refreshed with the Lincolniana of styling sovereign States "unlawful combinations," and warning a people standing on their own soil to return within twenty days to their "homes;" and, in Virginia, the Secessionists were hugely delighted at the strength Mr. Lincoln had unwittingly or perversely contributed to their cause. One after the other of the Border States refused the demands for their quotas in terms of scorn and defiance. Governor Rector, of Arkansas, repudiated the proclamation with an expression of concentrated defiance; Governor Magoffin, of Kentucky, replied, that that State would "furnish no troops for the wicked purpose of subduing her sister Southern States;" Governor Ellis, of North Carolina, telegraphed to Washington, "I can be no party to this wicked violation of the laws of

---

Subsequently the famous Hartford Convention was called. It assembled in the city of Hartford, on the 15th of December, 1814, and remained in session twenty days. It made a report accompanied by a series of resolutions The following is a part of the report, as adopted:

"In cases of deliberate, dangerous, and palpable infractions of the Constitution, affecting the sovereignty of a State and the liberties of the people, *it is not only the right, but the duty, of each State to interpose its authority for their protection in the manner best calculated to secure that end.* When emergencies occur which are either beyond the reach of judicial tribunals, or too pressing to admit of the delay incident to their forms, States, which have no common umpire, must be *their own judges and execute their own decisions.*"

This is the doctrine which the South had always held from the beginning, and for which the South is now pouring out her blood and treasure

this country, and especially to this war which is being waged upon a free and independent people;" Governor Jackson, of Missouri, replied directly to Mr. Lincoln, "Your requisition in my judgment, is illegal, unconstitutional, and revolutionary and, in its objects, inhuman and diabolical;" and even the unspirited governor of Virginia, John Letcher, constrained by the policy of the time-server to reflect the changes which had become apparent to him in the uprising indignation of the people, ventured upon a remonstrance to President Lincoln, reminding him that his proclamation was "not within the purview of the Constitution or the act of 1795." The only Southern governor that signified any degree of submission to the proclamation was the notorious Thomas Holladay Hicks, of Maryland; he gave verbal assurances to Mr. Lincoln that that State would supply her quota and give him military support; but, at the same time, with an art and effrontery that only a demagogue could attain, he published a proclamation to the people of Maryland, assuring them of his neutrality, and promising that an opportunity would be given them, in the election of congressmen, to determine, of their own free will, whether they would sustain the old Union, or assist the South ern Confederacy.

On the 17th day of April, the Virginia Convention passed an ordinance of secession. It was an important era in the history of the times. It gave the eighth State to the Southern Confederacy. The position of Virginia was a commanding one with the other Border States; she started, by her act of secession, the second important movement of the revolution; and she added to the moral influence of the event by the fact, that she had not seceded on an issue of policy, but on one of distinct and practical constitutional right, and that too in the face of a war, which had become absolutely inevitable and was frowning upon her own borders.

Virginia had been chided for her delay in following the Cotton States out of the Union, and, on the other hand, when she did secede, she was charged by the Northern politicians with being inconsistent and having kept bad faith in her relations with the Federal government. Both complaints were equally without foundation. The record of the State was singularly explicit and clear.

The Virginia Resolutions of '98 and '99 had for sixty years constituted the text-book of the State Rights politicians of the South. The doctrine of State sovereignty was therein vindicated and maintained, and the right and duty of States, suffering grievances from unjust and unconstitutional Federal legislation, to judge of the wrongs, as well as of "the mode and measure of redress," were made clear. The Virginia platform, as thus laid down in the elder Adams' time, was adopted by the "Strict Constructionist" party of that day, and has been reasserted ever since. Mr. Jefferson, the founder of the Democratic party in this country, was elected upon this platform, and his State Rights successors all acknowledged its orthodoxy. Whenever there arose a conflict between Federal and State authority, the voice of Virginia was the first to be heard in behalf of State Rights. In 1832–33, when the Tariff and Nullification controversy arose, Virginia, though not agreeing with South Carolina as to the particular remedy to which she resorted, yet assured that gallant State of her sympathy, and, at the same time, reasserted her old doctrines of State Rights. Her gallant and patriotic governor, John Floyd, the elder, declared that Federal troops should not pass the banks of the Potomac to coerce South Carolina into obedience to the tariff laws, unless over his dead body. Her Legislature was almost unanimously opposed to the coercion policy, and a majority of that body indicated their recognition of the right of a State to secede from the Union. The voice of Virginia was potential in settling this controversy upon conditions to which the Palmetto State could agree with both honor and consistency. At every stage of the agitation of the slavery question in Congress and in the Northern States, Virginia declared her sentiments and her purposes in a manner not to be misunderstood by friend or foe. Again and again did she enter upon her legislative records, in ineffable characters, the declaration that she would resist the aggressive spirit of the Northern majority, even to the disruption of the ties that bound her to the Union.

With almost entire unanimity, Virginia had resolved in legislative council, in 1848, that she would not submit to the passage of the Wilmot proviso, or any kindred measure. From the date of the organization of the Anti-Slavery party, her people, of áll parties, had declared that the election of an Abolitionist to the Presidency would be a virtual declaration of war against the South on the part of the North, and that Virginia and every other Slave State ought to resist it as such. The Legislature that assembled a few weeks after Lincoln's election declared in effect, with only four dissenting voices, that the interests of Virginia were thoroughly identified with those of the other Southern States, and that any intimation, from any source, that her people were looking to any combination in the last resort other than union with them, was unpatriotic and treasonable.

The sovereign Convention of Virginia, elected on the 4th of February, 1861, for a long time lingered in the hope that the breach that had taken place in the Union might be repaired by new constitutional guaranties. Nevertheless, that body, before it had yet determined to pass an ordinance of secession —while it was, in fact, hopeful that the Union would be saved through the returning sanity of the Northern people—adopted unanimously the following resolution :

" The people of Virginia recognize the American principle, that government is founded in the consent of the governed, and the right of the people of the several States of this Union, for just cause, to withdraw from their association under the Federal government, with the people of the other States, and to erect new governments for their better security ; and they never will consent that the Federal power, which is, in part, their power, shall be exerted for the purpose of subjugating the people of such States to the Federal authority."

The entire antecedents of Virginia were known to Mr. Lincoln and his Cabinet. They knew that she was solemnly pledged, at whatever cost, to separate from the Union in the very contingency they had brought about—namely, the attempt to subjugate her sister States of the South. They knew that the original " Union men," as well as the original Secessionists, were committed beyond the possibility of recantation to resistance to the death of any and every *coercive* measure of the Federal government. Nevertheless, Mr. Lincoln and his advisers had the temerity to make a call upon the State of Virginia to furnish her quota of seventy-five thousand men to subjugate the seceded States. They had but little right to be surprised at the course taken by the State, and still less to charge it with inconsistency or perfidy.

It was expected that Maryland might follow the heroic course of Virginia, and but two days after the secession of the latter State, there were indications in Maryland of a spirit of emulation of the daring and adventurous deeds that had been enacted South of the Potomac. On the 19th of April the passage of Northern volunteers, on their way to Washington, was intercepted and assailed by the citizens of Baltimore, and for more than two weeks the route through that city was effect- ually closed to Mr. Lincoln's mercenaries. The Baltimore " riot," as it was called, was one of the most remarkable col- lisions of the times. A number of Massachusetts volunteers, passing through Baltimore in horse cars, found the track bar- ricaded near one of the docks by stones, sand, and old anchors thrown upon it, and were compelled to attempt the passage to the depot, at the other end of the city, on foot. They had not advanced fifteen paces after leaving the cars when they found their passage blocked by a crowd of excited citizens, who taunted them as mercenaries, and flouted a Southern flag at the head of their column. Stones were thrown by a portion of the crowd, when the troops presented arms and fired. The crowd was converted into an infuriated mob; the fire was re- turned from a number of revolvers; the soldiers were attacked with sticks, stones, and every conceivable weapon, and in more than one instance their muskets were actually wrung from their hands by desperate and unarmed men. Unable to with- stand the gathering crowd, and bewildered by their mode of attack, the troops pressed along the street confused and stag- gering, breaking into a run whenever there was an opportunity to do so, and turning at intervals to fire upon the citizens who pursued them. As they reached the depot they found a crowd already collected there and gathering from every point in the city. The other troops of the Massachusetts regiment who had preceded them in the horse cars had been pursued by the people along the route, and the soldiers did not hesitate to stretch themselves at full length on the floors of the cars, to avoid the missiles thrown through the windows. The scene that ensued at the depot was terrific. Taunts, clothed in the most fearful language, were hurled at the troops by the panting crowd who, almost breathless with running, pressed up to the windows, presenting knives and revolvers, and cursing up in

the faces of the soldiers. A wild cry was raised on the plat
form, and a dense crowd rushed out, spreading itself along the
railroad track, until for a mile it was black with the excited,
rushing mass. The crowd, as they went, filled the track with
obstructions; the police who, throughout the whole affair, had
contended for order with the most devoted courage, followed
in full run removing the obstructions; as far as the eye could
reach the track was crowded with the pursuers and pursued, a
struggling and shouting mass of human beings. In the midst
of the excitement the train moved off; and as it passed from
the depot a dozen muskets were fired by the soldiers into the
people that lined the track, the volley killing an estimable
citizen who had been drawn to the spot only as a spectator.
The results of the riot were serious enough: two of the soldiers
were shot; several of the citizens had been killed, and more
than twenty variously wounded.

The excitement in Baltimore continued for weeks; the
bridges on the railroad to the Susquehanna were destroyed;
the regular route of travel broken up, and some twenty or
twenty-five thousand Northern volunteers, on their way to
Washington, detained at Havre de Grace, a portion of them
only managing to reach their destination by the way of Annap-
olis. On the night of the day of the riot, a mass-meeting was
held in Monument Square, and was addressed by urgent appeals for the secession of Maryland, and speeches of defiance
to the Lincoln government. Governor Hicks, alarmed by the
display of public sentiment, affected to yield to it. He addressed the crowd in person, condemning the coercive policy
of the government, and ending with the fervid declaration, " I
will suffer my right arm to be torn from my body before I will
raise it to strike a sister State." The same man, in less than a
month thereafter, when Maryland had fallen within the grasp
of the Federal government, did not hesitate to make a call
upon the people for four regiments of volunteers to assist that
government in its then fully declared policy of a war of invasion and fell destruction upon the South.

In the city of St. Louis there were collisions between the
citizens and soldiery as well as in Baltimore; but in Missouri
the indications of sympathy with the South did not subside or
allow themselves to be choked by spectral fears of the " crucial

experiment of secession"—they grew and strengthened in the face of all the Federal power could do.

The riots in Maryland and Missouri were, however, only inci dents in the history of the period in which they occurred That history is occupied with far more important and general events, indicating the increased and rapid preparations, North and South, for war; the collection of resources, and the policy and spirit in which the gathering contest was to be conducted.

Mr. Lincoln had, on the 19th of April, published his proclamation, declaring the ports of the Southern Confederacy in a state of blockade, and denouncing any molestation of Federal vessels on the high seas as piracy. The Provisional Congress at Montgomery had formerly recognized the existence of war with the North, and letters of marque had been issued by the Confederate authority. The theatre of the war on land was indicated in Virginia. General Lee, who had resigned a commission as colonel of cavalry in the old United States army, was put in command of all the Confederate States forces in Virginia.

That State was the particular object of the rancor of the government at Washington, which proceeded to inaugurate hostilities on her territory by two acts of ruthless vandalism. On the 19th day of April the Federals evacuated Harper's Ferry, after an attempt to destroy the buildings and machine-shops there, which only partially succeeded—the armory buildings being destroyed, but a train to blow up the machine-shop failed, and a large quantity of valuable machinery was uninjured. On the succeeding day, preparations were made for the destruction of the Navy Yard at Norfolk, while Federal reinforcements were thrown into Fortress Monroe. The work of vandalism was not as fully completed as the enemy had designed, the dry-dock, which alone cost several millions of dollars, being but little damaged; but the destruction of property was immense, and attended by a terrible conflagration, which at one time threatened the city of Norfolk.

All the ships in the harbor, excepting the old frigate the United States, were set fire to and scuttled. They were the Pennsylvania, the Columbus and Delaware, the steam-frigate Merrimac (she was only partially destroyed), the sloops Germantown and Plymouth, the frigates Raritan and Columbia, and the brig Dolphin. The Germantown was lying at the wharf under a large pair of shears, which were thrown across her decks by cutting loose the guys. The ship was nearly cut in two and sunk at the wharf. About midnight an alarm was given that the Navy Yard was on fire. A sickly blaze, that seemed neither to diminish nor increase, continued for several hours. Men were kept busy all night transferring every thing of value from the Pennsylvania and Navy Yard to the Pawnee and Cumberland, and both vessels were loaded to their lower ports. At length four o'clock came, and with it flood-tide. A rocket shot up from the Pawnee, and then, almost in an instant, the whole front of the Navy Yard seemed one vast sheet of flame. The next minute streaks of flame flashed along the rigging of the Pennsylvania and the other doomed ships, and soon they were completely wrapped in the devouring element. The harbor was now one blaze of light. The remotest objects were distinctly visible. The surging flames leaped and roared with mad violence, making their hoarse wrath heard at the distance of several miles. The people of Hampton, even those who lived beyond, saw the red light, and thought all Norfolk was on fire. It was certainly a grand though terrible spectacle to witness. In the midst of the brilliance of the scene, the Pawnee with the Cumberland in tow, stole like a guilty thing through the harbor, fleeing from the destruction they had been sent to accomplish.

The Lincoln government had reason to be exasperated towards Virginia. The second secessionary movement, commenced by that State, added three other States to the Southern Confederacy. Tennessee seceded from the Union, the 6th of May; on the 18th day of May, the State of Arkansas was formally admitted into the Southern Confederacy; and on the 21st of the same month, the sovereign Convention of North Carolina, without delay, and by a unanimous vote, passed an ordinance of secession.

The spirit of the rival governments gave indications to discerning minds of a civil war of gigantic proportions, infinite consequences, and indefinite duration. In every portion of the South, the most patriotic devotion was exhibited. Transportation companies freely tendered the use of their lines for transportation and supplies. The presidents of the Southern rail roads consented not only to reduce their rates for mail service and conveyance for troops and munitions of war, but voluntarily proffered to take their compensation in bonds of the Confederacy, for the purpose of leaving all the resources or the government at its disposal for the common defence. Under the act of the Provisional Congress authorizing a loan, proposals issued for the subscription of five millions of dollars were answered by the prompt subscription of more than eight millions by its own citizens; and not a bid was made under par. Requisitions for troops were met with such alacrity that the number in every instance, tendering their services, exceeded the demand. Under the bill for public defence, one hundred thousand volunteers were authorized to be accepted by the Confederate States government for a twelve months' term of service. The gravity of age and the zeal of youth rivalled each other to be foremost in the public service; every village bristled with bayonets; large forces were put in the field at Charleston, Pensacola, Forts Morgan, Jackson, St. Philip, and Pulaski; while formidable numbers from all parts of the Confederacy were gathered in Virginia, on what was now becoming the immediate theatre of the war. On the 20th day of May, the seat of government was removed from Montgomery, Alabama, to Richmond, Virginia, and President Davis was welcomed in the latter city with a burst of genuine joy and enthusiasm, to which none of the military pageants of the North could furnish a parallel.

It had been supposed that the Southern people, poor in manufactures as they were, and in the haste of preparation for the mighty contest that was to ensue, would find themselves but illy provided with arms to contend with an enemy rich in the means and munitions of war. This disadvantage had been provided against by the timely act of one man. Mr. Floyd, of Virginia, when Secretary of War under Mr. Buchanan's administration, had by a single order effected the transfer of 115,000 improved muskets and rifles from the Springfield armory and Watervliet arsenal to different arsenals at the South. Adding to these the number of arms distributed by the Federal government to the States in preceding years of our history, and those purchased by the States and citizens, it was safely estimated that the South entered upon the war with one hun dred and fifty thousand small-arms of the most approved modern pattern and the best in the world.

The government at Washington rapidly collected in that city a vast and motley army. Baltimore had been subdued; the route through it was restored; and such were the facilities of Northern transportation, that it was estimated that not less than four or five thousand volunteers were transported through the former Thermopylæ of Baltimore in a single day. The first evidences of the despotic purposes of the Lincoln government were exhibited in Maryland, and the characteristics of the war that it had commenced on the South were first displayed in the crushing weight of tyranny and oppression it laid upon a State which submitted before it was conquered.

The Legislature of Maryland did nothing practical. It was unable to arm the State, and it made no attempt to improve the spirit of the people, or to make preparations for any future opportunity of action. It assented to the attitude of submission indefinitely. It passed resolutions protesting against the military occupation of the State by the Federal government, and indicating sympathy with the South, but concluding with the declaration: "under existing circumstances, it is inexpedient to call a sovereign Convention of the State at this time, or take any measures for the immediate organization or arming of the militia." The government of Abraham Lincoln was not a government to spare submission or to be moved to magnanimity by the helplessness of a supposed enemy. The submission of Maryland was the signal for its persecution. By the middle of May, her territory was occupied by thirty thousand Federal troops; her quota of troops to the war was demanded at Washington, and was urged by a requisition of her obsequious governor; the city of Baltimore was invested by General Butler of Massachusetts, houses and stores searched for concealed arms, and the liberties of the people violated, with every possible addition of mortification and insult.

In a few weeks the rapid and aggravated progression of acts of despotism on the part of the Lincoln government reached its height in Maryland. The authority of the mayor and police board of the city of Baltimore was superseded, and their persons seized and imprisoned in a military fortress; the writ of *habeas corpus* was suspended by the single and unconsti tional authority of the President; the houses of suspected citizens were searched, and they themselves arrested by military force, in jurisdictions where the Federal courts were in uninterrupted operation; blank warrants were issued for domiciliary visits; and the sanctity of private correspondence was violated by seizing the dispatches preserved for years in the telegraph offices of the North, and making them the subject of inquisition for the purpose of discovering and punishing as traitors men who had dared to reproach the Northern government for an unnatural war, or had not sympathized with its rancor and excesses.

Such was the inauguration of "the strong government" of Abraham Lincoln in Maryland, and the repetition of its acts was threatened upon the "rebel" States of the South, with the addition that their cities were to be laid in ashes, their soil sown with blood, the slaves freed and carried in battalions against their masters, and "the rebels" doomed, after their subjection, to return home to find their wives and children in rags, and gaunt Famine sitting at their firesides.

CHAPTER III.

Confidence of the North.—Characteristic Boasts.—" Crushing out the Rebellion."—
Volunteering in the Northern Cities.—The New York " Invincibles."—Misrepresenta-
tions of the Government at Washington.—Mr. Seward's Letter to the French Govern-
ment.—Another Call for Federal Volunteers.—Opening Movements of the Campaign.—
The Federal Occupation of Alexandria.—Death of Col. Ellsworth.—Fortress Monroe.—
The BATTLE OF BETHEL.—Results of this Battle.—Gen. Joseph E. Johnston.—The Upper
Potomac.—Evacuation and Destruction of Harper's Ferry.—The Movements in the
Upper Portion of the Valley of Virginia.—Northwestern Virginia.—The BATTLE OF
RICH MOUNTAIN.—Carrock's Ford.—The Retreat of the Confederates.—General Mc-
Clellan.—Meeting of the Federal Congress.—Mr. Lincoln's Message.—Kentucky.—
Western Virginia.—Large Requisitions for Men and Money by the Federal Govern-
ment.—Its Financial Condition.—Financial Measures of the Southern Confederacy.—
Contrast between the Ideas of the Rival Governments.—Conservatism of the Southern
Revolution.—Despotic Excesses of the Government at Washington.

NOTHING could exceed the boastful and unlimited expressions
of confidence on the part of the Northern people, in the speedy
" crushing out of the rebellion," and of contempt for the means
and resources of the South to carry on any thing like a formidable war.   In the light of subsequent events, these expressions
and vaunts give a grotesque illustration of the ideas with which
the Northern people entered upon the war.

The New York people derided the rebellion.   The *Tribune*
declared that it was nothing " more or less than the natural
recourse of all mean-spirited and defeated tyrannies to rule or
ruin, making, of course, a wide distinction between the will
and power, for the hanging of traitors is sure to begin before
one month is over."   " The nations of Europe," it continued,
'may rest assured that Jeff. Davis & Co. will be swinging
from the battlements at Washington, at least, by the 4th of
July.   We spit upon a later and longer deferred justice."

The New York *Times* gave its opinion in the following
vigorous and confident spirit: " Let us make quick work.
The 'rebellion,' as some people designate it, is an unborn tad-
pole.   Let us not fall into the delusion, noted by Hallam, of
mistaking a 'local commotion' for a revolution.   A strong
active 'pull together' will do our work effectually in thirty
days.   We have only to send a column of 25,000 men across

the Potomac to Richmond, and burn out the rats there; another column of 25,000 to Cairo, seizing the cotton ports of the Mississippi; and retaining the remaining 25,000, included in Mr Lincoln's call for 75,000 men, at Washington, not because there is need for them there, but because we do not require their services elsewhere."

The Philadelphia *Press* declared that "no man of sense could, for a moment, doubt that this much-ado-about-nothing would end in a month." The Northern people were "simply invincible." "The rebels," it prophesied, "a mere band of ragamuffins, will fly, like chaff before the wind, on our approach."

The West was as violent as the North or the East. In the States of Iowa and Wisconsin, among the infidel Dutch, no rein was drawn upon the wild fanaticism. In Illinois, too, there was a fever of morbid violence. The Chicago *Tribune* insisted on its demand that the West be allowed to fight the battle through, since she was probably the most interested in the suppression of the rebellion and the free navigation of the Mississippi. "Let the East," demanded this valorous sheet, "get out of the way; this is a war of the West. We can fight the battle, and successfully, within two or three months at the furthest. Illinois can whip the South by herself. We insist on the matter being turned over to us."

The Cincinnati *Commercial*, in commenting upon the claims of the West, remarked that "the West ought to be made the vanguard of the war"—and proceeded: "We are akin, by trade and geography, with Kentucky, Tennessee, and Missouri, and in sentiment to the noble Union patriots who have a majority of three to one in all these States. An Ohio army would be received with joy in Nashville, and welcomed in a speech of congratulation by Andrew Johnson: Crittenden and Frank Blair are keeping Kentucky and Missouri all right. The rebellion will be crushed out before the assemblage of Congress —no doubt of it."

Not a paper of influence in the North, at that time, had the remotest idea of the conflict; not a journalist who rose to the emergencies of the occasion—all was passion, rant, and bombast.

In the Northern cities, going to the war for "three months," the term of the enlistment of volunteers, was looked upon almost as a holiday recreation. In New York and Philadelphia, the recruiting offices were besieged by firemen, rowdies, and men fished from the purlieus of vice, and every sink of degradation. There appeared to be no serious realization of the war. If a man ventured the opinion that a hundred thousand Southern troops might be gathered in Virginia, he was laughed at, or answered with stories about the Adirondack sharpshooters and the New York "roughs." The newspapers declared that the most terrible and invincible army that ever enacted deeds of war might be gathered from the "roughs" of the Northern cities. Nothing could compete with their desperate courage, and nothing could withstand their furious onslaught. A regiment of firemen and congenial spirits was raised in New York, and put under command of Colonel Ellsworth, of Chicago, a youth, who had some time ago exhibited through the country a company of young men drilled in the manual and exercises of the French Zouaves, who had made himself a favorite with the ladies at the Astor House and Willard's Hotel, by his long hair, gymnastic grace, and red uniform, and who boasted of a great deal of political influence as the pet and *protégé* of President Lincoln. To the standard of this young man, and also to that of a notorious bully and marauder, by the name of Billy Wilson, flocked all the vagrant and unruly classes of the great and vicious metropolis of New York. The latter boasted, that when his regiment was moved off, it would be found that not a thief, highwayman, or pickpocket would be left in the city. The people of New York and Washington were strangely enraptured with the spectacle of these terrible and ruthless crusaders, who were to strike terror to the hearts of the Southern people. Anecdotes of their rude and desperate disposition, their brutal speeches and their exploits of rowdyism, were told with glee and devoured with unnatural satisfaction. In Washington, people were delighted by anecdotes that Ellsworth's Zouaves made a practice of knocking their officers down; that their usual address to the sentinels was, "Say, fellow, I am agoin' to leave this ranch;' that on rainy days they seized umbrellas from citizens on the streets, and knocked them in the gutter if they remonstrated; that, "in the most entire good humor," they levied contributions of boots, shoes, liquors, and cigars on tradesmen; and that the "gallant little colonel," who controlled these unruly spirits, habitually wore a bowie knife two feet long. These freaks and eccentricities were not only excusable, they were admirable: the untamed courage of the New York firemen and rowdies, said the people, were to be so useful and conspicuous in the war; and the prophecy was, that these men, so troublesome and belligerent towards quiet citizens who came in contact with them, would be the first to win honorable laurels on the field of combat.

"Billy Wilson's" regiment was held up for a long time in New York as an inimitable scarecrow to the South. The regiment was displayed on every occasion; it was frequently marched up Broadway to pay visits to the principal hotels. On one of these occasions, it was related that Billy Wilson marched the companies into the hall and spacious bar-room of the hotel, and issued the order "Attention." Attention was paid, and the bystanders preserved silence. "Kneel down," shouted the colonel. The men dropped upon their knees. "You do solemnly swear to cut off the head of every d——d Secessionist you meet during the war." "We swear," was the universal response. "The gallant souls," said a New York paper, "then returned in good order to their quarters."

The newspaper extracts and incidents given above afford no little illustration of the spirit in which the North entered upon the war, and, in this connection, belong to the faithful history of the times. That spirit was not only trivial and utterly beneath the dignity of the contest upon which the North was to enter; it betrayed a fierceness and venom, the monstrous developments of which were reserved for a period later in the progress of events.

What was partly ignorance and partly affectation on the part of the Northern press and people, in their light estimation of the war, was wholly affectation on the part of the intelligent and better informed authorities at Washington. The government had a particular object in essaying to represent the Southern revolution as nothing more than a local mutiny. The necessity was plain for balking any thing like a European recognition of the Southern Confederacy, and Mr. Seward was prompt to rank the rebellion as a local and disorganized insurrection, amounting to nothing more than a passing and incidental "change" in the history of the Union. At the time that all the resources of the government were put out to encounter the gathering armies of the South, already within a few miles of the capital, Mr. Seward, in a letter of instructions to Mr. Dayton, the recently appointed minister to France, dated the 4th of May, urged him to assure that government of the fact that an idea of a permanent disruption of the Union was absurd; that the continuance of the Union was certain, and that too as an object of "*affection!*" He wrote: "The thought of a dissolution of this Union, peaceably or by force, has never entered into the mind of any candid statesman here, and it is high time that it be dismissed by the statesmen in Europe."

The government at Washington evidently showed, by its preparations, that it was secretly conscious of the resources and determined purposes of the revolution. Another proclamation for still further increasing his military forces had been made by Mr. Lincoln on the third of May. He called for forty-odd thousand additional volunteers to enlist for the war, and eighteen thousand seamen, besides increasing the regular army by the addition of ten regiments. It is curious that these immense preparations should have attracted such little notice from the Northern public. The people and soldiers appeared to be alike hilarious and confident in the prospect of a "short, sharp, and decisive" war, that was to restore the Union, open the doors of the treasury, give promotion and fame to those desirous of gain in those particulars, and afford new opportunities to adventurers of all classes.

The first and opening movements of the Northern campaign were decided to be a forward movement from the Potomac along the Orange and Alexandria and Central roads towards Richmond, while another invading army might be thrown into the Valley of Virginia from Pennsylvania and Maryland.

The first step of the invasion of Virginia was the occupation of Alexandria, which was accomplished on the 24th of May, by throwing some eight thousand Federal troops across the Potomac, the Virginia forces evacuating the town and falling back to the Manassas Junction, where General Bonham, of South Carolina, was in command of the Confederate forces.

The invasion was accomplished under cover of the night, and with such secrecy and dispatch, that a number of Virginia cavalry troops were found, unconscious of danger, at their quarters, and were taken prisoners.

The Federal occupation of the town was attended by a dramatic incident, the heroism and chivalry of which gave a remarkable lesson to the invader of the spirit that was to oppose his progress on the soil of Virginia. In the gray of the morning, Col. Ellsworth, who, with his Fire Zouaves, had entered the town, observed a Confederate flag floating from the top of an hotel called the Marshall House, and attended by a squad of his men, determined to secure it as his prize. He found his way into the hotel, ascended the stairs, and climbed, by a ladder, to the top of the house, where he secured the obnoxious ensign. As he was descending from the trap-door, with the flag on his arm, he was confronted by Mr. Jackson, the proprietor of the hotel, who, aroused from his bed by the unusual noise, half dressed and in his shirt-sleeves, with a double-barrel gun in his hands, faced Ellsworth and his four companions with a quiet and settled determination. "This is my trophy," said the Federal commander, pointing to the flag. "And you are mine," responded the Virginian, as, with a quick aim he discharged his gun full into the breast of Colonel Ellsworth, and the next instant sank by his side a breathless corpse, from a bullet, sped through the brain, and a bayonet-thrust at the hands of one of the soldiers.

The slayer of Colonel Ellsworth was branded, in the North, as an "assassin." The justice of history does not permit such a term to be applied to a man who defended his country's flag and the integrity of his home with his life, distinctly and fearlessly offered up to such objects of honor : it gives him the name which the Southern people hastened to bestow upon the memory of the heroic Jackson—that of " martyr." The character of this man is said to have been full of traits of rude, native chivalry. He was captain of an artillery company in his town. He was known to his neighbors as a person who united a dauntless and unyielding courage with the most generous impulses. A week before his death a " Union" man from Washington had been seized in the streets of Alexandria and a crowd threatened to shoot or hang him, when Jackson went to his rescue, threatened to kill any man who would molest him, and saved him from the vengeance of the mob. A day before the Federal occupation of the town, in a conversation in which some such movement was conjectured, his neighbors remonstrated with him about the danger of making his house a sign for the enemy's attack, by the flag which floated over it. He replied that he would sacrifice his life in keeping the flag flying—and by daybreak the next day the oath was fulfilled. He laid down his life, not in the excitement of passion, but coolly and deliberately, upon a principle, and as an example in defending the sacred rights of his home and the flag of his country. This noble act of heroism did not fail to move the hearts of the generous people of the South; a monument was proposed to the memory of the only hero of Alexandria; the dramatic story, and the patriotic example of "the martyr Jackson," were not lost sight of in the stormy excitements of the war that swept out of the mind so many incidents of its early history; and in most of the cities of the South practical evidences of regard were given in large, voluntary subscriptions to his bereaved family.

The Federal forces were not met in Alexandria with any of those demonstrations of "Union" sentiment which they had been induced, by the misrepresentations of the Northern press, to expect would hail the vanguard of their invasion of the South. The shouts and yells of the invaders fell upon the ears of a sullen people, who shut themselves up in their houses, as much to avoid the grating exultations of their enemies as contact with the rowdyism and riot that had taken possession of the streets. On coming into the town, the New York troops, particularly the Fire Zouaves, ran all over the city with their usual cry of "Hi," "Hi." Citizens closed their doors, and as the news of the tragedy at the Marshall House spread over the town, it assumed an aspect like that of the Sabbath. About the wharves and warehouses, where hitherto the life and excitement of the town had been concentrated, the silence was absolutely oppressive; and the only people to be seen were numbers of negroes, who stood about the wharves and on the street corners with frightened faces, talking in low tones to each other.

With Alexandria and Fortress Monroe in its possession, the

Federal Government held the most important passages into Virginia. General McDowell was charged with the command of the division of the forces thrown across the Potomac. General Butler was placed in command at Fortress Monroe. The town of Hampton was occupied by the Federal troops, and Newport News, at the mouth of the James River, invested by them. At Sewell's Point, some eight or ten miles distant on the other side, the Confederates had erected a powerful battery, which had proved its efficiency and strength by resisting an attack made upon it on the 19th of May, and continued for two days, by the Federal steamer Monticello, aided by the Minnesota.

The first serious contest of the war was to occur in the low country of Virginia. On the 10th of June the battle of Bethel was fought.

THE BATTLE OF BETHEL.

The Confederates, to the number of about eighteen hundred, under Colonel J. Bankhead Magruder, were intrenched at Great Bethel church, which was about nine miles on the road leading south from Hampton. A Federal force exceeding four thousand men, under General Pierce—a Massachusetts officer who was never afterwards heard of in the war—was moved towards Bethel in two separate bodies, a portion landing on the extreme side of the creek, some distance below, while the rest proceeded across the creek. The landing of the latter was effected without opposition, and presently the Federal troops, who had marched up from below, closed in on the Confederates almost simultaneously with those attacking their front.

The attack was received by a battery of the Richmond Howitzers, under command of Major Randolph; the action being commenced by a shot from the Parrott gun in our main battery aimed by himself. One of the guns of the battery being spiked by the breaking of a priming wire in the vent, the infantry supports were withdrawn, and the work was occupied for a moment by the enemy. Captain Bridges, of the 1st North Carolina regiment, was ordered to retake it. The charge of the North Carolina infantry, on this occasion, was the most brilliant incident of the day. They advanced calmly and coolly in the face of a sheet of artillery fire, and when within sixty yards of the enemy dashed on at the double quick. The Federals fell back in dismay.

The enemy continued to fire briskly, but wildly, with his ar tillery. At no time, during the artillery engagement, could the Confederates see the bodies of the men in the column or attack, and their fire was directed by the bayonets of the enemy. The position of the enemy was obscured by the shade of the woods on their right and two small houses on their left. The fire of the Confederates was returned by a battery near the head of the enemy's column, but concealed by the woods and the houses so effectually that the Confederates only ascertained its position by the flash of the pieces.

The earthworks were struck several times by the shots of the Federals. They fired upon us with shot, shell, spherical case, canister, and grape, from six and twelve pounders, at a distance of six hundred yards. The only injury received from their artillery was the loss of a mule. The fire on our part was deliberate, and was suspended whenever masses of the enemy were not within range. From 9 o'clock A. M. until 1:30 P. M. but ninety-eight shot were fired by us, every one of them with deliberation.

After some intermission of the assault in front, a heavy column, apparently a reinforcement or a reserve, made its appearance on the Hampton road and pressed forward towards the bridge, carrying the United States flag at its head. This column was under command of Major Winthrop, aid to General Butler. Those in advance had put on the distinctive badge of the Confederates—a white band around the cap. They cried out repeatedly, "don't fire." Having crossed the creek, they began to cheer most lustily, thinking that our work was open at the gorge, and that they might get in by a sudden rush. The North Carolina infantry, however, dispelled this illusion. Their firing was as cool as that of veterans; the only difficulty being the anxiety of the riflemen to pick off the foe, the men repeatedly calling to their officers, "May I fire? I think I can bring him."

As the enemy fell back in disorder and his final rout commenced, the bullet of a North Carolina rifleman pierced the breast of the brave Federal officer Major Winthrop, who had made himself a conspicuous mark by his gallantry on the field. " He was," says Colonel Hill, of the North Carolina regiment, in his official report of the action, " the only one of the enemy who exhibited even an approximation to courage during the whole day." The fact was, that he had fallen in circumstances of great gallantry. He was shot while standing on a log, waving his sword and vainly attempting to rally his men to the charge. His enemy did honor to his memory ; and the Southern people, who had been unable to appreciate the courage of Ellsworth, and turned with disgust from his apotheosis in the North, did not fail to pay the tribute due a truly brave man to the gallant Winthrop, who, having simply died on the battle-field, without the sensational circumstances of a private brawl or a bully's adventure, was soon forgotten in the North.

During the fight at the angle of our works, a small wooden house in front was thought to give protection to the enemy. Four privates in the North Carolina regiment volunteered to advance beyond our lines and set it on fire. One of them, a youth named Henry L. Wyatt, advanced ahead of his companions, and, as he passed between the two fires, he fell pierced by a musket-ball in the forehead, within thirty yards of the house. This was our only loss in killed during the entire engagement.

The results of the battle of Bethel were generally magnified in the South. It is true that a Confederate force of some eighteen hundred men, in a contest of several hours with an enemy more than twice their numbers, had repulsed them ; that the entire loss of the former was only one man killed and seven wounded, while that of the enemy, by their own acknowledgment, was thirty killed and more than one hundred wounded. The fact, however, was, that our troops had fought under the impenetrable cover of their batteries, the only instance of exposure being that of the North Carolina infantry, who, by their charge on the redoubt taken by the enemy early in the action, contributed, most of all, to the success and glory of the day. The battle had been the result of scarcely any thing more than a reconnoissance ; it was by no means to be ranked as a decisive engagement, and yet it was certainly a serious and well-timed check to the foe.

In one respect, however, the result was not magnified, and

that was in its contribution of confidence and ardor to the South. Thus regarded, it was an important event, and its effects of the happiest kind. The victory was achieved at a time when the public mind was distressed and anxious on account of the constant backward movements of our forces in Virginia, and the oft-recurring story of "surprise" and consequent disaster to our troops in the neighborhood of the enemy's lines. The surrender of Alexandria, the surprise and dispersion of a camp at Philippi by a body of Federal troops,*

---

* The disaster at Philippi was inconsiderable; but it was the subject of some recrimination at the time, and Colonel Porterfield, the Confederate commander, was subjected to a court-martial, which, in the main, exonerated him, and complimented him for his courage. Colonel Porterfield had been ordered to Grafton about the middle of May, 1861, with written instructions from General Lee to call for volunteers from that part of the State, and receive them into the service, to the number of five thousand; and to co-operate with the agents of the Baltimore and Ohio railroad; and with verbal orders to try to conciliate the people of that section, and to do nothing to offend them. Finding, soon after his arrival, that the country was in a state of revolution, and that there was a large and increasing Federal force at Camp Denison, in Ohio, opposite Parkersburg, and another in the vicinity of Wheeling, Colonel Porterfield wrote to the commanding general, that unless a strong force was sent very soon, Northwestern Virginia would be overrun. Upon directing the captains of organized volunteer companies to proceed with their companies to Grafton, they replied that not more than twenty in companies numbering sixty were willing to take up arms on the side of the State; that the others declared, if they were compelled to fight, it would be in defence of the Union. Colonel Porterfield succeeded in a week in getting together three newly-organized companies. This force was increased by the arrival of several other companies, two of which were unarmed cavalry companies—amounting in all to about 500 infantry and 150 cavalry. These troops had been at Grafton but a few days, when, or about the 25th of May, Colonel Porterfield was reliably informed of the force of the enemy and withdrew his command to Philippi. Orders were given for the destruction of the Cheat bridge, but were not executed. The enemy's force at Grafton was about eight thousand men. On the 3d of June, through the failure of the guard or infantry pickets to give the alarm, the command at Philippi was surprised by about five thousand infantry and a battery of artillery, and dispersed in great confusion, but with inconsiderable loss of life, through the woods. The command had no equipments and very little ammunition. Such was the inauguration of the improvident and unfortunate campaign in Western Virginia.

General Garnett succeeded Colonel Porterfield in the command in Northwestern Virginia, with a much larger force (about six thousand men), but one obviously inadequate, considering the extent of the district it was expected to defend, the hostile character of the country, and the invading forces of the enemy.

and the apparently uncertain movements of our forces on the Upper Potomac, had unpleasantly exercised the popular mind, and had given rise to many rash and ignorant doubts with respect to the opening events of the war. The battle of Bethel was the first to turn the hateful current of retreat, and sent the first gleam of sunlight through the sombre shadows that had hung over public opinion in the South.

It is certain that the movements on the Upper Potomac were greatly misunderstood at the time, especially with regard to the evacuation of Harper's Ferry. General Joseph E. Johnston, who had been a quartermaster-general in the old United States service, and had resigned to take part in the defence of his native State, Virginia, had assumed command at Harper's Ferry, on the 23d of May. On the 27th of the same month, General Beauregard had relinquished his command at Charleston, being assigned to duty at Corinth, Mississippi; but, the order being recalled, he was put in command at Manassas, our forces being divided into what was known as the armies of the Potomac and of the Shenandoah. At the time General Johnston took command at Harper's Ferry, the forces at that point consisted of nine regiments and two battalions of infantry, with four companies of artillery—a force which was certainly not sufficient, when we consider that it was expected to hold both sides of the Potomac, and take the field against an invading army. After a complete reconnoissance of the place and environs, General Johnston decided that it was untenable, but determined to hold it until the great objects of the government required its abandonment.

The demonstrations of the Federal forces in the direction of the Valley of Virginia were certainly thwarted by the timely falling back of our army from Harper's Ferry to Winchester. General Patterson's approach was expected by the great route into the Valley from Pennsylvania and Maryland, leading through Winchester, and it was an object of the utmost importance to prevent any junction between his forces and those of General McClellan, who was already making his way into the upper portions of the Valley. On the morning of the 13th of June, information was received from Winchester that Romney was occupied by two thousand Federal troops, supposed to be the vanguard of McClellan's army. A detachment was dispatched by railway to check the advance of the enemy; and on the morning of the 15th, the Confederate army left Harper's Ferry for Winchester.

The next morning, after the orders were issued for the evacuation of Harper's Ferry, brought one of those wild, fearful scenes which make the desolation that grows out of war. The splendid railroad bridge across the Potomac—one of the most superb structures of its kind on the continent—was set on fire at its northern end, while about four hundred feet at its southern extremity was blown up, to prevent the flames from reaching other works which it was necessary to save. Many of the vast buildings were consigned to the flames. Some of them were not only large, but very lofty, and crowned with tall towers and spires, and we may be able to fancy the sublimity of the scene, when more than a dozen of these huge fabrics, crowded into a small space, were blazing at once. So great was the heat and smoke, that many of the troops were forced out of the town, and the necessary labors of the removal were performed with the greatest difficulty.

On the morning of the day after the evacuation of Harper's Ferry, intelligence was received that General Patterson's army had crossed the Potomac at Williamsport; also that the Federal force at Romney had fallen back. The Confederate army was ordered to gain the Martinsburg turnpike by a flank movement to Bunker's Hill, in order to place itself between Winchester and the expected advance of Patterson. On hearing of this, the enemy crossed the river precipitately. Resuming his first direction and plan, General Johnston proceeded to Winchester. There his army was in position to oppose either McClellan from the West, or Patterson from the North-east, and to form a junction with General Beauregard when necessary.

Intelligence from Maryland indicating another movement by Patterson, Colonel Jackson with his brigade was sent to the neighborhood of Martinsburg to support Colonel Stuart, who had been placed in observation on the line of the Potomac with his cavalry. On the 2d of July, General Patterson again crossed the Potomac. Colonel Jackson, pursuant to instructions, again fell back before him; but, in retiring, gave him a severe lesson. With a battalion of the Fifth Virginia Regiment and Pendleton's Battery of Field Artillery, he engaged the enemy's advance. Skilfully taking a position where the smallness of his force was concealed, he engaged them for a considerable time, inflicted a heavy loss, and retired when about to be outflanked, scarcely losing a man, but bringing off forty-five prisoners.

Upon this intelligence, the force at Winchester, strengthened by the arrival of General Bee and Colonel Elzey and the Ninth Georgia regiment, were ordered forward to the support of Jackson, who, it was supposed, was closely followed by General Patterson. Taking up a position within six miles from Martinsburg, which town the enemy had invested, General Johnston waited for him four days, hoping to be attacked by an adversary double his number. Convinced at length that the enemy would not approach him, General Johnston returned to Winchester, much to the disappointment of his troops, who, sullen and discontented, withdrew in the face of the enemy.

On the 15th of July, Colonel Stuart, who, with his cavalry, remained near the enemy, reported the advance of General Patterson from Martinsburg. He halted, however, at Bunker's Hill, nine miles from Winchester, where he remained on the 16th. On the 17th, he moved his left to Smithfield. This movement created the impression that an attack was intended on the south of the Confederate lines; but, with a clear and quick intelligence, General Johnston had penetrated the designs of the enemy, which were to hold him in check, while "the Grand Army" under McDowell was to bear down upon General Beauregard at Manassas.

In the mean time, General McClellan's army had moved southwestward from Grafton. In the progress of the history of the war, we shall meet with frequent repetitions of the lesson of how the improvident spirit of the South, in placing small forces in isolated localities, was taken advantage of by the quick strategic movements and the overwhelming numbers of the North. The first of the series of these characteristic disasters was now to befall the South.

THE BATTLE OF RICH MOUNTAIN.

The main column of Federal troops under General McClellan was estimated to be twenty thousand strong; his movements were now directed towards Beverley, with the object of getting to the rear of General Garnett, who had been appointed to the command of the Confederate forces in Northwestern Virginia, and was occupying a strong position at Rich Mountain, in Randolph county.

The strength of General Garnett's command was less than five thousand infantry, with ten pieces of artillery, and four companies of cavalry. The disposition of these forces was in the immediate vicinity of Rich Mountain. Col. Pegram occupied the mountain with a force of about sixteen hundred men and some pieces of artillery. On the slopes of Laurel Hill, General Garnett was intrenched with a force of three thousand infantry, six pieces of artillery and three companies of cavalry.

On the 5th of July, the enemy took a position at Bealington, in front of Laurel Hill, and a day or two afterwards a large force appeared in front of Rich Mountain.

On the morning of the 11th instant, General Garnett received a note from Colonel Pegram at Rich Mountain, stating that his pickets had that morning taken a prisoner, who stated that there were in front of Rich Mountain nine regiments of seven thousand men and a number of pieces of artillery; that General McClellan had arrived in camp the evening before, and had given orders for an attack the next day; that General Rosecrans had started a night before with a division of the army three thousand strong, by a convenient route, to take him in the rear, while McClellan was to attack in front; that he had moved a piece of artillery and three hundred men to the point by which General Rosecrans was expected, and that he had requested Colonel Scott, with his regiment, to occupy a position on the path by which the enemy must come. As soon as General Garnett received this note, he sent a written order to Colonel Scott to move to the point indicated by Colonel Pegram, and to defend it at all hazards.

The attack on Colonel Pegram was met with the most gallant resistance. The fight lasted nearly three hours. The enemy advanced by a pathless route through the woods, the whole division moving in perfect silence through the brush, laurel, and rocks, while the rain poured down upon them in torrents. The expectation however of surprising the little force on the mountain was disappointed. As the enemy advanced, our artillery, posted on the top of the mountain, opened upon them, but with little effect, as their lines were concealed by the trees and brushwood. The earth of the mountain seemed to tremble under the thunders of the cannon. The tops of immense trees were cut off by our fire, which was aimed too high; the crash of the falling timber mingled with the roar of the cannon, and as our artillery again and again belched forth its missives of destruction, it seemed as if the forest was riven by living streams of lightning. While the cannonading progressed, an incessant fire of musketry was kept up in the woods, where the sharpshooters, wet to the skin in the rain, kept the advancing lines of the enemy at bay. For more than two hours the little army of Colonel Pegram maintained its ground. Its situation, however, was hopeless. Finding himself with three thousand of the enemy in his rear and five thousand in front, Colonel Pegram endeavored to escape with his command, after a small loss in the action. One part of the command, under Major Tyler, succeeded in escaping; the other, about five hundred in number, were compelled to surrender, when it was found that General Garnett had evacuated Laurel Hill. Among the prisoners taken by the enemy was Colonel Pegram himself. Thrown from his horse, which was wounded and had become unmanageable, he refused to surrender his sword to his captors, and a messenger had to ride six miles to find an officer to receive it from the hands of the ill-starred commander.

When Gen. Garnett heard of the result of the engagement at Rich Mountain, he determined to evacuate Laurel Hill as soon as night set in and retire to Huttonsville by the way of Beverley. This design was baffled, as Col. Scott with his regiment had retreated beyond Beverley towards Huttonsville, without having blocked the road between Rich Mountain and Beverley.* General Garnett was compelled by this untoward

---

* It is proper to state, that there was some controversy as to the precise orders given to Colonel Scott. That officer published a card in the newspapers

circumstance, and by the mistaken execution of another or der
by which the road was blocked from Beverley towards Laure
Hill, instead of that between the former place and Rich Moun
tain, to retreat by a mountain road into Hardy county.

The retreat was conducted in good order, amid distresses and
trials of the most extraordinary description. The road was
barely wide enough for a single wagon. In the morning, the
army arrived at a camp on the Little Cheat, and after resting
on the grass in the rain a few hours, took up their dreary line
of march through the forest. On the morning of the second
day of the retreat, soon after leaving the camp on the branch
of the Cheat River, the pursuing enemy fell upon the rear of
the distressed little army, and skirmishing continued during
the day. Four companies of the Georgia regiment were cut off.

At one of the fords, a sharp conflict ensued, in which the
enemy were held at bay for a considerable time.

This action, known as that of Carrock's Ford, more than
retrieved the disasters of the defeat. It was a deep ford,
rendered deeper than usual by the rains, and here some of the
wagons became stalled in the river and had to be abandoned.

The enemy were now close upon the rear, which consisted of
the 23d Virginia regiment, and the artillery ; and as soon as
the command had crossed, Colonel Taliaferro commanding the
23d was ordered to occupy the high bank on the right of the
ford with his regiment and artillery. On the right, this position was protected by a fence; on the left, only by low bushes;
but the hill commanded the ford and the approach to it by the
road, and was admirably selected for a defence. In a few
minutes, the skirmishers of the enemy were seen running along
the opposite bank, which was low and skirted by a few trees,
and were at first taken for the Georgians, who were known to
have been cut off, but our men were soon undeceived, and with
a simultaneous cheer for " Jeff. Davis" by the whole command,
they opened upon the enemy.

The enemy replied with a heavy fire from their infantry and
artillery. A large force was brought to the attack, but the

---

at the time, relieving himself from censure and showing that he occupied on
the day of the battle the position to which he was peremptorily ordered by
General Garnett at the instance of Colonel Pegram.

continued and well-directed fire of the Confederates kept them from crossing the river, and twice the enemy was driven back some distance from the ford. They again, however, came up with a heavy force and renewed the fight. The fire of their artillery was entirely ineffective, although their shot and shell were thrown very rapidly, but they all flew over the heads of the Confederate troops, without any damage except bringing the limbs of the trees down upon them.

After continuing the fight until nearly every cartridge had been expended, and until the artillery had been withdrawn by General Garnett's orders, and as no part of his command was within sight or supporting distance, as far as could be discovered, or, as was afterwards ascertained, within four miles of the ford, Col. Taliaferro, after having sustained a loss of about thirty killed and wounded, ordered the regiment to retire —the officers and men manifesting decided reluctance at being withdrawn.

The loss to the enemy in this gallant little affair must have been quite considerable, as they had, from their own account, three regiments engaged. The people in the neighborhood reported a heavy loss, which they stated the enemy endeavored to conceal by transporting the dead and wounded to Bealington in covered wagons, permitting no one to approach them.

At the second ford, about half-past one o'clock in the day, Gen. Garnett was killed by almost the last fire of the enemy. On reaching at this ford the opposite bank of the stream, Gen. Garnett desired one company from the 23d Virginia regiment to be formed behind some high drift wood. He stated that he would in person take charge of them, and did so—the company being the Richmond Sharpshooters, Capt. Tompkins. In a few minutes, Capt. Tompkins and all his men, but ten, came up to the regiment, stating that Gen. Garnett only wanted ten men. The inference was palpable—he had taken an extreme near position to the enemy. Very soon the firing commenced in the rear where Gen. Garnett was, and immediately the horse of the general came galloping past without a rider. He fell just as he gave the order to the skirmishers to retire, and one of them was killed by his side.

At the second ford, where Gen. Garnett was killed, the enemy abandoned the pursuit, and the command under Col.

Ramsey reached Monterey and formed a junction with Gen. Jackson.

The actual reverses of the retreat consisted of some thirty-odd killed and wounded, a number missing, many of whom afterwards reached the command, and the loss of its baggage a portion of which was used in blocking the road against the enemy's artillery. The conflict and the retreat, the hunger and fatigue of the men, many of whom dropped from the ranks from sheer exhaustion, were unequalled by any thing that had yet occurred in the war. Its success appeared as extraordinary as its hardships and privations. Surrounded by an army of twenty thousand men, without supplies, in a strange country, and in the midst of continuous and drenching rains, it was a wonder that the little army of three thousand men should have escaped annihilation. The command had marched sixty hours, resting only five hours, and had endured a march through the forest without food for men or horses.

Gen. McClellan announced to the government at Washington a signal victory. He summed up the results of the battle on the mountain and his pursuit of the retreating army as two hundred killed and wounded, a thousand taken prisoners, the baggage of the entire command captured, and seven guns taken. "Our success," he wrote to Washington, "is complete, and Secession is killed in this country."

The affair of Rich Mountain was certainly a serious disaster; it involved the surrender of an important portion of North-western Virginia; but with respect to the courage and discipline of our troops, it had exhibited all that could be desired, and the successful retreat was one of the most remarkable in history. It is certain that the unskilful disposition of our troops, as well as their inadequate numbers, had contributed to the success of the enemy, and doubts are admissible whether more advantage might not have been taken of the position at Carrock's Ford, with proper supports, considering its extraordinary advantages of defence, and how long it had been held against the forces of the pursuing enemy by a single regiment.

A feeling of deep sympathy, however, was felt for the unfortunate commander, whose courage, patriotic ardor, and gener-us, because unnecessary, exposure of his person to the bullets of the enemy, commended his memory to the hearts of his countrymen.

Whatever might have been the depression of the public mind of the South by the Rich Mountain disaster, it was more than recovered by news from other quarters. The same day that the unfavorable intelligence from Rich Mountain reached the government at Richmond, the telegraph brought, by a devious route, the news of the battle of Carthage in Missouri. The blow given to the enemy at this distant point, was the first of the brilliant exploits which afterwards made the Missouri campaign one of the most brilliant episodes of the war. It had gone far to retrieve the fortunes of an empire that was hereafter to be added to the Southern Confederacy, and assure the promise that had been made in the proclamation of the gallant Gen. Price of that State—"a million of such people as the citizens of Missouri were never yet subjugated, and, if attempted, let no apprehension be felt for the result." But of this hereafter.

On the anniversary of the Fourth of July, the Federal Congress met at Washington. Galusha A. Grow, a Pennsylvania Abolitionist, and an uncompromising advocate of the war, was elected Speaker of the House. The meeting of this Congress affords a suitable period for a statement of the posture of political affairs, and of the spirit which animated the North, with respect to existing hostilities.

In his message, Mr. Lincoln denounced the idea of any of the States preserving an armed neutrality in the war, having particular reference to the continued efforts of Governor Magoffin, of Kentucky, to maintain a condition of neutrality on the part of that State. Mr. Lincoln declared that if armed neutrality were permitted on the part of any of the States, it would soon ripen into disunion; that it would build impassable walls along the line of separation; and it would tie the hands of the Unionists, while it would free those of the Insurrectionists, by taking all the trouble from Secession, except that which might be expected from the external blockade. Neutrality, he said, gave to malcontents disunion without its risks, and was not to be tolerated, since it recognized no fidelity to the Constitution or obligation to the Union.

Kentucky was not unreasonably accounted a part of the

Northern government. But with an outrage of the plainest doctrines of the government, and a practical denial not only of every thing like the rights of States, but even of their territorial integrity, the Northwestern portion of Virginia, which had rebelled against its State government, was taken into the membership of the Federal Union as itself a State, with the absurd and childish addition of giving to the rebellious counties the name of "Virginia." A Convention of the disaffected Northwestern counties of Virginia had been held at Wheeling, on the 13th day of May, and after a session of three .days, decided to call another Convention, to meet on the 11th of June, subsequent to the vote of the State on the Ordinance of Secession. The Convention reorganized the counties as a member of the Federal Union: F. W. Pierpont was elected governor; and W. T. Willie and the notorious John S. Carlile, both of whom had already signalized their treason to their State by their course in the Convention at Richmond, were sent as representatives of "Virginia" to the United States Senate, in which absurd capacity they were readily received.

The message of the President gave indications of a determined and increased prosecution of hostilities. It called for an army of four hundred thousand men, and a loan of four hundred millions of dollars. This call was a curious commentary upon the spirit and resources of the people, who it had been thought in the North would be crushed out by the three months' levies before the Federal Congress met in July to decide upon what disposition should be made of the conquered States.

The statements of Mr. Lincoln's fiscal secretary were alarming enough; they showed a state of the treasury unable even to meet the ordinary expenditures of the government, and its resources were now to be taxed to the last point of ingenuity to make for the next fiscal year the necessary provision of four hundred and eighty millions of dollars, out of an actual revenue the first quarter of which had not exceeded five millions. The ordinary expenditures of the Federal government for the fiscal year ending June 30th, 1862, were estimated at eighty millions of dollars; the extraordinary expenditures, on the basis of increased military operations, at four hundred millions. To meet these large demands of the civil and war service, Secretary

Chase confessed to a receipt of but five millions per quarter from the "Morrill" tariff, showing that at this rate of the receipt of customs, the income of the government would be twenty millions per year against nearly five hundred millions of prospective outlay.

It was proposed in this financial exigency to levy specific duties of about thirty-three per cent. on coffee, tea, sugar, molasses, and syrup, which might yield twenty millions a year; it was hoped by some modification of the Morrill tariff, with respect to other articles, to increase its productiveness from twenty to thirty-seven millions; the revenue from the sale of public lands was estimated at three millions; and it was timidly proposed that a tax should be levied upon real property of one-third or one-fifth of one per cent., to produce twenty millions additional. Thus by means of—

The Tariff,	$37,000,000
Tea, Sugar, and Coffee,	20,000,000
Public Lands,	3,000,000
Direct Taxes,	20,000,000
Producing a total of	$80,000,000

The Northern government proposed to eke out the means of meeting its ordinary expenses, leaving the monstrous balance of four hundred millions of dollars to be raised by a sale of bonds.

The financial complications of the government of Mr. Lincoln were in striking contrast with the abundant and easy means which the Southern Confederacy had, at least so far, been able to carry on the war. The latter had been reduced to a paper currency, but it had for the basis of its currency the great staple of cotton,* which in the shape of a produce loan was practically pledged to the redemption of the public debt.

---

* The whole cotton crop of America, in 1860, was 4,675,770 bales and of this, 3,697,727 bales were exported, and 978,043 bales used at home. England alone took 2,582,000 bales, which amounted to about four-fifths of her entire consumption. The cotton-fields of the Southern States embrace an area of 500,000 square miles, and the capital invested in the cultivation of the plant amounts to $900,000,000. Seventy years ago, the exports of our cotton were only 420 bales—not one-tenth of the amount furnished by several countries to England. Now, the South furnishes five-sevenths of the surplus cotton product of the entire world

Prospects were entertained of a speedy raising of the blockade, the disappointment of which, at a later day, drove the Con federacy to other expedients of revenue, in a war tax, &c.; but, at the time of the comparison of the financial condition of the two governments, the Confederate currency was accounted quite as good as gold, as the cotton and tobacco once in the market would afford the Southern government the instant means to discharge every cent of its indebtedness.

The Federal Congress commenced its work in a spirit that essentially tended to revolutionize the political system and ideas of the North itself. It not only voted to Mr. Lincoln the men and supplies he asked for, but the first days of its session were signalized by a resolution to gag all propositions looking towards peace, or any thing else than a prosecution of the war; by another, to approve the acts done by the President without constitutional authority, including his suspension of the *habeas corpus;* and by the introduction of a bill to confiscate the property of " rebels."

The pages of history do not afford a commensurate instance of the wide opposition in the social and political directions of two nations who had so long lived in political union and intercourse as the North and the South. While the latter was daily becoming more conservative and more attached to existing institutions,* the North was as rapidly growing discontented,

---

* A type of the conservatism of the Southern revolution—its attachment to the past—was vividly displayed in the adoption of its national ensign, a blue union with a circle of stars, and longitudinal bars, red, white, and red, in place of "the stripes" of the flag of the old government. The present Confederate flag was balloted for in the Provisional Congress, and was selected by a majority of votes out of four different models. At the time of the early session of Congress at Montgomery, the popular sentiment was almost unanimous, and very urgent, that the main features of the old Federal Constitution should be copied into the new government, and that to follow out and give expression to this idea, the flag should be as close a copy as possible of the Federal ensign. A resolution was introduced in the Provisional Congress to the effect that the flag should be as little different as possible from that of the Federal government; which resolution was vigorously opposed by Mr. Miles, of South Carolina, who was then chairman of the Flag Committee. The design recommended by Mr. Miles, but voted down, has since been adopted as the battle flag of Generals Johnston and Beauregard. It is a blue *saltier* (or Maltese cross), with inner rows of stars, on a red field—the emblem of the *saltier* (*saltere*, to reap) being appropriately that of progress and power. The two other competing designs, from which our present flag was selected, were, one, an almost

restless, radical, and revolutionary. The people of the North had passed the stage of pure Democracy, and inaugurated military despotism. They, in effect, had changed their form of government, while vainly attempting to preserve their territorial ascendency. They charged the South with attempting revolution, when it was only fighting for independence; while they, themselves, actually perpetrated revolution rather than forego the advantages of a partial and iniquitous Union. The South, in the midst of a war of independence—a war waged not to destroy, but to preserve existing institutions—was recurring to the past, and proposing to revive conservative ideas rather than to run into new and rash experiments.

The war had already developed one great moral fact in the North of paramount interest. It was the entire willingness of the people to surrender their constitutional liberties to any government that would gratify their political passions.

This peculiarity of the condition of Northern society, was more significant of its disintegration and revolutionary destiny than all the other circumstances and consequences of the war combined, in loss of trade, prostration of commerce, and poverty and hunger of the people. It was the corruption of the public virtue. The love of constitutional liberty was degraded to political hatreds. While these were gratified, the Northern people were willing to surrender their liberties to their panderers at Washington. Without protest, without opposition, in silent submission, or even in expressions stimulating and encouraging the despot who stript them of their rights, to still further excesses, they had seen every vestige of constitutional liberty swept away, while they imagined that their greed of resentment towards the South was to be satisfied to its fill. They had seen the liberties of the people strangled, even in States remaining in the Union. They had seen the writ of *habeas corpus* denied, not only by the minions of Abraham Lincoln in Maryland, but by the commanding officers of Forts Hamilton and Lafayette. They had seen, not only the rights of free speech, but the sanctity even of private correspondence, violated by the seizure

---

exact reproduction of the Federal stars and stripes, the only variation being that of a blue stripe, and the other a simple blue circle or rim, on a red field. The consideration that determined the selection of the present flag was its similarity to that of the old government.

of dispatches in their own telegraph offices. They had seen the law of the drum-head not only established in Baltimore, but measures to subvert their own municipal liberties inaugurated by a system of military police for the whole Federal Union. They had suffered without protestation these monstrous viola tions of the Constitution under which they professed to live. They had not only suffered, but had indorsed them. They had not only done this, but they had applauded in this government of Abraham Lincoln violations of honor, morality, and truth, more infamous than excesses of authority.

CHAPTER IV.

The "Grand Army" of the North.—General McDowell.—The Affair of Bull Run.—
An Artillery Duel.—THE BATTLE OF MANASSAS.—" On to Richmond."—Scenery of the
Battle-field.—Crises in the Battle.—Devoted Courage of the Confederates.—THE ROUT.
—How the News was received in Washington.—How it was received in the South.—
General Bee.—Colonel Bartow.—The Great Error.—General Johnston's Excuses for
not advancing on Washington.—INCIDENTS OF THE MANASSAS BATTLE.

THE month of July found confronting the lines of the Potomac two of the largest armies that this continent had ever
seen. The confidence of the North in the numbers, spirit, and
appointments of its "Grand Army" was insolent in the extreme. It was thought to be but an easy undertaking for it to
march to Richmond, and plant the Stars and Stripes in Capitol
Square. An advance was urged not only by the popular
clamor of " On to Richmond," but by the pressure of extreme
parties in Congress; and when it was fully resolved upon, the
exhilaration was extreme, and the prospect of the occupation
of Richmond in ten days was entertained with every variety
of public joy.

Nothing had been left undone to complete the preparations
of the Northern army. In numbers it was immense ; it was
provided with the best artillery in the world; it comprised,
besides its immense force of volunteers, all the regulars east
of the Rocky Mountains, to the number of about ten thousand,
collected since February, in the city of Washington, from Jefferson Barracks, from St. Louis, and from Fortress Monroe.
Making all allowances for mistakes, we are warranted in saying that the Northern army consisted of at least fifty-five
regiments of volunteers, eight companies of regular infantry,
four of marines, nine of regular cavalry, and twelve batteries,
forty-nine guns. This army was placed at the command of one
who was acknowledged to be the greatest and most scientific
general in the North—General McDowell. This officer had a
reputation in the army of being a stoic philosopher—a reputation sought after by a certain number of West Point pupils.

General Beauregard was fully informed of the movements of

McDowell. The vaunting and audacious declaration of the enemy's purpose to force his position, and press on to Richmond, was met by firm and busy preparations for the crisis. It was no mean crisis. It was to involve the first important shock of arms between two peoples who, from long seasons of peace and prosperity, had brought to the struggle more than ordinary resources and splendors of war.

The decisive battle was preceded by the important affair of Bull Run, a brief sketch of which, as a precursor to the events of the 21st of July, furnishes an intelligent introduction to the designs of the enemy, and alike to the complicated plan and glorious issue of the great battle that, through the sultry heats of a whole day, wrestled over the plains of Manassas.

Bull Run constitutes the northern boundary of that county which it divides from Fairfax; and on its memorable banks, about three miles to the northwest of the junction of the Manassas Gap with the Orange and Alexandria railroad, was fought the gallant action of the 18th of July. It is a small stream, running in this locality, nearly from west to east, to its confluence with the Occoquan River, about twelve miles from the Potomac, and draining a considerable scope of country, from its source in Bull Run Mountain to within a short distance of the Potomac at Occoquan. Roads traverse and intersect the surrounding country in almost every direction. The banks of the stream are rocky and steep, but abound in long-used fords. At Mitchell's Ford, the stream is about equidistant between Centreville and Manassas, some six miles apart.

Anticipating the determination of the enemy to advance on Manassas, General Beauregard had withdrawn his advanced brigades within the lines of Bull Run. On the morning of the 17th of July our troops rested on Bull Run, from Union Mill's Ford to the Stone Bridge, a distance of about eight miles. The next morning the enemy assumed a threatening attitude. Appearing in heavy force in front of the position of General Bonham's brigade, which held the approaches to Mitchell's Ford, the enemy, about the meridian, opened fire with several 20-pounder rifle guns from a hill over one and a half miles from Bull Run. At first, the firing of the enemy was at random; but, by half-past 12 P. M., he had obtained the range of our position, and poured into the brigade a slower of shot, but without injury to us in men, horses, or guns. Our fire was reserved, and our troops impatiently awaited the opportune moment.

In a few moments, a light battery was pushed forward by the enemy, whereupon Kemper's battery, which was attached to Bonham's brigade, and occupied a ridge on the left of the Centreville road, threw only six solid shot, with the remarkable effect of driving back both the battery and its supporting force. The unexpected display of skill and accuracy in our artillery held the advancing column of the enemy in check, while Kemper's pieces and support were withdrawn across Mitchell's Ford, to a point previously designated, and which commanded the direct approaches to the ford.

In the mean time, the enemy was advancing in strong columns of infantry, with artillery and cavalry, on Blackburn's Ford, which was covered by General Longstreet's brigade. The Confederate pickets fell back, silently, across the ford before the advancing foe. The entire southern bank of the stream, for the whole front of Longstreet's brigade, was covered at the water's edge by an extended line of skirmishers. Taking advantage of the steep slopes on the northern bank of the stream, the enemy approached under shelter, in heavy force, within less than one hundred yards of our skirmishers. Before advancing his infantry, the enemy maintained a fire of rifle artillery for half an hour; then he pushed forward a column of over three thousand infantry to the assault, with such a weight of numbers as to be repelled with difficulty by the comparatively small force of not more than twelve hundred bayonets, with which Brigadier-general Longstreet met him with characteristic vigor and intrepidity. The repulse of this charge of the enemy was, as an exhibition of the devoted courage of our troops, the most brilliant incident of the day. Not one yard of intrenchment or one rifle-pit protected the men at Blackburn's Ford, who, with rare exceptions, were, on that day, the first time under fire, and who, taking and maintaining every position ordered, exceeded in cool, self-possessed, and determined courage the best-trained veterans. Twice the enemy was foiled and driven back by our skirmishers and Longstreet's reserve companies. As he returned to the contest

with increased numbers, General Longstreet had been rein
forced from Early's brigade with two regiments of infantry
and two pieces of artillery. Unable to effect a passage of the
stream, the enemy kept up a scattering fire for some time.
The fire of musketry was soon silenced, and the affair became
one of artillery. The enemy was superior in the character as
well as in the number of his weapons, provided with improved
munitions and every artillery appliance, and, at the same
time, occupying the commanding position. The results of the
remarkable artillery duel that ensued were fitting precursors
to the achievements of the twenty-first of July in this unexpectedly brilliant arm of our service. In the onset, our fire
was directed against the enemy's infantry, whose bayonets,
gleaming above the tree-tops, alone indicated their presence
and force. This drew the attention of a battery placed on a
high, commanding ridge, and the duel commenced in earnest.
For a time, the aim of the adversary was inaccurate, but this
was quickly corrected, and shot fell and shells burst thick and
fast in the very midst of our battery. From the position of
our pieces and the nature of the ground, their aim could only
be directed by the smoke of the enemy's artillery; how skilfully and with what execution this was done can only be realized by an eye-witness. For a few moments, the guns of the
enemy were silenced, but were soon reopened. By direction
of General Longstreet, his battery was then advanced, by hand,
out of the range now ascertained by the enemy, and a shower
of spherical case, shell, and round-shot flew over the heads of
our gunners. From this new position our guns fired as before,
with no other aim than the smoke and flash of their adversaries' pieces, and renewed and urged the conflict with such signal vigor and effect, that gradually the fire of the enemy slackened, the intervals between their discharges grew longer and
longer, finally to cease; and we fired a last gun at a baffled
flying foe, whose heavy masses in the distance were plainly
seen to break and scatter in wild confusion and utter rout,
strewing the ground with cast-away guns, hats, blankets, and
knapsacks, as our parting shell was thrown among them.

Thus ended the brilliant action of Bull Run. The guns engaged in the singular artillery conflict on our side were three
six-pounder rifle pieces and four ordinary six-pounders, all of

Walton's battery—the Washington Artillery of New Orleans. Our casualties were unimportant—fifteen killed and fifty-three wounded. The loss of the enemy can only be conjectured; it was unquestionably heavy. In the cursory examination, which was made by details from Longstreet's and Early's brigades, on the 18th of July, of that portion of the field immediately contested and near Blackburn's Ford, some sixty-four corpses were found and buried, and at least twenty prisoners were also picked up, besides one hundred and seventy-five stands of arms and a large quantity of accoutrements and blankets.

The effect of the day's conflict was to satisfy the enemy that he could not force a passage across Bull Run in the face of our troops, and led him into the flank movement of the 21st of July and the battle of Manassas.

THE BATTLE OF MANASSAS

General Scott having matured his plan of battle, ordered General McDowell to advance on Manassas on Sunday, the 21st of July—three days after the repulse at Bull Run. The movement was generally known in Washington; Congress had adjourned for the purpose of affording its members an opportunity to attend the battle-field, and as the crowds of camp followers and spectators, consisting of politicians, fashionable women, idlers, sensation-hunters, editors, &c., hurried in carriages, omnibuses, gigs, and every conceivable style of vehicle across the Potomac in the direction of the army, the constant and unfailing jest was, that they were going on a visit to Richmond. The idea of the defeat of the Grand Army, which, in show, splendid boast, and dramatic accessaries, exceeded any thing that had ever been seen in America, seems never to have crossed the minds of the politicians who went prepared with carriage-loads of champagne for festal celebration of the victory that was to be won, or of the fair dames who were equipped with opera-glasses to entertain themselves with the novel scenes of a battle and the inevitable rout of "rebels." The indecencies of this exhibition of morbid curiosity and exultant hate are simply unparalleled in the history of civilized nations. Mr Russell, correspondent of the London *Times*, an eye-witness of the scene, describes the concourse of carriages and gayly-dressed spectators in the rear of the army on tho morning of the battle of Manassas as like a holiday exhibitior. on a race-course.

The scene was an extraordinary one. It had a beauty and grandeur, apart from the revolting spectacle of the indecent and bedizened rabble that watched from a hill in the rear of the army the dim outlines of the battle and enjoyed the nervous emotions of the thunders of its artillery. The gay uniforms of the Northern soldiers, their streaming flags and glistening bayonets, added strange charms to the primeval forests of Virginia. No theatre of battle could have been more magnificent in its addresses to the eye. The plains, broken by a wooded and intricate country, were bounded as far as the eye could reach to the west by the azure combs of the Blue Ridge. The quiet Sabbath morning opened upon the scene enlivened by moving masses of men ; the red lights of the morning, however, had scarcely broken upon that scene, with its landscapes, its forests, and its garniture, before it was obscured in the clouds of battle. For long intervals nothing of the conflict was presented, to those viewing it at a distance, but wide and torn curtains of smoke and dust and the endless beat of tho artillery.

Orders had been issued by McDowell for the Grand Army to be in motion by two o'clock on the morning of the twenty-first, and *en route* for their different positions in time to reach them and be in position by the break of day. It was also ordered that they should have four days' rations cooked and stored away in their haversacks—evidently for the purpose of gaining Manassas and holding it, until their supplies should reach them by the railroad from Alexandria. Thus stood the arrangements of the Northern forces on the evening preceding the battle of the twenty-first.

It is a remarkable circumstance of the battle of Manassas, that it was fought on our side without any other plan than to suit the contingencies arising out of the development of the enemy's designs, as it occurred in the progress of the action. Several plans of battle had been proposed by General Beauregard, but had been defeated by the force of circumstances. He had been unwilling to receive the enemy on the defensive line of Bull Run, and had determined on attacking him at

Centreville. In the mean time, General Johnston had been ordered to form a junction of his army corps with that of General Beauregard, should the movement, in his judgment, be advisable. The best service which the army of the Shenandoah could render was to prevent the defeat of that of the Potomac. To be able to do this, it was necessary for General Johnston to defeat General Patterson or to elude him. The latter course was the most speedy and certain, and was, therefore, adopted. Evading the enemy by the disposition of the advance guard under Colonel Stuart, our army moved through Ashby's Gap to Piedmont, a station of the Manassas Gap railroad. Hence, the infantry were to be transported by the railway, while the cavalry and artillery were ordered to continue their march. General Johnston reached Manassas about noon on the twentieth, preceded by the 7th and 8th Georgia regiments and by Jackson's brigade, consisting of the 2d, 4th, 5th 27th and 33d Virginia regiments. He was accompanied by General Bee, with the 4th Alabama, the 2d and two companies of the 11th Mississippi. The president of the railroad had assured him that the remaining troops should arrive during the day.

General Johnston, being the senior in rank, necessarily assumed command of all the forces of the Confederate States then concentrating at Manassas. He, however, approved the plans of General Beauregard, and generously directed their execution under his command. It was determined that the two forces should be united within the lines of Bull Run, and thence advance to the attack of the enemy, before Patterson's junction with McDowell, which was daily expected. The plan of battle was again disconcerted. In consequence of the untoward detention on the railroad of some five thousand of General Johnston's forces that had been expected to reach Manassas prior to the battle, it became necessary, on the morning of the twenty-first, before daylight, to modify the plan accepted, to suit the contingency of an immediate attack on our lines by the main force of the enemy, then plainly at hand. It thus happened that a battle ensued, different in place and circumstance from any previous plan on our side.

Our effective force of all arms, ready for action on the field on the eventful morning, was less than thirty thousand men

Our troops were divided into eight brigades, occupying the defensive line of Bull Run. Brigadier-general Ewell's was posted at the Union Mill's Ford; Brigadier-general D. R. Jones' at McLean's Ford; Brigadier-general Longstreet's at Blackburn's Ford; Brigadier-general Bonham's at Mitchell's Ford; Colonel Cocke's at Ball's Ford, some three miles above, and Colonel Evans, with a regiment and battalion, formed the extreme left at the Stone Bridge. The brigades of Brigadier-general Holmes and Colonel Early were in reserve in rear of the right.

In his entire ignorance of the enemy's plan of attack, General Beauregard was compelled to keep his army posted along the stream for some eight or ten miles, while his wily adversary developed his purpose to him. The subsequent official reports of McDowell and his officers show that that commander had abandoned his former purpose of marching on Manassas by the lower routes from Washington and Alexandria, and had resolved upon turning the left flank of the Confederates.

The fifth division of his Grand Army, composed of at least four brigades, under command of General Miles, was to remain at Centreville, in reserve, and to make a false attack on Blackburn's and Mitchell's Fords, and thereby deceive General Beauregard as to its intention. The first division, composed of at least three brigades, commanded by General Tyler, was to take position at the Stone Bridge, and feign an attack upon that point. The third division, composed of at least three brigades, commanded by Heintzelman, was to proceed as quietly as possible to the Red House Ford, and there remain, until the troops guarding that ford should be cleared away. The second division, composed of three or four brigades, commanded by Hunter, was to march, unobserved by the Confederate troops, to Sudley, and there cross over the run and move down the stream to the Red House Ford, and clear away any troops that might be guarding that point, where he was to be joined by the third or Heintzelman's division. Together, these two divisions were to charge upon, and drive away any troops that might be stationed at the Stone Bridge, when Tyler's division was to cross over and join them, and thus produce a junction of three formidable divisions of the

Grand Army across the run, for offensive operations against the forces of Genera. Beauregard, which the enemy expected to find scattered along the run for seven or eight miles—the bulk of them being at and below Mitchell's Ford, and so situated as to render a concerted movement by them utterly impracticable.

Soon after sunrise, the enemy appeared in force in front of Colorel Evans' position at the Stone Bridge, and opened a light cannonade. The monstrous inequality of the two forces at this point was not developed. Colonel Evans only observed in his immediate front the advance portion of General Schenck's brigade of General Tyler's division and two other heavy brigades. This division of the enemy's forces numbered nine thousand men and thirteen pieces of artillery—Carlisle's and Ayres' batteries—that is, nine hundred men and two six-pounders confronted by nine thousand men and thirteen pieces of artillery, mostly rifled.

A movement was instantly determined upon by General Beauregard to relieve his left flank, by a rapid, determined attack with his right wing and centre on the enemy's flank and rear at Centreville, with precautions against the advance of his reserves from the direction of Washington.

In the quarter of the Stone Bridge, the two armies stood for more than an hour engaged in slight skirmishing, while the main. body of the enemy was marching his devious way through the "Big Forest," to cross Bull Run some two miles above our left, to take our forces in flank and rear. This movement was fortunately discovered in time for us to check its progress, and ultimately to form a new line of battle nearly at right angles with the defensive line of Bull Run.

On discovering that the enemy had crossed the stream above him, Colonel Evans moved to his left with eleven companies and two field-pieces to oppose his advance, and disposed his little force under cover of the wood, near the intersection of the Warrenton turnpike and the Sudley road. Here he was attacked by the enemy in immensely superior numbers.

The enemy beginning his detour from the turnpike, at a point nearly half-way between Stone Bridge and Centreville, had pursued a tortuous, narrow track of a rarely used road, through a dense wood, the greater part of his way until near the Sudley road. A division under Colonel Hunter, of the Federal regular army, of two strong brigades, was in the ad vance, followed immediately by another division, under Colonel Heintzelman of three brigades, and seven companies of regular cavalry, and twenty-four pieces of artillery—eighteen of which were rifled guns. This column, as it crossed Bull Run, numbered over sixteen thousand men, of all arms, by their own accounts.

Burnside's brigade—which here, as at Fairfax Court-house led the advance—at about 9.45 A. M., debouched from a wood in sight of Evans' position, some five hundred yards distant from Wheat's Louisiana battalion. He immediately threw forward his skirmishers in force, and they became engaged with Wheat's command. The Federalists at once advanced, as they report officially, the 2d Rhode Island regiment volunteers, with its vaunted battery of six thirteen-pounder rifle guns. Sloan's companies of the 4th South Carolina were then brought into action, having been pushed forward through the woods. The enemy, soon galled and staggered by the fire, and pressed by the determined valor with which Wheat handled his battalion, until he was desperately wounded, hastened up three other regiments of the brigade and two Dahlgren howitzers, making in all quite three thousand five hundred bayonets and eight pieces of artillery, opposed to less than eight hundred men and two six-pounder guns.

Despite the odds, this intrepid command, of but eleven weak companies, maintained its front to the enemy for quite an hour, and until General Bee came to their aid with his command.

General Bee moving towards the enemy, guided by the firing, had selected the position near the now famous " Henry House," and formed his troops upon it. They were the 7th and 8th Georgia under Colonel Bartow, the 4th Alabama, 2d Mississippi, and two companies of the 11th Mississippi regiments, with Imboden's battery. Being compelled, however to sustain Colonel Evans, he crossed the valley, and formed on the right and somewhat in advance of his position. Here the joint force, little exceeding five regiments, with six field pieces, held the ground against about fifteen thousand Federal troops. A fierce and destructive conflict now ensued—the fire was withering on both sides, while the enemy swept our short, thin lines with their numerous artillery, which, according to their official reports, at this time consisted of at least ten rifle guns and four howitzers. For an hour did these stout-hearted men, of the blended commands of Bee, Evans, and Bartow, breast an unintermitting battle-storm, animated surely by something more than the ordinary courage of even the bravest men under fire.

Two Federal brigades of Heintzelman's division were now brought into action, led by Rickett's superb light battery of six ten-pounder rifle guns, which, posted on an eminence to the right of the Sudley road, opened fire on Imboden's battery. At this time, confronting the enemy, we had still but Evans' eleven companies and two guns—Bee's and Bartow's four regiments, the two companies 11th Mississippi under Lieutenant-colonel Liddell, and the six pieces under Imboden and Richardson. The enemy had two divisions of four strong brigades, including seventeen companies of regular infantry, cavalry, and artillery, four companies of marines, and twenty pieces of artillery. Against this odds, scarcely credible, our advance position was still for a while maintained, and the enemy's ranks constantly broken and shattered under the scorching fire of our men; but fresh regiments of the Federals came upon the field, Sherman's and Keyes' brigades of Tyler's division, as is stated in their reports, numbering over six thousand bayonets, which had found a passage across the Run, about eight hundred yards above the Stone Bridge, threatened our right.

Heavy losses had now been sustained on our side, both in numbers and in the personal worth of the slain. The 8th Georgia regiment had suffered heavily, being exposed, as it took and maintained its position, to a fire from the enemy, already posted within a hundred yards of their front and right, sheltered by fences and other cover. The 4th Alabama also suffered severely from the deadly fire of the thousands of muskets which they so dauntlessly confronted under the immediate leadership of the chivalrous Bee himself.

Now, however, with the surging mass of over fourteen thousand Federal infantry pressing on their front and under the incessant fire of at least twenty pieces of artillery, with the fresh brigades of Sherman and Keyes approaching—the latter already in musket range—our lines gave back, but under orders from General Bee.

As our shattered battalions retired, the slaughter was deplorable. They fell back in the direction of the Robinson House, under the fires of Heintzelman's division on one side, Keyes' and Sherman's brigades of Tyler's division on the other, and Hunter's division in their rear, and were compelled to engage the enemy at several points on their retreat, losing both officers and men, in order to keep them from closing in around them. Under the inexorable stress of the enemy's fire the retreat continued. The enemy seemed to be inspired with the idea that he had won the field; the news of a victory was carried to the rear, and, in less than an hour thereafter, the telegraph had flashed the intelligence through all the cities in the North, that the Federal troops were completing their victory, and premature exultations ran from mouth to mouth in Washington.

If the enemy had observed the circumstances and character of this falling back of a portion of our lines, it would have been enough to have driven him in consternation from the field. With the terrible desperation that had sustained them so long in the face of fivefold odds and the most frightful losses, our troops fell back sullenly; at every step of their retreat staying, by their hard skirmishing, the flanking columns of the enemy.

The retreat was finally arrested just in rear of the Robinson House by the energy and resolution of General Bee, assisted by the support of the Hampton Legion, and the timely arrival of Jackson's brigade of five regiments. A moment before, General Bee had been well-nigh overwhelmed by superior numbers. He approached General Jackson with the pathetic exclamation, "General, they are beating us back;" to which the latter promptly replied, "Sir, we'll give them the bayonet." General Bee immediately rallied his over-tasked troops with the words, "There is Jackson standing like a stone wall. Let us determine to die here, and we will conquer."

In the mean time, the crisis of the battle and the full development of the enemy's designs had been perceived by our generals. They were yet four miles away from the immediate field of action, having p.aced themselves on a commanding hill in rear of General Bonham's left, to observe the movements of the enemy. There could be no mistake now of the enemy's intentions, from the violent firing on the left and the immense clouds of dust raised by the march of a large body of troops from his centre. With the keenest impatience, General Beauregard awaited the execution of his orders of the morning, which were intended to relieve his left flank by an attack on the enemy's flank and rear at Centreville. As the continuous roll of musketry and the sustained din of the artillery announced the serious outburst of the battle on our left flank, he anxiously, but confidently, awaited similar sounds of conflict from our front at Centreville. When it was too late for the effective execution of the contemplated movement, he was informed, to his profound disappointment, that his orders for an advance had miscarried.

No time was to be lost. It became immediately necessary to depend on new combinations, and to meet the enemy on the field upon which he had chosen to give us battle. It was plain that nothing but the most rapid combinations and the most heroic and devoted courage on the part of our troops could retrieve the field, which, according to all military conditions, appeared to be positively lost.

About noon, the scene of the battle was unutterably sublime. Not until then could one of the present generation, who had never witnessed a grand battle, have imagined such a spectacle. The hill occupied in the morning by Generals Beauregard, Johnston, and Bonham, and their staffs, placed the whole scene before one—a grand, moving diorama. When the firing was at its height, the roar of artillery reached the hill like that of protracted thunder. For one long mile the whole valley was a boiling crater of dust and smoke. Occasionally the yells of our men, in the few instances in which the enemy fell back, rose above the roar of artillery. In the distance rose the Blue Ridge, to form the dark background of a most magnificent picture.

The condition of the battle-field was now, at the least, desperate. Our left flank was overpowered, and it became necessary to bring immediately up to their support the reserves not already in motion. Holmes' two regiments and battery of artillery, under Captain Lindsey Walker, of six guns, and Early's brigade, were immediately ordered up to support our left flank. Two regiments from Bonham's brigade, with Kemper's four six-pounders, were also called for, and General Ewell, Jones (D. R.), Longstreet, and Bonham were directed to make a demonstration to their several fronts to retain and engross the enemy's reserves, and any forces on their flank, and at and around Centreville.

Dashing on at headlong gallop, General Johnston and General Beauregard reached the field of action not a moment too soon. They were instantly occupied with the reorganization of the heroic troops, whose previous stand in stubborn and patriotic valor has nothing to exceed it in the records of history. It was now that General Johnston impressively and gallantly charged to the front, with the colors of the 4th Alabama regiment by his side. The presence of the two generals with the troops under fire, and their example, had the happiest effect. Order was soon restored. In a brief and rapid conference, General Beauregard was assigned to th command of the left, which, as the younger officer, he claimed while General Johnston returned to that of the whole field.

The battle was now re-established. The aspect of affairs was critical and desperate in the extreme.

Confronting the enemy at this time, General Beauregard's forces numbered, at most, not more than six thousand five hundred infantry and artillerists, with but thirteen pieces of artillery, and two companies of Stuart's cavalry.

The enemy's force now bearing hotly and confidently down on our position—regiment after regiment of the best-equipped men that ever took the field—according to their own official history of the day, was formed of Colonels Hunter's and Heintzelman's divisions, Colonels Sherman's and Keyes' brigades of Tyler's division, and of the formidable batteries of Ricketts, Griffin, and Arnold regulars, and 2d Rhode Island, and two Dahlgren howitzers—a force of over twenty thousand infantry, seven companies of regular cavalry, and twenty four pieces of improved artillery. At the same time, perilous, heavy reserves of infantry and artillery hung in the distance, around the Stone Bridge, Mitchell's, Blackburn's, and

Union Mill's Fords, visibly ready to fall upon us at any moment.

Fully conscious of the portentous disparity of force, General Beauregard, as he posted the lines for the encounter, spoke words of encouragement to the men to inspire their confidence and determined spirit of resistance. He urged them to the resolution of victory or death on the field. The men responded with loud and eager cheers, and the commander felt reassured of the unconquerable spirit of his army.

In the mean time, the enemy had seized upon the plateau on which Robinson's and the Henry houses * are situated—the position first occupied in the morning by General Bee, before advancing to the support of Evans—Ricketts' battery of six rifle guns, the pride of the Federalists, the object of their unstinted expenditure in outfit, and the equally powerful regular light battery of Griffin, were brought forward and placed in immediate action, after having, conjointly with the batteries already mentioned, played from former positions with destructive effect upon our forward battalions.

About two o'clock in the afternoon, General Beauregard gave the order for the right of his line, except his reserves, to advance to recover the plateau. It was done with uncommon resolution and vigor, and at the same time Jackson's brigade pierced the enemy's centre with the determination of veterans and the spirit of men who fight for a sacred cause; but it suffered seriously. With equal spirit the other parts of the line made the onset, and the Federal lines were broken and swept back at all points from the open ground of the plateau. Rallying soon, however, as they were strongly reinforced by fresh regiments, the Federals returned, and, by the weight of numbers, pressed our lines back, recovered their ground and guns, and renewed the offensive.

By this time, between half-past 2 and 3 o'clock, P. M., our reinforcements pushed forward, and directed by General Johnston to the required quarter, were at hand just as General Beauregard had ordered forward to a second effort, for the recovery of the disputed plateau, the whole line, including his

---

* These houses were small wooden buildings, occupied at the time the one by the Widow Henry and the other by the free negro Robinson.

reserve, which, at this crisis of the battle, the commander felt called upon to lead in person. This attack was general, and was shared in by every regiment then in the field, including the 6th (Fisher's) North Carolina regiment, which had just come up. The whole open ground was again swept clear of the enemy, and the plateau around the Henry and Robinson houses remained finally in our possession, with the greater part of the Ricketts and Griffin batteries. This part of the day was rich with deeds of individual coolness and dauntless conduct, as well as well-directed, embodied resolution and bravery, but fraught with the loss to the service of the country of lives of inestimable preciousness at this juncture. The brave Bee was mortally wounded at the head of the 4th Alabama and some Mississippians, in the open field near the Henry house; and, a few yards distant, Colonel Bartow had fallen, shot through the heart. He was grasping the standard of his regiment as he was shot, and calling the remnants of his command to rally and follow him. He spoke after receiving his mortal wound, and his words were memorable. To the few of his brave men who gathered around him he said, "They have killed me, but never give up the field." The last command was gallantly obeyed, and his men silenced the battery of which he died in the charge. Colonel Fisher had also been killed. He had fallen at the head of the torn and thinned ranks of his regiment.

The conflict had been awfully terrific. The enemy had been driven back on our right entirely across the turnpike, and beyond Young's Branch on our left. At this moment, the desired reinforcements arrived. Withers' 18th regiment of Cocke's brigade had come up in time to follow the charge. Kershaw's 2d and Cash's 8th South Carolina regiments arrived soon after Withers', and were assigned an advantageous position. A more important accession, however, to our forces was at hand. A courier had galloped from Manassas to report that a Federal army had reached the line of the Manassas Gap railroad, was marching towards us, and was then about three or four miles from our left flank. Instead, however, of the enemy, it was the long-expected reinforcements. General Kirby Smith, with some seventeen hundred infantry of Elzey's brigade of the Army of the Shenandoah and Beckham's battery, had reached Manassas, by railroad, at noon. His forces were instantly marched across the fields to the scene of action.

The flying enemy had been rallied under cover of a strong Federal brigade, posted on a plateau near the intersection of the turnpike and the Sudley-Brentsville road, and was now making demonstrations to outflank and drive back our left, and thus separate us from Manassas. General Smith was instructed by General Johnston to attack the right flank of the enemy, now exposed to us. Before the movement was completed, he fell severely wounded. Colonel Elzey, at once taking command, proceeded to execute it with promptness and vigor, while General Beauregard rapidly seized the opportunity, and threw forward his whole line.

About 3.30 P. M., the enemy, driven back on their left and centre, and brushed from the woods bordering the Sudley road, south and west from the Henry house, had formed a line of battle of truly formidable proportions, of crescent outline, reaching, on their left, from the vicinity of Pittsylvania (the old Carter mansion), by Matthew's and in rear of Dogan's, across the turnpike near to Chinn's house. The woods and fields were filled with their masses of infantry and their carefully preserved cavalry. It was a truly magnificent, though redoubtable spectacle, as they threw forward in fine style, on the broad gentle slopes of the ridge occupied by their main lines, a cloud of skirmishers, preparatory for another attack.

Colonel Early, who, by some mischance, did not receive orders until 2 o'clock, which had been sent him at noon, came on the ground immediately after Elzey, with Kemper's 7th Virginia, Hay's 7th Louisiana, and Barksdale's 13th Mississippi regiments. This brigade, by the personal direction of General Johnston, was marched by the Holkham house, across the fields to the left, entirely around the woods through which Elzey had passed, and under a severe fire, into a position in line of battle near Chinn's house, outflanking the enemy's right.

The enemy was making his last attempt to retrieve the day He had re-formed to renew the battle, again extending hi right with a still wider sweep to turn our left. Colonel Early was ordered to throw himself directly upon the right flank of

the enemy, supported by Colonel Stuart's cavalry and Beckham's battery. As Early formed his line, and Beckham's
pieces played upon the right of the enemy, Elzey's brigade,
Gibbons' 10th Virginia, Lieut.-colonel Stuart's 1st Maryland,
and Vaughan's 3d Tennessee regiments, and Cash's 8th and
Kershaw's 2d South Carolina, Withers' 18th and Preston's 28th
Virginia, advanced in an irregular line, almost simultaneously.
The charge made by General Beauregard in front, was sustained by the resolute attack of Early on the right flank and
rear. The combined attack was too much for the enemy. He
was forced over the narrow plateau made by the intersection
of the two roads already mentioned. He was driven into the
fields, where his masses commenced to scatter in all available
directions towards Bull Run. He had lost all the artillery
which he had advanced to the last scene of the conflict; he
had no more fresh troops to rally on, and there were no combinations to avail him to make another stand. The day was
ours. From the long-contested hill from which the enemy had
been driven back, his retreating masses might be seen to break
over the fields stretching beyond, as the panic gathered in their
rear. The rout had become general and confused; the fields
were covered with black swarms of flying soldiers, while cheers
and yells taken up along our lines, for the distance of miles,
rung in the ears of the panic-stricken fugitives.

THE ROUT.

Early's brigade, meanwhile, joined by the 19th Virginia
regiment, of Cocke's brigade, pursued the now panic-stricken
fugitive enemy. Stuart, with his cavalry, and Beckham had
also taken up the pursuit along the road by which the enemy
had come upon the field that morning; but, soon cumbered by
prisoners who thronged the way, the former was unable to attack the mass of the fast-fleeing, frantic Federals. The want
of a cavalry force of sufficient numbers made an efficient pursuit a military impossibility.

But the pressure of close and general pursuit was not neces
sary to disorganize the flight of the enemy. Capt. Kemper
pursued the retreating masses to within range of Cub Run
Bridge. Upon the bridge, a shot took effect upon the horses

of a team that was crossing. The wagon was overturned directly in the centre of the bridge, and the passage was completely obstructed. The Confederates continued to play their artillery upon the train carriages and artillery wagons, and these were reduced to ruins. Cannons and caissons, ambulances and train-wagons, and hundreds of soldiers rushed down the hill into a common heap, struggling and scrambling to cross the stream and get away from their pursuers.

The retreat, the panic, the heedless, headlong confusion was soon beyond a hope. Officers with leaves and eagles on their shoulder-straps, majors and colonels who had deserted their comrades, passed, galloping as if for dear life. Not a field-officer seemed to have remembered his duty. The flying teams and wagons confused and dismembered every corps. For three miles, hosts of the Federal troops—all detached from their regiments, all mingled in one disorderly rout—were fleeing along the road. Army wagons, sutler's teams, and private carriages choked the passage, tumbling against each other amid clouds of dust, and sickening sights and sounds. Hacks containing unlucky spectators of the late affray were smashed like glass, and the occupants were lost sight of in the *debris*. Horses, flying wildly from the battle-field, many of them in death agony, galloped at random forward, joining in the stampede. Those on foot who could catch them rode them bareback, as much to save themselves from being run over as to make quick time.

Wounded men lying along the banks—the few either left on the field or not taken to the captured hospitals—appealed, with raised hands, to those who rode horses, begging to be lifted behind ; but few regarded such petitions. Then, the artillery, such as was saved, came thundering along, smashing and overpowering every thing. The regular cavalry joined in the *mêlée*, adding to its terrors, for they rode down footmen without mercy. One of the great guns was overturned and lay amid the ruins of a caisson. Sights of wild and terrible agony met the eye everywhere. An eye-witness of the scene describes the despairing efforts of an artilleryman, who was running between the ponderous fore and after wheels of his gun-carriage, hanging on with both hands and vainly striving to jump upon the ordnance. The drivers were spurring the horses; he could not cling much longer, and a more agonized expression never fixed the features of a drowning man. The carriage bounded from the roughness of a steep hill leading to a creek; he lost his hold, fell, and in an instant the great wheels had crushed the life out of him.

The retreat did not slacken in the least until Centreville was reached. There, the sight of the reserve—Miles's brigade—formed in order on the hill, seemed somewhat to reassure the van. The rally was soon overcome by a few sharp discharges of artillery, the Confederates having a gun taken from the enemy in position. The teams and foot-soldiers pushed on, passing their own camp and heading swiftly for the distant Potomac.

The men literally screamed with rage and fright when their way was blocked up. At every shot, a convulsion, as it were, seized upon the morbid mass of bones, sinews, wood, and iron, and thrilled through it, giving new energy and action to its desperate efforts to get free from itself. The cry of "cavalry" arose. Mounted men still rode faster, shouting out, "cavalry is coming." For miles the roar of the flight might be heard. Negro servants on led-horses dashed frantically past, men in uniform swarmed by on mules, chargers, and even-draught horses, which had been cut out of carts and wagons, and went on with harness clinging to their heels as frightened as their riders. "We're whipped," "we're whipped," was the universal cry. The buggies and light wagons tried to pierce the rear of the mass of carts, which were now solidified and moving on like a glacier; while further ahead the number of mounted men increased, and the volume of fugitives became denser.

For ten miles, the road over which the Grand Army had so ately passed southward, gay with unstained banners, and flushed with surety of strength, was covered with the fragments of its retreating forces, shattered and panic-stricken in a single day.

It is impossible to conceive of a more deplorable spectacle than was presented in Washington as the remnants of the army came straggling in. During Sunday evening, it had been supposed in the streets of the Federal city that its army had won a decisive and brilliant victory. The elation was extreme. At each echo of the peals of the cannon, men were seen on the street leaping up and exclaiming—"There goes another hundred of the d——d rebels." The next morning the news of defeat was brought by the tide of the panic-stricken fugitives. One of the boats from Alexandria came near being sunk by the rush of the panic-stricken soldiers upon its decks. Their panic did not stop with their arrival in Washington. They rushed to the depot to continue their flight from Washington. The government was compelled to put it under a strong guard to keep off the fugitives who struggled to get on the Northern trains. Others fled wildly into the country. Not a few escaped across the Susquehanna in this manner, compelling the negroes they met to exchange their clothes with them for their uniforms. For four or five days, the wild and terror-stricken excitement prevailed. Many of the fugitives, with garments nearly torn from them, and covered with the blood of their wounds, thronged the streets with mutinous demonstrations. Others, exhausted with fatigue and hunger, fear and dismay upon their countenances, with torn clothing, covered with dust and blood, were to be seen in all quarters of the city, lying upon the pavements, cellar-doors, or any other spot that offered them a place for the repose which nature demanded. Many of them had nothing of the appearance of soldiers left except their be smeared and tattered uniforms. They did not pretend to ob serve any order, nor did their officers seem to exercise the least authority over them. Some recounted to horror-stricken audiences the bloody prowess of the Confederate troops. The city of Washington was for days in trembling expectation of the advance of the Confederate army, flushed with victory and intent upon planting its flag upon the summits of the Northern capital.

We had, indeed, won a splendid victory, to judge from its fruits within the limits of the battle-field. The events of the battle of Manassas were glorious for our people, and were thought to be of crushing effect upon the *morale* of our hitherto confident and overweening adversary. Our loss was considerable. The killed outright numbered 369; the wounded, 1,483 making an aggregate of 1,852. The actual loss of the enemy will never be known; it may now only be conjectured. Their abandoned dead, as they were buried by our people where they fell, unfortunately were not enumerated, but many parts of the field were thick with their corpses, as but few battle-fields have ever been. The official reports of the enemy are expressly silent on this point, but still afford us data for an approximate estimate. Left almost in the dark, in respect to the losses or Hunter's and Heintzelman's divisions—first, longest, and most hotly engaged—we are informed that Sherman's brigade— Tyler's division—suffered in killed, wounded, and missing, 609 ; that is about 18 per cent. of the brigade. A regiment of Franklin's brigade—Gorman's—lost 21 per cent. Griffin's (battery) loss was 30 per cent. ; and that of Keyes' brigade, which was so handled by its commander, as to be exposed to only occasional volleys from our troops, was at least 10 per cent. To these facts add the repeated references in the reports of the more reticent commanders, to the " murderous" fire to which they were habitually exposed—the " pistol range" vol- leys, and galling musketry, of which they speak, as scourging their ranks, and we are warranted in placing the entire loss of the Federalists at over 4,500 in killed, wounded, and prisoners, 28 pieces of artillery, about 5,000 muskets, and nearly 500,000 cartridges ; a garrison flag and 10 colors were captured on the field or in the pursuit. Besides these, we captured 64 artillery horses, with their harness, 26 wagons, and much camp equipage, clothing, and other property, abandoned in their flight.

The news of our great victory was received by the people of the South without indecent exultations. The feeling was one of deep and quiet congratulation, singularly characteristic of the Southern people. A superficial observer would have judged Richmond, the Confederate capital, spiritless under the news. There were no bells rung, no bonfires kindled, no exul tations of a mob, and none of that parade with which the North had exploited their pettiest successes in the opening of the war. But there was what superficial observation might not have apprehended and could not have appreciated—a deep, serious, thrilling enthusiasm, which swept thousands of hearts, which was too solemn for wild huzzas, and too thoughtful to be uttered in the eloquence of ordinary words. The tremulous tones of deep emotion, the silent grasp of the hand, the faces of men catching the deep and burning enthusiasm of unuttered feelings from each other, composed an eloquence to which words would have been a mockery. Shouts would have marred the solem- nity of the general joy. The manner of the reception of the news in Richmond was characteristic of the conservative and poised spirit of our government and people. The only national recognition of the victory was the passage of resolutions in the Provisional Congress, acknowledging the interposition and mercies of Providence in the affairs of the Confederacy, and recommending thanksgiving services in all the churches of the South on the ensuing Sabbath.

The victory had been won by the blood of many of our best and bravest, and the public sorrow over the dead was called upon to pay particular tributes to many of our officers who had fallen in circumstances of particular gallantry. Among others, Gen. Bee, to whose soldierly distinction and heroic services on the field justice was never fully done, until they were especially pointed out in the official reports, both of General Johnston and General Beauregard, had fallen upon the field. The deceased general was a graduate of West Point. During the Mexican war, he had served with marked distinction, winning two brevets before the close of the war; the last that of captain, for gallant and meritorious conduct in the storming of Chapultepec. His achievements since that time in wars among the Indians were such as to attract towards him the attention of his State; and in his dying hand, on the field in which he fell, he grasped the sword which South Carolina had taken pride in presenting him.

Colonel Francis S. Bartow, of Georgia, who had fallen in the same charge in which the gallant South Carolinian had received his death-wound, was chairman of the Military Committee of the Provisional Congress, and that body paid a public tribute of more than usual solemnity and eloquence to his memory.*

---

* An eloquent tribute was paid to the memory of Colonel Bartow in Congress by Mr. Mason, of Virginia, in which some interesting recitals were given of Colonel Bartow's short, but brilliant experiences of the camp. The following extract is indicative of a spirit of confidence, which was peculiarly characteristic of the officers and men alike of our army:

"While in camp, and before the advance of Patterson's column into Virginia, but while it yet hovered on the border in Maryland, watched closely by Johnston's army, I said, casually, to Colonel Bartow, 'The time is approaching when your duties will call you to meet Congress at Richmond, and I look to the pleasure of travelling there with you.' He replied, 'I don't think I can go; my duties will detain me here.' I told him that if a battle was fought between the two armies, it certainly was not then imminent, and I thought his service in Congress, and especially as chairman of the Military

The results of the victory of Manassas were, on the first days of its full announcement, received in the South as indica tive of a speedy termination of the war. The advance of our army on Washington was impatiently expected. A few days passed, and it became known to the almost indignant disappointment of the people, that our army had no thoughts of an advance upon the Northern capital, and was content to remain where it was, occupying the defensive line of Bull Run.

Much has been said and written in excuse of the palpable and great error, the perniciousness of which no one doubted after its effects were realized, of the failure of the Confederate army to take advantage of its victory, and press on to Washington, where for days there was nothing to oppose them but

---

Committee, would be even more valuable to the country in Congress, than in the field. After a pause, and with a beaming eye, he said: 'No, sir; I shall never leave this army, until the battle is fought and won.' And, afterwards, while the two armies lay in front of each other, the enemy at Martinsburg, and Johnston with his command at Bunker Hill, only seven miles apart—the enemy we knew numbered some twenty-two thousand men, while on our side we could not present against them half that number, and the battle hourly expected. His head-quarters under a tree in an orchard, and his shelter and shade from a burning sun the branches of that tree, and his table a camp chest—I joined him at dinner. Little is, of course, known of the views and purposes of a general in command, but it was generally understood that Johnston was then to give the enemy battle, should he invite it. In conversation on the chances of the fight, I said to Bartow, 'of the spirit and courage of the troops I have no doubt, but the odds against you are immense.' His prompt reply was, 'they can never whip us. We shall not count the odds. We may be exterminated, but never conquered. I shall go into that fight with a determination never to leave the field alive, but in victory, and I know that the same spirit animates my whole command. How, then, can they whip us?'

"Am I here to tell you how gallantly and truthfully he made that vow good on the bloody plain at Manassas, and how nobly the troops under his command there redeemed the pledge made for them? The 'battle was fought and won,' as he vowed at Bunker Hill, and he sealed in death his first promise in the field of war. Will you call this courage—bravery? No, no. Bartow never thought of the perils of the fight. Bravery, as it is termed, may be nothing more than nervous insensibility. With him the incentives to the battle-field were of a far different type. The stern and lofty purpose to free his country from the invader; the calm judgment of reason, paramount on its throne, overruling all other sensations; resolution and will combined to the deed, the consequence to take care of itself. There is the column of true majesty in man. Such was Bartow, and such will impartial history record him He won immortality in Fame, even at the threshold of her temple."

an utterly demoralized army, intent upon a continuance of their flight at the approach of our forces. In his official report, General Johnston insists that "no serious thoughts" were ever entertained of advancing against the capital, as it was considered certain that the fresh troops within the works were, in number, quite sufficient for their defence; and that if not, General Patterson's army would certainly reinforce them soon enough. This excuse takes no account of the utterly demoralized condition of the Northern forces at Washington; and the further explanations of the inadequate means of our army in ammunition, provisions, and transportation are only satisfactory excuses, why the toil of pursuit was not undertaken immediately after the battle, and do not answer with complete satisfaction the inquiry why an advance movement was not made within the time when means for it might have been furnished, and the enemy was still cowed, dispirited, and trembling for his safety in the refuges of Washington.

The fact is, that our army had shown no capacity to understand the extent of their fortunes, or to use the unparalleled opportunities they had so bravely won. They had achieved a victory not less brilliant than that of Jena, and not more profitable than that of Alma. Instead of entering the gates of Sebastopol from the last-named field, the victors preferred to wait and reorganize, and found, instead of a glorious and unresisting prey, a ten months' siege.

The lesson of a lost opportunity in the victory of Manassas had to be repeated to the South with additions of misfortune. For months the world was to witness our largest army in the field confronting in idleness and the demoralizations of a stationary camp an enemy already routed within twenty miles of his capital; giving him the opportunity not only to repair the shattered columns of his Grand Army, but to call nearly half a million of new men into the field; to fit out four extensive armadas; to fall upon a defenceless line of sea-coast; to open a new theatre of war in the West and on the Mississippi, and to cover the frontiers of half a continent with his armies and navies.

INCIDENTS OF THE BATTLE.

A friend, Captain McFarland, who did service in the battle of Manassas as a private in Captain Powell's Virginia cavalry, has furnished us with a diary of some thrilling incidents of the action. We use a few of them in Captain McFarland's words:

"At 8 A. M. we proceeded to take position as picket guard and videttes in a little clump of timber, about three quarters of a mile, directly in front of the Confederate earth-works at Mitchell's Ford. The picket consisted of twelve infantry and three cavalry. Having secured our horses, we lay down in the edge of the timber, and with our long-range rifles commenced to pick off such of the enemy as were sufficiently presumptuous to show themselves clear of the heavy timber which crowned the distant hill. In a short time, the enemy, being very much annoyed by our sharp shooting, ran out from the woods, both in our front and on the left, two rifle pieces, and threw their conical shells full into our covert. The pickets, however, were not dislodged. But two of our horses became frantic from the whistling and explosion of the shells, and we found it necessary to remove them. Just at this moment, a detachment of the enemy's cavalry came dashing down the road, but halted before they came within range of the muskets of the infantry. The enemy then commenced a heavy firing with artillery on our earth-works at the ford, and we retired beyond Bull Run.

In the mean time, the thunder of battle was heard on our left, and from the heights above the stream could be seen the smoke from the scene of the conflict, which, as it shifted position, showed the varying tide of conflict. Occasionally, a small white cloud of smoke made its appearance above the horizon, indicating the premature explosion of a bomb-shell; while, at painfully regular intervals, the dull, heavy report of the enemy's thirty-two pounder told us that its position remained unassailed. In the mean time, the infantry in the trenches at Mitchell's Ford were impatiently awaiting the vainly looked-for advance upon our breastworks. The enemy threw their shells continuously into this locality, but during the whole day killed only three men, and these were standing up contrary to orders. This position was commanded by the brave Brigadier-general M. L. Bonham, of South Carolina.

About 11 o'clock, the cavalry were ordered to ride to the main field of action, in the vicinity of the Stone Bridge. We set off at a dashing gallop throwing down fences and leaping ditches, in our eagerness to participate in the then raging conflict. In crossing an open field, I was, with Lieutenant Timberlake, riding at the head of a detachment, consisting of Captain Wickham's light-horse troop, and Captain E. B. Powell's company of Fairfax cavalry, when a shell was thrown at the head of the column from a rifle piece stationed at the distance of not less than two miles, and as, hurrying onward, we leaned down upon our horses, the hurtling missile passed a few inche above us, burying itself harmlessly in the soft earth on our left.

On arriving near the scene of action, we took position below the Lewis house, under cover of an abruptly rising hill. Here we remained stationary for about an hour. The enemy in the mean time, knowing our position, endeavored to dislodge us with their shells, which for some time came hissing over our heads, and exploded harmlessly in our rear. Finally, however, they lowered their guns sufficiently to cause their shot to touch the crest of the hill, and *ricochet* into our very midst, killing one man, besides wounding several, and maiming a number of horses. But we still retained our position amid the noise of battle, which now became terrific.

From the distance came the roar of the enemy's artillery, while near by our field-pieces were incessantly vomiting their showers of grape and hurling their small shell into the very teeth of the foe. At intervals, as regiments came face to face, the unmistakable rattle of the musketry told that the small-arms of our brave boys were doing deadly work. At times, we could hear wild yells and cheers which rose above the din, as our infantry rushed on to the charge. Then followed an ominous silence, and I could imagine the fierce but quiet work of steel to steel, until another cheer brought me knowledge of the baffled enemy.

Meanwhile, our reinforcements were pouring by, and pressing with enthusiastic cheers to the battle-field. On the other hand, many of our wounded were borne past us to the rear. One poor fellow was shot through the left cheek ; as he came past me, he smiled, and muttered with difficulty, " Boys, they've spoilt my beauty." He could say no more, but an expression of acute pain flitted across his face, and shaking his clenched fist in the direction of the foe, he passed on. Another came by, shot in the breast. His clothing had been stripped from over his ghastly wound, and at every breath, the warm life-blood gushed from his bosom. I rode up to him, as, leaning on two companions, he stopped for a moment to rest. " My poor fellow," said I, " I am sorry to see you thus." " Yes! yes," was his reply, " they've done for *me* now, but my father's there yet! our army's there yet! our cause is there yet!" and raising himself from the arms of his companions, his pale face lighting up like a sunbeam, he cried with an enthusiasm I shall never forget, " and Liberty's there yet !" But this spasmodic exertion was too much for him, a purple flood poured from his wound, and he swooned away. I was enthusiastic before, but I felt then as if I could have ridden singly and alone upon a regiment, regardless of all but my country's cause.

Just then, the noble Beauregard came dashing by with his staff, and the cry was raised, that part of Sherman's battery had been taken. Cheer after cheer went up from our squadrons. It was taken up and borne along the whole battle-field, until the triumphant shout seemed one grand cry of victory. At this auspicious moment, our infantry who had been supporting the batteries were ordered to rise and charge the enemy with the bayonet. With terrific yells, they rushed upon the Federal legions with an impetuosity which could not be withstood, and terror-stricken, they broke and fled like deer from the cry of wolves. Our men followed hard upon them, shouting, and driving their bayonets up to the hilt in the backs of such of the enemy as by ill luck chanced to be hindmost in the flight.

At this moment, one of Gen. Beauregard's aids rode rapidly up and spoke to Col Radford, commander of our regiment of Virginia cavalry, who immediately turned to us and shouted, " Men, now is our time !" It was the happiest moment of my life. Taking a rapid gallop, we crossed Bull Run about three-quarters of a mile below the Stone Bridge, and made for the rear of the now flying enemy. On we dashed, with the speed of the wind, our horses wild with excitement, leaping fences, ditches, and fallen trees, until we came opposite to the house of Mrs. Spindle, which was used by the enemy as a hospital, and in front of which was a small cleared space, the fence which inclosed it running next the timber. Leaping this fence, we debouched from the woods with a demoniacal yell, and found ourselves on the flank of the enemy.

The remnant of Sherman's battery was passing at the time, and thus we threw ourselves between the main body of the enemy and Sherman's battery, which, supported by four regiments of infantry, covered the retreat of the Federal army. Our regiment had divided in the charge, and our detachment now consisted of Capt. Wickham's cavalry, Capt. E. B. Powell's troop of Fairfax cavalry, the Radford Rangers, Capt. Radford, the whole led by Col. Radford.

Our onslaught was terrific. With our rifles and shot-guns, we killed forty-nine of the enemy the first discharge, then drawing our sabres, we dashed upon them, cutting them down indiscriminately.

With several others, I rode up to the door of the hospital in which a number of terrified Yankees had crowded for safety, and as they came out, we shot them down with our pistols. Happening at this moment to turn round, I saw a Yankee soldier in the act of discharging his musket at the group stationed around the door. Just as he fired, I wheeled my horse, and endeavored to ride him down, but he rolled over a fence which crossed the yard. This, I forced my horse to leap, and drawing my revolver, I shouted to him to stop; as he turned, I aimed to fire into his face, but my horse being restive, the ball intended for his brain, only passed through his arm, which he held over his head, and thence through his cap. I was about to finish him with another shot (for I had vowed to spare no prisoners that day), when I chanced to look into his face. He was a beardless boy, evidently not more than seventeen years old. I could not find it in my heart to kill him, for he plead piteously; so seizing him by the collar, and putting my horse at the speed, leaping the fence, I dragged him to our rear-guard.

Just at this moment, I saw that the enemy had unlimbered two field-pieces, and were preparing to open upon us. Capt. Radford was near me, and I pointed to the cannon. He dashed the spurs into his horse, and shouted, " Charge the battery." But only twenty of our men were near, the rest having charged the rear of the main body of the flying Federals. Besides this, the cannon were supported by several regiments of infantry. We saw our situation at a glance, and determined to retreat to the enemy's flank. We were very close to the battery, and as I wheeled my horse, I fired a shot from my revolver at the man who was aiming the piece. He reeled, grasped at the wheel, and fell. I had thrown myself entirely on the left side of my horse. my foot hanging upon the croup of the saddle, and the grape consequently passed over me. Capt. Radford was in advance of me, his horse very unruly, plunging furiously. As I rode up, he uttered a cry, and put his hand to his side. At this instant, we came to a fence, and my horse cleared it with a bound. I turned to look for Capt. Radford, but he was not visible. A grape-shot had entered just above the hip, and tearing through his bowels, passed out of his left side. He fell from his steed, which leaped the fence and ran off. The captain was found afterwards by some of Col. Munford's cavalry. He lived till sunset, and died in great agony. By this discharge were killed, besides Capt. R., a lieutenant, two non-commissioned officers, and five privates.

Having gained the flank of the enemy, I dismounted and fired for some time with my rifle into the passing columns. Suddenly I found myself entirely alone, and remounting, I rode back until I found Col. Munford's column drawn up in the woods. Not being able to find my own company, I returned to the pursuit.

Kemper's battery had dashed upon the horror-stricken foe, and opened on their rear, which was covered by the remainder of Sherman's battery, including the thirty-two pound rifle-gun, known as "Long Tom." The havoc produced was terrible. Drivers were shot from their horses, torn to pieces by the shells and shot. Cannon were dismounted, wheels smashed, horses maimed, and the road strewn with the dead. This completed the rout, and the passage of Cub Run was blocked by wagons and caissons being driven into the fords above and below the bridge, and upon the bridge itself.

The route taken by the flying enemy was blocked with dead. I saw Yankees stone-dead, without a wound. They had evidently died from exhaustion or sheer fright. Along the route we found the carriage of Governor Sprague of Rhode Island, and in it his overcoat, with several baskets of champagne. The necks of the bottles were snapped in a trice, and we drank to our victory. But our delight and pride can scarcely be imagined, when we found "Long Tom," whose whistling shells had been falling continually among us from early dawn. It was hauled back to Bull Run amid the shouts of our men, and particularly Kemper's artillery boys, who acted so well their part in causing the Federals to abandon it.

* * * * * * * * The following morning, in the dark drizzling rain, I rode over the field of battle. It was a sorrowful and terrible spectacle to behold, without the stirring excitements of battle to relieve the horrors of the ghastly heaps of dead that strewed the field. At a distance, some portions of the field presented the appearance of flower-gardens, from the gay colors of the uniforms, turbans, &c., of the dead Zouaves. The faces of many of the dead men were already hideously swollen, blotched, and blackened, from the effects of the warm, wet atmosphere of the night.

In a little clump of second-growth pines, a number of wounded had crawled for shelter. Many of our men were busy doing them offices of kindness and humanity. There was one New York Zouave who appeared to be dying; his jaws were working, and he seemed to be in great agony. I poured some water down his throat, which revived him. Fixing his eyes upon me, with a look of fierce hatred, he muttered, "You d——d rebel, if I had a musket I would blow out your infernal soul." Another pale youth was lying in the wet undergrowth, shivering in the rain, and in the cold of approaching death. He was looking wistfully towards a large, warm blanket spread across my saddle, and said in his halting, shivering breath, "I'm so cold." I spread the blanket over him, and left him to that end of his wretchedness which could not be far distant.

CHAPTER V.

Results of the Manassas Battle in the North.—General Scott.—McClellan, "the Young Napoleon."—Energy of the Federal Government.—The Bank Loan.—Events in the West.—The MISSOURI CAMPAIGN.—Governor Jackson's Proclamation.—Sterling Price.—The Affair of Booneville.—Organization of the Missouri forces.—The BATTLE OF CARTHAGE.—General McCulloch.—The BATTLE OF OAK HILL.—Death of General Lyon.—The Confederate Troops leave Missouri.—Operations in Northern Missouri.— General Harris.—General Price's march towards the Missouri.—The Affair at Drywood Creek.—The BATTLE OF LEXINGTON.—The Jayhawkers.—The Victory of " the Five Hundred."—General Price's Achievements.—His Retreat and the necessity for it.—Operations of General Jeff. Thompson in Southeastern Missouri.—The Affair of Fredericktown.—General Price's passage of the Osage River.—Secession of Missouri from the Federal Union.—Fremont superseded.—The Federal forces in Missouri demoralized.—General Price at Springfield.—Review of his Campaign.—SKETCH OF GENERAL PRICE.—Coldness of the Government towards him.

THE Northern mind demanded a distinguished victim for its humiliating defeat at Manassas. The people and government of the North had alike flattered themselves with the expectation of possessing Richmond by midsummer ; their forces were said to be invincible, and their ears were not open to any report or suggestion of a possible disaster. On the night of the 21st of July, the inhabitants of the Northern cities had slept upon the assurances of victory. It would be idle to attempt a description of their disappointment and consternation on the succeeding day.

The Northern newspapers were forced to the acknowledgment of a disaster at once humiliating and terrible. They assigned various causes for it. Among these were the non-arrival of General Patterson and the incompetence of their general officers. The favorite explanation of the disaster was, however, the premature advance of the army under General Scott's direction ; although the fact was, that the advance movement had been undertaken from the pressure of popular clamor in the North.

The clamor was now for new commanders. It came from the army and the people indiscriminately. The commander-in-chief, General Scott, was said to be impaired in his faculties by age, and it was urged that he should be made to yield the command to a younger and more efficient spirit. The railing accusations against General Scott were made by Northern journals that had, before the issue of Manassas, declared him to be the " Greatest Captain of the Age," and without a rival among modern military chieftains. It was thought no alleviation of the matter that he was not advised, as his friends represented, of the strength of " the rebels." It was his business to have known it, and to have calculated the result.

General Scott cringed at the lash of popular indignation with a humiliation painful to behold. He was not great in misfortune. In a scene with President Lincoln, the incidents of which were related in the Federal House of Representatives by General Richardson, of Illinois, he declared that he had acted " the coward," in yielding to popular clamor for an advance movement, and sought in this wretched and infamous confession the mercy of demagogues who insulted his fallen fortunes.

The call for a " younger general" to take command of the Federal forces was promptly responded to by the appointment of General G. B. McClellan to the command of the Army of the Potomac. The understanding on both sides of the line was, that General Scott was virtually superseded by the Federal government, so far as the responsibility of active service was concerned, though he retained his nominal position and pay as lieutenant-general and commander-in-chief of the Army of the United States. The unfortunate commander experienced the deep humiliation and disgrace of being adjudged incompetent by the North, whose cause he had unnaturally espoused, and whose armies he had sent into the field as invaders of the land of his birth. The retribution was righteous. No penalties of fortune were too severe for a general who had led or directed an army to trample upon the graves of his sires and to despoil the homes of his kindred and country.

General McClellan had been lifted into an immense popularity by his successes in Northwestern Virginia, in the affair of Rich Mountain and the pursuit of General Garnett, which Northern exaggeration had transformed into great victories. For weeks he had been the object of a " sensation." His name was displayed in New York, on placards, on banners, and in newspaper headings, with the phrase, " McClellan—two victories in one day." The newspapers gave him the title of "the Young Napoleon," and in the South the title was derisively perpetuated. He was only thirty-five years of age—small in stature, with black hair and moustaches, and a remarkable military precision of manner. He was a pupil of West Point, and had been one of the American Military Commission to the Crimea. When appointed major-general of volunteers by Governor Dennison, of Ohio, he had resigned from the army, and was superintendent of the Ohio and Mississippi railroad, a dilapidated concern. There is no reason to suppose that the man who was appointed to the responsible and onerous command of the Army of the Potomac was any thing more than the creature of a feeble popular applause.

A leading Southern newspaper had declared, on the announcement of the complete and brilliant victory at Manassas, " the independence of the Confederacy is secured." There could not have been a greater mistake. The active and elastic spirit of the North was soon at work to repair its fortunes; and time and opportunity were given it by the South, not only to recover lost resources, but to invent new. The government at Washington displayed an energy which, perhaps, is the most remarkable phenomenon in the whole history of the war: it multiplied its armies; it reassured the confidence of the people; it recovered itself from financial straits which were almost thought to be hopeless, and while the politicians of the South were declaring that the Federal treasury was bankrupt, it negotiated a loan of one hundred and fifty millions of dollars from the banks of New York, Philadelphia, and Boston, at a rate but a fraction above that of legal interest in the State of New York.

While the North was thus recovering its resources on the frontiers of Virginia and preparing for an extension of the campaign, events were transpiring in the West which were giving extraordinary lessons of example and encouragement to the Southern States bordering on the Atlantic and Gulf. These events were taking place in Missouri. The campaign in that State was one of the most brilliant episodes of the war one of the most remarkable in history, and one of the most fruitful in the lessons of the almost miraculous achievements of a people stirred by the enthusiasm of revolution. To the direction of these events we must now divert our narrative.

THE MISSOURI CAMPAIGN.

The riots in St. Louis, to which reference has already been made, were the inaugurating scenes of the revolution in Missouri. The Federal government had commenced its programme of subjugation with a high hand. On the 10th of May, a brigade of Missouri militia, encamped under the law of the State for organizing and drilling the militia, at Camp Jackson, on the western outskirts of St. Louis, had been forced to surrender unconditionally on the demand of Captain (afterwards General) Lyon of the Federal Army. In the riots excited by the Dutch soldiery in St. Louis, numbers of citizens had been murdered in cold blood; a reign of terror was established; and the most severe measures were taken by the Federal authority to keep in subjection the excitement and rage of the people. St. Louis was environed by a line of military posts; all the arms and ammunition in the city were seized, and the houses of citizens searched for concealed munitions of war. The idea of any successful resistance of Missouri to the Federal power was derided. "Let her stir," said the Lincolnites, "and the lion's paw will crush out her paltry existence."

The several weeks that elapsed between the fall of Fort Sumter and the early part of June were occupied by the Secessionists in Missouri with efforts to gain time by negotiation and with preparations for the contest. At length, finding further delay impossible, Governor Jackson issued his proclamation, calling for fifty thousand volunteers. At the time of issuing this proclamation, on the 13th of June, 1861, the governor was advised of the purpose of the Federal authorities to send an effective force from St. Louis to Jefferson City, the capital of the State. He determined, therefore, to move at once with the State records to Booneville, situated on the south bank of the Missouri, eighty miles above Jefferson City. Before his departure from the latter place, he had conferred upon Sterling Price the position of major-general of the army of Missouri, and had also appointed nine brigadier-generals. These were Generals Parsons, M. L. Clark, John B. Clark, Slack, Harris, Stein, Rains, McBride, and Jeff. Thompson.

There was at the time of the issuance of this proclamation no military organization of any description in the State. Perhaps, there had not been a militia muster in Missouri for twelve or fifteen years, there being no law to require it. The State was without arms or ammunition. Such was her condition, when, with a noble and desperate gallantry that might have put to blush forever the stale and common excuse of "helplessness" for a cringing submission to tyranny, the State of Missouri determined alone and unaided to confront and resist the whole power of the North, and to fight it to the issue of liberty or death.

Orders were issued by General Price, at Jefferson City, to the several brigadiers just appointed, to organize their forces as rapidly as possible, and send them forward to Booneville and Lexington.

On the 20th June, General Lyon and Colonel F. P. Blair, with seven thousand Federal troops, well drilled and well armed, came up the river by vessels, and debarked about five miles below Booneville. To oppose them there the Missourians had but about eight hundred men, armed with ordinary rifles and shot-guns, without a piece of artillery, and with but little ammunition. Lyon's command had eight pieces of cannon and the best improved small-arms. The Missourians were commanded by Colonel Marmaduke, a graduate of West Point. Under the impression that the forces against him were inconsiderable, he determined to give them battle; but, upon ascertaining their actual strength, after he had formed his line, he told his men they could not reasonably hope to defend the position, and ordered them to retreat. This order they refused to obey. They declared that they would not leave the ground without exchanging shots with the enemy. The men remained on the field, commanded by their captains and by Lieutenant-colonel Horace Brand. A fight ensued of an hour and a half or more; the result of which was the killing and wounding of upwards of one hundred of the enemy, and a loss of three Missourians killed and twenty-five or thirty wounded, several of whom afterwards died. "The barefoot rebel militia," as they were sneeringly denominated, exhibited a stubbornness on the field of their first fight which greatly surprised their enemy, and, overpowered by his numbers, they retreated in safety, if not in order.

Governor Jackson and General Price arrived at Booneville, from Jefferson City, on the 18th June. Immediately after his arrival, General Price was taken down with a violent sickness, which threatened a serious termination. On the 19th, he was placed on board a boat for Lexington, one of the points at which he had ordered troops to be congregated. This accounts for his absence from the battle of Booneville.

A portion of the Missouri militia engaged in the action, from two hundred and fifty to three hundred in number, took up their line of march for the southwestern portion of the State, under the direction of Governor Jackson, accompanied by the heads of the State Department and by General J. B. Clark and General Parsons. They marched some twenty-five miles after the fight of the morning, in the direction of a place called Cole Camp, to which point it happened that General Lyon and Colonel Blair had sent from seven hundred to one thousand of their "Home Guard," with a view of intercepting the retreat of Jackson. Ascertaining this fact, Governor Jackson halted his forces for the night within twelve or fifteen miles of Camp Cole. Luckily, an expedition for their relief had been speedily organized south of Cole Camp, and was at that very moment ready to remove all obstructions in the way of their journey. This expedition, consisting of about three hundred and fifty men, was commanded by Colonel O'Kane, and was gotten up, in a few hours, in the neighborhood south of the enemy's camp. The so-called "Home Guards," consisting almost exclusively of Germans, were under the command of Colonel Cook, a brother of the notorious B. F. Cook, who was executed at Charlestown, Virginia, in 1859, as an accomplice of John Brown, in the Harper's Ferry raid. Colonel O'Kane approached the camp of the Federals after the hour of midnight. They had no pickets out, except in the direction of Jackson's forces, and he consequently succeeded in completely surprising them. They were encamped in two large barns, and were asleep when the attack was made upon them at daybreak. In an instant, they were aroused, routed, and nearly annihilated; two hundred and six of them being killed, a still larger number wounded, and upwards of one hundred taken prisoners. Colonel Cook and the smaller portion of his command made their escape. The Missourians lost four men killed and fifteen or twenty wounded. They captured three hundred and sixty-two muskets; thus partially supplying themselves with bayonets, the weapons for which they said they had a particular use in the war against their invaders. Of this success of the Missouri "rebels" there was never any account published, even in the newspapers of St. Louis.

Having been reinforced by Col. O'Kane, Governor Jackson proceeded with his reinforcements to Warsaw, on the Osage river in Benton county, pursued by Col. Totten of the Federal army, with fourteen hundred men, well armed and having several pieces of artillery. Upon the receipt of erroneous information as to the strength of Jackson's forces, derived from a German who escaped the destruction of Camp Cole, and per haps, also, from the indications of public sentiment in the country through which he marched, Col. Totten abandoned the pursuit and returned to the army under Gen. Lyon, at Booneville. Jackson's forces rested at Warsaw for two days, after which they proceeded to Montevallo, in Vernon county, where they halted and remained for six days, expecting to form a junction at that point with another column of their forces that had been congregated at Lexington, and ordered by Gen. Price to the southwestern portion of the State.

That column was under the command of Brigadier-generals Rains and Slack, and consisted of some twenty-five hundred men. Col. Prince, of the Federal army, having collected a force of four or five thousand men from Kansas, with a view of cutting them off, Gen. Price ordered a retreat to some point in the neighborhood of Montevallo. Gen. Price, still very feeble from his recent severe attack of sickness, started with one hundred men to join his forces. His object was to draw his army away from the base-line of the enemy, the Missouri river, and to gain time for the organization of his army. The column from Lexington marched forward, without blankets or clothing of any kind, without wagons, without tents, and, indeed, without any thing usually reckoned among the comforts of an army. They had to rely for subsistence on the country through which they passed—a friendly country it is true, but they had but little time to partake of hospitalities on their march, being closely pursued by the enemy. On the night of the 3d of July, the column from Lexington formed a junction with Jackson's forces in Cedar county.

That night, under orders from Governor Jackson, all the men belonging to the districts of brigadier-generals then present, reported respectively to their appropriate brigadier-generals for the purpose of being organized into companies, battalions, regiments, brigades, and divisions. The result was, that about two thousand reported to Brig.-gen. Rains, six hundred to Brig.-gen. Slack, and about five hundred each to Brigadier-generals J. B. Clark and Parsons; making an entire force of about three thousand six hundred men. Some five or six hundred of the number were, however, entirely unarmed; and the common rifle and the shot-gun constituted the weapons of the armed men, with the exception of the comparatively few who carried the muskets taken in the fight at Cole Camp. The army was organized by 12 o'clock, the 4th of July, and in one hour thereafter, it took up the line of march for the southwest.

Before leaving, Governor Jackson received intelligence that he was pursued by Gen. Lyon, coming down from a northeasterly direction, and by Lane and Sturgis from the northwest, their supposed object being to form a junction in his rear, with a force sufficiently large to crush him. He marched his command a distance of twenty-three miles by nine o'clock on the evening of the 4th, at which hour he stopped for the night. Before the next morning, he received authentic intelligence that a column of men, three thousand in number, had been sent out from St. Louis on the southwestern branch of the Pacific railroad for Rolla, under the command of Gen. Sigel, and that they had arrived at the town of Carthage, immediately in his front, thus threatening him with battle in the course of a few hours. Such was the situation of the undisciplined, badly-armed Missouri State troops, on the morning of the 5th of July; a large Federal force in their rear, pressing upon them, while Sigel in front intercepted their passage. But they were cheerful and buoyant in spirit, notwithstanding the perilous position in which they were placed. They resumed their march at two o'clock on the morning of the 5th, and proceeded, without halting, a distance of ten miles. At 10 o'clock A. M they approached a creek within a mile and a half of the enemy, whose forces were in line of battle under Sigel, in the open prairie, upon the brow of a hill, and in three detachments, numbering nearly three thousand men.

THE BATTLE OF CARTHAGE.

The Missourians arrived on their first important battle-field with a spirit undiminished by the toil of their march and their sufferings. The men were suffering terribly for water, but could find none, the enemy being between them and the creek The line of battle was formed with about twelve hundred men as infantry, commanded by Brigadier-generals J. B. Clark, Parsons, and Slack, and the remainder acting as cavalry under Brigadier-general Rains, the whole under the command of Governor Jackson. The infantry were formed, and placed in line of battle six hundred yards from the enemy, on the brow of the hill fronting his line. The cavalry deployed to the right and left, with a view of charging and attacking the enemy on his right and left wing, while the infantry were to advance from the front. Sigel had eight pieces of cannon. The Missourians had a few old pieces, but nothing to charge them with. While their cavalry were deploying to the right and left, Sigel's batteries opened upon their line with grape, canister, shell, and round-shot. The cannon of the Missourians replied as best they could. They were loaded with trace-chains, bits of iron, rocks, &c. It was difficult to get their cavalry up to the position agreed upon as the one from which a general charge should be commenced upon the foe. Sigel would turn his batteries upon them whenever they came in striking distance, causing a stampede among the horses, and subjecting the troops to a galling fire. This continued to be the case for an hour and thirty-five minutes. Owing to the difficulty of bringing the horses into position, the brigadier-generals ordered the infantry to charge the enemy, the cavalry to come up at the same time in supporting distance. They advanced in double-quick, with a shout, when the enemy retreated across Bear Creek, a wide and deep stream, and then destroyed the bridge over which they crossed. Sigel's forces retreated along the bank of the creek a distance of a mile or a mile and a half, and formed behind a skirt of timber. The Missourians had to cross an open field, exposed to a raking fire, before they could reach the corner of the woods, beyond which the enemy had formed. A number of the cavalry dismounted and acted with the infantry, thus bringing into active use nearly all the small-arms brought upon the field. They rushed to the skirt of timber, and opened vigorously upon the enemy across the stream, who returned the fire with great spirit. For the space of an hour, the fire on each side was incessant and fierce. The Missourians threw a quantity of dead timber into the stream, and commenced crossing over in large numbers, when the enemy again abandoned his position and started in the direction of Carthage, eight miles distant. A running fight was kept up all the way to Carthage, Sigel and his forces being closely pursued by the men whom they had expected to capture without a fight. At Carthage, the enemy again made a stand, forming an ambuscade behind houses, wood-piles, and fences. After a severe engagement there of some forty minutes, he retreated under cover of night in the direction of Rolla. He was pursued some three or four miles, till near nine o'clock, when the Missourians were called back and ordered to collect their wounded. They camped at Carthage that night (July 5), on the same ground that Sigel had occupied two nights before. The little army had done a brilliant day's work. They had fought an enemy from 10 A. M. to 9 P. M., killing and wounding a considerable number of his men, and driving him twelve miles on the route of his retreat. They afterwards ascertained that he continued to march all night, and did not halt till eleven o'clock the next day, nearly thirty miles from Carthage. The casualties of the day cannot be given with accuracy. The Missourians lost between forty and fifty killed, and from one hundred and twenty-five to one hundred and fifty wounded. The loss of the enemy was estimated at from one hundred and fifty to two hundred killed, and from three hundred to four hundred wounded—his killed and wounded being scattered over a space of upwards of ten miles. The Missourians captured several hundred muskets, which were given to their unarmed soldiers. The victory of Carthage had an inspiriting effect upon the Missourians, and taught the enemy a lesson of humility which he did not soon forget. It awakened the Federal commanders in Missouri to a sense of the magnitude of the work before them. When Sigel first got sight of the forces drawn up against him, he assured his men that there would be no serious conflict. He said they were coming into line like a worm-fence, and that a few grape, canister, and shell thrown into their midst, would throw them into confusion, and put them to flight. This accomplished, he would charge them with his cavalry and take them prisoners, one and all. But after carefully observing their movements for a time, in the heat of the action, he changed his tone. "Great God," he exclaimed, "was the like ever seen! Raw recruits, unacquainted with war, standing their ground like veterans, hurling defiance at every discharge of the batteries against them, and cheering their own batteries whenever discharged. Such material, properly worked up, would constitute the best troops in the world." Such was the testimony of Gen. Sigel, who bears the reputation of one of the most skilful and accomplished officers in the Federal service.

The next day, July 6th, General Price arrived at Carthage, accompanied by Brigadier-general McCulloch of the Confederate army, and Major-general Pierce of the Arkansas State forces, with a force of nearly two thousand men. These important arrivals were hailed with joy by the Missourians in camp. They were happy to see their beloved general so far restored to health as to be able to take command; and the presence of the gallant Generals McCulloch and Pierce with an effective force gave them an assurance, not to be mistaken, of the friendly feeling and intention of the Confederate government towards the State of Missouri.

On the 7th, the forces at Carthage, under their respective commands, took up the line of march for Cowskin Prairie, in McDonald county, near the Indian nation. It turned out that Lyon, Sturgis, Sweeny, and Sigel, instead of pursuing their foe, determined to form a junction at Springfield. The forces of Price and McCulloch remained at Cowskin Prairie for several days, organizing for the work before them. General Price received considerable reinforcements; making the whole numerical strength of his command about ten thousand. More than one half of the number, however, were entirely unarmed. Price, McCulloch, and Pierce decided to march upon Springfield, and attack the enemy where he had taken his position in force. To that end, their forces were concentrated at Cassville in Barry county, according to orders, and from that point they proceeded in the direction of Springfield, ninety miles distant, General McCulloch leading the advance.

Upon his arrival at Crane Creek, General McCulloch was informed by his pickets that the Federals had left Springfield, and were advancing upon him in large force, their advanced guard being then encamped within seven miles of him. For several days there was considerable skirmishing between the pickets of the two armies in that locality. In consequence of information of the immense superiority of the enemy's force, General McCulloch, after consultation with the general officers, determined to make a retrograde movement. He regarded the unarmed men as incumbrances, and thought the unorganized and undisciplined condition of both wings of the army suggested the wisdom of avoiding battle with the disciplined enemy upon his own ground, and in greatly superior numbers.

General Price, however, entertained a different opinion of the strength of the enemy. He favored an immediate advance. This policy being sustained by his officers, General Price requested McCulloch to loan a number of arms from his command for the use of such of the Missouri soldiers as were unarmed, believing that, with the force at his command, he could whip the enemy. General McCulloch declined to comply with the request, being governed, no doubt, by the same reasons which had induced him to decline the responsibility of ordering an advance of the whole command.

On the evening of the day upon which this consultation occurred, General McCulloch received a general order from General Polk, commander of the Southwestern division of the Confederate army, to advance upon the enemy in Missouri. He immediately held another consultation with the officers of the two divisions, exhibited the order he had received, and offered to march at once upon Springfield, upon condition that he should have the chief command of the army. General Price replied, that he was not fighting for distinction, but for the defence of the liberties of his countrymen, and that it mattered but little what position he occupied. He said that he was ready to surrender not only the command, but his life as a sacrifice to the cause. He accordingly did not hesitate, with a magnanimity of which history presents but few examples in military leaders, to turn over the command to General McCulloch, and to take a subordinate position in a contest in which, from the first, he was assured of victory.

On taking command, General McCulloch issued a general order, that all the unarmed men should remain in camp, and all those furnished with arms should get their guns in condition for service, provide themselves with fifty rounds of ammunition, and get in readiness to take up the line of march by twelve o'clock at night. The army was divided into three columns: the first commanded by General McCulloch, the second by General Pierce, and the third by General Price. They took up the line of march at the hour named, leaving the baggage train behind, and proceeded in the direction of Springfield. The troops were in fine condition and in excellent spirits, expecting to find the enemy posted about eight miles from their camp, on the Springfield road, where the natural defences are very strong, being a series of eminences on either side of the road. They arrived at that locality about sunrise, carefully approached it, and ascertained that the enemy had retired the previous afternoon. They followed in pursuit that day a distance of twenty-two miles, regardless of dust and heat; twelve miles of the distance without a drop of water—the troops having no canteens.

The weary army encamped on the night of the 8th at Big Spring, one mile and a half from Wilson's Creek, and ten miles and a half south of Springfield. Their baggage trains having been left behind, and their beef cattle also, the troops had not eaten any thing for twenty-four hours, and had been supplied with only half rations for ten days previous. In this exigency, they satisfied the cravings of hunger by eating green corn, without a particle of salt or a mouthful of meat. The wardrobe of the soldiers on that night was thus humorously described by one of the number: " We had not a blanket, not a tent, nor any clothes, except the few we had on our backs, and four-fifths of us were barefooted. Billy Barlow's dress at a circus would be decent in comparison with that of almost any one, from the major-general down to the humblest private."

On the next day, the army moved to Wilson's Creek and
.here took up camp, that they might be convenient to several
large fields from which they could supply themselves with
green corn, which, for two days, constituted their only repast.

Orders were issued by General McCulloch to the troops to
get ready to take up the line of march to Springfield by nine
o'clock P. M., with a view of attacking the enemy at four different points at daybreak the next morning. His effective force,
as stated by himself, was five thousand three hundred infantry,
fifteen pieces of artillery, and six thousand horsemen, armed
with flint-lock muskets, rifles, and shot-guns.

After receiving the order to march, the troops satisfied their
hunger, prepared their guns and ammunition, and got up a
dance before every camp-fire. When nine o'clock came, in
consequence of the threatening appearance of the weather, and
the want of cartridge-boxes to protect the ammunition of the
men, the order to march was countermanded, the commanding
general hoping to be able to move early the next morning.
The dance before the camp-fires was resumed and kept up
until a late hour.

THE BATTLE OF OAK HILL.

The next morning, the 10th of August, before sunrise, the
troops were attacked by the enemy, who had succeeded in
gaining the position he desired. General Lyon attacked them
on their left, and General Sigel on their right and in their
rear. From each of these points batteries opened upon them.
General McCulloch's command was soon ready. The Missourians, under Brigadier-generals Slack, Clark, McBride,
Parsons, and Rains, were nearest the position taken by General Lyon with his main force. General Price ordered them to
move their artillery and infantry rapidly forward. Advancing
a few hundred yards, he came upon the main body of the
enemy on the left, commanded by General Lyon in person
The infantry and artillery, which General Price had ordered
to follow him, came up to the number of upwards of two thousand, and opened upon the enemy a brisk and well-directed
fire. Woodruff's battery opened to that of the enemy under
Captain Totten, and a constant cannonading was kept up be-

tween these batteries during the action. Hebert's regiment of Louisiana volunteers and McIntosh's regiment of Arkansas mounted riflemen were ordered to the front, and, after passing the battery, turned to the left, and soon engaged the enemy with the regiments deployed. Colonel McIntosh dismounted his regiment, and the two marched up abreast to the fence around a large corn-field, where they met the left of the enemy already posted. A terrible conflict of small-arms took place here. Despite the galling fire poured upon these two regiments, they leaped over the fence, and, gallantly led by their colonels, drove the enemy before them back upon the main body. During this time, the Missourians, under General Price, were nobly sustaining themselves in the centre, and were hotly engaged on the sides of the height upon which the enemy was posted. Some distance on the right, General Sigel had opened his battery upon Churchill's and Green's regiments, and had gradually made his way to the Springfield road, upon each side of which the Confederates were encamped, and had established their battery in a strong position. General McCulloch at once took two companies of the Louisiana regiment which were nearest to him at the time, and marched them rapidly from the front and right to the rear, with orders to Colonel McIntosh to bring up the remainder. When they arrived near the enemy's battery, they found that Reid's battery had opened upon it, and that it was already in confusion. Advantage was taken of this, and soon the Louisianians gallantly charged upon the guns and swept the cannoneers away. Five guns were here taken, and Sigel's forces completely routed. They commenced a rapid retreat with a single gun, pursued by some companies of the Texas regiment and a portion of Colonel Major's Missouri regiment of cavalry. In the pursuit, many of the enemy were killed and his last gun captured. Having cleared their right and rear, it became necessary for the Confederate forces to direct all their attention to the centre, where General Lyon was pressing upon the Missourians with all his strength. To this point, McIntosh's regiment under Lieutenant-colonel Embry, and Churchill's regiment on foot, Gratiot's regiment, and McRae's battalion, were sent to their aid. A terrible fire of musketry was now kept up along the whole line of the hill upon which the enemy was posted. Masses of infantry fell back and again rushed forward. The summit of the hill was covered with the dead and the wounded. Both sides were fighting with desperation for the field. Carroll's and Green's regiments, led gallantly by Captain Bradfute, charged Totten's battery; but the whole strength of the enemy were immediately in the rear, and a deadly fire was opened upon them. At this critical moment, when the fortunes of the day seemed to be at the turning-point, two regiments of General Pierce's brigade were ordered to march from their position, as reserves, to support the centre. Reid's battery was also ordered to move forward, and the Louisiana regiment was again called into action on the left of it. The battle then became general, and probably, says General McCulloch, in his official report, "no two opposing forces ever fought with greater desperation; inch by inch the enemy gave way, and were driven from their position. Totten's battery fell back—Missourians, Arkansans, Louisianians, and Texans pushed forward—the incessant roll of musketry was deafening, and the balls fell thick as hailstones; but still our gallant Southerners pushed onward, and, with one wild yell, broke upon the enemy, pushing them back, and strewing the ground with their dead. Nothing could withstand the impetuosity of our final charge. The enemy fled, and could not again be rallied."

Thus ended the battle of Oak Hill, or of Wilson's Creek, as Gen. Sigel called it in his official report to the Federal authorities. It lasted about six hours. The force of the enemy was stated at from nine to ten thousand, and consisted for the most part of well-disciplined, well-armed troops, a large portion of them belonging to the old United States army. They were not prepared for the signal defeat which they suffered. Their loss was supposed to be about two thousand in killed, wounded, and prisoners. They also lost six pieces of artillery, several hundred stand of small-arms, and several of their standards. Major-general Lyon, their chief-in-command, was killed, and many of their officers were wounded—some of them high in rank. Gen. McCulloch, in his official report, stated the entire loss on the part of his command at two hundred and sixty-five killed, eight hundred wounded, and thirty missing. Of these, the Missourians, according to Gen. Price's report, lost one hundred and fifty-six killed, and five hundred and seventeen wounded.

The victory was won by the determined valor of each divi sion of the army. The troops from Texas, Arkansas, and Loui siana bore themselves with a gallantry characteristic of thei. respective States. The Missouri troops were mostly undisci- plined, but they had fought with the most desperate valor, never failing to advance when ordered. Repeatedly, during the action, they retired from their position, and then returned to it with increased energy and enthusiasm—a feat rarely per- formed by undisciplined troops. The efficiency of the double- barrel shot-gun and the walnut-stock rifle, was abundantly demonstrated—these being the only arms used by the Mis- sourians in this fight, with the exception of the four hundred muskets captured from the enemy on the two occasions already named.

Gen. Lyon, at the head of his regulars, was killed in an at- tempt to turn the wing mainly defended by the arms of the Missourians. He received two small rifle-balls or buckshot in the heart, the one just above the left nipple, the other immedi ately below it. He had been previously wounded in the leg His surgeon came in for his body, under a flag of truce, after the close of the battle, and Gen. Price sent it in his own wagon. But the enemy, in his flight, left the body unshrouded in Spring- field. The next morning, August 11th, Lieut.-col. Gustavus Elgin and Col. R. H. Mercer, two of the members of Brigadier- general Clark's staff, caused the body to be properly prepared for burial. He was temporarily interred at Springfield, in a metallic coffin procured by Mrs. Phelps, wife of John S. Phelps, a former member of the Federal Congress from that district, and now an officer in the Lincoln army. A few days after- wards, the body was disinterred and sent to St. Louis, to await the order of his relatives in Connecticut.

The death of Gen. Lyon was a serious loss to the Federals in Missouri. He was an able and dangerous man—a man of the times, who appreciated the force of audacity and quick decision in a revolutionary war. To military education and talents, he united a rare energy and promptitude. No doubts or scruples unsettled his mind. A Connecticut Yankee, without a trace of chivalric feeling or personal sensibility—one of those whc

submit to insult with indifference, yet are brave on the field—
he was this exception to the politics of the late regular army
of the United States, that he was an unmitigated, undisguised,
and fanatical Abolitionist.

Shortly after the battle of Oak Hill, the Confederate army
returned to the frontier of Arkansas, Generals McCulloch and
Price having failed to agree upon the plan of campaign in
Missouri.

In northern Missouri, the bold and active demonstrations of
Gen. Harris had made an important diversion of the enemy in
favor of Gen. Price. These demonstrations had been so successfully made, that they diverted eight thousand men from
the support of Gen. Lyon, and held them north of the river
until after the battle of Oak Hill, thus making an important
contribution to the glorious issue of that contest.

The history of the war presents no instance of a more heroic
determination of a people to accomplish their freedom, than
that exhibted by the people of northern Missouri. Occupying
that portion of the State immediately contiguous to the Federal
States of Kansas, Iowa, and Illinois, penetrated by two lines of
railroads, intersecting at right angles, dividing the country
north and south, east and west—which lines of railroads were
seized and occupied by the enemy, even before the commencement of hostilities ; washed on every side by large, navigable
rivers in possession of the enemy ; exposed at every point to
the inroads of almost countless Federal hosts, the brave people
of northern Missouri, without preparation or organization, did
not hesitate to meet the alternative of war, in the face of a foe
confident in his numbers and resources.

On the 21st June, 1861, a special messenger from Governor
Jackson overtook, at Paris, Monroe county, Thomas A. Harris,
who was then _en route_ as a private soldier to the rendezvous
at Booneville. The messenger was the bearer of a commission
by which Thomas A. Harris was constituted Brigadier-general
of the Missouri State Guard, and assigned to the duty of organizing the forces for the defence of that portion of the State
north of the Missouri river. The commission was accompanied
by orders from Gen. Sterling Price. At the date of the delivery of the commission and orders, the affair at Booneville had
transpired, and the governor and Gen. Price, with such of the

forces as had been hastily collected, were, as already stated, in full retreat before the enemy in the direction of southwestern Missouri.

Gen. Harris was without any organized force whatever; without military supplies of any kind; without money, or any authorized agent to pledge the credit of the State. He commenced recruiting an army in the face of the enemy. At a public meeting, called by him, he delivered a stirring and patriotic address, caused the oath of allegiance to the South to be administered to himself in the most public and impressive manner, and, in turn, administered the same oath to fifty-three men, and organized them into a company, directing them to return to their homes, collect their private arms, and join him without delay. When we consider that this bold action was within three hours' march of an enemy in force, and that it invited his bitter resentment, we can rightly appreciate the heroism and self-sacrificing patriotism of the participators.

A false report of the approach of the enemy caused the evacuation of the town of Paris, where quite a number of unarmed troops had assembled. General Harris retired into a stronghold in the knobs of Salt River. He was a brigadier-general, with a command of *three men*, and a few officers whom he had appointed upon his staff. Here, without blankets, tents, or any kind of army equipments, he commenced the organization of a guerrilla force, which was destined to render important service in the progress of the war in Missouri.

Gen. Harris adopted the policy of secretly organizing his force, the necessity for such secrecy being constantly induced by the continued presence and close proximity of the enemy. The fact, however, that Gen. Lyon was moving to the southwest in pursuit of Gen. Price, caused him to attempt a diversion, which was successful, as has been stated, in holding a large Federal force north of the Missouri river. Although the active duties of a guerrilla campaign necessarily involved a delay in organization, yet Gen. Harris was successful in raising a force of two thousand seven hundred and thirty men in the very face of the enemy, and in crossing them over the river; and after a march of sixty-two miles, in twenty-eight hours, he united his command with Gen. Price in time to par ticipate in the memorable battle of Lexington. T) follow Gen. Price's command, to that battle-field we must now turn.

Late in August, Gen. Price abandoned by the Confederate forces, took up his line of march for the Missouri river, with an armed force of about four thousand five hundred men, and seven pieces of cannon. He continued to receive reinforcements from the north side of the Missouri river.

Hearing that the notorious trio of Abolition bandits, Jim Lane, Montgomery, and Jenison, were at Fort Scott, with a marauding force of several thousand, and not desiring them to get into his rear, he detoured to the left from his course to the Missouri river, marching directly to Fort Scott for the purpose of driving them up the river. On the 7th of September, he met with Lane about fifteen miles east of Fort Scott, at a stream called Drywood, where an engagement ensued which lasted for an hour and a half, resulting in the complete rout of the enemy. Gen. Price then sent on a detachment to Fort Scott, and found that the enemy had evacuated the place. He continued his march in the direction of Lexington, where there was a Federal army strongly intrenched, under the command of Col. Mulligan.

Gen. Fremont, who had been appointed by the Federal government to take command in the Missouri department, had inaugurated the campaign with a brutality towards his enemy a selfish splendor in his camp, and a despotism and corruption more characteristic of an Eastern satrap than an American commander in the nineteenth century. He had published a proclamation absolutely confiscating the estates and slave property of " rebels," which measure of brutality was vastly pleasing to the Abolitionists of the North, who recognized the extinction of negro slavery in the South as the essential object of the war, but was not entirely agreeable to the government at Washington, which was not quite ready to declare the extremity to which it proposed to prosecute the war.

On the 10th of September, just as General Price was about to encamp with his forces for the day, he learned that a detachment of Federal troops were marching from Lexington to Warrensburg to seize the funds of the bank in that place, and to arrest and plunder the citizens of Johnson county, in accordance with General Fremont's proclamation and instruc-

tions. Although his men were greatly fatigued by several
days' continuous and rapid marching, General Price determined to press forward, so as to surprise the enemy, if possible, at Warrensburg. After resting a few hours, he resumed
his march at sunset, and continued it without intermission till
two o'clock in the morning, when it became evident that the
infantry, very few of whom had eaten any thing for twenty-
four hours, could march no further. He then halted them,
and went forward with the greater portion of his mounted men,
till he came, about daybreak, within view of Warrensburg,
where he ascertained that the enemy had hastily fled about
midnight, burning the bridges behind him. A heavy rain
commenced about the same time. This circumstance, coupled
with the fact that his men had been fasting for more than
twenty-four hours, constrained General Price to abandon the
pursuit of the enemy that day. His infantry and artillery
having come up, he encamped at Warrensburg, where the
citizens vied with each other in feeding his almost famished
soldiers.

A violent storm delayed the march next morning till the
hour of ten o'clock. General Price then pushed rapidly forward, still hoping to overtake the enemy. Finding it impossible to do this with his infantry, he again ordered a detachment of mounted men to move forward, and placing himself at
their head, continued the pursuit to within two and a half
miles of Lexington, where he halted for the night, having
learned that the enemy's forces had all gone within the city.

THE BATTLE OF LEXINGTON.

About daybreak the next morning, a sharp skirmish took
place between the Missouri pickets and the enemy's outposts.
A general action was threatened, but General Price, being unwilling to risk an engagement when a short delay would make
success, in his estimation, perfectly certain, fell back two or
three miles, and awaited the arrival of his infantry and cavalry.
These having come up, he advanced upon the town, driving in
the Federal pickets, until he came within a short distance of
the city. Here the enemy's forces attempted to make a stand,
but they were speedily driven from every position, and com

pelled to take shelter within their intrenchments. The enemy having strongly fortified the college building, the Missourians took their position within easy range of it, and opened a brisk fire from Bledsoe's and Parsons' batteries. Finding, after sunset, that his ammunition, the most of which had been left behind in the march from Springfield, was nearly exhausted, and that his men, most of whom had not eaten any thing in thirty-six hours, required rest and food, General Price withdrew to the Fair Ground, and encamped there. His ammunition wagons having been at last brought up, and large reinforcements having come in, he again moved into town on the 18th, and commenced the final attack upon the enemy's works. Brigadier-general Rains' division occupied a strong position on the east and northeast of the fortifications, from which position an effective cannonading was kept up on the enemy by Bledsoe's battery, and another battery commanded by Capt. Churchill Clark, of St. Louis. General Parsons took his position southwest of the works. Skirmishers and sharp-shooters were sent forward from both of these divisions to harass and fatigue the enemy, and cut them off from water on the north, east, and south of the college, and did great service in the accomplishment of the purposes for which they were detached. Colonel Congreve Jackson's division, and a part of General Stein's, were posted near General Rains and General Parsons as a reserve.

Shortly after entering the city on the 18th, Colonel Rives, who commanded the fourth division in the absence of General Slack, led his regiment and Colonel Hughes' along the river bank to a point immediately beneath and west of the fortifications, General McBride's command and a portion of General Harris's having been ordered to reinforce him. Colonel Rives, in order to cut off the enemy's means of escape, proceeded down the bank of the river to capture a steamboat which was lying immediately under their guns. Just at this moment, a heavy fire was opened upon him from a large dwelling-house, known as Anderson's house, on the summit of the bluff, which the enemy was occupying as a hospital, and from which a white flag was flying. Several companies of General Harris's command and the soldiers of the fourth division, who had won much distinction in previous battles, immediately rushed upon and took the place. The important position thus secured was within one hundred and twenty-five yards of the enemy's intrenchments. A company from Colonel Hughes' regiment then took possession of the boats, one of which was freighted with valuable stores. General McBride's and General Harris's divisions meanwhile stormed and occupied the bluffs immediately north of Anderson's house. The position of these heights enabled the assailants to harass the enemy so greatly, that, resolving to regain them, he made upon the house a successful assault, and one, said General Price, which would have been honorable to him had it not been accompanied by an act of savage barbarity, the cold-blooded and cowardly murder of three defenceless men who had laid down their arms, and surrendered themselves as prisoners. The position thus retaken by the enemy was soon regained by the brave men who had been driven from it, and was thenceforward held by them to the very end of the contest.

The heights on the left of Anderson's house were fortified by our troops with such means as were at their command. On the morning of the 20th, General Price caused a number of hemp bales to be transported to the river heights, where movable breastworks were speedily constructed out of them The demonstrations of the artillery, and particularly the continued advance of the hempen breastworks, attracted the attention and excited the alarm of the enemy, who made many daring attempts to drive back the assailants. They were, however, repulsed in every instance by the unflinching courage and fixed determination of men fighting for their homes. The hempen breastworks, said General Price, were as efficient as the cotton bales at New Orleans. In these severe encounters, McBride's and Slack's divisions, and Colonel Martin Green and his command, and Colonel Boyd and Major Winston and their commands, were warmly commended for their gallant conduct.

About two o'clock in the afternoon of the 20th, and after fifty-two hours of continuous fighting, a white flag was displayed by the enemy on that part of his works nearest to Col. Green's position, and shortly afterwards another was displayed opposite to Colonel Rives' position. General Price immediately ordered a cessation of all firing, and sent forward his staff officers to ascertain the object of the flag and to open negotiations with the enemy, if such should be his desire. It was agreed that the Federal forces should lay down their arms and surrender themselves prisoners of war.

The entire loss of the Missourians in this series of battles was but twenty-five killed and seventy-two wounded. The enemy's loss was considerably larger, but cannot be stated here with accuracy. The visible fruits of the victory to the Missourians were great: about three thousand five hundred prisoners—among whom were Cols. Mulligan, Marshall, Peabody, White, Grover, Major Van Horn, and one hundred and eighteen other commissioned officers; five pieces of artillery and two mortars; over three thousand stand of infantry arms, a large number of sabres, about seven hundred and fifty horses, many sets of cavalry equipments, wagons, teams, some ammunition, more than $100,000 worth of commissary stores, and a large amount of other property. In addition to all this, General Price obtained the restoration of the great seal of the State, of the public records, and about $900,000 of which the bank at Lexington had been robbed, in accordance with Fremont's instructions. General Price caused the money to be returned at once to the bank.

In his official report of the battle of Lexington, General Price paid a high compliment to the command that had achieved such rich and substantial fruits of victory. "This victory," he wrote, "has demonstrated the fitness of our citizen soldiery for the tedious operations of a siege, as well as for a dashing charge. They lay for fifty-two hours in the open air, without tents or covering, regardless of the sun and rain, and in the very presence of a watchful and desperate foe, manfully repelling every assault and patiently awaiting my orders to storm the fortifications. No general ever commanded a braver o better army. It is composed of the best blood and bravest men of Missouri."

During the siege, quite a number of citizens came in from the neighboring country, and fought, as they expressed it, " on their own hooks." A participator in the battle tells an anecdote of an old man, about sixty years of age, who came up daily from his farm, with his walnut-stock rifle and a basket of provisions, and went to work just as if he were engaged in hauling rails or some other necessary labor of his farm. He took his position behind a large stump upon the descent of the hill on which the fortification was constructed, where he fired with deadly aim during each day of the siege.

When the surrender was made, and the forces under Colonel Mulligan stacked their arms, General Price ordered that they were not to be insulted by word or act, assigning as the reason therefor, that they had fought like brave men, and were entitled to be treated as such. When Colonel Mulligan surrendered his sword, General Price asked him for the scabbard. Mulligan replied that he had thrown it away. The general, upon receiving his sword, returned it to him, saying, he disliked to see a man of his valor without a sword. Mulligan refused to be paroled, upon the ground that his government did not acknowledge the Missourians as belligerents. While awaiting his exchange, Colonel Mulligan and his wife became the guests of General Price, the general surrendering to them his carriage, and treating them with the most civil and obliging hospitality. The captive colonel and his lady were treated by all the officers and soldiers of the Missouri army with a courtesy and kindness which they seemed to appreciate.

After the first day's conflict at Lexington, while General Price was encamped at the Fair Grounds near the city, awaiting reinforcements and preparing the renewal of the attack, an episode occurred at some distance from the city, in which the Missourians again had the satisfaction of inflicting a terrible chastisement upon the bandits of the Lane and Montgomery organization.

Gen. Price was informed that four thousand men under Lane and Montgomery were advancing from the direction of St. Joseph, on the north side of the Missouri river, and Gen. Sturgis, with fifteen hundred cavalry, was also advancing from the Hannibal and St. Joseph railroad, for the purpose of relieving the forces under Mulligan. About twenty-five hundred Missourians, under the immediate command of Col. Saunders were, at the same time, hurrying to the aid of Gen. Price, from the same direction with the Lane and Montgomery Jayhawkers; and having reached the run at Blue Mills, thirty miles above Lexington, on the 17th September, crossed over their force, except some five hundred men, in a ferry-boat. While the remainder were waiting to cross over, the Jayhawkers attacked the five hundred Missourians on the north bank or the river. The battle raged furiously for one hour on the river bottom, which was heavily timbered and in many places covered with water. The Missourians were armed with only shot-guns and rifles, and taken by surprise: no time was given them to call back any portion of their force on the south side of the river; but they were from the counties contiguous to Kansas, accustomed in the border wars since 1854 to almost monthly fights with the Kansas "Jayhawkers," under Lane, and were fired with the most intense hatred of him and of them. Gen. D. R. Atchison, former President of the United States Senate, and well known as one of the boldest leaders of the State Rights party in Missouri, had been sent from Lexington by Gen. Price to meet our troops under Col. Saunders, and hasten them on to his army. He was with the five hundred, on the north side of the river, when they were attacked, and by his presence and example cheered them in the conflict. Charging the "Jayhawkers," with shouts of almost savage ferocity, and fighting with reckless valor, the Missourians drove the enemy back a distance of ten miles, the conflict becoming a hand-to-hand fight, between detached parties on both sides. At length, unable to support the fearful fire of the Missourians at the short distance of forty yards, the enemy broke into open flight. The loss of the Jayhawkers was very considerable. Their official report admitted one hundred and fifty killed and some two hundred wounded. The entire loss of the Missourians was five killed and twenty wounded. The intelligence of this brilliant victory of "the five hundred," was received with shouts of exultation by Price's army at Lexington.

On the second day after the battle of Blue Mills, Col. Saunders, with his command, joined the army at Lexington, and fought gallantly till the surrender of the Federal garrison. In the mean time, Sturgis with his cavalry appeared on the river bank opposite Lexington, expecting to cross over in the boats of Mulligan, and reinforce him to the extent of fourteen hundred men. It happened, however, that on the day before his arrival, Gen. Price's forces had captured all of the enemy's boats and Gen. Sturgis ascertaining this fact, retreated precipi

lately in the direction from which he came. Gen. Price had
sent across the river two thousand men under Gen. Parsons, to
meet the forces under Gen. Sturgis, and they succeeded in capturing all the tents and camp equipage of that distinguished
Yankee commander. The tents were most acceptable to the
Missourians, as they were the first they had obtained in the
war, except one hundred and fifty taken at Springfield. Gen.
Sturgis did not stop in his flight for three days and three
nights.

The capture of Lexington had crowned Gen. Price's command with a brilliant victory, and so far, the Missouri campaign
had proceeded, step by step, from one success to another. It
was at this period, however, that Gen. Price found his position
one of the greatest emergency. After the victory of Lexington, he received intelligence that the Confederate forces, under
Generals Pillow and Hardee, had been withdrawn from the
southeastern portion of the State. Gen. McCulloch had retired to Arkansas. In these circumstances, Gen. Price was
left with the only forces in Missouri, to confront an enemy
seventy thousand strong, and being almost entirely without
ammunition, he was reduced to the necessity of making a
retrograde movement.

Before leaving Springfield, Gen. Price had made arrangements for an ample supply of ammunition, then at Jacksons-
port, Arkansas, to be sent to him in Missouri, Gen. McCulloch
promising to send a safe escort for it. Gen. McCulloch subsequently declined to furnish the escort and stopped the train,
assigning as the reason therefor that, under the circumstances
then existing, it would be unsafe to send it, and that Gen.
Price would be compelled to fall back from the Missouri river,
before the overwhelming forces of the enemy moving against
him under the direction of Gen. Fremont.

Having no means of transportation, except for a limited
number of men, and surrounded by circumstances of the most
painful and unlooked-for misfortune, Gen. Price was compelled
to disband a considerable portion of his forces. No occasion
could be more fraught with mortifying reflections to the brave
generous, and hopeful spirit of such a commander as Gen. Price
He had marched from success to success ; he had raised a force
from hundreds to tens of thousands ; his army had been swelled

to twenty-three thousand during his stay at Lexington, not enumerating ten thousand volunteers who had collected on the north bank of the Missouri about the period when he com- menced a retreat, compelled by emergencies which the most daring valor could no longer hope to surmount. Gen. Price advised all who could not accompany him to take care of such arms as they had, to cherish a determined spirit, and to hold themselves in readiness for another opportunity to join his standard.

In southeastern Missouri, the operations of the partisan, Jeff. Thompson, in connection with Gen. Hardee's command, had attracted some public notice from its adventure, and some incidents of interest. But the campaign in the Ozark moun- tains was not productive of any important or serious results. Gen. Thompson and his "Swamp Fox Brigade" gave many rash illustrations of daring in the face of the enemy. At one time he burnt an important railroad bridge within fifty miles of the city of St. Louis, which was swarming with Federal troops. On a march towards Fredericktown, with a force of twelve hundred men, Gen. Thompson encountered a Federal force numbering ten thousand men, which he engaged with such skill and courage as to check the enemy's pursuit and move his little force out of danger. The feat showed extraordi- nary military skill, when we consider that the small force was extricated with only twenty killed, while the loss of the enemy was counted by hundreds; and that his pursuit was baffled only from the impression of a large force opposed to him, which was given by the skilful disposition of ambuscades.

Gen. Price commenced his retreat about the 27th of Septem- ber. He sent his cavalry forward, and directed them to make a demonstration in the neighborhood of Georgetown, fifty miles from Lexington, where Fremont was concentrating his forces with a view of surrounding him. With Sturgis on the north side of the river, Lane on the west, and himself on the east, each advancing upon Lexington, Fremont expected to cut off and capture the entire force of the Missourians. Gen. Price supplied his mounted men with provisions for several days, and directed them to make demonstrations on each of the divisions of the Federals, so as to gain time for the safe retreat of his infantry and artillery. By this means, he succeeded in deceiv ing the enemy as to his real purpose; inducing Fremont. Lane, and Sturgis to believe that he was about to attack each of them. Each of them fell back, and Fremont commenced ditching.

In the mean time, Price's infantry and artillery were making the best time they could towards the south. They had to encounter a very serious obstacle in crossing streams swollen by the recent rains. The whole command, fifteen thousand strong, crossed the Osage river in two common flat-boats, constructed for the occasion by men who could boast of no previous experience either as graduates of military schools, or even as bridge builders.

Subsequently, General Fremont was fifteen days engaged in crossing at the same place, upon his pontoon bridges. The superiority of the practical man of business, over the scientific engineer and "pathfinder," was demonstrated to the great satisfaction of the Missourians.

Gen. Price continued his retreat to Neosho, at which place the Legislature had assembled, under a proclamation from Governor Jackson.

At Neosho, Gen. Price again formed a junction with Gen. McCulloch, at the head of five thousand men. The Legislature had passed the Ordinance of Secession, and elected delegates to the Provisional Congress of the Southern Confederacy; and here Gen. Price had the satisfaction of firing one hundred guns in honor of the formal secession of Missouri from the United States, to which his services in the field had more than any thing else contributed.

Gen. McCulloch remained a day or two in Neosho, and then fell back with his forces to Cassville. Price remained ten days in Neosho, and then retreated also to Cassville, and from Cassville to Pineville, in McDonald county.

Meanwhile, General Fremont, with his grand army of sixty thousand men, equipped in the most splendid and costly manner, had concentrated his forces at Springfield, throwing forward an advance of ten thousand men under Gen. Sigel to Wilson's Creek. The Missouri forces at Springfield, under the command of Col. Taylor, were ordered by General Price to fall back upon the approach of the enemy; but in leaving the town they encountered Fremont's body-guard, three times their own number, armed with Colt's rifles and commanded by Col. Zagonyi. A conflict ensued, in which fifty of the enemy were killed, and twenty-five captured, including a major. The loss of the Missourians was one killed and three wounded.

At Pineville, General Price made preparations to receive Fremont, determined not to abandon Missouri without a battle. His troops were enthusiastic and confident of success, notwithstanding the fearful superiority of numbers against them. They were in daily expectation of being led by their commander into the greatest battle of the war, when they received the unexpected intelligence that Fremont had been superseded as commander of the Federal forces. This event had the effect of demoralizing the Federal forces to such an extent, that their numbers would have availed them nothing in a fight with their determined foe. The Dutch, who were greatly attached to Fremont, broke out into open mutiny, and the acting offi cers in command saw that a retreat from Springfield was not only a wise precaution, but an actual necessity. They accord ingly left that town in the direction of Rolla, and were pur sued by Gen. Price to Oceola. From Oceola, Gen. Price fell back to Springfield, to forage his army and obtain supplies and here, for the present, we must leave the history of his cam paign. We have now traced that history to a period about the first of December.

From the 20th of June to the 1st of December, General Price's army marched over 800 miles, averaging ten thousand men during the time. What they accomplished, the reader will decide for himself, upon the imperfect sketch here given. They fought five battles, and at least thirty skirmishes, in some of which from fifty to hundreds were killed on one side or the other. Not a week elapsed between engagements of some sort. They started without a dollar, without a wagon or team, without a cartridge, without a bayonet-gun. On the first of September, they had about eight thousand bayonet-guns, fifty pieces of cannon, four hundred tents, and many other articles needful in an army; for nearly all of which they were indebted to their own strong arms in battle and to the prodigality of the enemy in providing more than he could take care of in his campaign.

Notwithstanding the great exposure to which the Missouri

troops were subjected, not fifty died of disease during their six
months' campaign, and but few were on the sick list at the close
of it. The explanation is, that the troops were all the time in
motion, and thus escaped the camp fever and other diseases
that prove so fatal to armies standing all the time in a defensive position.

SKETCH OF GENERAL PRICE.

The man who had conducted one of the most wonderful
campaigns of the war—Sterling Price—was a native of Virginia. He was born about the year 1810 in Prince Edward
county, a county which had given birth to two other military
notabilities—General John Coffee, the "right-hand man" of
General Jackson in his British and Indian campaigns, and
General Joseph E. Johnston, already distinguished as one of
the heroes of the present war.

Sterling Price emigrated to Missouri, and settled in Charlton
county, in the interior of that State, in the year 1830, pursuing the quiet avocations of a farmer.

In the year 1844, Mr. Price was nominated by his party as
a candidate for Congress, and was elected by a decided
majority. He took his seat in December, 1845 ; but having
failed to receive the party nomination in the following spring,
he resigned his seat and returned home. His course in this
respect was dictated by that conscientious integrity and high
sense of honor which have ever distinguished him in all the
relations of life. He argued that his defeat was caused either
by dissatisfaction with his course on the part of his constituents, or else by undue influences which had been brought to
bear upon the people by ambitious aspirants for the seat, who
could labor to a great advantage in their work in supplanting
an opponent who was attending to his duties at a distance from
them. If the former was the case, he was unwilling to misrepresent his constituents, who, he believed, had the right to
instruct him as to the course he should pursue; if the latter,
his self-respect would not allow him to serve a people who had
rejected him without cause, while he was doing all in his power
to advance their interests.

At the time of Mr. Price's retirement from Congress, hostili-

GEN. STERLING PRICE.

war had broken out between the United States and Mexico, and volunteers from all parts of the South were flocking to the defence of their country's flag. Mr. Jefferson Davis, of Mississippi, bred a soldier, who, like Mr. Price, was serving his first term in Congress, resigned his seat about the same time, and was soon marching at the head of a Mississippi regiment to the field, from which he was destined to return loaded with many honors. So, too, did a brave Missouri regiment call to its head her own son, who had just doffed his civil robes to enter a new and untried field of duty and honor. The regiment to which Col. Price was attached was detailed for duty in what is now the Territory of New Mexico. It was by his own arms that that province was subdued, though not without several brilliant engagements, in which he displayed the same gallantry that has so distinguished him in the present contest.

Soon after the close of the Mexican war, a violent political excitement broke out in Missouri. The slavery agitation had received a powerful impetus by the introduction into Congress of the Wilmot Proviso and other sectional measures, whose avowed object was to exclude the South from any portion of the territory which had been acquired principally by the blood of Southern soldiers. The people of the South became justly alarmed at the spread of Abolitionism at the North, and no people were more jealous of any encroachment upon the rights of the South than the citizens of Missouri, a majority of whose leading statesmen were as sound on the slavery question as those of Virginia or South Carolina. In order to cause Col. Benton, who had become obnoxious to a large portion of the Democratic party by his course on the Texas question, the Wilmot Proviso, and other measures of public policy, to resign his seat, and for the purpose of casting the weight of the State against the surging waves of Abolitionism, a series of resolutions, commonly known as the "Jackson resolutions," was introduced into the Senate at the session of 1848-9, by Claiborne F. Jackson, the present governor of Missouri, which passed both houses of the General Assembly. These resolutions were substantially the same as those introduced the year before, by Mr. Calhoun, into the Senate of the United States. From the Legislature Col. Benton appealed to the people, and made a vigorous canvass against the Jackson resolutions through out the whole State, marked by extraordinary ability and bitterness towards their author and principal supporters. The sixth resolution, which pledged Missouri to "co-operate with her sister States in any measures they might adopt," to defend their rights against the encroachments of the North, was the object of his special denunciation and his most determined opposition. He denounced it as the essence of nullification, and ransacked the vocabulary of billingsgate for coarse and vulgar epithets to apply to its author and advocates. But his herculean efforts to procure the repeal of the resolutions proved abortive. Colonel Benton was defeated for the Senate the next year by a combination of Democrats and State-Rights Whigs; and the Jackson resolutions remain on the statute book unrepealed to this day. Their author is governor of the State; their principal supporters are fighting to drive myrmidons of Abolitionism from the soil of Missouri; and how nobly the State has redeemed her pledge to "co-operate with her sister States," the glorious deeds of her hardy sons, who have fought her battles almost single-handed, who have struggled on through neglect and hardship and suffering without ever dreaming of defeat, afford the most incontestible evidence.

In the canvass of 1852, the Anti-Benton Democrats put forward Gen. Sterling Price as their choice for the office of governor, and the Bentonites supported Gen. Thomas L. Price, at that time lieutenant-governor, and now a member of Lincoln's Congress and a brigadier-general in Lincoln's army. The Anti-Bentonites triumphed, and the nomination fell on Gen. Sterling Price, who, receiving the vote of the whole Democratic party, was elected by a large majority over an eloquent and popular whig, Colonel Winston, a grandson of Patrick Henry.

The administration of Gov. Price was distinguished for an earnest devotion to the material interests of Missouri. At the expiration of his term of office, he received a large vote in the Democratic caucus for the nomination for United States senator, but the choice fell on Mr. James Green.

In the Presidential election of 1860, in common with Major Jackson, who was the Democratic candidate for governor, and a number of other leading men of his party, Ex-Governor

Price supported Mr. Douglas for the Presidency, on the ground that he was the regular nominee of the Democratic party. He moreover considered Mr. Douglas true to the institutions of the South, and believed him to be the only one of the candidates who could prevent the election of the Black Republican candidate. The influence of these men carried Missouri for Douglas.

Upon the election of Abraham Lincoln, the Border States were unwilling to rush into dissolution until every hope of a peaceful settlement of the question had vanished. This was the position of Missouri, to whose Convention *not a single Secessionist was elected.* Governor Price was elected from his district as a Union man, without opposition, and, on the assembling of the Convention, was chosen its President. The Convention had not been in session many weeks before the radicalism of the Black Republican administration, and its hostility to the institutions of the South, became manifest to every unprejudiced mind. The perfidy and brutality of its officers in Missouri were particularly observable, and soon opened the eyes of the people to the true objects of the Black Republican party. The State authorities decided upon resistance to the Federal government; the Governor issued his proclamation for volunteers; and of the forces raised under this call, who were denominated the Missouri State Guard, Governor Price was appointed major-general, and took the field.

The period of history has scarcely yet arrived for a full appreciation of the heroic virtues of the campaign in Missouri, especially as illustrated in the character of the chieftain whom no personal jealousies could distract or unmerited slights turn from the single course of duty and devotion to his country. He had given the government at Richmond a valuable, but distasteful lesson in the conduct of the war. He did not settle down complacently into one kind of policy, refusing to advance because he was on the defensive, but he sought the enemy wherever he could find him, fought him when ready, and retreated out of his way when not prepared. His policy was both offensive and defensive, and he used the one which might be demanded by the exigencies of his situation. He was something better than a pupil of West Point—he was a general by nature, a beloved commander, a man who illustrated the Ro man simplicity of character in the nineteenth century. His troops not only loved him, they were wildly and enthusiastic ally devoted to him. His figure in the battle-field, clothed in a common brown linen coat, with his white hair streaming in the wind, was the signal for wild and passionate cheers, and there was not one of his soldiers, it was said, but who was willing to die, if he could only fall within sight of his commander.

It is not improbable that had General Price been supported after the battle of Lexington, he would have wrung the State of Missouri from the possession of the enemy. He was forced by untoward circumstances, already referred to, to turn back in a career just as it approached the zenith of success, and he could have given no higher proof of his magnanimity than that he did so without an expression of bitterness or a word of recrimination. He bore the cold neglect of the government at Richmond and the insulting proposition which President Davis was compelled by popular indignation to abandon, to place over him, as major-general in his department, a pupil of West Point his inferior in rank, with philosophic patience and without any subtraction from his zeal for his country. When his officers expressed resentment for the injustice done him by the government, he invariably checked them: stating that there should be no controversies of this kind while the war lasted, and that he was confident that posterity would do him justice. He was more than right; for the great majority of his living countrymen did him justice, despite the detractions of jealousy in Richmond.

CHAPTER VI.

WE must return here to the narrative of the campaign in Virginia. The campaign in the western portion of the State was scarcely more than a series of local adventures, compared with other events of the war. It was a failure from the beginning—owing to the improvidence of the government, the want of troops, the hostile character of the country itself, and a singular military policy, to which we 'shall have occasion hereafter to refer.

General Wise, of Virginia, was appointed a brigadier-general without an army. He rallied around him at Richmond a number of devoted friends, and explained to them his views and pu¬poses. Cordially favoring his plans, they went into the country, and called upon the people to rally to the standard of General Wise, and enable him to prevent the approach of the enemy into the Kanawha Valley.

About the first of June, General Wise left Richmond for the western portion of the State, accompanied by a portion of his staff. At Lewisburg, he was joined by several companies raised and organized in that region. From this point, he proceeded to Charleston, in the Kanawha Valley, where he undertook, with his rare and characteristic enthusiasm, to rally the people to the support of the State. A number of them joined his command ; but the masses continued apathetic, owing to a number of adverse influences, prominent among which was the political position of George W. Summers, the most influential politician of Western Virginia, the leader of the " Union" men .n the State Convention, and a prominent delegate to the Peace Conference at Washington.

This person threw the weight of his great influence in opposition to the uprising of the people. He advised them to a strict neutrality between the public enemy and the supporters of the Confederate government. Notwithstanding all the appeals made to his patriotism, he maintained an attitude of indifference, and, by reason of the high estimation in which he was generally held by the community in which he lived, as a wise and sagacious man, he succeeded in neutralizing the greater portion of Kanawha and the adjoining counties.

Despite, however, the obstacles in his way, General Wise succeeded in raising a brigade of two thousand five hundred infantry, seven hundred cavalry, and three battalions of artil lery. Of this force, western Virginia furnished about three fifths and the east about two-fifths. On his arrival at Charleston, General Wise found C. G. Tompkins in command of a number of companies, chiefly from Kanawha and the adjacent counties. These forces, combined with those of the Wise Legion, amounted to about four thousand men.

General Wise, anxious to give an assurance of support to the strong Southern sentiment reported to exist in Gilmer and Calhoun, sent an expedition into those counties to repress the excesses of the Union men. In the mean time, the enemy had landed considerable forces at Parkersburg and Point Pleasant on the Ohio river, and had military possession of the neighboring country. His superior facilities for raising troops in the populous States of Ohio and Indiana, and his ample means of transportation by railroad through those States, and by the navigation of the Ohio and Kanawha rivers, enabled him, in a short space of time, to concentrate a large force, with adequate supplies and munitions of war, in the lower part of the Kanawha Valley.

About the middle of July, the enemy advanced up the river into the county of Putnam, and, on the 17th, Captain Patton (afterwards Colonel Patton), with a small force, met and repulsed three regiments of the enemy at Scary Creek, in Put nam county, taking prisoners Cols. Norton and Villiers of the Ohio troops, and Cols. Woodroof and Neff of the Kentucky troops. The enemy retired, and our forces remained in possession of the field. On the evening of the day of the action, General Wise sent down two regiments under Colonels Tompkins and McCausland to reinforce the troops at Scary. Upon arriving at the opposite side of the river, they found that the enemy had fallen back to his main forces under the command of General Cox.

Being unprepared to hold the position, not having the adequate supplies of men and munitions of war, the Confederates fell back in the direction of Charleston. Capt. Patton had been dangerously wounded in the action, and could not be removed from the place. Col. Norton, one of the Federal officers captured, was also wounded. He and Capt. Patton were placed in the same house, Col. Norton entering into an arrangement by which Capt. Patton was to be released by the enemy in exchange for himself. Gen. Cox, on his arrival, repudiated the understanding. He, however, released Capt. Patton on parole as soon as he had partially recovered from his wound.

After the action of Scary, the enemy's forces, which had been largely increased, steadily advanced up the valley both by land and water. Gen. Wise, however, was ready to offer battle to the enemy, and was confident of his ability to repulse him. But just about this time the news of the disaster to Gen. Garnett's command at Rich Mountain reached the Kanawha Valley, and put a new aspect upon military operations in that section. The consequences of this disaster exposed the little army of Gen. Wise to imminent peril. He was in danger of being cut off in the rear by several roads from the north west, striking the Kanawha road at various points between Lewisburg and Gauley Bridge. Under these circumstances, Gen. Wise determined to fall back with his entire force to Lewisburg, a distance of one hundred miles. This he did in good order, destroying the bridges behind him, and reaching Lewisburg about the first of August. Remaining in that vicinity some ten days, laboriously engaged in organizing his brigade, and supplying it, as far as possible, with arms and the essential materials for an active campaign, he announced himself as again prepared to take up the line of advance

About this time, General Floyd arrived at the Greenbriei White Sulphur Springs with a brigade of three regiments of infantry and a battalion of cavalry. He had been ordered, in the first instance, to proceed with his command to Jackson River, with a view to the relief of the retreating forces of Gen. Garnett; but, on his arrival at the Sweet Springs from Southampton, Virginia, Gen. Floyd's direction was changed by authority to the Kanawha Valley. After consultation between Generals Floyd and Wise in Greenbrier county, the former, who was the ranking officer, resumed his march westward, the latter following in a few days.

Gen. Floyd commenced to skirmish with the enemy's pickets at Tyree's, on the west side of the Sewell Mountain, driving them back to their command, five miles distant, with a loss of four killed and seven wounded. Upon his approach, the army retreated from Locust Lane to Hamilton's, near Hawk's Nest, Floyd's command advancing and occupying the camp of the Federals the next night. The Wise Legion also came up and occupied the same ground. The two commands then advanced to Dogwood Gap, where the road from Summersville intersects the turnpike from Lewisburg to Charleston. There two pieces of artillery were posted to keep open the line, and prevent a flanking movement from Cox's command *via* Carnifax Ferry, where there was reported to be a Federal force of several thousand. The main command then moved down to Pickett's Mills, near Hamilton's, within a few miles of the enemy's camp. At this point, information was obtained that the rear of the Confederates was threatened by Matthews' and Tyler's commands, which had occupied Carnifax Ferry (on the Gauley river), and Cross Lanes, a few miles distant therefrom. Gen. Floyd at once ordered his brigade to strike tents, and at half-past one o'clock in the morning he took up the line of march, with the view of engaging the forces of his assailants, whose object was to cut off his trains and fall upon his rear.

Gen. Wise's command was left at Pickett's Mills to hold the turnpike, and prevent a flank movement from Hawk's Nest, where the main body of Cox's forces were stationed on New River, seven miles east of Gauley Bridge.

Floyd's brigade proceeded by a rapid march, and reached Carnifax Ferry about noon of the same day. On his arrival there, he learned that the enemy had drawn in his commands at Cross Lanes and Carnifax Ferry, in anticipation of an attack at Hawk's Nest. Gen. Floyd proceeded at once to raise the boats which the enemy had sunk in the river at the ferry, and to construct other boats for crossing the river immediately, so as to occupy the strong positions which the enemy had held on the opposite side of the Gauley. In the short space of twenty-four hours, he had constructed a small batteau to carry some ten men, and had raised a ferry-boat capable of carrying fifty men and transporting his wagons, and had succeeded in ferrying over all of his infantry and two pieces of artillery. He then undertook to transport his cavalry, when an accident occurred which caused the loss of the ferry-boat and four men The boat capsized and was drawn over the rapids. By this accident, Gen. Floyd's command was severed, most of his cavalry and four pieces of artillery being left on the eastern side of the stream, while his infantry and a small portion of his cavalry had reached the opposite shore. The stream had been so swollen by recent rains as to render ferrying extremely hazardous. Gen. Floyd, from the western side, ordered the quarter-master across the river to build boats on the other side, and to convey a message to Gen. Wise informing him of the condition of the command.

In twenty-four hours, a boat was built and launched from the west side of the river, and the remainder of the artillery and cavalry and such wagons as were needful were passed over. In the mean time, Gen. Floyd was engaged in strengthening his position. His scouts were thrown out in the direction of Gauley Bridge, by way of the Summersville and Gauley turnpike, and they reported the advance of the enemy in considerable strength from Gauley, in the direction of Cross Lanes. The next evening, the enemy had advanced to Cross Lanes, within two miles of Floyd's camp. The Federal officers had heard of the casualty at the ferry, and their "Union" friends in the neighboring country had reported to them that but two hundred of the infantry and cavalry had succeeded in crossing over.

Col. Tyler, who commanded the Federals, was confident of the capture of the whole force on the western side of the river. He was sadly disappointed. Gen. Floyd had drawn up his forces in line of battle on the evening of Sunday, August 25th, and prepared for an attack. His pickets had closely scented the enemy's position. Keeping his men in line of battle all night, at four o'clock the next morning he ordered an advance upon the enemy, whose strength was estimated at from fifteen hundred to two thousand. The order was promptly obeyed. The several Virginia regiments marched by the respective routes assigned them, and succeeded in completely surprising the Federals. Col. Tyler's line of pickets did not extend more than two or three hundred yards from his camp in the direction of Carnifax Ferry. His men were found preparing their breakfasts of green corn and fresh beef—roasting their corn by the fire and broiling their beef on sharp sticks. They were encamped in separate divisions, the rear being very near the church, in the direction of Gauley, in which building Col. Tyler had taken up his quarters. Their pickets were drawn in, and the division nearest to Floyd's forces took position behind a fence, where, for a time, they stubbornly resisted the attack. They were soon dislodged, and the whole command pushed over the hills, where they broke into the most disgraceful flight, the advance of which was conspicuously led by their colonel and field-officers. The flight was one of wild consternation, many of the enemy not only throwing away their arms, but divesting themselves of hats and coats to accelerate their flight, which was continued on an uninterrupted stretch for twelve or fifteen miles.

The commander of the Federals, Col. Tyler, was an Ohio man, and was familiar with the topography of the country he had come to invade, having visited it for years in the character of a fur-dealer. On his advent in the Kanawha Valley as the commander of an invading regiment, the coarse jest was made in some of the Northern papers that he would " drive a snug business" in *rebel skins*. The joke was turned against him by the Virginia soldiers at Cross Lanes, when they captured all the baggage of the Federal command, including the colonel's shirts, who had thus narrowly escaped with his own skin. As the flying enemy dashed on, the colonel led the retreat at a considerable distance ahead of it. One of his staff, a major, in leaping a fence got his horse astride it, and had to leave him there, trusting to the fleetness of his own heels for safety.

In the affair at Cross Lanes, the enemy's loss in killed wounded, and prisoners was about two hundred. That on our side in killed and wounded did not exceed a dozen men.

Gen. Floyd proceeded to strengthen his position on the Gauley. Having succeeded in throwing his forces between Cox and Rosecrans, he set to work to bring up ten days' supplies in advance, intending to throw a portion of his command into the Kanawha Valley below Cox, with a view of cutting off his retreat. Having secured supplies sufficient to justify an advance movement, Gen. Floyd was about this time apprised of the approach of Rosecrans, by way of Suttonsville, with a large force for the relief of Cox. On the evening previous to the contemplated advance of the Confederates against Cox, about three o'clock of the 10th of September, Rosecrans, by a rapid march of sixteen miles, threw his entire force of ten regiments and several heavy batteries of artillery about Floyd's intrenchments, and commenced a vigorous attack.

The successful resistance of this attack of the enemy, in the neighborhood of Carnifax Ferry, was one of the most remarkable incidents of the campaign in Western Virginia. The force of Gen. Floyd's command was 1,740 men, and from three o'clock in the afternoon until nightfall, it sustained, with unwavering determination and the most brilliant success, an assault from an enemy between eight and nine thousand strong, made with small-arms, grape, and round-shot, from howitzers and rifled cannon.

Upon the close of the contest for the night, Gen. Floyd determined at once to cross the Gauley river, and take position upon the left bank—Gen. Wise having failed to reinforce him, and it being only a question of time when he would be compelled to yield to the superiority of numbers. The retreat across the river was accomplished by aid of a hastily constructed bridge of logs, about four feet wide, without the loss of a gun, or any accident whatever. In a continued firing upon us, by cannon and small-arms, for nearly four hours, only twenty of our men had been wounded and none killed. We had repulsed the enemy in five distinct and successive assaults, and had held him in complete check until the river was placed between him and the little army he had come in the insolent confidence of overwhelming numbers to destroy. The loss fo the enemy had been considerable, Col. Lytle, of Cincinnati, and a number of other Federal officers, having fallen in their attempts to rally their men to a successful charge. The whole loss of the enemy cannot be stated here; it was very serious, by the admission of the Cincinnati *Commercial*, and other Federal newspapers; it, unquestionably, must have amounted to several hundred in killed and wounded. Gen. Floyd was wounded by a musket-shot in the arm. His flag, which was flying at head-quarters, and his tent were riddled with balls.

At the time that information had reached Gen. Floyd of the advance of the enemy towards his position, he had dispatched orders to Gen. Wise for reinforcements, which he failed to procure. In his official report of the action, Gen. Floyd wrote to the War Department at Richmond: "I am very confident that I could have beaten the enemy and marched directly to the Valley of the Kanawha, if the reinforcements from Gen. Wise's column had come up when ordered, and the regiments from North Carolina and Georgia could have reached me before the close of the second day's conflict. I cannot express the regret which I feel at the necessity, over which I had no control, which required that I should recross the river. I am confident that if I could have commanded the services of five thousand men, instead of eighteen hundred, which I had, I could have opened the road directly into the Valley of the Kanawha." Referring to the correspondence between himself and Gen. Wise, in which the latter had declined to send forward reinforcements, Gen. Floyd indicated to the government the urgent necessity of shaping the command in the Valley of the Kanawha, so as to insure in the future that unity of action, upon which alone can rest any hope of success in military matters.

While Gen. Floyd was at Carnifax Ferry, Gen. Wise marched down to Big Creek, in Fayette county, where the enemy were in considerable force, fortified his position, and offered them battle. He hoped to obtain a position upon the flank of the enemy, and with that view, sent Col. Anderson and his regiment by an obscure county road, but did not succeed in his object. Meanwhile, with two regiments of infantry and a battery of artillery, Gen. Wise remained within a quarter of a mile of the enemy. A sharp skirmish took place, the enemy opening upon Wise's forces with artillery, doing no execution, however. The artillery of the Wise Legion replied, throwing shell, with some effect, into the enemy's lines. But the attempt to bring on a general engagement was unsuccessful, the enemy declining the offer of battle.

Gen. Floyd retreated in good order from Carnifax Ferry to the summit of Big Sewell Mountain, where he remained for three days, when, in accordance with the decision of a council of officers called by him, he ordered a retreat to Meadow Bluff, a position which, it was said, guarded all the approaches to Lewisburg and the railroad. Gen. Wise, however, who had fallen back with Gen. Floyd to Big Sewell, declined to retreat to Meadow Bluff, and proceeded to strengthen his position, which he named Camp "Defiance."

The enemy had advanced to Tyree's—a well-known public house, on the turnpike-road, in Fayette county. This country tavern had been kept for a number of years by an ancient couple, whose fidelity and services to the South were remarkable. Of the courage and adventure of Mrs. Tyree, many well-authenticated anecdotes are told. Her husband, though a very old man, had gone into the ranks of the Confederate army at the commencement of the war. The enemy, who were well-advised of the enthusiastic attachment of Mrs. Tyree to the cause of the State of Virginia, soon made her an object of their annoyances. Their first attempt was to take away the only horse the old woman had. A Federal soldier came to her house, caught her horse without her knowledge, and was about to ride him off, when she discovered the thief and demanded his business. The soldier replied that he was directed to take the horse for the purpose of "jayhawking." The words were scarcely out of his mouth, when Mrs. Tyree knocked him down with a billet of wood, stretching the ambitious "jayhawker" almost lifeless upon the ground. The horse, for further security, was locked up in the old woman's smoke-house.

On another occasion, a file of Federal soldiers proceeded to the premises of Mrs. Tyree, with the intention of driving off her cow. Discovering them, she asked what they intended to do with her cow. "We intend to drive it to camp for a beef," was the reply. Instantly, wrenching a gun from the hands of one of the soldiers, Mrs. Tyree deliberately declared that she would shoot the first man who attempted to drive the cow from her premises. " The rest of you may then kill me," she said, " if you think proper." The soldiers were baffled, and Mrs. Tyree's cow was saved.

A few nights afterwards, a number of soldiers surrounded her house, under the shelter of which was herself, her daughter, and a few faithful servants, without any male protector whatever. They ordered the family to leave, as they intended to burn the house. Mrs. Tyree positively refused to leave the house, very coolly locked all the doors, and told them if they intended to burn the building, to apply the torch without further ceremony, as she and her family were resolved to be consumed with it. The villains, hesitating at such a work of fiendish assassination, were forced to leave without putting their threat into execution. The heroic spirit of such a woman, not only protected her household, but furnished many interesting incidents to the campaign in her neighborhood, which it is not now the time to relate. It is to be regretted that her home was left within the lines of the enemy.

Having traced to a certain period, the operations in the Valley of the Kanawha, we must turn to note the movements of the army in northwestern Virginia.

After the retreat of Gen. Garnett from Rich Mountain, and the death of that officer, Gen. Lee was appointed to succeed him, and, with as little delay as possible, to repair to the scene of operations. The most remarkable circumstance of this campaign was, that it was conducted by a general who had never fought a battle, who had a pious horror of guerrillas, and whose extreme tenderness of blood induced him to depend exclusively upon the resources of strategy, to essay the achievement of victories without the cost of life.

Gen. Lee took with him reinforcements, making his whole force, in conjunction with the remnant of Gen. Garnett's army that had fallen back from Rich Mountain to Monterey, about sixteen thousand men. Early in August, Gen. Lee reached with his command the neighborhood of Cheat Mountain, on the Staunton and Parkersburg turnpike, and found it strongly fortified by the enemy. The position was known to be an exceedingly strong one, and not easily turned. Nevertheless, Gen. Lee was confident that he would be able by strategic movements to dislodge the enemy from his stronghold, capture his forces, and then march his victorious army into the heart of northwestern Virginia, releasing the people there from the fetters with which, for two months, they had been bound. The prospect of such a conquest of the enemy was eminently pleasant. Rosecrans* was the ranking officer in northwestern Virginia, but Gen. Reynolds was in command of the troops on Cheat Mountain and in its vicinity, his force being estimated at from ten to twelve thousand men.

Gen. Lee felt his way cautiously along the road leading from Huntersville to Huttonsville, in the county of Randolph, and reaching Valley Mountain, he halted for some time, arranging his plans for attacking the enemy, who were about eight miles below him, in Randolph county, at Crouch's, in Tygart's Valley River, five or six thousand strong. His plans were arranged so as to divide his forces for the purpose of surrounding the enemy. After great labor and the endurance of severe hardships on the mountain spurs, where the weather was very cold, he succeeded in getting below the enemy, on Tygart's Valley River, placing other portions of his forces on the spurs of the mountain immediately east and west of the enemy, and marching another portion of his troops down the Valley River close to the enemy. The forces were thus arranged in position for making an attack upon the enemy at Crouch's, and remained there for some hours. It was doubtless in the plan of Gen. Lee for his forces to remain in position until the consummation of another part of his plan, viz. that some fifteen hundred of Gen. H. R. Jackson's forces stationed at Greenbrier

---

* Gen. Rosecrans is of German descent, a native of Ohio, and a graduate of West Point. He had devoted much study to chemistry and geology, and resided some time in Charleston, Kanawha, prosecuting some researches into the mineral riches of that region. He was also employed in some capacity for a time by some of the coal companies or some of the coal-oil manufacturers there. His last enterprise, previous to the war, was the establishment of an oil manufactory in Cincinnati. In this he failed pecuniarily. The war was a timely event to him, and his military education gave him a claim to consideration. In the South, he was esteemed as one of the best generals the North had in the field; he was declared by military critics, who could not be suspected of partiality, to have clearly out-generalled Lee in western Virginia, who made it the entire object of his campaign to "surround" the Dutch general; and his popular manners and amiable deportment towards our prisoners, on more than one occasion, procured him the respect of his enemy.

River should march around another position of the enemy, at the celebrated Cheat Mountain Pass, on the Staunton and Parkersburg road, where he was five or six thousand strong. Jackson's forces did march around this position, under command of Col. Rust, of Arkansas, through extraordinary diffi culties and perils and under circumstances of terrible exhaustion. The troops had to ascend the almost perpendicular mountain sides, but finally succeeded in obtaining a position in front of and to the west of the enemy. The attack of this force upon the enemy on Cheat Mountain was understood to be, in the plan of Gen. Lee, a signal for the attack by his forces upon the enemy at Crouch's. Col. Rust, however, discovered the enemy on the mountain to be safely protected by block-houses and other defences, and concluding that the attack could not be made with any hope of success, ordered a retreat. The signal was not given according to the plan of Gen. Lee, and no attack was made by his forces, which retreated without firing a gun back to Valley Mountain.

It is understood that Gen. Lee did not expect Col. Rust to make an attack with any certainty or even probability of success; his purpose being for Col. Rust to hold the enemy in position at Cheat Mountain Pass, while he was engaging them at Crouch's. The fact, however, is, that Cheat Mountain Pass was, by the nearest road to Crouch's, ten miles distant; and there are strong reasons for believing that, if Gen. Lee had made the attack upon the enemy at the latter position, they would have been captured to a man, notwithstanding the failure to hold the forces in check at Cheat Mountain. Such was the impression of the Federals themselves. If the enemy had been captured at Crouch's, a march of ten miles down the Valley River by Gen. Lee would have brought his forces in the rear of the enemy at Huttonsville, cutting off his supplies, and, with Jackson on the other side, compelling him to the necessity of surrender.

It is to be regretted that Gen. Lee failed to make the attack at Crouch's, and to realize the rich results of his well-matured plan. Had he defeated the enemy at Crouch's, he would have been within two days' march of the position from which Gen Garnett had retreated, and could have held Rosecrans in check, who was at that time making his way to Carnifax Ferry to oppose Floyd. There is reason to believe that if Gen. Lee had not allowed the immaterial part of his plan to control his action, a glorious success would have resulted, opening the whole northwestern country to us, and enabling Floyd and Wise to drive Cox with ease out of the Kanawha Valley. Regrets, however, were unavailing now. Gen. Lee's plan, finished drawings of which were sent to the War Department at Richmond, was said to have been one of the best-laid plans that ever illustrated the consummation of the rules of strategy, or ever went awry on account of practical failures in its execution.

Having failed in his plans for dislodging the enemy from Cheat Mountain, and thus relieving northwestern Virginia of his presence, Gen. Lee determined to proceed to the Kanawha region, with a view of relieving Generals Floyd and Wise, and possibly driving the enemy to the extreme western borders of Virginia. Accordingly, in the latter part of September, he ordered the principal portion of his command to take up a line of march in that direction.

It has already been stated that Gen. Floyd had fallen back with his forces to Meadow Bluff, while Gen. Wise stopped to the east of the summit of Big Sewell. In this position Gen. Lee found them on his arrival. He took up his head-quarters with Gen. Floyd, and, after examining his position, proceeded to Sewell, where Gen. Wise still remained in front of the enemy. He decided to fortify Wise's position. Gen. Floyd's command, except a garrison at Meadow Bluff, returned to Big Sewell. He had been largely reinforced since he had left the Gauley river. The position on Big Sewell was made exceedingly strong by a breastwork extending four miles.

The whole Confederate force here under the command of Gen. Lee was nearly twenty thousand. This formidable army remained for twelve or fifteen days within sight of the enemy, each apparently awaiting an attack from the other. Thus the time passed, when, one morning, Gen. Lee discovered, much to his surprise, that the enemy he had been so long hesitating to attack no longer confronted him. Rosecrans had disappeared in the night, and reached his old position on the Gauley, thirty-two miles distant, without annoyance from the Confederate army. Thus the second opportunity of a decisive

12

battle in western Virginia was blindly lost, Gen. Lee making no attempt to follow up the enemy who had so skilfully eluded him; the excuses alleged for his no⁺ doing so being mud, swol len streams, and the leanness of his artillery horses.

In withdrawing from the Cheat Mountain region, Gen. Lee had left a force of some twenty-five hundred men at Greenbrier River, and, while he was playing at strategy in the Kanawha valley, this little force had achieved a signal victory over an apparently overwhelming force of the enemy. The force on the Greenbrier at the foot of Cheat Mountain was under command of Gen. H. R. Jackson, of Georgia. A small force had also been left on the Alleghany Mountain, at Huntersville, and perhaps other localities in that region.

On the 3d of October, the enemy, thinking that he might strike a successful blow, in the absence of Gen. Lee and the 'arger portion of his command, came down from Cheat Mountain, five thousand strong, and attacked Jackson's position on the Greenbrier. The attack was gallantly repulsed. The most unusual and brilliant incident of the battle was the conduct of our pickets, who held the entire column of the enemy in check for nearly an hour, pouring into the head of it a galling fire not withdrawing until six pieces of artillery had opened briskly upon them, and full battalions of infantry were outflanking them on the right, and then retiring in such order, and taking such advantage of the ground, as to reach their camp with but a trifling loss.

The action was continued by a severe artillery engagement, when, after four hours' interchange of fire, in which we could not bring more than five pieces into action to return the fire of the enemy's eight, he began to threaten seriously our front and right, by heavy masses of his infantry. He had been repulsed at one point of the so-called river (in fact, a shallow stream, about twenty yards in width), by the 3d Arkansas regiment. As the designs of his column were fully developed, the 12th Georgia regiment were ordered to take position near the stream, while a battery commanded by Capt. Shumaker was directed to open fire upon the same column. The encounter was of but short duration. In a short time, the unmistakable evidences of the enemy's rout became apparent. Distinctly could their officers be heard, with words of mingled command, remonstrance, and entreaty, attempting to rally their batta.ions into line, and to bring them to the charge, but they could not be induced to re-form their broken ranks, nor to emerge from the cover of the woods, in the direction of our fire. Rapidly, and in disorder, they returned into the turnpike, and soon thereafter the entire force of the enemy, artillery, infantry, and cavalry, retreated in confusion along the road and adjacent fields.

The engagement lasted from seven in the morning to half-past two o'clock in the afternoon, at which time the enemy, who had come with artillery to bombard and demoralize the small force of Confederates; with infantry to storm their camp; with cavalry to rout and destroy them, and *with four days' cooked rations* in his haversacks, to prosecute a rapid march either towards Staunton, or towards Huntersville, was in precipitate retreat back to his Cheat Mountain fastnesses. His loss in killed and wounded was estimated at from two hundred and fifty to three hundred. That of the Confederates was very inconsiderable, not exceeding fifty in all.

The approaching rigors of a winter in the mountains, gave warning of a speedy termination of the campaign in western Virginia, in which, in fact, we had no reason to linger for any fruits we had gained. The campaign was virtually abandoned by the government, in recalling Gen. Lee shortly after he had allowed the opportunity of a decisive battle with Rosecrans to escape him. He was appointed to take charge of the coast defences of South Carolina and Georgia. Gen. Wise was ordered to report to Richmond ; Gen. Loring was sent with his command to reinforce Gen. T. J. Jackson ("Stonewall"), at Winchester; and Gen. H. R. Jackson was transferred to duty in the South. With the exception of Gen. Floyd's command, which still kept the field in the region of the Gauley, and a force of twelve hundred men on the Alleghany Mountain, the Confederate forces were withdrawn from western Virginia, after the plain failure of the campaign, and in the expectation that the rigors of the advancing winter season would induce the enemy to retire from the mountains to the Ohio.

The last incident of battle in the campaign was a brilliant one. On the 13th of December, the whole of the enemy's forces, under Gen. Reynolds, were brought out to attack the position commanded by Col. Edward Johnson, of Georgia, with his little force on the Alleghany. The enemy had been conducted to our position by a guide, a Union man. The Federals, on the flank, where the principal attack was made, numbered fully two thousand. They were gallantly met by our troops, who did not exceed three hundred at this time, being a portion of Hansborough's battalion, the 31st Virginia. These were reinforced by a few companies of Georgia troops, who came up with a shout, and joining the troops who had been forced back by overwhelming numbers, pressed upon the enemy with a desperate valor, and drove him from his almost impenetrable cover of fallen trees, brush, and timber. Many of the officers fought by the side of their men, and the enemy was pushed down the mountain, but with serious loss to the gallant little command. In describing the conduct of his men, Col. Johnson wrote to the War Department, " I cannot speak in terms too exaggerated of the unflinching courage and dashing gallantry of those five hundred men, who contended from a quarter past 7 A. M., until a quarter to 2 P. M., against an immensely superior force of the enemy, and finally drove them from their position and pursued them a mile or more down the mountain." The casualties in this small force amounted to twenty killed and ninety-six wounded.

Gen. Floyd was the last of the Confederate generals to leave the field of active operations in western Virginia. After the retreat of Rosecrans from Sewell Mountain, Gen. Floyd, at his own request, was sent with his brigade, by way of Richard's Ferry and Raleigh and Fayette Court House, to Cotton Hill, on the west side of the Kanawha. Here he again confronted Rosecrans and his whole force, encamped at Hamilton's, at Hawk's Nest, at Tompkins' farm, and at Stodin's, near the falls. Cotton Hill is in Fayette county, on the Kanawha, opposite the mouth of the Gauley ; the Raleigh and Fayette turnpike passes over the hill, crossing the Kanawha river at the ferry below the falls, where it intersects the Kanawha turnpike leading from Lewisburg to Charleston. From the position of Cotton Hill, the several camps of Rosecrans referred to could be distinctly seen, stretching to the distance of several miles. Gen. Floyd reached this point after a fatiguing march of eleven days, and occupied the landings of all the approaches to his position, at Bougen's Ferry, Matthews' Ferry, Mont-gomery's Ferry at the falls, and Loop Creek. For three weeks, he continued to challenge the enemy to battle, firing at him across the river, annoying him considerably, cutting off his communication with the Valley of the Kanawha, and holding in check his steamboats, which ran up to Loop Creek shoals at high tides. For several days, the communication of the Federals, between their corps on the opposite sides of the Gauley, was entirely suspended. Gen. Floyd continued to challenge, insult, and defy the enemy with his little six-pounders at Cotton Hill, while Rosecrans, before he would accept the challenge made to his already superior numbers, waited for heavy reinforcements from the Ohio.

At last, being largely reinforced by the way of Charleston, Rosecrans planned an attack upon Cotton Hill, and moved by several distinctly indicated routes, namely, Miller's, Montgomery's, and Loop Creek Ferries, all concentrating at Fayetteville, nine miles from Cotton Hill. He expected the most brilliant results from his overpowering numbers and well-conceived designs, and was confident of cutting off the retreat of Floyd and capturing his command. His force was fifteen thousand men; that of Floyd did not exceed four thousand effective men, his ranks having been reduced by sickness, and the old story of promised reinforcements never having been realized to him. In these circumstances, Gen. Floyd made a retreat, the success of which was one of the most admirable incidents of a campaign, which he, at least, had already distinguished by equal measures of vigor, generalship, and gallantry. He effected his retreat in perfect order, fighting the enemy for twenty miles, and bringing off his force, including sick, with a loss of not more than five or six men. In this loss, however, was Col. Croghan, of Kentucky, a gallant young officer, and a son of the late Col. Croghan, who had obtained historical distinction in the Northwestern campaign of the War of 1812. The enemy, after pursuing Gen. Floyd for twenty miles, turned back in the direction of Fayette Court House, leaving him to retire at his leisure to southwestern Virginia. It was from here that Gen. Floyd was transferred by the government to the now imposing theatre of war in Tennessee and Kentucky.

A minuter history of the campaign in western Virginia than

the plan of our work admits, would enable us to cite many in stances of individual gallantry and self-sacrifice. They would show the good conduct of small parties of Confederates on many occasions. In concluding the narrative of the general events of the war in western Virginia, we may add a very brief mention of some of these occurrences, which were only incidents of the campaign, which did not affect its general results, but which showed instances of gallantry that, on a larger scale of execution, might have accomplished very important results.

While the enemy had possession of the Kanawha Valley, Col. J. Lucius Davis' cavalry, of the Wise Legion, was sent to Big Coal River, thirty-five miles from Fayette Court House. On reaching Big Coal, they gave rapid chase to a marauding party of Federals, and overtook them at Tony's Creek, where a fight took place on the 11th September, which resulted in the total rout of the enemy, with a loss of about fifty killed and wounded, about the same number of prisoners, and the capture of all his provisions, munitions, &c. The Confederates sustained no loss whatever. The action lasted three hours, the remnant of the enemy having been pursued to a point within twelve miles of Charleston. The cavalry returned with their trophies, after having traversed, in twenty-four hours, a distance of seventy-five or eighty miles over steep mountain trails, bridle-paths, and rocky fords. Col. J. Lucius Davis, in his report of the affair, speaks of Lieut.-col. Clarkson as the hero of the expedition.

On the 25th September, Col. J. W. Davis, of Greenbrier, at the head of two hundred and twenty-five militia of Wyoming, Logan, and Boone counties, were attacked at Chapmansville, by an Ohio regiment commanded by Col. Pratt. The militia fought well, and were forcing the enemy from the field, when their gallant leader, Col. Davis, received a desperate, and as was thought at the time, a mortal wound. This unfortunate circumstance reversed the fortune of the field. The militia retreated and the enemy returned to the field. Col. Davis was taken by the Ohio troops, and remained in their hands till his partial recovery from his wounds, when he was paroled. The troops under Col. Davis lost but two killed and two wounded, while the loss of the Ohio troops in killed and wounded ex ceeded fifty, from the best information Col. D. was able to obtain.

Col. Jenkins' cavalry rendered efficient service in the Kanawha Valley, and kept the enemy all the time uneasy. On the 9th November, they made a gallant dash into the town of Guyandotte, on the Ohio river, and routed the forces of the enemy stationed there, killing and wounding a number of them, and taking nearly one hundred prisoners. Federal reinforcements afterwards came up to the town, and on the pretence that the Confederates had been invited to attack it by resident Secessionists, gratified a monstrous and cowardly revenge by firing the larger portion of the town, although many of the inhabitants had come out to meet them on the banks of the river, waving white flags and signifying the most unqualified submission. Women and children were turned into the street, many of them being forced to jump from the windows of their houses to escape the flames.

We have already adverted to the causes which contributed to make the campaign in western Virginia a failure. The cause which furnished the most popular excuse for its ineffectiveness—the disloyalty of the resident population—was, perhaps, the least adequate of them all. That disloyalty has been hugely magnified by those interested, in finding excuses in it for their own inefficiency and disappointment of public expectation. While Maryland, Kentucky, and other regions of the South, which not only submitted to Lincoln, but furnished him with troops, were not merely excused, but were the recipients of overflowing sympathy, and accounted by a charitable stretch of imagination " sister States" of the Southern Confederacy, an odium, cruelly unjust, was inflicted upon western Virginia, despite of the fact that this region was enthralled by Federal troops, and, indeed, had never given such evidences of sympathy with the Lincoln government as had been manifested both by Maryland and Kentucky in their State elections, their contributions of troops, and other acts of deference to the authorities at Washington. It is a fact, that even now, " Governor" Pierpont, the creature of Lincoln, cannot get one-third of the votes in a single county in western Virginia. It is a fact, that the Northern journals admit that in a large portion of this country, it is unsafe for Federal troops to show themselves unless in large bodies

The unfortunate results of the campaign in western V:rginia abandoned to the enemy a country of more capacity and grandeur than, perhaps, any other of equal limits on this continent; remarkable for the immensity of its forests, the extent of its mineral resources, and the vastness of its water-power, and possessing untold wealth yet awaiting the coal-digger, the salt dealer, and the manufacturer.

While the events referred to in the foregoing pages were transpiring in western Virginia, an inauspicious quiet, for months after the battle of Manassas, was maintained on the lines of the Potomac. A long, lingering Indian summer, with roads more hard and skies more beautiful than Virginia had seen for many a year, invited the enemy to advance. He steadily refused the invitation to a general action; the advance of our lines was tolerated to Munson's Hill, within a few miles of Alexandria, and opportunities were sought in vain by the Confederates, in heavy skirmishing, to engage the lines of the two armies. The gorgeous pageant on the Potomac, which, by the close of the year, had cost the Northern people three hundred millions of dollars, did not move. The "Young Napoleon" was twitted as a dastard in the Southern newspapers. They professed to discover in his unwillingness to fight the near achievement of their independence, when, however the fact was, the inactivity of the Federal forces on the northern frontier of Virginia only implied that immense preparations were going on in other directions, while the Southern people were complacently entertained with the parades, reviews, and pompous idleness of an army, the common soldiery of which wore white gloves on particular occasions of holiday display.

THE BATTLE OF LEESBURG.

The quiet, however, on the lines of the Potomac was broken by an episode in the month of October, which, without being important in its military results, added lustre to our arms. The incident referred to was the memorable action of Leesburg, in which a small portion of the Potomac army drove an enemy four times their number from the soil of Virginia, killing and taking prisoners a greater number than the whole Confederate force engaged.

Gen. Stone having been persuaded that no important force of the Confederates remained along the Upper Potomac, and in obedience to orders from head-quarters, commenced his passage of the river on Sunday, the 20th of October, at Harrison's Island, a point of transit about six miles above Edwards' Ferry, and nearly an equal distance from Leesburg. A force of five companies of Massachusetts troops, commanded by Col. Devins, effected a crossing at the ferry named above, and, a few hours thereafter, Col. Baker, who took command of all the Federal forces on the Virginia side, having been ordered by Stone to push the Confederates from Leesburg and hold the place, crossed the river at Conrad's Ferry, a little south of Harrison's Island.

The brigade of Gen. Evans (one of the heroic and conspicuous actors in the bloody drama of Manassas), which had occupied Leesburg, consisted of four regiments, viz. : the 8th Virginia, the 13th, the 17th, and the 18th Mississippi. Having a position on Goose Creek, they awaited the approach of the overwhelming numbers of the enemy, the force which he had thrown across the river being between seven and eight thousand strong. The enemy had effected a crossing both at Edwards' Ferry, and Ball's Bluff, and preparations were made to meet him in both positions. Lieut.-col. Jenifer, with four of the Mississippi companies, confronted the immediate approach of the enemy in the direction of Leesburg; Col. Hunton, with his regiment, the 8th Virginia, was afterwards ordered to his support, and, about noon, both commands were united, and became hotly engaged with the enemy in their strong position in the woods.

Watching carefully the action, Gen. Evans saw the enemy were constantly being reinforced, and at half-past two o'clock P. M., ordered Col. Burt to march his regiment, the 18th Mississippi, and attack the left flank of the enemy, while Colonels Hunton and Jenifer attacked him in front. On arriving at his position, Col. Burt was received with a tremendous fire from the enemy, concealed in a ravine, and was compelled to divide his regiment to stop the flank movement of the enemy.

At this time, about three o'clock, finding the enemy were in large force, Gen. Evans ordered Col. Featherston, with his regiment, the 17th Mississippi, to repair, at double quick, to the support of Col. Burt, where he arrived in twenty minutes, and the action became general along the whole line of the Confederates, and was hot and brisk for more than two hours

The Confederates engaged in the action numbered less than eighteen hundred men; the 13th Mississippi, with six pieces of artillery, being held in reserve. The troops engaged on our side fought with almost savage desperation. The firing was irregular. Our troops gave a yell and volley; then loaded and fired at will for a few minutes; then gave another yell and volley. For two hours, the enemy was steadily driven near the banks of the Potomac. The Federal commander, Col. Baker, had fallen at the head of his column, and his body was with difficulty recovered by his command. As the enemy continued to fall back, Gen. Evans ordered his entire force to charge and drive him into the river.

The rout of the enemy near the bluffs of the river was appalling. The crossing of the river had gone on until seven thousand five hundred men, according to the report of Gen. Stone, were thrown across it. Some of these never saw the field of battle. They had to climb the mud of the bluff, dragging their dismounted arms after them, before they could reach the field, expecting to find there a scene of victory. The difficult ascent led them to a horrible Golgotha. The forces that had been engaged in front were already in retreat; behind them rolled the river, deep and broad, which many of them were never to repass; before them glared the foe.

The spectacle was that of a whole army retreating, tumbling, rolling, leaping down the steep heights—the enemy following them, killing and taking prisoners. Col. Devins, of the 15th Massachusetts regiment, left his command, and swam the river on horseback. The one boat in the channel between the Virginia shore and the island was speedily filled with the fugitives. A thousand men thronged the banks. Muskets, coats, and every thing were thrown aside, and all were desperately trying to escape. Hundreds plunged into the rapid current, and the shrieks of the drowning added to the horror of sounds and sights. The Confederates kept up their fire from the cliff above. All was terror, confusion, and dismay One of the Federal officers, at the head of some companies, charged up the hill. A moment later, and the same officer, perceiving the hopelessness of the situation, waved a white

handkerchief and surrendered the main body of his regiment
Other portions of the column surrendered, but the Confed
erates kept up their fire upon those who tried to cross, and
many, not drowned in the river, were shot in the act of
swimming.

The last act of the tragedy was the most sickening and appalling of them all. A flat-boat, on returning to the island,
was laden with the mangled, the weary, and the dying. The
quick and the dead were huddled together in one struggling,
mangled mass, and all went down together in that doleful river,
never again to rise.

The Northern newspapers, with characteristic and persistent
falsehood, pretended that the Leesburg affair was nothing—
a mere reconnoissance, in which the Federals accomplished
their object—a skirmish, in which they severely punished the
" rebels"—an affair of outposts, in which they lost a few men,
nothing like so many as the " rebels," &c. But the truth at
last came out, stark and horrible. The defeat of Leesburg
was named in the Federal Congress as " most humiliating,"
" a great national calamity," and as another laurel added to
the chaplet of the " rebellion."

The Federal soldiers who had suffered most severely in this
action were from New York, Massachusetts, and Pennsylvania.
They had given an exhibition of cowardice, quite equal, in
degree at least, to its display at Manassas. There were no
instances among them of desperate stubbornness, of calm
front, of heroic courage. There was but one tint of glory to
gild the bloody picture, and that was in the circumstance of
the fall of their gallant commander, Col. Baker, who had been
shot several times through the body, and, at last, through the
head, in his desperate and conspicuous effort to rally his broken
forces.

Col. Baker was United States senator from Oregon. He
had served with distinction in the Mexican war ; was since a
member of Congress from Missouri ; emigrated to California.
where he long held a leading position at the bar, and, being
disappointed in an election to Congress from that State, removed to Oregon, where he was returned United States senator to Washington. In the opening of the war, he raised what
was called a " California" regiment, recruited in New York

aı d New Jersey, and at the last session of the Federal Con
gress had distinguished himself by his extreme views of the
subjugation of the South, and its reduction to a "territorial"
condition. He was a man of many accomplishments, of more
than ordinary gifts of eloquence, and, outside of his political
associations, was respected for his bravery, chivalry, and address.

Our loss in the action of Leesburg, out of a force of 1,709
men, was 153 in killed and wounded. The loss of the enemy
was 1,300 killed, wounded, and drowned; 710 prisoners captured, among them twenty-two commissioned officers; besides
1,500 stand of arms and three pieces of cannon taken. This
brilliant victory was achieved on our side by the musket alone,
over an enemy who never ventured to emerge from the cover,
or to expose himself to an artillery fire.

The battle of Leesburg was followed by no important consequences on the Potomac. It was a brilliant and dramatic
incident; it adorned our arms; and it showed a valor, a demonstration of which, on a grander scale and in larger numbers, might easily have re-enacted on a new field the scenes of
Manassas. But, like the Manassas victory, that of Leesburg
bore no fruits but those of a confidence on the part of the
South, which was pernicious, because it was overweening and
inactive, and a contempt for its enemy, which was injurious,
in proportion as it exceeded the limits of truth and justice,
and reflected the self-conceits of fortune.

CHAPTER VII.

The Position and Policy of Kentucky in the War.—Kentucky Chivalry.—Reminiscences of the "Dark and Bloody Ground."—Protection of the Northwest by Kentucky.—How the Debt of Gratitude has been repaid.—A Glance at the Hartford Convention.—The Gubernatorial Canvass of 1859 in Kentucky.—Division of Parties.—Other Causes for the Disloyalty of Kentucky.—The "Pro-Slavery and Union" Resolutions.—The "State Guard."—General Buckner.—The Pretext of "Neutrality," and what it meant.—The Kentucky Refugees.—A Reign of Terror.—Judge Monroe in Nashville.—General Breckinridge.—Occupation of Columbus by General Polk.—The Neutrality of Kentucky first broken by the North.—General Buckner at Bowling Green.—Camp "Dick Robinson."—The "Home Guard."—The Occupation of Columbus by the Confederates explained.—Cumberland Gap.—General Zollicoffer's Proclamation.—The Affair of Barboursville.—"The Wild-Cat Stampede."—The Virginia and Kentucky Border.—The Affair of Piketon.—Suffering of our Troops at Pound Gap.—The "Union Party" in East Tennessee.—Keelan, the Hero of Strawberry Plains.—The Situation on the Waters of the Ohio and Tennessee.—THE BATTLE OF BELMONT.—Weakness of our Forces in Kentucky.—General Albert Sidney Johnston.—Inadequacy of his Forces at Bowling Green.—Neglect and Indifference of the Confederate Authorities.—A Crisis imminent.—Admission of Kentucky into the Southern Confederacy.

If, a few months back, any one had predicted that in an armed contest between the North and the South, the State of Kentucky would be found acting with the former, and abetting and assisting a war upon States united with her by community of institutions, of interests, and of blood, he would, most probably, in any Southern company in which such a speech was adventured, have been hooted at as a fool, or chastised as a slanderer. The name of Kentucky had been synonymous with the highest types of Southern chivalry; her historical record was adorned by the knightly deeds, the hardy adventures, the romantic courage of her sons; and Virginia had seen the State which she had peopled with the flower of her youth grow up, not only to the full measure of filial virtue, but with the ornament, it was thought, of even a prouder and bolder spirit than flowed in the blood of the Old Dominion.

War discovers truths in the condition of society which would never otherwise have been known. It often shows a spirit of devotion where it has been least expected; it decides the claims of superior patriotism and superior courage often in favor of communities which have laid less claim to these qualities than others; and it not infrequently exposes disloyalty, rottenness, or apathy on the part of those who had formerly superior reputation for attachment to the cause which they are found to desert or to assail.

It is not to be supposed for a moment, that while the position of Kentucky, like that of Maryland, was one of reproach, it is to mar the credit due to that portion of the people of each, who, in the face of instant difficulties, and at the expense of extraordinary sacrifices, repudiated the decision of their States to remain under the Federal government, and expatriated themselves, that they might espouse the cause of liberty in the South. The honor due such men is in fact increased by the consideration that their States remained in the Union, and compelled them to fly their homes, that they might testify their devotion to the South and her cause of independence. Still, the justice of history must be maintained. The demonstrations of sympathy with the South on the part of the States referred to—Maryland and Kentucky—considered either in proportion to what was offered the Lincoln government by these States, or with respect to the numbers of their population, were sparing and exceptional; and although these demonstrations on the part of Kentucky, from the great and brilliant names associated with them, were perhaps even more honorable and more useful than the examples of Southern spirit offered by Maryland, it is unquestionably, though painfully true, that the great body of the people of Kentucky were the active allies of Lincoln, and the unnatural enemies of those united to them by lineage, blood, and common institutions.

A brief review of some of the most remarkable circumstances in the history of Kentucky is not inappropriate to the subject of the existing war.

Kentucky has been denominated "the Dark and Bloody Ground" of the savage aborigines. It never was the habitation of any nation or tribe of Indians ; but from the period of the earliest aboriginal traditions to the appearance of the white man on its soil, Kentucky was the field of deadly conflict between the Northern and Southern warriors of the forest.

When, shortly after the secession of the American colonies

from the British empire, this contested land was penetrated by the bold adventurous white men of Carolina and Virginia, who constituted the third party for dominion, its title of the "Dark and Bloody Ground" was appropriately continued. And when, after the declaration of American independence, Great Britain, with a view to the subjugation of the United States, formed an alliance with the Indian savages, and assigned to them the conduct of the war upon all our western frontier, the territory of Kentucky became still more emphatically the Dark and Bloody Ground. Nor did the final treaty of peace between Great Britain and the United States bring peace to Kentucky. The government of Great Britain failed to fulfil its obligations to surrender the western posts from which their savage allies had been supplied with the munitions of war, but still held them, and still supplied the Indians with arms and ammunition, inciting them to their murderous depredations upon the western border.

This hostile condition continued in Kentucky until the celebrated treaty of Jay, and the final victory over the savage enemy achieved by General Wayne, and the consequent treaty of peace which he concluded with them in 1795. By this treaty of peace, the temple of Janus was closed in Kentucky for the first time in all her history and tradition.

The battles in these wars with the savage enemy were not all in Kentucky, nor were they for the defence of the territory of her people only, but chiefly for the defence of the inhabitants of Ohio, who were unable to protect themselves against their barbarous foes. How this debt has been paid by the descendants of these Ohio people, the ravages of the existing war sufficiently demonstrate.

Peace was continued in Kentucky for about twenty years. There were commotions and grand enterprises which we cannot even mention here. But they were all terminated by the purchase of Louisiana by Mr. Jefferson in 1803. The ratification of the treaty by which this vast southern and western dominion was acquired at the price of fifteen millions of dollars, was opposed by the Northern politicians, whose descendants now seek to subjugate the people of the South, at the cost of a thousand millions of dollars, and of a monstrous, unnatural, and terrible expenditure of blood.

In the war of 1812 with Great Britain, the surrender of Hull having exposed the Michigan Territory and all the northern border of Ohio to the invasion of the British and the savages, who were now again the allies of that government, Kentucky sent forth her volunteers for the defence of her assailed Northern neighbors; and when so many of her gallant sons were sacrificed upon the bloody plains of Raisin, the Legislature of Kentucky requested the governor of the State to take the field, and at the head of his volunteer army to go forth and drive back the enemy. The request was promptly complied with. It was the army of Kentucky that expelled the savages from all Ohio and Michigan, and pursuing them into Canada, achieved over them and the British upon the Thames a victory more important than had been yet won upon land in that war, thus giving peace and security to Ohio and all the northwestern territory, whose people were confessedly powerless for their own defence.

It is these people, protected by the arms and early chivalry of Kentucky, who have now made her soil the Dark and Bloody Ground of an iniquitous civil war, waged not only upon a people bearing the common name of American citizens, but upon the eternal and sacred principles of liberty itself. In these references to the early history of Kentucky we must be brief. In indicating, however, the lessons of rebuke they give to the North with respect to the existing war, we must not omit to mention that in the war of 1812, in which Kentucky covered herself with such well-deserved and lasting glory, the New England States stood with the enemy, and the body of their politicians had resolved upon negotiation with Great Britain for a separate peace, and had, in fact, appointed a Convention to be assembled at Hartford, to carry into effect what would have been virtually a secession from the United States, and the assumption of neutrality between the belligerents, if not an alliance with the public enemy. These facts are not fully recorded in history, but they might be well collected from the public documents and journals of the day. Indeed, they are well known to men yet living in our land. The schemes of the New England traitors were defeated only by the battle of Orleans, and the consequent treaty of peace. Upon the happening of these events, the conspirators abandoned their

Convention *projet*, and denied that they had ever contemplated any thing revolutionary or treasonable. The whole matter was suffered to pass into oblivion. The conspirators were treated by the government and people of the United States as William the Third treated those around his throne who, within his knowledge, had conspired against him, and had actually served the public enemy of England. It was known in each case that the conspirators were controlled by their selfish interests, and that the best mode of managing them, was to cause them to see that it was to their interest to be faithful to their government. It needs no comment to indicate with what grace the vehement denunciation of the secession of the Southern States from a Union which had been prostituted alike to the selfishness of politicians and the passion of fanatics, comes from a people who had been not only domestic rebels, but allies to the foreign enemy in the war of 1812.

In tracing the political connections of Kentucky in the present war, it will be sufficient for our purposes to start at the election of its governor in 1859. Down to that period the body of the partisans now upholding the Lincoln government had been an emancipation party in the State. This party had lately suffered much in popularity. In the election of 1859, they determined to consult popularity, and took open pro-slavery ground. The State Rights candidate (Magoffin) was elected.

By their adroit movement, however, the Anti-State Rights party had made some advance in the confidence of the people, which availed them in the more important contests that followed. In the Presidential election of 1860 they supported Mr. Bell, and thus succeeded in their object of gaining the ascendency in the councils of the State. Emancipationists were urged to support Mr. Bell, upon the ground that from his antecedents and present position they had more to expect from him than from his principal competitor in the race in Kentucky, while the people at large were persuaded to support Mr. Bell as the candidate of the friends of "the Union, the Constitution, and the Laws."

The Anti-State Rights party (at least they may be known for the present by this convenient denomination), succeeded in carrying the State by a large plurality. They commenced at an early day to combat the movements of secession in the

South. Popular assemblies and conventions were called to pledge themselves to the support of the Union in every contingency. The party, as represented in these assemblies, united all the friends of Mr. Bell, and the great body of those of Mr Douglas and of Mr. Guthrie. By this combination an organization was effected which was able to control and direct public opinion in the subsequent progress of events.

It is certainly defective logic, or, at best, an inadequate explanation, which attributes the subserviency of a large portion of the people of Kentucky to the views of the Lincoln government to the perfidy of a party or the adroitness of its management. However powerful may be the machinery of party, it certainly has not the power of belying public sentiment for any considerable length of time. The persistent adhesion of a large portion of the Kentucky people to the Northern cause must be attributed to permanent causes; and among these were, first, an essential unsoundness on the slavery question, under the influences of the peculiar philosophy of Henry Clay, who, like every great man, left an impress upon his State which it remained for future even more than contemporary generations to attest; and, second, the mercenary considerations of a trade with both North and South, to which the State of Kentucky was thought to be especially convenient. These suggestions may at least assist to the understanding of that development of policy in Kentucky which we are about to relate.

On the meeting of the Legislature of Kentucky, after the election of Lincoln, the party in the interest of the North succeeded in obtaining the passage by that body of a singular set of resolutions, which, by a curious compost of ideas, were called "pro-slavery and Union" resolutions. They denounced secession, without respect to any cause which might justify the measure, deprecated any war between the North and the South, and avowed the determination of Kentucky to occupy in such an event a position of perfect neutrality.

At its regular session in 1859–'60, the Legislature had organized an active body of volunteer militia, denominated the State Guard, and General Buckner had been appointed its highest officer. This army, as it might be called, was found to consist of the finest officers and best young men in the State

It was necessarily, by the provisions of the Constitution, under the command of the governor; but as Governor Magoffin was supposed to be a Southern Rights man, and the fact appearing that nearly all of the State Guard were favorable to the same cause, and that they could not be made the soldiers of the despotic government of the North, he was in effect deprived of their command, and measures were taken for forcing out of their hands the public arms with which they had been furnished, and for the organization of a new corps, to be commanded by the officers and partisans of Abraham Lincoln. In the mean time, as if to make their professed determination of neutrality effective, the Legislature proceeded to arm with muskets their "Home Guards," as their new army was called. With this programme before the people, the Legislature took a recess, probably to await the progress of events, when the mask of neutrality might be thrown off, and their real purposes might safely be announced to the people.

Gov. Magoffin's refusal to furnish troops to answer the requisition of the Federal government (to which reference has already been made in another part of this work), appeared at the time to meet with the approval of the entire people of Kentucky. The enemies of the South acquiesced in the decision of the governor only until the period arrived when the farce of neutrality might be conveniently broken, and the next step ventured, which would be union with the North. With the pretence of neutrality, and the seductive promises of a trade with both belligerents, which would enrich Kentucky and fill her cities with gold, a considerable portion of the people were held blinded or willingly entertained, while the purposes of the Lincoln government with respect to their State were being steadily fulfilled.

In the election of members of the Congress called by Lincoln to meet in special session on the 4th of July, 1861, men of Northern principles were elected from every district in Kentucky save one; and in the same condition of the public mind, the members of the Legislature were elected in August the result being the return of a large majority of members os tensibly for the purpose of maintaining the ground of neu trality, but with what real designs was soon discovered. The election of the Lincoln rulers having been thus accomplished the measures all the time contemplated and intended were easily put in course of execution. In a short time every State Rights newspaper was suspended; every public man standing in defence of the South was threatened with arrest and prosecution; and the raising of a volunteer corps for the defence of the South was totally suppressed.

Immediately after the declaration of war by the Lincoln government, a number of young men in Kentucky, actuated by impulses of patriotism, and attesting the spirit of the ancient chivalry of their State, had commenced raising volunteer companies in the State for the Confederate service. They passed South in detachments of every number. This emigration was at first tolerated by the Unionists, if not actually desired by them, for the purpose of diminishing the opposition in the State to their sinister designs. By the removal of its members, and by the acts of the Legislature already mentioned, the admirable army of the "State Guard of Kentucky" was totally disorganized, and the command of it virtually taken from Governor Magoffin and General Buckner, and placed in the hands of the political partisans of the Lincoln government. General Buckner could not long occupy such a position, and therefore, as soon as practicable, he resigned his office, renounced the Lincoln government, and placed himself under the Confederate flag. The value of his accession to the Southern cause was justly appreciated, and he was speedily appointed a brigadier-general in the provisional army of the Confederacy.

The encouragement to emigration was not long continued by the party in power in Kentucky. It was determined by the Lincoln government to make examples of the small party remaining in Kentucky who sympathized with the South, and to arrest at once every public and influential man in the State known to be hostile to the North, or to the despotic purposes of the government at Washington. Ex-Governor Morehead was at a dead hour of the night arrested in his own house, a few miles from Louisville, in the presence of his afflicted family, by the Lincoln police, and hurried through the city and over the river, and out of his State and district, in violation of all law; and the benefit of the writ of *habeas corpus* was practically denied him in a mode which, at any period in the last two hundred years, would have aroused all England into commotion. The high-handed act, it might have been supposed, would have aroused Kentucky also to a flame of indignation at any other period since it became the habitation of white men. The people, however, seemed to be insensible, and the outrage was allowed to pass with no public demonstration of its disapproval. Encouraged by its experience of the popular subserviency in Kentucky to its behests, it was in convenient time determined by the Lincoln government to arrest or drive off from the State every prominent opponent of its despotic authority. It was determined at Louisville that John C. Breckenridge, late Vice-President of the United States, Col. G. W. Johnson, a prominent citizen, T. B. Monroe, Jr., Secretary of State, William Preston, late Minister to Spain, Thomas B. Monroe, Sr., for about thirty years District Judge of the United States, Col. Humphrey Marshall, ex-member of Congress, and a distinguished officer in the Mexican war, Capt. John Morgan (since " the Marion" of Kentucky), and a number of other distinguished citizens in different parts of the State, should be arrested at the same hour, and consigned to prison, or driven from their homes by the threats of such a fate. It is supposed that some of the Lincoln men, and perhaps some officers of the government, preferred the latter alternative, especially in respect to some of the individuals named. However this may be, it happened that all of them escaped, some in one direction, and some in another.

The venerable Judge Monroe, on his arrival at Bowling Green, whence he was on his next day's journey to pass out of his State and his district, executed in duplicate, and left to be transmitted by different modes of conveyance, his resignation of the office of Judge of the United States for Kentucky; and in conformity to the general expectation at the time, he placed upon historic record the declaration of his expatriation of himself from the dominion of the despotic government of Lincoln, and adopted himself a citizen of the Southern Confederacy. The proceedings occurred in the Confederate Court of Nashville on the 3d of October. The scene of the renunciation of allegiance to the government that would have enslaved him, by this venerable jurist, who had been driven from a long-cherished home, and was now on his way to the State of Virginia,

whose honored soil held the sacred ashes of a dozen genera
tions of his ancestors, was one of peculiar augustness and in
terest.   The picture of the scene alone was sufficient to illustrate and adorn the progress of a great revolution.   It was
that of a venerable patriot, a man of one of the greatest historical names on the continent, just escaped from the minions
of the despot, who had driven him from a State in which he
had lived, the light of the law, irreproachable as a man, beloved by his companions, honored by his profession, and venerable in years, voluntarily and proudly abjuring an allegiance
which no longer returned to him the rights of a citizen, but
would have made him an obsequious slave; and with all the
dignity of one thus honored and respected, and conscious of
his rectitude, appearing in the presence of a Confederate court
of justice, and with the pure eloquence of truth, offering the
remaining years of his life to the service of the new government, which had arisen as the successor of the old Union, as it
was in its purer and brighter days.

Mr. Breckenridge reached Nashville by a very circuitous
route, a few days after his departure from Lexington, and after
a brief sojourn in the former place, proceeded to Bowling
Green, and there entered into a compact with a number of his
old constituents who had taken refuge in the camp of General
Buckner, that they would take up their arms in defence of the
rights and liberties of their country, and never lay them down
till the invader was driven from the soil of Kentucky.   Shortly
afterwards, he received the appointment of brigadier-general
in the army of the Confederate States, and was assigned to the
command of a brigade of his fellow-citizens of Kentucky.   Col.
Humphrey Marshall received, at the same time, the appointment of brigadier-general, and was assigned to the district of
southeastern Kentucky and southwestern Virginia.   Colonel
Johnson was subsequently chosen Provisional Governor of
Kentucky by the friends of the Confederate government in
that State.

To reconcile the people of Kentucky to the Lincoln government, its partisans had told them at the outset that they had
the right to insist upon the strict observance of neutrality.   As
events progressed, they ascribed the violation of Kentucky's
neutrality to the acts of the Southern government, in the face

of facts about which there can be no dispute. The facts are, that the Federal forces were preparing to take possession of Columbus and Paducah, regarding them as important positions; and because Gen. Polk anticipated them and got prior possession of Columbus, they charged the Confederates with the responsibility of the first invasion of Kentucky. The Federals had commissioned Gen. Rouseau, at Louisville, to raise a brigade for the invasion of the South, but while the recruits were enlisted in Louisville, the camp was kept at Jeffersonville, on the Indiana side of the river, until the Lincoln commander became satisfied that the temper of the people of Louisville would tolerate a parade of Northern soldiers on their streets. Then, and not till then, were the Northern soldiers boldly marched across the State in the direction of Nashville. Gen. Buckner took possession of the railroad, and stationed himself at Bowling Green, in Southern Kentucky, about thirty miles from the Tennessee line. The partisans of Lincoln, still determined to blind the people by all sorts of false representations, established a camp called "Dick Robinson," near Lexington, and there made up an army comprised of recruits from Ohio, vagabonds from Kentucky, and Andrew-Johnson men from Tennessee. They insisted that no invasion was contemplated, that their forces were merely a "Home Guard" organization of a purely defensive character. They did not hesitate, however, to rob the arsenals of the United States of their muskets, bayonets, and cannon, and place them at the disposal of such infamous leaders as George D. Prentice, Tom Ward, and Garrett Davis. With these arms, "Dick Robinson's" camp was replenished, and at this memorable spot of the congregation of the most villanous characters, an army was raised in Kentucky for the invasion of the South.

The causes which led to the occupation of Kentucky by the Confederate States were plain and abundant. Finding that their own territory was about to be invaded through Kentucky, and that many of the people of that State, after being deceived into a mistaken security, were unarmed, and in danger of being subjugated by the Federal forces, the Confederate armies were marched into that State to repel the enemy, and prevent their occupation of certain strategic points which would have given them great advantages in the contest—a step which was

justified, not only by the necessities of self-defence on the part
of the Confederate States, but also by a desire to aid the people of Kentucky. It was never intended by the Confederate
government to conquer or coerce the people of that State; but,
on the contrary, it was declared by our generals that they
would withdraw their troops if the Federal government would
do likewise. Proclamation was also made of the desire to respect the neutrality of Kentucky, and the intention to abide by
the wishes of her people, as soon as they were free to express
their opinions.

Upon the occupation of Columbus by the Confederates, in
the early part of September, the Legislature of Kentucky
adopted resolutions calling upon them, through Governor
Magoffin, to retire. General Polk, who was in command of
the Confederates at Columbus, had already published a proclamation, clearly explaining his position. He declared in this
proclamation, that the Federal government having disregarded
the neutrality of Kentucky, by establishing camps and depots
of armies, and by organizing military companies within their
territory, and by constructing a military work on the Missouri
shore, immediately opposite and commanding Columbus, evidently intended to cover the landing of troops for the seizure
of that town, it had become a military necessity, involving the
defence of the territory of the Confederate States, that the Confederate forces should occupy Columbus in advance.

The act of Gen. Polk found the most abundant justification
in the history of the concessions granted to the Federal government by Kentucky ever since the war began. Since the election of Lincoln, she had allowed the seizure in her ports (Paducah) of property of citizens of the Confederate States. She
d, by her members in the Congress of the United States,
voted supplies of men and money to carry on the war against
the Confederate States. She had allowed the Federal government to cut timber from her forests for the purpose of building
armed boats for the invasion of the Southern States. She was
permitting to be enlisted in her territory troops, not only from
her own citizens, but from the citizens of other States, for th
purpose of being armed and used in offensive warfare against
the Confederate States. At camp "Dick Robinson," in the
county of Garrard, it was said that there were already ten

LT. GEN. POLK.

thousand troops, in which men from Tennessee, Ohio, Indiana, and Illinois were mustered with Kentuckians into the service of the United States, and armed by the government for the avowed purpose of giving aid to the disaffected in one of the Confederate States, and of carrying out the designs of that government for their subjugation. When Gen. Polk took possession of Columbus, he found that the enemy, in formidable numbers, were in position on the opposite bank of the river, with their cannon turned upon Columbus, that many of the citizens had fled in terror, and that not a word of assurance of safety or protection had been addressed to them.

In reply to the demand made through Governor Magoffin for the withdrawal of the Confederate troops from Kentucky, Gen. Polk offered to comply on condition that the State would agree that the troops of the Federal government be withdrawn simultaneously, with a guaranty (which he would give reciprocally for the Confederate government) that the Federal troops should not be allowed to enter, or occupy any part of Kentucky in the future. This proposition for a simultaneous withdrawal of forces, was derided by the partisans of Lincoln in Kentucky and elsewhere.

Gen. Polk had taken possession of Columbus on the 4th of September. The Federals were then occupying Paducah, at the mouth of the Tennessee river. The town of Cairo, at the mouth of the Ohio, had been previously occupied by a strong Federal force. New Madrid, on the Missouri side of the Mississippi, was occupied by Southern troops under the command of Gen. Jeff. Thompson.

Early in the summer, it was known that the Federals were threatening the invasion of East Tennessee by way of Cumberland Gap. To counteract their designs, the Confederate government sent Brigadier-general Zollicoffer, with a force of several thousand men, by way of Knoxville, East Tennessee, to the point threatened. On the 14th September, Gen. Zollicoffer telegraphed Governor Magoffin, of Kentucky, as follows : "The safety of Tennessee requiring, I occupy the mountain passes at Cumberland, and the three long mountains in Kentucky. For weeks, I have known that the Federal commander at Hoskins' Cross Roads was threatening the invasion of East Tennessee, and ruthlessly urging our people to destroy our own road and bridges. I postponed this precautionary movement until the despotic government at Washington, refusing to recognize the neutrality of Kentucky, has established formidable camps in the centre and other parts of the State, with the view, first to subjugate your gallant State, and then ourselves. Tennessee feels, and has ever felt, towards Kentucky as a twin-sister; their people are as one people in kindred, sympathy, valor, and patriotism. We have felt, and still feel, a religious respect for Kentucky's neutrality. We will respect it as long as our safety will permit. If the Federal force will now withdraw from their menacing position, the force under my command shall immediately be withdrawn."

At the same time Gen. Zollicoffer issued an order setting forth that he came to defend the soil of a sister Southern State against an invading foe, and that no citizen of Kentucky was to be molested in person or property, whatever his political opinions, unless found in arms against the Confederate government, or giving aid and comfort to the enemy by his counsels. On the 19th September, a portion of Gen. Zollicoffer's command advanced to Barboursville, in Kentucky, and dispersed a camp of some fifteen hundred Federals, without any serious struggle. He continued to advance cautiously in the direction of Somerset, driving the enemy before him. A large Federal force, chiefly from Ohio and Indiana, was sent forward to meet him. This expedition was speedily brought to a disgraceful and ruinous conclusion. Before getting near enough to Zollicoffer to confront him, Gen. Schoepff, the commander of the Yankee expedition, was induced to believe that Gen. Hardee was advancing from Bowling Green on his flank. What was known as the "Wild Cat Stampede" ensued. The retreat of the panic-stricken soldiers, which for miles was performed at the double-quick, rivalled the agile performances at Bull Run. For many miles the route of the retreat was covered with broken wagons, knapsacks, dead horses, and men who had sunk by the wayside from exhaustion. The flight of the Federals was continued for two days, although there was no enemy near them. Such was the result of the first expedition sent to capture Zollicoffer and to invade the South by way of Cumberland Gap.

Another design of the Federals was to invade southwestern

Virginia from eastern Kentucky, by way of Prestonsburg and Pound Gap, with the view of seizing upon the salt-works and lead-mines in this portion of Virginia, and of cutting off railroad communication between Richmond and Memphis. To thwart this design, there was raised in the neighborhood of Prestonsburg a force little exceeding a thousand men, who were placed under the command of Col. Williams. To capture the "rebels" at Prestonsburg, a considerable force was sent after them under the command of Gen. Nelson, of Kentucky. This somewhat notorious officer reported to the Lincoln government that his expedition had been brilliantly successful; his command, according to his account, having fallen upon the "rebels" at Piketon, captured upwards of a thousand of them, killed five hundred, or more, wounded a great number, and scattered the few remaining ones like chaff before the wind. This announcement caused intense joy in Cincinnati, and, indeed, throughout the North; but the rejoicings were cut suddenly short by the authentic account of the affair at Piketon, which occurred on the 8th of November, and in which the Confederates lost ten killed and fifteen wounded, while they ambushed a considerable body of Nelson's men on the river cliff, near that place, and killed and wounded hundreds of them. Owing to the superior force of the Federals, however, Col. Williams' little command fell back to Pound Gap.

He had not more than 1,010 men, including sick, teamsters, and men on extra duty. He described the little army that had held in check an apparently overwhelming force of the enemy, as an "unorganized, half-armed, and barefooted squad." He wrote to Richmond: "We want good rifles, clothes, greatcoats, knapsacks, haversacks, and canteens; indeed, every thing almost except a willingness to fight. Many of our men are barefooted, and I have seen the blood in their tracks as they marched."

There had long been unpleasant indications on the Tennessee border of disloyalty to the South. In what was called East Tennessee there was reported to be a strong "Union" party. This section was inhabited by an ignorant and uncouth population squatted among the hills. The Union faction in East Tennessee was the product of the joint influences of three men, differing widely in tastes, habits of thought, and political opinion, but concurring in a blind and bigoted devotion to the old Federal government. These men were Andrew Johnson, William G. Brownlow, and T. A. R. Nelson. The first of these was a man who recommended himself to the ignorant mountain people of Tennessee by the coarseness and vulgarity of his manners; but beneath his boorish aspect he had a strong native intellect, was an untiring political schemer, and for more than twenty years had exercised a commanding control over the rude mountaineers of Tennessee, who for an equal length of time had held the balance of power between the old Whig and Democratic parties in that State, voting first with one and then with the other political organization. Brownlow, "the parson," the haranguer of mobs in churches and at the hustings, and who, by his hatred of Andrew Johnson, had once made himself an ultra pro-slavery oracle of the Methodist Church, found Unionism so strong an element of popular partisan strength in East Tennessee, that he was forced to cooperate with his old enemy. The sincerest and most respectable of the trio was Nelson, an accomplished orator, a poet and dreamer besides, having no likeness to the people among whom he resided but in his apparel, and passing most of his time in the secluded occupations of a scholar, in which vocation he was both profound and classical. There could be no stranger combination of talent and character than in these three men, who had been brought together by a single sympathy in opposition to the cause of the South.

The Union party in Tennessee was for a long time occult; its very existence was for a considerable period a matter of dispute among Southern politicians; but it only awaited the operations of the enemy in Kentucky to assist and further their designs by a sudden insurrection among themselves. Their demonstrations were, however, premature. Early in November there was a conspiracy formed on the part of the Unionists for burning all the bridges on the East Tennessee and Virginia and Georgia and Tennessee railroads. The designs of the conspirators were consummated in part by the destruction of two or three bridges in East Tennessee, and of one in Georgia The bridge across the Holston, at Strawberry Plains, on the East Tennessee and Virginia road, was saved by the heroic and self-sacrificing act of an humble individual, named Edward

Keelan, at that time the sole guard at the place. He fought the bridge-burning party—more than a dozen in number—with such desperation and success, that they were forced to retire without accomplishing their object. One of the party was killed, and several badly wounded. Keelan was wounded in a number of places. Upon the arrival of friends, a few minutes after the occurrence, he exclaimed to them, "They have killed me, but I have saved the bridge." Luckily the wounds did not prove mortal, and the hero of Strawberry Plains still lives.

The Federal expedition to Pound Gap was of the same character with all the other invasions from the northwestern territory in this contest. The troops were from Ohio and other northwestern States, the occupiers of the lands bountifully granted by Virginia to the Federal government, and by that government liberally distributed among the ancestors of the people attempting the invasion of Virginia and the South. This territory had been won by a Virginia army, composed of volunteers from this State and from the district of Kentucky, then a part of the Old Dominion. The bold and successful enterprise of George Rogers Clark in the conquest of all that western territory, constitutes one of the most romantic and brilliant chapters of the history of the Revolution.

We turn from the operations on the Kentucky and Virginia border, which were in effect abandoned by the enemy, to the more active theatre of the war in Kentucky, in the neighborhood of the waters of the Ohio and Tennessee. It was to these waters that the enemy in fact transferred his plans of invasion of the South through Kentucky and Tennessee, by means of amphibious expeditions, composed of gunboats and land forces. Further on in the course of events we shall find the front of the war on the banks of the Tennessee instead of those of the Potomac, and we shall see that a war which the Southern people supposed lingered on the Potomac, was suddenly transferred, and opened with brilliant and imposing scenes on the Western waters. But it is not proper to anticipate with any comment the progress of events.

Gen. Polk had been completing his works for the defence of Columbus. While thus engaged, he was assailed on the 7th November by the enemy in strong force from Cairo.

THE BATTLE OF BELMONT.

Before daybreak on the morning of the 7th of November, Gen. Polk was informed that the enemy, who were under the command of Gen. Grant, had made their appearance in the river with gunboats and transports, and were landing a considerable force on the Missouri shore, five or six miles above Belmont, a small village. Gen. Pillow, whose division was nearest the point immediately threatened, was ordered to cross the river and to move immediately with four of his regiments to the relief of Col. Tappan, who was encamped at Belmont.

Our little army had barely got in position, when the skirmishers were driven in, and the shock took place between the opposing forces. The enemy were numerous enough to have surrounded the little Confederate force with triple lines. Several attempts were made by the enemy's infantry to flank the right and left wings of the Confederates; but the attempt on the right was defeated by the deadly fire and firm attitude of that wing, composed of the regiments of Colonels Russell and Tappan, the 13th Arkansas and the 9th Tennessee, commanded by Col. Russell, as brigade commander. The attempt to turn the left wing was defeated by the destructive fire of Beltzhoover's battery and Col. Wright's regiment, aided by a line of felled timber extending obliquely from the left into the bottom. The two wings of the line stood firm and unbroken for several hours, but the centre, being in the open field, and greatly exposed, once or twice faltered.

About this time, Col. Beltzhoover reported to Gen. Pillow that his ammunition was exhausted : Col. Bell had previously reported his regiment out of ammunition, and Col. Wright that one battalion of his regiment had exhausted its ammunition. The enemy's force being unchecked, and now emerging into the edge of the field, Gen. Pillow ordered the line to use the bayonet. The charge was made by the whole line, and the enemy driven back into the woods. But his line was not broken, and he kept up a deadly fire, and being supported by his large reserve, the Confederate line was forced back to its original position, while that of the enemy advanced. The charge was repeated the second and third time, forcing the

enemy's line heavily against his reserve, but with like result.
Finding it impossible longer to maintain his position without
reinforcements and ammunition, Gen. Pillow ordered the whole
line to fall back to the river-bank. In this movement his line
was more or less broken and his corps mingled together, so
that when they reached the river-bank they had the appearance of a mass of men rather than an organized corps.

The field was to all appearances lost. Reinforcements, however, had been sent for, and at the critical time when our
forces were being driven to the river, a regiment, the 2d Tennessee, commanded by Col. Walker, which had crossed the
river, came to their support. The opportunity was seized by
Gen. Pillow to engage afresh, with this timely addition to his
force, the advance of the enemy, while he made a rapid movement up the river-bank, with the design of crossing through
the fallen timber, turning the enemy's position and attacking
him in the rear.

As Gen. Pillow advanced the main body of his original
force in broken order up the river, to a point where he could
cross through the fallen timber to make the flank movement,
he was joined by two other regiments ordered by Gen. Polk to
his support. These fresh troops were placed under command
of Col. Marks, of the 11th Louisiana. He was directed to
lead the advance in double-quick time through the woods, and
to the enemy's rear, and to attack him with vigor. Col. Russell, with his brigade, was ordered to support the movement.

It was with great reluctance that Gen. Polk lessened the
force assigned to the immediate defence of Columbus, as an attack in his rear was every moment apprehended. It was obvious, however, from the yielding of our columns to the heavy
pressure of the masses of the enemy's infantry, and the fierce
assaults of their heavy battery, that further reinforcements
were necessary to save the field. Gen. Cheatham was ordered
to move across the river in advance of his brigade, to rally and
take command of the portions of the regiments within sight on
the shore, and to support the flank movement ordered through
Col. Marks.

About this time the enemy had fired our tents, and advancing his battery near the river-bank, opened a heavy fire on the
steamers which were transporting our troops. in some instances

driving shot through two of them at the same time. Captain Smith's Mississippi battery was ordered to move to the river bank, opposite the field of conflict, and to open upon the enemy's position. The joint fire of this battery and the heavy guns of the fort was for a few moments terrific. The enemy's battery was silenced, and it could be seen that they were taking up their line of march for their boats.

The Federals, however, had scarcely put themselves in motion, when they encountered Col. Marks first, and afterwards Gen. Cheatham, on their flank. The conjuncture was decisive. The enemy finding himself between two fires, that of Smith's artillery in front, and of Col. Marks' and Russell's column in the rear, after a feeble resistance, broke and fled in disorder.

Satisfied that the attack on Columbus for some reason had failed, Gen. Polk had crossed the river, and ordered the victorious commands to press the enemy to their boats. The order was obeyed with alacrity. The pursuit was continued until our troops reached the point where the enemy had made his surgical head-quarters, and depository of stores, of ammunition, baggage, &c. Here our troops found a yard full of knapsacks, arms, ammunition, blankets, overcoats, mess-chests, horses, wagons, and dead and wounded men, with surgeons engaged in the duties of their profession. The enemy's route of retreat was strewn likewise with many of these articles, and abundantly with blood, dead, and wounded men. "The sight along the line of the retreat," says an observer on the field, "was awful. The dead and wounded were at every tree. Some crawled into the creeks to get water, and died there."

On coming in sight of the enemy's gunboats and transports, our troops, as they arrived, were ordered to move as rapidly as possible through the cornfields to the bank of the river. The bank was thus lined for a considerable distance by our troops, who were ordered, as the boats passed up the river, to give the enemy their fire. The fire was hot and destructive. On the boats all was dismay. Under the fire from the bank, the Federals rushed to the opposite side of the boats, and had to be forced back by the bayonet to prevent capsizing. Many of the soldiers were driven overboard by the rush of those behind them. They did not take time to unloose the cables, but cut all loose, and were compelled to run through the fire of sharp-shooters lining the bank for more than a mile.

The day which at one time had been so inauspicious to our arms, closed upon a signal triumph. In his official report of the battle, Gen. Pillow declared, that no further evidence were needed to assure the fact, that "the small Spartan army" which withstood the constant fire of three times their number for nearly four hours (a large portion of them being without ammunition), had acted with extraordinary gallantry, than the length and character of the conflict, the great inequality of numbers, and the complete results that crowned the day.

That our loss should be severe in such a conflict might be expected. The list of our killed, wounded, and missing numbered 632. The loss of the enemy was stated in the official reports of our generals to have been more than treble ours. Of this, we had the most abundant evidence in the incidents of the field, in his flight, and his helpless condition, when assailed in his crowded transports with the fire of thousands of deadly rifles.

The victory of Belmont was esteemed as one of the most brilliant triumphs of the war.* In his congratulatory order, Gen. Albert Sydney Johnston, who had been appointed to

---

* The government at Washington, with a characteristic falsehood, stubborn to every other consideration but that of sustaining the spirits of its people, claimed the affair at Belmont as a victory to Northern arms. It is curious, and to some degree amusing, to notice the manner of this misrepresentation, and the gloze and insinuation by which it was effected in the Northern official reports of the battle. Gen. Grant, in his official report, declared that he had driven the Confederates to the river, burnt their camps, &c. So far, his report was ostentatiously fine, but not untrue. It has been shown, however, that the scale of battle was completely turned by a flank movement of our forces in heavy numbers, which routed the enemy, and converted his early successes of the morning into an ignominious defeat. In the Northern official reports of the battle, this portion of the day was dismissed with refreshing brevity and nonchalance. After describing in the most glowing terms his victory in pressing the Confederates to the river, Gen. Grant wrote to his friends, who communicated the letter to the newspapers, "on our return, *stragglers that had been left in our rear* fired into us, and more recrossed the river." In his official report, the flank movement of the Confederates, that was *the* event of the day and had decided it, was alluded to in a single sentence of casual mention, "The rebels recrossed the river, and *followed in the rear to our place of debarkation.*" Instances of this style and effrontery of falsehood abounded in all the Northern official reports of the events of the war; the above is furnished only as a characteristic specimen.

command in the Western Department, and had established his
head-quarters at Bowling Green, declared: "This was no ordi
nary shock of arms; it was a long and trying contest, in which
our troops fought by detachments, and always against superior
numbers. The 7th of November will fill a bright page in our
military annals, and be remembered with gratitude by the
sons and daughters of the South."

Despite the victory of Belmont, our situation in Kentucky
was one of extreme weakness and entirely at the mercy of the
enemy, if he had not been imposed upon by false representations of the number of our forces at Bowling Green. When
Gen. Johnston was about to assume command of the Western
Department, the government charged him with the duty of deciding the question of occupying Bowling Green, Kentucky,
which involved not only military, but political considerations.
At the time of his arrival at Nashville, the action of the Legislature of Kentucky had put an end to the latter consideration
by sanctioning the formation of companies menacing Tennessee,
by assuming the cause of the government at Washington, and
by abandoning the neutrality it professed ; and, in consequence
of their action, the occupation of Bowling Green became neces
sary as an act of self-defence, at least in the first step.

About the middle of September, Gen. Buckner advanced
with a small force of about four thousand men, which was increased by the 15th of October to twelve thousand, and though
other accessions of force were received, it continued at about
the same strength until the end of November, measles and
other diseases keeping down the effective force. The enemy's
force then was reported to the War Department at fifty thousand, and an advance was impossible.

Our own people were as much imposed upon as were the
enemy, with respect to the real strength of Gen. Johnston's
forces, and while they were conjecturing the brilliant results of
an advance movement, the fact was that inevitable disasters
might have been known by the government to have been in
store for the Southern cause in Kentucky and Tennessee, and
to be awaiting only the development of a crisis. The utter
inadequacy of Gen. Johnston's forces was known to the government. The authorities at Richmond appeared to hope for results without the legitimate means for acquiring them ; to look

for relief from vague and undefined sources; and to await, with dull expectation, what was next to happen. While the government remained in this blank disposition, events marched onward. It is easily seen, as far as our narrative has gone, that our troops had shown a valor that was invincible against largely superior numbers of the enemy; that had given striking illustrations of endurance in circumstances of the greatest adversity and suffering; and that promised with absolute certainty, as far as its agency could go, the achievement of our independence. It is hereafter to be seen that this valor and devotion, great as they were, could yet not withstand an enemy superior in force, when his numbers were multiplied indefinitely against them; that they could not resist armaments to which, for want of defences, they could only offer up useless sacrifices of life; and that some other agency than the natural spirit and hardihood of men was necessary in the conduct of a war, in the nineteenth century, against a nation which had given such unquestionable proofs, as the North had, of quick and abundant resource, mental activity, and unflagging hope.

It remains but to add here, mention of the political connection which was scarcely more than nominally effected between Kentucky and the Confederate States. On the 18th November, the opponents of the Lincoln rule in Kentucky assembled in Convention, at Russellville, in the southern part of the State, for the purpose of organizing a provisional government for Kentucky, and for taking steps for her admission into the Southern Confederacy. On the 20th November, the Convention unanimously agreed upon a report, presenting in a strong light the falseness of the State and Federal Legislature, and concluded with the declaration that " the people are hereby absolved from all allegiance to said government, and that they have the right to establish any government which to them may seem best adapted to the preservation of their lives and liberty." George W. Johnson, of Scott county, was chosen governor Commissioners were appointed to negotiate with the Confederate government for the earliest admission of Kentucky into the government of the Confederate States. The embassy of the commissioners to Richmond was successful, and before the middle of December, Kentucky was duly recognized as one of the States of the Southern Confederacy.

CHAPTER VIII.

Prospects of European Interference.—The selfish Calculations of England.—Effects of the Blockade on the South.—Arrest by Capt. Wilkes of the Southern Commissioners.—The Indignation of England.—Surrender of the Commissioners by the Lincoln Government.—Mr. Seward's Letter.—REVIEW OF AFFAIRS AT THE CLOSE OF THE YEAR 1861.—Apathy and Improvidence of the Southern Government.—Superiority of the North on the Water.—The Hatteras Expedition.—The Port Royal Expedition.—The Southern Privateers.—Their Failure.—Errors of Southern Statesmanship.—"King Cotton."—Episodes of the War.—The Affair of Santa Rosa Island.—The Affair of Dranesville.—Political Measures of the South.—A weak and halting Policy.—The Spirit of the War in the North.—Administration of the Civil Polity of the Southern Army.—The Quarter-master's Department.—The Hygiene of the Camps.—Ravages of the Southern Army by Disease.—The Devotion of the Women of the South.

SINCE the commencement of the war, the South had entertained prospects of foreign interference, at least so far as to involve the recognition of her government by England and France, and the raising of the blockade. Such prospects, continued from month to month, had an unhappy effect in weakening the popular sentiment of self-reliance, in turning the attention of the people to the result of external events, and in amusing their attention with misty illusions.

These prospects were vain. By the close of the year, the South had learned the lesson, that the most certain means of obtaining injury, scorn, and calumny from foreign people, was to attempt their conciliation or to seek their applause, and that not until she had proved herself independent of the opinions of Europe, and reached a condition above and beyond the help of England and France, was she likely to obtain their amity and justice.

It had been supposed in the South, that the interest of Europe in the staples of cotton and tobacco would effect a raising of the blockade, at least by the fall of the year. The statistics on these subjects were thought to be conclusive. France derived an annual revenue of $38,000,000 from her monopoly of the tobacco trade; and Great Britain and her people, a revenue of $350,000,000 per annum from American cotton. Five millions of souls, in England, were interested in one way or the other in the cotton manufacture; and the South calculated, with reason, that the blockade would be raised by foreign intervention, rather than that one-sixth of the population of the British Isles would be permitted to be thrown out of employment by a decree or fulmination of the Yankee govern ment at Washington.

Among the statesmen of Great Britain, however, a different calculation prevailed, and that was, as long as the possible contingencies of the future held out the least hope of avoiding the alternative of war with the Washington government, to strain a point to escape it. It was argued, that it would be cheaper for England to support, at the public expense, five millions of operatives, than to incur the cost, besides the unpleasantness of an embroilment in American affairs; and it was in this spirit of selfish calculation—the results of which were stated by Lord Palmerston in the declaration, that the "necessities" of England had not reached that point to require her to interfere, in any manner, in the American war—that it was ultimately decided by the British government to maintain her neutrality with reference to the blockade, as well as other incidents of the war.

About the fall of the year, the South had begun to feel se verely the effects of the blockade. Supplies of the usual goods, and even provisions, were becoming scarce. The evils were augmented every day in the results of a baneful spirit of speculation, which indulged in monstrous extortions and corrupted the public spirit, making opportunities for mercenary adventure out of the distresses and necessities of the country. There was great suffering among the poor, and especially among refugees, who had fled to the cities from districts occupied by the enemy.

The resources of the South were such, however, that any thing like famine or actual starvation, of any portion of the people, was not to be apprehended. The changes which happened in the circumstances and pursuits of people, were not always as unfortunate as they appeared, and, in the end, not unfrequently proved an advantage to them and to the prosperity of the country. Many new enterprises were started; many sources of profitable labor were sought out; and many instances of the diversion of popular industry were occasioned,

wh.ch promised to become of permanent advantage in de
veloping the resources of the country in minerals and manufac
tures, and introducing provision crops on an enlarged scale in
the Cotton States of the Confederacy.

In the month of December occurred an event which promised
the most fortunate consequences to the South, with respect to
foreign intervention and her release from the blockade. The
Confederate government had deputed Mr. James M. Mason, of
Virginia, and Mr. John Slidell, of Louisiana, commissioners,
respectively, to England and France. They had escaped the
blockade at Charleston on a Confederate vessel, and arriving
at the neutral port of Havana, had left there on the 7th day of
December in a British mail-steamer, the Trent, commanded by
Capt. Moir. The next day after leaving port, the British vessel, while in the Bahama channel, was intercepted by the Federal steam-frigate, San Jacinto, Commander Wilkes, being
brought to by a shotted gun, and boarded by an armed boat's
crew. The persons of the commissioners and their secretaries,
Messrs. Eustis and Macfarland, were demanded ; they claimed
the protection of the British flag, and refused to leave it except at the instance of actual physical force, which Lieut. Fairfax, who had boarded the vessel, then declared he was ready
to use. The Trent was an unarmed steamer, and as resistance
was hopeless, the commissioners were surrendered, under a
distinct and passionate protest against a piratical seizure of
ambassadors under a neutral flag.

This outrage done by a Federal vessel to the British flag,
when it was learned in the South, was welcome news, as it was
thought certain that the British government would resent the
insult, and as the boastful and exultant tone in the North, over
the capture of the commissioners, appeared to make it equally
certain that the government at Washington would not surrender its booty. War between England and the North was
thought to be imminent. Providence was declared to be in
our favor ; the incident of the Trent was looked upon almost
as a special dispensation, and it was said, in fond imagination,
that on its deck and in the trough of the weltering Atlantic
the key of the blockade had at last been lost.

These prospects were disappointed by the weakness of the
government at Washington, in surrendering the commissioners

and returning them to the British flag. The surrender was an exhibition of meanness and cowardice unparalleled in the political history of the civilized world, but strongly characteristic of the policy and mind of the North. The people of the North had, at first, gone into raptures over the arrest of the commissioners; the newspapers designated it as "worth more than a victory in the field;" the hospitalities of the city of New York were offered by its common council to Capt. Wilkes, and a dinner was given him by leading citizens of Boston, in honor of his brave exploit in successfully capturing, from the deck of an unarmed mail-steamer, four unarmed passengers. The government at Washington had given every indication of its approval of the arrest. The compliments of the Cabinet had been tendered to Capt. Wilkes, and a proposition introduced into Congress to distinguish his piratical adventure by a public vote of thanks. The subjects of the capture were condemned to close cells in Fort Warren.

Despite all this manifest indorsement by the government of the legality and value of the arrest of the commissioners, Mr. Seward did not hesitate to surrender them when the alternative of war with Great Britain was indicated to him, in the dispatches of that government demanding, in very simple and stern terms, the reparation of the outrage that had been committed upon its flag.

In a letter to Mr. Adams, the representative of the Washington government at London, Mr. Seward had advised him to make no explanations, as the Washington Cabinet thought it better that the ground taken by the British government should first be made known to them. The ground of its claims was never furnished by the British government. Its demand for reparation and apology was entirely naked, and evidently disdained to make a single argument on the law question. With unexampled shamelessness, Mr. Seward made the plea himself for the surrender of the commissioners; he argued that they could not be the subjects of a judicial proceeding to determine their status, because the vessel, the proper subject of such a proceeding, had been permitted to escape; and with a contemptible affectation of alacrity to offer, from a returning sense of justice, what all the world knew had been extorted from the alarms of cowardice, he declared that he "cheerfully" surrendered the commissioners, and did so in accordance with long-established American doctrine.

In surrendering the commissioners, the Washington government took the opportunity to declare its reassured hopes of the Union, and to express its contempt for the Southern revolution. In his letter to Earl Russell, Mr. Seward took particular pains to declare, that " the safety of the Union did not require the detention of the captured persons;" that an " effectual check" had been put to the " existing insurrection," and that its " waning proportions" made it no longer a subject of serious consideration.

The declaration was false and affected, but it contained an element of truth. There is no doubt that, at the time it was made, the power of the revolution in the South was declining; and a rapid survey of the political posture, and of events transpiring in the latter half of the year 1861, affords painful evidence of relaxation on the part of the Confederate government, and of instances of weakness and abuse that the people, who had pledged every thing and endured every thing in a contest for freedom, had no right to expect.

REVIEW OF AFFAIRS AT THE CLOSE OF THE YEAR 1861.

The justice of history compels us to state that two causes— the overweening confidence of the South in the superior valor of its people, induced by the unfortunate victory of Manassas, and the vain delusion, continued from month to month, that European interference was certain, and that peace was near at hand, conspired, about this time, to reduce the Southern cause to a critical condition of apathy.

Western Virginia had been abandoned to the enemy almost with indifference, and with an apathetic confidence in an army that was in danger of becoming demoralized, and in the prospects of European interference, which were no brighter than formerly, except in imagination, the South carelessly observed the immense preparations of the North, by sea and land, to extend the area of the contest from the coasts of Carolina to the States on the Mississippi, and to embrace her whole territory with the lengthening arms of the war.

While the enemy was busy making his immense naval prep

arations against our sea-coast, and building scores of gunboats on the upper Mississippi to drive our armies out ot
Kentucky and Tennessee, the Southern government had shown
the most extraordinary apathy; the spirit of our armies was
evidently decaying, and abuses of extraordinary magnitude
had crept into the civil administration of our affairs. No corresponding activity was manifested by us in the line of naval
enterprise adopted by the enemy. Means were not wanting for
at least some emulation in this respect. Large appropriations
had been made by Congress for the construction of gunboats
and objects of river defence; the State of Virginia had turned
over to the Confederate government the best navy-yard on the
continent, and two armories with their machinery; and with
the means and appliances at Gosport and Richmond, it is not
doubted that, with proper activity, the government might have
created a considerable fleet.

The North had improved the advantage of its possession of
a navy by increasing its numbers. Nearly a hundred vessels
of different descriptions were purchased by it, and fleets of
gunboats fitted out for operations on the coast and rivers.
Two naval expeditions had already, before the close of the
year, been sent down the Carolina coast, and without accomplishing much, had given serious indications of what was to be
expected from this arm of the service on the slight fortifications of our ocean frontier.

On the 29th of August, a naval expedition from Fortress
Monroe, under command of Commodore Stringham and Major-
general Butler, had reduced the two forts at Hatteras Inlet,
and had signalized their victory by the capture of fifteen guns
and 615 prisoners, among whom was Commodore Barron, the
Confederate officer in command.

The capture of Port Royal, on the South Carolina coast, on
the 7th of November, by the bombardment of Forts Walker
and Beauregard, gave to the enemy a point for his squadrons
to find shelter, and a convenient naval depot. The attack was
made on the 7th of November, by a Federal fleet, numbering
fifteen war-steamers and gunboats, under command of Capt.
Dupont, flag-officer of the south Atlantic blockading squadron.
The attack was easily successful by the bombardment of the
forts at the entrance of the sound. It may be imagined how

inefficient our defences must have been, when the fact is, tha*. they yielded after a bombardment which continued precisely four hours and thirty minutes; the condition of Fort Walker at this time being, according to the official report of General Drayton, who was in command, " all but three of the guns in the water front disabled, and only five hundred pounds of pow- der in the magazine." But these were only the first lessons of the enemy's power and our improvidence in defences, that were to be taught us on the coast.

The privateering service had yielded us but poor fruits. The Savannah, the first of the privateers, was captured, and her crew treated as pirates, at least so far as to load them with irons, and confine them in felons' cells. With the exception of the Sumter (an awkwardly rigged bark) and one or two others, the privateers of the South were pretty closely confined within their own harbors and rivers by the blockading fleets. The " militia of the seas," that, it was predicted in the early part of the war, would penetrate into every sea, and find splendid prizes in the silk ships of China, and the gold-freighted steam ers of California, had proved but an inconsiderable annoyance to the extensive commercial marine of the North; it had captured during the year but fifty prizes in smacks, schooners, and small merchantmen, and by this time the South had learned that its privateering resources were about as delusive as that other early and crude expectation of adventitious aid in the war—the power of " King Cotton."

It is curious, indeed, how the early expectations of the man- ner and conduct of a war are disappointed by the progress of its events, and its invariable law of success in the stern compe- titions of force, without reference to other circumstances. It was said, at the beginning of the war, that, while cotton would " bring Europe to its knees," the Southern privateers would cut up the commerce of the North, and soon bring the merce- nary and money-making spirits of that section to repentance. Neither result was realized. At the close of the year 1861, the South appeared to be fully convinced that it was waging a war in which it could no longer look for aid to external and adventitious circumstances; that it could no longer hope to obtain its independence from European interference, or from cotton, or from the annoyances of its privateers, or from the rupture of a financial system in the North; and that it had no other resource of hope but in the stern and bloody trials of the battle-field.

Beyond the events briefly sketched in this and the foregoing chapters, there were some incidents which were interesting as episodes in the progress of the war, up to the close of the year 1861, to which a full reference has been impossible in a work which professes to treat only the material parts of the important campaigns of the year.

The most interesting of these was probably the attack on Santa Rosa Island, in the harbor of Pensacola, on the night of the 8th October, and the storming, by picked companies from the Mississippi, Alabama, Georgia, Louisiana, and Florida regiments, of the camp which had been made on the island by the notorious Billy Wilson Zouaves. Landing from steamers and flats on the enemy's shore, within sight of his fleet, the small band of Confederates marched some three or four miles in the darkness of the night over an unknown and almost impassable ground, killing the enemy's pickets, storming his intrenched camp, driving off the notorious regiment of New York bullies, with their colonel flying at their head, and burning every vestige of their clothing, equipage, and provisions. This action was rendered remarkable by an instance of disgusting brutality on the part of the enemy—the murder of our wounded who had been left on the field on account of the necessity of rapidly retiring with our small force, before the enemy could rally from his surprise. Of thirteen dead bodies recovered, eleven were shot through the head, having, at the same time, disabling wounds on the body. This fact admits of but one inference.

The affair of Dranesville, on the line of the Potomac, had given a sharp and unexpected lesson to our immoderate confidence. This action occurred on the 22d day of December. Our whole force engaged was nearly 2,500 men, composed of Virginia, South Carolina, Kentucky, and Alabama troops, under command of Gen. Stuart. The expedition, which was attended by a train of wagons intended for foraging purposes, fell in with the enemy near Dranesville. On the appearance of the enemy, the 11th Virginia regiment charged them with a yell, and drove them back to their lines within sight of Dranes ville. Here the enemy rallied. In the confusion which ensued, the 1st Kentucky regiment fired upon the South Carolina troops, mistaking them for the enemy. Discovering his mistake, Colonel Taylor, of the 1st Kentucky, moved cautiously through the woods. Coming in sight of another regiment, and prompted to unusual caution by his previous mistake, he shouted to their commander to know who he was. "The colonel of the 9th," was the reply. "Of what 9th?" "Don't shoot," said the Yankees; "we are friends—South Carolinians." "On which side are you?" asked Col. Taylor. "For the Union," now shouted the Federals; at the same instant pouring a murderous volley into the ranks of the Kentuckians. The engagement now became general. The Federals had the advantage of position and largely superior numbers. Their field batteries swept our lines, and several regiments of their infantry, protected by the ground, had advanced within one hundred yards of us, keeping the air full of minié-balls. After sustaining the fire for some time, our troops were compelled to fall back. The retreat was executed in good order, as the enemy did not attempt any pursuit. Our loss on the field from which we were repulsed was about two hundred in killed and wounded. The next day, reinforcements having reached Gen. Stuart, the enemy had drawn off from the locality of the battle-field, and declined any further engagement.

The affair at Dranesville was no serious disaster, but it was a significant warning, and, in this respect, it had an importance beyond the size of the engagement and its immediate results. The Yankees were learning to stand fire, and, out of the material which was raw at Bull Run, McClellan was making troops who were no longer contemptible, and who were perceptibly improving in discipline, stanchness, and soldierly qualities.

Of the political measures adopted by the South in furtherance of the objects of the war, but a few words need be said. They are justly described as weak and halting responses to the really vigorous acts of the Northern government in its heartless, but strong and effective prosecution of the war. While the Washington government protected itself against disaffected persons and spies by a system of military police, extending over the whole North, the Provisional Congress, at Richmond, was satisfied to pass a law for the deportation of " alien enemies," the execution of which afforded facilities to the egress of innumerable spies. The Washington government had passed a law for the confiscation of the property of " rebels." The Congress at Richmond replied, after a weak hesitation, by a law sequestrating the property of alien enemies in the South, the operations of which could never have been intended to have effect ; for, by future amendments in the same Congress, the law was soon emasculated into a broad farce. The Washington government was actually collecting an army of half a million of men. The Richmond Congress replied to the threat of numbers, by increasing its army, on paper, to four hundred thousand men ; and the Confederate government, in the midst of a revolution that threatened its existence, continued to rely on the wretched shift of twelve months' volunteers and raw militia, with a population that, by the operation of conscription, could have been embodied and drilled into an invincible army, competent not only to oppose invasion at every point of our frontier, but to conquer peace in the dominions of the enemy.

The universal mind and energy of the North had been consolidated in its war upon the South. The patriotism of the nation was broadly invoked ; no clique arrogated and monopolized the control of affairs ; no favorites closed up against the million outside the avenues of patronage, of honor, and of promotion. It was a remarkable circumstance that the North had, at all stages of the war, adopted the best means for securing specific results. The popularity of Fremont, with the half million " Wide Awakes" of the North, was used to bring an army into the field. The great ship-broker ot New York, Morgan, and the great ship-owner, Vanderbilt, were patronized to create a navy. In the army, the popularity of Banks, Butler, Grant, and Baker were employed equally with the science of McClellan, Buell, and Halleck.* It had been thus that the

---

* The two most conspicuous Federal generals in the operations of the West were Generals Buell and Halleck. Don Carlos Buell was a native of Ohio. He had served in the Mexican war with distinction, having been twice brevetted for gallant conduct—the last time as major in the battle of Churubusco, in which he was severely wounded. At the close of the Mexican war, he was

Federal government had united the whole North, brought an army of half a million men into the field, and swelled the proportions of the war far beyond any expectations of the world.

The policy of monotonous defence had been perseveringly pursued by the authorities of the Confederacy. On the side of the enemy, it had more than repaired the damage inflicted upon them in many brilliant battles, and had left them at perfect leisure, in the very presence of our forces, to devise, mature, and make trial of any plan of campaign or assault which they thought expedient. A large portion of Virginia and important regions on the Southern seaboards were now occupied by the enemy, who would never have ventured forth to such distances, if they had been menaced nearer home. The strictly defensive policy was sustained by elaborate arguments.

---

appointed assistant adjutant-general, with rank of captain, but relinquished his rank in line in 1851. As a commander, he was courageous, energetic, and methodical, and he obtained the respect of the South for his chivalric disposition, his courteous behavior to prisoners, and his uniform recognition of the laws and amenities of civilized warfare.

Gen. Henry Wager Halleck, before the war, had been but little known, and that only as the author of some military works, and a prominent land lawyer, deeply versed in Mexican titles, at the bar of San Francisco, California. He was a pupil of West Point, and had been brevetted captain for meritorious services in California during the Mexican war. He was appointed Secretary of State of the province of California in the military government of Generals Kearney, Mason, and Riley, and was a member of the Convention to form and one of the committee to draft the State Constitution of California in 1849. He subsequently disappeared from public attention, and occupied himself with his innumerable Mexican clients in California as a lawyer and land speculator.

A correspondent gives the following account of the personnel of General Halleck: "In the field he is hardly the same person who might have been seen quietly gliding from the Planters' House to head-quarters in St. Louis He does not look a whit more military in appearance, but looks, in his new and rich, though plain uniform, as if he were in borrowed clothes. In truth, he bears a most striking resemblance to some oleaginous Methodist parson dressed in regimentals, with a wide, stiff-rimmed black felt hat sticking on the back of his head, at an acute angle with the ground. His demeanor in front of his tent is very simple and business-like. When on horseback, his Wesleyan character is more and more prominent. He neither looks like a soldier, rides like one, nor does he carry the state of a major-general in the field, but is the impersonation of the man of peace. His face is large, tabular and Teutonic; his eyes a kind of indistinct gray, not without expression, but of that deep welling kind that only reveal the emotion without indicating its character."

It is not within the design of our work to canvass the logical value of these arguments; but it is to recognize as a fact the natural and almost universal impression made upon the popular mind of the South, that it could not be good generalship which left the enemy at perfect leisure to mature all his preparations for aggression; and that it could not be a glorious system of warfare, which never ventured an aggressive movement, and which decimated its armies by inaction.

In the administration of the civil polity of the Southern army, as distinguished from its command, there were abuses and defects which were constant subjects of newspaper comment.

In the Quarter-master's department, however, the results accomplished by the energy of its directors were little less than surprising, and received the marked commendation of a committee of the Provisional Congress, appointed to inquire into the civil polity of the army. That the immense army now in the service of the Confederate States, suddenly collected, men and officers generally inexperienced in camp life and military duty, should be clothed, armed, and moved with the facility of a permanent organization, was not to be expected; and yet, with but few exceptions, this result was accomplished. Major Alfred M. Barbour, of Virginia, was appointed Chief Quarter-master of the army of the Potomac, our principal *corps d'armée* in the field; and his remarkable resources of judgment, his vast energy, and his untiring devotion to his extensive duties in the field, contributed most important results in the emergencies of the many sudden and rapid movements of our forces in Virginia, in the remarkable campaign in that State of the spring of 1862. Such contributions to the public service are not to be depreciated by the side of more visible, and, in the popular mind, more brilliant achievements of the war. The labors of the Quarter-master's department penetrate the entire military establishment, breathe life into the army, nurture its growth, and give it strength and efficiency in the field; vigilant, prepared, and present, it moves unnoticed amid the stirring events of the field, and obscured by the dust and smoke of the combat, it remains unobserved even while collecting the fruits of victory.

The most distressing abuses were visible in the ill-regulated

hygiene of our camps. The ravages of disease among the
army in Virginia were terrible ; the accounts of its extent were
suppressed in the newspapers of the day, and there is no doubt
that thousands of our brave troops disappeared from notice
without a record of their end, in the nameless graves that yet
mark the camping grounds on the lines of the Potomac, and
among the wild mountains of Virginia.

Our camps were scourged with fever, pneumonia, and diar
rhœa. The armies on the Potomac and in western Virginia
suffered greatly—those troops in Cheat Mountain and in the
vicinity of the Kanawha Valley most intensely. The wet and
changeable climate, the difficulty of transportation, exposure
to cold and rain without tents, the necessary consequence of
the frequent forward and retrograde movements, as well as the
want of suitable food for either sick or well men, produced
most of the sickness, and greatly aggravated it after its accession.

The regulations, requiring reports from the regiments as to
the number of sick, their diseases, and the wants of the medi
cal station, were, but in few instances, complied with. The
result of this neglect was, that upon a change of position in
the army, it was the unhappy consequence that the number of
sick greatly exceeded that indicated by the reports. They
were hurried to the rear, where the accommodations, both as
to food, shelter, and medical attendance, being all insufficient,
there was great suffering and great mortality.

The suffering of our army evoked, on the part of the Southern people, demonstrations of patriotic devotion and generosity,
such, perhaps, as the world had never seen. The patriotism
of our citizens at home was manifested in unremitting efforts
to supply the wants and relieve the sufferings of the soldiers,
sick and well. The supply of money, clothing, and hospital
stores, from this voluntary and generous source, is estimated
in millions of dollars.* It was the most cheering indication

---

* The following contributions (estimated in money) were listed at the Pass-
port Office, in Richmond, during the last three months of the year 1861. The
list comprises almost exclusively the donations made to the army of the Potomac. Of the voluntary supplies sent to the army in Missouri, Arkansas,
and Kentucky, there is no account whatever ; but, as the same patriotic devo
tion animated our people everywhere, there is no reason to doubt that an equal

ɔt the spirit of our people in the cause of independence. The women of the country, with the tenderness and generosity of their sex, not only loaded railroad cars with all those applian ces for the comfort of the sick which their patriotic ingenuity could devise, but also came to the rescue in clothing those who were well and bearing arms in the field. They made large pe cuniary contributions, took charge of the hospitals established by the States, and, as matrons of those institutions, carried cleanliness and comfort to the gallant soldier, far from home and kindred. A committee of the Provisional Congress placed on record the thanks of the country to the women of the South, for their works of patriotism and public charity, and declared that the government owed them " a public acknowledgment of their faithfulness in the glorious work of effecting our inde pendence."

amount of clothing, stores, &c., had been sent to those troops. With this cal culation, the whole amount of contributions for the last quarter of the year 1861 could not have fallen short of three millions of dollars :

North Carolina,	$325,417
Alabama,	317,600
Mississippi,	272,670
Georgia,	244,885
South Carolina,	137,206
Texas,	87,800
Louisiana,	61,950
Virginia,	48,070
Tennessee,	17,000
Florida,	2,350
Arkansas,	950

$1,515,898

CHAPTER IX.

Prospects of the Year 1862.—The Lines of the Potomac.—General Jackson's Expo-
dition to Winchester.—The BATTLE OF MILL SPRINGS IN KENTUCKY.—General Crittenden.—Death of General Zollicoffer.—Sufferings of Crittenden's Army on the
Retreat.—Comparative Unimportance of the Disaster.—The BATTLE OF ROANOKE
ISLAND.—Importance of the Island to the South.—Death of Captain Wise.—Causes of
the Disaster to the South.—Investigation in Congress.—Censure of the Government.—
Interviews of General Wise with Mr. Benjamin, the Secretary of War.—Mr. Benjamin
censured by Congress, but retained in the Cabinet.—His Promotion by President
Davis.—Condition of the Popular Sentiment.

THE year 1862 was to bring in a train of disasters to the
South. Taking a brief glance at the lines of the Potomac, we
shall thereafter have to find the chief interest of the war in
other directions—in the West and on the seacoast.

In December last, Gen. Thomas F. Jackson was sent from
Gen. Johnston's line to Winchester with a force at his disposal
of some ten thousand men. Had the same force been placed
at the command of Gen. Jackson in early autumn, with the
view to an expedition to Wheeling, by way of the Winchester
and Parkersburg road, the good effects would, in all probability, have shown themselves in the expulsion of the Federals
from northwestern Virginia.

On the 1st of January, 1862, Gen. Jackson marched with
his command from Winchester to Bath, in Morgan county,
and from the latter place to Romney, where there had been a
large Federal force for many weeks, and from which point
they had committed extensive depredations on the surrounding
country. Gen. Jackson drove the enemy from Romney and
the neighboring country without much fighting. His troops,
however, endured the severest hardships in the expedition.
Their sufferings were terrible in what was the severest portion
of the winter. They were compelled at one time to struggle
through an almost blinding storm of snow and sleet, and to
bivouac at night in the forests, without tents or camp equipage. Many of the troops were frozen on the march, and died
from exposure and exhaustion.

The heroic commander, whose courage had been so brilliantly illustrated at Manassas, gave new proofs of his iron will in this expedition and the subsequent events of his campaign in the upper portion of the valley of Virginia. No one would have supposed that a man, who, at the opening of the war, had been a professor in a State military institute—that at Lexington, Virginia—could have shown such active determination and grim energy in the field. But Gen. Jackson had been brought up in a severer school of practical experience than West Point, where he had graduated twenty years before; he had served in the memorable campaign from Vera Cruz to Mexico; and an iron will and stern courage, which he had from nature, made him peculiarly fitted to command.* But we must wait for a subsequent period to refer again to Gen. Jackson's operations in the Valley, or to other portions of the campaign in Virginia.

---

* At the siege of Vera Cruz, Jackson commanded a battery, and attracted attention by the coolness and judgment with which he worked his guns, and was promoted first lieutenant. For his conduct at Cerro Gordo, he was brevetted captain. He was in all Scott's battles to the city of Mexico, and behaved so well that he was brevetted major for his services. To his merits as a commander he added the virtues of an active, humble, consistent Christian, restraining profanity in his camp, welcoming army colporteurs, distributing tracts, and anxious to have every regiment in his army supplied with a chaplain. He was vulgarly sneered at as a fatalist; his habits of soliloquy were derided as superstitious conversations with a familiar spirit; but the confidence he had in his destiny was the unfailing mark of genius, and adorned the Christian faith, which made him believe that he had a distinct mission of duty in which he should be spared for the ends of Providence. Of the habits of his life the following description is given by one who knew him: "He is as calm in the midst of a hurricane of bullets as he was in the pew of his church at Lexington, when he was professor of the Institute. He appears to be a man of almost superhuman endurance. Neither heat nor cold makes the slightest impression upon him. He cares nothing for good quarters and dainty fare. Wrapped in his blanket, he throws himself down on the ground anywhere, and sleeps as soundly as though he were in a palace. He lives as the soldiers live, and endures all the fatigue and all the suffering that they endure. His vigilance is something marvellous. He never seems to sleep, and lets nothing pass without his personal scrutiny. He can neither be caught napping, nor whipped when he is wide awake. The rapidity of his marches is something portentous. He is heard of by the enemy at one point, and, before they can make up their minds to follow him, he is off at another. His men have little baggage, and he moves, as nearly as he can, without incumbrance. He keeps so constantly in motion that he never has a sick list, and no need of hospitals.'

THE BATTLE OF MILL SPRINGS IN KENTUCKY.

In a previous chapter, we noticed the expedition of Gen. Zollicoffer in Kentucky, and gave an account of the rout of the forces sent against him. The next expedition of the enemy against him was successful beyond their expectations.

Since the affair referred to, Gen. Zollicoffer had moved with a portion of his command to Mill Springs, on the southern bank of the Cumberland river, and soon after advanced across to Camp Beech Grove, on the opposite bank, fortifying this camp with earthworks. At Beech Grove, he placed five regiments of infantry, twelve pieces of artillery, and several hundred cavalry, and at Mill Springs he had two regiments of infantry and several hundred cavalry. About the first of January, Major-general Crittenden arrived and took the command, having been advanced, by President Davis, from a captaincy in the Federal army to a major-generalship in the Confederate army.

Our position at Beech Grove had but few advantages. From the face of the country in front there was a very bad range for artillery, and it could not be of very material benefit against an attacking infantry force; and, considering the extent of the front line and the number of works to be defended, there was within the camp an insufficient force. At the same time, for several weeks, bare existence in the camps was very precarious, from want of provisions and forage. Regiments frequently subsisted on one-third rations, and this very frequently of bread alone. Wayne county, which was alone productive in this region of Kentucky, had been exhausted, and the neighboring counties of Tennessee could furnish nothing for the support of the army. Only corn could be obtained for the horses and mules, and this in such small quantities that often cavalry companies were sent out on unshod horses which had eaten nothing for two days. The condition of the roads and the poverty of the intervening section rendered it impossible to transport from Knoxville, a distance of one hundred and thirty miles. The enemy from Columbia commanded the Cumberland river, and only one boat was enabled to come up with supplies from Nashville. With the channel of communication closed, the position became untenable without attack.

In these straits, when the entire army at Mill Springs had been reduced to a single ration of beef per day, and a half ration of corn, the latter eaten as parched corn, and not issued as meal, news reached Gen. Crittenden of an advance movement of the enemy, both from Columbia and from Somerset. On the 17th of January it was ascertained that a large Federal force, under Gen. Thomas, was moving on the road from Columbia, and, on the evening of that day, was camped about ten miles from Beech Grove. It was also ascertained that other reinforcements were moving from the direction of Columbia, under command of Gen. Schoëpff, and that the junction of these two forces was intended for an attack on Camp Beech Grove.

Under these circumstances, Gen. Crittenden determined to attack Gen. Thomas's force in his camp. The decision, which was sanctioned by a council of war, was a most adventurous one. It was proposed, with an effective force of four thousand men, to attack an enemy in his intrenchments, at least ten thousand strong; it is true, however, that a defence of our intrenchments was impracticable, and that to have awaited the enemy there, would only have given him time to have effected a junction of his forces. This consideration, however, gives but an imperfect vindication of the impetuous adventure determined upon by Gen. Crittenden. The fact was, that the avenues of retreat were open to our little army, and could only have been cut off by the enemy's crossing above and below Mill Springs.

In perfect silence, at midnight, the march began. The brigade of Gen. Zollicoffer moved in front. In the gray dawn, about six o'clock, two miles from their camp, the pickets of the enemy fired upon our advanced cavalry. The morning of the 19th was dark and rainy—a fit day for a sabbath battle. The 15th Mississippi regiment, in line of battle, was steadily advanced, under the constant fire of the enemy. The charge of Gen. Zollicoffer's brigade, in which this gallant regiment earned the most conspicuous distinction of the day, soon became impetuous. The Mississippi troops fought with a devotion never excelled by the soldiers of any battle-field; nearly half of the regiment (it numbered only 440) fell in the action; at times they fought with the enemy at ten or twelve paces, and, in one of their sweeping and exultant charges, for fifty yards, dashed over the dead bodies of Yankees. The enemy was steadily driven back before the charge of Gen. Zollicoffer's command. Already he was ascending the last hill to its crest, where the heaviest firing told the battle raged. He sent for reinforcements, and the brigade of Gen. Carrol was ordered up. In another moment, it was announced that Gen. Zollicoffer was killed. He had fallen on the crest of the hill, the stronghold of the enemy, which he had almost driven them from, and which once gained, the day was ours.

Gen. Zollicoffer fell very near the camp of the enemy. He was with Col. Battle's Tennessee regiment, this and the Mississippi regiment being the chief participants in the action, and in the ranks of which were his own home friends, born and brought up around him at Nashville. In front, and concealed in the woods, was a regiment of Kentucky renegades, com manded by Col. Fry. By some mistake, probably that of the Kentuckians for a regiment of his own command, Gen. Zolli coffer got very near them. Col. Fry was at the right of his regiment. Gen. Zollicoffer was within a few feet of the colonel. A gum coat concealed his uniform. The two parties mistook each other for friends, and discovered their mutual mistake almost at the same instant. One of General Zollicoffer's aids shot at Colonel Fry, but only wounded his horse. The next moment the Federal colonel fired at Zollicoffer, and the gen eral, raising his hand to his breast, fell, pierced by several balls.

At the announcement of the death of Gen. Zollicoffer, a sudden gloom pervaded the field and depressed the Tennessee troops, who had been devotedly attached to him. Gen. Crittenden essayed all that personal example could do to retrieve the sinking fortunes of the day. He, in person, rode up to the front of the fight, in the very midst of the fire of the enemy. To gain the disputed hill, the fight was still continued. Charge after charge was driven back by the heavy forces of the enemy. After a conflict of three and a half hours, our troops commenced to give way. The pursuit was checked by several stands made by the little army, and the intrenchments at Camp Beech Grove were reached in the afternoon, with a loss on our side of about three hundred killed and wounded, and probably fifty prisoners.

The advance of the enemy arrived late in the evening before

the Confederate intrenchments, and fired upon them with shot and shell. Night closing in, put a stop to further demonstrations. Our men, tired and worn out as they were, stood behind the breastworks until midnight, when orders came for them to retreat quietly across the river. A steamer, with three barges attached, commenced the work of transportation. Cannon, baggage wagons, and horses were abandoned; every thing was lost save what our men had on their backs, and yet the whole night was consumed in getting the army over the river, which was very high at the time. The line of retreat was taken up towards Monticello, Gen. Crittenden having determined to strike for the Cumberland at the highest point where boats could land with safety, in order to be in open communication with Nashville.

The retreat was one of great distress. Many of the troops had become demoralized, and, without order, dispersed through the mountain by-ways in the direction of Monticello. "We reached Monticello," writes an officer of one of the regiments in the retreat, "at night, and then we were threatened with starvation—an enemy far more formidable than the one we left beyond the river. Since Saturday night, we had but an hour of sleep, and scarcely a morsel of food. For a whole week, we have been marching under a bare subsistence, and I have at length approached that point in a soldier's career when a hand ful of parched corn may be considered a first-class dinner. We marched the first few days through a barren region, where supplies could not be obtained. I have more than once seen the men kill a porker with their guns, cut and quarter it, and broil it on the coals, and then eat it without bread or salt. The suffering of the men from the want of the necessaries of life, of clothing, and of repose, has been most intense, and a more melancholy spectacle than this solemn, hungry, and weary procession, could scarcely be imagined."

The enemy invested the abandoned camp of the Confederates on the morning following the day of the battle. Gen. Schoëpff's brigade had crossed the river preparatory to the attack which Gen. Thomas had intended to make on the intrenchments on Monday. Early in the morning, the steamer used by the Confederates in effecting their retreat was discovered lying in the river, and was burnt by the shells of the enemy. They con gratulated themselves that they had cut off the last hope of the escape of "the rebels." Long columns of troops filed away, and the artillery commenced to play on the intrenchments, in doubt for a moment whether their guns were replied to or not, when word came that the intrenchments were abandoned. As the enemy marched into the camp there was hardly a cheer. They had hoped to capture every man of the Confederates, and were bitterly disappointed. They secured, however, a rich spoil of victory—every thing in fact that made our poor soldiers an army. The property captured was of considerable value. It consisted of eight six-pounders and two Parrott-guns, with caissons filled with ammunition, about 100 four-horse wagons, and upwards of 1,200 horses and mules, several boxes of arms which had never been opened, and from 500 to 1,000 muskets.

The death of Gen. Zollicoffer was deeply lamented by his countrymen. It is doubtful whether the death of any man of the present generation ever produced such conspicuous grief among Tennesseeans. He was a man made of stern stuff, and possessed in a remarkable degree the confidence of his army and of the Tennessee people. He was devoted to the interests of the South, and, during a long career in Congress, was one of the few members of the Whig party who voted uniformly with Southern men on all questions involving her honor and welfare. Made a brigadier-general, he was assigned to the department of East Tennessee at an early period of the war, and had exhibited rare address and genuine courage and military talents in the administration of his responsible command. It was a melancholy mode which his army chose of testifying their appreciation of his ability as a commander, in giving up all for lost when he was shot down ; but it certainly afforded a marked testimony of their confidence in his generalship.

The body of General Zollicoffer fell into the hands of the enemy. His remains were treated by them with unusual respect. One of their officers, who had known him in Washington-asked to be permitted to see the corpse. A pistol-shot had struck him in the breast, a little above the heart. His face bore no expression such as is usually found upon those who fall in battle—no malice, no reckless hate, not even a shadow of physical pain. It was calm, placid, noble. "Poor fellow," wrote the officer who visited with respect his remains just after the battle, "I have never looked on a countenance so marked with sadness. A deep dejection had settled on it. 'The low cares of the mouth' were distinct in the droop at its corners, and the thin cheeks showed the wasting which comes through disappointment and trouble."

The reverse sustained by our arms in Southern Kentucky involved no important military consequences; and the government at Richmond found cause of congratulation in the circumstance that, if a defeat must needs have happened to it at this time, it could not have come upon it at a point of less comparative consequence than the battle-ground near Somerset, Kentucky. It was a hundred miles from the line of railroad connecting us with the great West; it was a still greater distance from Cumberland Gap, the nearest point of the Virginia line; and there intervened, on the road to Knoxville, rivers and mountain passes which an invading army could only traverse slowly and with great caution.

But a disaster to our arms was shortly to ensue, of the importance and gravity of which there could be no doubt, and with respect to which the government could find neither consolations nor excuses. While we have seen how matters stood on the Potomac in the opening of the year 1862, and what ominous indications had taken place in the West, we must now remove the attention of the reader to the sea-coast, where, along the low and melancholy scenery of the sea-border of North Carolina, one of the most extraordinary dramas of the war was to be enacted.

THE BATTLE OF ROANOKE ISLAND.

On the 21st of December, that part of North Carolina east of the Chowan river, together with the counties of Washington and Tyrrell, was, at the request of the proper authorities of North Carolina, separated from the remainder, and constituted into a military district, under Brigadier-general H. A. Wise, and attached to the command of Major-general Huger, commanding the department of Norfolk.

Immediately upon the secession of the State of North Carolina from the government of the United States, and the adoption of the Constitution of the Confederate States of America,

the authorities of that State commenced the construction of
fortifications at Hatteras and Oregon Inlets, and other points
upon her coast, which were not completed when the State
transferred her forts, arsenals, army, navy, and coast defence
to the Confederate government.   Shortly thereafter the attack
was made upon Forts Hatteras and Clark, and they were
taken, and the fortifications at Oregon Inlet were abandoned,
and the armament, stores, and ammunition were removed to
Roanoke Island.   The enemy immediately appeared in force
in Pamlico Sound, the waters of which are connected with Albemarle and Currituck sounds by means of the two smaller
sounds of Croatan and Roanoke.   The island of Roanoke being situated between these two latter sounds, commanding the
channels of each, became, upon the fall of Hatteras and the
abandonment of Oregon Inlet, only second in importance to
Fortress Monroe.   The island then became the key which unlocked all northeastern North Carolina to the enemy, and exposed Portsmouth and Norfolk to a rear approach of the most
imminent danger.

Such was the importance of Roanoke Island.   It was threatened by one of the most formidable naval armaments yet fitted
out by the North, put under the command of Gen. Burnside,
of Rhode Island.   It might have been placed in a state of defence against any reasonable force, with the expenditure of
money and labor supposed to be within the means of the government.   Ample time and the fullest forewarnings were given
to the government for the construction of defences, since, for a
full month, Gen. Wise had represented to the government,
with the most obvious and emphatic demonstrations, that the
defences of the island were wholly inadequate for its protection
from an attack either by land or water.

The military defences of Roanoke Island and its adjacent
waters on the 8th of February, the day of its surrender, consisted of three sand forts, a battery of two 32-pounders, and a
redoubt thrown across the road in the centre of the island, about
seventy or eighty feet long, on the right of which was a swamp,
on the left a marsh.   In addition to these defences on the
shore and on the island, there was a barrier of piles, extending
from the east side of Fulker Shoals, towards the island.   Its
object was to compel vessels passing on the west of the island

to approach within reach of the shore batteries; but up to the 8th of February, there was a span of 1,700 yards open opposite to Fort Bartow, the most southern of the defences, on the west side of the island.

The entire military force stationed upon the island prior to, and at the time of, the late engagement, consisted of the 8th regiment of North Carolina State troops, under the command of Col. H. M. Shaw; the 31st regiment of North Carolina volunteers, under the command of Col. J. V. Jordan; and three companies of the 17th North Carolina troops, under the command of Major G. H. Hill. After manning the several forts, on the 7th of February, there were but one thousand and twenty-four men left, and two hundred of them were upon the sick list. On the evening of the 7th of February, Brig.-gen. Wise sent from Nagg's Head, under the command of Lieut.-col. Anderson, a reinforcement, numbering some four hundred and fifty men. The whole force was under the command of Brig.-gen. Wise, who, upon the 7th and 8th of February, was at Nagg's Head, four miles distant from the island, confined to a sick-bed, and entirely disabled from participating in the action in person. The immediate command, therefore, devolved upon Col. H. M. Shaw, the senior officer present.

On the morning of the 7th of February, the enemy's fleet proceeded steadily towards Fort Bartow. In the sound between Roanoke Island and the mainland, upon the Tyrrell side, Commodore Lynch, with his squadron of seven vessels, had taken position, and at eleven o'clock the enemy's fleet, consisting of about thirty gunboats and schooners, advanced in ten divisions, the rear one having the schooners and transports in tow. The advance and attacking division again subdivided, one assailing the squadron and the other firing upon the fort with nine-inch, ten-inch, and eleven-inch shell, spherical case, a few round-shot, and every variety of rifled projectiles. The fort replied with but four guns (which were all that could be brought to bear), and after striking the foremost vessels several times, the fleet fell back, so as to mask one of the guns of the fort, leaving but three to reply to the fire of the whole fleet. The bombardment was continued throughout the day, and the enemy retired at dark. The squadron, under the command of Commodore Lynch, sustained their position

most gallantly, and only retired after exhausting all their am
munition, and having lost the steamer Curlew and the Forest
disabled.

In the mean time, the enemy had found a point of landing
out of the reach of our field-pieces, and defended by a swamp
from the advance of our infantry. The enemy having effected
a landing here, our whole force took position at the redoubt or
breastwork, and placed in battery their field-pieces with necessary artillerymen, under the respective commands of Captain
Schemerhorn, and Lieutenants Kinney and Seldon. Two companies of the Eighth and two of the Thirty-first were placed at
the redoubt to support the artillery. Three companies of the
Wise Legion, deployed to the right and left as skirmishers.
The remainder of the infantry were in position, three hundred
yards in the rear of the redoubt, as a reserve.

The enemy landed some fifteen thousand men, with artillery,
and, at 7 o'clock, A. M., of the 8th, opened fire upon the redoubt,
which was replied to immediately with great spirit, and the
action soon became general, and was continued without intermission for more than five hours, when the enemy succeeded
in deploying a large force on either side of our line, flanking
each wing. The order was then given by Col. Shaw to spike
the guns in the battery, and to retreat to the northern end of
the island. The guns were spiked, and the whole force fell
back to the camps.

During the engagement at the redoubt, the enemy's fleet attempted to advance to Croatan Sound, which brought on a
desultory engagement between Fort Bartow and the fleet,
which continued up to half-after 12 o'clock, when the commanding officer was informed that the land defences had been
forced, and the position of the fort turned; he thereupon ordered the guns to be disabled and the ammunition destroyed,
which was done, and the fort abandoned. The same thing was
done at the other forts, and the forces from all the forts were
marched in good order to the camp. The enemy took possession of the redoubts and forts immediately, and proceeded in
pursuit, with great caution, towards the northern end of the
island in force, deploying so as to surround our forces at the
camp.

Co. Shaw had arrived with his whole force at his camp in

time to have saved his whole command, if transports i.ad been furnished. But there were none. His situation was one of extreme exigency. He found himself surrounded by a greatly superior force upon the open island ; he had no field-works to protect him ; he had lost his only three field-pieces at the redoubt; and he had either to make an idle display of courage in fighting the foe at such immense disadvantage, which would have involved the sacrifice of his command, or to capitulate and surrender as prisoners of war. He determined upon the latter alternative.

The loss on our side was, killed, 23 ; wounded, 58 ; missing, 62. Our mortality list, however, was no indication of the spirit and vigor of our little army, as in its position it had but little opportunity of contest without a useless sacrifice of human life on their side. Among the killed was Captain O. Jennings Wise, of the Richmond Blues, son of General Wise, a young man of brilliant promise, refined chivalry, and a courage to which the softness of his manners and modesty of his behavior added the virtue of knightly heroism. His body, pierced by wounds, fell into the hands of the enemy, in whose camp, attended by every mark of respect, he expired. The disaster at Roanoke Island was a sharp mortification to the public. But for the unfortunate general, who was compelled to hear on a sick-bed—perhaps to witness from the windows of a sick-chamber—the destruction of his army and the death of his son, there was not a word of blame.

In a message to Congress, President Davis referred to the result of the battle at Roanoke Island as " deeply humiliating ;" a committee of Congress, appointed to investigate the affair, resented the attempt to attribute a disaster, for which the government itself was notoriously responsible, to want of spirit in our troops; declared that, on the contrary, the battle of Roanoke Island was " one of the most gallant and brilliant actions of the war ;" and concluded that whatever of blame and responsibility was justly attributable to any one for the defeat, should attach to Gen. Huger, in whose military department the island was, and to the Secretary of War, Judah P. Benjamin, whose positive refusal to put the island in a state of defence secured its fall. There was, in fact, but little room for the government to throw reflection upon the conduct of the troops. In the language of their commanding general, "both officers and men fought firmly, coolly, efficiently, and as long as humanity would allow."

The connection of the War Department with the Roanoke Island affair, which was with difficulty dragged to light in Congress, is decidedly one of the most curious portions of the history of the war. Gen. Wise had pressed upon the government the importance of Roanoke Island* for the defence of Norfolk. He assumed the command of the post upon the 7th of January. In making a reconnoissance of the island and its defences, on the 13th January, he addressed Secretary Benjamin, and declared that the island, which was the key of all the rear defences of Norfolk, and its canals and railroads, was "utterly defenceless." On the 15th of January, Gen. Wise addressed the secretary again. He wrote that twenty-four vessels of the enemy's fleet were already inside of Hatteras Inlet, and within thirty miles of Roanoke Island; that all there was to oppose him was five small gunboats, and four small land batteries, wholly inefficient; that our batteries were not casemated; and that the force at Hatteras, independent of the Burnside expedition, was "amply sufficient to capture or pass Roanoke Island in any twelve hours."

These written appeals for aid in the defences of the island were neglected and treated with indifference. Determined to leave nothing wanting in energy of address, Gen. Wise repaired in person to Richmond, and called upon the Secretary of War, and urged, in the most importunate manner, the absolute

---

* It (Roanoke Island) was the key to all the rear defences of Norfolk. It unlocked two sounds, Albemarle and Currituck; eight rivers, the North, West, Pasquotank, the Perquimmons, the Little, the Chowan, the Roanoke, and the Alligator; four canals, the Albemarle and Chesapeake, the Dismal Swamp, the Northwest Canal, and the Suffolk; two railroads, the Petersburg and Norfolk, and the Seaboard and Roanoke. It guarded more than four-fifths of all Norfolk's supplies of corn, pork, and forage, and it cut the command of General Huger off from all its most efficient transportation. It endangers the subsistence of his whole army, threatens the navy-yard at Gosport, and to cut off Norfolk from Richmond, and both from railroad communication with the South. It lodges the enemy in a safe harbor from the storms of Hatteras, gives them a rendezvous, and large rich range of supplies, and the command of the seaboard from Oregon Inlet to Cape Henry. It should have been defended at the expense of twenty thousand men, and of many millions of dollars."—*Report of Gen. Wise.*

necessity of strengthening the defences upon that island with additional men, armament, and ammunition. Mr. Benjamin replied verbally to his appeals for reinforcements, that he had not the men to spare for his command. Gen. Wise urged upon the secretary that Gen. Huger had about 15,000 men in front of Norfolk, lying idle in camp for eight months, and that a considerable portion of them could be spared for the defence of the rear of Norfolk, and especially as his (Gen. Wise's) district supplied Norfolk and his army with nearly or quite all of his corn, pork, and forage.

The reply to all these striking and urgent appeals was a peremptory military order from Secretary Benjamin, dated the 22d of January, requiring Gen. Wise to proceed immediately to Roanoke Island. With ready military pride the unfortunate general received the orders, without a murmur in public; it being known only to his most intimate friends the circumstances under which he left Richmond on the stern and unpropitious mission which promised nothing to himself but disaster, the mistaken calumnies of the public, and death in the midst of defeat.

The facts we have referred to are of record. The committee of Congress that investigated the affair of Roanoke Island declared that the Secretary of War, Mr. J. P. Benjamin, was responsible for an important defeat of our arms, which might have been safely avoided by him; that he had paid no practical attention to the appeals of Gen. Wise; and that he had, by plain acts of omission, permitted that general and an inconsiderable force to remain to meet at least fifteen thousand men, well armed and equipped. The committee referred to was open to any justification that might have been sought by the Secretary of War, or his friends: none was offered; and the unanimous conclusion of the committee, in sharp and distinct terms, was put upon the public record, charging a Cabinet officer with a matter of the gravest offence known to the laws and the interests of the country.

The effect of war is always, in some degree, public demoralization; and the gravest charges are often lost and swallowed up in the quick and feverish excitements of such times. But whatever may have been the charities of speedy oblivion with respect to the charges against Mr. Benjamin, the public were at least, not prepared for such an exhibition of trust and honor as was given him by the President, in actually promoting him, after the developments of the Roanoke Island disaster, and giving him the place in his cabinet of Secretary of State Whatever may have been the merits of this act of the President, it was at least one of ungracious and reckless defiance to the popular sentiment; and from the marked event of the surrender of Roanoke Island and its consequences, we must date the period when the people had their confidence weakened in the government, and found no other repose for their trust than in the undin'..ished valor and devoted patriotism of the troops in the field

CHAPTER X.

The Situation in Tennessee and Kentucky.—The affair at Woodsonville.—Death of Colonel Terry.—The Strength and Material of the Federal Force in Kentucky.—Condition of the Defences on the Tennessee and Cumberland Rivers.—The Confederate Congress and the Secretary of the Navy.—The Fall of Fort Henry.—Fort Donelson threatened.—The Army of General A. S. Johnston.—His Interview with General Beauregard.—Insensibility of the Confederate Government to the Exigency.—General Johnston's Plan of Action.—BATTLE OF FORT DONELSON.—Carnage and Scenery of the Battle-field.—The Council of the Southern Commanders.—Agreement to surrender. —Escape of Generals Floyd and Pillow.—The Fall of Fort Donelson develops the Crisis in the West.—The Evacuation of Nashville.—The Panic.—Extraordinary Scenes.—Experience of the Enemy in Nashville.—The Adventures of Captain John Morgan.—General Johnston at Murfreesboro.—Organization of a New Line of Defence South of Nashville.—The Defence of Memphis and the Mississippi.—Island No. 10.—Serious Character of the Disaster at Donelson.—Generals Floyd and Pillow "relieved from Command."—General Johnston's Testimony in favor of these Officers.-President Davis's Punctilio.—A sharp Contrast.—Negotiation for the Exchange o Prisoners.—A Lesson of Yankee Perfidy.—Mr. Benjamin's Release of Yankee Hostages.

THE unequivocal demonstrations of the Federals for an advance upon Tennessee through Kentucky, urged the Confederate government to send all the disposable forces at its command to strengthen the army of the southwestern division. Near the close of the year 1861, the Floyd Brigade and several regiments belonging to Tennessee and other Confederate States were sent from Virginia to Bowling Green, in southern Kentucky, the principal strategic point of the southwestern army. The command of that army was given, as we have seen, to General Albert Sidney Johnston.

Early in December, the Federal army occupied Muldraugh's Hill, Elizabethtown, Nolin, Bacon's Creek, and other points on the railroad, from forty to sixty miles below Louisville. Later in that month, a body of them advanced to Munfordville, on Green River, about seventy-five miles below Louisville, and about thirty-five miles above Bowling Green. A portion of this advance crossed the river at Munfordville to Woodsonville on the opposite shore, where they were attacked by the advance Confederate forces under Brig.-general Hindman and defeated with a loss of about fifty killed. The Confederates lost four killed and nine wounded. Their conduct was marked by the most impetuous valor. On charging the enemy, Col. Terry, of the Texas Rangers, was killed in the moment of victory. In the death of Col. Terry, said General Hardee, in his official report, "his regiment had to deplore the loss of a beloved and brave commander, and the whole army one of its ablest officers." His name was placed in the front rank of the gallant sons of Texas, whose daring and devoted courage had added to the lustre of our arms and to the fruits of more than one victory.

The fight at Woodsonville was on the 17th of December. When the enemy reached that place in force, the Confederates fell back some fifteen or twenty miles, in the direction of Bowling Green. For some weeks thereafter, the whole South was excited with reports to the effect that the Federals were advancing upon Bowling Green in three columns, of 20,000 each. But the unanticipated success of the Federals in two important movements at other points within the department of General Johnston, enabled them to accomplish their object without an attack upon Bowling Green, and forced upon the Confederates the necessity of evacuating that post.

The North had collected an immense army in Kentucky, under command of Major-general Buell, a general of great skill, remarkable for the caution of his operations, but having with this quality the rare combination of energy, courage, and unwearied activity. The whole force of the Federals in Kentucky consisted of about one hundred thousand infantry, eleven thousand cavalry, and three thousand artillerists, divided into some twenty odd batteries. It is remarkable that this immense army was composed almost entirely of Western men, and that the "Yankee" proper was scarcely represented in its ranks. Of the Eastern States, only Pennsylvania had troops in Kentucky, and those comparatively few. Every Western State, with the exception of Iowa, Missouri, and Kansas, was represented by more or less regiments.

A large force of the Federals had been collected at Paducah, at the mouth of the Tennessee river, with a view to offensive operations on the water. This river was an important stream. It penetrated Tennessee and Alabama, and was navigable for steamers for two or three hundred miles. The Provisiona

Congress, at Richmond, had appropriated half a million dollars for floating defences on the Tennessee and Cumberland rivers: but owing to the notorious inefficiency of the Navy Department, presided over by Mr. Mallory of Florida, who was remarkable for his obtuseness, slow method, and indifferent intellect, and whose ignorance even of the geography of Kentucky and Tennessee had been broadly travestied in Congress, both rivers were left open to the incursions of the enemy. On the Tennessee there was nothing to resist the enemy's advance up the stream but a weak and imperfectly constructed fort. The Cumberland was a still more important river, and the key to Nashville; but nothing stood in the way of the enemy save Fort Donelson, and from that point the Federal gunboats could reach Nashville in six or eight hours, and strike a vital point of our whole system of defences in the West.

On the 4th of February, the enemy's expedition up the Tennessee, under Gen. Grant, arrived at Fort Henry, the only fortification on the Tennessee river of any importance, situated near the lines of Kentucky and Tennessee, on the east bank of the stream. On the morning of the 6th, the fort was attacked.

Our works were untenable, but it concerned us to save our little army. To defend the position at the time, Gen. Tilghman, commanding division, had Col. Heiman's 10th Tennessee, Irish volunteers, eight hundred strong; Col. Drake's Mississippi volunteers, four hundred strong; Col. Hughes' Alabama volunteers, five hundred strong; and Lieut.-col. Gantt's Tennessee volunteers, cavalry, three hundred strong; one company of light artillery, commanded by Lieut. Culbertson, Confederate States artillery, and Captain Jesse Taylor's company of artillery, sixty strong, forming the garrison of Fort Henry, and manning its batteries of nine or ten guns.

A sudden rise in the river found Fort Henry, on the morning of the attack, completely surrounded by water, containing only Capt. Taylor's company of artillery. The two thousand men of all arms, who formed Gen. Tilghman's command, were half a mile off, beyond a sheet of back-water. Gen. Grant's army was on the direct road, between them and Fort Donelson, on the Cumberland, and within two miles of the fort, and already in motion to invest it. It was an embarrassing ques tion to determine what was to be done. Gen. Tilghman's little army was in the jaws of the lion, and the question was, how could it be extricated.

Gen. Tilghman at once solved the problem, by ordering it to retreat by the upper route. He remained with his sixty men in the fort, where he was surrounded by water, and unable to get away.

A few minutes before the surrender, the scene in and around the fort exhibited a spectacle of fierce grandeur. Many of the cabins and tents in and around the fort were in flames : added to the scene were the smoke from the burning timber, and the curling but dense wreaths of smoke from the guns; the con- stantly recurring spattering and whizzing of fragments of crashing and bursting shells ; the deafening roar of artillery ; the black sides of five or six gunboats, belching fire at every port-hole ; the volumes of smoke settled in dense masses along the surrounding back-waters ; and up and over that fog, on the heights, the army of Gen. Grant (10,000) deploying around our small army, attempting to cut off its retreat. In the midst of the storm of shot and shell, the small force outside of the fort had succeeded in gaining the upper road, the gunboats having failed to notice their movements until they were out of reach.

To give them further time, the gallant Tilghman, exhausted and begrimed with powder and smoke, stood erect at the middle battery, and pointed gun after gun. It was clear, how- ever, that the fort could not hold out much longer. A white flag was raised by the order of Gen. Tilghman, who remarked, " it is vain to fight longer ; our gunners are disabled ; our guns dismounted ; we can't hold out five minutes longer." As soon as the token of submission was hoisted, the gunboats came alongside the fort and took possession of it, their crews giving three cheers for the Union. Gen. Tilghman and the small gar- rison of forty were taken prisoners.

The fall of Fort Henry was the signal for the direction of the most anxious attention to Fort Donelson, on the Cumber land.

We have noticed before the extreme inadequacy of Gen Johnston's forces. It is doubtful whether he ever had over

23,000 effective troops at Bowling Green. Of these, after re-inforcing Fort Donelson, he had scarcely more than eleven thousand effective men. Shortly after the disaster at Mill Springs, Gen. Beauregard had been sent from the Potomac to Gen. Johnston's line in Kentucky. At a conference which took place between the two generals, Gen. Beauregard expressed his surprise at the smallness of Gen. Johnston's forces, and was impressed with the danger of his position. There is nothing more remarkable in the history of the war than the false impressions of the people of the South as to the extent of our forces at the principal strategic point in Kentucky, and the long and apathetic toleration, by the government in Richmond, of a prospect that promised nothing but eventual disaster. On establishing himself in Bowling Green early in October, General Johnston wrote to the War Department : " We have received but little accession to our ranks since the Confederate forces crossed the line—in fact, no such enthusiastic demonstration as to justify any movements not warranted by our ability to maintain our own communications." He repeatedly called upon the government for reinforcements. He made a call upon several States of the Southwest, including Tennessee, for large numbers of troops. The call was revoked at the instance of the authorities in Richmond, who declined to furnish twelve months' volunteers with arms ; and Gen. Johnston, thus discouraged and baffled by a government which was friendly enough to him personally, but insensible to the public exigency for which he pleaded, was left in the situation of imminent peril, in which Gen. Beauregard was so surprised to find him.

A memorandum was made of the conference between the two generals. In the plans of Gen. Johnston, Gen. Beauregard entirely concurred. It was determined to fight for Nashville at Donelson, and Gen. Johnston gave the best part of his army to do it, retaining only, to cover his front, fourteen thousand men, about three thousand of whom were so enfeebled by recent sickness that they were unable to march.

BATTLE OF FORT DONELSON.

On the 9th February, Gen. Pillow had been ordered to proceed to Fort Donelson and take command at that place, which it was supposed would be an immediate object of attack by Gen. Ulysses S. Grant and his combined land and naval forces No time was lost in getting the works in defensible condition. The armament of the batteries consisted of thirteen guns or different calibres. The site of the fortification was plainly unfavorable in view of a land attack, being commanded by the heights above and below the river, and by a continuous range of hills all around the work to its rear. A line of intrenchments about two miles in extent was occupied by the troops.

On the morning of the 13th of February, Gen. Floyd, who had been stationed at Russellville, reached the fort by orders transmitted by telegraph from Gen. A. S. Johnston, at Bowling Green. Soon after his arrival, the intrenchments were fully occupied from one end to the other, and just as the sun rose the cannonade from one of the enemy's gunboats announced the opening of the conflict, which was destined to continue for several days and nights. The fire soon became general along our whole lines.

During the whole day the enemy kept up a general and active fire from all arms upon our trenches. At several points along the line he charged with uncommon vigor, but was met with a spirit of courageous resistance, which by nightfall had driven him, discomfited and cut to pieces, back upon the position he had assumed in the morning. The results of the day were encouraging. The strength of our defensive line had been pretty well tested, and the loss sustained by our forces was not large, our men being mostly under shelter in the rifle pits.

The enemy continued his fire upon different parts of the intrenchments throughout the night, which deprived the Confederate troops of any opportunity to sleep. They lay that night upon their arms in the trenches. A more vigorous attack from the enemy than ever, was confidently expected at the dawn of day; but in this the Confederates were entirely mistaken. The day advanced, and no preparation seemed to be making for a general onset. The smoke of a large number of gunboats and steamboats on the river was observed a short distance below, and information at the same time was received within our lines of the arrival of a large number of new troops greatly increasing the strength of the enemy's forces, already said to be from twenty to thirty thousand strong.

About three o'clock in the afternoon the enemy's fleet ot gunboats, in full force, advanced upon the fort and opened fire They advanced in the shape of a crescent, and kept up a con stant fire for an hour and a half. Once the boats reached a point within a few hundred yards of the fort. The effects of our shot upon the iron-cased boats were now distinctly visible. Two or three well-directed shots from the heavy guns of the fort drove back the nearest boat; several shot struck another boat, tearing her iron case and splintering her timbers, and making them crack as if by a stroke of lightning, when she, too, fell back. A third boat received several severe shocks, making her metal ring and her timbers crack, when the whole line gave way and fell rapidly back from the fire of the fort, until they passed out of range.

The incidents of the two days had all been in our favor. We had repulsed the enemy in the battle of the trenches, broken the line of his gunboats, and discomfited him on the water.

In the mean time, however, reinforcements were continually reaching the enemy ; and it might have been evident from the first that the whole available force of the Federals on the western waters could and would be concentrated at Fort Donelson, if it was deemed necessary to reduce it. A consultation of the officers of divisions and brigades was called by General Floyd, to take place after dark. It was represented that it was an absolute impossibility to hold out for any length of time with our inadequate number and indefensible position ; that there was no place within our intrenchments but could be reached by the enemy's artillery from their boats or their batteries; that it was but fair to infer that, while they kept up a sufficient fire upon our intrenchments to keep our men from sleep and prevent repose, their object was merely to give time to pass a column above us on the river, and to cut off our communications; and that but one course was left by which a rational hope could be entertained of saving the garrison, and that was to dislodge the enemy from his position on our left, and thus to pass our troops into the open country lying southward towards Nashville.

It was thus determined to remove from the trenches at an early hour the next morning, and attack the enemy in his position. There was, in fact, no other alternative. The enemy had been busy in throwing his forces of every arm around the Confederates, extending his line of investment entirely around their position, and completely enveloping them. Every road and possible avenue of departure was intercepted, with the certainty that our sources of supply by the river would soon be cut off by the enemy's batteries placed upon the river above us.

The sufferings of our army had already been terrible. The day of the opening of the battle (Thursday) was very cold, the mercury being only ten degrees above zero, and during the night, while our troops were watching on their arms in the trenches, it sleeted and snowed. The distance between the two armies was so slight that but few of the dead of either could be taken off, and many of the wounded who could neither walk nor crawl remained for more than two days where they fell. Some of our men lay wounded before our earth-works at night, calling for help and water, and our troops who went out to bring them in were discovered in the moonlight and fired upon by the enemy. Many of our wounded were not recovered until Sunday morning—some of them still alive, but blue with cold, and covered with frost and snow. It would have been merciful if each army had been permitted, under a flag of truce, to bring off its wounded at the close of each day; but it was not so, and they lay in the frost and sleet between the two armies—many to hear, but none to help them.

For nearly a week a large portion of our troops had been guarding their earth-works, and from the day of the battle they had been out in force night and day. Many of them in the rifle-pits froze their feet and hands. The severity of the cold was such that the clothes of many of the troops were so stiff from frozen water, that could they have been taken off, they would have stood alone.

At the meeting of general officers called by Gen. Floyd on Friday night, it was unanimously determined to cut open a route of exit, and thus to save our army. The plan of attack agreed upon and directed by Gen. Floyd was, that Gen. Pillow assisted by Gen. Bushrod Johnson, having also under his command commanders of brigades, Col. Baldwin, commanding

Mississippi and Tennessee troops, and Col. Wharton and Col. McCausland, commanding Virginians, should, with the main body of the forces defending our left wing, attack the right wing of the enemy occupying the heights reaching to the bank of the river; that Gen. Buckner, with the forces under his command, and defending the right of our line, should strike the enemy's encampment on the Winn's Ferry road; and that each command should leave in the trenches troops to hold them.

The attack on the left was delayed, as Gen. Pillow moved out of his position in the morning. He found the enemy prepared to receive him in advance of his encampment. For two hours this principal portion of the battle-field was hotly and stubbornly contested, and strewn with piles of dead. The Federal troops in this quarter fought with a steadiness and determination rarely witnessed, and the exhibition of their courage on this field afforded a lesson to the South of a spirit that it had not expected in an enemy whose valor it had been accustomed to deride and sneer at since the battle of Manassas The Federals did not retreat, but fell back fighting us and con testing every inch of ground. Being forced to yield, they retired slowly towards the Winn's Ferry road, Buckner's point of attack.

On this road, where Gen. Buckner's command was expected to flank the enemy, it had been forced to retire from his battery, and as the enemy continued to fall back, Gen. Buckner's troops became united with the forces of Gen. Pillow in engaging the enemy, who had again been reinforced. The entire command of the enemy had been forced to our right wing, and in front of Gen. Buckner's position in the intrenchment. The advantage was instantly appreciated. The enemy drove back the Confederates, advanced on the trenches on the extreme right of Gen. Buckner's command, getting possession, after a stubborn conflict of two hours, of the most important and commanding position of the battle-field, being in the rear of our river batteries, and, advancing with fresh forces towards our left, drove back our troops from the ground that had been won in the severe and terrible conflict of the early part of the day

The field had been won by the enemy after nine hours of conflict. Night found him in possession of all the ground that had been won by our troops in the morning, and occupying the most commanding portion of our intrenched work, to drive him from which the most desperate assaults of our troops had been unsuccessful. The enemy had been landing reinforce ments throughout the day. His numbers had been augmented to eighty-two regiments. We had only about 13,000 troops all told. Of these we had lost in three different battles a large proportion. The command had been in the trenches night and day, exposed to the snow, sleet, mud, and ice-water, without shelter, without adequate covering, and without sleep. To re new the combat with any hope of successful result was obvi ously vain.

A council of general officers was called at night. It was suggested that a desperate onset upon the right of the enemy's forces on the ground might result in the extrication of a con siderable proportion of the command. A majority of the coun cil rejected this proposition. Gen. Buckner remarked, that it would cost the command three-fourths its present numbers to cut its way out, and it was wrong to sacrifice three-fourths to save one-fourth; that no officer had a right to cause such a sacrifice. The alternative of the proposition was a surrender of the position and command. Gen. Floyd and Gen. Pillow each, declared that they would not surrender themselves pris oners. The former claimed that he had a right individually to determine that he would not survive a surrender. He said that he would turn over the command to Gen. Buckner, if he (Gen. Floyd) could be allowed to withdraw his own particular brigade. To this Gen. Buckner consented. Thereupon, the command was turned over to Gen. Pillow, he passing it in stantly to Gen. Buckner, declaring that "he would neither sur render the command nor himself." Col. Forrest, at the head of an efficient regiment of cavalry, was directed to accompany Gens. Floyd and Pillow in what was supposed to be an effort to pass through the enemy's lines. Under these circumstances, Gen. Buckner accepted the command. He sent a flag of truce to the enemy for an armistice of six hours, to negotiate for terms of capitulation.* Before the flag and communication

* The following is a correct list of the Confederate prisoners taken at Fort Donelson. The number was reported in the newspapers of the time, South

were delivered, Gens. Pillow and Floyd had retired from the garrison, and by daylight were pursuing their retreat towards Nashville, the largest portion of the command of the latter toiling in their flight along the banks of the Tennessee, but without a pursuing enemy to harass them.

The surrender of Donelson was rendered memorable by the hardest fighting that had yet occurred in the war, and by one of the most terrible and sickening battle-fields that had yet marked its devastations, or had ever appealed to the horror-stricken senses of humanity. The conflict had run through four days and four nights; in which a Confederate force not exceeding 13,000, a large portion of whom were illy armed, had contended with an army at least three times its number. The loss of the Federals was immense, and the proofs of an undeniable courage were left in the numbers of their dead on the field. In his official report of the battle, Gen. Floyd conjectures that the enemy's loss in killed and wounded reached a number beyond 5,000. The same authority gives our loss at 1,500. Both statements are only conjectural.

The scene of action had been mostly in the woods, although there were two open places of an acre or two where the fight had raged furiously, and the ground was covered with dead. All the way up to our intrenchments the same scene of death was presented. There were two miles of dead strewn thickly, mingled with fire-arms, artillery, dead horses, and the paraphernalia of the battle-field. Federals and Confederates were promiscuously mingled, sometimes grappling in the fierce death throe, sometimes facing each other as they gave and received the fatal shot and thrust, sometimes huddled in grotesque shapes, and again heaped in piles, which lay six or seven feet deep. Many of the bodies were fearfully mangled. The artillery horses had not hesitated to tread on the wounded, dying,

as well as North, to have been much larger: Floyd's Virginia Artillery, 34; Gray's Virginia Artillery, 59; French's Virginia Artillery, 43; Murray's Battery, 97; Cumberland Battery, 55; Fiftieth Tennessee, 485; Fourteenth Mississippi, 326; Third Mississippi, 330; Seventh Texas, 354; Twenty-sixth Mississippi, 427; Twenty-seventh Alabama, 180; Third Tennessee, 627; Tenth Tennessee, 608; Forty-second Tennessee, 494; Forty-eighth Tennessee, 249; Forty-ninth Tennessee, 450; Twenty-sixth Tennessee, 65; Second Kentucky 136; Third Alabama, 34; Fiftieth Virginia, 10; Fifty-first Tennessee, 17 Total, 5,079.

and dead, and the ponderous artillery wheels crushed limbs and skulls. It was an awful sight to behold weak, wounded men lifting their feeble hands beneath the horses' hoofs. The village of Dover, which was within our lines, contained in every room in every house sick, wounded, or dead men. Bloody rags were everywhere, and a door could not be opened without hearing groans.

"I could imagine," says an eye-witness of the field of carnage, "nothing more terrible than the silent indications of agony that marked the features of the pale corpses which lay at every step. Though dead and rigid in every muscle, they still writhed and seemed to turn to catch the passing breeze for a cooling breath. Staring eyes, gaping mouths, clinched hands, and strangely contracted limbs, seemingly drown into the smallest compass, as if by a mighty effort to rend asunder some irresistible bond which held them down to the torture of which they died. One sat against a tree, and, with mouth and eyes wide open, looked up into the sky as if to catch a glance at its fleeting spirit. Another clutched the branch of an overhanging tree, and hung half-suspended, as if in the death-pang he had raised himself partly from the ground; the other had grasped his faithful musket, and the compression of his mouth told of the determination which would have been fatal to a foe had life ebbed a minute later. A third clung with both hands to a bayonet which was buried in the ground. Great numbers lay in heaps, just as the fire of the artillery mowed them down, mangling their forms into an almost undistinguishable mass."

The display of courage on the part of the Federal troops was unquestionable. The battle, however, was fought against us by Western men, there not being in the ranks of the enemy, as far as known, any men east of the Ohio. The Southern people, while contemning the fighting qualities of the New England "Yankee" and the Pennsylvania Dutchman, were constrained to give to the Western men credit for their bravery; and many of our own officers did not hesitate to express the opinion that the Western troops, particularly from southern Illinois, Minnesota, and Iowa, were as good fighting material as there was to be found on the continent. A Confederate officer relates a story of an extraordinary display of spirit on the field of Donelson by a regiment of Zouaves from southern Illinois—the "Egypt" regiment, as it was called. It had been completely shattered by the fire of artillery, and was scattered over the fields in what the Confederates supposed to be an irretrievable rout. A few sharp rallying words from their color-bearer, and the men, who a few minutes ago were fugitives, flocked to their colors, at the double quick, from different parts of the field, and re-formed in the very face of the advancing foe.

The fall of Fort Donelson developed the crisis in the West, which had long existed. The evacuation of Bowling Green had become imperatively necessary, and was ordered before and executed while the battle was being fought at Donelson. Gen. Johnston awaited the event opposite Nashville. The result of the conflict each day was announced as favorable. At midnight on the 15th February, Gen. Johnston received news of a glorious victory—at dawn of a defeat.

The blow was most disastrous. It involved the surrender of Nashville, which was incapable of defence from its position, and was threatened not only by the enemy's ascent of the Cumberland, but by the advance of his forces from Bowling Green. Not more than 11,000 effective men had been left under Gen. Johnston's command to oppose a column of Gen. Buell, of not less than 40,000 troops, while the army from Fort Donelson, with the gunboats and transports, had it in their power to ascend the Cumberland, so as to intercept all communication with the South. No alternative was left but to evacuate Nashville or sacrifice the army.

The evacuation of Nashville was attended by scenes of panic and distress on the part of the population unparalleled in the annals of any American city. The excitement was intensified by the action of the authorities. Governor Harris mounted a horse and galloped through the streets, proclaiming to everybody the news that Donelson had fallen; that the enemy were coming and might be expected hourly, and that all who wished to leave had better do so at once. He next hastily convened the Legislature, adjourned it to Memphis, and, with the legislators and the State archives, left the town.

An earthquake could not have shocked the city more. The congregations at the churches were broken up in confusion and dismay; women and children rushed into the streets, wailing with terror; trunks were thrown from three-story windows in the haste of the fugitives; and thousands hastened to leave their beautiful city in the midst of the most distressing scenes of terror and confusion, and of plunder by the mob.

Gen. Johnston had moved the main body of his command to Murfreesboro'—a rear-guard being left in Nashville under Gen. Floyd, who had arrived from Donelson, to secure the stores and provisions. In the first wild excitement of the panic, the store-houses had been thrown open to the poor. They were besieged by a mob ravenous for spoils, and who had to be dispersed from the commissariat by jets of water from a steam fire-engine. Women and children, even, were seen scudding through the streets under loads of greasy pork, which they had taken as prizes from the store-houses. It is believed that hundreds of families, among the lower orders of the population, secured and secreted government stores enough to open respectable groceries. It was with the greatest difficulty that Gen. Floyd could restore order and get his martial law into any thing like an effective system. Blacks and whites had to be chased and captured and forced to help the movement of government stores. One man, who, after a long chase, was captured, offered fight, and was in consequence shot and badly wounded. Not less than one million of dollars in stores was lost through the acts of the cowardly and ravenous mob of Nashville. Gen. Floyd and Col. Forrest exhibited extraordinary energy and efficiency in getting off government stores. Col. Forrest remained in the city about twenty-four hours, with only forty men, after the arrival of the enemy at Edgefield. These officers were assisted by the voluntary efforts of several patriotic citizens of Nashville, who rendered them great assistance.

These shameful scenes, enacted in the evacuation of Nashville, were nothing more than the disgusting exhibitions of any mob brutalized by its fears or excited by rapine. At any rate, the city speedily repaired the injury done its reputation by a temporary panic, in the spirit of defiance that its best citizens and especially its ladies, offered to the enemy. We discover, in fact, the most abundant evidence in the Northern newspapers that the Federals did not find the "Union" sentiment that they expected to meet with in the capital of Tennessee, and that, if there were any indications whatever of such sentiment, they were "found only among the mechanics and laboring classes of the city." The merchants and business men of Nashville, as a class, showed a firm, unwavering, and loyal attachment to the cause of the South. The ladies gave instances of patriotism that were noble testimonies to their sex. They refused the visits of Federal officers, and disdained their recognition; they collected a fund of money for the especial purpose of contributing to the needs of our prisoners; and, says a recipient of the bounty of these noble women, as soon as a Confederate prisoner was paroled, and passed into the next room, he found pressed in his hands there a sum of money given him by the ladies of Nashville. Many of the most respectable of the people had been constrained to leave their homes rather than endure the presence of the enemy. The streets, which, to confirm the predictions of Northern newspapers of the welcomes that awaited the "Union" army in the South, should have been gay and decorated, presented to the enemy nothing but sad and gloomy aspects. Whole rows of houses, which, but a short while ago, were occupied by families of wealth and respectability, surrounded by all the circumstances that make homes happy and prosperous, stood vacant, and the gaze of the passer-by was met, instead of, as in former days, with fine tapestry window-curtains and neatly polished marble steps, with panes of dust-dimmed glass.

On the whole, the experience of the enemy in Nashville was vastly instructive. The fact that, wherever he had gone, he had converted lukewarm Southern districts into Secession strongholds, or had intensified the sentiment of opposition to him, was as unexpected to him as it was gratifying to us. This experience was universal in the war, from the date of the occupation of Alexandria, which had voted overwhelmingly for the Union in the preliminary stages of the revolution, and was subsequently as thoroughly Southern as any town in the Confederacy, down to the occupation of Nashville, which had at first given some signs of weak submission to its fate, and afterwards spurned its invaders with a spirit of defiance, reckless of consequences.

In the neighborhood of Nashville, the enemy was constantly

harassed by local parties of adventurers, who shot his pickets, watched his movements, and attacked detached portions of his forces at various points. The whole country rang with the exploits of the gallant and intrepid cavalier, Captain John H. Morgan and his brave men, in the vicinity of Nashville. His squadron belonged to Gen. Hardee's command, and he had been left in command of the forces at Murfreesboro to watch the movements of the Federals, which he not only did effectually, but enacted a number of daring adventures within the lines of the enemy.

Scarcely a day passed without some such exploit of Capt Morgan and his intrepid partisans. Once he nearly succeeded in capturing a Federal general. Another day he attacked a party of scouts, and killed the captain. The next exploit was to rush into the camp of some regiment, and carry off a train of wagons. The most daring of his adventures was his sudden appearance in the rear of the enemy, entering with forty brave followers the town of Gallatin, twenty-six miles north of Nashville, on the Louisville and Nashville railroad. On entering the town, Capt. Morgan immediately seized upon the telegraph office and the depot. He had presented himself at the telegraph office, carelessly asking the operator what was the news, when that individual, never for a moment imagining who it was that addressed him, replied that there were rumors that "the rebel scoundrel" Morgan was in the neighborhood, and proceeded to illustrate his own valor by flourishing a revolver, and declaring how anxious he was to encounter the man who was creating so much uneasiness and alarm in the country. "You are now speaking to Captain Morgan" was the quiet reply of the partisan : "I am he!" At these words, the pistol dropped from the hands of the operator, who entreated the mercy of his captor. The poor fellow easily submitted to the task assigned to him of sending a dispatch, in the name of Capt. Morgan, to Prentice, the notorious editor of the Louisville *Journal*, politely offering to act as his escort on his proposed visit to Nashville. After this amusement, Capt. Morgan and his men awaited the arrival of the train from Bowling Green. In due time the train came thundering in ; Capt. Morgan at once seized it, and taking five Federal officers who were passengers and the engineer of the train prisoners, he burned to cinders all of the cars, with their contents, and then filling the locomotive with turpentine, shut down all the valves, and started it towards Nashville. Before it had run eight hundred yards, the accumulation of steam caused it to explode, shivering it into a thousand atoms. Capt. Morgan then started southward with his prisoners, and made his way safely to the Confederate camp.

On another occasion, while returning alone towards Murfreesboro, Capt. Morgan encountered a picket of six of the enemy, and captured them and their arms. It was accomplished by a bold adventure. He discovered the pickets in a house, and having on a Federal overcoat, assumed a bold front, and riding up to the sergeant rebuked him for not attending properly to his duty, and ordered that the whole party should consider themselves under arrest, and surrender their arms. The soldiers, not doubting for a moment that they were addressed by a Federal officer, delivered up their muskets. As they were marched into the road, with their faces turned from their camp, the sergeant said, "We are going the wrong way colonel." "We are not," was the reply. "I am Captain Morgan."

The name of Captain Morgan was fast becoming famous as that of a partisan leader. He was induced to abandon his present field of operations to accept promotion in the army, being appointed to a colonelcy in the regular military service, for which he had been urgently recommended by Gen. Hardee.

Since falling back to Murfreesboro, Gen. Johnston had managed, by combining Crittenden's division and the fugitives from Donelson, to collect an army of 17,000 men. His object was now to co-operate with Gen. Beauregard for the defence of the Valley of the Mississippi, on a line of operations south of Nashville. The line extending from Columbus, by way of Forts Henry and Donelson, had been lost. The disaster had involved the surrender of Kentucky, and a large portion of Tennessee to the enemy; and it had become necessary to reorganize a new line of defence south of Nashville, the object of which would be to protect the railroad system cf the Southwest, and to insure the defence of Memphis and the Mississippi.

The work of putting the Mississippi river in a state of com plete defence had been intrusted to General Beauregard. On abandoning Columbus, he had taken a strong position about forty-five miles below it, at Island No. 10. This locality was looked upon as the chief barrier to the progress of the Federals down the Mississippi. At the island, a bend occurs in the river of several miles extent. Around and upon this curve were located the towns of New Madrid and Point Pleasant. The distance around the bend was about thirty miles, whereas the distance across by land from Tiptonville below to the island above did not exceed five miles. It was calculated that even should the enemy hold Point Pleasant, and get possession of New Madrid by our evacuation of that post also, our communications by water to Tiptonville, and thence by land across the bend to Island No. 10, would still remain intact. The island was thought to be impregnable. It was flanked on the Missouri side by an extensive swamp, and on the other side by a lake of several miles extent, which rendered it impossible for the enemy to approach the position by land.

With this indication of the situation in the West, and the operations for the defence of Memphis and the Mississippi, to which the southward movement of Gen. Johnston towards the left bank of the Tennessee was expected to contribute, we must leave, for a short period, our narrative of the movements and events of the war in this direction.

The serious disaster at Donelson appears to have been fully appreciated by the Confederate government; and its announcement in Richmond was followed, to the surprise of the public, by a communication from President Davis to Congress, on the 11th of March, declaring the official reports of the affair incomplete and unsatisfactory, and "relieving from command" Gens. Floyd and Pillow. The main causes of dissatisfaction indicated by the President were, that reinforcements were not asked for by the commanding generals at Donelson, and that the senior generals "abandoned responsibility," by transferring the command to a junior officer. This act of President Davis was the subject of warm and protracted argument in Congress and in the newspapers. It was shown, by evidence produced before Congress, that no reinforcements had been asked for, because it was known how much the command of Gen. Johnston had already been weakened by sending Floyd's and Buckner's forces to Donelson; because an overwhelming force or the enemy was pressing on his rear; and because Gen. Johnston's troops were on the march between Bowling Green and Nashville, and could not reach Fort Donelson in time to change the fortunes of the day.

With reference to the second assignment of cause of the President's displeasure, it was agreed on all sides that the transfer of the command by the senior generals was irregular. In a letter, however, written to the President by Gen. Johnston himself, which was understood to be private and confidential, and was, therefore, wholly relieved from any suspicion of the gloze of an official report, that officer had directed no censure upon Gens. Floyd and Pillow. On the contrary, in the confidence of this private letter, he wrote to the President, "the command was irregularly transferred, and devolved on the junior general, but not apparently to avoid any just responsibility or from any want of personal or moral intrepidity;" and he expressed continued "confidence in the gallantry, the energy, and the devotion to the Confederacy," of both Gens. Floyd and Pillow, which was testified especially in the case of Gen. Floyd, by assigning him, after the fall of Donelson, to the important duty of proceeding to Chattanooga to defend the approaches towards northern Alabama and Georgia, and the communication between the Mississippi and the Atlantic. This was the private and unrestrained testimony of Gen. Johnston. With perhaps a superior military sensitiveness of "irregularity," Mr. Davis repudiated the explanations of the commanding general in the field; deprived Generals Floyd and Pillow of their commands; and offered the spectacle to the country of a President with one hand sacrificing two brave officers who had contributed to the country's glory and safety in more than one victory, for a military punctilio, and with the other elevating to the highest office in his gift a man who, as Attorney-general, Secretary of War, and. at last, Secretary of State, seemed to enjoy the monopoly of the lucre and honors of state, and who had been charged, by the official report of a general in the field, and by the deliberate and unanimous verdict of a committee of Congress, with the plain and exclusive responsibility of the disaster of Roanoke Island. The

contrast between these two acts needed no addition of argu
ment to convince the public mind that its government was not
above the errors of judgment or the partialities of human affec
tion.

The disposition of the Confederate prisoners taken at Fort
Donelson gave an exhibition of vile perfidy on the part of the
North, to which there is no parallel to be found in the history
of civilized warfare, or in all the crooked paths of modern
diplomacy. Instead of these prisoners being discharged by the
North according to the understanding existing between the
two governments, they were carried off into the Western
interior, where they were treated with indignities and made a
spectacle for mobs, who jeered at them because they did not
have uniforms and warm coats, because many of the poor
fellows had nothing better than horse blankets, rags, and coffee
sacks around their shoulders, and because the "rebels"—
whose true glory a just and generous spirit would have found
in their coarse and tattered garbs and marks of patient suffer
ing—lacked the fine and showy equipments of the Federal
troops. This act of bad faith on the part of the North is re
markable enough for a full and explicit history of the circum
stances in which it was committed.

Permission had been asked by the Northern government for
two commissioners, Messrs. Fish and Ames, to visit their
prisoners of war within the jurisdiction of the South. Our
government, while denying this permission, sought to improve
the opportunity by concerting a settled plan for the exchange
of prisoners; and for the execution of this purpose Messrs.
Conrad and Seddon were deputed as commissioners to meet
those of the Northern government under a flag of truce at
Norfolk.

Subsequently a letter from Gen. Wool was addressed to Gen.
Huger, informing him that he, Gen. Wool, had *full authority*
to settle any terms for the exchange of prisoners, and asking
an interview on the subject. General Howell Cobb was then
appointed by the government to mediate with Gen. Wool, and
to settle a permanent plan for the exchange of prisoners during
the war.

In the letter to General Huger, dated the 13th of February
1862, General Wool wrote:

"*I am alone clothed with full power* for the purpose of arranging for the exchange of prisoners. Being thus empowered, I am ready to confer with you on the subject, or the Honorable Messrs. Seddon and Conrad, or any other persons appearing for that purpose. I am prepared to arrange for the restoration of all the prisoners to their homes on fair terms of exchange, man for man, and officer for officer of equal grade, assimilating the grade of officers of the army and navy, when necessary, and agreeing upon equitable terms for the number of men or officers, of inferior grade, to be exchanged for any of higher grade when the occasion shall arrive. That all the surplus prisoners on either side be exchanged on parole, with the agreement that *any prisoners of war taken by the other party shall be returned in exchange as fast as captured,* and this system to be continued while hostilities continue.

"I would further inform you, or any other person selected for the purpose of making arrangements for the exchange of prisoners, that the prisoners taken on board of vessels, or otherwise in maritime conflict, by the forces of the United States, have been put, and are now held, only in military custody, and *on the same footing as other prisoners taken in arms.*"

The proposition, it appears, was readily accepted by our government, and a memorandum made as a basis for a cartel. It was proposed in this memorandum that the prisoners of war in the hands of each government should be exchanged, man for man, the officers being assimilated as to rank, &c.; that our privateersmen should be exchanged on the footing of prisoners of war; that any surplus remaining on either side, after these exchanges, should be released, and that hereafter, during the whole continuance of the war, prisoners taken on either side should be paroled within ten days after their capture, and delivered on the frontier of their own country.

General Wool promptly agreed to all the propositions except two. In lieu of the compensation basis of equivalents contained in one of the items of the memorandum, he proposed the cartel of equivalents adopted by Great Britain and the United States, in the war of 1812, and General Cobb accepted it.

He also objected to the provisions in another item, which required each party to pay the expense of transporting their prisoners to the frontier of the country of the prisoners. The provision met his entire approval, but he did not feel authorized, by his instructions, to incorporate it into the proposed cartel, and, therefore, desired time to consult his government on the subject.

The interview closed with the promise from General Wool that he would notify General Cobb, as soon as he could hear from his government, on that point.

On the first of March General Cobb held his second interview with him, in which he (General Cobb) proposed to enter into a *cartel*, containing the stipulations previously set forth. Gen. Wool then replied that his government would not agree to the proposition that each party should pay the expense of transporting their prisoners to the frontier, when General Cobb promptly waived it, thus leaving the cartel free from all his objections, and just what General Wool had himself proposed in his letter of the 13th February, to General Huger.

Upon this, General Wool informed General Cobb that his *government had changed his instructions*, and abruptly broke off the negotiation.

In the mean time our government, in a very curious or very foolish anticipation of the good faith of the North, had directed the discharge of the prisoners held by us as hostages for the safety and proper treatment of our privateersmen, who were confined in felons' cells and threatened with the gallows. Cols. Lee, Cogswell, and Wood, and Major Revere were sent to their own country; the remaining hostages were brought on parole from distant points to Richmond, on their way to be delivered up, at the expense of this government, and their surrender was only suspended on receipt of intelligence from General Cobb, that he saw reason to suspect bad faith on the part of the enemy.

The perfidy of the North was basely accomplished.* The

---

* This act of deception on the part of the North was but one of a long series of acts of Yankee perfidy, and of their abnegation of the rights of civilized war. When McDowell left Washington city to take Richmond, his army was supplied with handcuffs to iron rebels. After the battle of Bull Run they sent a white flag to ask permission to bury their dead. It was humanely granted. They left their dead to bury their dead, and attempted, under the protection of that white flag, to erect batteries for our destruction. On the battle-field of Manassas they unfurled a Confederate flag, and shouted to our troops not to fire upon them, that they were our friends, and then they fired upon our troops and fled. At Manassas and Pensacola they repeatedly and deliberately fired upon our hospitals, when over them a yellow flag was waving. In Hampton Roads they hung out a white flag, and then prostituted the protection it secured to them to the cowardly assassination of our brave seamen. At Newbern, in violation of the laws of war, they attempted to shell a city containing several thousand women and children, before either demanding a surrender, or giving the citizens notice of their intentions. A Kentuckian went into a Federal camp to reclaim a fugitive slave, and they tied him up

correspondence of the Federal authorities, to which we have alluded, on this subject, constitutes a chapter of diplomacy qualified to attract the scorn of all civilized and honorable nations. At the time when it was believed our government held the larger number of prisoners, the Federal government proposed to exchange all prisoners, and to place on parole, in their own country, the surplus held by either party; and our government agreed to the proposition. Before the agreement could be reduced to writing, and signed by the parties, the casualties of war, in the fall of Fort Donelson, reversed this state of things, and gave the Federal government the larger number of prisoners. With this change of things that govern ment changed its policy, and deliberately, and perfidiously, and shamelessly receded from the propositions to which it had been distinctly committed by every obligation of truth, honor, and good faith.

While Mr. Benjamin, Secretary of War, by a curious act of supererogation was releasing our most important prisoners of war *in advance* of the conclusion of negotiations, sending them North without waiting to have them regularly and safely exchanged under a flag of truce in Norfolk harbor, the enemy were conveying the prisoners captured at Fort Donelson to Chicago and other points more distant from their homes, and were parading the officers who fell into their power through the entire breadth of the land, from western Tennessee, to Fort Warren in Boston harbor, where they were incarcerated. For the prisoners so curiously, and with such unnecessary haste, dispatched to the North by Mr. Benjamin, not a single officer taken at Fort Donelson, nor a single captive privateersman, had been restored to his home. With an excess of zeal well calcu-

---

and gave him twenty-five lashes upon his bare back, in the presence of his runaway slave. It was repeatedly proposed by the people of the South to treat such an enemy without ceremony or quarter, by hanging out the black flag, and making the war a *bellum internecinum;* but while the South debated, talked, and threatened, the North acted, availing itself of the most ferocious and brutal expedients of the war, arming the slaves, breaking faith on every occasion of expediency, disregarding flags of truce, stealing private property, ravishing women, bombarding hospitals, and setting at defiance every law of civilized warfare. Such was the perfidy and brutality of the North, to which the South responded with the puerile threat of a black flag, which was never hoisted, and which did not even serve the purposes of a scarecrow to its bold and unscrupulous enemy

lateα to draw attention from his own part of the transaction, Mr. Benjamin proposed, as a retaliation upon the perfidy of the North, to discharge our own citizens who were subject to parole; but happily a counsel, which proposed to redress a wrong by an act disreputable to ourselves and in violation of what were the obligations of our own honor in the sight of the civilized world, was rejected alike by the government and the country, who were content to commit the dishonor of their enemy, without attempting to copy it under pleas of retaliation, to the justice of history and the future judgments of the world.

CHAPTER XI.

Organization of the permanent Government of the South.—The Policy of England. —Declaration of Earl Russell.—Onset of the Northern Forces.—President Davis's Message to Congress.—The Addition of New States and Territories to the Southern Confederacy.—Our Indian Allies.—The Financial Condition, North and South.—Deceitful Prospects of Peace.—Effect of the Disasters to the South.—Action of Congress. —The Conscript Bill.—Provisions vs. Cotton.—Barbarous Warfare of the North.—The Anti-slavery Sentiment.—How it was unmasked in the War.—Emancipation Measures in the Federal Congress.—Spirit of the Southern People.—The Administration of Jefferson Davis.—His Cabinet.—The Defensive Policy.—The NAVAL ENGAGEMENT IN HAMPTON ROADS.—Iron-clad Vessels.—What the Southern Government might have done.—The Narrative of General Price's Campaign resumed.—His Retreat into Arkansas.—The BATTLE OF ELK HORN.—Criticism of the Result.—Death of General McCulloch.—The BATTLE OF VALVERDE.—The Foothold of the Confederates in New Mexico.—Change of the Plan of Campaign in Virginia. – Abandonment of the Potomac Line by the Confederates.—The BATTLE OF KERNSTOWN.—Colonel Turner Ashby.— Appearance of McClellan's Army on the Peninsula.—Firmness of General Magruder. —The New Situation of the War in Virginia.—Recurrence of Disasters to the South on the Water.—The Capture of Newbern.—Fall of Fort Pulaski and Fort Macon.— Common Sense vs. " West Point."

THE permanent government of the Confederate States was organized on the 22d day of February, in a season of reverses to our arms and at a dark hour in our national fortunes.

All hopes of foreign interference were positively at an end. On the meeting of the British Parliament in the early part of February, Earl Russell had declared that the blockade of the American ports had been effective from the 15th of August, in the face of the facts that the dispatches of Mr. Bunch, the English consul at Charleston, said that it was not so; and that authentic accounts and letters of merchants showed that any ships, leaving for the South, could be insured by a premium of seven and a-half to fifteen per cent. England had accepted the Treaty of Paris, and yet did not hesitate to violate the principles that had been definitely consecrated by article four of that treaty, by declaring the Federal blockade effective, for no other reason than that " considerable prudence was necessary in the American question." In the House of Commons, Mr. Gregory asserted that the non-observation of the Treaty of

Paris was a deception for the Confederate States, and an ambuscade for the interests of commerce throughout the world.

The Northern army had remained quiet on the Potomac, amusing the Southern people with its ostentatious parades and gala-day sham fights, while the government at Washington was preparing an onset all along our lines from Hatteras to Kansas. Burnside had captured Roanoke Island in the east, while Fort Henry on the Tennessee and Fort Donelson on the Cumberland had sent the echo back to Albemarle. Buffeting sleet and storm, and by forced marches, the enemy had seized Bowling Green, while Sigel fell suddenly upon Springfield; the enemy's gunboats threatened Savannah, and Gen. Butler hurried off his regiments and transports to the Gulf, for an attack *via* Ship Island upon New Orleans.

In his message to Congress, President Davis declared that the magnified proportions of the war had occasioned serious disasters, and that the effort was impossible to protect by our arms the whole of the territory of the Confederate States, seaboard and inland. To the popular complaint of inefficiency in the departments of the government, he declared that they had done all which human power and foresight enabled them to accomplish.

The increase of our territory since the opening of the war was scarcely a cause for boast. The addition of new States and Territories had greatly extended our lines of defence. Missouri had been unable to wrest from the enemy his occupancy of her soil. Kentucky had been admitted into the Confederacy only to become the theatre of active hostilities, and, at last, to be abandoned to the enemy. The Indian treaties effected by the Provisional Congress, through the mediation of Gen. Albert Pike, had secured us a rich domain, but a troublesome and worthless ally.* It was possible, however, that

---

* In December last, Col. James McIntosh was sent from Arkansas into the Cherokee Nation to chastise the rebellious Creek chief Opoth-lay-oho-la, which he did with good effect. The results of the incursion were thus enumerated by Col. McIntosh: "We captured one hundred and sixty women and children, twenty negroes, thirty wagons, seventy yoke of oxen, about five hundred Indian horses, several hundred head of cattle, one hundred sheep, and a great quantity of property of much value to the enemy. The stronghold of Opoth lay-oho-la was completely broken up and his force scattered in every direction destitute of the simplest elements of subsistence."

ir this domain there might be secured a rich inheritance for posterity. It comprised an area of more than eighty thousand square miles, diversified by mountains filled with iron, coal, and other mineral treasures, and broad-reaching plains, with the Red River running along its southern border, the Arkansas river almost through its centre, and their tributaries reticulating its entire surface.

At the time of the inauguration of our permanent government, there was, however, one aspect of our affairs of striking encouragement. It was the condition of the finances of the government. We had no floating debt. The credit of the government was unimpaired among its own people. The total expenditures for the year had been, in round numbers, $170,000,000; less than one-third of the sum expended by the enemy to conquer us, and less than the value of a single article of export—the cotton crop of the year.

In the Federal Congress it was estimated that, at the end of the fiscal year (June, 1862), the public debt of the Northern government would be about $750,000,000, and that the demands on the treasury, to be met by taxation, direct and indirect, would not be less than $165,000,000 per annum.

The problem of the Northern finances was formidable enough. It was calculated that the Federal tax would be from four to six times greater for each State than their usual assessments heretofore, and doubts were expressed, even by Northern jour-

---

The Indian Territory (not including the Osage country—its extent being unknown—nor the 800,000 acres belonging to the Cherokees, which lie between Missouri and Kansas) embraces an area of 82,073 square miles—more than fifty-two millions of acres, to wit:

The land of the Cherokees, Osages, Quapaws, Senecas, and Senecas and Shawnees, 38,105 square miles, or 24,388,800 acres.

That of the Creeks and Seminoles, 20,531 square miles, or 13,140,000 acres.

That of the Reserve Indians, and the Choctaws and Chickasaws, 23,437 square miles, or 15,000,000 acres.

Total 82,073 square miles, or 52,528,800 acres.

Its population consists of Cherokees, 23,000 ; Osages, 7,500 ; Quapaws, 320 ; Creeks, 13,500 ; Seminoles, 2,500; Reserve Indians, 2,000 ; Choctaws, 17,500 ; and Chickasaws, 4,700—making an aggregate of 71,520 souls.

This Indian country is, in many respects, really a magnificent one. It is one of the brightest and fairest parts of the great West, and only needs the development of its resources to become the equal of the most favored lands on this continent.

nals in the interest of the government, if it could be raised in any other way than by practical confiscation.

The South, however, had already lingered too long in the delusive promise of the termination of the war by the breaking down of the finances of the Northern government, and had entertained prospects of peace in the crude philosophy and calculations of the newspaper article, without looking to those great lessons of history which showed to what lengths a war might be carried despite the difficulties of finance, the confines of reason, and the restraints of prudence, when actuated by that venom and desperation which were shown alike by the people and government of the North. The very extent of the Northern expenditure should have been an occasion of alarm instead of self-complacency to the South; it showed the tremendous energy of the North and the overpowering measure of its preparation; it argued a most terrible degree of desperation; and it indicated that the North had plunged so far into the war, that there was but little sane choice between striving to wade through it, and determining to turn back with certain and inevitable ruin in its face.

Fortunately, the lessons of its late disasters were not entirely lost upon the government of the Confederate States. They happily gave fresh impulses to the authorities, and were productive of at least some new and vigorous political measures. The most important of these was a conscript bill for increasing our forces in the field. The enlargement of the proportions of the war demanded such a measure; the conflict, in which we were now engaged, extended from the shores of the Chesapeake to the confines of Missouri and Arizona.

The measures and expressions of the government plainly intimated to the people, who had been so persistently incredulous of a long war, that it had become probable that the war would be continued through a series of years, and that preparations for the ensuing campaigns should be commensurate with such a prospect. In Congress, resolutions were passed urging the planters to suspend the raising of cotton, and to plant provision crops, so as to provide for the support of the army This change in the direction of our industry, besides increasing the capacity of the South to sustain itself, aimed a blow at the well-known selfish calculations of England to repay herself for past losses from the blockade, in the cheap prices expected from the excessive supply of two years' crops of cotton in the South. The South was not to be the only or chief loser in the diminished production of her great staple and the forced change in her industrial pursuits. For every laborer who was diverted from the culture of cotton in the South, perhaps, four times as many elsewhere, who had found subsistence in the various employments growing out of its use, would be forced also out of their usual occupations. The prospect of thus bringing ruin upon the industrial interests of other countries was not pleasing to our people or our government; although it was some consolation to know that England, especially, might yet feel, through this change of production in the South, the consequences of her folly and the merited fruits of her injustice to a people who had been anxious for her amity, and had at one time been ready to yield to her important commercial privileges.

In the growing successes of the Northern armies, the spirit of the Southern people came to the aid of their government with new power, and a generosity that was quite willing to forget all its shortcomings in the past. The public sentiment had been exasperated and determined in its resolution of resistance to the last extremity by the evidences of ruin, barbarism, and shameless atrocities that had marked the paths of the progress of the enemy. The newspapers were filled with accounts of outrages of the enemy in the districts occupied by him. By his barbarous law of confiscation, widows and orphans had been stripped of death's legacies; he had overthrown municipalities and State governments; he had imprisoned citizens without warrant, and regardless of age or sex; he had destroyed commerce, and beggared the mechanic and manufacturer; he had ripped open the knapsacks of our captured soldiery, robbing them of clothing, money, necessaries of life, and even of the instruments of their surgeons. The Southern people considered that they were opposing an enemy who had proved himself a foe to mankind, religion, and civilization.

The venomous spirit of Abolition had been free to develop itself in the growing successes of the Northern arms. It is a curious commentary on the faith of the people of the North, or rather a striking exposure of the subserviency of all the expressions of opinion on the part of that people to considerations of *expediency*, that, in the beginning of hostilities, even aftei the proclamation of war by President Lincoln, when it was yet thought important to affect moderation, fugitive slaves from Virginia were captured in the streets of Washington, and, by the direct authority of the Northern government, returned to their masters! A few months later, negro slaves were kidnapped from their masters by the Federal army, under the puerile and nonsensical pretence of their being "contraband of war." The anti-slavery purposes of the war rapidly developed from that point. The Northern journals declared that the excision of slavery was one of the important objects of the war ; that the opportunity was to be taken in the prosecution of hostilities to crush out what had been the main cause of difference, and thus to assure the fruit of a permanent peace. In his message to the Federal Congress in December, Mr. Lincoln had hinted that "*all indispensable means*" must be employed to preserve the Union. An order was published by the War Department making it the occasion of a court-martial for any army officer to return any negro slave within his lines to his master. It was followed by the explanation of Mr. Lincoln's former hint. In an executive message to the Federal Congress, the policy of "the gradual abolishment of slavery," with the pretence of "pecuniary aid" to States adopting such policy, was advised ; it was approved in the House of Representatives, by a vote of 88 to 31 ; and about the same time a bill was introduced into the Senate for the forcible emancipation of the negro slaves in the District of Columbia, which was subsequently passed.

These bitter exhibitions of the North had envenomed the war ; its sanguinary tides rose higher ; its battle-fields emu lated in carnage the most desperate in modern history ; flags of truce were but seldom used, and the amenities of intercourse between belligerents were often slighted by rude messages of defiance. Battles had become frequent and really bloody. But they were no longer decisive of a nation's fate. The campaign covered the whole of a huge territory, and could only be de cided by complicated movements, involving great expenditure of troops and time.

The Southern people, however, were again aroused, and

nothing was wanting but wisdom, energy, and capacity on the part of the government to have inaugurated another series of brilliant achievements, such as those which rendered illustrious the first months of the war. The rush of men to the battle-field, which was now witnessed in every part of the South, was beyond all former example; and if the government had met this mighty movement of the people with a corresponding amplitude of provision and organization, the cause of the South might have been reckoned safe beyond peradventure.

Unfortunately, however, President Davis was not the man to consult the sentiment and wisdom of the people; he desired to signalize the infallibility of his own intellect in every measure of the revolution, and to identify, from motives of vanity, his own personal genius with every event and detail of the re-markable period of history in which he had been called upon to act. This imperious conceit seemed to swallow up every other idea in his mind. By what was scarcely more than a constitutional fiction, the President of the Confederate States was the head of the army; but Mr. Davis, while he made himself the supreme master of the civil administration of the government, so far as to take the smallest details within his control, and to reduce his cabinet officers to the condition of head clerks, insisted also upon being the autocrat of the army, controlling the plans of every general in the field, and dictating to him the precise limits of every movement that was under-taken. Many of our generals fretted under this pragmatism of an executive, who, instead of attending to the civil affairs of the government and correcting the monstrous abuses that were daily pointed out by the newspapers in the conduct of the departments, was unfortunately possessed with the vanity that he was a great military genius, and that it was necessary for him to dictate, from his cushioned seat in Richmond, the de-tails of every campaign, and to conform every movement in the field to the invariable formula of "*the defensive policy*."*

---

* The following extract of terse criticism on offensive and defensive warfare is taken from a small work written by one of Napoleon's generals in 1815, and revised in 1855. The writer could not have written with more aptitude to the existing contest, if the errors and unfortunate demonstrations of President Davis's defensive policy had been before his eyes: "The offensive is the proper character which it is essential to give to every war; it exalts the courage of

In a revolutionary leader, something more is wanted than scholarly and polished intellect. The history of the world shows that, in such circumstances, the plainest men, in point o learning and scholarship, have been the most successful, and that their elements of success have been quick apprehension, practical judgment, knowledge of human nature, and, above all, a disposition to consult the aggregate wisdom of the people, and to increase their stores of judgment, by deigning to learn from every possible source of practical wisdom within their reach.

President Davis was not a man to consult, even in the smallest matter of detail, the wisdom of others, or to relax his purposes or personal preferences, at the instance of any consideration that might compromise him in respect of conceit or punctilio. About nothing connected with the new government had the popular will been so clearly and emphatically expressed, as the necessity of a reorganization of the Cabinet. Nobody expected those offices to be permanently filled by the provisional appointees. They were put there under an emergency; in some instances simply as compliments to certain States, and without the slightest expectation that they would be imposed on the country for seven long years. Had the Union continued, and Mr. Davis been elected to the Presidency, the selection of such a Cabinet of intellectual pigmies from the nation at large would have astounded the public. The two great branches of the administration—the War and the Navy Departments— were in the hands of men who had neither the respect, nor the confidence of the public. Mr. Benjamin, the Secretary of War, had been seriously injured, by a number of doubtful official acts, in the public estimation, which never held him higher

---

the soldier; it disconcerts the adversary, strips from him the initiative, and diminishes his means. Do not wait for the enemy in your own fireplaces, go always to seek him in his own home, when you will find opportunity at the same time to live at his expense, and to strip from him his resources. In penetrating his territory, commence by acting en masse with all forces, and be sure that the first advantages are yours. * * * * Never adopt the defensive, unless it is impossible for you to do otherwise. If you are reduced to this sad extremity, let it be in order to gain time, to wait for your reinforcements, drill your soldiers, strengthen your alliances, draw the enemy upon bad ground, lengthen the base of his operations; and *let an ulterior design to take the offensive be without ceasing the end of all your actions.*"

than a smart, expeditious, and affable official. Mr. Mallory, the Secretary of the Navy, had, in the old government, in which he was chairman of the Senate Committee on Naval Affairs, been the butt of every naval officer in the country for his ignorance, his *sang-froid*, his slow and blundering manner, and the engrossment of his mind by provisions to provide gratifications for his social habits.

President Davis refused to concede any thing to public sentiment with reference to the reorganization of his cabinet; although it is to be remarked that the demand for change was made not by a popular clamor, which a wise ruler would have done right to disregard and to contemn, but by that quiet, conservative, and educated sentiment which no magistrate in a republican government had the right to disregard. Mr. Mallory was retained at the head of the navy; Mr. Benjamin was promoted to the Secretaryship of the State, and the only material change in the cabinet was the introduction as Secretary of War of General Randolph, of Virginia, a gentleman whose sterling personal worth made him acceptable to all parties, and promised at least some change for the better in the administration of a government that had been eaten up by servility, and had illustrated nothing more than the imperious conceit of a single man.

The Confederate Congress had passed a bill to create the office of commanding general, who should take charge of the military movements of the war. The bill was vetoed by President Davis; but, at the same time, the unsubstantial show of compliance which had been made with reference to the Cabinet was repeated with reference to the commanding general, and Mr. Davis appointed Gen. Lee to the nominal office of commanding general, the order, however, which nominated him providing that he should " act under the direction of the president." Thus it was that Mr. Davis kept in his hands the practical control of every military movement on the theatre of the war; and it was very curious, indeed, that the servile newspapers, which applauded in him this single and imperious control of the conduct of the war, were unmindful of the plain and consistent justice of putting on his shoulders that exclusive responsibility for disasters which is inseparable from the honors of practical autocracy.

We have referred to the dark period and uncompromising auspices in which the permanent government of the Confederate States was inaugurated. Across the dreary tract of disaster there were, however, sudden and fitful gleams of light, such as the undaunted courage of our troops and the variable accidents of war might give in such circumstances of misgovernment as were adverse or embarrassing to a grand scale of successes. Of these, and of the disasters mingled with them, we shall proceed to treat in the progress of the narrative of the external events of the war.

THE NAVAL ENGAGEMENT IN HAMPTON ROADS.

In the progress of the war, attention had been directed, on both sides, to different classes of naval structure, composed of iron, such as floating batteries, rams, &c. On the 12th of October, an affair had occurred near the mouth of the Mississippi river, in which a partially submerged iron ram, the Manassas, attacked the Federal blockading fleet at the head of the Passes, sinking one of them, the Preble, and driving the remainder of the fleet out of the river. This, the first of our naval exploits, was to be followed by adventures on a larger and more brilliant scale.

As far back as the month of June, 1861, the little energy displayed by the Navy Department had been employed in building a single iron-clad naval structure. In the destruction of the navy-yard at Norfolk, at the commencement of the war, the steam-frigate Merrimac had been burned and sunk, and her engine greatly damaged by the enemy. However, the bottom of the hull, boilers, and heavy and costly parts of the engine were but little injured, and it was proposed of these to construct a casemated vessel with inclined iron-plated sides and submerged ends. The novel plan of submerging the ends of the ship and the eaves of the casement was the peculiar and distinctive feature of the Virginia, as the new structure was called. It was never before adopted. The resistance of iron plates to heavy ordnance, whether presented in vertical planes or at low angles of inclination, had been investigated in England before the Virginia was commenced; but, in the absence of accurate data, the inclination of the plates of the Virginia and their thickness and form had to be determined by actual experiment.

With the completion of the Virginia, the Confederate squadron in the James river, under command of Flag-officer Franklin Buchanan, was as follows: steamer Virginia, ten guns; steamer Patrick Henry, twelve guns; steamer Jamestown, two guns; and gunboats Teazer, Beaufort, and Raleigh, each one gun—total, 27 guns.

On the morning of the 8th of March, about eleven o'clock, the Virginia left the navy-yard at Norfolk, accompanied by the Raleigh and Beaufort, and proceeded to Newport News to engage the enemy's frigates Cumberland and Congress, and their gunboats and shore batteries. On passing Sewell's Point, Capt. Buchanan made a speech to the men. It was laconic. He said: "My men, you are now about to face the enemy. You shall have no reason to complain of not fighting at close quarters. Remember, you fight for your homes and your country. You see those ships—you must sink them. I need not ask you to do it. I know you will do it."

At this time, the Congress was lying close to the batteries at Newport News, a little below them. The Cumberland was lying immediately opposite the batteries. The Virginia passed the Congress, giving her a broadside, which was returned with very little effect, and made straight for the Cumberland. In the midst of a heavy fire from the Cumberland, Congress, gunboats, and shore batteries concentrated on the Virginia, she stood rapidly on towards the Cumberland, which ship Capt. Buchanan had determined to sink with the prow of the Virginia. On board the Yankee frigate, the crew were watching the singular iron roof bearing down upon them, making all manner of derisive and contemptuous remarks, many of them aloud, and within hearing of those on board the Virginia; such as: "Well, there she comes." "What the devil does she look like?" "What in h—ll is she after?" "Let's look at that great Secesh curiosity," etc. These remarks were cut short by a discharge from the Virginia's bow gun, which swept from one end of the Cumberland's deck to the other, killing and wounding numbers of the poor deluded wretches. In a few minutes thereafter, the Virginia had struck her on her starboard bow; the crash below the water was distinctly heard, and, in fifteen minutes thereafter, the Yankee vessel, against whom an old grudge had long existed for her participation in the burning of the navy-yard, sank beneath the water, her guns being fought to the last, and her flag flying at her peak.

Just after the Cumberland sunk, Commander Tucker was seen standing down James river under full steam, accompanied by the Jamestown and Teazer. Their escape was miraculous, as they were under a galling fire of solid shot, shell, grape, and canister, a number of which passed through the vessels without doing any serious injury, except to the Patrick Henry, through whose boiler a shot passed, scalding to death four persons and wounding others.

Having sunk the Cumberland, the Virginia turned her attention to the Congress. She was some time in getting her proper position, in consequence of the shoalness of the water. To succeed in this object, Captain Buchanan was obliged to run the ship a short distance above the batteries on James river in order to wind her. During all the time her keel was in the mud, and, of course, she moved but slowly. The vessel was thus subjected twice to all the heavy guns of the batteries in passing up and down the river.

It appears that while the Virginia was engaged in getting her position, it was believed on the Congress that she had hauled off. The Yankees left their guns and gave three cheers. Their elation was of short duration. A few minutes afterwards the Virginia opened upon the frigate, she having run into shoal water. The "Southern bugaboo," into whom the broadside of the Congress had been poured without effect, not even faizing her armor, opened upon the Yankee frigate, causing such carnage, havoc, and dismay on her decks, that her colors were in a few moments hauled down. A white flag was hoisted at the gaft and half-mast, and another at the main. Numbers of the crew instantly took to their boats and landed. Our fire immediately ceased. The Beaufort was run alongside, with instructions from Captain Buchanan to take possession of the Congress, secure the officers as prisoners, allow the crew to land, and burn the ship. Lieutenant Parker, commanding the Beaufort, received the flag of the Congress and her surrender from Commander William Smith and Lieutenant Pendergrast, with the side-arms of these officers. After having delivered themselves as prisoners of war on board the Beaufort, they were allowed, at their own request, to return to the Congress to assist in removing the wounded to the Beaufort. They never returned, although they had pledged their honor to do so, and in witness of that pledge had left their swords with Lieut. Alexander, on board the Beaufort.

The Beaufort had been compelled to leave the Congress under a perfidious fire opened from the shore, while the frigate had two white flags flying, raised by her own crew. Determined that the Congress should not again fall into the hands of the enemy, Captain Buchanan remarked : "That ship must be burned," when the suggestion was gallantly responded to by Lieutenant Minor, who volunteered to take a boat and burn her. He had scarcely reached within fifty yards of the Congress, when a deadly fire was opened upon him, wounding him severely and several of his men. On witnessing this vile treachery, Captain Buchanan instantly recalled the boat, and ordered the Congress to be destroyed by hot shot and incendiary shell. The illumination of the scene was splendid ; the explosion of the frigate's magazine a little past midnight, aroused persons asleep in Norfolk, and signalled to them the completeness of our victory.

In the perfidious fire from the shore, Captain Buchanan had been disabled by a severe wound in the thigh from a minié-ball, and the command of the ship had been transferred to Lieut. Catesby Jones, with orders to fight her as long as the men could stand to their guns. At this time the steam-frigate Minnesota and Roanoke, and the sailing-frigate St. Lawrence, which had come up from Old Point, opened their fire upon the Virginia. The Minnesota grounded in the North channel, where, unfortunately, the shoalness of the channel prevented the near approach of the Virginia. She continued, however, to fire upon the Minnesota, until the pilots declared that it was no longer safe to remain in that position, when she returned by the South channel (the middle ground being necessarily between the Virginia and Minnesota, and the St. Lawrence and Roanoke having retreated under the guns of Old Point), and again had an opportunity to open upon her enemy. Night falling about this time, the Virginia was anchored off Sewell's Point.

The next morning (Sunday) the contest occurred between the Monitor (the Ericsson battery) and the Virginia. The Yankee frigates, the Roanoke and St. Lawrence, had retreated to Old Point—"the apothecary shop," as it was facetiously styled by our men ; and the Monitor had gone up on Saturday night to assist the Minnesota, which was still aground. The daylight revealed lying near the Minnesota the celebrated iron battery, a wonderful-looking structure that was justly compared to a prodigious "cheese-box on a plank," said "cheese-box" being of a Plutonian blackness. At 8 o'clock the Virginia ran down to engage the Monitor. The contest continued for the space of two hours, the distance between the two vessels varying from half a mile to close quarters, in which the two iron vessels were almost side to side, belching out their fire, the heavy thugs on the iron sides of each being the only effect of the terrific cannonade. Again and again the strange-looking battery, with its black, revolving cupola, fled before the Virginia. It was, as one of our officers remarked, "like fighting a ghost." Now she ran down towards Old Point, now back towards Newport News, now approached to fire, and then ran away to load. The rapidity of the movements of the Monitor gave her the only advantage which she had in the contest. The great length and draft of the Virginia rendered it exceedingly difficult to work her. Once she got aground. It was a moment of terrible suspense to the noble ship, against which the combined batteries of the Minnesota and Monitor were now directed. The shot fell like hail, the shells flew like rain-drops, and slowly, steadily she returned the fire. There lay the Minnesota with two tugs alongside. Here, there, and everywhere, was the black "cheese-box." The Virginia still fired with the same deliberate regularity as before. Presently a great white column of smoke shot up above the Minnesota, higher and higher, fuller and fuller in its volume, and beyond doubt, carried death all along her decks, for the boiler of one of the tugs had been exploded by a shot, and that great white cloud canopy was the steam thus liberated.

In fifteen minutes the Virginia had got off and was again in motion. The pilots declared that it was impossible to get nearer the Minnesota, which was believed to be entirely disabled. The Virginia had twice silenced the fire of the Monitor, and had once brushed her, narrowly missing the coveted opportunity of sinking her with her prow, and the continuation of the contest being declined by the Monitor having run into shoal water, the Virginia ceased firing at noon and proceeded to Norfolk.

She steamed back amid the cheers of victory. In the direction of Newport News could be seen the spars of the Cumber land above the river she had so long insolently barred; but of her consort there was not even a timber-head visible to tell her story. This was not all the Virginia had done. The Minne sota was disabled and riddled with shot. Within eight and forty hours the Virginia had successfully encountered the whole naval force of the enemy in the neighborhood of Norfolk, amounting to 2,890 men and 230 guns; had sunk the Cumberland, probably the most formidable vessel of her class in the Federal navy, consigning to a watery grave the larger portion of her crew of 360 men; had destroyed the crack sailing-frigate Congress, with her enormous armament; and had crippled in the action the Minnesota, one of the best steamers of the enemy's navy. Our casualties were two killed and nineteen wounded, and the Virginia had come out of the action with the loss of her prow, starboard anchor, and all her boats, with her smoke-stack riddled with balls, and the muzzles of two of her guns shot away, but with no serious damage to her wonderful armor, that had sustained a cannonade such as never before was inflicted upon a single vessel.

The exploits of the Virginia created immense excitement in the North and a marked interest in Europe, as illustrating a novel and brilliant experiment in naval architecture. As an example of the sharp and practical energy of the Northern government, and its readiness to avail itself of all means in the prosecution of the war, it may be mentioned that in five days after the occurrence of the Confederate victory in Hampton Roads, a bill was introduced into the Senate at Washington, appropriating nearly fifteen millions of dollars for the construction of additional iron-clad vessels.

In Great Britain and France, and on the Continent generally, public attention was strained to a pitch of fearful anxiety on the subject of changes in naval architecture, and their adaptation to the new exigencies that had arisen in warfare on the water. All the European governments that had a strip of sea-coast busied themselves to turn to profit the lesson the Virginia had given them. Denmark voted a million of rix dollars for the construction of iron-plated vessels, while Sweden sent its Crown Prince to assist at the trial trip of the French frigate La Couronne, the largest iron war-steamer afloat. Italy had already some very fine iron vessels-of-war, and her citizens were hard at work on others. Austria was officially informed of the revolution in warfare at sea on the very day that an imperial commission reported her huge land fortresses as defiant of every known means of assault; and the Prussians, people and government, regarded the engagement in Hampton Roads as one of " the most important events of the day."

The Confederate States government might have learned some instructive lessons from the victory achieved by the Virginia. Instead of one such vessel, we might have had ten, had the Secretary of the Navy, Mr. Mallory, possessed the ability and zeal essential to his responsible position. The cost was not a matter of the slightest consideration. A vessel built at an ex pense of half a million was cheap enough, when in her first essay she had destroyed thrice her value of the enemy's property. The State of North Carolina and the Confederacy had spent at least a million of dollars already in futile attempts to defend the eastern coast of that State. If that sum had been expended in building iron-clad vessels suitable to the waters on the Carolina coast, all of our disasters in that direction might have been prevented, except, perhaps, the one at Hatteras, and our ports on that portion of our coast kept open, at least partially, if not entirely. In no possibly better manner could ten or twenty millions of dollars have been expended than by augmenting the power of our infant navy.

While the Virginia was achieving her memorable victory in Hampton Roads, a battle had commenced in the extreme northwest portion of the State of Arkansas, which had but one parallel as to its duration, and probably few as to its desperate character, since the opening of the war.

It will be recollected that, in a previous chapter, we left Gen. Price about the close of the year 1861 occupying Springfield, Missouri, for the purpose of being within reach of supplies, and protecting that portion of the State from domestic depredations and Federal invasion. About the latter part of January, it became evident that the enemy were concentrating in force at Rolla, and shortly thereafter they occupied Lebanon. Believing that this movement could be for no other purpose than to attack him, and knowing that his command was inadequate for such successful resistance as the interests of the army and the cause demanded, General Price appealed to the commanders of the Confederate troops in Arkansas to come to his assistance. He held his position to the very last moment. On the 12th of February, his pickets were driven in, and reported the enemy advancing upon him in force. Gen. Price commenced retreating at once. He reached Cassville with loss unworthy of mention in any respect. Here the enemy in his rear commenced a series of attacks, running through four days. Retreating and fighting all the way to the Cross Hollows, in Arkansas, the command of Gen. Price, under the most exhausting fatigue, all that time, with but little rest for either man or horse, and no sleep, sustained themselves, and came through, repulsing the enemy upon every occasion, with great determination and gallantry.

Gen. Van Dorn had recently been appointed to the command of the Confederate forces in the Trans-Mississippi district. A happy accord existed between him and Gen. Price, and a private correspondence that had ensued between these two military chieftains, on the occasion of Gen. Van Dorn's appointment by President Davis to take command in Arkansas and Missouri, not only showed a spirit of mutual appreciation and compliment highly honorable to both, but developed a singular similarity of views (considering that the letter of each was written without knowledge of that of the other) with reference to the conduct of the war.

Learning that Gen. Price had rapidly fallen back from Springfield before a superior force of the enemy, and was endeavoring to form a junction with the division of Gen. McCulloch at Boston Mountain, Gen. Van Dorn, who was then at Pocahontas, Arkansas, resolved to go in person to take command of the combined forces of Price and McCulloch. He reached their head-quarters on the 3d of March.

THE BATTLE OF ELK HORN.

The enemy, under the command of Gens. Curtis and Sigel had halted on Sugar Creek, fifty-five miles distant, where, with a force variously estimated at from seventeen to twenty-four thousand, he was awaiting still further reinforcements before he would advance. Gen. Van Dorn resolved to make the attack at once. He sent for Gen. Albert Pike to join him with his command of Indian warriors, and, on the morning of the 4th of March, moved with the divisions of Price and McCulloch, by way of Fayetteville and Bentonville, to attack the enemy's camp on Sugar Creek. The whole force under his command was about sixteen thousand men.

At Bentonville, General Sigel's division, seven thousand strong, narrowly escaped a surprise and fell back, our advance skirmishing with the rear-guard to Sugar Creek, about seven miles beyond.

On the morning of the 7th of March, Gen. Van Dorn made disposition for attack. Before eleven o'clock, the action had become general. The attack was made from the north and west, the enemy being completely surrounded. About two o'clock, Gen. Van Dorn sent a dispatch to Gen. McCulloch, who was attacking the enemy's left, proposing to him to hold his position, while Price's left advance might be thrown forward over the whole line, and easily end the battle. Before the dispatch was penned, Gen. McCulloch had fallen, and the victorious advance of his division upon the strong position of the enemy's front was checked by the fall of himself and Gen. McIntosh, also, in the heat of the battle and in the full tide of success. It appears that two musket-balls, by killing the gallant McCulloch and McIntosh, had prevented us from gaining a great victory. Notwithstanding the confusion that succeeded this untimely occurrence, Gen. Van Dorn pressed forward with the attack, sustained by the resistless charges of the Missouri division. At nightfall, the enemy had been driven back from the field of battle, and the Confederates held his intrenchments and the greater part of his commissary stores, on which our half-famished men fed. Our troops slept upon their arms nearly a mile beyond the point where the enemy had made his last stand, and Gen. Van Dorn's head-quarters for the night were at the Elk Horn tavern—from which locality the battle-field derived its name. We had taken during the day seven cannon and about two hundred prisoners.

On the morning of the 8th, the enemy, having taken a strong position during the night, reopened the fight. The action soon became general, and continued until about half-past nine o'clock, by which time Gen. Van Dorn had completed his arrangements to withdraw his forces. Finding that his right wing was much disorganized, and that the batteries were, one after another, retiring from the field, with every shot expended, Gen. Van Dorn had determined to withdraw his forces in the direction of their supplies. This was accomplished with almost perfect success. The ambulances, crowded with the wounded, were sent in advance; a portion of McCulloch's division was placed in position to follow, while Gen. Van Dorn disposed of his remaining force as best to deceive the enemy as to his intention, and to hold him in check while executing it. An attempt was made by the enemy to follow the retreating column. It was effectually checked, however, and, about 2 P. M., the Confederates encamped about six miles from the field of battle, all of the artillery and baggage joining the army in safety. They brought away from the field of battle 300 prisoners, four cannon, and three baggage wagons.

Our loss in killed and wounded was stated by Gen. Van Dorn to be about six hundred, as nearly as could be ascertained, while that of the enemy was conjectured to be more than seven hundred killed and at least an equal number wounded. Gen. Curtis, in his official report, gives no statement of his loss, but simply remarks that it was heavy. The entire engagement had extended over the space of three days, the 6th, 7th, and 8th of March. The gallantry of our soldiers had been unrivalled. More than half of our troops were raw levies, armed with shot-guns and country rifles. The enemy were armed with superior guns of the latest patents, such as revolving rifles, sabre bayonets, rifled cannon, mounted howitzers, &c. Our army had forced them by inches from one position to another, and, although compelled to fall back at last, were able to make their determination good never to permit the enemy to advance South.

The Indian regiments, under Gen. Pike, had not come up in time to take any important part in the battle. Some of the red-men behaved well, and a portion of them assisted in taking a battery; but they were difficult to manage in the deafening roar of artillery, to which they were unaccustomed, and were naturally amazed at the sight of guns that ran on wheels. They knew what to do with the rifle; they were accustomed to sounds of battle as loud as their own war-whoop; and the amazement of these simple children of the forest may be imagined at the sight of such roaring, deafening, crashing monsters as twelve-pounders running around on wheels. Gen. Van Dorn, in his official report of the battle, does not mention that any assistance was derived from the Indians—an ally that had, perhaps, cost us much more trouble, expense, and annoyance, than their services in modern warfare could, under any circumstances, be worth.

In the action, the Missouri troops, from the noble veteran, who had led them so long, down to the meanest private, behaved with a courage, the fire and devotion of which never, for a moment, slackened. The personal testimony of Gen. Van Dorn to their noble conduct, was a just and magnanimous tribute. He wrote to the government at Richmond: "During the whole of this engagement, I was with the Missourians under Price, and I have never seen better fighters than these Missouri troops, or more gallant leaders than Gen. Price and his officers. From the first to the last shot, they continually rushed on, and never yielded an inch they had won; and when at last they received orders to fall back, they retired steadily and with cheers. Gen. Price received a severe wound in the action, but would neither retire from the field nor cease to expose his life to danger."

Nor is this all the testimony to the heroism of Gen. Price on the famous battle-fields of Elk Horn. Some incidents are related to us by an officer of his conduct in the retreat, that show aspects of heroism more engaging than even those of reckless bravery. In the progress of the retreat, writes an officer, every few hundred yards we would overtake some wounded soldier. As soon as he would see the old general, he would cry out, "General, I am wounded!" Instantly some vehicle was ordered to stop, and the poor soldier's wants cared for

Again and again it occurred, until our conveyances were covered with the wounded. Another one cried out, ' General, I am wounded !' The general's head dropped upon his breast, and his eyes, bedimmed with tears, were thrown up, and' he looked in front, but could seen no place to put his poor soldier. He discovered something on wheels in front, and commanded : Halt! and put this wounded soldier up ; by G—d, I will save my wounded, if I lose the whole army !' This explains why the old man's poor soldiers love him so well."

Although, in the battle of Elk Horn, our forces had been compelled to retire, and the affair was proclaimed in all parts of the North as a splendid victory of their arms, there is no doubt, in the light of history, that the substantial fruits of victory were with the Confederates. The enemy had set out on a march of invasion, with the avowed determination to subjugate Arkansas, and capture Fort Smith. But after the shock of the encounter at Elk Horn, he was forced to fall back into Missouri, leaving several hundred prisoners in our hands, and more than two thousand killed and wounded on the field. The total abandonment of their enterprise of subjugation in Arkansas is the most conclusive evidence in the world, that the Federals were worsted by Gen. Van Dorn, and that this brave and honorable commander had achieved for his country no inconsiderable success.

The fall of Gen. Ben McCulloch was esteemed as a national calamity, and, in his official report of the battle, Gen. Van Dorn declared that no success could repair the loss of the gallant dead, who had fallen on the well-fought field. Gen. McCulloch's name was already historical at the time of the breaking out of the revolution. Twenty-six years ago he served in the battle of San Jacinto, afterwards passed his time on the Texan frontier, in a succession of hardships and dangers such as few men have seen, and subsequently, in the Mexican war on the bloody field of Buena Vista, received the public and official thanks of Gen. Taylor for his heroic conduct and services.

McCulloch, as a soldier, was remarkable for his singular capacities for partisan warfare, and, in connection with Walker, Hays, and Chevallie, had originated and rendered renowned the name of "Texas Ranger." These daring adventurers did much in achieving the independence of the Texan republic, and in defending its borders from the ruthless and enterprising Camanche. In the war of the United States with Mexico, they rendered invaluable service as daring scouts, and inaugurated the best and most effective cavalry service that has ever been known in the world.

The moment Lincoln's election became known, McCulloch identified himself as an unconditional secessionist, and repaired to Texas to take part in any movement that might grow out of the presence of over 3000 United States troops in that State. He was unanimously selected by the Committee of Public Safety to raise the men necessary to compel the surrender oi San Antonio, with its arsenal and the neighboring forts, four or five in number. Within four days, he had travelled one hundred and fifty miles, and stood before San Antonio with eight hundred armed men, his old comrades and neighbors. His mission succeeded. Texas looked to him with confidence as one of her strong pillars in case of war. She sent him abroad to procure arms; but, before he had fully succeeded, President Davis appointed him brigadier-general, and assigned him to the command of the Indian Territory.

He was killed in the brush on a slight elevation by one of the sharp-shooters of the enemy. He was not in uniform, but his dress attracted attention. He wore a dress of black velvet, patent-leather high-top boots, and he had on a light-colored, broad-brimmed Texan hat. The soldier who killed him, a private in an Illinois regiment, went up and robbed his body of a gold watch.

Gen. McIntosh, who had been very much distinguished all through the operations in Arkansas, had fallen on the battle-field, about the same time that McCulloch had been killed. During the advance from Boston Mountain, he had been placed in command of the cavalry brigade, and in charge of the pickets. He was alert, daring, and devoted to his duty. His kindness of disposition, with his reckless bravery, had attached the troops strongly to him, so that, after McCulloch fell, had he remained to lead them. all would have been well with the right wing; but, after leading a brilliant charge of cavalry and carrying the enemy's battery, he rushed into the thickest of the fight again at the head of his old regiment, and was shot through the heart.

A noble boy from Missouri, Churchill Clarke, commanded a battery of artil.ery, and, during the fierce artillery action of the 7th and 8th, was conspicuous for the daring and skill which he exhibited. He fell at the very close of the action.

While there was, in Richmond, great anxiety to construe aright the imperfect and uncertain intelligence which had arrived there, by devious ways, from Arkansas, news reached the Southern capital of a brilliant and undoubted victory still further to the West, in the distant territory of New Mexico. This victory had been achieved weeks before the slow intelligence of it reached Richmond. Although it had taken place on a remote theatre, and was but little connected with the general fortunes of the war, the victory of Valverde had a good effect upon the spirits of the Southern people, which had been so long depressed and darkened by a baleful train of disasters.

THE BATTLE OF VALVERDE.

The Confederates marched from Mesilla, in Arizona, upon Fort Craig, about 175 miles distant, and there fought the battle and won the victory of Valverde, on the 21st of March. Gen. Sibley, with his command, numbering, rank and file, two thousand three hundred men, left Fort Thorn, eighty miles below Fort Craig, about the 12th of February. On arriving in the vicinity of Fort Craig, he learned from some prisoners, captured near the post, that Gen. Canby was in command of the Federal forces in the fort; that he had twelve hundred regular troops, two hundred American volunteers, and five thousand Mexicans, making his entire force near six thousand four hundred men. Notwithstanding this superior force, he boldly advanced, and, on the 19th, crossed the river near Fort Craig, and, making a detour of some miles, arrived on the morning of the 21st March at Valverde, on the east bank of the Rio Grande, three miles above the fort, where a large body of the enemy were stationed to receive him. It seems that all the enemy's forces, with the exception of their artillery and reserve, were upon the same side of the river to which our troops were advancing. A portion of Col. Baylor's regiment, under command of Major Pyon, numbering 250 men, were the first to engage the enemy. Alone and unsupported for one hour they held their position amid a hail of grape, canister, and round-shot. At that time they were reinforced, and the battle became general. The enemy then made an attack upon our right wing, and were repulsed. A general movement was then made upon our line with more success, a portion of our left wing being compelled to fall back and take a new position. This was about 2 o'clock. The enemy now supposed they had gained the day, and ordered their battery across the river, which was done, and the battery planted upon the bank. As soon as the battery opened General Sibley knew it had crossed, and immediately ordered a general charge, which was performed only as Texans can do it. Starting at a distance of eight hundred yards, with their Camanche war-whoop, they reserved their fire until within thirty yards of the battery, when they poured a deadly fire, with double-barrelled shot-guns and pistols, immediately into the horror-stricken ranks of their foes. They sprung into the river, and in crossing, numbers were killed. Captain Teel's battery now coming up, closed this sanguinary contest with shell and grape, as they fled down the opposite side of the river to the fort. The battle lasted nine hours. It afforded one of the most remarkable instances of valor in the war—the taking of a field-battery with shot-guns and pistols. Our loss was thirty-eight killed, and one hundred and twenty wounded; that of the enemy, as given by themselves, was three hundred killed, four or five hundred wounded, and two thousand missing. The enemy suffered the most while retreating across the river, where the slaughter was for some moments terrible.

After the victory of Valverde, the small force of Texans not being in any condition to assault Fort Craig, pressed on to Albuquerque, about ninety miles north of the battle-field. This city, the second in size and importance in the territory, having a population of seven or eight thousand, the Federals had evacuated. The victorious Confederates still pressed towards Santa Fé, the capital city of the great central plateau of interior America, which the Federals had also evacuated, and fallen back on Fort Union, about sixty miles northeast of Santa Fé, and one of the strongest fortifications in America.

Thus the Texans had marched about three hundred miles

trom Mesilla, defeated the Federals and destroyed their army in a pitched battle, ejected them from their two chief cities, and driven them out of the territory to their outpost on its eastern limits.

The result of the battle of Valverde was encouraging, and the prospect was indulged that New Mexico was already conquered, and that the Confederate States held the Southern overland route to California.

Referring to the progress of the campaign in Virginia, we shall find its plans and locality widely changed, the line of the Potomac abandoned, and the long and persistent struggle of the Federals for the possession of Richmond transferred to a new but not unexpected theatre of operations.

Gen. Joseph E. Johnston had determined to change his line on the Potomac, as the idea of all offensive operations on it had been abandoned, and it had become necessary, in his opinion, that the main body of the Confederate forces in Virginia should be in supporting distance and position with the army of the Peninsula; and in the event of either being driven back, that they might combine for final resistance before Richmond.

The discretion of falling back from the old line of the Potomac was confided by President Davis entirely to the discretion of Gen. Johnston, who enjoyed a rare exemption from official pragmatism at Richmond, and was in many things very much at liberty to pursue the counsels of his own military wisdom.

For the space of three weeks before the army left its intrenchments at Manassas, preparations were being made for falling back to the line of the Rappahannock, by the quiet and gradual removal of the vast accumulations of army stores; and with such consummate address was this managed, that our own troops had no idea of what was intended until the march was taken up. The first intimation the enemy had of the evacuation of Manassas was the smoke of the soldiers' huts that had been fired by our army.

That the strategic plans of the enemy were completely foiled by the movement of Gen. Johnston, was quite evident in the tone of disappointment and vexation in which the Northern newspapers referred to the evacuation of Manassas, which, unless there had been some disconcert of their own strategy by such an event, they would have been likely to regard as a considerable advantage on their side in letting them further into the territory of Virginia.

THE BATTLE OF KERNSTOWN.

While our forces deserted the old line of the Potomac, it was determined not to leave the Valley of Virginia undefended, and the command of Gen. Jackson was left in the neighborhood of Winchester, to operate to the best advantage.

Near the town of Winchester occurred, on the 23d of March, what was known as the battle of Kernstown. The Federals were attacked by our forces under Gen. Jackson, the engagement having been brought on by the gallant Col. Ashby, who had been fighting the enemy wherever he had shown himself in the Valley. The Confederate forces amounted to six thousand men, with Capt. McLaughlin's battery of artillery and Colonel Ashby's cavalry. All the troops engaged were from Virginia, except a few companies from Maryland. It was thought that there would be but a very small force at the point of attack, but the enemy proved to be nearly eighteen thousand strong with a considerable number of field-pieces. They occupied a rising ground, and a very advantageous position.

Gen. Banks had concluded that there was no enemy in front except Ashby's force of cavalry; that Gen. Jackson would not venture to separate himself so far from the main body of the Confederate army as to offer him battle, and under these impressions he had left for Washington. On Sunday morning, Gen. Shields, who had been left in command of the Federals, satisfied that a considerable force was before him, concentrated his whole force, and prepared to give battle. The action commenced about four o'clock in the evening, and terminated when night closed upon the scene of conflict. Our men fought with desperation until dark, when the firing on both sides ceased. During the night, Gen. Jackson decided to fall back to Cedar creek, and prepare there to make successful opposition with his small force, should the enemy advance. The enemy was left in possession of the field of battle, two guns and four caissons, and about three hundred prisoners. Our loss was about one hundred killed, and probably twice that number wounded. The loss of the enemy was certainly more than

double. At one period of the fight our men had got possession of a stone wall, which formed the boundary of two fields,
and dropping on their knees, had fired deadly volleys into the
advancing lines of the enemy. The Confederates carried off
the greater portion of the wounded up the Valley. Their retreat was conducted in perfect order; and even Gen. Shields,
in his accounts of the affair, which were very much exaggerated, of course, for the purposes of popular sensation in the
North, testified of the Confederates, that "such was their gallantry and high state of discipline, that at no time during the
battle or pursuit did they give way to panic."

The enemy had but little reason to boast of the battle of
Kernstown. In fact, the affair was without general signification. It was an attack by the Confederates, undertaken on
false information, gallantly executed, and, although unsuccessful, was not disastrous. The Northern troops had made no advance in the Valley; from the Manassas line they had actually
retired; nor had they any considerable body of troops this side
of Centreville. Whether they would ever attempt to execute
their original plan, of a march through Piedmont to Richmond,
was now more than problematical.

The greater portion of our dead left on the field of battle
were buried under the direction of the mayor of Winchester.
Some fifty citizens collected the dead, dug a great pit on the
battle-field, and gently laid the poor fellows in their last resting-place. It was a sad sight, and sadder still to see women
looking carefully at every corpse to try to identify the bodies
of their friends. Scarcely a family in the county but had a
relative there. But their suffering did not mollify the noble
Southern women of Winchester. Every feeling, testified a
Federal officer who witnessed the sad and harrowing scenes of
the battle-field, seemed to have been extinguished in their intense hatred of "the Yankees." "They would say, 'You may
bring the whole force of the North here, but you can never
conquer us,—we will shed our last drop of blood,'" &c.

Col. Ashby covered the retreat of the army, and by his tire-
less energy, made himself, as on many other occasions, the
terror of the Yankees. The daring feats and heroic exploits of
this brave officer were universal themes of admiration in the
South, and were rehearsed by the people of the Valley, who

idolized him, with infinite gratification and delight. A few months before, when Winchester had been evacuated, under orders from the War Department, he had been unwilling to leave the town, and had lingered behind, watching the approach of the haughty and unprincipled foe into this ancient town of the Valley. He waited until the Federal columns had filled the streets, and, within two hundred yards of them, cheered for the Southern Confederacy, and then dashed off at full speed for the Valley turnpike. He reached it only to find his way intercepted by two of the enemy's pickets. Nothing daunted, he drew his pistol and shot down one of the pickets, and, seizing the other, dragged him off a prisoner, and brought him safely to the Confederate lines. It was adventures like these, as well as extraordinary gallantry in the field, that made the name of the brave Virginia cavalier conspicuous throughout the South, and a tower of strength with those for whose homes and firesides he had been struggling.

The personal appearance of Col. Ashby was not striking. He was of small stature. He wore a long black beard, and had dark, glittering eyes. It was not generally known that the man who performed such deeds of desperate valor and enterprise, and who was generally pictured to the imagination as a fierce, stalwart, and relentless adventurer, was as remarkable for his piety and devoutness as for his military achievements. His manners were a combination, not unusual in the truly re fined spirit, of gentleness with the most enthusiastic courage It was said of him, that when he gave his most daring commands, he would gently draw his sabre, wave it around his head, and then his clear, sounding voice would ring out the simple but thrilling words, "Follow me." In such a spirit we recognize the fine mixture of elements that the world calls heroism.

The Northern forces pursued neither the retreat of Johnston from Manassas, nor that of Jackson from Winchester. On the contrary, they withdrew the forces first advanced, and blocked the road between Strasburg and Winchester. It was known, however, about this time, that the camps at Washington had been rapidly diminished, and that McClellan had totally disappeared from the scene. At the same time an unusual confidence was expressed in the Northern journals that Richmond would now fall almost immediately into the hands of their generals. Then followed the daily announcements of fleets of transports arriving in Hampton Roads, and the vast extension of the long line of tents at Newport News. These were evi· dent indications of the intention of the enemy to abandon for the present other projects for the capture of Richmond, so as to make his great effort on the Peninsula formed by the York and James rivers.

General Magruder, the hero of Bethel, and a commander who was capable of much greater achievements, was left to confront the growing forces on the Peninsula, which daily menaced him, with an army of seventy-five hundred men, while the great bulk of the Confederate forces were still in motion in the neighborhood of the Rappahannock and the Rapidan, and he had no assurance of reinforcements. The force of the enemy was ten times his own; they had commenced a daily cannonading upon his lines; and a council of general officers was convened, to consult whether the little army of seven thousand five hundred men should maintain its position in the face of tenfold odds, or retire before the enemy. The opinion of the council was unanimous for the latter alternative, with the exception of one officer, who declared that every man should die in the intrenchments before the little army should fall back. "By G—, it shall be so!" was the sudden exclamation of Gen. Magruder, in sympathy with the gallant suggestion. The resolution demonstrated a remarkable heroism and spirit. Our little force was adroitly extended over a distance of several miles, reaching from Mulberry Island to Gloucester Point, a regiment being posted here and there, in every gap plainly open to observation, and on other portions of the line the men being posted at long intervals, to give the appearance of numbers to the enemy. Had the weakness of Gen. Magruder at this time been known to the enemy, he might have suffered the consequences of his devoted and self-sacrificing courage; but as it was, he held his lines on the Peninsula until they were reinforced by the most considerable portion of Gen. Johnston's forces, and made the situation of a contest upon which the attention of the public was unanimously fixed as the most decisive of the war.

It is not our purpose at this time to follow up the develop

ments of the situation on the Peninsula. We must, for the present, leave affairs there in the crisis to which we have brought them, while we refer to a serious recurrence of disasters about this time on our sea-coast and rivers, where again the lesson was repeated to us of the superiority of the enemy on the water, not by any mysterious virtue of gunboats, but solely on account, as we shall show, of inefficiency and improvidence in our government.

On the 4th of March, the town of Newbern, in North Carolina, was taken by the Federals, under command of General Burnside, after a feeble resistance. The day before, the Federals had landed about ten thousand troops fifteen miles below Newbern, and at the same time had ascended the river with a fleet of gunboats, which, as they advanced, shelled the woods in every direction. The next morning the fighting was commenced at early dawn, and continued until half-past ten o'clock, when our forces, being almost completely surrounded, were compelled to retreat. All the forts on the river were abandoned. Fort Thompson was the most formidable of these. It was four miles from Newbern, and mounted thirteen heavy guns, two of them rifled 32-pounders. The guns at Fort Ellis, three miles from Newbern, were dismounted and thrown down the embankment. Fort Lane, mounting eight guns, two miles from Newbern, was blown up. In the first attack upon our lines, at 7 o'clock, the enemy had been repulsed three times successively by our infantry, with the assistance of Fort Thompson; but having flanked our forces on the right, which caused a panic among the militia, he had changed the fortunes of the day. The railroad bridge across Neuse river was not burnt until after all our troops had crossed, except those whose escape had been effectually cut off by the enemy. The Federals achieved a complete victory after a contest of very short duration, having taken about five hundred prisoners, over fifty pieces of cannon, and large quantities of arms and ammunition.

The easy defeat of the Confederate forces at Newbern, the surrender of our fortifications, on which thousands of dollars had recently been expended, and the abandonment not only of our heavy guns, but of some of our field-guns also, was a subject of keen mortification to the South. The fact was known that our force at Newbern was very inadequate—not more than five thousand—a part of whom were militia, and had been left, despite of appeals to the government for reinforcements, to encounter whatever force Gen. Burnside should choose to bring against them. Gen. Branch, who was in command of the Confederate forces, and who displayed courage and judgment, was compelled to fight at Newbern. To have given it up without a struggle, after all that had been done there, would have brought him into discredit with the government, the people, and the troops. As it was, the enemy had gained an important position within easy reach of the Wilmington and Weldon road. But few persons remained in the town. Seven trains left for Goldsboro', all crowded to overflowing by fugitive soldiers and panic-stricken people. A shell from the enemy's gunboats fell within twenty-five feet of the last train as it moved off. Women and children were overtaken by the trains many miles from Newbern, some in vehicles of various kinds, and many on foot. The panic and disorganization extended for miles, and yet there was a nobility in the determination of the population of Newbern to fly anywhere rather than court security in their homes by submission to the enemy. The town of Newbern originally contained twelve hundred people; when occupied by the enemy, it contained one hundred people, male and female, of the old population.

On the 12th day of April one year ago, the guns and mortars of the South Carolina batteries opened upon the then hostile walls of Fort Sumter. Strangely enough, the first anniversary of the event was signalized by the startling and uncomfortable announcement that Fort Pulaski, the principal defence of the city of Savannah, had surrendered to the Yankees, after a brief bombardment. The news was all the more unpleasant, from the fact that the day before the public had been informed by telegraph that the enemy's batteries had been "silenced." It seems that they were not silent until our flag was struck. The surrender was unconditional, and the garrison, consisting of more than three hundred men, four of whom had been wounded and none killed, were made prisoners of war.

Another Confederate disaster on the coast shortly ensued, in the surrender of Fort Macon. This fort, on the North Carolina coast, was surrendered on the 25th of April, after a bombard-

ment from the enemy's land batteries of less than twelve hours
It commanded the entrance to Beaufort harbor, and was said
to be the most formidable fortification on the North Carolina
coast.

For these painful and almost humiliating disasters on our
coast and rivers, a ready but very silly excuse was always at
hand. A most pernicious and false idea appeared to have
taken possession of the public mind with reference to the essential superiority of the enemy on water. A very obvious reflection of common sense dissipates the idea of any *essential* advantage which the enemy had over us on the water. The failures
in our defences had been most unjustly attributed to the bug-
bear of gunboats, when they ought to have been ascribed to no
more unavoidable causes than our own improvidence and neg
lect.

The suggestion of common sense is, that if it was possible
to make a vessel ball-proof, it was certainly much easier to
make a fortification ball-proof. The excuse had been persistently made for our lack of naval defences, that it was difficult
to supply the necessary machinery, and almost impossible, with
the limited means at our disposal, to construct steam-engines.
But these excuses about lack of machinery and steam-engines
did not apply to our land defences. No machinery was necessary; no engine was necessary; and no consultation of curved
lines of naval architecture was required to make a land fortification ball-proof. The iron plate that was fitted on the side of
a gunboat had only to be placed on a dead surface, to make
the land fortification a match in invulnerability to the iron-
plated man-of-war. This was common sense. Unfortunately,
however, it was a common sense which the scientists of West
Point had been unable to appreciate. While the public mind
had been busy in ascribing so many of our late disasters to
some essential and mysterious virtue in iron-plated boats, it
seemed never to have occurred to it that it was much easier to
construct iron-plated batteries on land than the iron-plated
sides of a ship, besides giving the structure the power of loco-
motion, and that our defeats on the water, instead of being
charged to "gunboats," or to "the dispensations of Providence," had been but the natural results of human neglect and
human stupidity.

CHAPTER XII.

THE last period of our narrative of events in Tennessee, left Gen. Johnston making a southward movement towards the left bank of the Tennessee river, for the objects of the defence of Memphis and the Mississippi river, and indicated the important position of Island No. 10, forty-five miles below Columbus, as still in possession of the Confederates.

This important position in the Mississippi river was defended by General Beauregard with extraordinary vigor and success against the fleet of the enemy's gunboats, under the command of Flag-officer Foote. The works were erected with the highest engineering skill, were of great strength, and, with their natural advantages, were thought to be impregnable.

The bombardment of Madrid Bend and Island No. 10 commenced on the 15th of March, and continued constantly night and day. On the 17th a general attack, with five gunboats and four mortar-boats, was made, which lasted nine hours. The attack was unsuccessful. On the first of April, General Beauregard telegraphed to the War Department at Richmond that the bombardment had continued for fifteen days, in which time the enemy had thrown three thousand shells, expending about one hundred thousand pounds of powder, with the result on our side of one man killed and none seriously wounded. The gratifying statement was also made in General Beauregard's dispatches that our batteries were entirely intact. We had disabled one of the enemy's gunboats and another was reported to be sunk, and the results of the bombardment so far as it had continued, afforded room for congratulation that the fantasy of the invincible power of Yankee gunboats would at last be dispelled, and that the miserable history of the surrender of all our forts to this power was destined to wind up in a decisive and brilliant Confederate triumph on the waters of the Mississippi. The daily bulletin from Island No. 10, for many days, represented that the enemy, after an incessant bombardment of many hours, had inflicted no injury. The people of the South were constantly assured that the place was impregnable, and that the enemy never could pass it.

The bombardment had been one of unparalleled length in the war. Every day the mortars continued to boom, and still the cannon of the island replied with dull, sullen roar, wasting shot and temper alike. The very birds became accustomed to the artificial thunder, and alighted upon the branches of trees overhanging the mortars in the sulphurous smoke. The scenes of this long bombardment are described as affording some of the most magnificent spectacles—the tongues of flame leaping from the mouths of the mortars amid a crash like a thousand thunders, and then the columns of smoke rolling up in beautiful fleecy spirals, developing into rings of exquisite proportions. It is only necessary for one to realize the sublime poetry of war, as illustrated in the remarkable scenes at Island No. 10, to imagine a dozen of these monsters thundering at once, the air filled with smoke clouds, the gunboats belching out destruction and completely hidden from sight in whirls of smoke, the shells screaming through the air with an unearthly sound, and the distant guns of the enemy sending their solid shot above and around the island, dashing the water up in glistening columns and jets of spray.

While the people of the South were induced to anticipate a decisive and final repulse of the enemy on the waters of the Mississippi, the news reached them through Northern channels that the capture of Island No. 10 had been effected on the 8th of April, and that not only had the position been weakly surrendered, but that we had saved none of our cannon or munitions, had lost our boats, and had left about six hundred prisoners on the island in the hands of the enemy.

The evacuation of the island, which was effected in the greatest precipitation—our sick being abandoned, there being no concert of action whatever between the Confederates upon the island and those occupying the shore, the latter fleeing, leaving the former to their fate—had taken place but two days after Gen. Beauregard had left command of the post for important operations to check the movements of the enemy on the Tennessee river, which were developing a design to cut off his communication in west Tennessee with the eastern and southern States. Gen. Makall had been appointed to take command of the post. He assumed it on the 5th of April, in a flaming order, in which he announced to the soldiers : " Let me tell you who I am. I am a general made by Beauregard—a general selected by Gens. Beauregard and Bragg." In the mean time, the enemy was busy, and his operations were suffered to escape the vigilance of the Confederate commander. The Federals had cut a canal across the peninsula at New Madrid, through which the steamers and several barges were taken. The undertaking was an herculean one. The canal was twelve miles long, through heavy timber, which had to be sawed off by hand four feet under water.

One of the enemy's gunboats had succeeded in passing the island in a heavy fog. On the night of the 5th of April, the enemy, with a gunboat engaged Rucker's battery. While attention was engaged with this boat, a second gunboat slipped down unperceived, except by the men at one of the batteries, who fired two shots at her without effect. The situation was now serious ; the enemy had possession of the river below the island. On the night of April 6, Gen. Makall moved the infantry and Stewart's battery to the Tennessee shore, to protect the landing from anticipated attacks. The artillerists remained on the island. The enemy having effected a landing above and below the island in large force, its surrender might be considered as a military necessity. But there could be no excuse for the wretched management and infamous scenes that attended the evacuation. All our guns, seventy in number, varying in calibre from 32 to 100 pounders, rifled, were abandoned, together with our magazines, which were well supplied with powder, large quantities of shot, shell, and other munitions of war. The transports and boats were scuttled. Nothing seems to have been done properly. The guns were spiked with rat-tail files, but so imperfectly that several of them were rendered serviceable to the enemy in a very short time. The floating battery, formerly the Pelican Dock at New Orleans, of sixteen heavy guns, after being scuttled, was cut loose. At daylight it was found lodged a short distance above Point Pleasant, and taken possession of by the enemy. Four steamers afloat fell into the hands of the enemy, with all the stores on board.

The unhappy men on the island were abandoned to their fate, the Confederates on the mainland having fled with precipitation. On one of the hospital boats were a hundred poor wretches, half dead with disease and neglect. On the shore were crowds of our men wandering around among the profusion of ammunition and stores. A few of them effected their escape through the most remarkable dangers and adventures. Some trusted themselves to hastily constructed rafts, with which to float down the Mississippi, hoping to attract the attention and aid of the people living on the shore. Others gained the upper banks of the river, where, for several days and nights, they wandered, lost in the extensive cane-brakes, without food, and in severe toil. Some two or three hundred of the stragglers, principally from the forces on the mainland, succeeded in making their way to Bell's Station, on the Ohio railroad, and reached Memphis.

The disaster was considerable enough in the loss of Island No. 10; but the circumstances attending it, and the consequences in the loss of men, cannon, ammunition, supplies, and every thing appertaining to an army, all of which might possibly have been avoided, increased the regrets of the South, and swelled the triumph of her enemies. Our total loss in prisoners, including those taken on the mainland as well as those abandoned on the island, was probably not less than two thousand. The Federal Secretary of the Navy, Mr. Welles, had reason to declare, that "the triumph was not the less appreciated, because it was protracted, and finally bloodless.' No single battle-field had yet afforded to the North such visible fruits of victory as had been gathered at Island No. 10.

THE BATTLE OF SHILOH.

In the mean time, the movements of the enemy on the Tennessee river were preparing the situation for one of the grandest battles that had yet been fought in any quarter of the war, or had yet illustrated the exasperation and valor of the contestants. Gen. Beauregard had determined to foil the apparent designs of the enemy to cut off his communication with the south and east, by concentrating all his available forces at and around Corinth. This town is situated at the junction of the Memphis and Charleston and the Mobile and Ohio railroads, about ninety-two miles east of Memphis.

Gen. Johnston had taken up a line of march from Murfreesboro, to form a junction of his forces with those of General Beauregard. By the 1st of April, these united forces were concentrated along the Mobile and Ohio railroad from Bethel to Corinth, and on the Memphis and Charleston railroad from Corinth to Iuka. The army of the Mississippi had received other important accessions. It was increased by several regiments from Louisiana, two divisions of Gen. Polk's command from Columbus, and a fine corps of troops from Mobile and Pensacola. In numbers, in discipline, in the galaxy of the distinguished names of its commanders, and in every article of merit and display, the Confederate army in the vicinity of Corinth was one of the most magnificent ever assembled by the South on a single battle-field.

The enemy under Gen. Grant, on the west bank of the Tennessee, had obtained a position at Pittsburg and in the direction of Savannah. An advance was contemplated by him, as soon as he could be reinforced by the army under Gen. Buell, then known to be advancing for that purpose by rapid marches from Nashville by the way of Columbus. To prevent this demonstration, it was determined by Gen. Beauregard to press the issue without delay. By a rapid and vigorous attack on Gen. Grant, it was expected he would be beaten back into his transports and the river, or captured in time to enable the Confederates to profit by the victory, and remove to the rear all the stores and munitions that would fall into their hands, in such an event, before the arrival of Gen. Buell's army on the scene. It was never contemplated, however, to retain the position thus gained and abandon Corinth, the strategic point of the campaign.

It appears to have been Gen. Beauregard's plan to have attacked the enemy in their encampments on Saturday, the 5th. He, therefore, began the movement on Thursday, but the roads were heavy, and the men could not be got into position before Saturday. Had the attack been made on that day, the first day's fighting must have ended the conflict, for the enemy could have had no hope of aid from Buell. As it was, one day was lost, and the enemy were constantly inspirited by the almost momentary expectation of the arrival of Gen. Buell. In the mean time, courier after courier was sent by Gen. Grant for Buell to hasten on.

The Confederate forces did not reach the intersection of the roads from Pittsburg and Hamburg, in the immediate vicinity of the enemy, until late on Saturday afternoon. Their march had been tedious and wearisome. The roads were narrow and traversed a densely wooded country, and a severe rain-storm had rendered them almost impassable, and had drenched our troops in bivouac.

The morning of the 6th of April (Sunday) was to usher in the bloody scenes of a memorable battle. One camp of the enemy was near Shiloh church—a rude log chapel; and another stretched away in the direction of the road leading from Pittsburg Landing on the river to Corinth. The scene of the encampment was a very beautiful and magnificent one, there being but little undergrowth, and the thin ranks of the tall forest-trees affording open views, while the interlacing of their topmost boughs made a picturesque and agreeable canopy. In a military point of view, the battle-field might be described as a broken country, presenting opportunities for a great variety of manœuvres and independent operations by comparatively small bodies of men.

On the Saturday evening preceding the Sunday fight at Shiloh, there had been considerable skirmishing on our lines. Early Sunday morning, before sunrise, Gen. Hardee, in front of the enemy's camp, made an advance upon it. The enemy was taken completely by surprise, not expecting to be attacked under any circumstances, by our inferior force. Many of the

nen were undressed and in night attire, and the hot breakfasts
prepared by the messes were left untouched for the entertainment of our men. A line of battle was hastily formed by the
enemy, and, in the mean time, our forces were advancing in
every direction. The plan of the battle on our side was to
form three parallel lines—the front, centre, and rear—each line
having its centre and two flanks. The rear constituted the reserve, and the artillery was distributed between the first and
second lines. The front was commanded by Gen. Hardee, the
centre by Gen. Bragg, and the rear by Gen. Polk—Johnston
and Beauregard being with the latter.

From daylight until a little after six o'clock, the fighting
was principally between the pickets and skirmishers, but, at
the latter hour, a portion of our main body appearing in sight,
fire opened with artillery, and for an hour or more one heard
nothing but the incessant uproar of the heavy guns. Our men,
though many of them were unaccustomed to the iron hail, received the onset coolly, awaiting the orders to rise from their
recumbent position and advance. In due time these came, and
thenceforward through the day, brave and disciplined as were
the Federal troops, nothing seemed capable of resisting the
desperate valor of the Confedrates. The enemy fell like chaff
before the wind. Broken in ranks, they rallied behind trees
and in the underbrush, only to be again repulsed and driven
back.

The scenery of the battle-field was awfully sublime. Far up
in the air shells burst into flame like shattered stars, and passed
away in little clouds of white vapor, while others filled the air
with a shrill scream, and burst far in the rear. All along the
line the faint smoke of the musketry rose lightly, while, from
the mouths of the cannon, sudden gusts of intense white smoke
burst up all around. Every second of time had its especial
tone. Bullets shredded the air, and whistled swiftly by, or
struck into trees, fences, wagons, or with their peculiar "chuck"
into men. Every second of time had its especial tone, and the
forest, among whose branches rose the wreathing smoke, was
packed with dead.

The irresistible attack of our troops was compared by Gen.
Beauregard, in his official report of the battle, to "an Alpine
avalanche." The enemy were driven back by a series of dar-

ing, desperate, and successful charges, the various Confederate regiments and brigades rolling rapidly forward to the sound of enthusiastic cheers. In all of these, both general and field officers displayed a bravery that amounted to sheer recklessness, frequently leading the men into the very teeth of the opposing fire. It was these inspiring examples of personal valor which made our troops invincible.

At half-past two, Gen. Johnston, the commander-in-chief of the Confederates, fell. He was leading a charge upon the third camp of the enemy. The fatal wound was inflicted by a musket-ball on the calf of his right leg, and was considered by him as only a flesh wound. Soon after receiving it, he gave an order to Governor Harris, who was acting as volunteer aid to him, who, on his return to Gen. Johnston, in a different part of the field, found him exhausted from loss of blood, and reeling in his saddle. Riding up to him, Governor Harris asked: "Are you hurt?" To which the now dying hero answered: "Yes, and I fear mortally;" and then stretching out both arms to his companion, fell from his horse, and soon after expired. No other wounds were discovered upon his person.

Prudently the information of Gen. Johnston's fall was kept from the army. But the day was already secured. Amid the roar of artillery and the cheers of the victorious army, the commander-in-chief quietly breathed his last. Our forces were successfully pushing the enemy back upon the Tennessee river. It was after six o'clock in the evening when his last position was carried. The remnant of his army had been driven in utter disorder to the immediate vicinity of Pittsburg, under the shelter of the heavy guns of his iron-clad gunboats, and the Confederates remained undisputed masters of his well-selected, admirably provided cantonments, after over twelve hours of obstinate conflict with his forces, who had been beaten from them and the contiguous covert, but only by a sustained onset of all the men we could bring into action.

The substantial fruits of our victory were immense. We were in possession of all the enemy's encampments between Owl and Lick rivers, nearly all of his field artillery, about thirty flags, colors, and standards, over three thousand prisoners, including a division commander (General Prentiss) and several brigade commanders, thousands of small-arms, an im mense supply of subsistence, forage, and munitions of war, and a large amount of means of transportation. Never, perhaps, was an army so well provided as that of the enemy, and never, perhaps, was one so completely stripped on a single battle-field. On taking possession of the enemy's encampments, there were found therein the complete muster-rolls of the expedition up the river. It appeared that we had engaged the divisions of Gens. Prentiss, Sherman, Hurlbut, McClernand, and Smith, of 9,000 men each, or at least 45,000 men. Our entire force in the engagement could not have exceeded 38,000 men. The flower of the Federal troops were engaged, being principally Western men, from the States of Illinois, Indiana, Wisconsin, and Iowa. There were also quite a number of Missourians opposed to us, who are said to have fought with great spirit, opposite Gen. Gladden's brigade, on the extreme right. These men were accustomed to lives of hardihood and adventure. The captured Federal general, Prentiss, did not hesitate to testify to General Beauregard, "You have whipped our best troops to-day."

The enemy's artillery on the field, according to Gen. Prentiss' statement, numbered in all one hundred and eight pieces, or eighteen batteries of six pieces each. Their small-arms were of every description: Minié rifles, Enfield rifles, Maynard rifles, Colt's six-shooters, common muskets, &c., all of the best quality and workmanship. The Federal equipments left nothing to be desired. Their clothing was of the best quality and abundant, and the same may be said of their supplies. An abundance of excellent coffee was found in their tents— beef, pork, butter, cheese, navy biscuit, and sugar. The famous expedition to the plains of Manassas was not better fitted out or supplied.

On Sunday night, Gen. Beauregard established his headquarters at the little church of Shiloh, and our troops were directed to sleep on their arms in the enemy's encampment. The hours, however, that should have been devoted to the refreshment of nature were spent by many of the troops in a disgraceful hunt after the spoils. The possession of the rich camp of the enemy seemed to have demoralized whole regiments. All through the night and early the next morning the hunt after the spoils was continued. Cowardly citizens and rapacious soldiers were engaged alike in the wretched work. They might be seen everywhere, plundering the tents out of which the enemy had been driven, and loading them selves down with the spoils. The omission of discipline, which permitted these scenes, is not pardonable even in the license and indulgences which generally attend the victory of an army. The spoils of a victorious army should be carefully gathered up and preserved for the use of the army itself. They are the just possession of the conqueror, are frequently of great value, and should not be lost or carried off, where they can be of use. But, more than this, nothing could be more likely to demoralize troops than the indiscriminate pillage of an enemy's camp. It creates disorganization in the army; it so far stands in the way of a vigorous pursuit of the enemy; it demoralizes the spoiler himself, and lets him down at one step from an honorable soldier to a plundering brigand. It is no wonder that the troops which confronted the enemy next morning in the vicinity of Pittsburg Landing betrayed, however bravely they fought in comparison with the enemy, a diminution of spirit and visible signs of demoralization.

Sunday night found both armies in a critical situation. Gen. Beauregard hoped, from news received by a special dispatch, that delays had been encountered by Gen. Buell in his march from Columbia, and that his main force, therefore, could not reach the field of battle in time to save Gen. Grant's shattered fugitive forces from capture or destruction on the following day. The situation of Gen. Grant was that of the most extreme anxiety to himself. The enemy had supposed that the last act of the tragedy would have been completed on Saturday evening. The reserve line of the Federals was entirely gone. Their whole army was crowded into a circuit of half to two-thirds of a mile around the landing. They had been falling back all day. The next repulse would have put them into the river, and there were not transports enough to cross a single division before the Confederates would be upon them. As the lull in the firing of the Confederates took place, and the angry rattle of musketry died upon the ears of the fugitive Federals, they supposed that the pursuing army was preparing for the grand final rush that was to crown the day's success. But Gen. Beauregard had been satisfied to pursue the enemy to the river, and to leave him under the cover of his gunboats, with-out an attempt to penetrate it. When it was understood that pursuit was called off, Gen. Grant could ill conceal his exulta-tion. His anxiety was suddenly composed, and, in a tone of confidence, he exclaimed to the group of officers around him "to-morrow they will be exhausted, and then we will go at them with fresh troops." *

He was right. Looking across the Tennessee, he could see a body of cavalry awaiting transportation over. They were said to be Buell's advance; yet they had been there an hour or two alone. Suddenly there was a rustle among the gazers. They saw the gleaming of the gun-barrels, and they caught, amid the leaves and undergrowth down the opposite side of the river, glimpses of the steady, swinging tramp of trained sol-diers. A division of Buell's army was there, and was hailed with tremendous cheers by the men on the opposite bank of the river.

The enemy was reinforced on Monday morning by more troops than Gen. Beauregard could have counted upon. The divisions of Gens. Nelson, McCook, Crittenden, and Thomas, of Buell's army, had crossed the river, some 25,000 strong; also, Gen. L. Wallace's division of Gen. Grant's army had been moved up the river—making at least 33,000 fresh troops. Vigorous preparations were made by Gen. Beauregard to resist the as-sault, which was deemed almost certain on Monday. A hot fire of musketry opened about six o'clock in the morning from the enemy's quarter upon his advanced lines, and assured him of the junction of his forces. The battle soon raged with fury, the enemy being flushed by his reinforcements, and confident in his largely superior numbers.

---

* The evidence of a "lost opportunity" in the battle of Shiloh abundantly appeared in the statements of the Northern commanders. Gen. Prentiss is reported to have made the following statement: "Gen. Beauregard," he said, "asked me if we had any works at the river, to which I replied, 'you must consider us poor soldiers, general, if you suppose we would have neglected so plain a duty!' The truth is, however, we had no works at all. Gen. Beaure-gard stopped the pursuit at a quarter to six; had he used the hour still left him, he could have captured the last man on this side of the river, for Buell did not cross till Sunday night."

According to Buell's report, our shot were falling among the fugitives crouching under the river-bank when our troops were called off.

On the right and centre, the enemy were repulsed in every attempt he made with his heavy columns in that quarter of the field; on the left, however, and nearest to the point of arrival of his reinforcements, he drove forward line after line of his fresh troops, which were met with resolution and courage. Again and again our troops were brought to the charge, invariably to win the position at issue, invariably to drive back their foe. But hour by hour, thus opposed to an enemy constantly reinforced, the ranks of the Confederates were perceptibly thinned under the unceasing withering fire of the enemy. By noon, eighteen hours of hard fighting had sensibly exhausted a large number; Gen. Beauregard's last reserves had necessarily been disposed of, and the enemy was evidently receiving fresh reinforcements after each repulse; accordingly, about 1 P. M., he determined to withdraw from so unequal a conflict, securing such of the results of the victory of the day before as was then practicable.

The retreat was executed with uncommon steadiness, and the enemy made no attempt to follow. Gen. Breckinridge had been posted with his command so as to cover the withdrawal of the rest of the army. Gen. Beauregard had approached him and told him, that it might be necessary for him to sacrifice himself; for said he, "*This retreat must not be a rout!* You must hold the enemy back, if it requires the loss of your last man!" "Your orders shall be executed to the letter," said the chivalrous Breckinridge; and gathering his command, fatigued and jaded and decimated by the toils and terrors of a two days' battle, he and they prepared to devote themselves, if necessary, for the safety of the army. There, weary and hungry, they stood guard and vigil. The enemy, sorely chastised, did not indeed come as expected; but Breckinridge and his heroes deserve none the less praise.

Never did troops leave a battle-field in better order. Even the stragglers fell into the ranks, and marched off with those who had stood more steadily by their colors. The fact that the enemy attempted no pursuit indicates their condition. They had gained nothing; we had lost nothing. The Confederates left the field only after eight hours of incessant battle with a superior army of fresh troops, whom they had repulsed in every attack on their lines,—so repulsed and crippled, indeed, as to leave it unable to take the field for the campaign for which it was collected and equipped at such enormous expense, and with such profusion of all the appliances of war. The action of Monday had not eclipsed the glorious victory of the preceding day. Sunday had left the Confederate army masters of the battle-field, their adversary beaten, and a signal victory achieved after an obstinate conflict of twelve hours.

The result of the engagement was most honorable to the South, and was recognized as one of the most conspicuous triumphs to its arms. The exultations, however, of victory in the public mind were perceptibly tempered by the sad intelligence of the death of Gen. Albert Sidney Johnston.

The deceased commander had led, perhaps, one of the most eventful military lives on this continent. He was graduated at the West Point Academy in 1820, as lieutenant in the Sixth Infantry, and after serving in the Black Hawk war left the army, and in 1836 emigrated to Texas, arriving there shortly after the battle of San Jacinto. He entered the Texan army as a private soldier, and was soon promoted to succeed Gen. Felix Houston in the chief command—an event which led to a duel between them, in which Johnston was wounded. Having held the office of senior brigadier-general until 1838, he was appointed Secretary of War, and in 1839 organized an expedition against the Cherokees, who were totally routed in an engagement on the Neches. In 1840, he retired from office, and settled upon a plantation in Brazoria county. He was an ardent advocate for the annexation of Texas to the United States. In 1846, at the request of Gen. Taylor, he took the field against Mexico, as commander of the volunteer Texan rifle regiment, in which capacity he served six months. Subsequently, he was acting inspector-general to Gen. Butler, and for his services at the siege of Monterey received the thanks of his commander. In October, 1849, he was appointed paymaster by President Taylor, with the rank of major, and, upon the passage of the act of Congress authorizing the raising of additional regiments in the army, he was appointed colonel of the Second Cavalry. In the latter part of 1857, he received the command of the United States forces sent to coerce the Mormons into obedience to the Federal authority, and conducted the expedition in safety to Great Salt Lake City in the opening of the succeeding year. Since then he commanded the military district of Utah He resigned the Federal service as soon as the intelligence of the opening of the war reached him, and, travelling from California by the overland route, reached New Orleans in August last. Proceeding to Richmond, he was appointed, on his arrival there, general, to take command of the Department of the Mississippi.

It is known that Gen. Johnston was the subject of most unjust and hasty public censure in connection with his late retreat from Bowling Green and fall of Fort Donelson. He is said, but a few days before the battle in which he fell, to have expressed the determination to discharge his duties and responsibilities to his country, according to the best convictions of his mind, and a resolution to redeem his losses at no distant day. According to the official report, he fell in the thickest of the fight.

Keen regrets were felt by the friends of Gen Johnston on learning the circumstances of the manner of his death, as these circumstances appeared to leave but little doubt that his life might have been saved by surgical attention to his wound. His only wound was from a musket-ball that severed an inconsiderable artery in the thigh. He was probably unconscious of the wound, and never realized it until, from the loss of blood, he fell fainting and dying from his horse.

Gen. Johnston was in the natural vigor of manhood, about sixty years of age. He was about six feet in height, strongly and powerfully formed, with a grave, dignified, and commanding presence. His features were strongly marked, showing the Scottish lineage, and denoted great resolution and composure of character. His complexion, naturally fair, was, from exposure, a deep brown. His manner was courteous, but rather grave and silent. He had many devoted friends, but they had been won and secured rather by the native dignity and nobility of his character, than by his power of address.

Besides the conspicuous loss of the commander-in-chief, others had fallen whose high qualities were likely to be missed in the momentous campaign impending. Gen. Gladden, of South Carolina, had fallen, after having been conspicuous to his whole corps and the army for courage and capacity. Distinguished in Mexico, on the bloody fields of Contreras and

Churubusco, he received honorable wounds. Having become a citizen of Louisiana, and selected to command a noble brigade, he again accumulated honor upon his native State, illustrated its martial fame, served her, no less than Louisiana, with his life, and sealed the great cause with his best blood.

George M. Johnston, Provisional Governor of Kentucky, had gone into the action with the Kentucky troops. Having his horse shot under him on Sunday, he entered the ranks of a Kentucky company, commanded by Capt. Monroe, son of the venerable Judge Monroe. At night, while occupying the same tent with the captain, it occurred to him that he had not taken the oath which entitled him to be enrolled in that company. He, therefore, desired the oath to be administered, which was done with due solemnity; "and now," said the new recruit, "I will take a night's rest and be ready for a good day's fighting." Faithfully he kept his pledge, and fell mortally wounded in the thickest of the fight. In making official mention of his death, Gen. Beauregard declared that "not Kentucky alone, but the whole Confederacy had sustained a great loss in the death of this brave, upright, and able man." He was one of a family of heroes, the nephew of the dauntless chief in the battle of the Thames, and the man who, during a long public and private career, had been ever regarded one of the noblest of Kentucky chevaliers, true and worthy governor of all that was left of Kentucky.

The fearless deportment of the Confederate commanders in the action was remarkable, as they repeatedly led their commands personally to the onset upon their powerful adversary. Gen. Bragg had two horses shot under him. Gen. Breckinridge was twice struck by spent balls. Major-general Hardee had his coat rent by balls and his horse disabled, but escaped with a slight wound. Gen. Cheatham received a ball in the shoulder, and Gen. Bushrod Johnson one in the side. Gen. Bowen was wounded in the neck. Col. Adams, of the First Louisiana regulars, succeeded Gen. Gladden in the command of the right wing, and was soon after shot, the ball striking him just above the eye and coming out behind the ear. Col. Kitt Williams, of Memphis, and Col. Blythe, of Mississippi, formerly consul to Havana, were killed.

The casualties of the battle of Shiloh were terrible. In car nage, the engagement might have compared with some of the most celebrated in the world. Our loss, in the two days in killed outright, was 1,728; wounded, 8,012; missing, 959—making an aggregate of casualties of 10,699. The loss of the enemy in killed, wounded, and prisoners, unquestionably could not have been less than 15,000.

The suffering among the large numbers of our wounded was extreme. They continued to come in from the field slowly, but it was a long and agonizing ride that the poor fellows had to endure, over twenty-two or twenty-three miles of the roughest and ruttiest road in the Southern Confederacy. The weather was horrible, and a cold northeast storm pelted mercilessly down upon them. As they were carried, groaning, from the vehicle to the floor of the hospital, or laid in the depot, it was sad to see the suffering depicted upon their pinched and pallid features. Some of them had lain on the ground, in the mud, for two nights, and were wet to the skin and shivering with chills.

In view of the immense carnage of the battle of Shiloh, it was popularly esteemed *the* great battle of the war, and was declared by the Southern newspapers to take preference over the celebrated action of Manassas. Indeed, the rank which the Manassas battle held in the history of the war, was disputed by newspaper critics on every occasion when some other action presented a larger list of casualties or more prolonged scenes of conflict. But these circumstances, by themselves, certainly afford no standard for measuring the importance and grandeur of battles. It is true that the action of Shiloh was a brilliant Confederate success. But in dramatic situation, in completeness of victory, in interesting details, and in the grand historical tragedy of the enemy's rout, no battle has yet been fought in the war equal to that of Manassas, and, so far, it must hold its place in the history of the first year of the war as its grand battle, despite the efforts of interested critics to outrank its grandeur by that of other achievements, and to do violence to the justice of history.

There was one very remarkable circumstance in the battle of Manassas, which alone must give it an interest distinguished from that of any other engagement of the war. It was that, in the army which achieved that victory, there was rep resented, by troops, every State then in the Southern Confederacy.

At Shiloh, the troops engaged were principally Tennesseeans, Mississippians, Alabamians, Louisianians, Floridians, Texans, Arkansians, and Kentuckians. There was also a battery of Georgians in the field. The behavior of these troops had given us additional reason for the pride so justly felt in Southern arms and Southern prowess. Each and all of them fought so bravely that no distinction can be made between corps from different States. Battles are won, by each soldier feeling that the day depends upon his own individual efforts, and, on the field of Shiloh, this spirit was displayed, unless in rare instances of cowardice, or the more numerous exceptions of demoralization by the pillage which had unfortunately been permitted of the enemy's camp.

The misrepresentations of the North, with reference to the issue of the war, found a crowning example of falsehood and effrontery in the official declaration made at Washington of the action of Shiloh as a brilliant and glorious *Federal* victory. The Lincoln government had not hesitated to keep up the spirits of the people of the North by the most audacious and flaming falsehoods, which would have disgraced even the war bulletins of the Chinese, and which have always been found to be, in nations using this expedient in war, evidences not only of imperfect civilization, but of natural cowardice. The order of the War Department at Washington, signalizing its impostured victory at Shiloh, was as disgusting in profanity as it was brazen in falsehood. It declared that at meridian of Sunday next after the receipt of this order, at the head of every regiment in the armies of the United States, there should be offered by its chaplain a prayer, giving "thanks to the Lord of Hosts for the recent manifestation of His power in the overthrow of the rebels and traitors." One of the Federal generals who was incidentally complimented in this order—H. W. Halleck—for his "success" in the Missouri campaign, had written a voluminous letter to the Washington Cabinet recommending the *policy* of representing every battle in the progress of the war as a Federal victory. A government, which Mr. Seward had declared, in his letter to the British premier on the occasion of his cringing surrender to that power of the Southern commissioners, represented "a civilized and humane nation, a Christian people," had been persuaded to stoop to a policy which even the spirit and honor of brigands might have scorned, and which is never recognized but as a weapon of the vilest and most cowardly of humanity.

Gen. Beauregard retired to Corinth, in pursuance of his original design to make that the strategic point of his campaign. The Federals had sent several expeditions into North Alabama, and had succeeded in occupying Huntsville and Decatur; but the design of these expeditions did not appear to extend further than an attempt to cripple our resources by cutting off the Memphis and Charleston railroad, which runs through these towns.

In the mean time, it was decided by the government at Richmond to remove our forces from the Trans-Mississippi district, and to unite the armies of Van Dorn and Price with such force as Gen. Beauregard already had at Corinth. The order for leaving the limits of their States was responded to by the Missouri and Arkansas troops with ready and patriotic spirit. These brave men gave an example of gallantry and devotion, in leaving their homes and soil in the possession of the enemy, to fight for other parts of the Confederacy, which was made especially conspicuous from the contrast afforded by the troops of some other States which had made unusually large pretensions to patriotism and gallantry, regiments of which had openly mutinied at being ordered beyond the limits of their State, or had marched off with evident discontent, although no enemy held their territory, or was left in possession of their homes and the treasures they contained.

The noble "State Guard" of Missouri had a better appreciation of the duties of patriotism than many of their fellow-citizens of the Confederacy, whose contracted and boastful spirit had made them louder in professions of chivalry and devotion. They followed their beloved commander without a murmur across the waters of the Mississippi, turning their backs upon their homes, for which they had fought with a gallantry and devotion unequalled by any other struggle of the war. They felt that while they were fighting for the fortunes of the Confederacy, they were also contending for the ultimate restoration of Missouri, and that they would serve their State most effectually by following promptly and cheerfully Gens Var. Dorn and Price to Tennessee. Their leader had been made a major-general in the Confederate service; the tardy act of promotion having been at last done from motives of policy, after all efforts had been made in vain to wring it from the obtuse official sense of justice. His influence was used to lead the troops of Missouri to new and distant fields of service, and his noble, patriotic appeals could not but be effectual to men who loved him, who had suffered with him, and were almost as his children.*

---

* The annexed address of Gen. Price to the troops, who followed him across the Mississippi into the Confederate camp, will strike the reader as an admirable appeal. Comprehensive in its terms, Napoleonic in spirit, and glowing with patriotic fire, it challenges comparison with some of the military orders of the most celebrated commanders in history.

HEADQUARTERS, MISSOURI STATE GUARD,
Des Arc, Arkansas, April 3, 1862.

Soldiers of the State Guard:

I command you no longer. I have this day resigned the commission which your patient endurance, your devoted patriotism, and your dauntless bravery have made so honorable. I have done this that I may the better serve you, our State, and our country—that I may the sooner lead you back to the fertile prairies, the rich woodlands and majestic streams of our beloved Missouri, that I may the more certainly restore you to your once happy homes, and to the loved ones there.

Five thousand of those who have fought side by side with us under the grizzly bears of Missouri, have followed me into the Confederate camp. They appeal to you, as I do, by all the tender memories of the past, not to leave us now, but to go with us wherever the path of duty may lead, till we shall have conquered a peace, and won our independence by brilliant deeds upon new fields of battle.

Soldiers of the State Guard! veterans of six pitched battles and nearly twenty skirmishes! conquerors in them all! your country, with its "ruined hearths and shrines," calls upon you to rally once more in her defence, and rescue her forever from the terrible thraldom which threatens her. I know that she will not call in vain. The insolent and barbarous hordes which have dared to invade our soil, and to desecrate our homes, have just met with a signal overthrow beyond the Mississippi. Now is the time to end this unhappy war. If every man will but do his duty, his own roof will shelter him in peace from the storms of the coming winter.

Let not history record that the men who bore with patience the privations of Cowskin Prairie, who endured uncomplainingly the burning heats of a Missouri summer, and the frosts and snows of a Missouri winter; that the men who met the enemy at Carthage, at Oak Hills, at Fort Scott, at Lexington, and in numberless lesser battle-fields in Missouri, and met them but to

It was generally considered in the South that the victory of its arms at Shiloh fully compensated the loss of Island No. 10, and that the Mississippi river below Fort Pillow, with its rich and productive valley, might be accounted safe, with the great army at Corinth covering Memphis, and holding the enemy in check on the land. But a great disaster was to occur where it was least expected, and where it involved the most immense consequences—a disaster which was to astound the South, which was to shake the confidence of the world in the fortunes of the Confederacy, and which was to lead, by unavoidable steps, to the abandonment to the enemy of the great Valley of the Mississippi.

THE FALL OF NEW ORLEANS.

When it was known in Richmond that the Federal fleet, which had so long threatened New Orleans, had at last commenced an attack on the Mississippi river forts, Jackson and St. Philip, no uneasiness was felt for the result. The enemy's fleet, which was to be engaged in this demonstration, was of formidable size. It consisted of forty-six sail, carrying two hundred and eighty-six guns and twenty-one mortars; the whole under the command of Flag-officer Farragut, a renegade Tennesseean. But it was declared, with the most emphatic confidence, that New Orleans was impregnable; the forts, Jackson and St. Philip, were considered but as the outer line of defences; vast sums of money had been expended to line the shores of the river with batteries; the city itself was occupied by what was popularly supposed to be a large and disciplined Confederate force under Gen. Lovell, and in its harbor was a fleet consisting of twelve gunboats, one iron-clad steamer, and the famous ram Manassas.

The authorities at Richmond did not hesitate to express the most unlimited confidence in the safety of New Orleans, and

---

conquer them; that the men who fought so bravely and so well at Elk Horn; that the unpaid soldiery of Missouri were, after so many victories, and after so much suffering, unequal to the great task of achieving the independence of their magnificent State.

Soldiers! I go but to mark a pathway to our homes. Follow me!

STERLING PRICE.

refused even to entertain the probability of the enemy's penetrating the outer line of defence, constituted by the river forts, which were about sixty miles below the city. General Duncan, who was said to be the best artillerist in the Confederate service, was in command of the forts. On the 23d of April he had telegraphed the most encouraging account of their condition. The bombardment had then been continued for a week with extraordinary vigor. Nearly 25,000 thirteen-inch shell had been thrown by the enemy's mortar-boats, many thousands having fallen within the fort. But, in spite of this unremitting bombardment, the works were not at all damaged; only three guns had been dismounted, and the garrison had suffered only to the extent of five killed and ten wounded.

The public were inspired with confidence of a favorable result. The citizens cf New Orleans, never doubting the impregnability of the defences of their city, were occupied as usual with the avocations of business and trade. The morning succeeding the date of the encouraging telegram of General Duncan was to witness scenes of the most extraordinary consternation, and to usher in the appalling intelligence of the enemy's approach to the city.

At half-past three o'clock, on the morning of the 24th of April, the Federal fleet steamed up the river and opened on our gunboats and both the forts, Jackson and St. Philip. The fire was vigorously returned by our side, and in a very short time became perfectly furious, the enemy's fleet and our whole force being engaged. In about one hour several of the enemy's vessels passed the forts—the first one in the advance having our *night signal* flying, which protected her from the fire of our boats, until she ran up close and opened the fire herself.

The citizens of New Orleans were awakened from their dream of security to hear the tolling of the alarm bells announcing the approach of the foe. It was about 9 o'clock, on the morning of the 24th, that the intelligence was received. The whole city was at once thrown into intense commotion; every one rushed into the streets—to the public places—to head-quarters —to the City Hall—inquiring the meaning of the agitation which prevailed, the extent of the danger, and its proximity. It was soon announced, on authority, that the enemy's vessels had succeeded in passing the forts and were then on their way to the city. The number was not known, but was afterwards ascertained to amount to five heavy sloops-of-war and seven or eight gunboats.

The attempt of the enemy had been audacious, but was aided by various contingencies. The defences of the Mississippi consisted of the two forts already mentioned—Jackson and St. Philip—the former situated on the left bank, and the latter on the right bank of the river. About three-quarters of a mile below, the river had been obstructed by means of a raft consisting of a line of eleven dismasted schooners, extending from bank to bank, strongly moored, and connected together with six heavy chains. Unfortunately, a violent storm had rent a large chasm in the raft, which could not be closed in time.

It appears, too, that on the night of the attack, the river had not been lighted by fire-rafts, although General Lovell had several times requested that it should be done. Moreover, the person in charge of the signals neglected to throw up rockets on the approach of the fleet, and, by a strange coincidence, the enemy's signals, on that night, were identically the same as those used by our gunboats. The consequence was, that the advance of the enemy's vessels was not discovered until they were abreast of the forts.

The conflict between the Federal fleet and our fleet and forts, was of a desperate character. The forts opened fire from all their guns that could be brought to bear; but it was too late to produce much impression. The ships passed on, the Hartford, Commodore Farragut's flag-ship in the van, delivering broadsides of grape, shrapnell, and round-shot at the forts on either side. On arriving at this point they encountered the Confederate fleet, consisting of seventeen vessels in all, only about eight of which were armed. The Confederate gunboats carried, some of them, two guns, and others only one. Nevertheless, they fought with desperation against the enemy's overwhelming force, until they were all driven on shore and scuttled or burned by their commanders. The Manassas was not injured by the enemy's fire. She was run ashore and then sunk. The Louisiana, the great iron-clad vessel, built to compete with the success lately won by the famous Virginia, was not in good working order. She could not manœuvre, and only her three bow-guns could be used, although her full com plement consisted of eighteen She emerged from the action totally uninjured. The broadsides of the Pensacola, delivered three times, within a distance of ten yards, failed to loosen a single fastening, or to penetrate a single plate. The forts likewise, remained intact; but the garrisons lost 52, in killed and wounded. Commander McIntosh was desperately wounded. He and Commander Mitchell both stood on the deck of the Louisiana during the whole engagement.

Gen. Lovell arrived just in time to see the Federal fleet passing Fort St. Philip, and to witness the desperate but ineffectual attempt of the Confederate gunboats to check its progress up the river. Just at this moment, the Iroon, one of the enemy's vessels started in pursuit of the Doubloon, Gen. Lovell's boat, and was rapidly overhauling her, when the Governor Moore darted upon the Iroon, and ran into her three times. The Federal vessel managed to escape from this assault, and was again chasing the Doubloon, when the Quitman attacked her, ran into her amidships, and sank her. Thus General Lovell narrowly escaped capture. In the mean time, Captain Kennon, commanding the gunboat Governor Moore, sped down the river into the midst of the enemy's fleet, darting hither and thither, attacking first one and then another of his monstrous antagonists, until he had fired away his last round of ammunition. He then drove his vessel ashore, and applied the torch to her with his own hand. In this way the forts were eluded, the Confederate naval forces destroyed, and the great city of New Orleans placed at the mercy of the Federal squadron.

At 2 o'clock, P. M., on the 24th, General Lovell arrived at the city, having driven and ridden almost the whole way up along the levee. He was immediately called on by the mayor and many other citizens, and in reply to the inquiries of these gentlemen, stated that the intelligence already received was correct; that the enemy's fleet had passed the forts in force, and that the city was indefensible and untenable.

The hasty withdrawal of Gen. Lovell's army from the city drew upon him severe public censure; but the applications of this censure were made in ignorance of the facts, and the evidence which afterwards transpired showed that the evacuation had been made at the urgent instance of the civil authorities themselves of New Orleans, who had entreated the Confederate commander to retire from their midst, in order to save the city from the risk of bombardment. Gen. Lovell expressed a readiness and willingness to remain with all the troops under his command. But it was the undivided expression of public opinion that the army had better retire and save the city from destruction; and, accordingly, the general ordered his troops to rendezvous at Camp Moore, about seventy miles above New Orleans, on the Jackson railroad.

A demand was made by Farragut for the surrender of the command, which Gen. Lovell positively refused, but told the officer who bore the message, that if any Federal troops were landed he would attack them. Two days after he retired, it was said that the city had changed its purpose, and preferred a bombardment to occupation by the enemy. General Lovell promptly ordered a train and proceeded to New Orleans, and immediately had an interview with Mayor Monroe, offering, if such was the desire of the authorities and people, to return with his command and hold the city as long as a man and shot were left.

This offer not being accepted, it was decided that the safety of the large number of unprotected women and children should be looked to, and that the fleet would be permitted to take possession. The raw and poorly armed infantry could by this time have done nothing against the fleet.

The impression which prevailed, that General Lovell had a large army under his command, was singularly erroneous. His army had been stripped to reinforce that at Corinth, and, since the 1st of March, he had sent ten full regiments to Gen. Beauregard, besides many companies of cavalry and artillery. The morning report on the day of the evacuation of New Orleans showed his force to be about *twenty-eight hundred men*, two-thirds of whom were the volunteer and military companies which had recently been put in camp.

Notwithstanding, however, these facts, the circumstances in which Gen. Lovell agreed to evacuate the city under the persuasion of the civil authorities, appeared by no means to be in that desperate extremity that would have justified the step in military judgment; and it was thought by a considerable portion of the public, not without apparent reason, that the evacuation, at the time it was undertaken, was ill-advised, hasty, and the result of panic or selfish clamors in the com munity.

The evacuation was begun on the 24th of April. At this time the river forts had not fallen; but two of the enemy's gunboats actually threatened the city; and the works at Chalmette—five 32-pounders on one side of the river, and nine on the other—were still intact. But it is known that there were reasons other than those which were apparent to the public, which decided Gen. Lovell to evacuate the city, and which were kept carefully to himself for obvious reasons. Gen. Lovell was fully aware that a single frigate anchored at Kenner's plantation, ten miles above the city, where the swamp and the river approached within less than a mile of each other, and through which narrow neck the railroad passes, would have effectually obstructed an exit of troops or stores from the city by land.

This was doubtless the real or most powerful reason for the evacuation of the city.*

On the morning of the next day, the Federal ships appeared off the Chalmette batteries, which exchanged a few shots with them, but without effect. Passing the lower batteries, the ships came up the river under full headway, the Hartford leading, then the Brooklyn, the Richmond, the Pensacola, and six gunboats. On and on they came, until they had extended their line a distance of about five miles, taking positions at intervals of about 900 yards apart. The scene on the water and in the city was alike extraordinary. The Confederate troops were still busy in the work of evacuation, and the streets were thronged with carts, drays, vehicles of all descriptions, laden with the multifarious articles constituting the paraphernalia and implements of warfare. Officers on horseback were galloping hither and thither, receiving and executing orders. The streets were

---

* The water at Kenner's was so high that a ship's guns could have had a clear sweep from the river to the swamp, and there would have been no necessity of any bombardment; the people and the army of New Orleans would have been cut off and starved into a surrender in a short time. The failure of the enemy to occupy Kenner's, for which it is impossible to account, enabled Gen. Lovell to bring out of the city nearly all the portable government property necessary for war purposes, as well as a large part of the State property.

crowded with persons rushing about with parcels of sugar, buckets of molasses, and packages of provisions plundered from the public stores. Others were busying themselves with patriotic zeal to destroy property of value to the enemy, and huge loads of cotton went rumbling along on the way to the levee.

No sooner had the Federal fleet turned the point and come within sight of the city, than the work of destruction of property commenced. Vast columns of smoke ascended to the sky, darkening the face of heaven, and obscuring the noon-day sun; for five miles along the levee fierce flames darted through the lurid atmosphere, their baleful glare struggling in rivalry with the sunlight; great ships and steamers, wrapped in fire, floated down the river, threatening the Federal vessels with destruction by their fiery contact. In front of the various presses, and at other points along the levee, the cotton had been piled up and submitted to the torch. It was burned by order of the governor of Louisiana and of the military commander of the Confederate States. Fifteen thousand bales were consumed, the value of which would have been about a million and a half of dollars: The tobacco stored in the city, being all held by foreign residents on foreign account, was not destroyed. The specie of the banks, to the amount of twelve or fifteen millions, was removed from the city and placed in a secure place; so were nearly all the stores and movable property of the Confederate States. But other materials were embraced in the awful conflagration. About a dozen large river steamboats, twelve or fifteen ships, some of them laden with cotton, a great floating battery, several unfinished gunboats, the immense ram, the Mississippi, and the docks on the other side of the river, were all embraced in the fiery sacrifice. The Mississippi was an iron-clad frigate, a superior vessel of her class, and accounted to be by far the most important naval structure the Confederate government had yet undertaken.

On evacuating the city, Gen. Lovell had left it under the exclusive jurisdiction of Mayor Monroe. That officer, although he had appealed to Gen. Lovell to evacuate the city, so as to avoid such exasperation or conflict as might put the city in peril of bombardment, was not willing to surrender it to the enemy; but was content, after due protestations of patriotic fervor, that the enemy should perform, without interruption, the ceremony of surrender for himself in taking down the flags flying over all the public buildings of the city A correspondence ensued between the mayor and the flag-officer of the enemy's fleet. The correspondence was certainly of very unnecessary length on the part of the mayor, and was travestied in the Northern newspapers as a controversy between "*Farrago and Farragut.*" But the sentiments of the mayor, although tedious and full of vain repetitions, were just and honorable. He declared, with explanations that were not necessary to be given to the enemy, and at a length that showed rather too much the vanity of literary style, that the citizens of New Orleans yielded to physical force alone, and that they maintained their allegiance to the government of the Confederate States.

On the morning of the 26th of April, a force landed from the sloop-of-war Pensacola, lying opposite Esplanade-street and hoisted a United States flag upon the mint. It had not remained there long before some young men, belonging to the Pinckney battalion, mounted to the dome of the mint, tore it down and dragged it through the streets.

Whether Flag-officer Farragut was exasperated or not by this circumstance, is not known; but he seemed to have determined to spare no mortification to the city, which its civil officers had already assured him was unprepared to resist him, and to hesitate at no misrepresentation in order to vilify its citizens. In one of his letters to the mayor, he had sought to publish the fact to the world, that helpless men, women, and children had been fired upon by the citizens of New Orleans "for giving expression to their pleasure at witnessing the old flag;" when the fact was, that the cheering on the levee referred to had been, in defiance of the enemy, for "the Southern Confederacy," and the only firing in the crowd was that of incautious and exasperated citizens at the Federal fleet.

The *State* flag of Louisiana still floated from the City Hall. It was an emblem of nothing more than State sovereignty, and yet it too was required to be lowered at the unreasonable and harsh demand of the invader. A memorial, praying the common council to protect at least the emblem of State sovereignty from insult, was signed by a large number of the noble women of New Orleans, including many of the wealthiest, fairest, and highest in social position in the city. The reply of the council was feeble and embarrassed. They passed a resolution declaring that "no resistance would be made to the forces of the United States;" approving, at the same time, the "sentiments" expressed by the mayor, and requesting him "to act in the spirit manifested by them."

On the 28th of April, Flag-officer Farragut addressed his ultimatum to the mayor, complaining of the continued display of the flag of Louisiana on the City Hall, and concluding with a threat of bombardment of the city by notifying him to remove the women and children from its limits within forty-eight hours. The mayor replied with new spirit, that the satisfaction which was asked at the hands of a vanquished people, that they should lower with their own hands their State flag, and perform an act against which their natures rebelled, would not, under any circumstances, be given; that there was no possible exit from the city for its immense population of the women and children, and that if the enemy chose to murder them on a question of etiquette, he might do his pleasure.

In the delay of the enemy's actual occupation of the city while the correspondence referred to between the mayor and the enemy was in progress, the confidence of the people of New Orleans had, in a measure, been rallied. There were yet some glimmers of hope. They thought that, with the forts still holding out, and the enemy's transports unable to get up the river, the city might be saved. The fleet had no forces with which to occupy it, and there was no access for an army except by way of the lakes. They had determined to cut the levee below should Gen Butler, in command of the land forces, attempt an approach from Lake Borgne, and above the city, should he make the effort from Lake Pontchartrain. In the last resort, they were determined to man the lines around the city, armed with such weapons as they could procure, and fight the Federal land forces whenever they might make their appearance.

These hopes were suddenly dispelled by the unexpected news of the fall of Forts Jackson and St. Philip. Fort Jackson had been very little damaged in the bombardment. It yielded because of a mutiny of three or four hundred of the garrison, who refused to obey the commands of its brave officer, Gen. Duncan. He had no alternative but to give up the place. At the first signs of the mutinous disposition, he threatened to turn his guns on his own men, but found a large number or them spiked. He surrendered, in fact, to his own garrison. The post could, probably, have been held, if the men had stood to their guns. He stated this in an address on the levee to the people, and, while stating it, cried like a child.

The news of the surrender of the river forts effected a sudden change in the views of Flag-officer Farragut. He was evidently anxious lest Gen. Butler, to whose transports a way had now been opened to the city, should arrive before he could consummate the objects of his expedition. He had already involved himself in a maze of incongruities and contradictions. First, he demanded peremptorily that the flag should be taken down; then he insisted that it should be removed before 12 M. on Saturday, the 28th; on Monday, he repeated the demand, under a threat of bombardment, giving forty-eight hours for the removal of the women and children. On Tuesday morning, he reiterated his peremptory demand, but, within an hour, he agreed to waive every thing he had claimed, and reluctantly consented to send his own forces to take down the flag.

About noon, a Federal force, consisting of about two hundred armed marines and a number of sailors, dragging two brass howitzers, appeared in front of the City Hall, and the officer in command, mounting to the dome of the building, removed the flag of the State in sight of an immense crowd of the citizens of New Orleans. No interruption was offered to the small party of the Federals, and the idle utterances of curiosity were quelled by the sadness and solemnity of the occasion. Profound silence pervaded the immense crowd. Not even a whisper was heard. The very air was oppressive with stillness. The marines stood statue-like within the square, their bayonets glistening in the sunbeams, and their faces stolid with indifference. Among the vast multitude of citizens, the wet cheeks of women and the compressed lips and darkened brows of men betrayed their consciousness of the great humiliation which had overtaken them. But among them all there was not one spirit to emulate the devotion of the martyr-hero of Virginia, who, alone and unaided, on the steps of the Marshall

House, in Alexandria, had avenged with his life the first insult ever offered by the enemy to the flag of his country.

Thus was the surrender of the city of New Orleans completed. Gen. Butler took possession on the 1st of May, and inaugurated an administration, the despotism and insolence o which might have been expected from one of his vile personal character and infamous antecedents. He was a man who had all the proverbially mean instincts of the Massachusetts Yankee; he had been a disreputable jury lawyer at home; as a member of the old Democratic party, he had been loud in his professions of devotion to the South; but his glorification in this particular had been dampened in the Charleston Convention, where he pocketed an insult from a Southern delegate, and turned pale at the threat of personal chastisement. The war gave him an opportunity of achieving one of those easy reputations in the North which were made by brazen boastfulness, coarse abuse of the South, and aptitude in lying. We shall have future occasion to refer to the brutal and indecent despotism of this vulgar tyrant of New Orleans, who, in inviting his soldiers to treat as prostitutes every lady in the street who dared to show displeasure at their presence, surpassed the atrocities of Haynau, and rivalled the most barbarous and fiendish rule of vengeance ever sought to be wreaked upon a conquered people. If any thing were wanting to make the soldiers of the South devote anew whatever they had of life, and labor, and blood to the cause of the safety and honor of their country, it was the infamous swagger of Butler in New Orleans, his autocratic rule, his arrest of the best citizens, his almost daily robberies, and his "ingenious" war upon the helplessness of men and the virtue of women.

The narrative of the fall of New Orleans furnishes its own comment. Never was there a more miserable story, where accident, improvidence, treachery, vacillation, and embarrassment of purpose, each, perhaps, not of great importance in itself, combined under an evil star to produce the astounding result of the fall, after an engagement, the casualties of which might be counted by hundreds, of a city which was the commercial capital of the South, which contained a population of one hundred and seventy thousand souls, and which was the largest *exporting* city in the world.

The extent of the disaster is not to be disguised. It was a heavy blow to the Confederacy. It annihilated us in Louisiana; separated us from Texas and Arkansas; diminished our resources and supplies by the loss of one of the greatest grain and cattle countries within the limits of the Confederacy; gave to the enemy the Mississippi river, with all its means of navigation, for a base of operations; and finally led, by plain and irresistible conclusion, to our virtual abandonment of the great and fruitful Valley of the Mississippi.—It did all this, and yet it was very far from deciding the fate of the war.

CHAPTER XIII.

CONCLUSION.

Prospects of the War.—The Extremity of the South.—Lights and Shadows of the Campaign in Virginia.—Jackson's Campaign in the Valley.—The Policy of Concentration.—Sketch of the Battles around Richmond.—Effect of McClellan's Defeat upon the North.—President Davis's congratulatory Order.—The War as a great Money Job.—*Note:* Gen. Washington's Opinion of the Northern People.—Statement of the Northern Finances.—Yankee Venom.—Gen. Pope's Military Orders.—Summary of the War Legislation of the Northern Congress.—Retaliation on the part of the Confederacy.—The Cartel.—Prospects of European Interference.—English Statesmanship. —Progress of the War in the West.—The Defence of Vicksburg.—Morgan's great Raid.—The Tennessee-Virginia Frontier.—A Glance at the Confederate Congress.— Mr. Foote and the Cabinet.—The Campaign in Virginia again.—Rapid Movements and famous March of the Southern Troops.—*The signal Victory of the Thirtieth of August on the Plains of Manassas.*—Reflections on the War.—Some of its Characteristics.—A Review of its Military Results.—Three Moral Benefits of the War.—Prospects and Promises of the Future.

WE have chosen the memorable epoch of the fall of New Orleans, properly dated from the occupation of the enemy on the 1st of May, 1862, as an appropriate period for the conclusion of our historical narrative of the events of the first year of the war. Hereafter, in the future continuation of the narrative, which we promise to ourselves, we shall have to direct the attention of the reader to the important movements, the sorrowful disasters, and the splendid achievements, that more than compensated the inflictions of misfortune, in the famous summer campaign in Virginia. In these we shall find full confirmation of the judgment which we have declared, that the fall of New Orleans, and the consequent loss of the Mississippi Valley, did not decide the fate of the war; and, indeed, we shall see that the abandonment of our plan of frontier defence made the way for the superior and more fortunate policy of the concentration of our forces in the interior.

The fall of New Orleans and consequent loss of our command of the Mississippi river from New Orleans to Memphis, with all its immense advantages of transportation and supply; the retreat of Gen. Johnston's forces from Yorktown; the evacuation of Norfolk, with its splendid navy-yard—an event accomplished by a mere *brutum fulmen*, and without a blow; the stupid and unnecessary destruction of the Virginia, "the iron diadem of the South;"* the perilous condition of Charleston, Savan-

---

* The destruction of the Virginia was a sharp and unexpected blow to the confidence of the people of the South in their government.

How far the government was implicated in this foolish and desperate act, was never openly acknowledged or exactly ascertained; but, despite the pains of official concealment, there are certain well-attested facts which indicate that in the destruction of this great war-ship, the authorities at Richmond were not guiltless. These facts properly belong to the history of one of the most unhappy events that had occurred since the commencement of the war.

The Virginia was destroyed under the immediate orders of her commander, Commodore Tatnall, a little before five o'clock on the morning of the 11th of May, in the vicinity of Craney Island. During the morning of the same day a prominent politician in the streets of Richmond was observed to be very much dejected; he remarked that it was an evil day for the Confederacy.

On being questioned by his intimate friends, he declared to them that the government had determined upon, or assented to, the destruction of the Virginia, and that he had learned this from the highest sources of authority in the capital. At this time the news of the explosion of the Virginia could not have possibly reached Richmond; there was no telegraphic communication between the scene of her destruction and the city, and the evidence appears to be complete, that the government had at least a prevision of the destruction of this vessel, or had assented to the general policy of the act, trusting, perhaps, to acquit itself of the responsibility for it on the unworthy plea that it had given no *express* orders in the matter.

Again, it is well known that for at least a week prior to the destruction of the Virginia, the evacuation of Norfolk had been determined upon; that during the time the removal of stores was daily progressing; and that Mr. Mallory, the Secretary of the Navy, had within this period, himself, visited Norfolk to look after the public interests. The evacuation of this port clearly involved the question, what disposition was to be made of the Virginia.

If the government made no decision of a question, which for a week stared it in the face, it certainly was very strangely neglectful of the public interest. If Mr. Mallory visited Norfolk when the evacuation was going on, and never thought of the Virginia, or, thinking of her, kept dumb, never even giving so much as an *official nod* as to what disposition should be made of her, he must have been even more stupid than the people who laughed at him in Richmond, or the members of Congress who nicknamed without mercy, thought him to be.

It is also not a little singular that when a court of inquiry had found that the destruction of the Virginia was unnecessary and improper, Mr. Mallory should have waived the calling of a court-martial, forgotten what was due to the public interest on such a finding as that made by the preliminary court, and expressed himself satisfied to let the matter rest. The fact is indisputable, that the court-martial was called at the demand of Commodore Tatnall himself It resulted in his acquittal.

nah, and Mobile, and the menace of Richmond by one of the largest armies of the world, awakened the people of the South to a full appreciation of the crisis of the war, and placed their cause in an extremity which nothing could have retrieved but the undiminished and devoted spirit of their brave soldiers in the field.

We shall have, however, to mingle with this story of disasters, the triumphs, not indeed of the government, but of brave and adventurous spirits in the field. We shall tell how it was that the retreat from Yorktown, although undertaken without any settled plan as to the line of defence upon which it was to be reorganized, led to the successful battle of Williamsburg; we shall recount the events of the glorious battle of Seven Pines, the sound of whose guns was heard by the people of Richmond, and was followed by the speedy messages of a splendid victory; and we shall tell how it was that, while the news of the destruction of the Virginia was still the bitterest reminiscence of the people of the South, and while Secretary Mallory was making a drivelling show of alacrity to meet the enemy by advertising for "timber" to construct new naval defences, a powerful flotilla of Yankee gunboats was repulsed by a battery of four guns on the banks of James river, and the scale of war turned by even such a small incident as the action of Drury's Bluff. In this connection, too, we shall have to record the evidences of the heroic spirit that challenged the approaching enemy; the noble resolution of the citizens of Richmond to see their beautiful city consigned to the horrors of a bombardment, rather than to the hands of the enemy; and the brave resolution of the Virginia Legislature, which put the Confederate authorities to shame, and infused the hearts of the people with a new and lively spirit of courage and devotion.*

---

* " *Resolved by the General Assembly :* That the General Assembly hereby express its desire that the capital of the State be defended to the last extremity, if such defence is in accordance with the views of the President of the Confederate States; and that the President be assured that whatever destruction or loss of property of the State or individuals shall thereby result, will be cheerfully submitted to."—*Resolution Va. Legislature, May* 14.

" Some one said to me the other day, that the duty of surrendering the city would devolve either upon the President, the Mayor, or myself. I said to him

But we shall have occasion to tell of even more brilliant triumphs of Southern spirit, and to explain how, for some time at least, the safety of Richmond was trusted not so much to the fortunes of the forces that immediately protected it, as to the splendid diversion of the heroic Jackson in the Valley of Virginia.

We shall see how this brave general, whom the government had determined to recall to Gen. Johnston's lines, rejected the suggestions of the surrender of the Valley, and his personal ease, and adventured upon a campaign, the most successful and brilliant in the war. We shall trace with particular interest the events of this glorious expedition, and we shall find reason to ascribe its results to the zeal, heroism, and genius of its commander alone. We shall recount the splendid victory over Banks, the recovery of Winchester, the capture of four thousand prisoners, the annihilation of the invading army of the Valley, and the heroic deeds which threw the splendor of sunlight over the long lines of the Confederate host. The reader will have occasion to compare the campaign of General Jackson in the Valley of Virginia, with some of the most famous in modern history. We shall show that, in this brief, but brilliant campaign, a gallant Southern army fought four battles and a number of skirmishes; killed and wounded a considerable number of the enemy, took several thousand prisoners, secured millions of dollars of stores, destroyed many millions of dollars' worth for the enemy, and chased the Federal army, commanded by General Banks, out of Virginia and across the Potomac; and that all these events were accomplished within the period of three weeks, and with a loss scarcely exceeding one hundred in killed and wounded.

In this story of disaster, mingled with triumph, we shall be

---

if the demand is made upon me, with the alternative to surrender or be shelled, I shall reply, BOMBARD AND BE DAMNED."—*Speech of Gov. Letcher, May* 16.

"I say now, and will abide by it, when the citizens of Richmond demand of me to surrender the capital of Virginia and of the Confederacy to the enemy they must find some other man to fill my place. I will resign the mayoralty And when that other man elected in my stead shall deliver up the city, I hope I have physical courage and strength enough left to shoulder a musket and go into the ranks."—*Speech of Mayor Mayo, May* 16.

disappointed if we do not discover the substantial prospect of brighter fortunes and final triumph for the South.

Indeed, the fact will be shown to be, that events, although mixed and uncertain to the views taken of them at the time of their occurrence, were preparing the way for a great victory and a sudden illumination of the fortunes of the South.

The disasters on the Mississippi frontier and in other directions had constrained the government to adopt the policy of concentrating its forces in the interior of Virginia. The object of all war is to reach a decisive point of the campaign, and this object was realized by a policy which it is true the government had not adopted at the instance of reason, but which had been imposed upon it by the force of disaster. There were childish complaints that certain districts and points on the frontier had been abandoned by the Confederates for the purpose of a concentration of troops in Virginia. These complaints were alike selfish and senseless, and, in some cases, nothing more than the utterance of a demagogical, short-sighted, and selfish spirit, which would have preferred the apparent security of its own particular State or section to the fortunes of the whole Confederacy. The fact was, that there was cause of intelligent congratulation even in those districts from which the Confederate troops had been withdrawn to make a decisive battle, that we had at last reached a crisis, the decision of which might reverse all our past misfortunes, and achieve results in which every State of the Confederacy would have a share.

On the Richmond lines, two of the greatest and most splendid armies that had ever been arrayed on a single field confronted each other; every accession that could be procured from the most distant quarters to their numbers, and every thing that could be drawn from the resources of the respective countries of each, had been made to contribute to the strength and splendor of the opposing hosts.

Since the commencement of the war, the North had taxed its resources for the capture of Richmond; nothing was omitted for the accomplishment of this event; the way had to be opened to the capital by tedious and elaborate operations on the frontier of Virginia: this accomplished, the city of Richmond was surrounded by an army whose numbers was all that could be desired; composed of picked forces; having every advantage that science and art could bestow in fortifications and every appliance of war; assisted by gunboat flotillas in two rivers, and endowed with every thing that could assure success.

The Northern journals were unreserved in the statement that the commands of Fremont, Banks, and McDowell, had been consolidated into one army, under Major-general Pope, with a view of bringing all the Federal forces in Virginia, to co-operate with McClellan on the Richmond lines. A portion of this army must have reached McClellan, probably at an early stage of the engagements in the vicinity of Richmond. There is little doubt but that, in the memorable contest for the safety of Richmond, we engaged an army whose superiority in numbers to us was largely increased by timely reinforcements, and with regard to the operations of which the Northern government had omitted no conditions of success.

Of this contest, unparalleled in its duration; rich in dramatic incident and display ; remarkable for a series of battles, any one of which might rank with the most celebrated in history ; and distinguished by an obstinacy, on the part of the sullen and insolent enemy, that was broken only by the most tremendous exertions ever made by Southern troops, we shall have to treat in a future continuation of this work, with the utmost care as to the authenticity of our narrative, and with matured views as to the merits and importance of what is now supposed to be a great and decisive event.

For the present, merely for the purpose of extending the general record of events in this chapter to the present standpoint of intelligent reflection on the future of the war, we must content the reader with a very brief and summary sketch of the battles around Richmond. Such a sketch is necessarily imperfect, written amid the confusion of current events, and is limited to the design of acquainting the reader with the general situation at this writing, without venturing, to a great degree, upon statements of particular facts.

SKETCH OF THE BATTLES AROUND RICHMOND.

Upon taking command of the Confederate army in the field, after Gen. Johnston had been wounded in the battle of Seven Pines, Gen Lee did not hesitate to adopt the spirit of that commander, which had already been displayed in attacking the enemy, and which indicated the determination on his part that the operations before Richmond should not degenerate into a siege.

The course of the Chickahominy around Richmond affords an idea of the enemy's position at the commencement of the action. This stream meanders through the tide-water district of Virginia—its course approaching that of the arc of a circle in the neighborhood of Richmond—until it reaches the lower end of Charles City county, where it abruptly turns to the south and empties into the James. A portion of the enemy's forces had crossed to the south side of the Chickahominy, and were fortified on the Williamsburg road. On the north bank of the stream the enemy was strongly posted for many miles; the heights on that side of the stream having been fortified with great energy and skill from Meadow Bridge, on a line nearly due north from the city, to a point below Bottom's Bridge, which is due east. This line of the enemy extended for about twenty miles.

Reviewing the situation of the two armies at the commencement of the action, the advantage was entirely our own. McClellan had divided his army on the two sides of the Chickahominy, and operating apparently with the design of half circumvallating Richmond, had spread out his forces to an extent that impaired the faculty of concentration, and had made a weak and dangerous extension of his lines.

On Thursday, the 26th of June, at three o'clock, Major-general Jackson—fresh from the exploits of his magnificent campaign in the Valley—took up his line of march from Ashland, and proceeded down the country between the Chickahominy and Pamunkey rivers. The enemy collected on the north bank of the Chickahominy, at the point where it is crossed by the Brooke turnpike, were driven off, and Brigadier general Branch, crossing the stream, directed his movements

GEN. A.P. HILL.

From a Photograph taken from life.

for a junction with the column of Gen. A. P. Hill, which had crossed at Meadow Bridge. General Jackson having borne away from the Chickahominy, so as to gain ground towards the Pamunkey, marched to the left of Mechanicsville, while Gen. Hill, keeping well to the Chickahominy, approached that village and engaged the enemy there.

With about fourteen thousand men (Gen. Branch did not arrive till nightfall), Gen. Hill engaged the forces of the enemy until night put an end to the contest. While he did not succeed, in that limited time, in routing the enemy, his forces stubbornly maintained the possession of Mechanicsville and the ground taken by them on the other side of the Chicka hominy. Driven from the immediate locality of Mechanicsville, the enemy retreated during the night down the river to Powhite swamp, and night closed the operations of Thursday.

The road having been cleared at Mechanicsville, Gen. Longstreet's *corps d'armée*, consisting of his veteran division of the Old Guard of the Army of the Potomac, and Gen. D. H. Hill's division, debouched from the woods on the south side of the Chickahominy, and crossed that river. Friday morning the general advance upon the enemy began; Gen. A. P. Hill in the centre, and bearing towards Coal Harbor, while Gen. Longstreet and Gen. D. H. Hill came down the Chickahominy to New Bridge. Gen. Jackson still maintained his position in advance, far to the left, and gradually converging to the Chickahominy again.

The position of the enemy was now a singular one. One portion of his army was on the south side of the Chickahominy, fronting Richmond, and confronted by Gen. Magruder. The other portion, on the north side, had fallen back to a new line of defences, where McClellan proposed to make a decisive battle.

As soon as Jackson's arrival at Coal Harbor was announced, Gen. Lee and Gen. Longstreet, accompanied by their respective staffs, rode by Gaines's Mill, and halted at New Coal Harbor, where they joined General A. P. Hill. Soon the welcome sound of Jackson's guns announced that he was at work.

The action was now to become general for the first time on the Richmond lines; and a collision of numbers was about to take place equal to any that had yet occurred in the history of the war.

From four o'clock until eight the battle raged with a display of the utmost daring and intrepidity on the part of the Confederate army. The enemy's lines were finally broken, and his strong positions all carried, and night covered the retreat of McClellan's broken and routed columns to the south side of the Chickahominy.

The assault on the enemy's works near Gaines's Mills is a memorable part of the engagement of Friday, and the display of fortitude, as well as quick and dashing gallantry of our troops on that occasion, takes its place by the side of the most glorious exploits of the war. Gen. A. P. Hill had made the first assault upon the lines of the enemy's intrenchments near Gaines's Mills. A fierce struggle had ensued between his division and the garrison of the line of defence. Repeated charges were made by Hill's troops, but the formidable character of the works, and murderous volleys of grape and canister from the artillery covering them, kept our troops in check. It was past four o'clock when Pickett's brigade, from Longstreet's division, came to Hill's support. Pickett's regiments fought with the most determined valor. At last Whiting's division, composed of the "Old Third" and Texan brigades, advanced at a "double quick," charged the batteries, and drove the enemy from his strong line of defence. The works carried by these noble troops would have been invincible to the bayonet had they been garrisoned by men less dastardly than the Yankees.

To keep the track of the battle, which had swept around Richmond, we must have reference to some of the principal points of locality in the enemy's lines. It will be recollected that it was on Thursday evening when the attack was commenced upon the enemy near Meadow Bridge. This locality is about six miles distant from the city, on a line almost due north. This position was the enemy's extreme right. His lines extended from here across the Chickahominy, near the Powhite Creek, two or three miles above the crossing of the York River railroad. From Meadow Bridge to this railroad, the distance along the Chickahominy on the north side is about ten miles. The different stages between the points indicated, along which the enemy were driven, are Mechanicsville, about a mile north of the Chickahominy; further on, Beaver Dam Creek, emptying into the Chickahominy; then the New Bridge road, on which Coal Harbor is located; and then Powhite Creek, where the enemy had made his last stand, and been repulsed from the field.

The York River railroad runs in an easterly direction, intersecting the Chickahominy about ten miles from the city. South of the railroad is the Williamsburg road, connecting with the Nine Mile road at Seven Pines. The former road connects with the New Bridge road, which turns off and crosses the Chickahominy. From Seven Pines, where the Nine Mile road joins the upper one, the road is known as the old Williamsburg road, and crosses the Chickahominy at Bottom's Bridge.

With the bearing of these localities in his mind, the reader will readily understand how it was that the enemy was driven from his original strongholds on the north side of the Chickahominy, and how, at the time of Friday's battle, he had been compelled to surrender the possession of the Fredericksburg and Central railroads, and had been pressed to a position where he was cut off from the principal avenues of supply and escape. The disposition of our forces was such as to cut off all communication between McClellan's army and the White House, on the Pamunkey river; he had been driven completely from his northern line of defences; and it was supposed that he would be unable to extricate himself from his position without a victory or a capitulation. In front of him being the Chickahominy, which he had crossed—in his rear, were the divisions of Generals Longstreet, Magruder, and Huger, and, in the situation as it existed Saturday night, all hopes of his escape were thought to be impossible.

On Sunday morning, it appears that our pickets, on the Nine Mile road, having engaged some small detachments of the enemy, and driven them beyond their fortifications, found them deserted. In a short while, it became known to our generals that McClellan, having massed his entire force on this side of the Chickahominy, was retreating towards James river.

The intrenchments which the enemy had deserted, were found to be formidable and elaborate. That immediately across the railroad, at the six-mile post, which had been supposed to be light earth-work, designed to sweep the railroad, turned out to be an immense embrasured fortification, extending for hundreds of yards on either side of the track. Within this work were found great quantities of fixed ammunition, which had apparently been prepared for removal, and then deserted. All the cannon, as at other intrenchments, had been carried off. A dense cloud of smoke was seen issuing from the woods two miles in advance of the battery, and half a mile to the right of the railroad. The smoke was found to proceed from a perfect mountain of the enemy's commissary stores, consisting of sugar, coffee, and bacon, prepared meats, vegetables, &c., which he had fired. The fields and woods around this spot were covered with every description of clothing and camp equipage. No indication was wanting that the enemy had left this encampment in haste and disorder.

The enemy had been imperfectly watched at a conjuncture the most critical in the contest, and through some omission of our guard—the facts of which have as yet been but imperfectly developed—McClellan had succeeded in massing his entire force, and taking up a line of retreat, by which he hoped to reach the cover of his gunboats on the James. But the most unfortunate circumstance to us was, that since the enemy had escaped from us in his fortified camp, his retreat was favored by a country, the characteristics of which are unbroken forests and wide swamps, where it was impossible to pursue him with rapidity, and extremely difficult to reconnoitre his position so as to bring him to decisive battle.

On Sunday morning, the divisions of Generals Hill and Longstreet crossed the Chickahominy, and were, during the whole of the day, moving in the hunt for the enemy. The disposition which was made of our forces brought General Longstreet on the enemy's front, immediately supported by General Hill's division consisting of six brigades. The forces commanded by General Longstreet were his old division, consisting of six brigades.

The position of the enemy was about five miles northeast of Darbytown, on the New Market road. The immediate scene of the battle was a plain of sedge pines, in the cover of which the enemy's forces were skilfully disposed—the locality being known as Frazier's farm. In advancing upon the enemy, batteries of sixteen heavy guns were opened upon the advance columns of Gen. Hill. Our troops, pressing heroically forward, had no sooner got within musket range than the enemy, form, ing several lines of battle, poured upon them from his heavy masses a devouring fire of musketry. The conflict became terrible, the air being filled with missiles of death, every moment having its peculiar sound of terror, and every spot its sight of ghastly destruction and horror. It is impossible that in any of the series of engagements which had taken place within the past few days, and had tracked the lines of Richmond with fire and destruction, there could have been more desperate fighting on the part of our troops. Never was a more glorious victory plucked from more desperate and threatening circumstances While exposed to the double fire of the enemy's batteries and his musketry, we were unable to contend with him with artillery. But although thus unmatched, our brave troops pressed on with unquailing vigor and a resistless courage, driving the enemy before them. This was accomplished without artillery, there being but one battery in Gen. Hill's command on the spot, and that belonged to Longstreet's division, and could not be got into position. Thus the fight continued with an ardor and devotion that few battle-fields have ever illustrated. Step by step the enemy were driven back, his guns taken, and the ground he abandoned strewn with his dead. By half-past eight o'clock we had taken all his cannon, and, continuing to advance, had driven him a mile and a half from his ground of battle.

Our forces were still advancing upon the retreating lines of the enemy. It was now about half-past nine o'clock, and very dark. Suddenly, as if it had burst from the heavens, a sheet of fire enveloped the front of our advance. The enemy had made another stand to receive us, and, from the black masses of his forces, it was evident that he had been heavily reinforced, and that another whole *corps d'armée* had been brought up to contest the fortunes of the night. Line after line of battle was formed. It was evident that his heaviest columns were now being thrown against our small command, and it might have been supposed that he would only be satisfied with its annihilation. The loss here on our side was terrible.

The situation being evidently hopeless for any further pursuit of the fugitive enemy, who had now brought up such overwhelming forces, our troops retired slowly.

At this moment, seeing their adversary retire, the most vociferous cheers arose along the whole Yankee line. They were taken up in the distance by the masses which for miles and miles beyond were supporting McClellan's front.   It was a moment when the heart of the stoutest commander might have been appalled.   The situation of our forces was now as desperate as it well could be, and required a courage and presence of mind to retrieve it, which the circumstances which surrounded them were not well calculated to inspire.   They had fought for five or six hours without reinforcements.   All our reserves had been brought up in the action.   Wilcox's brigade, which had been almost annihilated, was re-forming in the rear.

Riding rapidly to the position of this brigade, Gen. Hill brought them, by great exertions, up to the front, to check the advance of the now confident, cheering enemy.   Catching the spirit of their commander, the brave, but jaded men, moved up to the front, replying to the enemy's cheers with shouts and yells.   At this demonstration, which the enemy, no doubt, supposed signified heavy reinforcements, he stopped his advance.   It was now about half-past ten o'clock in the night. The enemy had been arrested; and the fight—one of the most remarkable, long-contested, and gallant ones that had yet occurred on our lines—was concluded with the achievement of a field under the most trying circumstances, which the enemy, with the most overpowering numbers brought up to reinforce him, had not succeeded in reclaiming.

Gen. Magruder's division did not come up until 11 o'clock at night, after the fight had been concluded.   By orders from Gen. Lee, Magruder moved upon and occupied the battle-ground; Gen. Hill's command being in such a condition of prostration from their long and toilsome fight, and suffering in killed and wounded, that it was proper they should be relieved by the occupation of the battle-ground by a fresh *corps d'armée*.

Early on Tuesday morning the enemy, from the position to which he had been driven the night before, continued his retreat in a southeasterly direction towards his gunboats on James river.   At eight o'clock Magruder recommenced the pursuit, advancing cautiously, but steadily, and shelling the forests and swamps in front as he progressed.   This method of advance was kept up throughout the morning and until four o'clock, P. M., without coming up with the enemy.   But between four and five o'clock our troops reached a large open field, a mile long and three-quarters in width, on the farm of Dr. Carter. The enemy were discovered strongly intrenched in a dense forest on the other side of this field. Their artillery, numbering fifty pieces, could be plainly seen bristling over their freshly constructed earth-works. At ten minutes before five o'clock, P. M., Gen. Magruder ordered his men to charge across the field and drive the enemy from their position. Gallantly they sprang to the encounter, rushing into the field at a full run. Instantly, from the line of the enemy's breastworks, a murderous storm of grape and canister was hurled into their ranks, with the most terrible effect. Officers and men went down by hundreds; but yet, undaunted and unwavering, our line dashed on, until two-thirds of the distance across the field was accomplished. Here the carnage from the withering fire of the enemy's combined artillery and musketry was dreadful. Our line wavered a moment, and fell back to the cover of the woods. Twice again the effort to carry the position was renewed, but each time with the same result. Night, at length, rendered a further attempt injudicious, and the fight, until ten o'clock, was kept up by the artillery of both sides. To add to the horrors, if not to the dangers, of this battle, the enemy's gunboats, from their position at Curl's Neck, two and a half miles distant, poured on the field continuous broadsides from their immense rifle-guns. Though it is questionable whether any serious loss was inflicted on us by the gunboats, the horrors of the fight were aggravated by the monster shells, which tore shrieking through the forests, and exploded with a concussion which seemed to shake the solid earth itself.

The battle of Tuesday, properly known as that of Malvern Hill, was perhaps the most sanguinary of the series of bloody conflicts which had taken place on the lines about Richmond. It was made memorable by its melancholy monument of carnage. But it had given the enemy no advantage, except in the unfruitful sacrifice of the lives of our troops, and the line of his retreat was again taken up, his forces toiling towards the river through mud, swamp, and forest.

The skill and spirit with which McClellan had managed to retreat was, indeed, remarkable, and afforded no mean proofs of his generalship. At every stage of his retreat he had confronted our forces with a strong rear-guard, and had encountered

us with well-organized lines of battle, and regular dispo
sitions of infantry, cavalry, and artillery. His heavy rifled
cannon had been used against us constantly on his retreat. A
portion of his forces had now effected communication with the
river at points below City Point. The plan of cutting off his
communication with the river, which was to have been executed by a movement of Holmes' division between him and
the river, was frustrated by the severe fire of the gunboats,
and since then the situation of the enemy appeared to be that
of a division or dispersion of his forces, one portion resting
on the river, and the other, to some extent, involved by our
lines.

It had been stated to the public of Richmond, with great
precision of detail, that on the evening of Saturday, the 28th
of June, we had brought the enemy to bay on the south side of
the Chickahominy, and that it only remained to finish him in
a single battle. Such, in fact, appeared to have been the
situation then. The next morning, however, it was perceived
that our supposed resources of generalship had given us too
much confidence; that the enemy had managed to extricate
himself from the critical position, and, having massed his forces,
had succeeded, under cover of the night, in opening a way to
the James river.*

---

* A great deal was claimed for "generalship" in the battles around Richmond; and results achieved by the hardy valor of our troops were busily
ascribed by hollow-hearted flatterers to the genius of the strategist. Without
going into any thing like military criticism, it may be said that it is difficult
to appreciate the ascription of a victory to generalship, in the face of the
exposure and terrible slaughter of our troops in attacking, *in front*, the
formidable breastworks of the enemy. The benefit of "generalship" in such
circumstances is unappreciable : when troops are thus confronted, the honors
of victory belong rather to the spirit of the victors than the genius of the
commander.

With reference to McClellan's escape from White Oak Swamp to the river,
letters of Yankee officers, published in the Northern journals, stated that
when McClellan on Saturday evening sent his scouts down the road to Turkey
Island Bridge, he was astonished and delighted to find that our forces had not
occupied that road, and immediately started his wagon and artillery trains,
which were quietly passing down that road all night to the James river,
while our forces were quietly sleeping within four miles of the very road they
should have occupied, and should have captured every one of the enemy's one
thousand wagons, and four hundred cannon

Upon this untoward event, the operations of our army on the Richmond side of the Chickahominy were to follow the fugitive enemy through a country where he had admirable opportunities of concealment, and through the swamps and forests or which he had retreated with the most remarkable judgment, dexterity, and spirit of fortitude.

The glory and fruits of our victory may have been seriously diminished by the grave mishap or fault by which the enemy was permitted to leave his camp on the south side of the Chickahominy, in an open country, and to plunge into the dense cover of wood and swamp, where the best portion of a whole week was consumed in hunting him, and finding out his new position only in time to attack him under the uncertainty and disadvantage of the darkness of night.

But the successes achieved in the series of engagements which had already occurred were not to be lightly esteemed, or to be depreciated, because of errors which, if they had not occurred, would have made our victory more glorious and more complete. The siege of Richmond had been raised : an army of one hundred and twenty thousand men had been pushed from their strongholds and fortifications, and put to flight ; we had enjoyed the *eclat* of an almost daily succession of victories ; we had gathered an immense spoil in stores, provisions, and artillery ; and we had demoralized and dispersed, if we had not succeeded in annihilating, an army which had every resource that could be summoned to its assistance, every possible addition of numbers within the reach of the Yankee government, and every material condition of success to insure for it the great prize of the capital of the Confederacy, which is now, as far as human judgment can determine, irretrievably lost to them, and secure in the protection of a victorious army.

The Northern papers claimed that the movements of McClellan from the Chickahominy river were purely strategic, and that he had obtained a position, where he would establish a new

---

It is further stated in these letters, that if we had blocked up that only passage of escape, their entire army must have surrendered or been starved out in twenty-four hours. These are the Yankees' own accounts of how much they were indebted to blunders on our part for the success of McClellan's retreat—a kind of admission not popular with a vain and self-adulatory enemy.

base of operations against Richmond. Up to the first decisive stage in the series of engagements—Coal Harbor—there were certainly plain strategic designs in his backward movement. His retirement from Mechanicsville was probably voluntary, and intended to concentrate his troops lower down, where he might fight with the advantages of numbers and his own selection of position. Continuing his retreat, he fixed the decisive field at Coal Harbor. Again having been pushed from his strongholds north of the Chickahominy, the enemy made a strong attempt to retrieve his disasters by renewing a concentration of his troops at Frazier's farm.

From the time of these two principal battles, all pretensions of the enemy's retreat to strategy must cease. His retreat was now unmistakable; it was no longer a falling back to concentrate troops for action; it is, in fact, impossible to disguise that it was the retreat of an enemy who was discomfited and whipped, although not routed. He had abandoned the railroads; he had given up the strongholds which he had provided to secure him in case of a check; he had destroyed from eight to ten millions dollars' worth of stores; he had deserted his hospitals, his sick and wounded, and he had left in our hands thousands of prisoners, and innumerable stragglers.

Regarding all that had been accomplished in these battles; the displays of the valor and devotion of our troops; the expenditure of blood; and the helpless and fugitive condition to which the enemy had at last been reduced, there was cause for the keenest regrets that an enemy in this condition was permitted to secure his retreat. It is undoubtedly true, that in failing to cut off McClellan's retreat to the river, we failed to accomplish the most important condition for the completion of our victory. But although the result of the conflict had fallen below public expectation, it was sufficiently fortunate to excite popular joy, and grave enough to engage the most serious speculation as to the future.

The effect of the defeat of McClellan before Richmond was received at the North with ill-concealed mortification and anxiety. Beneath the bluster of the newspapers and the affectations of public confidence, disappointment, embarrassment, and alarm were perceptible. The people of the North had been so assured of the capture of Richmond, that it was diffi cult to reanimate them on the heels of McClellan's retreat. The prospects held out to them so long, of ending the war in "sixty days," "crushing out the rebellion," and eating victorious dinners in Richmond, had been bitterly disappointed and were not to be easily renewed. The government at Washington showed its appreciation of the disaster its arms had sustained by making a call for three hundred thousand additional troops; and the people of the North were urged by every variety of appeal, including large bounties of money, to respond to the stirring call of President Lincoln.

There is no doubt but that the North was seriously discouraged by the events that had taken place before Richmond. But it was a remarkable circumstance, uniformly illustrated in the war, that the North, though easily intoxicated by triumph, was not in the same proportion depressed by defeat. There is an obvious explanation for this peculiarity of temper. As long as the North was conducting the war upon the soil of the South, a defeat there involved more money expenditure and more calls for troops; it involved scarcely any thing else; it had no other horrors, it did not imperil their homes; it might easily be repaired by time. Indeed, there was some sense in the exhorta tions of some of the Northern orators, to the effect that defeat made their people stronger than ever, because, while it required them to put forth their energies anew, it enabled them to take advantage of experience, to multiply their means of success, and to essay new plans of campaign. No one can doubt but that the celebrated Manassas defeat really strengthened the North; and doubtless the South would have realized the same consequence of the second repulse of the enemy's movements on Richmond, if it had been attended by the same conditions on our part of inaction and repose.

In his congratulatory address to the army on their victory before Richmond, President Davis referred to the prospect of carrying the war into the North. His friends declared that the President had at last been converted from his darling military formulas of the defensive policy; that he was sensible that the only way to bring the war to a decisive point was to invade the North. But it was urged that our army was too feeble to undertake at present an aggressive policy; although the facts were that, counting in our immense forces under Gen. Bragg

in the West, which for months had been idly lying in Missis
sippi, we had probably quite as many troops in the field as the
North had; that delay could accomplish but little addition to
our forces, while it would multiply those of the North, its
resources of conscription and draft being intact; that if our
army was small, it was due to the neglect of the executive in
enforcing the Conscription Law, which should have furnished
three quarters of a million of men; and that if reduced and
demoralized by desertion and straggling, it was because of the
weak sentimentalism of our military authorities, which hesitated to enforce the death penalty in our armies, or to maintain
military discipline by a system much harsher than that or
moral suasion. Judgment must be taken subject to these facts
as to how far the government was responsible for lingering in
a policy which, though of its own choosing at first, it at last
confessed to be wrong, and from which, when discovered to be
an error and a failure, it professed to be unable to extricate
itself on account of a weakness of which itself was sole cause
and author. Happily, however, the valor and devotion of our
troops came to the rescue of the government, and opened a
way in which it had so long hesitated, and found paltry excuses
for its tame and unadventurous temper. But to this we shall
refer hereafter.

It is curious to observe how completely the ordinary aspects
of war were changed and its horrors diminished, with reference to the North, by the false policy of the South, in keeping
the theatre of active hostilities within her own borders. Defeat
did not dispirit the North, because it was not brought to her
doors. Where it did not immediately imperil the safety of
the country and homes of the Yankees, where it gave time for
the recovery and reorganization of the attacking party, and
where it required for the prosecution of the war nothing but
more money jobs in Congress and a new raking up of the scum
of the cities, the effects of defeat upon the North might well
be calculated to be the exasperation of its passions, the inflam
mation of its cupidity, and the multiplication of its exertions
to break and overcome the misapplied power of our armies.

Indeed, the realization of the war in the North was, in many
respects, nothing more than that of an immense money job.
The large money expenditure at Washington supplied a vast

fund of corruption; it enriched the commercial centres of the North, and by artificial stimulation preserved such cities as New York from decay; it interested vast numbers of politicians, contractors, and dissolute public men in continuing the war and enlarging the scale of its operations; and, indeed, the disposition to make money out of the war accounts for much of that zeal in the North, which was mistaken for political ardor or the temper of patriotic devotion.*

---

* The following is an extract from an unpublished letter from Gen. Washington to Richard Henry Lee, and, as an exposition of the character of the Northern people from a pen sacred to posterity, is deeply interesting. There can be no doubt of the authenticity of the letter. It has been preserved in the Lee family, who, though applied to by Bancroft, Irving, and others for a copy for publication, have hitherto refused it, on the ground that it would be improper to give to the world a private letter from the Father of his Country reflecting upon any portion of it while the old Union endured. But now, that "these people" have trampled the Constitution under foot, destroyed the government of our fathers, and invaded and desolated Washington's own county in Virginia, there can be no impropriety in showing his private opinion of the Massachusetts Yankees:

[Copy.]

CAMP AT CAMBRIDGE, Aug. 29, 1775.

Dear Sir : * * *

As we have now nearly completed our lines of defence, we have nothing more, in my opinion, to fear from the enemy, provided we can keep our men to their duty, and make them watchful and vigilant; but it is among the most difficult tasks I ever undertook in my life to induce these people to believe that there is or can be danger, till the bayonet is pushed at their breasts; not that it proceeds from any uncommon prowess, but rather from an unaccountable kind of stupidity in the lower class of these people, which, believe me, prevails but too generally among the officers of the Massachusetts part of the army, who are nearly of the same kidney with the privates, and adds not a little to my difficulties, as there is no such thing as getting officers of this stamp to exert themselves in carrying orders into execution. To curry favor with the men (by whom they were chosen, and on whose smiles possibly they may think they may again rely) seems to be one of the principal objects of their attention. I submit it, therefore, to your consideration, whether there is, or is not, a propriety in that resolution of the Congress which leaves the ultimate appointment of all officers below the rank of general to the governments where the regiments originated, now the army is become Continental? To me, it appears improper in two points of view—first, it is giving that power and weight to an individual Colony which ought of right to belong to the whole. Then it damps the spirit and ardor of volunteers from all but the four New England Governments, as none but their people have the least chance of getting into office. Would it not be better, therefore, to have the warrants, which the Commander-in-Chief is authorized to give *pro tempore,*

But while politicians plundered the government at Washington and cortractors grew rich in a single day, and a fictitious prosperity dazzled the eyes of the observer in the cities of the North, the public finances of the Yankee government had long ago become desperate. It is interesting at this point to make a brief summary of the financial condition of the North by a comparison of its public debt with the assets of the government.

The debt of the present United States, audited and floating, calculated from data up to June 30, 1862, was at least $1,300,000,000. The daily expenses, as admitted by the chairman of the Committee on Ways and Means, was between three and four millions of dollars; the debt, in one year from this time, could not be less than two thousand five hundred millions of dollars.

Under the census of 1860, all the property of every kind in all the States was estimated at less than $12,500,000,000. Since

---

approved or disapproved by the Continental Congress, or a committee of their body, which I should suppose in any long recess must always sit? In this case, every gentleman will stand an equal chance of being promoted, according to his merit: in the other, all offices will be confined to the inhabitants of the four New England Governments, which, in my opinion, is impolitic to a degree. I have made a pretty good slam among such kind of officers as the Massachusetts Government abounds in since I came to this camp, having broken one colonel and two captains for cowardly behavior in the action on Bunker's Hill, two captains for drawing more provisions and pay than they had men in their company, and one for being absent from his post when the enemy appeared there and burnt a house just by it. Besides these, I have at this time one colonel, one major, one captain, and two subalterns under arrest for trial. In short, I spare none, and yet fear it will not all do, as these people seem to be too inattentive to every thing but their *interest*.

    *   *   *   *   *   *   *

There have been so many great and capital errors and abuses to rectify—so many examples to make, and so little inclination in the officers of inferior rank to contribute their aid to accomplish this work, that my life has been nothing else (since I came here) but one continual round of vexation and fatigue. In short, no pecuniary recompense could induce me to undergo what I have; especially, as I expect, by showing so little countenance to irregularities and public abuses as to render myself very obnoxious to a great part of these people. But as I have already greatly exceeded the bounds of a letter I will not trouble you with matters relative to my feelings.

    Your affectionate friend and obedient servant,

           (Signed)   GEO. WASHINGTON

Richard Henry Lee, Esq.

the war commenced, the depreciation has been at least one-fourth, $3,175,000,000. From $9,375,000,000 deduct the property in the seceded States, at least one-third—$3,125,000,000; leaving in the present United States, $6,250,000,000.

It will thus be seen, that the present debt of the North is one-fifth of all the property of every kind it possesses; and in one year more it will be more than one-third. No people on earth has ever been plunged in so large a debt in so short a time. No government in existence has so large a debt in proportion to the amount of property held by its people.

In continuing the narrative of the campaign in Virginia, we shall have to observe the remarkable exasperation with which the North re-entered upon this campaign, and to notice many deeds of blackness which illustrated the temper in which she determined to prosecute the desperate fortunes of the war. The military authorities of the North seemed to suppose that better success would attend a savage war, in which no quarter was to be given and no age or sex spared, than had hitherto been secured to such hostilities as are alone recognized to be lawful by civilized men in modern times. It is not necessary to comment at length upon this fallacy. Brutality in war was mistaken for vigor. War is not emasculated by the observances of civilization; its vigor and success consist in the resources of generalship, the courage of troops, the moral ardors of its cause. To attempt to make up for deficiency in these great and noble elements of vigor by mere brutal severities—such as pillage, assassination, &c., is absurd; it reduces the idea of war to the standard of the brigand; it offends the moral sentiment of the world, and it excites its enemy to the last stretch of determined and desperate exertion.

The North had placed a second army of occupation of Virginia under command of Gen. Pope, who boasted that he was fresh from a campaign in the West, where he had "seen only the backs of rebels.* This brutal braggart threatened that fire,

* This notorious Yankee commander, Major-general John Pope, was a man nearly forty years of age, a native of Kentucky, but a citizen of Illinois. He was born of respectable parents. He was graduated at West Point in 1842, and served in the Mexican war, where he was brevetted a captain.

In 1849, he conducted the Minnesota exploring expedition, and afterwards acted as topographical engineer of New Mexico, until 1853, when he was as

famine, and slaughter should be the portions of the conquered. He declared that he would not place any guard over any private property, and invited the soldiers to pillage and murder. He issued a general order, directing the murder of peaceful inhabitants of Virginia as spies if found quietly tilling their farms in his rear, even outside of his lines; and one of his brigadier-generals, Steinwehr, seized upon innocent and peaceful inhabitants to be held as hostages, to the end that they might be murdered in cold blood, if any of his soldiers were killed by some unknown persons, whom he designated as "bushwackers."

---

signed to the command of one of the expeditions to survey the route of the Pacific railroad. He distinguished himself on the overland route to the Pacific by "sinking" artesian wells and government money to the amount of a million of dollars. One well was finally abandoned incomplete, and afterwards a perennial spring was found by other parties in the immediate vicinity. In a letter to Jefferson Davis, then Secretary of War, urging this route to the Pacific and the boring these wells, Pope made himself the *especial champion of the South.*

On the breaking out of the war, Pope was made a brigadier-general of volunteers. He held a command in Missouri for some time before he became particularly noted. When General Halleck took charge of the disorganized department, Pope was placed in command of the District of Central Missouri. He was afterwards sent to southeastern Missouri. The cruel disposition of the man, of which his rude manners and a vulgar bearded face, with coarse skin, gave indications, found an abundant field for gratification in this unhappy State. His proceedings in Missouri will challenge a comparison with the most infernal record ever bequeathed by the licensed murderer to the abhorrence of mankind. And yet it was his first step in blood, the first opportunity he had ever had to feast his eyes upon slaughter and regale his ears with the cries of human agony.

Having been promoted to the rank of major-general, Pope was next appointed to act at the head of a corps to co-operate with Halleck in the reduction of Corinth. After the evacuation of Corinth by General Beauregard, Pope was sent by Halleck to annoy the rear of the Confederate army, but Beauregard turned upon and repulsed his pursuit. The report of Pope to Halleck, that he had captured 10,000 of Beauregard's army, and 15,000 stand of arms, when he had not taken a man or a musket, stands alone in the history of lying. It left him without a rival in that respectable art.

Such was the man who took command of the enemy's forces in northern Virginia. His bluster was as excessive as his accomplishments in falsehood. He was described in a Southern newspaper as "a Yankee compound of Bobadil and Munchausen." His proclamation, that he had seen nothing of his enemies "but their backs," revived an ugly story in his private life, and gave occasion to the witty interrogatory, if the gentleman who cowhided him for offering an indignity to a lady, was standing with his back to him when he in

The people of the North were delighted with the brigandish pronunciamentos of Pope in Virginia. The government at Washington was not slow to gratify the popular passion ; it hastened to change the character of the war into a campaign of indiscriminate robbery and murder. A general order was issued by the Secretary of War, directing the military commanders of the North to take private property for the convenience and use of their armies, without compensation. The public and official expressions of the spirit of the North in the war were even more violent than the clamors of the mob. The abolitionists had at last succeeded in usurping complete control of the government at Washington, and in imparting to the war the unholy zeal of their fanaticism. Nine-tenths of the legislation of the Yankee Congress had been occupied in some form or other with the question of slavery. Universal emancipation in the South, and the utter overthrow of all property, was now the declared policy of the desperate and demented leaders of the war. The Confiscation Bill, enacted at the close of the session of Congress, confiscated all the slaves belonging to those who were loyal to the South, constituting nine-tenths at least of the slaves in the Confederate States. In the Border States occupied by the North, slavery was plainly doomed under a plan of emancipation proposed by Mr. Lincoln with the flimsy and ridiculous pretence of compensation to slaveholders.* Other violent acts of legislation were passed

---

flicted the chastisement. The fact was, that Pope had won his baton of mar shal by bragging to the Yankee fill. He was another instance, besides that of Butler, of the manufacture of military reputation in the North by cowardly bluster and acts of coarse cruelty to the defenceless.

* According to the census of 1860—

Kentucky had	225,490	slaves.
Maryland	87,188	"
Virginia	490,887	"
Delaware	1,798	"
Missouri	114,965	"
Tennessee	275,784	"

Making in the whole............1,196,112
At the proposed rate of valuation, these would amount to $358,833,600
Add for deportation and colonization $100 each, 119,244,533

And we have the enormous sum of $478,078,133

with the intention to envenom the war, to insult and torture the South, to suppress the freedom of public opinion in the North, and to keep the government in the hands of the fanatics and crusaders of Abolitionism. Disaffection was threatened with a long list of Draconian penalties. The political scaffold was to be erected in the North, while the insatiate and unbridled fury of its army was to sweep over the South. "Rebellion" was to be punished by a warfare of savages, and the devilish, skulking revenge, that pillages, burns, and assassinates, was to follow in the bloody footsteps of the invading armies.

To this enormous mass of brutality and lawlessness, the Confederate States government made but a feeble response. It proposed a plan of retaliation, the execution of which was limited to the *commissioned officers* of the army of Gen. Pope ; which, by declaring impunity to private soldiers, encouraged their excesses ; and which, in omitting any application to the army of Butler in New Orleans, who had laughed at female virtue in the conquered districts of the South, and murdered a citizen of the South for disrespect to the Yankee bunting,* was lamentably weak and imperfect. The fact was, that the gov-

---

It is scarcely to be supposed that a proposition could be made in good faith, or that in any event the proposition could be otherwise than worthless, to add this vast amount to the public debt of the North at a moment when the treasury was reeling under the enormous expenditures of the war.

* The act for which William B. Mumford was executed by Butler, was taking down the Yankee ensign from the Mint in that city on the 24th of April. This act of Mumford was committed *before* the city of New Orleans had surrendered. Indeed, the flag was hoisted in the city while negotiations were being conducted between the commander of the Yankee fleet and the authorities ; and under these circumstances the raising of the enemy's flag was a plain violation of the rules and amenities of war, and an outrage on the authorities and people of the city. Taking the harshest rule of construction, the act of Mumford, having been committed before the city of New Orleans had surrendered, was nothing more than an *act of war*, for which he was no more responsible than as a prisoner of war.

The unhappy man was hung in the open day by order of the Federal tyrant of New Orleans. The brutal sentence of death on the gallows was carried into effect in the presence of thousands of spectators. The crowd looked on, scarcely believing their senses, unwilling to think that even such a tyrant as Butler could really have the heart for such a wanton murder of a citizen of the Confederate States, and hoping every moment for a reprieve or a pardon : but none came, and the soul of the martyr was ushered by violent hands into the presence of its God.

ernment of President Davis had been weakly swindled in its military negotiation with the North. It was persuaded to sign a cartel for the exchange of prisoners, in which it made a present to its enemy of a surplus of about six thousand prisoners, and its weak generosity was immediately rewarded, not only by the barbarous orders of Pope, which were issued just at the time the cartel was signed, but by the practical proclamation in all the invaded districts of the South of the policy of the seizure and imprisonment of unarmed inhabitants. Our government had left out of the recent cartel any provisions for private citizens kidnapped by the enemy; it had left the North in the undisturbed enjoyment, in many places, of the privilege it claimed of capturing in our country as many political prisoners as it pleased; and it had, to a considerable extent, practically abandoned the protection of its own citizens.

Before the eyes of Europe the mask of civilization had been taken from the Yankee war; it degenerated into unbridled butchery and robbery. But the nations of Europe, which boasted themselves as humane and civilized, had yet no interference to offer in a war which shocked the senses and appealed to the common offices of humanity. It is to be observed, that during the entire continuance of the war up to this time, the British government had acted with reference to it in a spirit of selfish and inhuman calculation; and there is, indeed, but little doubt that an early recognition of the Confederacy by France was thwarted by the interference of that cold and sinister government, that ever pursues its ends by indirection, and perfects its hypocrisy under the specious cloak of extreme conscientiousness. No greater delusion could have possessed the people of the South than that the *government* of England was friendly to them. That government, which prided itself on its cold and ingenious selfishness, seemed to have discovered a much larger source of profit in the continuation of the American war, than it could possibly derive from a pacification of the contest. It was willing to see its operatives starving, and to endure the distress of a " cotton famine," * that it might have

---

* Great pains were taken alike by the Yankee and the English press to conceal the distress caused in the manufacturing districts of Europe by the withholding of Southern cotton; and the specious fallacy was being con-

the ultimate satisfaction, which it anticipated, of seeing both parties in the American war brought to the point of exhaustion and its own greatness enlarged on the ruins of a hated commercial rival. The calculation was far-reaching; it was characteristic of a government that secretly laughed at all sentiment, made an exact science of selfishness, and scorned the weakness that would sacrifice for any present good the larger fruits of the future.

In the regular continuation of our historical narrative, in which much that has been said here by way of general reflection will be replaced by the record of particular facts, and special comments upon them, we shall have occasion before

---

stantly put forward that the cotton product in the colonial dominions of Great Britain and elsewhere was being rapidly stimulated and enlarged; that it would go far towards relieving the necessities of Europe; and that one effect of the American war would be to free England from her long and galling dependence on the Slave States of the South for the chief article of her manufacturing industry.

The proofs in reply to the latter fallacy and falsehood are striking and unanswerable. The shipments of cotton from the British colonies, Egypt, Brazil, &c., are actually falling off, and were much less this last summer than for a corresponding period of the year before. The evidence of this fact is furnished in the cotton circulars of Manchester.

India seems to have been cleared out by the large shipments of last year, and the shipments to Europe, from the first of January to the last week in May, showed a decrease of 100,000 bales; the figures being 251,000 bales against 351,000 last year. From the large proportional consumption of Surat cotton, the stock at Liverpool of this description, which, on the 1st of January last, stood at 295,000 bales against 130,000 last year, was, about the close of May, reduced to 170,000 against 133,000 last year; while in the quantity afloat the figures were still more unfavorable, viz.: 184,000 bales against 258,000.

The downward progress of the stock of American cotton is illustrated roughly by the following quarterly table prepared from the Manchester circulars:

	March, 1861.	June.
In American ports	750,000	100,000
Afloat and at Liverpool	918,000	971,000
	1,668,000	1,071,000

	March, 1862.	May.
In American ports	30,000	20,000
Afloat and at Liverpool	160,000	108,000
	193,000	128,000

tracing the active prosecution of the campaign in Virginia, to direct the attention of the reader to the progress of events in the West.

We shall find many remarkable events to record in this direction. We shall see how it was that the evacuation of Corinth was determined upon; that the retreat was conducted with great order and precision; and that, despite the boasts of the North to the contrary, we lost no more prisoners than the enemy did himself, and abandoned to him in stores not more than would amount to one day's expense of our army.

We shall find in the defence of Vicksburg a splendid lesson of magnanimity and disinterested patriotism. We shall see how for several weeks this city resisted successfully the attack of the enemy's gunboats, mortar fleets, and heavy siege-guns; how it was threatened by powerful fleets above and below, and with what unexampled spirit the Queen City of the Bluffs sustained the iron storm that was rained upon her for weeks with continued fury.

New Orleans, Baton Rouge, Natchez, and Memphis were in the hands of the Yankees, and their possession by the enemy might have furnished to Vicksburg, in its exposed and desperate situation, the usual excuses of timidity and selfishness for its surrender. But the brave city resisted these vile and unmanly excuses, and gave to the world one of the proudest and most brilliant illustrations of the earnestness and devotion of the people of the South that had yet adorned the war.

The fact that but little hopes could be entertained of the eventual success of the defence of Vicksburg against the powerful concentration of the enemy's navy, heightened the nobility of the resistance she made. The resistance of an enemy in circumstances which afford but a feeble and uncertain prospect of victory, requires a great spirit; but it is more invaluable to us than a hundred easy victories; it teaches the enemy that we are invincible, and overcomes him with despair; it exhibits to the world the inspirations and moral grandeur of our cause; and it educates our people in chivalry and warlike virtues by the force of illustrious examples of self-devotion.

We shall have, however, the satisfaction of recording an unexpected issue of victory in the siege of Vicksburg, and have occasion to point to another lesson that the history of all

wars indicates, that the practical test of resistance affords the
only sure determination whether a place is defensible or not.
With a feeling of inexpressible pride did Vicksburg behold two
immense fleets, each of which had been heretofore invincible,
brought to bay, and, unable to cope with her, kept at a respectable distance, and compelled to essay the extraordinary
task of digging a new channel for the Mississippi.

In following the track of detachments of our forces in the
West, we shall refer to the brilliant movements across the
Mississippi that drove the enemy from Arkansas, and harassed
him on the Missouri border with ceaseless activity, and to the
dashing expedition of the celebrated John Morgan into Kentucky. We shall see that the expedition of this cavalier was
one of the most brilliant, rapid, and successful raids recorded
in history. He left Tennessee with a thousand men, only a
portion of whom were armed; penetrated two hundred and
fifty miles into a country in full possession of the Yankees;
captured a dozen towns and cities; met, fought, and captured
a Yankee force superior to his own in numbers; captured three
thousand stand of arms at Lebanon; and, from first to last,
destroyed during his raid, military stores, railroad bridges, and
other property to the value of eight or ten millions of dollars.
He accomplished all this, besides putting the people of Cincinnati into a condition, described by one of their newspapers, as
"bordering on frenzy," and returned to Tennessee with a
loss in all his engagements of fifteen men killed, and forty
wounded.

While some activity was shown in extreme portions of the
West, we shall see that our military operations from Greenbrier county, Virginia, all the way down to Chattanooga, Tennessee, were conducted with but little vigor. On the boundaries of East Tennessee, southwestern Virginia, and Kentucky,
we had a force in the aggregate of thirty thousand men, confronted by probably not half their number of Yankee troops;
yet the southwestern counties of Virginia, and the valley of
the Clinch, in Tennessee, were entered and mercilessly plundered by the enemy in the face of our troops.

Turning for a moment from the military events of this
period, we shall notice the reassembling of the Confederate
Congress on the 18th of August, 1862. We shall then find

occasion to review the conduct of this branch of the government, and to observe how it fell below the spirit and virtue of the people; what servility to the Executive it displayed, and what a singular destitution of talents and ability was remarkable in this body. Not a single speech that has yet been made in it will live. It is true, that the regular Congress elected by the people was an improvement upon the ignorant and unsavory body known as the Provisional Congress, which was the creature of conventions, and which was disgraced in the character of some of its members; among whom were conspicuous, corrupt and senile politicians from Virginia, who had done all they could to sacrifice and disgrace their State, who had toadied in "society," as well as in politics, to notabilities of New England, and who had taken a prominent part in emasculating, and, in fact, annulling the Sequestration Law, in order to save the property of relatives who had sided with the North against the land that had borne them and honored their fathers.

But the regular Congress, although it had no taint of disloyalty or Yankee toadyism in it, was a weak, sycophantic, and trifling body. It has made no mark in the history of the government; it was utterly destitute of originality. Its measures were those which were recommended by the Executive or suggested by the newspapers. It produced no great financial measure; it made not one stroke of statesmanship; it uttered not a single fiery appeal to the popular heart, such as is customary in revolutions. The most of the little ability it had was eaten up by servility to the Executive; and the ignorance of the majority was illustrated by a trifling and undignified style of legislation, in which whole days were consumed with paltry questions, and the greatest measures—such as the Conscript Law*—embarrassed by demagogical speeches made for home effect.

---

* The execution of the Conscript Law was resisted by Governor Brown, of Georgia. The correspondence between him and the President on this subject, which was printed and hawked in pamphlet-form through the country, is a curiosity. What will posterity think of a correspondence between such dignitaries, taking place at a time when the destinies of the country trembled in the balance, composed of about equal parts of hair-splitting and demagogueism, and illustrated copiously by Mr. Brown with citations from the Virginia and Kentucky Resolutions of 1798, and exhumed opinions of members of the

It is difficult, indeed, for a legislative body to preserve its independence, and to resist the tendency of the Executive to absorb power in a time of war, and this fact was well illus trated by the Confederate Congress. One of the greatest political scholars of America, Mr. Madison, noticed this dan ger in the political constitution of the country. He said :— " War is in fact the true nurse of Executive aggrandizement. In war a physical force is to be created, and it is the Executive will which is to direct it. In war the public treasures are to be unlocked, and it is the Executive hand which is to dispense them. In war the honors and emoluments of office are to be multiplied, and it is the Executive patronage under which they are to be enjoyed. It is in war, finally, that laurels are to be gathered, and it is the Executive brow they are to encircle."

There was but little opposition in Congress to President Davis ; but there was some which took a direction to his Cab- inet, and this opposition was represented by Mr. Foote of Ten- nessee—a man of acknowledged ability and many virtues of character, who had re-entered upon the political stage after a public life, which, however it lacked in the cheap merit of partisan consistency, had been adorned by displays of won- derful intellect and great political genius. Mr. Foote was not a man to be deterred from speaking the truth ; his quickness to resentment and his chivalry, which, though somewhat Quixotic, was founded in the most noble and delicate sense of honor, made those who would have bullied or silenced a weaker person, stand in awe of him. A man of such tem- per was not likely to stint words in assailing an opponent ; and his sharp declamations in Congress, his searching com- ments, and his great powers of sarcasm, used upon such men as Mallory, Benjamin, and Huger, were the only relief of the dulness of the Congress, and the only historical features of its debates.

---

old Federal Convention of 1787? The display was characteristic of Southern *politicians ;* in the most vital periods of the country's destiny they had an eye to making political capital for themselves, and in the fierce tumults of a revo- lution, refreshed the country with exhumations from the politicians of 1787 and the usual amount of clap-trap about our "forefathers," and the old political system that had rotted over our heads.

Returning to the history of the campaign in Virginia, we shall have occasion to enumerate another brilliant victory of our arms, achieved on that fortunate theatre of the war. We refer to the battle of Cedar Mountain. We shall find other topics to record in the events which, at the time of this writing, are developing themselves, and reaching to the most important consequences, both in Virginia and Tennessee. We shall see how the great army which McClellan had brought for the reduction of Richmond, and in sight of the church steeples of that city, was compelled to retire towards the Potomac, with its proud columns shattered, humiliated, and demoralized; how Pope, who had entered Virginia with a splendid army and the most insolent boasts, was ignominiously whipped on more than one occasion, and with what agony of cowardice he sought safety for his retreat; how considerable portions of Virginia and Tennessee were surrendered to the jurisdiction of the Confederacy; how the enemy in various quarters was pushed back to his old lines; and how intelligent men in the South saw for the first time certain and unmistakable indications of demoralization in the armies of the North, brought on by the remarkable train of victories in Virginia, extending from early June to September.

In these events we shall find bright and flattering prospects renewed to the South. Much of these we shall find already realized in the events in the midst of which we write this imperfect sketch. We shall trace the painful steps by which our worn troops advanced to meet another invading army in Virginia, reinforced not only by the defeated army of McClellan, but by the fresh corps of Generals Burnside and Hunter. We shall tell what hardships were endured by our troops, and what exploits of valor were performed by them on this celebrated expedition; how they were compelled to toil their way with inadequate transportation; how they crossed streams swollen to unusual height, and bore all the fatigues and distresses of forced marches; how their spirit and endurance were tested by repeated combats with the enemy; how at last they succeeded in turning his position; and how, having formed a junction of their columns in the face of greatly superior forces on the historic and blood-stained plains of Manassas, they achieved there the ever-memorable victory of the thirteenth of August

1862, the crowning triumph of their toil and valor. A nation's gratitude is evoked to repay all that is due to the valor of our troops and the providence of Almighty God.*

We do not trust ourselves to predict the consequences of current events; and the brilliant story of Manassas, grouped with contemporary victories in the West, must be left to the decisions of the future—trusting as we do that we may have occasion to record in another volume the consequences as well as the details of these events, and to find in the future the fulfilment of the promises of to-day.

* * * * A few general reflections on the material and moral phenomena of the war will appropriately conclude our work for the present.

It is a censurable practice to flatter the people. It is equally

---

* The vulgar and unintelligent mind worships success. The extraordinary and happy train of victories in Virginia seems to have had no other significance or interest to a number of grovelling minds in the South, than as a contribution to the personal fame of General Lee, who by no fault of his own (for no one had more modesty, more Christian dignity of behavior, and a purer conversation), was followed by toadies, flatterers, and newspaper sneaks in epaulets, who made him ridiculous by their servile obeisances and excess of praise. The author does not worship success. He trusts, however, that he has intelligence enough to perceive merit, without being prompted by the vulgar cry; he is sure that he has honesty and independence enough to acknowledge it where he believes it to exist. The estimation of General Lee, made in some preceding pages, was with reference to his unfortunate campaign in Western Virginia; it was founded on the events of that campaign, in which there is no doubt Gen. Lee blundered and showed an absurd misconception of mountain warfare; and so far as these events furnished evidence for the historian, the author believes that he was right, unprejudiced, and just in ascribing the failure of that campaign to the misdirection of the commanding general. If, however, it can be shown, as now seems to be likely from incomplete events, that on wider, clearer, and more imposing fields Gen. Lee has shown qualities which the campaign in the mountains of Virginia had not illustrated, the friends of this commander may be assured that the author will be honest and cordial in acknowledging the fact, and that in a future continuation of these annals, justice will be done to the recent extraordinary events in Virginia, fraught with so many critical issues of the war, and associated with so many reputations dear to the people of the South. In writing the facts of this war, the author takes no counsel of popular cries, and notions fashionable in the newspapers; he is neither the panegyrist nor the antagonist of any clique; he is more pleased to praise than to censure, but his aim is truth, and he is resolved to pursue it, no matter what popular prejudice or affection he is compelled to crush in its attainment.

censurable to withhold from them the plain recognition of their accomplishments. The present war will win the respect of the world for the masses of the people of the Confederate States With inferior numbers, with resources hampered on all sides, we are yet winning the issue of the great struggle in which we are involved. No one claims that this is owing to the wisdom of our government. No one ascribes it to the ability of our military chieftains; for blunders in our military management have been as common as in our civil administration. But there is a huge, unlettered power that wages the war on our side, overcoming everywhere the power of the enemy and the incumbrances of our own machinery. It is the determined, settled will of the people to be free, and to fight themselves free, that has constituted our strength and our safety.

The existing war has, doubtless, disappointed the world in its meagre phenomena of personal greatness, and, to some extent, has disappointed its own people in the bigotry of its policy and the official restraint put upon its spirit. It may be said with singular truth, that it has produced or exhibited but few great men—that it has not raised up to public admiration in the South a statesman, an orator, a poet, or a financier, all which are generally considered as much the natural products of war as military genius itself. For this disappointment, however, we may find an explanation in some degree satisfactory. It is, that the very circumstance of the almost universal uprising of the people of the South, and the equal measures of devotion shown by all classes and intellects, have given but little room for overshadowing names, and presented but little opportunity for marked personal distinctions of greatness.

After all, it is the spirit of the people that is most sure to achieve the victorious results of revolutions; and on this firm reliance, and not on the personal fortunes of master-spirits, or on adventitious aid, or on the calculations of any merely external events, do we rest, under Providence, the hopes of the Southern Confederacy. The verdict of the history of the world is, that no powerful nation has ever been lost except by its own cowardice. All nations that have fought for an independent existence, have had to sustain terrible defeats, live through deep, though temporary distress, and endure hours of profound discouragement. But no nation was ever subdued that really determined to fight while there was an inch of ground or a solitary soldier left to defend it.

As far as the war has been fought, its results, in a military point of view, are deeply humiliating to the North. The war was commenced by the North with the most intense expressions of contempt for its adversary; the idea of the contest being extended beyond a few months, was derided and spit upon; in that short time it was believed that the flag of the Union would float over the cities and towns of the South, and the bodies of "traitors" dangle from the battlements of Washington.

This was not affectation. It was calculated by many people, in a spirit of candor, that a contest so unequal in the material elements of strength as that between the North and the South would be speedily determined. The North had more than twenty millions of people to break the power of eight millions; it had a militia force about three times as strong as that of the South; it had the regular army; it had an immense advantage over the South in a navy, the value of which may be appreciated when it is known that its achievements in the war have been greater than those of the land forces, and that its strength, with proposed additions to its active war vessels, is estimated to-day in the North as equivalent to an army of half a million men.

Nor did the superiority of the North end here. While the South was cut off from the world by the restrictions of the blockade, without commerce, with but scanty manufactures and few supplies on hand, the North had all the ports of the world open to its ships; it had furnaces, foundries, and workshops; its manufacturing resources compared with those of the South were as five hundred to one; the great marts of Europe were open to it for supplies of arms and stores; there was nothing of material resource, nothing of the apparatus of conquest that was not within its reach.

These immense elements of superiority on the part of the North have not remained idle in her hands. They have been exercised with tremendous energy. Within the last fifteen months the government at Washington has put forth all its power to subjugate the South; it has contracted a debt six or seven times more than that of the South; it has called out more than half a million soldiers: it has put Europe under contribution to furnish it not only arms, but soldiers to use them ; it has left no resource untried and omitted no condition of success.

The result of all this immense and boasted superiority on the part of the North, coupled with the most immense exertions is, that the South remains unconquered. The result is humiliating enough to the warlike reputation of the North. It has not been separated from its feeble adversary by seas or mountains, but only by a geographical line; nature has not interfered to protect the weak from the strong; three "Grand Armies" have advanced in the Confederate territory; and yet to-day, the Yankees hold in Virginia and Tennessee only the ground they stand upon, and the South, in spirit, is more invincible than ever.

Nor has the war, so far as it has been waged, been without great moral benefits to the South. We may indicate at least three important and inestimable blessings which it has conferred upon our people.

It has made impossible the theory of the "reconstruction" of the old Union, which was no doubt indulged in the early formation of the Confederate government. It has carried a revolution, which, if no war had taken place, would probably have ended in "reconstruction," on the basis of concessions from the Northern States, which would in no way have impaired the advantages of the old Union to them, to a point where the demand for our independence admits of no alternative or compromise. It has revealed to us the true characteristics of the people of the North; it has repulsed us from a people whose vices and black hearts we formerly knew but imperfectly ; and it has produced that antagonism and alienation which were necessary to exclude the possibility a reunion with them.

Again: the war has shown the system of negro slavery in the South to the world in some new and striking aspects, and has removed much of that cloud of prejudice, defamation, falsehood, romance, and perverse sentimentalism through which our peculiar institution was formerly known to Europe. It has given a better vindication of our system of slavery than all the books that could be written in a generation. Hereafter there can be no dispute between facts plainly exhibited and the pictures of romance; and intelligent men of all countries will obtain their ideas of slavery from certain leading and indisputable facts in the history of this war, rather than from partisan sources of information and the literary inventions of the North. The war has shown that slavery has been an element of strength with us; that it has assisted us in the war; that no servile insurrections have taken place in the South, in spite of the allurements of our enemy; that the slave has tilled the soil while his master has fought; that in large districts unprotected by our troops, and with a white population consisting almost exclusively of women and children, the slave has continued at his work, quiet, cheerful, and faithful * and that, as

---

* The following is taken from the letter of an English nobleman, who visited the South while the war was in its active stages, and the result of whose observations there, at the time war was racking the country and many of our own whites were houseless and starving, was, that the condition of the negro slaves in the South was "better than that of any laboring population in the world."

*   *   *   *   *   *   *

"Among the dangers which we had heard at New York threatened the South, a revolt of the slave population was said to be the most imminent. Let us take, then, a peep at the cotton-field, and see what likelihood there is of such a contingency. On the bank of the Alabama river, which winds its yellow course through woods of oak, ash, maple, and pine, thickened with tangled copse of varied evergreens, lie some of the most fertile plantations of the State. One of these we had the advantage of visiting. Its owner received us with all that hospitality and unaffected *bonhomie* which invariably distinguish a Southern gentleman. Having mounted a couple of hacks, we started off through a large pine wood, and soon arrived at the "clearing" of about two hundred acres in extent, on most of which was growing an average cotton crop. This was a fair sample of the rest of the plantation, which consisted altogether of 7000 acres. Riding into the middle of the field, we found ourselves surrounded by about forty slaves—men, women, and children—engaged in "picking." They were all well dressed, and seemed happy and cheerful. Wishing to know what time of day it was, I asked Mr. —— the hour, where upon one of the darkies by my side took out a watch and informed me.

" 'Do your laborers wear watches, sir?' I inquired.

" 'A great many of them have. Why, sir, my negroes all have their cotton plats and gardens, and most of them have little orchards.'

" We found from their own testimony that they are fed well, chiefly upon pork, corn, potatoes, and rice, carefully attended to when sick, and on Sundays dress better than their masters. We next visited the 'station,' a street of cottages in a pine wood, where Mr. ——'s slaves reside. These we found clean and comfortable. Two of the men were sick, and had been visited that

a conservative element in our social system, the instⁱtution oɪ slavery has withstood the shocks of war and been a faithful ally of our arms, although instigated to revolution by every art of the enemy, and prompted to the work of assassination and pillage by the most brutal examples of the Yankee sol-- diery.

Finally, the war has given to the States composing the Con federacy a new bond of union. This was necessary. Com- merce and intercourse had been far more intimate between the Slave States on the Lower Mississippi and those on the Upper Mississippi and its tributaries, than between any portions of the Confederate States. The war has broken this natural affin- ity ; it has supplanted sympathy by alienation, interest by hate, between the people of Indiana, Illinois, and Ohio, and those of Tennessee, Louisiana, and Mississippi ; and by the prin- ciple of repulsion as well as union, by the tie of a common bloodshed, and the memory of a common labor and glory, the stability of our Confederacy has been strengthened and se- cured.

Such are the inestimable blessings which, although draped in sorrow and suffering, the war has conferred upon the people of the South.

The resolution of the South to achieve its independence has been greatly encouraged as the war has advanced. It is alike prompted by the spirit of her people, and strengthened by mo- tives which address the judgment. These motives are explained ⁱn the plain consequences of subjugation. The spirit of the North in the existing war has already been developed far enough to indicate the certain condition of the South, if her enemy should succeed in establishing his dominion over her people. That condition may be described in confiscation, brutality, military domination, insult, universal poverty, the beggary of millions, the triumph of the vilest individuals in these communities, the abasement of the honest and indus- trious, the outlawry of the slaves, the destruction of agriculture and commerce, the emigration of all thriving citizens, farewell to the hopes of future wealth, and the scorn of the world. The

---

morning by a doctor ; in the mean time they were looked after by the nurses of the establishment, of whom there were three to take care of the children and invalids."

resistance of such a destiny, properly conceived, will restore the worst fortunes of war, pluck victory from despair, and deserve the blessing of Providence, which " can save by many or by few," and which has never yet failed to reward a just and earnest endeavor for independence.

THE SECOND YEAR.

CHAPTER XIV.

THE fall of New Orleans was one of the most extraordinary triumphs which the enemy had obtained. It was the crowning stroke of that extraordinary campaign of the winter and spring of the year 1862, in which, by the improvidence of the Southern authorities, and a false military policy which divided their armies and weakened them by undue dispersion, they had lost much of their territory, most of the prestige of their arms, and had fallen upon a train of disasters well calculated to affect the general public, both at home and abroad. The close of this campaign, so ill-starred to the Confederacy, found it with scarcely more than three entire States—Texas, Alabama, and Georgia. Large portions of the territories of Virginia, the Carolinas, and Florida were occupied by the enemy, he had broken our line of defences in Tennessee, and held im portant positions on the Upper Mississippi; and now, by the capture of New Orleans, he had secured the great Southern depot of the trade of the immense central valley of the conti nent, obtained command of an extent of territory accessible by his gunboats greater than the entire country before lost to the Confederacy, and had good reason to hope, by the junction of his fleets on the Mississippi, to open its navigation, and give to the West an outlet to the ocean.

The conquests of the Federal arms made in the winter and spring of 1862, were not without their effect in Europe, and presented to the nations in that part of the world a sombre picture of the Confederacy. The dispatches of our ministers at the courts of England and France declared that the prospect of recognition, of which they had formerly given such warm and sanguine assurances, had been overclouded by the disaster at New Orleans. Mr. Slidell wrote from Paris that the French government declared that "if New Orleans had not fallen, our recognition could not have been much longer delayed." He added, however, that he had been assured that " even after that disaster, if we obtained decided successes in Virginia and Tennessee, or could hold the enemy at bay a month or two, the same result would follow"—a promise, to the breach of which, and to the unhappy expectations which it excited, we shall hereafter have occasion to refer. Mr. Mason, our minister at London, also referred to the opinion that at the time of the enemy's capture of New Orleans, our recognition was on the eve of accomplishment.

The immediate sufferers of the disaster at New Orleans were the people of that city. It was aptly rewarded for its easy submission by the scourge of a tyrant. The corrupt and merciless master of this great emporium, General Butler of Massachusetts, was a man who found no merit in submission, unless such as grovelled in the dust and paid personal court and pecuniary tribute to himself. The rule of this vulgar and drunken man excited the horror and disgust of the civilized world, and secured for him in the South the popular sobriquet of "the Beast." His order which stigmatized as prostitutes the ladies of New Orleans, who betrayed in the streets or from the balconies their indignation against the invaders of their city, while it made him the hero of the hour in the

North with a people who admired the coarse spirit of the bully, drew upon him the execrations of all humane and honorable people. In the British Parliament, Lord Palmerston declared the proclamation to be "infamous," and the condemnation of the indecent and dirty edict was echoed by the press of Europe.*

The acts of the tyrant of New Orleans surpassed all former atrocities and outrages of the war. In frequent instances, citizens, accused by Butler of contumacious disloyalty, were confined at hard labor, with balls and chains attached to their limbs; and sometimes this degrading punishment was inflicted upon men whose only offence was that of selling medicines to the sick soldiers of the Confederacy. Helpless women were torn from their homes and confined in prison. One of these— a Mrs. Phillips—was accused of laughing as the funeral train of a Yankee officer passed her doors; she was seized, and with an ingenious and devilish cruelty, her sentence was pronounced by Butler—imprisonment on an island of barren sand under a tropical sun. Various pretexts were invented for

---

* The "Order 28," which has stigmatized its brutal author throughout Christendom, was at first refused publication by all the newspapers in New Orleans. It was then copied on sheets of paper and surreptitiously posted on many of the principal corners of the streets in the immediate neighborhood of the St. Charles Hotel. The next day all of the newspaper offices were ordered to be closed for disobedience of orders. On this becoming known, the *True Delta* paper published the order, and the other newspapers timidly submitted to the *force* of circumstances, and published it also. The natural excitement and indignation that followed throughout the community is indescribable. Several lady subscribers sent to the newspaper offices and indignantly and positively forbade that such papers should longer be left at their dwellings. Mayor Monroe, with a party of influential citizens, at once called on the Beast and endeavored to obtain some qualification of the order; but they could get no satisfaction and were rudely dismissed. Mayor Monroe then wrote an indignant and reproachful communication to Butler, and again pressed him for a modification of the hateful order. Butler then sent for the Mayor. Mayor Monroe replied, "Tell General Butler my office is at the City Hotel, where he can see me, if desirable." Butler retorted, that unless the Mayor came at once to his headquarters, he would send an armed force to arrest and bring him there. Further opposition being useless, the Mayor chief of police, and several friends, then went to the St. Charles Hotel, where they found the Beast in a towering rage. Butler claimed to be much insulted at the conduct of the Mayor, and without ceremony or delay, sent Mr. Monroe and those who accompanied him to prison. In a few days they were all shipped down to Fort Jackson.

plundering the inhabitants of the conquered city; men were forced to elect between starvation by the confiscation of all their property and taking an oath of allegiance to the invaders of their country; fines were levied at pleasure, and recusants threatened with ball and chain.

The conduct of the negroes in New Orleans became intolerable to their owners. They were fed, clothed, and quartered by the Yankees, who fraternized with them generally in a shameful way. The planters in the neighborhood of the city were required to share their crops with the commanding general, his brother, Andrew J. Butler, and other officers; and when this partnership was refused, the plantations were robbed of every thing susceptible of removal, and the slaves taken from their owners and compelled to work under the bayonets of Yankee guards.

It would occupy many pages to detail what the people of New Orleans suffered at the hands of the invaders whom they had so easily admitted into their city, in insult, wrongs, confiscation of property, seizure of private dwellings, and brazen robbery. The Yankee officers, from colonel to lieutenant, as the caprice of each might dictate, seized and took possession of gentlemen's houses, broke into their wine-rooms, forced open the wardrobes of ladies and gentlemen, and either used or sent away from the city the clothing of whole families. Some of the private residences of respectable citizens were appropriated to the vilest uses, the officials who had engaged them making them the private shops of the most infamous female characters.

But while Butler was thus apparently occupied with the oppression of "rebels," he was too much of a Yankee to be lost to the opportunity of making his pecuniary fortune out of the exigencies which he had created. The banker and broker of the corrupt operations in which he was engaged was his own brother, who bought confiscated property, shipped large consignments from New Orleans, to be paid for in cotton, and speculated largely in powder, saltpetre, muskets, and other war material sold to the Confederacy, surreptitiously sent out from the city and covered by permits for provisions. Of the trade in provisions for cotton, Butler received his share of the gains, while the robbery was covered up by the pretence of consumption in New Orleans "to prevent starvation," or by reported actual issue to troops. The Yankee general did not hesitate to deal in the very life-blood of his own soldiers.

The rule of Butler in New Orleans is especially memorable for the deliberate murder of William B. Mumford, a citizen or the Confederate States, against whom the tyrant had invented the extraordinary charge that he had insulted the flag of the United States. The fact was, that before the city had surrendered, Mumford had taken down from the mint the enemy's flag. The ensign was wrongfully there; the city had not surrendered; and even in its worst aspects, the act of Mumford was simply one of war, not deserving death, still less the death of a felon. The horrible crime of murdering in cold blood an unresisting and non-combatant captive, was completed by Butler on the 7th of June. On that day, Mumford, the martyr, was publicly executed on the gallows. The Massachusetts coward and tyrant had no ear or heart for the pitiful pleadings made to save the life of his captive, especially by his unhappy wife, who in her supplications for mercy was rudely repulsed, and at times answered with drunken jokes and taunts. The execution took place in the sight of thousands of panic-stricken citizens. None spoke but the martyr himself. His voice was loud and clear. Looking up at the stars and stripes which floated high over the scene before him, he remarked that he had fought under that flag twice, but it had become hateful to him, and he had torn it and trailed it in the dust. "I consider," said the brave young man, "that the manner of my death will be no disgrace to my wife and child; my country will honor them."

The experience of New Orleans gave a valuable lesson to the South. It exhibited the consequences of submission to the enemy in confiscation, brutality, military domination, insult, universal poverty, the beggary of thousands, the triumph of the vilest individuals in the community, the abasement of the honest and industrious, and the outlawry of the slaves. The spirit of resistance in the South was fortified by the enemy's exhibitions of triumph, and the resolution gained ground that t was much better to consign the cities of the Confederacy to the flames than to surrender them to the enemy. A time was approaching when Yankee gunboats were to lose their prestige of terror, when cities were no longer to be abandoned or surrendered on the approach of a foe; and when the freemen of the South were to be taught how, by a spirit above fear and ready for all sacrifice, they might defy the most potent agencies of modern warfare.

With the bright month of May a new era was dawning on the fortunes of the Confederacy. This happy change of fortune was due not only to the improved resolution of the South. It is in a great degree to be attributed to two leading causes in the military administration. These were, first, the conscription law, with the consequent reorganization of the army; and, secondly, the abandonment of our plan of frontier defence, which made way for the superior and more fortunate policy of the concentration of our forces in the interior.

The first suggestion of a conscription law was made by the Richmond *Examiner*—a bold and vigilant leader of the newspaper press of the Confederacy. It was met with violent opposition from the administration, with the clamor of demagogical presses that the suggestion conveyed a reflection upon the patriotism of the country, and with the fashionable nonsense that it was a confession calculated to give aid and comfort to the enemy. But the early advocates of conscription enjoyed the singular triumph of converting public opinion completely to their side, and forcing the government at a future period to the confession that the system which it had at first frowned upon had proved the salvation of the country.

At the beginning of the war we had nothing that deserved the title of a military system. There was no lack of zeal or determination in the South; but the organization of the army was defective, its discipline was retarded by bad laws, and at a time that the forces of the enemy in Virginia had reached the highest state of efficiency, our own army was passing through successive stages of disorganization to dissolution. The army of the enemy was superior to our own in every respect, except courage and good cause; they had every guaranty of success that numbers, discipline, complete organization, and perfect equipments could effect.

The military system of the South dates from the passage of the conscription law. To this measure must be attributed that solidity in the organization of our army, and that efficiency which challenged the admiration of the world. The beneficial effects of this enactment were soon manifest as well to ourselves as to the world. It distributed over the Confederacy the levies in proportion to the inhabitants of each State and county; it centralized the organization of the army, and it introduced a regular system of recruiting, which guaranteed that the efficiency of the army would not be impaired by the lapse of time and the loss of health and life incident to warfare.

The conscription law came not a moment too soon. The acts of Congress providing for re-enlistments had failed to effect the desired object. Without decadence of the real valor of our people, or their invincible determination to achieve their independence, the spirit of volunteering had died out, and the resolution of our soldiers already in the field was not sufficient to resist the prospects, cherished for months amid the sufferings and monotony of the camps, of returning to their homes. The exigency was critical, and even vital. In a period of thirty days the terms of service of one hundred and forty-eight regiments expired. There was good reason to believe that a large majority of the men had not re-enlisted, and of those who had re-enlisted, a very large majority had entered companies which could never be assembled, or if assembled, could not be prepared for the field in time to meet the invasion actually commenced.

The first act of conscription was passed on the 16th of April, 1862. It was afterwards enlarged by another act (27th September), giving the Executive the power to call into service persons between the ages of thirty-five and forty-five. Although the rush of volunteers had comparatively ceased, and the ardor of the individual did not suffice for the proffer of self-devotion, yet the sentiments and convictions of the mass recognized as the most sacred obligation the stern duty of defending, if needs be, with their entire numbers, their imperilled liberty, fortune, and honor. The conscription law was, generally, cheerfully acquiesced in. In every State one or more camps of instruction, for the reception and training of conscripts was established; and to each State an officer, styled a commandant of conscripts, was appointed, charged with the supervision of the enrolment and instruction of the new levies.

The execution of the conscription law was unfortunately re sisted for a time by Governor Brown of Georgia. The cor respondence between him and the President on the subject, which was printed and hawked in pamphlet form through the country, was a curiosity. It was illustrated copiously by Mr Brown with citations from the Virginia and Kentucky resolu tions of 1798, and exhumed opinions of members of the old Federal Convention of 1787. In the most vital periods of the country's destiny, and in the fierce tumults of a revolution the people of the South were refreshed with exhumations from the politicians of 1787, and the usual amount of clap-trap about our "forefathers," and the old political system that had rotted over our heads.

The beneficial effect of the conscription law in the reorgani- zation of our army was assisted by some other acts of legisla- tion. That reorganization was advanced by the appointment of lieutenant-generals, some commanding separate depart- ments, and others heading army corps under a general in the field. The policy of organizing the brigades with troops and generals from the several States was pursued, as opportunities offered, without detriment to the public service. The greater satisfaction of the men from each State, when collected to- gether, the generous emulation for glory to their State, and the fair apportionment of officers assured to each State according to its contribution of defenders to the country, overbalanced the inconvenience of separating regiments or companies pre- viously associated, and the liability to State jealousies. Mili- tary courts were organized to secure the prompt administration of the military law, to check desertion and straggling, to re- strain license of all kinds, and to advance ten.perance, disci- pline, and subordination.

But it was not only the reorganization and improved morale of the army that came to the aid of the declining fortunes of the South in the war.

The disasters on the Mississippi frontier and in other direc- tions had constrained the government to adopt the policy ot concentrating its forces in the interior of Virginia. The ob ject of all war is to reach a decisive point of the campaign, and this object was realized by a policy which it is true the govern ment had not adopted at the instance of reason, but which had been imposed upon it by the force of disaster. There were childish complaints that certain districts and points on the frontier had been abandoned by the Confederates for the purpose of a concentration of troops in Virginia. An inflammatory appeal was made by Governor Rector of Arkansas to the States of the Trans-Mississippi, representing that the government had deserted them in transferring its troops to other portions of the Confederacy, and suggesting that they should form a new association for their safety. But the appeal was severely rebuked by public sentiment. The complaint of Governor Rector cost him his election, and the display of the demagogue consigned him to the reproaches of the public.

Such complaints were alike selfish and senseless, and in most cases nothing more than the utterances of a demagogical, short-sighted, and selfish spirit, which would have preferred the apparent security of its own particular State or section to the fortunes of the whole Confederacy. The fact was, that there was cause of intelligent congratulation, even in those districts from which the Confederate troops had been withdrawn to make a decisive battle, that we had at last reached a crisis, the decision of which might reverse all our past misfortunes and achieve results in which every State of the Confederacy would have a share.

But the first movements of the famous summer campaign in Virginia that was to change the fortunes of the war and adorn our arms, were not auspicious. The designs of some of these movements were not properly appreciated at the time, and some of the incidents that attended them were real disasters.

We have seen that by the happy boldness of General Magruder in keeping the enemy in check on the line between Yorktown, on York river, and Mulberry Island, on James river, the advance of the grand Federal army, destined for the capture of Richmond, was stayed until our forces were rescued by the consummate strategy of Gen. Johnston from the pressure of enveloping armies, who arrived in time to reinforce our lines on the Peninsula. It became necessary, however, in the judgment of that commander, to fall back in the direction of Richmond. It was easily seen by General Johnston that at Yorktown there was no prospect of a general action, as the attack on either side would have to be made under disadvan tages which neither army was willing to risk. The Yankees were in superior force, besides their additional strength in their gunboats, and in falling back so as to invest the line of the Chickahominy, General Johnston expected to force the enemy to more equal terms. The difficulty was to match the strength of the enemy on the water; and the best practical equivalent for this was considered to be the open field, where gunboats being out of the question, the position of our troops would be the same as if at Yorktown they had had a force of gunboats exactly equal to that of the enemy, thus neutralizing his advantage in respect of naval armament.

The retreat from Yorktown produced uneasiness in the public mind, and naturally shook the confidence of the many who were in ignorance of the plans of the cautious and taciturn strategist at the head of our forces in Virginia. It involved our surrender of Norfolk, with all the advantages of its contiguous navy-yard and dock. And it was accompanied by a disaster which, in so far as it was supposed to be unnecessary and wanton, occasioned an amount of grief and rage in the Confederacy such as had not yet been exhibited in the war.

This memorable disaster was the destruction of the famous mailed steamer Virginia—"the iron diadem of the South." This vessel, which had obtained for us our first triumph on the water, was an object of pride, and almost of affection, to the people of the South. She was popularly said to be worth fifty thousand troops in the field. Nor was this estimate excessive, when it is recollected that she protected Norfolk, the navy-yard, and James river; that no fleet of transports could safely land its troops, designed to attack those places, at any point from Cape Henry to the upper James, as far as she could ascend; that her presence at Norfolk had annihilated the land and water blockade at Newport News, passed the control of the James river into our hands, and protected the right flank of our army on the Peninsula.

The Virginia was destroyed under the immediate orders of her commander, Commodore Tatnall, on the morning of the 11th of May, in the vicinity of Craney Island. According to his statement, he had been betrayed into the necessity of destroying his vessel by firing her magazine, by the deceitful representations of his pilots, who at first assured him that they could take the ship, with a draft of eighteen feet of water within forty miles of Richmond, and after having lifted her so as to unfit her for action, then declared that they could not get her above the Jamestown flats, up to which point the shore on each side was occupied by the enemy. It is proper to add that this statement of facts was contested by the pilots, who resented the reflections made upon their loyalty or courage. Whatever may have been the merits of this controversy, it is certain that the vessel was destroyed in great haste by Commodore Tatnall, who, in the dead hour of night, aroused from his slumbers and acquainted with the decision of his pilots, ordered the ship to be put ashore, landed his crew in the vicinity of Craney Island, and blew to the four winds of heaven the only naval structure that guarded the water approach to Richmond.

The destruction of the Virginia was a sharp and unexpected blow to the confidence of the people of the South in their government. How far the government was implicated in this foolish and desperate act, was never openly acknowledged or exactly ascertained; but despite the pains of official concealment, there are certain well-attested facts which indicate that in the destruction of this great war-ship, the authorities at Richmond were not guiltless. These facts properly belong to the history of one of the most unhappy events that had occurred since the commencement of the war.

The Virginia was destroyed at 5 A. M. of the 11th of May. During the morning of the same day a prominent politician in the streets of Richmond was observed to be very much dejected; he remarked that it was an evil day for the Confederacy. On being questioned by his intimate friends, he declared to them that the Government had determined upon, or assented to, the destruction of the Virginia, and that he had learned this from the highest sources of authority in the capital. At this time the news of the explosion of the Virginia could not have possibly reached Richmond; there was no telegraphic communication between the scene of her destruction and the city, and the evidence appears to be complete, that the Government had at least a prevision of the destruction of this vessel, or had assented to the general policy of the act, trusting, perhaps, to acquit itself of the responsibility for it on the unworthy plea that it had given no *express* orders in the matter.

Again, it is well known that for at least a week prior to the destruction of the Virginia, the evacuation of Norfolk had been determined upon; that during this time the removal of stores was daily progressing; and that Mr. Mallory, the Secretary of the Navy, had within this period, himself, visited Norfolk to look after the public interests. The evacuation of this port clearly involved the question, what disposition was to be made of the Virginia. If the Government made no decision of a question, which for a week stared it in the face, it certainly was very strangely neglectful of the public interest. If Mr. Mallory visited Norfolk when the evacuation was going on, and never thought of the Virginia, or thinking of her, kept dumb, never even giving so much as an *official nod* as to what disposition should be made of her, he must have been more stupid than the people who laughed at him in Richmond, or the members of Congress who nicknamed without mercy thought him to be.

It is also not a little singular that when a court of inquiry had found that the destruction of the Virginia was unnecessary and improper, Mr. Mallory should have waived the calling of a court-martial, forgotten what was due to the public interest on such a finding as that made by the preliminary court, and expressed himself satisfied to let the matter rest. The fact is indisputable, that the court-martial, which afterwards sat in the case, was called at the demand of Commodore Tatnall himself. It resulted in his acquittal.

The evacuation of Norfolk was the occasion of great distress to its population. But it was the part of a wise policy, that our military lines should be contracted and that the troops of Gen. Huger should be consolidated with the army before Richmond.

The retreat from Yorktown to the Chickahominy was marked by spirited incidents and by one important engagement. McClellan becoming, through an accident, aware of the movement of General Johnston, immediately pursued our columns which recoiled on him at Williamsburg, on the 5th of May and drove back his army. During the whole of that day, General Longstreet's division, which brought up the rear, was engaged with the enemy from sunrise to sunset. The day was marked by signal successes, for we captured three hundred and fifty prisoners, took nine pieces of artillery, and left on the field, in killed and wounded, at least three thousand of the enemy. During the night our army resumed its movement towards Richmond, and half an hour after sunrise it had evacuated the town, under the necessity of leaving our killed and wounded in the hands of the enemy.

The following day, the insolence of the enemy was again checked on the route of our retreat. On the 7th of May he attempted a landing, under cover of his gunboats, at Barhamsville, near West Point. The attempt was ineffectual. The Yankees were driven back, after they had assaulted our position three different times—the last time being forced to the cover of their gunboats by the brave Texans of General Whiting's division, who, in the face of an artillery fire, pressed the fugitives so closely that many were driven into the river and drowned.

The investment of the lines of the Chickahominy brought the two opposing armies within sight of Richmond. After a desultory military experience, a useless and inglorious march to Manassas, a long delay on the banks of the Potomac and Chesapeake, and a vague abandonment of these lines for operations on the Peninsula, McClellan, who was the "Napoleon" of the Democratic party of the North, but a slow and contemptible blunderer in the estimation of the Republicans, found himself, by the fortune of circumstances, within sight of the steeples and spires of the long-sought capital of the Confederacy.

The proximity of the enemy was an occasion of great anxiety to the people of Richmond, and the visible tremor of the Confederate authorities in that city was not a spectacle calculated either to nerve the army or assure the citizens. The fact is, that the Confederate authorities had shamefully neglected the defences of Richmond, and were now making preparations to leave it, which were called prudent, but which naturally inspired a panic such as had never before been witnessed in the history of the war. The destruction of the Virginia had left the water avenue to Richmond almost undefended. The City Council had for months been urging upon the Confederate Government the necessity of obstructing the river, and failing to induce them to hurry on the work, had, with patriotic zeal undertaken it themselves. A newspaper in Richmond—th *Examiner*—had in good time pointed out the necessity of obstructing the river with stone, but the counsel was treated with such conceit and harshness by the government, that it was only at the risk of its existence that that paper continued for weeks to point out the insecurity of Richmond and the omissions of its authorities. The government was at last aroused to a sense of danger only to fall to work in ridiculous haste, and with the blindness of alarm. The appearance of the Yankee gunboats in James river was the signal for Mr. Secretary Mallory to show his alacrity in meeting the enemy by an advertisement for "timber" to construct new naval defences. The only obstruction between the city and the dread Monitor and the gunboats was a half-finished fort at Drewry's Bluff, which mounted four guns. Some of the Confederate officers had taken a "gunboat panic," for the line of stone obstructions in the river was not yet complete. They seized upon schooners at the wharves loaded with plaster of paris, guano, and other valuable cargoes, carried them to points where they supposed the passage of the river was to be contested, and in some instances sunk them in the wrong places.

There is no doubt that about this time the authorities of the Confederate States had nigh despaired of the safety of Richmond. The most urgent appeals had been made to Congress by the press and the people to continue its session in Richmond while the crisis impended. But its members refused to give this mark of confidence to the government, or to make any sacrifice of their selfish considerations for the moral encouragement of their constituents. They had adjourned in haste and left Richmond, regarding only the safety of their persons or the convenience of their homes.

Nor was the Executive more determined. In the President's mansion about this time all was consternation and dismay. A letter written by one of his family at a time when Richmond was thought to be imminently threatened, and intercepted by the enemy, afforded excessive merriment to the Yankees, an made a painful exhibition to the South of the weakness and fears of those intrusted with its fortunes. This letter, written with refreshing simplicity of heart, overflowed with pitiful

sympathy for the President, and amused the enemy with references to the sore anxieties of " Uncle Jeff." and to the prospect
of his sinking under the misfortunes of his administration.
The authenticity of this letter was never called into question
it is a painful and delicate historical evidence, but one to
which, in the interests of truth, allusion should not be spared.*

---

* The following is a portion of the letter referred to. The reflections which
it makes upon the courage of our noble, suffering soldiers were probably hasty,
and may be spared here :

. . . . "When I think of the dark gloom that now hovers over our
country, I am ready to sink with despair. There is a probability of General
Jackson's army falling back on Richmond, and in view of this, no lady is allowed
to go up on the railroad to Gordonsville for fear, if allowed to one, that many
others would wish to do it, which would incommode the army.

General Johnston is falling back from the Peninsula, or Yorktown, and Uncle
Jeff. *thinks we had better go to a safer place than Richmond.*

We have not decided yet where we shall go, but I think to North Carolina, to
some far off country town, or, perhaps, to South Carolina. If Johnston falls
back as far as Richmond, all our troops from Gordonsville and "Swift Run Gap"
will also fall back to this place, and make one desperate stand against McClellan.
If you will look at the map, you will see that the Yankees are approaching
Richmond from three different directions—from Fredericksburg, Harrisonburg,
and Yorktown. O God ! defend this people with thy powerful arm, is my
constant prayer. Oh, mother, Uncle Jeff. is miserable. He tries to be cheerful,
and bear up against such a continuation of troubles, but, oh, I fear he cannot
live long, if he does not get some rest and quiet.

Our reverses distressed him so much, and he is so weak and feeble, it makes
my heart ache to look at him. He knows that he ought to send his wife and
children away, and yet he cannot bear to part with them, and we all dread to
leave him too. Varina and I had a hard cry about it to-day.

Oh ! what a blow the fall of New Orleans was. It liked to have set us all
crazy here. Everybody looks depressed, and the cause of the Confederacy looks
drooping and sinking ; but if God is with us, who can be against us ? Our troops
are not doing as well as we expected . . . . The regiments that
are most apt to run are from North Carolina and Tennessee. I am thankful to
say that the Mississippi and Louisiana troops behave gloriously whenever called
on to fight.

Uncle Jeff. thinks you are safe at home, as *there will be no resistance at Vicksburg,*
and the Yankees will hardly occupy it ; and, even if they did, the army would
gain nothing by marching into the country, and a few soldiers would be afraid
to go so far into the interior.

P. S. We all leave here to-morrow morning for Raleigh. Three gunboats
are in James river, on their way to the city, and may probably reach here in a
few hours ; so we have no longer any time to delay. *I only hope that we have not
delayed too long already.* I shall then be cut off from all communication with
———, and I expect to have no longer any peace.

I will write again from Raleigh, and Fanny must write me a letter and direct
it to Raleigh ; perhaps I may get it. I am afraid that Richmond will fall into

It is true that President Davis, when invited by the Legislature of Virginia to express his intentions towards Richmond, had declared that he entertained the prospect of holding it. But his reply was full of embarrassment. While he declared his intention not to surrender the city, he at the same time suggested the fanciful possibility, that even with the loss of Richmond our struggle for independence might be protracted for many years in the mountains of Virginia. In the mean time, the acts of the Confederate officials gave visible and unmistakable signs of their sense of the insecurity of the capital. They added to the public alarm by preparations to remove the archives. They ran off their wives and children into the country. They gave the public every reason to believe that Richmond was to become the prey of the enemy, and the catastrophe was awaited with lively alarm, or dull and melancholy expectation.

In the early weeks of May the capital of the Confederacy presented many strange and humiliating spectacles. The air was filled with those rumors of treason and disloyalty which seem invariably to grow out of a sense of insecurity. Men who had been loudest in their professions of resistance and self-devotion when the Yankees were at a distance, were now engaged in secreting their property, and a few openly flattered themselves that they had not committed themselves in the war in a way to incur the enemy's resentment. Some of them had their cellars packed with manufactured tobacco. The railroad trains were crowded with refugees. At every extortioner's shop on Main street, even including the bookstores, an array of packing trunks invited attention, and suggested the necessity of flight from Richmond. At the railroad depots were to be seen piles of baggage, awaiting transportation. But the most abundant and humiliating signs of the panic were to be seen

the hands of the enemy, as there is no way to keep back the gunboats. James river is so high that all obstructions are in danger of being washed away; so that there is no help for the city. She will either submit or else be shelled, and I think the latter alternative will be resorted to.

Uncle Jeff. was confirmed last Tuesday in St. Paul's Church by Bishop Johns. He was baptized at home in the morning before church.

Do try to get a letter to me some way. Direct some to Raleigh and some to Richmond.   Yours, ever devotedly,
                                                    —— ——."

in the number of pine boxes about the departments ticketed "Columbia, South Carolina," and which contained the most valuable of the public archives.

In this condition of the public mind, a new appeal was made to it. When it was ascertained that the Monitor, Galena, and Aristook, were about to head for Richmond, the Legislature of Virginia passed resolutions calling upon the Confederate authorities to defend it to the last extremity, and to make choice of its destruction rather than that of surrender to the enemy. This resolution was worthy of the noble State of Virginia, and of a people who were the descendants of Washington's contemporaries, of Hampden's friends, and of King John's barons. Its terms were too explicit to admit of any doubt in their construction, or any wavering on the part of the Confederate authorities. They expressed the desire that Richmond should be defended to the last extremity, and declared that "the President be assured, that whatever destruction or loss of property of the State or individuals shall thereby result, will be cheerfully submitted to."

The resolutions of the Legislature were responded to in meetings of citizens. The magical effects of the spirit which they created will long be remembered in Richmond. The Confederate authorities were stimulated by the brave lesson; inert and speculative patriotism was aroused to exertion, mutual inspiration of courage and devotion passed from heart to heart through the community, and with the restoration of public confidence, came at last vigorous preparations. The James was rapidly filled up, the works at Drewry's Bluff were strengthened, and a steady defiance offered to the Yankee gunboats, which had appeared within a few miles of the city at a moment when the last gap in our river obstructions was filled up by a scuttled schooner.

On the 15th of May, the fleet of Yankee gunboats in the James opened an attack on our batteries at Drewry's Bluff. The sound of the guns was heard in the streets of Richmond, and various and uncertain reports of the fortunes of the contest agitated the public. In the midst of the excitement, an extraordinary scene occurred in the city. A meeting of citizens had been called at the City Hall on an accidental occasion, and at the enthusiastic call of the crowd, impromptu addresses

were made by the Governor of Virginia and the Mayor of the
city.   Each of these officials pledged his faith that Rich
mond should never be surrendered.   Gov. Letcher declared,
with a peculiar warmth of expression, that if the demand was
made upon him, with the alternative to surrender or be shelled,
he should reply, "bombard and be d——d."   Mayor Mayo
was not less determined in the language which he addressed to
the citizens.   He told them that even if they were to require
him to surrender the Capital of Virginia and of the Confederacy, he would, sooner than comply, resign the mayoralty;
and that, despite his age, he still had the nerve and strength
to shoulder a musket in defence of the city founded by one or
his ancestors.   These fervid declarations were responded to by
the citizens with wild and ringing shouts.   Nor were these the
demonstrations of a mob.   Among those who so enthusiastically approved the resolution of consigning Richmond to the
flames rather than to the possession of the enemy, were some
of the most wealthy and respectable citizens of the place,
whose stakes of property in the city were large, and whose
beautiful homes were exposed to the shot and shell of the
malignant foe.

The night brought the news of a signal victory.   Our batteries, under the skilful command of Capt. Farrand, had, after a
contest of four hours and a half, given a decisive repulse to
the gunboats, with the inconsiderable loss of five killed and
seven wounded.   The accuracy of our fire had astonished the
enemy, and carried dismay through his fleet.   Eighteen shots
went through the sides of the Galena, according to the enemy's
own account; and this river monster lost thirty of her crew in
killed and wounded.   Seventeen men were killed on another
of the boats by the explosion of a gun.   The boats had been
unable to advance in the face of the accurate and deadly fire
of our artillerists, and the next day they had dropped down
the stream, quite satisfied of the impracticability of the water
approach to Richmond.

Regarding all the circumstances in which this action had
taken place, there is no extravagance in saying, that the scale
of the war was turned in our favor by even so small an affair
as that of Drewry's Bluff.   It exploded the fanciful theories
of the enemy's invincibility on the water and went far to

assure the safety of the now closely threatened capital of the Confederacy.

But there were other causes about this time which conspired to renew the popular confidence in our arms, and to swell with gratitude and hope the hearts which had so long throbbed with anxiety in our besieged capital. We shall see how, for some time, at least, the safety of Richmond was trusted, not so much to the fortunes of the forces that immediately protected it, as to the splendid diversion of the heroic Jackson in the Valley of Virginia. To this famous expedition public attention was now turned, in the North as well as in the South, and its almost marvellous results, with marked unanimity, were ascribed to the zeal, heroism, and genius of its commander alone.

JACKSON'S CAMPAIGN IN THE VALLEY.

On the change of our military lines in Virginia, and the rapid shifting of the scene of active hostilities from the Potomac, Gen. Jackson had been assigned with a small force to guard the Valley of Virginia, and the approaches in that direction, to the armies of the enemy which enveloped Richmond.

Our first success was obtained in the upper portion of the Valley. On the morning of the 8th of May, our forces had approached the position of Milroy, the Yankee commander at McDowell. The brigade of General Johnson had secured an advantageous position on a hill, and the enemy, fearful of being surrounded, decided at last, after some signs of hesitation, to deliver battle. The action was not joined until about two hours of sunset. The fact was, that we engaged the enemy with not more than one-third of his own numbers, which were about twelve thousand. But the contest was easily decided by the brave troops of Johnson's brigade, composed of Virginia volunteers, with the 12th Georgia regiment. They had stood for nearly two hours, receiving with composed courage the cross-fire of the enemy's artillery; and then, as the sun was sinking, they made the charge decisive of the day, and drove the enemy in consternation and utter rout from the field.

Our loss in this action was considerable. Of three hundred and fifty killed and wounded, nearly two-thirds were Georgians.

The troops of this State on other occasions than this had left monuments of their courage in the mountains of Virginia The loss of the enemy at McDowell exceeded that of the Con federates, and was conjectured to be double our own.

It was probably at the suggestion of his own judgment, and at the instance of his own military instincts, that Gen. Jackson determined to act on the aggressive, and to essay the extraordinary task of driving the Yankees from the Valley. In pursuance of this determination, his resolution was quickly taken to make a dash at Fremont's advance, west of Staunton, and then to turn upon Banks with the adventurous purpose of driving him into Maryland.

Gen. Banks, one of the military pets of the more truculent party of the abolitionists, had entered Virginia with the airs of a conqueror. As early as the 24th of April he had telegraphed to his government the story of uninterrupted and triumphant progress; he announced that he had "advarced near Harrisonburg;" and, with a characteristic flourish, he added: "The rebel Jackson has abandoned the Valley of Virginia permanently, and is *en route* for Gordonsville by the way of the mountains."

The first intimation the obtuse Yankee general had of his mistake was the astounding news that reached him on the evening of May 23d, that the "rebel Jackson" had descended on the guard at Front Royal, Col. Kenly, 1st Maryland regiment, commanding, burned the bridges, driven the Federal troops towards Strasburg with great loss, captured a section of artillery, and taken about fourteen hundred prisoners.

It was now Banks's turn to betake himself to flight, or, in the official circumlocution of that commander, "to enter the lists with the enemy in a race or a battle, as he should choose, for the possession of Winchester, the key of the Valley." But he was not destined to reach his promised haven of security without disaster.

On the day following the sudden apparition of Jackson at Front Royal, the untiring commander had by a rapid movement succeeded in piercing Banks's main column while retreating from Strasburg to Winchester; the rear, including a body of the celebrated Zouaves d'Afrique, retreating towards Strasburg.

The Yankee general reached Winchester only to find fresh causes of alarm. The people of that ancient town, already sure of their deliverance, received the Yankees with shouts of derision and defiant cheers for Jackson. Some Confederate officers came into the enemy's camp with entire unconcern, supposing that their own troops occupied the town as a matter of course, and when captured gave the Yankees the delightful assurance that an attack would be made by the terrible Jackson at daybreak.

On the 25th of May, Gen. Jackson gave the crowning stroke to the rapid movements of the past two days by attacking Winchester and driving out the cowardly enemy almost without resistance. Gen. Banks speaks of his retreat with a shameless-ness that is at once simple and refreshing. He says, " Pursuit by the enemy was prompt and vigorous; but our movements were rapid ;" and he writes to the authorities at Washington of his crossing of the Potomac : " There never were more grateful hearts in the same number of men than when at mid-day on the 30th of May, we stood on the opposite shore." He had escaped with the loss of all the material and paraphernalia that constitute an army. He had abandoned at Winchester all his commissary and ordnance stores. He had resigned that town and Front Royal to the undisputed possession of the Confederates. He had left in their hands four thousand prisoners, and stores amounting to millions of dollars. And all these prizes had been obtained by the Confederates in the brief period of a few days, and with a loss not exceeding one hundred in killed and wounded.

When General Jackson fell back from Winchester, after routing Banks, he managed, with great address, boldness, and energy, to carry off his prisoners and spoils, and to bring off his army between the converging columns of Fremont, who approached his rear from the west, with eight brigades, and Shields, who approached from the east, with four brigades. If these brigades averaged twenty-five hundred men, the force of Fremont was twenty thousand and that of Shields ten thousand men. At Harrisonburg, Jackson left the main turn-pike-road of the Valley and marched towards Port Republic, the distance between these two places being about twelve miles. Port Republic is situated at the junction of South river, flow-

ing north, and North river, flowing east. Jackson could retire
no further without crossing North river, which was swollen,
and there was then no bridge over it except at Port Republic.
The two rivers uniting at that village form the Shenandoah,
which flows north, and which could not then be crossed by an
army.   On the east side of that stream was the army of Shields,
and on the west side were the armies of Fremont and Jackson.
The latter halted near North river without crossing it, and,
while in that position, his rear was approached and attacked
by Fremont's whole army, on the morning of Sunday, the 8th
of June, and, at the same time, Shields' force approached on
the east side of the Shenandoah near Port Republic.

That part of Jackson's army which engaged Fremont on
Sunday was commanded by General Ewell, while the rest of
the army under General Jackson held Shields in check with
artillery firing across the Shenandoah near Port Republic.
The battle of Sunday took place about five miles from that
village in the direction of Harrisonburg.

It began early in the morning and lasted all day, with occasional intervals.   It was mainly an artillery fight, but now and
then, here and there, the infantry became hotly engaged.
The force under Fremont was much larger than that under
Ewell, but the latter was strongly posted on eminences which
favored the effectiveness of artillery, and sheltered the infantry,
while the enemy could only approach through open fields.
Ewell's command was handled with remarkable skill, while
Fremont's generalship was indifferent.   Ewell's artillery was
served with admirable precision and effect, and his infantry,
whenever engaged, displayed great steadiness and gallantry.
The result was, that when night put an end to the contest,
Fremont had been driven back between one and two miles, with
a loss, in killed and wounded, of not less than two thousand,
and probably much larger, while our loss did not exceed three
hundred, and probably not two hundred.   The judicious selection of a position in which to receive the enemy favored this
result, but it was largely due to the superior fighting qualities
of our men.

Soon after nightfall, General Jackson began to withdraw
his men from this battle-field, and pass them over North river
by the bridge at Port Republic, with a view to attack Shields

the next morning. He left in front of Fremont a small force to amuse and detain him, and, after retiring before him to Port Republic, to burn the bridge behind him, and thus to prevent Fremont from rendering any aid to Shields. All this was accomplished.

On Monday morning, Jackson passed the greater part of his army across the South river (the smallest of the streams) by means of a bridge made of planks laid on wagons placed in the river. Early in the morning a sufficient number had crossed to commence the battle, and they were led to the field between one and two miles distant, on the east bank of the Shenandoah. The enemy's force was found drawn up awaiting the attack.

The enemy's line extended from the river about half a mile across a flat bottom, free from timber, and covered with wheat, grass, &c. His left rested on the point of a low ridge coming out from the woods which skirt the bottom. On a slight elevation there and in some small knolls in the bottom, he had his artillery commanding the road and the wide uncovered level plain, over which Jackson's army was obliged to advance. The level and exposed ground offered scarcely any suitable position for planting our artillery. The advantage of position belonged altogether to the enemy. The capital fault of his disposition for battle was that the battery on his extreme left was posted near the woods without any infantry in the woods to defend it. By availing himself of this circumstance, and by a brilliant manœuvre and charge, Jackson turned the fortune of the day at a critical moment.

For some two hours the battle raged with great fury. Our infantry, at first but few, advanced with marvellous intrepidity in the face of a withering fire of artillery and musketry. At one moment the enemy advanced a section of a battery several hundred yards, so as to enfilade our left wing, which already suffered terribly from the fire in front. It seemed that nothing could withstand the fury of the enemy's fire of all arms. His artillery was very fine, and was served with great effect by regulars. But other troops coming at double quick from Port Republic, came on the field, and, at the same time, the Louisiana brigade, under Taylor, emerged from the woods on the enemy's left. They had been sent by a considerable circuit through the woods, which extend all along the battle-field be tween the cleared ground and the neighboring mountain. By a slight error of direction they came out of the woods a little too soon, and found themselves almost in front of the battery. which instantly began to shower grape upon them. But, im- mediately rectifying their direction, they charged the battery with irresistible impetuosity, and carried it. The contest then was speedily ended. The enemy's whole line gave way and was presently retreating in disorder, pursued by our cavalry. The pursuit was kept up about ten or twelve miles, but the flight continued all that day and the next. About five hun- dred prisoners were taken that day, and others after that were brought in daily. The loss of the enemy in killed and wounded was heavy, and so was our own. Six splendid cannon were captured on the field, another was taken in the pursuit, and still another had been captured on Sunday. The force of the enemy engaged was about six or seven thousand, and ours a little larger. Shields was not present, but his troops were com manded by Gen. Tyler.

After the rout of the enemy had commenced, the last of our troops crossed over the bridge at Port Republic and burnt it. Fremont, cautiously following, appeared some time afterwards, and drew up his army in line of battle on the heights along the west bank of the Shenandoah, from which he overlooked the field of battle. While he stood there in impotent idleness, Jackson's army, having finally disposed of Shields, moved off at leisure to Brown's Gap, and there encamped, to rest for a few days from the fatigues of a month's campaign more ardu- ous and more successful than any month's operations of the war. The exhaustion of our men and the interposition of a river, no longer bridged, secured Fremont from a second bat- tle or a hasty flight. The next day he commenced his retreat down the Valley.

This famous campaign must, indeed, take a rank in the his- tory of the war, unrivalled by any other in the rapidity of its movements and in the brilliancy of the results accomplished, compared with the means at its command. Its heroic deeds revived the hopes of the South, and threw the splendor of sun- light over the long lines of the Confederate host. By a series of rapid movements, which occupied but a few weeks, General

Jackson had, with inferior numbers, defeated successively four generals, with as many armies, swept the Valley of Virginia of hostile forces, made the Federal authorities tremble in their capital, and frustrated the combinations by which the enemy had purposed to aid General McClellan and environ Richmond by large converging armies.

Our loss of life in this campaign was inconsiderable in numbers; but on the black list of killed, there was one name conspicuous throughout the Confederacy, and especially dear to Virginians. Colonel Turner Ashby, whose name was linked with so much of the romance of the war, and whose gentle and enthusiastic courage and knightly bearing had called to mind the recollections of chivalry, and adorned Virginia with a new chaplet of fame, had, on the 5th of June, fallen in a skirmish near Harrisburg.

"The last time I saw Ashby," writes a noble comrade in arms, Colonel Bradley T. Johnson of the Maryland Line, "he was riding at the head of the column with General Ewell—his black face in a blaze of enthusiasm. Every feature beamed with the joy of the soldier. He was gesticulating and pointing out the country and positions to General Ewell. I could imagine what he was saying by the motions of his right arm. I pointed him out to my adjutant. 'Look a Ashby; see how he is enjoying himself.'"

A few hours later, and the brave Virginian, so full of life, was a corpse. Our men had fallen upon a body of the enemy concealed in a piece of woods and under the cover of a fence. Ashby was on the right of the 58th Virginia. He implored the men to stop their fire, which was ineffectual, and to charge the enemy. They were too much excited to heed him, and turning towards the enemy he waved his hand—"Virginians, charge!" In a second his horse fell. He was on his feet in an instant. "Men," he cried, "cease firing—charge, for God's sake, charge!" The next instant he fell dead—not twenty yards from the concealed marksman who had killed him.

To the sketch we have briefly given of this campaign, it is just to add one word of reflection. It had been frequently and very unwarrantably asserted that the people of what was once the garden spot of the South, the Shenandoah Valley, were favorably inclined to the Union cause, and that many of them had shown a very decided spirit of disloyalty to the Confed erate authority. The best refutation of this slander is to be found in the enemy's own accounts of his experiences in that region.

The fact is, that the people of this Valley had suffered to a most extraordinary degree the fiery trials and ravages of war. Their country had been bandied about from the possession of the Confederates to that of the Yankees, and then back again, until it had been stripped of every thing by needy friends on the one side, and unscrupulous invaders on the other. Some portions of the country were actually overrun by three armies in two weeks. In such circumstances there were, no doubt, expressions of discontent, which had been hastily misinter- preted as disloyal demonstrations ; but, despite these, there is just reason to believe that a spirit of patriotism and integrity abided in the Valley of Virginia, and that it had been main- tained under trials and chastisements much greater than those which had befallen other parts of the Confederacy.

MEMOIR OF TURNER ASHBY.

The writer had proposed a record in another and more ex- tensive form of the principal events of the life of Turner Ashby ; but the disappointment of assistance to sources of information from persons who had represented themselves as the friends of the deceased, and from whom the writer had reason to expect willing and warm co-operation, has com- pelled him to defer the execution of his original and cherished purpose of giving to the public a worthy biography of one whose name is a source of immortal pride to the South, and an enduring ornament to the chivalry of Virginia. But the few incidents roughly thrown together here may have a certain interest. They give the key to the character of one of the most remarkable men of the war ; they afford an example to be emulated by our soldiers ; they represent a type of courage peculiarly Southern in its aspects ; and they add an unfading leaf to the chaplet of glory which Virginia has gathered on the blood-stained fields of the war.

It is not improper here to state the weight and significance given to the present revolution by the secession of Virginia It takes time for revolutions to acquire their meaning and proper significance. That which was commenced by the Cot ton States of the South, attained its growth, developed its purpose, and became instantly and thoroughly in earnest at the period when the *second secessionary movement*, inaugurated by Virginia, confronted the powers at Washington with its sublime spectacles.

Virginia did not secede in either the circumstances or sense in which the Cotton States had separated themselves from the Union. She did not leave the Union with delusive prospects of peace to comfort or sustain her. She did not secede in the sense in which separation from the Union was the primary object of secession. Her act of secession was subordinate ; she was called upon to oppose a practical and overt usurpation on the part of the Government at Washington in drawing its sword against the sovereignty of States and insisting on the right of coercion; to contest this her separation from the Union was necessary, and became a painful formality which could not be dispensed with.

A just and philosophical observation of events must find that in this second secessionary movement of the Southern States the revolution was put on a basis infinitely higher and firmer in all its moral and constitutional aspects; that at this period it developed itself, acquired its proper significance, and was broadly translated into a war of liberty. The movement of Virginia had more than any thing else added to the moral influences of the revolution and perfected its justification in the eyes of the world. It was plain that she had not seceded on an issue of policy, but one of distinct and practical constitutional right, and that, too, in the face of a war which frowned upon her own borders, and which necessarily was to make her soil the principal theatre of its ravages and woes. Her attach- ment to the Union had been proved by the most untiring and noble efforts to save it; her Legislature originated the Peace Conference, which assembled at Washington in February 1861; her representatives in Congress sought in that body every mode of honorable pacification ; her Convention sent delegates to Washington to persuade Mr. Lincoln to a pacific policy ; and in every form of public assembly, every expedient of negotiation was essayed to save the Union. When these efforts at pacification, which Virginia had made with an unselfishness without parallel, and with a nobility of spirit that scorned any misrepresentation of her office, proved abortive, she did not hesitate to draw her sword in front of the enemy, and to devote all she possessed and loved and hoped for to the fortunes of the war. It is not necessary to recount at length the services of this ancient Commonwealth in the war for Southern independence. She furnished nearly all of the arms, ammunition, and accoutrements that won the early battles; she gave the Confederate service, from her own armories and stores, seventy-five thousand rifles and muskets, nearly three hundred pieces of artillery, and a magnificent armory, containing all the machinery necessary for manufacturing arms on a large scale; and on every occasion she replied to the call for troops, until she drained her arms-bearing population to the dregs.

It is a circumstance of most honorable remark, that such has been the conduct of Virginia in this war, that even from the base and vindictive enemy tributes have been forced to the devoted courage and heroic qualities of her sons. The following extraordinary tribute from the Washington *Republican*, the organ of abolition at the Yankee capital, is a compliment more expressive than any thing a Virginian could say for his own State and its present generation of heroes.

"If there has been any decadence of the manly virtues in the Old Dominion, it is not because the present generation has proved itself either weak or cowardly or unequal to the greatest emergencies. No people, with so few numbers, ever put into the field, and kept there so long, troops more numerous, brave, or more efficient, or produced generals of more merit, in all the kinds and grades of military talent. It is not a worn-out, effete race which has produced Lee, Johnston, Jackson, Ashby, and Stuart. It is not a worn-out and effete race, which, for two years, has defended its capital against the approach of an enemy close upon their borders, and outnumbering them thirty to one. It is not a worn-out and effete race which has preserved substantial popular unity under all the straits and pressure and sacrifices of this unprecedented war. 'Let history,' as was said of another race, 'which records their unhappy fate as a people, do justice to their rude virtues as men.' They are fighting madly in a bad cause, but they are fighting bravely

They have few cowards and no traitors. The hardships of war are endured without a murmur by all classes, and the dangers of war without flinching, by the newest conscripts; while their gentry, the offshoot of their popular social system, have thrown themselves into the camp and field with all the dash and high spirit of the European *noblesse* of the middle ages, risking, without apparent concern, upon a desperate adventure, all that men value; and after a generation of peace and repose and security, which had not emasculated them, presenting to their enemies a trained and intrepid front, as of men born and bred to war."

What has been said here of Virginia and her characteristics in the present revolution, is the natural and just preface to what we have to say of the man who, more than any one else in this war, illustrated the chivalry of the Commonwealth and the virtues of her gentry. Turner Ashby was a thorough Virginian. He was an ardent lover of the old Union. He was brought up in that conservative and respectable school of politics which hesitated long to sacrifice a Union which had been, in part, constructed by the most illustrious of the sons of Virginia; which had conferred many honors upon her; and which was the subject of many hopes in the future. But when it became evident that the life of the Union was gone, and the sword was drawn for constitutional liberty, the spirit of Virginia was again illustrated by Ashby, who showed a devotion in the field even more admirable than the virtue of political principles.

Turner Ashby was the second son of the late Colonel Turner Ashby, of "Rose Bank," Fauquier county, and Dorothea F. Green, the daughter of the late James Green, Sr., of Rappahannock county. Colonel Ashby, at his death, left three sons and three daughters—the eldest of whom did not exceed twelve years of age at the time of his death—to the sole care of their devoted mother. To her excellent sense, generous disposition, and noble character, the Confederacy is indebted for two as noble and gallant men as have won soldiers' graves during this war.

The father of Turner Ashby was the sixth son, that reached manhood, of Captain Jack Ashby, a man of mark in the day in which he lived, and of whom many anecdotes are still extant, illustrative of his remarkable character. One of these belongs to the colonial times, and is interesting :

" When the news of the disastrous defeat and death of General Braddock reached Fort Loudoun (now Winchester. Virginia), John Ashby was there, and his celebrity as a horseman induced the British commandant of the post to secure his services as bearer of dispatches to the vice-royal governor at Williamsburg. Ashby at once proceeded on his mission, and in an incredibly short time presented himself before the commander at Fort Loudoun. This official, of choleric disposition, upon the appearance of Ashby, broke out in severe reproach for his delay in proceeding on his mission, and was finally struck dumb with astonishment at the presentation of the governor's reply to the dispatch ! The ride is said to have been accomplished in the shortest possible time, and the fact is certified in the records of Frederick county court."

Upon the breaking out of the Revolution of 1776, Captain Jack Ashby raised a company in his neighborhood in the upper part of Fauquier. It was attached to the third Virginia regiment, under command of General Marshall. He was in the battles of Brandywine, Germantown, and several other of the most desperately contested fields of the Revolution. From exposure and hardships endured upon the frontiers of Canada, he contracted disease, from which he was never entirely relieved to the day of his death. He continued in the service during the whole period of the Revolution, and after the proclamation of peace, quietly settled upon his beautiful farm not far from Markham station, upon the Manassas Gap railroad. Four of his sons, John, Samuel, Nimrod, and Thomson, served in the war of 1812.

The father of our hero died, as we have stated, leaving a family of children of tender age. Young Turner was put to school, where it does not appear that he showed any peculiar trait in his studies ; but he was remarkable among his young associates for his sedate manners, his grave regard for truth, and his appreciation of points of honor.

Turner Ashby never had the advantages of a college education, but he had a good, healthy mind ; he was an attentive student of human nature, and a convenient listener where information was to be gained ; and he possessed those ordinary stores of knowledge which may be acquired by a moderate use of books and an attentive intercourse with men. He was engaged for some time in merchandise at Markham's Depot. The old homestead of his father still stands near there, and not far from the homestead of the Marshalls. The tastes of Ashby were too domestic for politics. He was at one time Whig candidate for the Virginia Legislature from Fauquier, but was defeated by a small majority. This was his only public appearance in any political strife, and but little else is known of him as a politician beyond his ardent admiration of and personal attachment to Robert E. Scott.

Ashby's attachment to domestic life was enlivened by an extreme fondness for manly pastimes. He was a horseman from very childhood, and had the greatest passion for equestrian exercises. His delight in physical excitements was singularly pure and virtuous; he shunned the dissipations fashionable among young men, and while so sober and steady in his habits as sometimes to be a joke among his companions, yet he was the foremost in all innocent sports, the first to get up tournaments and fox-chases, and almost always the successful competitor in all manly games. His favorite horse was trained for tournaments and fox-hunting, and it is said to have been a common pastime of Ashby to take him into the meadow and jump him over hay-cocks and stone fences. Some of his feats of horsemanship are memorable, and are constantly related in his neighborhood. While at Fauquier Springs, which he frequently visited, and where he got up tournaments after the fashion of the ancient chivalry, he once displayed his horsemanship by riding into the ball-room, up and down steep flights of steps, to the mingled terror and admiration of the guests. No cavalier was more graceful. The reserve of his manner was thrown aside in such sports, and his black eyes and dark face were lighted up with the zeal of competition or. the excitement of danger.

The gravity so perceptible at times in Ashby's manner was not the sign of a melancholy or blank mind. He was too practical for reveries; he was rather a man of deep feelings. While he scorned the vulgar and shallow ambition that seeks for notoriety, he probably had that ideal and aspiration which *silent* men often have, and which, if called " ambition" at all is to be characterized as the noble and spiritual ambition that wins the honors of history, while others contend for the baubles of the populace.

"He was," writes a lady of his neighborhood, "a person of very deep feelings, which would not have been apparent to strangers, from his natural reserve of manner; but there was no act of friendship or kindness he would have shrunk to perform, if called on. While he was not a professor of religion, there was always a peculiar regard for the precepts of the Bible, which showed itself in his irreproachable walk in life. Often have I known him to open the Sabbath school at the request of his lady friends, in a little church near his home, by reading a prayer and a chapter in the Bible. Turner Ashby seldom left his native neighborhood, so strong were his local attachments, and would not have done so, save at his country'e call."

That call was sounded sooner than Ashby expected. At the first prelude to the bloody drama of the war—the John Brown raid—he had been conspicuous, and his company of horse then called "The Mountain Rangers," did service on that occasion. He appeared to have felt and known the consequences which were to ensue from this frightful crusade. Thenceforward his physical and intellectual powers were directed to the coming struggle. On the occasion of the irruption of John Brown and his felon band at Harper's Ferry, he remarked to Mr. Boteler, the member of Congress from that district, that a crisis was approaching, and that the South would be continually subject to such inroads and insults, unless some prevention was quickly effected. He continued, however, a strong Union man until the election of Lincoln: he was anxious that harmony should be effected between the States, and the legacies of the past should be preserved in a constitutional and fraternal Union; but this hope was instantly dispelled by the result of the election; and as soon as it was announced, he went quietly and energetically to work, drilling his men, promoting their efficiency, and preparing for that great trial of arms which he saw rapidly approaching.

The next time that Mr. Boteler met Ashby at Harper's Ferry was on the night of the 17th of April, 1861. Mr. Boteler took him aside, and said to him, " What flag are we going to fight under—the Palmetto, or what?" Ashby lifted his hat, and within it was laid a Virginia flag. He had had it painted at midnight, before he left Richmond. "Here," said he, "is the flag I intend to fight under." That night the flag was run up by the light of the burning buildings fired by the Yankees and the next morning the glorious emblem of the Old Domin ion was seen floating from the Federal flag-staff—the first ensign of liberty raised by Virginia in this war.

It was not long after the arrival of Capt. Ashby at Harper's Ferry, with his cavalry, that he was placed in command at Point of Rocks, by Gen. Johnston, supported by Capt. R. Welby Carter's company of cavalry and Capt. John Q. Winfield's infantry corps of "Brock's Gap Riflemen."

About the same time Col. Angus W. McDonald, senior, of Winchester, Virginia, was commissioned to raise a legion of mounted men for border service, the lieutenant-colonelcy of which was at once tendered to Capt. Ashby. Without final acceptance of this position, he, with his command, entered the legion, the organization of which was soon accomplished.

The original captains were Ashby, Winfield, S. W. Myers Mason, Shands, Jordan, Miller, Harper, and Sheetz.

This force was assembled at Romney, Hampshire county, very soon after the evacuation of Harper's Ferry by Gen. Johnston.

The difficulty which existed as to Capt. Ashby's acceptance of the lieutenant-colonelcy of the legion, consisted in the fact that he felt under special obligations to his company, who were unwilling to dispense with his personal command. The arrival of his brother, Richard Ashby, from Texas, who joined the company as an independent volunteer, appeared to open the way of relieving this difficulty, as the company was prepared to accept in him a captain, in order to secure the promotion of their beloved leader.

But a melancholy providence was to occur at this time, which was to color the life of Turner Ashby, and affect it more deeply than any thing he had yet experienced. The county of Hampshire had already been invaded by the enemy, and Colonel, now Major-general, A. P. Hill had already visited the county with several regiments of infantry, in order to repel the invader. This county was also chosen for the labor of the mounted legion.

It was shortly after the organization of the command, ? ¸ ¸
its active duty entered upon, that Capt. Ashby led a detachment to Green Spring station, on the Baltimore and Ohio rail
road, for the purpose of observation. He had with him eleven
men, and his brother Richard led another small band of six.
The latter was proceeding along the railroad westward, in the
direction of Cumberland—some ten miles away—when he was
ambuscaded at the mouth of a ravine just beside the railroad
there, running just between the river bank and the steep mountain side. The enemy's force consisted of about eighteen men,
commanded by Corporal Hays, of the Indiana Zouave regiment, which was stationed at Cumberland. His men, at
length compelled to fall back before superior numbers, hastened down the railroad to rejoin Turner Ashby. Covering their
retreat himself, he hastened to the rescue of one of his men,
severely wounded in the face by a sabre stroke, and in a hand
to hand fight with Corporal Hays, severely wounded him in
the head with his sabre. Following immediately his retreating
companions, the horse which he rode proved false, and fell into
a cattle-stop of the railroad with his unfortunate rider. He
was overtaken, beaten, bruised, wounded, and left for dead.
He was removed many hours afterwards, and lived for several
days, enjoying every kind attention, but his wounds proved
mortal. He was buried in the beautiful Indian Mound Cemetery at Romney, on the 4th of July, 1861.

During the engagement of his brother, Turner Ashby started
up the railroad to his rescue; but in passing along the river's
brink, his force was fired upon from Kelly's Island, on the
north branch of the Potomac, about twelve miles east of Cum
berland. The island lies some sixty feet from the Virginia
bank, which is precipitous, and directly laid with the railroad
track. On the other side of the island, which was reached
through water to the saddle girth, there is a gently rising
beach, some thirty yards to the interior, which is thickly
wooded, and contains a dense undergrowth. Here in ambush
lay, as was afterwards reported, about forty of the Indiana
troops, and about sixty of Merley's branch riflemen—Maryland
Union men of the vicinity—woodmen, skilled with the rifle,
and many of them desperate characters. After receiving the
enemy's fire, Turner Ashby and his eleven at once charged,

and after a sharp engagement, routed and dispersed their forces. It has been declared that not less than forty shots were fired at Ashby on that occasion, but not he nor his horse were harmed and at least five of the enemy were probably slain by his hand.

From the date of his brother's death, a change passed over the life of Turner Ashby. He always wore a sad smile after that unhappy day, and his life became more solemn and earnest to the end of his own evanescent and splendid career. "Ashby," said a lady friend, speaking of him after this period, "is now a *devoted man*." His behavior at his brother's grave, as it is described by one of the mourners at the same spot, was most touching. He stood over the grave, took his brother's sword, broke it and threw it into the opening; clasped his hands and looked upward as if in resignation; and then pressing his lips, as if in the bitterness of grief, while a tear rolled down his cheek, he turned without a word, mounted his horse and rode away. Thenceforth his name was a terror to the enemy.

Shortly after the death of his brother, his company consented to yield him up in order that he might accept the lieutenant colonelcy of the Legion, and elected First Lieut. William Turner (his cousin) captain in his stead. The Legion, numbering at that time nearly nine hundred effective men tolerably equipped and mounted, continued on duty in Hampshire until the 16th of July, 1861, when it started for Manassas, but did not arrive until after the battle. The command was immediately afterwards ordered to Staunton to join Gen. Lee's forces— subsequently to Hollingsworth, one mile south of Winchester. In the mean time, Col. Ashby, with several companies, was sent on detached duty to Jefferson, into which county the enemy was making frequent incursions from Harper's Ferry and Maryland.

In Jefferson, Ashby had command of four companies of cavalry and about eight hundred militia. Yankee raids were kept from the doors of the inhabitants, and the enemy made but little appearance in this portion of Virginia, until Banks crossed the Potomac in February, 1862.

It was about this time that Ashby's cavalry acquired its great renown. The Lincoln soldiers dreaded nothing so much as they did these hated troopers. Go where they would, out of sight of their encampments, they were almost sure to meet some of Ashby's cavalry, who seemed to possess the power or ubiquity. And, in truth, they had good cause both to hate and to fear Ashby's cavalry; for many a Federal horseman dropped from his saddle, and many a Federal soldier on foot dropped in his tracks, at the crack of Confederate rifles in the hands of Ashby's fearless sharpshooters.

During the time of the encampment at Flowing Springs, Col. Ashby rarely ever came into town, which was about a mile and a half distant. Nothing could seduce him from his duties; no admiration, no dinner parties or collations, could move him to leave his camp. He always slept with his men. No matter what hour of the night he was aroused, he was always wakeful, self-possessed, and ready to do battle. He was idolized by his men, whom he treated as companions, and indulged without reference to rules of military discipline. He had great contempt for the military arts, was probably incapable of drilling a regiment, and preserved among his men scarcely any thing more than the rude discipline of camp-hunters But though not a stickler for military rules, he would have no coward or eye-soldier in his command. If a man was dissatisfied, he at once started him off home. He allowed his men many liberties. A gentleman asked him one day where his men were. "Well," said he, "the boys fought very well yesterday, and there are not more than thirty of them here to-day."

Ashby's influence over his men was principally due to the brilliant and amazing examples of personal courage which he always gave them in front of the battle. His men could never find him idle. In battle his eye kindled up most gloriously. He wore a gray coat and pants, with boots and sash; he always looked like work, was frequently covered with mud, and appeared to be never fatigued or dejected. He would come and go like a dream. He would be heard of at one time in one part of the country, and then, when least expected, would come dashing by on the famous white horse, which was his pride.

When the fight occurred at Boteler's Mill, the militia were for the first time under fire. The enemy had encamped on the other side of the Potomac, opposite the mill. Our troops quietly crept upon them, and planted two pieces of cannon within range, and let drive at them with terrible effect, whereupon they fled. They afterwards returned in force, and ranged themselves on the other side with long-range guns. Ashby, to encourage the militia, who were raw, advanced to the bank of the river, and rode his white horse up and down within point-blank range of the enemy's fire. When the balls were hurtling thickest, he would rein in his horse and stand perfectly still, the very picture of daring and chivalry.

At Bolivar Heights, when the enemy were firing upon our men and had shot down the gunners at the cannon, he sprang from his horse and seized the rammer himself. He was conspicuous in action at every point. His friends used to implore him not to ride his white horse—for he had also a black one—but he was deaf to every caution that respected the safety of his person.

The key to Ashby's character was his passion for danger. He craved the excitement of battle, and was never happier than when riding his noble steed in the thickest of the storm of battle. There are some minds which find a sweet intoxication in danger, and Macaulay has named a remarkable instance in William III., the silent and ascetic king of England, who was transformed into gayety by the excitement of personal peril. "Danger," says the historian, "acted upon him like wine;" it made him full of animation and speech. Ashby's delight in danger was a royal one. It came from no brutal hardihood or animal spirits; and the Virginia cavalier is thus so far superior to other famous partisans in this war, that he united with the adventurousness of courage the courtesies of a gentleman and Christian, and the refinements of a pure and gentle soul. He was never rude; he was insensible to the humors of the vulgar; and he never even threw into the face of his enemy a coarse taunt or a specimen of that wit common in the army.

Turner Ashby was doubtless as perfect a specimen of modern chivalry as the South even has ever produced. His brilliant daring, his extreme courtesy to woman, his devotion to the *horse*, his open-hearted manner, and his scorn of mean actions, are qualities as admirable now as in the days of Froissart's Chronicles. After the battle of Winchester, the Yankee women and families of officers sometimes came to Ashby to get passes. They were surprised to find with what readiness permits were granted. They would say, " Colonel Ashby, you may search our baggage. We assure you we are carrying away nothing which we are not at liberty to do." His reply was, "I have no right to look into ladies' baggage, or to examine their trunks. Southern gentlemen do no such thing." They said, " Colonel, you may search our persons, and see if we carry away any thing contraband." The reply was, " Virginia gentlemen do not search the persons of ladies."

Few young men of Ashby's age could have resisted the intoxication of praise heaped upon him from every quarter. The fact was, no aged and stern devotee to duty was ever more insensible, in the performance of his task, to the currents of popular favor than the young Paladin of the South. The following copy of a letter, written at the height of his reputation to an elderly gentleman of Stafford county, illustrates the modesty which adorned the life of Turner Ashby, and the sense of duty which insured its most brilliant successes :

"My dear Sir : I have just received your exceedingly kind and most flattering letter. Let me assure you that it gives me no little pleasure to know that my course, while doing my duty to my country, meets your approval, whose age and experience make it more to be estimated. That I have not sought self-aggrandizement, or regarded any thing save what I believed to be my duty to my country in this war, I hope it is needless to assure you. When my course meets with the approval of the old patriots, I feel doubly satisfied that I have not mistaken what I believe to be my duty. What you are pleased to say of my brother (who fell as I, too, expect to fall, if my country needs it) is but too true. Had he been spared longer, he would doubtless have been of great value to our country. His fall, however, has not been without its lesson to the enemy, teaching them that Virginians know how to die as well as fight for their liberty. He died without a regret, feeling that his life was due to his country's cause. Please present me most kindly to all my friends in Stafford, and accept my highest respects for yourself.

"Your obedient servant,
"Turner Ashby."

We have already referred in the pages of this history to Ashby's share in the several glorious campaigns of Jackson in the Valley; to his participation in the battle of Kernstown to his famous adventure with the Yankee pickets at the bridge and to some other of his daring exploits on the front and flank of the enemy. It was on the occasion of the battle of Kernstown that his energy was exercised to an extraordinary degree in protecting the retreat and annoying the skirts of the enemy. In thirty-eight, out of forty-two days after this battle he was fighting the enemy, keeping him in check, or cutting off his communications. The terrible fatigues he incurred never seemed to depress him, or to tax his endurance. An acquaintance testifies that it was not an infrequent feat for him to ride daily over a line of pickets sixty or seventy miles in extent.

At a later period of the Valley campaign, when Banks returned from Strasburg and our troops were chasing him, Ashby would follow and charge the Yankees as the Rockbridge Artillery poured in their fire. At one time he was riding abreast of three hundred infantry, who were passing along the turnpike. All at once he wheeled his horse, and leaping the fence with drawn sword, cut his way right through them; then wheeling, he did the same thing a second time. Riding up to the standard-bearer, he seized it from him and dashed him to the earth. The terrified wretches never raised a weapon against him. Seventy-five of them, whom he cut off, laid down their arms, and sat down at his order in the corner of the fence, where they remained until his men came up to take care of them. The flag was that of a Vermont regiment. A few days after, Mr. Boteler asked Ashby of the exploit. He drew the flag from his bosom and gave it to him. It was presented by Mr. Boteler to the Library of the State, at Richmond, where it may now be seen—a testimony to one of the most brilliant deeds of Virginia's youthful hero.

A week after this adventure, Ashby was dead. But a few days before the termination of his brilliant career, he received the promotion which had been long due him from the government. Just before leaving Richmond, after the adjournmen of the first session of the permanent Congress, Mr. Boteler, who was a member of that body, and Ashby's constant friend, went to the president, told him that he was going home, and asked that one act of justice should be done to the people of the Valley, which they had long expected. He wished to be able to carry back to his people the assurance that Ashby should be commissioned a brigadier-general. The order for the commission was at once made out. When the announcement was made to Ashby, he exhibited no emotion, except that his face was lighted up by one of those sad smiles which had occasionally brightened it since the death of his brother.

The manner of Ashby's death has already been mentioned in the preceding pages of the brief historical narrative of the Valley campaign. The writer is indebted for the particulars of that sad event to Colonel Bradley T. Johnson, the brave Maryland officer whose command was conspicuous in the affair that cost Ashby his life, and earned an immortal honor in revenging his death. He takes the liberty of extracting from a letter of this officer an account of the engagement:

" On the morning of Friday, the 6th of June," writes Colonel Johnson, " we left Harrisonburg, not having seen the enemy for two days. To our surprise, in the afternoon his cavalry made a dash into our rear-guard, and was whipped most effectually their colonel, Sir Percy Wyndham, being taken prisoner. My regiment was supporting a battery a short distance behind this cavalry fight. In half an hour we were ordered forward—that is, towards the enemy retracing the march just made. Our infantry consisted only of Brigadier-general George H. Stewart's brigade, the 58th Virginia, 44th Virginia, two other Virginia regiments, and the Maryland Line—of the latter, only the 1st Maryland was taken back; the artillery and all the cavalry were left behind us. The 58th Virginia was first, my regiment (the 1st Maryland) next, then came the 44th and the rest.

" A couple of miles east of Harrisonburg we left the road and filed to the right, through the fields, soon changing direction again so as to move parallel to the road. General Ewell soon sent for two of my companies as skirmishers. Moving cautiously through the darkening shades of the tangled wood just as the evening twilight was brightening the trees in front of us in an opening, *spot, spot, spot,* began a dropping fire from the skirmishers, and instantly the 58th Virginia poured in a volley. Another volley was fired. The leaves began to fall, and the bullets hit the trees around. General Ewell came up in a gallop. 'Charge, colonel, charge to the left!' And I charged, got to the edge of the wood, and found a heavy body of infantry and cavalry supporting a battery on a hill six hun dred yards in front of me. But the Yankee balls came fast and thick on my flank. 'The 58th are firing into us,' the leading captain said. General Ewell and myself, the only mounted officers, plunged after them, and found it was not their fire. I got back. 'Up, men, and take that hill,' pointing to my right. They went in with a cheer. In less than five seconds the first rank of the second company went down. The color-sergeant, Doyle, fell. The corporal who caught them from him fell. The next who took them fell, when Corporal Shanks, a six-footer, seized them, raising them over his head at arm's length. Captain Robertson lay dead; Lieutenant Snowden shot to death; myself on the ground, my horse shot in three places. But still we went forward, and drove the Bucktails from the fence where they had been concealed. . . . ."

It was as the brave Marylanders were pressing on in this charge that Ashby, who was on the right of the 58th Virginia exhorting them, fell by an intelligent bullet of the enemy. His death was quickly avenged. As our troops reached the fence from which the shot had been fired, the line of Yankees melted away like mist before a hurricane.

"The account I have given you," writes Colonel Johnson, "of the manner of Ashby's death, is collated from the statements of many eye-witnesses of my skirmishing companies, who were all around him when he fell. I did not see it, though not thirty yards from him, but was busy with my own men; and I am specific in stating the source of his death, as there is a loose impression that he was killed by a shot from the 58th Virginia. I am persuaded this is not so, from the statements of two very cool officers, Captain Nicholas and Lieutenant Booth, who were talking to him the minute before he fell. . . . ."

"Ashby was my first revolutionary acquaintance in Virginia. I was with him when the first blow was struck for the cause we both had so much at heart, and was with him in his last fight, always knowing him to be beyond all modern men in chivalry, as he was equal to any one in courage. He combined the virtues of Sir Philip Sydney with the dash of Murat. I contribute my mite to his fame, which will live in the Valley of Virginia, outside of books, as long as its hills and mountains shall endure."

No word escaped from Ashby's lips as he fell.   It was not necessary.   No dying legend, spoken in death's embrace, could have added to that noble life.   Itself was a beautiful poem ; a sounding oration ; a sufficient legacy to the virtue of his coun trymen.

CHAPTER XV.

The Situation of Richmond.—Its Strategic Importance.—What the Yankees had done to secure Richmond.—THE BATTLE OF SEVEN PINES.—Miscarriage of Gen. Johnston's Plans.—THE BATTLES OF THE CHICKAHOMINY.—Storming of the Enemy's Intrenchments.—McClellan driven from his Northern Line of Defences.—The Situation on the other Side of the Chickahominy.—Magruder's Comment.—The Affair of Savage Station.—The Battle of Frazier's Farm.—A Terrible Crisis.—Battle of Malvern Hill.—The Enemy in Communication with his Gunboats.—The Failure to cut him off.—Glory and Fruits of our Victory.—Misrepresentations of the Yankees.—Safety of Richmond.—The War in other Parts of the Confederacy.—The Engagement of Secessionville.—The Campaign of the West.—The Evacuation of Corinth.—More Yankee Falsehoods.—Capture of Memphis.—The Prize of the Mississippi.—Statistics of its Navigation.—Siege of Vicksburg.—Heroism of "the Queen City."—Morgan's Raid into Kentucky.—The Tennessee and Virginia Frontier.—Prospects in the West.—Plan of Campaign there.

RICHMOND is the heart of the State of Virginia. It is hundreds of miles from the sea, yet with water communication to Old Point, to Washington, and to New York. It is the strategic point of the greatest importance in the whole Confederacy. If Richmond had fallen before McClellan's forces, the North expected that there would follow all of North Carolina except the mountains, part of South Carolina, and all of Tennessee that was left to us.

On the Richmond lines, two of the greatest and most splendid armies that had ever been arrayed on a single field confronted each other; every accession that could be procured from the most distant quarters to their numbers, and every thing that could be drawn from the resources of the respective countries of each, had been made to contribute to the strength and splendor of the opposing hosts.

Since the commencement of the war, the North had taxed its resources for the capture of Richmond; nothing was omitted for the accomplishment of this event; the way had to be opened to the capital by tedious and elaborate operations on the frontier of Virginia; this accomplished, the city of Richmond was surrounded by an army whose numbers was all that could be desired; composed of picked forces; having every advantage that science and art could bestow in fortifications and every appliance of war; assisted by gunboat flotillas in two rivers, and endowed with every thing that could assure success.

The Northern journals were unreserved in the statement that the commands of Fremont, Banks, and McDowell had been consolidated into one army, under Major-gen. Pope, with a view of bringing all the Federal forces in Virginia to co-operate with McClellan on the Richmond lines. A portion of this army must have reached McClellan, probably at an early stage of the engagements in the vicinity of Richmond. Indeed, it was stated at a subsequent period by Mr. Chandler, a member of the Federal Congress, that the records of the War Department at Washington showed that more than one hundred and fifty thousand men had been sent to the lines about Richmond. There is little doubt but that, in the memorable contest for the safety of the Confederate capital, we engaged an army whose superiority in numbers to us was largely increased by timely reinforcements, and with regard to the operations of which the Northern government had omitted no conditions of success.

THE BATTLE OF SEVEN PINES.

Having reached the Chickahominy, McClellan threw a portion of his army across the river, and, having thus established his left, proceeded to pivot upon it, and to extend his right by the right bank of the Pamunkey, so as to get to the north of Richmond.

Before the 30th of May, Gen. Johnston had ascertained that Keyes' corps was encamped on this side of the Chickahominy, near the Williamsburg road, and the same day a strong body of the enemy was reported in front of D. H. Hill. The following disposition of forces was made for the attack the next day, the troops being ordered to move at daybreak: Gen. Hill, supported by the division of Gen. Longstreet (who had the direction of operations on the right), was to advance by the Williamsburg road to attack the enemy in front; Gen. Huger, with his division, was to move down the Charles City road, in order to attack in flank the troops who might be engaged with Hill and Longstreet, unless he found in his front force enough to occupy his division; Gen. Smith was to march

GEN. J. E. JOHNSTON

to the junction of the New Bridge road and the Nine Mile road, to be in readiness either to fall on Keyes' right flank, or to cover Longstreet's left.

The next day hour after hour passed, while Gen. Longstreet in vain waited for Huger's division. At two o'clock in the afternoon he resolved to make the attack without these troops, and moved upon the enemy with his own and D. H. Hill's division, the latter in advance.

Hill's brave troops, admirably commanded and most gallantly led, forced their way through the abattis which formed the enemy's external defences, and stormed their intrenchments by a determined and irresistible rush. Such was the manner in which the enemy's first line was carried. The operation was repeated with the same gallantry and success as our troops pursued their victorious career through the enemy's successive camps and intrenchments. At each new position they encountered fresh troops belonging to it, and reinforcements brought on from the rear. Thus they had to repel repeated efforts to retake works which they had carried. But their advance was never successfully resisted. Their onward movement was only stayed by the coming of night. By night fall they had forced their way to the "Seven Pines," having driven the enemy back more than two miles, through their own camps, and from a series of intrenchments, and repelled every attempt to recapture them with great slaughter.

The attack on the enemy's right was not so fortunate. The strength of his position enabled him to hold it until dark, and the intervention of night alone saved him from rout. On this part of the field Gen. Johnston was severely wounded by the fragment of a shell.

In his official report of the operations of the day, General Johnston says: "Had Major-gen. Huger's division been in position and ready for action when those of Smith, Longstreet, and Hill moved, I am satisfied that Keyes' corps would have been destroyed instead of being merely defeated." The slow and impotent movements of Gen. Huger were excused by himself on account of the necessity of building a bridge to cross the swollen stream in his front, and other accidental causes of delay.

But notwithstanding the serious diminution of the fortunes

of the day by Huger's mishaps, they were yet conspicuous. We had taken ten pieces of artillery and six thousand muskets, besides other spoils. Our total loss was more than four thousand. That of the enemy is stated in their own newspapers to have exceeded ten thousand—an estimate which is no doubt short of the truth.

On the morning of the first of June, the enemy made a weak demonstration of attack on our lines. The 9th and 14th Virginia regiments were ordered to feel for the enemy, and while thus engaged suddenly came upon a body of fifteen thousand Yankees intrenched in the woods. Under the murderous fire poured into their ranks, our troops were forced to fall back, but were rallied by the self-devoted gallantry of their officers. Col. Godwin, the dashing and intrepid commander of the 9th, received a Minnié ball in the leg, and a moment later had his hip crushed by the fall of his horse, which was shot under him. He was thirty paces in advance of his regiment when the attack was made, encouraging his men. At last, reinforcements coming up, the attack of the enemy was vigorously repulsed. This was the last demonstration of the enemy, who proceeded o strengthen those lines of intrenchments from which he had not yet been driven.

THE BATTLES OF THE CHICKAHOMINY.

Upon taking command of the Confederate army in the field, after Gen. Johnston had been wounded in the battle of Seven Pines, Gen. Lee did not hesitate to adopt the spirit of that commander, which had already been displayed in attacking the enemy, and which indicated the determination on his part that the operations before Richmond should not degenerate into a siege.

The course of the Chickahominy around Richmond affords an idea of the enemy's position at the commencement of the action. This stream meanders through the Tide-water district of Virginia—its course approaching that of the arc of a circle in the neighborhood of Richmond—until it reaches the lower end of Charles City county, where it abruptly turns to th south and empties into the James. A portion of the enemy's forces had crossed to the south side of the Chickahominy, and were fortified on the Williamsburg road. On the north bank of the stream the enemy was strongly posted for many miles; the heights on that side of the stream having been fortified with great energy and skill from Meadow Bridge, on a line nearly due north from the city to a point below Bottom's Bridge, which is due east. This line of the enemy extended for about twenty miles.

Reviewing the situation of the two armies at the commencement of the action, the advantage was entirely our own. McClellan had divided his army on the two sides of the Chickahominy, and operating apparently with the design of half circumvallating Richmond, had spread out his forces to an extent that impaired the faculty of concentration, and had made a weak and dangerous extension of his lines.

On Thursday, the 26th of June, at three o'clock, Major-gen. Jackson—fresh from the exploits of his magnificent campaign in the Valley—took up his line of march from Ashland, and proceeded down the country between the Chickahominy and Pamunkey rivers. The enemy collected on the north bank of the Chickahominy, at the point where it is crossed by the Brooke turnpike, were driven off, and Brigadier-gen. Branch, crossing the stream, directed his movements for a junction with the column of Gen. A. P. Hill, which had crossed at Meadow Bridge. Gen. Jackson having borne away from the Chickahominy, so as to gain ground towards the Pamunkey, marched to the left of Mechanicsville, while Gen. Hill, keeping well to the Chickahominy, approached that village and engaged the enemy there.

With about fourteen thousand men (Gen. Branch did not arrive until nightfall) Gen. Hill engaged the forces of the enemy, until night put an end to the contest. While he did not succeed, in that limited time, in routing the enemy, his forces stubbornly maintained the possession of Mechanicsville and the ground taken by them on the other side of the Chickahominy. Driven from the immediate locality of Mechanicsville, the enemy retreated during the night down the river to Powhite swamp, and night closed the operations of Thursday

STORMING OF THE ENEMY'S INTRENCHMENTS.

The road having been cleared at Mechanicsville, Gen. Long-street's *corps d'armée*, consisting of his veteran division of the Old Guard of the Army of the Potomac, and Gen. D. H. Hill's division, debouched from the woods on the south side of the Chickahominy, and crossed that river. Friday morning the general advance upon the enemy began; Gen. A. P. Hill in the centre, and bearing towards Cold Harbor, while Gen. Long-street and Gen. D. H. Hill came down the Chickahominy to New Bridge. Gen. Jackson still maintained his position in advance, far to the left, and gradually converging to the Chick-ahominy again.

The position of the enemy was now a singular one. One portion of his army was on the south side of the Chickahom-iny, fronting Richmond, and confronted by Gen. Magruder. The other portion, on the north side, had fallen back to a new line of defences, where McClellan proposed to make a decisive battle.

As soon as Jackson's arrival at Cold Harbor was announced, Gen. Lee and Gen. Longstreet, accompanied by their respect-ve staffs, rode by Gaines' Mill, and halted at New Cold Har-bor, where they joined Gen. A. P. Hill. Soon the welcome sound of Jackson's guns announced that he was at work.

The action was now to become general for the first time on the Richmond lines; and a collision of numbers was about to take place eqral to any that had yet occurred in the history of the war.

From four o'clock until eight the battle raged with a display of the utmost daring and intrepidity on the part of the Con-federate army. The enemy's lines were finally broken, and his strong positions all carried, and night covered the retreat of McClellan's broken and routed columns to the south side of the Chickahominy.

The assault of the enemy's works near Gaines' Mill is a memorable part of the engagement of Friday, and the display of fortitude, as well as quick and dashing gallantry of our troops on that occasion, takes its place by the side of the most glorious exploits of the war. Gen. A. P. Hill had made the first assault upon the lines of the enemy's intrenchments near Gaines' Mill. A fierce struggle had ensued between his division and the garrison of the line of defence. Repeated charges were made by Hill's troops, but the formidable character of the works, and murderous volleys from the artillery covering them, kept our troops in check. Twenty-six pieces of artillery were thundering at them, and a perfect hailstorm of lead fell thick and fast around them. In front stood Federal camps, stretching to the northeast for miles. Drawn up in line of battle were more than three full divisions, commanded by McCall, Porter, and Sedgwick. Banners darkened the air; artillery vomited forth incessant volleys of grape, canister, and shell; and the wing of death waved everywhere in the sulphurous atmosphere of the battle.

It was past four o'clock when Pickett's brigade from Longstreet's division came to Hill's support. Pickett's regiments fought with the most determined valor. At last, Whiting's division, composed of the "Old Third" and Texan brigades, advanced at a double-quick, charged the batteries, and drove the enemy from his strong line of defence. The 4th Texas regiment was led by a gallant Virginian, Col. Bradfute Warwick. As the regiment was marching on with an irresistible impetuosity to the charge, he seized a battle-flag which had been abandoned by one of our regiments, and, bearing it aloft, he passed both of the enemy's breastworks in a most gallant style, and as he was about to plant the colors on a battery that the regiment captured, his right breast was pierced by a Minie ball, and he fell mortally wounded.

The works carried by our noble troops would have been invincible to the bayonet, had they been garrisoned by men less dastardly than the Yankees. All had been done on our side with the bullet and the bayonet. For four hours had our inferior force, unaided by a single piece of artillery, withstood over thirty thousand, assisted by twenty-six pieces of artillery.

To keep the track of the battle, which had swept around Richmond, we must have reference to some of the principal points of locality in the enemy's lines. It will be recollected that it was on Thursday evening when the attack was commenced upon the enemy near Meadow Bridge. This locality is about six miles distant from the city, on a line almost due north. This position was the enemy's extreme right. His lines extended from here across the Chickahominy, near the Powhite Creek, two or three miles above the crossing of the York River railroad. From Meadow Bridge to this railroad the distance along the Chickahominy on the north side is about ten miles. The different stages between the points indicated, along which the enemy were driven, are Mechanicsville, about a mile north of the Chickahominy; further on, Beaver Dam Creek, emptying into the Chickahominy; then the New Bridge road, on which Cold Harbor is located; and then Powhite Creek, where the enemy had made his last stand, and been repulsed from the field.

The York River railroad runs in an easterly direction, intersecting the Chickahominy about ten miles from the city. South of the railroad is the Williamsburg road, connecting with the Nine Mile road at Seven Pines. The former road connects with the New Bridge road, which turns off and crosses the Chickahominy. From Seven Pines, where the Nine Mile road joins the upper one, the road is known as the old Williamsburg road, and crosses the Chickahominy at Bottom's Bridge.

With the bearing of these localities in his mind, the reader will readily understand how it was that the enemy was driven from his original strongholds on the north side of the Chickahominy, and how, at the time of Friday's battle, he had been compelled to surrender the possession of the Fredericksburg and Central railroads, and had been pressed to a position where he was cut off from the principal avenues of supply and escape. The disposition of our forces was such as to cut off all communication between McClellan's army and the White House, on the Pamunkey river; he had been driven completely from his northern line of defences; and it was supposed that he would be unable to extricate himself from his position without a victory or capitulation.

On Sunday morning, it appears that our pickets, on the Nine Mile road, having engaged some small detachments of the enemy and driven them beyond their fortifications, found them deserted. In a short while it became known to our generals that McClellan, having massed his entire force on this side of the Chickahominy, was retreating towards James river.

The intrenchments, which the enemy had deserted, were

found to be formidable and elaborate. That immediately across the railroad, at the six-mile post, which had been supposed to be light earthwork, designed to sweep the railroad. turned out to be an immense embrasured fortification, extending for hundreds of yards on either side of the track. Within this work were found great quantities of fixed ammunition, which had apparently been prepared for removal and then deserted. All the cannon, as at other intrenchments, had been carried off. A dense cloud of smoke was seen issuing from the woods two miles in advance of the battery and half a mile to the right of the railroad. The smoke was found to proceed from a perfect mountain of the enemy's commissary stores, consisting of sugar, coffee, and bacon, prepared meats, vegetables, &c., which he had fired. The fields and woods around this spot were covered with every description of clothing and camp equipage. No indication was wanting that the enemy had left this encampment in haste and disorder.

The enemy had been imperfectly watched at a conjuncture the most critical in the contest, and through an omission of our guard—the facts of which are yet the subject of some controversy—McClellan had succeeded in massing his entire force, and taking up a line of retreat, by which he hoped to reach the cover of his gunboats on the James. But the most unfortunate circumstance to us was, that since the enemy had escaped from us in his fortified camp, his retreat was favored by a country, the characteristics of which are unbroken forests and wide swamps, where it was impossible to pursue him with rapidity, and extremely difficult to reconnoitre his position so as to bring him to decisive battle.

In an official report of the situation of forces on the Richmond side of the Chickahominy, Gen. Magruder describes it as one of the gravest peril. He states that the larger portion of the enemy was on that side of the Chickahominy; that the bridges had all been destroyed, and but one rebuilt—the New Bridge—which was commanded fully by the enemy's guns; and that there were but twenty-five thousand men between McClellan's army of one hundred thousand and Richmond. Referring to a situation so extremely critical, he says: "Had McClellan massed his whole force in column, and advanced it against any point of our line of battle, as was done at Austerlitz under similar circumstances, by the greatest captain of any age, though the head of his column would have suffered greatly its momentum would have insured him success, and the occupation of our works about Richmond, and, consequently, of the city, might have been his reward." Taking this view of the situation, Gen. Magruder states that his relief was great when it was discovered the next day that the enemy had left our front and was continuing to retreat.

The facts, however, are contrary to the theory of Gen. Magruder and to the self-congratulations which he derives from it. Our troops on the two sides of the river were only separated until we succeeded in occupying the position near what is known as New Bridge, which occurred before 12 o'clock m., on Friday, June 27, and before the attack on the enemy at Gaines' Mill. From the time we reached the position referred to, our communications between the two wings of our army may be regarded as re-establised. The bridge referred to and another about three-quarters of a mile above were ordered to be repaired before noon on Friday, and the new bridge was sufficiently rebuilt to be passed by artillery on Friday night, and the one above it was used for the passage of wagons, ambulances, and troops early on Saturday morning. Besides this all other bridges above New Bridge, and all the fords above that point, were open to us.

THE AFFAIR AT SAVAGE'S STATION.

During Sunday, a portion of the enemy was encountered upon the York River railroad, near a place called Savage's Station, the troops engaged on our side being the division of Gen. McLaws, consisting of Generals Kershaw and Semmes' brigades, supported by Gen. Griffith's brigade from Magruder's division. The Federals were found to be strongly intrenched, and as soon as our skirmishers came in view, they were opened upon with a furious cannonade from a park of field-pieces. Kemper's battery now went to the front, and for three hours the battle raged hotly, when the discomfited Yankees again resumed their retreat. Early in the day, on reaching the redoubts, Gen. Griffiths, of Mississippi, one of the heroes of Leesburg, was killed by the fragment of a shell. He was the only general officer killed on our side during the whole of the bloody week.

In this encounter with the enemy, the gallant 10th Georgia regiment suffered severely, engaging the enemy hand to hand, and leaving upon the field memorable evidences of their courage. The enemy, to use an expression of his prisoners, was "mowed down" by the close fire of our adventurous troops; and the failure of the attempt of McClellan to break through our lines at this point, left him to continue a hopeless retreat.

THE BATTLE OF FRAYSER'S FARM.

By daybreak on Monday morning, the pursuit of the enemy was actively resumed. D. H. Hill, Whiting, and Ewell, under command of Jackson, crossed the Chickahominy by the Grapevine bridge, and followed the enemy on their track by the Williamsburg road and Savage's Station. Longstreet, A. P. Hill, Huger, and Magruder pursued the enemy by the Charles City road, with the intention of cutting him off.

The divisions of Generals Hill and Longstreet were, during the whole of the day, moving in the hunt for the enemy. The disposition which was made of our forces, brought Gen. Longstreet on the enemy's front, immediately supported by Gen. Hill's division, consisting of six brigades. The forces commanded by Gen. Longstreet were his old division, consisting of six brigades.

The position of the enemy was about five miles northeast of Darbytown, on the New Market road. The immediate scene of the battle was a plain of sedge pines, in the cover of which the enemy's forces were skilfully disposed—the locality being known as Frayser's farm. In advancing upon the enemy, batteries of sixteen heavy guns were opened upon the advance columns of Gen. Hill. Our troops, pressing heroically forward, had no sooner got within musket range, than the enemy, forming several lines of battle, poured upon them from his heavy masses a devouring fire of musketry. The conflict became terrible, the air being filled with missiles of death, every moment having its peculiar sound of terror, and every spot its sight of ghastly destruction and horror. It is impossible that in any of the series of engagements which had taken place

within the past few days, and had tracked the lines of Rich
mond with fire and destruction, there could have been more
desperate fighting on the part of our troops. Never was a
more glorious victory plucked from more desperate and threat
ening circumstances. While exposed to the double fire of the
enemy's batteries and his musketry, we were unable to contend
with him with artillery. But although thus unmatched, our
brave troops pressed on with unquailing vigor and a resistless
courage, driving the enemy before them. This was accomplished without artillery, there being but one battery in Gen.
Hill's command on the spot, and that belonged to Longstreet's
division, and could not be got into position. Thus the fight
continued with an ardor and devotion that few battle-fields
have ever illustrated. Step by step the enemy were driven
back, his guns taken, and the ground he abandoned strewn
with his dead. By half-past eight o'clock we had taken all
his cannon, and, continuing to advance, had driven him a mile
and a half from his ground of battle.

Our forces were still advancing upon the retreating lines of
the enemy. It was now about half-past nine o'clock, and very
dark. Suddenly, as if it had burst from the heavens, a sheet
of fire enveloped the front of our advance. The enemy had
made another stand to receive us, and from the black masses
of his forces, it was evident that he had been heavily reinforced, and that another whole *corps d'armée* had been brought
up to contest the fortunes of the night. Line after line of
battle was formed. It was evident that his heaviest columns
were now being thrown against our small command, and it
might have been supposed that he would only be satisfied with
its annihilation. The loss here on our side was terrible.

The situation being evidently hopeless for any further pursuit of the fugitive enemy, who had now brought up such overwhelming forces, our troops retired slowly.

At this moment, seeing their adversary retire, the most
vociferous cheers arose along the whole Yankee line. They
were taken up in the distance by the masses which for miles
and miles beyond were supporting McClellan's front. It was
a moment when the heart of the stoutest commander might
have been appalled. The situation of our forces was now as
desperate as it well could be, and required a courage and

presence of mind to retrieve it, which the circumstances which surrounded them were not well calculated to inspire. They had fought for five or six hours without reinforcements. All our reserves had been brought up in the action. Wilcox's brigade, which had been almost annihilated, was re-forming in the rear.

Riding rapidly to the position of this brigade, Gen. Hill brought them by great exertions up to the front, to check the advance of the now confident, cheering enemy. Catching the spirit of their commander, the brave but jaded men moved up to the front, replying to the enemy's cheers with shouts and yells. At this demonstration, which the enemy, no doubt, supposed signified heavy reinforcements, he stopped his advance. It was now about half-past ten o'clock in the night. The enemy had been arrested; and the fight—one of the most remarkable, long-contested, and gallant ones that had yet occurred on our lines—was concluded with the achievement of a field under the most trying circumstances, which the enemy, with the most overpowering numbers brought up to reinforce him, had not succeeded in reclaiming.

Gen. Magruder's division did not come up until eleven o'clock at night, after the fight had been concluded. By orders from Gen. Lee, Magruder moved upon and occupied the battle-ground; Gen. Hill's command being in such a condition of prostration from their long and toilsome fight, and suffering in killed and wounded, that it was proper they should be relieved by the occupation of the battle-ground by a fresh *corps d'armee.*

THE BATTLE OF MALVERN HILL.

Early on Tuesday morning, the enemy, from the position to which he had been driven the night before, continued his retreat in a southeasterly direction towards his gunboats in James river.

General Magruder was directed to proceed by the Quaker road, and to form on the right of Jackson. On account of a misunderstanding as to which was the Quaker road, the wrong route was taken by General Magruder; and the direction of his movement was subsequently changed, so as to place his troops on the right of Huger, who in the mean time had formed on the right of Jackson.

The enemy had now placed himself in communication with his gunboats in the river. He was strongly posted on the crest of a hill, commanding an undulating field, which fell to our right into a plain or meadow. His batteries of artillery were numerous, and were collected into two large bodies, strongly supported by infantry, and commanded perfectly the meadow on our right, and the field in our front, except the open ravines formed by the undulations of the ground.

An order was dispatched by General Magruder to bring up from all the batteries thirty rifle pieces, if possible, with which he hoped to shatter the enemy's infantry. While delay was thus occasioned, he was ordered to make the attack. Returning rapidly to the position occupied by the main body of his troops, he gave Brigadier-general Jones the necessary orders for the advance of his division. While this was being done, a heavy and crushing fire was opened from the enemy's guns, or great range and metal.

General Armistead having repulsed, driven back, and followed up a heavy body of the enemy's skirmishers, an order was received from General Lee by Magruder, directing him " to advance rapidly, press forward his whole line and follow up Armistead's successes, as the enemy were reported to be getting off." In the mean time Mahone's and Ransom's brigades of Huger's division having been ordered up, General Magruder gave the order that Wright's brigade, supported by Mahone's, should advance and attack the enemy's batteries on the right, and that Jones' division, expected momentarily, should advance on the front, and Ransom's brigade should attack on the left. The plan of attack was to hurl about fifteen thousand men against the enemy's batteries and supporting infantry—to follow up any successes they might obtain; and if unable to drive the enemy from his strong position, to continue the fight in front by pouring in fresh troops; and in case they were repulsed, to hold strongly the line of battle where we stood.

At about 5 o'clock P. M., the order was given to our men to charge across the field and drive the enemy from their position. Gallantly they sprang to the encounter, rushing into

THE SECOND YEAR. 423

the field at a full run. Instantly, from the line of the enemy's breastworks, a murderous storm of grape and canister was hurled into their ranks, with the most terrible effect. Officers and men went down by hundreds; but yet, undaunted and unwavering, our line dashed on, until two-thirds of the distance across the field was accomplished. Here the carnage from the withering fire of the enemy's combined artillery and musketry was dreadful. Our line wavered a moment, and fell back to the cover of the woods. Twice again the effort to carry the position was renewed, but each time with the same result.

The hill was bathed with flames. Towards sunset the earth quivered with the terrific concussion of artillery and huge explosions. Shells raced athwart the horizon, exploding into deadly iron hail. The forms of smoke-masked men; the gleam of muskets on the plains, where soldiers were disengaged; the artistic order of battle; the wild career of wilder horsemen plunging to and fro across the field, formed a scene of exciting grandeur. In the forest, where eyes did not penetrate, there was nothing but the exhilarating and exhausting spasm of battle.

As the night fell the battle slackened. We had not carried the enemy's position, but we occupied the field, and during the night posted our pickets within one hundred yards of his guns. The brigades of Mahone and Wright slept on the battle-field in the advanced positions they had won, and Armistead's brigade and a portion of Ransom's also occupied the battle-field.

The battle of Tuesday, properly known as that of Malvern Hill, was perhaps the most sanguinary of the series of bloody conflicts which had taken place on the lines about Richmond. Although not a defeat, it broke the chain of our victories. It was made memorable by its melancholy monument of carnage, which was probably greater than Gen. Magruder's estimate, which states that our loss fell short of three thousand. But it had given the enemy no advantage, except in the unfruitful sacrifice of the lives of our troops; and the line of his retreat was again taken up, his forces toiling towards the river through mud, swamp, and forest.

The skill and spirit with which McClellan had managed to retreat was, indeed, remarkable, and afforded no mean proofs of his generalship. At every stage of his retreat he had confronted our forces with a strong rear-guard, and had encoun tered us with well-organized lines of battle, and regular dispo sitions of infantry, cavalry, and artillery. His heavy rifle cannon had been used against us constantly on his retreat. A portion of his forces had now effected communication with the river at points below City Point. The plan of cutting off his communication with the river, which was to have been executed by a movement of Holmes' division between him and the river, was frustrated by the severe fire of the gunboats, and since then the situation of the enemy appeared to be that of a division or dispersion of his forces, one portion resting on the river, and the other, to some extent, involved by our lines.

It had been stated to the public of Richmond, with great precision of detail, that on the evening of Saturday, the 28th of June, we had brought the enemy to bay on the South side of the Chickahominy, and that it only remained to finish him in a single battle. Such, in fact, appeared to have been the situation then. The next morning, however, it was perceived that our supposed resources of generalship had given us too much confidence; that the enemy had managed to extricate himself from the critical position, and, having massed his forces, had succeeded, under cover of the night, in opening a way to the James river.*

Upon this untoward event, the operations of our army on the Richmond side of the Chickahominy were to follow the fugitive enemy through a country where he had admirable opportunities of concealment, and through the swamps and forests

---

* With reference to McClellan's escape from White Oak Swamp to the river, letters of Yankee officers, published in the Northern journals, stated that when McClellan, on Saturday evening, sent his scouts down the road to Turkey Island bridge, he was astonished and delighted to find that our forces had not occupied that road, and immediately started his wagon and artillery trains, which were quietly passing down that road all night to the James river, whilst our forces were quietly sleeping within four miles of the very road they should have occupied, and should have captured every one of the enemy's one thousand wagons and four hundred cannon. It is further stated in these letters, that if we had blocked up that only passage of escape, their entire army must have surrendered or been starved out in twenty-four hours. These are the Yankees' own accounts of how much they were indebted to blunders on our part for the success of McClellan's retreat—a kind of admission not popular with a vain and self-adulatory enemy.

of which he had retreated with the most remarkable judgment, dexterity, and spirit of fortitude.

The glory and fruits of our victory may have been seriously diminished by the grave mishap or fault by which the enemy was permitted to leave his camp on the south side of the Chickahominy, in an open country, and to plunge into the dense cover of wood and swamp, where the best portion of a whole week was consumed in hunting him, and finding out his new position only in time to attack him under the uncertainty and disadvantage of the darkness of night.

But the successes achieved in the series of engagements which had already occurred were not to be lightly esteemed, or to be depreciated, because of errors which, if they had not occurred, would have made our victory more glorious and more complete. The siege of Richmond had been raised; an army of one hundred and fifty thousand men had been pushed from their strongholds and fortifications, and put to flight; we had enjoyed the *eclat* of an almost daily succession of victories; we had gathered an immense spoil in stores, provisions, and artillery; and we had demoralized and dispersed, if we had not succeeded in annihilating, an army which had every resource that could be summoned to its assistance, every possible addition to numbers within the reach of the Yankee government, and every material condition of success to insure for it the great prize of the capital of the Confederacy, which was now, as far as human judgment could determine, irretrievably lost to them, and secure in the protection of a victorious army.

The Northern papers claimed that the movements of McClellan from the Chickahominy river were purely strategic, and that he had obtained a position where he would establish a new base of operations against Richmond. Up to the first decisive stage in the series of engagements—Cold Harbor— there were certainly plain strategic designs in his backward movement. His retirement from Mechanicsville was probably voluntary, and intended to concentrate his troops lower down, where he might fight with the advantages of numbers and his own selection of position. Continuing his retreat, he fixed the decisive field at Cold Harbor. Again having been pushed from his strongholds north of the Chickahominy, the enemy made a strong attempt to retrieve his disasters by renewing a concentration of his troops at Frayser's farm.

From the time of these two principal battles, all pretensions of the enemy's retreat to strategy must cease. His retreat was now unmistakable; it was no longer a falling back to concentrate troops for action; it is, in fact, impossible to disguise that it was the retreat of an enemy who was discomfited and whipped, although not routed. He had abandoned the railroads; he had given up the strongholds which he had provided to secure him in case of a check; he had destroyed from eight to ten millions dollars' worth of stores; he had deserted his hospitals, his sick and wounded, and he had left in our hands thousands of prisoners and innumerable stragglers.

Regarding all that had been accomplished in these battles; the displays of the valor and devotion of our troops; the expenditure of blood; and the helpless and fugitive condition to which the enemy had at last been reduced, there was cause for the keenest regrets that an enemy in this condition was permitted to secure his retreat. It is undoubtedly true, that in failing to cut off McClellan's retreat to the river, we failed to accomplish the most important condition for the completion of our victory. But although the result of the conflict had fallen below public expectation, it was sufficiently fortunate to excite popular joy, and grave enough to engage the most serious speculation as to the future.

The mouth of the Yankee government was shut from any more promises of a speedy termination of the war; the powers of Europe saw that the Southern Confederacy was not yet crushed, or likely to be crushed, by its insolent foe; and the people of the South had again challenged the confidence of the world in the elasticity of their fortunes and the invincible destiny of their independence.

The fortune of events in other parts of the Confederacy, taking place about the time of the relief of Richmond, or closely following it, although less striking and dramatic, was not unpropitious. These events, a rapid survey of which takes us from the seacoast to the Mississippi frontier, added to the exultations which the victories of the Chickahominy had occasioned, and, although qualified by some disasters, enlarged and enlightened the prospects of the future.

A few days before the great battles had been joined around Richmond, a brilliant success over the Yankees had been obtained in an engagement on James Island in the neighborhood of Charleston. The battle of Secessionville, as it was called, occurred on the 16th of June. About four o'clock in the morning of that day, the enemy, taking advantage of the negligence of our pickets, drove them in, or captured them, some eight hundred yards in front of the battery at Secessionville, and, advancing rapidly upon this work in line of battle, arrived within a few hundred yards of it before we could open upon him. The men, however, were at their guns, which were at once well and rapidly served, while the infantry was moved promptly into position under the orders of Col. J. G. Lamar, the heroic commander of the post. It was not long after getting the infantry into position, that the enemy were driven back in confusion. They were soon, however, reinforced, and made another desperate charge, when they were again driven back; a third time they came, but only to meet with the most determined repulse. They then made a flank movement on our right, on the west of Secessionville, where they were gallantly met by the Charleston battalion, which was soon reinforced by the Louisiana battalion. Three times had the heroic band of Confederates repulsed (often at the point of the bayonet) a force thrice their strength, under the fire of three gunboats and four land batteries. About ten o'clock the enemy retreated in great confusion, leaving their dead and wounded on the field, a number lying in our trenches. The loss of the enemy was at least four hundred in killed, wounded, and prisoners. Their dead in front of the Secessionville works numbered one hundred and sixty-eight. Our loss was forty killed, and about twice that number wounded.

In the situation in the West some important changes had transpired in the early months of the summer.

The evacuation of Corinth was determined upon by Gen. Beauregard, after having twice offered the enemy battle outside of his intrenched lines, and was accomplished on the 30th of May. The transparent object of the Yankee commander was to cut off our resources, by destroying the Mobile and Ohio and Memphis and Charleston railroads. This was substantially foiled by the evacuation and withdrawal of our forces along the line of the former road. Remaining in rear of the Tus cumbia and its affluents, some six miles from Corinth, long enough to collect stragglers, Gen. Beauregard resumed his march, concentrating his main forces at Baldwin. On June 7th he left Baldwin, it offering no advantages of a defensive character, and assembled the main body of his forces at Tupelo.

On the morning of the evacuation of Corinth, our effective force did not exceed forty-seven thousand men of all arms; that of the enemy, obtained from the best sources of information, could not have been less than ninety thousand men of all arms. The story of the evacuation was flourished by the Yankees as a great success on their side, and coupled with an audacious falsehood reported by Gen. Pope to Gen. Halleck, then in command of the enemy's forces in the West, to the effect that he had taken ten thousand prisoners and fifteen thousand stand of arms. The facts are, that the retreat was conducted with great order and precision; and that, despite the boasts of the North to the contrary, we lost no more prisoners than the enemy did himself, and abandoned to him in stores not more than would amount to one day's expense of our army.

The capture of Memphis was another step towards the realization of the enemy's great object of opening the navigation of the Mississippi, which was persistently demanded by the Northwestern States, as the price of their contributions to the war, and their support of the administration at Washington.* This city had been formally surrendered to the Yankees after a naval engagement in front of it on the 6th of June, in which our loss was eighty killed and wounded and seventy-five taken prisoners, and four gunboats sunk.

---

* The Board of Trade of St. Louis published a paper on this subject, which assumed the ground that the object of the Confederacy was to hold the entire and exclusive control of the Mississippi. It went into detail to show how great a loss the present obstruction of that highway was to the "loyal" Western States. It was the natural outlet to the produce of the Upper Valley. During the year 1860, the shipments from Cairo and points above the Mississippi and its tributaries, by way of the lower Mississippi, amounted to a million of tons, o which 400,000 went from St. Louis. It averred that the difference in cost o freight by the river and the railroad was ten dollars a ton; also, that this, with the return freight, would amount to a total of $15,000,000 tax on the Western people by reason of the closing of the river.

The occupation of Memphis by the enemy was a serious disaster to the South, although it did not open the Mississippi, for it gave him extraordinary facilities for almost daily reinforcements of men and supplies, and for the preparation of expeditions to penetrate to the heart of the Confederacy.

But the enemy received a check on the Mississippi where he had least expected it. On the 24th of June, his combined fleet retired, and abandoned the siege of Vicksburg, without accomplishing any thing, after a siege of six weeks. No injury was sustained by any of the batteries at Vicksburg. The number of shells thrown into the city and at the batteries amounted to 25,000. The casualties in the city were one woman and one negro man killed, and among the soldiers on guard and at the batteries there were twenty-two killed and wounded. The lower bombarding fleet, under command of Coms. Farragut and Porter, consisted of 18 gun and mortar boats, 5 sloops-of-war and 70 transports; the upper fleet consisted of 11 gunboats and rams, and 13 transports, under command of Com. Davis.

The people of the South found in the defence of Vicksburg a splendid lesson of magnanimity and disinterested patriotism. For several weeks the city had resisted successfully the attack of the enemy's gunboats, mortar fleets, and heavy siege guns. She was threatened by powerful fleets above and below, and yet, with unexampled spirit, the Queen City of the Bluffs sustained the iron storm that was rained upon her for weeks with continued fury.

New Orleans, Baton Rouge, Natchez, and Memphis were in the hands of the Yankees, and their possession by the enemy might have furnished to Vicksburg, in its exposed and desperate situation, the usual excuses of timidity and selfishness for its surrender. But the brave city resisted these vile and unmanly excuses, and gave to the world one of the proudest and most brilliant illustrations of the earnestness and devotion of the people of the South that had yet adorned the war.

The fact that but little hopes could be entertained of the eventual success of the defence of Vicksburg against the powerful concentration of the enemy's navy heightened the nobility of the resistance she made. The resistance of the enemy in circumstances which afford but a feeble and uncertain prospect of victory requires a great spirit; but it is more invaluble to us than a hundred easy victories; it teaches the enemy that we are invincible and overcomes him with despair; it exhibits to the world the inspirations and moral grandeur of our cause; and it educates our people in chivalry and warlike virtues by the force of illustrious examples of self-devotion.

But the people of the South had the satisfaction of witnessing an unexpected issue of victory in the siege of Vicksburg, and had occasion to learn another lesson that the history of all wars indicates, that the practical test of resistance affords the only sure determination whether a place is defensible or not. With a feeling of inexpressible pride did Vicksburg behold two immense fleets, each of which had been heretofore invincible, brought to bay, and unable to cope with her, kept at a respectful distance, and compelled to essay the extraordinary task of digging a new channel for the Mississippi.

In the month of July occurred the remarkable expedition of the celebrated John Morgan into Kentucky. The expedition of this cavalier was one of the most brilliant, rapid, and successful raids recorded in history. Composed of a force less than one thousand, consisting of Morgan's own regiment, with some partizan rangers from Georgia, and a Texas squadron, to which was attached two companies of Tennessee cavalry, it penetrated as far as Cynthianna. It was Morgan's intention to make a stand at Richmond, Kentucky, to await reinforcements, as he was persuaded that nearly the whole people of that State was ready to rise and join him; but finding that the enemy were endeavoring to envelope him with large bodies of cavalry, he was compelled to fall back. On reaching Somerset, he took possession of the telegraph, and very coolly countermanded all the previous orders that had been given by Gen. Boyle at Louisville to pursue him.

He had left Knoxville on the fourth day of July with nine hundred men, and returned to Lexington on the 28th with nearly twelve hundred. In twenty-four days he had penetrated two hundred and fifty miles into a country in full possession of the Yankees; captured seventeen towns; met, fought and captured a Yankee force superior to his own in numbers captured three thousand stand of arms at Lebanon; and, from first to last, destroyed during his raid military stores, railroad bridges, and other property to the value of eight or ten millions of dollars. He accomplished all this, besides putting the people of Cincinnati into a condition, described by one of their newspapers, as "bordering on frenzy," and returned to Tennessee with a loss in all his engagements of not more than ninety men in killed, wounded and missing.

While some activity was shown in extreme portions of the West, we shall see that our military operations from Greenbrier county, Virginia, all the way down to Chattanooga, Tennessee, were conducted with but little vigor. On the boundaries of East Tennessee, Southwestern Virginia and Kentucky, we had a force in the aggregate of thirty thousand men, confronted by probably not half their number of Yankee troops; yet the Southwestern counties of Virginia and the valley of the Clinch, in Tennessee, were entered and mercilessly plundered by the enemy in the face of our troops.

But we shall have occasion to notice the campaign in the West on a broader arena. We shall see how movements in this direction pressed back the discouraged and retreating foe. We shall see how these movements of the Confederates were intended to repossess the country previously occupied by them and to go forward to the redemption of the State of Kentucky, and the attack of one or more of the leading cities of the West; how, in the prosecution of this plan, North Alabama and Mississippi were speedily cleared of the footsteps of the foe; how all of Tennessee, save the strongholds of Memphis and Nashville, and the narrow districts commanded by them, were retrieved, and, by converging armies, nearly the whole of Kentucky was occupied and held—and how, at last, all these achievements were reversed in a night's time, and the most valuable and critical points abandoned by our troops, or rather by the will of the unfortunate general who led them.

But our narrative does not yet open on the chequered page of the West. That important part of our history is prefaced by the brilliant story of the summer campaign of the upper Potomac, and is relieved by dazzling lights of glory on the old battle-grounds of Virginia.

CHAPTER XVI.

Effect of McClellan's Defeat in the North.—Call for more Troops.—Why the North was not easily dispirited.—The War as a Money Job.—*Note:* Gen. Washington's Opinion of New England.—The Yankee Finances.—Exasperation of Hostilities.—The Yankee Idea of a "Vigorous Prosecution of the War."—Ascendancy of the Radicals. —War Measures at Washington.—Anti-Slavery Aspects of the War.—Brutality of the Yankees.—The Insensibility of Europe.—Yankee Chaplains in Virginia.—Seizures of Private Property.—Pope's Orders in Virginia.—Steinwehrs Order respecting Hostages.—The Character and Services of Gen. John Pope.—The "Army of Virginia."— Irruption of the Northern Spoilsmen.—The Yankee Trade in Counterfeit Confederate Notes.—Pope's "Chasing the Rebel Hordes."—Movement against Pope by "Stone wall" Jackson.—BATTLE OF CEDAR MOUNTAIN.—McClellan recalled from the Peninsula.—The Third Grand Army of the North.—Jackson's Surprise of the Enemy at Manassas.—A Rapid and Masterly Movement.—Change of the Situation.—Attack by the Enemy upon Bristow Station and at Manassas Junction.—Marshalling of the Hosts.—Longstreet's Passage of Thoroughfare Gap.—The Plans of Gen. Lee.—Spirit of our Troops.—Their Painful Marches.—THE SECOND BATTLE OF MANASSAS.—A terrible Bayonet Charge.—Rout of the Enemy.—A hideous Battle-field.—Gen. Lee and he Summer Campaign of Virginia.—Jackson's Share in it.—Extent of the Great Victory of Manassas.—Excitement in Washington.—The Yankee Army falls back upon Alexandria and Washington.—Review of the Situation.—Rapid Change in our Military Fortunes.—What the South had accomplished.—Comparison of Material Strength between North and South.—Humiliating Result to the Warlike Reputation of the North.

THE effect of the defeat of McClellan before Richmond was received at the North with ill-concealed mortification and anxiety. Beneath the bluster of the newspapers, and the affectations of public confidence, disappointment, embarrassment and alarm were perceptible. The people of the North had been so assured of the capture of Richmond, that it was difficult to reanimate them on the heels of McClellan's retreat. The prospects held out to them so long, of ending the war in "sixty days," "crushing out the rebellion," and eating victorious dinners in Richmond, had been bitterly disappointed and were not to be easily renewed. The government at Washington showed its appreciation of the disaster its arms had sustained by making a call for three hundred thousand additional troops;[*]

---

[*] The Army *Register*, published at Washington, in its statement of the organization of the *regular* army, enumerates as its force six regiments of cavalry, five of artillery, ten of infantry (old army), and nine of infantry (new army).

and the people of the North were urged by every variety of appeal, including large bounties of money, to respond to the stirring call of President Lincoln.

There is no doubt but that the North was seriously discouraged by the events that had taken place before Richmond. But it was a remarkable circumstance, uniformly illustrated in the war, that the North, though easily intoxicated by triumph, was not in the same proportion depressed by defeat. There is an obvious explanation for this peculiarity of temper. As long as the North was conducting the war upon the soil of the South, a defeat there involved more money expenditure and more calls for troops; it involved scarcely any thing else; it had no other horrors, it did not imperil their homes; it might easily be repaired by time. Indeed, there was some sense in the exhortation of some of the Northern orators, to the effect that defeat made their people stronger than ever, because, while it required them to put forth their energies anew, it enabled them to take advantage of experience, to multiply their means of success, and to essay new plans of campaign. No one can doubt but that the celebrated Manassas defeat really strengthened the North; and doubtless the South would have realized the same consequence of the second repulse of the enemy's movements on Richmond, if it had been attended by the same conditions on our part of inaction and repose.

It is curious to observe how completely the ordinary aspects of war were changed and its horrors diminished, with reference to the North, by the false policy of the South, in keeping

---

The strength of this branch of the service in men, may be thus stated:

Total commissioned officers, ...	2,388
Total enlisted, ...	40,626
Aggregate,	43,014

The figures which are collected below, to show the organization of the *volunteer* army of the North, refer to the date of the *Register*, August 1, 1862.

It appears that at this date there were in the volunteer army of the North seventy regiments of cavalry, seventy of artillery, and eight hundred and sixty regiments of infantry.

These startling official figures give the following result:

Total commissioned officers, ...	39,922
Total rank and file, ...	1,052,480
Aggregate,	1,092,402

the theatre of active hostilities within her own borders. Defeat did not dispirit the North, because it was not brought to her doors. Where it did not immediately imperil the safety of the country and homes of the Yankees, where it gave time for the recovery and reorganization of the attacking party, and where it required for the prosecution of the war nothing but more money jobs in Congress and a new raking up of the scum of the cities, the effects of defeat upon the North might well be calculated to be the exasperation of its passions, the inflammation of its cupidity, and the multiplication of its exertions to break and overcome the misapplied power of our armies.

Indeed, the realization of the war in the North was, in many respects, nothing more than that of an immense money job. The large money expenditure at Washington supplied a vast fund of corruption; it enriched the commercial centres of the North, and by artificial stimulation preserved such cities as New York from decay; it interested vast numbers of politicians, contractors, and dissolute public men in continuing the war and enlarging the scale of its operations; and, indeed, the disposition to make money out of the war accounts for much of that zeal in the North, which was mistaken for political ardor or the temper of patriotic devotion.*

---

* The following is an extract from an unpublished letter from Gen. Washington to Richard Henry Lee, and, as an exposition of the character of the Northern people from a pen sacred to posterity, is deeply interesting. There can be no doubt of the authenticity of the letter. It has been preserved in the Lee family, who, though applied to by Bancroft, Irving, and others for a copy for publication, have hitherto refused it, on the ground that it would be improper to give to the world a private letter from the Father of his Country reflecting upon any portion of it while the Union endured. But now, that "these people" have trampled the Constitution under foot, destroyed the government of our fathers, and invaded and desolated Washington's own county in Virginia, there can be no impropriety in showing his private opinion of the Massachusetts Yankees:

[Copy.]

CAMP AT CAMBRIDGE, Aug. 29, 1775.

Dear Sir: * * *

As we have now nearly completed our lines of defence, we have nothing more, in my opinion, to fear from the enemy, provided we can keep our men to their duty, and make them watchful and vigilant; but it is among the most difficult tasks I ever undertook in my life, to induce these people to believe that there is or can be danger, till the bayonet is pushed at their breasts; not that it proceeds from any uncommon prowess, but rather from an unaccountable kind of stupidity in the lower class of these people, which, believe me, prevails but

But while politicians plundered the government at Washington, and contractors grew rich in a single day, and a fictitious prosperity dazzled the eyes of the observer in the cities of the North, the public finances of the Yankee government had long ago become desperate. It is interesting at this point to make a brief summary of the financial condition of the North by

---

too generally among the officers of the Massachusetts part of the army, who are nearly of the same kidney with the private, and adds not a little to my difficulties, as there is no such thing as getting officers of this stamp to exert themselves in carrying orders into execution. To curry favor with the men (by whom they were chosen, and on whose smiles possibly they may think they may again rely) seems to be one of the principal objects of their attention. I submit it, therefore, to your consideration, whether there is, or is not, a propriety in that resolution of the Congress which leaves the ultimate appointment of all officers below the rank of general to the governments where the regiments originated, now the army is become Continental? To me it appears improper in two points of view—first, it is giving that power and weight to an individual colony which ought of right to belong to the whole. Then it damps the spirit and ardor of volunteers from all but the four New England governments, as none but their people have the least chance of getting into office. Would it not be better, therefore, to have the warrants, which the Commander-in-chief is authorized to give *pro tempore*, approved or disapproved by the Continental Congress, or a committee of their body, which I should suppose in any long recess must always sit? In this case, every gentleman will stand an equal chance of being promoted, according to his merit; in the other, all offices will be confined to the inhabitants of the four New England governments, which, in my opinion, is impolitic to a degree. I have made a pretty good slam among such kind of officers as the Massachusetts government abounds in since I came to this camp, having broken one colonel and two captains for cowardly behavior in the action on Bunker's Hill, two captains for drawing more provisions and pay than they had men in their company, and one for being absent from his post when the enemy appeared there and burnt a house just by it. Besides these, I have at this time one colonel, one major, one captain, and two subalterns under arrest for trial. In short, I spare none, and yet fear it will not all do, as these people seem to be too inattentive to every thing but their *interest*.

* * * * * * * * *

There have been so many great and capital errors and abuses to rectify—so many examples to make, and so little inclination in the officers of inferior rank to contribute their aid to accomplish this work, that my life has been nothing else (since I came here) but one continual round of vexation and fatigue. In short, no pecuniary recompense could induce me to undergo what I have; especially, as I expect, by showing so little countenance to irregularities and public abuses as to render myself very obnoxious to a great part of these people. But as I have already greatly exceeded the bounds of a letter, I will not trouble you with matters relative to my own feelings.

Your affectionate friend and obedient servant,
(Signed) GEO. WASHINGTON.

Richard Henry Lee, Esq.

a comparison of its public debt with the assets of the govern ment.

The debt of the present United States, audited and float ing, calculated from data up to June 30, 1862, was at least $1,300,000,000. The daily expenses, as admitted by the Chairman of the Committee of Ways and Means, was between three and four millions of dollars; the debt, in one year from this time, could not be less than two thousand five hundred millions of dollars.

Under the census of 1860, all the property of every kind in all the States was estimated at less than $12,500,000,000. Since the war commenced, the depreciation has been at least one-fourth — $3,175,000,000. From $9,375,000,000 deduct the property in the seceded States, at least one-third — $3,125,000,000; — leaving, in the present United States, $6,250,000,000.

It will thus be seen, that the present debt of the North was one-fifth of all the property of every kind it possesses; and in one year more it would probably be more than one-third. No people on earth had ever been plunged in so large a debt in so short a time. No government in existence had so large a debt in proportion to the amount of property held by its people.

In continuing the narrative of the campaign in Virginia, we shall have to observe the remarkable exasperation with which the North re-entered upon this campaign, and to notice many deeds of blackness which illustrated the temper in which she determined to prosecute the desperate fortunes of the war. The military authorities of the North seemed to suppose that better success would attend a savage war, in which no quarter was to be given and no age or sex spared, than had hitherto been secured to such hostilities as are alone recognized to be lawful by civilized men in modern times. It is not necessary to comment at length upon this fallacy. Brutality in war was mistaken for vigor. War is not emasculated by the observ-ances of civilization; its vigor and success consist in the resources of generalship, the courage of troops, the moral ardors of its cause. To attempt to make up for deficiency in these great and noble elements of strength by mere brutal severities—such as pillage, assassination, &c.—is absurd; it reduces the idea of war to the standard of the brigand; it offends the moral sentiment of the world, and it excites its enemy to the last stretch of determined and desperate exertion

There had long been a party in the North who mistook brutality in war for vigor, and clamored for a policy which was to increase the horrors of hostilities by arming the slaves, and making the invaded country of the South the prey of white brigands and "loyal" negroes. This party was now in the ascendency. It had already obtained important concessions from the Washington government. Nine-tenths of the legislation of the Yankee Congress had been occupied in some form or other with the question of slavery. Universal emancipation in the South, and the utter overthrow of all property, was now the declared policy of the desperate and demented leaders of the war. The Confiscation Bill, enacted at the close of the session of Congress, confiscated all the slaves belonging to those who were loyal to the South, constituting nine-tenths at least of the slaves in the Confederate States. In the Border States occupied by the North, slavery was plainly doomed under a plan of emancipation proposed by Mr. Lincoln with the flimsy and ridiculous pretence of compensation to slaveholders.*

These concessions to the radical party in the North excited new demands. The rule which was urged upon the government, and which the government hastened to accept, was to

---

* According to the census of 1860—

Kentucky had	225,490	slaves.
Maryland	87,188	"
Virginia	490,887	"
Delaware	1,798	"
Missouri	114,965	"
Tennessee	275,784	"
Making in the whole	1,196,112	"

At the proposed rate of valuation, these would amount to...... $358,833,600
Add for deportation and colonization $100 each............... 119,244,533

And we have the enormous sum of $478,078,133

It is scarcely to be supposed that a proposition could be made in good faith, or that in any event the proposition could be otherwise than worthless, to add this vast amount to the public debt of the North at a moment when the treasury was reeling under the enormous expenditures of the war.

spare no means, however brutal, to contest the fortunes of the war, and to adopt every invention of torture for its enemy. The slaves were to be armed and carried in battalions against their masters. The invaded country of the South was to be pillaged, wasted, and burnt; the Northern troops, like hungry locusts, were to destroy every thing green; the people in the invaded districts were to be laid under contributions, compelled to do the work of slaves, kept in constant terror of their lives, and fire, famine, and slaughter were to be the portion of the conquered.

Before the eyes of Europe the mask of civilization had been taken from the Yankee war; it degenerated into unbridled butchery and robbery. But the nations of Europe, which boasted themselves as humane and civilized, had yet no interference to offer in a war which shocked the senses and appealed to the common offices of humanity. It is to be observed, that during the entire continuance of the war up to this time, the British government had acted with reference to it in a spirit of selfish and inhuman calculation; and there is, indeed, but little doubt that an early recognition of the Confederacy by France was thwarted by the interference of that cold and sinister government, that ever pursues its ends by indirection, and perfects its hypocrisy under the specious cloak of extreme conscientiousness. No greater delusion could have possessed the people of the South than that the *government* of England was friendly to them. That government, which prided itself on its cold and ingenious selfishness, seemed to have discovered a much larger source of profit in the continuation of the American war than it could possibly derive from a pacification of the contest. It was willing to see its operatives starving and to endure the distress of a "cotton famine," that it might have the ultimate satisfaction, which it anticipated, of seeing both parties in the American war brought to the point of exhaustion, and its own greatness enlarged on the ruins of a hated commercial rival. The calculation was far-reaching; it was characteristic of a government that secretly laughed at all sentiment, made an exact science of selfishness, and scorned the weakness that would sacrifice for any present good the larger fruits of the future.

This malevolent and venomous spirit of anti-slavery in the

war pervaded the whole of Northern society. It was not only the utterance of such mobs as, in New York city, adopted as their war-cry against the South, "*kill all the inhabitants;*" it found expression in the political measures, military orders and laws of the government; it invaded polite society, and was taught not only as an element of patriotism, but as a virtue of religion. The characteristic religion of New England, composed of about equal quantities of blasphemy and balderdash, went hand in hand with the war. Some of these pious demonstrations were curious, and bring to remembrance the fanaticism and rhapsodies of the old Puritans.*

The Yankee army chaplains in Virginia alternately disgusted and amused the country with the ferocious rant with which they sought to inspire the crusade against the South. One of these pious missionaries in Winchester, after the regular Sunday service, announced to the assembled Yankee troops an imaginary victory in front of Richmond, and then called for "three cheers and a tiger, and Yankee Doodle." In a sermon preached near the enemy's camp of occupation, the chaplain proclaimed the mission of freeing the negroes. He told them they were free, and that, as the property amassed by their masters was the fruit of the labors of the blacks, these had the best title to it

---

* No one affected the peculiarity of the Puritans more than Gov. Andrews, of Massachusetts. The following pious rant is quoted from one of his speeches at Worcester; in blasphemy and bombast it equals any of the fulminations of the "Pilgrim Fathers"—

" I know that the angel of the Lord, one foot on the earth and one on the sea, will proclaim in unanswerable language, that four millions of bondmen shall ere long be slaves no longer. We live in a war, not a riot; as we thought last year, with a half million in the field against an atrocious and rebellious foe. Our government now recognizes it as a war, and the President of the United States, fulminating his war-orders, has blown a blast before which the enemy must fly. Rebellion must fall, and they who have stood upon the necks of so many bondsmen shall be swept away, and four million souls rise to immortality.

" Ah, foul tyrants! do you hear him where he comes?
Ah, black traitors! do you know him as he comes?
In the thunder of the cannon and the roll of the drums,
    As we go marching on.

" Men may die and moulder in the dust—
Men may die and arise again from the dust,
Shoulder to shoulder in the ranks of the just,
    When God is marching on."

and should help themselves. At another place, near the scene of the execution of John Brown for violation of law, sedition, and murder, a sermon was preached by an army chaplain on ome text enjoining " the mission of proclaiming liberty ;" and the hymn given out and sung was—

> "John Brown's body hangs dangling in the air,
> Sing glory, glory, hallelujah !"

These, however, were but indications displayed of a spirit in the North, which, with reference to the practical conduct of the war, were serious enough.

By a general order of the Washington government, the military commanders of that government, within the States of Virginia, South Carolina, Georgia, Florida, Alabama, Mississippi, Louisiana, Texas, and Arkansas, were directed to seize and use any property, real or personal, belonging to the inhabitants of this Confederacy which might be necessary or convenient for their several commands, and no provision was made for any compensation to the owners of private property thus seized and appropriated by the military commanders of the enemy.

But it was reserved for the enemy's army in Northern Virginia to exceed all that had hitherto been known of the savage cruelty of the Yankees, and to convert the hostilities hitherto waged against armed forces into a campaign of robbery and murder against unarmed citizens and peaceful tillers of the soil.

On the 23d of July, 1862, Gen. Pope, commanding the forces of the enemy in Northern Virginia, published an order requiring that " all commanders of any army corps, divisions, brigades, and detached commands, will proceed immediately to arrest all disloyal male citizens within their lines, or within their reach, in rear of their respective commands. Such as are willing to take the oath of allegiance to the United States, and will furnish sufficient security for its observance, shall be permitted to remain at their homes and pursue in good faith their accustomed avocations. Those who refuse shall be conducted South, beyond the extreme pickets of this army, and be notified that, if found again anywhere within our lines, or at any point in rear, they shall be considered spies and subjected to the extreme rigor of military law. If any person, having taken the oath of allegiance as above specified, be found to have violated it, he shall be shot, and his property seized and applied to the public use."

By another order of Brigadier-general Steinwehr in Pope' command, it was proposed to hold under arrest the most prominent citizens in the districts occupied by the enemy as hostages, to suffer death in case of any of the Yankee soldiers being shot by "bushwhackers," by which term was meant the citizens of the South who had taken up arms to defend their homes and families.

The Washington government had found a convenient instrument for the work of villany and brutality with which it proposed to resume the active campaign in Virginia.

With a view to renewed operations against Richmond, large forces of Yankee troops were massed at Warrenton, Little Washington and Fredericksburg. Of these forces, entitled the "Army of Virginia," the command was given to Maj.-gen John Pope, who boasted that he had come from the West, where "he had only seen the *backs* of the enemy."

This notorious Yankee commander was a man nearly forty years of age, a native of Kentucky, but a citizen of Illinois. He was born of respectable parents. He was graduated at West Point in 1842, and served in the Mexican War, where he was breveted captain.

In 1849 he conducted the Minnesota exploring expedition, and afterwards acted as topographical engineer in New Mexico, until 1853, when he was assigned to the command of one of the expeditions to survey the route of the Pacific railroad. He distinguished himself on the overland route to the Pacific by "sinking" artesian wells, and government money to the amount of a million of dollars. One well was finally abandoned incomplete, and afterwards a perennial spring was found by other parties in the immediate vicinity. In a letter to Jefferson Davis, then Secretary of War, urging this route to the Pacific and the boring these wells, Pope made himself the *especial champion of the South.*

In the breaking out of the war, Pope was made a brigadier general of volunteers. He held a command in Missouri for some time before he became particularly noted. When Gen.

Halleck took charge of the disorganized department, Pope was placed in command of the District of Central Missouri. He was afterwards sent to Southeastern Missouri. The cruel disposition of the man, of which his rude manners and a vulgar bearded face, with coarse skin, gave indications, found an abundant field for gratification in this unhappy State. His proceedings in Missouri will challenge a comparison with the most infernal record ever bequeathed by the licensed murderer to the abhorrence of mankind. And yet, it was his first step in blood—the first opportunity he had ever had to feast his eyes upon slaughter and regale his ears with the cries of human agony.

Having been promoted to the rank of major-general, Pope was next appointed to act at the head of a corps to co-operate with Halleck in the reduction of Corinth. After the evacuation of Corinth by Gen. Beauregard, Pope was sent by Halleck to annoy the rear of the Confederate army, but Beauregard turned upon and repulsed his pursuit. The report of Pope to Halleck, that he had captured 10,000 of Beauregard's army, and 15,000 stand of arms, when he had not taken a man or a musket, stands alone in the history of lying. It left him without a rival in that respectable art.

Such was the man who took command of the enemy's forces in Northern Virginia. His bluster was as excessive as his accomplishments in falsehood. He was described in a Southern newspaper as " a Yankee compound of Bobadil and Munchausen." His proclamation that he had seen nothing of his enemies " but their backs," revived an ugly story in his private life, and gave occasion to the witty interrogatory, if the gentleman who cowhided him for offering an indignity to a lady was standing with his back to him when he inflicted the chastisement. The fact was, that Pope had won his baton of marshal by bragging to the Yankee fill. He was another instance, besides that of Butler, how easily a military reputation might be made in the North by bluster, lying, and acts of coarse cruelty to the defenceless. On what monstrous principles he commenced his career in Virginia, and what orders he issued, are still fresh in the public memory.

" I desire you to dismiss from your minds certain phrases (said Pope to his army), which I am sorry to find much in vogue among you. I hear constantly of taking strong positions and holding them; of lines of retreat and bases of supplies. Let us discard such ideas. The strongest position a soldier should desire to occupy is the one from which he can most easily advance upon the enemy. Let us study the probable line of retreat of our opponents, and leave our own to take care of itself. Let us look before, and not behind. Disaster and shame lurk in the rear."

On establishing his headquarters at Little Washington, the county seat of Rappahannock, Pope became a source of mingled curiosity and dread to the feeble villagers. They were in a condition of alarm and anguish from the publication of his order, to banish from their homes all males who should refuse to take the Yankee oath of allegiance. Dr. Bisphaw of the village was deputed to wait upon the Yankee tyrant, and ask that the barbarous order be relaxed.

He painted, at the same time, the agony of the women and children, and stated that the effect would be to place six new regiments in the rebel service. "We can't take the oath of allegiance," said the Doctor, "and we won't—man, woman, or child—but we will give a parol to attend to our own business, afford no communication with the South, and quietly stay upon our premises."

"I shall enforce the order to the letter," said Gen. Pope. "I did not make it without deliberation, and if you don't take the oath you shall go out of my lines."

In the short period in which Pope's army was uninterrupted in its career of robbery and villany in Northern Virginia, every district of country invaded by him, or entered by his marauders, was ravaged as by a horde of barbarians. This portion of Virginia will long bear the record and tradition of the irruption of the Northern spoilsmen. The new usage which had been instituted in regard to protection of Confederate property, and the purpose of the Washington government to subsist its troops upon the invaded country, converted the "Army of Virginia" into licensed brigands, and let loose upon the country a torrent of unbridled and unscrupulous robbers. The Yankee troops appropriated remorselessly whatever came within their reach. They rushed in crowds upon the smoke-houses of the farmers. On the march through a section of country, every spring-house was broken open; butter, milk eggs, and cream were ingulfed; calves and sheep, and, in fact, any thing and every thing serviceable for meat, or drink, or apparel, were not safe a moment after the approach of the Yankee plunderers. Wherever they camped at night, it would be found the next morning that scarcely an article, for which the fertility of a soldier could suggest the slightest use, remained to the owner. Pans, kettles, dishcloths, pork, poultry, provisions, and every thing desirable had disappeared. The place was stripped, and without any process of commissary or quartermaster.

Whenever the Yankee soldiers advanced into a new section, the floodgates were immediately opened, and *fac-simile* Confederate notes (this spurious currency being manufactured in Philadelphia, and sold by public advertisement for a few cents to Yankee soldiers) were poured out upon the land.* They were passed indiscriminately upon the unsuspecting inhabitants, poor as well as rich, old and young, male and female. In frequent instances, this outrage was perpetrated in return for kind nursing by poor, aged women.

These spurious notes passed readily, and seemed to be taken gladly for whatever was held for sale. Bank-notes and shinplasters were given for change. Horses and other valuable property were often purchased with this bogus currency. A party of Yankee soldiers entered a country store, fortified with exhaustless quantities of Philadelphia Confederate notes, and

---

* The Northern trade in this counterfeit money was open and undisguised; enticing advertisements of its profit were freely made in the Northern journals, and circulars were distributed through the Federal army proposing to supply the troops with "rebel" currency almost at the price of the paper on which the counterfeit was executed. We copy below one of these circulars found on the person of a Yankee prisoner; the curiosity being a court paper in the possession of Mr. Commissioner Watson, of Richmond:

"$20 *Confederate Bond ! !* I have this day issued a *fac-simile* $20 Confederate Bond—making, in all, fifteen different *fac-simile* Rebel Bonds, Notes, Shinplasters, and Postage Stamps, issued by me the past three months.

"Trade supplied at 50 cents per 100, or $4 per 1,000. All orders by mail or express promptly executed.

☞ "All orders to be sent by mail must be accompanied with 18 cents in postage stamps, in addition to the above price, to prepay the postage on each 100 ordered. Address, S. C. UPHAM,
403 Chesnut Street, Philadelphia.

" N. B.—I shall have a $100 Rebel Note out this week."

commenced trade. Forty pounds of sugar was first ordered, and the storekeeper, pleased with the sudden increase of business, called in his wife to assist in putting up the order in small parcels. Seventy-five cents a pound was the cost. That was a small matter. Matches were purchased. Twenty-five cents per box was the charge. Tobacco also found a ready market. Each man provided himself with a straw hat; but the crowning act of all was the abstraction from the till of money already paid to the dealer for his goods, and the purchase of more goods with the same spurious medium.

Such acts of villany and the daily robberies committed by Pope's soldiers were very amusing to the Northern people, and gave them a stock of capital jokes. "I not long ago saw," wrote a correspondent of a Yankee newspaper, "a dozen soldiers rushing headlong through a field, each anxious to get the first choice of three horses shading themselves quietly under a tree. The animals made their best time into the farthest corner of the field with the men close upon them, and the foremost men caught their prizes and bridled them as if they had a perfect immunity in such sort of things. A scene followed. A young lady came out and besought the soldiers not to take her favorite pony. The soldiers were remorseless and unyielding, and the pony is now in the army."

It is not within the design of these pages to pursue the stories of outrage, villany, and barbarism of the enemy's army in Virginia; but with what we have said, intended only to show the spirit of that army and the character of its leader, we shall hasten to describe the series of events which, at last, confronted it with an army of avengers on the historic Plains of Manassas, and culminated there in a victory, which liberated Virginia from its invaders, broke the "line of the Potomac" from Leesburg to Harper's Ferry, and opened an avenue for the first time into the territory of the North.

THE BATTLE OF CEDAR MOUNTAIN.

The Northern newspapers declared that Pope was right when he said that he was accustomed to see the backs of his enemy, and were busy in assuring their readers that his only occupation was to chase "the rebel hordes." It was said that

he had penetrated as far as Madison Court-house without seeing any enemy. The Southern troops, it was prophesied, would
keep on their retreat beyond the Virginia Central railroad
Pope's army was now as far in the interior, by overland
marches, as any of the Yankee troops had ever been. The
position of his advance was described as about ten miles east
of Port Republic, with an eye on the Shenandoah Valley; and
it was boasted that the second Napoleon of the Yankees had
already complete possession of the country north of the Rapidan river, and only awaited his leisure to march upon Richmond.

These exultations were destined to a sharp and early disappointment. The Confederate authorities in Richmond knew
that it was necessary to strike somewhere before the three hundred thousand recruits called for by the Washington government should be brought to the field to overwhelm them. It
was necessary to retain in the strong works around Richmond
a sufficient force to repulse any attack of McClellan's army;
but at the same time the necessity was clear to hold Pope's
forces in check and to make an active movement against him.
The execution of this latter purpose was intrusted to Jackson,
the brave, eccentric, and beloved commander,* who had
achieved so many victories against so many extraordinary
odds and obstacles; all the movements of the campaign being
directed by the self-possessed, controlling, and earnest mind of
Gen. Lee.

The insolent enemy received his first lesson at the hands of

---

* There have been a great many pen and ink portraits of the famous "Stonewall"
Jackson ; the singular features and eccentric manners of this popular hero affording a fruitful subject of description and anecdote. A gentleman, who was known
to be a rare and quick judge of character, was asked by the writer for a description of Jackson, whom he had met but for a few moments on the battle-field.
"He is a fighting man," was the reply; "rough mouth, iron jaw, and nostrils
big as a horse's." This description has doubtless much force in it, although
blunt and homely in its expression. The impression given by Jackson is that
of a man perhaps forty years old, six feet high, medium size, and somewhat
angular in person. He has yellowish-gray eyes, a Roman nose, sharp ; a thin,
forward chin, angular brow, a close mouth, and light brown hair. The expression of his face is to some extent unhappy, but not sullen or unsocial. He is
impulsive, silent, and emphatic. His dress is official, but very plain, his cap-front
resting nearly on his nose. His tall horse diminished the effect of his size, so
that when mounted he appears less in person than he really is

the heroic Jackson, on the wooded sides and cleared slopes of the mountainous country in Culpepper. In consequence of the advance of the Confederates beyond the Rapidan, Major-gen. Pope had sent forward two army corps, commanded by Gen. Banks, to hold them in check.

On the evening of the 8th of August, a portion of Gen Jackson's division, consisting of the 1st, 2d, and 3d brigades, under the command of Gen. Charles S. Winder, crossed the Rapidan river, a few miles above the railroad, and, having advanced a mile into Culpepper county, encamped for the night. The next morning, the enemy being reported as advancing, our forces, Ewell's division being in advance, moved forward on the main road from Orange Court-house to Culpepper Court-house, about three miles, and took position—our left flank resting on the Southwest Mountain, and our artillery occupying several commanding positions. At 12 M., our forces commenced cannonading, which was freely responded to by the enemy, who did not seem ready for the engagement, which they had affected to challenge. Indeed, some strategy seemed necessary to bring them to fight. About 3 P. M., Gen. Early's brigade (Ewell's division) made a circuit through the woods, attacking the enemy on their right flank, the 13th Virginia regiment being in the advance as skirmishers. At 4 o'clock the firing began, and soon the fight became general. As Gen. Jackson's division, then commanded by Gen. Winder, was rapidly proceeding to the scene of action, the enemy, guided by the dust made by the artillery, shelled the road with great precision. It was by this shell that the brave Winder was killed. His left arm shattered, and his side also wounded, he survived but an hour. At a still later period, a portion of Gen. A. P. Hill's division was engaged. The battle was mainly fought in a large field near Mrs. Crittenden's house, a portion being open, and the side occupied by the Yankees being covered with luxuriant corn. Through this corn, when our forces were considerably scattered, two Yankee cavalry regiments made a desperate charge, evidently expecting utterly to disorganize our lines. The result was precisely the reverse. Our men rallied, ceased to fire on the infantry, and, concentrating their attention on the cavalry, poured into their ranks a fire which emptied many a saddle, and caused the foe to wheel and retire, which, however, they effected without breaking their columns. For some time the tide of victory ebbed and flowed, but about dark the foe finally broke and retreated in confusion to the woods, leaving their dead and many of their wounded, with a large quantity of arms and ammunition, upon the field. Daylight faded, and the moon in her full glory appeared, just as the terrors of the raging battle gave way to the sickening scenes of a field where a victory had been won.

The battle of Cedar Mountain, as it was entitled, may be characterized as one of the most rapid and severe engagements of the war. In every particular it was a sanguinary and desperate struggle, and resulted in a complete and decisive victory for our arms. Our forces engaged amounted to about eight thousand, while those of the enemy could not have been less than fifteen thousand. Our loss was near six hundred killed, wounded, and missing; that of the enemy little, if any, less than two thousand. We captured nearly five hundred prisoners, over fifteen hundred stand of arms, two splendid Napoleon guns, twelve wagon-loads of ammunition, several wagon-loads of new and excellent clothing, and drove the enemy two miles beyond the field of battle, which we held for two days and nights.

The battle was remarkable for an extraordinary and terrific "artillery duel." In fact, the fire was conducted with artillery alone for more than three hours. The opposing batteries unlimbered so close to each other that, during the greater part of the firing, they used grape and canister. Those working our battery could distinctly hear the hum of voices of the infantry support of the Federal battery. The Louisiana Guard artillery and the Purcell battery were ordered to take position and open on the enemy from the crest of a hill. Here they found themselves opposed by five batteries of the enemy within short range. The battle raged fiercely, the enemy firing with great precision. The accuracy of our fire was proved by the fact that the enemy, though their guns were more than twice as numerous, were compelled to shift the position of their batteries five different times. Once during the fight, the enemy's sharpshooters, under cover of a piece of woods, crept up within a short distance of our batteries and opened on them, but were instantly scattered by a discharge of canister from one of the howitzers.

The battle of Cedar Mountain was the natural preface to that larger and severer contest of arms which was to baptize, for a second time, the field of Manassas with the blood of Southern patriots, and illuminate it with the splendid scenes of a decisive victory. It convinced the North of the necessity of a larger scale of exertion and a concentration of its forces in Virginia to effect its twice-foiled advance upon the capital of the Confederacy. It was decided by the Washington government to recall McClellan's army from the Peninsula, to unite his columns with those of Pope, to include also the forces at Fredericksburg, and, banding these in a third Grand Army more splendid than its predecessors, to make one concentrated endeavor to retrieve its unfortunate summer campaign in Virginia, and plant its banners in the city of Richmond.

Not many days elapsed before the evacuation of Berkeley and Westover, on the James river, was signalled to the authorities of Richmond by the large fleet of transports collected on the James and the Rappahannock. It became necessary to meet the rapid movements of the enemy by new dispositions of our forces; not a day was to be lost; and by the 17th of August, General Lee had assembled in front of Pope a force sufficient to contest his further advance, and to balk his threatened passage of the Rapidan.

After the battle of Cedar Mountain, the forces under Stonewall Jackson withdrew from the vicinity of the Rapidan, and were for some days unheard of, except that a strong force was in the vicinity of Madison Court-house, some twelve miles to the westward, in the direction of Luray and the Shenandoah valley; but it was supposed by the enemy that this was only a wing of the army under Ewell, intended to act as reserves to Jackson's army, and to cover his retreat back to Gordonsville. Not so, however. Those forces of Ewell, as afterwards discovered by the Yankees to their great surprise, were the main body of Jackson's army; *en route* for the Shenandoah valley.

It was probably the design of Gen. Lee, with the bulk of the Confederate army, to take the front, left, and right, and engage Gen. Pope at or near the Rapidan, while Jackson and Ewell were to cross the Shenandoah river and mountains, cut off his supplies by way of the railroad, and menace his rear. The adventure, on the part of Jackson, was difficult and des perate; it took the risk of any new movements of Pope, by which he (Jackson) himself might be cut off. It was obvious indeed, that if Pope could reach Gordonsville, he would cut off Jackson's supplies, but in this direction he was to be confronted by Gen. Lee with the forces withdrawn from Richmond. With the movement of Jackson the object was to keep Pope between the Rapidan and the Rappahannock rivers until Jackson had attained his position at Manassas, or perhaps at Rappahannock bridge; but Pope's retreat to the Rappahannock's north bank frustrated that design, and rendered it necessary for General Lee to follow up his advantage, and, by a system of feints, to take Pope's attention from his rear and divert it to his front.

On Monday, the 28th of August, at daybreak, Gen. Jackson's corps, consisting of Gen. Ewell's division, Gen. Hill's division, and Gen. Jackson's old division, under command of Gen. Taliaferro, and a force of cavalry under Gen. Stuart, marched from Jeffersonton, in Culpepper county, and crossed the Rappahannock eight miles above that place, and marched by Orleans to Salem, in Fauquier. The next day they passed through Thoroughfare Gap, of Bull Run Mountains, to Bristow and Manassas stations, on the Orange and Alexandria railroad, effecting a complete surprise of the enemy, capturing a large number of prisoners, several trains of cars, and immense commissary and quartermaster stores, and several pieces of artillery. The distance marched in these two days was over fifty miles. On Wednesday, Manassas station was occupied by Jackson's old division, while Ewell occupied Bristow, and Hill and Stuart dispersed the force sent from Alexandria to attack what the enemy supposed to be only a cavalry force.

The amount of property which fell into our hands at Manassas was immense—several trains heavily laden with stores, ten first-class locomotives, fifty thousand pounds of bacon, one thousand barrels of beef, two thousand barrels of pork, several thousand barrels of flour, and a large quantity of oats and corn. A bakery, which was daily turning out fifteen thousand loaves of bread, was also destroyed. Next to Alexandria, Manassas was probably the largest depot established for the Northern army in Virginia.

The movement of Jackson, which we have briefly sketched, is the chief element of the situation in which the decisive en gagements of Manassas were fought. In this connection it must be studied; it was the brilliant strategic preface to the most decisive victory yet achieved on the theatre of the war. The corps of Jackson, having headed off the Federal army under Pope, had now possession of Manassas Plains. It had accomplished its design, which was to force Pope back—deprive him completely of direct communication with Washington or Alexandria, and eventually induce his surrender or annihilation.

The principal and anxious topic in the North was, by what eccentric courses the famous Confederate commander had managed to get around the right wing of Pope's army, when it was supposed—and in fact the hasty exultation had already been caught up in the Yankee newspapers—that it was the "rebel" general who was cut off, and that he would probably make a desperate retreat into the mountains to escape the terrors of Pope. Indeed, it was some time before the full and critical meaning of the situation dawned upon the prejudiced mind of the Northern public. The idea was indulged that the capture of Manassas was only a successful raid by a body of rebel guerillas; and so it was dismissed by the newspapers, with a levity characteristic of their insolence and ignorance.

Weak and credulous as Gen. Pope was, it is probable that the moment he heard that Jackson was in his rear, he was satisfied that it was no raid. The situation had been changed almost in a moment. Pope had evacuated Warrenton Junction, and was moving along the railroad upon Manassas, anxious to secure his "line of retreat," and expecting, doubtless, with no little confidence, by rapid marches of a portion of his forces by the turnpike upon Gainesville, to intercept any reinforcements by the way of Thoroughfare Gap to Jackson, and to fall upon and crush him by the weight of numbers. A portion of the Confederate army now fronted to the South, and the Federal army towards Washington. The latter had been swollen by reinforcements, and the advance corps from Burnside was marching on rapidly from Fredericksburg to complete the amassment on the Federal side.

Although the situation of Gen. Pope was one unexpected by himself, and surrounded by many embarrassments, he yet had many circumstances of advantage in which to risk a great and decisive battle. The New York journals persisted in declaring that it was not the infallible Pope, but the "rebel" army that was "in a tight place." At any rate, Pope was not in the situation in which McClellan found himself when his right wing was turned by the Confederates in front of Richmond—that is, without supports or reinforcements. On the contrary, on his right, and on the way up from Fredericksburg, was the new army of the Potomac under Burnside; while advancing forward from Alexandria was the newly organized army of Virginia under McClellan. Such was the array of force that threatened the army we had withdrawn from Richmond, and in which the Northern populace indulged the prospect of a certain and splendid victory.

An encounter of arms of vital consequence was now to ensue on the already historic and famous Plains of Manassas—the beautiful stretch of hill and dale reaching as far as Centreville, varied by amphitheatres—an admirable battle ground; with the scenery of which the Southern troops associated the exciting thoughts of a former victory and a former shedding of the blood of their beloved and best on the memorable and consecrated spots that marked the field of battle.

THE ENGAGEMENT OF WEDNESDAY, THE TWENTY-SEVENTH OF AUGUST.

On Wednesday, the 27th, an attack was made by the enemy upon Bristow station, and also at Manassas Junction.

On the morning of that day, at about eleven o'clock, Gen. Taylor's brigade, of Major-gen. Slocum's division of the army of the Potomac, consisting of the first, second, third, and fourth New Jersey regiments, were ordered to proceed to Manassas by rail from their camp near Fort Ellsworth, Alexandria.

The brigade arrived at Bull Run bridge about seven o'clock in the morning. The troops landed and crossed the bridge with as little delay as possible, and marched towards Manassas. After ascending the hill emerging from the valley of Bull Run, they encountered a line of skirmishers of the Confederates, which fell back before them. The brigade marched on in the direction of Manassas, not seeing any of the enemy until within range of the circular series of fortifications around the Junction, when heavy artillery was opened upon them frcm all direc tions. Gen. Taylor retired beyond the range of our guns to the rear of a sheltering crest of ground, from which he was driven by our infantry. Crossing at Blackburn's ford, he was pursued by our horse artillery, which fired into him, creating the utmost havoc. The brigade retreated in a disorganized mass of flying men towards Fairfax; it was pursued by oui eager troops beyond Centreville, and the track of the flying and cowardly enemy was marked with his dead.

The flight of the enemy was attended by the most wild and terrible scenes, as he was pursued by our horse artillery, pouring canister into his ranks. The brigade was almost annihilated. Gen. Taylor himself, his son on his staff, and his nephew were wounded; also one-half of his officers.

At 3 o'clock, P. M., of the same day, the enemy attacked Gen. Ewell, at Bristow, and that general, after a handsome little fight, in which he punished the enemy severely, retired across Muddy Run, as had previously been agreed upon, to Manassas Junction. This attack was made by the division of the enemy commanded by Gen. Hooker, which was dispatched to that point and detached from the advancing forces of Pope, who, of course, claimed the result of the affair as a signal Federal success.

MOVEMENTS OF THURSDAY, THE TWENTY-EIGHTH OF AUGUST.

After sunset, on Thursday, Gen. Jackson accomplished one of the most beautiful and masterly strategic movements of the war. He found himself many miles in advance of the rest of our army. The enemy might throw his immense columns between him and Longstreet—Alexandria and Washington was to his rear when he turned to attack the enemy. He determined to throw himself upon the enemy's flank, to preserve the same nearness to Alexandria, to place himself within support of the remainder of our army, and to occupy a position from which he could not be driven, even if support did not arrive in time. All this he accomplished that night, after destroying the stores, buildings, cars, &c., and burning the rail road bridges over Muddy Run and Bull Run. He marched at night with his entire force from Manassas station to Manassas battle-field, crossing the Warrenton turnpike, and placing his troops in such position that he could confront the enemy should they attempt to advance by the Warrenton pike or by the Sudley road and ford, and have the advantage of communicating by the Aldie road with Longstreet, should he not have passed the Thoroughfare Gap, and at all events gain for himself a safe position for attack or defence. At seven o'clock, A. M., on Friday, Gen. Stuart encountered the enemy's cavalry near Gainesville, on the Warrenton pike, and drove them back; and during the morning the 2d brigade of Gen. Taliaferro's division, under Colonel Bradley Johnson, again repulsed them. It was now ascertained that the enemy's column was advancing (or retreating) from Warrenton, along the line of the railroad and by way of the Warrenton turnpike, and that they intended to pass a part of their force over the Stone bridge and Sudley ford. Gen. Jackson immediately ordered Gen. Taliaferro to advance with his division to attack their left flank, which was advancing towards Sudley Mill. Gen. Ewell's division marched considerably in the rear of the 1st division. After marching some three miles, it was discovered that the enemy had abandoned the idea of crossing at Sudley, and had left the Warrenton pike to the left, beyond Groveton, and were apparently cutting across to the railroad through the fields and woods. In a few minutes, however, he advanced across the turnpike to attack us, and Jackson's army was thrown forward to meet him.

From this sketch of the movements of the corps commanded by Gen. Jackson, it will be seen that though a portion of our forces, under Gens. Ewell and Jackson, were on Tuesday and a part of Wednesday, the 26th and 27th of August, on the Orange and Alexandria railroad, between Pope and Alexandria, on the approach of Pope from Warrenton they withdrew to the west, and halted in the vicinity of the Warrenton turnpike, expecting to be rejoined by Longstreet, where they awaited the approach of the enemy and delivered him battle.

THE BATTLE OF FRIDAY, THE TWENTY-NINTH OF AUGUST.

The conflict of Friday occurred near the village of Groveton, our right resting just above and near the village, and the left

O'Neill, N.Y.

LT. GEN. LONGSTREET.

From a Photograph taken from life.

upon the old battle-field of Manassas. The division of Gen. Anderson had not yet arrived, and the corps of Longstreet had not been fully placed in position. The enemy, probably aware of our movements, selected this opportunity to make an attack upon Jackson, hoping thereby to turn our left, destroy our combinations, and disconcert the plans which had already become apparent to the Federal commanders.

Gen. Longstreet's passage of the Thoroughfare Gap, in the face of a force of two thousand of the enemy, is one of the most remarkable incidents of the late operations in Northern Virginia. The Gap is a wild, rude opening through the Bull Run Mountains, varying in width from one hundred to two hundred yards. A rapid stream of water murmurs over the rocks of the rugged defile, along which runs a stony winding road. On either side arise the mountains, those on the left presenting their flat, precipitous faces to the beholder, with here and there a shrub jutting out and relieving the monotonous gray of the rocky mass; and those on the right covered thickly with timber, impassable to any but the most active men. The strong position afforded by this pass, which might have been held against almost any force by a thousand determined troops and a battery of artillery, had been possessed by the enemy, who had planted his batteries at various points and lined the sides of the mountains with his skirmishers. As it was, the passage was effected by Longstreet's division with the loss of only three men wounded. This result was accomplished by a decisive piece of strategy, by which a small column of three brigades—Pryor's, Wilcox's and Featherstone's, and two batteries of rifle pieces—were thrown through Hopewell Gap, some three miles to the left of Thoroughfare Gap, as we approached Manassas.

Under Jackson and Longstreet, the details of the plan of Gen. Lee had been so far carried out in every respect. For ten days or more the troops of both of these generals in the advance were constantly under fire. The former had been engaged in no less than four serious fights. Many of the men were barefooted, in rags; provided with only a single blanket as a protection against the heavy dews and severe cold at night; frequently they would get nothing from daylight to daylight; rations at best consisted of bread and water, with a rare and economical intermingling of bacon; and the troops were in what at any other time they would have characterized as a suffering condition. Notwithstanding these adverse circumstances not a murmur of complaint had been heard; marches of twenty and in one instance of thirty, miles a day had been patiently endured, and the spirit of the army, so far from being broken, was elevated to a degree of enthusiasm which foreboded nothing but the victory it won.

On the morning of the 29th, the Washington Artillery of New Orleans and several other batteries were planted upon a high hill that commanded the extensive ground over which the enemy were advancing, and just in front of this, perhaps a little to the left, the fight began. The Federals threw forward a heavy column, supported by field batteries, and under cover of their fire made a bold stroke to divide our line. The blow fell upon a portion of Ewell's troops, who were concealed behind the embankment of a railroad; but no sooner had the enemy appeared within close range, than they received a terribly galling fire, which drove them panic-stricken from that portion of the field. As they ran, our artillery opened upon the flying mass with shell and round shot. Every ball could be seen taking effect. The enemy fell by scores, until finally the once beautiful line melted confusedly into the woods. Again they renewed the attack, and gradually the fight became general along nearly the entire column of Jackson.

As the afternoon progressed, however, Gen. Lee discovered that strong Yankee reinforcements were coming up, and he accordingly ordered the division of Gen. Hood, belonging to Longstreet's corps, to make a demonstration on the enemy's left. This was done, perhaps an hour before dark, and the moment they became engaged the difference became perceptible at a glance. Jackson, thus strengthened, fought with renewed vigor, and the enemy, not knowing the nature of the reinforcements, and diverted by our onset, which compelled him to change his lines, was proportionately weakened. The result was, that at dark Hood's division had driven the forces in front of them three-quarters of a mile from our starting-point, and, had it not been for the lateness of the hour, might have turned the defeat into an utter rout.

The conflict had been terrific. Our troops were advanced

several times during the fight, but the enemy fought with des
peration, and did not retire until nine o'clock at night, when
they sullenly left the field to the Confederates. During the
night orders came from head-quarters for our troops to fall back
to their original positions, preparatory to our renewal of the
action in the morning. It might have been this simple retrograde movement which led to the mendacious dispatch sent by
Pope to Washington, stating that he had whipped our army,
and driven us from the field,* but confessing that the Federal
loss was eight thousand in killed and wounded.

THE BATTLE OF SATURDAY, THE THIRTIETH OF AUGUST.

The grand day of the prolonged contest was yet to dawn.
For two days each wing of our army under Generals Longstreet and Jackson had repulsed with vigor attacks made on
them separately. Gen. Pope had concentrated the greater
portion of the army under his command for a desperate renewal of the attack on our lines. Friday night found those of
our men who were not engaged in burying the dead and bring
ing away the wounded, sleeping upon their arms. All the
troops of Longstreet's corps, with the exception of Gen. R. H.
Anderson's, which was only three or four miles in the rear, had
taken their places in the line of battle, and every one looked
forward to the events of the coming day, the anticipations of
which had sustained our soldiers under the terrible fatigue,
discomforts, and deprivations of the ten days' tedious march,
by which reinforcements had at last reached the heroic and
unyielding Jackson.

With the first streak of daylight visible through the light
mist that ascended from the woods, our men were under arms.
The pickets of the two armies were within a few hundred yards
of each other. Every circumstance indicated that the battle
would commence at an early hour in the morning. The waking

---

* It appears that Gen. R. H. Anderson's division, which came down the turn
pike on their way to Sudley Church, where they had been ordered the day before, were stopped by our pickets. and told that the enemy were in strong force
immediately in front. The general countermarched his division, wagons, and
artillery, and fell back in rear of Longstreet for the night. It is probable that
the enemy, seeing this, supposed it to be the falling back of our whole army.

of a portion of our batteries into life soon after daylight, and the frequent cannonading thereafter, the almost incessant skirmishing in front, with its exciting volleys of musketry, all conspired to produce this impression.

Our line of battle was an obtuse crescent in shape, and at least five miles long. Jackson's line, which formed our left, stretched from Sudley, on Bull Run, along the partly excavated track of the Manassas Independent line of railroad, for a portion of the way, and thence towards a point on the Warrenton turnpike, about a mile and a half in rear or west of Groveton. His extreme right came within about six hundred yards of the turnpike.

Longstreet's command, which formed our right wing, extended from the point near the turnpike on which Jackson's right flank rested, and prolonged the line of battle far to the right, stretching beyond the line of the Manassas Gap railroad.

It is thus seen that a point on the Warrenton turnpike, a mile and a half west of Groveton, was the centre of our position, and the apex of our crescent, whose convexity was towards the west. It was here, in an interval between Jackson's right and Longstreet's left that our artillery was placed. Eight batteries were planted on a commanding elevation.

The enemy's line of battle conformed itself to ours, and took, therefore, a crescent form, of which the centre or more advanced portion was at Groveton, whence the wings declined obliquely to the right and left. Their batteries were in rear of their infantry, and occupied the hills which they had held in the fight of July, 1861, but pointed differently.

The disposition of the enemy's forces was, Gen. Heintzelman on the extreme right and Gen. McDowell on the extreme left, while the army corps of Generals Fitz John Porter and Seigel, and Reno's division of Gen. Burnside's army, were placed in the centre.

The elevation occupied by our artillery, under command of Col. Stephen D. Lee, of South Carolina, was the most commanding ground that could have been selected for the purpose. It was about the centre of the entire army. To the front, the land breaks beautifully into hill and dale, forming a sort of amphitheatre. Around the field, and occasionally shooting into it in narrow bands, are heavy woods.

Early in the morning the immense masses of the enemy's infantry were seen in line of battle, and far in the distance immense clouds of dust filled the heavens. During this time our batteries were pitching their shot and shell into the Federal ranks, and returning the fire of their artillery on the brow of an opposite hill. Sometimes it was fierce, but generally it was a deliberate interchange of fire.

About 1 A. M. a regiment advanced rapidly on the enemy's left, determined to drive out our pickets from an orchard, where all the morning they had been keeping up a brisk fire. This effort succeeded, and our brave sharpshooters retired through the orchard in good order. As soon as they got well out of the way, our batteries opened upon the enemy, and in ten minutes they were retreating, sheltering themselves in the ravines and behind a barn. At 2 o'clock the forces that had been moving almost the whole day towards our left, began to move in the opposite direction, and it appeared that they were retiring towards Manassas, two or three miles distant. Several attempts were now made to advance upon our left like those to drive in our pickets on our right, but a few shells served to scatter the skirmishers and drive them into the woods that skirted this beautiful valley on either hand. When it appeared more than probable that the enemy, foiled in his attempt to make us bring on the fight by these little advances on our right and left, was about to retire, and merely kept up the cannonading in order to conceal his retreat, suddenly, at 4 P. M., there belched forth from every brazen throat in our batteries a volley that seemed to shake the very earth.

It was at this instant that the battle was joined. As the sporting whirls of smoke drifted away the cause of the tumult was at once discerned. A dense column of infantry, several thousand strong, which had been massed behind and near a strip of woods, had moved out to attack Jackson, whose men were concealed behind an excavation on the railroad. As soon as they were discovered our batteries opened with tremendous power, but the Federals moved boldly forward, until they came within the range of our small-arms, where for fully fifteen minutes they remained desperately engaged with our infantry As the fight progressed, a second line emerged from the cover and went to the support of those in front, and finally a third line marched out into the open field below us and there halted hesitated, and soon commenced firing over the heads of their comrades beyond.

Jackson's infantry raked these three columns terribly. Repeatedly did they break and run, and rally again under the energetic appeals of their officers, for it was a crack corps of the Federal army—that of Generals Sykes and Morrell; but it was not in human nature to stand unflinchingly before that hurricane of fire. As the fight progressed, Lee moved his batteries to the left, until reaching a position only four hundred yards distant from the enemy's lines, he opened again. The spectacle was now magnificent. As shell after shell burst in the wavering ranks, and round shot ploughed broad gaps among them, one could distinctly see through the rifts of smoke the Federal soldiers falling and flying on every side. With the explosion of every bomb, it seemed as if scores dropped dead, or writhed in agony upon the field. Some were crawling on their hands and knees; some were piled up together; and some were lying scattered around in every attitude that imagination can conceive.

Presently the Yankee columns began to break and men to fall out to the rear. The retreating numbers gradually increase, and the great mass, without line or form, now move back like a great multitude without guide or leader. From a slow, steady walk, the great mass, or many parts of it, move at a run. Jackson's men, yelling like devils, now charge upon the scattered crowd; but it is easily seen that they themselves had severely suffered, and were but a handful compared with the overwhelming forces of the enemy. The flags of two or three regiments do not appear to be more than fifty yards apart. The brilliant affair has not occupied more than half an hour, but in that brief time more than a thousand Yankees have been launched into eternity, or left mangled on the ground.

The whole scene of battle now changes. It will be seen in referring to the disposition of our forces, that Jackson's line, which formed our left, stretched from Bull Run towards a point on the Warrenton turnpike. In his severe action with the enemy, his left, advancing more rapidly than his right, had swept around by the Pittsylvania House, and was pressing the Federals back towards the turnpike. It was now the golden op

portunity for Longstreet to attack the exposed left flank of the
enemy in front of it.

Hood's brigade charged next the turnpike. In its track it
met Sickles' Excelsior brigade, and almost annihilated it.
The ground was piled with the slain. Pickett's brigade was
on the right of Hood's, next came Jenkins' brigade, and next
was Kemper's, which charged near the Conrad House. Evans'
and Anderson's were the reserve, and subsequently came into
action.

Not many minutes elapsed after the order to attack passed
along our entire line before the volleys of platoons, and finally
the rolling reports of long lines of musketry, indicated that
the battle was in full progress. The whole army was now in
motion. The woods were full of troops, and the order for the
supports to forward at a quick step was received with enthusiastic cheers by the elated men. The din was almost deafening, the heavy notes of the artillery, at first deliberate, but
gradually increasing in their rapidity, mingled with the sharp
treble of the small-arms, gave one an idea of some diabolical
concert in which all the furies of hell were at work. Through
the woods, over gently rolling hills, now and then through an
open field we travel on towards the front. From an elevation
we obtain a view of a considerable portion of the field. Hood
and Kemper are now hard at it, and as they press forward,
never yielding an inch, sometimes at a double quick, you hear
those unmistakable yells, which tell of a Southern charge or a
Southern success.

Reaching the vicinity of the Chinn House, the eye at once
embraces the entire vista of battle—at least that portion of it
which is going on in front of Longstreet. Some of our men
are in the woods in the rear, and some in the open field where
stretches the undulating surface far away towards Bull Run.
The old battle-ground is plainly discernible less than two miles
distant, and to the right and left, as well as in front, the country is comparatively unobstructed by heavy woods. Just before you, only three or four hundred yards away, are the infantry of the enemy, and at various points in the rear are their
reserves and batteries. Between the armies, the ground is
already covered with the dead and wounded, for a distance
lengthwise of nearly a mile.

Our own artillery are likewise upon commanding positions, and you hear the heavy rush of shot, the terrible dumps into the ground, and the crash of trees through which they tear with resistless force on every side.

Nothing can withstand the impetuosity of our troops. Every line of the enemy has been broken and dispersed, but rallies again upon some other position behind. Hood has already advanced his division nearly half a mile at a double-quick, the Texans, Georgians, and Hampton Legion loading and firing as they run, yelling all the while like madmen. They have captured one or two batteries and various stands of colors, and are still pushing the enemy before them. Evans, at the head of his brigade, is following on the right, as their support, and pouring in his effective volleys. Jenkins has come in on the right of the Chinn House, and, like an avalanche, sweeps down upon the legions before him with resistless force. Still further to the right is Longstreet's old brigade, composed of Virginians—veterans of every battle-field—all of whom are fighting like furies. The First Virginia, which opened the fight at Bull Run on the 17th of July, 1861, with over six hundred men, now reduced to less than eighty members, is winning new laurels; but out of the little handful, more than a third have already bit the dust. Toombs and Anderson, with the Georgians, together with Kemper and Jenkins, are swooping around on the right, flanking the Federals, and driving them towards their centre and rear. Eschelman, with his company of the Washington artillery; Major Garnett, with his battalion of Virginia batteries, and others of our big guns, are likewise working around upon the enemy's left, and pouring an enfilading fire into both their infantry and artillery.

While the grand chorus of battle is thundering along our front, Jackson has closed in upon the enemy on their right, and Longstreet has similarly circumscribed them on their left. In other words, the V shaped lines with which we commenced the engagement have opened at the angle, while the two opposite ends of the figure are coming together. Lee has advanced his battalion of artillery from the centre, and from hill-top to hill-top, wherever he can effect a lodgment, lets loose the racing masses of iron that chase each other through the Federal ranks. Pryor, Featherstone, and Wilcox being on the extreme left of Longstreet's line, are co-operating with the army of Jackson.

It was at this point of the battle, when our infantry, pouring down from the right and left, made one of the most terrible and sublime bayonet charges in the records of war. There was seen emerging from the dust a long, solid mass of men, coming down upon the worn and disheartened Federals, at a bayonet charge, on the double-quick. This line of bayonets, in the distance, presented a spectacle at once awful, sublime, terrible, and overwhelming. "They came on," said a Northern account, referring to the Confederates, "like demons emerging from the earth." With grim and terrible energy, our men came up within good range of the enemy's columns; they take his fire without a halt; a momentary confusion ensues as the leaden showers are poured into our ranks; but the next moment the bugles sound the order to our phalanxes, and instantly the huge mass of Confederates is hurled against the enemy's left wing. The divisions of Reno and Schenck—the choicest veterans of the Federal army are swept away. Setting up a yell of triumph, our men push over the piles of their own dead and the corpses of many a Federal, using the bayonet at close quarters with the enemy.

The rout of the enemy was complete. It had been a task of almost superhuman labor to drive the enemy from his strong points, defended as they were by the best artillery and infantry in the Federal army, but in less than four hours from the commencement of the battle our indomitable energy had accomplished every thing. The arrival of R. H. Anderson with his reserves soon after the engagement was fairly opened, proved a timely acquisition, and the handsome manner in which he brought his troops into position showed the cool and skilful general. Our generals, Lee, Longstreet, Jackson, Hood, Kemper, Evans, Jones, Jenkins, and others, all shared the dangers to which they exposed their men. How well their colonels and the subordinate officers performed their duty is best testified by the list of killed and wounded.

In determining the fortunes of the battle our cavalry had in more than one instance played a conspicuous part.

As the columns of the enemy began to give way, Gen. Beverly Robinson was ordered by Gen. Longstreet to charge the

flying masses with his brigade of cavalry. The brigade num
bering a thousand men, composed of Munford's, Myers', Harman's, and Flourney's regiments, was immediately put in motion, but before reaching the infantry, Gen. Robinson discovered
a brigade of the enemy, fifteen hundred strong, drawn up on
the crest of a hill directly in his front. Leaving one of his
regiments in reserve, he charged with the other three full at
the enemy's ranks. As our men drew near, the whole of the
Yankee line fired at them a volley from their carbines, most of
the bullets, however, whistling harmlessly over their heads.
In another instant the enemy received the terrific shock of our
squadrons. There was a pause, a hand-to-hand fight for a
moment, and the enemy broke and fled in total rout. All
organization was destroyed, and every man trusted for his
safety only in the heels of his horse.

Night closed upon the battle. When it was impossible to
use fire-arms the heavens were lit up by the still continued
flashes of the artillery, and the meteor flight of shells scattering their iron spray. By this time the enemy had been forced
across Bull Run, and their dead covered every acre from the
starting-point of the fight to the Stone bridge. In its first
stages, the retreat of the enemy was a wild, frenzied rout; the
great mass of the enemy moving at a full run, scattering over
the fields and trampling upon the dead and living in the mad
agony of their flight. The whole army was converted into a
mob; regiments and companies were no longer distinguisha-
ble; and the panic-stricken fugitives were slaughtered at every
step of their retreat—our cavalry cutting them down, or our
infantry driving their bayonets into their backs.

In crossing Bull Run many of the enemy were drowned,
being literally dragged and crushed under the water, which was
not more than waist deep, by the crowds of frenzied men pressing and trampling upon each other in the stream. On reaching Centreville the flight of the enemy was arrested by the
appearance of about thirty thousand fresh Yankee troops—
Gen. Franklin's corps. The mass of fugitives was here rallied
into the extent of forming it again into columns, and with this
appearance of organization, it was resolved by Gen. Pope to
continue his retreat to the intrenchments of Washington.

Thus ended the second great battle of Manassas. We had

driven the enemy up hill and down, a distance of two and a half miles, strewing this great space with his dead, captured thirty pieces of artillery, and some six or eight thousand stand of arms. Seven thousand prisoners were paroled on the field of battle. For want of transportation valuable stores had to be destroyed as captured, while the enemy at their various depots are reported to have burned many millions of property in their retreat.

The appearance of the field of battle attested in the most terrible and hideous manner the carnage in the ranks of the enemy. Over the gullies, ravines, and valleys, which divided the opposite hills, the dead and wounded lay by thousands, as far as the eye could reach. The woods were full of them. In front of the Chinn House, which had been converted into a hospital, the havoc was terrible. The ground was strewn not only with men, but arms, ammunition, provisions, haversacks, canteens, and whatever else the affrighted Federals could throw away to facilitate their flight. In front of the positions occupied by Jackson's men, the killed were more plentiful. In many instances as many as eighty or ninety dead marked the place where had fought a single Yankee regiment. Around the Henry and Robinson Houses the dead were more scattered, as if they were picked off, or killed while running. The body of a dead Yankee was found lying at full length upon the grave of the aged Mrs. Henry, who was killed by the enemy's balls in the old battle that had raged upon this spot. Three others were upon the very spot where Bartow fell, and within a few feet of the death-place of Gen. Bee was still another group. A little further on a wounded Federal had lain for the last two days and nights, where by extending his hand on either side he could touch the dead bodies of his companions. His head was pillowed on one of these. Confederate soldiers were also to be found in the midst of these putrefying masses of death; but these were comparatively rare. The scenes of the battle-field were rendered ghastly by an extraordinary circumstance. There was not a dead Yankee in all that broad field who had not been stripped of his shoes or stockings—and in numerous cases been left as naked as the hour he was born Our barefooted and ragged men had not hesitated to supply their necessities even from the garments and equipments of the dead.

The enemy admitted a loss down to Friday night of 17,000 men, Pope officially stating his loss on that day to have been 8,000. In one of the Baltimore papers it was said that the entire Yankee loss, including that of Saturday, was 32,000 men—killed, wounded, and prisoners. This statement allows 15,000 for the loss on Saturday. That the loss of that particular day was vastly greater than the enemy admit, we take to be certain. They are not the persons to over-estimate their own losses, and, in the mean time, Gen. Lee tells us that over 7,000 of them were taken and paroled on the field. If they fought the battle with any thing like the desperation they pretend, considering that it lasted five hours, they certainly had more than 8,000 killed and wounded. Four days after the battle there were still three thousand wounded Yankees uncared for within the lines of Gen. Lee. It is very certain, if they were not cared for, it was because the number of wounded was so great that their turn had not come. Our own wounded, not exceeding, it is said, 3,000, could very well be attended to in a day, and then the turn of the Yankees would come. Yet so numerous were they, that at the end of four days three thousand of them had not received surgical assistance. This indicates an enormous list of wounded, and confirms the report of one officer, who puts down their killed at 5,000, and their wounded at three times that figure, making 20,000 killed and wounded, and of others who say that their killed and wounded were to us in the proportion of five, six, and even seven to one. As many prisoners were taken, who were not included in the 7,000 paroled men mentioned by Gen. Lee, we do not think we make an over-estimate when we set down the whole Yankee loss at 30,000 in round numbers. Their loss on Friday, estimated by Pope himself at 8,000, added to their loss on Saturday, makes 38,000. Previous operations, including the battle of Cedar Run, the several expeditions of Stuart, and the various skirmishes in which we were almost uniformly victorious, we should think would fairly bring the total loss of the enemy to 50,000 men, since our forces first crossed the Rapidan. This is a result almost unequalled in the history of modern campaigns.

The results of Gen. Lee's strategy were indicative of the resources of military genius. Day after day the enemy were beaten, until his disasters culminated on the plains of Manassas. Day after day our officers and men manifested their superiority to the enemy. The summer campaign in Virginia had been conducted by a single army. The same toil-worn troops who had relieved from siege the city of Richmond, had advanced to meet another invading army, reinforced not only by the defeated army of McClellan, but by the fresh corps of Generals Burnside and Hunter. The trials and marches of these troops are extraordinary in history. Transportation was inadequate; the streams which they had to cross were swollen to unusual height; it was only by forced marches and repeated combats they could turn the position of the enemy, and, at last succeeding in this, and forming a junction of their columns, in the face of greatly superior forces, they fought the decisive battle of the 30th of August, the crowning triumph of their toil and valor.

The route of the extraordinary marches of our troops presented, for long and weary miles, the touching pictures of the trials of war. Broken-down soldiers (not all "stragglers") lined the road. At night-time they might be found asleep in every conceivable attitude of discomfort—on fence rails and in fence corners—some half bent, others almost erect, in ditches and on steep hill-sides, some without blanket or overcoat. Daybreak found them drenched with dew, but strong in purpose; with half rations of bread and meat, ragged and barefooted, they go cheerfully forward. No nobler spectacle was ever presented in history. These beardless youths and gray-haired men, who thus spent their nights like the beasts of the field, were the best men of the land—of all classes, trades, and professions. The spectacle was such as to inspire the prayer that ascended from the sanctuaries of the South—that God might reward the devotion of these men to principle and justice by crowning their labors and sacrifices with that blessing which always bringeth peace.

The victory which had crowned the campaign of our armies in Virginia, illuminates the names of all associated with it. But in the achievement of that victory, and in the history of that campaign, there is one name which, in a few months, had mounted to the zenith of fame; which in dramatic associations, in rapid incidents, and in swift and sudden renown, challenged comparison with the most extraordinary phenomena in the annals of military genius. This remark is not invidious in its spirit, nor is it forced into the context of this sketch. A personal allusion may be spared in the narrative, when that allusion is to the most remarkable man in the history of the war.

We refer to Gen. Stonewall Jackson and that wonderful chapter of military achievements which commenced in the Valley of Virginia and concluded at Manassas. It was difficult to say what this man had not accomplished that had ever before been accomplished in history with equal means and in an equal period of time.

In the spring, Gen. Jackson had been placed in command of the small army of observation which held the upper valley of the Shenandoah and the country about Staunton. It was intended that he should remain *quasi* inactive, to watch the enemy and to wait for him; but he soon commenced manœuvring on his own responsibility, and ventured upon a scale of operations that threw the higher military authorities at Richmond into a fever of anxiety and alarm.

In less than thirty days he dashed at the Yankee advance and driving it back, wheeled his army, swept down the Valley and drove Banks across the Potomac. Returning to the upper Valley, he manœuvred around for three weeks—in the mean time dealing Fremont a heavy blow at Cross Keys and defeating Shields in the Luray valley—and then suddenly swept down the Virginia Central railroad, *via* Gordonsville, on McClellan's right, before Richmond. The part he played in winding up the campaign on the Peninsula is well known. Almost before the smoke had lifted from the bloody field of the Chickahominy, we hear of him again on his old stamping ground above Gordonsville. Cedar Mountain was fought and won from Pope before he knew his campaign was opened. Jackson fell back, but only to flank him on the right. Pope retired from the Rapidan to the Rappahannock, but Jackson swung still further round to the North, and outflanked him again. Yet again he gave up the Rappahannock and fell back south of Warrenton, and, for the third time, Jackson outflanked him through Thoroughfare Gap, and at last got in his rear. Pope now had to fight; and the victory which perched upon our banners was the most brilliant of the war.

It is curious to observe with what insolent confidence the North had anticipated a crowning triumph of its arms on the field of Manassas, even when the air around Washington was burdened with the signals of its defeat. The North did not tolerate the idea of defeat. On the very day of the battle, Washington was gay with exultation and triumph over an imagined victory. At thirty minutes past twelve o'clock, the Washington *Star* published a dispatch, declaring that it had learned from parties just from Fairfax county, that the firing had stopped; and added, "we trust the fact means a surrender of the rebels, and do not see how it can mean aught else." At a later hour of the afternoon, a dispatch was received at the War Department, from Major-gen. Pope, announcing a brilliant victory in a decisive battle with the Confederate forces on the old Bull Run battle-field. It was stated that he had defeated the Confederate army, and was driving it in discomfiture before him. This dispatch had a magical effect. The War Department, contrary to its usual custom, not only permitted, but officially authorized the publication of the dispatch. Citizens of every grade, of both sexes and of all ages, were seen in groups around the corners, and in the places of public resort, speculating upon the particulars and the consequences of the decisive victory reported. The triumph of the Federal arms was apparently shown to be more complete by reason of the announcement that Gen. Stonewall Jackson, with sixteen thousand of his troops, had been cut off and captured.

It was at this point of exultation that another dispatch was received from Gen. Pope, stating that the uncertain tide of battle had unfortunately turned against the Federal army, and that he had been compelled to abandon the battle-field during the evening. The revulsion was great; the untimely hallelu-iahs were interrupted, and the population of Washington, from its hasty and indecent exultations of the morning, was soon to be converted into a panic-stricken community, trembling for its own safety.

Indeed, the victory achieved by the Confederates was far more serious than the most lively alarm in Washington could at first imagine. The next morning after the battle, the last feeble resistance of the Federals at Centreville was broken. The finishing stroke was given by the Confederates under Gen.

A. P. Hill, who, on the first of September (Monday), encountered a large body of the enemy at Germantown, a small village in Fairfax county, near the main road leading from Centreville to Fairfax Court-house. The enemy, it appears, had
succeeded in rallying a sufficient number of their routed troops
at the point named, to make another show of opposition to
the advance of the victorious Confederates on their territory
On Sunday, the pursuit of Pope's army was commenced and
pressed with vigor on the Fairfax Court-house road, and on
Monday morning at daylight the enemy was discovered drawn
up in line of battle across the road, their right extending to
the village of Germantown. Gen. Hill immediately ordered
the attack, and after a brief but hotly contested fight, the
enemy withdrew. During the night, the enemy fell back to
Fairfax Court-house and abandoned his position at Centreville.
The next day, about noon, he evacuated Fairfax Court-house,
taking the road to Alexandria and Washington.

Thus were realized the full and glorious results of the second
victory of Manassas; thus were completed the great objects of
the brilliant summer campaign of 1862 in Virginia; and thus,
for a second time, on the famous borders of the Potomac, the
gates were thrown wide open to the invasion of the North, and to
new fields of enterprise for the victorious armies of the South.

The rapid change in the fortunes of the Confederacy, and
the sharp contrast between its late forlorn situation and what
were now the brilliant promises of the future, were animating
and suggestive topics.

Little more than three months had elapsed since the columns
of a hostile army were debouching on the plains near Richmond, when the evacuation of the city and a further retreat of
the Confederate army were believed by nearly all official persons the most prudent and politic steps that the government
could take under the circumstances. Little more than three
months had elapsed since our armies were retreating weak and
disorganized before the overwhelming force of the enemy,
yielding to them the sea-coast, the mines, the manufacturing
power, the grain fields, and even entire States of the Confederacy. Now we were advancing with increased numbers, improved organization, renewed courage, and the prestige of
victory, upon an enemy defeated and disheartened.

As the opposing armies of the war now stood, the South had causes for congratulation and pride such, perhaps, as no other people ever had in similar circumstances. The North had a population of twenty-three millions against eight millions serving the South, and of these eight millions nearly three millions were African slaves. The white population of New York and Pennsylvania was greater than that of the Confederate States. Manufacturing establishments of all descriptions rendered the North a self-sustaining people for all the requirements of peace or war, and, with these advantages, they retained those of an unrestricted commerce with foreign nations. The North had all the ports of the world open to its ships; it had furnaces, foundries, and workshops; its manufacturing resources, compared with those of the South, were as five hundred to one; the great marts of Europe were open to it for supplies of arms and stores; there was nothing of material resource, nothing of the apparatus of conquest that was not within its reach.

The South, on the other hand, with only a few insignificant manufactories of arms and materials of war, textile fabrics, leather, &c., had been cut off by an encircling blockade for fifteen months from all those supplies upon which she had depended from the North and from Europe, in the way of arms, munitions of war, clothing, medicines, and many of the essentials of subsistence. The South was without the vestige of a navy, except a straggling ship or two, while that of the North in this war was equal to a land force of three or four hundred thousand men. The South was nearly exhausted of the commonest articles of food, while the Northern States had a superabundance of all the essentials and luxuries of life. The Northern troops, *en masse*, were better armed, equipped, and subsisted than those of any other nation, while those of the South were armed with all sorts of weapons—good, bad, and indifferent—clothed in rags and fed upon half rations.

The result of all this immense and boasted superiority on the part of the North, coupled with the most immense exertions, was that the South remained unconquered. The result was humiliating enough to the warlike reputation of the North. It had not been separated from its feeble adversary by seas or mountains, but only by a geographical line; nature had not interfered to protect the weak from the strong. Three " grand armies" had advanced against Richmond ; and yet not only was the South more invincible in spirit than ever, but her ar mies of brave and ragged men were already advancing upon the Northern borders, and threatening, at least so far as to alarm their enemy, the invasion of Ohio and Pennsylvania, and the occuvation of the Northern capital.

CHAPTER XVII.

THE close of the summer found the long-harassed soil of Virginia cleared of the footsteps of the invader. The glorious victory of Manassas was followed by other propitious events in this State of lesser importance, but which went to complete the general result of her freedom from the thraldom of the Yankee.

In the early part of September the campaign of Gen. Loring in the valley of the Kanawha was consummated by a vigorous attack on the enemy at Fayette Court-house, and the occupation of Charlestown by our troops. On the 10th of that month we advanced upon the enemy's front at Fayette Court-house, while a portion of our forces made a detour over the mountain so as to attack him in the rear. The fighting continued from noon until night, our artillery attacking desperately in front; and the enemy took advantage of the darkness to effect his escape, not, however, without leaving his trains in our hands.

The Yankees made a stand at Cotton Hill, seven miles further on. A few hours' fighting dislodged them, and we pursued on to Kanawha Falls, where they again made a stand: but a few hours' contest made us again masters of the field, with more than a million dollars' worth of stores and some prisoners.

The advance of our troops to Charlestown was the signal to the enemy for an inhuman attempt to burn the town, the women being driven from their homes on fifteen minutes' notice. As our troops approached the town, dense clouds of black smoke were seen to hang over it, mingled with the lurid glare of burning buildings, while the shrieks of frightened women and children filled the air. The sight stung to madness our troops. Two regiments of Kanawha valley men, beholding in plain view the homes of their childhood blazing, and catching the cries of distress of their mothers, wives, and sisters, rushed, furious and headlong, to the rescue. Happily they were not too late to arrest the conflagration, and a few public buildings and some private residences were all that fell under the enemy's torch.

The campaign of the Kanawha was accomplished by us with a loss of not more than a hundred men. The results were apparently of great importance, as we had secured the great salines of Virginia,* driven the enemy from the valley of the Kanawha, and put our forces in position to threaten his towns on the bank of the Ohio. But unhappily we shall have occasion hereafter to see that these results were ephemeral, and that this unfortunate part of Virginia was destined to other experiences of the rigor of the enemy.

For the present the progress of events takes us from the old battle-fields of the South and introduces us to a novel theatre of the war—that theatre being located for the first time on the soil and within the recognized dominions of the enemy.

On the fourth day of September, Gen. Lee, leaving to his right Arlington Heights, to which had retreated the shattered army of Pope, crossed the Potomac into Maryland.

The immediate designs of this movement of the Confederate

---

* But few persons, even in the South, have adequate ideas of the resources and facilities for the production of salt in the Kanawha valley, and of the value of that small strip of Confederate territory. In Kanawha county alone forty furnaces were in operation; some operated by gas and some by coal. Salt by the million of bushels had been sold here from year to year at twelve cents and twenty cents per bushel, filling the markets of the West and South. Ships for Liverpool had formerly taken out salt as ballast; and yet, at one time in the war, owing to the practical cutting off of the saline supplies in Virginia, this article, formerly of such cheap bulk, had been sold in Richmond at a dollar and a half *a pound.*

commander were to seize Harper's Ferry and to test the spirit
of the Marylanders; but in order to be unmolested in his plans,
he threatened Pennsylvania from Hagerstown, throwing Gov.
Curtin almost into hysterics, and animating Baltimore with
the hope that he would emancipate her from the iron tyranny
of Gen. Wool.

After the advance of our army to Frederick, the Northern
journals were filled with anxious reports of a movement of our
troops in the direction of Pennsylvania. While the people of
the North were agitated by these reports, the important movement undertaken for the present by Gen. Lee was in the direction of Virginia. It appears that for this purpose our forces
in Maryland were divided into three corps, commanded by
Generals Jackson, Longstreet, and Hill. The forces under
Jackson having recrossed the Potomac at Williamsport and
taken possession of Martinsburg, had then passed rapidly behind Harper's Ferry, that a capture might be effected of the
garrison and stores known to be there. In the mean time, the
corps of Longstreet and Hill were put in position to cover the
operations of Jackson, and to hold back McClellan's forces,
which were advancing to the relief of Harper's Ferry.

Gen. McClellan had resumed the chief command of the
Federal armies on the second day of September. On the
fourteenth of that month, he fought his first battle in Maryland, called the battle of Boonesboro', or of South Mountain.

THE BATTLE OF BOONESBORO'.

When Jackson had diverged to the left from the line of
march pursued by the main body of the Confederates, recross-
ing the Potomac and moving rapidly upon Harper's Ferry,
Gen. Longstreet had meanwhile continued his march to Hagerstown, and there awaited the result. To frustrate this design, and relieve Gen. Miles and the ten or twelve thousand
men who occupied Harper's Ferry, the enemy moved their
entire force upon the Gap in the mountains, to which we have
alluded, and there sought to break through the barrier we were
so jealously guarding, divide our lines, and defeat our armies
in detail. Foreseeing this intention on the part of the Federals, Gen. Lee had posted the division of Gen. D. H. Hill in

and around the Gap, on the opposite side and summit, with instructions to hold the position at every hazard, until he was
notified of the success of the movement of Jackson and his
co-operates. It was certainly no part of the original plan to
fight a pitched battle here, except to secure this one desirable
result.

The pass is known as Boonesboro' Gap, being a continuation
over the broad back of the mountain of the national turnpike.
The road is winding, narrow, rocky, and rugged, with either a
deep ravine on one side and the steep sides of the mountain on
the other, or like a huge channel cut through a solid rock.
Near the crest are two or three houses, which, to some extent,
overlook the adjacent valleys, but elsewhere the face of the
mountain is unbroken by a solitary vestige of the handiwork
of man.

The battle commenced soon after daylight, by a vigorous
cannonade, under cover of which, two or three hours later, first
the skirmishers and then the main bodies became engaged. A
regular line of battle on our part, either as regards numbers
or regularity, was impossible, and the theatre of the fight was
therefore limited. The fortunes of the day, which were desperate enough in the face of the most overwhelming numbers,
were stubbornly contested by the Confederates. The brigade
of Gen. Garland of Virginia, the first engaged, lost its brave
commander. While endeavoring to rally his men, he fell,
pierced in the breast by a musket ball, and died upon the field.

While our lines were giving way under the pressure of the
enemy's numbers, the welcome sounds of reinforcements were
borne on the air. The corps of Gen. Longstreet was at Hagerstown, fourteen miles distant, and at daylight commenced
its march towards the scene of action. Hurrying forward
with all speed, stopping neither to rest nor eat, the advance
arrived at the pass about four o'clock, and were at once sent
into the mountain. Brigade after brigade, as rapidly as it
came up, followed, until by five o'clock nearly the entire command, with the exception of the brigade of Gen. Toombs,
which had been left at Hagerstown, was in position, and a portion of it already engaged. Evans was assigned to the extreme
left, Drayton to the right. and Hood, with his " ragged Texans," occupied the centre.

The accession of fresh numbers at once changed the tone and temper of the combat. The ominous volleys of musketry rolled down the mountain in almost deafening succession. But advance we could not. The enemy in numbers were like a solid wall. Their bayonets gleamed from behind every rock and bush. Retreat we would not, and thus we fought, doggedly giving and taking the fearful blows of battle, until long after nightfall.

The cessation of firing left the respective forces, with some exceptions, in nearly the same relative situation as at the commencement of the battle. The enemy gained nothing and we lost nothing. On the contrary, our object had been obtained. We had encountered a force of the enemy near fivefold our own, and after a bloody day, in which our killed and wounded were quite twenty-five hundred and those of the enemy probably more, we had held him in check until Gen. Jackson was heard from and the success of his enterprise rendered certain.

THE CAPTURE OF HARPER'S FERRY.

While the action of Boonesboro' was in progress, and the enemy attempting to force his way through the main pass on the Frederick and Hagerstown road, the capture of Harper's Ferry was accomplished by the army corps of Gen. Jackson.

During the night of the 14th of September, Gen. Jackson planted his guns, and in the morning opened in all directions on the Federal forces drawn up in line of battle on Bolivar Heights. The white flag was raised at twenty minutes past seven. At the moment of surrender, Col. Miles, the Federal commander, was struck by a piece of shell, which carried away his left thigh. "My God, I am hit," he exclaimed, and fell into the arms of his aid-de-camp.

The extent of the conquest is determined by the fact that we took eleven thousand troops, an equal number of small-arms, seventy-three pieces of artillery, and about two hundred wagons. The force of the enemy which surrendered consisted of twelve regiments of infantry, three companies of cavalry, and six companies of artillery. The scene of the surrender was one of deep humiliation to the North. It was indeed a repetition of the revolutionary glories of Yorktown, to see here the proud.

gayly-dressed soldiers of the oppressor drawn up in line, stack
ing their arms, and surrendering to the ragged, barefoot, half-
starved soldiers of liberty.*

---

* OFFICIAL REPORT OF OPERATIONS OF GEN. JACKSON'S COMMAND, from
September 5th to September 27th, 1862.

Headquarters 2d Corps A. N. V.,
April 23d, 1863.

General,—I have the honor to submit a report of the operations of my command from the 5th to the 27th of September, 1862, embracing the capture of
Harper's Ferry, the engagement at Shepherdstown, and so much of the battle
of Sharpsburg as was fought by my command.

My command comprised A. P. Hill's division, consisting of the brigades of
Branch, Gregg, Field (Col. Brockenbrough commanding), Pender, Archer, and
Col. Thomas, with the batteries of the division, under Lieut.-col. R. L. Walker ;
Ewell's division, under Brigadier-gen. Lawton, consisting of the brigades of
Early, Hays (Col. Strong), Trimble (Col. Walker), and Lawton (Col. Douglas),
with the artillery under Major Courtney ; and Jackson's division, under Briga
dier-gen. Starke, consisting of the brigades of Winder (Col. Grigsby), Jones (Col.
B. T. Johnson), Taliaferro (Col. Warren), and Starke (Col. Stafford), with the
artillery under Major Shumaker, Chief of Artillery.

On the 5th of September my command crossed the Potomac at White's ford,
and bivouacked that night near the Three Springs, in the State of Maryland.
Not having any cavalry with me except the Black Horse, under Capt. Randolph,
I directed him, after crossing the Potomac, to take a part of his company and
scout to the right, in order to prevent a surprise of the column from that direction.   For the thorough and efficient manner in which this duty was performed,
and for the valuable service rendered generally whilst attached to my headquarters, I desire to make special mention of this company and of its officers,
Capt. Randolph, and Lieuts Paine, Tyle, and Smith, who frequently transmitted orders, in the absence of staff-officers.

The next day we arrived in the vicinity of Frederick City.   Jackson's division
encamped near its suburbs, except the brigade of Gen. Jones (Col. Bradley T.
Johnson commanding), which was posted in the city as a provost guard.   Ewell's
and Hill's divisions occupied positions near the railroad bridge, on the Monocacy, guarding the approaches from Washington city.   In obedience to instructions from the commanding general, and for the purpose of capturing the Federal forces and stores then at Martinsburg and Harper's Ferry, my command
left the vicinity of Frederick City on the 10th, and passing rapidly through
Middletown, Boonesborough, and Williamsport, recrossed the Potomac into Vir
ginia, at Light's ford, on the 11th.   Gen. Hill moved with his division on the
turnpike direct from Williamsport to Martinsburg.   The divisions of Jackson
and Ewell proceeded towards the North Mountain depot, on the Baltimore and
Ohio railroad, about seven miles northwest of Martinsburg.   They bivouacked
that night in the vicinity of the depot.   In order to prevent the Federal forces
then at Martinsburg from escaping westward unobserved, Major Myers, commanding the cavalry, sent part of his troops as far south as the Berkeley and
Hampshire turnpikes.   Brigadier-gen. White, who was in command of the
Federal forces at Martinsburg, becoming advised of our approach, evacuated

THE BATTLE OF SHARPSBURG.

On the 17th of September Gen. Lee had retired to unite his forces, as far as possible, to confront the still advancing forces

---

the place on the night of the 11th, and retreated to Harper's Ferry. On the morning of the 12th, our cavalry entered the town, as in the course of the day did the main body of my command. At this point, abandoned quartermaster, commissary, and ordnance stores fell into our hands. Proceeding thence towards Harper's Ferry, about 11 o'clock, A. M., on the following morning (13th), the head of the column came in view of the enemy drawn up in force at Bolivar Heights. Gen. Hill, who was in the advance, went into camp near Hallstown, about two miles from the enemy's position. The two other divisions encamped near by.

The commanding general, having directed Major-gen. McLaws to move with his own and Gen. R. H. Anderson's division, to take possession of the Maryland Heights, overlooking Harper's Ferry, and Brigadier-gen. J. G. Walker, pursuing a different route, to cross the Potomac, and move up that river on the Virginia side, and occupy the Loudon Heights, both for the purpose of co-operating with me, it became necessary, before making the attack, to ascertain whether they were in position. Failing to learn the fact by signals, a courier was dispatched to each of these points for the required information. During the night the courier from the Loudon Heights returned, with a message from Gen. Walker, that he was in position. In the mean time, Gen. McLaws had attacked the Federal force posted to defend the Maryland Heights, had routed it, and taken possession of that commanding position. The Potomac river flowed between the positions respectively occupied by Gen. McLaws and myself, and the Shenandoah separated me from Gen. Walker; and it became advisable, as the speediest mode of communication, to resort to signals. Before the necessary orders were thus transmitted, the day was far advanced. The enemy had, by fortifications, strengthened the naturally strong position which he occupied along Bolivar Heights, extending from near the Shenandoah to the Potomac. McLaws and Walker, being thus separated from the enemy by intervening rivers, could afford no assistance, beyond the fire of their artillery, and guarding certain avenues of escape to the enemy. And from the reports received from them by signals, in consequence of the distance and range of their guns, not much could be expected from their artillery, so long as the enemy retained his advanced position on Bolivar Heights.

In the afternoon (14th), Gen. Hill was ordered to move along the left bank of the Shenandoah, turn the enemy's left, and enter Harper's Ferry. Gen. Lawton, commanding Ewell's division, was directed to move along the turnpike for the purpose of supporting Gen. Hill, and of otherwise operating against the enemy to his left.

Gen. J. R. Jones, commanding Jackson's division, was directed, with one of his brigades, and a battery of artillery, to make a demonstration against the enemy's right, whilst the remaining part of his command, as a reserve, moved along the turnpike. Major Massie, commanding the cavalry, was directed to keep upon our left flank, for the purpose of preventing the enemy from escaping. Brig.-gen. Walker guarded against an escape across the Shenandoah river.

of McClellan, which, having obtained possession of Crampton's Gap, on the direct road from Frederick City to Sharpsburg, were pressing our forces, and seemed determined on a decisive

---

Fearing lest the enemy should attempt to escape across the Potomac, by means of signals I called the attention of Major-gen. McLaws, commanding on the Maryland Heights, to the propriety of guarding against such an attempt. The demonstration on the left against the enemy's right was made by Winder's brigade (Col. Grigsby commanding). It was ordered to secure a commanding hill to the left of the heights, near the Potomac. Promptly dispersing some cavalry, this eminence, from which the batteries of Poague and Carpenter subsequently did such admirable execution, was secured without difficulty. In execution of the orders given Maj.-gen. Hill, he moved obliquely to the right until he struck the Shenandoah river. Observing an eminence, crowning the extreme left of the enemy's line, occupied by infantry, but without artillery, and protected only by an abatis of fallen timber, Pender, Archer, and Brockenbrough were directed to gain the crest of that hill, while Branch and Gregg were directed to march along the river, and during the night to take advantage of the ravines, cutting the precipitous banks of the river, and establish themselves on the plain to the left and rear of the enemy's works. Thomas followed as a reserve. The execution of the first movement was intrusted to Brig.-gen. Pender, who accomplished it with slight resistance; and during the night, Lieut.-col. Walker, chief of artillery of Hill's division, brought up the batteries of Captains Pegram, McIntosh, Davidson, Braxton, and Crenshaw, and established them upon the position thus gained. Branch and Gregg also gained the positions gained for them, and daybreak found them in rear of the enemy's line of defence.

As directed, Brig.-gen. Lawton, commanding Ewell's division, moved on the turnpike in three columns—one on the road, and another on each side of it—until he reached Hallstown, where he formed line of battle, and advanced to the woods on School-house Hill. The division laid on their arms during the night, Lawton and Trimble being in line on the right of the road, and Hays on his left, with Early immediately in his rear. During the night, Col. Crutchfield, my chief of artillery, crossed ten guns of Ewell's division over the Shenandoah, and established them on its right bank, so as to enfilade the enemy's position on Bolivar Heights, and take his nearest and most formidable fortifications in reverse. The other batteries of Ewell's division were placed in position on School-house Hill and Bolivar Heights, on each side of the road.

At dawn, Sept. 15th, Gen. Lawton advanced his division to the front of the woods, Lawton's brigade (Col. Douglas commanding) moved by flank to the bottom between School-house Hill and Bolivar Heights, to support the advance of Maj.-gen. Hill.

Lieut.-col. Walker opened a rapid enfilade fire from all his batteries at about one thousand yards' range. The batteries on School-house Hill attacked the enemy's line in front. In a short time the guns of Capts. Brown, Garber, Latimer, and Dement, under the direction of Col. Crutchfield, opened from the rear. The batteries of Poague and Carpenter opened fire upon the enemy's right. The artillery upon the Loudon Heights of Brig.-gen. Walker's command, under Capt. French, which had silenced the enemy's artillery near the superin-

battle. Sharpsburg is about ten miles north of Harpe.'s Fcrry, and about eight miles west of Boonesboro'.

This town lies in a deep valley. The country around it is broken. Ascending a hill just on the outer edge of the town,

---

tendent's house, on the preceding afternoon, again opened upon Harper's Ferry, and also some guns of Maj.-gen. McLaws, from the Maryland Heights. In an hour the enemy's fire seemed to be silenced, and the batteries of Gen. Hill were ordered to cease their fire, which was the signal for storming the works. Gen. Pender had commenced his advance, when, the enemy again opening, Pegram and Crenshaw moved forward their batteries and poured a rapid fire into the enemy. The white flag was now displayed, and shortly afterwards, Brig.-gen. White (the commanding officer, Col. D. S. Miles having been mortally wounded), with a garrison of about 11,000 men, surrendered as prisoners of war.

Under this capitulation we took possession of 73 pieces of artillery, some 13,000 small-arms, and other stores. Liberal terms were granted Gen. White and the officers under his command in the surrender, which I regret to say, do not seem, from subsequent events, to have been properly appreciated by their government.

Leaving Gen. Hill to receive the surrender of the Federal troops, and taking the requisite steps for securing the captured stores, I moved, in obedience to orders from the commanding general, to rejoin him in Maryland with the remaining divisions of my command. By a severe night's march, we reached the vicinity of Sharpsburg on the morning of the 16th.

By direction of the commanding general I advanced on the enemy, leaving Sharpsburg to the right, and took position to the left of Gen. Longstreet, near a Dunkard church, Ewell's division (Gen. Lawton commanding), forming the right, and Jackson's division (Gen. J. R. Jones, commanding), forming the left of my command. Major-gen. Stuart, with the cavalry, was on my left.

Jackson's division (Gen. Jones commanding), was formed partly in an open field and partly in the woods, with its right resting upon Sharpsburg and Hagerstown turnpike, Winder's and Jones' brigades being in front, and Taliaferro's and Starke's brigades a short distance in their rear, and Poague's battery on a knoll in front.

Ewell's division followed that of Jackson to the wood on the left of the road near the church. Early's brigade was thus formed on the left of the line of Jackson's division to guard its flank, and Hays' brigade was formed in its rear : Lawton's and Trimble's brigades remaining during the evening with arms stacked near the church.

A battery of the enemy, some five hundred yards to the front of Jackson's division, opening fire upon a battery to the right, was silenced in twenty minutes by a rapid and well-directed fire from Poague's battery ; other batteries of the enemy opened soon after upon our lines and the firing continued until after dark.

About 10 P. M., Lawton's and Trimble's brigades advanced to the front to relieve the command of Brigadier-general Hood (on the left of Major-general D. H. Hill), which had been more or less engaged during the evening. Trimble's brigade was posted on the right, next to Ripley's, of D. H. Hill's division, and Lawton's on the left.

and looking towards the Blue Ridge, the eye ranges over the greater portion of the eventful field. To the right and left is a succession of hills, which were occupied by the Confederates. In front is the beautiful valley of the Antietam, divided longitu-

---

The troops slept that night upon their arms, disturbed by the occasional fire of the pickets of the two armies, who were in close proximity to each other. At the first dawn of day, skirmishing commenced in front, and in a short time the Federal batteries, so posted on the opposite side of the Antietam as to enfilade my line, opened a severe and damaging fire. This was vigorously replied to by the batteries of Poague, Carpenter, Brockenbrough, Raine, Caskie, and Wooding. About sunrise the Federal infantry advanced in heavy force to the edge of the wood on the eastern side of the turnpike, driving in our skirmishers. Batteries were opened in front from the wood with shell and canister, and our troops became exposed, for near an hour, to a terrific storm of shell, canister, and musketry. Gen. Jones having been compelled to leave the field, the command of Jackson's division devolved upon Gen. Starke. With heroic spirit our lines advanced to the conflict and maintained their position in the face of superior numbers. With stubborn resolution, sometimes driving the enemy before them and sometimes compelled to fall back, before their well-sustained and destructive fire. Fresh troops from time to time relieved the enemy's ranks, and the carnage on both sides was terrific. At this early hour Gen. Starke was killed, Col. Douglas (commanding Lawton's brigade) was also killed ; Gen. Lawton, commanding division, and Col. Walker, commanding brigade, were severely wounded. More than half of the brigades of Lawton and Hays were either killed or wounded, and more than a third of Trimble's, and all the regimental commanders in those brigades except two were killed or wounded. Thinned in their ranks and exhausted of their ammunition, Jackson's division and the brigades of Lawton, Hays, and Trimble retired to the rear, and Hood, of Longstreet's command, again took the position from which he had been before relieved.

In the mean time, Gen. Stuart moved his artillery to a position nearer to the main command and more in our rear. Early being now directed, in consequence of the disability of Gen. Lawton, to take command of Ewell's division, returned with his brigade (with the exception of the 13th Virginia regiment, which remained with Gen. Stuart), to the piece of wood where he had left the other brigades of his division when he was separated from them. Here he found that the enemy had advanced his infantry near the wood in which was the Dunkard church, and planted a battery across the turnpike near the edge of the wood and an open field, and that the brigades of Lawton, Hays, and Trimble had fallen back some distance to the rear. Finding here Cols. Grigsby and Stafford with a portion of Jackson's division, which formed on his left, he determined to maintain his position there if reinforcements could be sent to his support, of which he was promptly assured. Col. Grigsby, with his small command, kept in check the advance of the enemy on the left flank while Gen. Early attacked with great vigor and gallantry the column on his right and front. The force in front was giving way under this attack, when another heavy column of Federal troops were seen moving across the plateau on his left flank. By this time the expected reinforcements, consisting of Semmes'

dinally by the river, which empties into the Potomac on your right, and behind, forming a background to the picture; only two miles distant are the steep, umbrageous sides of the Blue Ridge.

---

and Anderson's brigades, and a part of Barksdale's of McLaw's division, arrived, and the whole, including Grisby's command, now united, charged upon the enemy, checking his advance, then driving him back with great slaughter entirely from and beyond the wood, and gaining possession of our original position. No further advance, beyond demonstrations, was made by the enemy on the left. In the afternoon, in obedience to instructions from the commanding general, I moved to the left with a view of turning the Federal right, but I found his numerous artillery so judiciously established in their front and extending so near to the Potomac, which here makes a remarkable bend, which will be seen by reference to the map herewith annexed, as to render it inexpedient to hazard the attempt. In this movement Major-gen. Stuart had the advance and acted his part well. This officer rendered valuable service throughout the day. His bold use of artillery secured for us an important position, which, had the enemy possessed, might have commanded our left. At the close of the day my troops held the ground which they had occupied in the morning. The next day we remained in position awaiting another attack. The enemy continued in heavy force west of the Antietam on our left, but made no further movement to the attack.

I refer you to the report of Major-gen. A. P. Hill for the operations of his command in the battle of Sharpsburg. Arriving upon the battle-field from Harper's Ferry at half-past two o'clock of the 17th, he reported to the commanding general, and was by him directed to take position on the right. I have not embraced the movements of his division, nor his killed and wounded of that action in my report.

Early on the morning of the 19th we recrossed the Potomac river into Virginia, near Shepherdstown. The promptitude and success with which this movement was effected reflected the highest credit upon the skill and energy of Major Harman, chief quartermaster. In the evening the command moved on the road leading to Martinsburg, except Lawton's brigade (Col. Lamar, of the 61st Georgia, commanding), which was left on the Potomac Heights.

On the same day the enemy approached in considerable force on the northern side of the Potomac, and commenced planting heavy batteries on its heights. In the evening the Federals commenced crossing under the protection of their guns, driving off Lawton's brigade, and Gen. Pendleton's artillery. By morning a considerable force had crossed over. Orders were dispatched to Gens. Early and Hill, who had advanced some four miles on the Martinsburg road, to return and drive back the enemy.

Gen. Hill, who was in the advance, as he approached the town, formed his line of battle in two lines, the first composed of the brigades of Pender, Gregg, and Thomas, under the command of Gen. Gregg; and the second of Lane's, Archer's, and Brockenbrough's brigades, under command of Gen. Archer. Gen. Early, with the brigades of Early, Trimble, and Hays, took position in the wood on the right and left of the road leading to the ford. The Federal infantry lined the high banks of the Virginia shore, while their artillery, formidable

The morning of the 17th found Gen. Lee strongly posted, but with no more than forty-five thousand men when the battle commenced. The force of the enemy could not have been much short of one hundred and fifty thousand men, of whom one hundred thousand were trained soldiers, disciplined in camp and field since the commencement of the war.

The forces of the enemy were commanded by McClellan in person, and numbered the whole command of Gen. Burnside, recently augmented by the addition of several new regiments; the army corps lately under Gen. McDowell, now under command of Gen. Hooker; Gen. Sumner's corps; Gen. Franklin's corps; Gen. Banks' corps, commanded by Gen. Williams; and Sykes' division of Fitz John Porter's corps. Their line of battle was between four and five miles long, with their left stretching across the Sharpsburg road. Burnside was on the extreme left; Porter held a commanding eminence to the right

---

in numbers and weight of metal, crowned the opposite heights of the Potomac. Gen. Hill's division advanced with great gallantry against the infantry, in the face of a continued discharge of shot and shell from their batteries. The Federals massing in front of Pender, poured a heavy fire into his ranks, and then extending with a view to turn his left. Archer promptly formed on Pender's left, when a simultaneous charge was made, which drove the enemy into the river, followed by an appalling scene of the destruction of human life. Two hundred prisoners were taken. This position on the banks of the river we continued to hold that day, although exposed to the enemy's guns and within range of his sharpshooters posted near the Chesapeake and Ohio Canal. Our infantry remained at the river until relieved by cavalry under Gen. Fitzhugh Lee. On the evening of the 20th the command moved from Shepherdstown and encamped near the Opequon, in the vicinity of Martinsburg. We remained near Martinsburg until the 27th, when we moved to Bunker Hill, in the county of Berkeley. The official lists of the casualties of my command during the period embraced in this report, will show that we sustained a loss of 38 officers killed, 171 wounded; of 313 non-commissioned officers and privates killed, 1,859 wounded; and missing 57—making a total loss of 2,438, killed, wounded, and missing.

For these great and signal victories our sincere and humble thanks are due unto Almighty God. Upon all appropriate occasions we should acknowledge the hand of Him who reigns in heaven and rules among the powers of the earth. In view of the arduous labors and great privations which the troops were called on to endure, and the isolated and perilous position which the command occupied while engaged with the greatly superior force of the enemy, we feel the encouraging consolation that God was with us and gave to us the victory, and unto His holy name be all gratitude and praise.

I am, general, very respectfully,

Your obedient servant,

T. J. JACKSON, Lieutenant-general.

of Burnside, though Warren's brigade of Porter's corps was subsequently posted in the woods on the left in support of Burnside's men; Sumner's corps was on an eminence next to the right, or north from Porter, and Gen. Hooker had the extreme right.

On the afternoon of Tuesday, the 16th, the enemy opened a light artillery fire on our lines. At three next morning every man was at his post, and awaited in solemn silence the day dawn. No sooner did the light break in the east than the picket firing began, and increased in fury until about sunrise, when artillery and infantry together grappled in the terrible fight.

Large masses of the Federals, who had crossed the Antietam above our position, assembled on our left. They advanced in three compact lines. The divisions of Generals McLaws, R. H. Anderson, A. P. Hill and Walker, who were expected to have joined Gen. Lee on the previous night, had not come up. Generals Jackson's and Ewell's divisions were thrown to the left of Generals Hill and Longstreet. The enemy advanced between the Antietam and the Sharpsburg and Hagerstown turnpike, and was met by Gen. D. H. Hill's and the left of Gen. Longstreet's divisions, where the conflict raged, extending to our entire left.

When the troops of D. H. Hill were engaged, the battle raged with uncommon fury. Backwards, forwards, surging and swaying like a ship in storm, the various columns are seen in motion. It is a hot place for the enemy. They are directly under our guns, and we mow them down like grass. The raw levies, sustained by the veterans behind, come up to the work well, and fight for a short time with an excitement incident to their novel experiences of a battle; but soon a portion of their line gives way in confusion. Their reserves come up, and endeavor to retrieve the fortunes of the day. Our centre, however, stands firm as adamant, and they fall back.

Prior to the arrival of the divisions of McLaws, Anderson and Walker, who had been advanced to support the left wing and centre, as soon as they had crossed the Potomac on the morning of the 17th, that portion of our line was forced back by superior numbers. As soon, however, as these forces could be brought into action, the enemy was driven back, our line was restored, and our position maintained during the rest of the day.

Time and again did the Federals perseveringly press close up to our ranks—so near, indeed, that their supporting batteries were obliged to cease firing, lest they should kill their own men, but just as often were they driven back, by the combined elements of destruction which we brought to bear upon them. It was an hour when every man was wanted. And nobly did our brave soldiers do their duty. "It is beyond all wonder," writes a Federal officer, "how men such as the rebel troops are can fight as they do. That those ragged wretches, sick, hungry, and in all ways miserable, should prove such heroes in fight, is past explanation. Men never fought better. There was one regiment that stood up before the fire of two or three of our long-range batteries and of two regiments of infantry; and though the air around them was vocal with the whistle of bullets and the scream of shells, there they stood and delivered their fire in perfect order."*

In the afternoon the enemy advanced on our right, where Gen. Jones' division was posted, and he handsomely maintained his position. The bridge over the Antietam creek was guarded by Gen. Toombs' brigade, which gallantly resisted the approach of the enemy; but their superior numbers enabling them to extend their left, they crossed below the bridge, and forced our line back in some confusion.

Our troops fought until they were nearly cut to pieces, and then retreated only because they had fired their last round. It was at this juncture that the immense Yankee force crossed the river, and made the dash against our line, which well-nigh

---

* There are some characteristic anecdotes of the close quarters in which the battle of Sharpsburg was fought, and the desperate valor shown in such straits. At one passage of the battle, Col. Geary, of the famous Hampton Legion, one of the most celebrated corps of the army, found himself confronted by an overwhelming force of the enemy. An officer came forward and demanded his surrender. "Surrender! Hell!" exclaimed the intrepid South Carolinian, as with the spring of a tiger he seized the officer and clapped a pistol to his head, "if you don't surrender your own command to me this instant, you infernal scoundrel, I'll blow your brains out." The astonished and affrighted Yankee called out that he surrendered. But his men were not as cowardly as himself, and the flag of the regiment he commanded was only taken after the color-bearer had been cut down by our swords.

proved a success. But it was at this moment also that welcome and long-expected reinforcements reached us. At four o'clock in the afternoon Gen. A. P. Hill's division came up and joined the Confederate right. It was well that Gen. Burnside's advance on the Federal left was so long delayed, and was eventually made with overwhelming numbers. The day closed with Gen. Burnside clinging closely to the bridge, beyond which he could not advance, with Gen. Jackson on the same ground as the Confederates held in the morning, upon as level and drawn a battle as history exhibits. But it was fought for half the day with 45,000 men on the Confederate side, and for the remaining half with no more than an aggregate of 70,000 men, against a host which is admitted to have consisted of 130,000, and may have been more.

It is certain that if we had had fresh troops to hurl against Burnside at the bridge of Antietam, the day would have been ours. The anxious messages of this officer to McClellan for reinforcements were again and again repeated as the evening wore on, and the replies of that commander showed that he understood where was the critical point of the battle. As the sun was sinking in the west, he dispatched orders to Gen. Burnside, urging him to hold his position, and as the messenger was riding away he called him back—"Tell him if he *cannot* hold his ground, then the bridge, to the last man!—always the bridge! If the bridge is lost, all is lost."

The enemy held the bridge, but of other portions of the field we retained possession. Varying as may have been the successes of the day, they left us equal masters of the field with our antagonist. But our loss had been considerable; it was variously estimated from five to nine thousand; and we had to deplore the fall of Gens. Branch and Starke, with other brave and valuable officers. The loss of the enemy was not less than our own.* They had fought well and been ably

---

* The New York *Tribune* said: "The dead lie in heaps, and the wounded are coming in by thousands. Around and in a large barn about half a mile from the spot where Gen. Hooker engaged the enemy's left, there were counted 1,250 wounded. In Sumner's corps alone, our loss in killed, wounded and missing amounts to five thousand two hundred and eight. The 15th Massachusetts regiment went into the battle with five hundred and fifty men, and came out with one hundred and fifty-six. The 19th Massachusetts, of four

commanded. But they had the advantage not only of num bers, but of a position from which they could assume an offensive or defensive attitude at will, besides which their signal stations on the Blue Ridge commanded a view of our every movement.

The battle-field of Sharpsburg will long be remembered from the terrible and hideous circumstances that so many of the dead were left unburied upon it. Some of them laid with their faces to the ground, whither they had turned in the agony of death, and in which position they had died; others were heaped in piles of three and four together, with their arms interlocked, and their faces turned upwards towards the sky. Scores of them were laid out in rows, as though the death-shot had penetrated their breasts as they were advancing to the attack. Covered with mud and dust, with their faces and clothes smeared with blood and gore, there they rotted in the sun!

The close of this great battle left neither army in a condition to renew the conflict, although our own brave troops were desperately ready to do so. But the next morning McClellan had disappeared from our front, and, knowing the superiority of the enemy's numbers, and not willing to risk the combinations he was attempting, Gen. Lee crossed the Potomac without molestation, and took position at or near Shepherdstown.

The enemy claimed a victory, but the best evidence, if any were wanting, to prove that he was really defeated and his army crippled, is found in the fact that he did not renew the fight on the succeeding day, and on the next permitted Gen. Lee to recross the Potomac without an attempt to obstruct him. The pretence of victory on this occasion cost McClellan his command. On the 20th of September he made a feint or a weak and hesitating attempt to cross the Potomac at Shepherdstown, when the column which had crossed was fallen upon by A. P. Hill and pushed into the river, which was filled with the dead and wounded attempting to escape.

The charges against McClellan consequent upon his pre-

---

hundred and six, lost all but one hundred and forty-seven. The 5th New Hampshire, about three hundred strong, lost one hundred and ten enlisted men and fourteen officers. Massachusetts, out of eight regiments engaged, loses upwards of fifteen hundred, and Pennsylvania has suffered more than any other State."

tended victory, were sustained by the official testimony of the Yankee commander-in-chief. The report of Gen. Halleck accused McClellan of disobedience of orders, in refusing to advance against the enemy after the battle of Sharpsburg, upon the plea that the army lacked shoes, tents, stores, and other necessaries, which Gen. Halleck held to be entirely unfounded, asserting that all the wants of the army were duly cared for, and that any causes of delay that might have occurred were trivial and speedily remedied. He furthermore charged McClellan with willful neglect of a peremptory order of the 6th of October to cross the Potomac immediately, to give battle to the Confederates or to drive them south.

A fatal consequence to the Yankees of the campaign in Maryland was the sacrifice to popular clamor and official envy of him whom they had formerly made their military pet and "Napoleon," and who, although the extent of his pretensions was ridiculous, was really esteemed in the South as the ablest general in the North. The man who succeeded him in the command of the army of the Potomac was Gen. Ambrose Burnside, of Rhode Island. He had served during the Mexican war as a second lieutenant; and at the time he was raised to his important command, the captain of the company with which he had served in Mexico, Edmund Barry, was a recruiting agent in Richmond for the "Maryland Line."

We have perhaps imperfectly sketched the movements of the Maryland campaign.* But we have sought to determine

---

* It would be difficult to find a more just summary of the campaign in Northern Virginia and on the Upper Potomac, or one the statements of which may be more safely appropriated by history than the following address of Gen. Lee to his army :

HEADQUARTERS ARMY NORTHERN VIRGINIA, }
October 2d, 1862. }

General Orders, No. 116.

In reviewing the achievements of the army during the present campaign, the commanding general cannot withhold the expression of his admiration of the indomitable courage it has displayed in battle, and its cheerful endurance of privation and hardship on the march.

Since your great victories around Richmond you have defeated the enemy at Cedar Mountain, expelled him from the Rappahannock, and, after a conflict of three days, utterly repulsed him on the Plains of Manassas, and forced him to take shelter within the fortifications around his capital.

Without halting for repose you crossed the Potomac, stormed the heights of

its historical features without any large enumeration of details. It was mixed with much of triumph to us; it added lustre to our arms; it inflicted no loss upon us for which we did not exact full retribution; it left the enemy nothing but barren results; and it gave us a valuable lesson of the state of public opinion in Maryland.

There is one point to which the mind naturally refers for a just historical interpretation of the Maryland campaign. The busy attempts of newspapers to pervert the truth of history were renewed in an effort to misrepresent the designs of Gen. Lee in crossing the Potomac, as limited to a mere incursion, the object of which was to take Harper's Ferry, and that accomplished, to return into Virginia and await the movements of McClellan. It is not possible that our commanding general can be a party to this pitiful deceit, to cover up any failure of his, or that he has viewed with any thing but disgust the offer of falsehood and misrepresentation made to him by flatterers.

Harper's Ferry, made prisoners of more than eleven thousand men, and captured upwards of seventy pieces of artillery, all their small arms and other munitions of war.

While one corps of the army was thus engaged, the other insured its success by arresting at Boonesboro' the combined armies of the enemy, advancing under their favorite general to the relief of their beleaguered comrades.

On the field of Sharpsburg, with less than one-third his numbers, you resisted, from daylight until dark, the whole army of the enemy, and repulsed every attack along his entire front, of more than four miles in extent.

The whole of the following day you stood prepared to resume the conflict on the same ground, and retired next morning, without molestation, across the Potomac.

Two attempts, subsequently made by the enemy to follow you across the river, have resulted in his complete discomfiture, and being driven back with loss.

Achievements such as these demanded much valor and patriotism. History records few examples of greater fortitude and endurance than this army has exhibited; and I am commissioned by the President to thank you, in the name of the Confederate States, for the undying fame you have won for their arms.

Much as you have done, much more remains to be accomplished. The enemy again threatens us with invasion, and to your tried valor and patriotism the country looks with confidence for deliverance and safety. Your past exploits give assurance that this confidence is not misplaced.

R. E. LEE,
General Commanding.

Let it be freely confessed, that the object of Gen. Lee in crossing the Potomac was to hold and occupy Maryland; that his proclamation issued at Frederick, offering protection to the Marylanders, is incontrovertible evidence of this fact; that he was forced to return to Virginia, not by stress of any single battle, but by the force of many circumstances, some of which history should blush to record; that, in these respects, the Maryland campaign was a failure. But it was a failure relieved by brilliant episodes, mixed with at least one extraordinary triumph of our arms, and to a great extent compensated by many solid results.

In the brief campaign in Maryland, our army had given the most brilliant illustrations of valor; it had given the enemy at Harper's Ferry a reverse without parallel in the history of the war; it had inflicted upon him a loss in men and material greater than our own; and in retreating into Virginia, it left him neither spoils nor prisoners, as evidence of the successes he claimed. The indignant comment of the New York *Tribune* on Lee's retirement into Virginia is the enemy's own record of the barren results that were left them. "He leaves us," said this paper, "the *debris* of his late camps, two disabled pieces of artillery, a few hundred of his stragglers, perhaps two thousand of his wounded, and as many more of his unburied dead. Not a sound field-piece, caisson, ambulance, or wagon, not a tent, a box of stores, or a pound of ammunition. He takes with him the supplies gathered in Maryland, and the rich spoils of Harper's Ferry." The same paper declared, that the failure of Maryland to rise, or to contribute recruits (all the accessions to our force, obtained in this State, did not exceed eight hundred men), was the defeat of Lee, and about the only defeat he did sustain; that the Confederate losses proceeded mainly from the failure of their own exaggerated expectations; that Lee's retreat over the Potomac was a masterpiece; and that the manner in which he combined Hill and Jackson for the envelopment of Harper's Ferry, while he checked the Federal columns at Hagerstown Heights and Crampton Gap, was probably the best achievement of the war.

The failure of the people of Maryland to respond to the proclamation of Gen. Lee issued at Frederick, inviting them to his standard, and generously assuring protection to all classes

of political opinion, admits of some excuse; but the explanations commonly made on this subject do not amount to thei.
vindication. It is true that when Gen. Lee was in Frederick,
he was forty-five miles from the city of Baltimore—a city
surrounded by Federal bayonets, zealously guarded by an armed
Federal police, and lying in the shadow of Fort McHenry
and of two powerful fortifications located within the limits of
the corporation. It is true that our army passed only through
two of the remote counties of the State, namely Frederick
and Washington, which, with Carroll and Alleghany, are well
known to contain the most violent "Union" population in
Maryland. It is true that the South could not have expected
a welcome in these counties or a desperate mutiny for the
Confederacy in Baltimore. But it was expected that Southern
sympathizers in other parts of the State, who so glibly ran the
blockade on adventures of trade, might as readily work their
way to the Confederate army as to the Confederate markets;
and it was not expected that the few recruits who timidly advanced to our lines would have been so easily dismayed by the
rags of our soldiers and by the prospects of a service that promised equal measures of hardship and glory.

The army which rested again in Virginia had made a history
that will flash down the tide of time a lustre of glory. It had
done an amount of marching and fighting that appears almost
incredible, even to those minds familiar with the records of
great military exertions. Leaving the banks of James river,
it proceeded directly to the line of the Rappahannock, and
moving out from that river, it fought its way to the Potomac,
crossed that stream, and moved on to Fredericktown and Hagerstown, had a heavy engagement at the mountain gaps below, fought the greatest pitched battle of the war at Sharpsburg, and then recrossed the Potomac back into Virginia.
During all this time, covering the full space of a month, the
troops rested but four days. Of the men who performed these
wonders, one-fifth of them were barefoot, one-half of them in
rags, and the whole of them half famished.

The remarkable campaign which we have briefly sketched
extending from the banks of the James river to those of the
Potomac, impressed the world with wonder and admiration,
excited an outburst of applause among living nations, which

anticipated the verdict of posterity, and set the whole of Europe ringing with praises of the heroism and fighting qualities of the Southern armies. The South was already obtaining some portion of the moral rewards of this war, in the estimation in which she was held by the great martial nations of the world. She had purchased the rank with a bloody price. She had extorted homage from the most intelligent and influential organs of public opinion in the Old World, from men well versed in the history of ancient and modern times, and from those great critics of contemporary history, which are least accustomed to the language of extravagant compliment.

The following tribute from the London *Times*—the great organ of historic precedent and educated opinion in the Old World—was echoed by the other journals of Europe:

"The people of the Confederate States have made themselves famous. If the renown of brilliant courage, stern devotion to a cause, and military achievements almost without a parallel, can compensate men for the toil and privations of the hour, then the countrymen of Lee and Jackson may be consoled amid their sufferings. From all parts of Europe, from their enemies as well as their friends, from those who condemn their acts as well as those who sympathize with them, comes the tribute of admiration. When the history of this war is written, the admiration will doubtless become deeper and stronger, for the veil which has covered the South will be drawn away and disclose a picture of patriotism, of unanimous self-sacrifice, of wise and firm administration, which we can now only see indistinctly. The details of extraordinary national effort which has led to the repulse and almost to the destruction of an invading force of more than half a million men, will then become known to the world, and whatever may be the fate of the new nationality, or its subsequent claims to the respect of mankind, it will assuredly begin its career with a reputation for genius and valor which the most famous nations may envy."

It is at first appearance strange, that while such was the public opinion in England of our virtues and abilities, that that government should have continued so unjust and obstinate with respect to our claims for recognition. But the explanation is easy. The demonstrations of the conflict which awakened such generous admiration of us in the breasts of a majority of the

English people were to the government the subjects only of jealous and interested views. We had trusted too much to manifestations of public opinion in England; we had lost sight of the distinction between the people and government of that country, and had forgotten that the latter had, since the beginning of this war, been cold and reserved, had never given us any thing to hope from its sympathies or its principles, and had limited its action on the American question to the unfeeling and exacting measures of selfishness.

The bloody and unhappy revelation which the war has made of enormous military resources has naturally given to Europe, and especially to England, an extraordinary interest in its continuation. It is probable that she would not have hesitated to recognize the South, unless firmly persuaded of our ability and resolution to carry on the war, and unless she had another object to gain besides that of a permanent division in the nationality and power of her old rival. That object was the exhaustion of both North and South. England proposed to effect the continuation of the war, as far as possible, to the mutual ruin of the two nations engaged in it, by standing aside and trusting that after vast expenditures of blood and waste of resources the separation of the Union would be quite as surely accomplished by the self-devotion of the South, as by the less profitable mode of foreign intervention.

In this unchristian and inhuman calculation, England had rightly estimated the resolution and spirit of the South. We were prepared to win our independence with the great prices of blood and suffering that she had named. But we understood what lurked behind the mask of British conscience, and we treasured the lesson for the future.

OUR FOREIGN RELATIONS IN THE WAR.

It is not amiss in this connection to make a summary in reference to the relations between the Confederacy and the neutral powers of Europe during the progress of the war to the present period of our narrative.

The confederation of the Southern States in 1861 was the third political union that had been formed between the States of North America. The first act of secession dates as far back

the old articles of confederation made in 1778, seceded and
formed a second union. When in 1861 eleven of the States
again seceded and united themselves under the style of the
Confederate States of North America, they exercised a right
which required no justification, and which in a former instance
had not been contested by any party at home, or made the subject of discussion with any third power.

On every attempt for the opening of formal diplomatic intercourse with the European powers, the commissioners of the
Confederate States had met with the objection that these powers could not assume to judge between the conflicting representations of the two parties as to the true nature of their previous
mutual relations ; and that they were constrained by interna-
tional usage and the considerations of propriety to recognize
the self-evident fact of the existence of a war, and to maintain
a strict neutrality during its progress.

On this neutrality, two remarks are to be made :

First. It was founded upon the grave error that the separate
sovereignty and independence of the States had been merged
into one common sovereignty ; an error easily induced by the
delegation of power granted by these States to the Federal government to represent them in foreign intercourse, but one that
should have been as easily dispelled by appeals to reason and
historical fact.

Secondly. The practical operation of this falsely assumed and
falsely named " neutrality " was an actual decision against the
rights of the South, and had been but little short of active hostilities against her.

By the governments of England and France, the doctrines
announced in the treaty of Paris were ignored, and the monstrous Yankee blockade, by some forty or fifty vessels, of a
coast line nearly three thousand miles in extent, came to be
acknowledged and respected. When this recognition of the
blockade was made, it is very certain that the whole Yankee
navy, if employed on that service and nothing else, could not
furnish vessels enough to pass signals from point to point along
the coast. At the time this paper blockade was declared and
acknowledged, the Navy Register shows that the Federal Government had in commission but forty vessels, all told   These

were scattered over the world : some of them were in the China seas, some in the Pacific, some in the Mediterranean, some in our own part of the world, and some in another. The actual force employed in the blockading service did not give one vessel for every fifty miles of coast. In addition to these considerations, it had been shown by unquestionable evidence, furnished in part by the officials of the European powers themselves, that the few Southern ports really guarded by naval forces of the Yankees had been invested so inefficiently that hundreds of entries had been effected into them since the declaration of the blockade.

During nearly two years of struggle had this boasted " neutrality" of the European powers operated as active hostility against us, for they had helped the enemy to prevent us, with a force which was altogether inadequate, from obtaining supplies of prime necessity.

Nor was this all. We had no commerce; but in that the enemy was rich. We had no navy ; in that he was strong. Therefore, when England and her allies declared that neither the armed cruisers nor the prizes of either of the belligerents should have hospitality and protection in neutral ports, the prohibition, directed against both belligerents, was in reality effective against the Confederate States alone, for they alone could find a hostile commerce on the ocean.

Thus it was that, in the progress of the war, the neutral nations of Europe had pursued a policy which, nominally impartial, had been practically most favorable to our enemies and most detrimental to us.

The temper which this injustice produced in the South was fortunate. The South was conscious of powers of resistance of which the world was incredulous; and the first feverish expectations of recognition by the European powers were replaced by a proud self-reliance and a calm confidence, which were forming our national character, while contributing at the same time to the immediate successes of our arms.

The recognition by France and England of Lincoln's paper blockade, had by no means proved an unmitigated evil to us. It had forced us into many branches of industry, into which, but for that blockade, we should have never entered. We had excellent powder-mills of our own, and fine armories which turned out muskets, rifles, sabres, &c. The war found no more than half a dozen furnaces in blast in the whole Confed eracy, and most of those had been destroyed by the enemy. But the government had given such encouragement to the iron men that new mines had been opened in other parts of the Confederacy, and furnaces enough were already up or in the course of erection, to supply the wants of the government. In the last spring we had planted not more than one-fourth of the usual breadth of land in cotton, and our surplus labor was directed to breadstuffs and provisions. All these were the fruits to us of a blockade which threatened England especially with a terrible reaction of her own injustice, and was laying up a store of retribution for Europe.

CHAPTER XVIII.

Movements in the West.—The splendid Programme of the Yankees.—Kentucky
the critical Point.—Gen. Kirby Smith's Advance into Kentucky.—THE BATTLE OF
RICHMOND.—Reception of the Confederates in Lexington.—Expectation of an Attack
on Cincinnati.—Gen. Bragg's Plans.—Smith's Movement to Bragg's Lines.—Escape
of the Yankee Forces from Cumberland Gap.—Affair of Munfordsville.—Gen. Bragg
between the Enemy and the Ohio.—An Opportunity for a decisive Blow.—Buell's
Escape to Louisville.—The Inauguration of Governor at Frankfort.—An idle Ceremony.—Probable Surprise of Gen. Bragg.—THE BATTLE OF PERRYVILLE.—Its Immediate Results in our Favor.—Bragg's failure to concentrate his Forces.—His Resolution of Retreat.—Scenes of the Retreat from Kentucky.—Errors of the Campaign.—
A lame Excuse.—Public Sentiment in Kentucky.—The Demoralization of that
State.—The Lessons of Submission.

On the same day that victory perched on our banners on
the plains of Manassas, an important success was achieved by
our brave troops in another part of the Confederacy. A victory gained at Richmond in Kentucky gave a companion to
Manassas, and opened in the West a prospect of the advance
of our troops simultaneous with the dawn of new hopes and
aspirations in the East.

A few paragraphs are sufficient for the rapid summary of
events necessary to the contemplation of the situation in the
West, in which the battle of Richmond was won.

The North had prepared a splendid programme of operations in the country west of the Alleghanies. But few persons
on the Southern seaboard had adequate ideas of the grandeur
of the enemy's preparations, or of the strength of the forces
concentrating on the march in the Western country. These
preparations exceeded in magnitude all military movements
designed or attempted since the commencement of the war;
for they contemplated not only the expulsion of our forces
from Kentucky and Tennessee and the States west of the Mississippi, but the penetration through the Gulf States of the
heart of the South. The army, now well on its way into Middle Tennessee, had Northern Alabama and Georgia for its
ultimate destination; that of Grant was already advanced into
Mississippi; that of McClernand, organizing at Columbus and

Memphis, was intended to operate on the Mississippi; another army was already operating in Missouri and Arkansas; and a gunboat fleet had been placed on the waters of the Mississippi which was said to be terrible in destructiveness, and impreg nable in strength. Such was the extent of the enemy's plans of campaign in the West.

The situation left the South but little choice than that of making an aggressive movement by which North Alabama and Middle and East Tennessee might be cleared of the forces of the enemy, and they compelled to fall back to assist Gen. Buell in Kentucky—this State being fixed as the critical point in the West, and the field of the active campaign. The brief retirement of Gen. Beauregard from active command on account of ill health, which was made shortly after his evacuation of Corinth, left the way open to the promotion of Gen. Bragg, a favorite of the administration, who had a certain military reputation, but, as an active commander in the field, had the confidence neither of the army nor of the public. The first steps of the campaign were easily decided by this commander: it was to use the forces of Gen. Kirby Smith to threaten Cincinnati, and thus distract the attention and divide the forces of the enemy; while Gen. Bragg himself, co-operating with Smith, was to fulfil the great purpose of the campaign, which was the expulsion of the enemy from Kentucky and the capture of Louisville—thus subjecting the whole of that great grain-growing and meat-producing commonwealth, with all its rich stores, to our control.

Early in the month of August, Gen. McQown, under the orders of Gen. Smith, moved his division from London to Knoxville in East Tennessee. Thence our troops moved to the gaps in the Cumberland mountains, being joined by Claiborne's division at the lower gap, when the whole force was ordered through, with the trains and artillery. From this time our troops made forced marches until they reached Barboursville, which is on the main thoroughfare by which the Yankees received their supplies at the gap by way of Lexington. Halting there long enough only to get water, our wearied army was pushed on to the Cumberland ford. Here a few days' rest was allowed to the troops, who had performed their hard march over stony roads, with their almost bare feet, and with green corn garnished with a small supply of poor beef for their food.

THE BATTLE OF RICHMOND.

On the 29th of August our troops were in striking distance of the enemy at Richmond. Until our advance descended the Big Hill, it met with no opposition from the enemy. Here, on the morning of the 29th, the enemy was discovered to be in force in our front, and a bold reconnoissance of the cavalry under Colonel Scott, in the afternoon, indicated a determination to give us battle. Although Churchill's division did not get up until quite late in the afternoon, and then in an apparently exhausted state, Gen. Smith determined to march to Richmond the next day, even at the cost of a battle with the whole force of the enemy. The leading division, under Gen. Claiborne, was moved early the next morning, and, after advancing two or three miles, they found the enemy drawn up in line of battle in a fine position, near Mount Zion church, six miles from Richmond. Without waiting for Churchill's division, Claiborne at once commenced the action, and by half-past seven o'clock in the morning, the fire of artillery was brisk on both sides. As our force was almost too small to storm the position in front, without a disastrous loss, Gen. Churchill was sent with one of his brigades to turn the enemy's right. While this movement was being executed, a bold and well-conducted attempt on the part of the enemy, to turn Claiborne's right, was admirably foiled by the firmness of Col. Preston Smith's brigade, who repulsed the enemy with great slaughter In the mean time Gen. Churchill had been completely successful in his movement upon the enemy's right flank, where, by a bold charge, his men completed a victory already partially gained by the gallantry of our troops on the left.

The Yankees having been repulsed and driven in confusion from this part of the field, might have retreated without risk ing another passage at arms, had they not misapprehended our movements.

Gen. Smith having ordered the cavalry to go around to the north of Richmond and attempt to cut off the retreat of the enemy, our artillery ceased firing, and the enemy, thinking our army was preparing for a retreat, had the foolhardiness to rally on their own retreat and attempt a charge upon the Texas and Arkansas troops under McCray, who, to the great astonishment of the enemy, instead of running away, met them on the half-way ground. This gallant brigade of Texans and Arkansians had to fight the battle alone. Although the odds opposed to them were fearful, yet by reserving their own fire, under the deafening roar of the enemy's guns, and by a well-timed and dashing charge upon the advancing lines, they completely routed and put to flight the hosts of the enemy. They fled in the wildest confusion and disorder. Their knapsacks, swords, pistols, hats, and canteens, scattered along the road, would have marked the route they travelled, even if their dead and dying had not too plainly showed the way.

In passing a deserted camp of the enemy, Gen. Smith found from some of the wounded that Gen. Nelson, the Yankee commander, with reinforcements, had arrived after the second battle. A march of two miles brought us within sight of the town, in front of which, and on a commanding ridge, with both flanks resting upon woods, Nelson had determined to make a final stand. Churchill, with a brigade, was sent off to the left, when a deafening roar of musketry soon announced the raging of a furious combat. In the mean while, Preston Smith, bringing up his division at a double-quick, formed in front of the enemy's centre and left. Almost without waiting the command of the officers, this division coolly advanced under the murderous fire of a force twice their number, and drove them from the field in the greatest confusion, and with immense slaughter. The exhausted condition of our men, together with the closing in of night, prevented the pursuit of the enemy more than a mile beyond Richmond.

The results of the day were gratifying enough. With less than half his force, Gen. Smith had attacked and carried a very strong position at Mount Zion church, after a hard fight of two hours. Again, a still better position at White's farm, in half an hour, and finally, in the town of Richmond, just before sunset, our indomitable troops deliberately walked (they were too tired to run) up to a magnificent position, manned by ten thousand of the enemy, many of them perfectly fresh, and carried it in fifteen minutes. In the last engagement, we took prisoners from thirteen regiments. Our loss in killed and wounded was about four hundred; that of the enemy was about one thousand, and his prisoners five thousand. The immediate fruits of the victory were nine pieces of artillery and ten thousand small-arms, and a large quantity of supplies. These latter were greatly increased by the capture of Richmond and Frankfort, the whole number of cannon taken being about twenty.

On the 1st day of September Gen. Smith took up the line of march for Lexington; and on the morning of the fourth day of that month, our forces, consisting of a Texas brigade and an Arkansas brigade, under the command of Gen. Churchill, and Gen. Claiborne's division and Gen. Heath's division, all under the command of Gen. Kirby Smith, marched through the city amidst the hearty and generous welcome of thousands of men, women, and children.

The entrance of our troops into Lexington was the occasion of the most inspiriting and touching scenes. Streets, windows, and gardens were filled with ladies and little girls with streamers of red and blue ribbons and flags with stars. Beautiful women seized the hard brown hands of our rough and ragged soldiers, and with tears and smiles thanked them again and again for coming into Kentucky and freeing them from the presence and insults of the hated and insolent Yankees. For hours the enthusiasm of the people was unbounded. At every corner of the streets, baskets of provisions and buckets of water were placed for the refreshment of our weary soldiers, and hundreds of our men were presented with shoes and hats and coats and tobacco from the grateful people. Private residences were turned for the time into public houses of entertainment, free to all who could be persuaded to go and eat. But if the reception of the infantry was enthusiastic, the tears, the smiles, and shouts and cheers of wild delight which greeted Gen. John Morgan's cavalry as they came dashing through the streets amidst clouds of dust, was without a parallel. The wildest joy ruled the hours. The bells of the city pealed forth their joyous welcome, whilst the waving of thousands of white handkerchiefs and tiny Confederate flags attested the gladness and delight of every heart.

It would have been well if the enthusiasm which welcomed Gen. Smith in this town could have been confirmed as a true token of the public sentiment of Kentucky. But while this sentiment was developing itself, the exultation which greeted our troops at Lexington was reflected in other parts of the Confederacy; and from the results already achieved in the Western campaign, the Southern public was raised to the pinnacle of hopeful expectation. When it was known at the seat of government in Virginia that Gen. Smith, after crushing the force opposed to him at Richmond, had gone on and captured Lexington, Paris, and Cynthiana, and established his lines almost in sight of Cincinnati, the public indulged the prospect of the speedy capture of this great city of the West, with its valuable stores and yards for building gunboats. What might have been the result of a sudden attack on this city (for one of our brigades was in striking distance of it) is left to conjecture. The order was to menace, not to attack; and the purposes of the campaign projected by Gen. Bragg required that Smith's command, after making its demonstration on the Ohio should fall back into the interior to co-operate with the splendid army he had already brought into Kentucky.

Gen. Bragg had entered the State by the eastern route from Knoxville and Chattanooga. The direct route by the way of Nashville would have brought him on Buell's front; but he chose to make the crossing of the Cumberland river several miles above Nashville, apparently with the design of making a flank movement on Buell. The immediate effect of this movement was to cause the Yankees to evacuate East Tennessee, and to relieve North Alabama from Federal occupation; but the enemy, learning that Cincinnati was not in immediate danger, had abundant time to remove the forces collected for the defence of that city, to be united with Buell's army in Kentucky.

The sudden disappearance of Smith from in front of Cincinnati, and the rapidity of his movement, intimated clearly enough that he was making a forced march to reach Bragg and strengthen him before a decisive trial of his strength with Buell. But the movement deprived us of a victory that might have been cheaply won; for it gave opportunity of escape to the Yankee Gen. Morgan, who had been completely hemmed in at Cumberland Gap, with an army of ten or twelve thousand men and abundance of arms and equipments.

The distance to the Ohio river is about two hundred and fifty miles, and includes the most mountainous portions of Kentucky. There are scarcely fifty miles of the entire route in which there are not defiles and passes where a small force could have kept the enemy at bay. The famous cavalry commander, John H. Morgan, had been sent with a portion of his command to harass the retreating enemy; and this intrepid officer, with seven hundred and fifty men, arrested the Yankee army for five days, and might have captured them with the half of Marshall's infantry, who were within little more than a day's march. But reinforcements were not sent forward, and no alternative was left to Morgan but—after inflicting such damage as he could upon the enemy—to rejoin Smith's march, which had now taken the direction of Frankfort.

On the 17th of September, Gen. Bragg captured about five thousand of the enemy at Munfordsville, with the inconsiderable loss on our side of about fifty men in killed and wounded. He had thrown his lines between Buell's force at Bowling Green and Louisville, and it was confidently expected that he would engage him, drive him across the Ohio or the Mississippi, or at least disconcert his hopes of preparations and increase of forces at Louisville. Buell's entire force at this time was not computed at over thirty-five thousand, for which our army, in the best possible spirits and confidence, was an overmatch.

It is probable that at this juncture the struggle in Kentucky might have been decided by a fight on a fair field with an army our inferior in all respects. Viewed in the light of subsequent events, it is difficult to determine what good object Gen. Bragg could have had in declining a contest with the enemy but a few miles distant. It is still more inexplicable that after the success of Munfordsville he should have stood idly by and suffered Buell and his wagon trains to pass between him and the Ohio river, almost in sight of his lines. He had passed Buell to enter Kentucky, and having accomplished it, his reasons for allowing his enemy to repass him and enter Louisville are inadmissible to any justification that can be offered by practical good sense. Whatever explanations have been made of them, it is certain that at this time the public has not abandoned its opinion, that General Bragg's failure to deliver battle at the important conjuncture which placed him between the enemy and the Ohio, was the fatal error of the Kentucky campaign.

On the 4th of October, Gen. Bragg joined Smith's army at Frankfort, where was conducted the inauguration of the Provisional Governor of Kentucky, Mr. Hawes. This ceremony, however, was scarcely any thing more than a pretentious farce. Scarcely was it completed, when the Yankees threatened the State capital, and the newly installed Governor had to flee from their approach. The delusion, that Buell's army was quietly resting in Louisville, was dispelled by the news received at Frankfort on the inauguration day, to the effect that the Yankees were in large force within twelve miles of the place. But the apparent movement on Frankfort was a mere feint, while the enemy was concentrating to force our left wing near Perryville.

THE BATTLE OF PERRYVILLE.

Having arrived at Harrodsburg from Frankfort, Gen. Bragg, finding the enemy pressing heavily in his rear near Perryville, determined to give him battle there, and ordered Gen. Polk to make the attack next day. But he had made an unfortunate disposition of his forces, for on the day before the division of Withers had been sent to Salvisa to reinforce Gen. Kirby Smith and cut off Sill's division. Hardee's and Buckner's divisions were marched to Perryville, leaving Gen. Cheatham's at Harrodsburg, which, however, came up to Perryville on the night of the 7th of October, before the engagement. Withers failed to intercept Gen. Sill's division, but captured the rearguard, consisting of seven hundred and fifty men, with an ammunition train; and on the morning of the 9th, Gen. Withers' and Gen. Kirby Smith's forces reached Harrodsburg, having been too late to participate in the decisive events of the preceding day.

The morning of the 8th of October found not more than fifteen thousand Confederate troops confronting an enemy three times their numbers. The forces opposed to us at Perryville

consisted of the right wing of the " Army of the Ohio," com
posed of Buell's veteran army, with Major-gen. Geo. W. Thomas
as commander-in-chief of the field, and Gen. Alex. McCook
commanding the first corps. We fought nine divisions of the
Abolition army, composed at least of five thousand each, making forty-five thousand men.

Gen. Buckner's division, which was posted on our extreme
right, with Anderson's division, formed the left wing of the
army of the Mississippi, under Major-gen. Hardee. Cheatham's and Withers' divisions formed the right wing, under
Major-gen. Polk. Thus we had but three divisions in the
field.

The action opened a little past noon. It was only skirmishing for a considerable time, Col. Powell's brigade holding the
extreme left of our lines, and gallantly driving the enemy
back for about a mile against superior forces. It was about
this time, towards 4 P. M., when Gen. Smith's brigade, belonging to Cheatham's division, was ordered back to our assistance,
that Gen. Adams, with his brave Louisianians, was holding the
enemy in check against fearful odds, when he was forced to fall
back from his position. Gen. Hardee, seeing the importance
of holding the point, ordered Gen. Adams to retake it, telling
him he would be supported by reinforcements. It was while
advancing again, and anxiously looking for the reinforcements,
that Gen. Adams, seeing some soldiers firing at what he supposed to be our own men, ordered them to cease firing. " I
tell you, sir, they are Yankees," cried one of the officers. " I
think not, and you had better go forward first and ascertain,"
replied Adams. "I'll go, sir, but I don't think it necessary,
for I know they are Yankees," insisted the officer. " Well,"
said Adams, " I'll go myself," and dashing forward on his
charger, he had not proceeded one hundred yards when a furious storm of Minié balls whizzed by his ears from the enemy.
The general turned immediately, and riding up, shouted to
our troops to pour in their fire. Towards six o'clock the firing
became incessant on both sides. There stood Adams, with his
little brigade, holding back a division of the enemy, left, as it
were, alone to his fate, until, seeing no chance of being reinforced, he gradually fell back, in most excellent order, but not
without considerable loss.

Towards night the engagement subsided. Fearfully out-numbered, our troops had not hesitated to engage at any odds, and despite the checks they had encountered at times, the enemy was driven two miles from his first line of battle. As darkness fell, the conflict was over. A few shots from long range guns were exchanged. The full round moon rose in the east and lighted the dismal scene. In half an hour the picket fires of the opposing armies were visible five hundred yards distant, and our wearied men laid down on their arms.

The immediate results of the battle of Perryville were in our favor. We had captured fifteen pieces of artillery by the most daring charges, had inflicted the loss of four thousand men on the enemy, and held several hundred of his prisoners. Our own loss was estimated at twenty-five hundred in killed, wounded, and missing. The enemy had lost one of their best generals on the field—Jackson. Seeing his men wavering, he had advanced to the front line, and, waving his sword, cheered and urged them on. While thus displaying an extraordinary courage he was struck in the right breast by a piece of an ex-ploded shell, and fell from his horse. It is said by those near him that he said only, "O God!" and died without a struggle.

But the success of Perryville was of no importance to us; it was merely a favorable incident and decided nothing. It is probable Gen. Bragg had it in his power here, by concentrat-ing his troops, to crush the enemy's force in Kentucky; but he allowed himself to be deceived as to the disposition of the enemy's forces, scattered his own, and engaged and defeated the head of the Yankee column with less than fifteen thousand men.* Had he fallen with his whole available force, forty thousand men, on the enemy at Perryville, it is not improba-ble that he might have dispersed the Yankee army and given it such a blow that it would not have made a stand this side the Ohio river.

---

* It is proper to state, that an apology for Gen. Bragg, in this matter, was offered in the public prints, to the effect that before the battle of Perryville Gen. Kirby Smith had communicated to Gen. Bragg his positive belief that the real attack was threatened upon him, whilst the feint was upon Perryville, and urged reinforcements; and that this was the reason why Gen. Withers' di-vision was sent to Gen. Kirby Smith and was not sent to Generals Polk and Hardee.

Unfortunately the battle of Perryville was another experience of Shiloh, without any decisive results. Had we have had five thousand more men, or had Withers been there, we might have completely routed the enemy, leaving us the way clear to Louisville. No troops in the world ever fought with more desperate courage than ours. Whole regiments of our men went into that fight barefooted, fought barefooted and had marched barefooted from Chattanooga. The brunt of the battle was borne by Gen. Cheatham's gallant Tennesseeans. No soldiers of the Confederacy ever fought with greater bravery.

Ascertaining that the enemy was heavily reinforced during the night, Gen. Bragg withdrew his force early the next morning to Harrodsburg, where he was joined by. Smith and Withers. On the 10th, all our forces fell back to Camp Breckinridge (Dick Robinson), the cavalry holding the enemy in check at Danville. It was supposed that Gen. Bragg would have made a stand here, as the place was very defensible and gave him the opportunity of sweeping the country and driving off by private enterprise or cavalry force vast herds of cattle, so much needed by our army. The camp is in an acute angle formed by the junction of Kentucky and Dick's rivers, with high and impassable and perpendicular cliffs for long distances up these rivers, except at a few crossings ; and the upper line of the angle has high and commanding hills, suited for artillery defences. It was said that it was impregnable to any other attack than that of famine.

But moved by various considerations, and excited by the superiority of Buell's numbers, it was determined by Gen. Bragg that the whole army should make its exodus from·Kentucky ; and in order to secure the immense quantity of captured stores, goods, clothing, &c., much of which had also been purchased, with some five thousand head of cattle, horses, mules, &c., that the retreat should commence on the night of the 12th. On that day, Sunday, orders were received to cook four days' rations for the march. Major-gen. McCowan, with Gen. Hilliard's Legion, and a cavalry force and artillery, was ordered to defend Fishing Ford, across Dick's river, and commanding the road to Camp Breckinridge, in our rear, to the last extremity.

The distress of those people of Kentucky who were friendly

to the South, on learning that they were to be abandoned by our troops, was the most affecting circumstance of the sad retreat. When our troops abandoned Lexington, the terror, dismay, and anguish of the inhabitants were extreme. The women ran through the streets crying and wringing their hands, while families hastily gathered their clothing, packed their trunks, and obtained wagons to depart, the greatest distress prevailing.

The retreat commenced on Sunday night, the 12th October, Major Adrain's cavalry conducting the advance train of Gen. Kirby Smith. That night piles of goods, clothes, &c., were burned that could not be carried off from the warehouse. Long before day on the morning of the 13th, the whole camp was astir. If any one doubted that we were actually retreating, the burning piles of abandoned stores, gun-carriages, &c., was sufficient to convince him of the deplorable fact.

At gray dawn the troops reached Bryantsville, about two miles from the camp, where the whole command of conducting the retreat was turned over to Gen. Polk. Already train after train of wagons had passed, and others were still forming and joining in the immense cavalcade. Ammunition trains and batteries of captured artillery had preceded. Then followed trains of goods, wares, and merchandise, provision trains of army stores, trains of captured muskets, escorts of cavalry, artillery drawn by oxen. Then came private trains of refugee families, flying with their negroes for safety—ladies and children in carriages, stage-coaches, express wagons, omnibuses, buggies, ambulances, jersey wagons, and every conceivable vehicle imaginable, and following, came the wagons of the different brigades of Gen. Smith's army, with infantry, cavalry, and artillery in the rear. Intermixed with the throng were thousands of head of cattle, horses, and mules.

The effect of our retreat along the road everywhere was sinking and depressing in the extreme. No miniature banners waved, no white kerchiefs greeted our troops with approving smiles from lovely women, and no wild cheer was heard responsive to the greetings which had attended their march into Kentucky. Trembling women stole to the doors to look upon the strange, mystified scene before them, and as the truth gradually forced itself upon them, their eyes filled with tears, and they shrank back, fearing even to make the slightest demonstration of friendliness—all was sullen, downcast, and gloomy.

The enemy was in pursuit, and making a strong effort to flank us, so as to cut off our trains, and it was necessary to urge on the teams night and day for fear of capture. For some portion of the way the road lay along the bed of Dick's river, a miserable rocky branch, which our troops had to cross and recross for six miles in a dark and hazy night. Scenes of terrible confusion and delay occurred along this road. Wagons broke down, were overturned, and frequently stalled, and in the former case were often abandoned. The bawling of the teamsters to their mules, the cracking of their whips, and volleys of oaths in the most outlandish gibberish, which none but the mules could understand, were kept up all night. In the daytime more cheerful scenes relieved the retreat. The foliage of the forest trees and brushwood enlivened the wayside with their rich hues of dark maroon splendor to brilliant crimson.

The retreat was admirably covered by Gen. Wheeler. From the battle-field at Perryville to Cumberland Gap this general conducted his movements in the same masterly manner that had characterized him in the previous part of the campaign. He retarded the enemy by various means. When he reached the hilly country he obstructed the road by felled trees. By all such ingenious devices, he, with a small force, enabled the baggage trains and straggling infantry to escape capture. From Altamont to Cumberland Gap he encountered the enemy twenty-nine times, seriously damaged him, and saved much of our infantry from capture. At Rock Castle the enemy abandoned the pursuit; our whole train of stores being up, and not even a wagon lost, except those abandoned on account of breaking down.

We must leave here an account of the movements of Gen. Bragg until the time shall come for us to see how his retreat from Kentucky through Cumberland Gap transferred the most important scenes of the war in the West to the memorable lines of Nashville. Deplorable as was this retreat, it was not without some circumstances that palliated it, or relieved the grief of the public mind. It is certain that it was a disappointment to the enemy, who had expected to crush our forces in Kentucky, and were not prepared for the news of their liberation from the coils which they flattered themselves had been so industriously and elaborately woven around them.

It is probable, too, that under the circumstances, after oui own army had blundered so badly in the first steps of the campaign, its retreat from Kentucky, without the burden of defeat and without material losses, was preferable to alternatives which otherwise would have probably befallen it. It had entered into Gen. Beauregard's plan of campaign in the West, before he had been superseded, to regain the control of the Tennessee and Cumberland rivers, and thus prepare for future operations. The construction of works on the Cumberland and Tennessee rivers so as to command them, was plainly an important concern ; and, according to Gen. Beauregard's idea, should have been preliminary to the active campaign in the West. With these works, it appears probable that an advance might have been made with safety into Kentucky ; and even had we failed in the taking of Louisville and Cincinnati, which was a part of Gen. Beauregard's plan, and been compelled to fall back, it is thought not improbable that we could have made a successful stand on the Cumberland. But Gen. Bragg had failed to adopt these suggestions. Had he succeeded, after our victory at Perryville, in driving the enemy back to Louisville, unless he had been able to take that place, he would have been compelled to retreat so soon as the Tennessee and Cumberland rivers should have risen sufficiently to have admitted the entrance of the enemy's gunboats and transports. Taking this view, it may be said that as we did not have command of these rivers, it was fortunate that our army left Kentucky when it did, otherwise it might have found great difficulty, after the winter rains commenced, in getting away at all.

For the failure of Gen. Bragg's campaign in Kentucky, the excuse was offered that the people of that State had been unfriendly, that they had not joined his standard in considerable numbers, and that they had disappointed his own and the common expectation of the Southern public with respect to their political sentiments. It is scarcely necessary to remark how little applicable such an excuse is to positive blunders in the conduct of an army, and to those imperfections of judgment and faults of strategy which, whatever may be their remote connection, are the immediate occasions and responsible causes of disaster.

But it is to be admitted that the South was bitterly disappointed in the manifestations of public sentiment in Kentucky; that the exhibitions of sympathy in this State were meagre and sentimental, and amounted to but little practical aid of our cause. Indeed, no subject was at once more dispiriting and perplexing to the South than the cautious and unmanly reception given to our armies, both in Kentucky and Maryland. The references we have made to the sentiment of each of these States, leaves but little room to doubt the general conclusion, that the dread of Yankee vengeance, and love of property, were too powerful to make them take risks against these in favor of a cause for which their people had a mere preference, without any attachment to it higher than those of selfish calculation.

There must, indeed, be some explanation for the extraordinary quiet of the people of Maryland and Kentucky under the tyranny that ruled them, and for that submission the painful signs of which we had unwillingly seen. This explanation was not to be found in the conduct of the United States. It is a remarkable fact that the Lincoln government had not taken any pains to change the opinions and prejudices of the people in these two States. It had made no attempt to conciliate them; it had performed no act calculated to awaken their affection; it had done nothing to convert their hearts to the support of an administration to which they were originally hostile.

It would be a foolish and brutal explanation to attribute the submission of these States to cowardice. The people of these States were brave; they were descended from noble ancestries, and they had the same blood and types of race that were common to the South. The sons of Kentucky and Maryland who had fought under the Confederate flag were as noble specimens of the Southern soldier as any to be found in our armies. But the people of these States, who had stayed at home and been schooled in the lessons of submission, appeared to have lost the spirit and stature of their ancestors, and dragged the names of Maryland and Kentucky in the dust.

The only just explanation that can be furnished of the abject attitude of these States is, that having taken the first steps of submission to a pitiless despotism, they had been easily corrupted into its subjects. The lessons of history furnish many exhibitions of how easily the spirit of a community is crushed by submission to tyranny; how the practice of non-resistance makes of men crawling creatures. The mistake is in making the first step of submission; when that is accomplished, demoralization becomes rapid, and the bravest community sinks into emasculation. Under the experience of non-resistance to the rule of a despot, men become timid, artful, and miserly; they spend their lives in consulting the little ends of personal selfishness. This corruption in Kentucky, as well as in Maryland, had gone on with visible steps. Their history was a lesson which the South might well remember, of the fatal consequences of any submission to despotic will; for however specious its plea, all records of man's experience have shown that it undermines the virtues of a people, and degenerates at last into servile acquiescence in its fate.

CHAPTER XIX.

The crisis in Kentucky was probably hastened by certain disastrous events which had taken place on our lines in the Southwest. A large Confederate force had been left in North Mississippi when Gen. Bragg moved into Kentucky, and the speculation was not remote that, with the Memphis and Charleston railroad open from Chattanooga to a point near the position of our army in Mississippi, that portion of our forces in the West might render important assistance to, or, in some emergency, effect a co-operation with the armies that had been marched into Kentucky.

But the story of the Southwest was one of almost unbroken disaster, owing less, perhaps, to inadequate numbers than to the blind and romantic generalship which carried them into the jaws of destruction. There was one golden link in the chain of events here, and that was the heroic defence of Vicksburg. But while this famous town so nobly disputed the palm of the Mississippi, her example of victorious resistance was obscured, though not overshadowed, by other events in the Southwest.

On the 5th of August, an attack made by Gen. Breckenridge with less than three thousand men on Baton Rouge, was severely repulsed by an enemy nearly twice his numbers, fighting behind fortifications which were almost impregnable, and assisted by a fleet of gunboats in the river. The unequal attack was made by our troops with devoted courage; they succeeded in driving the enemy to the arsenal and tower, and to the cover of his gunboats; but they were compelled to withdraw with diminished and exhausted numbers before a fire which it was impossible to penetrate.

This check (for it deserves no more important or decisive title) was in a measure occasioned, or, at least, was accompanied, by a disaster of real importance. This was the destruction of the great Confederate ram Arkansas, already famous for having run the gauntlet of the hostile fleet at Vicksburg, and the promises of whose future services had given to the South many brilliant but illusory hopes. The Arkansas left Vicksburg to co-operate in the attack upon Baton Rouge. After passing Bayou Sara her machinery became deranged or disabled. But two alternatives were left—to blow her up or suffer her to be captured by the Yankee gunboats. The former was resorted to, and this proud achievement of naval architecture floated a wreck on the Mississippi river.

The failure of another enterprise of attack on the enemy, made by Gen. Price at Iuka on the 20th of September, was much more disastrous than the affair of Baton Rouge. Overmatched by numbers, Gen. Price was, after some partial and temporary success, forced back, with a loss greater than that of the enemy. In this engagement our loss was probably eight hundred in killed and wounded. But never had troops fought with more terrible resolution or wilder energy than the soldiers of Price. The fighting was almost hand to hand; and as an instance of the close and deadly combat, it may be mentioned that an Ohio battery was taken by our men four different times, and as often retaken by greatly superior numbers of the enemy. The desperation of our soldiers astonished those who, by the weight of numbers alone, were able to resist them. Several of our men endeavored to tear the colors from the hands of the Yankees by main force, and either perished in the attempt or were made prisoners. In one spot next morning, there were counted seventeen Confederate soldiers lying dead around one of their officers. Sixteen feet square would cover the whole space where they died.

But there was yet to ensue the great disaster which was to react on other theatres of the war and cast the long shadow of misfortune upon the country of the West. It was destined to take place at Corinth, where Major-gen. Rosecrans, command- ing the Yankee army of the Mississippi and Tennessee, was stationed with at least forty thousand men.

THE BATTLE OF CORINTH.

The armies of Generals Van Dorn and Price—under Gen. Van Dorn as the ranking officer—having formed a junction at Ripley, marched thence for the purpose of engaging the enemy in battle, though it was well known that the battle must be waged under the serious disadvantages of great disparity in numbers and strength of position.

On the 2d of October our forces marched from Pocahontas to Chewalla, points on the Memphis and Charleston railroad, thus moving from the west on Corinth, the stronghold of the enemy. That night the soldiers rested on their arms, in eager and confident expectation of meeting the foe in battle array on the ensuing morning.

On Friday, October 3d, the order of battle was formed—the right being held by Gen. Van Dorn's troops, composing only one division, under Gen. Lovell; while the left was occupied by Gen. Price's troops, composed of two divisions—the extreme left under Gen. Herbert, and the right under Gen. Maury, whose division, as thus placed, formed the centre of the whole force. Advancing in this order, at half past 7 o'clock in the morning Gen. Lovell's division arrived within long range of the enemy, who had marched out some miles in front of the extreme outer lines of his fortifications. Immediately the artillery of Gen. Villipigue, whose brigade was in the advance, opened fire upon the enemy, who in a short time began to give way and fall back, and continued to do so for two hours, under a heavy and effective fire from the advancing batteries of Gen. Lovell's division.

At half-past 9 o'clock, the enemy having made a stand one half mile in front of his fortifications, Gen. Lovell advanced his infantry and poured a destructive musketry fire into the ranks of the Yankees, who replied with spirit; and now, Gen. Price having ordered up his divisions under Generals Maury and Herbert, the battle raged all along the line—the enemy suffering terribly. At length a charge was ordered, Gen. Lovell's division leading. In double-quick time our soldiers, pressing forward with loud cheers, drove the enemy behind his intrenchments. Simultaneously almost, the divisions of Gen. Maury and Herbert, the one after the other, charged the enemy in front of them with equal success.

There was now a strange lull in the battle. The Yankees had withdrawn entirely behind their fortifications, their fire had dropped off, and the tumult of the fierce strife died away. The unexpected quiet lasted for a whole hour. By that time, the Yankees having brought several field batteries in front, opened from these, and at the same time from his heavy artillery, a most tremendous cannonade. This fire was directed chiefly, if not wholly, against the right wing under Gen. Lovell, and, though so tremendous in sound, produced but little effect. Our soldiers remained silent and stood firm. They were waiting for orders. Presently the second charge was ordered. Gallantly was it made by Gen. Lovell's division, and as gallantly was it supported by charges all along the centre and right wing by the divisions of Generals Maury and Herbert. On, on our glorious columns swept through the leaden rain and iron hail; the first line of fortifications is reached and passed; and the Yankees do not stop until they have reached the next line of intrenchments.

On Friday night the news of a great victory was dispatched by Gen. Van Dorn to Richmond. This announcement was made with an exultation so hasty and extreme, that it is to be supposed that this commander was entirely unaware of the strength of the enemy's works at Corinth, and, consequently, of the supreme trial which yet remained for the courage and devotion of his troops.

The next morning the general relation of our troops to each other and to the enemy remained as it was on the previous day—Gen. Van Dorn, in supreme command, occupying the centre, Gen. Price the left wing, and Gen. Lovell the right wing. Gen. Lovell's division held ground west of Corinth and just south of the Memphis and Charleston railroad. Gen. Maury's division was posted north of the Memphis and Charleston railroad, and between it and the Memphis and Ohio railroad. Gen. Herbert's division was on the left, east of the Memphis and Ohio railroad—thus advancing from the north upon Corinth.

The battle was commenced by Gen. Price early in the morning, one half-hour before daylight. The artillery having been moved forward, opened upon the enemy in his intrenchments at a distance of four hndred yards. The enemy replied, and a heavy cannonading, by both sides, ensued for one hour. Our troops suffered but little damage from this fire, and the artillery was withdrawn with the view of advancing the infantry. Now heavy skirmishing followed all along the line, which was kept up until about 10 o'clock. Then beginning with Gen. Lovell's division, who were immediately seconded by Gen. Price's army—Gen. Herbert's division first, and then Gen. Maury's,—our whole line advanced upon the intrenchments of the enemy.

Here occurred one of the most terrible struggles of the war. The shock of the tremendous onset was terrible. One portion of our lines rushed pell-mell into Corinth, losing in their confidence of victory almost every semblance of order, infantry and cavalry being crowded together in a dense mass, wild with excitement, and rending the air with fierce and exulting yells. But the batteries of the enemy were situated to command the village as well as the approaches to it.

The serried ranks of the enemy, now prepared to receive us, afforded convincing proof that victory was yet distant from our grasp, and that a hard and bloody fight was at hand. A portion of Maury's division was ordered to charge the formidable fort on College Hill. This was the forlorn hope. Disappointed in gaining a lodgment in the village, we must confess to a defeat, if that battery be not taken. Once in our possession, the town is ours. The men, massed in single column, eight deep, moved forward in silence, regardless of the shower of bullets which whistled about their ears and decimated their ranks. The decisive moment—the turning point of the engagement—had arrived. Every battery of the enemy bearing on the column was double charged with grape and canister which burst over the heads of our troops. Scores were killed at every discharge, but they moved steadily on, maintaining the silence of the grave. As fast as one soldier fell, his comrade behind stepped forward and took his place. They charged up to the battery, reserving their fire until they reached the parapets. Twice repulsed, the third time they reached the outer works, and planted their flag upon the escarpment. It was shot down and again planted, but shot down again.

These devoted troops now held partial possession of the works. But the triumph was of short duration. According to previous instructions, the enemy's gunners fell back behind the works, and the next instant from their batteries threw a murderous fire into our ranks at the shortest possible range. Nothing human could withstand such a fire; the confusion it produced was irretrievable; our men were driven back and the day lost.

But the attack was not abandoned without instances of wild and terrible courage that were almost appalling. In their madness and desperation, our men would rush up to the very mouths of the cannon, and many were blown to pieces by the rapid and constant discharges. Such spectacles of courage were curious and terrible to behold. An officer, standing a little way out from his men, was shouting, "Give it to the scoundrels." The words had but passed from his lips, when the first shell from a Parrott gun struck his left shoulder, tearing off his whole side. He turned his head a little to one side, his mouth opened, his eyes glared, and he fell dead.

The attack on the enemy's batteries was rash and magnificent. The intensity of the fight may be judged from the fact that two hundred and sixty dead bodies were found in and about the trenches, within a distance of fifty feet of the works. It is impossible to enumerate the examples of daring which adorn the story of this attack. The Second Texas Infantry, under Col. Rogers, led the charge, and the colonel himself fell on the enemy's breastworks, with the colors of his regiment in his hand. A piece of paper was found under his clothing, giving his name and rank and the address of his friends. As Gen. Cabell mounted the enemy's parapet, the first man he encountered was a Yankee colonel, who cried out, "Kill that d——d rebel officer." The next instant a blow from the general's sabre placed his antagonist at his feet. In the brigade of this brave officer, J. H. Bullock, adjutant of the 13th Arkansas regiment, a noble specimen of the Southern soldier—for, though blessed in estate and family, a son-in-law of Chief justice Parsons, of North Carolina, and the master of a beautiful and prosperous home, he had volunteered as a private and been advanced for merit—made a display of courage to animate his men that was a splendid picture of heroism, as he stood out and exposed himself to the enemy's fire until his clothing was pierced by balls, his life being saved only by that unseen shield with which Providence protects its agents. The gallant commander of this ever-glorious regiment, Col. Daly, had fallen, while himself engaged in the animation of his men—cheering and leading them on to the attack.

Under the necessities of the case, our troops had fallen back; and though in doing so they were exposed to a terrible and destructive fire, there was no panic, no rout—the wounded, except those who fell right at the intrenchments, having been nearly all brought away. Our army retired to the woods at a distance of only six hundred yards, and there, while our artillery resumed fire and kept it up for a short time, formed again in order of battle. But the enemy appearing indisposed to renew the conflict, Gen. Van Dorn, at three o'clock, drew off his whole force, being most ably supported in doing so by Gen. Price and the other general officers.

The next morning, at half past eight o'clock, our advance, consisting of Gen. Phifer's brigade, and Col. Whitfield's Legion, with one battery—not exceeding one thousand five hundred in all—crossed the Davis bridge at Hatchie river, to engage the enemy, a large body of whom, from Bolivar, had the day before reached that point, and had there been held in check by Col. Slemmon's and Adams' cavalry, with one battery. Our advance having crossed the bridge and gone a little distance, received a heavy fire at short range from a concealed battery, which was followed directly by a charge from a largely superior force. Our troops retreated in a good deal of confusion across the bridge—having suffered a loss, perhaps, of three hundred killed, wounded, and missing. The reinforcements arriving, our troops formed in line, and a fight with musketry ensued and was kept up for some time across the river, but with very little loss on our side. Meanwhile, our field-pieces opened upon the enemy—and they replying, cannonading was continued during the greater part of the day. During this time our advance was gradually withdrawn, and following the other troops, with the long wagon train of supplies, wounded, &c.—the artillery having also been brought off—made a successful crossing of Hatchie river, some miles higher up the stream. The retreat was eventually halted at a point a little north of Ripley.

Our loss in all the three days' engagements was probably quite double that of the enemy. In killed and wounded it exceeded three thousand; and it was estimated, besides, that we had left more than fifteen hundred prisoners in the hands of the enemy.

The defeat of Corinth was followed by swift news of disaster and discouragement. The military prospect was not dark, but it had lost much of the brightness it had only a few weeks before. Kentucky had been gloomily abandoned. In Virginia the hopes of conquering a peace on the Potomac had for the time been given up; the Kanawha Valley had again been mostly surrendered to the enemy; and Marshall's forces, back again in Southwestern Virginia, were consuming the substance of the country with but little return of other service. In other parts of the Confederacy, the prospect was not much relieved.

THE DEPARTMENT OF THE TRANS-MISSISSIPPI.

The events in the department of the Trans-Mississippi were too distant to affect the general fortunes of the war; they were but episodes to the great drama of arms that passed over the broad and imposing theatres of Virginia, Kentucky, and Tennessee; but they were replete with romance, and if their interest is at present partial, it is so, perhaps, for the reason that they are imperfectly known.

Missouri had the better of other seats of hostility for the real romance of war. The remote geography of the country, the rough character of the people, the intensity and ferocity of the passions excited, and the reduction of military operations to a warfare essentially partisan and frontier, gave to the progress of the war in this quarter a wild aspect, and illustrated it with rare and thrilling scenes.

Gen. Schofield, the Yankee commander, who had been left by Halleck with the brief and comprehensive instructions "to take care of Missouri," found the power of the Confederates broken in nearly three-fourths of that State, but the South-western portion threatened by the active movements of Gen. Hindman, in command of State forces raised in Arkansas and Texas. But in no part of Missouri was the spirit of the people broken. Guerrilla bands made their appearance in all parts of the State; and their numbers rapidly augmented under the despotic edict of Schofield, calling out the militia of the State to murder their own countrymen.

The dark atrocities of the Yankee rule in Missouri, enacted as they were in a remote country, and to a great extent re-moved from observation, surpassed all that was known in other parts of the Confederacy of the cruelty and fury of the enemy. The developments on this subject are yet imperfect; but some general facts are known of the inordinate license of the enemy in Missouri, while others of equal horror have es-caped the notice of the public.

In other parts of the Confederacy many of the excesses of the enemy were performed under certain formalities, and to some extent regulated by them. But in Missouri there was no "red tape," no qualification of forms; the order of the day was open robbery, downright murder, and freedom to all crimes of which "rebels" were the victims. Citizens were plundered with barefaced audacity. Those citizens of St. Louis county alone, who were suspected by Gen. Schofield to sympathize with the South, were taxed five hundred thousand dollars to arm, clothe, and subsist those who were spilling the blood of their brothers, and threatening their own homes with the torch and with outrages to which death is preferable.

The sanguinary guerrilla warfare in Missouri may be said to have commenced in the month of July, by the assembling of bands under Porter, Poindexter, Cobb, and others. The principal theatre of guerrilla operations was at this time the northeastern division of Missouri, where the almost devilish cruelties of the Yankee commander, the notorious Colonel McNeil, had lashed the people into incontrollable fury.

On the 6th of August, Porter's band was attacked at Kirksville by McNeil with a large force of cavalry and six pieces of artillery. This gallant partisan made a resistance of four hours against overwhelming numbers, and retired only after such a demonstration of valor, leaving the Yankees to claim as a victory an affair in which they had sustained a loss of more than five hundred in killed and wounded, probably double our own.

The day after the action, a party of Yankee scouts succeeded in capturing, near Edina, Col. F. McCullough, who was attached to Porter's command, and at the time of his capture was quite alone. The next morning a train with an armed escort proceeded from Edina to Kirksville. McCullough was sent along. On arriving at Kirksville, the news of the capture of this famous partisan excited the most devilish feeling among the Yankee troops. He was confined a brief time with the prisoners. Meantime a court-martial was held, and he was sentenced to be shot that very afternoon. He received the information of his fate with perfect composure, but protested against it. Leaning against the fence, he wrote a few lines to his wife. These, with his watch, he delivered to the officer, to be given to her. Upon the way to his execution, he requested the privilege to give the command to fire, which was granted. All being ready, he said: "What I have done, I have done as a principle of right. Aim at the heart. Fire!"

The command taking the soldiers by surprise, one fired sooner than the rest. The ball entering his breast, he fell, while the other shots passed over him. Falling with one leg doubled under the body, he requested to have it straightened out. While this was being done he said: "I forgive you for this barbarous act." The squad having reloaded their pieces, another volley was fired—this time into his body, and he died.

On the 15th of August occurred the more important action of Lone Jack. Large Yankee forces were moved from Lexington, with orders to effect a junction near Lone Jack and attack the forces under Hughes and Quantrell, supposed to be somewhere in Jackson county. The disaster which met the Yankees here was the most serious of the guerrilla campaign. Their command was defeated, with a loss of three hundred killed and wounded, two pieces of their artillery captured on the field, their routed forces turned back upon Lexington, and that place put in imminent peril. The timely reinforcement of Lexington by all the available forces of the enemy in north-eastern Missouri alone saved the place from capture by the Confederates, and disconcerted their plans of relieving their comrades north of the river.

The guerrilla campaign of Missouri is made memorable by the fearful story of the "Palmyra massacre." The important incidents of this tragedy are gathered from the enemy's own publications, and it was from Yankee newspapers that the people of the South first learned the barbarous and exultant news that McNeil had executed ten Confederate prisoners because a tory and spy had been carried off a captive by our forces.

From the enemy's own accounts, it appears that the missing man, Andrew Allsman, was a legitimate prisoner of war; that on the descent of the Confederate forces upon Palmyra he was captured by them; that he belonged to the Federal cavalry, but that being too old to endure all the hardships of active duty, he was detailed as a spy, being "frequently," as one of the Yankee papers states, "called upon for information touching the loyalty of men, which he always gave to the extent of his ability."

When McNeil returned to Palmyra in October, he caused a notice to be issued that unless Allsman was returned in ten days he would shoot ten Confederate prisoners as "a meet reward for their crimes, among which was the illegal restraining of said Allsman of his liberty." The ten days elapsed, and the prisoner was not returned. The following account of what ensued, is condensed from the Palmyra *Courier*, a "Union" journal, without any variation from the language in which it describes the deed of the demons with whom it was in sympathy:

"The tenth day expired with last Friday. On that day ten rebel prisoners, already in custody, were selected to pay with their lives the penalty demanded. A little after 11 o'clock,

a. m., the next day, three government wagons drove to the jail. One contained four, and each of the others three rough board coffins. The condemned men were conducted from the prison and seated in the wagons, one upon each coffin. A sufficient guard of soldiers accompanied them, and the cavalcade started for the fatal grounds. The ten coffins were removed from the wagons and placed in a row, six or eight feet apart, forming a line north and south. Each coffin was placed upon the ground with its foot west and head east. Thirty soldiers of the 2d M. S. M. were drawn up in a single line, extending north and south, facing the row of coffins. The arrangements completed, the men knelt upon the grass between their coffins and the soldiers. At the conclusion of a prayer by the army chaplain, each prisoner took his seat upon the foot of his coffin, facing the muskets which in a few moments were to launch them into eternity. They were nearly all firm and undaunted. The most noted of the ten was Captain Thomas A. Sidner of Monroe county, whose capture at Shelbyville, in the disguise of a woman, we related several weeks since. He was now elegantly attired in a suit of black broadcloth, with a white vest. A luxurious growth of beautiful hair rolled down upon his shoulders, which, with his fine personal appearance, could not but bring to mind the handsome but vicious Absalom. There was nothing especially worthy of note in the appearance of the others. A few moments after 1 o'clock the chaplain in attendance shook hands with the prisoners. Two of them accepted bandages for the eyes, the rest refused. A hundred spectators had gathered around the amphitheatre to witness the impressive scene. The stillness of death pervaded the place. The officer in command now stepped forward, and gave the word of command—'Ready! aim! fire!' The discharges, however, were not made simultaneously—probably through want of a perfect understanding of the orders to fire. Two of the rebels fell backwards upon their coffins and died instantly. Capt. Sidner sprang forward and fell with his head towards the soldiers, his face upwards, his hands clasped upon his breast, and the left leg drawn half way up. He did not move again, but died immediately. He had requested the soldiers to aim at his heart, and they obeyed but too implicitly. The other seven were not killed outright; so the reserves were called in who dispatched them with their revolvers."

The "Palmyra massacre" was destined to a long and painful remembrance by the people of the South, not only because of its tragic interest, but because it was a comment scrawled in blood on that weak and remiss policy of our government, which had so long submitted to the barbarous warfare of the enemy and hesitated at the rule of retaliation.

THE MILITARY AND POLITICAL SITUATION.

A slight survey of the military situation at this time adds something to the list of our disasters, and is necessary to understand the proportions of the crisis at which the fortunes of the South had arrived.

The capture of Galveston on the coast of Texas, on the 9th of October, was another repetition of the almost invariable story of disaster at the hands of the enemy's naval power. It was made almost without resistance. In the early part of the war, the defenceless condition of Galveston had been represented to the government, as in fact there was no ordnance available there but a lot of old cannon captured from the United States. These representations in the letters and petitions of the people of Galveston were made without effect, until at last, some time in the summer of 1861, a deputation of citizens waited upon the authorities at Richmond, begging piteously a few cannon to defend them from the enemy. The whole extent of the response of the government to this and other appeals was to send to Galveston eleven or thirteen guns, two of which were rifled; and transportation for these was only given to New Orleans, whence they had to be dragged over piney hills and through swamps to their destination. The consequence was, that the enemy had made an easy prize of one of our principal seaports; when, after threatening it for eighteen months, he at last found it practically defenceless.

The fall of Galveston again turned the perplexed attention of the people of the South to the enormous and rapid increase of the enemy's naval power in this war as one of its most painful subjects of interest. This arm had grown to such size as to threaten us in many respects more seriously than the enemy's land forces. It was calculated that, with the completion of their vast number of naval structures already on the stocks, the Yankees would have 388 vessels, mounting 3,072 guns—nearly nine guns to the vessel. Of these, thirty were iron-clad, mounting ninety of the heaviest guns in the world, each weighing 42,240 pounds, and throwing a solid shot, fifteen inches in diameter, weighing 480 pounds.

It is not wonderful that in view of these vast preparations in the North, the people of the South should have watched with intense interest the long lines of their sea-coast, and been on the tiptoe of expectation for the fleets of the Yankees, which were to sweep upon them in numbers and power yet unequalled by any naval demonstration of the enemy in this war. It was easy to see that the South would have to look to its foundries to set-off the naval power of the enemy. When we could match their naval armaments with our batteries on shore, we might expect to hold our sea-coast against their fleets. The authorities at Richmond were instructed that there was but one way of replying to the Yankee iron-clads on equal terms; and that was by iron-clad batteries, with powerful guns in them, and with the use of steel-pointed or wrought-iron projectiles.

In the Southwest, the strong tenure which we maintained of Vicksburg was a stumbling-block to the Yankee schemes for the conquest of Mississippi. The fate of that State was also confidently intrusted to the brave troops under the command of Gen. Pemberton, who was assisted by Van Dorn and Price and an increasing army.

But it was to Tennessee that the minds of the intelligent were turned to look for the earliest and severest conflict of the campaign in the West. The enemy already held the western portion of the State and a part of the middle, and evidently desired to obtain possession of the eastern portion. He was reported to be coming down from Kentucky for the purpose, in heavy columns, under Gen. Rosecrans, by way of Nashville; and there was reason to suppose that he would endeavor to make a flank movement on Knoxville, and, at the same time, capture Chattanooga, as the key of North Alabama and Georgia.

In Virginia a lull had followed the famous summer campaign,

and our army in the northern part of the State quietly recruited, and was daily improving in organization and numbers
The only incident that had broken the monotony of our camp
was the renewal in the North of the phantom of " invasion by
the rebels" by a raid into Pennsylvania, accomplished by the
rapid and brilliant commander of our cavalry, Gen. J. E. B.
Stuart, with about two thousand men. The expedition penetrated to Chambersburg, which was occupied for a short time
by our troops on the 10th of October. It met with no resistance, accumulated no stores, and accomplished nothing beyond
the results of a reconnoissance, and the wonder of one of the
most rapid marches on record.

This expedition left to the Yankees a remarkable souvenir
of Southern chivalry. Private property was uniformly respected by our troops; Yankee civilians were treated with
scrupulous regard; and many kindnesses were shown the
alarmed people in a knightly style, which would have been
creditable to us had it not been made ridiculous by excess of
courtesy and a tender and ceremonious politeness which was
in very absurd contrast to the manners of our enemy. On entering Chambersburg, " the soft-mannered rebels," as Col.
McClure, the Yankee commander of the post, described them,
treated him with the most tender politeness. Indeed, the narrative of this officer's experience furnishes a curious leaf in
the history of the war. To the great amusement of the people of the North, Col. McClure gave a long account in the
newspapers of the strained chivalry of our troops. He related how they had " thanked him for being candid," when he
told them that he was a Republican; how he was politely asked
for food by the officers; and how a private in Stuart's terrible
command had, " with a profound bow, asked for a few coals to
light a fire."

The story of these courtesies and salaams to our enemy is
not one for our amusement. It affords an instructive illustration that is valuable in history, of the over-amiable disposition
and simple mind of the South; and it places in stark and horrible contrast an agreeable picture with that of the devilish
atrocities and wanton and mocking destruction of the Yankee
armies on the soil of the Confederacy.

While the war lagged, we are called upon to notice new

sources of resolution and power in the South, which were perhaps more valuable than victories in the field. In this depart ment of interest, which is quite equal to that of battles and sieges, it will be necessary to pass in review some political acts of the rival governments, and some events of moral importance.

At last the Abolitionists of the North had had their wild and wicked will. On the 22d day of September, President Lincoln issued his celebrated proclamation of "emancipation"* of the slaves of the South, to take effect after the 1st of next January, thus unmasking the objects of the war, and exhibiting to the world the sublime of administrative madness.

---

* The following is a copy of this remarkable document:

BY THE PRESIDENT OF THE UNITED STATES—A PROCLAMATION.

Washington, Sept. 22, 1862.

I, Abraham Lincoln, President of the United States of America, and Commander-in-Chief of the army and navy thereof, do hereby proclaim and declare, that hereafter, as heretofore, the war will be prosecuted for the object of practically restoring the constitutional relation between the United States and the people thereof, in which States that relation is, or may be, suspended or disturbed; that it is my purpose, upon the next meeting of Congress, to again recommend the adoption of a practical measure tendering pecuniary aid to the free acceptance or rejection of all the slave States, so called, the people whereof may not then be in rebellion against the United States, and which States may then have voluntarily adopted or thereafter may voluntarily adopt the immediate or gradual abolishment of slavery within their respective limits; and that the efforts to colonize persons of African descent, with their consent, upon the continent or elsewhere, with the previously obtained consent of the governments existing there, will be continued; that on the 1st day of January, in the year of our Lord one thousand eight hundred and sixty-three, all persons held as slaves within any State, or any designated part of a State, the people whereof shall then be in rebellion against the United States, shall be thenceforward and forever free; and the executive government of the United States, including the naval and military authority thereof, will recognize and maintain the freedom of such persons, and will do no act or acts to repress such persons, or any of them, in any efforts they may make for their actual freedom; that the Executive will, on the 1st day of January, aforesaid, by proclamation, designate the States and parts of States, if any, in which the people thereof respectively shall then be in rebellion against the United States; and the fact that any State, or the people thereof, shall on that day be in good faith represented in the Congress of the United States by members chosen thereto at elections wherein a majority of the qualified voters of such State shall have participated, shall, in the absence of strong countervailing testimony, be deemed conclusive evidence that such State and the people thereof have not been in rebellion against the United States.

Since the commencement of the war, the Abolitionists had gradually compassed their ends at Washington, or rather the real objects and inherent spirit of the war had been gradually developed. They had legislated slavery forever out of the Territories; they had abolished it in the District of Columbia; they had passed laws confiscating the property of "rebels" and emancipating their slaves, and declaring all fugitive slaves free within their military lines; they had made it a crime on the part of their military officers to restore or aid in restoring any fugitive slave to his master; and finally, they had procured from President Lincoln a proclamation declaring all the slaves in the Confederate States, beyond the lines of their land and naval forces, " henceforward and forever free."

This infamous proclamation, while regarded by the South as a fulmination of exasperated passion, was in the North a source of weakness and division. It divided the North and strengthened the enemies of Mr. Lincoln's administration without creating any enthusiasm among its friends. The few in the North who still had some regard for the written constitution under which they lived, contended that the President could not proclaim emancipation except under the pressure of military necessity, and what sort of a military necessity, it was asked, was that which admitted of a delay of a hundred days. The *fulmen brutum* issued to appease the anti-slavery party proved a firebrand at home. Many, even of this party, were dissatisfied, and decried the proclamation because of its tardiness. "There was a time," said the New York *Tribune,* "when even this bit of paper could have brought the negro to our side; but now slavery, the real rebel capital, has been surrounded by a Chick-

---

And I do hereby enjoin upon and order all persons engaged in the military and naval service of the United States to observe, obey, and enforce within their respective spheres of service the act and sections above recited.

And the Executive will in due time recommend that all citizens of the United States, who shall have remained loyal thereto throughout the rebellion, shall (upon the restoration of the constitutional relation between the United States and their respective States and people, if the relation shall have been suspended or disturbed) be compensated for all losses by acts of the United States, including the loss of slaves.

In witness whereof, I have hereunto set my hand and caused the seal of the United States to be affixed.

ABRAHAM LINCOLN.

ahominy swamp of blunders and outrages against that race which no *paper spade* can dig through."

To the South the fulmination of Lincoln was a crowning proof of the true principles of the party that had elevated him to the Presidency, and that on its accession to power had made perfidious use of the most solemn pledges.* It was a public confession of the fact that conquest, extermination, and emancipation were the real objects of the war—a fact which the enemy for a while had affected to deny. It attempted to accomplish by the horrors of servile insurrection what our enemy had failed to accomplish by military operations. It confessed to the world his inability and failure to accomplish his pur-

* One of the most singular juxtapositions between the professions of the North at the commencement of hostilities and its present ideas, is afforded in Mr. Seward's famous letter, written to the French government on the 22d April, 1861, and his subsequent circular to the Yankee ministers in Europe. It is one of the most singular of all the juggleries and summersaults of Yankee diplomacy.

In the first pronunciamento of Secretary Seward, written "by the direction of the President," occurs the following passage:

"The condition of slavery in the several States will remain just the same, whether it succeeds or fails. The rights of the States, and the condition of every human being in them, will remain subject to exactly the same laws and form of administration, whether the revolution shall succeed or whether it shall fail. Their constitutions, and laws, and customs, habits, and institutions, in either case will remain the same. It is hardly necessary to add to this incontestable statement, the further fact that the new President, as well as the citizens through whose suffrages he has come into the administration, has always repudiated all designs whatever, and wherever imputed to him and them, of *disturbing the system of slavery as it is existing under the constitution and laws*. The case, however, would not be fully presented were I to omit to say that any such effort on his part would be *unconstitutional*, and all his acts in that direction would be prevented by the judicial authority, even though they were assented to by Congress and the people."

Within eighteen months after Seward declares officially to one of the ministers of the government that the President has no wish and no right to interfere with the institutions of the "rebellious" States, he writes another letter, also directed to the ministers abroad, announcing the adoption of a policy which, if it could be carried out, would make a complete revolution in the social organization of the South. Utterly regardless of his former position and declaration, he undertakes to justify the "emancipation" proclamation of the Yankee President. But this is not all. What shall we say of the effrontery of the lie, when Seward asserts that the abolition proclamation is not only a ʻust and proper act, but avows his belief that the world will recognize "*the moderation and magnanimity with which the government proceeds in a matter so solemn and important!*"

poses by regular and honorable hostilities. It was, in short, the diabolical attempt of an infatuated ruler, unworthy of authority, in a fit of disappointed malice, to inflict the worst horrors known to human nature upon eight millions of people who had wisely rejected his authority.

The "emancipation" proclamation not only strengthened the South and nerved her to greater exertions in the war, but it fortunately gave occasion to the world for a more interested observation and closer study of the peculiar institution of the Confederacy. The sympathies of Europe with the anti-slavery party in America were depressed by the conduct of that party, its exhibitions of ferocity, and by the new manifestations which the war had made of the nature and moral condition of negro slavery in the South.

Indeed, the war had shown the system of slavery in the South to the world in some new and striking aspects, and had removed much of that cloud of prejudice, defamation, false-hood, romance, and perverse sentimentalism through which our peculiar institution had been formerly known to Europe. It had given a better vindication of our system of slavery than all the books that could be written in a generation. It had shown that slavery was an element of strength with us; that it had assisted us in our struggle; that no servile insurrections had taken place in the South, in spite of the allurements of our enemy; that the slave had tilled the soil while his master had fought; that in large districts unprotected by our troops, and with a white population consisting almost exclusively of women and children, the slave had continued at his work quiet, cheer-ful, and faithful; and that, as a conservative element in our social system, the institution of slavery had withstood the shocks of war, and been a faithful ally of our arms, although instigated to revolution by every art of the enemy, and prompted to the work of assassination and pillage by the most brutal examples of the Yankee soldiery.*

---

* The missionary settlements of the Yankees on the coast of South Caro-lina were an acknowledged failure, so far as the proposed education and exalta-tion of the blacks were concerned. The appearance of the ancient town of Beaufort, since it had fallen into the enemy's possession, indicated the peculiari-ties of Yankee rule, and afforded an interesting exhibition of their relations with the negro. The inhabitants had taken nothing away with them but their

Since the commencement of the war the North had had almost exclusive access to the ear of the world, and had poured into it whatever of slander or of misrepresentation human ingenuity could suggest. This circumstance, which was at first thought to be a great disadvantage to us, had not only proved a harmless annoyance, but had resulted in invaluable benefit. It had secured sympathy for us; it had excited the inquiries of the intelligent, who, after all, give the law to public opinion; and it had naturally tempted the North to such lying and bravado as to disgust the world.

At the beginning of the war the North had assured the world that the people of the South were a sensual and barbarous people, demoralized by their institution of slavery, and depraved by self-will and licentiousness below the capacity for administrative government. The best reply to these slanders, was our conduct in this war. Even the little that was known in Europe of the patriotic devotion, the dignity and cultivated humanity of the people of the South, as shown in the war, had been sufficient to win unbounded encomiums for them. We had not only withstood for nearly two years a power which had put thirteen hundred thousand men in the field; but we had

---

personal property and their valuable domestic slave servants. The furniture was left untouched in the houses. These houses were owned by the Barnwells, the Rhetts, the Cuthberts, the Phillipses, and other distinguished families of North Carolina. The elegant furniture, the libraries, the works of art, had nearly all disappeared. They had been sent North from time to time by Yankee officers, and many of these officers of high rank. The elegant dwelling-houses had been converted into barracks, negro quarters, hospitals, and storehouses. The best houses had been put in complete order, and were occupied by the officers of the department and the abolitionist missionaries from Boston and elsewhere. The efforts of these missionaries to teach the negroes their letters and habits of cleanliness met with no success. Beaufort was full of negroes, well clothed, at government expense, fat, saucy, and lazy. The town looked dirty and disorderly, and had the appearance of a second-class Mexican village. Some of the missionaries had been elevated to the position of planters, and occupied the estates of the old Carolinians. The labor on these estates was performed by contraband negroes. These abolition lords assumed all the hauteur and dignity of the Southern planter. The only difference to the black laborer was that he had the name of freeman; his labor was as unrelenting as ever. Massachusetts missionaries and Massachusetts speculators enjoyed the larger share of government patronage here. The department of Hunter appeared to be experimenting in attempts to elevate a negro to equality with the white man. Military operations were secondary considerations.

shown that we were a people able in public affairs, resolute, brave, and prudent.

Another characteristic Yankee misrepresentation, made to the world about this time on the subject of the war, was, that it was to be concluded at an early day by the force of destitution and suffering in the South. The delusion of conquering the "rebels" by famine easily caught the vulgar ear. The North made it a point to exaggerate and garble every thing it could find in Southern newspapers, of the ragged condition of our armies, the high prices of the necessaries of life, and the hardships of the war. The Yankees were pleasantly entertained with stories of our suffering. Their pictorials were adorned with caricatures of "secesh" in skeleton soldiers and gaunt cavalrymen with spurs strapped to their naked heels. Their perfumed fops and dainty ladies had the fashion of tittering at the rags of our prisoners. They had an overwhelming sense of the ludicrous in the idea of Southern women cutting up the carpets in their houses to serve for blankets and garments for the soldiers.

The fact was that our sufferings were great; but their mute eloquence, which the enemy misinterpreted as a prospect of craven submission, was truly the sign of self-devotion. Whatever was suffered in physical destitution was not to be regretted. It practised our people in self-denial; it purified their spirit; it brought out troops of virtues; it ennobled our women with offices of charity; it gave us new bonds of sympathy and love, and it trained us in those qualities which make a nation great and truly independent.

In the whirl of passing events, many strange things were daily happening around us that at a remoter period of history will read like romance. The directions of our industry were changed. Planters raised corn and potatoes, fattened hogs and cultivated garden vegetables, while cotton was by universal consent neglected. Our newspapers were of all sizes and colors, sometimes containing four pages, sometimes two, and not a few were printed on common brown wrapping paper. Politics were dead. A political enemy was a curiosity only read of in the records of the past. Our amusements had been revolutionized. Outside of Richmond, a theatre was remembered only as an institution of by-gone times. Most of our people did their own playing and their own singing; and the ladies spent the mornings in sewing coarse shirts or pantaloons for the soldiers to wear, and sung in public at night to gain money for the soldiers' equipments.

The footprints of the enemy, in Virginia especially, had marked lines of desolation such as history seldom records. Starting from Fortress Monroe and running westward to Winchester, scarcely a house within fifty miles of the Potomac but bore evidence of Yankee greed and spoliation. In nearly every county the court-house in which the assizes for each county used to be held, was rudely demolished, doors and windows torn down; while within, upon the white walls in every phase of handwriting, were recorded the autographs of the vandals, whose handiwork surrounded the beholder.

While the people of the South suffered, the resources of the country were developed by harsh necessity; and about the period where our narrative reaches, we are called upon to notice that happy change in the administration of our government, in which short-sighted expectations of peace were replaced by the policy of provision and an amassment of stores for a war of indefinite duration. Measures were adopted to afford adequate supplies of ordnance, arms, and munitions for the army. Of small-arms the supply was more adequate to the regiments of the army than at any other time. They had increased from importation and capture not less than eighty thousand. Establishments for making ordnance were founded in different parts of the South; a nitre corps was organized for service; and former dread of deficiency of the munitions of war no longer existed. The manufacturing resources of the country, especially in iron, were liberally patronized by the government, by large advances and liberal contracts; but in this the public service met great embarrassment from the temptations constantly offered to contractors to prefer the superior profits which they could command by supplying the general market. The quartermaster's department was under the direction of Gen. Myers, of South Carolina, whose contributions to the cause of the South, in the zeal and ability which he brought into his important office, must take a high rank in all the histories of the war. He contended against the great obstacles of the blockade, the difficulties of railroad transportation, and the constant losses in the enemy's ravages of the country, and performed wonders under the most unfavorable circumstances. Woollens and leather were imported from Europe through trains of difficulties, the most devoted exertions were made to replenish the scant supplies of blankets and shoes in the army, and by using to the utmost our internal resources, by the establishment of factories and the organization of workshops; and by greater economy in the use of our supplies, the sufferings of our soldiers were alleviated and their zeal refreshed for the campaign.

CHAPTER XX.

The Heroism of Virginia.—Her Battle-fields.—Burnside's Plan of Campaign.—Calculations of his Movement upon Fredericksburg.—Failure to surprise Gen. Lee.—THE BATTLE OF FREDERICKSBURG.—The Enemy crossing the River.—Their Bombardment of the Town.—Scenes of Distress.—The Battle on the Right Wing.—The Story of Marye's Heights.—Repulse of the Enemy.—The old Lesson of barren Victory.—Death of Gen. Cobb.—Death of Gen. Gregg.—Romance of the Story of Fredericksburg.—Her noble Women.—Yankee Sacking of the Town.—A Specimen of Yankee Warfare in North Carolina.—Designs of the Enemy in this State.—The Engagements of Kinston.—Glance at other Theatres of the War.—Gen. Hindman's Victory at Prairie Grove.—Achievements of our Cavalry in the West.—The Affair of Hartsville.—Col. Clarkson's Expedition.—Condition of Events at the Close of the Year 1862.

VIRGINIA had borne the brunt of the war. Nearly two-thirds of her territory had been overrun by the enemy, and her richest fields had been drenched with blood or marked by the scars of the invader. The patriotic spirit and the chivalrous endurance of this ancient and admirable commonwealth had not only supported these losses and afflictions without a murmur, but these experiences of the war were the sources of new inspiration, and the occasions of renewed resolution and the reinforcement of courage by the sentiment of devotion. When we add to the consideration of the grand spirit of this State the circumstances that the flower of the Confederate army was naturally collected on this the most critical theatre of the war, and that the operations in Virginia were assisted by the immediate presence of the government, we shall naturally look here for the most brilliant and decisive successes of the war.

When the Confederate army fell back into Virginia, after its short but eventful campaign in Maryland, Gen. Lee, by the skilful disposition of his forces in front of Winchester, rendered it impracticable for McClellan to invade the Valley of the Shenandoah, and forced him to adopt the route on the east side of the Blue Ridge. The Federal commander accepted this alternative the more readily, since he hoped, by an ostentatious display of a part of his forces near Shepherdstown, to deceive Gen. Lee and gain his flank and rear at Warrenton

On his arrival at this latter place, however, much to his surprise and dismay, he found the forces of Lee quietly awaiting him on the south bank of the Rappahannock.

McClellan having been superseded by Burnside, that officer undertook a plan of campaign entirely on his own responsibility, in opposition to the suggestions of Halleck and to what were known to be the predilections of the military authorities at Washington. The plan of Gen. Burnside was to concentrate the army in the neighborhood of Warrenton, to make a small movement across the Rappahannock as a feint, with a view to divert the attention of the Confederates and lead them to believe he was going to move in the direction of Gordonsville, and then to make a rapid movement of the whole army to Fredericksburg, on the north side of the Rappahannock.

In moving upon Fredericksburg, Gen. Burnside calculated that his army would all the time be as near Washington as would the Confederates, and that after arriving at Fredericksburg it would be at a point nearer to Richmond than it would be even if it should take Gordonsville.

This novel enterprise against the Confederate Capital was hailed by the Northern newspapers with renewed acclamations of "on to Richmond;" and the brazen and familiar prophecy of the fall of the city "within ten days" was repeated with new emphasis and bravado. In the mean time the plans of Burnside, so far as they contemplated a surprise of the Confederates, had failed, and at Fredericksburg, as at Warrenton, his army found itself, by the active movements of Gen. Lee, confronted by a force sufficient to dispute its advance and to deliver battle on a scale commensurate with the stake.

THE BATTLE OF FREDERICKSBURG.

Gen. Burnside having concentrated his army at Fredericksburg, employed himself for several days in the latter part of November in bringing up from Aquia Creek all the pontoons he could for building the bridges which were necessary to throw his forces across the river. Several councils of war were called to decide about crossing the Rappahannock. It was finally determined to cross at Fredericksburg, under the impression that Gen. Lee had thrown a large portion of his force down the river and elsewhere, thus weakening his defences in front.

On the night of the 10th of December the enemy commenced to throw three bridges over the Rappahannock—two at Fredericksburg, and the third about a mile and a quarter below near the mouth of Deep Run. In the prosecution of this work, the enemy was defended by his artillery on the hills of Stafford, which completely commanded the plain on which Fredericksburg stands. The narrowness of the Rappahannock, its winding course, and deep bed, afforded opportunity for the construction of bridges at points beyond the reach of our artillery, and the banks had to be watched by skirmishers. The houses of Fredericksburg afforded a cover for the skirmishers at the bridges opposite the town, but at the lowest point of crossing no shelter could be had.

The 17th Mississippi regiment, Barksdale's brigade, being on picket within the town, were ordered to the bluff overlooking the site of the old railroad bridge. The moon was brilliant, and by its light our men could distinguish the enemy's forces working on a pontoon bridge stretching from the Stafford bank towards the foot of the bluff. In the course of an hour the bridge had been stretched within sixty yards of the southern shore. The work was going bravely on, when the two companies of the 17th, who were lying on the extreme verge of the bluff, were ordered to fire. The order was deliberately given and executed. At the crack of our rifles, the bride-builders scampered for the shore; but the next moment there was opened upon the bluff a terrific fire of shell, grape, and musketry, which was kept up until our troops retired. Twice again, at intervals of half an hour, the enemy renewed the attempt to complete the bridge, but was in each instance repulsed. After the third repulse of the enemy, the whole of Barksdale's brigade was ordered to the support of the 17th regiment, and were put into position, some in the rear of the bluff and others higher up and lower down the stream. At this juncture the enemy's fire from cannon and small-arms became so tremendous and overwhelming, that our troops were only preserved from destruction by lying flat on their faces. In every instance in which a man ventured to raise his head from the earth, he was instantly riddled by bullets or torn to pieces by grapeshot.

The emergency may be understood when it is borne in mind that the position occupied by our men was swept by the enemy' batteries and sharpshooters not two hundred yards distant on the opposite heights.

Towards five o'clock in the afternoon of the 11th of December, three rousing cheers from the river bank beneath the bluff announced that the enemy had completed the bridge, and that his troops had effected a landing on the southern bank. About this time the order for a retreat was received by our men. The regiments of the brigade fell back by different streets, firing as they retreated upon the enemy, who closely followed them. The brigade rendezvoused at the market-house and faced the enemy. A sharp skirmish ensued, but our troops, acting under orders, again fell back and left the town in possession of the enemy.

It having become evident to Gen. Lee that no effectual opposition could be offered to the construction of the bridges or passage of the river, it only remained that positions should be selected to oppose the enemy's advance after crossing. Under cover of the darkness of the night of the 12th and of a dense fog, a large force passed the river, and took position on the right bank, protected by their heavy guns on the left.

The effects of the enemy's bombardment upon the unfortunate town were deplorable. The majority of the population had long ago fled the city at the prospect of its destruction; and the touching spectacles of their misery and suffering were seen for miles around the city, where houseless women and children were camped out or roaming shelterless and hungry through the fields. A number of citizens who had returned to the town under the delusion that it would not be attacked, left it during the day the enemy crossed the river, single or in families, and sought for refuge and safety in the country. They were scattered about—some in cabins, some in the open air, and others wandering vacantly along the railroads. Little children with blue feet trod painfully the frozen ground, and those whom they followed knew as little as themselves where to seek food and shelter. Hundreds of ladies wandered homeless over the frozen highway, with bare feet and thin clothing, knowing not where to find a place of refuge. Delicately nurtured girls, with slender forms, upon which no rain had ever

heat, which no wind had ever visited too roughly, walked hurriedly, with unsteady feet, upon the road, seeking only some
place where they could shelter themselves. Whole families
sought sheds by the wayside, or made roofs of fence-rails and
straw, knowing not whither to fly, or to what friend to have
recourse. This was the result of the enemy's bombardment.
Night had settled down, and though the roar of the batteries
had hushed, the flames of burning houses still lit up the land-
scape.

The sun of the 13th of December rose clear, but a dim fog
shrouded the town of Fredericksburg and the circumjacent
valleys, and delayed the opening of the antagonistic batteries.
At two o'clock in the morning our troops were all under arms,
and batteries in position to receive the expected attack of the
enemy.

The Rappahannock, in its course from west to east, is skirted
just at the point where Fredericksburg stands on its southern
bank, by low crests of hills, which on the northern bank run
parallel and close to the river, and on the southern bank trend
backward from the stream, and leave a semicircular plain six
miles in length and two or three in depth, inclosed within their
circumference before they again approach the river in the
neighborhood of Massaponax creek. Immediately above the
town, and on the left of the Confederate position, the bluffs
are bold and bare of trees; but south of the railroad, beginning near the town and running to a point at Hamilton's crossing, and also parallel with the river, is a range of hills covered
with dense oak forest, fringed on its northern border by pine
thickets. Our forces occupied the whole length of this forest.
Longstreet's corps occupied the highlands above, opposite and
for a mile below the town. Jackson's corps rested on Longstreet's right, and extended away to the eastward, the extreme
right, under A. P. Hill, crossing the railroad at Hamilton's
crossing, and stretching into the valley towards the river.
Our front was about six miles in length. Most of the batteries
of both corps were posted in the skirts of the forest, along
the line of the railroad, the seven batteries in Col. Lindsey
Walker's regiment and Stuart's horse artillery being stationed
in the valley, between the railroad at Hamilton's crossing and
the river. The enemy's forces occupied the valley north of

the railroad from Fredericksburg to within half a mile of our extreme right. His light batteries were posted over the southern extremity of the valley, at from a quarter of a mile to a mile from the railroad, while the hills on the northern banks of the river from Falmouth to Fitzhugh's farm, five miles below Fredericksburg, were studded at intervals of half a mile with his batteries of heavy guns.

At noon the fog had cleared away, but there was a thick haze in the atmosphere. About this time the enemy's infantry moved forward from the river towards our batteries on the hills. As they pressed forward across the valley, Stuart's horse artillery from our extreme right opened upon them a destructive enfilading fire of round-shot. This fire, which annoyed them sorely, was kept up in spite of six batteries which were directed against the horse artillery as soon as it was unmasked. By one o'clock the Yankee columns had crossed the valley and entered the woods south of the railroad. The batteries on both sides slackened their fire, and musketry, at first scattering, but quickly increasing to a crash and roar, sounded through the woods. Dense volumes of smoke rose above the trees, and volley succeeded volley, sometimes so rapidly as to blend into a prolonged and continuous roar. A. P. Hill's division sustained the first shock of battle. The rest of Jackson's corps were in different lines of reserves. D. H. Hill's division was drawn up in J. L. Marye's field, under a long hill, in rear of our line of battle. Here they remained during the most of the day, being moved from time to time to the right or left, as the exigencies of battle dictated. Shortly after the infantry fight began, a brigade of this division was moved at a double-quick a mile and a half to the right, and posted in a dense clump of pines, in supporting distance of Stuart's horse artillery. In ten minutes they were brought back to their original position. The celerity of this movement made a singular and exciting spectacle. A long black line shoots from the position of the reserves, crosses the railroad at Hamilton's station, skims across the valley, and in a few moments is lost in the pines nearly two miles away. After scarcely a breathing spell, the same line emerges from the pines and retraces its steps to its original position. As this brigade resumed its position in reserve, the fire of musketry directly in its front slackened. A few crackling shots were heard to our left, along Longstreet's division, and then a succession of volleys, which were kept up at intervals during the remainder of the evening. The musketry fire on our right was soon renewed, and the battle raged with increased fury. Our batteries along our whole front again reopened, and Col. Walker's artillery regiment, composed of Latham's, Letcher's, Braxton's, Pegram's, Crenshaw's, Johnson's and McIntosh's batteries, stationed in the open low grounds, to the east of the railroad at Hamilton's station, moved forward several hundred yards in the direction of Fredericksburg. Hill's and Early's troops had driven the enemy from the woods and across the railroad in the direction of their pontoon bridges near Deep Run. Our men pursued them a mile and a half across the bottom land, and fell back only when they had gotten under the shelter of their batteries. Again the enemy rallied and returned to renew the contest, but were again driven back. All the batteries of Jackson's corps were at this time in full play, and in the approaching twilight the blaze of the guns and the quick flashes of the shells more distinctly visible, constituted a scene at once splendid and terrific.

On the right wing the enemy had been driven back with great loss. Gen. Stuart had well redeemed his grim dispatch—that he was " going to crowd 'em with artillery." The enormous strength of this military arm had been used with desperation on one side and devoted courage on the other. The enemy had twenty thousand men engaged on this wing, while, altogether, from first to last, we had not more than ten thousand in the line of fire.

But while the battle was dashing furiously against the lines of Jackson, the enemy was crossing troops over his bridges at Fredericksburg and massing them in front of Longstreet, in the immediate neighborhood of the town.

On reference to the positions of the battle-field, it will be apparent that the left of the Confederate army—a portion of it stationed not more than four hundred yards from Fredericksburg—occupied a much stronger position than the centre and right. There was not sufficient room for the Yankee troops destined for the attack of the nearest Confederate batteries to deploy and form, except under a deadly Confederate fire, whereas, the Yankee troops who attacked the Confederate centre and right, had a large plain on which to deploy, and had much fewer disadvantages of ground to contend with, inasmuch as they advanced against lower hills and had the long spurs of copse to assist them as points of attack, calculated to protect and serve as *points d'appui* to the Yankees if they could once have succeeded in carrying and holding them.

In this part of the field the enemy displayed a devotion that is remarkable in history. This display does not adorn the Yankees; it was made by a race that has left testimonies of its courage in such stories as Waterloo and Fontenoy. To the Irish division, commanded by Gen. Meagher, was principally committed the desperate task of bursting out of the town of Fredericksburg, and forming under the withering fire of the Confederate batteries, to attack Marye's Heights, towering immediately in their front. The troops were harangued in impassioned language by their commander, who pointed to the heights as the contested prize of victory.

The heights were occupied by the Washington Artillery and a portion of McLaws' division. As the enemy advanced, the artillery reserved their fire until he arrived within two hundred and fifty yards, when they opened on the heavy masses with grape and canister. At the first broadside of the sixteen guns of the battalion, hundreds of the enemy went down, and at every successive discharge, great furrows were plowed through their ranks. They staggered repeatedly, but were as often rallied and brought forward. Again and again they made frantic dashes upon our steady line of fire, and as often were the hill-sides strewn for acres with their corpses. At last, no longer able to withstand the withering fire, they broke and fled in confusion. They were pressed into town by our infantry. Our victory was complete all along the line. When the voices of our officers in the darkness ordered the last advance, the combat had terminated in the silence of the foe.

The enemy left behind him a ghastly field. Some portions of it were literally packed with his dead. At the foot of Marye's Heights was a frightful spectacle of carnage. The bodies which had fallen in dense masses within forty yards of the muzzles of Col. Walton's guns, testified to the gallantry of the Irish division, and showed what manner of men they were who pressed on to death with the dauntlessness of a race whose courage history has made indisputable. The loss of the enemy was out of all comparison in numbers with our own; the evidences of its extent do not permit us to doubt that it was at least ten thousand; while our own killed and wounded, during the operations since the movements of the enemy began at Fredericksburg, amounted to about eighteen hundred.

At the thrilling tidings of Fredericksburg the hopes of the South rose high that we were at last to realize some important and practical consequences from the prowess of our arms. We had obtained a victory in which the best troops of the North —including Sumner's grand division—had been beaten; in which defeat had left the shattered foe cowering beneath the houses of Fredericksburg; and in which he had been forced into a position which left him no reasonable hope of escape, with a river in his rear, which, though threaded by pontoon bridges, would have been impassable under the pressure of attack. It is remarkable that, so far as the war had progressed, although fought on an almost unparalleled scale in numbers, it was yet not illustrated by the event so common in the military history of Europe, of the decisive annihilation of any single army. But it was thought that Fredericksburg, at least, would give an illustration of a decisive victory in this war. The Southern public waited with impatience for the completion of the success that had already been announced, and the newspapers were eagerly scanned for the hoped-for intelligence that Gen. Lee had, by the vigor of a fresh assault, dispatched his crippled enemy on the banks of the river. But no such assault was made. While the public watched with keen impatience for the blow, the announcement came that the enemy, after having remained entirely at his leisure one day in Fredericksburg, had the next night crossed the Rappahannock without accident or a single effort at interruption on our part, and that the army of Burnside, which was a short while ago thought to be in the jaws of destruction, was quietly reorganizing in perfect security on the north bank of the river. It was the old lesson to the South of a barren victory. The story of Fredericksburg was incomplete and unsatisfactory; and

there appeared no prospect but that a war waged at awfu,
sacrifices was yet indefinitely to linger in the trail of bloody
skirmishes.

The victory, which had only the negative advantage of having checked the enemy without destroying him, and the vulgar
glory of our having killed and wounded several thousand men
more than we had lost, had been purchased by us with lives,
though comparatively small in numbers, yet infinitely more
precious than those of mercenary hordes arrayed against us.
Two of our brigadier-generals—Gen. Thomas R. R. Cobb of
Georgia and Gen. Maxcy Gregg of South Carolina—had fallen
on the field.   The loss of each was more conspicuous from extraordinary personal worth than from mere distinctions of
rank.   Gen. Cobb was the brother of Gen. Howell Cobb, and
was an able and eloquent member of the Provisional Congress,
in which body he had served in the important capacity of
chairman of the committee on military affairs.

Of the virtues and services of Gen. Maxcy Gregg it is not
necessary to remind any portion of the people of the South
by a detailed review of incidents in his career.   His name was
familiarly coupled with the first movements of the war, he
having been appointed to the command of the 1st South Carolina regiment, the first force from the State which arrived in
Virginia, and whose advent at Richmond had been hailed with
extraordinary demonstrations of honor and welcome.   The term
of the service of this regiment having expired, it returned to
South Carolina, but its commander, Col. Gregg, remained in
Virginia, and subsequently reorganized the regiment, which
had since been constantly and conspicuously in service.   Its
commander was subsequently made a brigadier-general.

Gen. Gregg, although the occupations of his life were principally professional, had a large and brilliant political reputation in his State.   He was a leading member of the bar, and
practised his profession with distinction and success for a
period of more than twenty years in Columbia.   In politics he
was an extreme State Rights man, and stood, with others, at
the head of that party in South Carolina.   He took a promi
nent part in favor of the policy of reopening the slave-trade
which had been the subject of some excited and untimely dis
cussion in the South some years ago; he and ex-Governor

Adams, of South Carolina, being associated as the leading representatives of that idea in the cotton States.

Gen. Gregg was remarkable for his firm and unflinching temper. In the army he had an extraordinary reputation for self-possession and *sang froid* in battle. He was never disconcerted, and had the happy faculty of inspiring the courage of his troops, not so much by words as by his cool determination and even behavior.

The romance of the story of Fredericksburg is written no less in the quiet heroism of her women than in deeds of arms. The verses of the poet rather than the cold language of a mere chronicle of events are most fitting to describe the beautiful courage and noble sacrifices of those brave daughters of Virginia, who preferred to see their homes reduced to ashes, rather than polluted by the Yankee, and who in the blasts of winter, and in the fiercer storms of blood and fire, went forth undismayed, encouraging our soldiers, and proclaiming their desire to suffer privation, poverty, and death, rather than the shame of a surrender or the misfortune of a defeat. In all the terrible scenes of Fredericksburg, there were no weakness and tears of women. Mothers, exiles from their homes, met their sons in the ranks, embraced them, told them their duty, and with a self-negation most touching to witness, concealed their want, sometimes their hunger, telling their brave boys they were comfortable and happy, that they might not be troubled with domestic anxieties. At Hamilton's crossing, many of the women had the opportunity of meeting their relatives in the army. In the haste of flight, mothers had brought a few garments, or perhaps the last loaf of bread for the soldier boy, and the lesson of duty whispered in the ear gave to the young heart the pure and brave inspiration to sustain it in battle. No more touching and noble evidence could be offered of the heroism of the women of Fredericksburg than the gratitude of our army; for, afterwards, when subscriptions for their relief came to be added up, it was found that thousands of dollars had been contributed by ragged soldiers out of their pittance of pay to the fund of the refugees. There could be no more eloquent tribute than this offered to the women of Fredericksburg—a beautiful and immortal souvenir of their sufferings and virtues.

What was endured in the Yankee sacking of the town, finds scarcely anywhere a parallel in the history of civilized races. It is impossible to detail here the murderous acts of the enemy, the arsons, the robberies, the torture of women, and the innumerable and indescribable villanies committed upon helpless people. The following extract from the New York *Tribune*, written by one of its army correspondents in a tone of devilish amusement, affords a glimpse of Burnside's brigands in Fredericksburg, and of the accustomed barbarities of the enemy :

"The old mansion of Douglas Gordon—perhaps the wealthiest citizen in the vicinity—is now used as the headquarters of General Howard, but before he occupied it, every room had been torn with shot, and then all the elegant furniture and works of art broken and smashed by the soldiers, who burst into the house after having driven the rebel sharpshooters from behind it. When I entered it early this morning, before its occupation by Gen. Howard, I found the soldiers of his fine division diverting themselves with the rich dresses found in the wardrobes; some had on bonnets of the fashion of last year, and were surveying themselves before mirrors, which, an hour or two afterwards, were pitched out of the window and smashed to pieces upon the pavement; others had elegant scarfs bound round their heads in the form of turbans, and shawls around their waists.

"We destroyed by fire nearly two whole squares of buildings, chiefly used for business purposes, together with the fine residences of O. McDowell, Dr. Smith, J. H. Kelly, A. S. Cott, William Slaughter, and many other smaller dwellings. Every store, I think, without exception, was pillaged of every valuable article. A fine drug-store, which would not have looked badly on Broadway, was literally one mass of broken glass and jars."

The records of the Spanish and Moorish struggles, the wars of the Roses, and the thirty years' war in Germany, may be safely challenged for comparisons with the acts of barbarity of the Yankees. Their worst acts of atrocity were not committed in the mad intoxication of combat, but in cold and cowardly blood on the helpless and defenceless. While the lawless and savage scenes in Fredericksburg, to which we have referred, were still fresh in the public mind, the enemy in another department of the war, was displaying the same fiendish temper, stung by defeat and emboldened with the prospect of revenging his fortunes on the women and children of the South. The Yankee incursions and raids in North Carolina in the month of December are companion pieces to the sack of Fredericksburg.

" On entering Williamstown, North Carolina," says an eyewitness, " the Yankees respected not a single house—it mattered not whether the owner was in or absent. Doors were broken open and houses entered by the soldiers, who took every thing they saw, and what they were unable to carry away they broke and destroyed. Furniture of every description was committed to the flames, and the citizens who dared to remonstrate with them were threatened, cursed, and buffeted about. . . . . The enemy stopped for the night at Mr. Ward's mill. Mr. Ward was completely stripped of every thing, they not even leaving him enough for breakfast. While on a sick-bed, his wife was, in his presence, searched and robbed of five hundred dollars. The Yankees went about fifteen miles above Hamilton, when, for some cause, they suddenly turned and marched back, taking, with some slight deviations in quest of plunder, the same route they had come. The town of Hamilton was set on fire and as many as fifteen houses laid in ashes. During the time the Yankees encamped at Williamstown every thing which they left unharmed when last there was demolished. Every house in town was occupied and defaced. Several fine residences were actually used as horse-stables. Iron safes were broken open, and in the presence of their owners rifled of their contents. Several citizens were seized and robbed of the money on their persons. . . . . On Sunday morning Williamstown was fired, and no effort made to arrest the flames until several houses were burnt. No attempt was made by the Yankee officers, from Gen. Foster down, to prevent the destruction of property. On the contrary, they connived at it, and some of the privates did not hesitate to say that they were instructed to do as they had done. Two ladies at Williamstown went to Gen. Foster to beseech protection from his soldiers, and were rudely and arrogantly ordered from his presence '

Referring to the same scenes, a correspondent writes: " Fam ilies who fled in dismay at the approach of the invader, re- turned and found, as well as the few who remained at home, clothes, beds, bedding, spoons, and books abstracted ; costly furniture, crockery, doors, harness, and vehicles demolished ; locks, windows, and mirrors broken ; fences burned ; corn, po- tatoes, and peas gathered from the barns and fields consumed; iron safes dug to pieces and thrown out of doors, and their con- tents stolen."

The object of the enemy's movements in North Carolina, long a subject of anxious speculation, was at last developed, in time for a severe check to be given it. At the time that the enemy assaulted our lines in front of Fredericksburg, following his favorite policy of simultaneous attack in different depart- ments, he had planned a movement upon the Wilmington and Weldon railroad ; and on the same day that the battle of Fred- ericksburg was fought, occurred an important passage of arms in North Carolina.

On the 13th of December, Brigadier-gen. Evans encoun tered, with two thousand men, the advancing enemy, and with this small force held him in check at Southwest creek, beyond Kinston. The Yankee force, commanded by Foster, consisted of fifteen thousand men and nine gunboats. Having delayed their advance for some time, Gen. Evans succeeded in with- drawing his force, with small loss, to the left bank of the Neuse river at Kinston. He held the Yankees at bay until the 16th, when they advanced on the opposite side of the river, and made an attack at Whitehall bridge, about eighteen miles below Goldsboro'; in which they were driven back by Gen. Robertson, with severe loss.

The important object on our side was to protect the railroad bridge over the Neuse, and the county bridge about half a mile above; and to effect this, reinforcements having reached us, a rapid disposition of our forces was made. During the 17th, the enemy appeared in force before Gen. Clingman's three regiments, and he withdrew, across the county bridge, to this side of the river. The artillery of the enemy was playing upon the railroad bridge; and Evans' brigade had at last to move forward by the county road, and cross, if at all, the bridge a half mile above the railroad. About two o'clock in the after-noor one bold and daring incendiary succeeded in reacling the bridge, and covered by the wing wall of the abutment, lighted a flame which soon destroyed the superstructure, leaving the masonry, abutments, and pier intact.

It was very important for us now to save the county bridge, the only means remaining of crossing the river in the vicinity. Evans' and Clingman's brigades were ordered to cross, supported by Pettigrew's brigade; and the Mississippi brigade, just coming in, was ordered to move forward at once. The enemy were driven back from their position on the line of the railroad, but on account of the lateness of the hour, the nature of the ground, and the fact that our artillery, cavalry, and a large portion of the reinforcements had not yet arrived, it was not deemed advisable to attack their strong second position that evening. During the night the enemy made a hurried retreat to their fortifications and gunboats, moving with such celerity that it was useless to attempt pursuit with any other arms than cavalry, of which, at that time, unfortunately, we had none.

Our loss in these engagements was inconsiderable—seventy-one killed and two hundred and sixty-eight wounded. The enemy's occupation of Kinston, and the bridge there, prevented a body of our men, about five hundred in number, from escaping. The greater part were taken prisoners and paroled, and some few succeeded in escaping higher up on the river.

The substantial achievements of the grand army of invasion were, that they burned the superstructure of two bridges, which cost originally less than ten thousand dollars. They had utterly failed to attempt to take advantage of the temporary and partial interruption of our railroad line, for the purpose of striking a decisive blow at any important point before we could thoroughly re-establish our communication without it.

In other quarters of the war less important than Virginia or North Carolina, the early months of the winter were distinguished by some combats of various importance. The feeble campaign in the country west of the Mississippi was marked by one engagement, the dimensions of which were large for that campaign, but the situation of which was too distant to affect the general condition of the Confederacy.

On the 27th of November, Gen. Hindman came up with the enemy at Prairie Grove, near Fayetteville, Arkansas, with a force of about nine thousand men. The enemy, under the command of Gen. Blount, was already largely superior in numbers; and it was the object of Hindman to cut off rein forcements of seven or eight thousand, which were on the march. In this he failed; but, nothing daunted, brought on the attack at daylight, capturing, in the first charge of Gen. Marmaduke's cavalry, a whole regiment, and twenty-three wagons heavily laden with quartermaster and medical stores. Soon after sunrise the fight commenced in good earnest, and with no cessation the artillery continued until nightfall. Our whole line of infantry were in close conflict nearly the whole day with the enemy, who were attempting, with their force of eighteen thousand men, to drive us from our position. In every instance they were repulsed, and finally driven back from the field; Gen. Hindman driving them to within eight miles of Fayetteville, when our forces fell back to their supply depot, between Cane Hill and Van Buren. We captured three hundred prisoners and vast quantities of stores. The enemy's loss in killed and wounded was about one thousand; the Confederate loss, in killed, wounded, and missing, about three hundred. In one of the charges of the engagement, Gen. Stein, of the Missouri State Guard, was killed, a ball passing directly through his brain.

The close of the year 1862 leaves little to record of events of importance sufficient to affect the fortunes of the war, beyond what has been related in these pages with more or less particularity of detail. In that large expanse of country between the Mississippi and the tributaries of the Atlantic, events, since our last reference to these theatres of the war, were of little apparent importance, although they were preparing for a grand tragedy of arms upon which we shall find that the first page of the new year opens. There were daring forays, brilliant skirmishes and enterprises of our cavalry, to which a brief reference is only possible in these pages. Such were the exploits of Generals Forrest and Morgan, our distinguished cavalry commanders in West Tennessee, in which they annoyed the enemy, destroyed railroad bridges and Federal property, and captured several towns in successful raids. On the 7th of December a single expedition, sent out under Morgan from Gen. Bragg's lines, attacked an outpost of the enemy at Hartsville, on the Cumberland, killed and wounded two hundred, captured eighteen hundred prisoners, two pieces of artillery, and two thousand small-arms, and all other stores at the position. Nor in our slight record of indecisive but gallant incidents of the war, must we neglect to mention the brave enterprise of Col. Clarkson, another choice spirit of Southern chivalry, who, with a detachment of the Virginia State line, penetrated into Kentucky, captured the town of Piketon on the 8th of December, secured a large amount of stores, and nipped an important enterprise of the enemy in the bud.

In the mean time some important new assignments of military command had been made in preparation for the winter campaign, and happily inspired the country with renewed confidence in the fortunes of the war. Gen. Gustavus W. Smith, whose patriotism was as enthusiastic as his military genius was admirable (for he had broken ties as well as restraints in escaping from the North to join the standard of his native South), had taken command in North Carolina. Gen. Beauregard had been assigned to the important care of the defences of Charleston and Savannah, threatened by the most formidable armadas that the warlike ingenuity and lavish expenditure of the enemy had yet produced. Gen. Pemberton had relieved Van Dorn of the army of the Southwest at Holly Springs, which had been taken by surprise on the 20th of December, and was now in our possession ; and that latter officer, ill-starred by fortune, but whose gallantry and enterprise were freely acknowledged, was appropriately appointed to take command of the cavalry forces in the West. The command of all the forces between the Alleghany and the Mississippi was intrusted to Gen. Joseph E. Johnston, whose matchless strategy had more than once enlightened the records of the war, and whose appointment to this large and important command was hailed with an outburst of joy and enthusiastic confidence in all parts of the South.

CHAPTER XXI.

The eastern Portion of Tennessee.—Its Military Importance.—Composition of Bragg's Army.—THE BATTLE OF MURFREESBORO'.—The Right Wing of the Enemy routed.—Bragg's Exultations.—The Assault of the 2d of January.—"The bloody crossing of Stone River."—The Confederates fall back to Tullahoma.—Review of the Battle-field of Murfreesboro'.—Repulse of the Enemy at Vicksburg.—THE RECAPTURE OF GALVESTON.—The Midnight March.—Capture of the "Harriet Lane."—Arkansas Post taken by the Yankees.—Its Advantages.—The affair of the Rams in Charleston Harbor.—Naval structure of the Confederacy.—Capture of the Yankee gunboat "Queen of the West."—Heroism of George Wood.—Capture of the "Indianola."—The War on the Water.—The Confederate Cruisers.—Prowess of the "Alabama."

THE eastern portion of Tennessee abounds in hills, rocks, poverty, and ignorance. But its military situation was one of great importance to the Confederacy. The enemy already held West and Middle Tennessee. It required but to occupy East Tennessee to have entire possession of one of the most valuable States of the Confederacy. They also felt bound in honor and duty to render the long-promised assistance to the Unionists of East Tennessee. Tennessee would be more thoroughly theirs than Kentucky, when once they filled this eastern portion of it with their armies. The essential geographical importance of this country to the Confederacy was too obvious to be dwelt upon. It covered Georgia and involved the defences of the cotton region of the South. Through it ran a great continental line of railroad, of which the South could not be deprived without unspeakable detriment. The importance of this road to the supply of our armies was no less considerable than to the supply of our general population.

The gallant and heroic army of the Confederacy, commanded by Gen. Braxton Bragg, composed of Floridians, Louisianians, South Carolinians, Georgians, and Kentuckians, numbering between thirty and forty thousand men, had occupied Murfreesboro' for over a month, in confidence and security, never dreaming of the advance of the enemy. President Davis had visited and reviewed the brave veterans of Fishing creek,

GEN. BRAXTON BRAGG.

Pensacola, Donelson, Shiloh, Perryville, and Hartsvil'e, and, satisfied of their ability to resist any foe who should have the temerity to attack them, he withdrew from our forces Stevenson's division, of Kirby Smith's corps, numbering about eight thousand men, leaving scarcely thirty thousand men to defend what was left to us of Tennessee.

Balls, parties, and brilliant festivities relieved the ennui of the camp of the Confederates. On Christmas eve scenes of revelry enlivened Murfreesboro', and officers and men alike gave themselves up to the enjoyment of the hour, with an abandonment of all military cares, indulging in fancied security.

The enemy's force at Nashville, under command of Rosecrans, was not believed to have been over forty thousand, and the opinion was confidently entertained that he would not attempt to advance until the Cumberland should rise, to afford him the aid of his gunboats. Indeed, Morgan had been sent to Kentucky to destroy the Nashville road and cut off his supplies, so that he might force the enemy to come out and meet us. Yet, that very night, when festivity prevailed, the enemy was marching upon us!

THE BATTLE OF MURFREESBORO'.

The grounds in front of Murfreesboro' had been surveyed and examined a month before, in order to select a position for battle in case of surprise, and our troops were thrown forward to prevent such a misfortune. Polk's corps, with Cheatham's division, occupied our centre, Maney's brigade being thrown forward towards Lavergne, where Wheeler's cavalry was annoying the enemy. A portion of Kirby Smith's corps, McCown's division, occupied Readyville on our right, and Hardee's corps occupied Triune on our left, with Wharton's cavalry thrown out in the vicinity of Franklin.

Festival and mirth continued on Christmas day, but the day following, Friday, the 26th, was a most gloomy one. The rain fell in torrents. That same evening couriers arrived and reported a general advance of the enemy. All was excitement and commotion, and the greatest activity prevailed. The enemy had already driven in our advance front. Hardee's corps fell back from Triune. Major-gen. McCown's division was ordered to march to Murfreesboro' at once, having received the order at midnight. Heavy skirmishing by Wheeler and Wharton's cavalry had continued since the 25th. On the 27th the ground for our line of battle was selected in front of the town, about a mile and a half distant on Stone's river. The enemy had now advanced beyond Triune, his main body occupying Stuart's creek, ten miles from town. On the 28th our troops took up their position in line of battle. Polk's corps, consisting of Withers' and Cheatham's divisions, formed our left wing, and was posted about a mile and a half on the west side of Stone's river, its right resting on the Nashville road, and its left extending as far as the Salem pike, a distance of nearly six miles. Hardee's corps, consisting of Breckinridge's and Cleburne's divisions, was formed on the east bank of the river, its left resting near the Nashville road, and its right extending towards the Lebanon pike, about three miles in length, making our line of battle about nine miles in length, in the shape of an obtuse angle. McCown's division formed the reserve, opposite our centre, and Jackson's brigade was held in reserve on the right flank of Hardee. Stone's river crosses the Salem pike about a mile and a half on the south side of the town, making a curve below the pike about a mile further south, and then runs nearly north and south in front of Murfreesboro', crossing the Nashville pike and extending towards the Lebanon pike, some half a mile, when it makes another turn or bend and runs nearly east and west, emptying into the Cumberland river. The river, at the shoals, where it crosses the Nashville pike, was fordable, and not over ankle deep. The banks above and below were rather steep, being some five to eight feet high, with rocky protrusions. The nature of the country was undulating, but mostly level in our front, with large, open fields. To the right or the west side the ground was more rolling, with rocky upheaval and croppings of limestone and thick cedar groves. On the side of the river towards the Lebanon pike were thin patches of woods and rocky projections.

On the 29th there was continued skirmishing by our cavalry forces, the enemy gradually advancing. On the 30th the enemy had advanced by three columns and took up his position about a mile in our front. At noon he shelled our right and centre, in order to feel our reserves. At 3 P. M. the enemy made an advance on our left, and attempted to drive us back in order to occupy the ground for his right wing. A spirited engagement immediately commenced, Gen. Polk having ordered forward a portion of Withers' division. Robinson's battery held the enemy in check, keeping up a most deadly and destructive fire. Three times the enemy charged this battery, but were repulsed by the gallant one hundred and fifty-fourth Tennessee. Col. Loomis, commanding Gardner's brigade, and the brigade formerly Duncan's, with the South Carolinians, Alabamians, and Louisianians, were most hotly engaged, and though suffering considerably, succeeded in driving back the enemy with great slaughter. It was now clear that the enemy intended to mass his forces on our left, in order to make a flank movement the next day, and obtain, if possible, the Salem pike, which, if successful, would give him possession of the Chattanooga railroad. Cleburne's division, of Hardee's corps, and Major-gen. McCown's division, were immediately ordered over towards the Salem pike to reinforce our extreme left wing. Wheeler's cavalry had already gained the enemy's rear, and had captured a train of wagons and a number of prisoners. A cold, drizzling rain had set in, and our troops were greatly exposed, being without shelter, and bivouacking by their camp fires.

On the morning of the 31st, the grand battle was opened. At the break of day on the cold and cloudy morning, Gen. Hardee gave the order to advance, and the fight was opened by McCown's division, with Cleburne, advancing upon the enemy's right wing under Gen. McCook. The charge was of the most rapid character. The alarm given by the enemy's pickets scarcely reached his camp before the Confederates were upon it. The sight of our advance was a most magnificent one. Two columns deep, with a front of nearly three-fourths of a mile, the line well preserved and advancing with great rapidity, on came the Confederate left wing, the bayonets glistening in a bright sun, which had broken through the thick fog.

The enemy was taken completely by surprise, their artillery horses not even being hitched up. Such was the impetuosity of the charge, that the enemy fell back in disn.ay, our troops pouring in a most murderous fire. With such rapidity did our men cross the broken ploughed fields, that our artillery could not follow them. Wharton's cavalry had charged a battery, the horses not being harnessed, and driving back the infantry supporting it, succeeded in capturing it. The enemy having gradually recovered, now disputed our further advance, and the battle raged with terrific violence. They continued to fall back, however, under our fire, until we had swung round nearly our whole left on their right, as if on a pivot, driving the enemy some six miles towards his centre, when Withers and Cheatham also hurled their divisions on the foe with such terrible effect, that battery after battery was taken, and their dead lay in heaps upon the field. The enemy was now driven towards the Nashville road, about a mile in front of our centre, and took a commanding position on an eminence overlooking the plain, and which was protected by rocks and a dense cedar wood.

The battle had been terrific; crash upon crash of musketry stunned the ear; the ground trembled with the thunder of artillery; the cedars rocked and quivered in the fiery blast, and the air was rent with the explosion of shells. The enemy at several points offered a most gallant resistance, but nothing human could withstand the impetuosity of that charge. A spirit of fury seemed to possess our men, from the commanders down to the common soldiers, and on they swept, shot and shell, canister, grape, and bullets tearing through their ranks, until the way could be traced by the dead and dying. Still on they went, overturning infantry and artillery alike, driving the enemy like the hurricane scatters the leaves upon its course, capturing hundreds of prisoners, and literally blackening the ground with the dead. Such a charge was never before witnessed. For miles, through fields and forests, over ditches, fences, and ravines, they swept. Brigade after brigade, battery after battery, were thrown forward to stay their onward march; but another volley of musketry, another gleaming of the bayonet, and like their predecessors they were crushed into one common ruin.

It was now about noon. Our charge had been one of splendid results. We had already captured some five thousand prisoners, nearly thirty pieces of cannon, some five thousand stand of arms, and ammunition wagons. We had broken the enemy's right, having driven him for nearly five hours on a curve, a distance of over five miles from our extreme left to the enemy's centre, and backwards about three miles from our centre. The Yankees had made a stand only where the natural advantages of the ground sheltered them.

Rosecrans had not been dismayed by the events of the morning, and had watched them with an air of confidence which his subordinate officers found it difficult to understand. Referring to his adversary, he said : "I'll show him a trick worth two of his." Gen. Rosecrans was well aware of the danger of advancing reinforcements from his left or centre. The Confederates lay in his front, within sight and almost within hearing. He knew that they were anxiously watching his movements, and waiting to see which part of his line would be weakened. But though he declined to send McCook reinforcements, Rosecrans employed himself in so preparing his line as to aid McCook to get safely on his right. His preparations were to halt the Confederates on his defeated right without exposing his left and centre to imminent danger. For this purpose he quickly determined to mass his artillery on the position occupied by the centre. These movements were masked by immense cedar forests. Thus prepared, at the proper moment the centre of the enemy was advanced a few hundred yards, and soon after the Confederates appeared in force pursuing his right wing.

The position of the enemy was on an oval-shaped hill not very high, but furnishing an excellent position for his artillery It was determined to carry this stronghold at all hazards, and the brigades of Chalmer and Donelson, supported by Manley's and Stewart's brigades, with Cobb's, Byrne's, Chas. Smith's, and Slocomb's batteries, were ordered to prepare for the charge. It was a forlorn hope, but our men faced the mighty whirlwind of shot and shell with heroic firmness, and did not fall back till they had captured two batteries. The brigades of Generals Adams and Jackson, of Breckinridge's division, who held our right, were now ordered across the river to relieve our broken columns, and advanced towards the enemy's grand battery with a like coolness and heroism, but they were also repulsed and fell back under the enemy's terrible fire.

A portion of Gen. Hardee's command bivouacked for the night in the cedars, within five hundred yards of the enemy's lines. That night it was cold to freezing. Upon the battle-field lay thousands of the enemy's dead and wounded, who froze stiff, presenting a ghastly scene by moonlight.

The scene in the cedars was fearful and picturesque. A brilliant winter moon shed its lustre amid the foliage of the forest of evergreens, and lighted up with silver sheen the ghastly battle-field. Dismounted cannon, scattered caissons, glittering and abandoned arms strewed the forest and field. The dead lay stark and stiff at every step, with clenched hands and contracted limbs in the wild attitudes in which they fell, congealed by the bitter cold. It was the eve of the new year. Moans of the neglected dying, mingled with the low peculiar shriek of the wounded artillery horses, chanted a *miserere* for the dying year.

Amid the dim camp-fires, feebly lighted to avoid attracting the artillery of the enemy, groups of mutilated and shuddering wounded were huddled, and the kneeling forms of surgeons bending in the firelight over the mangled bodies of the dying, added to the solemnity of the night.

The appearance of the dead on the field was remarkable, for the large proportion was evidently slain by artillery. The bodies of many of the Confederates who had advanced to the assault on the enemy's masked batteries were literally torn to pieces. The cross-fire of the artillery had had this terrible effect. " I saw," says a spectator of this terrible seen, " an officer, whose two legs, one arm, and body lay in separate parts of the field. I saw another whose dislocated right arm lay across his neck, and more than half his head was gone."

On the day succeeding the fight, Gen. Bragg telegraphed to Richmond the news of a great victory, presented his compliments to the authorities, and wrote " God has granted us a happy new year." His exultations were over hasty, for though we had routed on the morning of the preceding day the right wing of the enemy, the final contest was yet to be decided.

In the mean time, Rosecrans fearing that his position might be flanked, or from some suspicion that it was not secure, abandoned it that night, only to take up a still stronger one in the bend of the river, towards the Lebanon pike, on a couple of hillocks, which he again crowned with his strongest batteries.

Many of his generals felt despondent; some favored retreat; but the constancy of Rosecrans remained untouched. One of his staff-officers remarked, "Your tenacity of purpose, general, is a theme of universal comment." "I guess," he replied, "that the troops have discovered that Bragg is a good dog, but hold-fast is better."

The first of the year found the enemy strongly intrenched, with his right drawn up a little on the south side of the Nashville pike, while his left remained fortified in the bend of the river, already described. Our position was greatly advanced on the left and centre, but otherwise remained the same. On that day Gen. Bragg issued the following address to his army:

"The general commanding is happy to announce to the troops the continued success of our arms yesterday. Generals Wheeler and Wharton, with the cavalry, again assaulted the enemy's line of communication, capturing over two hundred wagons and other stores. Twice have we now made the circuit of the enemy's forces, and destroyed his trains, and not less than six hundred wagons, and three thousand mules have fallen into our hands. . . . . . Our success continues uninterrupted. One more struggle, and the glorious victory already achieved will be crowned by the rout of the enemy, who are now greatly demoralized. The general commanding has every confidence that his gallant troops will fully meet his expectations."

It was confidently believed that the enemy would retreat on the night of the 31st, but as he did not, it was concluded to wait and see if he would make any attack. The day consequently passed off quietly, excepting some slight skirmishing.

On the 2d of January, the ill-omened Friday, the attitude of the two armies remained the same during the morning, and without incident, except some shelling on our right.

By three o'clock it was determined to assault the enemy's stronghold on the bend of the river. It was a desperate determination. Unfortunately, Gen. Bragg had given the enemy nearly two days to reorganize and concentrate his baffled army, so that he might the more effectually make a stubborn resistance.

The enemy had taken up a position at a point near the bend of the river where it takes a westerly course. Here rises a high ridge covered by a skirt of woods, on which the enemy had planted their artillery, supported by a line of infantry. Behind this ridge, and in the woods and rocky ravines, lay concealed also a large force of the enemy. Further to the enemy's left was another skirt of woods, which the enemy also occupied, out-flanking our front nearly one thousand yards. Near the first skirt of woods mentioned is a ford of the river, the opposite banks of which, from its elevated position, over-looks and commands the ridge above described on this side, or the south and east bank of the river, while one mile further down the river is another ford. It was at this commanding position in the river bend where the enemy had made his cita-del, having massed his batteries of artillery and infantry in such a skilful manner as to protect his centre on the Nashville pike, and his extreme left, which now extended on our side of the river. Such was the position of the enemy on our extreme right on the morning of that memorable day of slaughter, the 2d of January.

Gen. Breckinridge was ordered to carry, by assault, the po-sition of the enemy on the ridge already described. He form-ed his division in two lines, changing front from his former position to nearly a right angle, and facing in the direction of the river. Gen. Hanson's brigade, with Palmer's, now com-manded by Gen. Pillow, formed the first line, with Pillow on the right; the second line being formed by Preston's and Gib-son's, two hundred yards in the rear. Col. Hunt's regiment, of Hanson's brigade, was left to support Cobb's battery on the hill. From the enemy's commanding position across the river, he was enabled to see all of our movements, and consequently prepared to resist us. Between Gen. Breckinridge's division and the enemy's batteries on the ridge was an intervening space of eight hundred yards, extending over an open field skirted by woods, along which the enemy's skirmishers were in such force as almost amounted to a line of battle.

The attack was to be made at four o'clock, and a signal gun was to announce the hour. In those battalions stood the noble soldiers of Florida, Alabama, Kentucky, Louisiana, Tennessee, and North Carolina in battle array, firm and inflexible, await-

·ng the signal for combat. The report of a cannon had not died upon the ear before the bugle from Hanson's brigade sounded a charge. The brigades moved rapidly forward through the thinned woods until gaining the open fields, the men having been instructed not to deliver their fire until close upon the enemy, and then to charge with the bayonet. On came Pillow, followed by Preston; forward hurried Hanson, followed by Gibson. From the moment of gaining the field the enemy's artillery from the ridge opened a sweeping fire, and a whirlwind of Minnie balls from their infantry, with shot and shell, filled the air. Our men were ordered to lie down for a few minutes to let the fury of the storm pass. Then the cry from Breckinridge—" Up, my men, and charge !"—rang out. With the impetuosity of a torrent they rushed forward to the woods sloping the ridge. On dashed Wright's battery of Preston's brigade at a furious gallop, and soon opened fire upon one of the enemy's batteries about three hundred yards to our right. The enemy, awed by the mad bravery of our men, recoiled ; their ranks thinned rapidly, notwithstanding they received reinforcement after reinforcement. Their left wing, which already out-flanked us on our right, was driven back towards the river bank, the 20th Tennessee capturing some two hundred prisoners. The contest now raged fierce and bloody. It was one continuous roar of musketry and artillery. Facing the storm of death, our heroes charged with fury, and so effective was the firing of our lines, that we carried the ridge with a wild demoniac yell, driving the enemy from it, with his artillery, down the hill-side and across the river. Capt. Wright soon reached the top of the ridge with his battery, and opened on the enemy with spherical case. At this time the concentrated fire of the enemy became terrible and appalling. A sheet of flame was poured forth from their artillery on the hills on the opposite side of the river overlooking our left and front, and from their batteries on the river bank, while the opposite side also swarmed with their infantry, who poured in on us a most murderous fire. Still our men never quailed, but pressed forward and crossed the river, the enemy making frightful gaps in our ranks, but which were immediately closed up. Here it was that in less than half an hour over two thousand of our brave soldiers went down ! The utter hopelessness of carrying the opposite heights, and of con tending against the overwhelmingly superior numbers of the enemy, without artillery or reinforcements to support us, hav ing been fully tested, Gen. Breckinridge ordered his division to fall back. It was nearly dark when the conflict closed, and during the night he occupied a portion of the field in advance of that he occupied during the day.

It was after the capture of the enemy's position on the ridge, when our men drove him across the river with terrible slaughter of his forces, that the noble Hanson fell mortally wounded, exclaiming, "Forward — forward, my brave boys, to the charge ;" and afterwards, when brought from the field, he said with his flickering breath, "I am willing to die with such a wound received in so glorious a cause." We had held the enemy's position on the ridge for about half an hour, Capt. E. E. Wright's battery doing admirable execution, when that gallant officer fell at his guns mortally wounded, the enemy having charged within seventy-five yards of his pieces.

The final repulse of Breckenridge was a sad blow to our hopes. The prudence of this terrible attack upon the impregnable position of the enemy has been seriously questioned, and military critics of the battle of Murfreesboro' have also found room for censuring the neglect of Gen. Bragg in not previously securing the hillocks in the bend of Stone's river, which he permitted the enemy to occupy. As it happened, it was a bad repulse, and the vivid recollections of the " bloody crossing of Stone's river," in which in less than one hour two thousand of our men were killed and wounded, long survived in our army. It lost us the vantage ground we had gained over the enemy on the 31st and greatly depressed our troops. But for this we would still have held Murfreesboro'. On the 3d the rain fell in torrents, and as our troops were worn out and nearly exhausted, it was determined to fall back that night, and not run the risk of meeting the enemy's reinforcements, which, it was reported, he was receiving. Every thing had previously been provided for the retreat. It was conducted with order and composure.*

* In his official report of the battle, Gen. Bragg makes the following statement on the subject of the first day's operations, relative to their check and the failure to break the enemy's centre :

Sunday morning Rosecrans moved into Murfreesboro', and Gen. Bragg retired to the position of Tullahoma. This place is in Coffee county, Tennessee, situated on Rock creek, and offers admirable means of defence. It is seventy-one miles from Nashville and thirty-two from Murfreesboro', and lies immediately on the Nashville and Chattanooga railroad, where it is intersected by the McMinnville and Manchester road. As a base of operations, and as a position of defence, the place offered great advantages.

So far as the relative amount of carnage affects the question of victory, no doubt can be entertained to which side in the battle of Murfreesboro' is to be ascribed the superiority. In the first day's fight, the number of the enemy's killed and wounded was probably six or seven thousand; in the engagement which succeeded, our loss was disproportionate to the enemy's; but at the close of the whole affair, the Yankees were doubtless greater losers in life than ourselves. In point of cap-

---

"To meet our successful advance, and retrieve his losses in the front of his left, the enemy early transferred a portion of his reserve from his left to that flank, and by two o'clock had succeeded in concentrating such a force in Lieutenant-gen. Hardee's front as to check his further progress. Our two lines had by this time become almost blended, so weakened were they by losses, exhaustion, and extension to cover the enemy's whole front. As early as 10 o'clock, A. M., Major-gen. Breckenridge was called on for one brigade, and soon after for a second, to reinforce or act as a reserve to Lieutenant-gen. Hardee. His reply to the first call represented the enemy crossing Stone's river in heavy force, in his immediate front, and on receiving the second order, he informed me that they had already crossed in heavy force, and were advancing to attack his lines. He was immediately ordered not to await attack, but to advance and meet him. About this same time a report reached me that a heavy force of the enemy's infantry was advancing on the Lebanon road, about five miles in Breckenridge's front. Brigadier-gen. Pegram, who had been sent to that road to cover the flank of the infantry with his cavalry brigade, save two regiments detached with Wheeler and Wharton, was ordered forward immediately to develop any such movement. The orders for the two brigades from Breckenridge were countermanded, whilst dispositions were made, at his request, to reinforce him. Before they could be carried out, the movements ordered disclosed the fact that no force had crossed Stone's river; that the only enemy in our immediate front then was a small body of sharpshooters; and that there was no advance on the Lebanon road. These unfortunate misapprehensions on that part of the field, which with proper precaution could not have existed, withheld from active operations three fine brigades until the enemy had succeeded in checking our progress, had re-established his lines, and had collected many of his broken battalions."

tures and with respect to the number of prisoners taken, the battle of Murfreesboro' may be accounted a Confederate success. The ground which the North has for claiming a victory is, that our forces fell back, and that their positions were occupied. But the occupation of Murfreesboro' was no important consideration; the works were neither extensive nor strong; and the new line of defence reorganized by Gen. Bragg was, as we shall see, quite sufficient to hold the enemy in check. The truth is, that the Yankees, although their claims to the victory of Murfreesboro' are questionable, had great reasons to congratulate themselves that an army which, in the first day's battle, had its right wing broken and one-third of its artillery lost, should have escaped destruction and extricated itself in a manner to assure its further safety.

But however the issue of Murfreesboro' is to be decided, the South had reason to expect considerable material advantages from events in other parts of the West. The siege of Vicksburg by land was for the time virtually abandoned. Some engagements had taken place before this town, which were exaggerated by the telegraph; but they were mere skirmishes, intended to feel the strength of the defences. Being satisfied that they were too strong to be attacked with safety, and probably learning that Grant's army would never effect a junction with it, the Yankee force before Vicksburg re-embarked, with a great loss of material employed in the intrenchments preparatory to the siege.

THE RECAPTURE OF GALVESTON.

While the new year had doubtfully opened in Tennessee, a brilliant success marked the same period in the distant State of Texas. An expedition was skilfully planned and gallantly executed by the brave and energetic Magruder, the results of which were the capture of the city and harbor of Galveston, a large quantity of arms, ammunition, stores, &c., the famous Yankee steamer Harriet Lane, and some other craft of less importance.

On the night of the 31st of December, Gen. Magruder silently marched along the road to Galveston city. Our forces consisted of several regiments of infantry and about twenty-two pieces of artillery, though the principal attack was to be made by the artillery, as there were only about three hundred of the enemy in the city, and they were behind a barricade at the outer end of the wharf.

Our troops reached the suburbs of the city about three o'clock. The streets were completely deserted ; the few inhabitants who had remained in the city were sleeping soundly, and had our men not awaked and warned them of their danger, they would have slept on until the cannon's roar had startled them. The march of our troops through the city was a quiet procession.

The scene, the dead hour of night, and the fact that this was to be the first battle of many of them, all conspired to make them serious. Then, too, the great heavy waves came tumbling and roaring in from the Gulf, chanting out upon the still night air, as they dashed along, something that sounded like a funeral dirge. But onward our men stole, through long, lonely streets, now around this corner and now turning that, until at length they reached Strand-street, which runs parallel with the water, and is the next one to the wharves. The moon was now down, and every thing was enveloped in darkness ; the guns were noiselessly placed in position and loaded, the men looking like so many shadows as they took their places in the gloom. There, within three hundred yards lay the Harriet Lane, the Owasso, the Clifton, and two other boats, with their broadsides turned towards our troops, and ready to open upon them the moment they fired. This they knew, for the Yankees had been ashore the day before and told the people that they knew all about the plans of the " rebels," and were waiting for them. In fact, they were so certain of victory that they allowed our men to place their guns in position without firing upon them.

Gen. Magruder opened the attack by firing the first gun. In a few moments the bright flashes, the booming reports, and whizzing shells told plainer than words that the action had begun in earnest ; for the next hour the roar of cannon was incessant. The clear keen crack of our little rifled guns, the dull sound of our sea-coast howitzers, and the mighty thundering bass of the columbiads and 100-pound Parrott guns on the gunboats, combined to form a piece of music fitted for Pandemonium.

The fight raged furiously on both sides, but it was fast becoming evident that our land forces alone were no match for the Yankee boats, with their great guns and mortars, which vomited a half bushel of grape and canister at every discharge. Early in the engagement a charge was made by three hundred of our infantry on three companies of the 42d Massachusetts regiment, stationed behind a barricade at the end of Kuhn's wharf. The enemy had torn up the planks from the wharf, and made a breastwork of them. Our men rushed out into the waters with their scaling ladders and dashed up to them, but the position was too strong and they had to retire, leaving our artillery to shell them out. We lost some ten or fifteen in this charge, and would have lost more, but it was pitch dark and the Yankees fired very wildly.

Daylight at length arrived, and every one was anxiously looking for our boats, which ought to have been up two hours before. They had come down within sight at about 12 o'clock, and, hearing nothing of our troops, retired five or six miles, under the impression that the land attack had been postponed. There they waited until about three o'clock, when the land attack began. As soon as Major Smith, who commanded the expedition, saw that the work had begun, he ordered all steam to be put on and started back. He was then a considerable distance from the city, and was unable to reach it until daylight. At that time the Bayou City and Neptune, followed in the distance by the John F. Can and Lucy Gwinn, hospital boats, bore steadily down upon the Harriet Lane, then lying at the end of the wharf, opposite the Cotton Press.

The Harriet Lane had for some time directed her fire at them, but fortunately without effect; but when within about fifty yards, the Neptune received several balls, damaging her considerably. She kept steadily on her way, however, and in a few moments more ran into the Lane amidship. The enemy's decks were soon cleared with the buckshot from the double-barrel guns of the Neptune's crew, who would have boarded her, but it was discovered that the Neptune was rapidly sinking, in consequence of the damages she had received. She was accordingly run into shoal' water, about fifty yards from the Lane, where she sunk immediately. In the mean time the Yankee crew, seeing the predicament of the Neptune, came

up on deck again, and were preparing to give her a broadside
when the Bayou City fortunately interfered with their prepa
rations, by running into the Lane's wheel-house. Another
volley of buckshot again cleared her decks. The next instant
the crew of the Bayou City were aboard of her, Major Smith
gallantly leading the way, and shooting the Lane's commanding officer (Capt. Wainwright) as he leaped upon the deck.
The vessel was immediately surrendered, and down came the
Stars and Stripes and up went our flag. It was found that the
captain and first lieutenant of the boat were both killed, and
about thirty of her crew killed or wounded. Our loss on the
boats was about sixteen killed, and thirty wounded.

The Yankee boats, the Clifton and Owasso, saved themselves
by beating out of the harbor, while the Bayou City was in
some way entangled with her prize. The Westfield was burnt,
as she was fast aground. Our prize was one of which we
might well be proud. The Harriet Lane was a vessel of six
hundred tons burden, was originally built for the revenue ser
vice, but at the beginning of the war with the South she was
turned over to the navy, and at once underwent such altera
tions as were thought necessary to adapt her to her new ser
vice. At the time of her capture, she mounted eight guns ot
heavy calibre, her bow gun being a fifteen-inch rifle.

The recapture of Galveston and the advantages which ensued, were perhaps outbalanced by a disaster which shortly
followed and overshadowed much of the prospect in the remote
regions west of the Mississippi. This was the forcible occupation by the Yankees of Arkansas Post and the surrender of its
entire garrison.

The troops garrisoning Arkansas Post at the time of attack,
consisted of three brigades, mostly Texans, and commanded
respectively by Cols. Garland, Deshler, and Dunnington, the
whole forming a division under the command of Brigadier-
gen. T. J. Churchill, and numbering, on the day of the fight,
not more than thirty-three hundred effective men. On the 9th
day of January a scout from below brought intelligence to
Gen. Churchill of a Yankee gunboat having made its appearance in the Arkansas river, some thirty miles below the Post.
Some hours later, on the same day, another scout brought news
of other gunboats, followed by transports, making their way

up the river. Upon the receipt of this intelligence, Gen. Churchill ordered every thing in readiness for an attack, and ere night closed in, all the troops were distributed along the line of intrenchments, where they remained all night, in a pelting storm of rain. The enemy, in the mean time, had landed a force about two miles below the fort, but they made no demonstration until about nine or ten o'clock the next morning, when they commenced shelling the fort from their advance gunboats, that were cautiously and slowly feeling their way up the river.

Our troops held the position first taken by them until about four o'clock, P. M., when the general, fearing a flank movement on our left, ordered the men to fall back to a line of intrenchments near the yet unfinished fort, which line was speedily completed and all the troops properly distributed before night set in. Just as darkness was drawing near, four gunboats approached the fort and commenced their bombardment, our guns from the fort answering gallantly; and after two hours' terrific shelling, the gunboats retired, one of them, the Eastport, badly disabled. Our loss up to this time consisted of only three killed and some three or four wounded.

The next morning, at ten o'clock, the enemy renewed the attack with gunboats and land forces combined. They had also erected a battery on the opposite side of the river, by means of which they kept up a terrible cross-fire that swept the whole area of ground occupied by our men. The firing continued until about four o'clock in the evening, when Gen. Churchill, seeing his defences exposed to a raking fire and storming parties closing upon his rear, surrendered, Gen. McClernand taking the whole force, making more than three thousand men prisoners. Our loss in killed and wounded was not two hundred men.

The results of this success of the Yankees were many thousand prisoners of war, and a fortified point guarding the navigation of the Arkansas river, and shutting out its commerce from the Mississippi. But the prospect which they indulged of ascending without interruption to Little Rock and taking full possession of the Arkansas capital, was rather premature.

There is nothing yet important to record of the operations of the immense fleets of the enemy collected on our coast in the winter of 1862. The armadas were as yet silent. For months a large fleet of the enemy had been at the mouth of Charleston harbor, or picketed off the coast.

On the 30th of January the Confederate rams in the harbor of Charleston, under command of Capt. Ingraham, had made a sally towards the enemy's fleet. The success of this sally was ignorantly exaggerated by the Confederates, and a claim made that the blockade had been raised, which pretension was afterwards abandoned. The fact was, that one of the Yankee vessels—the Mercedita—was seriously injured, and another—the Keystone State—got a shot through her steam-drum, causing the death of twenty one persons. The Mercedita was saved by the treachery of the Yankees, who represented the ship to be in a sinking condition, thus deceiving the Confederates as to the extent of the damage they had inflicted. She steamed down to Port Royal, after our rams had left her, under the supposition that she was sinking in shoal water. Her commander had called out, "We are in a sinking condition," and the reply of Capt. Ingraham was that she could only sink as far as her rails, and we could not take her crew aboard. A mean and cowardly falsehood saved the vessel, but in Yankee estimation the triumphs of such villany were quite equal to the congratulations of a victory.

Our victory at Galveston, of which we have given some account, was the precursor of other captures of the enemy's vessels, which were important accessions to our little navy. That arm of service, in which we were so deficient, and had shown such aptitude for self-destruction, was not entirely powerless; for we not only had rams for harbor defences and three fleet privateers at sea, but our power on the water was enlarged even beyond our expectations, as we shall see, by captures from the enemy.

The Yankee gunboat Queen of the West, having succeeded in running our batteries at Vicksburg, had for some weeks been committing ravages, penetrating the country of the Red river. On the 14th of February she encountered in this river and captured a small Confederate steamer, the Era. The crew and passengers of the Era were taken prisoners, and all were guarded on board the Era by a band of soldiers, save Mr. George Wood, the pilot, who was ordered aboard the Queen of the West, and, with threats, directed to her pilot-wheel to assist her pilot in directing her onward to the capture of our fort on the river. On they glided, but not distrustful, and much elated at their success, till they came in reach of our battery at five P. M., when the vessel commenced firing, still advancing. She had come within a quarter of a mile of our battery and on the opposite shore in full range for our guns, when the gallant Wood, who directed her wheel, had her rounded, ran her aground, breaking her rudder and thus crippling her and turning her broadside to give our guns a fair chance. This gallant man, in the confusion, made good his escape. Thus crippled and disabled by the hand that drove her on to her destiny, she lay like a wounded falcon, at the mercy of her adversaries.

The night was dark and stormy, the heavens overhung with clouds, which now and then pealed forth their muttering thunder, and drenched the earth with rain. Thus in the rain-storm this crippled Queen lay beaten by the tempest. She was well barricaded with cotton bales. On seeing all hope of success gone, the commanding officer, Col. Ellett, made his escape, with nearly all his crew, by getting on cotton bales and floating down the river. She raised the white signal, as the storm abated, as it was seen by the light of a burning warehouse, but it was not answered till next morning. Thirteen of the crew remained in silence till daylight, then her white banner was still afloat, and then, and not till then, our soldiers crossed the river and took possession of her.

The fog which had enabled the Queen of the West to get by Vicksburg had also availed for the passage of another gunboat, the Indianola. This vessel had also continued for weeks to go at large, preying on the boats that were transporting our supplies, and harassing our forces in every way. Seeing the great injury and havoc that she might do, a council was held, and the capture of the Indianola at every sacrifice was determined upon.

Accordingly an expedition was fitted out, consisting of two gunboats—the Queen of the West and the Webb—and two steamers—the Era and Dr. Batey. The expedition was commanded by Major Walker, with Captain Hutton as executive officer of the fleet. All being ready, the expedition started out from the mouth of the Red river in pursuit of the Indian-ola. Coming up the Mississippi to Grand Gulf, it was learned that the Indianola was not far off, and a halt was ordered that all the vessels might come up. All being in line, the expedition put up the river, and on the 24th of February came upon the Indianola, overhauling her about five miles below New Carthage, and some thirty below Vicksburg. It was about nine o'clock at night. The enemy had received no information of the movement, and was not aware of our approach until we were within a half mile of her. Seeing the rapid approach of the vessels, the Indianola at once knew that it was an attempt to capture her, and she immediately rounded her broadside to, lashing a coal barge alongside her to parry the blows that might be made to run in and sink her. On the vessels nearing, fire was opened, and a most terrific and desperate engagement ensued, lasting over an hour. Putting on all her steam, the Queen of the West made a blow at the Indianola, cleaving the barge in two and striking her with such tremendous force that the Indianola's machinery was badly injured. Here the action on both sides became desperate. The blow of the Queen of the West was quickly followed up by the Webb with a terrific "butt" at full speed. This finished the work. The Indianola was discovered to be in a sinking condition, and was put for the shore on the Louisiana side. Seeing this, the Dr. Batey was ordered to board her. On bearing alongside her, the Indianola surrendered, and all her officers and crew—numbering in all about one hundred and twenty men—were made prisoners.

These additions to our naval structures on the Mississippi were important. We now possessed some power in the interior waters of the Confederacy; to our harbor defences we had already added some rams; and our deficiency in a navy was not a laughing-stock to the North as long as our few privateers were able to cruise in the Atlantic, and carry dismay to the exposed commerce of the Gulf.

The few ships the North possessed that were the equals in point of speed of the Confederate privateers, the Alabama and Florida, were, with a single exception, purchased vessels, built for the merchant service, and exceedingly liable to be disabled in their machinery on account of its being nearly all above the

water-line.   Taking, as samples of vessels of this class, the
Vanderbilt, Connecticut, and Rhode Island, the North had
three ships which, for the purpose they were intended, were
without superiors; but the chances were that, if coming under
the fire of the Alabama or Florida, they would be, by a well-
directed shot or shell at close quarters, crippled and become an
easy prize.

The exploits of our cruisers were sufficient to show the value
and efficiency of the weapon of privateering, and to excite
many regrets that our means in this department of warfare
were so limited.   One national steamer alone—-the Alabama—
commanded by officers and manned by a crew who were de-
barred by the closure of neutral ports from the opportunity
of causing captured vessels to be condemned in their favor as
prizes, had sufficed to double the rates of marine insurance in
Yankee ports, and consigned to forced inaction numbers of
Yankee vessels, in addition to the direct damage inflicted by
captures at sea.   The Northern papers paid a high tribute to
the activity and daring of our few privateers in the statement
that, during one month of winter, British steamers had carried
from San Francisco to Europe six and a quarter millions of
gold, whilst during the same time from the same port there
had arrived in New York only two hundred and fifty thousand dollars of the precious metal.   In view of such results,
it would be difficult to over-estimate the effects, if we had
had a hundred of private armed vessels, and especially if we
could have secured from neutral Europe the means of dis-
posing of such prizes as we might make of the commerce of
the enemy.

CHAPTER XXII.

An extraordinary Lull in the War.—An Affair with the Enemy on the Black-water.—Raids in the West.—Van Dorn's Captures.—THE MEETING OF CONGRESS.—Character of this Body.—Its Dulness and Servility.—Mr. Foote and the Cabinet.—Two Popular Themes of Confidence.—Party Contention in the North.—Successes of the Democrats there.—Analysis of the Party Politics of the North.—The Interest of New England in the War.—How the War affected the Northwestern Portions of the United States.—Mr. Foote's Resolutions respecting the Northwestern States.—How they were received by the Southern Public.—New War Measures at Washington.—Lincoln a Dictator.—Prospect of Foreign Interference.—Action of the Emperor Napoleon.—Suffering of the Working Classes in England.—The Delusions of an early Peace.—The Tasks before Congress.—Prostrate Condition of the Confederate Finances.—President Davis's Blunder.—The Errors of our Financial System.—The Wealth of the South.—The Impressment Law of Congress.—Scarcity of Supplies.—Inflated Prices.—Speculation and Extortion in the Confederacy.—Three Remarks about these.—The Verdict of History.

THE battle of Murfreesboro' was followed by an extraordinary lull of the movements of the war. For months the great armies in Tennessee and Virginia were to stand agaze of each other. The events of this period are slight, and easily recounted.

While the lines of the Rappahannock remained undisturbed, our forces on the Blackwater had an engagement of outposts on the 31st of January, which was unduly magnified into a battle. The success of the affair was not wholly unimportant, as a loss of some hundreds was inflicted upon the enemy before our forces fell back to Carrsville, which they were compelled to do in the face of superior numbers.

In Tennessee there was a series of exploits of our cavalry, the details of which it is impossible now to recount. The most remarkable of these successes was probably that of Van Dorn, who, on the 1st day of March, at Thompson's station, between Columbia and Franklin, captured five regiments of the enemy's infantry, comprising twenty-two hundred officers and men.

THE MEETING OF CONGRESS.

The reader will be interested in turning from the unimportant military events of this period to notice the reassem-

bling of the Confederate Congress, and its proceedings in the
early months of 1863. It is not to be disguised that this body
fell below the spirit and virtue of the people, and was remarkable for its destitution of talents and ability. Not a single
speech that has yet been made in it will live. It is true that
the regular Congress, elected by the people, was an improvement upon the ignorant and unsavory body known as the Provisional Congress, which was the creature of conventions, and
which was disgraced in the character of some of its members;
among whom were conspicuous corrupt and senile politicians
from Virginia, who had done all they could to sacrifice and
degrade their State, who had "toadied" in society, as well as
in politics, to notabilities of New England, and who had taken
a prominent part in emasculating, and, in fact, annulling the
Sequestration Law, in order to save the property of relatives
who had sided with the North against the land that had borne
them and honored their fathers.

But the regular Congress, although it had no taint of disloyalty or Yankee toadyism in it, was a weak body. It had
made no mark in the history of the government; it was destitute of originality; its measures were, generally, those which
were recommended by the Executive, or suggested by the newspapers; it had produced no great financial measure; it made
not one stroke of statesmanship; it uttered not a single fiery
appeal to the popular heart, such as is customary in revolutions. It afforded, perhaps, a proof of the frequent assertion
that our democratic system did not produce great men. The
most of the little ability it had was occupied with servility to
the Executive and demagogical displays.

It is difficult, indeed, for a legislative body to preserve its
independence, and to resist the tendency of the Executive to
absorb power in time of war, and this fact was well illustrated
by the Confederate Congress. One of the greatest political
scholars of America, Mr. Madison, noticed this danger in the
political constitution of the country. He said:—"War is in
fact the true nurse of Executive aggrandizement. In war a
physical force is to be created, and it is the Executive will
which is to direct it. In war the public treasures are to be
unlocked, and it is the Executive hand which is to dispense
them. In war the honors and emoluments of office are to be

multiplied, and it is the Executive patronage under which they are to be enjoyed. It is in war, finally, that laurels are to be gathered, and it is the Executive brow they are to encircle."

There was but little opposition in Congress to President Davis; but there was some which took a direction to his cabinet, and this opposition was represented by Mr. Foote of Tennessee—a man of acknowledged ability and many virtues of character, who had re-entered upon the political stage after a public life, which, however it lacked in the cheap merit of partisan consistency, had been adorned by displays of wonderful intellect and great political genius. Mr. Foote was not a man to be deterred from speaking the truth; his quickness to resentment and his chivalry, which, though somewhat Quixotic, was founded in the most noble and delicate sense of honor, made those who would have bullied or silenced a weaker person stand in awe of him. A man of such temper was not likely to stint words in assailing an opponent; and his sharp declamations in Congress, his searching comments, and his great powers of sarcasm, used upon such men as Mallory, Benjamin, and Northrop, were the only relief of the dulness of the Congress, and the only historical features of its debates.

Mr. Foote was of a temperament that easily indulged the prospects of peace which so generally existed when Congress resumed its session in the opening of the new year. At an early period of the session resolutions were introduced by him inviting the Northwestern States to abstention from the war, and expressing a lively and friendly confidence in the negotiation which the Emperor of the French had just undertaken for a qualified mediation in the war in America. Of these two popular themes of confidence some explanation is due.

Since the commencement of the war, there had been some few people in the North who had opposed its prosecution, and many more who were averse to its policy and measures. The removal of McClellan added a bitter feud to animosities already existing, and the enunciation at Washington of the policy of emancipation contributed to the party divisions in the North. The result of the Northern elections in the fall o 1862 was apparently an emphatic and impressive popular verdict against the Abolition party, which had ruled the government at Washington. In the face of a majority of 107,000 against them in 1860, the Democrats had carried the State of New York. The metropolis of New York was carried by a Democratic majority of 31,000—a change of 48,000 votes in twelve months. Within the great States of New Jersey, New York, Pennsylvania, Ohio, Indiana, and Illinois, the results of the popular elections were a more or less emphatic avowal of opposition to the schemes of those who were using the power of the government to advance and fasten upon the country their political vagaries, regardless of right and written constitutions. These six States contained a majority of the free State population. They furnished the majority of the troops in the field against us. They had two-thirds of the wealth of the North. It was clear that the Washington government needed men and money to carry on the war, and to have a united North the Democratic States must furnish more than half of either.

Under these circumstances, it is not surprising that the people of the South should have convinced themselves that an important reaction was taking place in public sentiment in the North, and that it naturally tended to a negotiation for peace. But in one-half of this opinion they were mistaken. There was a reaction in the North; but it had scarcely any thing more than a partisan significance. It was a struggle between those in power and those out of power; the issues of which were feigned and exaggerated; in which much that was said against the war was not really meant; and at the close of which the passions it had excited suddenly evaporated. Mr. Van Buren, who, in the Democratic campaign in New York, had made speeches quite warm enough for Southern latitudes, was after the elections an advocate of the war and a mocker of "the rebellion." Many more followed the distinguished lead of the demagogue in raising a clamor about the administration merely for party purposes, and having served those purposes, in returning to the advocacy of a war, in which, by giving false encouragement to the North, and holding out hopes of "reconstruction," they were enemies more fatal to the South than the blind and revengeful radicals who sought her destruction.

It is probable that the movements in the Northwestern States against the administration were better founded in principle than those that had taken place in other parts of the

North, and that they denoted a sincere aversion to the war. The opposition of Mr. Vallandigham, who assumed to represent this sentiment of the Northwest in Congress, was apparently superior to the demagogical clamor of such men as Van Buren and Seymour of New York. The sentiment was undoubtedly sincere, whatever the merits or demerits of its officious representative.*

The pecuniary interest of New England in the war was plain enough. The demand for the products of her industry for objects of this war was greater than at any former period in the history of this continent. Her workshops were in full blast. Ships and locomotives were to be built, the weapons of war were to be created, and the ironmongers of New England found a vast and profitable employment in answering these demands. The spinners and weavers and blanket-makers and artisans were kept busy at their avocations, and everywhere in these avaricious districts of the North arose the hum of profitable industry.

But while New England rioted in the gains of the war, it was stark ruin to the agricultural States of the Northwest.

---

* There is unavoidable reason for doubting the virtue of Mr. Vallandigham. It is difficult to discover the motives of the Yankee. The people of the South have reason to know, from former political association with this faithless race, how indirect are their courses and how affected their zeal. What appears to be the inspiration of virtue, may be the deep design of a selfish ambition; singularity of opinion may prove nothing but an itch for a cheap reputation; and an extraordinary display of one's self before the public may, at best, be but the ingenious trick of a charlatan.

When Mr. Vallandigham was exiled for obstructing enlistments in the North, he had an opportunity, in his travels in the Confederacy, of learning the sentiments of the people, and of these he gave the following report in an address to the people of Ohio:

"Travelling a thousand miles and more through nearly one-half of the Confederate States, and sojourning for a time at widely different points, I met not one man, woman, or child, who were not resolved to perish rather than yield to the pressure of arms, even in the most desperate extremity. . . .
. . . . *Neither, however, let me add, did I meet any one, whatever his opinion or station, political or private, who did not declare his readiness, when the war shall have ceased and invading armies be withdrawn, to consider and discuss the question of reunion.* And who shall doubt the issue of the argument ?"

A man who can be guilty of such a deliberate falsehood, and one evidently planned to catch votes for his political hobby, can certainly make no pretension to heroism, and may even have his claims to honesty justly doubted.

The people there were growing poorer every day in the midst of plenty. The great Southern market which their resources supplied had been closed, and there was no new demand for their agricultural products. The corn, wheat, and bacon of Indiana and Illinois were scarcely worth the cost of transportation to the Atlantic coast. The railroads connecting the West with the seaboard were principally in the hands of the Eastern capitalists, and the rates of freight were so enormous, that the surplus agricultural product of the Northwestern farmers was in many instances left to rot on their lands, or be used as fuel.

This violent contrast between New England and the West, in the effects on each of the war, was developed in a formidable opposition of opinion. Indications of this opposition had already been given in the press of St. Louis and Chicago. The jealousy of the agricultural States of the North was being inflamed by the unequal profits of the war and the selfish policy of the Abolitionists; and the opinion plainly grew in the press and public discussion that the West had not a single interest in the war beyond securing the free navigation of the Mississippi.

How far statesmanship in the South might have profited by this disaffection in the Northwestern States is left a matter of conjecture and controversy. The efforts made in the Confederate Congress by Mr. Foote in this direction, tendering to these States a complete assurance of the free navigation of the Mississippi, and proposing an alliance with the Confederacy, without political complications, met with feeble encouragement in that body, a doubtful response from the army, and divided comments of the press. Whatever may have been the merits of Mr. Foote's proposition, it admitted of no delay. While our government treated it with hesitation, the authorities at Washington were making anxious and immense preparations to overcome the disaffection of the people and to carry on the war; and the means to do this were supplied by an act suspending the *habeas corpus*, and making Lincoln absolute dictator; by new measures of finance, and by a conscription law which called into the field three million of men.

The prospect of a termination of the war by any action of foreign governments, was more distant than that afforded by party elections and movements in the North. This action was limited to the French Emperor alone; it had not progressed further at this time than an invitation to England and Russia made in November, 1862, to unite in proposing an armistice to the Washington government, which should merely give an opportunity for discussion, without affecting in any way the present military interests and positions of the belligerents. Mild as the French proposition was, it was rejected by Russia and England. Lord Russell replied for his government that the time was not ripe for such mediation as was proposed, and that it would be better to watch carefully the progress of opinion in America, and wait for some change in which the three Courts could offer their friendly counsel with a prospect of success. The British statesman had nothing to plead for the mass of suffering humanity in his own land, which the war he was implored to stop or to ameliorate had occasioned; for humanity was easily outweighed by political reasons, which are as often worked out through the blood and tears of its own people as through the misfortunes of others.*

---

* In a letter of Mr. Cobden, published during the early winter in an English journal, he declares that in travelling from Manchester to Blackburn, over a country covered with snow, he found hundreds of wasted victims of cold and want. He says: "Hitherto the distressed population have felt little more than the want of food. Now and from henceforth blankets, fuel, and clothing are as essential to health as bread and soup." He argues that it is useless to save people from dying by hunger, only that they may perish by fever, or by the exhaustion consequent on cold and insufficient food.

The early advent of winter enhanced the misery of the suffering. In many districts there was no fuel, no means of warmth except the scanty allowance of coals distributed in some places by the Relief Committees. Everywhere the people had too little to eat, and that little was not sufficiently nutritious; everywhere they suffered from cold yet more cruelly than from hunger; and nowhere was there a fund sufficient to provide for their necessities.

The humane shuddered with horror as they read the frightful accounts of the suffering of the poor published day after day in the London *Times*. A letter from Stockport described the people there as " suffering all the horrors of a protracted famine." The same writer says: " One poor man upon whom I called this morning, having stripped the walls of every little ornament to purchase bread for his wife and three little children, took the fender and sold it for a shilling." The cases of distress reported in the newspapers merely represented the average condition of the unemployed. An aged couple, we are told, had saved thirty-six pounds; this is gone, their furniture is pawned, the husband is in the infirmary, and the old woman living on a charitable dole of half a crown per week, with some soup and bread. In another case five persons, among them a sick woman, are living on seven shillings a week. One

But while the prospect of an early peace dissolved before the eyes of Congress, a subject of instant and practical importance was sorely pressing upon its attention. The vast volume of Treasury notes issued by the government had occasioned a rapid depreciation of our currency, inflated prices, and produced serious financial difficulties. So crude and short-sighted had been our notions of public finance, that at the meeting of Congress in August, 1862, we find President Davis recommending to it that the public creditors should not be paid in bonds, but that unlimited issues of currency should be made. He then said in his written message to Congress: "The legislation of the last session provided for the purchase of supplies with the bonds of the government, but the preference of the people for Treasury notes has been so marked, that legislation is recommended to authorize an increase in the issue of Treasury notes, which the public service seems to require. No grave inconvenience need be apprehended from this increased issue, as the provision of law by which these notes are convertible into eight per cent. bonds, forms an efficient and per-

---

family of six—considered to be particularly well off—have seven shillings, an allowance of coals and some soup and bread from their former employer. Another family of six or seven had lived for twelve months on six shillings a week.

The University of Oxford had subscribed about £4000 towards the relief of the suffering people. A meeting was held to promote further action, at which the following facts were stated by the Hon. E. L. Stanley of Baliol College:

"They received from America before the blockade five-sixths of their cotton; five days of the week they worked on what came from America; only one day on what came from other countries. That supply was now practically at an end. The few ships that ran the blockade made no noticeable difference, and even if other countries should double their production, we should be only supplied with material for one-third of our usual work. The country, then, was losing two-thirds of the industry engaged in this trade, and two-thirds of the capital were making no return. And this trade was such a main part of the industry of the nation, that what affected it must affect all. A Parliamentary return gave the persons actually engaged in the mills at near 500,000. If they reckoned their families, the traders who supplied them, the colliers, machinists, builders, and shipping interest engaged in supplying cotton, they would probably not overstate the number of dependents on cotton only at 3,000,000. These people were now deprived of fully two-thirds of their subsistence."

Such is a picture of the "Cotton Famine" in England. The most remarkable circumstance in connection with it was the profound indifference of the English Ministry to the distress of near a million of those for whose lives and happiness they were responsible.

manent safeguard against any serious depreciation of the currency.

The consequences of this ignorant and wild financial policy were, that, by the next meeting of Congress, the volume of currency was at least four times what were the wants of the community for a circulating medium; that prices were inflated more than an equal degree, for want of confidence in the paper of the government had kindled the fever of speculation; that the public credit, abused by culpable ignorance and obstinate empiricism, had fallen to an ebb that alarmed the country more than any reverse in the military fortunes of the war; and that the government was forced to the doubtful and not very honorable expedient of attempting to restore its currency by a system of demonetizing its own issues.

The redundancy of the currency was the chief cause of its depreciation. The amount of money in circulation in the South, in time of peace, was $80,000,000. In January, 1863, it was $300,000,000. In September, 1861, Confederate notes were about equal to specie; before December, specie was at 20 per cent. premium; before April, 1862, it was at 50 per cent.; before last September, at 100; before December, at 225; before February, at 280; and in the spring of 1863, at the frightful premium of 400 per cent., while bank bills were worth 190 cents on the dollar.

Since the foundation of the Confederate government, its finances had been grossly mismanaged. The Treasury note was a naked promise to pay; there was no fund pledged for its redemption; and the prospect of the rigid liquidation of the enormous debt that this class of paper represented six months after the restoration of peace, depended solely on the speculative prospect of a foreign loan to the amount of many hundred millions of dollars. At the commencement of the war the South had the elements for the structure of one of the most successful and elastic schemes of finance that the world had seen. The planters were anxious to effect the sales of their cotton and tobacco to the Confederate States; these would have supplied the government with a basis of credit which would have been extended as the prices of these staples advanced, and therefore kept progress with the war; but this scheme was opposed by the Secretary of the Treasury, Mr.

Memminger, and defeated by his influence. He was unfortu nately sustained by an Executive grossly incompetent on sub ¹ects of finance; which was ignorant of the principle of political economy, that there are no royal ways of making money out of nothing, that governments must raise money in the legitimate way of taxation, loans, &c.; which relied upon the manufacture of a revenue out of naked paper obligations; and which actually went to the foolish extremity of recommending that the creditors of the government should take their payment in currency rather than in the public stocks. It appears, indeed, that our government was ignorant of the most primitive truths of finance, and that it had not read in history or in reason the lesson of the *fatal connection between currency and revenue.*

It is true that some appreciation of this lesson was at last shown by Congress in its new tax-bill; for the theory of that bill was, by an enormous weight of taxation, to pay, at least measurably, the expenses of the war as it progressed, and to risk no further connection between the two distinct financial concerns of revenue and currency. But on the other hand, its system of forcing the funding of treasury notes by arbitrary reductions of interest, betrayed the ignorance of Congress; left incomplete and embarrassed a system of finance which might have otherwise been carried to a point of extraordinary suc- cess; and aimed a direct blow at the integrity of the public credit.

It was easy to see that slight differences in rates of interest would afford but feeble inducements for the conversion of the treasury note into the bond, when money was easily doubled or quadrupled in the active commercial speculations peculiar to the condition of the South in the war, unless the bond could be readily used as a medium of exchanges; and in that event there would only be a change in the form of the paper, the volume of the currency would be undiminished, and its depre- ciation therefore remain the same. But while the analysis of this system of funding shows it to be a transparent juggle, it was by no means certain that it did not contain the germ of many positive evils. The right of a government to make ar- bitrary changes in any of the terms of its obligations which affe t their value, is questionable, and the commercial honor of such an expedient is more than doubtful. While it introduced the shadow of repudiation only to weak and suspicious minds, it is yet to be regretted that even whispers on that subject were ever heard in the South. But as far as our foreign credit was concerned, there is no doubt that the empirical action of Congress, which involved, even to the smallest extent, the integrity of our obligations, was of serious prejudice. It might indeed have been logically and certainly expected that the general confidence in Europe in the military fortunes of the Confederacy would have been productive of unlimited credit to us abroad, had the faith of Europe in the management of our finances equalled that in the success of our arms.*

On the subject of the financial management of the new Confederacy, one general reflection at least admits of no doubt. The attentive reader will recognize as the most remarkable circumstance of this war, that within two years the public finances of the Confederacy should have been brought to the brink of ruin. The sympathy of the people with the revolution was unbounded. The disposition of all classes towards the government was one of extreme generosity. The property of the States of the Confederacy was greater per capita than that of any community on the globe. No country in the world had export values comparable in magnitude to those of the South, and the exports of all other countries were produced at a cost in labor four times that of ours. In such circumstances it is highly improbable that the government of the Confederacy

---

* It is true that a small foreign loan has been negotiated in Europe; but it affords no test of our credit in present circumstances, as it was made on a pledge of cotton. It shows, however, what might have been done, if the cotton had been purchased by the government and mobilized, for the whole crop might have been secured in 1861 at seven cents a pound. But against this scheme the government had set its face as flint, and when it did become distrustful of its former conclusion, it had only the nerve to make a very limited experiment in the application of this staple to support a credit almost hopelessly abused by paper issues.

It was estimated that there remained in the States of the Confederacy at this time 3,500,000 bales of cotton, which could be exported in the event of the port being opened to trade. This estimate is made after deducting from the crop of 1861 and 1862 the quantity of cotton which had run the blockade, the amount destroyed to prevent capture by the Yankees, and the quantity used for home consumption, which, since the commencement of the war, had enormously increased, being now fully 500,000 bales per annum.

could, within two years, have wrecked its credit with its own people, unless by the most ignorant trifling with great questions and the childish management of its treasury.

At an early period of the war it had been our boast that we had spent only fifteen millions, while the Yankees had spent ten or fifteen times that amount. But we find that the debt of the general government of the Confederate States in January last was $556,000,000, with the prospect, at the current rate of expenditure, that it would reach nine hundred millions by the close of the fiscal year on the first of July; and it is curious to observe what miscalculations were made of public debt both in the North and in the South. The newspapers of the two nations flourished the estimates of their debt in enumerations only of the obligations of the general government of each, and made complacent comparisons of these sums with the debts of European governments. But according to the estimates of Europe, and the calculations of plain reason, the true volume of the debt of each of these nations was represented not only by what was owed by the Richmond and Washington governments, but by the aggregate amount of the indebtedness of the several States composing each confederation. Here could be the only true and just measure of the national debt of either the South or the North, in comparison with the debts of other governments, to which the system of the division of powers between a central authority and States was unknown. The debt of each member of the Southern Confederacy, as well as that of a central authority, was a burden on the nation, for the problem of its payment was at last to resolve itself into a tax upon the people. It is only by a calculation of these aggregates that just comparisons could be made between our financial condition and that of the North or European nations; and although such comparisons on our side were to the disadvantage of our enemies, yet they exhibited facts which were unpleasant enough to ourselves.

The law of impressment enacted by Congress affords the evidence of the scarcity of supplies in the South. The question of food with that of finance divided the attention of the government. The grain-growing and provision-raising country, which stretches from the Potomac at Harper's Ferry to Memphis on the Tennessee, was now exhausted of its provisions. Much of the productive portions of North Carolina and the Gulf States had been also exhausted. The great and true source of meat supply, the State of Kentucky, which contained more hogs and cattle, two or three to one, than were left in all the South besides, had fallen into the undivided possession of the Yankees. The general scarcity of all sorts of supplies was attested by the high prices of every thing eatable. The advance in prices induced by the scarcity of supplies, was still further enormously enhanced by the greedy commercial speculation which distressed the South, and threw a shadow of dishonor upon the moral aspects of our struggle.

It is a subject of extraordinary remark, that the struggle for our independence should have been attended by the ignoble circumstances of a commercial speculation in the South unparalleled in its heartlessness and selfish greed. War invariably excites avarice and speculation; it is the active promoter of rapid fortunes and corrupt commercial practices. But it is a matter of surprise that more than an ordinary share of this bad, avaricious spirit should have been developed in the South during a war which involved the national existence, which presented so many contrasts of heroic self-sacrifice, and which was adorned with exhibitions of moral courage and devotion such as the world had seldom seen.

But of this social and moral contradiction in our war for independence, some explanation may be offered. It may, in some measure, be found in three facts: first, that a distrust of the national currency prevailed in the country; secondly, that the initiative (for it is the first steps in speculation which are more responsible) was made by Jews and foreign adventurers who everywhere infested the Confederacy; and thirdly, that the fever of gain was greatly inflamed by the corruptions of the government, the abuse of its pecuniary patronage, and a system of secret contract, in which officials who were dishonest shared the profits, and those who were incompetent were easily overreached in the negotiation. The only serious blot which defaced our struggle for independence was, at least to some extent, the creature of circumstances; and that is lost to the eye of humane and enlightened history in the lustre of arms and virtues shed on the South in the most sublime trials of the war.

CHAPTER XXIII.

Character of Military Events of the Spring of 1863.—Repulse of the Enemy at Fort McAllister.—The Siege of Vicksburg.—The Yazoo Pass Expedition.—Confederate Success at Fort Pemberton.—The Enemy's Canals, or " Cut-offs."—Their Failure.—Bombardment of Port Hudson.—Destruction of " The Mississippi."—A Funeral Pyre.—Happy Effects of our Victory.—A Review of the line of inland Hostilities.—Hooker's hesitation on the Rappahannock.—The Assignment of Confederate commands west of the Mississippi.—The Affair of Kelly's Ford.—Death of Major Pelham.—Naval Attack on Charleston.—Destruction of " The Keokuk."—Scenery of the Bombardment.—Extent of the Confederate Success.—Events in Tennessee and Kentucky.—Pegram's Reverse.—The Situation of Hostilities at the close of April, 1862.

ALTHOUGH but little is to be found of a decisive character in the military events of the Spring of 1862, there was yet a series of interesting occurrences which went far to prove the inefficiency of the most boasted naval structures of the enemy, and the progress we had made in defensive works on the lines of our harbors and the banks of our rivers.

The first of these may be mentioned as the repulse of the enemy at Fort McAllister on the 3d of March. This fort is on the outer line of the defences of Savannah. Off the Georgia coast, and eighteen miles to the southward of the Savannah river, is Ossabaw sound. Into this sound flows the Ogechee river, a stream navigable some distance up—some thirty miles —to vessels of a larger class. On the Ogechee river, four miles above the sound, is situate Fort McAllister. The fort stands on the mainland, directly on the river bank, and commands the river for a mile and a half or two miles.

The attack of the enemy on this fort was made with three iron-clads and two mortar-boats. The result of a whole day's bombardment was, that one gun was dismounted, but the fort remained uninjured, and no loss of life was sustained on our side. The iron-clad Montauk was struck with solid shot eventy-one times, and was lifted clear out of the water by the explosion of a torpedo under her bow, but the Yankees stated that she was not seriously injured. Indeed, they declared that the whole affair was nothing more than an *experimentum crucis*, to ascertain the power of their new iron-clads to resist cannon-shot, and that the result of the encounter was all that they had hoped. If the enemy was pleased with the result, the Confederates had certainly no reason to dispute his satisfaction, as long as they had the solid gratification of having resisted a bombardment of eight hours, without injury to their works or the loss of a single life.

While the enemy menaced the seaboard, he had found another theatre for his naval power on the waters of the Mississippi river. His operations there were even more important than those on our sea lines, for they were an essential part of the campaign in the West. In fact, Vicksburg was for a long time the point on which depended the movements in Tennessee and the resolution of the great crisis in the West.

THE SIEGE OF VICKSBURG.

The siege of Vicksburg furnishes a most remarkable instance of the industry and physical perseverance of the Yankees. Ever since December, 1862, they had been busily engaged in the attempt to circumvent our defences, even to the extremity of forcing our internal navigation of swampy lagoons and obstructed creeks for a distance of four hundred and fifty miles.

The enemy's operations in other directions kept him quiet directly in front of Vicksburg, but his purpose was all the same—the capture and occupation of the place. The enemy had three distinct projects for compassing the capture of Vicksburg: First, the canal across the isthmus opposite the city; secondly, the project of getting through the Yazoo Pass; third, the Lake Providence canal project. It had been all the time the principal aim of the Yankees to get in the rear or below Vicksburg. Their present plan, and one on which they were now at work, was to get through the Yazoo Pass, in the hope of getting in our rear and cutting off our supplies. Their idea was to flank Vicksburg, capture Jackson, cut off Grenada, and destroy all possibility of our obtaining supplies throughout that rich country, by this one bold stroke.

The route mapped out by the Yankees commences near Helena, Arkansas, where the Yazoo Pass connects the Mississippi with the Coldwater river, through Moon lake. The distance from the Mississippi to the Coldwater, by this pass, is about twenty miles—a very narrow and tortuous channel, only navigable when the Mississippi is quite high and its waters overflow the low lands of this region. The Coldwater river empties into the Tallahatchie, and the Tallahatchie into the Yazoo. The whole distance by this route from the Mississippi to the mouth of the Yazoo, in the neighborhood of Vicksburg, is some five hundred miles, and over one-half of it, or to the mouth of the Tallahatchie, it is easily obstructed. The Yankees met with no obstruction on their ascent of the Tallahatchie, except the overgrowth and tortuousness of the stream —which prevented the gunboats, in some instances, from making more than three and four miles a day—until reaching the mouth of the Tallahatchie, or its neighborhood, where they encountered the batteries known as Fort Pemberton, which stood as the barrier against the entrance of their fleet into the Yazoo river, formed by the confluence of the Tallahatchie and Yalabusha rivers.

This fort was nothing more than an indented line of earthworks, composed of cotton bales and mud, thrown up on the neck of a bend of the Tallahatchie river, where the river was only two hundred and fifty yards wide. The site was selected by Major-gen. Loring as the best position on the Yazoo or Tallahatchie river.

It was here, on the 13th of March, that the Yazoo expedition was intercepted and driven back by our batteries, which achieved a splendid victory over the Yankee gunboats. The Yalabusha river unites with the Tallahatchie in the bend, forming the Yazoo, so that the right flank of our works rested upon the Tallahatchie, and the left upon the Yazoo, both, however, being really the same stream. The left flank was opposite Greenwood, which is situated on the east side of the Yazoo. The Tallahatchie, under the guns of the fort, was obstructed by an immense raft, behind which the Star of the West was sunk in the channel. The intervention of the point above the bend masked the whole of our line except the left, upon which, consequently, the fire of the enemy's boats was directed. The fire was terrific, uninterrupted for four hours, from ten to sixteen heavy calibre guns on gunboats, two heavy guns on land and one mortar. Yet the line of our batteries was maintained. The loss of the enemy in this unsuccessful attack is not known; but his gunboats and batteries were constantly hit, and large quantities of burning cotton were struck from them.

The defeat of the enemy at Fort Pemberton prevented his fleet from passing by to the lower Yazoo. But this was not the only canal project of the Yankees. One at Lake Providence, was intended to afford a passage from the Mississippi to the head-waters of the Red river, by which they might command a vast scope of country and immense resources. This canal, which it was said was to change the bed of the Mississippi and turn its mighty current in the Atchafalaya river on its way to the Gulf of Mexico, was also a failure. The canal had been opened, and an enormous extent of country submerged and ruined, but it was found that no gunboats or transports could ever reach the Mississippi below Vicksburg by that route. Snags and drift choked up the tortuous streams formed by the flood from the cut levees, and even if navigation had been possible, the channel might have been rendered impassable in a hundred places by a score of active guerrillas.

In the mean time, there was every reason to believe that the Yankees were content to abandon the project of cutting a ditch through the mainland opposite Vicksburg, by which it was hoped to force the current of the Mississippi into an unaccustomed course, through which to pass their vessels without going within range of our batteries.

It was thus that the enemy was apparently brought to the point of necessity of either attacking our fortifications at Snyder's Bluff on the Yazoo, or our batteries in front of the city. These were the only two points left against which he could operate, and they were the same which he had been trying to avoid for the last three months. When he first arrived, these were the only points susceptible of assault, but wishing to flank them, he had wasted three months' time, lost a number of gunboats and transports, and many thousands of his troops.

An attack directly in front of the city plainly threatened the most serious disaster to the enemy. From a point of the river above, where high land begins, there is a high and precipitous bluff, which would not afford any landing-place for the troops—only about two acres of ground are to be found where a landing could be effected, and upon this a formidable battery was ready to receive them, and in the rear there were numberless other batteries to protect it. The whole bluff, extending a distance of two miles, was also frowning with guns, all of which would bear upon an enemy in the river.

The expedition of the enemy on the Tallahatchie, which met such unexpected and disgraceful defeat from the guns of a hastily made fort, is memorable as another of those Yankee raids which, unable to accomplish military results, was left to gratify itself with the plunder of citizens and the cowardly atrocities of marauders. From the barbarity of the Yankee, Mississippi was a distinguished sufferer as well as Virginia. Two-thirds of Sherman's army was composed of new troops from Indiana, Illinois, and Wisconsin, and they had come down the Mississippi with the intention of burning and destroying every thing they could lay their hands on. The whole line of their march was one continued scene of destruction. Private dwellings were burned, women and children driven out of their houses, and even the clothes stripped from their backs, to say nothing of acts committed by the soldiery which might make the blackest-hearted libertine blush for shame.*

Another attempt of the enemy to force our strongholds on the Mississippi, which we have to relate at this time, was made

---

* The following is a private confession taken from the letter of a Yankee officer, attached to Sherman's command : "I have always blamed Union generals for guarding rebel property, but I now see the necessity of it. Three weeks of such unbridled license would ruin our army. I tell you the truth when I say we are about as mean a mob as ever walked the face of the earth. It is perfectly frightful. If I lived in this country, I never would lay down my arms while a 'Yankee' remained on the soil. I do not blame Southerners for being secessionists now. I could relate many things that would be laughable if they were not so horribly disgraceful. For instance, imagine two privates in an elegant carriage, belonging to some wealthy Southern nabob, with a splendid span of horses riding in state along the road we are marching over, with a negro coachman holding the reins in all the style of an English nobleman, and then two small drummer-boys going it at a two-forty pace, in an elegant buggy, with a fast horse, and the buggy loaded with a strange medley of household furniture and kitchen utensils, from an elegant parlor mirror to a pair of fire-dogs, all of which they have 'cramped' from some fine house, which, from sheer wantonness, they had rifled and destroyed."

on Port Hudson on the 15th of March. We have seen how fatal, so far, had been the enemy's attempts to run our batteries and to get to the south of Vicksburg. His first attempt was with the Queen of the West, his second with the Indianola; but though successful in these two cases in running our batteries, the boats were soon captured by our men, and the enemy completely foiled in his design. It was now proposed that the enemy's fleet should attack Port Hudson and attempt to force a passage up the river.

THE BOMBARDMENT OF PORT HUDSON.

Port Hudson is a strongly fortified position on the lower Mississippi—about sixteen miles above Baton Rouge and three hundred below Vicksburg. It is situated on a bend in the river, and its great strength as a place of defence against a fleet consists in the height of its cliffs and the peculiar formation of the river at that place. The cliffs are very high, and also very steep—in fact, almost perpendicular. The river, just at the bend opposite the town, suddenly narrows, so that the rapid current strikes against the west bank, and then sweeps through a narrow channel just at the base of the cliff. Our batteries were located on a bluff at the elbow of the river, and commanded a range of three miles above and below, compelling any vessel which might attempt the passage to run the gauntlet of a plunging fire.

Six vessels were to comprise the enemy's expedition, divided into two divisions. The vanguard was to consist of the flagship Hartford, a first-class steam sloop-of-war, carrying twenty-six eight and nine inch Paixhan guns, leading, followed by the Monongahela, a second-class steam sloop, mounting sixteen heavy guns, and the Richmond, a first-class steam sloop of twenty-six guns, principally eight and nine inch columbiads. The rear-guard was composed of the first-class steam sloop Mississippi, twenty-two guns, eight and nine inch, and the gunboats Kinnes and Genesee, each carrying three columbiads and two rifled thirty-two pounders. The Mississippi was a side-wheel steamer. All the others were screw propellers. The vanguard was commanded by Admiral Farragut in person, on board the Hartford. The rear was under command of

Captain Melancthon Smith, flying his pennant from the Mississippi. They were to proceed up the stream in a single file, the stern of the one following close upon the stern of another, and keeping their fires and lights well concealed until they should be discovered by our batteries, when they were to get by the best they could, fighting their passage; and once above, they believed they would have the stronghold on both sides, their guns covering every part of the encampment.

Shortly before midnight, the boats having formed the line of battle as described, their decks cleared for action, and the men at their quarters, the Hartford led the way and the others promptly followed her direction. At the moment of their discovery, a rocket was to be sent up from the admiral's flag-ship, as the signal for the Essex and her accompanying mortar-boats to commence work.

Although there had been no indications of such a determined night attack by Farragut, the usual vigilant precautions were in force at our batteries. Every gun was ready for action, and around each piece slept a detachment of gunners. So dark was the night, however, and so slightly had the armed craft nosed their way up, that the flag-ship had passed some or our guns, and all the fleet were within easy range before their approach was known. Almost at the same time a rocket from our signal corps, and the discharge of muskets by an infantry picket, aroused our line. Quick as a flash, while the falling fire of our alarm rocket was yet unextinguished, there shot up into the sky, from the Hartford's deck, another. Then came one grand, long, deafening roar, that rent the atmosphere with its mighty thunder, shaking both land and water, and causing the high battery-crowned cliffs to tremble, as if with fear and wonder.

The darkness of the night gave extraordinary sublimity to the scene of bombardment. The sheets of flame that poured from the sides of the sloops at each discharge lit up nearly the whole stretch of river, placing each craft in strong relief against the black sky. On the long line of bluff, the batteries, but a moment before silent as the church-yard, now resounded to the hurrying tread of men, while the quick, stern tones of command were heard above the awful din, and the furtively glancing rays of light from the battle-lanterns revealed the huge instruments of death and destruction, and showed the half-covered way to magazines.

Minute after minute passed away, and the fleet kept its unchecked course up the stream. The feeling of its officers was one of amazement at the silence of the batteries. The question was seriously propounded, had not the Confederates deserted them? But only too soon did the enemy discover that we were but waiting to bring their whole fleet irretrievably under our guns before we went to work.

For fifteen minutes had they plied at their monster cannon, and now they were commencing to relax from sheer vexation, when a flash of light from the crest of a cliff lights the way for a shell to go plunging through the Hartford's deck. This was the monitor, and at once the enemy saw a cordon of vivid light as long as their own.

Now commenced the battle in all its terrible earnestness. Outnumbered in guns and outweighed in metal, our volleys were as quickly repeated, and the majority of them unerring in their aim. As soon as the enemy thus discovered our batteries, they opened on them with grape and canister, which was more accurately thrown than their shells, and threw clouds of dirt upon the guns and gunners; the shells went over them in every conceivable direction except the right one.

The Hartford, a very fast ship, now made straight up the river, making her best time, and trying to divert the aim of our gunners by her incessant and deafening broadsides. She soon outstripped the balance of the fleet. Shot after shot struck her, riddling her through and through, but still she kept on her way.

Every craft now looking out for itself and bound to make its very best time to get by, the fleet lost its orderly line of battle, and got so mixed up, it was difficult, and sometimes impossible to distinguish one from another. It was speedily apparent to the enemy that the fire was a great deal hotter and more destructive than had been expected, and the captains of the two gunboats and of the Monongahela, doubtless resolved quickly that it would be madness to attempt to run such a terrific gauntlet of iron hail. Whether the commanders of the Richmond and Mississippi had already arrived at the same determination, or came to it soon after, is not known; but they all, except the Hartford, undertook to put about and return the way they came.

For this purpose the Richmond came close in to the left bank, under the batteries, and then circled round, her course reaching nearly up to the opposite point. In executing this manœuvre, she gave our batteries successively a raking position, and they took excellent advantage of it, seriously damaging her, as the crashing of her timbers plainly told.

The Mississippi undertook to execute the same manœuvre, of turning round and making her escape back to the point she started from. She had rounded and just turned down stream, when one of our shots tore off her rudder, and another went crushing through her machinery. Immediately after came the rushing sound of steam escaping from some broken pipe, and the now unmanageable vessel drifted aground directly opposite our crescent line of batteries. Her range was quickly gained, and she was being rapidly torn to pieces by our missiles, when her commander gave the order for all hands to save themselves the best way they could. At the same time fire broke out in two places. At this time her decks were strewn with dead and wounded. Some fifty-five or sixty persons saved themselves by jumping overboard and swimming to the shore.

The dead and wounded were left upon the Mississippi, which soon floated off and started down with the current. All the other vessels were now out of range, and the spectacle of the burning ship was a grand and solemn one, yet mingled with painful thoughts of the horrible fate of those mangled unfortunates who were being burned to death upon this floating funeral pyre. As the flames would reach the shells lying among her guns, they exploded one by one, adding to the novel grandeur of the sight. The light of the burning wreck could be seen, steadily increasing its distance, for two hours and a half. At five minutes past five o'clock, when the Mississippi was probably within five miles of Baton Rouge, a sudden glare lit up the whole sky. The cause was well known to be the explosion of the magazine. After a considerable interval of time, a long rumbling sound brought final proof that the Mississippi, one of the finest vessels of the United States navy, which had earned an historical fame before the commencement of the present war, for her usefulness in the Gulf during the Mexican war, and as the flag-ship of the Japan expedition, was a thing of the past.

The victory of Port Hudson forms one of the most satisfactory and brilliant pages in the history of the war. The fleet, with the exception of the Hartford, had been driven back by our batteries, and a grateful surprise had been given to many of our people, who had acquired the disheartening conviction that gunboats could treat shore batteries with contempt. So far our strongholds on the Mississippi had bid defiance to the foe, and months of costly preparation for their reduction had been spent in vain.

While these events were transpiring on the Mississippi, the long line of inland hostilities remained unvaried and almost silent. In Virginia and in Tennessee, the powerful armies of Lee and Hooker, Bragg and Rosecrans, had camped for months in close proximity, without a cannonade, and almost without a skirmish. To some extent the elements had proclaimed a truce, while the hesitating temper of the enemy betrayed a policy strangely at variance with the former vigorous campaign in the same season of the last year. Especially was the hesitation remarkable in Virginia, where the new commander-in-chief of the enemy—Hooker—was a violent member of the Abolitionist party. He was the chief of that clique among the Yankee officers who made the war, not to realize the dream of a restored Union, but for the subjugation and destruction of the Southern social system, the massacre or exile of the inhabitants of the Southern country, and the confiscation of their entire real and personal property.

Beyond the Mississippi there was scarcely any thing to remark but a new assignment of military commands. We had now west of the Mississippi Lieutenant-gen. Kirby Smith, Gen. Price, Gen. Magruder, and Gen. Sibley. Gen. Smith had been placed at the head of the department, and had already issued an order announcing that fact; Gen. Price was assigned to lead the field movements for the redemption of Arkansas and his own State, Missouri; Gen. Sibley was moving to other important points; and Gen. Magruder's field of operations was Texas.

We have to record but a single incident in the spring of 1863, to break the long silence of the lines of the Rappahan-

nock.   On the morning of the 17th of March the enemy crossed the river at Kelly's ford, with both a cavalry and artillery
force, numbering probably three thousand men.   They advanced within six miles of Culpepper Court-house, where they
were engaged by the brigade of Gen. Fitzhugh Lee.   The
fight was severe and lasted several hours.   The Yankees were
finally repulsed, and fell back routed and panic-stricken, after
having inflicted a loss upon us of about one hundred in killed
and wounded.   They had fought with some advantages at first,
bravely contesting their ground, and it is not improbable that
a report of reinforcements coming up to us was the occasion of
their retreat.   When the retreat was ordered, they fled in
dismay and confusion.

This affair—if it was worth any thing—cost us the life of
one of the most brilliant artillery officers in the army.   Major
Pelham, of Alabama, who had acquired the title of "the gallant Pelham" from the hands of Gen. Lee in the official report
of the battle of Fredericksburg, was killed by the fragment of
a shell.   At Fredericksburg, he had distinguished himself by
sustaining the concentrated fire of a number of the enemy's
batteries.   In that terrible trial he had stood as a rock.   In
the affair which cost him his life, he had just risen in his saddle to cheer a troop of cavalry rushing to the charge, when
the fatal blow was given.   He was only twenty-two years of
age, and had been through all the battles in Virginia.   Unusual honors were paid his remains, for they were laid in the
capitol, and tributes of rare flowers strewn upon the bier of
" the young Marcellus of the South."

NAVAL ATTACK ON CHARLESTON.

The city of Charleston had long been the object of the
enemy's lust ; it was considered a prize scarcely less important
than the long-contested one of Richmond ; and with more than
their customary assurance, the Yankees anticipated the glory
and counted the triumphs of the capture of the cradle of the
revolution.   It was thought to be an easy matter for Admiral
Dupont's iron-clad fleet to take the city, and the Yankee newspapers for months had indulged the prospect of the capture of
Charleston as a thing of the future that only awaited their
pleasure.

On Sunday morning, the 5th of April, four "monitors," the Ironsides (an armor-plated frigate with an armament of twenty-two 10, 11, and 15-inch guns), and thirty vessels of various sizes, were seen off the bar. Four monitors and thirty-five wooden vessels were added to the fleet on the following day, thirty-five vessels, for the most part transports, appeared in the Stono, and the enemy landed a force of about six thousand men on Coles' and Battery Islands. These facts, with other indications, led Gen. Beauregard to count upon an attack on Tuesday, and the expectations of that sagacious and vigilant commander were not disappointed.

The atmosphere early on Tuesday morning, 7th of April, was misty, but as the day advanced, the haze lightened, and the monitors and the Ironsides were seen lying off Morris Island. Between two and three o'clock in the afternoon, a dispatch from Col. Rhett, commandant of Fort Sumter, informed Gen. Beauregard that five monitors and the Ironsides were approaching the fort. The fleet were seen rounding the point of Morris Island, the Keokuk in the advance. It was a happy moment for the defenders of Charleston. So long had suspense reigned in that city, that the booming of the signal gun and the announcement that at last the battle had begun was a positive relief. A thrill of joy came to every heart, and the countenances of all declared plainly that a signal victory over the mailed vessels was reckoned upon without doubt or misgiving. The long-roll beat in Fort Sumter; the artillerists in that work rushed to their guns. The regimental flag of the 1st South Carolina Artillery, and "the stars and bars" of the Confederate States, flaunted out from their flagstaffs on the fort, and were saluted as the enemy advanced with an outburst of "Dixie" from the band and the deep-mouthed roar of thirteen pieces of heavy artillery.

On came the mailed monitors. Their ports were closed, and they appeared deserted of all living things. They moved northwardly towards Sullivan's Island, and at a distance from its batteries of about 1,200 yards they began to curve around towards Sumter. A flash, a cloud of smoke, a clap of thunder, herald a storm of heavy shot, which bursts from the island upon the side of the frigate. The ships move on silently. The deep-mouthed explosions of Sumter in the next instant burst upon the advancing ships, and hurl tremendous bolts of wrought iron against the armor of the Ironsides. The frigate halts. At a distance of about twelve hundred yards from that work she delivers from seven guns a broadside of 15-inch shot that dashes against the sea-face of Sumter with a heavy crash. Bricks fly from the parapet and whirl from the traverse. A shell smashes a marble lintel in the officers' quarters, hustles through a window on the other side, and, striking the parapet, hurls a tornado of bricks far to the rear. The works on Morris Island burst into the deafening chorus—on land and on sea, from all the batteries of the outer circle, from all the turrets of the inner circle.

It was manifest that the Ironsides was appointed to test the strength of the fort. Fort Sumter acknowledged the compliment by pouring the contents of her biggest guns into that pride of the Yankee navy. Advancing on her circling course, the Ironsides made way for her attendant warriors; and one by one, as their turrets moved in the solemn waltz, they received the fire, sometimes diffused, sometimes concentrated, of the surrounding circle of batteries. The first division of the ships curved on its path under an iron storm that rended the air with its roar, and burst upon their mail in a quick succession of reports; sometimes with the heavy groan of crushing, sometimes with the sharp cry of tearing. Delivering a fire of shot and shell as they passed the works on Morris Island, the Ironsides and her monitors moved slowly out of range. As the Ironsides withdrew from the action, taking position to the south of Fort Sumter, steam was seen issuing from her in dense volumes, and it was believed that she was seriously damaged.

The Keokuk, a double-turreted iron-clad, led into the fight four monitors. More bold than even the Ironsides, she advanced under a tornado of shot to a position within about nine hundred yards of Fort Sumter. Halting at that distance, she discharged her 15 inch balls from her turrets against the sea-face of that fort. Crushing and scattering the bricks on the line of her tremendous fire, she failed, however, to make any serious impression on the walls. A circle of angry flashes radiated towards her from all sides, while a tempest of iron bolts and round-shot crashed against her sides. For about twenty minutes she stood still, in apparent helplessness. At the expiration of that time she moved slowly on, and after receiving the fire of the works on Morris Island, passed out of range. She was fairly riddled, for she had been the target of the most powerful guns the Confederates could command. Great holes were visible in her sides, her prow, her after-turret, and her smoke-stack. Her plates were bent and bolts protruded here and there all over her. She was making water rapidly, and it was plain to see that she was a doomed ship.

After the Keokuk and her companions had passed out of range, the circular movement was not renewed. The ships retired outside the harbor to their anchorage; and after about two hours and a half of a most terrible storm of shot and thunder of artillery, Fort Sumter and its supporting batteries settled down under sluggish clouds of smoke into triumphs of quiet.

Our victory was one of unexpected brilliancy, and had cost us scarcely more than the ammunition for our guns. A drummer boy was killed at Fort Sumter and five men wounded. Our artillery practice was excellent, as is proved by the fact that the nine Yankee vessels were struck five hundred and twenty times. The Keokuk received no less than ninety shots. She did not outlive the attack on Fort Sumter twelve hours. The next day her smoke-stack and one of her turrets were visible during low water off Morris Island, where she had sunk.

The battle had been fought on the extreme outer line of fire, and the enemy had been defeated at the very threshold of our defences. Whether his attack was intended only as a reconnoissance, or whether what was supposed to be the preliminary skirmish was in fact the whole affair, it is certain that our success gave great assurances of the safety of Charleston; that it had the proportions of a considerable victory; and that it went far to impeach the once dreaded power of the iron-clads of the enemy.*

---

* It is a question of scientific interest whether, in the construction of iron-clads, the Confederate plan of slanted sides is not superior to the Yankee plan of thick-walled turrets—the Virginia-Merrimac, and not the Monitor, the true model. The Yankee monitor is an upright, cylindrical turret. If a shot strikes the centre line of this cylinder, it will not glance, but deliver its full force. On the contrary, the peculiarity of the Virginia-Merrimac was its roof-shaped sides,

The month of April has but few events of military note be-yond what has been referred to in the foregoing pages. The check of Van Dorn at Franklin, Tennessee, and the reverse of Pegram in Kentucky, were unimportant incidents; they did not affect the campaign, and their immediate disasters were inconsiderable. The raid of the latter commander into Ken-tucky, again revived reports of the reaction of public sentiment in that unhappy State in favor of the Confederacy. It was on his retreat that he was set upon by a superior force of the en-emy near Somerset, from which he effected an escape across the Cumberland, after the loss of about one hundred and fifty men in killed, wounded, and prisoners.

This period, properly the close of the second year of hostili-ties, presents a striking contrast with the corresponding month of the former year with respect to the paramount aspects of the war. In April, 1862, the Confederates had fallen back in Virginia from the Potomac beyond the Rappahannock, and were on the point of receding from the vicinity of the lower Chesapeake before the advancing army of McClellan. Now they confronted the enemy from the Rappahannock and hov-ered upon his flank within striking distance to the Potomac, while another portion of our forces manœuvred almost in the rear and quite upon the flank of Norfolk. Twelve months ago the enemy threatened the important Southern artery which links the coast of the Carolinas with Virginia; he was master of Florida, both on the Atlantic and the Gulf; and Mobile trembled at every blast from the Federal bugles of Pensacola. Now his North Carolina lines were held exclusively as lines of occupation; he was repulsed on the seaboard; his operations in Florida were limited to skirmishing parties of negroes; and Mobile had become the nursery of cruisers in the very face of his blockading squadron. A year ago the grasp of the enemy

---

on which the shot glances. The inventor of that noble naval structure, Com-mander Brooke, claimed the slanted or roof-shaped sides as constituting the original feature and most important merit of his invention. We may add now that to the genius of this accomplished officer the Confederacy was variously indebted; for it was a gun of his invention—"the Brooke gun"—that fired the bolt which pierced the turret of the Keokuk, and gave the first proof in the war that no thickness of iron, that is practical in the construction of such a machine, is sufficient to secure it

was closing on the Mississippi from Cairo to the Gulf; but while Butler was enjoying his despotic amusements and building up his private fortunes in the Crescent City, the strongholds of Vicksburg and Port Hudson were created, and held at bay the most splendid expeditions which the extravagance of the North had yet prepared. A year ago the enemy, by his successes in Kentucky and Tennessee, held the way almost into the very heart of the Confederacy, through Eastern Tennessee and Western Virginia. Now the fortunes of the war in that whole region were staked upon the issues of impending battle.

For three months the "grand hesitation" of the North had continued. With some seven or eight hundred thousand soldiers in the field and countless cruisers swarming on our coasts, the enemy had yet granted us a virtual suspension of arms since the great battles of Fredericksburg and Murfreesboro', interrupted only by petty engagements and irresolute and fruitless bombardments. He had shown that he possessed no real confidence in the success of his arms; he had so far failed to reduce any one of "the three great strongholds of the rebellion," Richmond, Charleston, and Vicksburg; and he had ceased to map out those plans of conquest of which he was formerly so prolific.

CHAPTER XXIV.

THE second year of the war, having commenced with the fall of New Orleans, 1st of May, 1862, properly closes with the events recorded in the preceding chapter. Of succeeding events, which have occurred between this period and that of publication, we do not propose to attempt at this time a full narrative; their detail belongs to another volume. It is proposed at present only to make an outline of them, so as to give to the reader a stand-point of intelligent observation, from which he may survey the general situation at the time these pages are given to the public.

The next volume of our history will open on that series of remarkable raids and enterprises on the part of the enemy's cavalry, which, in the months of April and May, disturbed many parts of the Confederacy. We shall find that the extent of these raids of Yankee horsemen, their simultaneous occurrence in widely removed parts of the Confederacy, and the circumstances of each, betrayed a deliberate and extensive purpose on the part of the enemy and a consistency of design deserving the most serious consideration.

We shall relate how the people of Richmond were alarmed by the apparition of Yankee cavalry near their homes. But we shall find causes of congratulation that the unduly famous expedition of Stoneman was not more destructive. The damage which it inflicted upon our railroads was slight, its hurried pillage did not amount to much, and the only considerable capture it effected was a train of commissary wagons in King William county.

Other parts of the Confederacy, visited about the same time

by Yankee cavalry, were not so fortunate. The State of Mississippi was ransacked almost through its entire length by the Grierson raid. Starting from Corinth, near the northern boundary of Mississippi, a body of Yankee horsemen, certainly not exceeding two thousand, rode down the valley of the Tombigbee, penetrated to a point below the centre of the State, and then making a detour, reached the Mississippi Gulf coast in safety. This force, so insignificant in numbers, made the entire passage of the State of Mississippi, from the northeast to the southwest corner; and the important town of Enterprise was barely saved by reinforcements of infantry which arrived from Meridian just fifteen minutes before the Yankees demanded the surrender of the place.

We shall have to add here cotemporary accounts of another Yankee raid in Georgia. That adventure, however, was happily nipped in the bud by Forrest, who captured the Yankee commander, Stuart, and his entire party, at Rome, Georgia, after one of the most vigorous pursuits ever made of an enemy.

The interest of these raids was something more than that of the excursions of brigands. That of Stoneman was an important part of the great battle which signalized the opening of the month of May on the banks of the Rappahannock, and broke at last the " grand hesitation" of the enemy, which had been the subject of so much impatience in the South.

SKETCH OF THE BATTLES OF THE RAPPAHANNOCK.

The plan of attack adopted by Gen. Hooker may be briefly characterized as a feint on our right, and a flank movement in force on our left. It was determined to throw a heavy force across the river just below the mouth of Deep Run, and three miles below Fredericksburg, and pretend to renew the attempt in which Burnside had previously been unsuccessful. The object of this movement was two-fold—first, to hold the Confederate forces at that point; and second, to protect Hooker's communications and supplies, while the other half of the army should make a crossing above the fortifications, and sweeping down rapidly to the rear of Fredericksburg, take a strong position and hold it until they could be reinforced by the portion of the army engaged in making the feint, which was to withdraw from its position, take the bridges to the point of the river which had been uncovered by the flank movement, and the whole army was thus to be concentrated in the rear of Fredericksburg.

The execution of this plan was commenced on Monday, the 26th of April. Three *corps d'armée*—the Fifth, Eleventh, and Twelfth—were ordered to march up the river with eight days' rations to Kelly's ford, on the north bank of the Rappahannock, near the Orange and Alexandria railroad. This force, under the command of Gen. Slocum, of the Twelfth corps, reached the point at which it was to cross the Rappahannock on Tuesday night. On the same night three other corps—the First, Third, and Sixth—were sent to the mouth of Deep Run, three miles below Fredericksburg, to be ready to undertake the crossing simultaneously with the other corps at Kelly's ford on Wednesday morning, before day. The movement was successfully conducted at both points, and without serious opposition from the Confederates.

The Second corps, under Couch, which had remained at Banks' ford, four miles above the town, was moved up to the United States ford, just below the point of confluence of the Rappahannock and Rapidan, and crossed to join Gen. Slocum, who had crossed the Rappahannock several miles higher up at Kelly's ford, and the Rapidan at Germania Mills and Ely's ford, and marched down to Chancellorsville. These movements occupied Wednesday and Thursday. Hooker now assumed command of the right wing of his army. He took his position across the plank-road and turnpike at Chancellorsville, eleven miles from Fredericksburg, in order to cut off our anticipated retreat in the direction of Gordonsville, and strengthened his naturally formidable position by a series of elaborate abatis and field-works.

The North eagerly seized upon the different circumstances of the existing situation as indicative of victory. Gen. Hooker had made himself conspicuous in the eyes of the Yankees. He was confident, when examined before the Congressional Committee on the conduct of the war, that he could have marched into Richmond at any time at his ease had he been at the head of the Army of the Potomac instead of Gen McClellan; and if he had had command instead of Burnside he would have achieved wonders. He had recently stated that the army he led was "the finest on the planet," "an army of veterans," as the Tribune remarked, "superior to that of the Peninsula;" and so large was it that Northern journals asserted that Hooker had more troops than he knew what to do with. Nor was this all. He was allowed by Lee to cross the Rappahannock, without opposition and without loss, and to secure a position deemed impregnable—one which, according to the order he issued on Thursday the 30th of April, had rendered it necessary that "the enemy must either ingloriously fly, or come out from behind his defences and give us (the Yankee army) battle on our own ground, where certain destruction waits him."

In the mean time, Gen. Lee was not slow to meet the dispositions of his adversary. The enemy continued to pour across the river at Deep Run, until three entire corps, numbering between fifty and sixty thousand men under Gen. Sedgwick, had crossed to the south side. Lee calmly watched this movement, as well as the one higher up the river under Hooker, until he had penetrated the enemy's design, and seen the necessity of making a rapid division of his own forces, to confront him on two different fields, and risking the result of fighting him in detail.

About noon on Wednesday, the 29th, information was received that the enemy had crossed the Rappahannock in force at Kelly's and Ellis' fords above, and were passing forward towards Germania Mills and Ely's ford on the Rapidan. Two brigades of Anderson's division, Posey's Mississippians, and Mahone's Virginians, numbering about 8,000 men, and one battery of four guns, were, and had been for several weeks, stationed in the neighborhood of Ely's ford on the Rapidan, and United States ford on the Rappahannock, guarding the approaches to Fredericksburg in that direction. It was apparent that this small force would be entirely inadequate to arrest the approach of Hooker's heavy column, and Wright's brigade was ordered up to their support. At daylight on Thursday morning, the head of Wright's brigade reached Chancellorsville, at which point Posey and Mahone had concentrated their forces with a view of making a stand. Majorgen. Anderson having also arrived in the latter part of the

night, and having obtained further information of the number
of the Yankee forces, upon consultation with his brigade commanders, determined to fall back from Chancellorsville in the
direction of Fredericksburg, five miles, to a point where the
Old Mine road, leading from the United States ford, crosses
the Orange and Fredericksburg turnpike and plank-road.
The turnpike and plank-road were parallel to each other
from Chancellorsville to the point where the Old Mine road
crosses them, and from there to Fredericksburg they make one
road.

Chancellorsville is eleven miles above Fredericksburg, and
about four miles south of the point of confluence of the Rapidan with the Rappahannock, and consists of a large two-story
brick house, formerly kept as a tavern, and a few out-houses.
It is situated on the plank-road leading from Fredericksburg
to Orange Court-house, and is easily approached by roads
leading from Germania Mills, and Ely's, United States, and
Banks' fords.   Between Chancellorsville and the river and
above lies the Wilderness, a district of country formerly
covered with a scrubby black-jack, oaks, and a thick, tangled
under-growth, but now somewhat cleared up.   The ground
around Chancellorsville is heavily timbered, and favorable for
defence.   Seven miles from Chancellorsville, on the road to
Fredericksburg, and four miles from the latter place, is Salem
Church.

During the night of Thursday, Gen. Lee ordered Jackson to
march from his camp below Fredericksburg, with A. P. Hill's
and Rhodes' (formerly D. H. Hill's) division, to the relief of
Anderson. Gen. Lee brought up the divisions of Anderson
and McLaws. He occupied the attention of the enemy in
front, while Gen. Jackson, with the divisions of Hill, Rhodes,
and Trimble, moved by the road that leads from the Mine
road, behind the line-of-battle, to the road that leads to Ger-
mana ford. This movement of General Jackson occupied
nearly the whole of Saturday, May 2d, so that he did not get
into position at the Wilderness Church until near sunset of
that day.

While Jackson was gaining the enemy's rear, McLaws and
Anderson had successfully maintained their position in front.
Hooker had been felicitating himself upon his supposed good

fortune in gaining our rear. What must have been his surprise, then, to find Stonewall Jackson on his extreme right and rear. Jackson's assault was sudden and furious. In a short time he threw Siegel's corps (the 11th) of Dutchmen into a perfect panic, and was driving the whole right wing of the Yankee army fiercely down upon Anderson's and McLaw's sturdy veterans, who, in turn, hurled them back, and rendered futile their efforts to break through our lower lines, and made it necessary for them to give back towards the river.

There was an intermission of about one hour in the firing from three until nine o'clock. It was at this time that Jackson received his death wound from his own men, who mistook him for the enemy. Gen. Hill, upon whom the command now devolved, was soon afterwards wounded also, when Gen. Rhodes assumed command until Gen. Stuart could arrive upon that part of the field. Stewart renewed the fight at nine o'clock, night as it was, in accordance with Gen. Jackson's original plan, and did not withhold his blows until the enemy's right had been doubled in on his centre in and around Chancellorsville.

At daylight Sunday morning, our army, which now surrounded the enemy on all sides except towards the river, commenced advancing and closing in upon him from all points. The enemy had dug rifle-pits and cut abatis in front and along his whole line, while his artillery, well protected by earthworks, covered every eminence and swell of rising ground, so as to get a direct and enfilading fire upon our advancing columns. But on our gallant men moved, their ranks played upon by an incessant fire of shell, grape, and canister, from the front, the right, and left. On they pressed through the wood, over the fields, up the hills, into the very mouths of the enemy's guns and the long line of rifle-pits. With a terrible shout they sprang forward, and rushing through the tangled abatis, they gained the bank in front of the rifle-pits, when the foe gave way in great confusion and fled.

An extraordinary victory appeared to be in our grasp. The capture or destruction of Hooker's army now appeared certain.

Gen. Lee, finding the enemy still in force towards the river, ordered the army to form on the plank-road above Chancellorsville, extending his line in a southeasterly direction down the turnpike below Chancellorsville, with his centre resting about the latter point. Just then, news was received that Sedgwick, taking advantage of our weakness, had crossed the river at Fredericksburg, driven Barksdale from the town, and occupied Marye's hill, after capturing several pieces of the Washington Artillery. It was also stated that Sedgwick was advancing up the plank-road upon Lee's rear. This movement of the enemy was all that saved Hooker from destruction.

The story of the reverse at Fredericksburg is easily told. Our forces in defence of the line, commencing at Marye's hill and terminating at Hamilton's crossing, consisted of Gen. Barksdale's brigade and Gen. Early's division. Gen. Barksdale held the extreme left. His line had its beginning at a point two hundred yards north of Marye's heights, and extended a mile and a half to a point opposite the pontoon bridge on the left of Mansfield. This brigade, on the morning of the battle, did not exceed two thousand in numbers, rank and file, and throughout the entire length of its line had no other support than six pieces of the Washington Artillery, which were posted on Marye's heights, and Read's battery, which was placed in position on the hill to the left of Howison's house.

Against this position the enemy brought to bear the command of Gibbins on the left flank, and about twenty thousand of Sedgwick's corps. The first assault was made in front of the stone wall, as in the case of last December, and was signally repulsed. This was repeated three times, and on each occasion the handful of men behind the wall, with shouts of enthusiasm and deadly volleys, drove back the assailants. The first charge was made before sunrise, and the others in as rapid succession as was possible after rallying and reinforcement. About nine o'clock in the morning the enemy adopted the ruse of requesting a flag of truce, for the alleged purpose of carrying off the wounded, but for the real object of ascertaining our force. The flag was granted, and thereby our insufficient defence was exposed, the bearer coming up on the left flank from a direction whence our whole line was visible. Immediately after the conclusion of the truce, the enemy reinforced their front, and threw the whole of Gibbins' division on our left, defended by the 21st Mississippi regiment alone, commanded by Col. B. J. Humphreys. This regiment faced the advancing host without quailing, and, after firing until but a few feet in tervened between them and the foe, they clubbed muskets and successfully dashed back the front line of their assailants. The enemy, by the force of overwhelming numbers, however, broke through our line, and Marye's hill was flanked about eleven o'clock Sunday morning.

The turn which events had taken in front of Fredericksburg made it necessary for Gen. Lee to arrest the pursuit of Hooker, and caused him to send back to Fredericksburg the divisions of Anderson and McLaws to check the advance of Sedgwick. Gen. McLaws moved down the plank-road to reinforce Barksdale and Wilcox, the latter of whom had been observing Banks' ford, and who had been driven back to Salem Church. McLaws reaching Salem Church in time to relieve Wilcox from the pressure of overwhelming numbers, checked the advance of Sedgwick, and drove him back, with great loss to both parties, until night closed the conflict.

The enemy, however, was not yet defeated. One more struggle remained, and to make that the enemy during the night massed a heavy force against McLaws' left in order to establish communication with Hooker along the river road. Anderson moved rapidly to the support of McLaws, and reached the church about 12 M., having marched fifteen miles. Gen. Lee having arrived on the field, ordered Anderson to move round the church and establish his right on Early's left, (Early having come up from Hamilton's crossing, in rear of the enemy). The enemy having weakened his left in order to force McLaws and gain the river road, Gen. Lee massed a heavy force upon this weakened part of the enemy, and at a concerted signal, Anderson and Early rushed upon the enemy's left.

The signal for the general attack was not given until just before sunset, when our men rushed upon the enemy like a hurricane. But little resistance was made, the beaten foe having fled in wild confusion in the direction of Banks' ford. At dark a short pause ensued; but as soon as the moon rose, the enemy was speedily driven to Banks' ford, and on that night of the 4th of May ended this remarkable series of battles on the lines of the Rappahannock.

The enemy being driven from every point around Fredericksburg, Gen. Lee determined to make short work of Hooker at United States ford.   Therefore, Tuesday noon Anderson was ordered to proceed immediately back to Chancellorsville, while McLaws was instructed to take up his position in front of United States ford, at or near the junction of the Old Mine and River roads.   But a drenching storm of wind and rain set in and continued without cessation until Wednesday forenoon, when it was discovered that Hooker, taking advantage of the darkness and the storm, had also retreated across the river the preceding night.

Our forces engaged in the fight did not exceed fifty thousand men.   The enemy's is variously estimated at from one hundred thousand to one hundred and fifty thousand.   Yet the greater gallantry of our troops, even despite the emergency into which their commander had brought them, enabled him not only to beat this immense army, but to capture several thousand prisoners, thirty or forty thousand small-arms, several stands of colors, and an immense amount of personal property, and to kill and wound some twenty-five thousand men.   It was a glorious week's work.*

We have not at present those lights before us necessary for a just criticism of the military aspects of these battles of the Rappahannock.   They were undoubtedly a great victory for the Confederacy.   But there were two remarkable misfortunes which diminished it.   The breaking of our lines at Fredericksburg withdrew pursuit from Hooker.   When thereupon our

---

* The army which accomplished this work was, according to the Yankee description of it, a curiosity.   Some of the military correspondence of the Yankee journals was more candid than usual, and admitted a shameful defeat by the " ragged rebels."   One of these correspondents wrote:

"We had men enough, well enough equipped and well enough posted, to have devoured the ragged, imperfectly armed and equipped host of our enemies from off the face of the earth.   Their artillery horses are poor, starved frames of beasts, tied on to their carriages and caissons with odds and ends of rope and strips of raw hide.   Their supply and ammunition trains look like a congregation of all the crippled California emigrant trains that ever escaped off the desert out of the clutches of the rampaging Camanche Indians.   The men are ill-dressed, ill-equipped, and ill-provided—a set of ragamuffins that a man is ashamed to be seen among, even when he is a prisoner and can't help it.   And yet they have beaten us fairly, beaten us all to pieces, beaten us so easily that we are objects of contempt even to their commonest private soldiers, with no shirts to hang out of the holes in their pantaloons, and cartridge-boxes tied round their waists with strands of rope."

O'Neill, N.Y.

LT GEN. T. J. JACKSON.

From a Photograph taken a few days before his death.

forces were turned upon Sedgwick, a second misfortune robbed us of a complete success; for he managed to secure his retreat by Banks' ford, which exit might possibly have been cut off, and the exclusion of which would have secured his surrender. Of these events there is yet no official detail.

But a shadow greater than that of any partial misfortunes on the field rested on the Confederate victory of Chancellorsville. It was the death of Gen. Jackson. This event is important enough to require, even in the contracted limits of these supplementary pages, a separate title and a notice apart from our general narrative.

THE DEATH OF "STONEWALL" JACKSON.

It was about eight o'clock on Saturday evening, 2d of May, when Gen. Jackson and his staff, who were returning on the front of our line of skirmishers, were fired upon by a regiment of his own corps, who mistook the party for the enemy. At the time the general was only about fifty yards in advance of the enemy He had given orders to fire at any thing coming up the road, before he left the lines. The enemy's skirmishers appeared ahead of him and he turned to ride back. Just then some one cried out, "Cavalry! charge!" and immediately the regiment fired. The whole party broke forward to ride through our line to escape the fire. Captain Boswell was killed and carried through the line by his horse, and fell amid our own men. The general himelf was struck by three balls: one through the left arm, two inches below the shoulder joint, shattering the bone and severing the chief artery; another ball passed through the same arm, between the elbow and wrist, making its exit through the palm of the hand; a third ball entered the palm of the right hand about its middle, and passing through, broke two of the bones. As Gen. Jackson was being borne from the field, one of the litter-bearers was shot down, and the general fell from the shoulders of the men, receiving a severe contusion, adding to the injury of the arm, and injuring the side severely. Th enemy's fire of artillery on the point was terrible. Gen. Jack son was left for five minutes, until the fire slackened, then placed in an ambulance and carried to the field hospital at

Wilderness Run. He lost a large amount of blood, and at one time told Dr. McGuire he thought he was dying, and would have bled to death, but a tourniquet was immediately applied. For two hours he was nearly pulseless from the shock.

Amputation of the arm was decided upon, and the operation was borne so well that hopes of a speedy recovery were confidently entertained. A few days had elapsed, and his physicians had decided to remove the distinguished sufferer to Richmond, when symptoms of pneumonia were unfortunately developed. The complication of this severe disease with his wounds, left but little hope of his life, and on Sunday, the eighth day of his suffering, it was apparent that he was rapidly sinking, and he was informed that he was dying. The intelligence was received with no expression of disappointment or anxiety on the part of the dying hero; his only response was, "It is all right," which was repeated. He had previously said that he considered his wounds "a blessing!" as Providence had always a good design in whatever it ordained, and to that Providence in which he had always trusted he had committed himself with uninterrupted confidence. But once he regretted his early fall, and that was with reference to the immediate fortunes of the field. He said: "If I had not been wounded, or had had an hour more of daylight, I would have cut off the enemy from the road to the United States ford, and we would have had them entirely surrounded, and they would have been obliged to surrender or cut their way out; they had no other alternative. My troops sometimes may fail in driving the enemy from a position, but the enemy always fail to drive my men from a position." This was said with a sort of smiling playfulness.

The following account of the dying moments of the hero is taken from the authentic testimony of a religious friend and companion:

"He endeavored to cheer those who were around him. Noticing the sadness of his beloved wife, he said to her tenderly, 'I know you would gladly give your life for me, but I am perfectly resigned. Do not be sad—I hope I shall recover. Pray for me, but always remember in your prayer, to use the petition, Thy will be done.' Those who were around him noticed a remarkable development of tenderness in his manner and feelings during his illness, that was a beautiful mellowing of that iron sternness and imperturbable calm that characterized him in his military operations. Advising his wife, in th event of his death, to return to her father's house, he remarked, 'You have a kind and good father; but there is no one so kind and good as your Heavenly Father.' When she told him that the doctors did not think he could live two hours, although he did not himself expect to die, he replied, 'It will be infinite gain to be translated to Heaven and be with Jesus.' He then said he had much to say to her, but was too weak.

"He had always desired to die, if it were God's will, on the Sabbath, and seemed to greet its light that day with peculiar pleasure, saying, with evident delight, 'It is the Lord's day;' and inquired anxiously what provision had been made for preaching to the army; and having ascertained that arrangements were made, he was contented. Delirium, which occasionally manifested itself during the last two days, prevented some of the utterances of his faith, which would otherwise have doubtless been made. His thoughts vibrated between religious subjects and the battle-field; now asking some questions about the Bible, or church history, and then giving an order—'Pass the infantry to the front.' 'Tell Major Hawks to send forward provisions to the men.' 'Let us cross over the river, and rest under the shade of the trees,'—until at last his gallant spirit gently passed over the dark river and entered on its rest."

It is not proposed here, nor could space be found within the limits of a supplementary chapter to make a record of the life and services of Gen. Jackson. A very brief sketch is all that is possible; and indeed it is scarcely necessary to do more, as so much of his military life is already spread on the pages of this volume and intermixed with the general narrative of the war.

Gen. Thomas Jonathan Jackson was born in Harrison county, Virginia, in 1825, and graduated at West Point in 1846. His first military services were in the Mexican war, and he behaved so well that he was breveted major for his services. The Army Register and the actual history and facts of the Mexican war do not furnish the name of another person entering the war without position or office, who attained the high rank of major in the brief campaign and series of battles from Vera Cruz to the city of Mexico.

At the close of the Mexican war Jackson resigned his position in the army, and obtained a professorship in the Virginia Military Institute. His services were not conspicuous here. Col. Gilham was considered as the military genius of the school, and Thomas Jackson was but little thought of by the small hero-worshippers of Lexington. The cadets had but little partiality for the taciturn, praying professor.

Perhaps none of the acquaintances of Jackson were more surprised at his brilliant exhibitions of genius in this war, than those who knew his blank life at the Institute, and were familiar with the stiff and uninteresting figure that was to be seen every Sunday in a pew of the Presbyterian Church at Lexington. But true genius awaits occasion commensurate with its power and aspiration. The spirit of Jackson was trained in another school than that of West Point or Lexington, and had it been confined there, it never would have illuminated the page of history.

In the early periods of the war, Jackson, commissioned colonel by the Governor of Virginia, was attached to Gen. Johnston's command, on the Upper Potomac. At Falling Waters, on the 2d of July, 1861, he engaged the advance of Patterson, and gave the Yankees one of the first exemplifications of his ready-witted strategy; as Patterson never knew that, for several hours, he was fighting an insignificant force, skilfully disposed to conceal their weakness, while Johnston was making his dispositions in the rear.

The first conspicuous services of Jackson in this war were rendered at Manassas, in 1861; although the marks of active determination he had shown on the Upper Potomac, and the affair at Falling Waters, had already secured for him promotion to a brigadier-generalship. The author recollects some paragraphs in a Southern newspaper expressing great merriment at the first apparition of the future hero on the battle-field. His queer figure on horseback, and the habit of settling his chin in his stock, were very amusing to some correspondents, who made a flippant jest in some of the Southern newspapers of the military specimen of the Old Dominion. The jest is forgiven and forgotten in the tributes of admiration and love which were to ensue to the popular hero of the war.

We have already given in another part of this work (the first volume), an account of the remarkable expeditic n of Jack· son in the depth of the winter of 1861–2, to Winchester, where he had been sent from Gen. Johnston's lines. The expedition was successful, and the march was made through an almost blinding storm of snow and sleet, our troops bivouacking at night in the forest, where many died from cold and exhaustion.

Without doubt, the most brilliant and extraordinary passages in the military life of General Jackson was the ever famous campaign of the summer of 1862 in the Valley of Virginia. From the valley he reached by rapid marches the lines of the Chickahominy in time to play a conspicuous part in the splendid conclusion of the campaign of the Peninsula.

Since the battles of the Chickahominy, the military services of General Jackson are comparatively fresh in the recollections of the public. We have already seen in these pages that the most substantial achievements and brilliant successes of last summer's campaign in Virginia are to be attributed to him.

The participation of Jackson in the campaign of Maryland, and that of the Rappahannock, shared their glory, but without occasion for observation on those distinct and independent movements which were his *forte*, and for the display of which he had room in the valley campaign, and that against Pope.

The most noble testimony of the services of the departed hero in the battle of Chancellorsville is to be found in the note of Gen. Lee, which is characteristic of his own generosity and worth. Gen. Lee wrote him :

" General : I have just received your note informing me that you were wounded. I cannot express my regret at the occurrence. Could I have dictated events, I should have chosen for the good of the country to have been disabled in your stead.

" I congratulate you upon the victory which is due to your skill and energy."

Jackson's response to his attendants on hearing the note read is said to have been, " Gen. Lee should give the glory to God." It was an expression of his modesty and reverence.

A friend relates that a few nights before this battle, an equally characteristic incident occurred that is worthy of

record. He was discussing with one of his aids the probability and issue of a battle, when he became unusually excited.
After talking it over fully, he paused, and with deep humility
and reverence said, " My trust is in God ;" then, as if the
sound of battle was in his ear, he raised himself to his tallest
stature, and, with flashing eyes and a face all blazoned with the
fire of the conflict, he exclaimed, " I wish they would come."

A strong religious sentiment combined with practical energy,
and an apparent dash of purpose qualified by the silent calculations of genius, were the remarkable traits of the character
of Jackson. It was his humble Christian faith combined with
the spirit of the warrior that made that rare and lofty type of
martial prowess that has shrined Jackson among the great
heroes of the age.

From all parts of the living world have come tributes to his
fame. " He was," says the London *Times*, " one of the most
consummate generals that this century has produced. . . .
That mixture of daring and judgment, which is the mark of
' Heaven-born' generals, distinguished him beyond any man
of his time. Although the young Confederacy has been
illustrated by a number of eminent soldiers, yet the applause
and devotion of his countrymen, confirmed by the judgment
of European nations, have given the first place to Gen. Jackson. The military feats he accomplished moved the minds of
the people with astonishment, which it is only given to the
highest genius to produce. The blows he struck at the enemy
were as terrible and decisive as those of Bonaparte himself."

It is proposed already that the State of Virginia shall build
for him a stately tomb, and strike a medal to secure the
memory of his name. These expressions of a nation's gratitude may serve its own pleasure. But otherwise they are unnecessary.

> " Dear son of memory, great heir of fame,
> What need'st thou such weak witness of thy name !"

CHAPTER XXV.

WE find it necessary to give another chapter to the extension of our narrative beyond its appropriate limit. We shall proceed rapidly with a general reference to such events as may exhibit the condition of the Confederacy at the time of this writing, reserving details for another volume that will properly cover the period of the *third* year of the War. That year has opened with disasters, at which we can now glance only imperfectly, for upon them the lights of time have scarcely yet developed.

DEPARTMENT OF THE MISSISSIPPI.

As the attention of the reader returns to the busy scenes of the war, it is taken by one of those sudden translations, so common in this history, from Virginia to the distant theatres of the West. The smoke of battle yet lingered on the Rappa nock, when the attention of the public was suddenly drawn to the Valley of the Mississippi by the startling announcement that an army of the enemy was on the overland march against Vicksburg, that had so long defied an attack from the water.

We have at this time only very uncertain materials for the history of the campaign in Mississippi. We must at present trust ourselves to a very general outline that will exclude any considerable extent of comment; satisfied that what we can do at present to interest the reader is simply to put certain leading occurrences of the campaign in their natural succession, and make a compact resume of events which, up to this time, have been related in a very confused and scattering style.

By running the gauntlet of our batteries at Vicksburg with his transports, Grant avoided the necessity of the completion of the canal, and secured a passage of the river, after leading his troops over the narrow peninsula below Vicksburg, at any point above Port Hudson which he might select. It appears that the defences at Grand Gulf, twenty-two miles south of Warrenton, at the mouth of Black river, were only constructed after the enemy had succeeded in getting some of his vessels between Port Hudson and Vicksburg. The Black river being navigable for some distance, they were intended to obstruct the passage of a force to the rear of Vicksburg by this route.

The abandonment of our works there, after a severe bombardment, opened the door to the enemy, and the battle of Port Gibson, fought on the 1st day of May, put them still further on their way to Vicksburg. The evacuation of Port Gibson by Gen. Bowen was followed by that of Bayou Pierre, and his forces were withdrawn across the Big Black within twenty miles of Vicksburg.

So far in the campaign the enemy had a remarkable advantage. Our generals were wholly unable to penetrate his designs, and were compelled to wait the progressive steps of their development.

It was impossible to foresee the precise point at which the blow would be struck, or to form any probable conjecture of the immediate objects of the enemy's enterprise. When Grant's transports had succeeded in passing the batteries at Vicksburg he had a river front of more than a hundred miles where h could land. The point of his landing having been determined at Grand Gulf, it was still uncertain whether he meant to approach Vicksburg by the river, under cover of his gunboats, or whether he would attempt to circumscribe the place and cut our communications east. It subsequently appeared that the latter enterprise was selected by the enemy, and that Jackson was the immediate point of attack.

On the 14th of May the enemy took possession of Jackson. Gen. Johnston was intrusted with the active command of the Confederate forces in the southwest too late to save those disastrous results which had already occurred; and the very first step to which he was forced by existing circumstances was the evacuation of Jackson. But the enemy's occupation of the capital of Mississippi seems to have been but an unimportant incident, and it is probable that, even with inferior forces on our side, a battle would have been risked there if Jackson had been of greater importance than as a point of railroad in possession of the enemy.

Although Gen. Bowen, in the engagement of Port Gibson, failed to check the rapid advance of the enemy, it was understood that he had been able to evacuate in good order his position south of the Big Black, and establish a line of defence, extending along that stream east from the Mississippi, so as to secure Vicksburg against assault from the south. This, the main line of our defence, was occupied by Gen. Pemberton with heavy reinforcements from Vicksburg.

On the 16th of May occurred the bloody battle of Baker's creek (on the Jackson and Vicksburg road), in which the force under Pemberton was defeated, with considerable loss of artillery. On the following day the Confederates again sustained a disaster at Big Black bridge; and on the 18th Vicksburg was closely invested by the enemy, and the right of his army rested on the river above the town.

It is probable that it was to give time for reinforcements to arrive in the enemy's rear, who, flushed with victory at Grand Gulf, Port Gibson, and Jackson, had turned back from the latter on the rear defences of Vicksburg, that Gen. Pemberton, perhaps unwisely, advanced from his works to meet Grant in the open field and hold him in check, and thus, from greatly inadequate forces, suffered the disheartening disasters of Baker's creek and Big Black bridge. As a last resort he retired behind his works with a weakened and somewhat dispirited but still glorious little army. The unfortunate commander appeased the clamor against himself by an apparently noble candor and memorable words of heroism. He said that it had been declared that he would sell Vicksburg, and exhorted his soldiers to follow him to see the price at which he would sell it—for it would not be less than his own life and that of every man in his command. Those words were not idle utterances; they deserve to be commemorated; they were heroic only in proportion as they were fulfilled and translated into action.

The events of the 19th, 20th, and 21st of May wearied the Yankees, who imagined that they saw in their grasp the palm of the Mississippi. So fully assured were they of victory, that they postponed it from day to day. To storm the works was to take Vicksburg, in their opinion; and when it was known, on the morning of the 21st, that at ten o'clock next morning the whole line of Confederate works would be assaulted, the credulous and vain enemy accounted success so certain that it was already given to the wings of the telegraph.

Indeed, there is no doubt that at one hour of this famous day, McClernand, the Yankee general who made the assault on the left, sent a dispatch to Grant that he had taken three forts, and would soon be in possession of the city. But the success was a deceitful one. The redoubts carried by the enemy brought him within the pale of a devouring fire. At every point he was repulsed; and with reference to completeness of victory, exhibitions of a devoted courage, and the carnage accomplished in the ranks of the enemy, these battles of Vicksburg must be accounted among the most famous in the annals of the war.

But despite the discouragements of the repulse, there still remained to the enemy the prospects of a siege under circumstances of peculiar and extraordinary advantage. Although Grant's attack was made from Grand Gulf, that place was not long his base; and when he gained Haines' Bluff and the Yazoo, all communication with it was abandoned. He was enabled to rely on Memphis and the river above Vicksburg for food and reinforcements; his communications were open with the entire West; and the Northern newspapers urgently demanded that the utmost support should be given to a favorite general, and that the Trans-Mississippi should be stripped or troops to supply him with reinforcements.

But the South still entertained hopes of the safety of Vicksburg. It was stated in Richmond by those who should have been well informed, that the garrison numbered considerably more than twenty thousand men, and was provisioned for a siege of six months. Nearly every day the telegraph had some extravagance to tell concerning the supreme safety of Vicksburg and the confidence of the garrison. The heroic promise of Pemberton that the city should not fall until the last man had fallen in the last ditch was called to the popular remembrance. The confidence of the South was swollen even to insolence by these causes; and although a few of the intelligent doubted the extravagant assurances of the safety of Vicksburg, the people at large received them with an unhesitating and exultant faith.

Under these circumstances the surprise and consternation of the people of the South may be imagined, when, without the least premonition, the announcement came that the select anniversary of *the Fourth of July* had been signalized by the capitulation of Vicksburg, without a fight; the surrender of twenty odd thousand troops as prisoners; and the abandonment to the Yankees of one of the greatest prizes of artillery that had yet been made in the war. The news fell upon Richmond like a thunder-clap from clear skies. The day of our humiliation at Vicksburg had been ill-selected. But it was said that Gen. Pemberton was advised that the enemy intended to make a formidable assault on the next day, and that he was unwilling to await it with an enfeebled garrison, many of whom were too weak to bear arms in their hands. The condition of the garrison, although certainly not as extreme as that which Pemberton had heroically prefigured as the alternative of surrender, and although holding no honorable comparison with the amount of privation and suffering borne in other sieges recorded in history, was yet deplorable. Our troops had suffered more from exhausting labors than from hunger; and their spirit had been distressed by the melancholy isolation of a siege in which they were cut off from communication with their homes, and perhaps by other causes which are not now certainly known. Patience is not a virtue of Southern soldiers, and for it at least the garrison of Vicksburg will not be conspicuous in history.

It is not possible at this time to determine the consequences of the fall of Vicksburg. That it was the ostensible key to a vast amount of disputed territory in the West, and that it involved a network of important positions, were universally admitted in the South. But this estimate of its importance is intricate and uncertain, and awaits the development of events. The army of Johnston was saved, instead of being risked in an attack on Grant's rear at Vicksburg, and is still disputing the enemy's encroachments in the Southwest. We must leave its movements to more convenient and future narration.

But we must recognize the fact of various disasters which have immediately ensued from the fall of Vicksburg. It compelled the surrender of Port Hudson as its necessary consequence.* It neutralized in a great measure a remarkable series

---

* The fall of Port Hudson did not take place until after a prolonged and gallant resistance, the facts of which may be briefly commemorated here. On the morning of the 22d of May, the enemy, under command of Gen. Banks, pushed his infantry forward within a mile of our breastworks. Having taken his position for the investment of our works, he advanced with his whole force against the breastworks, directing his main attack against the left, commanded by Col. Steadman. Vigorous assaults were also made against the extreme left of Col. Miles and Gen. Beale, the former of whom commanded on the centre, the latter on the right. On the left the attack was made by a brigade of negroes, composing about three regiments, together with the same force of white Yankees across a bridge which had been built over Sandy creek. About five hundred negroes in front advanced at double-quick within one hundred and fifty yards of the works, when the artillery on the river bluff, and two light pieces on our left, opened upon them, and at the same time they were received with volleys of musketry. The negroes fled every way in perfect con¯usion, and, according to the enemy's report, six hundred of them perished. The repulse on Miles' left was decisive.

On the 13th of June a communication was received from Gen. Banks, demanding the unconditional surrender of the post. He complimented the garrison in high terms for their endurance. He stated that his artillery was equal to any in extent and efficiency; that his men outnumbered ours five to one, and that he demanded the surrender in the name of humanity, to prevent a useless sacrifice of life. Gen. Gardner replied that his duty required him to defend the post, and he must refuse to entertain any such proposition.

On the morning of the 14th, just before day, the fleet and all the land batteries, which the enemy had succeeded in erecting at one hundred to three hundred yards from our breastworks, opened fire at the same time. About daylight, under cover of the smoke, the enemy advanced along the whole line, and

of successes on the Lower Mississippi, including the victory of Gen. Taylor at Ashland, Louisiana, which broke one of the points of investment around Vicksburg, and his still more glorious achievement in the capture of Brashear City. The defence of the cherished citadel of the Mississippi had involved exposure and weakness in other quarters. It had almost stripped Charleston of troops; it had taken many thousand men from Bragg's army; and it had made such requisitions on his force for the newly organized lines in Mississippi, that that general was compelled or induced, wisely or unwisely, to fall back from Tullahoma, to give up the country on the Memphis and Charleston railroad, and practically to abandon the defence of Middle Tennessee.

While people in Richmond were discussing the story of Vicksburg, the grief and anxiety of that disaster were suddenly swallowed up by what was thought to be even more

---

in many places approached within ten feet of our works. Our brave soldiers were wide awake, and, opening upon them, drove them back in confusion, a great number of them being left dead in the ditches. One entire division and a brigade were ordered to charge the position of the 1st Mississippi and the 9th Alabama, and by the mere physical pressure of numbers some of them got within the works, but all these were immediately killed. After a sharp contest of two hours, the enemy were everywhere repulsed, and withdrew to their old lines.

During the remainder of the month of June, there was heavy skirmishing daily, with constant firing night and day from the gun and mortar boats. During the siege of six weeks, from May 27th to July 7th, inclusive, the enemy must have fired from fifty to seventy-five thousand shot and shell, yet not more than twenty-five men were killed by these projectiles. They had worse dangers than these to contend against.

About the 29th or 30th of June, the garrison's supply of meat gave out, when Gen. Gardner ordered the mules to be butchered, after ascertaining that the men were willing to eat them. At the same time the supply of ammunition was becoming exhausted, and at the time of the surrender there were only twenty rounds of cartridges left, with a small supply for artillery

On Tuesday, July 7th, salutes were fired from the enemy's batteries and gunboats, and loud cheering was heard along the entire line, and Yankees who were in conversing distance of our men told them that Vicksburg had fallen. That night about ten o'clock Gen. Gardner summoned a council of war, who, without exception, decided that it was impossible to hold out longer, considering that the provisions of the garrison were exhausted, the ammunition almost expended, and a large proportion of the men sick or so exhausted as to be unfit for duty. The surrender was accomplished on the morning of the 9th. The number of the garrison which surrendered was between five and six thousand, of whom not more than half were effective men for duty.

painful news from the army of Gen. Lee. For once it appeared to the popular imagination that a great disaster in the West had a companion in the East. The fall of Vicksburg was preceded but one day by the battle of Gettysburg. To that battle-field we must translate the reader by a very rapid summary of the operations which led to it.

THE CAMPAIGN IN PENNSYLVANIA AND MARYLAND.

By a series of rapid movements, Gen. Lee had succeeded in manœuvring Hooker out of Virginia. On the extreme left, Jenkins with his cavalry, began the movement by threatening Milroy at Winchester, while, under the dust of Stuart's noisy cavalry reviews, designed to engage the attention of the enemy, Ewell's infantry marched into the valley by way of Front Royal. Advancing by rapid marches across the Blue Ridge, Gen. Ewell, the successor to Jackson's command, fell like a thunder-bolt upon Milroy at Winchester and Martinsburg, capturing the greater part of his forces, many guns, and heavy supplies of grain, ammunition, and other military stores. The Yankees' own account of their disaster indicated the magnitude of our success. The New York *Herald* declared, "not a thing was saved except that which was worn or carried upon the persons of the troops. Three entire batteries of field artillery and one battery of siege guns—all the artillery of the command, in fact—about two hundred and eighty wagons, over twelve hundred horses and mules, all the commissary and quartermaster's stores, and ammunition of all kinds, over six thousand muskets and small arms without stint, the private baggage of the officers and men, all fell into the hands of the enemy. Of the seven thousand men of the command, but from sixteen hundred to two thousand have as yet arrived here, leaving to be accounted for five thousand men."

After accomplishing his victory at Winchester, Gen. Ewell moved promptly up to the Potomac, and occupied such fords as we might desire to use, in the event it should be deemed proper to advance into the enemy's country. The sudden appearance of Ewell in the valley of the Shenandoah, coupled with the demonstration at Culpepper, made it necessary for Hooker to abandon Fredericksburg entirely, and to occupy the strong positions at Centreville and Manassas, so as to interpose his army between us and Washington, and thus prevent a sudden descent from the Blue Ridge by Gen. Lee upon the Yankee capital. Meanwhile, Longstreet and Hill were following fast upon Ewell's track, the former reaching Ashby's and Snicker's Gaps in time to prevent any movement upon Ewell's rear, and the latter (Hill) getting to Culpepper in good season to protect Longstreet's rear, or to co-operate with him in the event of an attack upon his flank, or to guard against any demonstration in the direction of Richmond.

Having gained over the Yankee commander the important advantage of the military initiative, and firmly established his communications in the rear of his base of operations on the other side of the Potomac, Gen. Lee was in a position to hurl his forces wherever he might desire; and it was soon announced in the North that Hooker had declined a battle in Virginia, and that the second invasion of the Northern territory had been commenced by the Confederates under auspices that had not attended the first. It was soon known that the light horsemen of Lee had appeared upon his war path in the southern region of Pennsylvania. For weeks the dashing and adventurous cavalry of Jenkins and Imboden were persistently busy in scouring the country between the Susquehannah and the Alleghanies, the Monocacy and the Potomac, and from the lines before Harrisburg to the very gates of Washington and Baltimore their trumpets had sounded.

The North was thrown into paroxysms of terror. At the first news of the invasion, Lincoln had called for a hundred thousand men to defend Washington. Governor Andrews offered the whole military strength of Massachussetts in the terrible crisis. Governor Seymour of New York, summoned McClellan to grave consultations respecting the defences of Pennsylvania. The bells were set to ringing in Brooklyn. Regiment after regiment was sent off from New York to Philadelphia. The famous Seventh regiment took the field and proceeded to Harrisburg. The Dutch farmers in the valley drove their cattle to the mountains, and the archives were removed from Harrisburg.

Nor did the alarm exceed the occasion for it. It was obvious to the intelligent in the North that their army of the Potomac was the only real obstacle which could impede the triumphant march of the army of Lee into the very heart of the Yankee States, and in whatever direction he might choose to push his campaign. The press attempted some ridiculous comfort by writing vaguely of thousands of militia springing to arms. But the history of modern warfare afforded better instruction, for it taught clearly enough that an invading army of regular and victorious troops could only be effectively checked by the resistance of a similar army in the field, or of fortified places strong enough to compel a regular siege. In certain circumstances, a single battle had often decided the fate of a long war; and the South easily indulging the prospect of the defeat of Hooker's forces, was elated with renewed anticipations of an early peace.

While the destruction of Hooker's army was the paramount object of Gen. Lee's campaign, he had unfortunately fallen into the error of attempting to conciliate the people of the North and to court the opinions of Europe by forswearing all acts of retaliation and omitting even the devastation of the enemy's country. The fertile acres of the Pennsylvania valley were untouched by violent hands; all requisitions for supplies were paid for in Confederate money; and a protection was given to the private property of the enemy, which had never been afforded even to that of our own citizens. So far as the orders of Gen. Lee on these subjects restrained pillage and private outrage, they were sustained by public sentiment in the South, which, in fact, never desired that we should retaliate upon the Yankees by a precise imitation of their enormities and crimes. But retaliation is not only the work of pillagers and marauders. Its ends might have been accomplished, as far as the people of the South desired, by inflicting upon the enemy some injury commensurate with what they had suffered at his hands; the smallest measure of which would have been the devastation of the country, which, done by our army in line of battle, would neither have risked demoralization nor detracted from discipline. Such a return for the outrages which the South had suffered from invading hordes of the Yankees, would in fact have been short of justice, and so far have possessed the merit of magnanimity. But Gen. Lee was resolved on more exces sive magnanimity; and at the time the Yankee armies, particularly in the Southwestern portion of the Confederacy, were enacting outrages which recalled the darkest days of mediæval warfare, our forces in the Pennsylvania valley were protecting the private property of Yankees, composing their alarm, and making a display of stilted chivalry to the amusement of the Dutch farmers and to the intense disgust of our own people.*

If Gen. Lee had supposed that his moderate warfare would conciliate the Yankees, he was greatly mistaken; for it is precisely this warfare which irritates a people without intimidating them. The simple object of his campaign appears to have been the defeat of Hooker, which would uncover Washington and Baltimore. The critical conjuncture which had been so long sought was the battle of Gettysburg.

We must spare here many of the details of those movements which brought the two armies in contact, and trust ourselves to a brief and general account of this great engagement in Pennsylvania, followed, as it is, by a rapid current of events there and elsewhere.

---

* A letter from our lines in Mississippi thus describes the outrages of the enemy there, which were cotemporary with Lee's civilities in Pennsylvania:

"I thought the condition of Northern Mississippi, and the country around my own home in Memphis, deplorable. There robberies were committed, houses were burned, and occasionally a helpless man or woman was murdered; but here, around Jackson and Vicksburg, there are no terms used in all the calendar of crimes which could convey any adequate conception of the revolting enormities perpetrated by our foes. Women have been robbed of their jewelry and wearing apparel—stripped almost to nakedness in the presence of jeering Dutch; ear-rings have been torn from their ears, and rings from bleeding fingers. Every house has been pillaged, and thousands burned. The whole country between the Big Black and the Mississippi, and all that district through which Grant's army passed, is one endless scene of desolation. This is not the worst; robbery and murder are surely bad enough, but worse than all this, women have been subjected to enormities worse than death.

"Negroes, men and women, who can leave their homes, are forced or enticed away. The children alone are left. Barns and all descriptions of farmhouses have been burned. All supplies, bacon and flour, are seized for the use of the invading army, and the wretched inhabitants left to starve. The roads along which Grant's army has moved, are strewn with all descriptions of furniture, wearing apparel, and private property. In many instances husbands have been arrested and threatened with instant death by the hangman's rope, in order to make their wives reveal the places of concealment of their valuable effects. The poor women are made to ransom their sons, daughters, and husbands. The worst slaves are selected to insult, taunt and revile their masters, and the wives and daughters of their masters."

Having crossed the Potomac at or near Williamsport, the Confederates marched to Hagerstown, to Greencastle, and thence to Chambersburg. Ewell, who held the advance, went as far as Carlisle, some twelve miles from Harrisburg. Meanwhile, Hooker, having withdrawn his forces from Stafford, moved to and across the Potomac, and took up a line extending from Washington to Baltimore, expecting Gen. Lee to offer him battle in Maryland. Finding himself disappointed in this, and compelled by pride or by his superiors, he relinquished his command to Mead, who, finding out that Lee had deflected in his march through Pennsylvania, and was moving down the Baltimore turnpike from Chambersburg, moved from Baltimore on the same road to meet him. The two armies which had ceased to confront each other since the breaking up of the Fredericksburg lines, found themselves again face to face near Gettysburg, on Wednesday, July 1st.

The action of the 1st July was brought on by Gen. Reynolds, who held the enemy's advance, and who thought himself in superior force to the Confederates. He paid the penalty of his temerity by a defeat; he was overpowered and outflanked, and fell mortally wounded on the field.

In this fight the corps of A. P. Hill was generally engaged; but, about one hour after its opening, Gen. Ewell, who was moving from the direction of Carlisle, came up and took a position on our extreme left. Two divisions of this corps, Rhodes' and Early's, advanced upon and engaged the enemy in front. Longstreet, who was not engaged in the fight of the first day, swung around his column to A. P. Hill's right, but did not take position for action until Thursday morning. The result of the first day was that the enemy was repulsed at all points of the line engaged, and driven over the range of hills to the south of Gettysburg, through the town and about half a mile beyond. At this point is a mountain which commands the ground in front for a mile on all sides. This the enemy retreated to after their repulse, and immediately fortified, their line occupying the mountain, and extending on the right and left of it.

The early part of Thursday, the 22d of July, wore away without any positive demonstration of attack on either side. Late in the afternoon an artillery attack was made by our forces on the left and centre of the enemy, which was rapidly followed by the advance of our infantry, Longstreet's corps on our side being principally engaged. A fearful but indecisive conflict ensued, and for four hours the sound of musketry was incessant. In the fight we lost a number of officers, among them Gen. Barksdale of Mississippi, whose brave and generous spirit expired, where he preferred to die, on the ensanguined field of battle. Of this "haughty rebel," who had fallen within their lines, the Yankees told with devilish satisfaction the story that his end was that of extreme agony, and his last words were to crave as a dying boon a cup of water and a stretcher from an ambulance boy. The letter of a Yankee officer testifies that the brave and suffering hero declared with his last breath that he was proud of the cause he died fighting for; proud of the manner in which he received his death; and confident that his countrymen were invincible.

The third day's battle was commenced by the Confederates. The enemy's position on the mountain was apparently impregnable, for there was no conceivable advance or approach that could not be raked and crossed with the artillery. The reserve artillery and all the essentials to insure victory to the Yankees were in position at the right time. All the heights and every advantageous position along the entire line where artillery could be massed or a battery planted, frowned down on the Confederates through brows of brass and iron. On the slopes of this mountain occurred one of the most terrific combats of modern times, in which three hundred cannon were belching forth their thunders at one time, and nearly two hundred thousand muskets were being discharged as rapidly as men hurried with excitement and passion could load them.

The battle of Friday had commenced early in the morning. With the exception from ten o'clock in the morning to one in the afternoon, it lasted all day. The Confederates did not succeed in holding any of the crests, although one or two were reached; and night again closed on the smoke-wrapped field.

The most glorious incident of Gettysburg, and the one upon which the eye of history will beam, was the charge of our devoted men upon the deadly heights where turned the tide of battle. The principal stronghold of the enemy was known as McPherson's heights, where his centre rested. In Thursday's

fight this important position had for a short time been in pos
session of a single one of our brigades—Wright's noble Geor
gians—who had charged it with the bayonet and captured the
heavy batteries on the crest, but were unable to hold it for
want of timely support.

In Friday's contest, a more formidable and elaborate attempt
was to be made to wrest from the enemy the crest which was
the key of his position. Pickett's division being in the advance, was supported on the right by Wilson's brigade, and on
the left by Heth's division, commanded by Pettigrew. The
steady movement of Pickett's men into the tempest of fire and
steel, against a mountain bristling with guns, had nothing to
exceed it in sublimity on any of the battle-fields of the revolution. Into the sheets of artillery fire advanced the unbroken
lines of our men. The devoted Confederates are struggling
not only against the enemy's artillery, but against a severe fire
from heavy masses of his infantry, posted behind a stone fence.
But nothing checks their advance; they storm the fence, they
shoot the gunners, and Kemper's and Armistead's banners are
already planted on the enemy's works.

There is no doubt but that at this auspicious moment a
proper amount of support to Pickett would have secured his
position, and carried the fortunes of the day. But that support was not at hand. Pettigrew's division had faltered, and
that gallant commander in vain strove to rally the raw troops.
In the mean time, the enemy had moved around strong flanking bodies of infantry, and was rapidly gaining Pickett's rear.
With overwhelming numbers in our front, almost hemmed in
by the enemy, the order is given to fall back. The retreating
line is pressed heavily. It does not give way; but many noble
spirits who had passed safely through the fiery ordeal of the
advance and charge, now fall on the right and on the left.

In this great battle, though unfavorable to us, the enemy's
loss probably exceeded our own, as the Yankees were closely
crowded on the hills, and devoured by our artillery fire. The
information of the enemy's loss is perhaps most accurately obtained from the bulletin furnished by his Surgeon-general,
which stated that he had something over 12,000 Yankees
wounded under his control. Counting one killed for four
wounded, and making some allowance for a large class of

wounded men who had not come under the control of the official referred to, we are justified in stating the enemy's loss, in casualties at Gettysburg, as somewhere between fifteen and eighteen thousand. Our loss, slighter by many thousands in comparison, was yet frightful enough. On our side, Pickett's division had been engaged in the hottest work of the day, and the havoc in its ranks was appalling. Its losses on this day are famous, and should be commemorated in detail. Every brigadier in the division was killed or wounded. Out of twenty-four regimental officers, only two escaped unhurt. The colonels of five Virginia regiments were killed. The 9th Virginia went in two hundred and fifty strong, and came out with only thirty-eight men, while the equally gallant 19th rivalled the terrible glory of such devoted courage.

The recoil at Gettysburg was fatal, not necessarily, but by the course of events, to Gen. Lee's campaign; and the return of his army to its defensive lines in Virginia, was justly regarded in the South as a reverse in the general fortunes of the contest. Yet the immediate results of the battle of Gettysburg must be declared to have been to a great extent negative. The Confederates did not gain a victory, neither did the enemy. The general story of the contest is simple. Lee had been unable to prevent the enemy from taking the highlands, many of them with very steep declivities, and nearly a mile in slope. The battle was an effort of the Confederates to take those heights. The right flank, the left flank, the centre, were successively the aim of determined and concentrated assaults. The Yankee lines were broken and driven repeatedly. But inexhaustible reserves, and a preponderant artillery, advantageously placed, saved them from rout.

The first news received in Richmond of Gen. Lee's retreat was from Yankee sources, which represented his army as a disorganized mass of fugitives, unable to cross the Potomac on account of recent floods, and at the mercy of an enemy immensely superior in numbers and flushed with victory. This news and that of the fall of Vicksburg reached the Confederate capital the same day. Twenty-four hours served to dash the hope of an early peace, and to overcloud the horizon of the war. The temptation of despair was again whispered to weak minds. It was the second period of great disaster to the

South, and renewed a grief similar to what had been expended a year ago upon the sorrowful stories of Donelson and New Orleans.

But happily in this instance the public despondency was of short duration. A few days brought news from our lines, which exploded the falsehoods of the Yankees, and assured the people of the South that the engagements of Gettysburg had resulted in worsting the enemy, in killing and wounding a number exceeding our own, and in the capture of a large number of prisoners. The public was yet further satisfied that the falling back of our army, at least as far as Hagerstown, was a movement dictated by general considerations of strategy and prudence. It consoled itself that the subsequent retirement of our forces into Virginia was the excess of safety; and it found reason for congratulation that the retreat of Lee to his old lines was accomplished with a dexterity and success that foiled the enemy, and disappointed the greater portion of his triumph.

But notwithstanding these causes of moderate thankfulness, it must be confessed that the retreat from Hagerstown across the Potomac was an inconsequence and a mystery to the intelligent public. Lee's position there was strong; his force was certainly adequate for another battle; preparations were made for aggressive movements; and in the midst of all came a sudden renouncement of the campaign, and the retreat into Virginia. The history of this untimely retreat has not been developed; but there is one fact to assist the explanation of it, and that is that the authorities at Richmond were much more alarmed than Gen. Lee, and much less capable than the commander himself of judging the military situation from which his army was recalled. The troops availed themselves of no other refuge than that of their own soil; they had not been defeated or seriously worsted; and so far the public had its secondary wish for the safety of the army. But this did not exclude mortification on the part of those who believed that Gen. Lee had abandoned the enemy's territory, not as a consequence of defeat, but from the undue timidity or the arrogant disposition of the authorities who controlled him. The grounds of such a belief are not certainly stated; but its existence in the public mind is a fact to be recognized by the historian, and to be determined by evidence, when time and occasion shall produce it.

* * * * * * * * * *

The check at Gettysburg and the fall of Vicksburg, which we have seized upon as the prominent events of the summer of 1863, and of which we hope hereafter, in another volume, to give a more minute and faithful account, in connection with many contemporary or closely consequent events, which are here omitted, afford a natural pause in which we may well review the events of the revolution, and speculate on its distant or ultimate future.

The disasters to which we have briefly referred, although considerable, were far from being desperate, and were scarcely occasions of any serious alarm in the South, as to the ultimate issue of the struggle. The military condition of the country was certainly far better than at the former unhappy period of the spring of 1862. Then our armies were feeble, and, in a great measure, disorganized; the conscription law had not gone into operation, and our reduced forces were scattered along an extended frontier. Now well-disciplined and seasoned armies hold with compact forces the critical positions in the Confederacy. The loss of territory, which in a European campaign, where inland fortresses and great cities give convenient footholds to an invading army, would have been estimated as a fatal disadvantage, had a very different signification in a war between the two great American powers. Indeed it may be said that the armies of our enemy scarcely did more than hold the ground they stood upon, and that in a war now passing into its third year, they had failed to touch the vitals of the Confederacy. The temporary cession of large bodies of territory to them, was really to their disadvantage in military respects; for it occasioned the necessity of extending their lines of communication, exposing their rear, and subjecting themselves, on every side, to the dangers of a hostile country, where there were no great fortresses or citadels to protect them.

But it must be confessed that there were to be found at this time but few subjects of congratulation in the internal condition of the Confederacy. The civil administration, in many of the departments, was ignorant, defective, and, in some instances, oppressive. The appendage of Congress might well have been dispensed with in our revolution, for it accomplished nothing; all its legislation was patch-work, and its measures but the weak echoes of the newspapers. The extraordinary cabinet of Mr. Davis still survived as a ridiculous cipher; for its members never dared to raise their voices on any public measure, or to assert their existence beyond signing their names to certify the laws and orders of the government, or the will of the President.

The military pragmatism of the President was his worst failing. He had treated Price, among the earliest heroes of the war, with cold and insolent neglect. He had constrained Gustavus Smith to resign, and deprived the country of one of its most brilliant generals. He had taken the unfair opportunity of a sick furlough on the part of Beauregard, to deprive him of his command in the West and give it to a favorite. He had even attempted to put Jackson in leading-strings; for it was the Presidential order that set bounds to his famous Winchester expedition, and that would have timidly recalled him from his splendid campaign in the valley. Nor was this all. There was reason to suppose that Lee's return from the territory of the North was constrained by the views of the Executive, and that the President, who had once defeated the capture of Washington, by his interference at the first field of Manassas, had again repeated his intermeddling, removed a decisive victory from the grasp of our army, and turned back the war for years.

While such was the envious or ignorant interference of the President with our most meritorious generals, he was not without favorites. While he quarrelled with such men as Price, Beauregard, Gustavus Smith, and Johnston, he maintained such favorites as Holmes, Heth, Lovell, and Pemberton. No man was ever more sovereign in his likes and dislikes. Favorites were elevated to power, and the noblest spirits consigned to obscurity by the fiat of a single man in the Confederacy, and that man one of the strongest prejudices, the harshest obstinacy, and the most ungovernable fondness for parasites.

In this war Mr. Davis has evidently been anxious to appear in the eyes of Europe as the military genius of the Confederacy as well as the head of its civil administration. He has been careless of public opinion at home. But this has been no proof

of stoicism or of greatness ; it has merely shown his conceit to
be in a different direction. This conceit has been that of
" provincialism "—the courting of that second-hand public
opinion which is obtained from the politicians and journalists
of Europe ; the bane of political and civil society in the South.
No man of equal public station on this continent has ever
courted the opinions of Europe more assiduously than the
President of this Confederacy. The proclamations of the Executive, the general orders of the army, the pronunciamentoes
of chivalry which have denied the rights of retaliation, bilked
the national conscience, and nursed a viperous enemy with the
milk of kindness, have all been composed with an eye to European effect. Compromises of dignity and self-respect have
been made to conciliate foreign nations. Consuls drawing their
exequaturs from the Washington government—a standing dero-
gation to the Confederacy which has received them—have been
sheltered and endured here ; and Europe, which denies our
rights over our territory, has received at our hands the safety
of her citizens.

We have referred in other pages to the low condition of the
finances of the Confederacy in the opening months of this year.
It had since declined much further. In February, 1862, President Davis had made the most extravagant congratulations to
the country on our financial condition, and pointed with an
air of triumph to the failing fortunes of the enemy's treasury.
In less than eighteen months thereafter, when gold was quoted
in New York at twenty-five per cent. premium, it was selling
in Richmond at nine hundred per cent. premium ! Such have
been the results of the financial wisdom of the Confederacy,
dictated by the President, who advised Congress to authorize
illimitable issues of treasury notes, and aggravated, no doubt,
by the ignorance of his Secretary, who invented a legerdemain
of funding which succeeded not only in depreciating the currency, but also in dishonoring the government.

The experiments of Mr. Memminger on the currency was
the signal of multiplied and rapid depreciation. While the
eccentric and pious Secretary was figuring out impossible
schemes of making money, or ransacking the bookstores for
works on religious controversy, unprincipled brokers in the
Confederacy were undermining the currency with a zeal for

the destruction of their country not less than that of the Yankees. The assertion admits of some qualification. Sweeping remarks in history are generally unjust. Among those engaged in the business of banking and exchange in the South, there were undoubtedly some enlightened and public-spirited men, who had been seduced by the example or constrained by the competition of meaner and more avaricious men of the same profession, to array themselves against the currency, and to commit offences from which they would have shrunk in horror, had they not been disguised by the casuistry of commerce and gain.

It was generally thought in the South reprehensible to refuse the national currency in the payment of debts. Yet the broker, who demanded ten dollars in this currency for one in gold, really was guilty of nine times refusing the Confederate money. It was accounted shocking for citizens in the South to speculate in soldiers' clothing and bread. Yet the broker, who demanded nine or ten prices for gold, the representative of all values, speculated alike in every necessary in the country. Nor was this the greatest of their offences. With unsurpassed shamelessness brokers in the Confederacy exposed the currency of the North for sale, and demanded for it four hundred per cent. premium over that of the Confederacy! This act of benefit to the Yankees was openly allowed by the government. A bill had been introduced in Congress to prohibit this traffic, and to extirpate this infamous anomaly in our history; but it failed of enactment, and its failure can only be attributed to the grossest stupidity, or to sinister influences of the most dishonorable kind. The traffic was immensely profitable. State bonds and bank bills to the amount of many millions were sent North by the brokers, and the rates of discount were readily submitted to when the returns were made in Yankee paper money, which, in the Richmond shops, was worth in Confederate notes five dollars for one.

One—but only one—cause of the depreciation of the Confederate currency was illicit trade. It had done more to demoralize the Confederacy than any thing else. The inception of this trade was easily winked at by the Confederate authorities; it commenced with paltry importations across the Potomac: it was said that the country wanted medicines, surgical instruments, and a number of trifles, and that trade with the Yankees in these could result in no serious harm. But by the enlarged license of the government it soon became an infamy and a curse to the Confederacy. What was a petty traffic in its commencement soon expanded into a shameless trade, which corrupted the patriotism of the country, constituted an anomaly in the history of belligerents, and reflected lasting disgrace upon the honesty and good sense of our government. The country had taken a solemn resolution to burn the cotton in advance of the enemy; but the conflagration of this staple soon came to be a rare event; instead of being committed to the flames it was spirited to Yankee markets. Nor were these operations always disguised. Some commercial houses in the Confederacy counted their gains by millions of dollars since the war, through the favor of the government in allowing them to export cotton at pleasure. The beneficiaries of this trade contributed freely to public charities and did certain favors to the government; but their gifts were but the parings of immense gains; and often those who were named by weak and credulous people or by interested flatterers as public-spirited citizens and patriotic donors, were, in fact, the most unmitigated extortioners and the vilest leeches on the body politic.

In this war we owe to the cause of truth some humiliating confessions. Whatever diminution of spirit there may have been in the South since the commencement of her struggle, it has been on the part of those pretentious classes of the wealthy, who, in peace, were at once the most zealous "secessionists," and the best customers of the Yankees, and wh. now, in war, are naturally the sneaks and tools of the enemy. The cotton and sugar planters of the extreme South who prior to the war were loudest for secession, were at the same time known to buy every article of their consumption in Yankee markets, and to cherish an ambition of shining in the society of Northern hotels. It is not surprising that many of these affected patriots have found congenial occupation in this war in planting in copartnership with the enemy, or in smuggling cotton into his lines. The North is said to have obtained in the progress of this war, from the Southwest and Charleston, enough cotton at present prices to uphold its whole system of currency--a damning testimony of the avarice of the planter. Yet it is nothing more than a convincing proof, in general, that property, though very pretentious of patriotism, when identified with selfishness, is one of the most weak and cowardly things in revolutions and the first to succumb under the horrors of war.

It is pleasing to turn from the exhibition of ignorance and weakness in the government, and the vile passions of its favorites, to the contemplation of that patriotic spirit which yet survives in the masses of the people and keeps alive the sacred animosities of the war. We rejoice to believe that the masses are not only yet true, but that a haughtier and fiercer spirit than ever animates the demand of our people for independence, and insures their efforts to obtain it. The noble people and army who have sustained and fought this war will have cause to rejoice. Society in the South is being upheaved by this war, and with our independence will be re-established on new orders of merit. The insolent and pampered slave-holding interest of the South; the planters' aristocracy, blown with conceit and vulgar airs of patronage; the boast of lands and kin, give way before new aspirants to honor. The republic gives new titles to greatness. Many of those who were esteemed great politicians before the war, are now well-nigh forgotten. The honors of State, the worship of society, the rewards of affection, are for the patriots of the revolution that will date our existence. Such are the great prizes, intertwined with that of independence, which stir our people and army with noble desires and beckon them to victory.

It is not only in the present external situation of the war that encouragement is to be found for the South. With considerable additions to her material elements of success, the South has in the second year of the war abated none of that moral resolution which is the vital and essential principle of victory, whatever co-operation and assistance it may derive from external conditions. That resolution has been strengthened by recent developments; for as the war has progressed, the enemy has made a full exposure of his cruel and savage purposes, and has indicated consequences of subjugation more terrible than death.

He has, by the hideous array of the instruments of torture

which he has prepared for a new inauguration of his authority among those who have disputed it, not only excited the zeal of a devoted patriotism to war with him, but has summoned even the mean but strong passions of selfishness to oppose him. The surrender to an enemy as base as the Yankee, might well attract the scorn of the world, and consign the South to despair. The portions of such a fate for the South are gibbets, confiscation, foreign rule, the tutelage of New England, the outlawry of the negro, the pangs of universal poverty, and the contempt of mankind.

War is a thing of death, of mutilation and fire; but it has its law of order; and when that law is not observed, it fails in effecting the purpose for which it is waged, and the curse it would inflict recoils upon itself. It is remarkable in the present war, that the policy of the Washington government has been an increase in every feature of the first cause of the revolt. But this has been fortunate for the South. The consequences of such despotic and savage violences, as the emancipation proclamation, the arming of slaves, and the legalization of plunder, have been the growth of new hostility to the Union, and an important and obvious vindication to the world of the motives of the South, and the virtues of her cause.

Regarding the condition of events in which this record closes; the broad lustre of victories covering the space of so many months; the numbers of our forces in the field, unequalled at any other period of the war; and the spirit animated by the recollections of victorious arms, and stung by the fresh cruelties of an atrocious enemy, we may well persuade ourselves that there is no such word as "fail" in this struggle. Even beneath the pall of disaster, there is no place for such a word. The banners of the Confederacy do not bear the mottoes and devices of a doubtful contest. That brave phrase we may apply to ourselves, which is the law of progress and success; which summons the energies of mankind and works out the problems of human existence; which is at once an expression of the will of the Creator, and the power of the creature; and which beautifully harmonizes the dispensations of Providence with the agency of men—"FORTUNA FORTIBUS."

CHAPTER XXVI.

REVIEW—POLITICAL IDEAS IN THE NORTH, &c.

The Dogma of Numerical Majorities.—Its Date in the Yankee Mind.—Demoralization of the Idea of the Sovereignty of Numbers.—Experience of Minorities in American Politics.—Source of the Doctrine of "Consolidation."—The Slavery Question the logical Result of Consolidation.—Another Aspect of Consolidation in the Tariff.—Summary of the Legislation on the Tariff.—A Yankee Picture of the Poverty of the South.—John C. Calhoun,—President Davis' Opinion of his School of Politics.—"Nullification," as a Union Measure.—Mr. Webster's "Four Exhaustive Propositions."—The True Interpretation of the Present Struggle of the South.—The Northern Idea of the Sovereignty of Numbers.—Its Results in this War.—President Lincoln's Office.—The Revenge of the Yankee Congress upon the People.—The easy Surrender of their Liberties by the Yankees.—Lincoln and Cromwell.—Explanation of the Political Subserviency in the North.—Superficial Political Education of the Yankee.—His "Civilization."—The Moral Nature of the Yankee unmasked by the War.—His new Political System.—Burnside's "Death Order."—A Bid for Confederate Scalps.—A new Interpretation of the War.—The North as a Parasite.—The Foundations of the National Independence of the South.—Present Aspects of the War.—Its external Condition and Morals.—The Spirit of the South and the Promises of the Future.

THE chief value of history is the moral discoveries it makes. What is discovered in the records of the old Union and the events of the present war, of that portion of the American people commonly known as the Yankees, furnishes not only food for curiosity, but a valuable fund of philosophy.

In exploring the character and political experience of the people of the North, much of what is generally thought to be a confusion of vices may be traced to the peculiar idea that people have of the nature and offices of government. Their idea of government may be briefly stated as the *sovereignty of numbers*. This conception of political authority is of no late date with the people of the North; it came in their blood and in their traditions for centuries; it was part of the Puritanical idea; it was manifest in the Revolution of 1776 (the issues of which were saved by the conservatism of the South); and it is to-day exhibited in the passionate and despotic populace that wages war upon the Confederacy.

The peculiarities of this idea of government are very inter

esting, and its consequences are visible in every part and fibre of the society of the North. It excludes all the elements of virtue and wisdom in the regulation of political authority; it regards numbers as the great element of free government; it represents a numerical majority as infallible and omnipotent; and it gives opportunity to the flattery of demagogues to proclaim the divine rights and sagacity of numbers, and to denounce all constitutions which restrict liberty as most unrighteous inventions.

It is unnecessary to comment at length upon the error and coarseness of this idea of government. According to the interpretation of the Yankees, the body politic ought simply to have a political organization to bring out and enforce the will of the majority; and such an organization was supposed to be the general government made by our forefathers. But while it is unnecessary to discuss the fallacy of this view, it is entertaining and instructive to observe the train of demoralization it introduced into the society of the North and the consequences it involved.

The Northern idea of government was materialistic; it degraded political authority, because it despoiled it of its moral offices and represented it as an accident determined by a comparison of numbers. It destroyed the virtue of minorities; compelled them to servile acquiescence; and explains that constant and curious phenomenon in much of American politics—the rapid absorption of minorities after the elections. It laid the foundations of a despotism more terrible than that of any single tyrant; destroyed moral courage in the people; broke down all the barriers of conservatism; and substituted the phrase, "*the majority must govern,*" for the conscience and justice of society.

This idea, carried out in the early political government of America, soon attained a remarkable development. This development was the absurd doctrine of CONSOLIDATION. It denied the rights of the States; refused to interpret the Union from the authority of contemporaries, or from the nature of the circumstances in which it was formed, or from the objects which it contemplated; and represented it as a central political organization to enforce the divine pleasure of a numerical majority. The Union was thus converted, though with diffi-

culty, into a remorseless despotism, and the various and con
flicting interests and pursuits of one of the vastest political
bodies in the world were intrusted to the arrogant and reckless
majority of numbers.

The slavery question was the logical and inevitable result o
Consolidation. It is remarkable how many minds in America
have proceeded on the supposition that this agitation was accidental, and have distracted themselves with the foolish inquiry
why the Yankees assailed the domestic institutions of the South,
while they neglected to attack the similar institutions of Cuba
and Brazil. These minds do not appreciate the fact that the
slavery agitation was a *necessity* of the Northern theory of
government. Duty is the correlative of power; and if the
government at Washington in Yankee estimation was a consolidated organization, with power to promote the general
welfare by any means it might deem expedient, it was proper
that it should overthrow the hated institution of slavery in
the South. The central government was responsible for its
continuance or existence, in proportion to its power over it.
Under these circumstances, the duty of acting upon the subject of slavery was imperious, and amounted to a moral ne
cessity.

But the slavery agitation was not the only remarkable consequence of the Northern idea of the divine rights of majorities. It may be said that every political maxim of the
North has its practical and selfish application as well as its
moral and sentimental aspect. The same idea of the power of
numerical majorities that kindled the slavery disputes, gave
birth to the tariff and other schemes of legislation, to make the
Southern minority subservient and profitable to those who were
their masters by the virtue of numbers.

The slavery and tariff issues are singularly associated in
American politics; for one at least was an important auxiliary
to the other. It was necessary for the Northern people to
make their numerical power available to rule the Union; and
as slavery was strictly a sectional interest, it only had to be
made the criterion of the parties at the North to unite this
section and make it master of the Union. When the power of
the North could thus be united, it was easy to carry out its
measures of sectional ambition, encroachment, and aggrandize-

ment. The history of the enormous despotism of Yankee tariffs is easily summed up.

The war of 1812 left the United States with a debt of one hundred and thirty millions. To provide for the payment of this debt, heavy duties were laid on foreign goods; and as in the exigencies of the war some home manufactures had sprung up, which were useful and deserving, and which were in danger of sinking under foreign competition, on the return of peace it was proposed to regulate the tariff so as to afford them some assistance. Protection was an incidental feature in the tariff of 1816, and as such was zealously recommended even by John C. Calhoun, who was a conspicuous advocate of the bill. But the principle of protection once admitted, maintained its hold and enlarged its demands. In the tariffs of 1820, '24, and '28, it was successively carried further; the demand of the North for premiums to its manufacturing interests becoming more exacting and insolent.

In 1831 the public debt had been so far diminished as to render it certain that, at the existing rate of revenue, in three years the last dollar would be paid. The government had been collecting about twice as much revenue as its usual expenditures required, and it was calculated that if the existing tariff continued in operation, there would be, after three years, an annual surplus in the treasury of twelve or thirteen millions. Under these circumstances, the reduction of the tariff was a plain matter of justice and prudence; but it was resisted by the North with brazen defiance. Unfortunately, Mr. Clay was weak enough to court popularity in the North by legislative bribes, and it was mainly through his exertions that enough was saved of the protection principle to satisfy the rapacity of the Yankee; for which the statesman of Kentucky enjoyed a brief and indecent triumph in the North.

As an engine of oppression of the South, the tariff did its work well; for it not only impoverished her, but fixed on her a badge of inferiority, which was an unfailing mark for Yankee derision. The South had no great cities. Their growth was paralyzed, and they were scarcely more than the suburbs or Northern cities. The agricultural productions of the South were the basis of the foreign commerce of the United States; yet Southern cities did not carry it on. The resources of this unhappy part of the country were taxed for the benefit of the Northern people, and for forty years every tax imposed by Congress was laid with a view of subserving the interests of the North.

The blight of such legislation on the South was a source of varied gratification to the Yankee; especially that it gave him the conceit that the South was an inferior. The contrast between the slow and limited prosperity of the South and the swift and noisy progress of the North, was never more remarkable than at the period of the great tariff controversy of 1831-2. The condition of the country at this time is described by Parton, the Yankee biographer of Andrew Jackson, with flippant self-complacency. He says:

"The North was rushing on like a Western high-pressure steamboat, with rosin in the furnace, and a man on the safety-valve. All through Western New York, Ohio, Indiana, and Illinois, the primeval wilderness was vanishing like a mist, and towns were springing into existence with a rapidity that rendered necessary a new map every month, and spoiled the gazetteers as fast as they were printed. The city of New York began already to feel itself the London of the New World, and to calculate how many years must elapse before it would be the London of the world.

"The South meanwhile was depressed and anxious. Cotton was down, tobacco was down. Corn, wheat, and pork were down. For several years the chief products of the South had either been inclining downward, or else had risen in price too slowly to make up for the (alleged) increased price of the commodities which the South was compelled to buy. Few new towns changed the Southern map. Charleston languished, or seemed to languish, certainly did not keep pace with New York, Boston, and Philadelphia. No Cincinnati of the South became the world's talk by the startling rapidity of its growth. No Southern river exhibited at every bend and coyne of vantage a rising village. No Southern mind, distracted with the impossibility of devising suitable names for a thousand new places per annum, fell back in despair upon the map of the Old World, and selected at random any convenient name that presented itself, bestowing upon clusters of log huts such titles as Utica, Rome, Palermo, Naples, Russia, Egypt, Madrid, Paris, Elba, and Berlin. No Southern commissioner, compelled to find names for a hundred streets at once, had seized upon the letters of the alphabet and the figures of arithmetic, and called the avenues A, B, C, and D, and instead of naming his cross streets, numbered them."

For forty years the North reaped the fruits of partial legislation, while the South tasted the bitterness of oppression The shoemakers, the iron men, the sailmakers, and the cotton and woollen spinners in the North, clamored for protection against their English, Swedish, and Russian competitors, and easily obtained it. The South paid duties upon all articles that the tariff kept out of the country; but these duties, instead of going into the treasury as revenue, went into the purses of manufacturers as bounty. After paying this tribute money to the North, the South had then to pay her quota for the support of the government. The North, for there was perfect free trade between the States, had a preference over all the world for its wares in the markets of the South. This preference amounted to 20 or 30, or 40 or 50 per cent., and even more, according to the article and the existing tariff. It extended over a country having twelve millions of customers. The sum of the Yankee profits out of the tariff was thus enormous. Had the South submitted to the "Morrill tariff," it would have exacted from her something like one hundred million dollars as an annual tribute to the North. But submission has some final period, and the South has no longer a lot in the legislation at Washington.

In the tariff controversy of 1831–2, we find the premonitions of the present revolution. It is a curious circumstance that in the excitement of that period some medals were secretly struck, bearing the inscription, "*John C. Calhoun, First President of the Southern Confederacy.*" The name of the new power was correctly told. But the times were not ripe for a declaration of Southern independence, and even the public opinions of Mr. Calhoun resisted the suggestion of a dissolution of the Union.

The "nullification" doctrine of the statesmen of North Carolina, is one of the most interesting political studies of America; for it illustrates the long and severe contest in the hearts of the Southern people between devotion to the Union and the sense of wrong and injustice. Mr. Calhoun either did not dare to offend the popular idolatry, or was sincerely attached to the Union; but at the same time he was deeply sensible of the oppression it devolved upon the South. Nullification was simply an attempt to accommodate these two facts. It professed to find a remedy for the grievances of States without disturbing the Union; and the nullification of an unconstitutional law within the local jurisdiction of a State, was proposed as the process for referring the matter to some constitutional tribunal other than the Supreme Court, whose judgments should be above all influences of political party. It was a crude scheme, and only remarkable as a sacrifice to that peculiar idolatry in American politics which worshipped the name of the Union.

The present President of the Southern Confederacy—Mr. Jefferson Davis—has referred to the political principles of Mr. Calhoun, in some acute remarks made on the interesting occasion of his farewell to the old Senate at Washington. He says:

"A great man, who now reposes with his fathers, and who has often been arraigned for a want of fealty to the Union, advocated the doctrine of nullification, because it preserved the Union. It was because of his deep-seated attachment to the Union, his determination to find some remedy for existing ills short of a severance of the ties which bound South Carolina to the other States, that Mr. Calhoun advocated the doctrine of nullification, which he proclaimed to be peaceful; to be within the limits of State power, not to disturb the Union, but only to be the means of bringing the agent before the tribunal of the States for their judgment."

In defending, in the speech referred to, the action of the State of Mississippi in separating herself from the Union, Mr. Davis remarks with justice, that Secession belongs to another class of remedies than that proposed by the great South Carolinian. The Kentucky and Virginia resolutions of 1798, long the political text of the South, bore the seeds of the present revolution, for they laid the foundation for the right of secession in the sovereignty of the States; and Mr. Calhoun's deduction from them of his doctrine of nullification was narrow and incomplete.

But we shall not renew here vexed political questions. We

have referred at some length to the details of the old United States' tariffs and the incidental controversies of parties, because,we shall find here a peculiar development of the political ideas of the North. To all the ingenious philosophy of State rights; to the disquisitions of Mr. Calhoun and Mr. Tyler; to the discussions of the moral duties of the government, the North had but one invariable reply, and that was the sovereignty of the will of the majority. It recognized no sovereign but numbers, and it was thought to be a sufficient defence of the tariff and other legislation unequal to the South, that it was the work and the will of the majority.

It was during the agitation of the tariff that the consolidation school became firmly established. Mr. Webster, the mouth-piece of the manufacturing interest in the North, attempted by expositions of the Constitution to represent the government as a central organization of numbers, without any feature of originality to distinguish it from other rude democracies of the world. In his attempt to simplify it, he degraded it to the common-place of simple democracy, and insulted the wisdom of those who had made it. The political opinions or Mr. Webster were summed up in what he arrogantly called "Four Exhaustive Propositions." These propositions were famous in the newspapers of his day, and may be reproduced here as a very just summary of the political ideas of the North.

MR. WEBSTER'S FOUR EXHAUSTIVE PROPOSITIONS.

1. "That the Constitution of the United States is not a league, confederacy, or compact between the people of the several States in their sovereign capacity; but a government founded on the adoption of the people, and creating direct relations between itself and individuals."

2. "That no State authority has power to dissolve these relations; that nothing can dissolve them but revolution; and that, consequently, there can be no such thing as secession without revolution."

3. "That there is a supreme law, consisting of the Constitution of the United States, acts of Congress passed in pursuance of it, and treaties; and that in cases not capable of assuming the character of a suit in law or equity, Congress must

judge of, and finally interpret this supreme law, as often as it has occasion to pass acts of legislation; and in cases capable of assuming the character of a suit, the Supreme Court of the United States is the first interpreter."

4. "That the attempt by a State to abrogate, annul, or nullify an act of Congress, or to arrest its operation within her limits, on the ground that, in her opinion, such law is unconstitutional, is a direct usurpation on the just powers of the general government, and on the equal rights of other States; a plain violation of the Constitution; and a proceeding essentially revolutionary in its character and tendency."

It is in the light of these propositions that the present assertion of the independence of the South is denounced by the North as rebellion. And it is with reference to them and their savage doctrine of the power of numbers in a union of sovereign States, that we may in turn challenge the world to declare if the South in this struggle is not enlisted in the cause of free government, which is more important to the world than " the Union," which has disappeared beneath the wave of history.

In the present war the North has given faithful and constant indications of its dominant idea of the political sovereignty, as well as the military omnipotence of numbers. It is absurd to refer to the person of Abraham Lincoln as the political master of the North; he is the puppet of the vile despotism that rules by brute numbers. We have already referred to some of the characteristics of such despotism. We shall see others in this war, in the timidity and subservient hesitation to which such a government reduces party minorities, and in that destitution of honor which invariably characterizes the many-headed despotism of the people.

Mr. Lincoln was elected on a principle of deadly antagonism to the social order. His party found him subservient to their passions, and with the President in the hollow of their hand, for two years they have reigned triumphantly in the Congress at Washington. Such has been the stupendous lunacy and knavery of this body, that it will be regarded in all coming time as a blotch on civilization and a disgrace to the common humanity of the age.

There are some minds in the South which are prejudiced by

the impression that the power of the Lincoln party was broken by the fall elections of 1862 ; that it has lost the majority oi numbers in the North ; and that thereby the despotism which we have described as characteristic of the North is rapidly approaching the period of its dissolution or an era of reaction. But this reply to our theory does not take into account all the facts. The Republican party in the North still has the *majority of force*—a majority more dangerous and appalling than that of numbers, as it finds more numerous objects of revenge among its own people.

The Yankee Congress rejected at the polls has taken fearful revenge on the people who ventured an opinion hostile to the ruling dynasty. They have passed the bank, conscription, and *habeas corpus* suspension bills, thus placing every life and every dollar, and, indeed, every right of twenty millions of freeborn people at the absolute mercy of Abraham Lincoln. They have abated none of their legislation against the interests of humanity and the written and unwritten law of civilization in this war. They have added to it. They are organizing insurrections in South Carolina ; they have sent a negro army into Florida ; they are organizing black regiments in Tennessee But a few months ago the infamous law was passed at Washington known as " the Plunder Act," in which the Secretary of the Treasury was authorized to appoint agents to go South, collect all property, send it North, and have it sold. In different parts of the Confederacy the Yankee troops are now destroying all farming implements, seizing all provisions, and preventing the planting of crops, with the avowed determination of starving the Southern people into submission. Such a warfare contemplates the extermination of women and children as well as men, and proposes to inflict a revenge more terrible than the tortures of savages and the modern atrocities of the Sepoys.

It is, perhaps, not greatly to be wondered at that a people like the Yankees should show a brutal rage in warfare upon an enemy who has chastised their insolence and exasperated their pride, and that they should therefore be generally ready to give their adhesion to any train of measures calculated for revenge upon the South. But it is a matter of grave and solicitous inquiry that this people should so easily tolerate measures in the government which have been plainly directed against their own liberties, and which, while they have been applauding a " vigorous prosecution of the war," have established a savage despotism at home. It is yet more remarkable that the erection of this despotism should be hailed with a certain applause by its own victims. History has some instances of the servile and unnatural joys of a people in the surrender of their liberties; but none grosser than that in which has been inaugurated the throne of Abraham Lincoln at Washington.

There are numerous examples in history where great abilities or some scattered virtues in the character of a despot have won the flattery of minds not ignoble and unconscious of their humiliation. Milton in his Latin superlatives spoke of Cromwell very much after the same manner in which Mr. Lincoln is spoken of in Yankee vernacular. *Eum te agnoscunt omnes, Cromuelle, ea tu civis maximus et gloriosissimus, dux publici consilii, exercitum, fortissimorum imperator, pater patriæ gessisti.* But the Western lawyer and tavern-jester is not a Cromwell. No attractions of genius are to be found in the personal composition of Abraham Lincoln. His person in fact is utterly unimportant. He holds the reins for a higher power; and that power is the many-headed monster of Fanaticism, which by numbers or by force constrains the popular will and rules with the rod of iron.

The disposition generally of the Northern people to submit to or tolerate the assaults of the Washington government on their own liberties and the destruction of their civil rights, must proceed from permanent and well-defined causes. We have already hinted in these pages an explanation of this servile acquiescence in the acts of the government. It is doubtless the fruit of the false political education in the North, that gives none other but materialistic ideas of government, and inculcates the virtue of time-serving with all political majorities. It is to be attributed to the demoralization of the Yankee; to the servile habit of his mind; to his long practice of ubmission to the wild democracy of numbers,—all proceeding from that false idea of government which recognizes it only as the organ of an accidental party, and not as a self-existent principle of right and virtue. It is a melancholy fact that the

people of the North have long ceased to love cr to value lib
erty. They have ceased to esteem the political virtues; to
take any account of the moral elements of government; or to
look upon it else than as a physical power, to be exercised at
the pleasure of a party, and to be endured until reversed by
the accident of numbers.

The superficial political education of the people of the North
explains much that is curious in their society. Time-serving
of power gave them wealth, while it degraded their national
character. In the old government they easily surrendered their
political virtue for tariffs, bounties, &c.; and the little left of
it is readily sacrificed on the devilish altars of this war. Their
habit of material computation made them boastful of a "civilization" untouched by the spirits of virtue and humanity, consisting only of the rotten, material things which make up the
externals and conveniences of life, and the outer garments of society. Their wealth was blazed out in arts and railroads; common schools, the nurseries of an insolent ignorance; and gilded
churches, the temples of an impure religion. No people has
ever established more decisively the fact of the worthlessness
of what remains of "civilization," when the principle of liberty
is subtracted, or more forcibly illustrated how much of phos-
phorescent rottenness there is in such a condition.

"Their much-loved wealth imparts
Convenience, plenty, elegance, and arts;
But view them closer, craft and fraud appear,
Even liberty itself is bartered here;
At gold's superior charms all freedom flies,
The needy sell it and the rich man buys;
A land of tyrants and a den of slaves."

The present war has sufficiently demonstrated the mistake of
the North in the measure of its civilization, and convinced the
world that much of what it esteemed its former strength was
"but plethoric ill." It has done more than this, for it has unmasked the moral nature of the Yankee. It has exposed to
the detestation of the world a character which is the product
of materialism in politics and materialism in religion—the
spawn of the worship of power and the lust of gain. The
Yankee—who has followed up an extravagance of bluster by
the vilest exhibitions of cowardice—who has falsified his prate

of humanity by the deeds of a savage—who, in the South, has been in this war a robber, an assassin, a thief in the night, and at home a slave fawning on the hand that manacles him—has secured for himself the everlasting contempt of the world. The characteristics of a people who boasted themselves the most enlightened of Christian nations, are seen in a castrated civili-.ation; while the most remarkable qualities they have displayed in the war are illustrated by the coarse swagger and drunken fumes of such men as Butler, and the rouged lies of such "military authorities" as Halleck and Hooker.

All vestiges of constitutional liberty have long ago been lost in the North. The very term of "State rights" is mentioned with derision, and the States of the North have ceased to be more than geographical designations. No trace is left of the old political system but in the outward routine of the government. The Constitution of the United States is but "the skin of the immolated victim," and the forms and ceremonies of a republic are the disguises of a cruel and reckless despotism.

During the two miserable and disastrous years that Mr. Lincoln has held the presidency of the United States, he has made the institutions of his country but a name. The office of president is no longer recognized in its republican simplicity; it is overlaid with despotic powers, and exceeds in reality the most famous imperial titles. Not a right secured by the Constitution but has been invaded; not a principle of freedom but has been overthrown; not a franchise but has been trampled under foot. The infamous "death order" published by Burnside, more bloody than the Draconian penalty and more cruel than the rude decrees of the savage, is without a parallel in the domestic rule, or in the warfare of any people making the feeblest pretence to civilization. It assigns the penalty of death to "writers of letters sent by secret mails," and to all persons who "feed, clothe, or in any manner aid" the soldiers of the Confederacy. This infamous decree will live in history; it is already associated with a memorable martyrdom—that of Clement Vallandigham.

It is remarkable that the North finds great difficulty in assigning to the world the objects of the present mad and inhuman war. The old pretences made by the Yankees of fighting for a constitutional Union, and contesting the cause of free government for the world, are too absurd and disgusting to be repeated. They are unwilling to admit that they are fighting for revenge, and prosecuting a war, otherwise hopeless, for the gratification of a blind and fanatical hate. They have recently changed the political phrases of the war, and the latest exposition of its object is, that the North contends for "the life of the nation." If this means that a parasite is struggling for existence, and that the North desires the selfish aggrandizements of the Union, and its former tributes to its wealth, we shall not dispute the theory. But the plain question occurs, what right has the North to constrain the association of a people who have no benefit to derive from the partnership, and who, by the laws of nature and society, are free to consult their own happiness? The North has territory and numbers and physical resources enough for a separate existence, and if she has not virtue enough to sustain a national organization, she has no right to seek it in a compulsory union with a people who, sensible of their superior endowments, have resolved to take their destinies in their own hands.

There is one sense, indeed, in which association with the South does imply the national welfare of the North. The South gave to the old government all its ideas of statesmanship; it leavened the political mass with its characteristic conservatism; and it combated, and, to some extent, controlled the brutal theory that represented numbers as the element of free government. The revolutionary and infidel society of the North was moderated by the piety and virtues of the South, and the old national life was in some degree purified by the political ideas and romantic character of that portion of the country now known as the Confederacy. It is in this sense that the Southern element is desirable to the North, and that the Union involves "the life of the nation;" and it is precisely in the same sense that an eternal dissociation and an independent national existence are objects to the South not only of desire, but of vital necessity.

We can never go back to the embraces of the North. There is blood and leprosy in the touch of our former associate. We can never again live with a people who have made of this war a huge assassination; who have persecuted us with savage and cowardly hate; who gloat over the fancies of starving women and children; who have appealed to the worst passions of the black heart of the negro to take revenge upon us; and who, not satisfied with the emancipation proclamation and its scheme of servile insurrection, have actually debated in their State Legislatures the policy of paying negroes premiums for the murder of white families in the South.*

While we congratulate ourselves on the superiority of our political ideas over those of the North, and the purer life of our society, we do not forget that, although we have carried away much less of the territory and numbers of the old Union than have been left to our enemy, we still have a sufficiency of the material elements of a national existence.

The South has attempted to lay the foundations of national independence, with a territory as great as the whole of Europe, with the exception of Russia and Turkey; with a population four times that of the continental colonies; and with a capacity for commerce equivalent to nearly four-fifths of the exports of the old Union.

It is only necessary to glance at the contemporary aspects of the war to reassure our confidence in its destiny, and to renew our vows upon its altars. The hope of reconstruction is a vanity of the enemy. To mobocratic Yankees; to New England

---

* The following is taken from an Abolition pamphlet (1863), entitled "Interesting Debate," etc., in the Senate of Pennsylvania. It is characteristic of the blasphemous fanaticism of the Yankee and his hideous lust for blood:

"Mr. LOWRY—I believed then and now that He who watches over the sparrow will chastise us until we will be just towards ourselves and towards four millions of God's poor, down-cast prisoners of war. I said that I would arm the negro—that I would place him in the front of battle—and that I would invite his rebel master with his stolen arms to shoot his stolen ammunition into his stolen property at the rate of a thousand dollars a shot. I said further, that were I commander-in-chief, by virtue of the war power and in obedience to the customs of civilized nations, and in accordance with the laws of civilized nations, I would confiscate every rebel's property, whether upon two legs or four, and that I would give to the slave who would bring me his master's disloyal scalp one hundred and sixty acres of his master's plantation; nor would I be at all exacting as to where the scalp was taken off, so that it was at some point between the bottom of the ears and the top of the loins. This, sir, was my language long before Fremont had issued his immortal proclamation. The logic of events is sanctifying daily these anointed truths. Father, forgive thou those who deride and vilify me, because I enunciated them: they know not what they do."

" majorities ;" to the base crews of Infidelity and Abolitionism; to the savages who have taken upon their souls the curse of fratricidal blood and darkened an age of civilization with unutterable crime and outrage, the South can never surrender, giving up to such a people their name, their lands, their wealth, their traditions, their glories, their heroes newly dead, their victories, their hopes of the future. Such a fate is morally impossible. We have not paid a great price of life for nothing. We have not forgotten our dead. The flower of our youth and the strength of our manhood have not gone down to the grave in vain. We are not willing for the poor boon of a life dishonored and joyless to barter our liberties, surrender our homes to the spoiler, exist as the vassals of Massachusetts, or become exiles, whose title to pity will not exceed the penalty of contempt. Any contact, friendly or indifferent, with the Yankee, since the display of his vices, would be painful to a free and enlightened people. It would be vile and unnatural to the people of the South if extended across the bloody gulf of a cruel war, and unspeakably infamous if made in the attitude of submission.

SOUTHERN HISTORY OF THE WAR.

Very Truly & Respectfully Yours

Edwd A Pollard

SOUTHERN HISTORY

OF

THE WAR.

BY

E. A. POLLARD,

EDITOR OF THE "RICHMOND EXAMINER."

TWO VOLUMES IN ONE.

VOL. II.

————————

CONTENTS.

CHAPTER I.

CHAPTER II.

CHAPTER III.

CHAPTER IV.

CHAPTER V.

CHAPTER VI.

CHAPTER VII.

CHAPTER VIII.

CHAPTER IX.

CHAPTER X.

CHAPTER XI.

CHAPTER XII.

CHAPTER XIII.

AMERICAN IDEAS: A REVIEW OF THE WAR.

CHAPTER XIV.

CHAPTER XV.

CHAPTER XVI.

CHAPTER XVII.

CHAPTER XVIII.

CHAPTER XIX.

CHAPTER XX.

CHAPTER XXI.

CHAHTER XXII.

CHAPTER XXIII.

CHAPTER XXIV.

CHAPTER XXV.

CHAPTER XXVI.

APPENDIX No. I.

I.

Political Iconoclasm in America.—The two idols of "the Constitution" and "the Union."—Extravagant praises of the Constitution.—Its true value.—It contained a noble principle and glaring defects.—Character of the founders of the Constitution. —Hamilton.—Franklin.—His cookery-book philosophy.—His absurdities in the Convention.—The call for the Convention that formed the Constitution.—Three parties in the Convention.—The idea of a "national" government.—Conflict between the small and large States.—The result of this, the distinguishing feature of the Constitution.—That feature an accident, and not an *a priori* discovery.—Enumeration of defects in the Constitution.—The weakness and ignorance of its framers. —Its one conspicuous virtue and original principle.—Combination of State-rights

II.

III.

IV.

SOUTHERN HISTORY OF THE WAR.

THE THIRD YEAR.

CHAPTER I.

In the close of a former volume, we proposed to open the Third Year of the War with a revised and extended account of the battles fought between Fredericksburg and Chancellorsville, on the 1st, 2d, 3d and 4th of May, 1863. On examination, however, of what has already been written of these events, we find so little of authentic detail to add to it, that we shall content ourselves with a general reference to this impor tant series of engagements (known collectively as the battle of Chancellorsville), and a concise statement of results.

We have here again the old story of a great and bloody battle, defective in conclusion and barren in practical results. The Confederates had failed to capture Sedgwick's corps by not seizing Banks' Ford. The capture of his whc.e corps would then have been inevitable, for we held the access to Fredericksburg guarded. As it was, Hooker was able to cross the river under cover of night with all of his army but what had been lost in the casualties of the fight; and the Southern public were again treated to the old excuse that we had neither the men nor the facilities to pursue him.

But, notwithstanding these deficiencies of our victory, it was a great and brilliant one, and it gave the Confederacy occasion of pride second to none in the war. The Confederates had whipped what Hooker entitled "the finest army on the planet." They had done this with an effective fighting force which, compared with that of the enemy, was as three to ten. They had put thirty thousand of the enemy *hors du combat,* while our own casualties did not foot up more than one-third of that number. This battle, more than anything else, confirmed the fame of General Lee; for, however it had failed in accomplishing all that was possible, it was at least a victory won against an enemy of superior numbers, who had the advantage of the initiative and naturally secured that of position.

General Hooker had come with eight days' rations and a plan of battle combining all that was essential on paper to a complete success. General Lee had to watch the movements of Hooker until they were developed; to arrest his progress by attack; to engage him at the same time with a flank movement with a portion of his forces; and then to transfer his blows to Sedgwick. All this was done with a readiness of combination that showed a high order of military ability. Hooker was defeated by two critical circumstances: the flank movement of Jackson, executed with signal rapidity and decision, and the failure of Sedgwick to effect a junction. It was these movements and interpositions directed by Lee which ranked him among the greatest of modern strategists. He was now recognized as the master military mind of the Confederacy.

General Lee had, by a perceptible progress, risen to be one of the most remarkable men of the revolution. His military life had been one of steady advancement. He had graduated at West Point in 1829, at the head of his class; and it is said that, in that severe school and early test of the soldier, he had never been marked with a demerit or had received a repri

GEN. S. COOPER.

ir and. He had twice been brevetted in the Mexican war. For thirty years he had served the United States, and the period of disunion found him lieutenant-colonel of that famous regiment of cavalry of which Sydney Johnson was colonel.

Upon the secession of Virginia he was appointed commander in-chief of her forces, and organized an army with a system and rapidity that at once surprised and gratified the public. When President Davis made his appointments of generals, he was the third on the list: General Cooper being first, and General Sydney Johnson second. The appointments were made with reference to the rank held by each officer in the old army. The unfortunate campaign of General Lee in Western Virginia in the first year of the war threw a shadow on his fame; it disappointed his admirers and occasioned a very general denunciation of his ability. The battles around Richmond secured his fame. There was, in fact, but little military merit in them; but there was a great success, and results alone are the standards of popular appreciation. It was when General Lee moved out to the line of the Rappahannock that the true display of his abilities commenced; and his title to a substantial and abiding fame he had now crowned with the victory of Chancellorsville.

No one had ever accused General Lee of "genius." A sedate, methodical man, putting duty before everything else, illustrating the unselfish and Christian orders of virtue, almost sublime in his magnanimity, and uniting with these qualities a fair intellectual ability and an excellent practical judgment, this modern copy of Washington had nothing with which to dazzle mankind, but much with which to win its sober admiration. It has often been remarked how entirely limited by professional routine was the circle of intellectual accomplishments in the old army of the United States. Thirty years in this school had not made General Lee an "Admirable Crichton." Outside of his profession, his conversation was limited to a few commonplaces; he knew nothing of literature, and never attempted to draw an illustration from history. But the stranger who was at first shocked at such poverty of accomplishments in one so famous was soon won to admiration by the charming simplicity of a man who knew but little outside of the line of his duty, but in that was pre-eminently able and thoroughly heroic. It may be said of him that he was one of those few self-depreciating men whose magnanimity was not sentimental, and whose modesty was not unmanly.

In taking up the thread of our story after the battle of Chan cellorsville, we must now follow this great commander in on of the most extraordinary movements of the war, and to one of its most critical and imposing fields.

A great battle had now been twice fought on the line of the Rappahannock with no other effect than driving the enemy back to the hills of Stafford. The position was one in which he could not be attacked to advantage. It was on this reflection that General Lee resolved to maneuver Hooker out of Virginia, to clear the Shenandoah Valley of the troops of the enemy, and to renew the experiment of the transfer of hostilities north of the Potomac. It was a blow to the summer campaign of the enemy, calculated to disarrange it and relieve other parts of the Confederacy, but, above all, aimed at the prize of a great victory on Northern soil, long the aspiration of the Southern public.

The movement commenced on the 3d of June. The army of Northern Virginia had been thoroughly reorganized, and the question of Stonewall Jackson's successor had been deter mined to the satisfaction of the country. About the 20th of May the President commissioned both Major-generals R. S. Ewell and A. P. Hill as lieutenant-generals in the army of Northern Virginia. To each of these generals a corps was assigned, consisting of three divisions, General Longstreet, for this purpose, parting with one of his divisions (Anderson's), and A. P. Hill's old division being reduced by two brigades, was assigned to Major-general W. D. Pender. The two brigades thus taken from A. P. Hill's division, were united with Pettigrew's and another North Carolina brigade, and assigned to Major-general Heth, who, with Major-general Pender, was promoted from the rank of brigadier-generals. General A. P. Hill was assigned to the command of this corps, whilst General Ewell retained General Jackson's old corps, consisting of Early's division; Early having been made a Major-general in February, and receiving command of Ewell's old division; Rode's division and Trimble's division, to which General Edward Johnson, then just promoted to a major-gen eralslup, was assigned. Five of the six major-generals in the infantry department of this army, and the two corps generals, received their promotion within the twelve months past.

On the 3d of June McLaw's division of Longstreet's corps left Fredericksburg for Culpepper Court-house, and Hood's division, which was occupied on the Rapidan, marched to the same place. General Ewell's corps took up the line of march from its camps near Fredericksburg on the morning of June 4th, moving in the direction of Culpeper Court-House. On the same evening Longstreet's corps moved in the same direction. On Friday, June 5th, the enemy crossed a force below Fredericksburg, near the Bernard House, as if they intended to move once more upon our lines, stretching from Hamilton's crossing up to Fredericksburg. Ewell and Longstreet were halted at or near Locust Grove, in Orange county, to await the issue of the movement. Hooker having made this diversion in our front, set himself to work in removing his stores and in retiring his troops from the Stafford heights.

The forces of Longstreet and Ewell reached Culppeper Court-house by the 8th, at which point the cavalry, under General Stuart, was also concentrated. On the 9th a large force of Federal cavalry, strongly supported by infantry, crossed the Rappahannock at Beverly's and Kelly's fords, and attacked General Stuart. A severe engagement ensued, continuing from early in the morning until late in the afternoon, when the enemy was forced to recross the river with heavy loss, leaving four hundred prisoners, three pieces of artillery, and several colors in our hands.

This affair, popularly known as that of Brandy Station, was distinguished by an extraordinary exploit of Confederate troops. In one of the charges the Eleventh Virginia cavalry, under Colonel Lomax, captured, the third and last time, a battery of three pieces, the Sixth regiment and Thirty-fifth battalion having done so before them. Pushing his success, he divided his regiment, sending a squadron after the fugitives east of the railroad, while, with the remainder of his regiment, he assailed three regiments of cavalry, awaiting him at the depot. He routed this whole force completely.

THE CAPTURE OF WINCHESTER.

General Jenkins, with his cavalry brigade, had been ordered to advance towards Winchester to co-operate with the infantry in the proposed expedition into the Lower Valley, and at the same time General Imboden was directed, with his command, to make a demonstration in the direction of Romney, in order to cover the movement against Winchester, and prevent the enemy at that place from being reinforced by the troops on the line of the Baltimore and Ohio railroad. Both of these officers were in position when General Ewell left Culpepper Court-house, on the 16th. Crossing the Shenandoah near Front Royal, he detached Rodes' division to Berryville with instructions, after dislodging the forces stationed there, to cut off the communication between Winchester and the Potomac. With the divisions of Early and Johnson, General Ewell advanced directly upon Winchester, driving the enemy into his works around the town on the 13th. On the same day the troops at Berryville fell back before General Rodes, retreating to Winchester. Lieutenant-general Ewell, after consultation with Major-general Early, determined upon a flank movement, in order to reduce the town, as preferable to an assault in front. General Early at once began to move to attack a work of the enemy on the Pughtown road, on a hill commanding their main fort.

About an hour before sunset, on the evening of the 14th of June, General Early, without encountering scout or picket, was in easy cannon range of the enemy's work, which it was his purpose to assault. He at once set to work making disposition of his forces preparatory to the attack. Twenty pieces of artillery were placed in position. Hay's Louisiana brigade was now ordered to prepare for the charge. Our artillery opened a vigorous and well-directed fire on the enemy's works and guns. They responded with considerable spirit. Then Hay's Lousianians moved forward to the music of our cannon, which were still playing upon the works of the enemy. No Yankee dared show his head above the parapet. When our men got within two hundred yards of the enemy's works, suddenly our artillery ceased. And now Hay's men charge over an abattis,

LT. GEN. R. S. EWELL.

capturing the work and taking six pieces of artillery. The enemy vainly attempted, under cover of the guns of their main fort, to form in the bottom, between the two hills, and retake the works, but Hay's men manned and turned the enemy's own guns upon them. A few well-directed shots quickly broke them in confusion, and they retreated to the inner fort.

General Edward Johnston had been ordered to move to the Martinsburg road, and intercept the expected retreat of the enemy. His dispositions had scarcely been made when the Yankees charged, with loud yelling, hoping to break through our lines and escape. The battle raged for nearly an hour, our troops (but little over twelve hundred men) being greatly outnumbered. Just, however, as the last of our cartridges gave out, General Walker came up. The enemy had by this time divided into two columns, for the purpose of endeavoring to turn both of our flanks simultaneously. General Walker charged the party attempting to turn our right flank, and they surrendered. General Johnson moved the two Louisiana regiments, held in reserve, against the body of the enemy attempting to pass our left flank, and captured the greater part of them. Though Milroy and three hundred cavalry, besides some straggling infantry, made their escape, our captures here amounted to some twenty-five hundred men. The unfortunate Yankee commander fled to Harper's Ferry with his small party of fugitives.

General Rodes marched from Berryville to Martinsburg, entering the latter place on the 14th, where he took seven hundred prisoners, five pieces of artillery and a considerable quantity of stores. These operations cleared the valley of the enemy, those at Harper's Ferry withdrawing to Maryland Heights. More than four thousand prisoners, twenty-nine pieces of artillery, two hundred and seventy wagons and ambulances, with four hundred horses, were captured, besides a large amount of military stores. Our loss was small. On the night that Ewell appeared at Winchester, the Federal troops in front of A. P. Hill, at Fredericksburg, recrossed the Rappahannock, and the next day disappeared behind the hills of Stafford.

The onward movement of General Lee had now fairly commenced. The success of Winchester was a brilliant introduction to the campaign. The men who had achieved this success and who had been trained in marching, fighting and endurance, under Stonewall Jackson, were appropriately placed in the van of the imposing movement that now threatened the territory of the agitated and alarmed North.

The whole army of General Hooker withdrew from the line of the Rappahannock, pursuing the roads near the Potomac, and no favorable opportunity was offered for attack. It seemed to be the purpose of General Hooker to take a position which would enable him to cover the approaches to Washington City.

With this view, he occupied strong positions at Centreville and Manassas, so as to interpose his army between us and Washington, and thus prevent a sudden descent from the Blue Ridge by General Lee upon the Yankee capital. Meanwhile, Longstreet and Hill were following fast upon Ewell's track, the former reaching Ashby's and Snicker's gaps in time to prevent any movement upon Ewell's rear, and the latter (Hill) getting to Culpepper in good season to protect Longstreet's rear, or to co-operate with him in the event of an attack upon his flank, or to guard against any demonstration in the direction of Richmond.

When Longstreet occupied the mountain gaps, the cavalry, under General Stuart, was thrown out in his front to watch the enemy, now reported to be moving into Loudon. On the 17th, his cavalry encountered two brigades of ours, under General Stuart, near Aldie, and was driven back with loss. The next day the engagement was renewed, the Federal cavalry being strongly supported by infantry, and General Stuart, in turn, was compelled to retire.

The enemy advanced as far as Upperville and then fell back. In these engagements General Stuart took about four hundred prisoners and a considerable number of horses and arms.

In the meantime, a portion of Ewell's corps had crossed the Potomac at Williamsport. No report had been received that the Federal army had crossed the Potomac, and the absence of the cavalry rendered it impossible to obtain accurate information. In order, however, to retain it on the east side of the mountains after it should enter Maryland, and thus leave open our communication with the Potomac, through Hagerstown and Wiliiamsport, General Ewell had been instructed to send a division eastwards from Chambersburg to cross the South Mountains. Early's division was detached for this purpose, and proceeded as far east as York, while the remainder of the corps proceded to Carlisle.

On the 24th, the whole of A. P. Hill's corps crossed the Potomac at Shepherdstown, that of Longstreet having previously reached the Maryland shore by the Williamsport ford—the corps of General Longstreet being composed of the divisions of McLaws, Pickett and Hood, whilst that of Hill consisted of Pender, Heth and Anderson. The columns reunited at Hagerstown, and advanced thence into Pennsylvania, encamping near Chambersburg on the 27th.

The invasion of Pennsylvania had now progressed to a crisis, which was the signal of unbounded excitement in the North. On the 29th, Brigadier-general Jenkins and command went within sight and artillery range of Harrisburg, with a view, it was thought, of attack. The light horsemen of the Confederates scoured the southern region of Pennsylvania. For weeks the dashing and adventurous cavalry of Jenkins and Imboden were persistently busy in scouring the country between the Susque-hannah and the Alleghanies, the Monocacy and the Potomac, and from the lines before Harrisburg their trumpets had sounded.

At the first news of the invasion, Lincoln had called for a hundred thousand men to defend Washington. Governor Andrews offered the whole military strength of Massachusetts in the terrible crisis. Governor Seymour, of New York, summoned McClellan to grave consultations respecting the defences of Pennsylvania. The bells were set to ringing in Brooklyn. Regiment after regiment was sent off from New York to Philadelphia. The famous Seventh regiment took the field, and proceeded to Harrisburg. The Dutch farmers in the valley drove their cattle to the mountains, and the archives were removed from Harrisburg.

Hooker had declined a battle in Virginia. This hesitation was to cost him his command; it was the theme of bitter reproach in the North. Lee had been allowed to obtain the important advantage of the military initiative, and had gained time enough to firmly establish his communications in the rear of his base of operations on the other side of the Potcmac. Having brought up and consolidated his forces with consummate address he was in a position to hurl them wherever he might desire.

On crossing the Potomac, Hooker had taken up a line extending from Washington to Baltimore, expecting General Lee to offer him battle in Maryland. Finding himself disappointed in this, and compelled by his superiors at Washington, or smarting under their distrust, he relinquished his command to George C. Meade, who, finding that Lee had deflected in his march through Pennsylvania, moved towards Chambersburg to meet him.

General Lee had proposed to attack Harrisburg. On the 30th, as General Ewell was preparing to march to Harrisburg, twenty miles distant, an order came to him to unite his corps with the rest of the army near Gettysburg. Major-general Early, of this corps, who, after crossing the river, had moved to York, and who was then at that place, was at once notified, and the corps immediately took up the line of march.

Important news had been received. On the night of the 29th, information was brought to General Lee's head-quarters that the Federal army, having crossed the Potomac, was advancing northwards, and that the head of the column had reached the South Mountain. As our communications with the Potomac were thus menaced, it was resolved to prevent his further progress in that direction by concentrating our army on the east side of the mountains. Accordingly, Longstreet and Hill were directed to proceed from Chambersburg to Gettysburg, to which point General Ewell had been also instructed to march.

A day pregnant with a momentous issue was at hand. The two armies which had ceased to confront each other since the breaking up of the Fredericksburg lines found themselves again face to face near Gettysburg, on Wednesday, July 1st.

Before turning to the bloody page of Gettysburg, the curiosity of the reader naturally inquires into the conduct of the Confederate army on the long march which had at last penetrated the fruitful fields of Pennsylvania. Considering what the country and homes of the Confederacy had suffered from the ferocity of the enemy, it might have been supposed that

Lee's army would have improved their grand opportunity in Pennsylvania, not indeed by an imitation of the enemy's outrages in the South, but by that eminently justifiable retaliation which, while it scorns to mete out in kind the enemy's crime, in arson, pillage and innocent blood, insists upon doing him some commensurate injury by severe acts of war, done with deliberation and under the authority of superiors. Such expectations were disappointed. Every just and intelligent reader of the records of this war must wonder that General Lee gave a protection to the citizens of Pennsylvania which had never been accorded to our own people; that, with an obtuseness that is inexplicable, he confounded two very different classes of retaliation; and that, while forbidding the irregular pillage of the country, and threatening marauders with death (which admirable orders were heartily approved by all people in the South), he also restrained his army from laying waste the country in line of battle, or destroying the enemy's subsistence. Such tenderness, the effect of a weak and strained chivalry, or more probably that of deference to European opinion, is another of the many instances which the war has furnished of the simplicity and sentimental facility of the South.

General Lee attempted conciliation of a people who were little capable of it, but were always ready to take counsel of their fears. The effect of his moderate warfare on such a people was to irritate them without intimidating them; in fact, to compose their alarms and to dissuade them from what had been imagined as the horrors of invasion. In this respect, his movement into Pennsylvania gave to the enemy a certain moral comfort, and encouraged the prosecution of the war.

With reference, now, to the military features of the movement, it must rank with the most remarkable marches on record. 'Looking back to the Rappahannock, we now see what Lee had accomplished. When he set out upon the northern expedition, he was confronted by one of the largest and best-appointed armies the enemy ever had in the field. Winchester, Martinsburg, Harper's Ferry and Berryville were garrisoned by hostile forces. The cavalry of the enemy were in splendid condition. General Lee marched over the Blue Ridge and across the Shenandoah and Potomac rivers. The mountain passes and the fords of the rivers might have been effectually blockaded. The whole of the lower valley was in possession of the enemy. And yet, starting from Culpepper Court-house, General Lee conducted his army across the mountains, along the valley and over the rivers, without encountering serious opposition. Except a few cavalry engagements, the army marched from Culpepper Court-house to Gettysburg, in Pennsylvania, without resistance.

The conjuncture which had been reached was the most critical of the war. Meade's army was the only real obstacle which could impede the triumphant march of the army of Lee into the very heart of the Yankee States, and in whatever direction he might choose to push his campaign. The press attempted some ridiculous comfort by writing vaguely of thousands of militia springing to arms. But the history of modern warfare afforded better instruction, for it taught clearly enough that an invading army of regular and victorious troops could only be effectively checked by the resistance of a similar army in the field, or of fortified places strong enough to compel a regular siege. In Richmond, the garish story of the newspapers prepared the public mind for a great victory. There was the renewed and feverish anticipation of an early peace. The elated public of the Confederate capital little imagined that, in a few days, events were to occur to turn back the war for years.

THE BATTLE OF GETTYSBURG.

The march towards Gettysburg was conducted slowly. At 10 o'clock A. M., on the 1st instant, Heth's division, of Hill's corp, being ahead, encountered the enemy's advance line, the Eleventh corps, about three miles west of Gettysburg. Here a sharp engagement ensued, our men steadily advancing and driving the enemy before them to the town, and to a range of hills or low mountains running out a little east of south from the town.

General Reynolds, who commanded the enemy's advance, rode forward to inspect the ground and select a position for his line of battle. The Confederates, distinguishing him from his uniform to be an officer of high rank, opened upon him with heavy volleys of infantry fire. He was struck by several balls, and died instantly without uttering a word.

About an hour after the opening of the engagement, which was principally of artillery, General Ewell, who was moving from the direction of Carlisle, came up and took a position on our extreme left. Rodes came into the engagement on the flank of the enemy, who were confronting A. P. Hill, and occupied the most commanding point of the very ridge with artillery which the enemy were upon. This ridge runs in the shape of a crescent around Gettysburg, following the windings of a creek which is between it and the town.

After our artillery had been engaged for some half an hour, with admirable effect, the enemy were observed to be moving rapidly from Hill's front to that of Rodes, and to be advancing their new columns against Rodes from the town. Rodes, his dispositions having been made, advanced his whole line. It had first to cross a field, six hundred yards wide, and enter woods—immediately upon entering which it became hotly engaged.

The Alabama brigade (Rodes' old command) advanced somewhat confusedly, owing, it is said, to a misconception as to the direction which it should take, and, whilst confused, became engaged, and was forced back with its lines broken, though reinforced by the Fifth Alabama, which uncovered Lawson's brigade. This brigade was thought to have behaved badly ; it was reported to General Rodes, in the midst of the fight, that one of the regiments had raised the white flag, and gone over in a body to the enemy. The only foundation for this report was, that two of the regiments were almost entirely surrounded, in consequence of the giving way of the Alabama brigade and the concentration of the enemy at that point, and were either killed or captured almost to a man. The gallant resistance, however, which they made is shown by a statement coming from General Rodes himself : that, riding along behind where their line had been, he thought he observed a regiment lying down, as if to escape the Yankee fire. On going up, however, to force them into the fight, he found they were all corpses.

As the battle wavered General Early came up, and got his artillery into position so as to enfilade and silence batteries which were then occupied in an attempt to enfilade Rodes'

battery. As the enemy attempted a flank movement, Gordon's
brigade of gallant Georgians was ordered to make a charge.
They crossed a small stream and valley, and entered a long
narrow strip of an opposite slope, at the top of which the enemy
had a strong force posted. For five minutes nothing could be
heard or seen save the smoke and roar proceeding from the
heavy musketry, and indicating a desperate contest; but the
contest was not long or uncertain. The Yankees were put to
flight, and our men pressed them, pouring a deadly fire at the
flying fugitives. Seeing a second and larger line near the
town, General Early halted General Gordon until two other
brigades (Hayes' and Hoke's) could come up, when a second
charge was made, and three pieces of artillery, besides several
entire regiments of the enemy, were captured.

There should not be lost from the records of the individual
heroism of the Confederacy an incident of this battle. During
a lull in the engagement, when the enemy were reforming and
awaiting reinforcements, Lieutenant Roberts, of the Second Mississippi, observing, some distance off, but nearer the enemy's than
our own fires, two groups, each consisting of from seven to ten
men, and each guarding a stand of colors, called for volunteers
to take them. Four gallant spirits from his own, and an equal
number from the Forty-second Mississippi regiment, readily responded, and soon a dash is made for the colors. A hand-to-hand
fight ensued, in which all on both sides were either killed or
wounded, except Private McPherson, who killed the last
Yankee color-bearer and brought off the colors, Lieutenant
Roberts being killed just as he was seizing one of the colors.

The result of the day's fight may be summed up thus: We
had attacked a considerable force; had driven it over three
miles; captured five thousand prisoners, and killed and
wounded many thousands. Our own loss was not heavy,
though a few brigades suffered severely.

Unfortunately, however, the enemy, driven through Gettysburg, got possession of the high range of hills south and east
of the town. Here was the fatal mistake of the Confederates.
In the engagement of the 1st instant, the enemy had but a
small portion of his force up, and if the attack had been pressed
in the afternoon of that day there is little doubt that our forces
could have got the heights and captured this entire detach-

ment of Meade's army. But General Lee was not aware of the enemy's weakness on this day. In fact, he had found himself unexpectedly confronted by the Yankee army. He had never intended to fight a general battle so far from his base. He was forced to deliver battle where prudence would have avoided it; he could obtain no certain information of the disposition of Meade's forces; and the inaction of an evening—the failure to follow up for a few hours a success—enabled the Yankee commander to bring up his whole army, and post it on an almost impregnable line which we had permitted a routed detachment of a few thousand men to occupy.

During the night, General Meade and staff came up to the front. Before morning all his troops but the Sixth corps, commanded by General Sedgwick, arrived on the field. The forces of the enemy were disposed on the several hills or ridges, so as to construct a battle-line in the form of a crescent.

The town of Gettysburg is situated upon the northern slope of this ridge of hills or mountain range, and about one and a half or two miles from its summit. The western slope of this range was in cultivation, except small "patches," where the mountain side is so precipitous as to defy the efforts of the farmer to bring it into subjection to the ploughshare. At the foot of the mountain is a narrow valley, from a mile to two miles in width, broken in small ridges running parallel with the mountain. On the western side of the valley rises a long, high hill, mostly covered with heavy timber, but greatly inferior in altitude to the mountain range upon which the enemy had taken position, but running nearly parallel with it. The valley between this ridge and the mountain was in cultivation, and the fields were yellow with the golden harvest. About four or five miles south from Gettysburg, the mountain rises abruptly to an altitude of several hundred feet. Upon this the enemy rested his left flank, his right being upon the crest of the range about a mile or a mile and a half from Gettysburg.

Our line of battle was formed along the western slope of the second and inferior range described above, and in the following order: Ewell's corps on the left, beginning at the town with Early's division, then Rodes' division; on the right of Rodes' division was the left of Hill's corps, commencing with Heth's, then Pender's and Anderson's divisions. On the right of Anderson's division was Longstreet's left, McLaw's div sion being next to Anderson's, and Hood on the extreme right of our line, which was opposite the eminence upon which the enemy's left rested.

THE SECOND DAY.

The preparations for attack were not completed until the afternoon of the 2d. Late in the afternoon an artillery attack was made by our forces on the left and centre of the enemy, which was rapidly followed by the advance of our infantry, Longstreet's corps on our side being principally engaged. A fearful but indecisive contest ensued, and for four hours the sound of musketry was incessant. The main object of the attack of the Confederates was the famous Cemetery Hill, the key of the enemy's position. The enemy's artillery replied vigorously. The roar and thunder and flame and smoke of artillery, and the screech of shells, so completely filled the heavens that all else seemed forgotten.

General Ewell had been ordered to attack directly the high ground on the enemy's right, which had already been partially fortified. It was half an hour of sunset when Johnson's infantry were ordered forward to the attack. In passing down the hill on which they had been posted, and whilst crossing the creek, they were much annoyed by the fire to which they were subjected from the enemy's artillery, which, from Cemetery Hill poured nearly an enfilade fire upon them. The creek was wide, and its banks steep, so that our men had to break ranks in order to cross it. Having passed the creek, General Jones' brigade was thrown into disorder and retired a short distance.

On the extreme left, General G. H. Stewart's brigade was more successful. Pushing around to the enemy's left, he enfiladed and drove the enemy from a breastwork they had built in order to defend their right flank, and which ran at right angles to the rest of their lines up the mountain side. The enemy, however, quickly moved forward a force to retake it, but were repulsed, our troops occupying their own breastworks in order to receive their attack. General Stewart made no further effort to advance. Night had nearly fallen, and the ground was new to him.

General Early, upon hearing General Johnson's infantry engaged, sent forward Hayes' Louisiana and Hoke's North Carolina brigades. The troops, advancing as a storming party, quickly passed over a ridge and down a hill. In a valley below they met two lines of the Federals posted behind stonewalls. These they charged. At the charge the Federals broke and fled up the hill closely pursued by our men. It was now dark; but Hayes and Avery, still pursuing, pushed the enemy up the hill and stormed the Cemetery heights.

The contest here was intensely exciting and terrible. The gloom of the falling night was lighted up by the flashes of the enemy's guns. Thirty or forty pieces, perhaps more, were firing grape and canister with inconceivable rapidity at Early's column. It must have been that they imagined it to have been a general and simultaneous advance, for they opened on our men in three or four directions besides that which they were attacking.

Hayes' and Hoke's brigades pressed on and captured two or three lines of breastworks and three or four of their batteries of artillery. For a few moments every gun of the enemy on the heights was silenced; but, by the time General Hayes could get his command together, a dark line appeared in front of them and on either flank a few yards off. The true situation soon became clear. The Yankees were bringing up at least a division to retake the works. General Hayes, being unsupported by the troops on his right (which were from Hill's corps), was compelled to fall back.

Major-general Rodes commenced to advance simultaneously with General Early. He had, however, more than double the distance of Early to go, and being unsupported by the troops on his right, who made no advance, he consequently moved slower than he would have done had he been supported. Before reaching the enemy's works Early had been repulsed, and so General Rodes halted, thinking it useless to attack since he was unsupported.

When the second day closed this was the position of Ewell's corps. Johnson's left had gained important ground, part of it being a very short distance from the top of the mountain, which, if once gained, would command the whole of the enemy's position; but his right had made no progress. Early's attack, almost a brilliant success, had produced no results, and he occupied nearly his former position. Rodes, having advanced nearly half-way to the enemy's works, and finding there good cover for his troops, remained in his advanced position.

But we must take the reader's attention to another part of the field, where a more dramatic circumstance than Early's momentary grasp of victory had occurred.

General Hill had been instructed to threaten the centre of the Yankee line, in order to prevent reinforcements being sent to either wing, and to avail himself of any opportunity that might present itself to attack.

On the right of Hill's corps and the left of Longstreet, being joined on to Barksdale's brigade of McLaw's division, was Wilcox's brigade, then Perry's, Wright's, Posey's, Mahone's. At half-past five o'clock Longstreet commenced the attack, and Wilcox followed it up by promptly moving forward; Perry's brigade quickly followed, and Wright moved simultaneously with him. The two divisions of Longstreet's corps soon encountered the enemy, posted a little in rear of the Emmetsburg turnpike, which winds along the slope of the range upon which the enemy's main force was concentrated. After a short but spirited engagement, the enemy was driven back upon the main line upon the crest of the hill. McLaw's and Hood's divisions made a desperate assault upon their main line; but, owing to the precipitate and very rugged character of the slope, were unable to reach the summit.

After Barksdale's brigade, of McLaw's division, had been engaged for some time, Wilcox, Wright, and Perry, were ordered forward, encountering a line of the enemy, and soon putting them to rout. Still pressing forward, these three brigades met with another and stronger line of the enemy, backed by twelve pieces of artillery. No pause was made. The line moved rapidly forward and captured the artillery.

Another fresh line of battle was thrown forward by the enemy. Wright had swept over the valley under a terrific fire from the batteries posted upon the heights, had encountered the enemy's advance line, and had driven him across the Emmetsburg pike, to a position behind a stone wall, or fence, which runs parallel with the pike, and about sixty or eighty yards in front of the batteries on the heights, and immediately under them. Here the enemy made a desperate attempt to retrieve his fortunes. The engagement lasted for fifteen or twenty minutes. Charging up the steep sides of the mountains, the Confederates succeeded in driving the enemy from behind the wall at the point of the bayonet. Rushing forward with a shout, they gained the summit of the heights, driving the enemy's infantry in disorder and confusion into the woods beyond.

The key of the enemy's position was for a moment in our hands. But the condition of the brave troops who had wrested it by desperate valor, had become critical in the extreme. Wilcox, Perry, and Wright, had charged most gallantly over a distance of more than three-quarters of a mile, breaking two or three of the enemy's lines of battle, and capturing two or three batteries of artillery. Of course, our lines were greatly thinned, and our troops much exhausted. No reinforcements were sent this column by the Lieutenant-general commanding. The extent of their success was not instantly appreciated. A decisive moment was lost.

Wright's little brigade of Georgians had actually got in the enemy's entrenchments upon the heights. Perceiving, after getting possession of the enemy's works, that they were isolated—more than a mile from support—that no advance had been made on their left, and just then seeing the enemy's flanking column on their right and left flanks rapidly converging in their rear, these noble Georgians faced about, abandoning all the guns they had captured, and cut their way back to our main lines, through the enemy, who had now almost entirely surrounded them.

The results of the day were unfortunate enough. Our troops had been repulsed at all points save where Brigadier-general Stewart held his ground. A second day of desperate fighting and correspondingly frightful carnage was ended. But General Lee still believed himself and his brave army capable of taking these commanding heights, and thus to be able to dictate a peace on the soil of the free States.

THE THIRD DAY.

The third day's battle was again to be commenced by the Confederates. At midnight a council of war had been held by the enemy, at which it was determined that the Confederates would probably renew the attack at daylight on the following morning, and that for that day the Yankees had better act purely on the defensive.

The enemy's position on the mountain was well-nigh impregnable, for there was no conceivable advance or approach that could not be raked and crossed with the artillery. All the heights and every advantageous position along the entire line where artillery could be massed or a battery planted, frowned down on the Confederates through brows of brass and iron. On the slopes of the mountain was to occur one of the most terrific combats of modern times, in which more than two hundred cannon were belching forth their thunders at one time, and nearly two hundred thousand muskets were being discharged as rapidly as men hurried with excitement and passion could load them.

Early in the morning preparations were made for a general attack along the enemy's whole line, while a large force was to be concentrated against his centre, with the view of retaking the heights captured and abandoned the day before. Longstreet massed a large number of long-range guns (fifty-five in number) upon the crest of a slight eminence just in front of Perry's and Wilcox's brigades, and a little to the left of the heights, upon which they were to open. Hill massed some sixty guns along the hill in front of Posey's and Mahone's brigades, and almost immediately in front of the heights. At twelve o'clock, while the signal-flags were waving swift intelligence along our lines, the shrill sound of a Whitworth gun broke the silence, and the cannonading commenced.

The enemy replied with terrific spirit, from their batteries posted along the heights. Never had been heard such tremendous artillery firing in the war. The warm and sultry air was hideous with discord. Dense columns of smoke hung over the beautiful valley. The lurid flame leaps madly from the cannon's mouth, each moment the roar grows more intense; now chime in volleys of small arms. For one hour and a half this most terrific fire was continued, during which time the shrieking of shells, the crashing of falling timber, the fragments of rock flying through the air, shattered from the cliffs by solid shot, the heavy mutterings from the valley between the opposing armies, the *splash* of ·bursting shrapnel, and the fierce neighing of wounded artillery-horses made a picture terribly grand and sublime.

But there was now to occur a scene of moral sublimity and heroism unequalled in the war. The storming party was moved up—Pickett's division in advance, supported on the right by Wilcox's brigade, and on the left by Heth's division, commanded by Pettigrew. With steady measured tread the division of Pickett advanced upon the foe. Never did troops enter a fight in such splendid order. Their banners floated defiantly in the breeze as they pressed across the plain. The flags which had waved amid the wild tempest of battle at Gaines' Mill, Frazer's Farm, and Manassas, never rose more proudly. Kemper, with his gallant men, leads the right; Garnett brings up the left; and the veteran Armistead, with his brave troops, moves forward in support. The distance is more than half a mile. As they advance the enemy fire with great rapidity—shell and solid shot give place to grape and canister—the very earth quivers beneath the heavy roar—wide gaps are made in this regiment and that brigade. The line moves onward, cannons roaring, grape and canister plunging and ploughing through the ranks, bullets whizzing as thick as hail-stones in winter, and men falling as leaves fall in the blasts of autumn.

As Pickett got well under the enemy's fire, our batteries ceased firing, for want, it is said, of ammunition. It was a fearful moment—one in which was to be tested the pride and mettle of glorious Virginia. Into the sheets of artillery fire advanced the unbroken lines of Picketts' brave Virginians. They have reached the Emmettsburg road, and here they meet a severe fire from heavy masses of the enemy's infantry, posted behind the stone fence, while their artillery, now free from the annoyance of our artillery, turn their whole fire upon this devoted band. Still they remain firm. Now again they advance. They reach the works—the contest rages with intense fury—men fight almost hand to hand—the red cross and the "stars and stripes" wave defiantly in close proximity. A Federal officer dashes forward in front of his shrinking columns, and with flashing sword, urges them to stand. General Pickett, seeing the splendid valor of his troops, moves among them as if courting death. The noble·Garnett is dead, Armistead wounded, and the brave Kemper, with hat in hand, still cheering on his men falls from his horse. But Kemper and Armistead have already planted their banners in the enemy's works. The glad shout of victory is already heard.*

But where is Pettigrew's division—where are the supports? The raw troops had faltered and the gallant Pettigrew himself had been wounded in vain attempts to rally them. Alas, the victory was to be relinquished again. Pickett is left alone to contend with the masses of the enemy now pouring in upon him on every side. Now the enemy move around strong flanking bodies of infantry, and are rapidly gaining Pickett's rear. The order is given to fall back, and our men commence the movement, doggedly contesting for every inch of ground. The enemy press heavily our retreating line, and many noble spirits who had passed safely through the fiery ordeal of the advance and charge, now fall on the right and on the left.

This division of Virginia troops, small at first, with ranks now torn and shattered, most of the officers killed or wounded, no valor able to rescue victory from such a grasp, annihilation or capture inevitable, slowly, reluctantly, fell back. It was

---

* A correspondent of a Yankee paper thus alludes to the traces of the struggle at the Cemetry :

"Monuments and headstones lie here and there overturned. Graves, once carefully tended by some loving hand, have been trampled by horses' feet until the vestiges of verdure have disappeared. The neat and well-trained shrubbery has vanished, or is but a broken and withered mass of tangled brushwood. On one grave lies a dead artillery horse fast decomposing under a July sun. On another lie the torn garments of some wounded soldier, stained and saturated with his blood. Across a small headstone, bearing the words "To the memory of our beloved child, Mary," lie the fragments of a musket, shattered by a cannon shot. In the centre of the space enclosed by an iron fence and containing a half-dozen graves, a few rails are still standing where they were erected by our soldiers and served to support the shelter tents of a bivouacking squad. A family shaft has been broken to fragments by a shell, and only the base remains, with a portion of the inscription thereon. Stone after stone felt the effect of the *feu d'enfer* that was poured upon the crest of the hill. Cannon thundered, and foot and horse soldiers trampled over the sleeping-places of the dead. Other dead were added to those who are resting there, and many a wounded soldier still lives to remember the contest above those silent graves."

not given to these few remaining brave men to accomplish human impossibilities. The enemy dared not follow them beyond their works. But the day was already lost.

The field was covered with Confederates slowly and sulkily retiring in small broken parties under a heavy fire of artillery. There was no panic. Never did a commanding general behave better in such trying circumstances than did Lee. He was truly great in disaster. An English colonel who witnessed the fight, says: "I joined General Lee, who had, in the meanwhile, come to the front on becoming aware of the disaster. General Lee was perfectly sublime. He was engaged in rallying and encouraging the broken troops, and was riding about a little in front of the wood quite alone—the whole of his staff being engaged in a similar manner further to the rear. His face, which is always placid and cheerful, did not show signs of the slightest disappointment, care, or annoyance, and he was addressing to every soldier he met a few words of encouragement, such as, 'All this will come right in the end; we'll talk it over afterwards; but, in the meantime, all good men must rally. We want all good and true men just now,' &c. He spoke to all the wounded men that passed him, and the slightly wounded he exhorted 'to bind up their hurts and take up a musket' in this emergency. Very few failed to answer his appeal, and I saw many badly wounded men take off their hats and cheer him."

"It is difficult," says the same intelligent spectator, "to exaggerate the critical state of affairs as they appeared about this time. If the enemy or their general had shown any enterprise there is no saying what might have happened. General Lee and his officers were evidently fully impressed with a sense of the situation; yet there was much less noise, fuss, or confusion of orders, than at any ordinary field day; the men, as they were rallied in the wood, were brought up in detachments and lay down quiet and coolly in the positions assigned to them."

At night the Confederate army held the same position from which it had driven the enemy two days previous. The starry sky hung over a field of hideous carnage. In the series of engagements a few pieces of artillery were captured by the Confederates and nearly seven thousand prisoners taken, two thousand of whom were paroled on the field. Our loss in killed, wounded, and prisoners, was quite ten thousand. The enemy's loss probably exceeded our own, as the Yankees were closely crowded on the hills, and devoured by our artillery fire. The information of the enemy's loss is perhaps most accurately obtained from the bulletin furnished by his Surgeon-general, which stated that he had something over twelve thousand Yankee wounded under his control. Counting one killed for four wounded, and making some allowance for a large class of wounded men who had not come under the control of the officers referred to, we are justified in stating the enemy's loss in casualties at Gettysburg as somewhere between fifteen and eighteen thousand. Our loss, slighter by many thousands in comparison, was yet frightful enough. On our side Pickett's division had been engaged in the hottest work of the day, and the havoc in its ranks was appaling. Its losses on this day are famous, and should be commemorated in detail. Every brigadier in the division was killed or wounded. Out of twenty-four regimental officers, only two escaped unhurt. The Ninth Virginia went in two hundred and fifty strong and came out with only thirty-eight men.

Conspicuous in our list of casualties was the death of Major-general Pender. He had borne a distinguished part in every engagement of this army, and was wounded on several occasions while leading his command with admirable gallantry and ability. Brigadier-generals Barksdale and Garnett were killed, and Brigadier-general Semmes mortally wounded, while leading their troops with the courage that had always distinguished them. The brave and generous spirit of Barksdale had expired, where he preferred to die, on the ensanguined field of battle. Of this "haughty rebel," who had fallen within their lines, the Yankees told with devilish satisfaction the story that his end was that of extreme agony, and his last words were to crave, as a dying boon, a cup of water, and a stretcher from an ambulance boy. The letter of a Yankee officer testifies that the brave and suffering hero declared with his last breath that he was proud of the cause he died fighting for; proud of the manner in which he received his death; and confident that his countrymen were invincible.

The fearful trial of a retreat from a position far in the enemy's country was now reserved for General Lee. Happily he had an army with zeal unabated, courage intrepid, devotion unchilled; with unbounded confidence in the wisdom of that great chieftian who had so often led them to victory. The strength of the enemy's position; the reduction of our ammunition; the difficulty of procuring supplies, these left no choice but retreat.

On the night of the 4th, General Lee's army began to retire by the road to Fairfield, without any serious interruption on the part of the enemy. In passing through the mountains, in advance of the column, the great length of the trains exposed them to attack by the enemy's cavalry, which captured a number of wagons and ambulances; but they succeeded in reaching Williamsport without serious loss.

They were attacked at that place on the 6th, by the enemy's cavalry, which was gallantly repulsed by General Imboden. The attacking force was subsequently encountered and driven off by General Stuart, and pursued for several miles in the direction of Boonsboro'. The army, after an arduous march, rendered more difficult by the rains, reached Hagerstown on the afternoon of the 6th and morning of the 7th July.*

---

* The following official communication from General Lee illustrates the unreliability of despatches emanating from Yankee generals :

HEADQUARTERS ARMY NORTHERN VIRGINIA, }
21st July, 1863. }

GENERAL S. COOPER, *Adjutant and Inspector-General C. S. A.*, Richmond, Va. :

General—I have seen in Northern papers what purported to be an official despatch from General Meade, stating that he had captured a brigade of infantry, two pieces of artillery, two caissons, and a large number of small arms, as this army retired to the south bank of the Potomac, on the 13th and 14th inst.

This despatch has been copied into the Richmond papers, and as its official character may cause it to be believed, I desire to state that it is incorrect. The enemy did not capture any organized body of men on that occasion, but only stragglers and such as were left asleep on the road, exhausted by the fatigue and exposure of one of the most inclement nights I have ever known at this season of the year. It rained without cessation, rendering the road by which our troops marched to the bridge at Falling Waters very difficult to pass, and causing so much delay that the last of the troops did not cross the river at the bridge until 1 P. M. on the 14th. While the column was thus detained on the road, a number of men, worn down with fatigue, lay down in barns and by the roadside, and though officers were sent back to arouse them, as the troops moved on, the darkness and rain prevented them from finding all, and many were in this way left behind. Two guns were left in the road. The horses that drew them became exhausted, and the officers went forward to procure others. When they returned, the rear of the column had passed the guns so far that it was deemed unsafe to send back for them, and they were thus lost. No arms, cannon, or prisoners were taken by the enemy in battle, but only such as were left

The enemy in force reached our front on the 12th. A position had been previously selected to cover the Potomac from Williamsport to Falling Waters, and an attack was awaited during that and the succeeding day. This did not take place, though the two armies were in close proximity, the enemy being occupied in fortifying his own lines. Our preparations being completed, and the river, though still deep, being pronounced fordable, the army commenced to withdraw to the south side on the night of the 13th. The enemy offered no serious interruption, and the movement was attended with no loss of material, except a few disabled wagons and two pieces of artillery, which the horses were unable to move through the deep mud.

The following day the army marched to Bunker Hill, in the vicinity of which it encamped for several days. It subsequently crossed the Blue Ridge, and took position south of the Rappahannock.

Any comment on Gettysburg must necessarily be a tantalizing one for the South. The Pennsylvania campaign had been a series of mishaps. General Lee was disappointed of half of his plan, in the first instance, on account of the inability or unwillingness of the Richmond authorities to assemble an army at Culpepper Court-house under General Beauregard, so as to distract the enemy and divide his force by a demonstration upon Washington. Johnston was calling for reinforcements in Mississippi; Bragg was threatened with attack; Beauregard's whole force was reported to be necessary to cover his line on the sea-coast; and the force in Richmond and in North Carolina was very small. Yet with what force Lee had, his campaign proposed great things—the destruction of his adversary, which would have uncovered the Middle and Eastern States of the North; for, behind Meade's array, there was nothing but militia mobs and home-guards incapable of making any resistance to an army of veterans. It was in

---

behind under the circumstances I have described. The number of stragglers thus lost, I am unable to state with accuracy, but it is greatly exaggerated in the despatch referred to.

> I am, with great respect,
>   Your obedient servant,
>   R. E. LEE, General.

anticipation of this great stake that Richmond was on the tiptoe of expectation. For once in the Confederate capital gold found no purchasers, prices declined, speculation was at its wits' end, and men consulted their interests as if on the eve of peace.

The recoil at Gettysburg was fatal, perhaps, not necessarily, but by the course of events, to General Lee's campaign; and the return of his army to its defensive lines in Virginia was justly regarded in the South as a reverse in the general for tunes of the contest. Yet the immediate results of the battle of Gettysburg must be declared to have been to a great extent negative. The Confederates did not gain a victory, neither did the enemy. The general story of the contest is simple. Lee had been unable to prevent the enemy from taking the highlands, many of them with very steep declivities, and nearly a mile in slope. The battle was an effort of the Confederates to take those heights. The right flank, the left flank, the centre, were successively the aim of determined and concentrated assaults. The Yankee lines were broken and driven repeatedly. But inexhaustible reserves and a preponderant artillery, advantageously placed, saved him from rout.

The first news received in Richmond of General Lee's retreat was from Yankee sources, which represented his army as a disorganized mass of fugitives, unable to cross the Potomac on account of recent floods, and at the mercy of an enemy immensely superior in numbers and flushed with victory. A day served to dash the hope of an early peace, and to overcloud the horizon of the war.

A few days brought news from our lines, which exploded the falsehoods of the Yankees, and assured the people of the South that the engagements of Gettysburg had resulted in worsting the enemy, in killing and wounding a number exceeding our own, and in capturing a large number of prisoners; and that the falling back of our army, at least as far as Hagerstown, was a movement dictated by general considerations of strategy and prudence.

And here it must be confessed that the retreat from Hagerstown across the Potomac was an inconsequence and a mystery to the intelligent public. Lee's position there was strong; his force was certainly adequate for another battle; preparations were apparently made for aggressive movements; and in the midst of all came a sudden renouncement of the campaign and the retreat into Virginia. The public had its secondary wish for the safety of the army. But this did not exclude mortification on the part of those who believed that General Lee had abandoned the enemy's territory, not as a consequence of defeat, but from the undue timidity or arrogant disposition of the authorities who controlled him.

But news of an overshadowing calamity, undoubtedly the greatest that had yet befallen the South, accompanied that of Lee's retreat, and dated a second period of disaster more frightful than that of Donelson and New Orleans. The same day that Lee's repulse was known in Richmond, came the astounding intelligence of *the fall of Vicksburg*. In twenty-four hours two calamities changed all the aspects of the war, and brought the South from an unequalled exaltation of hope to the very brink of despair.

CHAPTER II.

Vicksburg, "the Heroic City."—Its Value to the Confederacy.—An Opportunity Lost by Butler. — Lieutenant-general Pemberton.—A Favorite of President Davis.—The President's Obstinacy.—Blindness of Pemberton to the Enemy's Designs.—His Telegram to Johnston.—Plan of U. S. Grant.—Its Daring.—THE BATTLE OF PORT GIBSON.—Exposure of General Bowen by Pemberton.—The First Mistake.—Pemberton's Disregard of Johnston's Orders.—Grant's advance against Jackson.—Johnston's Evacuation of Jackson.—His Appreciation of the Situation.—Urgent Orders to Pemberton.—A Brilliant Opportunity.—Pemberton's Contumacy and Stupidity.—His Irretrievable Error.—Yankee Outrages in Jackson.—THE BATTLE OF BAKER'S CREEK, &c.—Stevenson's Heroic Fight.—Alleged Dereliction of General Loring.--His Division Cut Off in the Retreat.—Demoralization of Pemberton's Troops.—The Enemy's Assault on the Big Black.—Shameful Behavior of the Confederates.—A Georgia Hero.—Pemberton and the Fugitives.—His Return to Vicksburg.—Recriminations as to the Disaster of the Big Black.—How Pemberton Was in the Wrong.—Johnston Orders the Evacuation of Vicksburg.—Pemberton's Determination to Hold It.

VICKSBURG had already become famous in the history of the war, from the cupidity of the enemy and the gallantry of its resistance. The habitual phrase in the Yankee newspapers was—"the three strongholds of the rebellion, Richmond, Vicksburg, and Charleston." The possession of Richmond would have given an important *éclat* to the enemy, and some strategic advantages. That of Charleston would have given him a strip of sea-coast and an additional barrier to the blockade. Vicksburg was a prize almost as important as Richmond, and much more so than Charleston. It was the key of the navigation of the Mississippi, and the point of union between the positions of the Confederacy on the different sides of this river.

At the time of the fall of New Orleans, the defence of Vicksburg was not even contemplated by the authorities at Richmond; and the city was given up for lost by President Davis, as appears by an intercepted letter from one of his family. It was a characteristic want of appreciation of the situation by the Confederate Administration. It is not improbable, that if Butler had had the enterprise and genius to direct a land attack against Vicksburg, it might have readily fallen, on ac-

count of the feeble nature of its defences and the insufficiency
of its garrison. But the tyrant of New Orleans was a man
utterly destitute of military ability, whose ferocious genius
was expended in a war upon non-combatants. He let slip the
golden opportunity which the pre-occupation of Beauregard
with Halleck gave him to operate upon Vicksburg, and at once
complete the Yankee victory, which had been gained at the
mouth of the Mississippi.

The time the enemy gave for strengthening the defences of
Vicksburg was improved; and we have seen in another volume
how it passed comparatively unscathed through one bombardment; how it resisted Sherman's expedition of 1862; and how
it defied the gigantic enterprises of the enemy to encompass it
with the waters of the Mississippi turned from their channel.
But, unfortunately, the battle of Corinth had placed its destinies in the hands of a commander who had not the confidence
of the army; who encountered a positive hostility among the
people within the limits of his command; and whose haughty
manner and military affectation were ill-calculated to win the
regard of the soldier or reconcile the dislike of the civilian.

But a short time after the battle referred to, Major-general
Earl Van Dorn was removed from command, and Major-general Pemberton was placed in command of the Department of
Mississippi and East Louisiana, and, in consequence of his being outranked by both General Van Dorn and General Lovell,
was soon after appointed a Lieutenant-general. He was raised
by a single stroke of President Davis's patronage from the obscurity of a major to the position of a lieutenant-general. He
had never been on a battle-field in the war, and his reputation
as a commander was simply nothing. He was entirely the
creature of the private and personal prejudices of President
Davis. Never was an appointment of this president more self-
willed in its temper and more unfortunate in its consequences
It might have been supposed that the fact that Pemberton did
not command the confidence of his troops or of any considerable portion of the public would, of itself, have suggested to the
President the prudence of a change of commanders, and dis-
suaded him from his obstinate preference of a favorite. But
it had none of this effect. The Legislature of Mississippi
solicited the removal of Pemberton. Private delegations from

Congress entreated the President to forego his personal prejudices and defer to the public wish. But Mr. Davis had that
conceit of opinion which opposition readily confirms; and the
effect of these remonstrances was only to increase his obstinacy
and intensify his fondness for his favorite. To some of them
he replied that Pemberton was "a great military genius," not
appreciated by the public, and destined on proper occasion to
astonish it.

General Pemberton took command amid the suppressed
murmurs of a people to whom he was singularly unwelcome.
The first evidence of his want of comprehension was his ignorance and bewilderment as to the enemy's designs. We have
referred to the failure of the canal projects. The enemy, after
long-continued and streneous efforts to reach the right flank of
Vicksburg, by forcing a passage through the upper Yazoo
river, finally relinquished his design, and on the nights of the
4th and 5th of April, re-embarked his troops, and before daylight was in rapid retreat. About the same time a heavy force
of the enemy, which had been collected at Baton Rouge, was
mostly withdrawn and transferred to western Louisiana, leaving but one division to occupy that place.

So blind was Pemberton to the designs of the enemy, that
for many weeks he continued to believe that the object of the
movements of Ulysses S. Grant—the last commander sent from
Washington to contest the prize of the Mississippi—was not
Vicksburg, but Bragg's army in Tennessee. In this delusion,
and the self-complacent humor it inspired, he telegraphed to
General Johnston, on the 13th of April: "I am satisfied that
Rosecrans will be reinforced from Grant's army. Shall I
order troops to Tullahoma?" The aberration was soon dispelled. A few days after this despatch, information obtained
from Memphis indicated that Grant's retrogade movement
was a ruse; and thus suddenly Pemberton was called upon to
prepare for one of the most extraordinary and audacious games
that the enemy had yet attempted in this war.

We know that it is customary to depreciate an adversary in
war, by naming his enterprise as desperation, and entitling his
success as luck. We shall not treat with such injustice the
enemy's campaign in Mississippi. In daring, in celerity of
movement, and in the vigor and decision of its steps it was the

most remarkable of the war. The plan of Grant was, in brief, nothing else than to gain firm ground on one of the Confederate flanks, which, to be done, involved a march of about one hundred and fifty miles, through a hostile country, and in which communication with the base of supplies was liable at any moment to be permanently interrupted. In addition, a resistance to his advance could be anticipated, of whose magnitude nothing was certainly known, and which, for aught he knew, might at any time prove great enough to annihilate his entire army.

The plan involved the enterprise of running a fleet of transports past the batteries, crossing the troops from the Louisiana shore, below Vicksburg, to Mississippi, and then marching the army, by the way of Jackson, through the heart of the Confederacy, so to speak, to the rear of Vicksburg. On the night of the 22d of April, the first demonstration was made, in accordance with the newly-formed plan, by the running past our batteries of three gunboats and seven transports.

Grand Gulf is situated on the east bank of the Mississippi river, immediately below the mouth of the Big Black river. It was not selected as a position for land-defence, but for the protection of the mouth of the Big Black, and also as a precautionary measure against the passage of transports, should the canal before referred to prove a success, which then seemed highly probable. The necessary works were constructed under the direction of Brigadier-general Bowen, to defend the batteries against an assault from the river front, and against a direct attack from or across Big Black.

THE BATTLE OF PORT GIBSON.

The enemy having succeeded in getting his transports past Vicksburg, an attack on Grand Gulf was anticipated. Twelve miles below this, at the mouth of the Bayou Pierre, is Brainsburg, and at this point the enemy landed in heavy force, on the 30th of April, and prepared for an advance movement.

As soon as General Bowen received information of the landing of the enemy, he crossed Bayou Pierre, and advanced towards Port Gibson, situated several miles south-east of Grand

Gulf. In the vicinity of this place General Bowen met the enemy advancing in full force, and immediately prepared for battle, having previously telegraphed to Vicksburg for rein-forcements. He was left with a few thousand men to confront an overwhelming force of the enemy, as Pemberton had in sisted upon putting the Big Black between the enemy and the bulk of his own forces, which he declared were necessary to cover Vicksburg.

Early on the morning of the 1st of May, General Green, who had been sent out on the Brainsburg road with about a thousand men, encountered the enemy. He was joined by General Tracy, with not more than fifteen hundred men. The enemy's attack was sustained with great bravery until between nine and ten o'clock, when, overwhelmed by numbers and flanked on the right and left, General Green had to fall back. Courier after courier had been sent for General Baldwin, who was on the way with some reinforcements, but his troops were so utterly exhausted that he could not get up in time to prevent this. Just as the retreat was taking place General Baldwin arrived, and was ordered to form a new line about one mile in rear of General Green's first position. General Baldwin had no artillery, and that ordered up from Grand Gulf had not arrived. Colonel Cockrell, with three Missouri regiments came up soon after. General Bowen now had all the force at his command on the field, excepting three regiments and two battalions, which occupied positions which he could not re-move them from until the last moment. He ordered them up about one o'clock, but only one of them arrived in time to cover the retreat and burn the bridges. Between twelve and one o'clock General Bowen attempted, with two of Colonel Cockrell's regiments, to turn the enemy's right flank, and nearly succeeded. The enemy formed three brigades in front of a battery, to receive our charge. The first was routed, the second wavered, but the third stood firm, and after a long and desperate contest, our troops had to give up the attempt. It is probable, however, that this attack saved the right from being overwhelmed, and kept the enemy back until nearly sunset. All day long the fight raged fiercely, our men everywhere maintaining their ground. Just before sunset a desperate attack was made by the enemy, they having again received fresh troops. Our right was forced to give ground, and General Bowen was reluctantly compelled to fall back. The order was given and executed without confusion. The enemy attempted no pursuit.

Though unsuccessful, the bloody encounter in front of Port Gibson nobly illustrated the valor and constancy of our troops, and shed additional lustre upon the Confederate arms. In his official report, General Bowen declared that the enemy's force engaged exceeded twenty thousand, while his own did not number over fifty-five hundred.

It was the first mistake with which Pemberton had opened his chapter of disasters. On the 28th of April he ascertained that the enemy was landing troops at Hard Times, on the west bank of the river; he became satisfied that neither the front nor right (north) of Vicksburg would be attacked, and he turned his attention to the left (south) of Vicksburg; but unfortunately he did not concentrate "*all*" his troops on that side of Vicksburg. On the 29th of April he telegraphed General Johnston that the enemy were at Hard Times, and "can cross to Brainsburg;" and on the 1st of May that "a furious battle has been going on all day below Port Gibson." On the 2d of May General Johnston replied: "If General Grant crosses unite all your troops to beat him. Success will give back what was abandoned to win it." Unfortunately it was not done. His explanation why it was not done, was, that to have marched an army across Big Black of sufficient strength to warrant a reasonable hope of successfully encountering his very superior forces, would have stripped Vicksburg and its essentially flank defences of their garrisons, and the city itself might have fallen an easy prey into the eager hands of the enemy. His apprehensions for the safety of Vicksburg were morbid. While he was gazing at Vicksburg, Grant was turning towards Jackson.

The battle of Port Gibson won, Grant pushed his columns directly towards Jackson. Pemberton's want of cavalry did not permit the interruption of Grant's communications, and he moved forward unmolested to Clinton. General Pemberton anticipated "a raid on Jackson," and ordered the removal of "the staff department and all valuable stores to the east;" but he regarded Edwards' Depot and the Big Black Bridge as the objects of Grant's movement to the eastward.

The movement of the enemy was one of extreme peril On one flank was General Joseph E. Johnston with a force whose strength was unknown to General Grant; and on the other was Lieutenant-general Pemberton. To have remained at Grand Gulf would have ruined the Federal army, and, with this knowledge, Grant determined to make certain movements on the west bank of the Big Black, while he marched rapidly on Jackson, Mississippi, with his main force. The object of the Yankee commander was to make sure of no enemy being in his rear when he marched on Vicksburg.

By glancing at a map it will be seen that the country included between Grand Gulf, Jackson and Big Black river, at the railroad crossing, forms a triangle. In moving forward, Grant's forces kept upon the line which leads from Grand Gulf to Jackson; but, instead of all going to Jackson, as might have been expected, the advance only continued toward that point, while the remainder of the army turned off to the left, at intervals, and proceeded along lines which converged until they met in the angle of the triangle located at the Big Black railroad crossing.

Many persons have doubtless been astonished at the ease with which Grant's forces advanced upon and took possessior. of Jackson. Its importance as a railroad centre and a depot for Confederate supplies warranted the anticipation that the place would be vigorously defended and only surrendered in the last extremity.

Unfortunately such a resistance could not be made. General Johnston had arrived too late to prepare a defence of the capital of Mississippi. On reaching Jackson, on the night of the 13th of May, he found there but two brigades numbering not more than six thousand men; and, with the utmost that could be relied upon from the reinforcements on the way, he could not expect to confront the enemy with more than eleven thousand men. But he comprehended the situation with instant and decisive sagacity. He ascertained that General Pemberton's forces, except the garrison of Port Hudson (five thousand) and of Vicksburg, were at Edwards' Depot—the general's headquarter's at Bovina; and that four divisions of the enemy, under Sherman, occupied Clinton, ten miles west of Jackson, between Edwards' Depot and ourselves.

Not a moment was to be lost. A despatch was hurried to Pemberton on the same night (13th), informing him of John ston's arrival, and of the occupation of Clinton by a portion of Grant's army, urging the importance of re-establishing com munications, and ordering him to come up, if practicable, on Sherman's rear at once, and adding, "to beat such a detach-ment would be of immense value." "The troops here," wrote Johnston, "could co-operate. All the strength you can quickly assemble should be brought. Time is all-important."

It appears from General Pemberton's official report that he had preconceived a plan of battle; that he expected to fight at Edwards' Depot; and that he was unwilling to separate him-self further from Vicksburg, which he regarded as his base. He had the choice of disobeying Johnston's orders, and falling back upon his own matured plan, or of obeying them, and taking the brilliant hazard of crushing an important detach-ment of the enemy. He did neither. He attempted a middle course—a compromise between his superior's orders and his own plans, the weak shift and fatal expedient of military in-competency. He telegraphed to Johnston, "I comply at once with your order." Yet he did not move for twenty-eight hours. A council of war had been called, and a majority of officers approved the movement indicated by General Johnston. Pem-berton opposed it; but he says, "I did not, however, see fit to put my own judgment and opinion so far in opposition as to prevent a movement altogether." So he determined upon *an advance*, not to risk an attack on Sherman, but, as he says, to cut the enemy's communications. He abandoned his own former plans; he disobeyed Johnston's order, and invented a compro-mise equally reprehensible for the vacillation of his purpose and the equivocation of his despatch. He moved, not on Sher-man's rear at Clinton, but in another direction toward Ray-mond. The purpose of General Johnston's order was to unite the two armies and attack a detachment of the enemy. The result of General Pemberton's movement towards Raymond was to prevent this union, and to widen the distance between the two armies.

In a moral view, it is difficult to find any term but that of the harshest censure for this trifling compromise of General Pemberton between the orders of his superior and the prefer ences of his own mind. In a military view it was equally reprehensible. When the several corps of the enemy were separated into two or more distinct columns, separated by twelve or fifteen miles, it would be naturally supposed that the true opportunity of Pemberton would have been to strike at one separately, rather than to wait until all the enemy's forces concentrated, and attacked him on his uncertain march.

The error was irretrievable. While General Pemberton was in " council of war," on the 14th, the enemy, from Clinton and Raymond, marched on Jackson and compelled its evacuation. Had General Pemberton promptly obeyed General Johnston's order, and boldly marched on Clinton, the enemy could not have marched to Jackson, as that would have been to facilitate the union of Johnston and Pemberton and to have encountered their concentrated armies. The audacity of Johnston's order, if executed, might have reversed the fate of Vicksburg. The vacillation of General Pemberton, and his loss of a day and a half, caused the evacuation of Jackson, and opened the way to Vicksburg.

The occupation of Jackson was the occasion of the usual scenes of Yankee outrage. The watchword of McPherson's corps, which first entered it, was plunder. The negroes were invited to assist and share in the pillage. Supposing that the year of jubilee had finally come, the blacks determined to enjoy it, and, with this end in view, they stole everything they could carry off. " Nothing," says a Yankee spectator, " came amiss to these rejoicing Africans ; they went around the streets displaying aggregate miles of double-rowed ivory, and bending under a monstrous load of French mirrors, boots, shoes, pieces of calico, wash-stands and towels, hoop-skirts, bags of tobacco, parasols, umbrellas, and fifty other articles equally incongruous."

McPherson left Jackson on the afternoon of the 15th, and, in the morning of the next day, Sherman's corps took up its line—the whole moving westward along the south side of the railroad to Vicksburg. As the enemy left Jackson it resembled more the infernal regions than the abode of civilization. Vast volumes of smoke lay over it, through which, here and there, rolled fiercely up great mountains of flame, that made infernal music over their work of destruction. The Confederate

State-house—a large new wooden building—the Penitentiary, several private house and several government buildings were all in flames. It was the first step of that catalogue of horrors of invasion in which Mississippi was to rival Virginia, and the Big Black was to be associated with the Potomac in the ghastly romances of ruin and desolation.

We return to Pemberton and his ill-starred march. On the 15th, at the head of a column of seventeen thousand men, he had taken the direction of Raymond. On the morning of the 16th, at about six and a half o'clock, he ascertained that his pickets were skirmishing with the enemy on the Raymond road, some distance in his front. At the same moment a courier arrived and handed him a despatch from General Johnston announcing the evacuation of Jackson, and indicating that the only means by which a union could now be effected between the two forces was that Pemberton should move directly to Clinton, whither Johnston was retiring. The order of counter-march was given by Pemberton. It was too late. Just as this reverse movement commenced, the enemy drove in his cavalry pickets, and opened with artillery, at long range, on the head of his column on the Raymond road. The demonstrations of the enemy soon becoming more serious, orders were sent by General Pemberton to the division commanders to form in line of battle on the cross-road from the Clinton to the Raymond road—Loring on the right, Bowen in the centre, and Stevenson on the left. The enemy had forced the Confederates to give battle on the ground of his own selection, under the disadvantages of inferior numbers and in circumstances which had all the moral effect of a surprise.

THE BATTLE OF BAKER'S CREEK, ETC.

But the ground itself was not unfavorable to our troops. The line of battle was quickly formed, in a bend of what is known as Baker's creek, without any interference on the part of the enemy; the position selected was naturally a strong one, and all approaches from the front well covered. The enemy made his first demonstration on our right, but, after a lively artillery duel for an hour or more, this attack was relinquished and a large force was thrown against our left, where skirmishing became heavy about ten o'clock, and the battle began in earnest along Stevenson's entire front about noon.

At this time Major-general Loring was ordered to move forward, and crush the enemy in his front, and General Bowen was directed to co-operate with him in the movement. The movement was not made by Loring. He replied that the enemy was too strongly posted to be attacked, but that he would avail himself of the first opportunity of successful assault. The opportunity never came to him.

Stevenson's troops sustained the heavy and repeated attacks of the enemy. Six thousand, five hundred men held in check four divisions of the enemy, numbering, from his own statement, twenty-five thousand men. Such endurance has its limits. The only reinforcements that came to the relief of these devoted men were two brigades of Bowen, among them Cockrell's gallant Missourians. This was about half-past two o'clock. The combined charge of these forces for a moment turned the tide of battle. But the enemy still continued to move troops from his left to his right, thus increasing his vastly superior forces against Stevenson's and Bowen's divisions. Again orders were despatched to General Loring to move to the left as rapidly as possible leaving force enough only to cover the bridge and ford at Baker's Creek. He did not come. He seems still to have been engaged with the movements of the enemy in his front, and to have supposed that they were endeavoring to flank him.

In the mean time the contest raged along Stevenson's lines, the enemy continuing his line movement to our left. Here were displays of gallantry, which, unable to retrieve the disaster, adorned it with devotion. Here fell the gallant Captain Ridley, commanding a battery, refusing to leave his guns, single-handed and alone fighting until he fell, pierced with six shots, receiving, even from his enemies, the highest tribute of admiration. Nothing could protect the artillery horses from the deadly fire of the enemy; almost all were killed, and along the whole line, the pieces, though fought with desperation, on the part of both officers and men, almost all fell into the hands of the enemy. In this manner the guns of Corput's and Johnston's batteries, and Waddell's section, were lost.

Double shotted, they were fired until, in many instances, swarms of the enemy were in amongst them. Officers and men stood by them to the very latest moment that they could be served.

About 5 o'clock P. M., a portion of Stevenson's division broke and fell back in disorder. General Pemberton rode up to Stevenson and told him that he had repeatedly ordered two brigades of Loring to his assistance. The brave commander, who had fought the enemy since morning, replied that the relief would be too late and that he could no longer hold the field. "Finding," says General Pemberton, "that the enemy's vastly superior numbers were pressing all my forces engaged steadily back into old fields, where all advantages of position would be in his favor, I felt it too late to save the day even should Brigadier-general Featherstone's brigade of General Loring's division come up immediately. I could, however, learn nothing of General Loring's whereabouts; several of my staff officers were in search of him, but it was not until after General Bowen had personally informed me that he could not hold his position, and not until I had ordered the retreat, that General Loring, with Featherstone's brigade, moving, as I subsequently learned, by a country road, which was considerably longer than the direct route, reached the position on the left, known as Champion's Hill, where he was forming line of battle when he received my order to cover the retreat. Had the movement in support of the left been promptly made, when first ordered, it is not improbable that I might have maintained my position, and it is possible the enemy might have been driven back, though his vastly superior and constantly increasing numbers would have rendered it necessary to withdraw during the night to save my communications with Vicksburg."*

---

* In a correspondence which ensued between the Richmond authorities and General Pemberton as to the cause of the defeat, the Secretary of War wrote, in a letter dated October 1st, 1863: "I should be pleased to know if General Loring had been ordered to attack before General Cummings' brigade gave way; and whether, in your opinion, had Stevenson's division been promptly sustained, the troops with him would have fought with so little tenacity and resolution as a portion of them exhibited? Have you had any explanation of the extraordinary failure of General Loring to comply with your reiterated orders to attack? And do you feel assured your orders were received by him?

But the disaster of the day was not yet complete. The retreat of the Confederates was by the ford and bridge of Baker's
Creek. Bowen's division was directed to take position on the
left bank, and to hold the crossing until Loring's division.
which was directed to bring up the rear, had effected the passage. The intelligence of the approach of Loring was awaited
in vain. Probably another unfortunate misapprehension had
occurred. He had covered the retreat with great spirit. It
was in this part of the contest that Brigadier-general Lloyd
Tilghman, one of the bravest officers in the Confederate army,
fell, pierced through his manly breast with a fragment of a
shell. He was serving with his own hands a twelve-pound
howitzer, trying to dislodge a piece which was annoying the
retreat. It is said that General Loring was under the impression that a force of the enemy had got in the rear of the
bridge, and that Stevenson had been compelled to continue his
retreat in the direction of Edwards' Depot. At any rate, he
resolved to make his retreat through the east, turn Jackson,
and effect a junction with the forces of General Johnston, then
supposed to be near Canton. He succeeded, but with the loss
of his artillery.

Pemberton had retired from the battle-field with a demoralized army. It had lost nearly all of its artillery; it was weakened by the absence of General Loring's division; it had
already shown the fatal sign of straggling; and, worse than
all, it had conceived a distrust of its commander, who had carried his troops by a vague and wandering march on the very
front of the concentrated forces of the enemy.

On Sunday morning, the 17th of May, the enemy advanced
in force against the works erected on the Big Black. The
river, where it is crossed by the railroad bridge, makes a bend
somewhat in the shape of a horse-shoe. Across this horse-shoe,

His conduct, unless explained by some misapprehension, is incomprehensible
to me."

To this General Pemberton replied, on the 10th of November: "General
Loring had been ordered to attack before General Cummings' brigade gave way
and the order had been again and again repeated; and, in my opinion, 'had
Stevenson's division been promptly sustained,' his troops would have deported
themselves gallantly and creditably. I have received no explanation of 'the
extraordinary failure of General Loring to comply with my reiterated orders to
attack;' and I do feel 'assured that my orders were received by him.'"

at its narrowest part, a line of rifle-pits had been constructed, making an excellent cover for infantry, and, at proper intervals, dispositions were made for field artillery. The line of pits ran nearly north and south, and was about a mile in length. North of, and for a considerable distance south of the railroad, and of a dirt-road to Edwards' Depot, nearly parallel with it extended a bayou, which, in itself, opposed a serious obstacle to an assault upon the pits. This line abutted north on the river, and south upon a cypress brake, which spread itself nearly to the bank of the river. In addition to the railroad bridge, which had been floored for the passage over of artillery and wagons, a steamer, from which the machinery had been taken, was converted into a bridge, by placing her fore-and-aft across the river. Between the works and the bridge, about three-quarters of a mile, the country was open, being either clear or cultivated fields, affording no cover should the troops be drawn from the trenches. East and north of the railroad, the country over which the enemy must necessarily pass was similar to those above described; but north of the railroad, and about three hundred yards in front of the rifle-pits, a copse of wood extended from the road to the river. Our line was manned on the right by the gallant Cockrell's Missouri brigade, the extreme left by Brigadier-general Green's Missouri and Arkansas men, both of Bowen's division, and the centre by Brigadier-general Vaughan's brigade of east Tennesseeans, in all about four thousand men, as many as could be advantageously employed in defending the line with about twenty pieces of field artillery.

The position was one of extraordinary strength, yet this position was abandoned by our troops, almost without a struggle, and with the loss of nearly all that remained of our artillery.

It would be well if this page could be omitted from our martial records, and its dishonor spared. But it is easily told, and the charitable reader is already prepared for it. Early in the morning the enemy opened his artillery at long range, and very soon pressed forward, with infantry, into the copse of wood north of the railroad; about the same time he opened on Colonel Cockrell's position with two batteries, and advanced a line of skirmishers, throwing forward a column of infantry, which was quickly driven back by our batteries. Pretty heavy skirmishing was, for awhile, kept up along our whole line, but presently the enemy, who had massed a large force in the woods immediately north of the railroad, advanced at a run with loud cheers. Our troops in their front did not remain to receive them, but broke and fled precipitately.

The retreat was disgraceful. It soon became a matter of *sauve qui peut*. A strong position, with an ample force of infantry and artillery to hold it, was shamefully abandoned, almost without resistance. Between the troops occupying the centre and the enemy there was an almost impassable bayou. They fled before the enemy had reached that obstacle. In this precipitate retreat but little order was observed, the object with all being to reach the bridge as rapidly as possible. Many were unable to do so, but effected their escape by swimming the river; some were drowned in the attempt. A considerable number, unable to swim, and others too timid to expose themselves to the fire of the enemy by an effort to escape, remained in the trenches, and were made prisoners. A captain, who disgraced the Confederate uniform, laid down in the rifle-pits, and was captured by the enemy. Another behaved more bravely. Captain Osborne, of the Thirty-sixth Georgia, took his place just behind his line, and, with drawn revolver, swore he would shoot the first unwounded man who turned his back. The consequence was that his company, and the fragment of another, were soon left alone in the field where the steady line of the enemy were advancing under the smoke of their own murderous fire. Completely flanked, and in peril of capture, he gave the order to "march a retreat," but still with revolver and voice checking any unwise or unbecoming haste. When satisfied with his distance, he halted his company, and dressed the line; just then General Cumming rode up, and, taking off his hat, said: "Captain, I compliment you upon having the only organized body of men on the field."

Lieutenant-general Pemberton rode up and down the lines trying to rally the men; but his courage was not well rewarded. One of his staff threatened to shoot a runaway with his pistol. "Bigger guns than that, back there," said the soldier, and went on.

General Pemberton told a fellow to stop and to go back, and, to give force to the order, said : "I am Lieutenant-general Pemberton, commanding this department." The fellow looked up and said, "You are !"—and proceeded the same way.

Who could have recognized in the flying mob the same men whose heroic defence of Vicksburg had attracted the attention and won the applause of the world!

About ten o'clock, Sunday night, the main body of Pemberton's army entered Vicksburg. A scene of terror ensued. Many planters living near the city with their families, abandoned their homes and entered our lines with the Confederate forces. The stillness of the Sabbath night was broken in upon, and an uproar in which the blasphemous oath of the soldier and the cry of the child mingled, heightened the effect of a scene which the pen cannot depict. There were many gentle women and tender children, torn from their homes by the advance of a ruthless foe and compelled to fly to our lines for protection; and mixed up with them, in one vast crowd, were the gallant men who had left Vicksburg three short weeks before in all the pride and confidence of a just cause, and returning to it under the shame of a defeat, and with the panic of a mob.

It is not necessary to enter at length into the recrimination which ensued between Pemberton and Johnston, as to the memorable disaster of the Big Black. It was argued on Pemberton's side that had it not been for Johnston's order to move on the enemy at Canton, he never would have advanced *in any direction* beyond the Big Black. To this the reply of General Johnston was neat and conclusive. "It was," he said, "a new military principle that when an officer disobeys a positive order of his superior, that superior becomes responsible for any measure his subordinate may choose to substitute for that ordered."

Pemberton had neither obeyed the order referred to, nor fallen back upon his original plan; he had supplanted both by a new movement which concluded in one of the worst disasters of the war. The order of the 13th directed truly a "hazardous movement," but it was nevertheless a great conception —it was one of those bold and audacious moves that characterize military genius, and is a practical illustration of Napo-

leon's maxim, that " a great captain supplies all deficiencies by
his courage, and marches boldly to meet the attack." It was
a wise order, for it tended to concentration and the union of
both detachments of his army; and, if promptly and boldly
executed, might have resulted in saving Vicksburg. For if
Sherman had been defeated between Clinton and Jackson
Grant could not have invested Vicksburg.

As it was, the fall of Vicksburg had become but a question
of time. General Johnston was convinced of the impossibility
of collecting a sufficient force to break the investment of the
city, should it be completed. He appreciated the difficulty of
extricating the garrison. It was with this foresight that, on
learning that Pemberton had been driven from the Big Black,
he ordered the *evacuation of Vicksburg.* He wrote: "If
Haynes' Bluff be untenable, Vicksburg is of no value and
cannot be held. If, therefore, you are invested in Vicksburg,
you must ultimately surrender. Under such circumstances,
instead of losing both troops and place, you must, if possible,
save the troops. If it is not too late, evacuate Vicksburg and
its dependencies, and march to the northeast."

It was a grave order. It commanded the surrender of valuable stores and munitions of war; the surrender of the Mississippi
river; and the severance of the Confederacy. But Johnston
had presented to his mind a given alternative: that of the loss
of Vicksburg, and that of the loss of Vicksburg *and* an army
of twenty-five thousand men, and he had the nerve to accept
with promptness the lesser of two evils. It required the greatest moral courage to come to such a conclusion; for so deluded were the Confederate people as to the safety of Vicksburg, and so firmly persuaded were they that Grant was a
desperate fool "who would butt his brains out against the
stockades of Vicksburg," that had this order of Johnston been
known at the time it would have produced from one end of
the Confederacy to the other an outbreak of indignation, and
have probably made him the victim of an incorrigible popular
passion and ignorance.

Pemberton received the order with dismay; he called a coun
cil of war. It was unanimous for its rejection; but the reason given was peculiar and but little creditable. It was decided that it was impossible to withdraw the army with such

morale and material as to be of future service to the Confeder
acy; and this, although there were eight thousand fresh troops
in Vicksburg.   Pemberton replied: "I have decided to hold
Vicksburg as long as possible, with the firm hope that the
Government may yet be able to assist me in keeping this obstruction to the enemy's free navigation of the Mississippi
river.   I still conceive it to be the most important point in the
Confederacy."   While the council of war was assembled, the
guns of the enemy opened on the works.

CHAPTER III.

THE line of defence around the city of Vicksburg consisted of a system of detached works (redans, lunettes, and redoubts) on the prominent and commanding points, with the usual profile of raised field works, connected, in most cases, by rifle-pits. The strength of the city towards the land was equally as strong as on the river side. The country was broken, to a degree affording excellent defensive positions. In addition to this, the ravines intervening the ridges and knolls, which the Confederates had fortified, were covered with a tangled growth of cane, wild grape, &c., making it impossible for the enemy to move his troops in well-dressed lines.

To man the entire line of fortifications, General Pemberton was able to bring into the trenches about eighteen thousand five hundred muskets; but it was absolutely necessary to keep a reserve always ready to reinforce any point heavily threatened. It became indispensable, therefore, to reduce the number in the trenches to the minimum capable of holding them until a reserve could come to their aid. It was also necessary that the reserve should be composed of troops among the best and most reliable. Accordingly, Bowen's division (about twenty-four hundred) and some other forces were designated for that purpose, reducing the forces in the trenches to little over fifteen thousand five hundred men.

Fortunately, the army of Vicksburg had speedily recovered from its demoralization, reassured, as the troops were, of a prospect of Johnston's co-operation, and inspired by a remarkable appeal from Pemberton. This unfortunate commander appeased the clamor against himself by an apparently noble candor and memorable words of heroism. He said that it had been declared that he would sell Vicksburg, and exhorted his soldiers to witness the price at which he would sell it, for it would not be less than his own life, and that of every man in his command. Those words deserve to be commemorated in relation to the sequel.

The stirring words of Pemberton were circulated through the Confederacy, and satisfied the public that either Vicksburg was safe, or that the catastrophe would be glorious. They called to mind Leyden and Genoa, Londonderry and Saragossa, and the people of the Confederacy expected that a name no less glorious would be added to the list of cities made immortal by heroism, endurance, suffering, and, as they hoped, triumph. Much of this elation, it is true, was from ignorance of the true situation; but even the intelligent refused to entertain a sequel so humiliating and disastrous to the South as that which was to ensue.

The troops of Grant were flushed with victory, and had proposed to finish their work by a single assault. The events of the 19th, 20th, and 21st of May, wearied those who imagined that they saw in their grasp the palm of the Mississippi. So fully assured were they of victory, that they postponed it from day to day. To storm the works was to take Vicksburg, in their opinion, and when it was known on the morning of the 21st, that at ten o'clock next morning the whole line of Confederate works would be assaulted, the credulous and vain enemy accounted success so certain, that it was already given to the wings of the telegraph.

On the 22d, the fire from the enemy's artillery and sharpshooters in the rear was heavy and incessant until noon, when his gunboats opened upon the city, while a determined assault was made along Moore's, Hebert's, and Lee's lines. At about one o'clock P. M., a heavy force moved out to the assault on the lines of General Lee, making a gallant charge. They were allowed to approach unmolested to within good musket range, when every available gun was opened upon them with grape and canister, and the men, rising in the trenches, poured into their ranks volley after volley, with so deadly an effect that, leaving the ground literally covered in some places with their dead and wounded, they precipitately retreated. The angle of one of our redoubts having been breached by their artillery previous to the assault, when the repulse occurred, a party of about sixty of the enemy, under the command of a Lieutenant-colonel, made a rush, succeeded in effecting a lodgment in the ditch at the foot of the redoubt, and planted two colors on the parapet. It was of vital importance to drive them out, and, upon a call for volunteers for that purpose, two companies of Waul's Texas legion, commanded respectively by Captain Bradley and Lieutenant Hogue, accompanied by the gallant and chivalrous Colonel E. W. Pettus, of the Twentieth Alabama regiment, musket in hand, promptly presented themselves for the hazardous service. The preparations were quietly and quickly made, but the enemy seemed at once to divine the purpose, and opened upon the angle a terrific fire of shot, shell, and musketry. Undaunted, this little band, its chivalrous commander at its head, rushed upon the work, and, in less time than it requires to describe it, it and the flags were in our possession. Preparations were then quickly made for the use of our hand-grenades, when the enemy in the ditch, being informed of the purpose, immediately surrendered.

On other parts of our lines the enemy was repulsed, although he succeeded in getting a few men into our exterior ditches at each point of attack, from which they were, however, driven before night. Our entire loss in this successful day was comparatively very small, and might be counted in a few hundreds So accustomed had the population of Vicksburg become to the fire and rage of battle, that the circumstance is no less true than curious that throughout the day stores in the city were open and women and children walked the streets, as if no missile of death were filling the air and bursting and scattering the fragments around. There is no reliable account of the enemy's loss this day; but, in killed and wounded, it was several thousands. Two thousand had fallen in front of General Forney's lines alone, according to the report of that commander. The dead lay before our works, while thousands of wounded men were carried off as soon as they fell.

The result of this engagement was a lesson to the temerity of the enemy. After this decided repulse, the enemy seemed to have abandoned the idea of taking Vicksburg by assault, and went vigorously at work to thoroughly invest and attack by regular approaches. The weakness of our garrison prevented anything like a system of sallies, but, from time to time, as opportunities offered, and the enemy effected lodgments too close to our works, they were made with spirit and success. But these were unimportant incidents. The patience of Southern soldiers—a virtue for which they are not remarkable—was now to be tried by the experiences of a siege: exhausting labors, scant rations, a melancholy isolation, and the distress of being entirely cut off from their homes and friends.

The siege was established by the enemy under circumstances of peculiar and extraordinary advantage. Although Grant's attack was made from Grand Gulf, that place was not long his base; and, when he gained Haines' Bluff and the Yazoo, all communication with it was abandoned. He was enabled to rely on Memphis and the river above Vicksburg for food and reinforcements; his communications were open with the entire West; and the Northern newspapers urgently demanded that the utmost support should be given to a favorite general, and that the Trans-Mississippi should be stripped of troops to supply him with reinforcements.

But the South still entertained hopes of the safety of Vicksburg. It was stated in Richmond, by those who should have been well informed, that the garrison numbered considerably more than twenty thousand men, and was provisioned for a siege of six months. Nearly every day the telegraph had some extravagance to tell concerning the supreme safety of Vicksburg and the confidence of the garrison. The heroic promise of Pemberton, that the city should not fall until the last man had fallen in the last ditch, was called to the popular remembrance. The confidence of the South was swollen even to insolence by these causes ; and, although a few of the intelligent doubted the extravagant assurances of the safety of Vicksburg, the people at large received them with an unhesitating and exultant faith.

The prospect of Johnston's relief to Vicksburg was a delusion of its unhappy garrison and of an ignorant public. Indeed, on learning of the Baker creek disaster, Johnston had given up Vicksburg for lost, and considered that Pemberton had made a fatal mistake in determining to be besieged in Vicksburg, rather than maneuvering, in the first instance, to prevent a siege. The fact is, that at no time after the disaster referred to did General Johnston have at his disposal half the troops necessary to risk an assault on Grant. After the evacuation of Jackson he had retired to Canton, and the force he had collected there, including reinforcements to the amount of eight thousand men from Bragg's army in Tennessee, and above six thousand from Charleston, scarcely exceeded twenty-four thousand men. Grant's army was estimated at sixty thousand or eighty thousand men, and drawn, as they were, principally from the Northwestern States, they were of the best material. His great excess of force was being daily enlarged by reinforcements, while the Richmond authorities refused to give or to promise more troops to Johnston. On the 5th of June, Mr. Seddon, the Confederate Secretary of War, telegraphed to Johnston : " You must rely on what you have, and the irregular forces Mississippi can afford."

The fact is, that the resources of the Confederacy were at this time in the most critical condition. In Virginia we were outnumbered by the enemy more than two to one ; and with reference to Bragg's condition in Tennessee, General Johnston did not hesitate to declare that, to take from him a force sufficient to oppose Grant, would involve the yielding of that State. He advised the Richmond authorities that it was for them to decide between Mississippi and Tennessee. He informed Pemberton that it was impossible for him (Johnston) with the force at his command to raise the siege of Vicksburg, and all that he could attempt was to extricate the garrison by a simultaneous attack on some part of the enemy's lines.

On the 15th of June, General Johnston communicated to the government his opinion that, without some great blunder of the enemy, we could not hold both Mississippi and Tennessee, and that he considered saving Vicksburg hopeless. Indeed such an attempt had now become utterly desperate. Grant had entrenched his position, and protected it by powerful artillery. His reinforcements alone equalled Johnston's whole force. The Big Black covered him from attack, and would cut off our retreat, if Johnston had been defeated in his mad enterprise of attack.

And now ensued a series of extraordinary communications from Richmond, remarkable even among the curiosities of the secret correspondence of officials. A favorite of the Richmond Administration had entangled himself in a hopeless siege, and the proposition was to be recklessly made to General Johnston to effect the relief of the favorite, or to cover his disaster by an attempt, which he (General Johnston) had declared would be tantamount to the sacrifice of himself and army, and which all the circumstances of the situation plainly denounced as hopeless. The authorities essayed the dictatorial style, and declared that the aim justified " any risk and all probable consequences." General Johnston could not be convinced. They attempted the persuasions of flattery : " The eyes and the hopes of the whole Confederacy are upon you," wrote Mr. Seddon to Johnston, " with the full confidence that you will act." General Johnston could not be cajoled. The Richmond authorities were left to await the development of that for which they themselves were most responsible.

The situation revealed in this correspondence was a close secret to the public. It was known to Pemberton, but most studiously kept from his troops, who, whenever a courier reached Vicksburg, imagined certain tidings of Johnston's approach. At times, the unhappy men listened for the sound of his guns. The hardships of the siege were telling upon them. The enemy were mining at different points, and it required the active and constant attention of our engineers to repair at night the damage inflicted upon our works during he day, and to meet his different mines by countermining The same men were constantly in the trenches. The enemy bombarded day and night from seven mortars on the opposite side of the peninsula. He also kept up a constant fire on our lines by artillery and sharpshooters. Many officers and men were lost by this fire. Among the first, was the brave Briga dier-general Green, of Missouri, who was shot in the neck by a minie ball. His wish was gratified—"he lived not to see Vicksburg fall."

But although General Johnston despaired of the ability of his army to save Vicksburg, he was busy with efforts to extri cate the garrison or to cut the enemy's communications, hop ing, from day to day, there might possibly be some new de velopment of the situation. On arriving in Mississippi he had informed General Kirby Smith, commanding the forces west of the Mississippi river, of the condition of Vicksburg and Port Hudson, and requested his aid and co-operation. Gen eral Smith did send troops to give all possible aid to Vicks burg. General Taylor was sent with eight thousand men to co-operate from the west bank of the Mississippi, to throw in supplies and to cross with his force if expedient and practi cable. On the 27th of June General Johnston telegraphed Pemberton that these troops "had been mismanaged, and had fallen back to Delhi." All prospect of relief from this quarter was thus terminated.

A few days before this disappointment Pemberton had com municated to Johnston the suggestion, that he (Johnston) should make to Grant propositions to pass the army of Vicks burg out with all its arms and equipages. He renewed the hope, however, of his being able, by force of arms, to act with Johnston, and expressed the opinion that he could hold out for fifteen days longer. Johnston was reassured by this spirit of determination. He still had some hopes of the co-operation of Kirby Smith. He replied to Pemberton, that *something might yet be done to save Vicksburg*, and to postpone the modes suggested of merely extricating the garrison.

This despatch never reached Vicksburg. "Had I received," said General Pemberton, "General Johnston's despatch of the 27th of June, in which he encouraged the hope that both Vicksburg and the garrison might be saved, I would have lived upon an ounce a day, and have continued to meet the assaults of all Grant's army, rather than have surrendered the city until General Johnston had realized or relinquished that hope; but I did not receive his despatch until the 20th day of August, in Gainesville, Alabama, nor had I the most remote idea that such an opinion was entertained by General Johnston; he had for some weeks ignored its possibility."

Whatever may be the merit of this declaration, Johnston's reassurance was too late. The very day it was penned, Pemberton had proposed a capitulation.

Forty-five days of incessant duty, with short rations, had had a marked effect upon the troops of Vicksburg. The trials of the siege were extraordinary. The men had been exposed to burning suns, drenching rains, damp fogs, and heavy dews, and had never had, by day or by night, the slightest relief. The extent of our works required every available man in the trenches, and even then they were, in many places, insufficiently manned. It was not possible to relieve any portion of the line for a single hour. Confined to the narrow limits of a trench, with their limbs cramped and swollen, without exercise, constantly exposed to a murderous storm of shot and shell, while the enemy's unerring sharpshooters stood ready to pick off every man visible above the parapet, the troops had suffered many combinations of hardship which had told upon their health and spirits. It is undoubtedly true, that in the condition in which the troops were, they would not have been able to cut their way through the enemy's lines, without the abandonment of a large number of sick, and the loss of, probably, half their effective strength. Such an enterprise was discouraged by all the division commanders. But however unequal the condition of the troops to an enterprise of such vigor and hardihood, it is certain that it was yet equal to sustain for many days longer the fatigues and hardships of a siege. The condition of the garrison was certainly not as extreme as that which Pemberton had heroically prefigured as the alternative of surrender; and it must be said, in the severe interest of truth, that it holds no honorable comparison with the amount of privation and suffering borne in other sieges recorded in history.

On the 3d of July, Pemberton proposed terms of capitulation for the morrow, to " save the further effusion of blood,' " feeling himself fully able to maintain his position for a yet indefinite period." There was but little dispute about terms:

the parole of the garrison, Grant's persistent refusal to make any stipulation with regard to the treatment of citizens, and the surrender of this latter point by Pemberton.

On the morning of Saturday, the Fourth of July, the anniversary of American Independence, the troops of Vicksburg marched from the lines of entrenchments they had defended and held for nearly two months, and, after stacking their arms and lowering their standards which had proudly floated upon many a battle-field, returned inside of the works, prisoners of war to a detested and exultant foe. At the hour of noon the Yankee flag was raised over the Court-house amid the shouts and cheers of Grant's troops. Demoralized as was Pemberton's army, there were yet those whose hearts throbbed or eyes filled with tears as they saw the hated ensign floating over a city which the Confederacy had boasted to be impregnable, and which had at last been surrenderred to signalize an American holiday.

The public confidence of the South with regard to the safety of Vicksburg had been abused by the silly mendacities of the telegraph, which, to the last, reported the garrison in supreme spirits and the enemy in woful plight. Under these circumstances the surprise and consternation of the people of the South may be imagined, when, without the least premonition, the announcement came that the select anniversary of the Fourth of July had been signalized by the capitulation of Vicksburg, without a fight: the surrender of twenty odd thousand troops as prisoners; and the abandonment to the Yankees of one of the greatest prizes of artillery that had yet been made in the war. The news fell upon Richmond like a thunder-clap from clear skies. It was at first denounced as an invention of speculators in sugar. The people were unwilling to reconcile themselves to a misfortune so unexpected in its announcement, and so monstrous in its particulars.

The authorities of Richmond maintained a sullen silence. But the truth, at last, came out stark and unwelcome. We had surrendered to the enemy a force of more than twenty-three thousand men, with three major-generals, and nine brigadiers; upwards of ninety pieces of artillery, and about forty thousand small arms, large numbers of the latter having been taken from the enemy during the siege.

The statement that the garrison of Vicksburg was surren
dered on account of an inexorable distress, in which the soldiers had to feed on mules, with the occasional luxury of rats,
is either to be taken as a designing falsehood, or as the crudities of that foolish newspaper romance so common in the war
In neither case does it merit refutation.   A citizen of Vicksburg declares that the only foundation for the rat story is that
a pie spiced with this vermin was served up in some of the
officers' messes as a practical joke, and that for days after the
surrender he himself had dined on excellent bacon from Pemberton's stores.   In his official report Pemberton declares that
he had at the time of the surrender of Vicksburg about
40,000 pounds of pork and bacon, which had been reserved for
the subsistence of his troops in the event of attempting to cut
his way out of the city.   Also 51,241 pounds of rice, 5,000
bushels of peas, 112,234 pounds of sugar, 3,240 pounds of
soap, 527 pounds of tallow candles, 27 pounds of star candles,
and 428,000 pounds of salt.*

There appears, then, to have been no immediate general occasion for the surrender of Vicksburg other than Pemberton's
desire " to save the further effusion of blood."   The explanation of his motives for selecting the Fourth of July as the day
of surrender implies a singular humiliation of the Confederacy ;
as he was willing to give this dramatic gratification to the
vanity of the enemy in the hope of thus conciliating the ambition of Grant, and soliciting the generosity of the Yankees.
He says : " If it should be asked why the Fourth of July was

---

* But it must be stated that Pemberton's supplies of Vicksburg, which he
had a year to provide, were criminally scant ; and that as the failure of supplies would in all probability have decided the fate of Vicksburg, had he not
anticipated it by a surrender, he cannot be acquitted of blame in this particular.   He declined to provision Vicksburg in prospect of a siege.   When one of
the Confederate generals, from Mississippi, pointed out to him vast supplies in
certain counties of the State accessible to his garrison, he dismissed the advice
with a haughtiness that almost amounted to personal insult.

As proof of the abundance of the country around Vicksburg, we have Grant's
official report of his Mississippi campaign, in which he states that, with a view
of rapid movement and surprise, having calculated that twenty days would
place him before Vicksburg, he permitted his troops to take only four days'
provisions, trusting to the country for the other sixteen days' supply, and, in
fact, supplied his army (50,000 men), from the country lying about the line of
his march.

selected as the day for the surrender, the answer is obvious; I believed that, upon that day, I should obtain better terms. Well aware of the vanity of our foes, I knew they would attach vast importance to the entrance, on the Fourth of July, into the stronghold of the great river, and that, to gratify their national vanity, they would yield then what could not be extorted from them at any other time." Such an incident of humiliation was alone wanting to complete the disaster and shame of Vicksburg.

What the Confederacy had proudly entitled its "heroic city," was now destined to the experience of Yankee despotism, and, what was worse, to the shame of those exhibitions of cowardly submission which suited the interests of those who were left to herd with their country's destroyers. The citizens of Vicksburg had suffered little more than mere inconvenience from the siege. There had been but little loss of life among them in the bombardment. The city was filled with groups of caves on every hill-side. In these caves the women and children were sheltered during the nights, and occasionally in the daytime when the firing was very severe. The excava tions branched out in various directions after passing the entrance. They were not very desirable bed-chambers, but they seemed to have answered a very good purpose. In one or two instances shells entered them, and two women and a number of children were thus killed during the siege.

On the same day the Yankees entered Vicksburg, several places of business were opened. Signs were hoisted on express offices, book and fruit stores, informing the new customers that the proprietors were in and ready to serve them. A well-known citizen of Vicksburg took the oath of allegiance and accommodated General Grant with headquarters at his residence. The Jewish portion of the population, composed principally of Germans, with but one honorable exception, went forward and took the oath of allegiance to the United States.

These tokens of submission were rewarded in the enemy's usual way. At first the citizens were placed under very little restraint. They were permitted to come in and go out of the lines almost at pleasure. In a few days, however, the reins were tightened. Vicksburg found a second edition of Beast Butler in General Osterhaus, a tawny Dutchman, who peremptorily stopped the ingress and egress of the people; forbid citizens from purchasing provisions without first registering their names; re-enacted much of the ingenious despotism of New Orleans; and declared that the height of his ambition was to get our people to hate and abhor him.

A Mississippi paper declared that it had no word of excuse or charity for the men who had remained in Vicksburg under the enemy's flag. To quote from their own slang dialect, "the Confederacy was about gone up, and there was no use in following its fortunes any further." But it repeated the characteristic story of the conquered cities of the South. The spirit of the women of Vicksburg was unbroken; and amid all its shameful spectacles of subserviency, female courage alone redeemed the sad story of a conquered and emasculated city. There was but a single exception to the compliment; and she a Northern school-teacher who was first to sing "the Bonnie Blue Flag" in Vicksburg, at the commencement of the war, to raise the means to clothe our soldiers. She forgot the "hope-crowned past," and attended a social gathering at MacPherson's headquarters, where during the evening a sword was presented "in honor of the surrender of Vicksburg."

The city had been accounted one of the most beautiful of the South, of commanding situation, and adorned with a profusion of shrubbery; but the rain of shot and shell had sadly marred its beauty. But few buildings were entirely demolished; yet there was scarcely a house in Vicksburg that remained unscathed; in all of them were frightful looking holes in the walls and floors. The streets had been ploughed up by shells. In walking along the pavement one had to exercise care not to tumble into a pit dug by a projectile from a thirteen-inch mortar, or from a Parrott gun. The yards, gardens, and open lots were cut up with shot holes. Nearly every gate in the city was crowned with unexploded thirteen-inch shells placed a-top of each post, and the porches and piazzas were adorned with curious collections of shot and shell that had fallen within the inclosures. Everywhere were to be found evidences of the fiery ordeal through which the city had passed.

It is impossible to recount with precision the various interests involved in the fate of Vicksburg. It compelled, as its necessary consequence, the surrender of other posts on the

Mississippi, and cut the Confederacy in twain. It neutralized successes in Lower Louisiana, to which we shall presently refer. Its defence had involved exposure and weakness in other quarters. It had about stripped Charleston of troops; it had taken many thousand men from Bragg's army; and it had made such requisitions on his force for the newly organized lines in Mississippi, that that general was compelled or induced, wisely or unwisely, to fall back from Tullahoma, to give up the country on the Memphis and Charleston railroad, and practically to abandon the defence of Middle Tennessee.

The fall of Vicksburg was followed by the enemy's re-occupation of Jackson, the capitulation of Port Hudson, the evacuation of Yazoo city, and important events in Arkansas, which resulted in the retreat of our army from Little Rock and the surrender to the enemy of the important valley in which it is situated. To these events we must now direct the attention of the reader.

THE YANKEE RE-OCCUPATION OF JACKSON.

General Grant advanced his forces on Jackson, to which point Johnston retreated so soon as he learned the Vicksburg disaster. His policy was to march rapidly to the capture or discomfiture of General Johnston's army. On the evening of the 9th of July, his advance drove in our outer line of pickets. The troops employed in this expedition were Sherman's army corps, the Fifteenth, commanded by General Steele; the Thirteenth army corps, General Ord, commanding, with Lauman's division of Sixteenth army corps attached, a portion of the Sixteenth and Ninth army corps, commanded by General Parker, and McArthur's division of General McPherson's corps—in all about four army corps.

The works thrown up for the defence of Jackson consisted of a line of rifle-pits, prepared at intervals for artillery. These extended from a point north of the town, a little east of the Canton road, to a point south of the town, within a short distance of Pearl river, and covered most of the approaches west of the river; but were badly located and constructed, presenting but a slight obstacle to a vigorous assault.

The troops promptly took their assigned positions in the

intrenchments on the appearance of the enemy, in expectation of immediate assault: Major-general Loring occupying the right; Major-general Walker the right of the centre; Major-general French the left of the centre, and Major-general Breckinridge the left. The cavalry, under Brigadier-general Jackson, was ordered to observe and guard the fords of Pearl river, above and below the town.

But the enemy, instead of attacking, as soon as he arrived, commenced intrenching and constructing batteries. On the 10th, there was spirited skirmishing with slight cannonading, continuing throughout the day. This was kept up with varying intensity. Hills commanding and encircling the town, within easy cannon range, offered favorable sites for batteries. A cross-fire of shot and shell reached all parts of the town, showing the position to be entirely untenable against a powerful artillery.

On the 12th, besides the usual skirmishing, there was a heavy cannonade from the batteries near the Canton and sonth of the Clinton roads. The missiles reached all parts of the town. An assault, though not a vigorous one, was also made on Major-general Breckinridge's line. It was quickly repelled, however, principally by the direct fire of Cobb's and Slocumb's batteries, and a flank attack of the skirmishers of the First, Third and Fourth Florida and Forty-seventh Georgia regiments. The enemy's loss in killed, wounded, and prisoners, was at least five hundred.*

On the 16th, General Johnston obtained information that a large train from Vicksburg, loaded with ammunition, was near the enemy's camp. This, and the condition of the enemy's batteries, made it probable that Sherman would the next day concentrate upon Jackson the fire of near two hundred guns.

---

* During the heavy bombardment Colonel Withers was killed by the explosion of a shell near his own residence. He had just returned from the front when he was killed. He was buried at night by his faithful slave, who was fired upon by the enemy during the interment. This boy's conduct to his deceased master was a rebuke to the enemy. In the face of the enemy's position, at night, within easy range of the enemy's sharpshooters, he, with the assistance of two Confederate officers, and by the flickering light of a lamp—which was shot out of his hand while he was performing his sacred duty—carried the body of his dead master and interred it with as much affection and tende care as if it were his own child.

The evacuation of Jackson was determined on and effected on the night of the 16th. The evacuation was not discovered by the enemy until the next day; and Johnston retired by easy marches to Morton, distant about thirty-five miles from Jackson.

When Sherman's troops entered Jackson, exasperated by the losses which their ranks had sustained, they commenced a destruction of the houses by fire, which was kept up until there was but little left of the town but ashes. Jackson has been an ill-fated place. When it was captured before there was a great destruction. Now, where was but lately a thriving and pretentious town of between four and five thousand inhabitants, with a State-house, lunatic asylum, and many other public buildings, there was a heap of ruins.

The country between Vicksburg and Jackson was completely devastated. A letter from our lines in Mississippi thus described the outrages there:

"I thought the condition of northern Mississippi and the country around my own home in Memphis deplorable. There robberies were committed, houses were burned, and occasionally a helpless man or woman was murdered; but here, around Jackson and Vicksburg, there are no terms used in all the calendar of crimes which could convey any adequate conception of the revolting enormities perpetrated by our foes. Women have been robbed of their jewelry and wearing apparel—stripped almost to nakedness in the presence of jeering Dutch; ear-rings have been torn from their ears, and rings from bleeding fingers. Every house has been pillaged, and thousands burned. The whole country between the Big Black and the Mississippi, and all that district through which Grant's army passed, is one endless scene of desolation. This is not the worst; robbery and murder are surely bad enough, but worse than all this, women have been subjected to enormities worse than death.

"Negroes, men and women, who can leave their homes, are forced or enticed away. The children alone are left. Barns and all descriptions of farm-houses have been burned. All supplies, bacon and flour, are seized for the use of the invading army, and the wretched inhabitants left to starve. The roads, along which Grant's army has moved, are strewn with all descriptions of furniture, wearing apparel, and private property. In many instances husbands have been arrested, and threatened with instant death by the hangman's rope, in order to make their wives reveal the place of concealment of their valuable effects. The poor women are made to ransom their sons, daughters, and husbands. The worst slaves are selected to insult, taunt, and revile their masters, and the wives and daughters of their masters."

We must remember that these enormities were contemporary with Lee's civilities in Pennsylvania. It was bad enough for that commander to make such return for what he had experienced in Virginia ; but the enemy's warfare in distant and remote parts of the Confederacy exceeded in atrocity what had been known on the lines of the Potomac. It appears to have been aggravated in proportion to its distance from the centres of intelligence. In the Southwest it was not denied that the policy of the enemy was the destruction of all resources of live lihood, but on the border (in Missouri, for instance), the enemy was bold enough to announce the policy of the extermination of the inhabitants.* But to this subject we shall have occasion to refer again.

THE FALL OF PORT HUDSON, ETC.

The fate of Port Hudson was necessarily involved in that of Vicksburg. But it did not fall until after a prolonged and gallant resistance, the facts of which may be briefly commemorated. On the morning of the 22d of May, the enemy, under

---

* For instance, a Missouri paper, speaking of the policy of General Ewing (the Yankee general in command of that department), towards the secessionists of that country, says :

"General Ewing's policy towards these wretches from the very start has been simply *extermination*—nothing less. His orders have been *to take no prisoners from them, and the orders have been strictly obeyed.*"

Again, the St. Louis *Democrat,* an abolition sheet, says, in referring to the troubles on the Missouri border :

"The Seventh Missouri State militia are burning all the houses of rebel sympathizers all along the border. A fearful state of things exists in all the border counties, and general devastation is observable."

One of these ruffians, a Yankee colonel, declared that he would hang every man without "protection papers." He said that "the whole duty" of his regiment (the Fifteenth) would be " to kill rebels ;" and closed with the following atrocious boast : "We carry the flag ; kill with the sabre ; and hang with the gallows."

command of General Banks, pushed his infantry forward
within a mile of our breastworks. Having taken his position
for the investment of our works, he advanced with his whole
force against the breastworks, directing his main attack against
the left, commanded by Colonel Steadman. Vigorous assaults
were also made against the extreme left of Colonel Miles and
General Beale, the former of whom commanded on the centre,
the latter on the right. On the left the attack was made by a
brigade of negroes, composing about three regiments, together
with the same force of white Yankees, across a bridge which
had been built over Sandy creek. About five hundred negroes
in front advanced at double-quick within one hundred and fifty
yards of the works, when the artillery on the river bluff, and
two light pieces on our left, opened upon them, and at the
same time they were received with volleys of musketry. The
negroes fled every way in perfect confusion, and, according to
the enemy's report, six hundred of them perished. The repulse
on Miles' left was decisive.

On the 13th of June a communication was received from
General Banks, demanding the unconditional surrender of the
post. He complimented the garrison in high terms for their
endurance. He stated that his artillery was equal to any in
extent and efficiency; that his men outnumbered ours five to
one; and that he demanded the surrender in the name of
humanity, to prevent a useless sacrifice of life. General Gardner replied that his duty required him to defend the post, and
he must refuse to entertain any such proposition.

On the morning of the 14th, just before day, the fleet and
all the land batteries, which the enemy had succeeded in
erecting at one hundred to three hundred yards from our
breastworks, opened fire at the same time. About daylight,
under cover of the smoke, the enemy advanced along the
whole line, and in many places approached within ten feet of
our works. Our brave soldiers were wide-awake, and, opening
upon them, drove them back in confusion, a great number of
them being left dead in the ditches. One entire division and
a brigade were ordered to charge the position of the First Mississippi and the Ninth Alabama, and by the mere physical
pressure of numbers some of them got within the works, but
all these were immediately killed. After a sharp contest of two

hours, the enemy were everywhere repulsed, and withdrawn to their old lines.

During the remainder of the month of June there was heavy skirmishing daily, with constant firing night and day from the gun and mortar boats. During the siege of six weeks, from May 27th to July 7th, inclusive, the enemy must have fired from fifty to seventy-five thousand shot and shell, yet not more than twenty-five men were killed by these projectiles. They had worse dangers than these to contend against. About the 29th or 30th of June, the garrison's supply of meat gave out, when General Gardner ordered the mules to be butchered after ascertaining that the men were willing to eat them. At the same time the supply of ammunition was becoming exhausted, and at the time of the surrender there were only twenty rounds of cartridges left, with a small supply for artillery.

On Tuesday, July 7th, salutes were fired from the enemy's batteries and gunboats, and loud cheering was heard along the entire line, and Yankees, who were in conversing distance of our men, told them that Vicksburg had fallen. That night about ten o'clock, General Gardner summoned a council of war, who, without exception, decided that it was impossible to hold out longer, considering that the provisions of the garrison were exhausted, the ammunition almost expended, and a large proportion of the men sick or so exhausted as to be unfit for duty. The surrender was accomplished on the morning of the 9th. The number of the garrison which surrendered, was between five and six thousand, of whom not more than half were effective men for duty.

A few days later, and another disaster is to be noticed in Mississippi: the enemy's capture of Yazoo city. He advanced against Yazoo city, both by land and water, on the 13th of July. The attack of the gunboats was handsomely repulsed by our heavy battery, under the command of Commander Isaac N. Brown of the navy. The De Kalb, the flag-ship of the hostile squadron, an iron-clad, mounting thirteen guns, was sunk by a torpedo. To the force advancing by land no resistance was made by the garrison, commanded by Colonel Creasman, of the 29th North Carolina regiment.

The greatest misfortune of this event was our loss in boats

and material of a character much needed. Some twenty vessels were scuttled and destroyed; and of the fine fleet of boats that had sought refuge in the Yazoo river, not more than four or five were saved, which were up the Tallahatchie and Yellobusha.

THE BATTLE OF HELENA.—THE TRANS-MISSISSIPPI.

The Vicksburg disaster was attended with a grave misfortune on the other side of the Mississippi: the repulse of the Confederates at Helena. Our army arrived within five miles of Helena on the evening of the 3d of July, when General Holmes assumed immediate command, detached Marmaduke's division and left Price but two brigades—McRae's Arkansians and Parsons' Missourians—with which he was ordered to assume position, assault and take what was known as the Graveyard Hill the next morning.

The route lay for the greater part of the way across abrupt hills and deep ravines, over which it was utterly impossible to move artillery during the darkness. General Price ordered his artillery to be left behind until daybreak, and moved forward with details from each battery accompanying the infantry, in order to command the guns which he expected to capture.

Within half a mile of the enemy's works, Price's troops were formed into two columns of divisions, Parsons' brigade occupying the right, moving in front. Both brigades moved forward rapidly, steadily, unflinching, and in perfect order under a storm of grape, canister, and minie balls, which were poured upon them not only from the Graveyard Hill in their front, but from the fortified hills upon the right and left, both of which were in easy range. The enemy gave way before the impetuous assault of the attacking columns, which entering the works almost simultaneously, planted the Confederate flag on the summit of the Graveyard Hill.

In the meantime, however, the attack of the enemy's works on Price's left, which was to have been made by General Fagan, had been repeatedly repulsed; although the men fought gallantry, and more than once drove the enemy from his rifle pits, under a heavy enfilading fire from one of the

enemy's strongest forts and a gunboat in front of the town
General Price had ordered McRae's brigade to reinforce Fa
gan; but it soon became obvious that it had been so much
weakened by losses, and by the straggling of men overcome
by thirst and the intense heat of the day, or disheartened by
the failure of the other assaulting column, that it could not be
detached without too greatly endangering General Price's own
position.   Under these circumstances, an order came from
General Holmes to Price to withdraw his division.   The attack was abandoned after a loss to the Confederates of about
five or six hundred killed and wounded, and probably twice
that number of prisoners.

But the result was important in other respects than that of
the casualties of the fight.   It, in connection with the fall of
Vicksburg, terminated all hope of the connection of the Trans-
Mississippi with the eastern portions of the Confederacy, and
was the first step of the retreat which, at last abandoning
Little Rock, was to surrender into the hands of the enemy the
most valuable portion of Arkansas.

It was supposed that the worst consequences of these events
would be to estrange the Trans-Mississippi, and easily subject it
to the arms or to the persuasions of the enemy.   Never were
fears of Confederate statesmen so little realized.   They found
in this distant section of the Confederacy a virtue which had
been maintained under all disasters, and which should be commemorated here in a brief review of the history of this section.

The spirit of the Trans-Mississippi was most conspicuous and
noble in view of the peculiar sufferings it had endured.   It
had made a proud record of patriotic integrity.   In another
volume we have seen how the Confederate forces, in anticipation of a grand contest near Corinth, were moved east of the
Mississippi by order of General Albert Sidney Johnson, then
commanding the Western Department.   We may look back
to that dark period.   The Confederates took with them from
Arkansas all material of war and public property, of every
description.   Immediately afterwards, Brigadier-general Pike
retreated southward, to the vicinity of Red river.   Thus Missouri was left hopeless of early succor, Arkansas without a
soldier, and the Indian country undefended, except by its own
inhabitants.   A Federal force, five thousand strong, was organ-

ized at Fort Scott, under the name of the " Indian expedition," and with the avowed intention to invade the Indian country and wrest it from our control. Hostile Indians began collecting on the border, and Federal emissaries were busy among the Cherokees and Creeks, inciting disaffection. Detachments of Federal cavalry penetrated, at will, into various parts of the upper half of Arkansas, plundering and burning houses, stealing horses and slaves, destroying farming utensils, murdering loyal men or carrying them into captivity, forcing the oath of allegiance on the timid, and disseminating disloyal sentiments among the ignorant. Tory bands were organized in many counties, not only in the upper, but in the lower half of the State likewise, and depredations and outrages upon loyal citizens were of constant occurrence. Straggling soldiers, belonging to distant commands, traversed the country, armed and lawless, robbing the people of their property, under the pretence of "impressing" it for the Confederate service. The governor and other executive officers fled from the capital, taking the archives with them. The courts were suspended, and civil magistrates almost universally ceased to exercise their functions. Confederate money was openly refused, or so depreciated as to be nearly worthless. This, with the short crop of the preceding year, and the failure, on all the uplands, of the one then growing, gave rise to the cruelest extortion in the necessaries of life, and menaced the poor with actual starvation.

But it was not only the omissions of the Richmond Administration of which the Trans-Mississippi had to complain. There were perpetrated upon it such positive outrages of the Confederate authority as had never been ventured or imagined in other portions of the country. The excesses of Major-general Hindman, who assumed, by a certain color of authority from Richmond, to be commanding-general of the Trans-Mississippi, had been severely censured by members of the Confederate Congress, and were the subject of an investigation in that body. They were such as might have moved any people from their allegiance, whose patriotism was not paramount to all other considerations. He suspended the civil authority, and instituted what he called "a government *ad interim*." In the summer of 1863, he had proclaimed martial law. To make this declaration effective, a provost martial was appointed in each county, and all the independent companies therein were placed under his control. Over these were appointed provost marshals of districts which included several counties. The provost marshal general, at General Hindman's headquarters, had command over all.

Whatever may have been the good intentions or the pallia tive circumstances of this singular usurpation, it certainly could not be agreeable to a people accustomed to civil liberty; and it was an excrescence of the war, after the fashion of Yankee "vigor," which did serious dishonor to the Confederacy. We have referred to it here to illustrate the virtues of a people, whose steadfast patriotism could survive such trials.

As we have elsewhere seen, General Holmes assumed command of the Trans-Mississippi Department in the latter part of 1862. His operations had been feeble and unsuccessful. The fall of Vicksburg and the defeat at Helena, were irreparable disasters. Communication was interrupted between the two sections of the Confederacy, and each thrown on its own resources. It was supposed that this division of the efforts of the Confederacy would tend to weakness and jealousies. But these fears were dismissed, when it was known that the governors of the States of the Trans-Mississippi had made the recent disasters an occasion of official conference, in which they had taken the noble resolution to do their respective parts in the war, and to take care that the common cause of our independence should not suffer by a division of the efforts to obtain it. They declared that, instead of such division of effort being occasion of jealousy, it should be that of noble and patriotic rivalry.

It is not to be denied that it was unfortunate that the Eastern States and those of the Trans-Mississippi had been constrained to separate efforts in the war. But it was an especial subject of congratulation and pride that the spirit and unanimity of the South were unaffected by such an event, and that the most distant people of the Confederacy, not only faithfully kept, but fondly cherished their attachment to the vital prin iple of our struggle and the common cause of our arms.

CHAPTER IV.

THE most remarkable quality displayed by the Southern mind in this war has been its elasticity under reverse, its quick recovery from every impression of misfortune. This, more than any thing else, has attested the strength of our resolution to be free, and shown the utter insignificance of any " peace party," or element of submission or compromise in the Confederacy. Great as were the disasters of Vicksburg and Gettysburg they were the occasions of no permanent depression of the public mind ; and as the force of misfortune could scarcely, at any one time, be expected to exceed these events, it may be said they taught the lesson that the spirit of the Confederacy could not be conquered unless by some extremity close to annihilation. A few days after the events referred to President Davis took occasion, in a proclamation of pardon to deserters, to declare that a victorious peace, with proper exertions, was yet immediately within our grasp. Nor was he extravagant in this. The loss of territory which we had sustained, unaccompanied as it was by any considerable adhesion of its population to the enemy, though deplorable indeed, was not a

vital incident of the war : it had reduced the resources of sub
sistence, but it had multiplied the spirit of resistance, and it
was yet very far from the centre of our defence.   While Mr.
Seward was making to Europe material calculations of Yankee success in the square miles of military occupation and in
the comparative arithmetic of the military power of the belligerents, the Confederacy had merely postponed its prospect of
a victorious peace, and was even more seriously confident of
the ultimate issue than when it first declared its independence.

But it must not be disguised that one, and perhaps the most
important of the disasters referred to—the fall of Vicksburg—
while no occasion of despair to the Confederacy, was yet that
of another great decline of popular confidence in the Administration of President Davis.   Happily, every page of the history of this war attests that the dissatisfaction of the Confederate people with the Richmond Administration was compa-
tible with steady attachment to that cause for which they
fought and which was impersonal and sublime.   It is the fact
of these two existing conditions in the Confederacy, a puzzle
to many, that gives the sublimest quality to this war, and contains its most valuable lesson.

Never had the obstinate adhesion of President Davis to his
favorites been more forcibly illustrated than in the case of
Pemberton.   The criticism of the public had no charity for
this commander, and his recent campaign, culminating in the
surrender of Vicksburg, was denounced by the intelligent as a
series of blunders, and by others less just and more passionate
as the device of treason.   President Davis had retained him in
command in spite of the most powerful remonstrance ever
made by a people against the gratification of a personal conceit in their ruler.   Indeed, the President went further than
mere opposition to the public sentiment.   He defied and almost insulted it; for after the disaster of Vicksburg, Pemberton, with the public reproaches clinging to him, and public
sentiment clamoring in vain for an inquiry into his conduct,
was ostentatiously entertained as the President's guest in Richmond, and given the distinction of one of his suite in the sub
sequent official visit of the President to our armies in the
West !   It was said by Mr. Foote, in public session of Congress, that when the President, with a peculiar hardihood, es-

sayed to ride down the lines of our troops, with Pemberton at his side, angry exclamations assailed them, and passed from lip to lip of the soldiers.

There were certain events which aided in relieving the im pression of the Vicksburg disaster, or, at least, served to divert the public mind. Of these were the operations of the Confederate general, Taylor, in Lower Louisiana, some of which had preceded the fall of Vicksburg, and, at one time, had kindled in the South the hope of the recapture of New Orleans.

HEE CAMPAIGN IN LOWER LOUISIANA.

Information received from Southwest Louisiana had determined General Taylor to organize an attack upon Brashear City and its forts. Colonel Majors, who commanded a brigade of cavalry on the Atchafalaya, was to push boldly through the Grosse Tete, Marangoin and Lafourche country, to Donaldsonville, thence to Thibodeaux, cut off the railroad and telegraph communication, then push rapidly to Bœuf river, in the rear of Brashear City, while a force under Generals Mouton and Green was to co-operate in front of the enemy's position, on Berwick's Bay.

On the 22d of June General Mouton had succeeded in collecting some thirty-seven skiffs and other row-boats, near the mouth of the Teche, with a view to co-operate, from the west side of the Atchafalaya, with Colonel Majors' command, then on the Lafourche. An expedition, numbering three hundred and twenty-five gallant volunteers, under Major Sherod Hunter, started at 6 o'clock P. M., to turn the enemy's stronghold at Brashear City. It was a hazardous mission to cross the lake (twelve miles) in these frail barks, to land at midnight on the enemy's side, in an almost impenetrable swamp, and await the dawn of day, to make the desperate attempt which would insure victory or a soldier's death.

The boat-expedition having got off, General Thomas Green, with the Fifth Texas mounted volunteers, the Second Louisiana cavalry, Waller's Texas battalion, and the Valverde and Nicholls' batteries, advanced, under cover of night, to opposite the enemy's camp. The Seventh and Fourth Texas regiments were thrown across the Atchafalaya, to Gibbons' Island, during the night. General Green was to attract the enemy's attention and fire, while the troops on Gibbons' Island were to be thrown across to the support of Major Hunter, as soon as the boats returned from the latter's landing-point, in rear of the enemy's position.

Immediately after daylight, General Green fired the first gun from the Valverde battery, at a gunboat of the enemy, which was steaming up the bay in the direction of the upper fort (Buchanan). Instantly the whole bay was in a blaze, our guns playing upon the long lines of the enemy's tents. The Yankees were completely surprised. Their heavy guns, from three forts, opened on Green. There was a keen anxiety on our side for the sound of Colonel Majors' guns, for it only remained for him to occupy the Bœuf crossing, to cut off completely the enemy's communication. At last the long-distant sound of artillery told that Majors was there; and at the same moment the storming party of Major Hunter made its appearance on the edge of a piece of woods. With a real Texas yell the latter dashed at once, with bayonets fixed and pistols drawn, full at the threatening walls of the proud fort—in twenty minutes they had climbed its walls, dispersed its garrison, torn down the stars and stripes, and hoisted the Confederate flag over its ramparts. This heroic charge was made at the point of the bayonet, with unloaded muskets. In half an hour Generals Taylor, Mouton, and Green, with their respective staffs, had their headquarters in the city of Brashear.

The immediate fruits of the capture were one thousand prisoners, ten heavy guns, and a large amount of stores of all descriptions. The position obtained by General Taylor, with that of Thibodeaux, gave him command of the Mississippi river above New Orleans; enabled him, in a great measure, to cut off Banks' supplies, and, it was hoped, might eventually force Banks to the choice of losing New Orleans or abandoning his operations against Port Hudson.

But the plan which General Taylor had arranged for an attack on New Orleans unfortunately fell through, in consequence of his disappointment of reinforcements. His active force, not including the garrison at Berwick's Bay, was less than four thousand. He had obtained from New Orleans in-

telligence of the fall of Vicksburg, and this, with the consequent fate of Port Hudson, rendered his position in the La
fourche extremely hazardous, and not to be justified on military
grounds.

On the 28th of June General Green had been repulsed in
an attack on Donaldsonville, after a desperate struggle, with
two hundred and sixty casualties. On the 12th of July, after
the fall of Port Hudson, the enemy, over four thousand strong,
advanced six miles from Donaldsonville, where he was met by
General Green, with his own and a part of Majors' brigade
(in all twelve hundred men), and driven from the field, with a
loss of about five hundred in killed and wounded, some three
hundred prisoners, three pieces of artillery, many small arms,
and the flag of a New York regiment. The gallant Green
dismounted from his horse, placed himself at the head of his
old regiment, captured the enemy's guns, and drove his forces
into the fort, and under the guns of the fleet.

These operations in Lower Louisiana were not followed by
the important consequences which were at one time anticipated : for, as we have seen, Taylor's force was not competent to
hold the Lafourche country against the overwhelming forces
of the enemy released from the siege of Port Hudson. Yet
the events we have briefly narrated, had afforded a certain encouragement to the South ; for they were, at least, some relief
from the unwelcome news we had hitherto had from an ill-
starred portion of the Confederacy.

But one must look in another direction for the first important wave of the returning tide of victory that was to cover
the popular recollection of Vicksburg, and again exalt the
hopes and confidence of the Confederacy.

THE SIEGE OF CHARLESTON.

The enemy had prepared to follow up the achievements of
the summer campaign, by a vigorous attempt upon Charleston.
It had been determined by General Gilmore, in command of
the Yankee forces, to take Folly Island, as the base of siege
operations against Charleston, and to possess, if possible, Morris Island, under the belief that it was the key to Charleston.

This latter island is an outer strip of land, lying directly on the ocean. It is some three and a half miles in length, and the northern end, crowned by Cummings' Point Battery, was the goal aimed at by the enemy, as it bore directly on Fort Sumter and the channel leading by it to the city. At the southern extremity of the island was another battery, pointing out towards the north end of Folly Island, where the Yankees had been encamped for many months, and constructing heavy works. It was known and reported to the Confederate government, that Folly Island was occupied in force since the 7th of April, and, as a consequence, that Morris Island was threatened. The changes of land and naval commanders of the enemy were reported as presages of impending hostilities. But in vain. All ideas of attack were scouted at Richmond, as late even as the first week in July.

General Beauregard's force at Charleston had been greatly reduced by the authorities, under the persistent belief that the city and adjoining coast were safe from any serious military operations of the enemy. He was left to provide against attacks upon Charleston in no less than five different directions. There is no doubt that he had been seriously embarrassed in his attempts to put Morris Island in condition to meet the attack of the enemy, by the want of labor to carry out the plans for its defence; want of armament for the works necessary to that end; and last, but not least, want of men to hold and fight any works which might have been thrown up at the south end of Morris Island, without stripping other important positions of the feeble supports left them.

But although General Beauregard must have had a general expectation of attack in this direction, it is not to be disguised, that he was surprised in the time and manner of its development. It is said, that he had not force enough left to venture upon a thorough reconnoissance of the enemy's outposts on Folly Island. For a number of weeks the enemy had been busily engaged on this point of land, in building sand batteries and mounting heavy guns within eight hundred yards of our works on Morris Island. The work was all performed under cover of the night. Screened from observation by the nature of the ground, hundreds of men were engaged night after night, silently and industriously throwing up earthworks, and mounting heavy guns so near to the Confederates that a loud word might have revealed the work. Shortly before daylight brush would be so disposed as to conceal the work of the previous night, without exciting the suspicions of the Confederates. The morning light would dawn upon a quiet and deserted scene—not a soul to be seen—not a sound to be heard—not a thing to indicate offensive operations that the night had concealed. In this manner batteries were thrown up, and guns and mortars put in position.

On the evening of the 9th, a division of the enemy was sent up Stono river to effect a landing on James Island, near a place called Stevens' Point. This movement was partially intended to occupy the attention of our forces, and conceal from them the real object of the large fleet of vessels hovering about Stono Inlet, and movements of the enemy on Folly Island. At nightfall small boats, loaded with armed men, began to dash out from either shore. These men were to make their way up the narrow creek, which makes into Morris Island, and there wait till morning, when on a given signal they would assault the battery. This force was under General Strong.

At daybreak on the following morning, the brush and boughs, which had served to conceal the battery on Folly Island from observation, were hastily removed, and the guns exposed to the Confederates. At five o'clock the first gun was heard from the enemy's battery. The battery was somewhat screened from view by a grove of trees, but the incessant cannonade, and the dense white smoke, which rose above the tall pines, told how fearfully the contest raged.

In the meantime the assaulting column of the enemy, consisting of three regiments, moved on slowly and silently up the beach, until they arrived within two hundred yards of Fort Wagner, when the Confederate pickets were encountered. The order to charge was given. The fort opened with three eight-inch howitzers, heavily charged with grape and canister. The Seventh Connecticut, which was in the advance, pressed through the fort, but the Pennsylvania and New York regiments, which were to support them, staggered back and lost their distance, when all three regiments broke into a shameful run, scattering down the beach.

The assault of the enemy was a shameful failure. The loss of life was inconsiderable, as two of the regiments kept out of the fire, and we may imagine how many were "missing" when the casualties in the storming party were officially enumerated by the enemy as three hundred and thirty-four. But as our lower battery had been abandoned, the Yankees had succeeded in getting possession of the lower end of the island. They had gained a foothold, and were now to direct all their energies to get possession of Fort Wagner. This strong earthwork was near midway of the island, and had to be reduced before the enemy could reach Cummings' Point, and operate from there on Fort Sumter.

The enemy having once obtained a foothold on Morris Island, it might have been easily foreseen that he would eventually compel an evacuation by the operations of siege, and the impossibility of defending forever a small island cut off from communication by an enormous fleet. But it was not to be given up without a brilliant incident of arms; for General Beauregard had determined to hold it, while works were elsewhere erected, and until the door of honorable retreat was open.

In about a week the Yankees had occupied Black Island—a small spot between James and Morris Islands—and thrown up a battery; they had erected two or three additional batteries on Morris Island, about one and three-quarter miles from Fort Wagner, and they had concentrated their fleet, consisting of four monitors, the Ironsides, a frigate, and four gunboats, some of which threw shell from mortars. Altogether, the circle of fire embraced not far from seventy guns. At daylight, of the 18th August, these opened, first deliberately; but as the morning wore on the fire increased. Two monitors, two mortar boats, and the Ironsides, had by ten o'clock formed a line nearly in front of Battery Wagner, and about noon these were joined by two additional monitors. Until six o'clock in the evening the firing was incessant. There was scarcely an interval that did not contain a reverberation of the heavy guns, and the shock of the rapid discharges trembling through the city called hundreds of citizens to the battery, wharves, steeples, and various look-outs, where, with an interest never felt before, they looked on a contest that might decide the fate of their fair city. Above Battery Wagner, bursting high in air, striking the sides of the work or plunging into the beach, and throwing up pillars of earth, were to be seen the quickly succeeding shells and round shot of the enemy's guns. Battery Gregg at Cummings' Point and Fort Sumter took part in the thundering chorus. As the shades of evening fell upon the scene the entire horizon appeared to be lighted up with the fitful flashings of the lurid flames that shot out from monster guns on land and sea.

As night began to fall the bombardment relaxed. But it was known to our officers commanding that such a demonstration on the part of the enemy was not without its object; and every man was ordered, by General Taliaferro, who commanded our side, to the parapet to prepare for the expected assault of the enemy.

At dusk two brigades of the enemy were formed in line on the beach. The regiments were disposed in columns, except a Massachusetts regiment of blacks, which, for peculiar reasons, was given the post of extreme honor and extreme danger in the advance, and was drawn up in line of battle, exposing its full front to our fire.

The enemy moved forward at quick time and in deep silence. As they reached the vicinity of our rifle-pits, our batteries opened, and grape and canister was thrown into their ranks with fearful precision and execution. Checked for an instant only, they closed up the ragged gaps in their lines and moved steadily on until within less than eighty yards.

Barely waiting for the Yankees to get within a destructive range our infantry opened their fusilade, and from a fringe of fire that lined the parapet leaped forth a thousand messengers of death. Staggering under the shock, the first line seemed for a moment checked, but, pushed on by those in the rear, the whole now commenced a charge at a "double-quick." Our men could not charge back; but they gave a Southern yell in response to the Yankee cheer, and awaited the attack. On they came over the sand-hills, tripping and stumbling in the huge pits their own shells had dug, until they reached the ditch of the battery; then it was but a moment's work for those who survived our terrible fire of musketry to clamber up the sloping sides of the fortification and attempt to effect a

lodgment. But the men who met them on the parapet were as
desperate as themselves, and the contest that ensued was brief
and bloody. The antagonists were breast to breast, and Southern rifles and Southern bayonets made short work of human
life. We could stop to take no prisoners then. The parapet
was lined with dead bodies, white and black, and every second
was adding to the number. It was one of those rencounters in
which one side or the other must quickly yield or fly. The
enemy took their choice.

In less than five minutes probably, the first line had been
shot, bayoneted, or were in full retreat—rolling into the ditch
or dragging their bloody bodies through the sand-hills on their
hands and knees. But another line came, and another and
another, each reinforcing its predecessor, until the battle waxed
hot, fierce, and bloody. Finally, however, the whole were
driven back, either into the broad trench at the base of the
battery, out of reach of our guns, or scampering out of view in
the darkness of the night.

There was now a comparative lull in the firing, but in fifteen
or twenty minutes a second column of Yankees filed down on
the beach towards the left of the fort in much the same manner
as that pursued by the first. These repeated the experiment
that had just before terminated so disastrously to their companions, and, with a bravery that was worthy of a better
cause, dashed upon the work. The first assault failed utterly,
but with the reinforcements that joined the defeated party,
they came again with such strength and impetuosity that
between the extreme darkness of the night, which had now
enveloped the entire scene, the difficulty of distinguishing
friend and foe, and the confusion incident to such an occasion,
some two or three hundred, as is estimated, effected a lodgment in the vicinity of the chambers occupied by two of our
guns. Most of these were taken prisoners.

About midnight the enemy gave the order to retire. His
repulse had been terribly disastrous in loss of life. His killed
and wounded, according to his own accounts, was fifteen
hundred and fifty ; and the next day we buried six hundred of
his dead left on the field. Our own loss was comparatively
light, not more than one hundred in killed and wounded.

While the enemy was constrained to fall back upon siege

operations against Fort Wagner, it was determined by Gilmore to employ his batteries in the reduction of Fort Sumter, over the heads of both Wagner and Gregg.

But there was an episode, which was an introduction to these operations against Sumter, and which must not be omitted here. On the 21st of August, Gilmore addressed to General Beauregard a demand, which was curiously without signature, for the evacuation of Morris Island and Fort Sumter; stating that Sumter was already doomed to swift and complete demolition, and that, if the Confederate commander did not comply with his demand *within four hours,* a fire would be opened on the city of Charleston from batteries already established *within easy and effective reach of the heart of the city.* In the following night and without further notice fire was opened on the city from Morris Island batteries. Twelve eight-inch shells fell in the city; several flew in the direction of St. Michael's steeple; but fortunately no one was injured.

Of this atrocious and cowardly episode General Beauregard said in a letter addressed to Gilmore: "It would appear, Sir, that, despairing of reducing these works, you now resort to the novel means of turning your guns against the old men, the women and children, and the hospitals of a sleeping city; an act of inexcusable barbarity from your own confessed point of sight, inasmuch as you allege that the complete demolition of Fort Sumter within a few hours by your guns seems to you a matter of certainty; and your omission to attach your signature to such a grave paper must show the recklessness of the course upon which you have adventured, while the fact that you knowingly fixed a limit for receiving an answer to your demand, which made it almost beyond the possibility of receiving any reply within that time, and that you actually did open fire and threw a number of the most destructive missiles ever used in war into the midst of a city taken unawares, and filled with sleeping women and children, will give you a bad eminence in history—even in the history of this war."

The same day that Gilmore made his feeble attempt to execute the threat he had so fiercely and confidently breathed against Charleston, he opened heavily against the east face of Fort Sumter from his land batteries enfilading it. The cannonade was continued throughout the day, nine hundred and forty-three shots being fired. The effect was to batter the eastern face heavily, doing considerable damage, and to disable one ten-inch gun and a rifled forty-two pounder. On the 22d the enemy threw six hundred and four shots at the fort, disabling some of the barbette guns, demolishing the arches of the north-west face, and scaling the eastern face severely. The next day the fire from the enemy's land batteries was kept up on Sumter, disabling the only ten-inch columbiad that remained, and the three rifled forty-two-pounders in the northern salient of the second tier. The eastern face was badly scaled, and the parapet seriously injured. The flag-staff was twice shot away, but the flag each time immediately replaced.

On the 24th of August General Gilmore announced in despatches to Washington that "Fort Sumter was a shapeless and harmless mass of ruins." His chief of artillery reported its destruction so far complete that it was no longer of any avail in the defence of Charleston. But in this there was some mistake. Fort Sumter was in one respect stronger than ever; for the battering down of the upper walls had rendered the casemated base impregnable, and the immense volume of stone and debris which protected it was not at all affected by the enemy's artillery. It had been held through the siege and cannonade by the First South Carolina artillery, under Colonel Alfred Rhett, until its armament had been disabled; and the services of the artillerymen being elsewhere required, General Beauregard determined that it should be held by infantry. On the night of the 4th of September, the Charleston battalion, under Major Blake, relieved the garrison; Major Stephen Elliot relieving Colonel Rhett in command of the post.

In the mean time the enemy's operations on Morris Island had fearfully progressed. His sappers had advanced up to the very moat of Wagner. On the night of the 4th September the enemy kept up a continual fire, and on the morning of the 5th the Ironsides combined her fire with the enemy's land batteries, all concentrated on Wagner. The effect was to severely injure the traverses and communications, and to disable the guns and equipments still more effectually. But Wagner was not the only object of this bombardment. During the night of the 5th the enemy displayed from the deck of a monitor off Morris Island an immense calcium light, and several monitors soon after moved up and opened on battery Gregg. Moultrie and Gregg replied with spirit. At a quarter to two a rocket was thrown up, and ere many minutes elapsed, the enemy were discerned approaching Morris Island at a point between Gregg and Wagner. They had come down in barges through a creek west of Morris Island, obviously with the design of assaulting Gregg in the rear. Advancing in line of battle they were permitted to come very near, when a nine inch Dahlgren opened upon them at short range, with double canister. Our howitzers then commenced a fire of shrapnel and canister, while our infantry, admirably posted, poured into them a fire of musketry. This the Yankees could not withstand, and though for a very short while they maintained a fire of musketry and grape shot from their barges, they were soon forced to withdraw.

For three days and nights battery Wagner had been subjected to the most terrific fire that any earthwork had undergone in all the annals of warfare. In these nights the whole of Charleston harbor had been lighted up in a scene of terrible beauty. From Moultrie almost to Secessionville a whole semicircle of the horizon was lit up by incessant flashes from cannon and shell. As peal on peal of artillery rolled across the waters, one could scarcely resist the belief that not less than a thousand great guns were in action. All this went on beneath a waning September moon, which, with its warm Southern light, mellowed by a somewhat misty atmosphere, brought out softly, yet distinctly, the most distant outlines of the harbor.

The effect of the fire on Wagner had been terrible. The immense descending force of the enormous Parrott and mortar shells of the enemy had nearly laid the wood work of the bombproofs entirely bare, and had displaced the sand to so great a degree that the sally-ports were almost entirely blocked up. Wagner and battery Gregg had now been held under a continued and furious cannonade, by land and sea, for fifty-seven days; two assaults had been signally and gloriously repulsed; the enemy had been forced to expend time, men and material, most lavishly in approaching the first; but at this time he was within a few yards of the salient; most of the guns of the fort were injured, transportation and supply had become most difficult with the inefficient means at our disposal, the possibility of throwing heavy reinforcements in time to resist an assault by the enemy's overwhelming forces, issuing from his trenches only a few yards distant, out of the question, and the practicability of keeping a sufficient force on the island for the purpose, under the furious cannonade from land and sea, without protecting shelter, scarcely less so. This matter had been some time under consideration by General Beauregard, and after receiving reports concerning the state of the works, and our capabilities for reinforcing the garrison, it was determined not to subject those brave men, the flower of our force, to the desperate chances of assault. Orders were accordingly given, on the morning of the 6th, to prepare for evacuation.

It commenced about 9 p. m., and was concluded at about twelve. The guns of the batteries were spiked and implements generally destroyed. Matches were fixed to explode the magazines, but, from some unfortunate cause, both those at Wagner and Gregg failed to explode. The enemy threw his calcium light on Wagner during the whole night, and one of the most furious bombardments on record, even during this war, was continuously kept up while the movements were progressing; but he did not ascertain the evacuation until the last of the boats were leaving. Then his guard-boats discovered the movement of our boats engaged in the embarkation, and creeping up upon the rear succeeded in cutting off and capturing three barges.

Thus ended the defence of Morris Island—one relieved by much of glory to Confederate arms, and its conclusion, as we shall soon see, an empty advantage to the enemy. The defence had been prolonged far beyond what was deemed possible at first, and the brave garrisons who had held it deserved the admiration of their countrymen. The aggregate of casualties in the struggle for the Island have been on our side about seven hundred—killed, wounded, and missing. The enemy's loss was estimated at several thousand.

The occupation of Morris Island was the signal to the enemy of great but temporary exultation. The Yankee newspapers flattered their readers that it was the key of Charleston. But the fact was that no one point in its fortification could be so called. In the system of Vaughan there was always such a point;—once taken, it commanded the rest. But the excellence of the new system of defence, illustrated at Comorn and Sebastopol, and repeated at Charleston, was the necessity of a siege for every battery, in which the besiegers were always exposed to the fire of others. It was easily seen by the Confederates that such a defence, if conducted with courage, by an army which could not be surrounded and starved, might be easily rendered interminable.

But such was not the opinion of Gilmore. On his occupation of the island he announced to the exultant authorities at Washington: "The city and harbor of Charleston are now completely covered by my guns." Now was the time, declared the newspapers, for the famous *Greek fire* to pour destruction upon "the secession city." "General Gilmore," said the Baltimore *American*, "may be expected to roll his fire-shells through the streets of Charleston." That commander had already been experimenting in liquid fire, and in a new style of bombs filled with fuses. During the bombardment of Sumter, in one of his official despatches he had declared with devilish complacency: "the projectiles from my batteries entered the city of Charleston, and General Beauregard himself designates them as the most destructive missiles used in war."

But the enemy's fleet was now to appear upon the scene to accomplish the reduction of Charleston. General Gilmore had proposed—firstly, the occupation of the southern portion of Morris Island; secondly, the capture of Wagner and Gregg; thirdly, the reduction of Sumter. At that point Admiral Dahlgren was to take up the work, for it was calculated that if Gilmore succeeded in his designs, the navy would find it a comparatively easy task to ascend the harbor of Charleston.

But had the condition as to Sumter been fulfilled? On the 7th of September Admiral Dahlgren sent in a flag of truce demanding a surrender of the fort. General Beauregard telegraphed to Major Elliot to reply that the Yankees could have Fort Sumter when they took it and held it, and that, in the mean time, such demands were puerile and unbecoming.

Dahlgren was left to complete the programme in Charleston Harbor, and the North waited to hear that the possession of 'the shapeless mass of ruins" that had once been Fort Sum ter was readily accomplished, and that Charleston, the cyno-sure of Yankee hatred, was at last the prize of the costly and protracted operations. It remained for the Yankee admiral to accept the invitation to assault Sumter, and he proposed to do so by an elaborate surprise. A special force of picked men from all the fleet was organized for a night attack.

It was midnight of the 8th of September, when the expedi-tion, consisting of over twenty boats, and with thirty-four officers and four hundred and thirteen men, of which one hundred and twenty were marines, all under the command of Commander Stevens, pulled its way silently and cautiously towards Fort Sumter. The plan was to assail the fort on three sides—one party landing on the gorge-wall, and attempting to ascend the debris and gain the parapet; a second was to at-tempt to gain entrance through the lower embrasures, and a third was to act as a reserve.

At half-past one in the morning the first line of boats was close upon the fort. The enemy had supposed it to be feebly garrisoned, and had hoped to find an unguarded moment. The garrison consisted of the Charleston Battalion, command by Major Stephen Elliot. They were not asleep. As the Yankee boats crept up to the huge and shapeless mass of shivered walls, all was dark and still; the great black rifted mound seemed some long-deserted ruin, where the lizards had crept into their holes for the night, and the very bats and owls had gone to bed. They approached with beating hearts. It appeared, indeed, that the hour of doom for Sumter and for Charleston was come.

Suddenly a "fire of hell" streamed from out of the night. The stilly ruin becomes as a throat of the bottomless pit; the bay is lighted with signals; and on the instant, from Fort Moultrie and from a gunboat in the harbor, hail of shot and shell comes crashing around the barges.

Major Elliot had caused his fire to be reserved until the enemy was within a few yards of the southern and eastern faces upon which the landing was attempted. A close fire of musketry devoured those who had landed; while three of the boats were torn to pieces by hand grenades or shells from the distant batteries. The garrison lined the walls of Sumter, and as the Yankees landed on the rocks, received them with sharp volleys of musketry, which added confusion to their already bewildered movements. A strong party of the enemy now hastily gathered and made an attempt to climb over the ruin of the sally-port, which had been torn down by the tremendous fire of their land batteries. Our men received them breast to breast, pelting them with brickbats and pouring in a spattering shower of balls. Some bolder than the others, dashed forward, and seizing Yankees, one in each hand, dragged them by main force inside. Thus the fight raged for twenty or thirty minutes, when the Yankees, finding themselves overpowered, and likely to be cut to pieces, threw down their arms, retreated to the shelter of the walls and surrendered. Those who remained in the boats, not already landed, made their escape under the cover of the night, followed, however, by the spiteful balls of the batteries of Moultrie and of the gunboat Chicora.

Not a life was lost on our side. Major Elliot succeeded in securing five boats, five stand of colors, twelve officers, and one hundred and nine men, including two officers and seventeen men wounded. Amongst the captured colors was a worn and torn garrison-flag, reported by some of the prisoners as being that which Major Anderson was permitted to take from the fort, on the occasion of his being compelled to surrender, in April, 1861. This had been brought to hoist on the fort, and to be made the subject of boast and Yankee "sensation," had the assault succeeded. " It was," says a Charleston paper, " the identical ' gridiron' carried from Fort Sumter in 1861 : exhibited to a monster mass meeting in New York shortly after ; talked, cheered, and prayed over until almost sanctified ; wrapped around the gouty limbs of General Scott, and finally brought back under oath that it should be victoriously replanted on the walls where it was first lowered in recognition of the Southern Confederacy."

This unsuccessful attempt to open the way to Charleston, leaves but little to record of the operations of the enemy against this famous city. Those operations were to be nominally continued for many long and weary months ; there were daily bulletins of bombardments ; but the more intelligent persons of the North were not to be deceived by the noisy and expensive display, and readily came to the conclusion that the

siege of Charleston was a failure, and that, despite Dahlgren s
noisy protest, it was virtually abandoned. Months were to
pass, and the Yankee admiral was to make no attempt to
move up the harbor and complete not only the remaining part
of the expedition, but that which he had promised to do when
he assumed command of the fleet.

It is unnecessary to pursue here the desultory record of a
fruitless bombardment. The Yankee public had had such a
series of emotions, surprises, and disappointments about
Charleston, that it sickened of the name, and seemed to be
fast progressing to the opinion that the monitors were a failure, that their Parrott guns and monster artillery had been
greatly overrated, and that sand-bank fortifications were substantially impregnable to their vaunted artillery. " How
many times," asked an indignant Philadelphia paper, " has
Fort Sumter been taken? How many times has Charleston
been burned? How often have the people been on the eve of
starvation and surrender? How many times has the famous
Greek fire poured the rain of Sodom and the flames of hell
upon the secession city? We cannot keep the count—though
those can who rang the bells and put out the flags, and
invoked the imprecations, and rejoiced at the story of conflagration and ruin."

We must leave here the story of Charleston : the city safe
beneath the pale autumn sky, with the waters of its beautiful
bay unvexed by the busy keel of commerce, yet sleeping
quietly ; while across them might be seen the Yankee flag
floating from the parapet of Wagner, then the enemy's batteries, still beyond these the white tents of the enemy, and
further yet, over the woods of James Island, the masts of the
fleet. A large besieging force was in sight of the spires of
Charleston, and yet the city was safe, and proclaimed to the
Confederacy new lessons of brilliant courage and hope.

We have referred to the period which this chapter traverses
as one of encouraging events for the South. The reader's
attention must be turned back from the coast to the fields of
the West, for another in the list of successes which made this
period fortunate.

Jno H Morgan

From a Photograph from life.

MORGAN'S EXPEDITION INTO INDIANA AND OHIO.

The command of General Morgan, consisting of detachments from two brigades, numbering two thousand and twenty-eight effective men, with four pieces of artillery—two Parrotts and two howitzers—left Sparta, Tennessee, on the 27th of June, and crossed the Cumberland near Burkesville on the 2d July.

On the 4th of July, the expedition took up the line of march for Green river bridge. An attack was here made upon the enemy, who were found to be posted in a strong position, protected by well constructed stockades. On account of the superior strength of the works our forces failed to carry the position.

From Green river bridge Morgan next directed his attention to the town of Lebanon. He encamped within five miles of the place on the night of the 4th. He at once demanded the surrender of the place, which was refused by the Yankee officer in command of the post. A heavy engagement ensued next day, which lasted, with considerable spirit, for some hours, the Yankees stubbornly resisting, firing from the houses. Finally a charge was ordered, and· the town was captured, together with the whole Yankee force, consisting of about six hundred effective men, together with a large amount of stores, arms, &c. In the charge was killed Lieutenant Thos. Morgan, a brother of the general, who was shot through the heart. He fell at the very first volley. His only words were, " Brother Cally, they have killed me."

The commandant of the post was Colonel Hanson, a brother of General Hanson, who had fallen on our side at Murfreesboro'. He had behaved with extraordinary gallantry. When a surrender was demanded by Morgan, at his first approach, Colonel Hanson quietly remarked, "If it was any other day he might consider the demand, but the 4th of July was a bad day to talk about surrender, and he must, therefore, decline." His command had been raised in the heart of the Blue Grass region, and among them were brothers and other near relatives of Morgan's own men. This unnatural encounter between men of the same blood and same family—a painful incident of all the Kentucky campaigns—was heightened in its horrible ferocity by the death of General Morgan's brother, a favorite of his comrades, who undertook to revenge his death, and who were with difficulty restrained by their officers from the indiscriminate slaughter of the enemy and pillage of the town.

It is to be remarked that, in all his expeditions, General Morgan restrained his men from all outrages, and was very severe upon those bad men inseparable from adventures of his sort, and who accompanied them simply for plunder. But the day before the Lebanon fight, a terrible incident had occurred in his little army. An officer of the expedition, whose journal lies before us, writes of this occurrence: "About three o'clock, as I rode on about forty yards in advance, I heard the general exclaim something in a very excited tone which I could not understand; and heard at the same time the report of a pistol. I turned, and, great God! to my horror, I saw Captain Magennis falling from his horse, with the blood rushing out of his mouth and breast. His only remark was, 'Let me down easy.' In another moment his spirit had fled. He was killed by Captain Murphy, because Magennis, by the direction of General Morgan, had ordered Murphy to restore a watch taken from a prisoner."

Leaving Lebanon, Morgan proceeded to Bardstown, where he captured some cavalry, advanced then upon the Louisville and Nashville railroad, and next reached Garnettsville, when a feint was made upon the city of Louisville, whilst preparations were on foot to effect a crossing of the Ohio river. A scouting party was sent to the river at Brandensburg, at which point two steamers were captured. Here the command effected a crossing of the river, after a severe fight with the enemy. They captured about one hundred Home Guards, one rifled twelve-pounder piece, and successfully repulsed two gunboats.

On the 8th of July, Morgan's little command stood on the soil of Indiana. He immediately took up the line of march for the town of Corydon, where he captured about 600 militia and some few regular soldiers. Salem was the next point which invited his attention, where an immense amount of damage was inflicted upon the enemy by the destruction of railroad property, bridges, depots, stores, &c.

The expedition from this point visited the interior of the State, and was enabled to find any quantity of work to perform, which embraced the destruction of vast amounts of public property, such as railroads, bridges, depots, and government stores generally.

At Salem, Morgan first learned from the telegraph wires of the tremendous excitement his unexampled invasion had created, and the station and numbers of the enemy around for the hunt. He discovered that Indianapolis was running over with them—that New Albany contained 10,000—that 3,000 had just arrived at Mitchell—and, in fact, 25,000 men were armed and ready to meet the "bloody invader."

Morgan moved rapidly forward to Lexington, thence to Vernon, and from Vernon to Versailles, scattering destruction and dismay along the route. Near the latter place, an amusing and characteristic incident occurred. A Presbyterian chaplain, in Morgan's command, captured an entire company of militia. He was moving ahead, when he found that he had flanked the advance, and run upon a full company of State militia. Imitating his commander's demeanor, he boldly rode up to the company and inquired for the captain. Being informed that there was a dispute as to who should lead them, he volunteered his services, expatiating largely upon the part he had played as an Indiana captain at Shiloh, and was soon elected to lead the valiant Hoosiers against "the invading rebs." Twenty minutes spent in drilling, inspired complete confidence; and when the advance guard of Morgan's command had passed without Captain P. permitting the Hoosiers to fire, he ordered them into the road, and surrendered them to our command. Crest-fallen, indeed, were the Yankees; but General Morgan treated them kindly, and, returning to them their guns, advised them to go home and not come hunting such game again, as they had every thing to lose and nothing to gain by it.

Leaving the State of Indiana, General Morgan struck the Ohio line at a place called Harrison. Here he completely destroyed a very long bridge of great strength and value. A feint was here made upon Cincinnati. The whole Ohio country, in this direction, is chequered over with railroads, and the attention of the expedition was particularly directed to these. Immense damage was thus inflicted upon the enemy. The Mississippi and Ohio railroad was greatly injured. The command approached within eight miles of the city of Cincinnati, and it is said that some of Morgan's scouts were within the suburbs of the city.

On the march, the command bore to the left of the city, striking the little Miami railroad, capturing a valuable train of cars soon after reaching the road, together with about 200 Federal soldiers. The train was, of course, destroyed, which was the usual disposition made of such captures.

After passing Cincinnati, Morgan next went in the direction of Camp Denison, upon which point he made another feint for the purpose of deceiving the enemy, who were at this time harassing him as he proceeded. Leaving the neighborhood of Camp Denison, he proceeded through the interior of the State, operating upon an extensive scale, in destroying the railroads in which that section abounds.

Upon arriving near the town of Pomeroy, another feint was here resorted to. The numerous roads in this section were generally very effectively blockaded, and much difficulty was experienced in overcoming these obstacles. Near Pomeroy General Morgan encountered a force of the enemy of several thousand men, consisting of infantry, cavalry, and artillery. Whilst the skirmishers were engaged at this point, the main body of the command moved around the town to the left, with the view of reaching the river, which they accomplished about daylight on the morning of the 18th of July, at Buffington Island. Here the enemy came up with them, with a strong force, assisted by gunboats in the river, which prevented a crossing at this point.

The rear guard of the expedition held the enemy in check, whilst the main body was enabled to move off from the river, to a point further up, called Belleville. Here another effort was made to cross. About two hundred of the command had succeeded in crossing the river when the gunboats again made their appearance, and also a force of cavalry and infantry, evidently the same which had opposed them at Buffington. Only two men were drowned of the number which attempted to cross the river. Morgan being thus prevented from crossing his whole command, those who effected a crossing succeeded in keeping the gunboats at bay until he could remove his force to a point higher up the river. The enemy claimed to have taken seventeen hundred prisoners in the running fight. At any rate, the few hundred who had crossed the Ohio, thus cut off from the main body, had no other alternative left them but to make their way as they best could to the Confederate lines, which they succeeded in doing—passing through the mountains of West Virginia to Lewisburg, near which place they encamped.

Morgan and about two hundred of his men had broken through the enemy's lines, on the north side of the Ohio. He had by some means got into a carriage. A Yankee major saw him, and, galloping up, reached for him. Morgan jumped out at the other side of the carriage, leaped over a fence, seized a horse, and galloped off as fast as horse-flesh could carry him.

The fugitive commander, with the remainder of his scattered forces, pressed three citizens of Salineville into their service as guides, and continued their flight on the New Lisbon road. One of the impressed guides made his escape and rode back, conveying intelligence of the route taken, which it was believed was with the ultimate design of reaching the Ohio river higher up. Forces were immediately despatched from Wellesville to head him off, whilst another force followed hotly in his rear, and a strong militia force from New Lisbon came down to meet him.

About two o'clock, in the afternoon, these various detachments closed in around Morgan in the vicinity of West Point, about midway between New Lisbon and Wellesville. The Confederates were driven to a bluff from which there was no escape, except by fighting their way through or leaping from a lofty and almost perpendicular precipice. Finding themselves thus cooped, Morgan surrendered himself and the remnant of his command.

We shall have occasion elsewhere to refer to the enemy's treatment of this distinguished captive. It is sufficient to conclude for the present our narrative of this remarkable expedition to say, that its brave and generous leader and his officers were confined in felons' cells in the Ohio Penitentiary; were subjected to cruelties at which the blood runs cold; and that on the 20th day of November, Morgan and six of his officers escaped from the confinement and torture of their infamous prison. They had dug out of their cells with small knives, after weeks of constant toil. Morgan left behind to his enemy an account of his toil and escape, "with two small knives," with this legend : " *La patience c'est amère, mais son fruit es doux.*" " Patience is bitter, but its fruit is sweet."

So far from Morgan's expedition being accounted a failure, on account of its termination in a surrender, it is to be taken as one of the most fruitful and brilliant of Confederate successes. There were persons who accused him of rashness in crossing the Ohio. But those who preferred this flippant accusation probably did not know that although the passage of the Ohio was not, at the outset, a part of General Morgan's programme, it created an important diversion of Burnside's army, large detachments of which were drawn after Morgan into and through Kentucky; prevented the Yankee general from marching on Knoxville and getting in rear of Bragg's army, then menaced in front by Rosecrans, at Shelbyville; thus disconcerted the Yankee campaign in the West, and delayed its operations for many valuable weeks.

It is true that Morgan lost about two thousand prisoners. But for this number added to the Yankee exchange list, he had exacted an immense and brilliant compensation. With twenty-five hundred men he traversed two enormous States from end to end—occupied their towns almost at pleasure—cut their principal arteries of communication, burnt depots, destroyed engines, sunk steamboats innumerable. He threw several millions of people into frantic consternation for the safety of their property, turned entire populations into fugitives, and compelled several thousand men to leave their occupations for weeks and go under arms—only as an equivalent to him and his twenty-five hundred troops. He paroled near six thousand Yankees, they obligating themselves not to take up arms during the war. He destroyed thirty-four important bridges, destroying the track in sixty places. His loss was by no means slight : twenty-eight commissioned officers killed, thirty-five wounded, and two hundred and fifty men killed and wounded. By the Yankee accounts he killed more than two hundred, wounded at least three hundred and fifty, and captured, as before stated, near six thousand. The damage to railroads, steamboats, and bridges, added to the destruction ot public stores and depots, was not less than ten millions of dollars.

This brilliant expedition taught Confederates the value of adventure. Want of enterprise had been the curse of the South in war as in peace; and the counsels of the war in the Confederacy had been too much to the effect that it must do nothing but parry—that it must never presume to thrust. However unwelcome the ultimate misfortune of General Morgan, it did not rob his expedition of its glory, or its profit to the Confederacy.

CHAPTER V.

TENNESSSEE was a conspicuous theatre of the war, but one of strange misfortune to the Confederates. We have in preceding volumes of this work, and at different periods in the history of the war, referred to the marked and striking contrast between our military fortunes in the East and in the West. True, the picture was not entirely free from lights and shadows on either side. Roanoke Island somewhat marred the one, while the first day of Shiloh, the brilliant forays of Morgan, Wheeler, and Forrest, and the unexpected success with which, for more than a year, Vicksburg defied three successive expeditions, until an evil star shed its malignant influence over her, lighted up the sombre tints of the other. The steady tendency and actual result on each side was, however, clear and unmistakable. Two years ago our army was encamped at Bowling Green, and our batteries, on the beetling cliff of Columbus, scowled defiance to Cairo. From the time General Johnston fell back from

Bowling Green, a dark and bloody struggle ensued, which culminated in the disasters of Bragg's Kentucky campaign. The battle of Murfreesboro', in which we won a brilliant victory, on the 31st of December, 1862, afterwards proved but a drawn battle, and on the night of the 2d of January following, th Confederates had retreated to Tullahoma.

The remarkable and persistent contrast between our military affairs in the West and those east of the Alleghanies, especially on the grand theatre of Virginia, affords a curious study for the future and elaborate historian of the war. But some partial explanation of it is to be found in obvious circumstances. The army of Virginia was undoubtedly superior in composition to that of the West. The Virginia troops—it may be said without invidiousness, where there is so much of common glory for every member of the Confederate army—were especially complimented by General Lee for a remarkable union of spirit and *tractability*, which made them the best soldiery in the world. And it may be said emphatically, that no other State, whose soil was the theatre of war, had exhibited such happy accord, and such thorough and generous co-operation with the Confederate authority as had Virginia. It is in the circumstance of this zealous and devoted co-operation of Virginia with the Confederate authority—in contrast with the conduct of certain other States, in whose borders was pitched the theatre of war— that we shall especially find an explanation for those triumphs of the common arms of the South, which so frequently and so uniformly graced her soil.

No embarrassments of party politics, no indecent bickerings of demagogues, chilled the zeal of Virginia, or divided her efforts in the war. From the beginning of the contest she had poured out a lavish stream of contributions to every necessity of the general government. In the fall of 1863, it was officially reported in her legislature, that she had already furnished 102,915* soldiers to the Confederate service, and that, in addition, thirty thousand conscripts had just passed through the camp of instruction, and that she had issued in this time, 103,840 muskets, 399 pieces of cannon, and other arms in proportion.

---

* *Statement of the Number of Troops Furnished the Confederate States by th*

In adverting to the fortunes involved by the fall of Vicksburgh, we have already said, that General Bragg's army in Tennessee had been considerably weakened by drafts upon it to reinforce the lines in the Southwest. He was in a critical condition at Tullahoma. Rosecrans had nearly double his numbers in his front, and Burnside, who commanded what the Yankees called the Army of the Cumberland, was in a position, by an advance towards Knoxville, to threaten his rear.

Rosecrans, whose name is coupled with so much of the military history of the West, enjoyed a divided reputation in the Confederacy, being esteemed by many as the most skilful and formidable of Yankee generals, and by others, as a lucky military adventurer, who would soon run his career of good fortune. In the early stages of the war, he had made great reputation by his successes over Lee in Western Virginia, the latter being taken quite out of his element, in a contracted mountain warfare, and being easily bewildered by a man who, as an itinerary speculator, a peddler in "oil springs," had made himself minutely familiar with these mountains. He was now at the head of the class in President Lincoln's academy, for the graduation of young and sudden field-marshals. In the Department of Tennessee his star had been in the ascendant; h had yet to sustain a defeat; but such fortune, said those who disputed his generalship, was simply that likely to attend the march of a much superior army of well-disciplined western troops, against a small army of brave and patient, but badly handled Confederates. The Chattanooga *Rebel* quoted against

---

State of Virginia, as taken from the first Rolls on file in the Adjutant and Inspector-general's Office.

Sixty-four regiments infantry	52,496
Twenty regiments cavalry	14,175
Two regiments artillery	1,779
Twenty-eight battalions, cavalry, infantry and artillery	11,717
Nine battalions artillery, Army Northern Virginia	4,500
Two hundred and fourteen unattached companies, artillery, infantry and cavalry	18,248
Total number of men	102,915

The above statement does not embrace the recruits or conscripts furnished y the State of Virginia.
October, 1863.

him a vulgar, but trite axiom, among the backwoodsmen of Tennessee: "There is no telling the luck of a lousy calf—he lives all the winter, and dies in the spring."

Rosecrans was now to test his generalship by one of the most extensive movements in the West: the occupation of East Tennessee, and a movement thence into the heart of the cotton States. This military Hercules, said a Northern paper, had, of all others, been selected to "drive a wedge into the centre of the Confederacy."

Since his retreat to Tullahoma General Bragg had advanced to Wartrace and Shelbyville, and was apparently ready to give the enemy battle. A portion of his forces having been withdrawn to Mississippi, he considered that he was left as a mere army of observation. The enemy at last succeeded in surprising our forces at Liberty and Hoover's Gaps by a flank movement, and General Bragg, to save his army, fell back, on the 27th of June, to Chattanooga. The enemy followed at leisure to the banks of the Tennessee.

The enemy's advance on Chattanooga was in two columns, on a double line of operations—Rosecrans moving on Chattanooga, and Burnside moving on Knoxville. It was thought to be necessary that the exposed left flank of Rosecrans' army should be covered while he made a right swinging movement on Chattanooga, and this appeared to be the whole purpose of the co-operation of Burnside's column. The possession of Knoxville, under the circumstances, was not supposed to be of vital moment, for, Chattanooga in the enemy's possession, Knoxville and the whole line was turned and fell of its weight.

On the 20th of August, it was ascertained certainly that Rosecrans had crossed the mountains to Stevenson and Bridgeport. His force of effective infantry and artillery amounted to fully 70,000, divided into four corps. About the same time General Burnside advanced from Kentucky towards Knoxville, East Tennessee, with a force estimated by the General commanding that department at over 25,000. In view of the great superiority of numbers brought against him, General Buckner concluded to evacuate Knoxville, and with a force of about 5000 infantry and artillery, and his cavalry, took position in the vicinity of Loudon. Two brigades of his command, Frazier's at Cumberland Gap and Jackson's in Northeast Tennessee, were thus severed from us. The enemy having already obtained a lodgment in East Tennessee by another route, the continued occupation of Cumberland Gap became very hazardous to the garrison and comparatively unimportant to us. Its evacuation was accordingly ordered, but on the appeal of its commander, stating his resources and ability for defence, favorably endorsed by Major-General Buckner, the orders were suspended on the 31st of August. The main body of our army was encamped near Chattanooga, whilst the cavalry force, much reduced and enfeebled by long service on short rations, was recruiting in the vicinity of Rome, Georgia.

THE SURRENDER OF CUMBERLAND GAP.

We may anticipate our narrative to say here that Cumberland Gap was surrendered on the 9th of September by General Frazier; a garrison, consisting of four regiments, about two thousand men, and fourteen pieces of artillery being unconditionally surrendered to the enemy without firing a gun.

The first demand for a surrender was made on the 5th by the Yankee General Shackelford; and Colonel De Courcy having come up with a brigade on the Kentucky side, renewed the demand on the evening of the 9th September. General Frazier replied under flag of truce, asking De Courcy the number of forces to which he was ordered to surrender. De Courcy replied nearly twelve o'clock at night, refusing to give the number of forces under his command, stating that it was from motives entirely disconnected with the attack upon the gap that he did so. General Frazier then refused to surrender, and it was understood that the fight would open at twelve o'clock the next day. A council of the commanding officers of regiments was called, which resulted in the refusal of all to be surrendered. A majority preferred the risk of cutting their way through the Yankee lines to being surrendered on any terms. A fight was therefore confidently expected. Near twelve o'clock on Wednesday, the 9th, when all was in anxious expectation for the fight to open, General Frazier received from Burnside, under flag of truce, a demand for the unconditional surrender of himself and his command. Very soon after its reception, one of General Frazier's aid-de-camps came in great haste down the mountain and ordered the battle-flag down, and a white one to be hoisted in its stead.*

This surrender was declared by the Richmond *Dispatch* to be "one of the most disgraceful occurrences of the war." In a message to Congress President Davis said of it: "The country was painfully surprised by the intelligence that the officer in command of Cumberland Gap had surrendered that important and easily defensible pass without firing a shot, upon the summons of a force still believed to have been inadequate to its reduction, and when reinforcements were within supporting distance, and had been ordered to his aid. The entire garrison, including the commander, being still held prisoners by the enemy, I am unable to suggest any explanation of this disaster, which laid open eastern Tennessee and south-western Virginia to hostile operations, and broke the line of communication between the seat of government and middle Tennessee."

---

* The following communication with respect to this surrender was published in the Richmond newspapers from Major McDowell, one of the officers of the garrison.

"Various statements have been made in regard to the conduct of the troops composing the command at Cumberland Gap. I assert most positively that I have yet to see troops in finer spirits, or more determined to hold their ground than the troops in the gap. I have learned that an attempt is being made to justify the surrender of the gap upon the ground that the troops in the gap would not fight, and that some of them shouted when the flag was ordered down. The last charge was made against the Sixty-second North Carolina regiment. The first is false, and the second not only false, but is a base and cowardly effort to protect those that may be guilty at the expense of the innocent, brave, patriotic and true. We were surrendered, then, to General Burnside on Wednesday, the 9th, at 4 o'clock P. M. Many made their escape after the surrender. We had when we were surrendered provisions upon which we could have subsisted thirty days. We had all the ammunition on hand that we had when the gap was first invested. My regiment had 150 rounds to the man, and I presume other regiments had the same. If the surrender was a matter of necessity, it was from causes other than a want of provisions, ammunition, or a willingness on the part of the men to do their duty."

THE BATTLES OF CHICKAMAUGA.

Before proceeding to discuss those movements, by which the forces of Rosecrans and of Bragg at last joined in decisive bat tle, a topographical *coup d'œil* is necessary.

The Cumberland range is a lofty mass of rocks, separating the waters which flow into the Cumberland from those which flow into the Tennessee, and extending from beyond the Ken tucky line in a south-westerly direction nearly to Athens, Alabama. The Sequatchie Valley is along the river of that name, and is a cañon or deep cut splitting the Cumberland range parallel to its length.

Chattanooga commands the southern entrance into Tennessee, and is one of the great gateways through mountains to the champaign counties of Georgia and Alabama. It is situated on the Tennessee river, at the mouth of the Chattanooga Valley—a valley following the course of the Chattanooga creek, and formed by Lookout Mountain and Missionary Ridge. The former is a vast palisade of rocks, rising twenty-four hundred feet above the level of the sea, in abrupt rocky cliffs, from a steep, wooded base. East of Missionary Ridge, and running parallel with it, is another valley—Chickamauga Valley—following the course of Chickamauga creek, which, with the Chattanooga creek, discharges its waters into the Tennessee river—the first above, and the last below the town of Chattanooga, and has with it a common source in McLemore's Cove—the common head of both valleys, and formed by Lookout Mountain on the west, and Pigeon Mountain to the east. Wills' Valley is a narrow valley lying to the west of Chattanooga, formed by Lookout Mountain and Sand Mountain, and traversed by a railroad, which takes its name from the valley, and which, branching from the Nashville and Chattanooga Railroad, where the latter crosses the valley, has its present terminus at Trenton, and future at Tuscaloosa, Alabama. The wagon-road from Chattanooga to Rome, known as the Lafayette road, crosses Missionary Ridge into Chickamauga Valley at Rossville, and, proceeding in a south westerly direction, crosses Chickamauga creek, eleven miles from Chattanooga, at Lee and Gordon's Mills, and, passing to

the east of Pigeon Mountain, goes through Lafayette, distant
some twenty-two miles from Chattanooga, and Summerville
within twenty-five miles of Rome.

Immediately after crossing the mountains to the Tennessee
the enemy threw a corps by the way of Sequatchie Valley to
strike the rear of General Buckner's command, whilst Burnside occupied him in front. One division, already ordered to
his assistance, proving insufficient to meet the force concentrating on him, Buckner was directed to withdraw to the
Hiawassee with his infantry, artillery, and supplies, and to
hold his cavalry in front, to check the enemy's advance. As
soon as this change was made, the corps threatening his rear
was withdrawn, and the enemy commenced a movement in
force against our left and rear. On the last of August it became known that he had crossed his main force over the Tennessee river at or near Caperton's Ferry, the most accessible
point from Stevenson. By a direct route, he was now as near
our main depot of supplies as we were, and our whole line of
communication was exposed, while his own was partially
secured by mountains and the river. By the timely arrival of
two small divisions from Mississippi, our effective force,
exclusive of cavalry, was now a little over thirty-five thousand,
with which it was determined to strike on the first favorable
opportunity. Closely watched by our cavalry, which had
been brought forward, it was soon ascertained that the
enemy's general movements were towards our left and rear, in
the direction of Dalton and Rome, keeping Lookout Mountain
between us. The nature of the country, and the want of supplies in it, with the presence of Burnside's force on our right,
rendered a movement on the enemy's rear, with our inferior
force, extremely hazardous, if not impracticable. It was now,
therefore, determined to meet him in front whenever he should
emerge from the mountain gorges. To do this and hold Chattanooga was impossible, without such a division of our small
force as to endanger both parts. Accordingly, our troops
were put in motion on the 7th and 8th of September, and took
position from Lee and Gordon's Mills to Lafayette, on the road
leading south from Chattanooga, and fronting the east slope of
Lookout Mountain.

On Monday, September 7th, Lieutenant-general D. H. Hill

was ordered to move with his corps to Lafayette, and General Polk to Lee and Gordon's Mills, and Major-general Buckner, with the army of East Tennessee, and Major-general Walker, with his division from the army of Mississippi, to concentrate at Lafayette, and Brigadier-general Pegram to cover the rail road with his cavalry. These dispositions having been made of the Confederate forces, Major-general Crittenden command ing the left wing of Rosecrans' army, which had not moved with the right and centre, but had been left in the Sequatchie Valley, crossed the Tennessee river at the mouth of Battle creek, and moved upon Chattanooga. Major-general McCook, commanding the right wing, was thrown forward to threaten Rome, and the corps of Major-general Thomas was put in motion over Lookout Mountain, in the direction of Lafayette.

During the 9th of September it was ascertained that a column of the enemy had crossed Lookout Mountain into the cove by the way of Stevens' and Cooper's. Thrown off his guard by our rapid movement apparently in retreat, when in reality we had concentrated opposite his centre, and deceived by information from deserters and others sent into his lines, the enemy pressed on his columns to intercept us, and thus exposed himself in detail.

A splendid opportunity was now presented to Bragg. The detached force in McLemore's cove was Thomas's corps. Being immediately opposite Lafayette, at and near which General Bragg had all his forces concentrated, it was completely at the mercy of the latter. It was only necessary that General Bragg should fall upon it with such a mass as would have crushed it; then turned down Chattanooga Valley, thrown himself in between the town and Crittenden, and crushed him; then passed back between Lookout Mountain and the Tennessee river into Wills' Valley, and cut off McCook's retreat to Bridgeport; thence moved along the Cumberland range into the rear of Burnside, and disposed of him.

No time was to be lost in taking advantage of a blunder of the enemy, into which he had fallen in his stupid conceit that the Confederates were retreating. Instant orders were given to Major-general Hindman to prepare his division to move against Thomas, and he was informed that another division from Lieutenant-general D. H. Hill's command, at Lafayette, would move up to him and co-operate in the attack.

General Hill received his orders on the night of the 9th He replied that he could not undertake the movement; that the orders were impracticable; that Cleburne, who commanded one of his divisions, was sick; and that both the gaps, Dug and Catlett's, through which he was required to move, were impassable, having been blocked by felled timber.

Early the next morning, Hindman was promptly in position to execute his part of the critical movement. Disappointed at Hill's refusal to move, General Bragg, with desperate haste, despatched an order to Major-general Buckner to move from his present position at Anderson, and execute, without delay, the orders issued to Hill.

It was not until the afternoon of the 10th, that Buckner joined Hindman, the two commands being united near Davis's Cross-roads in the cove. The enemy was still in flagrant error moving his three columns, with an apparent disposition to form a junction at or near Lafayette. To strike in detail these isolated commands, and to fall upon Thomas, who had got the enemy's centre into McLemore's Cove, such rapidity was necessary as to surprise the enemy before he discovered his mistake.

Lieutenant-general Polk was ordered to Anderson's, to cover Hindman's rear, who, at midnight of the 10th of September, again received orders, at all hazards to crush the enemy's centre, and cut his way through to Lafayette. The indomitable Cleburne, despite the obstructions in the road, had moved up to Dug Gap; was in position at daylight; and only waited the sound of Hindman's guns to move on the enemy's flank and rear.

Courier after courier sped from Dug Gap to urge Hindman on. *But it was too late.* The enemy had discovered the mistake that had well-nigh proved his ruin. He had taken advantage of our delay, retreated to the mountain passes; and so the movement upon Thomas, which promised such brilliant results, was lost by an anachronism by which the best laid military schemes are so frequently defeated.

But it was not easy for Rosecrans to repair his error wholly, and extricate himself from the meshes of a bad military movement. The movement upon Thomas in McLemore's Cove having failed, he having effected his escape up the mountain, Rosecrans, who, by this time, had discovered Bragg's whereabouts, recalled McCook into Wills' Valley, and ordered him to follow Thomas, who was again put in motion over the mountain into the cove. But the third corps, under Crittenden, moving from the direction of Chattanooga, was yet in position to be attacked; and dispositions were rapidly made by General Bragg to fall upon it, and thus retrieve in some measure the miscarriage of his other plans.

Crittenden had moved on towards Ringgold, with the hope of cutting off Buckner. On reaching the point on the Georgia railroad at which Buckner crossed, he discovered he was too late, and turned towards Lafayette to follow him. He moved up the Chickamauga, on its east side, in the direction of Lafayette, and was confronted by the cavalry under Generals Pegram and Armstrong. After skirmishes with them, in which there were some brilliant dashes on the part of our cavalry, the latter retired slowly before the enemy, falling back towards Lafayette. To meet this movement, General Bragg ordered a force of two divisions, under Lieutenant-general Polk, to move to the front. These divisions, Cheatham's and Walker's, were put in motion, and were in line of battle before daylight, covering the three roads on which the enemy's three divisions were marching. Hindman came up after daylight, and Buckner was thrown forward as a supporting force to guard Polk's left against Thomas and McCook in the cove. Crittenden, finding himself confronted, declined battle, and retired during the night, falling back on the Chickamauga, which he crossed at Lee and Gordon's Mills. This placed the whole of Rosecrans' three corps on the east side of the Chickamauga, and in easy supporting distance.

Thus had failed the preliminary plans to take the enemy in a flagrant error of generalship, and at vital disadvantage; and nothing remained but to fight out the issue against his concentrated forces on the banks of the Chickamauga.*

---

* To avoid recriminations, which resulted in Generals Hill and Polk being deprived of their commands in Bragg's army, we annex here what has never been published in the Confederacy: General Bragg's official letters and orders

On Saturday, the 19th September, General Bragg had moved his army by divisions and crossed it at several fords of the Chickamauga and bridges north of Lee and Gordon's Mills. Reinforcements had reached him. Johnston had arrived with

---

with respect to the alleged dereliction of these officers. General Polk was also blamed in subsequent operations, as we shall see.

. . . . Major-general Hindman received verbal instructions on the 9th to prepare his division to move against this force [Thomas's corps], and was informed that another division from Lieutenant-general Hill's command, at Lafayette, would join him. That evening, the following written orders were issued to Generals Hindman and Hill:

HEADQUARTERS ARMY TENNESSEE, }
Lee and Gordon's Mills, 11¾ P. M., Sept. 9th, 1863. }

GENERAL :—You will move your division immediately to Davis's X roads on the road from Lafayette to Stevens' Gap. At this point you will put yourself in communication with the column of General Hill, ordered to move to the same point, and take command of the joint forces, or report to the officer commanding Hill's column, according to rank. If in command you will move upon the enemy, reported to be 4,000 or 5,000 strong, encamped at the foot of Lookout Mountain, at Stevens' Gap. Another column of the enemy is reported to be at Cooper's Gap, number not known.

I am, General, &c.,
Signed,   KINLOCK FALCONER, A. A. General.

To MAJOR-GENERAL HINDMAN,
Commanding Division.

HEADQUARTERS ARMY TENNESSEE, }
Lee and Gordon's Mills, 11¾ P. M., Sept. 9th, 1863. }

GENERAL :—I enclose orders given to General Hindman. General Bragg directs that you send or take, as your judgment dictates, Cleburne's division to unite with General Hindman at Davis's X roads to-morrow morning. Hindman starts at 12 o'clock to-night and he has thirteen miles to make. The commander of the column thus united will move upon the enemy encamped at the foot of Stevens' Gap, said to be 4,000 or 5,000. If unforeseen circumstances should prevent your movement, notify Hindman. A cavalry force should accompany your column. Hindman has none. Open communications with Hindman with your cavalry, in advance of the junction He marches on the road from Dr. Anderson's to Davis's X roads.

I am, General, &c., &c.,
KINLOCK FALCONER, A. A. General.

LIEUTENANT-GENERAL HILL,
Commanding.

On the receipt of his order, during the night, General Hill replied that the movement required by him was impracticable, as General Cleburne was sick, and both the gaps—Dug and Catlett's—had been blocked by felling timber, which would require twenty-four hours for its removal. Not to lose this favorable opportunity, Hindman, by prompt movement, being ready in position, the

two brigades from Mississippi, and reinforcements from General Lee's lines in Virginia were hurrying up to what was to be the scene of one of the most critical and magnificent actions of the war. The latter reinforcements consisted of five brig-

---

following orders were issued at 8 o'clock, A. M., on the 10th, for Major-general Buckner to move with his two divisions, and report to Hindman.

HEADQUARTERS ARMY TENNESSEE, ⎫
Lee and Gordon's Mills, 8 o'clock A. M., Sept. 10th, 1863. ⎰

GENERAL :—I enclose orders issued last night to Generals Hill and Hindman. General Hill has found it impossible to carry out the part assigned to Cleburne's division. The general commanding desires that you will execute without delay the order issued to General Hill. You can move to Davis's X roads by the direct road from your present position at Anderson's, along which General Hindman has passed.

I am, General, &c., &c.,
Signed, 　　　　　GEO. W. BRENT, A. A. General.

MAJOR-GENERAL BUCKNER,
　　　Anderson's.

And both Hindman and Hill were notified. Hindman had halted his division at Morgan's, some three or four miles from Davis's X roads, in the cove, and at this point Buckner joined him during the afternoon of the 10th. Reports fully confirming previous information in regard to the position of the enemy's forces, were received during the 10th, and it became certain that he was moving his three columns to form a junction upon us at or near Lafayette. The corps near Colonel Winston's moved on the mountain towards Alpine, a point twenty miles south of us. The one opposite the cove continued its movement and threw forward its advance to Davis's X roads, and Crittenden moved from Chattanooga on the roads to Ringgold and Lee and Gordon's Mill. To strike these isolated commands in succession was our obvious policy. To secure more prompt and decided action in the movement ordered against the enemy's centre, my Headquarters were removed to Lafayette, where I arrived about 11½ on the 10th,—and Lieutenant-general Polk was ordered forward with his remaining division to Anderson's, so as to cover Hindman's rear during the operations in the cove. At Lafayette I met Major Nocquet, engineer officer on General Buckner's staff, sent by General Hindman after a junction of their commands, to confer with me and suggest a change in the plan of operations. After hearing the report of this officer, and obtaining from the active and energetic cavalry commander in front of our position, Brigadier general Martin, the latest information of the enemy's movements and position, I verbally directed the major to return to General Hindman, and say that my plans could not be changed, and that he would carry out his orders. At the same time the following written orders were sent to the general by a courier:

HEADQUARTERS ARMY TENNESSEE, ⎫
Lafayette, Ga., 12 P. M., Sept. 10th, 1863. ⎰

GENERAL :—Headquarters are here and the following is the information : Crittenden's corps is advancing on us from Chattanooga. A large force from the South has advanced to within seven miles of this point. Polk is left at

ades of Longstreet's corps; and these were without artillery and transportation. The Virginia troops landed from the railroad at Ringgold, and were moved rapidly forward to the Chickamauga.

Rosecrans' army was distributed from the head of McLe-

Anderson's to cover your rear. General Bragg orders you to attack and force your way through the enemy to this point, at the earliest hour you can see him in the morning.

Cleburne will attack in front the moment your guns are heard.

I am, General, &c.,

Signed,   GEO. W. BRENT, A. A. General

MAJOR-GENERAL HINDMAN,
    Commanding, &c.

Orders were also given for Walker's reserve corps to move promptly and join Cleburne division at Dug Gap to unite in the attack. At the same time Cleburne was directed to remove all obstructions in the road in his front, which was promptly done, and by daylight he was ready to move. The obstructions in Catlett's Gap were also ordered to be removed to clear the road in Hindman's rear. Breckinridge's division, Hill's corps, was kept in position south of Lafayette to check any movement the enemy might make from that direction.

At daylight I proceeded to join Cleburne at Dug Gap, and found him waiting the opening of Hindman's guns to move on the enemy's flank and rear. Most of the day was spent in this position, waiting, in great anxiety, for the attack by Hindman's column. Several couriers and two staff officers were despatched at different times, urging him to move with promptness and vigor. About the middle of the afternoon the first gun was heard, when the advance of Cleburne's division discovered the enemy had taken advantage of our delay and retreated to the mountain passes. The enemy now discovered his error and commenced to repair it by withdrawing his corps from the direction of Alpine to unite with the one near McLemore's Cove, while that was gradually extended towards Lee and Gordon's Mills. Our movement having thus failed in its justly anticipated results, it was determined to turn upon the third corps of the enemy approaching us from the direction of Chattanooga. The forces were accordingly withdrawn to Lafayette, and Polk's and Walker's corps were moved immediately in the direction of Lee and Gordon's Mills. The one corps of the enemy in this direction was known to be divided—one division having been sent to Ringgold. Upon learning the dispositions of the enemy from our cavalry commander in that direction on the afternoon of the 12th, Lieutenant general Polk, commanding the advance forces, was directed in the following note.

HEADQUARTERS ARMY TENNESSEE, }
Lafayette, Ga., 6 P. M., 12th Sept. }

GENERAL:—I enclose you a despatch from General Pegram. This presents you a fine opportunity of striking Crittenden in detail, and I hope you will avail yourself of it at daylight to-morrow. This division crushed and the

more's Cove, along and down the west side of the Chickamauga Valley, as far as Lee and Gordon's Mills, Chickamauga
creek separating it from the army of the Confederates.

The enemy commenced the affair of the 19th by a vigorous
attack on Major-general Walker's corps. Our line was formed
with Buckner's left resting on the Chickamauga about one

---

others are yours. We can then turn again on the force in the cove. Whee
ler's cavalry will move on Wilden so as to cover your right.

I shall be delighted to hear of your success.

Very truly, Yours,

Signed,   BRAXTON BRAGG.

LIEUTENANT-GENERAL POLK.

Upon further information the order to attack at daylight on the 13th, was re
newed in two notes, at later hours of the same day, as follows:

HEADQUARTERS ARMY TENNESSEE, }
Lafayette, 8 P. M., Sept. 12th, 1863. }

GENERAL:—I enclose you a despatch marked "A" and I now give you the
orders of the commanding general, viz.: to attack at day-dawn to-morrow the
infantry column reported in said despatch at ¾ of a mile beyond Pea-vine
church, on the road to Graysville from Lafayette.

Signed,   GEO. W. BRENT, A. A. General.

LIEUTENANT-GENERAL POLK,
Commanding Corps

HEADQUARTERS ARMY TENNESSEE, }
Lafayette, Georgia, Sept. 12th, 1863. }

GENERAL:—The enemy is approaching from the South, and it is highly
important that your attack in the morning should be quick and decided. Let
no time be lost.

I am, General, &c.,

Signed,   GEO. W. BRENT, A. A. General.

LIEUTENANT-GENERAL POLK,
Commanding Corps.

At 11 P. M. a despatch was received from the general stating that he had
taken a strong position for defence, and requesting that he should be heavily
reinforced. He was promptly ordered not to defer his attack, his force being
already superior to the enemy, and was reminded that his success depended
upon the promptness and rapidity of his movements. He was further informed that Buckner's corps would be moved within supporting distance the
next morning. Early on the 13th I proceeded to the front, ahead of Buckner's
command, to find that no advance had been made on the enemy, and that his
forces had formed a junction and recrossed the Chickamauga.

. . . .

BRAXTON BRAGG, General.

To GENERAL S. COOPER,
Adjutant and Inspector General, Richmond, Va.

mile below Lee and Gordon's Mills. On his right came Wood with his own and Johnston's divisions, with Walker on the extreme right,—Cheatham's division being in reserve. General Walker found a largely superior force of the enemy opposed to him. He drove them handsomely, however, and captured several batteries of artillery in most gallant charges Before Cheatham's division, ordered to his support, could reach him, he had been pressed back to his first position by the extended lines of the enemy assailing him on both flanks.

The two commands united were soon enabled to force the enemy back again, and recover our advantage, though we were yet greatly outnumbered.

These movements on our right were in a direction to leave an opening in our line between Cheatham and Hood. Stewart's division forming Buckner's second line was thrown to the right to fill this, and it soon became hotly engaged, as did Hood's whole front.

The enemy, whose left was at Lee and Gordon's Mills when our movement commenced, had rapidly transferred forces from his extreme right, changing his entire line, and seemed disposed to dispute with all his ability our effort to gain the main road to Chattanooga in his rear.

Lieutenant-general Polk was ordered to move his remaining division across at the nearest ford and to assume the command in person on our right. Hill's corps was also ordered to cross below Lee and Gordon's Mills and join the line on the right. Whilst these movements were being made our right and centre were heavily and almost constantly engaged.

Stewart by a vigorous assault broke the enemy's centre and penetrated far into his lines, but was obliged to retire for want of sufficient force to meet the heavy enfilade fire which he encountered from the right.

Hood, later engaged, advanced from the first fire and continued to drive the force in his front until night.

Cleburne's division of Hill's corps, which first reached the right, was ordered to attack immediately in conjunction with the force already engaged. This veteran command, under its gallant chief, moved to its work after sunset, taking the enemy completely by surprise, driving him in great disorder for nearly a mile, and inflicting a very heavy loss.   Night found us masters of the ground, after a series of very obstinate contests with largely superior numbers.

For the grand and decisive work of the next day, the forces of Bragg's army were divided into two wings.

The right wing was placed under Lieutenant-general Polk, and the left under Lieutenant-general Longstreet.   The former was composed of Lieutenant-general Hill's corps, of two divisions, Major-general Cleburne's and Major-general Breckinridge's; of the division of Major-general Cheatham, of Lieutenant-general Polk's corps, and the division of Major-general W. H. T. Walker.

The left was composed of the divisions of Major-general Stewart, and Brigadier-general Preston and Bushrod Johnson, of Major-general Buckner's corps; Major-general Hindman, of Lieutenant-general Polk's corps, and Benning's, Lane's and Robertson's brigades, of Hood's division, and Kershaw's and Humphrie's brigades, of McLaw's division, of his own (Lieutenant-general Longstreet's) corps.

The front line of the right wing consisted of three divisions —Breckinridge and Cleburne, of Hill's corps, and Cheatham, of Polk's corps—which were posted from right to left in the order named.   Major-general Walker was held in reserve.

The left wing was composed of Major-general Stewart's division on the right with Hood's on the left.   On Hood's left was Hindman's division of Lieutenant-general Polk's corps, with Preston's division of Buckner's corps on the extreme left.

Orders were given to Lieutenant-general Polk to commence the attack at daylight.   The left wing was to await the attack by the right, take it up promptly when made, and the whole line was then to be pushed vigorously and persistently against the enemy throughout its extent.

"Before the dawn of day," writes General Bragg in his official report, "myself and staff were ready for the saddle, occupying a position immediately in rear of and accessible to all parts of the line.   With increasing anxiety and disappointment I waited until after sunrise without hearing a gun; and at length despatched a staff officer to Lieutenant-general Polk to ascertain the cause of the delay, and urge him to a prompt and speedy movement. This officer not finding the general with his troops, and learning where he had spent the night, proceeded across Alexander's Bridge, to the east side of the Chickamauga, and there delivered my message. Proceeding in person to the right wing, I found the troops not even prepared for the movement. Messengers were immediately despatched for Lieutenant-general Polk, and he shortly after joined me. My orders were renewed and the general was urged to their prompt execution, the more important as the ear was saluted throughout the night with the sounds of the axe and falling timber as the enemy industriously labored to strengthen his position by hastily constructed barricades and breastworks. A reconnoissance made in the front of our extreme right during this delay crossed the main road to Chattanooga, and proved the important fact that this greatly desired position was open to our possession. The reasons assigned for this unfortunate delay by the wing commander, appear in part in the reports of his subordinates. It is sufficient to say they are entirely unsatisfactory."

But it was said, on the other side of the story, that Polk's delay was due to circumstances beyond his control; that, prior to giving the order to move forward to the attack, General Polk discovered that owing to the want of precaution on the part of the proper authority in the formation of the general line of battle, a portion of the line of the left wing had been formed in front of his line—a portion amounting to a whole division—and that had the order to make the attack at daylight been obeyed, this division, from its position, must inevitably have been slaughtered. It was saved by an order to halt Cheatham's division, and by orders to the left of Cleburne advising it of its whereabouts.

The action was opened upon the right of the Confederates about ten o'clock in the morning by a forward movement of Breckinridge, followed and accompanied by Cleburne. The enemy had during the night thrown up breastworks of heavy timber, cut down from the forest, behind which he had entrenched himself. These lay chiefly in Cleburne's front. He moved direct upon them, while Breckinridge swung round to flank them. The assault was a desperate one. General Polk

being informed by General Hill that the enemy was threatening his right flank, Polk ordered Walker immediately to move
to the right and form an echelon upon Breckinridge, over-
lapping his right. It was then ascertained that no enemy was
there. But the forward movement of the front line had resulted
in a severe conflict, desperately contested, which drove the
enemy around on the extreme left a mile or more across the
Chattanooga road.

For two hours the fight raged with sublime fury. Again
and again, as we struck the enemy, did his stately lines of
soldiers crumble into masses of terror-stricken fugitives.
Thomas commanded the Yankee's left. Heavy reinforcements
being sent from the enemy's right to him, he was enabled to
regain a portion of the ground he had lost. Never did Yankees
fight better than just here. They drove back Cleburne's magnificent division, and it appeared at one time as if our right
and centre were giving way before Thomas's extraordinary
attack.

But while such were the operations on our right wing, the
tide of battle running from right to left had reached Longstreet's extreme left about eleven o'clock. Hood and others
were ordered to make a vigorous assault in front; Buckne
was made to execute a successful flank movement; and under
the vigor of the combined attack Rosecrans found his lines
steadily giving way, and McCook and Crittenden forced far to
the right. He had moved most of his strength to the left
where Thomas had fought so brilliantly, but with the advantage
of superior numbers. Negley, hard pressed on the left, reported
to Rosecrans. "Tell General Negley I can't help him," was
the reply.

The Yankees in Longstreet's front had sought a position on
a high ridge. From this position they were driven, with heavy
loss in killed, wounded, prisoners, artillery, small-arms and
colors, after a desperate struggle, by the brigades of Kershaw
and Humphries, under the command of Brigadier-general
Kershaw, in the absence of Major-general McLaws, reinforced
by Gracise's, Kelley's, and Trigg's brigades, of Major-general
Preston's division, Major-general Hindman completing the
general work of the line to the left by driving the enemy on
his front before him along with those driven from the ridge by

Preston and Kershaw. Rosecrans, perceiving what was taking place on his right, ordered up reinforcements from his left to support his retiring or rather frightened battalions, which, finding a good position, awaited their arrival, turning upon their pursuers with the fierceness of a temporary and desperate energy. Brigadier-general Law, commanding Hood's division, perceiving this movement, ordered a battery of ten guns to a position from which he could enfilade the reinforcing column as it advanced. The battery opened just as it was about wheeling into position, and, at the same time, Stewart's division, posted on the extreme right, was thrown forward on its flank. The shock was terrible. The enemy halted, staggered backwards, and fell into confusion.

It was late in the evening when the whole Confederate line was revised and posted, and a forward movement in all its length ordered. The right swung round with an extended sweep, with its firm supports, and the left rallied once more to the charge of the works, before which it had suffered so severely in the morning. Never did troops move up to their work with more resolution; the daring Breckinridge with his Kentuckians and Louisianians, and Cleburne with his Arkansians and Alabamians, and Walker with his South Carolinians, Mississippians, and Georgians, and Cheatham with his Tennesseeans—all moved forward in one mighty tide amidst the thunders of some twenty batteries, and the roar of thousands of muskets and rifles. The scene was one of surpassing sublimity and grandeur. Sweeping forward as the flood of a mighty river, it carried every thing before it, nothing being able to stand in the resistless line of its path. The enemy's works, which opposed such a stubborn resistance in the morning, succumbed before the torrent, and the brave men of Cleburne's division, which had been repulsed in the morning, had, by their extraordinary gallantry in the evening, the opportunity of avenging the experiences of the earlier part of the day. The whole field was carried triumphantly, and the enemy driven as chaff before the wind. He withstood as long as human powers of endurance could bear up against such a pressure, then yielded, and fell back partly upon and into the hands of the right wing, where several hundred were captured, the residue crossing the Chattanooga road and retreating in the direction of Missionary Ridge. Night interposed, and though it brought with it a magnificent moon, no orders were received to pursue, and the troops were halted, giving expression to their sense of the glorious victory won, and unconquerable desire to pursue it to an absolute success in the enemy's utter annihilation, in such long, loud and triumphant cheering, as would almost seem to rend the heavens.

Never was a more disorderly retreat of an enemy. Longstreet, who had contributed so much to the fortunes of the day, now saw that by a forward movement of the whole army, Rosecrans' whole force might be captured in twenty-four hours, and that no obstacle was between us and the Ohio, and perhaps peace. He sent word to Wheeler, who was on his left, to dash forward between Chattanooga and the enemy and cut him to pieces; but just as Wheeler was about to execute this movement, he received an order from Bragg directing him to pick up arms and stragglers. It was said that Longstreet had not heard from Bragg but once during the day, and then it was to say that he was beaten on the right. He now sent to beg him to advance; but the General-in-chief declined to do so.

General Forrest had climbed a tree and from his lofty perch watched the retreating enemy. He saw the blue uniforms swarming over the fields, and the disorganized masses of the enemy choked with flight, and struggling in mortal panic as sounds of feeble pursuit followed on their heels. He shouted to a staff officer: "Tell General Bragg to advance the whole army; the enemy is ours."

Bragg did not catch the inspiration. He tells us in his official report: "The darkness of the night and the density of the forest rendered further movements uncertain and dangerous, and the army bivouacked on the ground it had so gallantly won."

But granting that reasons, substantive reasons, existed for not pursuing on Sunday night, what hindered General Bragg from pursuing on Monday morning at daylight? Chattanooga was only ten miles from the battle-field, and unfortified; our pursuing cavalry could see their head of column, and urged General Bragg by repeated messages to pursue, that every hour's delay would be equal to the loss of a thousand men. Citizens along the road reported that many of the Yankee commands passed their dwellings in the utmost disorder, without arms or accoutrements, and many without hats, as a confused and routed mob, not as troops in column, everything in Chattanooga and on the road inviting rather than forbidding attack. Even if they had had good defensive works, with the condition as reported above, by a prompt pursuit our army would have gone into Chattanooga with theirs, and thus broken the effect of their fire; and if such could have been the result with good defensive works, what might not the result have been without them, and the enemy panic-stricken because of the knowledge that none such existed? What hindered General Bragg from pursuing is not known, but it is known that, while pursuit seems to have been invited, he did not pursue. He simply sent out detachments to the battle-field to gather up the fruits of victory, in arms large and small, to be secured and sent to the rear, and caused the captured banners to be collected to be sent to Richmond, and prisoners to be counted and sent to the rear.

The enemy's immediate losses in the battle of Chickamauga were immense. It was officially stated that we captured over eight thousand prisoners, fifty-one pieces of artillery, fifteen thousand stand of small arms, and quantities of ammunition, with wagons, ambulances, teams, medicines, hospital stores, &c., in large quantities.

The enemy's loss in killed and wounded have been by many thousands greater than ours; and General Bragg, in his official report, makes the appalling confession that, on this " River of Death," he lost " *two-fifths* " of his troops. Our loss in general officers was conspicuous. Brigadier-general B. H. Helm,* Preston Smith, and James Deshler, had died on the field. The

---

* Brigadier-general Helm was a grandson of Ben Hardin, well known to the oldest inhabitants of Kentucky, as a leading public-spirited gentleman of high moral worth in the earlier days of the Warrior State. General Helm was born in Hardin County, Kentucky, in 1831—graduated at West Point, and afterwards retired from the army of the United States to take up the study of law. He entered the Southern army without a commission, but from the rank of private he was soon made colonel, and commanded the first Kentucky cavalry in the Confederate service. He was made brigadier-general in March, 1862. The Kentucky brigade, which he commanded in the battle of Chicka-

lion-hearted Hood, the luminary of Texas chivalry and courage, was so severely wounded that he had to suffer amputation of the thigh. The notice of his extraordinary gallantry by Longstreet, who with generous ardor communicated it in a special letter to his government, obtained for him the commission of a Lieutenant-general, and ranged him with the popular heroes of the war.

The day following this terrible conflict, General Bragg ordered the troops under arms, and marched them down the Chattanooga road until they came near to Rossville, where Forest and Pegram were thundering away with their batteries at the retreating enemy, there had them filed to the right, and thrown down the Chickamauga creek, that they might rest from their fatigues and be in a good position to move upon Burnside or flank Rosecrans, as future contingences might dictate. On Wednesday, the 23d of September, an order was issued for the whole army to move upon Chattanooga. It moved up to and over Missionary Ridge, where it was halted. And there it was to remain halted for many long weeks.

Chickamauga had conferred a brilliant glory upon our arms, but little else. Rosecrans still held the prize of Chattanooga, and with it the possession of East Tennessee. Two-thirds of our nitre beds were in that region, and a large proportion of the coal which supplied our foundries. It abounded in the necessaries of life. It was one of the strongest countries in the world, so full of lofty mountains, that it had been called, not unaptly, the Switzerland of America. As the possession of Switzerland opened the door to the invasion of Italy, Germany and France, so the possession of East Tennessee gave easy access to Virginia, North Carolina, Georgia and Alabama.

---

mauga, went into the fight with seventeen hundred and sixty-three men, and came out with only four hundred and thirty-two.

General Helm's wife was a half-sister of Mrs. Lincoln. Immediately after the fall of Fort Sumter, in 1861, President Lincoln sent him a commission as major in the regular army of the United States ; and apprehending that he might not be willing to be employed to murder his own people, the Yankee Secretary of War proposed, as a salve for any scruples, to send him as pay master to New Mexico. The gallant Kentuckian spurned the bribe, gave his services, and at last his life, to the Confederacy, and fell in the numerous throng of brave defenders of truth, justice and liberty. His wife lives, known as one of the most enthusiastic and devoted patriot women of the South

Rosecrans found occasion after the battle to congratulate his army on their retention of Chattanooga. He said, "You have accomplished the great work of the campaign; you hold the key of East Tennessee, of Northern Georgia, and of the enemy's mines of coal and nitre." He claimed that he held in his hands the substantial fruits of victory, and sought to persuade his government that the battle of Chickamauga was merely an incident to the concentration of his forces and his cover of Chattanooga. He lost no time in reorganizing his army at Chattanooga. He assumed a fortified line about a mile and a half in length, covering the pontoons, stores and hospitals, and commanding all the south-east and eastern approaches to the place, leaving Bragg no chance to dislodge him by direct attack, only by long and toilsome maneuvers and marches threatening his communications.

Bragg's awkward pause before Chattanooga was the occasion of new propositions of the campaign on our side. Of one of these General Bragg communicated as follows to the War Department at Richmond.

"The suggestion of a movement by our right immediately after the battle, to the north of the Tennessee, and thence upon Nashville, requires notice only because it will find a place in the files of the Department. Such a movement was utterly impossible for want of transportation. Nearly half our army consisted of reinforcements just before the battle, without a wagon or an artillery horse, and nearly, if not quite, a third of the artillery horses on the field had been lost. The railroad bridges too had been destroyed to a point south of Ringgold, and on all the roads from Cleveland to Knoxville. To these insurmountable difficulties were added the entire absence of means to cross the river, except by fording at a few precarious points too deep for artillery, and the well known danger of sudden rises by which all communication would be cut, a contingency which did actually happen a few days after the visionary scheme was proposed. But the most serious objection to the proposition was its entire want of military propriety. It abandoned to the enemy our entire line of communication, and laid open to him our depots of supplies, while it placed us with a greatly inferior force beyond a difficult, and at times impassable river, in a country affording no subsistence to men or animals. It also left open to the enemy, at a distance of only ten miles, our battle-field, with thousands of our wounded, and his own, and all the trophies and supplies we had won. All this was to be risked and given up, for what? to gain the enemy's rear and cut him off from his depot of supplies, by the route over the mountains, when the very movement abandoned to his unmolested use the better and more practicable route half the length, on the south side of the river.

"It is hardly necessary to say the proposition was not even entertained, whatever may have been the inferences drawn from subsequent movements."

The plan preferred by General Bragg was to invest Chattanooga, and starve the enemy out. Rosecrans' shortest and most important road to his depot at Bridgeport lay along the south bank of the Tennessee; and, as Bragg held this, the enemy was forced to a road double the length, over two ranges of mountains, by wagon transportation, upon which long and difficult route our cavalry might operate with advantage. Looking to a speedy evacuation of Chattanooga, for want of wood and forage, General Bragg declared that he " held the enemy at his mercy, and that his destruction was only a question of time." Alas, we shall see hereafter how vain were the sanguine expectations and the swollen boast of this ill-starred and unfortunate commander!

General Bragg has burdened the story of Chickamauga with recriminations of his officers: a resource to which he showed, on all occasions, a characteristic and ungenerous tendency. His course, in this respect, invites and justifies severe criticism of himself. Whatever may have been the faults of his subordinate officers in the action of Chickamauga, it is certain that the military opinion of the Confederacy indicated two important errors of his own in the conduct of this famous battle.

1. That he failed to cut off the enemy's exit to Chattanooga, which it is considered he might have done, if he had marched his army by the right flank, and crossed lower down on the Chickamauga; at such point throwing his army across the creek and valley, forming it at right angles to the Lafayette and Chattanooga road, and so covering the exit from the valley in the direction of Chattanooga. As it was, he crossed his

army north of Lee and Gordon's Mills, ordered a demonstration there, which might have been well used as a cover for the proper movement, and utterly failed, as his critics say, to grasp the situation.

2. That he failed to pursue a routed and disorganized enemy, threw away the opportunity of completing his victory, realized no substantial fruit from it, and, after one of the most splendid successes in the record of Confederate arms, left his enemy *in statu quo*, reorganizing at leisure.

In this latter respect, Chickamauga must indeed be confessed to be a second and enlarged edition of the famous Bull Run. It will stand conspicuous among the various fruitless victories gained by the Confederates—among the least pardonable blunders and shortcomings of history.*

---

* We may place here, in conjunction with Chickamauga, some interesting passages from a private letter of a distinguished general officer in the West, reviewing the campaign there, and criticising with great intelligence, the general military policy of the Confederacy :

. . . . It would be a laborious task to review the campaigns even of the Army of Tennessee. Yet what profound lessons do they teach ? What errors have been committed ? What opportunities have been lost ? The man who does not see these, and who has not learned from them powerful lessons for the future, is totally unfit for any responsible military position in the pregnant future, on which the destiny of untold millions now trembles.

We lost Donelson, and as a consequence Middle Tennessee, from the want of rapid combination and concentration. We lost Shiloh first by delay, then by want of persistence in the first day's fight, then for the want of the proper distribution of troops at the close of that day. We threw away the golden moments at Mumfordsville, in Kentucky, and further neglected to make security doubly sure by concentrating the two armies, Smith's and Bragg's ; and yet again these two armies, for the want of proper generalship and energy together, precipitately and ingloriously abandoned the broad territory between the Ohio and the Cumberland rivers. It is remarkable, that this campaign in Kentucky presented more glorious opportunities for great results, than any other in this, or, perhaps, any other war, and all was lost for the want of the simplest combinations. Again, Nashville, garrisoned by a few thousand Federals, was not taken, simply because the attack was prohibited. God knows how often this city might have been taken before the battle of Murfreesboro', while the two armies were lying idle or being slowly moved, without any decided plan or purpose. How often before and subsequent to the battle of Murfreesboro', did the dispersed condition of the Yankee forces offer the opportunity for a good general to make a vigorous and rapid movement, such as would have destroyed its fragments in detail ? Murfreesboro' was lost by want, first, of proper combination on the field, and then by want of persistence in the fight, especially on the left. In six weeks after the battle of Murfreesboro', our army in Tennessee was as strong as when it fought that battle, and could have driven Rosecrans from Tennessee with ordinary generalship. From March till June, in 1863, we remained idly stretching from Shelbyville to the right, while the Yankees, holding a line from Franklin to Woodbury, again and again afforded us an opportunity to fall, by rapid combinations, upon detached masses, and thus destroy their army. In July we occupied a strong ridge, stretching from Bell-Buckle towards Bradyville, very strong by nature on the right, and made strong by fortifications on the left, in front of Shelbyville. An injudicious disposition of forces left Hoover's Gap undefended by our army. Rosecrans advanced upon Hoover's Gap. Three brigades of Confederates moved rapidly up and held them in the gap for over forty hours. A rapid concentration of our forces at Hoover's Gap, or one half of them, by moving on the enemy's flank and rear, to a commanding position, which lay invitingly before us, would have routed the enemy, and planted us still more firmly in Tennessee. But we were ordered to retreat, and we retired before the scattered forces of the enemy, when a rapid combination and a vigorous attack, with a sudden change from a retrograde to an advance movement on some one of the enemy's masses in motion, might have insured victory. In that retrograde movement we also abandoned some remarkably strong positions without taking advantage of them, or making an effort to repulse the enemy, even when we could have done so without danger to our army.

At Chickamauga, the world knows, we lost the fruits of the victory for want of vigorous pursuit. On the night of the 20th of September there should have been no sleep and no repose. A vigorous, persistent, onward movement would have destroyed Rosecrans' army. How deplorable has been the consequences of our want of energy, want of activity, and want of persistence! The army of Tennessee being tied to no special line of operations, and embarrassed by no important point, such as Richmond, requiring to be defended, had greatly the advantage over the army of Virginia, yet the former has constantly yielded up territory to a conquering foe, and the latter has overthrown every army that came against it.

I have meant merely to allude to the errors on our line of operations. There are greater errors than these, greater because they pertain to the management of all the Confederate forces. They are errors in what is usually denominated grand strategy.

We now have, I may say, numerous independent armies in the field, each acting almost without reference to all the others, and rarely co-operating with any other army.

The Allied Armies, in 1814, entered France with 400,000 men, and had a numerous force hovering on the borders of that empire. Napoleon had but 120,000 in the field, exclusive of the forces shut up in fortifications and operating beyond the boundaries of France. We know how nearly he came to vanquishing the Allied Powers, and even his enemies have demonstrated how he could have completely overthrown the armies against which he contended. A rapid concentration of forces upon detached armies, is a well-established means by which inferior forces must conquer superior numbers. Superior mobility in strategy, and the concentrated, swift, lightning stroke in the hour of battle, must compensate for inferiority of numbers. Napoleon, Frederick the Great, and Charles the XII., have illustrated these facts, and they have become the most familiar lessons of the soldier. But, with proper strategy, in my opinion, we need seldom fight superior forces. Look at the position of all our armies now. We are remaining listlessly waiting for the enemy to mass his forces and men upon us. Can any one contemplate this attitude of our armies, and not feel utterly astonished at our policy, and the repose into which we have sunk on every hand? Where is that activity which should belong to inferior forces? It is rather to be found among our enemies, whose superior numbers would entitle them to the repose which we have quietly assumed.

CHAPTER VI.

Political Movements in the Fall of 1863.—The "Peace Party" in tl e North.—The Yankee Fall Elections.—The War Democrats in the North.—The South's Worst Enemies.—Yankee Self-Glorification.—Farragut's Dinner-Party.—The Russian Banquet.—Russia and Yankeedom.—The Poles and the Confederates.—The Political Troubles in Kentucky.—Bramlette and Wickcliffe.—The Democratic Platform in Kentucky.—Political Ambidexterity.—Burnside's Despotic Orders.—The Kentucky "Board of Trade."—An Election by Bayonets.—The Fate of Kentucky Sealed.—Our European Relations.—Dismissal of the Foreign Consuls in the Confederacy.— Seizure of the Confederate "Rams" in England.—The Confederate Privateers.— Their Achievements.—British Interests in Privateering.—The Profits of So-called "Neutrality."—Naval Affairs of the Confederacy.—Embarrassments of Our Naval Enterprise.—The Naval Structures of the Confederates.—Lee's Flank Movement in Virginia.—Affair of Bristoe Station.—Failure of Lee's Plans.—Meade's Escape to Centreville.—Imboden's Operations in the Valley.—Capture of Charlestown. —Operations at Rappahannock Bridge.—Kelley's Ford.—Surprise and Capture of Hayes' and Hoke's Brigades.—Gallantry of Colonel Godwin.—Lee's Army on the Rapidan.—The Affair of Germania Ford.—Meade Foiled.—The "On-to-Richmond" Delayed.

We must take the reader's attention from military campaigns to certain political movements, which, in the fall of 1863, apparently involved more or less distinctly the fortunes of the war.

The long-continued delusion, indulged by Southern men, of "a peace party" in the North, which would eventually compel peace on the terms of the Confederacy, is to be compared to that similar delusion of Northern politicians, which insisted that "a Union party" existed in the South, and that it was only temporarily suppressed by a faction. There was not the least foundation in fact for either of these opinions; and the agreeable confidence of the South, in its supposed friends in the North, was to be rudely dispelled by events that admitted of but one construction. The South had mistaken for substantial tokens of public sentiment the clamors and exaggerations of party elections. The Democratic party in the North went into the fall elections of 1863, on the issue of a general opposition to the Lincoln Administration; at the same time, promising a vigorous "constitutional" prosecution of the war, while their vague allusions to an impossible peace and platitudes of fraternal sentiment were merely intended to catch favor in the South, and really meant nothing. Even Mr. Seymour, of New York, managed, while cozening the South, to maintain, on the other hand, a cordial understanding with the authorities at Washington; and he found it necessary to conclude one of his finest speeches by saying, "never have I embarrassed the Administration, and I never will."

But even on its moderate issues, with reference to the war, which, as we have seen, proposed only certain constitutional limitations, the Democratic party in the North was badly beaten in the fall elections. From Minnesota to Maine, the Democrats were defeated. In the latter, which was supposed to be the least fanatical of the New England States, the Republicans carried the election by an overwhelming majority. In Ohio, Vallandigham was defeated. He was still in exile. Voorhies, who had proclaimed doctrines somewhat similar to his, in a neighboring State, narrowly escaped being lynched by the soldiers. The elections were followed by a remarkable period of political quiet in the North. Those who had the courage to confront the administration of Lincoln, had either been suppressed by the strong hand of lawless power, or had supinely sought safety in silence. The overthrow of free government in the North was complete.

The South was not easily imposed upon by that organized hypocrisy, the War Democracy of the North. While it professed constitutional moderation in the conduct of the war, it aimed at the reconstruction of the Union, which was only a different phrase for the military conquest of the South. It must be observed that so far as questions of the constitutional conduct of the authorities at Washington were made in the North, they were questions entirely between their domestic parties, which did not properly interest the people of the Confederacy, inasmuch as their demand for independence, simple and absolute, had nothing to do with the modifications of the different parties which opposed it. Indeed, with regard to this demand, the War Democrat at the North was a far more dangerous enemy to the Confederacy than the open and avowed Abolitionist. The former was more plausible; his programme of reconstruction carried an appearance of possibility to entice the popular faith which that of naked conquest did not possess. But both programmes—that of the War Democrat and that of the Abolitionist—were equally fatal to the Confederacy : as it mattered not what was the formula of subjugation, if the people of the South once placed themselves within the power of their treacherous enemies, and submitted to any form of their authority.

The North had yet shown no real disposition to abandon the war. The Yankees were still busy with the game of self-glorification. Their conceit, their love of display, their sensations amused the world. Their favorite generals were all Napoleons; in the cities mobs of admirers chased them from hotel to hotel; in the New England towns deputations of school-girls kissed them in public. Farragut, their successful admiral, was entertained in New York with feasts, where a plaster of ice-cream represented the American Eagle, and miniature ships, built of sticks of candy, loaded the table. These childish displays and vain glory had culminated in an immense banquet given to a Russian fleet in the harbor of New York, at which distinguished Yankee orators declared that the time had come when Russia and the United States were to be taken as twins in civilization and power, to hold in subjection all others of Christendom, and to accomplish the " destiny" of the nineteenth century.

And really this festive fervor but gave insolent expression to an idea that had long occupied thoughtful minds in distant quarters of the world. Christendom was called upon to witness two political murders. While twenty millions of Yankees sought to strangle the Southern Confederacy, fifty millions of Muscovites combined to keep ten or twelve millions of Poles under a detested yoke. In their infamous attempt upon Poland, Russians tried to pass themselves off as the defenders of liberal ideas against Polish aristocracy; and it was declared that the Polish nobility was in rebellion in order not to be forced to emancipate the serfs. "Russia and the United States," said a French writer of the time, "proclaim the liberty of the serf and the emancipation of the slave, but in return both seek to reduce to slavery all who defend liberty and independence."

Liberty of the press, of speech, of public meetings, even the venerable privilege of *habeas corpus*, inherited from England had already been put under the feet of Abraham Lincoln.

While the Democratic party was timidly protesting in the Northern States, Mr. Lincoln had prefaced the farce of the fall elections in the North by an outrage upon the ballot in Kentucky, which Yankee Democrats were too weak or too dishonest to resent.

A history of the Kentucky troubles, in some details, is the best commentary we can choose from events, upon the condition to which the whole system of political liberty had fallen in the North.

THE POLITICAL TROUBLES IN KENTUCKY.

In the last days of August, 1862, the Hon. Beriah Magoffin resigned his office as Governor of the State of Kentucky. From causes into which it is not necessary now to enter, he had incurred the suspicion of a great majority of the Union party, and through the Legislature they had succeeded in divesting him of all real power in the government. The executive control of the State had rapidly fallen into the hands of the military officers of the United States, and for months the people had been subject to martial law in all its oppressiveness, without its declaration in form. Under these circumstances, and for the purpose of relieving the people, and especially that portion of them known as "Southern-rights Men," who had been the peculiar objects of persecution, Mr. Magoffin, in a published letter, declared his willingness to resign whenever he could be assured of the election of a successor of conservative views, who, commanding the confidence at the same time of the Administration at Washington and of the people of Kentucky, would be able and willing to secure every peaceful citizen in the exercise of the rights guaranteed to him by the Constitution and laws. James F. Robinson, then a member of the Senate, was indicated to him, and he consented to resign in his favor.

For the August election of 1863, Thomas E. Bramlette was offered as a candidate for governor. Mr. Bramlette maintained generally the rightfulness of the suspension of the writ of *habeas corpus*, and the extension of martial law over States where war did not exist, and gave in a *quasi* adhesion to Mr. Lincoln's policy.

A number of Kentucky Democrats presented a ticket in opposition, headed by C. A. Wickcliffe for governor, and published the following expressions of their views, as comprising the issues of the approaching election.

"We cannot consent to the doctrine that the Constitution and laws are inadequate to the present emergency; that the constitutional guarantees of liberty and property can be suspended by war.

"Our fathers certainly did not intend that our Constitution should be a fair-weather document, to be laid away in a storm, or a fancy garment to be worn only in dry weather. On the contrary, it is in times like the present that constitutional restraints on the power of those in authority are needed.

"We hold the Federal government to be one of limited powers, that cannot be enlarged by the existence of civil commotion.

"We hold the rights reserved to the States equally sacred with those granted to the United States. The government has no more right to disregard the Constitution and laws of the States than the States have to disregard the Constitution and laws of the United States.

"We hold that the Administration has committed grave errors in confiscation bills, lawless proclamations, and military orders setting aside constitutions and laws, and making arrests outside of military lines where there is no public danger to excuse it.

"It is now obvious that the fixed purpose of the Administration is to arm the negroes of the South to make war upon the whites, and we hold it to be the duty of the people of Kentucky to enter against such a policy a solemn and most emphatic protest.

"We hold as sacred and inalienable the right of free speech and a free press—that the government belongs to the people and not the people to the government.

"We hold this rebellion utterly unjustifiable in its inception, and a dissolution of the Union the greatest of calamities. We would use all just and constitutional means adapted to the suppression of the one and the restoration of the other."

Notwithstanding these resolutions, which so carefully sounded in "loyalty," and exhibited the usual ambidexterity of the War Democracy, it soon became evident that the authorities at Washington were determined to interfere in the Kentucky election, and force it exactly to their purpose. Messrs. Wolfe and Trimble, candidates for Congress in the First and Fifth districts, and Mr. Martin, candidate for the Legislature in Lyon and Livingston counties, were arrested by the provost-marshals.

On the 31st of July, Burnside declared martial law in Kentucky. The following is a summary of the most outrageous of the despotic orders which followed in quick succession the declaration of martial law.

1. By way of precaution, the people are informed that whenever any property is needed for the use of the United States army, it will be taken from *rebel sympathizers*, and receipts given for the same marked " disloyal," and to be paid at the end of the war, on proof that the holder is a loyal man.

2. Rebel sympathizers are defined to be not only those who are in favor of secession, but also those who are not in favor of a vigorous prosecution of the war, and of furnishing men and money unconditionally for that purpose. "Loyalty" is to be proved by the vote given at the election.

3. County judges are required to appoint none but "loyal" men as judges of election, notwithstanding the provisions of our laws, which require the officers of election to be taken equally from each political party.

4. Persons offering to vote, whose votes may be rejected by the judges, are notified that they will be immediately arrested by the military.

5. The judges of election are notified that they will be arrested and held responsible by the military, should they permit any disloyal men to vote.

In addition to all this there was at work beneath the surface a potent machinery, whose labors could be traced only by results, for the work was done in darkness and in secret.

In every city, town, and considerable village in the commonwealth, there had long been organized, under the authority of the Secretary of the Treasury, a body of men known as a "Board of Trade," an innocent title, little expressive of their true functions. Under the same regulations of the Secretary, no shipments of goods to the interior of the State could be made without the *permit* of the United States custom-house officers at Cincinnati or Louisville. In order to obtain such a permit, the individual applying must have procured the recommendation of the "Board of Trade" located nearest to his place of business, and the recommendation was given to none but "loyal" men, each Board establishing its own test of "loyalty." Without such recommendation no merchant could hope to add to his stock by importation—no mechanic to replenish the materials necessary in his calling. These inquisitorial bodies, therefore, held in their hands the absolute fate of every tradesman and mechanic in the State. The prosperous merchant

and needy shopkeeper were alike at their mercy. The tradesman and mechanic were thus left to choose between a vote for
Bramlette and the utter ruin of their business.

Such were the circumstances under which the election of
August 3d was begun. In twelve counties not a single vote
was permitted to be cast for Wickliffe. In eight others he received less than ten votes to the county. In fifteen others he
received less than fifty votes to the county. In sixteen others
he received less than one hundred votes to the county. These
fifty-one counties embraced many of the strongest Democratic
counties in the State. In only twenty-eight counties of the
State did Bramlette receive a majority of the population entitled to vote. Less than two-fifths of the population entitled
to vote made him Governor of Kentucky. Thus was the fate
of Kentucky sealed, and, on the 1st of September, Bramlette
entered upon the duties of the office into which he had been
foisted by bayonets.

We have briefly seen what little comfort there was for the
Confederates in the fall elections of 1863, and the contemporary
political movements in the North. We naturally glance from
this part of the situation, external to the military campaigns,
to the European relations of the Confederacy. Here there wa
quite as little encouragement for the South as in that other
alternative of hope outside the war—Yankee politics.

OUR EUROPEAN RELATIONS.

Some feeble attempt was made by the Confederacy in the
fall of 1863 to reassert its dignity by the dismissal of the
foreign consuls, who had been, oddly enough, allowed for
nearly three years to reside in the Confederate States, and exercise super-consular powers under authority granted by the
government with which we were at war. The force of this proceeding was, however, much impaired by the fact that it was
attributed to certain objectionable action of the British consuls
in the Confederacy, and not based, as it should have been, upon
the conduct and bearing towards us of the British Government
itself. Put upon that ground, the dismissal would have marked
distinctly our sense of British injustice.

We have referred in former pages to the prejudicial effect

of so called British " neutrality " with respect to the Confederate States. Another instance was now to be afforded of its
unequal and unjust disposition in the seizure by the British
Government of two two-thousand-ton iron-clads, combining the
ram and monitor principles, which were being built for the
Confederacy by the Messrs. Laird, at Birkenhead. The seizure
was made without any evidence to justify it. The Messrs.
Laird were forbidden to allow these vessels to leave their yard
" without an ample explanation of their destination and a sus-
tainable reference to the owner or owners for whom they are
constructed." It was curiously held by Lord Russell that
" Messrs. Laird were bound to declare—and sustain on unim-
peachable testimony such declaration—the government for
whom the steam rams have been built." In other words, without an affidavit or other legal foundation for proceedings
against them, these gentlemen were required to come forward
and prove their innocence.

The animus displayed in this proceeding was in keeping with
the whole conduct of the British ministry towards this country.
They suspended, to our great detriment, the law of nations
which allowed captures at sea to be taken into neutral ports for
condemnation. They ignored and violated their own solemn
engagement in the Treaty of Paris, requiring that a blockade,
to be acknowledged and binding, should be such as actually to
exclude ships from ingress or egress. They allowed their
Foreign Enlistment Act to be inoperative against our enemy,
permitting them not only to supply themselves with vast quantities of arms and ammunition, but even to recruit their armies
from British dominions. But they had revived against us a
law practically obsolete, and, in order to give it force and
make it applicable, they had reversed a principle of law to be
found in the codes of all free countries.

But, notwithstanding the invidiousness of foreign powers,
especially against the naval efforts of the Confederacy, it was
a matter of surprise how much we had accomplished upon the
sea against an enemy whose navy was his particular boast. A
few solitary ships, hunted by vast navies, had maintained in
foreign seas a warfare that required not only the loftiest courage, but the most consummate skill, the most sleepless vigilance,
and the most perfect self-reliance.

Two years had passed since Semmes commenced his cruise in the *Sumter*, since which time about one hundred and fifty Yankee vessels, valued, with their cargoes, at ten million dollars, had been captured by vessels under the Confederate flag. From the first appearance of the little schooner, *Jeff Davis*, the Confederate navy had been the terror of the entire Yankee mercantile marine.*

The effect of our privateering on Yankee commerce and tonnage was already immense. Since the commencement of the war, three hundred and eighty-five vessels, with an aggregate tonnage of more than one hundred and sixty-six thousand tons, had been transferred to foreigners at the port of New York alone, most of which were sailing under the flag of Great Britain, the most prominent commercial rival of the Yankee. At other ports the same practice had prevailed, and it would be fair to estimate the loss of Yankee tonnage under it, during the past two years, at three hundred thousand tons. This loss to the North, as a matter of course, involved a consequent increase of the tonnage and power of its rivals.

In the first six months of the year 1860 the number of vessels cleared at New York for foreign ports was seventeen hundred and ninety-five, of which eleven hundred and thirty-three were American and six hundred and sixty-two foreign—a difference of nearly one hundred per cent. in favor of American vessels; while, during the same period of the present year, there had been twenty-one hundred and ninety-seven clearances, of which fourteen hundred and fifty were foreign and only seven hundred and forty-seven American—showing an increase in the number of foreign vessels, and a difference in their favor, as compared with the first named period, of about two hundred per cent.

The Yankees had a navy which was daily increasing, and one which, in war-making power, already exceeded vastly any navy in the world. Yet it was impotent against a few Con-

---

* A report was made to the Yankee Congress of captures by Confederate cruisers up to the 30th of January, 1864. The list, which was not complete, foots up 193, with a tonnage of 89,704. At fifty dollars a ton, the vessels are valued at $4,485,200 ; the cargoes, at one hundred dollars a ton, are estimated at $8,970,400. Total value, $13,455,500. Sixty-two were captured by the Alabama, twenty-six by the Sumter, and twenty-two by the Florida.

federate cruisers which defied its power, and burnt Yankee vessels even within sight of their commercial marts.

NAVAL AFFAIRS OF THE CONFEDERACY.

We take occasion here to make a brief summary of what had been accomplished in the naval affairs of the Confederacy since the commencement of the war. At that time, but seven steam war vessels had been built in the States now forming the Confederacy since the war of 1812, and the engines of only two of these had been contracted for in these States. All the labor or materials requisite to complete and equip a war vessel could not be commanded at any one point of the Confederacy.

To these disadvantages was to be added the notorious incompetency of the Confederate Secretary of the Navy. His contracts were injudicious; and there was traced more or less directly to his mismanagement, the destruction of the Virginia-Merrimac, the Louisiana, the Mississippi, the vessels in Lake Ponchartrain, bayou St. John, the Yazoo and Mississippi rivers, and elsewhere.

Yet the department, with all its drawbacks, could now exhibit results of no mean order. It had erected a powder-mill, which supplied all the powder required by our navy; two engine-boilers and machine-shops, and five ordnance work-shops. It had established eighteen yards for building war vessels, and a rope-walk, making all cordage, from a rope-yarn to a nine-inch cable, and capable of turning out eight thousand per month.

Of vessels not iron-clad, the department had purchased and otherwise acquired and converted to war vessels, forty-four.

Had built and completed as war vessels, twelve.

Had partially constructed and destroyed to save from the enemy, ten.

And had now under construction, nine.

Of iron-clad vessels, it had completed and had now in commission, fourteen.

Had completed and destroyed, or lost by capture, four.

Had in progress of construction and in various stages of forwardness, twenty.

It had, also, one iron-clad floating battery, presented to the Confederate States by the ladies of Georgia ; and one iron-clad ram partially completed and turned over to the Confederacy by the State of Alabama.

Taking into consideration the poverty of our means, and the formidable naval power and boundless resources of our enemy, at the beginning of this war, our people had no sufficient cause for shame or discouragement in the operations of our navy.

LEE'S FLANK MOVEMENT IN VIRGINIA.

We must return from the discussion of these general subjects to the military campaign of the later months of 1863, and take up the long-suspended story of Lee's army in Virginia.

Since its campaign into Pennsylvania, it had rested on the Rapidan. In October General Lee was prepared to put into execution a campaign which promised the most brilliant results, as its ultimate object appears to have been to get between Meade and Washington.

With the design of bringing on an engagement with the Yankee army, which was encamped around Culpepper Court-house, and extending thence to the Rapidan, Lee's army crossed that river on the 9th instant, and advanced by way of Madison Court-house. Our progress was necessarily slow, as the march was by circuitous and concealed roads, in order to avoid the observation of the enemy.

General Fitz Lee, with his cavalry division and a detachment of infantry, remained to hold our lines south of the Rapidan; General Stuart, with Hampton's division, moved on the right of the column. With a portion of his command he attacked the advance of the enemy near James City, on the 10th, and drove them back towards Culpepper. Our main body arrived near that place on the 11th instant, and discovered that the enemy had retreated towards the Rappahannock, removing or destroying his stores. We were compelled to halt during the rest of the day to provision the troops, but the cavalry, under

General Stuart, continued to press the enemy's rear guard towards the Rappahannock. A large force of Federal cavalry, in the mean time, had crossed the Rapidan, after our move ment begun, but was repulsed by General Fitz Lee, and pur sued towards Brandy Station.

Near that place the commands of Stuart and Lee united, on the afternoon of the 11th, and, after a severe engagement, drove the enemy's cavalry across the Rappahannock, with heavy loss.

On the morning of the 12th, the army marched in two columns, with the design of reaching the Orange and Alexandria railroad, north of the river, and interrupting the retreat of the enemy.

After a skirmish with some of the Federal cavalry at Jeffersonton, we reached the Rappahannock at Warrenton Springs, in the afternoon, where the passage of the river was disputed by cavalry and artillery. The enemy was quickly driven off by a detachment of our cavalry, aided by a small force of infantry and a battery. Early next morning, 13th, the march was resumed, and the two columns united at Warrenton in the afternoon, when another halt was made to supply the troops with provisions. The enemy fell back rapidly along the line of the railroad, and early on the 14th the pursuit was continued, a portion of the army moving by way of New Baltimore towards Bristoe Station, and the rest, accompanied by the main body of the cavalry, proceeded to the same point by Auburn Mills and Greenwich. Near the former place a skirmish took place between General Ewell's advance and the rear guard of the enemy, which was forced back and rapidly pursued.

The retreat of the enemy was conducted by several direct parallel roads, while our troops were compelled to march by difficult and circuitous routes. We were consequently unable to intercept him. General Hill arrived first at Bristoe Station, where his advance, consisting of two brigades, became engaged with a force largely superior in numbers, posted behind the railroad embankment.

The action of Bristoe Station was a disastrous affair for the Confederates. Hill's brigades were repulsed with considerable loss in killed and wounded, and the loss of five pieces of artillery. The Yankees reported their loss at fifty-one killed and three hundred twenty-nine wounded, and claimed to have captured four hundred and fifty prisoners.

The repulse at Bristoe proved the end of General Lee's plans, so far as they embraced the view of getting on Meade's communications, or reaching Centreville before him. Before the rest of the troops could be brought up to Hill's assistance and the position of the enemy ascertained, Meade retreated across Broad Run. The next morning he was reported to be fortifying beyond Bull Run, extending his line towards the Little River Turnpike.

The vicinity of the entrenchments around Washington and Alexandria rendered it useless to turn his new position, as it was apparent that he could readily retire to them, and would decline an engagement unless attacked in his fortifications. A further advance was therefore deemed unnecessary, and after destroying the railroad from Cub Run southwardly to the Rappahannock, the army returned on the 18th to the line of that river, leaving the cavalry in the enemy's front.

The fall campaign in Virginia must be confessed a failure. It was an attempt by Lee to flank Meade and get between him and Washington. Unfortunately the enemy appears to have become cognizant of the plan at the moment of its execution, and to have retreated with sufficient deliberation to destroy all their stores that they did not carry off to the fortifications of Centreville. It was impossible to follow them, for the country was a desert in which our army could not live, while the enemy would be at the door of the magazines in Washington.

But while General Lee's flank movement had thus terminated in disappointment, a contemporary and accompanying operation in the Valley district had been most fortunate. When the movement of the army from the Rapidan commenced, General Imboden was instructed to advance down the Valley and guard the gaps of the mountains on General Lee's left. This duty was well performed by that officer, and on the 18th October he marched upon Charlestown, and succeeded by a well-concerted plan in surrounding the place. Imboden found the enemy occupying the court-house, jail, and some contiguous buildings, in the heart of the town, all loop-holed for musketry, and the court-house yard enclosed by a heavy wall of oak timber. To his demand for a surrender, Colonel Simp son, the Yankee commander, requested an hour for consider ation. Imboden offered him five minutes, to which he replied "Take me, if you can." Imboden immediately opened on the building with artillery at less than two hundred yards, and with half a dozen shells drove out the enemy into the streets, where he formed and fled towards Harper's Ferry. At the edge of the town he was met by the Eighteenth cavalry and Gilmore's battalions.

One volley was exchanged, when the enemy threw down his arms and surrendered unconditionally. The Colonel, Lieutenant-colonel, and five others who were mounted, fled at the first fire, and ran the gauntlet, and escaped towards Harper's Ferry. The force captured was the Ninth Maryland regiment and three companies of cavalry, numbering between four and five hundred, men and officers.

As was expected, the Harper's Ferry forces, infantry, artillery, and cavalry, appeared at Charlestown in a few hours after Imboden had fired the first gun. The brave Confederate retired, fighting back this largely superior force, bringing off his prisoners and captured property, and inflicting considerable damage upon the pursuing column.

In the course of these operations in Virginia, in the month of October, two thousand four hundred and thirty-six prisoners were captured, including forty-one commissioned officers; of the above number, four hundred and thirty-four were taken by General Imboden.

OPERATIONS AT RAPPAHANNOCK BRIDGE.

After the return of General Lee's army to the Rappahannock, it was disposed on both sides of the Orange and Alexandria railroad, General Ewell's corps on the right and General Hill's on the left, with the cavalry on each flank. To hold the line of the Rappahannock at this part of its course, it was deemed advantageous to maintain our communication with the north bank, to threaten any flank movement the enemy might make above or below, and thus compel him to divide his forces, when it was hoped that an opportunity would be presented to concentrate on one or the other part. For this purpose a point was selected a short distance above the site of the railroad bridge, where the hills on each side of the river afforded protection to our pontoon bridge and increased the means of defence. The hill on the north side was converted into a *tete-de-pont*, and a line of rifle trenches extended along the crest on the right and left, to the river bank. The works on the south side were remodelled, and sunken batteries for additional guns constructed on an adjacent hill to the left. Higher up, on the same side and east of the railroad, near the river bank, sunken batteries for two guns, and rifle-pits, were arranged to command the railroad embankment, under cover of which the enemy might advance.

Four pieces of artillery were placed in the *tete-de-pont*, and eight others in the works opposite.

The defence of this position was intrusted to Lieutenant-general Ewell's corps, and the troops of Johnson's and Early's divisions guarded them alternately, Rodes' division being stationed near Kelley's ford.

The enemy began to rebuild the railroad as soon as we withdrew from Bristoe's Station, his army advancing as the work progressed. His movements were regularly reported by our scouts, and it was known that he had advanced from Warrenton Junction a few days before the attack.

His approach towards the Rappahannock was announced on the 6th of November, and about noon next day his infantry was discovered advancing to the bridge, while a large force moved in the direction of Kelley's ford, where the first attack was made.

General Rodes had the Second and Thirtieth North Carolina regiments, of Ramseur's brigade, on outpost duty at the river. As soon as he perceived that the enemy was in force, he ordered his division to take position in rear of the ford. While it was getting into line, the enemy's artillery opened upon the Second North Carolina, and soon drove it to shelter. The Thirtieth North Carolina was advanced to the assistance of the Second, but in moving across the open ground, was broken by the concentrated fire of the enemy's artillery, and took refuge behind some buildings, at the river. The enemy, being unopposed except by the party in the rifle-pits, crossed at the rapids above the ford, and captured the troops defending it, together with a large number of the Thirtieth North Carolina, who refused to leave the shelter of the houses.

It was not intended by General Lee to attack the enemy until he should have advanced from the river, where it was hoped, that by holding in check the force at the bridge, we would be able to concentrate upon the other. With this view, General Johnson's division was ordered to reinforce General Rodes.

In the mean time a large force was displayed in our front, at the bridge, upon receiving information of which, General A. P. Hill was ordered to get his corps in readiness, and Anderson's division was advanced to the river, on the left of the railroad. The artillery was also ordered to move to the front. General Early put his division in motion towards the bridge, and hastened thither in person. The enemy's skirmishers advanced in strong force, with heavy supports, and ours were slowly withdrawn into the trenches.

Hoke's brigade, of Early's division, under Colonel Godwin (General Hoke being absent with one regiment on detached service), reinforced General Hayes, whose brigade occupied the north bank. No other troops were sent over, the two brigades mentioned being considered sufficient to man the works, and though inferior to the enemy in numbers, the nature of the position was such, that he could not attack with a front more extended than our own.

It was not known whether the demonstration of the enemy was intended as a serious attack, or only to cover the movement of the force that had crossed at Kelley's ford, but the lateness of the hour and the increasing darkness induced the belief that nothing would be attempted until morning. It was believed that our troops on the north side would be able to maintain their position if attacked, and that, in any case, they could withdraw under cover of the guns on the north, the location of the pontoon bridge being beyond the reach of a direct fire from any position occupied by the enemy.

As soon, however, as it became dark enough to conceal his movements, the enemy advanced in overwhelming numbers against our rifle-trenches. It was a simultaneous advance, under cover of the darkness, of the entire force of the enemy. The first line of the enemy was broken and shattered by our fire, but the second and third lines continued to advance at a double-quick, arms at a trail, and a column formed by companies, moving down the railroad, was hurled upon our right, which, after a severe struggle, was forced back, leaving the battery in the hands of the enemy. General Hayes ordered a charge of the Ninth Louisiana regiment, for the purpose of retaking the guns; but his centre having been broken, and the two forces opposed to his right and centre having joined, rendered the execution of his purpose impracticable. Forming a new line after this junction, facing up the river, the enemy advanced, moving behind our works, towards our left, while a line which he had formed in a ravine, above our extreme left, moved down the stream, thus enclosing Hoke's brigade, and the Seventh and Fifth Louisiana regiments, in a manner that rendered escape impossible. Nothing remained but surrender. Many of our men effected their escape in the confusion—some by swimming the river, and others by making their way to the bridge, amidst the enemy, and passing over under a shower of balls. General Hayes owed his escape to the fact, that after he was completely surrounded, and was a prisoner, his horse took fright and ran off, and as the enemy commenced firing on him, he concluded to make the effort to escape across the bridge, and was successful.

Unfortunately no information of this attack was received on the south side of the river until too late for the artillery, there stationed, to aid in repelling it. Indeed, the darkness of the night, and the fear of injuring our own men who had surrendered, prevented General Early from using artillery.

Colonel Godwin's efforts to extricate his command, were made with a gallant desperation, that has adorned with glory this disaster. He continued to struggle, forming successive lines as he was pushed back, and did not for a moment dream of surrendering; but, on the contrary, when his men had dwindled to sixty or seventy, the rest having been captured, killed, wounded, or lost in the darkness, and he was completely surrounded by the enemy, who were, in fact, mixed up with his men, some one cried out that Colonel Godwin's order was for them to surrender. He immediately called for the man who made the declaration, and threatened to blow his brains out if he could find him, declaring his purpose to fight to the last moment, and calling upon his men to stand by him. He was literally overpowered, by mere force of numbers, and was taken with his arms in his hands.

Of this unfortunate surprise, which cost us the greater portion of two brigades, there is to be found some excuse in the circumstances that the enemy was aided by a valley in our front in concealing his advance from view, and that a very high wind effectually prevented his movements from being heard. General Lee declared, with characteristic generosity, that " the courage and good conduct of the troops engaged had been too often tried to admit of question." Our loss in prisoners was very considerable. General Rodes reported three hundred of his men missing. General Early's loss in prisoners was sixteen hundred and twenty-nine.

The loss of the position at Rappahannock Bridge made it necessary for General Lee to abandon the design of attacking the force that had crossed at Kelley's ford; and his army was withdrawn to the only tenable line between Culpepper Court-house and the Rappahannock, where it remained during the succeeding day. The position not being regarded as favorable, it returned the night following to the south side of the Rapidan.

THE AFFAIR OF GERMANIA FORD.

We shall complete here the record of General Lee's army for 1863 with a brief account of another affair which occurred at Germania ford, on the Rapidan, on the 27th of November.

This affair appears to have been an attempt by Meade of a flank movement on General Lee's position, his immediate object being to get in the rear of Major-general Johnson's division. This division was composed of the Stonewall brigade, under Brigadier-general J. A. Walker, and Stuart's, J. M. Jones's, and Stafford's brigades, with four pieces of Anderson's artillery. These were the only troops engaged in the affair on our side. Opposed to them were Major-general French's corps (the Third), and one division of the Fifth corps. The enemy were in position, and opened the attack before our forces knew of their presence. Their object was to make a sudden attack from their concealed position upon our flank, disperse the troops and capture our wagon train. They not only failed of their object, but were driven from the field with considerable slaughter. Our loss in killed and wounded was about four hundred and fifty ; that of the enemy was certainly double.

If Meade had designed a general battle—and the fact that. before this movement, his army had supplied itself with eight days' rations argues such design—this repulse and the heavy rains appear to have damped his ardor ; and the " on-to-Richmond " was reserved for another year.

CHAPTER VII.

WE left Rosecrans in Chattanooga and General Bragg hopefully essaying the investment of that place. The defeat of Rosecrans at Chickamauga had, despite all his attempts to qualify it, cost him his command, and added him to the long list of the victims of popular disappointment.*

---

* In an official statement on the Tennessee campaign, the Yankee commander-in-chief, General Halleck, attributed the defeat of Chickamauga to a disobedience of his orders. He stated that Burnside was ordered to connect his right with Rosecrans' left, and, if possible, to occupy Dalton and the passes into Georgia and North Carolina, so that the two armies might act as one body, and support each other. Rosecrans was not to advance into Georgia or Alabama at that time, but to fortify his position and connect with Burnside. If his weak point—his right and the communications with Nashville—were threatened, he was to hand over Chattanooga to Burnside, and swing round to cover that flank. At the same time forces were ordered up from Memphis and other quarters to guard that side, as well as his long line of communications. General Burnside, as alleged by Halleck, entirely disobeyed or neglected his orders, and did not connect with the Army of the Cumberland, leaving a great gap be-

On the 18th of October General Ulysses S. Grant assumed command of the Military Division of the Mississippi, comprising the Departments of the Ohio, the Cumberland, and the Tennessee. He was invested with plenary powers, and a military autocracy that extended from the Alleghanies to the Mississippi. Thomas was placed in command of the Cumberland, and Burnside commanded at Knoxville.

Grant proceeded directly to Chattanooga. He had telegraphed Thomas to hold the place to the last extremity, and the latter had replied, somewhat ominously, that he should do so until his army "starved." The fact was, the Yankee forces at Chattanooga were practically invested, the Confederate lines extending from the Tennessee river above Chattanooga to the river at and below the point at Lookout Mountain, below Chattanooga, with the south bank of the river picketed to near Bridgeport, our main force being fortified in Chattanooga Valley, at the foot of and on Missionary Ridge and Lookout Mountain, and a brigade in Lookout Valley. The enemy's artillery horses and mules had become reduced by starvation. It was estimated that ten thousand animals perished in supplying half-rations to the Yankee troops by the long and tedious route from Stevenson and Bridgeport to Chattanooga over Waldron's Ridge.

While Bragg thus held the Yankees in Chattanooga at the point of starvation, his cavalry had not been idle in their rear. General Wheeler had crossed the river in the face of a division of the enemy at Cotton Port Ford, and proceeded in the direction of McMinneville, when after a sharp fight he captured a large train and seven hundred prisoners. The train was loaded with ammunition and other stores, and supposed to consist of seven hundred wagons, all which were burned. He then attacked McMinneville, capturing five hundred and thirty prisoners, and another large train, destroyed several bridges, an engine and a train of cars. He then moved to Shelbyville, where he captured a large amount of stores and burned them. The amount of property destroyed by him was almost without precedent in the annals of raiding.

tween the two armies. It was claimed by General Halleck that had the instructions of the department been strictly followed, the disaster of Chickamauga would not have occurred.

On arriving at Chattanooga, General Grant seems to have at once appreciated the situation. It was decided that Hooker's command at Bridgeport should be concentrated; the plan agreed upon being for it to cross to the south side of the river, and to move on the wagon road, by the way of Whitesides, to Wauhatchie in Lookout Valley. On the 28th of October Hooker emerged into Lookout Valley at Wauhatchie, with the Eleventh army corps under Major-general Howard, and Geary's division of the Twelfth army corps.

In the mean time Grant had planned an expedition to seize the range of hills at the mouth of Lookout Valley, which easily succeeded. Hooker proceeded to take up positions for the defence of the road from Whitesides, over which he had marched, and also the road leading from Brown's Ferry to Kelly's Ferry; and Major-general Palmer, who had moved up to Whitesides, also took position to hold the road passed over by Hooker. By these movements Grant calculated to secure two good lines for supplies from the terminus of the railroad at Bridgeport; that at Whitesides and Wauhatchie, and that by Kelly's Ferry and Brown's Ferry.

THE AFFAIR OF LOOKOUT VALLEY.

The Confederates were not idle observers of these movements. On the night of the 29th October, a night attack was made by a portion of Longstreet's forces, with the hope of opening the way to the possession of the lines which had been lost to us by surprise, and with the immediate object of capturing Hooker's wagon-train. The expedition unexpectedly found itself fighting a whole Yankee corps, the Twelfth, under command of Slocum. Our force consisted of but six regiments. By the vigor of our attack the enemy's lines were broken. At one time the Yankees had fallen back in front, and on the right and left flanks, until wagon-trains and prisoners were captured in the rear. But the pressure of the Yankee columns from Brown's Ferry, where it was known there were at least two corps, threatened the integrity of our position. It had become critical in the extreme; and an order was given to retire. In this action Jenkins's brigade suffered severely; its loss in killed and wounded was said to be three hundred and sixty-one.

Grant's possession of the lines of communication south of the Tennessee river was no longer disputed. By the use of two steamboats he was enabled to obtain supplies with but eight miles of wagoning. His relief of Chattanooga was to be taken as an accomplished fact.

THE BATTLE OF MISSIONARY RIDGE.

President Davis had visited General Bragg's lines, and on his return therefrom made, in public, certain mysterious allusions to a campaign that was to retrieve our fortunes in the West. The country was shortly afterwards surprised to learn that Bragg had detached Longstreet from his front, and moved him in the direction of Knoxville, to attack Burnside.

Of this event, so untoward for the Confederates, Grant says, in his official report: "Ascertaining from scouts and deserters that Bragg was despatching Longstreet from the front, and moving him in the direction of Knoxville, Tennessee, evidently to attack Burnside, and feeling strongly the necessity for some move that would compel him to retain all his forces and recall those he had detached, directions were given for a movement against Missionary Ridge, with a view to carrying it and threatening the enemy's communication with Longstreet, of which I informed Burnside by telegraph on the 7th November."

Lookout Mountain was evacuated by the Confederates, on the 24th of November, being no longer important to us after the loss of Lookout or Wills' Valley, and no longer tenable against such an overwhelming force as General Grant had concentrated around Chattanooga. General Bragg abandoned also the whole of Chattanooga Valley, and the trenches and breastworks running along the foot of Missionary Ridge and across the valley to the base of Lookout, and moved his troops up to the top of the ridge. It was found necessary to extend his right well up towards the Chickamauga, near its mouth, in consequence of the heavy forces which the enemy had thrown up the river in that direction. The ridge varies in height from four to six hundred feet, and is crossed by several roads leading out from Chattanooga. The western side next to the enemy was steep and rugged, and in some places almost bare, the timber having been cut away for firewood. Our pickets occupied the breastworks below, while the infantry and artillery were distributed along the crest of the ridge from McFarlan's Gap almost to the mouth of the Chickamauga, a distance of six miles or more. In addition to the natural strength of the position we had thrown up breastworks along the ridge wherever the ascent was easy.

Determined to make his attack upon Bragg's reduced numbers as formidable as possible, Grant waited for Sherman to come up: Sherman, strengthened by a division from Thomas's command, to cross the Tennessee river below the mouth of Chickamauga, to form a junction with Thomas, and advance towards the northern end of Missionary Ridge. On the night of the 23d November, Sherman, with four divisions, commenced crossing the river. By daylight of the 24th, eight thousand Yankees were on the south side of the Tennessee, and fortified in rifle-trenches. By noon the remainder of Sherman's force was over, and before night the whole of the northern extremity of Missionary Ridge was in his possession. In the mean time, Hooker scaled the western slope of Lookout Mountain. On the night of the 24th, the Yankee forces maintained an unbroken line, with open communications, from the north end of Lookout Mountain, through Cheat Valley, to the north end of Missionary Ridge.

On the 25th of November, the enemy prepared for his grand assault. The Yankee army was marshalled under Grant, Thomas, Hooker, and Sherman, and did not number less than eighty-five thousand veteran troops. The Confederate army, under Bragg, Hardee and Breckinridge, did not number half so many. Longstreet's Virginia divisions and other troops had been sent to East Tennessee. Had these been present, with their steady leader at the head of them, we might have won a victory. As it was, we ought to have won the day; especially considering the advantages of our position, by which the ranks of the enemy were exposed to an artillery fire while in the plain, and to the infantry fire when they attempted the ascent of the hill or mountain.

Grant deployed his immense masses in two heavy lines of battle, and sometimes in three, supported by large reserve forces. The spectacle was magnificent as viewed from the crest of Missionary Ridge. He advanced first against our right wing, about ten o'clock, where he encountered Hardee, who commanded on the right, while Breckinridge commanded on the left. Hardee's command embraced Cleburne's, Walker's (commanded by General Gist, General Walker being absent), Cheatham's and Stevenson's divisions. Breckinridge's embraced his old division, commanded by Brigadier-general Lewis, Stewart's, part of Buckner's, and Hindman's commanded by Patton Anderson. The enemy's first assault upon Hardee was repulsed with great slaughter, as was his second, though made with double lines, supported with heavy reserves.

The attack on the left wing was not made until about noon. Here, as on the right, the enemy was repulsed; but he was obstinate, and fought with great ardor and confidence, returning to the charge again and again in the handsomest style, until one of our brigades in the centre gave way, and the Yankee flag was planted on Missionary Ridge. The enemy was not slow in availing himself of the great advantages of his new position. In a few minutes he turned upon our flanks and poured into them a terrible enfilading fire, which soon threw the Confederates on his right and left into confusion. Under this confusion, the gap in our lines grew wider and wider, and the wider it grew the faster the multitudinous foe rushed into the yawning chasm. A disgraceful panic ensued. The whole left wing of the Confederates became involved, gave way, and scattered in unmitigated rout. The day was lost, and shamefully lost. Hardee still maintained his ground; but no success of the right wing could restore the left to its original position. With cheers answering cheers the Yankees swarmed upwards. Color after color was planted on the summit, while muskets and cannon poured their deadly thunder upon the flying Confederates. Grant was surprised at the ease with which he had won a victory such as he had never before obtained, and attributed it to the dismay of the Confederates at his " audacity," and the " purposeless aiming " of our artillery from the crest of the ridge.

Our casualties were shamefully small. Granted stated his

O'Neill N.Y.

LT. GEN. HARDEE.

own loss as about five thousand in killed and wounded. He claimed to have taken over six thousand prisoners, forty pieces of artillery, and seven thousand stand of small arms.

The disaster of Missionary Ridge was not only a great misfortune, but a grievous disgrace. Of the unhappy event, President Davis said: " After a long and severe battle, in which great carnage was inflicted on the enemy, some of our troops inexplicably abandoned positions of great strength, and, by a disorderly retreat, compelled the commander to withdraw the forces elsewhere successful, and finally to retire with his whole army to a position some twenty or thirty miles to the rear. It is believed that if the troops who yielded to the assault had fought with the valor which they had displayed on previous occasions, and which was manifested in this battle on the other parts of the line, the enemy would have been repulsed with very great slaughter, and our country would have escaped the misfortune, and the army the mortification of the first defeat that has resulted from misconduct by the troops."

On the night of the 25th of November, Bragg was in full retreat; and all of his strong positions on Lookout Mountain, Chattanooga Valley and Missionary Ridge were in the hands of the enemy. His army was put in motion on the road to Ringgold, and thence to Dalton.

The disgrace of this retreat was somewhat relieved by the spirit of the brave and undaunted Cleburne. He had been left to bring up the rear. The Yankee pursuing column, numbering, it is estimated, about ten thousand men of all arms, assaulted him before he reached Tunnel Hill. This column consisted of picked troops, who moved rapidly and fought gallantly; but Cleburne succeeded in restraining them whenever he encountered them. After some desultory fighting, he succeeded in ambuscading Thomas's advance at Taylor's Ridge. He managed to conceal his forces, including his artillery, until the enemy got within a few paces of his guns, when they poured grape and canister into them with the most destructive effect. The road was filled with their dead and wounded. Our infantry then sprang forward from their covert on either side of the road, and literally mowed them down by their well-directed shot. The enemy fled in confusion, leaving two hundred and fifty prisoners and three flags (the latter taken by the artille

rists) in our hands, and from one thousand to fifteen hundred
killed and wounded in the road. Grant desisted from pursuit,
convinced by Cleburne's lesson, that the Confederates were not
demoralized, and impressed with the necessity of despatching
reinforcements to aid Burnside, at Knoxville.

LONGSTREET'S EXPEDITION AGAINST KNOXVILLE.

We must turn, to follow the fortunes of Longstreet's ill-advised and worse-furnished expedition against Knoxville.

It is an indisputable fact that, when Longstreet was sent from
General Bragg's lines, he was furnished with no subsistence
whatever; and in way of transportation, was provided only
with some refuse teams by Bragg's quartermaster. Despite
these difficulties, he succeeded in subsisting his army, and in
capturing an aggregate amount of stores from the enemy, which
alone was a valuable result of the campaign. At Lenoir Station
he captured a train of eighty-five wagons, many of them loaded
with valuable medical stores. At Bean Station he captured
thirty wagons, a quantity of forage, and some horses. In the
Clinch Valley he captured forty other wagons—a particularly
rich spoil, as they were mostly laden with sugar and coffee.

He had been disappointed in the force which was placed
at his command. When he started on his expedition, Stevenson's division was then at Loudon, some thirty miles from
Knoxville. Stevenson was hastily recalled to Chattanooga by
Bragg, who was suddenly awakened to the danger of an attack
on his front; and the first train which carried Longstreet's
troops through to Loudon, returned with those of Stevenson.
It appears that Longstreet's movement was thus uncovered, and
that he was left with only eleven thousand infantry to conduct
the campaign, arduous in all respects, against an enemy twice
his numbers.

On the 18th of November, Longstreet drove the enemy from
his advance lines, in front of Knoxville, close under his works.
This sortie was the occasion of one of those dashing feats of individual gallantry which demands a passing notice. A breastwork was charged by our infantry. They winced under the
galling fire of the enemy, and wavered, when Captain Stephen

Northrop, an Englishman, formerly Captain of Her Britannic Majesty's 22d foot, who had joined our ranks, and was on duty in Alexander's artillery battalion, stationed several hundred yards from the scene of conflict, mounted his horse, and dashing across the plain—the only horseman in the melee—rode in advance of the wavering line, up to the very works of the enemy; a hundred rifles were lowered upon him, but he moved on, and rallied the wavering line; the work was carried, and Northrop borne away, with a minie ball through his shoulder, his sword-scabbard broken by another, and the point of his sword cut off by yet another. His escape was miraculous.

Longstreet's investment of Knoxville was nearly complete. The enemy could only procure supplies from one side of the river, and the Yankees were already restricted in their rations.

But in the mean time news had come of Bragg's disaster, and nothing remained for Longstreet but to trust to the vigor of a decisive assault. It is not improbable that a few days more might have starved the Yankees into a surrender; but we could not wait for the event. The enemy's cavalry were already on the line of the railroad between Knoxville and Chickamauga. Communication with General Bragg had been severed, and Loudon was threatened.

Knoxville was well fortified. College Hill was fortified with a heavy fort, carrying a siege-piece of artillery. Another fort was thrown up on the hills, near the Summit House. The hill on the right of the street leading from the public square to the depot, had a strong fort. Near the Humphrey's was another. The hill known as Temperance Hill, had two heavy forts. Another rise had two batteries. The heights south of Knoxville were also fortified, and connected with these immense fortifications was one continuous line of rifle-pits and breastworks, from the extreme east of Knoxville, on the river, to the west, on the river. The point of attack was a strong work on the north-west angle of the enemy's line (the salient angle north-west the immediate point to be assailed). The fort was on a hill of considerable eminence, near the Kingston road, known as Fort Sanders.

The force which was to attempt an enterprise which ranks with the most famous charges in military history, should be mentioned in detail. It consisted of three brigades of McLaw's

division : that of General Wolford, the Sixteenth, Eighteenth,
and Twenty-fourth Georgia regiments, and Cobb's and Phillips's
Georgia legions; that of General Humphrey, the Thirteenth,
Seventeenth, Twenty-first, Twenty-second and Twenty-third
Mississippi regiments, and a brigade composed of General Anderson's and Bryant's brigades, embracing, among others, the
Palmetto State Guard, the Fifteenth South Carolina regiment,
and the Fifty-first, Fifty-third and Fifty-ninth Georgia regiments.

The signal gun broke the silence of the early dawn of the
29th of November. The assaulting column of the Confederates
moved up to the attack over the slope, in front of the fort, in
a direction oblique to the Loudon road. A heavy artillery-
fire was opened upon them at the first advance. Despite the
storm of canister which howled around them, on came the devoted men, with brigade front, slowly pouring over the railroad cut, and anon quickening in motion as the ground presented less obstruction, until at last, emerging from the nearest
timber, they broke into the charge.

Across the open space which intervened between the timber
and the fort, and which was crossed with logs and the stumps
of felled trees, the Confederates came at impetuous speed. But
the enemy had prepared for them a device quite worthy of
Yankee ingenuity. Among the stumps which covered the
slope, the Yankees had woven a *network of wire*. Lines of
telegraph wire had been stretched through the low brush, and
coiled from stump to stump, out of ordinary view. The foremost of the assaulting column stumbled, one falling over another, and were thrown into some confusion, until the cause of
the obstruction was discovered. The enemy took advantage of
the momentary halt and confusion to pour a devouring fire upon
the broken lines. The embrasures of the fort, and the whole
line of the parapet blazed at once with discharges. But still
the gallant Confederates pressed on, their battle-flags of red,
with cross of blue, floating triumphantly above their heads.
Rallying over the temporary obstruction, leaping the stumps
and logs, and pushing through the brush, they were soon within
pistol shot of the fort. The enemy reserved his fire. He had
treble-shotted some of his guns, and others were loaded with
terrible canister.

Suddenly all the enemy's guns launched forth their missiles of death. Our lines were shattered; but with a terrible courage, some of the Confederates sprang into the ditch, clambered up the glacis, and almost side by side with the Yankee flag planted their own. But the rear of the assaulting column had given way. Others remained with their officers, who valiantly kept the lead to the very fort itself, and in the attempt to scale the glacis. There was a spatter of blood and brains as each head appeared above the parapet. A Confederate captain, with an oath, demanded the surrender of the garrison, as he pushed his body through one of the embrasures, and faced the very muzzle of the cannon. The answer to him was the discharge of the piece, when, rent from limb to limb, his mangled corpse, or what was left of it, was hurled outward into the air. His comrades, yet essaying to get within the work, were now subjected to the fire of hand-grenades, extemporized by cutting short the fuses, and the shells being then tossed over the edge of the parapet. Baffled at every point, and unsupported by the rest of the charging column, these brave men surrendered, and were hauled within the fort; but not until the trench was filled with the dead and dying.

In this terrible ditch the dead were piled eight or ten feet deep. In comparatively an instant of time, we lost seven hundred men in killed, wounded, and prisoners. Colonel McElroy of the Thirteenth Mississippi and Colonel Thomas of the Sixteenth Georgia, had both fallen mortally wounded in the ditch. The Yankees lost in the action not more than twenty men killed and wounded.

Never—excepting Gettysburg—was there in the history of the war a disaster adorned with the glory of such devoted courage as Longstreet's repulse at Knoxville. It left him, considering the consequences of Bragg's defeat at Missionary Ridge, with no other alternative than to raise the siege and occupy a new line of operations. A retreat to Bragg's line was not contemplated, and he decided to transfer his base to a point where he could threaten Knoxville from the opposite side of the town, and establish communications with Bristol, Lynchburg, and Richmond. These intentions, it is said, were known to President Davis in advance, who, it is further said, advised with General Longstreet on the subject, and left to his discretion the plan of campaign to be pursued in the future.

It was in the exercise of an independant judgment, that Longstreet made his retreat to Russellville. It was one of the most fortunate retreats of the war. It was made without the slightest loss. It evaded a large column of the enemy at Loudon. Its immediate object was Rogersville, where Longstreet expected to get supplies and milling for his army. Our forces, however, being pressed by the enemy, who followed them to Bean Station, on the Cumberland Gap road, turned upon the Yankees, inflicted upon them a severe defeat, and drove them twelve lines before Russellville.

By an admirable movement, Longstreet selected a position in Northeastern Tennessee, where he could hold communication with his superiors in Richmond, and intrenching himself against all possibility of surprise, he proceeded to carry out what remained of his military plans. The Army of the Ohio was weak, and he knew it. It was strong enough to hold Knoxville, as he had learned by sad experience. The reinforcements which were sent from Chattanooga, were withdrawn. He, therefore, organized his forces for conquest, not necessarily of territory, but of material for the subsistence of his troops. In this way he managed to overrun the entire section of the State east of a line drawn from Cumberland Gap to Cleveland ; to gather within his lines all that was valuable in supplies of food ; and to make his army quite self-subsisting in a tract of country where it was thought it was impossible for him to remain without external aid.

While events of dominant importance were taking place on the lines of Generals Lee and Bragg, there were distant and minor theatres of the contest, which, at various times in the fall of 1863, exhibited some remarkable episodes in the war. We shall make a rapid *résumé* of these minor events, taking the reader's attention from the Gulf Coast to the distant regions of the Trans-Mississippi, and thence to the frontiers of some of the eastern States of the Confederacy.

THE AFFAIR AT SABINE PASS, TEXAS.—THE TRANS-MISSISSIPPI.

An engagement with the Yankee navy had occurred at Sabine Pass, the dividing line between Louisiana and Texas, on the 8th of September. A brilliant victory was won by the little Confederate garrison of Sabine Pass against the fleet of the enemy. Attacked by five gunboats, the fort, mounting but three guns of small calibre, and manned by the Davis Guards, Lieutenant R. M. Dowling, assisted by Lieutenant Smith, of the engineers, supported by about two hundred men, the whole under command of Captain F. A. Odlum. steadily resisted their fire, and at last forced the surrender of the two gunboats Clifton and Sachem, badly crippling another, which with the others escaped over the bar. The result of this gallant achievement was the capture of two fine gunboats, fifteen heavy guns, over two hundred prisoners (among them the commodore of the fleet), and over fifty of the enemy killed and wounded, while not a man was lost on our side, or a gun injured.

This demonstration of the Yankees, under command of General Franklin, was part of an expedition from General Banks' lines against Texas. A column under Washburne had moved by railroad to Brashear and Bayou Bœuf; and another Yankee column had been taken by steamboats to the mouth of Red River to go to Simmsport. But Franklin's disaster at Sabine Pass caused him to abandon his part of the movement; and on this account, and also, it is said, the low state of water, an expedition elaborately and ambitiously planned by Banks was wholly abandoned.

In the upper portions of the Trans-Mississippi, Confederate operations had assumed an irregular character. The States beyond the great river possessed many advantages for the maintenance of their defence. In provisions they abounded beyond any other part of the Confederacy. In the various equisites for establishing and supplying an army they were by no means destitute. Through Mexico they had been enabled to make good their deficiencies, to some extent, by importation.

Great activity seemed to pervade the Trans-Mississippi, and brilliant actions performed by small bodies of men characterized it, instead of sanguinary and resultless battles. The nature of the country and the requirements of the situations had no doubt wrought a considerable change in the character of the warfare carried on in that region; but although no signal indications of strategic skill might be traceable, marks of dash and daring were plainly discernible.

But while Texas and Arkansas still maintained formidable military organizations, in unhappy Missouri the Confederates were well nigh driven to the wall. Quantrell, the famous partisan chief, was compelled, in the fall of 1863, to make his exodus from Missouri.

Towards the middle of September the guerillas reunited at Blackwater, and were ready in a few hours to leave their rendezvous for their march South. Cold nights and occasional frost had warned them to leave Missouri, and like poor houseless birds of passage, beaten by the pitiless storm, they sought a more genial clime, where the grass was green and Yankees less numerous. Missouri would afford no shelter of safety after winter had set in; the bare and leafless forests no hiding places, and the pure driven snow would afford to the enemy the best means of tracking the hunted and hungry guerillas whenever they should leave their holes in search of food. Outlawed by an order of General Blount, proscribed by every Yankee official, the citizens warned against furnishing food or shelter under the cruelest and severest penalties, the very earth almost denying them a resting-place, the gallant three hundred broke up their rendezvous and left for the plains of Texas.

The romantic adventures of these men in the Indian country were of thrilling interest. At one time, they came upon a party of Yankees near Fort Smith, who mistook them for comrades. The little Confederate command was drawn up in line of battle, motionless as statues, with Quantrell at their head on his war-horse, looking grimly at a brilliant cavalcade of horsemen forming beautifully about three hundred yards in front. The whisper ran through the line, "It is old Blount, and he thinks we are Yankees coming out to give him a reception!" It was true. There rode General Blount and staff, glittering in blue cloth and gold lace, and about two hundred of his body guard; just then the cavalcade moved, and the band commenced playing Yankee Doodle. Quantrell moved also; but the quick eye of Blount discovered something wrong and called a halt. But the guerillas by this time were under full gallop, and down they swept upon the brilliant cortege like an avalanche and hurled them to the earth. The struggle was short and fierce; the shock terrific, as guerilla rode over both horse and his rider, and dashed out the brains of the latter as he passed. Again and again they turned and fired, charged and recharged, until the ground was strewn with the dead, ambulances overturned, and horses flying madly in every direction.*

THE VIRGINIA-TENNESSEE FRONTIER.

The frontier in which we include the vast body of land lying generally between General Lee's lines in Virginia and East Tennessee, was one of the most important of the minor theatres of the war.

What was known as the Department of West Virginia and East Tennessee, was under the command of Major-general Sam

---

* A stirring episode of this engagement is told by one who participated in it. We give it, in his words, as a characteristic incident of the romance of partisan warfare:

"Lieutenant-colonel Curtis, adjutant-general on General Blount's staff, rode a magnificent horse, richly caparisoned, and was himself dressed in the richest uniform of his rank. He was a remarkably handsome man, fair, and rosy, eyes blue as those of the fairest blonde of his own clime; pale, fair, tall, slender figure—with features as beautiful as those of a woman. He was well armed with pistol and sabre, and used them gallantly. He sees that his force is defeated, and determines to escape. But as he turns his horse's head he encounters the fierce eye of a young guerilla as handsome, as brave and as well mounted as himself, bearing right down upon him. He observes the adjutant-general endeavoring to escape; calls to him to stop and fight. He does turn to meet the guerilla now swooping down upon him like an eagle on its prey. The Yankee fires a long-range gun, but misses his aim; he draws his six-shooter and rapidly, nervously discharges the contents at his adversary, who all this time is gaining on him and dashing straight at him.

"As an eagle swoops down on his prey, gracefully and grandly ferocious, beautiful even in the act of destruction, so does Peyton Long, the young hero, gallantly bear down on the "cute" Yankee; he reserves every shot, while Curtis is wasting his; he dashes upon him—both pause for an instant as if in mutual admiration—but only for a moment. Peyton Long watches his antagonist, and sways his body to the left to escape the sabre cut of the Yankee; the next instant the inevitable six-shooter of the guerilla is pointed at the head of the splendid-looking fellow; it is the work of an instant; Peyton strikes like an eagle, and all is over! A shout of triumph rose from the throng of guerillas, who had ceased the fight to watch the encounter between this well-matched couple."

Jones, one of the most active of Confederate commanders. Of events in his department we must make a rapid summary, which, however, will admit some detail of his most interesting operations.

For many months operations had been active in this Department to cope with raids under the energetic direction of the somewhat famous Yankee commander General Averill. On the 26th of August a portion of General Jones's forces encountered the enemy about a mile and a half from Dublin, on the road leading to the Warm Springs. Every attack made by the enemy was repulsed. At night each side occupied the same position they had in the morning. The next morning the enemy made two other attacks, which were handsomely repulsed, when he abandoned his position and retreated towards Warm Springs, pursued by cavalry and artillery. The troops engaged were the first brigade of Jones's army, Colonel George S. Patton commanding. The enemy were about three thousand strong, with six pieces of artillery, under Brigadier-general Averill. Our loss was about two hundred killed and wounded. The enemy's loss was not known. We took about one hundred and fifty prisoners and a piece of artillery.

On the 6th November occurred an affair at Rogersville, East Tennessee, which was a considerable success for the Confederates. Information of a reliable character was received by General Ransom of the exact position, numbers and condition of the Yankees at Big Creek, four miles east of Rogersville. The nearest supporting force being at Greenville, he conceived the idea of cutting them off by a rapid night march of cavalry upon their front and rear. The attack was successful. Among the fruits of the expedition were eight hundred and fifty prisoners, four pieces of artillery, sixty wagons, and several hundred animals.

BATTLE OF DROOP MOUNTAIN.

On the same day (6th November) occurred an important action between another portion of General Jones's forces, and the redoubtable Averill.

At nine o'clock on the morning of the 6th of November

Echols' brigade, consisting of a regiment and battalion of infantry, and six pieces of artillery, came up to the support of Colonel Wm. L. Jackson, commanding Confederate forces in the Northwest (who was closely pushed by General Averill), on Droop Mountain, in the county of Pocahontas, twenty-eight miles north-east of Lewisburg. The entire forces of the two commands thus united, amounted to about fifteen hundred infantry and dismounted cavalry, and eight pieces of artillery. The position of our men, naturally a very strong one, was selected with great judgment by Colonel Jackson, on the western extremity of Droop Mountain. At ten o'clock, the enemy, who had remained in the front of Colonel Jackson since daybreak, with a force amounting to seven thousand five hundred mounted infantry and cavalry, and eight pieces of artillery, commenced his advance upon us, by posting his long-range guns on an eminence to our right, and by advancing his line of skirmishers upon our right and left; and brisk skirmishing then ensued, which continued from time to time until the fight became general between our infantry and dismounted cavalry and those of the enemy.

The monstrously unequal combat was kept up for several hours. Our men fought with the utmost gallantry and determination, and stubbornly maintained their position against an enemy five times their number until they were well nigh surrounded. Human endurance could hold out no longer; the troops on the right gave away before overwhelming numbers, while the enemy were rapidly flanking those on the left. Just at this stage of proceedings, General Echols, seeing that if he remained longer his retreat would be cut off, withdrew the troops from the field and ordered a retreat in the direction of Lewisburg. Our loss in killed and wounded was about three hundred. Although the action terminated in the retreat of the Confederates, yet they had given an exhibition of spirit among the proudest in the war. Our little army had wrestled in deadly conflict with an enemy five times its strength for seven long hours; and when they did retreat, succeeded in bringing off all of our quartermaster and commissary stores together with our trains and artillery, leaving to the enemy no trophies over which to exult, save the bodies of our gallant dead.

So far as the beneficial results of the expedition to the enemy could be estimated they amounted to nothing. They came with two large forces, amounting, in the aggregate, to nearly ten thousand men, with the expectation of capturing the command of Colonel Jackson and General Echols' brigade, and of moving then upon our interior lines of railroad. By fighting, however, so far from the interior, and by being so checked and damaged and baffled as they were, they failed in the one object and abandoned the other.

But the great raid of Averill seems to have been reserved for December. He came from New Creek, a depot on the Baltimore and Ohio railroad, in the county of Hardy, along the western base of the Shenandoah mountains, through Covington to Salem, burning and destroying what he could in his path. His command consisted of four regiments of mounted infantry, a battalion of cavalry, and a battery. On the 16th of December he cut the Virginia and Tennessee railroad at Salem. Here three depots were destroyed, the contents of which were officially stated by Averill to have been 2,000 barrels of flour, 10,000 bushels of wheat, 100,000 bushels of shelled corn, 50,000 bushels of oats, 2,000 barrels of meat, several cords of leather, and 1,000 sacks of salt.

On his retreat, the adventurous Yankee had to run the gauntlet of different Confederate commands, arranged in a line extending from Staunton to Newport upon all the available roads to prevent his return. Having captured a despatch from General Jones to General Early, Averill deflected from the line of his retreat and instead of passing through Buchanan, moved towards Covington.

Colonel William L. Jackson moved his command down to Jackson's river depot, and directed the bridge to be burned as soon as it was ascertained that the enemy were advancing towards it. Jackson then took a strong position near the Jackson's river depot, at the point where the Rich Patch road connects the Covington turnpike. He then directed his mounted men, under Captain Sprague, to move on the Rich Patch road until they met the enemy's advance, and to attack them desperately, and cut the column in two, if possible. At four o'clock on Saturday evening, the 19th December, a courier from Captain Sprague announced the approach of the enemy by that road, and that he had commenced a skirmish with Averill's advanced forces. Jackson immediately ordered an advance of the Twentieth Virginia Regiment by a blind road, so as to attack the enemy obliquely. He also ordered the Nineteenth Virginia Regiment to advance on the Covington turnpike road, and to attack the enemy directly. At that point Jackson conceived the idea of taking a detachment of about fifty men, and move forward with them for the purpose of striking the enemy vigorously, and cutting his column in two. In this he succeeded perfectly. One half of the Yankees were thus separated from the other half, which was under the immediate command of Averill, and who rapidly passed forward towards the Island Ford bridge. Persons entrusted with the burning of the Island Ford bridge failed to do so, however, owing to the rapid advance of the enemy upon that point. The advance, under Averill in person, thus managed to make their escape across the bridge.

There remained in Jackson's hand about two hundred prisoners. Averill continued his retreat to Pocahontas county. On the 22d December he wrote to the War Department at Washington : " My command has marched, climbed, slid and swam three hundred and fifty miles since the 8th instant."

THE NORTH CAROLINA SWAMPS.

We have referred in this chapter to the occult romances of warfare in the Trans-Mississippi. But there was a district much nearer the capital of the Confederacy, to which all eyes were turned to witness certain thrilling scenes, a drama of cruelty such as the world had seldom seen, even in the wars and outrages of barbarians.

We refer to the north-eastern parts of North Carolina. In Camden and Currituck counties, and in the country lying generally between Franklin on the Blackwater and the Roanoke river, a series of atrocities was committed by the enemy at which the blood runs cold. It is difficult to find words of description for the pictures of the wild and terrible consequences of the negro raids in this obscure theatre of the war. The country was traversed by negro banditti; they burned houses; they entered the parlors of their masters ; they compelled ladies to entertain them on the piano, cursed and abused them, stripped them of their jewelry and clothing, and offered them indignities which it would offend delicacy to describe.

The fiat seemed to have gone forth for stern and terrible work on the North Carolina frontier, in this dark and melancholy country of swamps, overrun with negro banditti, and now the especial theatre of the war's vengeance. The country was a rich one, comparing favorably with the Mississippi bottoms, and one of the most important sources of meat supplies which was at this time accessible to our armies. To protect this country as far as possible, forces were raised, under authority of the Government of North Carolina, for local defence and to repel invasion ; they were duly organized, and their officers were commissioned by the governor, and for a year or more had been in the regular service of the State. The Yankees found it convenient to designate these forces as "guerillas," in order to justify the fiendish warfare of negro partisans and white banditti, who were invited to prey upon the population.

In December, a force of negroes, under the command of Brigadier-general Wild, who emulated the brutal disposition and ferocious cowardice of his master, "Beast" Butler, invaded the north-eastern parts of North Carolina. In the county of Pasquotank, forty miles from Norfolk, he hung Daniel Bright at his own house. He seized more than one hundred thousand dollars' worth of personal property in the adjoining counties; stripped the farmers of every living thing, and brought it all away, leaving hundreds of inhabitants without a pound of meat or a peck of meal.

Daniel Bright was a member of the Sixty-second Georgia regiment, under command of Colonel J. R. Griffin, and had received authority from the Governor of North Carolina to raise a company in the county for local defence. Failing in the effort, he had retired to his farm, and was there seized, carried off and executed. He was hung on the side of the public road, and a placard fastened upon his back.

But the most brutal of all the outrages of Wild was the seizure, as "hostages" for two of his negroes who had been captured, of two most respectable married ladies, Mrs. Phœbe Munden, wife of Lieutenant W. J. Munden, and Mrs. Elizabeth

Weeks, wife of Private Pender Weeks, of Captain John T Elliot's company. The first was arrested at her own house, in the presence only of her three children, of whom the oldest was ten years of age, conveyed a few miles to Elizabeth City, confined in a room without fire, bed or bedding, with several male prisoners, and tied by the feet and hands. A negro guard was placed in charge of the prisoners. The succeeding day, the other lady, Mrs. Weeks, was placed in the same room. They were constantly guarded, and neither was allowed to leave the room for the most necessary duty, but in company with an armed negro soldier. Mrs. Munden was in delicate health, and forced from a home immediately laid in ashes, with all it contained, without other apparel than she wore upon her person, and passed several nights in the cheerless and cold apartment to which she was confined at that inclement season, before the humanity of her captors was so far softened as to permit blankets to be furnished for her use. They were kept some days and then removed to Norfolk. When Mrs. Munden was carried off, her wrists were bleeding with the stricture of the cord with which she was bound, and it is said that a negro was allowed by Wild to hold the cord that bound her, and thus drive her into Norfolk.

Such were the scenes which illustrated the Yankee idea of prosecuting the war with "vigor," and gratified the vile and cowardly revenge of those who, in luxurious cities and comfortable homes, clamored for the blood of "rebels," and even claimed women and children as their victims.

CHAPTER VIII.

The President's Declaration to the Confederate Congress of 1863–64.—"Want of Capacity" in the Confederate Authorities.—Character of Jefferson Davis.—Official Shiftlessness at Richmond.—Early Prognostications of the War.—The "Statesmanship" of the Confederates.—Ludicrous Errors of Confederate Leaders.—What "King Cotton" might have done.—Gross Mismanagement of the Confederate Finances.—Mr. Memminger's Maladministration.—The Moral Evils of an Expanded Currency.—The Military Situation in December.—Secretary Seddon's Shameful Confession.—"Demagogueism" in the Confederate War Department.—Seddon's Propositions.—Military "Substitutes."—An Act of Perfidy.—Bullying in Congress.—Spirit of the Confederate Soldiery.—LINCOLN'S "PEACE PROCLAMATION."—Its Stupidity, Insolence, and Outrage.—How the Confederates Replied to it.—A New Appeal Against "Reconstruction."—THE SLAVERY QUESTION IN THE· WAR.—A French Opinion.—The Abolitionists Unmasked.—Decay of European Sympathy with Them.—Review of Lincoln's "Emancipation" Policy.—The Arming of the Blacks.—The Negro Colonization Schemes.—Experiments of New England "Civilization" in Louisiana.—Frightful Mortality of "Freedmen."—The Appalling Statistics of Emancipation.—The Contraband Camps in the Mississippi Valley.—Pictures of Yankee Philanthropy.—"Slavery" Tested by the War.—The Confederates the True Friends of the African Laborer.—The System of Negro *Servitude* in the Confederacy.—The "War-to-the-Knife" Party in the North.—HISTORY OF THE "RETALIATION" POLICY.—The Outrages of Yankee Warfare.—President Davis's Sentimentalism.—The Record of his Unpardonable and Unparalleled Weakness.—A Peep into Yankee Prisons.—The Torture-Houses of the North.—Captain Morgan's Experience Among "the Convict-Drivers."—President Davis's Bluster.—His Two Faces.—Moral Effects of Submission to Yankee Outrage.—The Rival Administrations in December 1863.—Richmond and Washington.—Mr. Lincoln's Gaiety.—New Issues for the Confederacy.

At the meeting of the Confederate Congress, in December, 1863, President Davis said: "We now know that the only reliable hope for peace is in the vigor of our resistance, while the cessation of their [the enemy's] hostility is only to be expected from the pressure of their necessities." The Confederate Administration had at last arrived at the correct comprehension of the war. But it had reached this conclusion only after a period of nearly three years of ignorance, short-sighted conceit and perversity.

The careful and candid reader of the pages of two volumes of the history of the war, by this writer, will bear him witness that at no time has he reflected upon the patriotism or the public integrity of President Davis. The accusation, which has run through these volumes, is simply this: *want of capacity* in the administration of public affairs.

It is not possible that any historian of this war can overlook certain admirable qualities of the President of the Confederacy: his literary abilities, his spruce English, his ascetic morals, the purity of his private life, and the extraordinary facility of his manners. But he was not a statesman; he had no administrative capacities; he lacked that indispensable and practical element of success in all political administrations—knowledge of the true value of men; and he was—probably, unconsciously through his vanity—accessible to favorites. In the old government, Mr. Davis had never been accounted as a statesman, but was quite as obtuse as most of the public men of that day. He it was, of Southern politicians, who declared in a public letter, in 1858, that the "Kansas Conference bill" was "the triumph of *all* for which we contended." He had failed to see the origin and occasion of the revolution which he assumed to conduct.

His choice of favorites in the field had been as unapt as his selection of political advisers in the Cabinet. This President, who depreciated Price as a militiaman, and held (or probably affected) a light opinion of Beauregard, was convinced that Pemberton was a genius who should be raised by a single stroke of patronage from the obscurity of a major to the position of a Lieutenant-general; recognized Heth as a young Napoleon; selected Lovell as the natural guardian of the Mississippi; declared that Holmes, who had let the enemy slip out of his fingers at Richmond, was the appointed deliverer of Missouri and Arkansas, and competent to take charge of the destinies of an empire; and prophesied with peculiar emphasis of mystery, but a few weeks before the session of Congress, in a public speech in a Southern city, that Bragg by that time would be in the heart of Tennessee, and on the pinnacles of victory!

The civil administration of Mr. Davis had fallen to a low ebb. There are certain minds which cannot see how want of capacity in our government, official shiftlessness and the mismanagement of public affairs yet consist with the undeniable facts of the successes of our arms and the great achievements of the Confederacy. But it is possible that these two conditions may consist--that, in a revolution, the valor and determinaticn of a people may make considerable amends for the faults of its governors. If the history of this war has proved one proposition clearly it is this: that in all its subjects of congratulation, the "statesmanship" of Richmond has little part or lot. Let those who deny the justice of this historical judgment, which refuses to attribute to the official authorities of this government such success as we have had in this war, say what they have contributed to it.

The evidences of the "statesmanship" of Richmond were not to be found in our foreign relations: these were absurdities. They were not to be found in our provisions for the war: these were make-shifts from month to month. They were not to be found in our financial calculations: these had proved the most ridiculous failures in the monetary annals of the world. We owe this melancholy confession to history, that we do not know of any real and substantial particulars in which the administration of Mr. Davis has contributed to this war. The reverse of the proposition need not be repeated here.

It is mortifying, indeed, to look back upon the currents of our history, to observe the blindness and littleness of mind, the conceit, the perversity, the short-sighted management on all which we have drifted into this present vastness of war and depths of distress. In Montgomery, at the period of the provisional inauguration of the Confederacy, any one who had the hardihood to insist upon the probability of a war, became a butt of raillery or the object of suspicion. The war once begun, the next idea in the minds of the Confederate leaders was that it was to be despatched in a few months by mere make-shifts of armies and money, and with the scant supply of munitions already on hand. Months intervened between Lincoln's declaration of war and the actual establishment of the blockade. But no use was made of this golden opportunity, and our importations of army supplies from Europe during all these months, actually may be counted in a few thousand stand of small arms. Secretary Mallory laughed off contractors in New Orleans, who offered to sell to the government a large amount of navy supplies. Judah P. Benjamin, at the head of the War Department, wrote to a friend in the first winter o the war, that within sixty days the country would be at peace

Later still, in the winter of 1862, President Davis, in a speech before the Legislature of Mississippi, had pronounced the solemn opinion that the war would soon come to an end. Yet we find the same eminent personage now declaring to the Congress of 1863, his belief in an indefinite prolongation of the war, and his despair of his many brilliant former prospects of peace, through instrumentalities other than that of our arms.

Able and candid journals of the North, have repeatedly confessed that they were puzzled by the extraordinary want of foresight and judgment displayed by the Confederate leaders, in their calculation at different periods of the war of the course likely to be pursued by Europe and the North. These errors might have been expected from men of little education, to whom self-interest in its lowest sense was the key to all political problems, but by no means from persons who had studied politics in books. "The notion," said the New York *Times*, "that the North, being a commercial community, devoted to the pursuit of gain, was, for that reason, sure not to fight, was rather the conclusion of a backwoodsman than of a student. The lesson of history is that commercial communities are among the most pugnacious and ambitious and most obstinate of belligerents: witness Carthage, Venice, Genoa, Holland, and England."

The utter failure of the calculations of the Confederate Administration, regarding France and England, had exhibited a hasty and passionate reasoning, of which Mr. Davis and his associates might well be ashamed. The idea is ludicrous now that at the very beginning of the American revolution, France and England, with their centuries of vast and varied experience, in peace and war, would fling themselves into a convulsion which their great politicians easily saw was the most tremendous one of modern times. Yet this idea was entertained by President Davis; and as proof of it, the Confederate commissioners were instructed to apply to Earl Russell for recognition in England after the first battle of Manassas!

At the commencement of the war, cotton was pronounced "King;" and the absurd and puerile idea was put forward by the politicians of the Davis school, that the great and illustrious power of England would submit to the ineffable humiliation of acknowledging its dependency on the infant Confed-

eracy of the South, and the subserviency of its empire, its
political interests, and its pride, to a single article of trade that
was grown in America! And what indeed is the sum of
advantages which the Confederacy drew from the royal resources of cotton? It is true that these resources could not
compel the political interests and pride of England. But,
properly used, they might have accomplished much for the
interests of the Confederacy. In point of fact they accomplished nothing. For one year after the war commenced, the
blockade was so slight that the whole of the cotton might have
been shipped to Europe, and there sold at two shillings sterling a pound, giving the government, purchasing at twenty
cents, a clear profit of *six hundred millions of dollars!* We
may even suppose one-fifth of this captured by the enemy, and
we would still have had a balance in our favor, which would
have enabled us to have drained every bank in Europe of its
specie! Or if we had drawn for this sum as we needed it, our
treasury notes would have been equal to gold, and confidence
in our currency would have been unshaken and universal.

The Confederacy had thus the element at ready hand for the
structure of one of the most successful schemes of finance in
the world. But the government was too grossly ignorant to
see it. The purchase of the cotton to the government was
decried by Mr. Memminger, as a scheme of " soup-house legislation ;" and the new government was started without a basis
of credit; without a system of revenue; on the monstrous delusion that money might be manufactured at will out of paper,
and that a naked " promise to pay," was all sufficient for the
wants of the war!

It is to be frankly admitted that the South commenced the
war with *financial* advantages which the North did not have—
that is, without reference to commercial incidents of the blockade, but with respect to the sustention of its credit at home.
The South had the cotton and the tobacco. It had the unbounded sympathies of its people. It had larger taxable values
per capita than any other country in the world. It is not possible that with these advantages it could have wrecked its
credit with its own people, unless through a great want of
capacity in the administration of the government. It is not
possible, that, with these advantages, its currency should have

declined with its own people ten times faster than that of the North with its people, unless through a gross mismanagement of public affairs. These are logical conclusions which are not to be disputed.

At the organization of the permanent government of the Confederacy, in February, 1862, President Davis had made the most extravagant congratulations to the country, on our financial condition in comparison with that of the North. In less than eighteen months thereafter, when gold was quoted in New York at twenty-five per cent. premium, it was selling in Richmond at nine hundred per cent. premium; and by the time that the Confederate Congress met, in December, 1863, gold in Richmond was worth about two thousand per cent. premium, and was publicly sold, one for twenty in Confederate notes! Such had been the results of the financial wisdom of the Confederacy. It had been dictated by the President, who advised Congress (as late as August, 1862) to authorize illimitable issues of treasury notes, without fear of their depreciation, and aggravated, no doubt, by the ignorance of his secretary, who invented the legerdemain of "funding," that had given the last stab to the currency, and who opened the doors of the treasury to brokers, blockade-runners, and the vast tribes of those who lived on the depreciation of the public credit.*

---

* The experiments of Mr. Memminger on the currency was the signal of multiplied and rapid depreciation. While the eccentric and pious Secretary was figuring out impossible schemes of making money, or ransacking the book-stores for works on religious controversy, unprincipled brokers in the Confederacy were undermining the currency with a zeal for the destruction of their country not less than that of the Yankees. The assertion admits of some qualification. Sweeping remarks in history are generally unjust. Among those engaged in the business of banking and exchange in the South, there were undoubtedly some enlightened and public-spirited men who had been seduced by the example or constrained by the competition of meaner and more avaricious men of the same profession, to array themselves against the currency, and to commit offences from which they would have shrunk in horror, had they not been disguised by the casuistry of commerce and gain.

It was generally thought in the South reprehensible to refuse the national currency in the payment of debts. Yet the broker, who demanded eighteen or twenty dollars in this currency for one in gold, really was guilty of so many times refusing the Confederate money. It was accounted shocking for citizens in the South to speculate in soldiers' clothing and bread. Yet the broker, who

Of all the features of maladministration in the Confederacy, which we have unwillingly traced, that of the currency was, certainly, the most marked, and, perhaps, the most vital. Nothing could be more absurd than the faith of Mr. Davis and Mr. Memminger in the virtues of paper money, and no empiricism more ignorant and destructive than that which made the mere emission of paper issues a system of revenue. In the old government, we had had many emphatic lessons on the subject of paper money. Indeed, it is a curious and interesting fact, that in sixty years of our past history, the banking

demanded twenty prices for gold, the representative of all values, speculated alike in every necessary in the country. Nor was this the greatest of their offences. With unsurpassed shamelessness, brokers in the Confederacy exposed the currency of the North for sale, and demanded for it ten hundred per cent. premium over that of the Confederacy! This act of benefit to the Yankees was openly allowed by the government. A bill had been introduced in Congress to prohibit this traffic and to extirpate this infamous anomaly in our history; but it failed of enactment, and its failure can only be attributed to the grossest stupidity, or to sinister influences of the most dishonorable kind. The traffic was immensely profitable. State bonds and bank bills to the amount of many millions were sent North by the brokers, and the rates of discount were readily submitted to when the returns were made in Yankee paper money, which, in Richmond shops, was worth in Confederate notes ten dollars for one

One—but only one—cause of the depreciation of the Confederate currenc. was illicit trade. It had done more to demoralize the Confederacy than any thing else. The inception of this trade was easily winked at by the Confederate authorities; it commenced with paltry importations across the Potomac; it was said the country wanted medicines, surgical instruments, and a number of trifles, and that trade with the Yankees in these could result in no serious harm. But by the enlarged license of the government it soon became an infamy and a curse to the Confederacy. What was a petty traffic in its commencement soon expanded into a shameless trade, which corrupted the patriotism of the country, constituted an anomaly in the history of belligerents, and reflected lasting disgrace upon the honesty and good sense of our government. The country had taken a solemn resolution to burn the cotton in advance of the enemy; but the conflagration of this staple soon came to be a rare event; instead of being committed to the flames it was spirited to Yankee markets. Nor were these operations always disguised. Some commercial houses in the Confederacy counted their gains by millions of dollars since the war, through the favor of the government in allowing them to export cotton at pleasure. The beneficiaries of this trade contributed freely to public charities, and did certain favors to the government; but their gifts were but the parings of immense gains; and often those who were named by weak and credulous people or by interested flatterers as public-spirited citizens and patriotic donors, were, in fact, the most unmitigated extortioners and the vilest leeches on the body politic.—" *The Second Year of the War*,"—pp. 304, 305

ir.stitutions of America had been, more or less, in a state of suspension for one-third of the time.

But despite the protest of historical facts, against all systems of paper expansion, Mr. Memminger had succeeded by the time of the meeting of Congress, in putting afloat some seven hundred millions of currency; although at another time, he himself had declared that the business of the country could not conveniently absorb more than one hundred and fifty millions.* And even that estimate of absorption was ridiculously excessive. It was so for this particular reason: that in the state of war, with its commerce cut off by the blockade, with no merchant ships, with few manufactures, with few enterprises open to capital, the South afforded but little scope for the profitable employment of its currency. The difficulty was that of stagnant capital, as well as that of an expanded currency.

At least one reason for the comparative financial prosperity of the North, during the war, was its capacity of absorbing large amounts of currency in the various functions of its active commercial life: in its trade open with all the world; in its shipping whitening every sea; in its immense internal trade, borne over immense lines of railroad and navigable waters; in its manufactures, enjoying the monopoly given them by a tariff, which shut out foreign competition; in its stocks, which made fortunes by the million in Wall street.†

---

* Before the war the paper money of the whole country, North and South, was two hundred and twelve millions; the gold and silver, say one hundred and fifty millions—total circulation, three hundred and sixty-two millions.

† The hey-day of "Wall street" is thus described in a New York paper (August, 1863): "Stocks have advanced on an average fully three hundred per cent. For example, the Erie formerly sold for five; it is now one hundred and twenty. The Galena and other roads of the same kind, which were down to thirty and forty, are now up to one hundred and thirty and one hundred and forty. The Harlem railroad, that nobody would take at six, has risen to one hundred and seventy. Formerly the average receipts of the Erie railroad were five millions; now they are eleven millions. The receipts of the New York Central formerly averaged seven millions; now they average eleven and a half millions. Formerly the Hudson River never could pay its debts; this year it is making thirty per cent. The Fort Wayne road formerly received two and a half millions annually; its receipts this year are five millions. The Central Illinois increased its receipts last week, by fifty thousand dollars, and it will earn this month four hundred thousand dollars."

But the agricultural South was inundated with a currency for which there was no outlet except in that pernicious and unproductive speculation whose sphere of trade is within itself, and whose operations can be only those of engrossing and extortion. The evils of the expanded currency of the Confederacy, were not only financial; they were also moral. The superabundance of paper money was the occasion of a wild speculation, which corrupted the patriotism of the country; introduced extravagance and licentiousness into private life; bestowed fortune upon the most undeserving; and above all, bred the most grave and dangerous discontents in the army. As long as there was a spirit of mutual sacrifice and mutual accommodation in the war, our soldiers were content and cheerful. But when they had to compare their condition—the hardships of the camp; the pittance of eleven dollars a month, that could scarcely buy a pair of socks; the poverty of the dear home left behind them—with the easy and riotous wealth of those who had kept out of the army merely to wring money out of the necessity and distress of the country; who, in snug shops in Richmond, made thousands of dollars a day, or, by a single stroke of speculation, became rich for life; it is not to be wondered, that bitter conclusions should have been drawn from the contrast, and that the soldier should have given his bosom to the bullets with less alacrity and zeal, when he reflected that his martyrdom was to protect a large class of men grown rich on his necessities, and that too, with the compliance and countenance of the Government he defended!

At the period of the assembling of Congress, the military situation in the Confederacy, which in the early part of 1863 had encouraged, not without apparent reasons, hopes of an early and honorable peace, had become overshadowed, critical, and, to some extent, truly alarming. At the time of the fall of Vicksburg, the enemy had also obtained an important and permanent success in Arkansas. The greater portion of the Southwest he had now overrun. Missouri, Kentucky and Northwestern Virginia, were exclusively occupied by the forces of the enemy. North Carolina, South Carolina and Alabama, were partially invaded by him. He had passed the barrier of the Cumberland mountains, established his dominion in East Tennessee, and from his lines in the central West, now huped to inundate South Carolina, Georgia, and South Alabama.

In the face of this critical military situation, came the astounding disclosure from the Confederate Secretary of War Mr. James Seddon, that the effective force of the army was "not more than a half, never two-thirds of the soldiers in the ranks."

In stating this deplorable fact, the Secretary avoided attributing it to its paramount causes—the fault of his own administration ; the remissness of discipline ; the weak shunning of the death-penalty in our armies, and that paltry quackery which proposed to treat the great evil of desertion with "proclamations" and patriotic appeals. He did what was worse than this insincerity ; for he proposed to repair that evil of absenteeism, which the government itself had occasioned, by new and violent measures to replenish the army. These were an extension of the conscription, which endangered the exhaustion of the military reserves of the country ; the *ex post facto* annulment of all contracts for substitution, which was to the scandal of the moral world, and to the lively dissatisfaction of more than seventy thousand persons, many of whom were indispensable in civil employments and by their wealth and social position, commanded an influence which the government could not afford to despise ;—and, to crown all, the supersedure of all exemptions by a system of details in the War Department, which would have transferred the question of all relief with respect to the burdens of the war, from the proper constitutional jurisdiction and collective wisdom of Congress, to the exclusive discretion, caprice or malice of a single official.*

---

* There is a little piece of official history which may be properly given here. On the 8th of January, 1864, Mr. Dargan, of Alabama, referred in the House of Representatives to "*acts of merciless cruelty*" on the part of the authorities, with reference to exemptions, which it was then proposed, by a certain demagogical bill in the House, to entrust exclusively and omnipotently to the Executive. He illustrated the epithets applied by an instance where a man had been mercilessly put in the military service, who had never walked and never been able to walk a quarter of a mile in any one day in his life, and all the efforts made by Mr. Dargan with the Secretary of War to procure his release had so far been unavailing.

Yet it appears, from a certain record, that the same official who had been so

Such measures were finished pieces of demagoguism. The various propositions made to Congress for further military drafts, at the expense of the public faith and the gravest interests of the citizen and producer, were calculated to find favor, of course, in the army, which, as designing politicians knew, contained the great body of voters in the country, and was destined to hold the balance of political power in the Confederacy.

The vice of our public men was an inordinate passion for an ephemeral and worthless popularity. The entire legislation of the country, Confederate and State, was demoralized by a peculiar demagoguism. All the legislative bodies of the country were filled with schemes of agrarianism for the benefit of the soldier, and assaults on the most important civil rights

---

exacting to the cripple, and who solicited from Congress plenary powers on the subject of exemptions, had given, over his own name, a special, secret exemption to a man who professed to him that he was writing a history of the war; in which it was, of course, expected that Mr. James Seddon would be one of the figure-heads in the gallery of celebrities.

This little piece of nefarious traffic in an official's vanity is of record: else it might be doubted whether, even in our Democratic system, a man occupying Mr. Seddon's position could be so easily and shamefully used.

We copy the extraordinary paper below, omitting the name of its beneficiary, because it is not necessary to history, and because we are anxious to spare all private feelings which are not materially involved in a public issue:

CONFEDERATE STATES OF AMERICA,
WAR DEPARTMENT,
RICHMOND, October 20, 1863.

Mr. ———, not being a native or naturalized citizen of the Confederacy, AND MOREOVER, *being engaged in compiling a work of interest to our people, and advantageous to our cause,* is exempt until further orders from conscription.

JAMES A. SEDDON,
Secretary of War.

Of this curious paper two remarks are to be made:

1. If Mr. ——— had relied for exemption upon his alienage (a plea we must suppose him unwilling to admit, after his literary exploits for the Confederacy), then it was quite unnecessary for the Secretary to assign "moreover" his literary adventure as a cause of exemption.

2. If Mr. ——— had relied for exemption upon his alienage, it was not for the Secretary of War, but for the consular authority of the courts, to give him he benefit of that plea.

This record may appear to be a small matter for history. It is not: it is one evidence, selected because it is indisputable, of the spirit that is fast reducing the administration of the Confederate affairs to schools of demagoguism and paltry inventions of personal vanity.

and interests at the instance of the blind passions of the army.

The annulment, by the Confederate Congress, of contracts heretofore concluded for military substitutes, was an act of unparalleled infamy. In making the assertion, that the substitution was not a contract, but a privilege accorded by the authorities, the government adopted the argument of the despot to this effect, that the rights of the people is the pleasure of the sovereign, to be enjoyed with becoming humility. In assuming to break the contract as to the principal, and, at the same time, maintain it in force against the substitute, the government stultified itself, and violated the plainest and justest of legal maxims, that a contract broken on one side, is broken on all sides. In attempting this violence in the face of the admitted fact, that nearly half of the army were out of the ranks, the government avoided the plain duty of replenishing the army with these absentees; proposed to replace seasoned veterans by raw malcontents; and, for a nominal accession to its military forces, to sacrifice recorded pledges; to wound the confidence and affections of the people; and to perpetrate a great moral evil, for which the compensation in any practical benefit was utterly disproportionate.

If such an act of perfidy had been accomplished by the Lincoln government, the Southern newspapers would have exclaimed against it as an unequalled example of despotism. But when it was perpetrated by their own government, Southern journals, with few honorable exceptions, were base enough to sustain or disguise it; and one Southern Senator, at least—a man of the name of Brown—was ready in his official seat, and in the security of his own exemption from military service, to bully the people with an insufferable insolence, and to flourish from the shelter of his parliamentary position, the vulgar and detestable threat of "military power."

But it is not necessary to pursue here the legislation of the Confederate Congress on military subjects. We have forborne to say here that the condition of our arms was desperate: it was critical, but there was no real occasion for despair, or for that violent anxiety which approaches it. There was yet much room for hope. We have stated that the amount of absenteeism in the army was, at least in great part, the fault of the au thorities, and it is therefore not to be taken as the indication of decay in the spirit of our soldiery. That spirit was yet brave and resolute. The displacement of Bragg from his command, which was at last unwillingly made by the President, had composed a dangerous discontent in the armies of the West, and was the occasion of the re-organization of our forces there, and a reassurance of the spirits of the troops. In Virginia, Lee still held the enemy at bay, and possessed the unanimous and enthusiastic confidence of the country and the army. At Charleston, Beauregard had checked the enemy, broken the line of his successes on the coast, and was advanced even in his former reputation as a skilful commander. If the prospect was chequered in the West, it was without a serious shadow in the East; and, although a large portion of the Confederacy had passed into the possession of the enemy, the general condition, at least, externally, was not so serious as when, in 1862, Richmond was threatened, and there were two hundred and ten thousand Federal soldiers in Virginia alone.

LINCOLN'S "PEACE" PROCLAMATION.

In the mean time there came a new and powerful appeal to the patriotism and resolution of the Confederacy. The Yankee Congress had assembled simultaneously with that of the Confederacy, and, for the first time in the war, the conditions upon which peace would be made with the South were officially announced. They were contained in the message and proclamation of Abraham Lincoln.* They were briefly these:

---

* The following are the material portions of this remarkable proclamation:

Whereas, In and by the Constitution of the United States, it is provided that the President shall have power to give reprieves and pardons for offences against the United States, except in cases of impeachment, and

Whereas, a rebellion now exists whereby the loyal State Governments of several States have for a long time been subverted, and many persons have committed, and are now guilty, of treason against the United States, and

Whereas, with reference to said rebellion and treason, laws have been enacted by Congress declaring forfeitures and confiscations of property and liberation of slaves, all upon terms and conditions therein stated; and also declaring that the President was thereby authorized at any time thereafter, by proc

the forcible emancipation of the slaves; the perpetuity of confiscations; pardon on condition of an oath of allegiance to the
government, to the Union, *and to the Abolition party of the
North;* the exception from this pardon of all important ranks
in the army, and conditions in political life; and finally, the
monstrous republican anomaly that *one-tenth* of the voters in
any of the Confederate States, declaring for these terms, "should
be recognized as the true government of the State." In pro-

---

lamation, to extend to persons who may have participated in the existing rebellion in any State, or part thereof, pardon and amnesty, with such exceptions,
and at such times, and on such conditions as he may deem expedient for the
public welfare, and

Whereas, the Congressional declaration for limited and conditional pardon
accords with the well-established judicial exposition of the pardoning power.
and

Whereas, with reference to the said rebellion the President of the United
States has issued several proclamations and provisions in regard to the liberation of slaves, and

Whereas, it is now desired by some persons heretofore engaged in said rebellion, to assume their allegiance to the United States, and to reinaugurate
loyal State Governments within and for their respective States;

Therefore, I, Abraham Lincoln, President of the United States, do proclaim,
declare, and make known to all persons who have directly or by implication
participated in the existing rebellion, except as hereinafter excepted, that
a full pardon is hereby granted to them and each of them, with restor
ation of all rights of property *except as to slaves,* and in property cases
where *the rights of third parties shall have intervened,* and upon the condition that every such person shall take and subscribe an oath, and thenceforward keep and maintain such oath inviolate, and which oath shall be registered for permanent preservation, and shall be of the tenor and effect following, to wit:

"I, ———, do solemnly swear in the presence of Almighty God, that I will
henceforth faithfully support, protect, and defend the Constitution of the Uni
ted States and the Union of the States thereunder, and that I will in like man
ner abide by and *faithfully support all acts of Congress passed during the ex
isting rebellion with reference to slaves,* so long and so far as not repealed, modified, or held void by Congress or by decision of the Supreme Court, and that
I will, in like manner, abide and faithfully support all proclamations of the
President made during the existing rebellion having reference to slaves, so far
as not modified or declared void by decision of the Supreme Court. So help
me God."

The persons excepted from the benefits of the foregoing provisions are all
who are or shall have been civil or diplomatic officers or agents of the so-called
Confederate Government; all who have left judicial stations under the United
States to aid in the rebellion; all who are or shall have been military or naval
officers of said so-called Confederate Government above the rank of Colonel in

posing these utterly infamous terms, this Yankee monster of inhumanity and falsehood had the audacity to declare, that in some of the Confederate States the elements of reconstruction were ready for action; that those who controlled them differed, however, as to the plan of action; and that, "by the pro clamation, a plan is presented which may be accepted by them as a *rallying point*, and which they are assured in advance will not be rejected here."

This insulting and brutal proposition of the Yankee government was the apt response to those few cowardly factions which in North Carolina, and in some parts of Georgia and Alabama, hinted at "reconstruction." It was as the sound of a trumpet to every brave man in the South to meet and to contest a question of life and death. Appeals had formerly been made in the Confederacy against "reconstruction," on such arguments as the conduct of the enemy in the war; his political prostitution; his vandalism; and sentimental motives of vengeance. There were truth and eloquence in those appeals. But now there was another added to them which

---

the army, of Lieutenant in the navy; all who left seats in the United States Congress to aid the rebellion:

All who resigned commissions in the army or navy of the United States, and afterwards aided the rebellion, and all who have engaged in any way in treating colored persons or white persons in charge of such, otherwise than lawfully as prisoners of war, who have been found in the United States service as soldiers, seamen, or in any other capacity.

And I do further proclaim, declare, and make known, that whenever, in any of the States of Arkansas, Texas, Louisiana, Mississippi, Tennessee, Alabama, Georgia, Florida, South Carolina, and North Carolina, a number of persons, not less than *one-tenth* in number of the votes cast in such States, at the Presidential election of the year of our Lord, 1860, each having taken the oath aforesaid, and not having since violated it, and being a qualified voter by the election law of the State existing immediately before the so-called act of secession, and excluding all others, shall re-establish a State Government, which shall be republican, and in no wise contravening said oath, such shall be recognized as the true Government of the State, and the State shall receive thereunder the benefit of the Constitutional provision which declares that

"The United States shall guarantee to every State in the Union a Republican form of Government, and shall protect each of them against invasion, on application of the Legislature, or of the Executive, when the Legislature cannot be convened, against domestic violence."

•   •   •   •   •   •   •   •   •   •   •   •

addressed us not only in our passions, but in every fibre of our selfishness, and in every ramification of our interests. It was the authoritative exposition to the South of the consequences of its submission. These could no longer be misconstrued: they were gibbets, proscription, universal poverty, the subversion of our social system, a feudal allegiance to the Abolitionists and the depths of dishonor.

THE SLAVERY QUESTION IN THE WAR.

The proclamation of President Lincoln was made under certain affectations of benevolent zeal for the negro. He declared that his former "emancipation" proclamation had "much improved the tone of public sentiment in foreign countries," and he insisted that to abandon it would be to the negro "a cruel and astounding breach of faith."

In view of these pretensions, it is not out of place here to make a brief summary of the true questions of the war, and its real relations to negro slavery in the South.

A French pamphlet on the American war, published at Paris, holds the following language:

"The pride of the North will never stoop to admit the superiority of Southern men; and yet it is from these that the Union drew its best statesmen and a majority of its presidents. The pride of the North will bend only to necessity, because it has not kept pace with the progress of the age. To-day the Americans of the North are as completely foreign to the family of nations as they were twenty years ago. They understand nothing but the narrowest and most mechanical mercantilism, the art of purchase and sale; and they long to annihilate the Confederate States in order that the South, by its intelligence, its enterprise, and the talent of its statesmen, may not throw down the rampart it has built up against Europeanism. . . . . The Federals are so well aware of this that the war which they are waging is really and mainly a war of interest. The producing, agricultural South was the commercial vassal of the North, which insists upon keeping its best customer: emancipation is merely a skilful device for entrapping the sympathies of European liberalism. . . . . The Northern idea of the abolition of slavery by making the negro food for powder, or by exiling him from his home to die of hunger, is now thoroughly understood in Europe. Our notions of philanthropy and our moral sense alike revolt from these ferocious exaggerations of the love of liberty."

The above is an admirable summary of the questions of the war—especially of the "*slavery question*." There is no doubt that the Anti-Slavery party in the North had, through the violence of its measures, and the exposure of its hollow pretensions for the negro, lost much of that sympathy in Europe which it had formerly obtained; while the war had also given occasion to intelligent persons in all parts of the world for a more thorough, a more interested, and a more practical study of slavery in the South. The old stories which the newspapers of the enemy revived of fiendish masters in the South, and pandemoniums on the cotton plantations, had now come to be objects of scepticism or derision in Europe.

In connection with the subject of the relations of slavery to the war, it becomes interesting to inquire what real benefits to the negro were accomplished by the political measures of the Lincoln government. The famous "emancipation" proclamation extended "freedom" to the negro merely to subject him to a worse fate, and to transfer him from the peaceful service of the plantation to that of the military camp. It was followed by various acts of Congress to enlist the negro in the military service. It was stated by Mr. Seward, in a diplomatic circular, dated August the 12th, 1863, that nearly seventy thousand negroes were at that time employed in the Yankee armies, of whom twenty-two thousand were actually bearing arms in the field; and at a later date (that of the meeting of the Yankee Congress in December), the whole number of these African allies of the North was said to exceed one hundred thousand. The employment, as soldiers, against the Confederacy, of this immense number of blacks, was a brutality and crime in sight of the world; it was the ignoring of civilization in warfare; it was a savage atrocity inflicted on the South;—but it, certainly, was no benefit to the negro. It could be no benefit to him that he should be exposed to the fury of the war, and translated from a peaceful and domestic sphere of labor to the hardships of the camp and the mortal perils of the battle-field.

The scheme of the colonization of the negro in the invaded districts of the South was alike destitute of benefit to him, and destructive of the white "civilization" under whose auspices it was conducted. Wherever this new system of labor was introduced, the negro suffered, the plantation relapsed into weeds, the garden disappeared, and desolation and ruin took up their abodes. It had converted the rice coasts of South Carolina into barrens. It had been instituted on a grand scale in Louisiana. The result was, to use the language of a Yankee writer, this beautiful State was fast becoming "an alligator pleasure-ground." Where formerly had flourished rich and teeming plantations, were to be seen here and there some show of cultivation, some acres of corn and cane; but these were "government" plantations; the able-bodied negroes had been forced into the Yankee military service, and a few aged and shiftless negroes, who poked lazily through the weed-growth, were the only signs of labor in the vast districts occupied by the enemy. In Louisiana, where the Yankees had indulged such hopes of "infusing new life" by free labor and the scientific farming of Massachusetts, the development of the country, its return in crops, in wealth, amounted to little more than nothing. The negro had merely exchanged his Southern master for a Massachusetts shoe-maker, who was anxious to become a Louisiana sugar-maker. His condition was not improved, his comforts were decreased; and the country itself, redeemed by the most tedious labors from the waters of the Mississippi, and brought to a point of fertility unexampled in American soils, was fast reverting to the original swamp. Louisiana had taken more than fifty years to raise the banks of the Mississippi, to drain and redeem the swamp lands, and to make herself a great producing State. But, said the New York *World*, "it has required only a few months for the Administration at Washington to prepare the State for its return to its original worthlessness; to 'restore' it to barbarism; to re-people it, in spots, with half-bred bastards; to drive out every vestige of civilization, and to make the paradise of the South a rank, rotten, miasmatic, alligator and moccasin swamp-ground again."

The fact is indisputable, that in all the localities of the Con federacy where the enemy had obtained a foothold, the negroes had been reduced by mortality during the war to not more than one-half their previous number.

To this statement, the deliberate assertion of President Davis to the Confederate Congress, we may make an official addition of the most melancholy interest. In the winter of 1863–64, the Governor of Louisiana, in his official message, published to the world the appalling fact, that *more negroes had perished in Louisiana from the cruelty and brutality of the public enemy than the combined number of white men, in both armies, from the casualties of war.* In illustration he stated, that when the Confederate forces surprised and cap tured Berwick's Bay, last summer, they found about two thousand negroes there in a state of the most utter destitution —many of them so emaciated and sick that they died before the tender humanity of the Confederates could be applied to their rescue from death.

The fate of these poor wretches was to be attributed to sheer inhumanity. The Yankees had abundant supplies of food, medicines and clothing at hand, but they did not apply them to the comfort of the negro, who, once entitled to the farce of "freedom," was of no more consequence to them than any other beast with a certain amount of useful labor in his anatomy.

The practice of the enemy in the parts of the Confederacy he had invaded, was to separate the families of the blacks without notice. Governor Moore officially testified to this practice in Louisiana. The men were driven off like so many cattle to a Yankee camp, and were enlisted in the Yankee army. The women and children were likewise driven off in droves, and put upon what are called "Government planta-tions"—that is, plantations from which the lawful owners had been forced to fly, and which the Yankees in Louisiana were cultivating.

The condition of the negroes at the various contraband camps in the Mississippi valley furnishes a terrible volume of human misery, which may some day be written in the fright-ful characters of truth. Congregated at these depots, without employment, deprived of the food to which they had been ac·

customed, and often without shelter or medical care, these helpless creatures perished, swept off by pestilence or the cruel ties of the Yankees.

We may take from *Northern* sources some accounts of these contraband camps, to give the reader a passing picture of what the unhappy negroes had gained by what the Yankees called their " freedom."

A letter to a Massachusetts paper said :—" There are, between Memphis and Natchez, not less than fifty thousand blacks, from among whom have been culled all the able-bodied men for the military service. Thirty-five thousand of these, viz., those in camps between Helena and Natchez, are furnished the shelter of old tents and subsistence of cheap rations by the Government, but are in all other things in extreme destitution. Their clothing, in perhaps the case of a fourth of this number, is but one single worn and scanty garment. Many children are wrapped night and day in tattered blankets as their sole apparel. But few of all these people have had any change of raiment since, in midsummer or earlier, they came from the abandoned plantations of their masters. Multitudes of them have no beds or bedding—the clayey earth the resting place of women and babes through these stormy winter months. They live of necessity in extreme filthiness, and are afflicted with all fatal diseases. Medical attendance and supplies are very inadequate. They cannot, during the winter, be disposed to labor and self-support, and compensated labor cannot be procured for them in the camps. They cannot, in their present condition, survive the winter. It is my conviction that, unrelieved, the half of them will perish before the spring. Last winter, during the months of February, March and April, I buried, at Memphis alone, out of an average of about four thousand, twelve hundred of these people, or twelve a day."

Another Yankee correspondent wrote as follows respecting the negroes who had come into Vicksburg after the surrender of General Pemberton :—

" About the 1st of August the military authorities became alarmed lest a pestilence should break out among them and extend to the army. Peremptory orders were issued to at once remove across the river all negroes, of every age and sex, whether sick or well, who were not in some employment.

" One morning I went out to inform a certain Lieutenant W——, who, with an inadequate force, was executing the order, that one of them in the Baptist church was dead, and that another, a woman, was lying behind a fence, dying. He told me that he had detailed, for the purpose of removing the negroes, 20 army wagons; that he had hauled them, well, sick and dead, with all their traps, to the river, where he had a steamer to convey them across to a point opposite the lower part of the city; that he had one wagon to haul the dead, and that some days he found as many as twenty; that in one house he found six dead bodies, with living ones sitting and lying around them, apparently unconscious of their situation. Holes were dug on the river's bank and the dead buried. The searching out and removal of these negroes consumed about fifteen or twenty days. About three hundred were thus removed to the low grounds opposite Vicksburg, and there left in the weeds without any shelter, under the care of a man who was appointed to organize them into a camp, and separate small-pox cases from the rest.

" The chaplain told me that these negroes had suffered and were still suffering untold want and wretchedness; that nearly four hundred had died since he had taken charge of them; that from sixteen to twenty died daily. Sometimes they would crawl off into the woods and die, where their bodies would be found only by the stench which arose from their decay. That there was no white man with them but a nephew of his; that rations were furnished them by the Government, but sometimes he had difficulty in getting them over the river; that once they were five days without receiving any food, and the negroes in their despair threatened to kill him, thinking the fault was his. He also stated that they had no tents or shelter except brush to shield them from the sun, or storm, or dews of night. Captain A—— stated to me that there were in his camp two thousand; at Young's Point, eight thousand five hundred and fifty-one; on Papaw Island, where he purposed gathering most of them, two thousand eight hundred; and on Black's plantation, on the Yazoo, two thousand four hundred—in all over sixteen thousand. One morning I went among the wretched masses where they were hauled to the bank of the river, preparatory to being sent across. I tried in vain to find some women who were able to work, as we wished their labor at our house. All were either sick or taking care of the sick. I saw nothing but one sad scene of misery."

The war had tested slavery in the South with results that could not escape the intelligent attention of the world. While it had exhibited the horrors of "emancipation" on the one side, it had shown, on the other, the docility and fidelity of the slave in his proper condition of servitude. It is true that the negroes, in cases of invasion, had flocked to the standards of the Yankee; but such a course was to be ascribed purely to their ignorance and tractability, seduced as they were by the word "liberty," by bribes and by frauds. It was no evidence of any real discontent, still less of hostility to the masters they deserted. The majority of negroes lost by us were those allured to the Yankees by promises of freedom, no work, and bountiful supplies of good things. Deceived in their anticipation of *otium cum dignitate*, and finding the spade and the musket in health, and cold neglect in sickness, in lieu of it—their wives and children, their old and infirm, subjected to privations and sufferings never experienced from their masters—as many as could returned home.

In all the war there had been no servile insurrection in the South—not a single instance of outbreak among the slaves—a conclusive evidence that the negro was not the enemy of his master, but, in his desertion of him, merely the victim of Yankee bribes. Assured, through a thousand channels, as these negroes were, that they were the victims of the most grinding and cruel injustice and oppression; assured of the active assistance of the largest armies of modern times, and of the countenance and sympathy of the rest of the world; assured that such an enterprise would not only be generous and heroic, but eminently successful, our enemies had heretofore failed to excite one solitary instance of insurrection, much less to bring on a servile war.

It was thus that the war itself had greatly cleared up our moral atmosphere, and swept away much mist and darkness of doubt and delusion. After nearly three years of bloody struggle, we had at least already attained this result: the assurance that it was we, the Confederates, who had in charge the cause of freedom in the Western continent against the wild anarchy of ignorant mobs—we, who were saving civilization from the frenzy of democracy run mad—we, above all, who were guarding the helpless black race from utter annihilation at the hands of a greedy and bloody "philanthropy," which sought to deprive them of the care of humane masters only that they might be abolished from the face of the earth, and leave the fields of labor clear for that free competition and demand-and-supply, which reduced even white workers to the lowest *minimum* of a miserable livelihood, and left the simple negro to compete, as he best could, with swarming and hungry millions of a more energetic race, who were already eating one another's heads off, and who regarded *him* and his claims as an intrusion and superfluity upon earth—to be retrenched and got rid of in the most summary manner.

The affectation of the Yankee for the good of the negro was intended, as we have seen, to solicit the sympathies of Europe in the war. It was not very effectual in this respect. But, at least, it could no longer hope to impose upon the South, and it did not hesitate to unmask to it its brutal and ferocious insincerity. In the mean time, the "war-to-the-knife" party in the North, with the large accession of so many blacks to its armies, and a recent confirmation at the polls of its party strength, was preparing for new careers of atrocity and crime.*

---

* In referring to the condition of the negro in this war, we use the term "*slavery*" in these pages under strong protest. For there is no such thing in the South; it is a term fastened upon us by the exaggeration and conceit of Northern literature, and most improperly acquiesced in by Southern writers. There is a system of African *servitude* in the South; in which the negro, so far from being under the absolute dominion of his master (which is the true meaning of the vile word "slavery"), has, by *law* of the land, his personal rights recognized and protected, and his comfort and "right" of "happiness" consulted, and by the *practice* of the system, has a sum of individual indulgences, which makes him altogether the most striking type in the world of cheerfulness and contentment. And the system of servitude in the South has this peculiarity over other systems of servitude in the world: that it does not debase one of God's creatures from the condition of free-citizenship and membership in organized society and thus rest on acts of debasement and disenfranchisement, but elevates a savage, and rests on the solid basis of human improvement. The European mind, adopting the nomenclature of our enemies, has designated as "slavery" what is really the most virtuous system of servitude in the world.

HISTORY OF THE "RETALIATION" POLICY.

While thus the war waxed in the hands of the North, the Administration at Richmond had nothing to respond to its ferocity but a feeble sentimentalism and a weak protest for the rights of humanity, which amused the enemy and disgusted the stern spirit of a people fighting for their liberties. "Retaliation" had by this time become a lost word in our vocabulary. In the year now well nigh past, the Yankees had enacted barbarities greater than those of former years, in proportion as they were encouraged by impunity. They had burned the town of Darien, and this, one of the oldest towns in Georgia, the New Inverness of Oglethorpe's time, was now a plain of ashes and blackened chimneys. They had, in a raid on the Combahee, committed to the flames the beautiful town of Bluffton. They had attempted to destroy Charleston by an incendiary composition. They had made a desert of the whole country between the Big 'Black and the Mississippi, and in every district of the South which they had penetrated, houses had been either pillaged or burnt, crops laid waste, and enormities committed which exhausted the calendar of crimes.

Yet we have seen that when General Lee invaded the territory of the North he had omitted even the devastation of the enemy's country, had paid the Yankees' own prices for their supplies, and had, in fact, given a protection to their property which had never been afforded that of our citizens, either from the rapacity of the soldier or that of the impressment agent.

It is true that of this singular behavior President Davis said in his message to Congress: "Though the forbearance may have been unmerited and unappreciated by the enemy, it was imposed by their [our soldiers'] own self-respect, which forbade their degenerating from Christian warriors into plundering ruffians." But herein the President sought to impose upon the public mind not only a wretched piece of sentimentalism, but a glaring fallacy, alike unworthy of his intellect. The punishment of the Yankees for what they had done in the South certainly did not mean an imitation of the wrong—a retaliation *in kind*. The Southern people had almost unanimously applauded General Lee's orders in Pennsylvania restraining pillage and private outrage. But there were penalties other than those of marauding which might have been measured out to the enemy, and have inflicted upon him some injury commensurate with what we had suffered at his hands. It would not have been unjust, it would not have been immoral, it would not have detracted from our "self-respect," it would not have endangered the discipline of our troops, it would not have been an act unbecoming "Christian warriors," to have laid waste the enemy's country, if done under the justification of retaliation, with the deliberation of official orders, and by the army acting in line of battle. But no such orders were given; no such line of battle carried with it the chastisements of *real* war; and the fertile acres of the Pennsylvania Valley were untouched by the "Christian warriors."

The subject of "retaliation" brings to the mind a number of specific acts in which the Confederate government had failed, alike, in the execution of justice and in the protection of its own people. The record of these affords an exhibition of weakness that is, positively, without parallel in the history of governments. In contrasting the rival administrations of the North and South, it is indispensable here to make a brief review of the incidents to which we have referred in the history of the "retaliation" policy. They are rapidly grouped in the summary which follows:

1. Shortly after the capture of New Orleans, General Butler executed a citizen of the Confederacy, William B. Mumford, for the extraordinary crime of "disrespect" to the Yankee flag.

Instead of making prompt retaliation, the Confederate government found a conveniently circuitous course in addressing, several months after the event, the singularly gratuitous inquiry to the Lincoln government, whether the act of Butler was "approved" by it?

The authorities at Washington returned this answer:

HEADQUARTERS OF THE ARMY,
WASHINGTON, Aug. 9, 1862.

GEN'L R. E. LEE, Comd'g, &c.:

General :—Your two communications of the 2d inst., with inclosures, are received. As these papers are couched in language *exceedingly insulting* to the Government of the United

States, I must respectfully *decline to receive them.* They are returned herewith.

   Very respectfully,

     Your ob't serv't,

       H. W. HALLECK, Gen'l-in-Chief U. S. Army.

And here ended the whole matter.

2. At Palmyra, in Missouri, General McNeil murdered, in cold blood, ten soldiers of the Confederacy.

Although the Confederate government must have had prompt official intelligence of this outrage, it was only several months thereafter, when "the Palmyra massacre" had been inconveniently noised in the newspapers, that President Davis ordered by telegraph the execution in retaliation, of ten Yankee prisoners, in the Department of the Trans-Mississippi.

The bloody telegram, communicated by the Richmond authorities to the press with peculiar liberality of information, quieted it and consoled the public. But that was all; the telegraphic order was never executed; it was a dead letter, that died in the public mind; and the Palmyra massacre was not only unavenged, but justice itself was cheated by a false and most unworthy *show* of compliance with its demands.

3. Under the "Death Order" of Burnside, two Confederate officers, Captains Corbin and McGraw, had been executed for recruiting white soldiers in Kentucky, a part of our own territory embraced in our political system and represented in our Congress; at a time when the Yankees were recruiting *negro* soldiers in our political jurisdiction, and in the circle of our homes.

By the order of the Confederate government, two Yankee prisoners were selected by a formal lot at Richmond, upon whom retaliation was to be visited. The day of their execution was fixed. But instead of hanging them, President Davis arranged a back-door of mercy by commissioning a personage no less considerable than Mr. Stephens, Vice-president of the Republic, to make arrangements in Washington "to temper the present cruel character of the contest." The "back-door of mercy" was closed in his face. Mr. Stephens went as far as Hampton Roads, where he was stopped by the enemy's admiral, with the curt information from Washington, that the enemy wished no further communication with the Confederacy than it already had through the ordinary military channels.

In the mean time, the Yankee government, without troubling itself with a selection by lot, had summarily designated two of the most important prisoners in its hands as victims to repay with their lives the tragedy that had been appointed at Richmond. The consequences were, that the tragedy did not come off, but the Confederate government replied with some brave words, that it was not dismayed by the threat, but would, *at its convenience*, execute the penalties it had pronounced. The day of execution passed; there was no public notice of respite or pardon; there was no other day of execution appointed; and the convenient silence of the authorities was evidence enough that the matter was dropped, and that they desired it to pass out of the public mind. Thus terminated this issue of "retaliation."

4. A notorious renegade, Rucker, was taken in the ranks of the enemy in Western Virginia, and committed as a spy and murderer. The Yankees threatened the life of one of our prisoners of war, if he should be executed.

The criminal was kept fifteen months without a trial, and at last conveniently escaped. There was no possible occasion for the extraordinary delay of a trial, unless that the Confederate authorities feared to risk its conclusion, for the evidence was ready, abundant, and immediately at hand to convict him.

5. The Yankees imprisoned women for waving handkerchiefs at our prisoners. For offences not much more considerable, they put them in political jails, and subjected them to the vilest indignities, and to penalties which made no distinction of sex.

In the summer of 1863, a Mrs. Patterson Allen, a Yankee woman, was detected in Richmond holding the most brutal and treasonable communication with the enemy; pointing out to him objects for his resentment; and proposing to betray into his hands as prisoner a minister of Christ, under whose roof, at the time the letter was written, the Yankee spy and traitress was herself a guest, and a sick child of the minister was dying in the absence of its father.

By special direction of the Confederate Secretary of War Mr. Seddon, Mrs. Patterson Allen, a fashionable woman, was sent, not to prison, but to the Asylum, Francis de Sales, in Richmond. Her trial had not yet taken place; and for nearly six months the vulgarity of a legal prison was spared her, and a romantic confinement in a charitable institution was the chivalric invention of the Confederacy for the crime of treason !

6. It had been estimated by the Confederate Commissioner of Exchange, in the fall of 1863, that the enemy held in imprisonment not less than one thousand *citizens* of the Confederacy, who had been captured in peaceful employments, and were in no way amenable as combatants in the war.

In a correspondence on the subject of exchange of prisoners, the Confederate government protested against the outrageous practice of the enemy in arresting non-combatants and kidnapping private citizens within his military lines or elsewhere within his reach. But the enemy continued these arrests, and no retaliation was ever attempted. At the time unarmed citizens of the Confederacy were torn from their homes in Mississippi and sent to the jails of Memphis, General Lee protected the citizens of Pennsylvania, and allowed them even to avow their political animosity in his camps.

7. When General Morgan was captured by the enemy, he was carried to Cincinnati, and thence he and twenty-eight of his officers were taken to Columbus, Ohio, where they were shaved, their hair cut close by a negro convict, and then locked up in cells. Seven days afterwards, forty-two more of General Morgan's officers were conveyed from Johnston's Island to the penitentiary, and subjected to the same indignities.

A correspondence ensued between the Commissioners of Exchange on the subject of these cruelties and indignities, in which the excuse was made by the enemy that the Federal authority was not responsible for them, implying that the *State* of Ohio having these captives in her custody, had chosen to associate them with convicts.

Yet, at this time, our government was, in deference to " general orders" at Washington, treating as prisoners of war *negroes* captured in arms, who were clearly responsible to the authority of the *States*, under State laws, as criminals. No surrender of these criminals was made to any of the *States* of the Confederacy, and when South Carolina made some motion

in the matter, it was strangely hushed up, and the negro ma..
efactors retained to this day by the Confederate authority in
full enjoyment of the privileges accorded them by Yankee
edict, as " prisoners of war."

8. The enemy had violated the cartel. Under this cartel,
for many months, we had restored to the enemy many thousands of prisoners in excess of those whom he held for exchange. But in July, when the fortune of war favored the
Yankees, and they held the excess of prisoners, they had broken the cartel; they had refused to return to our lines the
prisoners taken at Gettysburg; and they had gone further
even than this treachery, for they had not only retained the
prisoners captured by them, but they had declared null the
paroles given by the prisoners captured by us in the same
series of engagements.

What were the returns of the Confederate government for
this outrage? It allowed the prisoners in our hands comforts
not enjoyed by the men who captured them in battle. It permitted the Yankee captives in Richmond to receive stores
from the North to the amount of half a million of dollars. It
indulged them in a festival; and while our prisoners were
sighing in the dungeons and penitentiaries of the North, or at
Johnston's Island, were (to use President Davis's own statement), dying from the slow tortures of cold, " exposed to the
piercing cold of the Northern lakes, by men who cannot be
ignorant of, even if they do not design, the probable result," a
table d'hote was spread in the Libby Prison at Richmond, with
all the luxuries that the teeming markets of the Northern
cities could afford. And this licentiousness, with its awful
and terrible contrast to our own people, went by the name of
Christian charity in Richmond, and was a pleasant humanity
to be told to Europe!

9. The Confederacy treated prisoners of war according to
the rules of war; consulted their comfort as well as their security; enacted a law allowing them the same rations as Confederate soldiers in the field; and, in fine, considering the
scarcity of supplies in the South, made a provision for prisoners of war of extreme generosity.

It is true that statements were made by the North much to
the contrary; that Yankee newspapers circulated ghastly

romances of their starving prisoners; and that pictorial illustrations of the horrors of Libby Prison and Belle Isle were manufactured into a public document by a Yankee Congress for circulation throughout Christendom. However, these stories were but little entitled to the credit or sympathy of the world; so often had it been imposed upon by Yankee fictions, and so little reason had it to suppose that a people false in one particular were even tolerably truthful in another.

It was not to be supposed, indeed, that in a war in which the favorite object of the Yankee was to plunder and starve the Confederacy, and in which the first men of the Confederacy were forced to live scantily on bread and beef, and to deny themselves such luxuries as tea, coffee, sugar, and vegetables, Yankee prisoners of war could have many of the comforts which they had been accustomed to obtain from their own bountiful commissariat. But it is seriously true that they fared as well as our own worn and hardened soldiers in the field. They were allowed, in many instances, to receive supplies from friends in the North, and it frequently happened that the occupants of the Libby actually lived better than the cabinet ministers of the Confederacy.

What was the Yankee treatment of prisoners of war in comparison with these humanities of the Confederacy? Their system of imprisonment was essentially a *penal* one. They assumed the right to *punish* prisoners of war; to enact the part of *magistrate* over soldiers and citizens of the Confederacy; to sentence them to terms of years, to add ball and chain, to subject them to penalties of the felon, and to employ upon them the tortures of the common penitentiary. Even women, accused of sympathy with the South, were required to employ their time in prison with "sewing for Union soldiers." The right to *punish* prisoners of war was assumed quite as much as that to secure their persons.

We have already referred to the outrageous incarceration of General Morgan and his command. We may refer here to the experience at length of one of these unfortunate captives which was personally narrated to the writer of these pages.

This statement was taken from the lips of Captain Calvin C Morgan, a brother of the famous General Morgan.

Captain Morgan was among those of his brother's expedi

tion who, in last July, were incarcerated in the penitentiary of Ohio. On entering this infamous abode, Captain Morgan and his companions were stripped in a reception room and, their naked bodies examined there. They were again stripped in the interior of the prison, and washed in tubs by negro convicts; their hair cut close to the scalp, the brutal warden, who was standing by, exhorting the negro barber to "cut off every lock of their rebel hair." After these ceremonies, the officers were locked up in cells, the dimensions of which were thirty-eight inches in width, six and a-half feet in length, and about the same in height. In these narrow abodes our brave soldiers were left to pine, branded as felons, goaded by "convict-drivers," and insulted by speeches which constantly reminded them of the weak and cruel neglect of that government, on whose behalf, after imperilling their lives, they were now suffering a fate worse than death. But even these sufferings were nothing to what was reserved for them in another invention of cruelty without a parallel, unless in the secrets of the infernal.

It appears that, after General Morgan's escape, suspicion alighted on the warden, a certain Captain Merion, who, it was thought, might have been corrupted. To alleviate the suspicion (for which there were really no grounds whatever), the brute commenced a system of devilish persecution of the unfortunate Confederate prisoners who remained in his hands. One part of this system was solitary confinement in dungeons. These dungeons were close cells, a false door being drawn over the grating, so as to exclude light and air. The food allowed the occupants of these dark and noisome places, was three ounces of bread and half a pint of water per day. The four walls were bare of every thing but a water-bucket, for the necessities of nature, which was left for days to poison the air the prisoner breathed. He was denied a blanket; deprived of his overcoat, if he had one, and left standing or stretched with four dark, cold walls around him, with not room enough to walk in to keep up the circulation of his blood, stagnated with the cold, and the silent and unutterable horrors of his abode.

Confinement in these dungeons was the warden's sentence for the most trivial offences. On one occasion one of our prisoners was thus immured because he refused to tell Merion which one of his companions had *whistled contrary to the prison rules.* But the most terrible visitation of this demon's displeasure remains to be told.

Some knives had been discovered in the prisoners' cells, and Merion accused the occupants of meditating their escape. Seven of them, all officers, were taken to the west end of the building and put in the dark cells there. They were not allowed a blanket or overcoat, and *the thermometer was below zero.* There was no room to pace. Each prisoner had to struggle for life, as the cold benumbed him, by stamping his feet, beating the walls, now catching a few minutes of horrible sleep on the cold floor, and then starting up to continue, in the dark, his wrestle for life.

"I had been suffering from heart disease," says Captain Morgan, speaking of his own solitary confinement on another occasion. "It was terribly aggravated by the cold and horror of the dungeon in which I was placed. I had a wet towel, one end of which I pressed to my side; the other would freeze, and I had to put its frozen folds on my naked skin. I stood this way all night, pressing the frozen towel to my side and keeping my feet going up and down. I felt I was struggling for my life."

Captain Morgan endured this confinement for eighteen hours, and was taken out barely alive. The other prisoners endured it for *sixteen days and nights.* In this time they were visited at different periods by the physician of the penitentiary —Dr. Loring—who felt their pulses, and examined their condition, to ascertain how long life might hold out under the exacting torture. It was awful, this ceremony of torture, this medical examination of the victims. The tramp of the prisoners' feet, up and down (there was no room to walk), as they thus worked for life, was incessantly going on. This black tread-mill of the dungeon could be heard all through the cold and dreary hours of the night. Dr. Loring, who was comparatively a humane person, besought Merion to release the unhappy men; said they had already been taxed to the point of death. The wretch replied, "They did not talk right yet." He wished them to humble themselves to him. He went into the cell of one of them, Major Webber, to taunt him. "Sir," said the officer, "I defy you. You can kill me, but you can add nothing to the sufferings you have already inflicted. Proceed to kill me; it makes not the slightest difference."

At the expiration of sixteen days the men were released from the dungeons. Merion said "he would take them out this time alive, but next time they offended, they would be taken out feet foremost." Their appearance was frightful; they could no longer be recognized by their companions. With their bodies swollen and discolored, with their minds bordering on childishness, tottering, some of them talking foolishly, these wretched men seemed to agree but in one thing—a ravenous desire for food.

"I had known Captain Coles," says Captain Morgan, "as well as my brother. When he came out of his dungeon, I swear to you I did not know him. His face had swollen to two or three times its ordinary size, and he tottered so that I had to catch him from falling. Captain Barton was in an awful state. His face was swollen and the blood was bursting from the skin. All of them had to be watched, so as to check them in eating, as they had been starved so long."

We had had in this war many examples of Yankee cruelty. But the statement given above, may be said to take precedence of all that had ever yet been narrated of the atrocities of the enemy; and it is so remarkable, both on account of its matter and the credit that must naturally attach to its authorship that we doubt whether the so-called civilized world of this generation has produced anywhere any well-authenticated story of equal horror.

. . . . . In his message to Congress, President Davis eloquently adverted to the savage ferocity of the enemy and his crimes. But he had not a word to say of what had become of all his proclamations, pronunciamentos, gloomy appeals and terrible threatenings with respect to retaliation. The truth was they had never resulted in one solitary performance; they were a record of bluster and an exhibition of weakness and shame upon which the President might well turn his back. It is remarkable that Mr. Davis in all these proceedings touching questions of retaliation should have shown a character so different from that which he exhibited in the domestic controversies and intrigues of his administration. In his controversies with his military officers, he was very obstinate, very bitter; in his attachment to certain favorites and to certain measures of domestic policy he was immovable and defiant. It was only when his duty brought him in contact with the enemy that these imperious traits of character disappeared, and were replaced by halting timidity and weak hesitation.

It was unfortunate that the Confederate President ever made any threats of retaliation, since he had not the resolution to perform them. They had been ineffectually repeated until they had become the sneer of the enemy. But the most unfortunate consequence of the want of a proper response to the cruel assumptions of power by the North was the moral effect it had upon our own people; for it implied a certain guilt, a certain moral inferiority in the South, of which the enemy had the right to take advantage. It converted the relations between us and our foes to those of the malefactor and the constable; it depressed our sense of right; and it gave to the soldier the bitter reflection that his government cared but little for him, in that martyrdom on the gallows or captivity in dungeons with the terrors of which the enemy assailed him.

Finally, there is this to be said of the rival administrations of Richmond and Washington: that if in the former there were to be found many evidences of weakness, these, at least, were not crimes, while if in the latter there were to be seen vigor and decision, they were associated with the insolence of the reprobate and the inhumanity of the savage. If the history of the retaliation policy and other questions which we have traced, exhibits imbecility on the part of the Confederate authorities, it has this compensation: that it has inseparably connected with it a fearful record of the inhumanity and crime of the enemy.

In this conflict, which, as to goverments, was that between the weakly good and the resolutely evil, the people of the Confederacy had but little to expect from their political authorities; but it was precisely the condition in which they had much to expect from the resources of their own righteous and aroused passions.

In connection with his "peace" proclamation, the Yankee President pointed with an air of triumph to the great resources of the North for the prosecution of the war. There was an actual surplus in its treasury. While the Confederacy had collected only one hundred millions from its tax and revenue system, the receipts of the Yankee treasury were nine hundred millions. The Yankee army was increased. The Yankee navy now numbered nearly six hundred vessels, and seventy-five of them were iron-clads or armored steamers. The Yankee political parties had accommodated their differences and no longer embarrassed the authorities at Washington. "The crisis which threatened to divide the friends of the Union is past," said Mr. Lincoln.

The Washington government had now a united people, an unexhausted treasury, enlarged military resources, and a confidence more insolent than ever.

Richmond, in December, 1863, was a sombre city. An air of gloom pervaded the public offices. In Congress, Mr. Foote told his endless story of official corruption and imbecility, and had his savage jokes on " the pepper-doctor from North Carolina," who governed the commissariat of the Confederacy. There were no social gaieties, although disreputable balls and gambling "hells" still amused those immoral mobs, at all times inseparable from a metropolis. In the streets there was the perpetual juggle of bargain and sale, apparently unconscious of the war, simply because engrossed in individual avarice; the clatter of the auction sales; the levity of the thoroughfare. But there was the seriousness of anxiety, if not the gloom of despair, in the home, in the private sanctuary, in the public office—in every place where thoughtful minds contemplated the future, and looked beyond the circle of the twenty-four hours.

Washington was gay, in the mean time, not with thoughtlessness, but with exultations over the prospects of the war, and the promises of its government. Balls, "diamond" weddings, presidential levees, social parties, with splendid arrays of silks and jewels, with all the fantasy of wealth, the insolence of licentiousness, and the fashionable commerce of lust, amused the hours. Mr. Lincoln was jocose again. He snapped his fingers at "the rebellion." He attended the theatre nightly. This piece of human jacquerie chattered incessantly over the success of his schemes. The Northern newspapers indulged the almost immediate prospect of a peace, which was to irradiate the Yankee arms, humiliate the South, and open the door to the prosperity of the conquerors in an indiscriminate plunder, and the lasting vassalage of the vanquished. The New York *Herald* declared, that even if this event did not happen in the festivities of the Christmas season of 1863, it would certainly be celebrated in the early part of the ensuing year.

. . . . . Intelligent men of the South, understood the approaching issues. The war was to be prosecuted by the North with certain important accessions to its former advantages; and, on the side of the South, there was a demand for a new measure of that devotion in the minds of the people, which wins success on unequal terms—and without which all expedients of States, all violence of legislation, and all commands of authority are utterly in vain.

CHAPTER IX.

The Importance of the Winter Campaigns of the War.—A Series of Remarkable Events.—Encouragement of the Confederacy.—Rosser's Raid.—A Magnificent Prize.—Pickett's Expedition against Newbern.—The Fight on Bachelor's Creek.—Destruction of the Yankee Gunboat " Underwriter."—The Brilliant Exploit of Commander Wood.—Results of the Expedition.—The Affair of John's Island.—General Wise's Fight.—The Battle of Ocean Pond.—History of the Yankee Expeditions into Florida.—Lincoln's Designs upon Florida.—Their Utter Defeat.—Political Jugglery of Seymour's Expedition.—Price of " Three Electoral Votes."—Sherman's Expedition in the Southwest.—What it Contemplated.—Grant's Extensive Designs.—The Strategic Triangle.—Grant's *Proposed Removal of the Mississippi River.*—Polk's Retreat into Alabama.—Forrest's Heroic Enterprise.—His Defeat of Smith's and Grierson's Columns.—Sherman's Retreat to Vicksburg.—His Disgraceful Failure.—The Yankee Campaign in the West Disconcerted.—The Lines in North Georgia.—Repulse of the Yankees.

So far in the history of the war, the winter had been comparatively an uninteresting period. That of 1863–64 was not an exception to this observation. But although there was, in this period, no battles on the dominant military lines in Virginia and North Georgia, there was a series of remarkable events, running through several months, each one a marked success for the Confederacy, and, collectively, an important sum of victory which did much to raise the hopes of the Confederacy and relieve the dark days in which the year 1863 had expired. These events transpired at considerable distances from each other, and they have no other connection than a chronological one, and their singular concurrence in uniform success. In this connection we shall treat them.

ROSSER'S RAID.

On the 30th of January, a brilliant expedition of General Rosser in the Valley district culminated in the capture of a train of ninety-three wagons loaded with commissary stores and forage on the way from New Creek to Petersburg, and was prosecuted in a few days thereafter to a most unexpected and gratifying success. The incidents of this expedition were of unusual interest.

For several months past the enemy had kept a garrison at the village of Petersburg, in Hardy county, as an outpost to their defences of the Baltimore and Ohio Railroad. Petersburg was some forty-two miles from New Creek, their principal depot for supplies and operations.

General Early, who had lingered in the Valley since the Averill raid, concluded to go over and capture this party at Petersburg, numbering about one thousand, and strongly fortified. He sent General Rosser's brigade (cavalry) and four pieces of McClannahan's battery (Imboden's command) through Brock's Gap, and pushed on himself with Thomas's brigade of infantry from New Market, by Orkney Springs, to the same destination—Moorefield, in Hardy. Moorefield is between Petersburg and the railroad, eleven miles from the former place. Rosser and the artillery arrived first. The plan was for Early to remain with the infantry at Moorefield, preventing the enemy's escape to the railroad by that route, while Rosser passed over Patterson Creek mountain —fifteen miles across—and took position on the turnpike lead ing from Petersburg to New Creek. When Rosser reached Moorefield he learned that the road from that place across Patterson Creek mountain to the turnpike had been blockaded by felling numberless trees and cutting away the road itself. He also learned that a large train of wagons were coming up from New Creek to Petersburg, heavily guarded by infantry. He started across the mountain with his brigade and the four pieces. In the gap he met one or two hundred of the enemy, perfecting the blockade and guarding the pass. They were charged by the Twelfth cavalry and fled. The pioneers went to work heartily. Never did axes fly more rapidly. The train was near the point on the turnpike opposite the mouth of the gap. If it passed that place, the probability was of its escape within the breastworks at Petersburg, which was only ten miles distant. The fortifications were strong, and the chances were against the capture of this place, being reinforced by the wagon guard. In an hour the obstructions were cleared away, and the horsemen and cannon rushed into the turnpike, and saw, with exultation, a long line of snowy-covered wagons slowly moving towards them. Our position was difficult. If the twelve hundred infantry guarding the wagons should make a stubborn resistance, the force at Petersburg might come up and fall upon our rear. Rosser had only about eight hundred cavalry. The dispositions were soon made. Colonel White's (Lige) battalion and three pieces were sent towards Petersburg —the balance of the brigade and one piece of artillery advanced upon the train. The enemy were so certain of success, that they never even turned their wagons around, but stopped them facing us in the pike.

The Yankees were posted at right angles with the pike, behind a ten-rail fence. The long-range guns were dismounted and advanced as infantry. A squadron of cavalry were sent to the left to flank the enemy, while another was placed in the pike. The piece opened. The dismounted men trudged through a miry meadow, sinking to their ankles, right up a hill to meet twelve hundred Yankees with their guns resting upon the fence. Four hundred cavalry, on foot, in an open field, with boots and spurs, and without the advantage of order, faced such odds and such position! The enemy's artillery, which had accompanied the train from New Creek, thinking all safe, turned back a few miles below, hence they were without cannon. We had only one piece. It being placed in a flat, and firing up hill, the recoil came almost directly against the axle, and it broke. Still it continued to fire, carrying dismay among the wagoners and the enemy's line.

The action lasted about twenty minutes. The squadron on the left charged a Yankee squadron up hill, some on foot leading their horses, and as each one reached the plateau mounted and spurred after the frightened enemy, who fled without making but a feeble resistance. Meanwhile the party behind the fence were routed and fled; but being too swift for boots and spurs, the cavalry on the pike charged upon them. The immense train, now in a mass of confusion, so blocked the pike as to prevent overtaking the fugitives. The whole train was now in our hands.*

---

* The prize is thus described by a correspondent who participated in the affair : "There stood ninety-three six-mule wagons, loaded to the very sheet with commissary stores, new gear, new wagons, new everything. Contents,

After securing his prize, Rosser moved rapidly on to co-operate with Early in the capture of Petersburg. But information of the advance had been received, and the garrison evacuated the place during the night. They had powerful works and six pieces of cannon, and, if they had been less cowardly, might have given us a terrible reception.

Rosser, when he had discovered the escape of the Yankees, wheeled and moved upon the railroad, destroying two bridges —one over Patterson creek, the other the North Branch of the Potomac.

The expedition got back safely into the valley. Rosser brought off two hundred and seventy prisoners, fifty wagons and teams, twelve hundred cattle and five hundred sheep.

PICKETT'S EXPEDITION AGAINST NEWBERN.

The town of Newbern, situated at the junction of the Trent and Neuse, was a place of some note in North Carolina. Soon after the fall of Roanoke Island, on the 14th day of February, 1862, it fell into the hands of the Yankees, since which time it had been in their possession, and had been the seat of some of their most important military operations. Immediately after occupation, extensive fortifications were erected, and the lines extended over some twenty miles of surrounding country. The regiments stationed here had been composed principally of men from Massachusetts and New York, the blackest of Abolitionists, full of schemes and plans for negro emancipation, equalization and education. Negro regiments had been organized; companies of disloyal Carolinians put in service against us; the most tyrannical rule established; and both men and officers had been guilty of the grossest outrages and atrocities. For many months they had occupied the town securely, retaining undisturbed possession, scarcely dreaming of the possibility of an attack. In the river some two or three gunboats were

---

'in part,' corn, oats, flour, bacon, *ad infinitum ;* coffee, two thousand pounds nicely roasted; candles (adamantine), fifty boxes; sugar, by the barrel; fresh oysters, one thousand cans; brandy peaches, five hundred cans; cheese, hats, &c., &c., 'too numerous to mention.' One bushel of pocket-knives."

generally lying, either anchored off the town or cruising up or down the Neuse or Trent, to the great terror of the inhabitants living near their banks.

General Pickett's demonstration upon Newbern, which surprised the Yankees, on the 1st of February, appears to have followed just in the retiring footsteps of a Yankee raiding party which had been sent out from the town. He had with him two brigades only—Clingman's and Hoke's—while General Barton had been sent up the Trent to fall upon the town simultaneously with those in front. An expedition of boats, under command of Commander Wood, of the Confederate Navy, was to make a demonstration upon the enemy's gunboats, and to essay, if possible, their capture or destruction.

Early on the morning of 1st February, the Yankee outposts at Bachelor's creek were attacked by the Confederates. The force of the enemy here occupied a strong line of fortifications along the edge of the creek, on both flanks of a powerful blockhouse, which commanded the approach to the bridge.

While a furious shower of shot and shell was kept up near the bridge, the right of our line succeeded in pushing through the marsh and effected a crossing, flanking the enemy. A vigorous attack was made by the Confederates, and the Yankees were driven out, and began falling back. Those of our men on the other side of the creek rushed upon the bridge, laid the pontoon planks, crossed, and joined the fight. Charging with a yell, they broke the line of the enemy, and pursued them to the cover of the fortifications of Newbern.

The night passed without a general attack; but not without a bold achievement by the Confederates.

The Yankee gunboat, Underwriter, had passed up the Neuse river near Fort Stephenson, throwing out her anchors and placing all her guns, to be in readiness for any service in case of an attack on the town. About one o'clock at night, the sentinel saw some boats approaching, and, hailing them, received no reply. They were Wood's boats. As they came up the Yankees greeted them with a volley of musketry, which flashed in the very faces of the daring Confederates, the balls whistling unpleasantly into the boats or into the water beyond. But the boats were soon at the side of the steamer, the grapnels thrown on, and a hand-to-hand combat joined between the boarding-party and the crew. But the Yankees soon cried for quarter, and the steamer was ours. The Confederate engineer Gill was lying in the gangway, shot in four places and mortally wounded, and midshipman Saunders, cut down in a hand-to-hand fight, was breathing his last upon the decks.

The Underwriter was moored, head and stern, to the shore, under three of the largest batteries, and hardly a stone's throw from the wharf. The flash of the guns and the report of musketry had aroused the soldiers on shore, and they were now witnesses of the scene, but determined not to be inactive ones; for, regardless of their own prisoners on board, they fired a shell into the steamer, which, striking the upper machinery and exploding on the deck, produced a terrible shock. To spare the prisoners and wounded, Captain Wood ordered them to be put into the boats and the ship made ready for firing. As the steam was down, it was found it would be impossible to take time to get it up under the heavy fire of batteries not one hundred yards away; and so, the wounded and prisoners being put into the boats, the vessel was fired. In a few minutes the Underwriter was one mass of flame, burning up the dead bodies of the Yankees killed in action.

General Pickett having ascertained the strength of the fortifications of Newbern, concluded that it would be useless to risk an assault upon them, and appears to have been satisfied with the results his expedition had already accomplished. Indeed, he represented to the War Department that he had attempted nothing more than a "reconnoissance in force." But the results of the reconnoissance was not a mean victory. Pickett had met the enemy in force at Bachelor's creek, killed and wounded about one hundred in all, captured thirteen officers and two hundred and eighty prisoners, fourteen negroes two rifled pieces and caissons, three hundred stand of small arms, four ambulances, three wagons, fifty-five animals, a quantity of clothing, camp and garrison equipage, and two flags. The destruction of the Underwriter was an important part of the success. She was the largest and best of the Yankee gunboats in the sounds; had engines of eight hundred horse power, the largest the Yankees had taken across Hatteras swash; mounted four guns—two large eight-inch shell guns one twelve-pound rifle, and one twelve-pound howitzer.

THE AFFAIR OF JOHN'S ISLAND.

An incident "worthy of note" was at last to occur in what for months had been the dull vicinity of famous Charleston.

On the 9th of February the enemy came over in force from Folly to Kiawah Island, and thence crossed over at a place called the Haulover, to John's Island, killing, wounding, and capturing some nine men of Major Jenkins's command. With about one hundred and fifty men only, he fought them until night, when Colonel Tabb reinforced him, and the Colonel im- mediately attacked the enemy at night, with but a battalion, and staggered them so that they paused and did not advance again until Colonel Page reinforced them with another battal- ion of the 26th Virginia, the next morning.

General Wise sent forward more troops, and went in person on the 10th, and got there just as five hundred and fifty in- fantry, with one battery and two hundred cavalry were drawn up in line under the fire of two thousand, at least, of the enemy. Seeing they were about to turn our left flank, Gen- eral Wise ordered our forces to fall back to a point called the "Cocked Hat." There we took a position and awaited rein- forcements. They came up in time to increase our numbers to about one thousand infantry, and two batteries of artillery.

The enemy did not advance until the 11th. By 3 P. M. they came up to our front. Just at this moment General Colquitt reinforced us with nine hundred men. At 3.25 P. M. we opened upon the enemy with six pieces, the Marion battery, and one section of Charles's, at about three-quarters of a mile distance. The enemy replied with three pieces—Parrott's and Blakely's. They ceased firing at forty minutes past 5 P. M., and retreated rapidly, leaving some of their dead. Four bod- ies were found on the ground. General Wise's men were too much broken and fatigued to follow them. The enemy retired in confusion to Haulover, burnt the Seabrook houses there, and before day crossed back to Kiawah, burning the bridge behind them.

THE BATTLE OF OCEAN POND.

But the month of February was to be distinguished by an important battle, and that in a part of the Confederacy which had yet attracted but little notice in the war.

The Yankees had invaded Florida in the spring of 1862, when they occupied Jacksonville. They then said they came to protect the city against the reprehensible incendiarism of some of our own people; and, after this profession of protection, and making great promises of an intention to hold the place forever, thus duping a good many disaffected citizens to take sides with them in some sort of a State government which they proposed, and finding much less of Union sentiment than they expected, but more of a military demonstration in their front than they looked for, they departed, after a three weeks' stay in the " water-oak city."

They came again in October, 1862. But this expedition turned out to be a very heavy negro trade; and General Brannon, who commanded it, after collecting a large number of " contrabands," took his departure.

Again, in March, 1863, the Yankees invaded Florida, to try the experiment there of recruiting blacks. They were only partially successful; and the third experiment of invasion ended, leaving its malignant track in the burning of two churches, and laying waste a number of squares of private residences in the beautiful little city of Jacksonville.

The fourth invasion was designed at Washington, and con templated nothing less than the taking and holding of the whole State of Florida, reincorporating it into the Union, and erecting a State government there under the auspices of Mr. Lincoln's private secretary, who was sent to Florida to engineer the political part of the movement. The times were thought to be ripe for so extensive a design upon Florida. The operations against Charleston were virtually abandoned; surplus troops were on hand; and deserters and fugitives had persuaded the Yankees that the pathway was open, and that all there was to resist them was a local force of not more than a dozen companies scattered broadcast over the State. It was soon known that a force of six or seven thousand Yankee

troops, under command of Major-general Seymour, had left
Charleston harbor in eighteen transports for what was supposed
to be the easy conquest of Florida.

The State was in General Beauregard's military department,
and that alert commander had hastened General Colquitt down
to meet the movement of the enemy. General Finnegan was
in command of a small force at Camp Finnegan, where the
enemy had expected to surprise him. He eluded him by withdrawing his forces through the woods. The enemy advanced
twenty miles on the railroad, and took the junction of the other
railroad crossing it, the place or village known as Baldwin.
Our rail lines in their hands, our case seemed desperate. The
enemy advanced still westward towards Lake City, which had
long been the head-quarters of the Eastern Department. His
advance cavalry had come within three miles of Lake City.
But troops were pouring in to Finnegan. General Colquitt
and his brigade were *en route*. The celebrated Chatham artillery of Savannah, which stood the brunt of Fort Wagner for
long weeks, arrived. They were hurried down. Body after
body of troops arrived. Clinch's cavalry were expected to
enter the State in the rear of the enemy, and thus cut off their
retreat while the main body of the troops pushed them back.
Our forces concentrated and fortified at Oulustre, a spot pre
serving its Indian name. It was the headwaters of a creek of
that name, being a continuous swamp on the right of the railroad, inclining southward, Ocean Pond, or one of the inland
lakes of Florida, lying not far north, thus forming a good defensible position. Our forces there concentrated about five
thousand men. Our rifle-pits and redoubts connected with
the swamp on the south, and Ocean Pond on the north.

On the morning of the 20th February, General Finnegan
was notified that the enemy was approaching. About 12
M., they were reported as distant four miles. The command
was then moved out to meet them.

When we had marched three miles from camp, our cavalry
was discovered falling back rapidly. Our line of battle
was formed at once, but so rapidly did the enemy advance that
a furious fire commenced before the line was completed. The
fire soon became general. The battle opened at 2 o'clock P. M.
For two hours the enemy was steadily pushed back, though

they resisted most obstinately. We had captured in this time five pieces of artillery, and the enemy were at their last line. Just then our ammunition became exhausted. It was a trying time to all our troops. Their conduct, however, was above praise. They remained steadfast in line under a heavy fire, to which there was scarcely any reply. But as soon as cartridges were distributed, the men moved forward, and drove them again.

Just at sunset, the Twenty-seventh Georgia, commanded by Colonel Zachry, made a furious attack upon the centre. This movement was seconded by a flank attack of the Sixth Georgia, Colonel Lofton, upon the enemy's right. They now broke and fled in great confusion. We pursued until dark. The Yankees did not halt until they had placed the St. Mary's river in their rear, twenty miles from the battle-field. The fruits of the victory were five pieces of artillery, two stands of colors, two thousand small arms, and five hundred prisoners. The enemy left upon the field three hundred and fifty dead. They also abandoned the severely wounded.

Our loss amounted to eighty killed and six hundred and fifty wounded. The fight was in the open pine woods peculiar to Florida. This accounts for the large number wounded in pro portion to the killed. The enemy could not have lost less than two thousand killed and wounded. General Finnegan reported that the roads for three miles were strewn with the enemy's dead and wounded. More than one half of the two negro regiments that Seymour had placed in front were said to have been killed and wounded.

The enemy fell back to Jacksonville, forty-five miles from where they fought the battle. Our forces followed them along the road, and stragglers and wounded were picked up as they went. A lady reported that General Seymour passed along, looking haggard and pale, saying he had lost half of his troops.

The victory was a subject of extraordinary congratulation. Had the enemy been successful at Ocean Pond, there were not five hundred men between them and the capital, and, with the capture of our rolling stock at Lake City, they would soon have reached Tallahassee and fallen back on St. Mark's as a base, and by water held their communications perfectly. Viewed in this respect, it was one of the decisive battles of the war, and had preserved the State of Florida to the Confederacy.

The Yankee journals (probably for political reasons) were
more candid in their admissions of defeat at Ocean Pond than
on any other occasion of disaster to them in the war. An investigation was ordered in the Yankee Congress. The New
York *Herald* declared that the whole movement grew out of
the political jugglery for the next Presidency, and the whole
thing was a trick to secure the electoral vote of Florida. It
said that " a thousand lives were lost in the attempt to get
three electoral votes."

SHERMAN'S EXPEDITION IN THE SOUTHWEST.

In the winter of 1864, the enemy had planned a grand military combination in the Southwest, which, properly viewed,
was one of the greatest projects of the war. It was imperfectly known by the Confederates at the time, who, for many
weeks vainly imagined the object of Sherman's movement into
Mississippi at the head of an infantry column of thirty-five
thousand men.

Events developed the scheme, and indicated Grant, the Yankees' present military idol, as its originator. It was the con
ceit of this General that the " rebellion " presented its most
formidable front in North Georgia and that he was so circum-
stanced as to render it extremely difficult to turn his advantage, in the possession of Chattanooga, to account. His disadvantages were the enormous prolongation of the line connect
ing the front of operations with the base of supplies, the imperfect character of the communications, and the difficulty of
accumulating sufficient supplies for a long and severe campaign
in the Gulf States.

A New York paper declared that it had been recognized as
a necessary condition to any advance from Chattanooga, looking to great and decisive results, that a water base be opened
up, whence a powerful column should march to connect with,
and support, the Union army advancing from Chattanooga.
A possible point from which a water base could be opened up
was Mobile.

It was known by the beginning of February that three distinct Yankee columns, from as many different points, were now

under way in the Southwest. A very powerful cavalry column, under command of Generals Smith and Grierson, had started from Corinth and Holly Springs. An infantry column, composed of the two corps of Hurlbut and McPherson, under command of General Sherman, was under way from Vicksburg. A combined land and naval expedition was moving from New Orleans.

While Mobile was the plain objective point at which the latter force aimed, it is probable that Sherman did not design to make an overland march from Vicksburg to Mobile—about three hundred miles. There is reason to believe that he expected, when he marched out of Vicksburg, to reach Selma, in Alabama. The heavy column of cavalry that started from Memphis, and constituted an important part of his forces, was to move rapidly across Mississippi and Alabama, cut the interior railway lines, destroy the bridges and Government workshops, lay waste the country, and gain the rear of General Polk, harass and delay his retreat, and, if possible, force him down towards Mobile, while Sherman rushed upon him in front. Had General Polk retreated upon Mobile, the attack upon which by the Federal fleets was calculated if not designed to draw him in that direction, Sherman would have occupied Meridian, Demopolis, and Selma, and thus have rendered his escape impossible, and the fall of Mobile, from lack of provisions and without a blow, a matter of absolute certainty. The possession of Mobile and Selma would have given the Federal commander two important water bases, the one on the Mississippi, at Vicksburg, the other at Mobile, on the Gulf, two navigable rivers communicating with the latter—the Alabama and Tombigbee—and two railways ready to hand, viz.: the Mobile and Ohio, and the Vicksburg and Jackson roads. Once in possession of these important points and his army firmly established in the triangle formed by the Alabama and Tombigbee rivers, and the railroad leading from Selma to Demopolis and Meridian, and we should no more have been able to dislodge him from his position than we had been to drive the enemy from the Virginia Peninsula and Fortress Monroe.

It must be confessed that there were in these combinations the marks of a bold, brilliant, original conception. General Grant had contemplated, so to speak, the removal of the Mississippi river from Vicksburg and New Orleans to Montgomery and Mobile; while at the same time the organization of this line would have operated as a flank movement upon General Johnston's army, and might have resulted in the fall of Atlanta, and the occupation by the legions of the enemy of the northern half of the great State of Georgia. He proposed thus to get possession of the only remaining line of defence which it was possible for the Confederates to take up when he should advance from Chattanooga. Military men of the North had recognized that, if the Confederates were once turned at Atlanta, the line of the Tombigbee was the only available position left them. The other line led directly into a cul-de-sac, ending in Florida. If, therefore, the present movements were successful, it would clutch this single position at which the Confederates could have hoped to make any protracted stand.

But Grant—and it will be found to be his characteristic fault—had overtasked himself. His formidable combination was to fail because too much was attempted, and because it was to be met by the Confederates with consummate skill and courage. The co-operating columns were too widely separated, were exposed to too many chances of failure, and were entrusted to too many different heads.

The expedition so largely planned was inaugurated by the moving of the first two columns. Sherman left Vicksburg the 1st of February, at the head of thirty-five thousand infantry, two or three thousand cavalry, and from sixty to eighty pieces of artillery. Almost simultaneously Grierson or Smith began their march through North Mississippi with about ten thousand cavalry and mounted infantry. Mobile, at the same time, was threatened by water with the enemy's fleet of gunboats, and by land from Pensacola and Pascagoula.

General Polk had recently been placed by the Confederate authorities in command of the Department of the Southwest. He assumed command late in December, and scarcely had more than familiarized himself with the command, and had but little time to organize his troops and collect together all the energies of his department.

General Polk took the field. Forrest was still detached from the main army, and remained so as to watch the movements of Grierson and his command. Sherman with his thirty five thousand men could only be opposed by Loring, French, and Lee.

From Vicksburg the enemy moved very rapidly and vigorously on to Jackson, and from that point they threatened Meridian, the railroad centre of the Southwestern Department. At this time General Polk borrowed from the Mobile garrison two or three brigades to retard the enemy in order to enable him to save his supplies, which had accumulated at different points of the railroads for the past two years. It would have been the height of folly to have given the enemy battle under the circumstances. Our force, when strengthened by the reinforcements from Mobile, did not reach over half that of the enemy, inclusive of our cavalry.

With the additional force from Mobile the enemy was checked, enabling General Polk to save his accumulated stores and protect his supplies. The little army fell back from Brandon in perfect order—slowly and successfully. The enemy moved his bodies of infantry, artillery and cavalry, with caution and prudence. Lee hung upon his flanks and compelled him to move in compact column, giving him but little time to forage or to depredate upon the country. In the mean time General Polk, with all his acknowledged energy, was moving all his stores from points of the different railroads likely to fall into the enemy's hands.

On Sunday, the 14th, Lieutenant-general Polk evacuated Meridian, with his little army, heavily pressed by an enemy thirty-five thousand strong. Before the evacuation, however, every article belonging to the different departments of the Government had been moved. The rolling stock of four important railroads had been saved—not a car was left, and scarcely a wheel left. The locomotives and cars belonging to the Mobile and Ohio road were safely housed in Mobile. Those of the other roads were brought to the Tombigbee and safely placed upon the other side of the river. It was a literal and positive evacuation of this great railroad centre. The little town of Meridian stood lonely amid the silence of pine barrens, without a noise to disturb its solitude or to arouse its inhabitants. The garrison belonging to Mobile had been safely returned to their duties there, and Mobile was as safe as the department at Richmond intended it to be. General Polk retired to Demopolis, Alabama, and prepared for the gathering emergency.

The enemy's cavalry column under Smith and Grierson was to pass through one of the richest districts of the Confederacy to the assistance of Sherman.

From Pontotoc, Mississippi, to the southern boundary line of Noxubee county, a distance of eighty or ninety miles from forty to fifty in width, there was an area of country rich as the Delta of the Nile. Magnificent plantations were spread on either side of the Mobile and Ohio Railroad, level as the sea, and dotted with abodes of wealth and intelligence. Pontotoc, Aberdeen, Columbus, and Macon, were the centres of local trade for all this region. These towns had an aggregate population of perhaps thirty thousand, and the narrow territorial limits of their trade illustrated the fact that this district was the richest granary of the South.

Owing to the exhaustion of his horses, the want of arms and munitions, and other causes, Forrest could array a force of only two thousand four hundred men to confront Smith and Grierson's column of seven thousand of the best equipped cavalry the Yankees had ever put in the field. Forrest's men, too, were mostly new and untried, especially in the cavalry service. He had recently recruited them in West Tennessee. It seemed the extreme of rashness and recklessness, to attempt with such a force to arrest the march of a column of seven thousand splendidly mounted and equipped men, led by experienced officers, whose march thus far had been uninterrupted, who were buoyant and confident, and were charged with such an important mission. The junction of this cavalry force with Sherman at Meridian, was the key of the Yankee plan for the occupation and subjugation of the Southwest. If successful, Sherman would have been in a condition to advance upon Demopolis and Selma, and these important points, as well as the rich countries adjacent, would have been at the mercy of the enemy.

General Polk, with his scant infantry force, quickly perceived the momentous issue which depended upon the result of the cavalry movement from Memphis, and after securing his small army on the east side of the Tombigbee, and removing all his supplies and munitions and returning to Mobile the troops he had borrowed from General Maury, sent imperative orders to Lee and Forrest to unite their forces, and at every cost to crush and drive back Smith and Grierson's cavalry.

Lee did not receive these orders in time to reach Forrest with his force, which was already greatly exhausted by the continual skirmishing with Sherman's column. Forrest, therefore, was left alone with his two thousand four hundred men to perform this immense undertaking. Confronting the enemy on the broad prairies near West Point, on the Tibbee river, he prepared for action. The enemy formed in a long and most imposing line, outflanking Forrest and threatening the instant demolition of his small and imperfectly organized force. The charge was given, and the Yankees advanced with great boldness and an air of certain victory. Great was their surprise when, as they approached Forrest's line, they observed his men slip from their horses, converting themselves into infantry, each man taking the most favorable position, availing themselves of every advantage the ground afforded, and awaiting with the utmost coolness the impetuous charge of the Yankee chivalry. On came the splendidly mounted dragoons, under those far-famed Yankee chiefs, Smith and Grierson, with such fierce displays of valor and determination as augured badly for Forrest's infantry scouts, scattered through the bushes and over the prairie in rather an irregular and unmilitary style. But these valorous horsemen did not advance far before the balls of two thousand riflemen began to rattle through their ranks with fearful effect. Scores of men and horses fell at the first fire, and their onward movement was checked, and before they could recover and reform the volley was repeated—again and again—until dismay and terror began to prevail in their ranks, and they soon broke into confusion and fled.

Having discovered the small force of Forrest, several attempts were made by Smith and Grierson to rally their men and resume the offensive. Their efforts were successful on the hills, just beyond Okalona, when the last grand charge was made by them on the 21st of February. The fight commenced late in the evening, and was obstinate, as the enemy were forced to make repeated stands to hold us in check, and to save their pack mules, &c., from a stampede. It closed with a grand cavalry charge of the enemy's whole force. We repulsed them with heavy loss, and completely routed them.

General Forrest's command was too tired to continue the pursuit. General Gholson, with six or seven hundred State troops, arrived and went in pursuit. The enemy never halted for a moment in his retreat, and when last heard from, the remnant of this splendid force was hastening fast to Memphis, in far different plight from that in which it had so recently emerged from its fortifications.

The disastrous retreat of Grierson and Smith upon Memphis was decisive of the campaign. Their retreat naturally interrupted Sherman's communications all along the line of the Mobile and Ohio Railroad, and deprived his army of an important source of supply, without which he was incapable of maintaining his ground. Worse still, the falling back of these two officers took away from him the cavalry force upon which he relied to prosecute his operations. He was left to retrace his steps in disappointment and disgrace, and to retire to Vicksburg. Back there he dragged his weary, broken-down column, in a demoralized state ; having accomplished not a single military result in his campaign, and having achieved no other glory than that of warfare upon private property and inoffensive people, a cheap triumph of the ruffian and the plunderer.

In a congratulatory order to his army, General Polk said : "The concentration of our cavalry on the enemy's column of cavalry from West Tennessee formed the turning point of the campaign. That concentration broke down his only means of subsisting his infantry. His column was defeated and routed, and his whole force compelled to make a hasty retreat. Never did a grand campaign, inaugurated with such pretension, terminate more ingloriously. With a force three times that which was opposed to its advance, they have been defeated and forced to leave the field with a loss of men, small arms and artillery."

The Yankees made an absurd attempt to cover up Sherman's defeat with the stereotyped lie, that the expedition had "accomplished all that was intended." It could hardly be possible that the object of an expedition of such magnitude as that conducted by Sherman through Mississippi was simply to march over a sterile country one hundred and fifty miles, take possession of a comparatively insignificant point, and then march back again.

The truth was, Grant's grand combination in the West had completely broken down; and Sherman's defeat had given the Confederacy two months more time to prepare for the great campaign of 1864.

While the events we have been narrating were transpiring in the Southwest, as part of the grand plan, there had been a movement on the lines in North Georgia. Thomas, in immediate command of the Yankee forces there, had attempted an advance on the 25th of February. For a whole day he attempted to penetrate our lines, but was compelled suddenly to fall back upon his base at Chickamauga. The "On-to-Atlanta" was a programme all parts of which had been disconcerted, and to amend which the campaign in the West had to be put over until the fighting month of May.

CHAPTER X.

Auspicious Signs of the Spring of 1864.—Military Successes of the Confederates.—
Improvements in the Internal Polity of the Confederacy—Two Important Measures
of Legislation.—Revolution of our Finances.—Enlargement of the Conscription.—
Theory of the New Military Law.—A Blot on the Political Record of the Confederacy.—Qualified Suspension of the *Habeas Corpus.*—An Infamous Edict, but a " Dead-
letter."—An Official Libel upon the Confederacy.—The Real Condition of Civil
Liberty in the South.—The Conscription not properly a Measure of Force.—Impressments but a System of Patriotic Contribution.—Development of the Yankee
Government into Despotism.—An Explanation of this.—The Essence of Despotism
in One Yankee Statute.—MILITARY RESOURCES OF THE CONFEDERACY.—Its Military
System, the Best and Most Elastic in the World.—The War Conducted on *A Voluntary Basis.*—Supplies.—Scarcity of Meat.—The Grain Product.—Two Centres of Sup-
plies.—A Dream of Yankee Hate.—Great Natural Resources of the North.—Summary
of the Yankee Military Drafts.—Tonnage of the Yankee Navy.—The Yankee War
Debt.—Economic Effects of the War.—Its Effects on European Industry.—Yankee
Conquest of the South an Impossibility.—A Remarkable Incident of the War.—
DAHLGREN'S RAID AROUND RICHMOND.—Kilpatrick's and Custar's Parts of the Expedition.—Dahlgren and his Negro Guide.—His " Braves" Whipped by the Richmond
Clerks and Artisans.—Death of the Marauder.—Revelation of his Infamous Designs.
—Copy and History of " the Dahlgren Papers."—A Characteristic Yankee Apothe-
osis.—Ridiculous and Infamous Behavior of the Confederate Authorities.—A Bru-
tal and Savage Threat.—President Davis in Melodrama.

THE auspicious signs of the spring of 1864 was the theme
everywhere of the Confederate press. We have seen how a
current of success had set in for the South. Mr. Lincoln's
shocking experiment in Florida; Thomas's disastrous repulse
in North Georgia; Sherman's magnificent failure, were glad
auguries for the Confederate arms in the coming campaigns.
The situation was being rapidly improved. Not to speak just
yet of our achievements in Texas, in Western Louisiana, and
along the banks of the Mississippi, we could refer with satisfaction to Longstreet's exploits in East Tennessee, subsequent to
the raising of the siege of Knoxville, and fancied permanent
occupation of East Tennessee by the enemy. The siege of
Charleston had proven only a running sore, where the strength
and wealth of the enemy were wasted without the slightest
prospect of advancing one step beyond the landward beach of
Morris Island. Florida had afforded nothing but disaster to
them and glory to us. The rainy season would soon render it

as uninhabitable to a Northern army as it has hitherto been unconquerable. "Dixie," said the Yankee papers, was " in fine feather."

This period of military success was coincident, too, with certain important improvements in the internal polity of the Confederacy. The Confederate Congress of 1863–64, had accomplished two important measures of legislation. It had revolutionized the Confederate finances by a law which required the currency to be funded, under the penalty, within certain dates, of thirty-three and a third per cent., stopped further issues of paper money, and provided for the public revenues by heavy taxation, and the sale of five hundred millions of six per cent. bonds. It had enlarged the conscription and qualified it by a system of details, the administration of which, though it properly resided in Congress, and should not have been delegated to the Executive branch of the Confederacy, which was notoriously corrupted by favoritism, was especially designed to compose and protect the vexed industry and resources of the country.

The new military law was designed to devote to the army, directly or indirectly, the whole physical power and energy of the country. Providing, first, recruits for the ranks by an extended conscription, it then organized the remaining labor of the country, for the sole use and benefit of the army and the country's cause. The great pervading principle of this military bill was that every man owed to his country the duty of defending it, either *in or out* of the ranks, and the law provided for the discharge of this paramount duty by putting in the ranks all men capable of bearing arms, except certain persons who could be of more service to the cause out of, than in the army. Exemptions and details were to be permitted upon the great and important principle of promoting the public service. Recognizing the absolute dependence of the country's cause upon the great agricultural interest, the Confederate Congress, while protecting this great interest, had made it contribute to the support of the army, for the privilege of its exemption— thus protecting the production of the country, without depriving the army of the recruits necessary to its reinforcement.

It is, however, to be confessed, with pain, that the Confederate Congress of 1863–64, marred the work of this legislative

year by a base imitation of the Washington despotism in a sus
pension of the *habeas corpus.* It was an act of criminal stupidity, the fruit of an inferiority of mind in our legislators that
aped the precedents of the Yankee. It is true that the law
authorizing the suspension of the great writ of liberty was
qualified by a stringent bill of particulars.*   But what can be

---

* The following is a copy of this unfortunate law:

A bill to suspend the privilege of the writ of HABEAS CORPUS *in certain cases.*

Whereas, the Constitution of the Confederate States of America provides, in
article 1, section 9, paragraph 3, that " the privilege of the writ of *habeas corpus*
shall not be suspended, unless when, in case of rebellion or invasion, the public
safety may require it ;" and, whereas the power of suspending the privilege of
said writ, as recognized in said article 1, is vested solely in the Congress, which
is the exclusive judge of the necessity of such suspension ; and, whereas, in the
opinion of the Congress, the public safety requires the suspension of said writ
in the existing case of the invasion of these States by the armies of the United
States ; and, whereas the President has asked for the suspension of the writ of
habeas corpus, and informed Congress of conditions of public danger which render the suspension of the writ a measure proper for the public defence against
invasion and insurrection ; now, therefore :

1. That during the present invasion of the Confederate States, the privilege
of the writ of *habeas corpus* be, and the same is hereby, suspended ; but such
suspension shall apply only to the cases of persons arrested or detained by order
of the President, Secretary of War, or the general officer commanding the
Trans-Mississippi Military Department, by the authority and under the control
of the President. It is hereby declared that the purposes of Congress in the
passage of this act is to provide more effectually for the public safety by suspending the writ of *habeas corpus* in the following cases, and no other :

I. Of treason or treasonable efforts or combinations to subvert the Government of the Confederate States.

II. Of conspiracies to overthrow the Government, or conspiracies to resist the
lawful authority of the Confederate States.

III. Of combining to assist the enemy or of communicating intelligence to
the enemy, or giving him aid and comfort.

IV. Of conspiracies, preparations and attempts to incite servile insurrection.

V. Of desertions or encouraging desertions, of harboring deserters, and of
attempts to avoid military service ; Provided, that in cases of palpable wrong
and oppression by any subordinate officer, upon any party who does not legally
owe military service, his superior officer shall grant prompt relief to the oppressed party, and the subordinate shall be dismissed from office

VI. Of spies and other emissaries of the enemy.

VII. Of holding correspondence or intercourse with the enemy, without necessity, and without the permission of the Confederate States.

VIII. Of unlawful trading with the enemy and other offences against th
laws of the Confederate States, enacted to promote their success in the war.

IX. Of conspiracies, or attempts to liberate prisoners of war held by the Confederate States.

most said, to wipe from the record of the Confederacy the stain of this infamous edict, is, that it was never put into practice. It was not put into practice for the simple reason that there was no occasion for it; no one doubted the integrity and patriotism of our judiciary; that branch of the government was practically permitted to continue its dispensations of law and justice; and the worst that can be said of the law suspending the *habeas corpus* was, that it was a stain upon our political history. It was an uncalled for libel upon the Confederacy; but although it might blacken our reputation, yet it is a satisfaction to know that it did not practically affect our system of liberties.

In contrasting the political systems of the North and South in this war, we find an invariable superiority in the latter with respect to all questions of civil liberty. This, indeed, is to be taken as the most striking and significant moral phenomenon of the war.

Despite the conscription and other harsh necessities of legislation, the principles of liberty were yet substantially secure in the Confederacy. The spirit of the devotion of the people was, in most instances, in advance of the demands of the gov-

---

X. Of conspiracies, or attempts or preparations to aid the enemy.

XI. Of persons aiding or inciting others to abandon the Confederate cause, or to resist the Confederate States, or to adhere to the enemy.

XII. Of unlawfully burning, destroying, or injuring, or attempting to burn, destroy, or injure any bridge or railroad, or telegraph line of communication, or other property with the intent of aiding the enemy.

XIII. Of treasonable designs to impair the military power of the Government by destroying or attempting to destroy the vessels, or arms, or munitions of war, or arsenals, foundries, workshops, or other property of the Confederate States.

SEC. 2. The President shall cause proper officers to investigate the cases of all persons so arrested or detained, in order that they may be discharged if improperly detained, unless they can be speedily tried in the due course of law.

SEC. 3. That during the suspension aforesaid, no military or other officer shall be compelled, in answer to any writ of *habeas corpus*, to appear in person, or to return the body of any person detained by him by the authority of the President, Secretary of War, or the general officer commanding the Trans-Mississippi Department; but upon the certificate, under oath, of the officer having charge of any one so detained that such person is detained by him as a prisoner under the authority aforesaid, further proceedings under the writ of *habeas corpus*, shall immediately cease and remain suspended so long as this act shall continue in force.

SEC. 4. This act shall continue in force for ninety days after the next meeting of Congress, and no longer.

ernment. The people of the Confederacy were more heartily willing than the Yankees to contribute of their substance and convenience to the war, but much less willing than they to sacrifice their civil liberties to its fancied necessities. In the Confederacy the impressments of property were, in fact, in the majority of instances, voluntary contributions. In the Confederacy, the conscription was not, in effect, a measure of force, but was rather to be regarded as a measure to organize the proffer of patriotic devotion, and to equalize its service. It was the purer spirit and superior motives of the Confederacy in the war that made its administration so superior to that of the enemy, with regard to the constitutional standards of liberty, and the well recognized principles of conservatism.

The North presented a different picture. The process by which the Yankee Government had developed itself into one of the vilest despotisms on the earth is one of the most interesting problems of the history of the war. In an address of the Confederate Congress, which met in the spring of 1864, a reference was made to Yankee despotism as " engendered in a desperate warfare upon the liberties of another and kindred people." The language of this reference contains the key of the problem. The unholy passions of this war, its hate, its greed, its dire revenge, its desperation, induced the people of the North to compromise their constitutional rights. They were willing to purchase the gratification of their passions at the expense of their liberty, and those who gainsayed the price were denounced as disloyal persons, and threatened as traitors.

Personal liberty was no longer a thing of any account in the eyes of " the best government the world ever saw." There was a law on the statute-book of the Government at Washington, which not only undertook to deprive the judicial tribunals of the States of all cognizance, civil and criminal, over proceedings instituted against persons who had done any act injurious to a citizen, by order of President Lincoln, but which also made the order of the President, or of any one acting under his authority, *a full and perfect defence*, in all courts, in any civil or any criminal proceeding in which the act was drawn in question. This law annihilated the liberties of th citizen ; perfected the despotism at Washington ; and gav

Abraham Lincoln a power above all judicial redress in the country, and as irresponsible as any autocracy on earth.

MILITARY RESOURCES OF THE CONFEDERACY.

The military system of the South was, perhaps, the most admirable and elastic in the world. The conscription, which, as we have seen, was not regarded in the Confederacy as an edict of violence, but was in fact merely an organized form of public spirit, was constantly and harmoniously in operation; and it had the especial merit of avoiding that agitation and public demoralization inseparable from a system of periodical drafts. It provided a class of reserves, from sixteen to eighteen years of age, which was constantly passing within the limits of the active military age. The army was thus steadily replenished. It was qualified by a system of details, the administration of which was to be constantly concerned in adjusting the demands of the military service to precise necessities, and accommodating the conscription, either enlarging or contracting it, to the state of the country. The military system of the Confederacy had thus an elasticity which was indeed its most valuable quality.

Ignorant minds appear to have been much impressed with the idea that the Confederacy would break down for the want of men. There had been yearly repetitions of this idea since the commencement of the war; and yet, strange to say, for all this time the Confederate armies had not declined in numbers. Fighting on the defensive, their losses were much less than those of the Yankees; occupying interior and shorter lines, and commanded by generals who carefully economized human life, they did not require the same numbers as the enemy; and, even if they were decreasing, there was this compensation: that while they declined in numbers, the Yankee army was declining, at a much more rapid rate, in a *personnel*, which had come to be mostly composed of negroes and foreigners, and in those measures of courage and devotion which best insure victory.

The advantage which the Confederacy had in the conduct of the war was that every thing was, really and substantially, on the *voluntary basis*. The impressment law, though violent in form, like the conscription, was, in fact, the *conduit* of patriotic contributions. Every thing that was asked for the war was generally given with cheerful consent; and supplies poured in upon the Government, from private sources, much faster than the transportation of rail-cars, boats, and wagons could dispose of them.

The scarcity of meat was a difficulty which could be comparatively endured. There was an impression, long prevalent with us, that the South was dependent upon the North for a large portion of the meat we consumed. We actually reared and slaughtered more animals in proportion to population than the North, and it was simply owing to the fact of our almost wasteful use of meat, in which they economized, that we became annual purchasers of this article to so great an extent. Thrown upon our own resources, diverting our agriculture from the production of our great commercial staples to that of breadstuffs, and, along with it, to raising animals, hogs especially, since the war began, in sections undisturbed by the march of armies, or not affected by epidemics among our stock, the supplies of meat were far more bountiful than ever before.

But although it must be confessed that our meat supplies which would otherwise have been superabundant, had been sadly diminished by the enemy's occupation of Kentucky and Tennessee, and the isolation of the Trans-Mississippi, yet none but the most ignorant could doubt our sufficiency of other subsistence in a country where the cereals might be produced on every acre of arable land. The difficulty was in the ready equalization of supplies by transportation, not in the want of them. There were two centres of supplies in the Confederacy, inaccessible to the enemy, either of which was sufficient to subsist our entire army and people; one whose lines radiated through north-western Carolina and the southern tier of counties in Virginia, and the other in the unequalled grain districts of south-western Georgia and Alabama. To "starve" the South was the atrocious dream of Northern hate, scarcely the calculation of Yankee shrewdness and intelligence.

The North had great material resources, but it was wasting them in a war the advance of which was more than doubtful, and the object of which morally unattainable. It had put two millions of soldiers in the field.* The tonnage of its navy was but little short of half a million. But while Yankee pride took delight in the exhibits, they were not merely displays of power, they were also evidences of debt.

The expenditures of the Yankee Government during the war had constantly exceeded the official estimates, while the receipts had fallen off.

Mr. Chase estimated the expenses for 1864 at $750,815,088; Congress had already appropriated $1,104,000,000 *for the War Department alone!* The rate at which the debt had accumulated, and the amount of claims yet to be adjusted, made it certain that the public debt was not far from $3,000,000,000.†

---

* The following is a list, compiled from official sources, of Mr. Lincoln's enormous calls for troops:

April 16, 1861	75,000
May 4, 1861	64,748
From July to December, 1861	500,000
July 1, 1862	300,000
August 4, 1862	300,000
Draft, summer of 1863	300,000
February 1, 1864	500,000
Total	2,039,748

† The following figures, which we find compiled to our hand, show the various loans and liabilities of the Yankee Government thus far authorized by various acts of Congress:

Loan of 1842	$242,621
Loan of 1847	9,415,250
Loan of 1848	8,908,341
Texas indemnity loan of 1850	3,461,000
Loan of 1858	20,000,000
Loan of 1860	7,622,000
Loan of 1861	18,415,000
Treasury notes, March 1861	512,910
Oregon war loan, 1861	1,016,000
Another loan of 1861	50,000,000
Three years treasury notes	139,679,000
Loan of August, 1861	320,000
Five-twenty loan	400,000,000
Temporary loans	104,933,103
Certificates of indebtedness	156,918,437
Unclaimed dividends	114,115
Carried over	921,557,777

Mr. Chase's statement of his administration exhibited the fcl lowing interesting figures:

Government expenses, 72 years, 1789 to 1861, $1,458,790,786
Government expenses, 4 years, 1861 to 1865,   2,692,086,941

Excess in four years $1,238,294,155

So we find that, accepting the figures and estimates of the Yankee Secretary of the Treasury, the expenditures of the Government during the administration of Abraham Lincoln would nearly double those of the whole period from the establishment of the government to the inauguration of the " age of purity."

It is impossible, with the imperfect materials at present at hand, to make a pecuniary estimate of the losses due to the shock and derangement of the war. These losses were not only shared by the North and South; the whole commercial world was involved in the misfortunes of the war, and dragged into its vortex.

The South, with a population of ten millions, of whom four millions were slaves, with about one million of these engaged in the production of our great commercial staples, with but little artificial labor, but with only the simplest implements of husbandry, her peculiar social institution and her climate, had yet furnished all the vitality, had actually created and brought into existence the greater part of all the great wealth-producing artificial labor in other nations. Her productions, which could be supplied or substituted from no other avenue without enormous additional expense, were indispensable to the capital invested and the labor developed. English factories had already many of them suspended, or were reduced greatly in the'r operations. Northern newspapers informed us that not a

Brought over................................	921,557,777
Demand treasury notes.....................	500,000
Legal tenders, 1862........................	397,767,114
Legal tenders, 1863........................	104,969,937
Postal and fractional currency............	50,000,000
Old treasury notes outstanding............	118,000
Ten-forty bonds............................	900,000,000
Interest-bearing treasury notes............	500,000,000
Total........	$2,774,912,828

spindle at Lowell was in operation. The manufacturers of France were already clamorous. The only wonder was, that civilized nations could so long remain unmoved by such catastrophes—so long remain disinterested spectators of a war upon the South for the destruction of our system of natural labor, whether for a mere sentiment or for any other cause, that of necessity involved the loss to them of an immense invested capital, and was destructive of artificial labor equivalent, in operatives, to many hundred-fold the number of our slaves.

And what of the results of conquest? what of the indications of final success? what of the signs of conclusion had the war accomplished? Eight hundred thousand square miles was too large an area for decisive war. When we imagine the toilsome marches, the mighty mountains, the dense and unhealthy swamps, the innumerable and impassable rivers and inlets, when we see a resolute people enduring outrage and destitution, ever ready to sting the heel of the invader, it is obvious that no human force can traverse those distances, subdue that people, and establish any other government than what such a people shall approve. A territory so extensive could not be held by the policy of plunder and extermination. The miserable gains of the thief, the marauder, the ruffian, and the plunderer—the achievements of banditti, might discourage any government and dissatisfy any soldiery.*

---

* A curious attempt was that of the Yankees to represent to the world the extent and permanency of their conquests by bogus State organizations ; altogether, one of the vilest cheats of the war. Arkansas, Louisiana, and other States, were made to play false parts upon paper, and were claimed as acquisitions for "the Union," when a Yankee dared not show his face in his new dominions outside of his picket lines. It was by the management of bayonets that bogus delegates met at Little Rock, and concocted a paper which they termed a "Constitution," declaring that slavery should not exist in the State of Arkansas, and sent men to Washington to ask to be received back into the Union.

In Louisiana the farce of a State election had just been completed. How far such an election represented the franchise or free will of the people we may infer from the following extract from General Order No. 23, issued by General Banks, and paraded in every Government paper the morning of the election :

"Open hostility cannot be permitted. Indifference will be treated as a crime, and faction as treason. Men who refuse to defend their country with the ballot-box have no just claim to the benefits of liberty regulated by law

We leave these discussions to follow the current of military
events.

DAHLGREN'S RAID AROUND RICHMOND.

In the month of March, 1864, was to occur one of the most
remarkable incidents of the war; inasmuch as it was the occasion of certain documentary evidence of the savage and
atrocious spirit of our enemies, which heretofore, though it had
been the constant assertion of the Confederates, had been persistently denied in Yankee prints, and concealed from the
world by brazen lies, audacious recrimination, and the stereotypes of Yankee hypocrisy.

On the 28th of February, a raid was undertaken towards
Richmond by the Yankee cavalry under General Kilpatrick.
Colonel Ulric Dahlgren, a son of the Yankee admiral of
Charleston "sensation," was second in command. After
reaching Beaver Dam and destroying the water station and
tearing up a few hundred yards of the track at that point, the
force divided, Kilpatrick with his command passing through
the upper part of Hanover into Louisa, where he took the
mountain road, which he followed until he struck the Brook
turnpike, which led into Richmond.

After the force was divided, Dahlgren's command proceeded
to Frederick Hall, in Louisa county, where they captured several of our officers who were holding a court-martial at the
time. Among these officers was Captain Dement, of a Baltimore battery, who was compelled to follow the expedition.
After tearing up the railroad for some distance, Dahlgren proceeded rapidly towards the James River Canal, which he
struck in Goochland county. He burnt a grist-mill here, some
barns, injured some of the locks on the canal, and did other

. . . . Whoever is indifferent or hostile, must choose between
the liberty which foreign lands afford, the poverty of the rebel States, and the
innumerable and inappreciable blessings which our Government confers upon
its people."

Thirty-five thousand Louisianians had already gone to partake of the "poverty of the rebel States," and about eleven thousand played the farce of voting
to continue "the blessings which the Yankee Government confers upon its
people."

trifling damage. His men were allowed to amuse themselves for some hours at the farm-houses, in hacking up furniture and stealing silver spoons. His purpose was to cross the James river here, get into Richmond by a surprise on the south side, and do his peculiar work in that city of the Confederacy.

He had employed a negro to guide him to a ford of the river. He had paid him for the proposed service with what appeared to be a five-dollar bill, but was in fact a barber's "token," in the shape of a bank note, after the ingenious fashion of Yankee advertisements. The negro conducted him to a ford, but finding the water too high to cross, and imagining that he had been duped, Dahlgren turned upon the helpless black, had him instantly hanged, and to expedite the horrible deed, furnished a rein from his own bridle to strangle his victim.

Finding that he could not cross the river, Dahlgren directed his movements to make a junction with Kilpatrick. But in the mean time all the other parts of the expedition had failed.

One part had been to distract attention by a movement of General Custer, with cavalry and artillery, in the direction of Charlottesville. It had come to grief. It had reached the vicinity of Rio Mills, where Stuart's horse artillery, under Major Beckham, was stationed. As soon as the enemy crossed the Rivanna river, the artillery, supported by some furloughed and dismounted men, opened on the advancing column. This seemed entirely unexpected, some of the Yankees exclaiming, "By ——, the Secesh have been reinforced; let's go back," which they did at a double-quick; nor did they halt to camp until they reached their infantry supports at Madison Court-house.

Kilpatrick's part of the expedition had manifested a similar ludicrous cowardice. He had reached the outer line of the Richmond fortifications at a little past ten on the morning of the 1st of March. A desultory fire was kept up for some hours, in which the Yankees who had proposed a desperate inroad into Richmond never once got within range of our artillery, and, satisfied to boast that they had been within sight of the city, withdrew, and took up their line of march down the Peninsula.

Unapprised of these dastardly events, Dahlgren, on the

night of the 1st of March, pursued his way towards Richmond, following the Westham plank-road, with some seven or eigh hundred horsemen. An exhibition of cowardice was reserved for him, unequalled even by that of Custer, or Kilpatrick.

All that stood in the darkness of that night between Dahl gren and Richmond, between the ferocious Yankee and the revenge he had plotted to pour in blood and fire upon the devoted capital of the Confederacy, was a force of local soldiery, composed of artisans from the Richmond Armory, and clerks, many of them young boys, from the departments of the government. Such was the force that was to give to Dahlgren's " braves" a lesson for their temerity.

The Armory battalion was on the enemy's flank, and appears to have been surprised. But when the enemy came in contact with Henly's battalion (the clerks), the valorous cavalry broke at the first fire. The first volley of musketry seems to have done all the disaster that occurred, and to have finished the business. Eleven of Dahlgren's Yankees were killed and thirty or forty wounded, while the rest scattered in shameful flight.

After this disgraceful affair, Dahlgren seemed to be anxious only for his retreat. He divided his forces so as to increase the chances of escape. The force under his immediate command moved down the South bank of the Pamunkey, and crossed the river at Dabney's Ferry. From the ferry they proceeded by the most direct route to Ayletts on the Mattapony, watched closely at every step by scouts detached from Lieutenant James Pollard's company of Lee's Rangers, then on picket duty and recruiting service in King William County, the residence of most of it members. Pollard, himself, while passing through the streets of Richmond, had chanced to see at a newspaper office a bulletin giving some account of the retreat of Dahlgren's party, and declaring that he would make them "pay toll" on their route, had posted to intercept the fugitives.

The ferry-boat on the Mattapony having been previously removed, and Pollard's arrangements for disputing the passage of the Yankees when they reached the King and Queen side being suspected, they dashed across the river as precipitately as possible under the fire of a small squad of rangers.

The Yankees had no sooner reached King and Queen County than they were harassed, both front and rear, by the Rangers, showing fight as they advanced, until Pollard was reinforced by Captain Fox of the Fifth Virginia Cavalry and some of his men then on furlough in the county, some members of Lieutenant-colonel Robins' cavalry, and a few home guards.

While Dahlgren, with his party of fugitives constantly slipping from him by straggling, and with sinking spirits, pursued the road to Walkerton, the improvised force of Confederates kept pressing him, while a detachment, making a rapid circuit, got ahead of him, and awaited his approach in the darkness of the night. Seeing some figures ahead on the road, Dahlgren rode towards them, requiring for his protection that Captain Dement, the prisoner he had taken at Frederick Hall, should ride by his side. "Surrender," he shouted, to what he supposed was a few skulkers, who would instantly accede to the command. "Fire," was the reply. "Give 'em hell, boys," yelled Pollard; and the woods were lighted up with a volley from Confederate muskets. It was enough. Dahlgren fell dead from his horse, two bullets in the head, two in the body, and one in the hand. Captain Dement's horse was shot under him. The woods were filled with fugitive Yankees, who had fled at the first volley, and who might be heard in the darkness of the night imploring the Confederates to have the kindness to come up and accept their surrender. The remnant of Dahlgren's party captured here in the night was one hundred and forty negroes and Yankees.

On the body of their leader were found the remarkable documents to which we have referred: papers showing the fiendish purpose of his expectation, and revealing to the startled sensibilities of the people of Richmond, the horrors which they had narrowly escaped.

The following address to the officers and men of the command was written on a sheet of paper having in printed letters on the upper corner, "Headquarters Third Division, Cavalry Corps, ——, 1864 :"

Officers and Men :
  You have been selected from brigades and regiments as a picked command to attempt a desperate undertaking—an undertaking which, if successful, will

write your names on the hearts of your countrymen in letters that can never be erased, and which will cause the prayers of our fellow soldiers now confined in loathsome prisons to follow you and yours wherever you may go.

We hope to release the prisoners from Belle Island firs⁺ and having seen them fairly started we will cross the James river into Richmond, destroying the bridges after us, and exhorting the released prisoners to *destroy and burn the hateful city, and do not allow the rebel leader Davis, and his traitorous crew to escape.* The prisoners must render great assistance, as you cannot leave your ranks too far, or become too much scattered, or you will be lost.

Do not allow any personal gain to lead you off, which would only bring you to an ignominious death at the hands of citizens. Keep well together and obey orders strictly, and all will be well, but on no account scatter too far ; for in union there is strength.

With strict obedience to orders, and fearlessness in the execution, you will be sure to succeed.

We will join the main force on the other side of the city, or perhaps meet them inside.

Many of you may fall ; but if there is any man here not willing to sacrifice his life in such a great and glorious undertaking, or who does not feel capable of meeting the enemy in such a desperate fight as will follow, let him step out, and he may go hence to the arms of his sweetheart, and read of the braves who swept through the city of Richmond.

We want no man who cannot feel sure of success in such a holy cause.

We will have a desperate fight ; but stand up to it when it does come, and all will be well.

Ask the blessing of the Almighty, and do not fear the enemy.

U. DAHLGREN, Colonel Commanding.

The following special orders were written on a similar sheet of paper, and on detached slips, the whole disclosing the diabolical plans of the leaders of the expedition :

"Guides—Pioneers (with oakum, turpentine, and torpedoes)—Signal Officer —Quartermaster—Commissary :

"Scouts and pickets—men in rebel uniform :

"These will remain on the north bank and move down with the force on the south bank, not getting ahead of them ; and if the communication can be kept up without giving alarm, it must be done ; but everything depends upon a surprise, and NO ONE must be allowed to pass ahead of the column. Information must be gathered in regard to the crossings of the river, so that should we be repulsed on the south side we will know where to recross at the nearest point. All *mills* must be *burned,* and the *canal destroyed ;* and also every thing which can be used by the rebels must be destroyed, including the boats on the river. Should a ferry-boat be seized, and can be worked have it moved down. Keep the force on the south side posted of any important movement of the enemy, and, in case of danger, some of the scouts must swim the river and bring us information. As we approach the city, the party must take great care that they do not get ahead of the other party on the south side, and must conceal themselves and watch our movements. We will try and secure the bridge to the city (one mile below Belle Isle), and release the prisoners at the same time. If we do not succeed, they must then dash down, and we will try and carry the bridge from each side.

"When necessary, the men must be filed through the woods and along the river bank. The bridges once secured, and the prisoners loose and over the river, the bridges will be secured and the city destroyed. The men must keep together and well in hand, and once in the city, it must be destroyed, and *Jeff Davis and Cabinet killed.*

"Pioneers will go along with combustible material. The officer must use his discretion about the time of assisting us. Horses and cattle, which we do not need immediately, must be shot rather than left. Every thing on the canal and elsewhere, of service to the rebels, must be destroyed. As General Custer may follow me, be careful not to give a false alarm.

"The signal-officer must be prepared to communicate at night by rockets, and in other things pertaining to his department.

"The Quartermasters and Commissaries must be on the lookout for their departments, and see that there are no delays on their account.

"The engineer officer will follow to survey the road as we pass over it, &c.

"The pioneers must be prepared to construct a bridge or destroy one. They must have plenty of oakum and turpentine for burning, which will be rolled in soaked balls and given to the men to burn when we get in the city. Torpedoes will only be used by the pioneers for destroying the main bridges, &c. They must be prepared to destroy railroads. Men will branch off to the right with a few pioneers and destroy the bridges and railroads south of Richmond, and then join us at the city. They must be well prepared with torpedoes, &c. The line of Falling Creek is probably the best to work along, or, as they approach the city, Goode's Creek; so that no reinforcements can come up on any cars. No one must be allowed to pass ahead, for fear of communicating news. Rejoin the command with all haste, and, if cut off, cross the river above Richmond and rejoin us. Men will stop at Bellona Arsenal and totally destroy it, and anything else but hospitals; then follow on and rejoin the command at Richmond with all haste, and, if cut off, cross the river and rejoin us. As General Custer may follow me, be careful and not give a false alarm."

The exhibition of these papers, disclosing a Yankee plot of incendiarism and murder that challenged comparison with the atrocities of the darkest ages, produced a profound sensation in Richmond. Our people, although already familiar with outrages of the enemy, were scarcely prepared to imagine such extremity of excess; while these bloody papers were to the world an important evidence of the spirit of Yankee warfare.*

---

* Yankee newspapers, with persistent hardihood, disputed the authenticity of these papers. The writer, whose relative was engaged in the affair, and who himself was familiar with all the incidents relating to these papers, may assert most positively that there is not a shadow of ground to question their authenticity. He saw the originals. In half an hour after they were found on Dahl

It is partly amusing to notice that flimsy and flippant hypo crisy which, in Yankee newspapers, declared that Dahlgren who had come on such an errand, when killed in a fight with our troops was "assassinated," or which, through the offices of an alliterative strong-minded woman, the peculiar creature of Yankeedom—one "Grace Greenwood"—apotheosized, through public lectures to Yankee soldiers, one of the worst of their kind, and proclaimed him as "the young hero of the North." The dramatic account of the stripping of the body of the marauder, and the cutting off the joint of a finger to get from it a diamond ring, is, however revolting to a tender humanity, nothing but an ordinary circumstance in a war where both sides have admitted what is indeed a deplorable practice—that of "*peeling*" on the battle-field.

But there were some acts of the Confederate authorities in relation to the Dahlgren affair, which deserved a severe censure, and which were wholly indefensible. Many persons in the Confederacy very justly thought that Dahlgren's raiders were not entitled to the privileges of prisoners of war, but should be turned over to the State authorities as thieves, incendiaries, and felons in all respects. The Confederate authorities, from motives which could only have been fear of the enemy's displeasure, declined to accede to this demand. But popular clamor was to be appeased; and to do so the old game of "retaliation" was to be played, and its plain demands put off by melodramatic expedients honorable to tell, but in reality amounting to nothing.

---

gren's body they were placed in the hands of General FitzHugh Lee; and the soiled folds of the paper were then plainly visible. The words referring to the murder of the President and his cabinet were not interlined, but were in the regular context of the manuscript. The proof of the authenticity of the papers is clinched by the circumstance that there was also found on Dahlgren's body a private note-book, which contained a rough draft of the address to his soldiers, and repetitions of some of the memoranda copied above. The writer has carefully examined this note-book—a common memorandum pocket-book, such as might be bought in New York for fifty cents—in which are various notes, some in ink and some in pencil; the sketch of the address is in pencil, very imperfect, written as one who labored in composition, crossed and recrossed. It does not differ materially in context or language from the more precise composition, except that the injunction to murder the Confederate leaders is in the rough draft made with this additional emphasis, "*killed on the spot.*"

Dahlgren's body was buried out of sight, with the puerile mystery of a concealed grave. The Libby Prison was undermined, several tons of powder put under it, and the threat made that if any demonstration on Richmond, such as Dahlgren's, was ever again to occur, the awful crime, the appaling barbarity would be committed of blowing into eternity the hundreds of helpless men confined in a Confederate prison. No one can believe that such an atrocity was ever intended, under any circumstances, to be executed by the Confederacy, or that it was any thing more than the melodrama by which our weak authorities had been accustomed to avoid the real and substantial issues of "retaliation." This was not the first instance in which the Confederacy had needlessly blackened its reputation by exaggerated pretences of retaliation, which it was thought necessary to make very ferocious in their conception, in proportion as they were to be failures in execution.

CHAPTER XI.

The Current of Confederate Victories.—THE RED RIVER EXPEDITION.—Banks' Ambitious Designs.—Condition of the Confederates West of the Mississippi.—Banks' Extensive Preparations.—A Gala Day at Vicksburg.—Yankee Capture of Fort De Russy.—Occupation of Alexandria.—Porter's Warfare and Pillage.—Banks' Continued Advance.—Shreveport, the Grand Objective Point.—Kirby Smith's Designs.—General Green's Cavalry Fight.—BATTLE OF MANSFIELD.—Success of the Confederates.—BATTLE OF PLEASANT HILL.—The Heroic and Devoted Charge of the Confederates.—The Scene on the Hill.—Banks Fatally Defeated.—Price's Capture of Yankee Trains.—Grand Results of Kirby Smith's Campaign.—Banks in Disgrace.—Yankee Tenure of Louisiana.—FORREST'S EXPEDITION INTO KENTUCKY.—His Gallant Assault on Fort Pillow.—The Yankee Story of "Massacre."—Capture of Union City.—Confederate Occupation of Paducah.—Chastisement of the Yankees on their own Theatre of Outrages—CAPTURE OF PLYMOUTH, N. C.—General Hoke's Expedition.—Capture of "Fort Wessel."—Exploit of the "Albemarle."—The Assaults upon the Town.—Fruits of its Capture.—The Yankees in North Carolina.

THE current of victory for the Confederacy was still to enlarge. The spring campaign of General Kirby Smith in the Trans-Mississippi was to terminate for us in one of the most decisive and fruitful successes of the war. On account of the remoteness of the theatre of action and its very imperfect communications with Richmond, we have now at hand but scant materials for composing the history of these events, which terminated in the overwhelming defeat of Banks, and the complete demolition of his extensive schemes in Western Louisiana and Texas.

THE RED RIVER EXPEDITION.

To understand the importance of Banks' great expedition up the Red River, it is necessary to review the military situation in the beginning of March. Sherman had returned to Vicksburg from his grand but disappointed expedition into Mississippi, and instead of directing his forces towards Mobile, the point of the greatest concern to the Confederates, he detached a portion of them to General Banks assistance, who, it appears, had predetermined on scattering or demolishing the Confederate force in West Louisiana, operating against Texas, and opening to Yankee spoliation and theft one of the richest cotton regions of the South. A very general impression existed in the North that the Confederate cause west of the Mississippi was particularly hopeless. General Steele had captured Little Rock, and was thought to have control of almost the entire country north of the Red river. General Banks had captured Brownsville, and occupied several points on the Texas coast, with Yankee forces. The discouragement of the Confederate leaders was said to be so complete that the story found believers among the Yankees that Kirby Smith had determined to pay off his army, furlough his men for an indefinite period, and then retire with his principal officers into Mexico.

The preparations of Banks, however, showed that he either contemplated a much greater resistance than what vulgar opinion in the North anticipated, or that he was determined to insure success by that exaggeration of means which timidity always suggests. The expedition had been the occasion of a complete change in his plan of military operations in the Department of the Gulf. Altogether, it was the most important military enterprise ever attempted west of the Mississippi, and the largest army ever assembled in that section (amounting, besides the fleet, to at least forty thousand men), was entrusted with its execution.

About the 1st of March the columns under General Franklin proceeded from New Orleans to Brashear City, and thence took up the line of march along the Bayou Teche. The forces under General A. J. Smith, from the Department of Tennessee, comprising the brigades under Generals F. S. Smith, Thomas, and Ellet, embarked at Vicksburg on the 10th of March, and proceeded down to the mouth of Red river, where they found a fleet of twenty gunboats ready for the ascent. The twenty transports, preceded by the twenty gunboats, started from the Mississippi on the 10th. As for the naval force of the expedition, a Northern paper stated that a more formidable fleet was never under a single command than that now on the western rivers under Admiral Porter.

The day of the embarkation at Vicksburg was a gala one for the Yankees. "The scene on the Mississippi river, opposite Vicksburg," says a Yankee correspondent, "was sublime. From the deck of this steamer, the flagship of the expedition, went up the long, shrill whistle, the signal for our departure, which was instantly answered by the immense fleet, each steamer's whistle screaming a reply, ' All ready,' in notes ranging from C sharp to B flat. In five minutes the gigantic flotilla was in motion, the variegated lights swinging to and fro from the mastheads, while the crowded decks glistened with loyal bayonets, and the cabin windows reflected a brilliant light upon the rushing waters. Add to this picture the lively music of several brass bands, the cheering of the soldiers, eager for the approaching conflict, and their simple shelter-tents spread in miniature encampments on the upper decks of the steamers, while from the monster black chimneys the sparks fell in golden showers over the whole scene, and perhaps a slight idea will be conveyed of the romantic beauty of this rare war spectacle."

The imposing expedition proceeded up the Red river without serious opposition ; and its first achievement was the capture, on the 14th of March, of Fort De Russy. The fort was easily taken by General Smith's advance, as it was garrisoned by only two or three companies of Confederates. Had it been fully manned it would have been a difficult point to capture. The fort was intended for a large force. It consisted of a very strong water-battery, mounting four guns, and a bomb-proof battery of three guns, only two of which were really mounted. Both these batteries fully commanded the approaches, and were connected with a strong fort, about a quarter of a mile to the rear, by a causeway, protected by high breastworks, thus enabling the men to pass from the battery to the fort in action with comparative safety. The bomb-proof was covered with two feet of solid timber and two layers of railroad iron of the T style, fitted into each other.

Porter's gunboats were not engaged ; and the garrison of the fort missed the coveted opportunity of testing the power of their superb water-battery. The Yankees took here two hundred and eighty-three prisoners and several heavy guns Among the prisoners taken was Lieutenant-colonel Byrd, formerly in command of the fort. He was put in double irons, and sent to the penitentiary at Baton Rouge!

Fort De Russy having fallen, Porter had no difficulty in steaming up to Alexandria, a place of about fifteen hundred inhabitants, and the county-seat of Rapides parish. It was situated on the Red river, about one hundred and fifty miles above its confluence with the Mississippi. The advance of General A. J. Smith's forces in transports, and Admiral Porter's fleet of iron-clad gunboats, anchored before the red clay bluffs of Alexandria on the evening of the 16th March.

The Yankees had now penetrated the famous cotton district of the Red river; and Porter, who had already obtained in the South the unenviable title of "the Thief of the Mississippi," took the initiative in a system of pillage that might have disgraced the most ruthless and ferocious banditti. Many of the planters applied the torch to their cotton rather than it should fall into the hands of the rapacious enemy. Porter reported to his Government that upwards of four thousand bales of cotton had been confiscated and rescued by his gunboats: a boastful estimate, much above the truth. If cotton could not be found, the Yankees had no hesitation in making prizes of other property; and when disappointed of plunder, they could at least give vent to their feelings in a spirit of destruction and wanton ferocity.

Alexandria was occupied without resistance; and from that point Smith continued his advance towards Shreveport, one hundred and seventy miles higher up Red river. In the meantime, Franklin was making his way with all haste across the country *via* Franklin, New Iberia, and Opelousas, with the intention of joining Smith at Alexandria; but he arrived at that place too late for the purpose. Smith's forces had already gone up the river, and, therefore, in order to consummate the junction, it was necessary for Franklin to move towards Shreveport over land. The Yankee army, now under command of General Banks, passed Grand Ecore, sixty miles from Alexandria, the fleet having, meanwhile, got within one hundred miles of Shreveport.

This latter place, on the Louisiana boundary, appears to have been the grand objective point of Banks' campaign. The Trans-Mississippi district might be considered as having its

centıe oı supplies and resources at Shreveport, and it was an
obvious base of operations against Texas. Appreciating its
importance, and with a view of sustaining and uniting with
Price, who was falling back in Arkansas, General Kirby
Smith, in command of the Confederates, in giving up Fort De
Russy and the adjoining country had resolved to make a stand
to cover Shreveport, and had merely designed to draw Banks
to a decisive point of the campaign.

On the 7th of April, Banks encountered a body of Confederate cavalry, under General Green, about two miles beyond
Pleasant Hill. A desultory fight ensued, in which Green's
cavalry, fighting in the strips of woods along the road, severely
harassed the Yankees. The appearance of this force had
probably taken Banks by surprise. He despatched a courier
to Franklin urging him to "hasten up," and announcing that
he was "surrounded by rebel cavalry."

BATTLE OF MANSFIELD.

Four miles from the town of Mansfield, on the 8th of April,
General Banks found himself encountered by a considerable
Confederate army, composed of forces under Kirby Smith,
Dick Taylor, Mouton, Green, and some of Price's men. The
Yankee cavalry were cautiously advancing, when the Confed-
erates suddenly assailed the enemy's front in strong force.
The contest continued fiercely for several hours, when the
Yankees were driven back with great loss, and both wings of
Banks' army flanked. A retreat appeared to be inevitable,
should the Confederates continue to assault the enemy's front.
The Yankee artillery played furiously upon the Confederate
lines. But they continued to advance boldly, our devoted
men evincing a desperate determination to conquer or perish
in the attempt. An order of retreat was at last given by
Banks. But the retreating force found the road blocked up
by their trains, which had got into confusion. The retreat
soon became a route and a panic ensued. The Confederates
pushed on in pursuit, capturing eighteen guns, all of General
Lee's wagon trains, and driving the panic-stricken mass of
fugitive Yankees for ten miles to Pleasant Hill. Here

O'Neill N.Y.

LT. GEN. KIRBY SMITH.

Franklin, who had at last come up, opened his line of battle and allowed the latter to pass. The Yankees reported their loss about fifteen hundred killed, wounded, and missing. Among the Confederates, General Mouton had fallen in the action, his body pierced by four balls.

BATTLE OF PLEASANT HILL.

The next day Banks had his forces well in hand; during the night General A. J. Smith having arrived with fresh troops. The place he had selected for a decisive battle was a large open field, once cultivated, but now overgrown with trees and bushes. In the centre of the field was a slight elevation, from which the name, Pleasant Hill, was taken; and a semicircular belt of timber ran around the field on the Shreveport side.

The engagement of the two armies was scarcely more than skirmishing until about five o'clock in the afternoon. One of the most thrilling scenes of mortal contest was now to take place. The Confederates reached the open ground and moved on to the attack in three lines of battle. The Yankee batteries and infantry opened with terrible effect, making great slaughter with grape and canister, while the Confederate artillery, being in the woods and in bad position, did scarcely any damage. The fighting was terrific. The Confederates pressed furiously on. The Yankees were pushed back, Taylor's battery taken, and the enemy's line pushed up the hill. As the second line of Confederates appeared on the crest of the hill, the death-signal was sounded, and from the long line of cannon and crouching forms of men there leaped a terrible and destroying fire. Thousands of rifles blazed away, and cannon loaded nearly to the muzzles belched forth destruction. Finding it impossible to force the enemy further, the Confederates fought their way slowly and steadily back to their original line. The enemy could not be rallied after such proof of valor. In vain General Smith ordered a charge. Night was near at hand, and the engagement dwindled into desultory skirmishing.

The loss of the enemy in this engagement is not exactly known, though probably much greater than he reported—two thousand. After the battle Banks fell back to the line of the Red River, and took position at Grand Ecore, near Nachitoches. Thus ended the fearful and bloody struggle for the control of Western Louisiana, and the important destinies it involved.

Some days later there was an exchange of fire between Porter's gunboats and a force of Confederate mounted infantry about twenty-five miles above Grand Ecore, in which, unhappily, the brave General Green was killed by the fragment of a shell.

The Yankees made various pretences to conceal the extent of their disaster. It was declared that the redoubtable Banks had only fallen back for "rest and rations," and that Steele was pushing forward from Arkansas with fifteen thousand men. The fact was that the latter commander had left Little Rock with twelve thousand infantry, and three thousand cavalry; but Price, whom he imagined he was driving helplessly before him, had turned at Camden, and captured all his trains. The Yankee version of this event was that Steele had *broken through Price's lines* and got back to Little Rock to save it from Marmaduke who was advancing upon it.

The results of the campaign of Kirby Smith were for us the most substantial ever achieved in the Trans-Mississippi. The expedition of Banks had proved a failure, and nothing was left for him but to retreat to Alexandria, after losing several thousand prisoners, and thirty-five pieces of artillery. The expedition of Steele into Western Arkansas had, as we have seen, ended in a complete disaster. The immediate points of our victories, as summed up in the official report of General Kirby Smith, were eight thousand killed and wounded, six thousand prisoners, thirty-five pieces of artillery, twelve hundred wagons, one gunboat, and three transports. These wagons comprised the whole of Steele's train, which had been captured in Arkansas. It was supposed, at one time, that the portion of Porter's fleet, above the falls at Alexandria, would have to be abandoned; but they were released from their unpleasant position by building a tree-dam of six hundred feet across the river at the lower falls, which enabled all the vessels to pass— the back-water of the Mississippi reaching Alexandria, and enabled the vessels to pass over all the shoals and the obstructions planted by the Confederates, to a point of safety.

It was late in the month of May, when Banks arrived at
h w Orleans, with the remnants of his army. In moving
across the country, during his retreat from Alexandria, he left
the Red River at Fort De Russy, and struck for Semmesport,
where he crossed the Atchafalaya, and then marched to Mor-
ganza, on the Mississippi. The complete failure of the expedition was beyond disguise, and was the topic of severe criticism in the North. Although Banks was still permitted to
remain in command of his department, as were Rosecrans and
Steele, he was placed under the order of General Canby, whose
first business was to resupply the troops brought back by General Steele and General Banks from the disastrous campaign
of the Red River, and to reorganize from these disjected materials the army of the Trans-Mississippi.

Banks' splendid empire west of the Mississippi was now
practically reduced to the tenure of New Orleans, the banks of
the river, and a strip of coast. "If," said a "loyal" observer,
at New Orleans, "our friends at the North choose to amuse
themselves with the idea that Louisiana is reclaimed, and again
loyal, we ought not to complain of so cheap an entertainment.
In truth, under the mild sway of Governor Hahn, who was
elected by several thousand majority, there is just so much of
Louisiana in the Union as is covered by our pickets. Outside
of New Orleans, no Union officer or citizen can ride alone in
safety two miles from the Mississippi, except where our organized soldiery move."

Banks had stripped the coast and frontier for his expedition
towards Shreveport. He had played a heavy stake in his
campaign, and he had plainly and irrevocably lost it.

FORREST'S EXPEDITION INTO KENTUCKY.

On the other side of the Mississippi we left Forrest, the famous cavalry chief of the West, driving back the Yankee
cavalry that had threatened to descend through Northern Mississippi with fire and sword. The unwearied Confederate was
on the war path again.

By long and rapid marches, Forrest and his men found themselves, in the month of April, on the waters of the Ohio, sweep-

ing the enemy before them, wherever they could meet the Yankees, capturing hundreds of prisoners, and valuable and needed stores in the quartermaster and ordnance departments.

On the 12th of April, at Fort Pillow, near Columbus, Kentucky, our brave men, in the face of a murderous fire from two Yankee gunboats and six pieces of artillery, stormed the works, and killed or captured the entire garrison, a motley herd of negroes, traitors, and Yankees.

The attack was made with a part of Bell's and McCullogh's brigades, under Brigadier-general J. R. Chalmers. After a short fight, we drove the enemy, seven hundred strong, into the fort under cover of their gunboats, and demanded a surrender, which was denied by Major L. W. Booth, commanding the Yankee forces. General Forrest then stormed the fort, and after a contest of thirty minutes captured the entire garrison, killing five hundred, and taking one hundred horses and a large amount of quartermaster's stores. The officers in the fort were all killed, including Major Booth. General Forrest sustained a loss of twenty killed and sixty wounded. Over one hundred citizens, who had fled to the fort from conscription, ran into the river and were drowned.

Yankee newspapers entitled this affair "the Fort Pillow Massacre." There is no doubt that, for some moments, the Confederate officers lost control of their men, who were maddened by the sight of negro troops opposing them. It is to be remarked, too, that the Yankees and negroes in Fort Pillow neglected to haul down their flag. In truth, relying upon their gunboats, the Yankee officers expected to annihilate our forces after we had entered the fortifications. They did not intend to surrender.

At the first fire, after Forrest's men scaled the walls, many of the negroes threw down their arms, and fell as if they were dead. They perished in the pretence, or could only be restored at the point of the bayonet. To resuscitate some of them, more terrified than the rest, they were rolled into the trenches made as receptacles for the fallen. This is the extent of the Yankee story of " burying negroes alive."

The fall of Fort Pillow was soon followed by the news of the surrender of Union City, and five hundred and fifty "tories," to a force under command of Colonel Falker, of Kentucky. In the meantime, Forrest had pressed rapidly to Paducah, which place was reached about ten o'clock in the morning of the 25th of April.

The Yankee force here was two thousand infantry, one negro regiment and two gunboats of large size, carrying heavy siege pieces and rifled six pounders. Two siege pieces were mounted at the fort, and a battery of light artillery inside. The attack began at once, not, however, with the object of capturing or routing the enemy here; for it was well known that he would take shelter behind his fortifications, which were strong and made impregnable by abattis, ditches and spikes; but for the purpose of getting possession of the town, and capturing or destroying the immense quantities of commissary, quartermaster, ordnance and medical supplies. The enemy was immediately driven into and beyond the town, behind his fortifications, where he was kept until night, while the Confederates were capturing or destroying his stores.

Our forces retiring at nightfall, the enemy immediately set fire to two blocks of buildings behind which our men had been fighting, fearing that the attack would be renewed in the morning. Nearly the whole town was thus burned to ashes, and great damage done to the remainder by shelling.

The results of this expedition across the State of Kentucky were especially gratifying to the Confederacy, not only for its valuable results in captures, but for the well merited chastisement it had inflicted upon the enemy in a quarter where, with his convenient allies in white "tories" and negro banditti, he had long practised with impunity the most infamous outrages. The Yankees liberally applied to this expedition the epithets of "assassination," "massacre," &c.; but these were nothing more than their usual terms for those Confederate successes under which they especially smarted.

CAPTURE OF PLYMOUTH, NORTH CAROLINA.

The detached military events of the latter part of the winter of 1863–64, and the ensuing spring—all of them successes for the Confederacy—were to be crowned with an important victory in North Carolina.

After some hesitation by the Confederate authorities, Brigadier-general Hoke, a young and energetic North Carolinian, was permitted to organize and lead an expedition against Ply mouth, on the south bank of the Roanoke, about one hundred and twenty-five miles below Weldon.

Our forces consisted of Ransom's and Hoke's North Carolina brigades, commanded by General Ransom and Colonel Mercer, of the Twenty-first Georgia; Kemper's Virginia brigade, commanded by Colonel Terry; Colonel Dearing's regiment of cavalry, and seven batteries of field artillery, under Lieutenant-colonel Branch and Major Reid—General Hoke, as senior brigadier, commanding the entire force.

For nearly twelve months the Yankees had been busy with pick and spade at Plymouth. They had thrown up a very heavy fortification in front, extending from the river to Conoby creek—a distance of a mile—with a deep ditch in front. At short intervals along this line were siege and field guns in embrasure; and in the centre was the "Williams Fort," mounting six very heavy siege and three field guns in batteries. This fort occupied a commanding elevation; was exceedingly strong, with a deep ditch and impenetrable stockade surrounding it, enclosed on all sides, and, in case of assault, was protected with a heavy gate and drawbridge, thus closing the only entrance into the fort. Inside of this line were three other forts, mounting two to four siege guns in barbette, protecting their left flank and rear. Immediately upon the river was one two-hundred-pound Parrott rifle in position. On the right flank, about six hundred yards in advance of the main line, was "Fort Wessell," similar to Fort Williams—not so large—and mounting two guns. One mile higher up the river was "Fort Warren," of like construction, mounting one one-hundred-pound Parrott, and several other guns of heavy calibre, all commanding the river and any land attack. In addition were four gunboats to co-operate with these forts.

The force in the town and at Warren Neck consisted of the Sixteenth Connecticut, Eighty-fifth New York, One Hundred and First and One Hundred and Third Pennsylvania, two companies of Massachusetts heavy artillery, one battery of light artillery, and two squadrons of cavalry, the whole commanded by Brigadier-general Wessell, of the old United States army.

On the 17th of April, our forces were within two miles of

Plymouth, having marched through swamps and across swollen creeks a distance of seventy-five miles without the knowledge of the enemy. Kemper's brigade, with a battery of twelve pounder Napoleons and three twenty-pounder Parrotts, was detached to attack Warren Neck, a strong position on the river a mile above the town, which the enemy thought, and we feared, would effectually stop the passage of our " ram "—the Albemarle—and so deprive us of her valuable aid.

About sunset, Dearing and Reid, with their rifle artillery, opened a brisk fire upon Fort Warren, at fifteen hundred yards, with marked effect, soon cutting down the garrison flag-staff. The gunboats steamed up to the assistance of the fort. One was speedily sunk and another seriously damaged.

Early the next morning, our artillery under Colonel Branch opened a heavy fire upon the enemy's works, which they vigor-ously responded to. That afternoon General Hoke determined to carry " Fort Wessell " with his and Kemper's brigades, and one battery under Major Reid ; he ordered Ransom, with his brigade, and Branch, with fourteen pieces of artillery, to make a heavy demonstration simultaneously with his attack.

Ransom's brigade, with the 8th North Carolina, was drawn up in the woods, facing the works on the Washington, Lee's Mill, and Bath roads. A heavy line of skirmishers was thrown out, and advancing rapidly with the peculiar gait of the sharp-shooters, and the yell with which Confederate troops go to the charge, drove the enemy back into his works, and approached within two hundred and fifty yards of the fort, earnestly de-manding to be led into the place. Meanwhile, Pegram's bat-tery dashed forward at a run, supported by the infantry, and unlimbering, delivered a furious fire upon the devoted place. Three times the infantry advanced, each time nearer, until within good charging distance ; but the artillery had it all to themselves. The movement was merely a demonstration to call off the enemy's attention from Hoke's attack upon Fort Wessel.

The enemy being now fully engaged on the right, General Hoke made a vigorous attack upon Fort Wessell with artillery and infantry—the enemy opposing a spirited resistance. Our infantry again and again charged the fort, the enemy hurling at them hand-grenades ; but the strong stockade, deep ditch, and high parapet prevented our men from scaling it. During one of these charges, the intrepid Colonel Mercer, commanding Hoke's brigade, fell mortally wounded at the head of his command. Finally, our infantry surrounded the fort, the artillery advanced to within two hundred yards of it, and Colonel Dearing, in behalf of General Hoke, demanded a surrender of the place, which was immediately complied with, and fifty-two prisoners marched to the rear.

About two o'clock the next morning, our iron-clad, the Albemarle, mounting two Brooke rifled guns, and commanded by Captain Cooke, passed easily over the obstructions from the high water, passed Fort Warren without eliciting a shot, our sharpshooters so closely investing the fort that the cowardly cannoniers would not man their guns. Steaming just below Plymouth, she met the Miami, commanded by Flusser, and the Southfield, under French. They were side by side of each other and connected by heavy iron cables, with the hope of entangling the Albemarle and running her ashore, or breaking her propeller, and then boarding her. Each of these boats carried eight guns of very heavy calibre, and were regarded equal to any in the waters of Eastern Carolina. The gallant Cooke headed directly for the Southfield, gave her the contents of his bow gun, and striking her forward with his prow, she immediately began to sink, and with such rapidity, that before the Albemarle could disengage herself she was well nigh carried down, water running in at her ports. This occasioning some delay, the Miami fled, but not until she was severely punished, her commander, Flusser, and many of her crew being killed.

Having obtained possession of Fort Wessell, General Hoke arranged his forces for an assault upon the town, sending Ransom on the right to make a demonstration or attack as he thought best, while Hoke, with his and Kemper's brigades, would attack on the left.

At early dawn on the morning of the 28th, our infantry moved forward, and our artillery, consisting of Blount's, Marshall's, and Lee's batteries, under Colonel Branch, dashed forward at a full gallop into position, and opened immediately upon the town and forts at about twelve hundred yards. The enemy by this time had concentrated a most terrific fire from their siege and field guns. Just at this time General Hoke opened, with his artillery, a very rapid and tremendous fire, and his infantry sent up yell after yell as if charging. Ransom caught the sound, and rising in his stirrups, from the head and right of the line, in a clear and ringing voice gave the command, "Charge, boys, and the place is yours."

In ten minutes the two outer forts, with eight guns, were captured, our infantry scaling their parapets, and the artillery within one hundred and fifty yards of the forts, horses and limbers blown up and cannoniers shot down, and yet those remaining stood to their guns, without shelter, confident of victory and to avenge their dead. The whole command, officers and men, infantry and artillery, seemed enthused with the inspiration of certain victory. Several hundred prisoners were captured in these forts, which were immediately sent to the rear, and now began the contest for the town, more than half a mile in length, the enemy's infantry slowly retiring, and stubbornly resisting our advance; Fort Williams dealing out grape and spherical case; their field-pieces, at the further extremities of the broad, straight streets, raking them with a murderous fire; their infantry, in the houses and cellars, and behind fences, delivering galling charges of minies; but all of no avail; our men were aroused, confident, and irresistible. They pressed on steadily, without halt or hesitation, tearing down fences, hedges, and every obstacle that they met, capturing the enemy at every step.

The town was ours. But still Wessell, shut up in his stronghold, Fort Williams, refused to yield. A heavy cannonade was opened upon the fort, and the garrison was galled by our sharpshooters. At last some of the Confederates, creeping forward through the intrenchments, got an enfilading fire upon them, which soon brought them to terms, and hundreds of them rushed out of the fort without arms and surrendered. Just at this time a shell burst directly on the magazine, and when the smoke cleared away, the hated flag was fluttering rapidly down to the ground.

The fruits of this capture were sixteen hundred prisoners, twenty-five pieces of artillery, vast quantities of commissary and quartermaster supplies, and immense ordnance stores. Our loss in killed and wounded was about three hundred. We had also destroyed two gunboats, and with all, had obtained the strong position of Plymouth, which protected the whole Roanoke valley.

The Yankees now held but two places on the North Carolina coast, Washington, at the mouth of Tar river, and Newbern, at the mouth of the Neuse. The latter was strongly garrisoned, but the larger part of the forces at Washington had been moved up to Plymouth. It was supposed that General Hoke would prosecute his campaign against Newbern; but his forces were suddenly to be recalled to more imposing scenes, and to a participation in the great crisis of 1864 in Virginia.

CHAPTER XII.

Close of the Third Year of the War.—Sketch of the Subsequent Operations in Virginia and Georgia.—GRANT's "ON-TO-RICHMOND."—The Combination Against the Confederate Capital.—THE BATTLES OF THE WILDERNESS.—A Thrilling Crisis.—Grant on the Verge of Rout.—His First Design Baffled.—THE BATTLES OF SPOTTSYLVANIA COURT-HOUSE.—Death of General Sedgwick.—THE CARNAGE OF MAY THE 12TH.—Five Battles in Six Days.—Grant's Obstinacy.—" The Butcher."—Sheridan's Expedition.—Death of General "Jeb" Stuart.—Butler's Operations on the South Side of the James.—" The Beast" at the Back-Door of Richmond.—He is Driven to Bermuda Hundred by Beauregard.—Defeat of Sigel in the Valley.—Grant's Movement Down the Valley of the Rappahannock.—His Passage of the Pamunkey.—Re-organization of General Lee's Lines.—Grant's Favorite Tactics.—Yankee Exultation at his Approach to Richmond—Caricatures of the Confederacy.—A Hasty Apotheosis.—A True Theory of Grant's " Flank Movements."—His Occupation of McClellan's Old Lines.—THE BATTLE OF THE CHICKAHOMINY OR COLD HARBOR.—A Confederate Victory in Ten Minutes.—What Had Become of Yankee Exultation.—Review of the Rival Routes to Richmond.—Grant Crosses the James River.—His Second Grand Combination Against Richmond.—Hunter's Capture of Staunton.—THE BATTLES OF PETERSBURG.—General Wise's Heroic Address.—Engagement of 16th June.—Grand Assault of 18th June.—on " the Cockade City."—A Decisive defeat of the Yankees.—Engagement at Port Walthal Junction—Sheridan's Defeat Near Gordonsville.— Hunter's Repulse at Lynchburg.—Two Affairs on the Weldon Railroad.—Grant's Second Combination a Complete Failure.—Discouragement of the North.—The Gold Barometer.—Secretary Chase's Declaration.—SHERMAN's " ON-TO-ATLANTA."—His Flanking Movement.—Engagement in Resaca Valley.—Johnston's Retreat —Engagement at New Hope.—Johnston's Telegram to Richmond.—Defeat of Sturgis's Expedition in Mississippi.—BATTLE OF KENESAW MOUNTAIN.—Sherman's Successful Strategy.—The Confederates Fall Back to Atlanta.—THE BATTLES OF ATLANTA.—Hood's Gallant Defence.— . . . . The Military Situation in July, 1864.—Grant's Failure.—His Consumption of Troops.—Review of Yankee Atrocities in the Summer Campaign of 1864.—Sherman's Character.—His Letter on " Wild Beasts."—His War on Factory Girls.—Sufferings of Confederate Women and Children.—Ravages in Georgia.—Hunter's Vandalism in Virginia.—" The Avengers of Fort Pillow."—Sturgis and his Demons.—The Spirit of the Confederates.— . . . Some Words on " Peace Negotiations."—A Piratical Proposition and an Infamous Bribe.—The Heroic Choice of the Confederates.

THE third year of the war closes properly at the month of May, according to our arrangement of dates in preceding volumes. But on account of the magnitude of what is closely subsequent, it is thought advisable to give a summary and very general SKETCH of the material events of the enemy's two grand campaigns of the summer of 1864—the parallel operations of Grant and Sherman in Virginia and in Georgia;—at least, so

far as to bring the reader to a stand-point of intelligent observation, with reference to questions of peace and negotiation
which were agitating the public mind at the time these pages
were committed to the press. We shall follow their campaigns
only to what appear to be their decisive stages in June and
July. The period we shall thus rapidly traverse we hope to
go over in another volume with a more perspicuous narrative,
and certainly with much more abundant detail.

GRANT'S " ON-TO-RICHMOND."*

General Ulysses S. Grant was now to answer the eager expectation of the public by a campaign of unrivalled importance
in Virginia. He had hitherto been known in the North as the
great General of the West, and the Yankee newspapers had
entitled him the hero of Fort Donelson, Shiloh, and Vicksburg. His elevation had been rapid. Four years ago the
man who commanded all the armies of the North had been a
tanner, and at the beginning of the war had been accidentally
selected to lead a regiment of raw recruits.

From the moment of receiving his commission as Lieutenant-
General, Grant had transferred his personal presence to the
Army of the Potomac, leaving Sherman as his vicegerent to
carry out the Western campaign. Warren, Sedgwick, and
Hancock, were made the corps commanders of this army, and
Burnside was given a separate army corps. Butler at Fortress
Monroe was reinforced by the Tenth corps from Charleston
under Gilmore, and the Eighteenth from the West, under
"Baldy" Smith. To the infamous hero of New Orleans was
allotted the task of cutting off the city of Richmond from its
southern lines of communication; while Sigel operating in the
Shenandoah Valley was to cut the railroad which by way or
Gordonsville connected Lee's army with his principal base of
supplies at Lynchburg.

Thus were the preparations completed for the most momen
tous campaign in American history. On Wednesday, May 4,
just eight weeks from the day Grant received his commission, his two grand columns were ready to move—the one

---

* This, and the subsequent sketches of battles in this chapter, are treated
more fully in chapters xiv., xv., and xvi.

well in hand on the north bank of the Rapidan, seventy miles north of Richmond, and the other at Fortress Monroe, one day's sail from Richmond on the James.

THE BATTLES OF THE WILDERNESS.

At dawn on the 5th of May, the Army of the Potomac, closely succeeded by that of Burnside, had crossed the Rapidan river; the Second corps at Ely's, the Fifth and Sixth corps at Germania ford. Having crossed the river, the first demonstration of the enemy was an attempt to turn the right flank of Lee's army, between the Orange Court-house pike and the river. The assault was sustained by Heth and Wilcox's divisions of the Confederate Army, during the entire day; and that it was successfully sustained even the Northern accounts do not hesitate to admit. "No cheer of victory," says a Northern correspondent," swelled through the Wilderness that night."

During the day Hancock, Second corps, had come up, and the Federal forces were concentrated. On the morning of the 6th their lines were consolidated and freshly posted; the three corps sustaining their respective positions—Warren in the centre, Sedgwick on the right, and Hancock on the left.

The attack was made by the Confederates; Hill and Longstreet's corps attacking both of Hancock's flanks with such fury, that the whole line of command thus assaulted is broken in several places. The effort, however, of the Confederates to pierce the enemy's centre is stayed, the Yankees having secured their line of battle behind their entrenchments.

But with the expiration of the day was to occur a thrilling and critical conjuncture. Just at dusk (the Confederates' favorite hour of battle) a column of Lee's army attacked the enemy's left, captured Seymour and a large portion of his brigade, and excited a panic which put Grant's whole army on the verge of irretrievable rout. Unfortunately, the Confederates had no idea of the extent of their success, and could not imagine how fraught with vital issue were those few moments of encounter. The Yankee supply trains were thought to be immediately threatened, and artillery was posted to bear upon the Confederate advance in that direction. But the Confederates did not press their advantage. As it was, Generals Shaler and Seymour, with the greater part of their commands, were taken prisoners.

Such had been the two days' battle of the Wilderness : a marked success for the Confederates, disputed by the Northern newspapers, of course, but manifest in the face of the facts. The enemy confessed to a loss of twelve thousand. The immediate consequence of these engagements was, that Grant being clearly outgeneralled in his first design of reaching Lee's rear and compelling him to fight a battle with his communications cut off, which would be decisive of the campaign, was forced to change his plans, and with it his position ; falling back to his entrenched line, between the Wilderness and Trigg's Mill, nearly coincident with the Brock road, leading from the Wilderness to Spottsylvania Court-house.

On the 7th, with some desultory fighting, Grant continued his movement towards Fredericksburg, with the evident view of attempting the Fredericksburg road to Richmond. It was in consequence of this change of front that General Lee took up a new line on the Po. It will amuse the candid reader to find how this movement was interpreted by the mendacious press of the North ; for, in the newspapers of New York and Boston it was entitled, in flaming capitals, " A Waterloo Defeat of the Confederates," " The Retreat of Lee to Richmond," &c. For a few days the North was vocal with exultation, and for the hundredth time it had the Rebellion "in a corner," to be conveniently strangled. But this imagination of easy conquest was to be dissipated as the many that had preceded it.

THE BATTLES OF SPOTTSYLVANIA COURT-HOUSE.

On the 8th of May two engagements were fought at Spottsylvania Court-house, between Longstreet's corps, under Anderson (General Longstreet having been wounded in the battle of the 6th) and the Fifth corps, under Warren, supported by cavalry. The enemy was repulsed, with heavy loss, in both instances.

On the 9th, which was marked by some skirmishing, General John Sedgwick, one of the most valuable corps commanders in the Yankee army, was killed, probably by a stray bullet. He had just been bantering his men about dodging and ducking their heads at the whistle of Confederate bullets in the distance. "Why," said he, "they couldn't hit an elephant at this distance." The next moment a ball entered his face, just below the left eye, and pierced his brain, causing instant death.

On Thursday, the 12th of May, occurred what may be entitled as the great battle of Spottsylvania Court-house. The enemy had planned an attack on what was supposed to be a vital section of the Confederates, a salient angle of earthworks held by Johnson's division of Ewell's corps. The storming column advanced silently, and without firing a shot, up to the angles of the breastworks, over which they rushed, taking the forces within in flank, surrounding them, capturing nearly the entire division of Johnson's, with its commander, and also a brigade or two of other troops, Brigadier-general George H. Stuart in command.

But the surprise was only momentary. For long hours a battle raged over those intrenchments, the intense fury, heroism, and horror of which it is impossible to describe. From dawn to dusk the roar of guns was ceaseless; a tempest of shell shrieked through the forest and ploughed the field. Ewell's corps held the critical angle with a courage that nothing could subdue. General Hill moved down from the right, joined Ewell, and threw his divisions into the struggle. Longstreet came on from the extreme left of the Confederate line. Column after column of the enemy was hewn down, or repulsed and sent back like a broken wave. At all points the enemy was repulsed with enormous loss. The ground in front of the Confederate lines was piled with his slain.

The sixth day of heavy fighting had been ended. "It would," says an intelligent critic of this period, "not be impossible to match the results of any one day's battle with stories from the wars of the old world; but never, we should think, in the history of man were five such battles as these compressed into six days." Grant had been foiled; but his obstinacy was apparently untouched, and the fierce and brutal consumption of human life, another element of his generalship, and which had already obtained for him with his soldiers the soubriquet of " the butcher," was still to continue. He te.e graphed to Washington : " I propose to fight it out on this line, if it takes all summer."

But we must turn for a few moments from this dominant field of action and interest to notice other movements, which were parts of Grant's combination, and of the great military drama in Virginia.

While Grant was engaged on the Rapidan, a cavalry expedition of the enemy, commanded by General Sheridan, moved around Lee's right flank to the North Anna river ; committed some damage at Beaver Dam ; moved thence to the South Anna and Ashland station, where the railroad was destroyed ; and finally found its way to the James at Turkey Island, where it joined the forces of Butler. The damage inflicted by this raid was not very considerable ; but it was the occasion of a severe fight, on the 10th May, at Yellow Tavern, on the road to Richmond, where Sheridan encountered a Confederate cavalry force, in which engagement was lost the valuable life o. General J. E. B. Stuart, the brilliant cavalry commander, who had so long made Virginia the theatre of his daring and chiv alric exploits.

The column of Butler, the important correspondent to Grant's movement, intended to operate against Richmond on the south side, had raised the hopes of the North merely to dash them by a failure decisive in its character, and ridiculous in all its circumstances. On the 5th of May, Butler proceeded with his fleet of gunboats and transports, and the Tenth and Eighteenth army corps, up the James river, landing at Wilson's Wharf a regiment of Wild's negro troops, and two brigades of the same color at Fort Powhatan ; thence up to City Point, where Hinks' division was landed ; and at Bermuda Hundred, just below the mouth of the Appomattox, the entire army was disembarked.

On the 7th, five brigades, under General Brooks, struck for the Petersburg and Richmond Railroad, and succeeded in destroying a bridge seven miles north of Petersburg. In the mean time, Butler, after intrenching himself, closed about the defences of Drury's Bluff. The Yankee general seemed confi-

O'Neill, N.Y.

GEN. J. E. B. STUART.

From a Photograph taken from life.

dent that he could, by a little fighting, in conjunction with the powerful flotilla upon the James, easily overcome the main barrier to his approach to the rear of the Confederate capital, presented in the defences of Drury's Bluff. It was already announced to the credulous public of the North that Butler had cut Beauregard's army in twain; that he had carried two lines of the defences of Drury's Bluff; and that he held the keys to the back-door of Richmond.

On Monday, the 16th of May, General Beauregard fell upon the insolent enemy in a fog, drove Butler from his advanced positions back to his original earthworks, and inflicted upon him a loss of five thousand men in killed, wounded, and captured. He had fallen upon the right of the Yankee line of battle with the force of an avalanche, completely crushing it backward and turning Butler's flank. The action was decisive. The day's operations resulted in Butler's entire army being ordered to return from its advanced position, within ten miles of Richmond, to the line of defence known as Bermuda Hundred, between the James and Appomattox rivers.

While Butler had thus come to grief, the failure of Sigel, who threatened the valley of Virginia, was no less complete. On the 15th his column was encountered near Newmarket by General Breckinridge, who drove it across the Shenandoah, captured six pieces of artillery and nearly one thousand stand of small arms, and inflicted upon it a heavy loss; Sigel abandoning his hospitals and destroying the larger portion of his train.

We left Grant defeated in the action of the 12th in front of Spottsylvania Court-house. On the 14th, he moved his lines by his left flank, taking position nearer the Richmond and Fredericksburg railroad. On the 18th he attempted an assault on Ewell's line, which was easily repulsed. It was admitted by the enemy that the object of this attack was to turn Lee's left flank, and that their line got no further than the abattis, when it was "*ordered*" back to its original position.

A new movement was now undertaken by Grant: to pass his army from the line of the Po, down the valley of the Rappahannock. It thus became necessary for General Lee to evacuate his strong position on the line of the Po; and by an admirable movement he had taken a new position between the

North and South Anna, before Grant's army had arrived at the former stream. Having cut loose from Fredericksburg as a base (and established depots on the Lower Rappahannock), on the 21st Grant's forces occupied Milford Station and Bowling Green, and were moving on the well known high roads to Richmond. But they were again intercepted; for Lee had planted himself between Grant and Richmond, near Hanover Junction.

On the 23d, and on the 25th, Grant made attempts on the Confederate lines, which were repulsed, and left him to the last alternative. Another flanking operation remained for him, by which he swung his army from the North Anna around and across the Pamunkey. On the 27th, Hanovertown was reported to be occupied by the Yankee advance under General Sheridan; and on the 28th Grant's entire army was across the Pamunkey.

In the mean time, General Lee also reformed his line of battle, north and south, directly in front of the Virginia Central railroad, and extending from Atlee's Station, south, to Shady Grove, ten miles north of Richmond. In this position he covered both the Virginia Central and the Fredericksburg and Richmond railroads, as well as all the roads leading to Richmond, west of, and including the Mechanicsville pike.

The favorite tactics of Grant appear to have been to develope the left flank; and by this characteristic maneuver, he moved down the Hanover Court-house road, and on the first day of June took a position near Cold Harbor.

Grant was now within a few miles of Richmond. The vulgar mind of the North readily seized upon the cheap circumstance of his proximity in miles to the Confederate capital, and exclaimed its triumph. The capture of Richmond was discounted as an event of the next week. The Yankee periodicals were adorned with all those illustrations which brutal triumph could suggest; Grant drubbing Lee across his knee; the genius of Yankee liberty holding aloft an impersonation of the Southern Confederacy by the seat of the breeches, marked "Richmond;" Jefferson Davis playing his last card, ornamented with a crown of death's heads, and with his legs well girt with snakes; and a hundred other caricatures alike characteristic of the vulgar thought and fiendish temper of the Yankee.

To such foolish extremity did this premature celebration go that a meeting was called in New York to render the thanks of the nation to Grant, and twenty-five thousand persons completed the hasty apotheosis.

But for the candid and intelligent, the situation of Grant was one of sinister import to him, implied much of disaster, and was actually a consequence of his repeated disappointments. The true theory of it was defeat, not victory. He did nothing more than hold the same ground as that occupied by General McClellan in his first peninsular campaign. This position, had he come by that point, a day's sail from Washington, he could have occupied without the loss of a single man. But he had occupied it by a devious route; with a loss variously estimated at from sixty to ninety thousand men; with the consumption of most of his veteran troops, whom he had put in front; with the disconcert and failure of those parts of the drama which Butler and Sigel were to enact; and with that demoralization which must unavoidably obtain in an army put to the test of repeated defeats and forced marches.

What was represented by the enemy as the retreat of General Lee's army to Richmond, was simply its movement from a position which its adversary had abandoned, to place itself full before him across the new road on which he had determined to travel. In this sense, it was Grant who was pursued. He had set out to accomplish Mr. Lincoln's plan of an overland march upon Richmond. Mr. Lincoln's scheme as detailed by himself, in his famous letter to General McClellan, was to march by the way of the Manassas railroad. The first movement of General Grant was to give up that route, and fall back upon the line by which Generals Burnside and Hooker attempted to reach the Confederate capital—that is, the Fredericksburg and Richmond line. But, repulsed at Spottsylvania, this route proved untenable, and General Grant was forced east and south, and adopted a new base at Port Royal and Tappahannock, on the Rappahannock river, which conformed in a measure to General McClellan's first plan of a march upon Richmond by way of Urbana. The next change Grant was compelled to make was, after finding how strong the Confederates were, as posted on the South Anna, to cross the Pamunkey and make his base at the White House, bearing thereafter still further east and south to the precise ground of McCle.lan's operations.

The significance of all these movements was, that Grant had utterly failed in his design of defeating Lee's army far from its base, and pushing the fragments before him down to Rich mond, and had been forced to cover up his failure by adopting the derided scheme of McClellan. The event of the 12th or May at Spottsylvania Court-house, had settled the question whether he could beat Lee in the field and put him in a dis-astrous retreat. Unable to remove the obstacle on the thresh-old of his proposed campaign, nothing was left but to abandon it. Grant makes his way down the valley of the Rappahan-nock; turns aside to Hanover Junction, to find a repetition of Spottsylvania Court-house; deflects to the headwaters of the York; and at last, by a monstrous circuit, reaches a point where he might have landed on the 1st of May, without loss or opposition. We may appreciate the amount of gaseous non-sense and truculent blackguardism of Yankee journals, when we find them declaring that these movements were a footrace for Richmond, that Grant was across the last ditch, and that the end of the rebellion was immediately at hand.

THE BATTLE OF THE CHICKAHOMINY, OR COLD HARBOR.

But we must return to the events on the Richmond lines. The position occupied by Grant on Wednesday, 1st of June, had been obtained after some fighting, and by the enemy's own admission had cost him two thousand men in killed and wounded. An important and critical struggle was now to ensue. Grant had secured a position, the importance of which was that it was the point of convergence of all the roads, radi-ating whether to Richmond—his objective point, or to White House—his base of supplies. He was now to essay the pas-sage of the Chickahominy, and we were to have another deci-sive battle of Cold Harbor.

There is good evidence that Grant's intention was to make it the decisive battle of the campaign. The movements of the preceding days, culminating in the possession of Cold Harbor —an important strategic point—had drawn the enemy's lines close in front of the Chickahominy, and reduced the military problem to the forcing of the passage of that river—a problem which, if solved in Grant's favor, would decide whether Richmond could be carried by a *coup de main*, if a decisive victory should attend his arms, or, whether he should betake himself to siege operations or some other recourse.

Early on the morning of Friday, June 3d, the assault was made, Hancock commanding the left of the Yankee line of battle, and leading the attack. The first Confederate line was held by Breckinridge's troops, and was carried. The reverse was but momentary, for the troops of Millegan's brigade and the Maryland battalion, soon dashed forward, to retrieve the honors which the Yankees had snatched.

On every part of the line the enemy was repulsed by the quick and decisive blows of the Confederates. Hancock's corps, the only portion of the Yankee army that had come in contact with the Confederate works, had been hurled back in a storm of fire; the Sixth corps had not been able to get up further than within two hundred and fifty yards of the main works; while Warren and Burnside, on the enemy's right and right centre, were staggered on the lines of our rifle pits. The decisive work of the day was done *in ten minutes*. Never were there such signal strokes of valor; such despatch of victory. It was stated in the accounts of the Confederates that fourteen distinct assaults of the enemy were repulsed, and that his loss was from six to seven thousand. No wonder that the insolent assurance of the capture of Richmond was displaced in the Yankee newspapers by the ominous calculation that Grant could not afford many such experiments on the entrenched line of the Chickahominy, and would have to make some other resort to victory.

The battle of Cold Harbor was sufficient to dispel the delusion of weakness and demoralization in Lee's army; for this derided army, almost in the time it takes to tell the story, had repulsed at every point the most determined assault of the enemy, and in the few brief moments of a single morning had achieved an unbroken circuit of victories. Grant and his friends were alike dismayed. The latter insisted that he should have half a million more of men to accomplish his work. "We should," said a Boston paper, "have a vigorous and overwhelming war, or else peace without further effusion of blood." A certain portion of the Yankee press maintained th unbroken lie, and told the story of an uninterrupted series o victories.

An object of most curious and constant interest in the war was the rivalry of the different routes to Richmond. McClellan had chosen the peninsular approach, while Mr. Lincoln dissented in favor of an advance from the Lower Rappahannock, Burnside had chosen Fredericksburg as his base; Hooker had acted on the same choice. Meade had selected the Rapidan, as Pope had done before him. Grant came to his command, unembarrassed and untrammeled by the precedents and comments of others. He had hunted up the roads to Richmond, through the Wilderness and Spottsylvania Courthouse, and avowed his unchangeable purpose to adhere to that as his true line. He had now wandered around to McClellan's old base. But the battle of July 3d, decided that Richmond could no longer be approached with advantage from the North, and the disconcerted, shifting commander, with his stock of expedients well-nigh exhausted, found nothing now left for him but to transfer his entire army to the south side of the James river.

On the 5th of June Hunter had obtained a success at Piedmont, in Western Virginia, and had effected the capture of Staunton; the saddest circumstance of which affair was the loss of General W. E. Jones, one of the most distinguished cavalry commanders of the Confederacy.

After occupying Staunton, Hunter had formed a junction with the combined forces of Crook and Averill, and on the 13th of June was reported to be moving with his whole command against Lynchburg. On the 7th, Sheridan had crossed the Pamunkey, and was moving eastward in the direction of the Gordonsville railroad. The main movement of the new combination—that of Grant across the James—commenced Sunday night the 12th of June.

The first plan of the enemy had comprehended the advance of Sigel down the Shenandoah, and the capture of Petersburg, if nothing more, by Butler, while General Grant engaged Lee's army between the Rapidan and Richmond. That plan having signally failed, the second comprised the capture of

Lynchburg by Hunter, of Gordonsville and Charlottesville by Sheridan, and of Petersburg by Meade. It was thus hoped to isolate the Confederate capital by cutting off its communications on every side.

It was, perhaps, not Grant's design to cross the river until he had made some attempt on the Central and New Market roads leading into Richmond from the direction of Malvern Hill. On the 13th June, he caused a reconnoissance in force to be made from the Long Bridge toward the Quaker road, and in an affair near the intersection of this road with the Charles City road was repulsed, and drew off his forces, well satisfied that the Confederates held with heavy forces all the roads by which Richmond could be reached from the southeast.

The Eighteenth Yankee corps had proceeded by water to Bermuda Hundred. The remaining corps had crossed the Chickahominy at James Bridge and Long Bridge; and after the reconnoissance of the 13th, proceeded down the James, and crossed in the neighborhood of City Point.

THE BATTLES OF PETERSBURG.

Petersburg had already sustained a considerable attack of the enemy. An expedition from Butler's lines had essayed its capture on the 9th of June.

Approaching with nine regiments of infantry and cavalry, and at least four pieces of artillery, the enemy searched our lines, a distance of nearly six miles. Hood's and Batles' battalions, the Forty-sixth Virginia, one company of the Twenty-third South Carolina, with Sturdevant's battery, and a few guns in position, and Talliaferro's cavalry, kept them at bay The Yankees were twice repulsed, but succeeded at last in penetrating a gap in our line; when reinforcements coming up drove back the insolent foe from approaches which their footsteps for the first time polluted.

The fortunate issue of this first attack on Petersburg encour aged the raw troops and militia who had been put under arms for the defence of "the Cockade City." General Wise addressed the troops of his command in a memorable and thrill ing order; "Petersburg," said he, "is to be, and shall be defended on her outer walls, on her inner lines, at her corporation bounds, in every street, and around every temple of God, and altar of man."

The resolution of the gallant city—with its defences reinforced by the fortunate Beauregard—was now to be put to a much more severe test, for it was to encounter the shock of the bulk of Grant's army.

Smith's corps having disembarked at Bermuda Hundred on the 14th, moved rapidly upon Petersburg, and made an assault on the batteries covering the approaches to the city on the north-east. Having got possession of this line of works, held principally by Confederate militia, Smith waited the coming up of the Second corps.

On the evening of the 16th, an attack was ordered on the Confederate line of works in front of Petersburg, Smith's corps being on the right, on the Petersburg and City Point road, west of the railroad, the Second corps in the centre, and Burnside on the left, reaching the Prince George Court-house road. The assault was not only repulsed at every point, but our troops, assuming the aggressive, drove the Yankees from their breastworks, at Howlett's House, captured some of their guns, and opened upon them an enfilading fire, under which they fled precipitately.

The most furious assault of the enemy had been made on General Hoke's front, whose division occupied a position facing batteries from Nine to Twelve inclusive. Three different charges were repulsed by these heroic troops. In the final repulse of the enemy, a large portion of a Yankee brigade, being exposed to an enfilading artillery fire from our guns, sought shelter in a ravine, and surrendered to the Sixty-fourth Georgia regiment.

On Friday, 17th June, fighting was renewed without result. The next day, it was resolved by the enemy to make an assault along the whole line for the purpose of carrying the town. It was thus that the action of the 18th was designed to be decisive of operations on the present position.

Three different assaults were made by the enemy during the day—at four in the morning, at noon, and at four in the afternoon. Each one was repulsed. Hancock and Burnside in the centre suffered severely. After severe losses on the part of all the Yankee corps, night found the Confederates still in possession of their works covering Petersburg.

The disaster of this day left Grant without hope of making any impression on the works in his front, and placed him under the necessity of yet another change of operations. The series of engagements before Petersburg had cost him at least ten thousand men in killed and wounded, and had culminated in another decisive defeat.

The misfortune of the enemy appeared, indeed, to be overwhelming. Pickett's division had given him another lesson at Port Walthal Junction. It was here the heroes of Gettysburg repulsed a force under Gilmore engaged in destroying the railroad, took two lines of his breastworks and put him to disastrous flight.

Nor was there any compensation to be found in the auxiliary parts of Grant's second grand combination. Sheridan had failed to perform his part. He was intercepted by Hampton's cavalry at Trevillian station on the Gordonsville road, defeated in an engagement on the 10th, and compelled to withdraw his command across the North Anna. Hunter had come to similar grief, and his repulse at Lynchburg involved consequences of the gravest disaster to the enemy.

On the 18th of June, Hunter made an attack upon Lynchburg from the south side which was repulsed by troops that had arrived from General Lee's lines. The next day, more reinforcements having come up, preparations were made to attack the enemy, when he retreated in confusion. We took thirteen of his guns, pursued him to Salem, and forced him to a line of retreat into the mountains of Western Virginia. The attempt of the Yankees to whitewash the infamous and cowardly denouement was more than usually refreshing. Hunter officially announced that his expedition had been "extremely successful;" that he had left Lynchburg because "his ammunition was running short;" and that as to the singular line he had taken up, he was now "ready for a move in any direction."

But the measure of misfortune in Grant's distracted campaign appeared to be not yet full. On the 22d he made a movement on his left to get possession of the Weldon railroad, but found the Confederates had extended their right to meet him. While the Second and the Sixth corps of Grant's army were attempting to communicate in this movement, the Confederates, under General Anderson, pierced the centre, captured a battery of four guns and took prisoners one entire brigade, General Pearce's, and part of another.

Another attempt or raid on the railroad, by Wilson's and Kautz's divisions of cavalry was terminated in disaster. In the neighborhood of Spottswood river, twenty-five miles south of Petersburg, on the 28th, the expedition was attacked, cut in two, the greater part of its artillery abandoned and its wagon trains left in the hands of the Confederates. The enemy had been encountered by Hampton's cavalry, and Finnegan's and Mahone's infantry brigades; and the results of the various conflicts were enumerated as one thousand prisoners, thirteen pieces of artillery, thirty wagons and ambulances, and many small arms.

It was evident that the spirit of the North had commenced to stagger under this accumulation of disaster. Gold had already nearly touched three hundred. The uneasy whispers in Washington of another draft gave new suggestions to popular discontent. The Confederate Congress had adjourned after the publication of an address referring to recent military events and the confirmed resolution of the South, and deprecating the continuance of the war. These declarations were eagerly seized upon by Northern journals, who insisted that no time should be lost in determining whether they might not possibly signify a willingness on the part of the South to make peace on the basis of new constitutional guaranties. The finances at Washington were becoming desperate. Mr. Chase, the Secretary of the Treasury, had peremptorily resigned. His last words of official counsel were, that nothing could save the finances but a series of military successes of undoubted magnitude.

SHERMAN'S " ON-TO-ATLANTA."

Simultaneously with Grant's advance on Richmond, Sherman moved on Dalton in three columns: Thomas in front, Schofield from Cleveland on the north-east, while McPherson

threw himself on the line of communication south-west at Resaca, fifteen miles south of Dalton. On the 7th of June
Thomas occupied Tunnel Hill, ten miles north-west of Dalton
and took up a strong position at Buzzard's Roost. By the
flank movement on Resaca, Johnston was forced to evacuate
Dalton.

On the 14th the first important battle of the campaign was
ought in Resaca valley. Two efforts were made to carry the
breastworks of the Confederates, without success, when Johnston in the afternoon assumed the offensive and drove the enemy some distance, with a loss which his own bulletins stated
to be two thousand.

On the 15th, there was desultory fighting, and on the 16th
General Johnston took up at leisure his line of retrograde
movement, in the direction of the Etowah river, passing
through Kingston and Cassville. At both places the enemy
was held in check. From Cassville, Sherman, having sent
the right of his army by way of Rome, moved his centre and
left across the Etowah west of the railroad, and then marched
towards Dallas.

On the 28th, General Cleburne's division of Johnston's army
engaged the advance corps of the enemy under General Mc-
Pherson at New Hope, and signally repulsed him, with heavy
loss. So far, the retrograde movement of Johnston was, in
some respects, a success; it had been attended with at least
two considerable victories; it had been executed deliberately,
being scarcely ever under the immediate pressure of the enemy's advance; and it had now nearly approached the decisive
line of the Chattahoochee or whatever other line he, who was
supposed to be the great strategist of the Confederacy, should select for the cover of Atlanta. The events of the campaign, so far,
were recounted with characteristic modesty by General Johnston. On the 1st of June, he telegraphed to Richmond of his
army: "In partial engagements it has had great advantages,
and the sum of all the combats amounts to a battle."

In the mean time, the two armies continued to maneuver
for position. Sherman held both Altoona and Ackworth with
out a battle, the latter about twelve miles from Marietta. It
was said that these positions would enable him to maintain his
lines of communications with Chattanooga by railway intact,

and clear his rear of Confederates; but he found Johnston opposing him with a strong rear-guard, and drawn close to his supplies in Atlanta and Augusta.

While these events were transpiring in Georgia, an important event had taken place in the Southwest: the defeat of the Yankee expedition under Sturgis on its way from Memphis to operate in Sherman's rear. In this action, at Guntown, Mississippi, Sturgis lost most of his infantry and all of his artillery and trains, and the Confederates, under Forrest, achieved a victory that had an important influence on the campaign in Georgia. Forrest took two thousand prisoners, and killed and wounded an equal number.

BATTLE OF KENESAW MOUNTAIN.

On the 27th of June, General Sherman directed an attack on Johnston's position at Kenesaw Mountain. This mountain was the apex of Johnston's lines. Both armies were in strong works, the opposite salients being so near in some places that skirmishers could not be thrown out. The assault of the enemy was made in three columns, about eight o'clock in the morning. It was repulsed on every part of the Confederate line. The loss of the enemy was considerable, even as stated in his own official reports. General McPherson reported his loss about five hundred, and Thomas, his, about two thousand.

In consequence, however, of a flanking movement of the enemy on the right, Johnston on the 3d of July abandoned the mountain defence and retired toward Atlanta.

It is true that Johnston's retreat to the immediate lines of Atlanta, was consummated without any considerable military disaster. But it was a sore disappointment to the public; for it had given up to the Yankees half of Georgia, abandoned one of the finest wheat districts of the Confederacy, almost ripe for harvest, and at Rome and on the Etowah river, had surrendered to the enemy iron-rolling mills, and government works of great value.

THE BATTLES OF ATLANTA.

But a lesson was reserved for Sherman on the Atlanta lines by the gallant and impulsive Lieutenant-general Hood, who had taken command of the army that Johnston had, by a long and negative campaign, brought back to Atlanta.

We shall not attempt here the details of the great battles of Atlanta.

On the 20th of July, Hood attacked the enemy's right on Peach-tree creek, near the Chattahoochee, driving him from his works, and capturing colors and prisoners.

On the 22d of July, Hood's army shifted its position fronting on Peach-tree creek, and Stewart's and Cheatham's corps formed line of battle around the city. Hardee's corps made a night march and attacked the enemy's extreme left at one o'clock, on the 22d, and drove him from his works, capturing sixteen pieces of artillery and five stands of colors. Cheatham attacked the enemy at four o'clock in the afternoon, with a portion of his command, and drove the enemy, capturing six pieces of artillery. During the engagement we captured about two thousand prisoners.

After the battle of the 22d, Sherman's army was transferred from its position on the east side of Atlanta to the extreme right of Hood's army, on the west side, threatening the Macon road. Lieutenant-generals Stewart and Lee were directed by Hood to hold the Lickskillet road for the day with their commands. On the 28th, a sharp engagement ensued, with no advantage to either side; the Confederate loss fifteen hundred killed and wounded.

The results of these battles were, on the whole, a most encouraging success for the Confederates; revived their hopes on what had been considered a doubtful theatre of action; and left Sherman, although still holding his lines of investment, in a most critical condition, with an army, several hundred miles in its country, having its rear exposed, and depending upon a single line of railroad for its communications.

We may take leave here of the military situation; satisfied

that a pause had now been given to the parallel operations of
the enemy in Virginia and Georgia : aimed, the one at Richmond, which the Yankees entitled the heart and brains of the
Confederacy ; and the other at Atlanta, the centre of important manufacturing enterprises, and the door to the great
granary of the Gulf States.   Both movements were now
unmistakably in check ; and the interlude of indecision afforded a curious commentary on the boastful confidence that had
recorded the fall of Richmond and the capture of Atlanta as
the expectations of each twenty-four hours.

There was reason, indeed, for the North to be depressed.
The disappointment of the Yankees was with particular reference to the campaign of Grant in Virginia.   The advance
from the Rapidan, which we have followed to its recoil before
Petersburg, had been made under conditions of success which
had attended no other movement of the enemy.   It was made
after eight months' deliberate preparation.   In the Congress
at Washington it was stated that, in these eight months, the
Government had actually raised seven hundred thousand men
—an extent of preparation which indicated an intention to
overwhelm and crush the Confederacy by a resistless combined attack.   Nor was this all.   One hundred thousand
three-months' men were accepted from Ohio and other States,
for defensive service, in order that General Grant might avail
himself of the whole force of trained soldiers.   The result of
the campaign, so far, did not justify the expectations on which
it had been planned.   The Yankee Government which, since
the commencement of the war, had called for a grand total of
twenty-three hundred thousand men, and had actually raised
eighteen hundred thousand men, of an average term of service
.f three years, to crush the Confederacy, saw in the fourth
year of the war the Confederacy erect and defiant, and Richmond shielded by an army which had so far set at nought the
largest preparations and most tremendous exertions of the
North.

We cannot close this brief sketch of important parts of the
summer campaign of 1864, in Virginia and in the West, without adverting to the barbarities of the enemy, which especially
marked it, and which, indeed, by regular augmentatio
became more atrocious as the war progressed.   In this year

they exceeded all that was already known of the brutal.ty of our enraged enemy.

General Sherman illustrated the campaign in the West, by a memorable barbarity, in a letter of instructions to General Burbridge, commanding in the Department of Kentucky, charging him to treat all partisans of the Confederates in that State as "*wild beasts.*" It was the invariable and convenient practice of the Yankees to designate as "guerillas," whatever troops of the Confederates were particularly troublesome to them; and the opprobrious term was made, by General Sherman, to include the regularly commissioned soldiers of General Morgan's command, and whatever bodies of Confederate cavalry chose to roam over territory which the enemy disputed.*

Some expressions, in the orders referred to, were characteristic of the Yankee, and indicated those notions of constitutional law which had rapidly demoralized the North. General Sherman declared that he had already recommended to Governor Bramlette of Kentucky, "at one dash to arrest every man in the country who was dangerous to it." "The fact is," said this military Solomon, "in our country personal liberty has been so well secured that public safety is lost sight of in our laws and institutions; and the fact is we are thrown back one hundred years in civilization, laws, and every thing else,

---

* Burbridge was not slow to carry out the suggestions or instructions of his masters. The following is a copy of a section of one of his orders:

HEADQUARTERS DISTRICT KENTUCKY,)
FIFTH DIVISION, TWENTY-THIRD ARMY CORPS, }
LEXINGTON, Kentucky, July 16, 1864.)

Rebel sympathizers living within five miles of any scene of outrage committed by armed men, not recognized as public enemies by the rules and usages of war, will be arrested and sent beyond the limits of the United States.

In accordance with instructions from the major-general commanding the military district of the Mississippi, so much of the property of rebel sympathizers as may be necessary to indemnify the Government or loyal citizens for losses incurred by the acts of such lawless men, will be seized and appropriated for this purpose.

Whenever an unarmed Union citizen is murdered, four guerillas will be selected from the prisoners in the hands of the military authorities, and publicly shot to death in the most convenient place near the scene of outrage. By ommand of

Brevet Major-general S. G. BURBRIDGE.
J. B. DICKSON, Captain and A. A. General.

and will go right straight to anarchy and the devil, if some-
body don't arrest our downward progress. We, the military,
must do it, and we have right and law on our side. . . . .
Under this law everybody can be made to stay at home and
mind his or her own business, and, if they won't do that, can
be sent away." These sage remarks on American liberty were
concluded with the recommendation that all males and
females, in sympathy with so-called " guerillas," should be
arrested and sent down the Mississippi to some foreign land,
where they should be doomed to perpetual exile.

As Sherman advanced into the interior of Georgia he laid
waste the country, fired the houses, and even did not hesitate
at the infamous expedient of destroying the agricultural implements of all those who produced from the soil subsistence for
man. He declared to the persecuted people that this time he
would have their property, but, if the war continued, next
year he would have their lives. Four hundred factory girls
whom he captured in Georgia he bundled into army wagons,
and ordered them to be transported beyond the Ohio, where
the poor girls were put adrift far from home and friends, in a
strange land.*

---

* The following announcement appeared in the Louisville newspapers :—

" ARRIVAL OF WOMEN AND CHILDREN FROM THE SOUTH.—The train which arrived
from Nashville last evening brought up from the South two hundred and forty-nine
women and children, who are sent here by order of General Sherman, to be transferred north of the Ohio river, there to remain during the war. We understand that
there are now at Nashville fifteen hundred women and children, who are in a very
destitute condition, and who are to be sent to this place to be sent North. A number of them were engaged in the manufactories at Sweet Water, at the time that
place was captured by our forces. These people are mostly in a destitute condition,
having no means to provide for themselves a support. Why they should be sent
here to be transferred North is more than we can understand."

It was also stated in these same papers that, when these women and children
arrived at Louisville, they were detained there and advertised to be hired out
as servants, to take the place of the large number of negroes who have been
liberated by the military authorities and are now gathered in large camps
throughout Kentucky, where they are fed and supported in idleness and
viciousness at the expense of the loyal taxpayers. Thus, while these negro
women are rioting and luxuriating in the Federal camps, on the bounty of the
Government, the white women and children of the South are arrested at their
homes, and sent off as prisoners to a distant country, to be sold in bondage as
the following advertisement fully attests :—

' NOTICE.—Families residing in the city or the country, wishing seamstress.

From Chattanooga to Marietta there was presented to the eye one vast scene of misery. The fugitives from ruined villages or deserted fields sought shelter in the mountains. Cities were sacked, towns burnt, populations decimated. All along the roads were great wheat-fields, and crops sufficient to feed all New England, which were to be lost for want of laborers. The country had been one of the most beautiful of the Confederacy. One looked upon the gentle undulations of the valleys, terminating in the windings of the rivers, and flanked by the majestic barriers of the mountains. This beautiful country had been trodden over by both armies. In every town the more public buildings and the more conspicuous residences had been devoured by fire, or riddled with shot and shell. Every house used as headquarters, or for Confederate commissary stores, or occupied by prominent citizens, had been singled out by the enemy for destruction. In some instances churches had not escaped. They had been stripped for fire-wood or converted into barracks and hospitals. Fences were demolished, and here and there a lordly mansion stood an unsightly ruin.

The vandalism of Hunter in Virginia drew upon him the censure of the few journals in the North which made any pretension to the decencies of humanity. At Lexington, he had burned the Virginia Military Institute with its valuable library, philosophical and chemical apparatus, relics and geological specimens; sacked Washington College, and burned the house of ex-Governor Letcher, giving his wife only ten minutes to save a few articles of clothing.

In the Southwest, the hellish crimes of the enemy were enough to sicken the ear. The expedition of Sturgis, defeated, as we have seen, in Mississippi by Forrest, flourished the title of the "Avengers of Fort Pillow." "Before the battle," says a correspondent, "fugitives from the counties through which Sturgis and his troops were advancing, came into camp detailing incidents which made men shudder, who are accustomed to scenes of violence and bloodshed. I cannot relate the stories of these poor frightened people. Robbery, rapine, and the assassination of men and women, were the least crimes com

servants, can be suited by applying at the refugee quarters on Broadway, between Ninth and Tenth. This is sanctioned by Captain Jones, Provost Marshal."

mitted, while the 'Avengers of Fort Pillow' overran and desolated the country. Rude unlettered men, who had fought at Shiloh, and in many subsequent battles, wept like children when they heard of the enormities to which their mothers, sisters, and wives had been subjected by the negro mercenaries of Sturgis."

Such enormities were monstrous enough; they shocked the moral sentiment of the age; yet they did not affright the soul of the South. The outrages practised upon helpless women, more helpless old age, and hopeless poverty, assured the people of the Confederacy of the character of their enemies, and the designs of the war, and awakened resolution to oppose to the last extremity the mob of murderers and lawless miscreants who desecrated their soil and invaded their homes. The war had obtained this singular hold on the minds of the Confederates; that every man considered that he had in it the practical, individual stake of his personal fortunes. When such a sentiment pervades a nation in war, who can say when or how it may be conquered!

. . . . . At the time these pages are given to the press, it appears that the great disappointment of the North in the results of the summer campaign of 1864, has given rise to a certain desire to end the war by negotiations, and that this desire has found some response in the South. The undignified and somewhat ridiculous overtures for peace made in this summer by parties, who, on each side, anxiously disclaimed that they had any authority from their governments, but, on each side, by a further curious coincidence, represented that they were acquainted with the wishes and views of their governments, cannot be altogether a story of egotistical adventures. They betray the incipiency, though an obscure one, of negotiations; and the times are rapidly making developments of the tendency of an appeal to compose the war.

We cannot anticipate what bribes may be offered the South to confederate again with the North. But one has been already suggested in the North: it is, to find an atrocious compensation for the war in a combined crusade against foreign nations.

The New York *Herald* declares: "With a restored Union, prosperity would once more bless the land. If any bad blood remained on either side, it would soon disappear, or be purged by a foreign war. With a combined veteran army of over a million of men, and a fleet more powerful than that of any European power, we could order France from Mexico, England from Canada, and Spain from Cuba, and enforce our orders if they were not obeyed. The American continent would then belong to Americans. The President at Washington would govern the New World, and the glorious dreams and prophecies of our forefathers would at length be realized."

To a proposition of such infamy of infamies, the attention of the civilized world should be called. What a commentary upon that European policy which has lavished so much of sympathy and material comfort upon the North, and, on the other hand, has rejected the cause of a people, who as they are resolute in maintaining their own rights, are as equally, indeed expressly and emphatically, innocent of any designs on the right and welfare of others! The suggestion is, that of a huge and horrible Democracy, eager to prey upon the rights of others, and to repair by plunder and outrage the cost of its feuds and the waste of its vices.

The people of the Confederacy do not easily listen to suggestions of dishonor. Yet none are more open to the cunning persuasion which wears the disguise of virtuous remonstrance and friendly interest. It is here where the Yankee peacemaker is to be resisted and unmasked.

It will be for the Confederacy to stand firm in every political conjuncture, and to fortify itself against the blandishments and arts of a disconcerted and designing enemy. It will remember that enemy's warfare. It will remember that an army, whose *personnel* has been drawn from *all parties* in the North, has carried the war of the savage into their homes. It will remember how Yankees have smacked their lips over their carnage and the sufferings of their women and little ones. It will remember how New England clergymen have advised that "rebels," men, women and children, should be sunk beneath the Southern sod, and the soil "salted with Puritanical blood, to raise a new crop of men." To hate let us not reply with hate. We reply with the superiority of contempt, the resolution of pride, the scorn of defiance. Surely, rather than reunite with such a people; rather than cheat the war of "independence," and make its prize that cheap thing in American history--a paper guarantee; rather than cheat our dead of that for which they died; rather than entitle ourselves to the contempt of the world, the agonies of self-accusation, the reproof of the grave, the curses of posterity, the displeasure of the merciful God who has so long signified His providence in our endeavors, we are prepared to choose more suffering, more trials, even utter poverty and chains, and exile and death.

CHAPTER XIII.

AMERICAN IDEAS: A REVIEW OF THE WAR.

Sentimental Regrets concerning American History.—The European Opinion of 'State" Institutions.—Calhoun, the Great Political Scholar of America.—His Doctrines.—*Conservatism* of "Nullification."—Its "Union" Sentiment.—Brilliant Vision of the South Carolina Statesman.—Webster, the Representative of the Imperfect and Insolent "Education" of New England.—Yankee Libels in the shape of Party Nomenclature.—Influence of State Institutions.—How they were Auxiliary to the Union.—*The Moral Veneration of the Union Peculiarly a Sentiment of the South.*— What the South had done for the Union.—Senator Hammond's Speech.—The States, not Schools of Provincialism and Estrangement.—The Development of America, a North and South, not Hostile States.—Peculiar Ideas of Yankee Civilization.—Ideas Nursed in "Free Schools."—Yankee Materialism.—How it has Developed in the War.—Yankee Falsehoods and Yankee Cruelties.—His Commercial Politics.—Price of his Liberties.—Ideas of the Confederates in the War.—How the Washington Routine was introduced. — The Richmond Government, Weak and Negative.— No Political Novelty in the Confederacy.—The Future of Confederate Ideas.— Intellectual Barrenness of the War.—Material of the Confederate Army.—The Birth of Great Ideas.—The Old Political Idolators.—The Recompense of Suffering.

It has been a sentimental regret with certain European students of American History that the colonies of America, after acquiring their independence, did not establish a single and compact nationality. The philosophy of these optimists is that the State institutions were perpetual schools of provincialism, selfishness, and discontent, and that they were constantly educating the people for the disruption of that Union which was only a partial and incomplete expression of the nationality of America. These men indulge the idea that America, as a nation, would have been colossal; that its wonderful mountains and rivers, its vast stretch of territory, its teeming wealth, and the almost boundless military resources, which the present war has developed and proved, would then have deen united in one picture of grandeur, and in a single movement of sublime, irresistible progress.

These are pretty dreams of ignorance. Those who ascribe to the State institutions of America our present distractions, and discover in them the nurseries of the existing war, are essentially ignorant of our political history. They are strangers to the doctrines of Calhoun of South Carolina—the first name in the political literature of our old government—the first man who raised the party controversies of America to the dignity of a political philosophy and illuminated them with the lights of the patient and accomplished scholar.

The great political discovery of Mr. Calhoun was this : that the rights of the States were the only solid foundation of the Union ; and that, so far from being antagonistic to it, they con stituted its security, realized its perfection, and gave to it all the moral beauty with which it appealed to the affections ot the people. It was in this sense that the great South Carolina statesman, so frequently calumniated as "nullifier," agitator, &c , was indeed the real and devoted friend of the American Union. He maintained the rights of the States—the sacred distribution of powers between them and the general government—as the life of the Union, and its bond of attachment in the hearts of the people. And in this he was right. The State institutions of America, properly regarded, were not discordant ; nor were they unfortunate elements in our political life. They gave certain occasions to the divisions of industry ; they were instruments of material prosperity ; they were schools of pride and emulation ; above all, they were the true guardians of the Union, keeping it from degenerating into that vile and short-lived government in which power is consolidated in a mere numerical majority.

Mr. Calhoun's so-called doctrine of Nullification is one of the highest proofs ever given by any American statesman ot attachment to the Union. The assertion is not made for para doxical effect. It is clear enough in history, read in the severe type of facts, without the falsehoods and epithets of that Yankee literature which has so long defamed us, distorted our public men, and misrepresented us, even to ourselves.

The so-called and miscalled doctrine of Nullification marked one of the most critical periods in the controversies of America, and constitutes one of the most curious studies for its philosophic historian. Mr. Calhoun was unwilling to offend the popular idolatry of the Union ; he sought a remedy fo existing evils short of disunion, and the consequence was what was called, by an ingenious slander, or a contemptible stupidity, Nullification. His doctrine was, in fact, an accommodation of two sentiments: that of Yankee injustice and that of reverence of the Union. He proposed to save the Union by the simple and august means of an appeal to the sovereign States that composed it. He proposed that should the general government and a state come into conflict, the power should be invoked that called the general government into existence, and gave it all of its authority. In such a case, said Mr. Calhoun, "the States themselves may be appealed to, three-fourths of which, in fact, form a power whose decrees are the Constitution itself, and whose voice can silence all discontent. The utmost extent, then, of the power is, that a State acting in its sovereign capacity, as one of the parties to the constitutional compact, may compel the government created by that compact to submit a question touching its infraction to the parties who created it." He proposed a peculiar, conservative, and noble tribunal for the controversies that agitated the country and threatened the Union. He was not willing that vital controversies between the sovereign States and the general government should be submitted to the Supreme Court, which properly excluded political questions, and comprehended those only where there were parties amenable to the process of the court. This was the length and breadth of Nullification. It was intended to reconcile impatience of Yankee injustice, and that sentimental attachment to the Union which colors so much of American politics; it resisted the suggestion of revolution; it clung to the idolatry of the Union, and marked that passage in American history in which there was a combat between reason and that idolatry, and in which that idolatry made a showy, but ephemeral conquest.

The doctrine, then, of Mr. Calhoun was this: he proposed only to constitute a conservative and constitutional barrier to Yankee aggression; and, so far from destroying the Union, proposed to erect over it the permanent and august guard of a tribunal of those sovereign powers which had created it. It was this splendid, but hopeless vision of the South Carolina statesman, which the North slandered with the catch-word of Nullification; which Northern orators made the text of indignation; on which Mr. Webster piped his schoolboy rhetoric;

and on which the more modern schools of New England have exhausted the lettered resources of their learned blacksmiths and Senatorial shoemakers. Mr. Webster, the representative of that imperfect and insolent education peculiar to New England, appears never to have known that Mr. Calhoun's doctrine was not of his own origination; that its suggestion, a least, came from one of the founders of the republic. We refer to that name which is apostolic in the earliest party divisions of America, and the enduring ornament of Virginia—Thomas Jefferson, the Sage of Monticello. At a late period of his life, Mr. Jefferson said: "With respect to our State and Federal governments, I do not think their relations are correctly understood by foreigners. They suppose the former subordinate to the latter. This is not the case. They are co-ordinate departments of one simple and integral whole. But you may ask if the two departments should claim each the same subject of power, where is the umpire to decide between them? In cases of little urgency or importance, the prudence of both parties will keep them aloof from the questionable ground; but, if it can neither be avoided nor compromised, a Convention of the States must be called to ascribe the doubtful power to that department which they may think best."

Here was the first suggestion of the real safety of the Union; and it was this suggestion, reproduced by Calhoun, which the North slandered as Nullification, insulted as heresy, and branded as treason.

It is a remarkable circumstance that the South should have tamely allowed the Yankees to impose upon her political literature certain injurious terms, and should have adopted them to her own prejudice and shame. The world takes its impression from names; and the false party nomenclature which the North so easily fastened upon us, and which survives even in this war, has had a most important influence in obscuring our history, and especially in soliciting the prejudices of Europe.

The proposition of Mr. Calhoun to protect the Union by a certain constitutional and conservative barrier, the North designated Nullification, and the South adopted a name which was both a falsehood and a slander. The well-guarded and moderate system of negro servitude in the South, the North called Slavery; and this false and accursed name has been permitted to pass current in European literature, associating and carrying with it the horrors of barbarism, and defiling us in the eyes of the world. The Democratic party in the South, which claimed equality under the Constitution, as a principle, and not merely as a selfish interest, was branded by the North as a pro-slavery party, and the South submitted to the designation.

How little that great party deserved this title was well illustrated in the famous Kansas controversy; for the history of that controversy was simply this: the South struggled for the principle of equality in the Territories, without reference to the selfish interests of so-called Slavery, and even with the admission of the hopelessness of those interests in Kansas; while the North contended for the narrow, selfish, practical consequence of making Kansas a part of her Free-soil possessions. The proofs of this may be made in two brief extracts from these celebrated debates. These are so full of historical instruction that they supply a place here much better than any narrative or comment could do:

Mr. ENGLISH, of Indiana.—I think I may safely say that there is not Southern man within the sound of my voice who will not vote for the admission of Kansas as a Free state, if she brings here a Constitution to that effect Is there a Southern man here who will vote against the admission of Kansa as a Free State, if it be the undoubted will of the people of that Territory tha it shall be a Free State?

MANY MEMBERS.—Not one.

At another stage of the Kansas debate occurs the following:

Mr. BARKSDALE, of Mississippi.—I ask you, gentlemen, on the other side of the House, of the Black Republican party, would you vote for the admission of Kansas into the Union, with a Constitution tolerating Slavery, if a hundred thousand people there wished it?

Mr. GIDDINGS, of Ohio.—I answer the gentleman that I will never associate, politically, with men of that character, if I can help it. I will never vote to compel Ohio to associate with another Slave State, if I can prevent it.

. . . .

Mr. STANTON.—I will say, if the gentleman will allow me, that the Republican members of this House, so far as I know, will never vote for the admission of any Slave State north of 36° 30'.

We return to the influence of State institutions on America. We contend that they were not hostile to the Union, or malignant in their character; that, on the contrary, they were auxiliary to the Union; that they stimulated the national progress; that, in fact, they interpreted the true glory of America; and that it was especially these modifications of our national life which gave to the Union that certain moral sublimity so long the theme of American politicians. From these propositions we advance to a singular conclusion. It is that the moral veneration of the Union, which gives the key to so much of American history, was peculiarly a sentiment of the South; while in the North it was nothing more than a mere affectation.

This may sound strange to those who have read American history in the smooth surface of Yankee books; who remember Webster's apostrophes to the glorious Union, and Everett's silken rhetoric; whose political education has been manufactured to hand by the newspapers, and clap-traps of Yankee literature about " nullification" and treason. But it is easy of comprehension. The political ideas of the North excluded that of any peculiar moral character about the Union; the doctrine of State Rights was rejected by them for the prevalent notion that America was a single democracy; thus, the Union to them was nothing more than a geographical name, entitled to no peculiar claims upon the affections of the people. It was different with the South. The doctrine of State Rights gave to the Union its moral dignity; this doctrine was the only real possible source of sentimental attachment to the Union; and this doctrine was the received opinion of the Southern people, and the most marked peculiarity of their politics. The South did not worship the Union in the base spirit of commercial idolatry, as a painted machinery to secure tariffs and bounties, and to aggrandize a section. She venerated the Union because she discovered in it a sublime moral principle; because she regarded it as a peculiar association in which sovereign States were held by high considerations of good faith; by the exchanges of equity and comity; by the noble attractions of social order; by the enthused sympathies of a common destiny of power, honor, and renown. It was this galaxy which the South wore upon her heart, and before the clustered fires of whose glory she worshipped with an adoration almost Oriental. That Union is now dissolved; that splendid galaxy of stars is no more in the heavens; and where once it shone, the fierce comet of war has burst, and writes a red history on the azure page.

But let this be said by the historian of this war: that the South loved the Union; dissolved it unwillingly; and, though she had had the political administration of it in her hands during most of its existence, surrendered it without a blot on its fame. "Do not forget," said a Southern Senator, when Mr. Seward boasted in the United States Senate that the North was about to take control at Washington, "it can never be forgotten—it is written on the brightest page of human history— that we, the slaveholders of the South, took our country in her infancy, and, after ruling her for sixty out of the seventy years of her existence, we shall surrender her to you without a stain upon her honor, boundless in prosperity, incalculable in her strength, the wonder and the admiration of the world. Time will show what you will make of her; but no time can ever diminish our glory or your responsibility."

But there is one conclusive argument which we may apply to the common European opinion, and the half-educated notion of this country that the State institutions of America were schools of provincialism and estrangement. If such had been the case, the dissolution of the Union would have found the States that composed it a number of petty principalities opposed to each other, or, at least, diverse and heterogeneous. But this war has found no such thing. It has found the people of Virginia and Tennessee, the people of Missouri and South Carolina, entertaining the same political ideas, pursuing a single, common object in the war, and baptizing it in a common bloodshed on its fields of contest and carnage. The States of the Southern Confederacy offer to the world the example of its inhabitants as one people, homogeneous in their social systems, alike in their ideas, and unanimous in their resolves; and the States of the North afford similar illustrations of national unity. The war has found not discordant States, but two distinct nations, in the attitude of belligerents, differing in blood, in race, in social institutions, in systems of popular instruction, in political education and theories, in ideas, in manners; and the whole sharpened by a long and fierce political controversy, that has arrayed them at last as belligerents, and interposed the gage of armed and bloody contest. The development of America has been a North and a South; not discordant States, but hostile nations. The present war is not for paltry theories of political parties, or for domestic institutions, or for rival administrations, but for the vital ideas of each belligerent, and the great stakes of national existence.

What have been the ideas which the North has developed or illustrated in this war? We will answer briefly.

The North presents to the world the example of a people corrupted by a gross material prosperity; their ideas of government, a low and selfish utilitarianism; their conceptions of civilization, prosperous railroads, penny newspapers, showy churches. Their own estimates of their civilization never penetrated beyond the mere surface and convenience of society; never took into account its unseen elements; the public virtue, the public spirit, the conservative principle, the love of order, the reverence of the past, all which go to make up the grand idea of human civilization.

It is amusing to the student of history to hear Mr. Sumner of Massachusetts, asserting, with scholarly flourishes, that the South is barbarous, because she has no free schools: the source of that half education in the North, which have been nurserie. of insolence, irreverence of the past, infidelity in religion, and an itch for every new idea in the mad calendar of social reforms. It is yet more amusing to hear his Senatorial peer— "the Natick cobbler." When, on the eve of the downfall of the government at Washington, a Southern Senator depicted the wealth that the South had poured into the lap of the Union, the elements it had contributed to its civilization, and the virtues it had brought to its adornment, Mr. Wilson, of Massachusetts, had this reply: "Massachusetts has more religious newspapers than all the slaveholding States of the Union."

The people of the North have never studied politics as a moral science. They have no idea of government as an independent principle of truth, virtue and honor; to them it is merely an engine of material prosperity—a mere auxiliary appendage to a noisy, clattering world of trade, and steam, and telegraphs. It is this low commercial sense of government which developed all the old Yankee theories of tariffs, and bounties, and free farms.

Indeed, the most fruitful study in American politics is the peculiar materialistic idea of the Yankee. Its developments are various, but all held together by the same leading idea: superficial notions of civilization; agrarian theories; the subordination of the principles of government to trade; mercantile "statesmanship;" the exclusion of moral ideas from politics; the reduction of the whole theory of society to the base measure of commercial interests. Such are some of the developments of the materialistic idea: the last and fullest is the present war.

This war, on the part of the Yankee, is essentially a war of interest: hence its negation, on his part, of all principles and morals; hence its adoption of that coarse maxim of commercial casuistry, "*the end justifies the means;*" hence its treachery, its arts of bad faith, its "cuteness" on all belligerent questions; hence its atrocities which have debased the rules of civilized warfare to a code of assassins and brigands. It is true that the North has affected in this war such sentiments as love of the Union, reverence of the American nationality, a romantic attachment to the old flag. But we repeat that the proof that the North has fought for coarse, material interests in this war is the conduct of the war itself.

War is horrible; but it has its laws of order and amelioration. Civilization has kindled the dark cloud of horrors with the vestal observances of honor; and the undying lights of humanity have irradiated its aspects—softened the countenance of the Giant who

> " On the mountain stands,
> His blood-red tresses deepening in the sun,
> With death-shot glowing in his fiery hands."

But where, in this war of the Yankee, shall we find exhibitions of the chivalry and amenity of modern belligerents. A ghostly echo comes shrieking from fields blackened by fire, and scarred and tormented by the endless scourge of the tyrant. The characteristics of the Yankee war are precisely those which arise out of the materialistic idea: treachery dignified as genius, and cruelty set up to gaze as the grandeur of power.

The crooked woof of treachery—the scarlet thread of the lie—
have been woven by the Yankee into every part of this war.*
It is not necessary to unravel here the whole story of Yankee
falsehood. One instance will suffice. The government which
at the commencement of hostilities, played at the game of con
ciliation by affecting to arrest on the streets of its capital,
Washington, fugitive slaves, and to return them to their masters; which, in the first months of the war, declared that it
" repudiated all designs whatever, and wherever imputed to it,
of disturbing the system of slavery; " that any such effort
would be " unconstitutional; " and that " all acts of the President in that direction would be prevented by the judicial authority, even though they were assented to by Congress and
the people "—for such was the solemn assurance of Mr. Sew-

---

* It is a curious fact, in the indisputable records of American History, that
the separation of the Southern States from the Union, is defensible, in all respects; that is, as an assertion of *State rights*, and, again, as an assertion of the
still higher principle of self-government—on grounds taken by our enemies,
when it suited them to take those grounds.

With reference to the ground of State Rights:

At the third session of the Eleventh Congress, in 1811, the dissolution of the
Union was spoken of for the first time, by a member from the State of Massachusetts. The bill to form a Constitution and State Government for the Territory of Orleans, and the admission of such State, under the name of Louisiana,
into the Union, was under consideration.

" Mr. Quincy, of Massachusetts, in opposition to the bill, said : ' I am compelled to declare it as my deliberate opinion, that if this bill passes, the bonds
of this Union are virtually dissolved; that the States which compose it are free
from their obligations, and that, as it will be the right of all, so it will be the
duty of some, to prepare definitely for a separation—amicably, if they can;
violently, if they must.'

" Mr. Quincy was here called to order by Mr. Poindexter.

" Mr. Quincy repeated and justified the remark he had made, which, to save
all misapprehension, he committed to writing in the following words : 'If
this bill passes, it is my deliberate opinion that it is virtually a dissolution of
this Union; that it will free the States from their moral obligations, and, as it
will be the right of all, so it will be the duty of some, definitely to prepare for
a separation—amicably, if they can; violently, if they must.' "

In 1844, the Legislature of Massachusetts resolved that the annexation of
Texas would be cause of dissolution of the Union.

With reference to the other, higher ground of Self-Government:

Abraham Lincoln, now President at Washington said : " Any people, anywhere, being inclined and having the power, have the right to rise up and
shake off the existing Government, and form a new one that suits them better
Nor is this right confined to cases where the people of an existing Government

ard's diplomatic circular of 1861; which promised the South "the Constitution as it was," and recited poetry in Congress entreating South Carolina to return to the bosom of the Union is to-day found making the boast—rather, we may say, indulging the fiendish exultation—that it has Abolitionized every district it has invaded ; that it has forced into military service one hundred thousand blacks, stolen from their masters; that it has forcibly consigned them from peaceful occupations to the perils of the battle-field ; and that it has whetted their ignorant and savage natures with an appetite for the blood of the white man of the Confederacy. And this stupendous lie is called the genius of Yankee statesmanship, and the world is asked to applaud it.

But it is in the atrocious warfare of the enemy that we find the most striking instances of his exclusion of that noble spirituality common to the great conflicts of civilized nations, and the most characteristic evidence of the brutal selfishness of his hostilities. The Yankee has never shown mercy in this war, and not one touch of refinement from his hand has relieved its horrors. The track of his armies has been marked by the devouring flame, or by the insatiate plunder and horrid orgies of a savage and cowardly foe. The weed-growth of Louisiana, where once flourished the richest plantations of the South; the desert that stretches from the Big Black to the

---

may choose to exercise it. Any portion of such people that can, may revolutionize, putting down a minority intermingled with or near about them, who may oppose them."

In 1860, the New York *Tribune* declared: "Whenever a portion of this Union large enough to form an independent, self-sustaining nation shall see fit to say authentically to the residue, 'We want to get away from you,' we shall say—and we trust self-respect, if not regard for the principle of self-government, will constrain the residue of the American people to say—Go!"

At the beginning of the secession movements, Secretary Seward used the following language to Mr. Adams, the United States Minister at London "For these reasons he would not be disposed to reject a cardinal dogma o theirs (the Secessionists), namely, that the Federal Government could not reduce the seceding States to obedience by conquest, even although he were disposed to question that proposition. But in fact the President willingly accepts it as true. Only an imperial or despotic government could subjugate thoroughly disaffected and insurrectionary members of the State. This Federal Republican system of ours is, of all forms of government, the very one most unfitted for such a labor."

Mississippi, once a beautiful expanse of happy homes; the black, mangled belt of territory that, commencing at Harper's Ferry, extends to Fortress Monroe, bound like a ghastly pall with the silver fringe of the Potomac; these are the hideous monuments of partial conquest which the Yankee has committed to the memory of the world and to the inscriptions of history. What has been safe in this war from the grasp of his plunder or the touch of his desecration? In the districts of the Confederacy where his soldiers have penetrated they have appropriated or destroyed private property; they have stolen even works of art and ornament; they have plundered churches; they have desecrated the grave and despoiled the emblems which love has consecrated to honor. And all this has been done according to a peculiar theory of hostilities which makes of war a sensual selfishness, and contemplates its objects as a savage gain of blood and plunder. This is the true and characteristic conception of the Yankee. He is taught by his political education, by his long training in the crooked paths of thrift, that all the principles of civilized usage are to be set at nought, when convenience and present policy interfere with their fulfilment.

It is in this sense of narrow, materialistic expediency that the Yankee has surrendered his liberties in this war, and proclaimed the enormous doctrine, that the Constitution under which he lives, and all his other monuments of liberty, are suspended by the paramount necessity of conquering and despoiling the South. He has carried his commercial politics into the war, and trades his own liberties for the material rewards of an otherwise vain and fruitless conquest.

But we leave the subject of the Yankee to turn to the other side of the question, and inquire what new political ideas the South has developed in this war. Here is an extraordinary blank. In the new government of the Confederacy we do not discover any statesmanship, any financial genius, any ideas beyond what are copied from the old effete systems that, it was thought, the revolution replaced. There must be some explanation of this absence of new ideas, this barren negation in our revolution.

By a misfortune, not easily avoided, the new government of the Confederacy fell into the hands of certain prominent partisans but mediocre politicians, who made a servile copy of the o d Yankee Constitution ; who had no ideas of political administration higher than the Washington routine ; and who, by their ignorance and conceit, have blindfolded and staggered the revolu tion from its commencement. This observation gives the key to the political history of the Confederacy in this war. A servile copy of old political ideas, an ape of the Washington administration, without genius, without originality, rejecting the counsels of the intelligent, and living in its own little circle of conceit, the Confederate government has fallen immeasurably below the occasion of this revolution, and misrepresents alike its spirit and its object.

But this weak, negative government of the Confederacy is but the early accident of this revolution ; and the people endure the accident of their present rulers merely from patriotic scruples which contemplate immediate exigencies. We stand but on the threshold of this revolution, and the curtain falls over a grand future of new ideas. Those who expect that it will terminate with the mere formality of a treaty with the public enemy, and that we shall then have a plodding future of peace, a repetition of old political ideas and manners, have got their pleasant philosophy from newspaper articles and street talk ; they have never read the exalted and invariable lesson of history, that, on commotions as immense as this war— no matter what its particular occasion—there are reared those new political structures which mark the ages of public progress. If it was true that this war, with its immense expenditures of blood and treasure, was merely to determine the status of negroes in the South—merely to settle the so-called Slavery question—there is not an intelligent man in the Confederacy but would spit upon the sacrifice. If it was true that this terrible war was merely to decide between two political administrations of the same model, then the people of the Confederacy would do right to abandon it.

Political novelty will come soon enough : it is the inevitable offspring of such commotions as this war. We repeat, that the Confederacy is now barren of political ideas, because those who are accidentally its rulers are, without originality or force, copyists of old rotten systems, and the apes of routine ; and because the public mind of the South is now too forcibly engrossed with the public enemy, either to replace their authority or to chastise their excesses. It is under these peculiar restraints that the Confederacy has produced such little political novelty in this war.

But the revolution is not yet past. Those exalted historical inspirations, which, with rapt souls and kindled blood, we read in the printed pages of the past, are this day, with trumpet sound, at our doors. We live in great times; we are in the presence of great events; we stand in the august theatre of a national tragedy. This struggle cannot pass away, until the great ideas, which the public danger alone holds in abeyance, have found a full development and a complete realization; until the South vindicates her reputation for political science and eliminates from this war a system of government more ingenious than a Chinese copy of Washington.

But while we thus reflect upon the intellectual barrenness of this war, we must not forget that, while the Confederacy in this time has produced but few new ideas, it has brought out troops of virtues. In this respect, the moral interest of the war is an endless theme for the historian; and we may be pardoned for leaving our immediate subject to say a few words of those fields of grandeur in which the Confederacy has found compensation for all other short-comings, and stands most conspicuous before the world.

We have put into the field soldiers such as the world has seldom seen—men who, half-clothed and half-fed, have, against superior numbers, won two-thirds of the battles of this war. The material of the Confederate army, in social worth, is simply superior to all that is related in the military annals of mankind. Men of wealth, men accustomed to the fashions of polite society, men who had devoted their lives to learned professions and polished studies, have not hesitated to shoulder their muskets and fight as privates in the ranks with the hard-fisted and uncouth laborer, no less a patriot than themselves. Our army presents to the world, perhaps, the only example of theoretical socialism reduced to practice it has ever seen, and realizes, at least in respect of defensive arms, the philosopher's dream of fraternal and sympathetic equality.

The hero of this war is the private soldier: not the officer whose dress is embroidered with lace, and whose name gar nishes the gazette, but the humble and honest patriot of the South in his dirt-stained and sweat-stained clothes, who toils through pain and hunger and peril; who has no reward but in the satisfaction of good deeds; who throws his poor, unknown life away at the cannon's mouth, and dies in that single flash of glory. How many of these heroes have been laid in unmarked ground—the nameless graves of self-devotion. But the ground where they rest is in the sight of Heaven. Nothing kisses their graves but the sunlight; nothing mourns for them but the sobbing wind; nothing adorns their dust but the wild flowers that have grown on the bloody crust of the battlefield. But not a Southern soldier has fallen in this war without the account of Heaven, and Death makes its registry of the pure and the brave on the silver pages of immortal life.

It is said that some of our people in this war have cringed beneath disaster, and compromised with misfortune. These are exceptions: they may be sorrowful ones. But in this war the people of the Confederacy, in the mass, have shown a fortitude, an elasticity under reverse, a temperance in victory, a self-negation in misfortune, a heroic, hopeful, patient, enduring, working resolution, which challenge the admiration of the world. It is not only material evils which have been thus endured: the scourge of tyranny, the bitterness of exile, the dregs of poverty. But the most beautiful circumstance of all is the strange resignation of our people in that worst trial and worst agony of war—the consignment of the living objects of their love to the bloody altars of sacrifice. These are the real horrors of war, and patriotism has no higher tribute to pay than the brave and uncomplaining endurance of such agony.

How have we been resigned in this war to the loss of our loved ones! How many noble sorrows are in our hearts! How many skeletons are in our closets! War may ruin and rifle the homestead; may scatter as chaff in the wind the property of years; may pronounce the doom of exile—but all these are paltry afflictions in comparison with the bereavement of kindred, whose blood has been left on the furze of the field and the leaves of the forest, and whose uncoffined bones are scattered to the elements.

The virtues and passions of the South in this war are not idle sentimentalisms. They are the precursors of new and illus-

trious ideas—the sure indications of a new political growth
In the warmth of such passions are born noble and robust ideas
Thus we await the development of this war in ideas, in politi
cal structures, in laws, which will honor it, and for which we
shall not unduly pay the dreadful price of blood.

It is impossible that a nation should have suffered as the
South has in this struggle; should have adorned itself with
such sacrifices; should have illustrated such virtues, to relapse,
at the end, into the old routine of its political existence. We
have not poured out our tears—we have not made a monument of broken hearts—we have not kneaded the ground with
human flesh, merely for the poor negative of a peace, with
nought higher or better than things of the past. Not so does
nature recompense the martyrdom of individuals or of nations
it pronounces the triumph of resurrection.

We believe that a new name is to be inscribed in the Pan·
theon of history; not that of an old idolatry. All now is ruin
and confusion, but from the scattered elements will arise a new
spirit of beauty and order. All now is dark, but the cloud will
break, and in its purple gates will stand the risen Sun.

THE LAST YEAR.

CHAPTER XIV.

THE spirit of the Southern Confederacy was scarcely ever more buoyant than in the month of May, 1864. The confidence of its people in the ultimate accomplishment of their independence was so firm and universal, that any other conclusion was but seldom referred to in general conversation or in the prevision of one's private affairs; and in Richmond and elsewhere the hope was freely indulged that the campaign of 1864 was to be decisive of the war, and to crown the efforts of the South with peace and independence.

There had been abundant occasion for this revival of confidence in the public mind of the Confederacy. The winter just past had been one of a large aggregate of success to the Confederate arms. Several brilliant expeditions had been planned and accomplished by them; while on the enemy's side all the work he had cut out for the winter had come to grief, and every one of his elaborate enterprises in that season had failed, with a concurrence of disaster most remarkable in the history of the war.

The invasion of Florida had been a shocking failure. Thomas had been repulsed in North Georgia, and was held completely in check there. Sherman's grand expedition in the Southwest and his famous experiment of " the strategic triangle" had come to the most absurd and disastrous conclusion—" Half of his army," said this chieftain, " went to Memphis .and half went to h—ll." Banks's proposed conquest of the Trans-Mississippi had been to the Confederates the occasion of that celebrated Red River campaign, the most glorious in the pages of their history, in which they not only reclaimed the coast and frontier of the Trans-Mississippi, but left the Massachusetts hero scarcely more of Louisiana than was covered by his pickets. And there had been other positive successes on the Confederate side. Forrest, by long and rapid marches, had spread terror along the banks of the Mississippi, and cut a swath across the State of Kentucky ; and on the eastern frontier the expeditions of Pickett and of Hoke had been brilliant events for the Confederacy, leaving the enemy only two places, Washington and Newbern, on the coast of North Carolina.

No wonder that the events of this winter were accepted by the Confederates as happy auguries for the ensuing campaign, and fresh occasions of hope and confidence. Their internal affairs, too, had improved along with this current of military success. The army had been replenished by an enlarged conscription ; a happy revolution was already going on in the finances under the operation of the law which curtailed the currency thirty-three per cent.; supplies had been accumulated during the winter, and the storehouses of Richmond were filled to bursting with the subsistence that had been gathered, through the course of several months, for the great campaign in Virginia.

Such were the extraordinary prospects with which the Confederacy entered upon the summer campaign of 1864. A general opinion had taken possession of the public mind that the North would make its grand effort in this year for the conquest of the South; and that even negative results would be fatal to the enemy, as they would be insufficient to appease the growing popular impatience of the war in the North, or sustain any new demand of the government at Washington for men and means.

This opinion was right, at least so far as it contemplated an extraordinary exertion on the part of the North. Two grand campaigns for the summer of 1864 had been elaborately planned at Washington. They were the parallel operations of Grant and Sherman in Virginia and in Georgia.

GRANT'S "ON TO RICHMOND."

General Ulysses S. Grant had hitherto been known in the North as the great general of the West, and the Yankee newspapers had entitled him the hero of Fort Donelson and Vicksburg. He was now to answer the eager expectation of the public by a campaign of unrivalled importance in Virginia. His elevation had been rapid. Four years ago the man who commanded all the armies of the North had been occupied with the obscure experiments of life in the successive callings of farmer, auctioneer, and tanner; and at the beginning of the war, having at first been refused an active military command by Governor Yates of Illinois, he was accidentally selected to lead a regiment of raw recruits.

The grade of lieutenant-general in the armies of the United States had been conferred by brevet only on General Scott, but as an actual rank in time of war had only been bestowed on General Washington. It was revived by the Federal Congress, and the commission conferred on General Grant, the hero of the West, who, despite the gap in his successes at Shiloh in 1862, and his narrow escape on that occasion from being consigned to obscurity by the ungenerous and characteristic changes in the fickle popular idolatry of the North, had had a long run of success, and was in advance of all his contemporaries in the coarse Yankee measure of greatness. The commission bore date March 2, 1864; and on the 9th of that month President Lincoln presented to Grant in person this commission, assuring him of his own cordial personal concurrence in the measure. General Halleck, hitherto general-in-chief, was relieved from duty and made chief of staff to the army at Washington.

The armies put under the command of Grant presented one of the most imposing arrays in modern history. They dotted the country from the Potomac to the Rio Grande, and thence around and along the sea-coast, and back to the Chesapeake. It was said that the Yankee lines might be traced by the smoke of camp-fires through a zig-zag journey of five thousand miles.

A few words may be bestowed here upon the character of the man, the designation of whom as the military idol of the North was not extravagant. General Grant had but little education, and was a man of not much more than ordinary ability; but he had a Scotch pertinacity of character which was a constant and valuable assistance in his military campaigns. As a commander he possessed a rare faculty of combination. He was a man who gathered his forces, who could "afford to wait," who dealt deliberate and heavy strokes; but he lacked that quickness of perception which decides single fields and illustrates military genius. His heart was certainly not a bad one, and his disposition was above most of the little tricks of the Yankee. On particular occasions he did some noble things, as we shall see in other parts of this volume. He was one of the few Yankee notabilities who, without affectation and in sincerity, avoided sensations and displays, had a horror of being "lionized," and lived for history rather than for the gazette. He had an imperturbable good-humor. In his appearance and manners he was very plain; but it was not a plebeian plainness; it was the plainness of a man trained to habits of self-reliance, who never lost the dignity and self-poise which come from a consciousness of one's merits without vanity.

From the moment of receiving his commission as lieutenant general, Grant had transferred his personal presence to the Army of the Potomac, leaving Sherman as his vicegerent to carry out the Western campaign. Warren, Sedgwick, and Hancock were made the corps commanders of this army, and Burnside was given a separate army corps. Butler, at Fortress Monroe, was reinforced by the Tenth Corps from Charleston under Gillmore, and the Eighteenth from the West under "Baldy" Smith. To the infamous hero of New Orleans was allotted the task of cutting off the city of Richmond from its southern lines of communication; while Sigel, operating in the Shenandoah Valley, was to cut the railroad which by way of

Gordonsville connected Lee's army with his principal base of supplies at Lynchburg.

Thus were the preparations completed for the most moment-ous campaign in American history. On Wednesday, May 4, eight weeks from the day Grant received his commission, his two grand columns were ready to move—the one well in hand on the north bank of the Rapidan, seventy miles north of Richmond; and the other at Fortress Monroe, one day's sail from Richmond on the James.

THE BATTLES OF THE WILDERNESS.

At dawn on the 5th of May, the Army of the Potomac, closely succeeded by that of Burnside, had crossed the Rapidan River; the Second Corps at Ely's, the Fifth and Sixth corps at Germania Ford. Having crossed the river, the first demon-stration of the enemy was an attempt to turn the right flank of Lee's army between the Orange Courthouse pike and the river.

The enemy's attack on the line of the turnpike was sustained by the division of General Edward Johnson of Ewell's corps. After a brief struggle the enemy succeeded in forcing back part of Jones's brigade, which had been formed across the turn-pike; but the gap in our lines was speedily closed by Stewart's brigade, and the Yankees driven back with the loss of some guns. In the mean time Gordon's gallant brigade of Georgians crushed through the enemy's first lines, and driving furiously on, struck back the Yankee front in confusion upon its sup-ports. Another advance of the enemy upon Johnson's left flank was gallantly repulsed by Pegram's Virginians and Hays's Louisianians; and the day's work on the left witnessed the Confederates still holding their advanced lines.

Hill had been ordered to march from Lee's left, and with Heth's division in advance had moved along the plank-road in a direction somewhat parallel with the turnpike, eventually effecting a junction with Gordon's brigade, on Ewell's extreme right. The line of battle, thus completed, presented a front of six miles.

About 3 o'clock in the afternoon, the attack on Ewell having

been repulsed, the enemy commenced a more decided demonstration in front of Hill. Heth's division bore at first the whole
brunt of the attack, but about four o'clock Wilcox's division
was moved up from Ewell's right. For more than three hours
the dreadful conflict continued, the enemy attempting to force
his way rather by constant pressure than by dashing enterprise
Never was a more gallant spectacle than these two divisions
of Confederates holding at bay the Yankee onslaught from
three o'clock until half-past seven, firm and unbroken in all
that long and dreadful monotony of conflict. Night closed
upon the Confederate line in the position it had originally
taken. That the day was an unsuccessful one for the Yankees
even their own accounts did not hesitate to admit. "No cheer
of victory," says a Northern correspondent, "swelled through
the Wilderness that night."

During the day Hancock, Second Corps, had come up, and
the Federal forces were concentrated. On the morning of the
6th their lines were consolidated and freshly posted; the three
corps sustaining their respective positions—Warren in the
centre, Sedgwick on the right, and Hancock on the left.

The attack was made by the Confederates, Hill and Longstreet's corps attacking both of Hancock's flanks with such
fury that the whole line of command thus assaulted was broken
in several places. The effort, however, of the Confederates to
pierce the enemy's centre was stayed, the Yankees having secured their line of battle behind their intrenchments.

But with the expiration of the day was to occur a thrilling
and critical conjuncture. Just at dusk (the Confederates' favorite hour of battle) a column of Lee's army attacked the enemy's left, captured Seymour and a large portion of his brigade, and excited a panic which put Grant's whole army on
the verge of irretrievable rout. Unfortunately, the Confed-
edrates had no idea of the extent of their success, and could
not imagine how fraught with vital issue were those few moments of encounter. The Yankee supply-trains were thought
to be immediately threatened, and artillery was posted to bear
upon the Confederate advance in that direction. But the Confederates did not press their advantage. As it was, Generals
Shaler and Seymour, with the greater part of their commands,
were taken prisoners.

Such had been the two days' battle of the Wilderness—a marked success for the Confederates, disputed by the Northern newspapers, of course, but manifest in the face of the facts. The enemy confessed to a loss of twelve thousand.* The immediate consequence of these engagements was, that Grant, being clearly out-generalled in his first design of reaching Lee's rear and compelling him to fight a battle with his communications cut off, which would be decisive of the campaign, was forced to change his plans, and with it his position ; falling back to his intrenched line, between the Wilderness and Trigg's Mill, nearly coincident with the Brock road, leading from the Wilderness to Spottsylvania Courthouse.

On the 7th, with some desultory fighting, Grant continued his movement towards Fredericksburg, with the evident view of attempting the Fredericksburg road to Richmond. It was in consequence of this change of front that General Lee took up a new line on the Po. It will amuse the candid reader to find how this movement was interpreted by the mendacious press of the North ; for in the newspapers of New York and Boston it was entitled, in flaming capitals, " A Waterloo Defeat of the Confederates," " The Retreat of Lee to Richmond," &c. For a few days the North was vocal with exultation, and for the hundredth time it had the rebellion " in a corner," to be conveniently strangled. But this imagination of easy conquest was to be dissipated as the many that had preceded it.

---

* A correspondent of the London *Herald,* who witnessed the two days' battle, writes : " The results to the enemy in some parts of the field cannot be described by any word less forcible than massacre. Eleven hundred and twenty-five Federal dead were buried in front of Ewell's line, lying to the left of the turnpike. Five hundred more were buried on the right of that road ; and, in addition to about one hundred dead officers, whose bodies must have been removed, the number of corpses lying on the field, within range of the enemy's sharpshooters, is estimated at fully three hundred. The Federal killed in the struggle on the right may, therefore, be declared positively to number as many as two thousand. I have no data on which to estimate the breadth of the slaughter in the fierce conflicts of the right ; but from the stubbornness and volume of these, feel quite confident that they must have added to the slain as awful an account as that rendered in front of Ewell. With three thousand prisoners and four thousand dead, the usual proportion of six or seven to one for the wounded, would show that the losses of Grant in the battle of the Wilderness cannot have been less than thirty thousand men."

THE BATTLES OF SPOTTSYAVANIA COURTHOUSE.

On the 8th of May two engagements were fought at Spott sylvania Courthouse, between Longstreet's corps, under Anderson (General Longstreet having been wounded in the battle of the 6th) and the Fifth Corps, under Warren, supported by cavalry. The enemy was repulsed, with heavy loss, in both instances.

On the 9th, which was marked by some skirmishing, General John Sedgwick, one of the most valuable corps commanders in the Yankee army, was killed, probably by a stray bullet. He had just been bantering his men about dodging and ducking their heads at the whistle of Confederate bullets in the distance. "Why," said he, "they couldn't hit an elephant at this distance." The next moment a ball entered his face, just below the left eye, and pierced his brain, causing instant death.

On Thursday, the 17th of May, occurred what may be entitled as the great battle of Spottsylvania Courthouse. The enemy had planned an attack on what was supposed to be a vital section of the Confederates, a salient angle of earthworks held by Johnson's division of Ewell's corps. The storming column advanced silently, and without firing a shot, up to the angle of the breastworks, over which they rushed, taking the forces within in flank, surrounding them, capturing nearly the entire division of Johnson's, with its commander, and also a brigade or two of other troops, Brigadier-General George H. Stuart in command.

But the surprise was only momentary. One of the most thrilling scenes of the war was to occur. In a moment when all was excitement, and when it could be easily seen that unless the Confederates could check the enemy's advance, the consequence would be disastrous in the extreme, General Lee rode forward in front of the Confederate line, his position being opposite at the time to the colors of the Forty-ninth regiment of Pegram's brigade. Not a word did he say. He simply took off his hat. "As he sat on his charger," says a near eyewitness of him, "I never saw a man look so noble or witnessed a spectacle so impressive."

At this interesting moment General Gordon, spurring his

foaming charger to the front, seized the reins of General Lee's horse, and turning him around, said, "General, these are Virginians! These men have never failed! They never will! Will you, boys?" Loud cries of "No, no!" "General Lee to the rear!" "Go back!" "Go back!" "General Lee to the rear!" burst from along the lines; and as one led the general's horse to the rear, General Gordon gave the command, "Forward, charge!" And with a shout and yell the brigades dashed on, through bog and swamp, and briers and undergrowth, to the breastworks. For long hours a battle raged over the intrenchments, the intense fury, heroism, and horror of which it is impossible to describe. From dawn to dusk the roar of guns was ceaseless; a tempest of shell shrieked through the forest and ploughed the field. Ewell's corps held the critical angle with a courage that nothing could subdue. General Hill moved down from the right, joined Ewell, and threw his divisions into the struggle. Longstreet came on from the extreme left of the Confederate line. Column after column of the enemy was stricken down, or repulsed and sent back like a broken wave. The ground in front of the Confederate lines was piled with his slain.

The works which the Yankees had captured in the morning contained an angle in the form of an A, with the point towards the enemy. At the close of the day the enemy maintained possession of about three hundred yards of our works in that quarter. The loss in Johnson's division was probably between 3,000 and 3,500, including over 2,000 prisoners. Our whole loss, during the day, amounted to between six and seven thousand. The enemy stated their loss at from 18,000 to 25,000. They captured twenty pieces of artillery. This was their "great victory."

The sixth day of heavy fighting had been ended. "It would," says an intelligent critic of this period, "not be impossible to match the results of any one day's battle with stories from the wars of the old world; but never, we should think, in the history of man were five such battles as these compressed into six days." Grant had been foiled; but his obstinacy was apparently untouched, and the fierce and brutal consumption of human life, another element of his generalship, and which had already obtained for him with his soldiers the

soubriquet of "the butcher," was still to continue. He telegraphed to Washington: "I propose to fight it out on this
line, if it takes all summer."

But we must turn for a few moments from this dominant
field of action and interest to notice other movements, which
were parts of Grant's combination, and of the great military
drama in Virginia.

While Grant was engaged on the Rapidan, a cavalry expedition of the enemy, commanded by General Sheridan, moved
around Lee's right flank to the North Anna River; committed
some damage at Beaver Dam; moved thence to the South
Anna and Ashland Station, where the railroad was destroyed;
and finally found its way to the James at Turkey Island,
where it joined the forces of Butler. The damage inflicted by
this raid was not very considerable; but it was the occasion
of a severe fight, on the 10th of May, at Yellow Tavern, on the
road to Richmond, where Sheridan encountered a Confederate
cavalry force, in which engagement was lost the valuable life
of General J. E. B. Stuart, the brilliant cavalry commander,
who had so long made Virginia the threatre of his daring and
chivalric exploits.

The column of Butler, the important correspondent to
Grant's movement, intended to operate against Richmond on
the south side, had raised the hopes of the North merely to
dash them by a failure decisive in its character, and ridiculous
in all its circumstances. On the 5th of May, Butler proceeded
with his fleet of gunboats and transports, and the Tenth and
Eighteenth army corps, up the James River, landing at Wilson's Wharf a regiment of Wild's negro troops, and two
brigades of the same color at Fort Powhatan; thence up to
City Point, where Hinks's division was landed; and at Bermuda Hundred, just below the mouth of the Appomattox, the
entire army was disembarked.

On the 7th, five brigades, under General Brooks, struck for
the Petersburg and Richmond Railroad, and succeeded in
destroying a bridge seven miles north of Petersburg. In the
mean time, Butler, after intrenching himself, closed about the
defences of Drury's Bluff. The Yankee general seemed confident that he could by a little fighting, in conjunction with
the powerful flotilla upon the James, easily overcome the main

barrier to his approach to the rear of the Confederate capital, presented in the defences of Drury's Bluff. It was already announced to the credulous public of the North that Butler had cut Beauregard's army in twain; that he had carried two lines of the defences of Drury's Bluff; and that he held the keys to the back-door of Richmond.

On Monday, the 16th of May, General Beauregard fell upon the insolent enemy in a fog, drove Butler from his advanced positions back to his original earthworks, and inflicted upon him a loss of several thousand men in killed, wounded, and captured. He had fallen upon the right of the Yankee line of battle with the force of an avalanche, completely crushing it backward and turning Butler's flank. The action was decisive. No result but that of victory could be expected in Richmond when Butler was the combatant. The Richmond *Examiner* designated the fight as that of "the Buzzard and the Falcon." The day's operations resulted in Butler's entire army being ordered to return from its advanced position, within ten miles of Richmond, to the line of defence known as Bermuda Hundred, between the James and Appomattox rivers.

THE ENEMY'S OPERATIONS IN WESTERN VIRGINIA.

While Butler had thus come to grief, the failure of Sigel, who threatened the Valley of Virginia was no less complete.

Grant had made an extraordinary combination in Virginia. His plan of campaign was clearly not limited to the capture of Richmond. He might capture it without capturing the government machinery and without overthrowing Lee's army. In such event further operations were necessary; and these were already provided for in the ambitious and sweeping plan of the campaign.

The movement of Sigel up the Shenandoah Valley towards Staunton was designed with the view, first, of taking possession of the Virginia Central Railroad, and ultimately effecting a lodgment upon the Virginia and Tennessee Railroad at Lynchburg. Averill was to move towards the same great railroad with a design of striking it at Salem. General Crook was to move with a strong force and large supplies from Charlestown towards Dublin Depot; and a fourth movement—which, however, was not actively developed until the period, some weeks later, of the second combination of forces in this part of Virginia—was designed on the Virginia side of the Big Sandy towards Abingdon on the same railroad.

The invasion thus planned for Western Virginia comprehended a heavy aggregate of forces. There were the six thousand of Crook, which came from the Lower Kanawha. These last were joined by Averill, with twenty-five hundred cavalry, coming from Northwest Virginia; and there was the army of Sigel, whose strength was variously estimated, but was not less than twelve thousand. The design was that these different corps should strike the Lynchburg and Tennessee and the Central railroads simultaneously at Abingdon, Wytheville, Dublin Depot, and Staunton, and should afterwards unite, west of Lynchburg, and march against that city. Grant was strongly impressed with the importance of this city. In subsequent attempts against it, his orders were that it should be taken and held at any loss and at all hazards.

In pursuance of the plan of operations in Western Virginia, at the very moment that Grant crossed the Rapidan it was announced that Sigel was in motion upon Staunton, Crook upon Dublin Depot, and Averill upon Wytheville, with design, after destroying that town and the lead mines, to unite with Crook at Dublin for a march towards Lynchburg; but no news came of a movement at that early day of Major-General Burbridge upon Abingdon and Saltville. The sequel proved that we were poorly prepared to meet this concerted assault. Breckinridge had been ordered away from Dublin in a hurry, with all the troops he could collect at short notice, and sent down the Valley to confront Sigel, leaving nothing but a few scattered troops, afterwards collected together by McCausland, to oppose Crook at Dublin.

On the 15th of May, Sigel's column was encountered near Newmarket by General Breckinridge, who drove it across the Shenandoah, captured six pieces of artillery and nearly one thousand stand of small-arms, and inflicted upon it a heavy loss, Sigel abandoning his hospitals and destroying the larger portion of his train.

But while Breckinridge defeated Sigel, and drove him back

in dismay and rout, McCausland was left at Dublin with only 1,500 men to resist Crook's 6,000. He fought bravely, however, and so shattered Crook's army as to destroy his design of proceeding towards Lynchburg, and compel a retreat as far as Meadow Bluff, in Greenbrier, for the purpose of recruiting his disorganized army and repairing damages. Crook left several hundred prisoners and all his wounded, but succeeded, before leaving the region of the battle, in destroying the important bridge over New River.

It so happened that the Confederates had a larger force at that time in the extreme Southwest than anywhere else on the line of the Lynchburg and Tennessee Railroad. The fact was fortunate, for it enabled General W. E. Jones, then commanding there, to spare General Morgan's command for services further east. Thus it happened that General Morgan, making a forced march from Saltville, arrived at Wytheville with his mounted men in time to save that town from Averill, and to completely defeat that boasted cavalry officer, with a heavy loss of killed, wounded, prisoners, and horses. This defeat was very important, for it prevented Averill from joining Crook before the battle at Dublin, and before that general had found it necessary to fall back to Meadow Bluff. Averill arrived in Dublin two days after Crook had gone. It was still further fortunate that General Morgan, at the same time that he marched from Saltville with his mounted men against Averill, at Wytheville, was able to send his dismounted men by the railroad to Dublin, which force arrived there just in time to take part with McCausland in the fight which sent Crook back to Meadow Bluff.

These occurrences took place in the early part of May, simultaneously with Grant's operations in Spottsylvania. Morgan's fight at Wytheville, McCausland's at Dublin, and Breckinridge's at Newmarket, all occurred about the same time with each other, and simultaneously with the great battles of the Wilderness between Lee and Grant.

We left Grant defeated in the action of the 12th in front of Spottsylvania Courthouse. On the 14th he moved his lines by his left flank, taking position nearer the Richmond and Fredericksburg railroad. On the 18th he attempted an assault on Ewell's line, which was easily repulsed. It was admitted by the enemy that the object of this attack was to turn Lee's left flank, and that their line got no further than the abattis, when it was "*ordered*" back to its original position.

A new movement was now undertaken by Grant—to pass his army from the line of the Po, down the valley of the Rappahannock. It thus became necessary for General Lee to evacuate his strong position on the line of the Po ; and by an admirable movement he had taken a new position between the North and South Anna, before Grant's army had arrived at the former stream. Having cut loose from Fredericksburg as a base and established depots on the lower Rappahannock, on the 21st Grant's forces occupied Milford Station and Bowling Green, and were moving on the well-known high roads to Richmond. But they were again intercepted ; for Lee had planted himself between Grant and Richmond, near Hanover Junction.

On the 23d and on the 25th Grant made attempts on the Confederate lines, which were repulsed, and left him to the last alternative. Another flanking operation remained for him, by which he swung his army from the North Anna around and across the Pamunkey. On the 27th, Hanovertown was reported to be occupied by the Yankee advance unde General Sheridan ; and on the 28th Grant's entire army was across the Pamunkey.

In the mean time, General Lee also reformed his line of battle, north and south, directly in front of the Virginia Central Railroad, and extending from Atlee's Station south to Shady Grove, ten miles north of Richmond. In this position he covered both the Virginia Central and the Fredericksburg and Richmond railroads, as well as all the roads leading to Richmond, west of and including the Mechanicsville pike.

The favorite tactics of Grant appear to have been to develop the left flank ; and by this characteristic manœuvre he moved down the Hanover Courthouse road, and on the first day of June took a position near Cold Harbor.

Grant was now within a few miles of Richmond. The vulgar mind of the North readily seized upon the cheap circumstance of his proximity in miles to the Confederate capital, and exclaimed its triumph. The capture of Richmond was accounted as an event of the next week. The Yankee periodicals were adorned with all those illustrations which brutal triumph could suggest;—Grant drubbing Lee across his knee the genius of Yankee Liberty holding aloft an impersonation o₁ the Southern Confederacy by the seat of the breeches, marked "Richmond;" Jefferson Davis playing his last card, ornamented with a crown of death's heads, and with his legs well girt with snakes; and a hundred other caricatures alike characteristic of the vulgar thought and fiendish temper of the Yankee. To such foolish extremity did this premature celebration go, that a meeting was called in New York to render the thanks of the nation to Grant, and twenty-five thousand persons completed the hasty apotheosis.

But for the candid and intelligent, the situation of Grant was one of sinister import to him, implied much of disaster, and was actually a consequence of his repeated disappointments. The true theory of it was defeat, not victory. He did nothing more than hold the same ground as that occupied by General McClellan in his first peninsular campaign. This position, had he come by another route, a day's sail from Washington, he could have occupied without the loss of a single man. But he had occupied it by a devious route; with a loss variously estimated at from sixty to ninety thousand men; with the consumption of most of his veteran troops, whom he had put in front; with the disconcert and failure of those parts of the drama which Butler and Sigel were to enact; and with that demoralization which must unavoidably obtain in an army put to the test of repeated defeats and forced marches.

What was represented by the enemy as the retreat of General Lee's army to Richmond was simply its movement from a position which its adversary had abandoned, to place itself full before him across the new road on which he had determined to travel. In this sense, it was Grant who was pursued. He had set out to accomplish Mr. Lincoln's plan of an overland march upon Richmond. Mr. Lincoln's scheme, as detailed by himself in his famous letter to General McClellan, was to march by the way of the Manassas Railroad. The first movement of General Grant was to give up that route, and fall back upon the line by which Generals Burnside and Hooker attempted to reach the Confederate capital—that is, the Fredericksburg and Richmond line. But, repulsed at Spottsylvania, this route proved untenable, and General Grant was forced east and south, and adopted a new base at Port Royal and Tappahannock, on the Rappahannock River, which conformed in a measure to General McClellan's first plan of a march upon Richmond by way of Urbana. The next change Grant was compelled to make was, after finding how strong the Confederates were, as posted on the South Anna, to cross the Pamunkey and make his base at the White House, bearing thereafter still further east and south to the precise ground of McClellan's operations.

The significance of all these movements was, that Grant had utterly failed in his design of defeating Lee's army far from its base, and pushing the fragments before him down to Richmond, and had been forced to cover up his failure by adopting the derided scheme of McClellan. The event of the 12th of May at Spottsylvania Courthouse had settled the question whether he could beat Lee in the field and put him in a disastrous retreat. Unable to remove the obstacle on the threshold of his proposed campaign, nothing was left but to abandon it. Grant makes his way down the valley of the Rappahannock; turns aside to Hanover Junction, to find a repetition of Spottsylvania Courthouse; deflects to the head-waters of the York; and at last, by a monstrous circuit, reaches a point where he might have landed on the 1st of May, without loss or opposition. We may appreciate the amount of gaseous nonsense and truculent blackguardism of Yankee journals, when we find them declaring that these movements were a foot-race for Richmond, that Grant was across the last ditch, and that the end of the rebellion was immediately at hand.

CHAPTER XV.

Grant essays the passage of the Chickahominy.—BATTLE OF COLD HARBOR.—A brilliant and extraordinary victory for the Confederates.—Grant's stock of expedients. —He decides to move to the south side of the James.—OPERATIONS IN WESTERN VIRGINIA.—Shocking improvidence of the Richmond authorities.—Hunter captures Staunton.—Death of General Jones.—Grant's new combination.—Hunter's part.—Sheridan's part.—THE BATTLES OF PETERSBURG.—Butler attempts to steal a march upon "the Cockade City."—Engagements of the 16th, 17th, and 18th of June.—Port Walthal Junction.—Defeat of Sheridan at Trevillian Station.—Defeat of Hunter near Lynchburg.—Morgan draws Burbridge into Kentucky.—Two affairs on the Petersburg and Weldon Railroad.—THE GREAT MINE EXPLOSION.—A scene of infernal horror.—Yankee comments on Grant's failures.—Great depression in the North.—Mr. Chase's declarations.—General Lee's sense of success. —His singular behavior.—THE SINKING OF THE PRIVATEER ALABAMA.—A Yankee trick of concealed armor.—The privateer service of the Confederates.—Interesting statistics.

WE return to the events on the Richmond lines. The position occupied by Grant, on Wednesday, June 1st, had been obtained after some fighting, and, by the enemy's own admission, had cost him two thousand men in killed and wounded. An important and critical struggle was now to ensue. Grant had secured a position, the importance of which was that it was the point of convergence of all the roads radiating, whether to Richmond, his objective point, or to White House, his base of supplies. He was now to essay the passage of the Chickahominy, and we were to have another decisive battle of Cold Harbor.

THE BATTLE OF COLD HARBOR.

There is good evidence that Grant's intention was to make it the decisive battle of the campaign. The movements of the preceding days, culminating in the possession of Cold Harbor —an important strategic point—had drawn the enemy's lines close in front of the Chickahominy, and reduced the military problem to the forcing of the passage of that river—a problem which, if solved in Grant's favor, would decide whether Richmond could be carried by a *coup de main*, if a decisive victory should attend his arms, or, whether he should betake himself to siege operations or some other recourse.

Early on the morning of Friday, June 3d, the assault was made, Hancock commanding the left of the Yankee line of battle, and leading the attack. The first Confederate line was held by Breckinridge's troops, and was carried. The reverse was but momentary, for the troops of Milligan's brigade, and the Maryland battalion, soon dashed forward to retrieve the honors which the Yankees had snatched.

This engagement was on the right; Breckinridge's division, with Field's, constituting a part of Longstreet's corps. On the left, General Early engaged the enemy. On every part of the line the enemy was repulsed by the quick and decisive blows of the Confederates. Hancock's corps, the only portion of the Yankee army that had come in contact with the Confederate works, had been hurled back in a storm of fire; the Sixth Corps had not been able to get up further than within two hundred and fifty yards of the main works; while Warren and Burnside, on the enemy's right and right centre, were staggered on the lines of our rifle-pits. The decisive work of the day was done in a few minutes. Never were there such signal strokes of valor, such dispatch of victory. It was stated in the accounts of the Confederates, that fourteen distinct assaults of the enemy were repulsed, and that his loss was from six to seven thousand.* No wonder that the insolent assurance of the capture of Richmond was displaced in the Yankee newspapers by the ominous calculation, that Grant could not afford many such experiments on the intrenched line of the Chickahominy, and would have to make some other resort to victory.

The battle of Cold Harbor was sufficient to dispel the delusion of weakness and demoralization in Lee's army; for this derided army, almost in the time it takes to tell the story, had

---

* The lowest estimate of their own loss, in the Yankee newspapers, was five thousand; and the report of the adjutant-general at Washington stated the loss in three days' operations on the Chickahominy at seven thousand five hundred. Yet Grant dispatched to Washington: "Our loss was not severe, nor do I suppose the enemy to have lost heavily. We captured over three hundred prisoners, mostly from Breckinridge."

repulsed at every point the most determined assault of the enemy, and, in a few brief moments of a single morning, had achieved an unbroken circuit of victories. Grant and his friends were alike dismayed. The latter insisted that he should have half a million more of men to accomplish his work. "We should," said a Boston paper, "have a vigorous and overwhelming war, or else peace without further effusion of blood." A certain portion of the Yankee press maintained the unbroken lie, and told the story of an uninterrupted series of victories.

An object of most curious and constant interest in the war was the rivalry of the different routes to Richmond. McClellan had chosen the peninsular approach, while Mr. Lincoln dissented in favor of an advance from the Lower Rappahannock; Burnside had chosen Fredericksburg as his base; Hooker had acted on the same choice. Meade had selected the Rapidan, as Pope had done before him. Grant came to his command, unembarrassed and untrammelled by the precedents and comments of others. He had hunted up the roads to Richmond, through the Wilderness and Spottsylvania Court-house, and avowed his unchangeable purpose to adhere to that as his true line. He had now wandered around to McClellan's old base. But the battle of July 3d decided that Richmond could no longer be approached with advantage from the north, and the disconcerted, shifting commander, with his stock of expedients well-nigh exhausted, found nothing now left for him but to transfer his entire army to the south side of the James River.*

---

* A Richmond paper (the *Dispatch*) made the following estimate of Grant's enormous losses up to the time of crossing the James; still leaving him, however, a tremendous force in hand, compared with Lee's numbers: "Grant had had first his own original army, 150,000; second, 25,000 veteran reinforcements; third, 40,000 hundred days' men; fourth, 20,000 from Butler—total, 225,000 men, under his own eye. Of these, he had lost 125,000 before he left Cold Harbor. He crossed the river with 110,000 men, and there united his operations with those of Butler, who had with him about 20,000 men, besides those he had sent to Grant."

OPERATIONS IN WESTERN VIRGINIA.

We have already referred to the failure in May of the operations in Western Virginia. They were to be enlarged by the augmentation of the Yankee forces by several thousand troops, drawn from the extreme Northwestern States, and by the appointment of General Hunter, an officer of higher rank, to command—the same Hunter, by the by, who inaugurated negro enlistments and miscegenation in the department of Beaufort, South Carolina, as early as he first winter of the war.

This second combination in Western Virginia was imposing enough. Crook and Averill were refitting and preparing at Meadow Bluff for an advance on Staunton and Lynchburg; Hunter was organizing at Winchester heavy reinforcements for a second advance upon Lynchburg by way of Staunton; and Burbridge, in Kentucky, was getting ready to descend upon extreme Southwestern Virginia, so as to prevent any advance from that direction upon the rear of the combined armies about to move on Lynchburg.

It is almost incredible how inadequate the preparations of the Confederates were to meet these formidable enterprises of the enemy. Breckinridge, with the only army that could be called such, which we had west of the Blue Ridge, was ordered elsewhere, leaving nothing to confront some twenty-seven thousand troops but a few small brigades of inferior cavalry, about two regiments of infantry, and a small brigade (Vaughan's) of dismounted troops acting as infantry. To supply the place of Breckinridge, McCausland's little force, from Dublin, was sent to the front of Staunton, and General William E. Jones was ordered to take all the troops he could move from Southwestern Virginia to the same position in the lower valley. Accordingly, General Jones not only got together all the infantry west of the New River, but dismounted Vaughan's brigade of cavalry also, and took all to Staunton, leaving nothing in the extreme southwest but a few disjointed bodies of cavalry and Morgan's command to meet Burbridge coming in from Kentucky.

On the 5th of June, Hunter had obtained a success at Piedmont, in Western Virginia, and had effected the capture of Staunton; the saddest circumstance of which affair was the loss of General Jones, one of the most distinguished cavalry commanders of the Confederacy.*

After occupying Staunton, Hunter had formed a junction with the combined forces of Crook and Averill, and on the 13th of June was reported to be moving with his whole command against Lynchburg. On the 7th, Sheridan had crossed the Pamunkey, and was moving eastward in the direction of the Gordonsville Railroad. The main movement of the new combination—that of Grant across the James—commenced Sunday night the 12th of June.

The first plan of the enemy had comprehended the advance of Sigel down the Shenandoah, and the capture of Petersburg, if nothing more, by Butler, while General Grant engaged Lee's army between the Rapidan and Richmond. That plan having signally failed, the second comprised the capture of Lynchburg by Hunter, of Gordonsville and Charlottesville by Sheridan, and of Petersburg by Meade. It was thus hoped to isolate the Confederate capital by cutting off its communications on every side.

It was, perhaps, not Grant's design to cross the river until he had made some attempt on the Central and New Market roads, leading into Richmond from the direction of Malvern

---

* A correspondent thus writes of this officer—whose eccentricities were almost as well-known to Virginians as those of Stonewall Jackson: "General Jones was a captain in the United States Army, ranking Stuart. A small, thin, black-eyed and whiskered man, he dressed very plainly, bordering on shabbiness; never shaved, never in uniform, no insignia of office. He had a fine, squeaking voice; was misanthropic, despising parade and every man that indulged in it; never courting any man's favor; never, perhaps, speaking to a congressman or the President, since the war commenced; fearing no man—reverencing no man; speaking freely, if not curtly, to and of everybody. He was a widower. When stationed in Texas he lost his wife, an accomplished lady, by shipwreck in Galveston Bay; since which he has never married again, and has seemed, if not to wish for death, at least to hold his life very cheaply. He was cool in a fight, and the bravest of the brave. With hat in hand, he was cheering his men when he fell, pierced through his head by a minnie ball. The enemy refused his body. Some citizens buried him in a neat coffin, and marked the spot."

Hill. On the 13th of June he caused a reconnoissance in force to be made from the Long Bridge towards the Quaker road, and in an affair, near the intersection of this road with the Charles City road, was repulsed, and drew off his force, well satisfied that the Confederates held, with heavy forces, all the roads by which Richmond could be reached from the southeast.

The Eighteenth Yankee corps had proceeded by water to Bermuda Hundred. The remaining corps had crossed the Chickahominy at James Bridge and Long Bridge; and after the reconnoissance of the 13th, proceeded down the James, and crossed it in the neighborhood of City Point.

THE BATTLES OF PETERSBURG.

Petersburg had already sustained a considerable attack of the enemy. An expedition from Butler's lines had essayed its capture on the 9th of June.

Approaching with nine regiments of infantry and cavalry, and at least four pieces of artillery, the enemy searched our lines a distance of nearly six miles. Hood's and Battles' battalions, the Forty-sixth Virginia, one company of the Twenty-third South Carolina, with Sturdevant's battery, and a few guns in position, and Talliaferro's cavalry, kept them at bay. The Yankees were twice repulsed, but succeeded, at last, in penetrating a gap in our line; when reinforcements coming up drove back the insolent foe from approaches which their footsteps for the first time polluted.

The fortunate issue of this first attack on Petersburg encouraged the raw troops and militia who had been put under arms for the defence of " the Cockade City." General Wise addressed the troops of his command in a memorable and thrilling order. " Petersburg," said he, " is to be, and shall be, defended on her outer walls, on her inner lines, at her corporation bounds, in every street, and around every temple of God and altar of man."

The resolution of the gallant city—with its defences reinforced by the fortunate Beauregard—was now to be put to a much more severe test, for it was to encounter the shock of the bulk of Grant's army.

Smith's corps, having disembarked at Bermuda Hundred on the 14th, moved rapidly upon Petersburg, and made an assault on the batteries covering the approaches to the city on the northeast. Having got possession of this line of works, held principally by Confederate militia, Smith waited the coming up of the Second Corps.

On the evening of the 16th an attack was ordered on the Confederate line of works in front of Petersburg, Smith's corps being on the right, on the Petersburg and City Point road, west of the railroad, the Second Corps in the centre, and Burnside on the left, reaching the Prince George Courthouse road. The assault was not only repulsed at every point, but our troops, assuming the aggressive, drove the Yankees from their breastworks at Howlett's House, captured some of their guns, and opened upon them an enfilading fire, under which they fled precipitately.

The most furious assault of the enemy had been made on General Hoke's front, whose division occupied a position facing batteries from Nine to Twelve inclusive. Three different charges were repulsed by these heroic troops. In the final repulse of the enemy, a large portion of a Yankee brigade, being exposed to an enfilading artillery fire from our guns, sought shelter in a ravine, and surrendered to the Sixty-fourth Georgia regiment.

On Friday, June 17th, fighting was renewed without result. The next day it was resolved by the enemy to make an assault along the whole line for the purpose of carrying the town. It was thus that the action of the 18th was designed to be decisive of operations in the present position.

Three different assaults were made by the enemy during the day—at four in the morning, at noon, and at four in the afternoon. Each one was repulsed. Hancock and Burnside in the centre suffered severely.

After severe losses on the part of all the Yankee corps, night found the Confederates still in possession of their works covering Petersburg.

The disaster of this day left Grant without hope of making any impression on the works in his front, and placed him under the necessity of yet another change of operations. The series of engagements before Petersburg had cost him at least ten thousand men in killed and wounded, and had culminated in another decisive defeat.

The misfortune of the enemy appeared, indeed, to be overwhelming. Pickett's division had given him another lesson at Port Walthal Junction. It was here the heroes of Gettysburg repulsed a force under Gillmore engaged in destroying the rail road, took two lines of his breastworks, and put him to disastrous flight.

Nor was there any compensation to be found in the auxiliary parts of Grant's second grand combination. Sheridan had failed to perform his part. He was intercepted by Hampton's cavalry at Trevillian Station on the Gordonsville road, defeated in an engagement on the 10th, and compelled to withdraw his command across the North Anna. Hunter had come to similar grief, and his repulse at Lynchburg involved consequences of the gravest disaster to the enemy.

On the 18th of June, Hunter made an attack upon Lynchburg from the south side, which was repulsed by troops that had arrived from General Lee's lines. The next day, more reinforcements having come up, preparations were made to attack the enemy, when he retreated in confusion. The Confederates took thirteen of his guns, pursued him to Salem, and forced him to a line of retreat into the mountains of Western Virginia. The attempt of the Yankees to whitewash the infamous and cowardly *dénouement* was more than usually refreshing. Hunter officially announced that his expedition had been " extremely successful ;" that he had left Lynchburg because " his ammunition was running short ;" and that as to the singular line he had taken up, he was now " ready for a move in any direction."

In the mean time General Morgan had done his part in breaking up the enemy's combination in Western Virginia. General Jones being ordered from the extreme Southwest, together with all the troops he could transport, to Staunton at the very time that Southwest Virginia was about to be invaded by Burbridge, General Morgan held a brief and hasty conference with him on the eve of his departure, in which it was agreed by both generals that it would be in vain to meet Burbridge in front, and that, as the enemy had much more to lose in Kentucky than we had in Virginia, the only chance of saving the Southwest was by Morgan's dashing boldly into the heart of Kentucky, and in that way drawing Burbridge away. This plan was carried into effect, and completely succeeded. Burbridge was lured back, his army scattered and crippled, Southwest Virginia saved for the time, and the discomfited general set to reorganizing his command,—a task which occupied him until the necessities of General Sherman rendered all available reinforcements from Kentucky needful at Chattanooga.

These latter movements all took place in the first part of June, after the date of the battle of Cold Harbor. They were designed by Grant as auxiliary to his own movement upon Petersburg, and were a material part of the comprehensive plan he had formed for completely isolating Richmond. When these important movements west of the Blue Ridge, which had their focus at Lynchburg, are considered in connection with Sheridan's great raid in the same central direction, and with the enterprises of Wilson and Kautz against the Danville and Weldon railroads, all of them auxiliary to Grant's attempt upon Petersburg, we are obliged to accord to the enemy's plan of campaign for June, the merit of unusual grasp and ability. Thanks to the miracles of Providence wrought for us on the west of the Blue Ridge, and to the valor of our soldiers and skill of our generals, so eminently displayed on the east, these formidable movements, to encircle and overwhelm the capital of the Confederacy and the State of Virginia, had completely failed.

And yet the measure of misfortune in Grant's distracted campaign appeared to be not yet full. On the 22d of June he made a movement on his left to get possession of the Weldon Railroad, but found the Confederates had extended their right to meet him. While the Second and the Sixth corps of Grant's army were attempting to communicate in this movement, the Confederates, under General Anderson, pierced the centre, captured a battery of four guns, and took prisoners one entire brigade, General Pearce's, and part of another.

Another attempt or raid on the railroad, by Wilson's and Kautz's divisions of cavalry, terminated in disaster. In the neighborhood of Spottswood River, twenty-five miles south of Petersburg, on the 28th, the expedition was attacked, cut in two, the greater part of its artillery abandoned, and its wagon-trains left in the hands of the Confederates. The enemy had been encountered by Hampton's cavalry, and Finnegan's and Mahone's infantry brigades; and the results of the various conflicts were enumerated as one thousand prisoners, thirteen pieces of artillery, thirty wagons and ambulances, and many small-arms.

THE GREAT MINE EXPLOSION.

But some weeks later another remarkable and desperate attempt was to be made by Grant upon Petersburg, the artifice and elaboration of which were among the greatest curiosities of his campaign. A citizen of Petersburg had, early in July, printed what was supposed to be a crazy letter, stating that he had certain information, at which General Lee would probably laugh, and which he preferred to communicate to the more credulous quarter of the newspapers, to the effect that Grant designed to mine the city of Petersburg, blow it into the air, and thus accomplish its destruction.

Although the scheme of the Yankees was not quite so extensive, it was elaborate and formidable enough. For six weeks Grant had been preparing a mine on the slopes of Cemetery Hill, with the view of opening the way to an assault on the second line of works that crowned its crest. From day to day, by the aid of the shovel and the pick, the Yankee lines had been insidiously advanced by zigzags and covered ways, until the outlying pickets of both armies scarcely averaged 500 yards' distance between them. Along portions of the line, the interval between the rifle-pits was scarcely 150 yards. The crest of Cemetery Hill frowning with guns was not more than 800 yards distant from the advanced works of the Yankees, and its gently sloping sides were welted with long rows of earthworks, pitted with redoubts and redans, and ridged with serried salients and curtains, and other skilful defences.

To draw off the attention of the Confederates from his real business, Grant had ordered the Second corps to cross to the north side of the James; and at the same time an empty train of four hundred wagons crossed the Appomattox in view of the Confederate signal stations.

It was appointed that the mine, which contained eight tons of powder, should be exploded at three o'clock in the morning of the 30th July, and that thereupon Burnside, who com manded the Yankee centre, should pierce the works in front of him. Simultaneously with the advance of the infantry, every piece of siege artillery posted along the line was ordered to open upon the Confederates; and all the field artillery which could be got into position, after the opening of the battle, was to advance, as opportunity offered, and bring their batteries into play. It was naturally expected that the shock of the explosion, and of the suddenness of this awful fire, would have a demoralizing effect, and so make the way of the infantry easier.

The mine was not exploded until half-past four o'clock in the morning. The earth was rent along the entire course of the excavation, exhibiting a yawning chasm; in some places it heaved slowly and majestically to the surface; in others, where the charge in the burrow was heaviest, immense masses of dull, red earth were thrown high in air, and human forms, and gun-carriages, and small-arms, might be seen shooting up in this fountain of horror.

But the explosion had only demolished a six-gun battery It was followed immediately by such a thunder of artillery as had seldom been heard before. Ninety-five pieces niched in every hill-side, commanding the position of the Confederates, belched out their sheets of flame and milk-white smoke, while screeching and howling shell sped forward in their work of destruction. But the Confederates were not dismayed. In a few moments their own pieces were replying, and banks of angry smoke partially veiled the field from both sides.

In the midst of the shock of artillery, through the dense clouds of flying dust, the assaulting column of the Yankees passed through the crater, fifty feet in length, and half as many wide, in what was supposed to be the easy attempt of carrying the second line of Confederate works. But there were men there ready to receive them who had never flinched from death, and who were not to be alarmed by loud and furious noises. Some colored troops, under General White's command, were pushed forward, but the poor creatures, unwilling to be thus sacrificed, were soon panic-stricken and past control. They crushed into the ranks of the white troops and broke through to the rear. The demoralization was rapid. The whole mass of Yankees, broken and shattered, swept back like a torrent into the crater, which was soon choked with the flying and the dead. An order was given to retreat to the old lines, but to do this an open space had to be traversed, and this again was closely dotted with Yankee dead.

The action was very brief, very terrible, very decisive. Nothing in the war exceeded it in point of severity, and probably no conflict had ever been attended with all the appointments of war displayed in such graphic prominence. The explosion of the mine, the tremendous peals of artillery and musketry, the effort of the attacking column, the carnage, and finally the retreat of the Yankees to their old lines, all composed a scene of terrible and thrilling interest.

The Yankee loss was quite five thousand; that of the Confederates was trivial in comparison. It was thus stated in detail: Mahone's division, four hundred and fifty; Elliot's South Carolina brigade, which was in the blown up fort, three hundred; Ransom, Clingman, and Wise, whose commands were under musketry and artillery firing for some time, three hundred.

The ghastly failure of this last of Grant's attempts upon Petersburg appeared to be almost sufficient to persuade the Yankee public that his whole campaign had been a failure. Some intelligent Yankee newspapers made peculiar comments upon it. The Intelligencer, published in Washington, said: "After a loss of more than five thousand men, the army has made no advance towards the capture of that city, which is itself only an outpost of the city of Richmond. The delay in springing the mine, the want of concert and promptitude in following up the explosion with a dash by our assaulting column, and the inaptitude which ordered that this assaulting column should be selected from the least trustworthy and homogeneous corps in the army, are a sufficient explanation perhaps of this calamity." The New York Times was yet more querulous and explicit. It said: "Under the most favorable circumstances, with the rebel force reduced by two great detachments, we failed to carry their lines. Will they not conclude that the twenty-five thousand men that held Grant in check are sufficient to garrison the works of Petersburg? Will they not conclude that, if they were able thus to

hold their own with the force of from eighteen to twenty thou
sand men sent to the north side of the James River neutral
ized, this force is available for active operations elsewhere ?"

It was evident that the spirit of the North had commenced
to stagger under this accumulation of disaster. Gold had al
ready nearly touched three hundred. The uneasy whispers in
Washington of another draft gave new suggestions to popular
discontent. The Confederate Congress had adjourned, after the
publication of an address referring to recent military events
and the confirmed resolution of the South, and deprecating the
enemy's continuance of the war. These declarations were
eagerly seized upon by Northern journals, who insisted that
no time should be lost in determining whether they might not
possibly signify a willingness on the part of the South to make
peace on the basis of new constitutional guaranties. The
finances at Washington were becoming desperate. Mr. Chase,
the Secretary of the Treasury, had peremptorily resigned. His
last words of official counsel were, that nothing could save the
finances but a series of military successes of undoubted magnitude.

The brilliant and so far successful campaign of General Lee
in Virginia added, if that were possible, to the popular confidence and devotion which were concentrated upon him more
than any other man of the South. He had indulged in no
terms of exultation. He had written the history of his great
summer campaign of 1864, in brief telegrams in which there
was never a stray word, and the fullest expressions of which
were ascriptions of success to the providence of God. Now in
the highest moments of Confederate confidence and expectation,
when indeed the people of the South had reason to suppose
that they stood on the threshold of peace, and were about to
crown their hopes with triumph, General Lee was still the
modest and reserved commander, never raising his voice in a
note of triumph, or spending a comment upon the situation of
affairs.

A newspaper printed in Virginia complained that " General
Lee never speaks," and with playful but sagacious comment
continued : " What does he think about ? None of us can read
the thoughts of that impenetrable bosom. It is appropriate
that the hero of this story should not be garrulous ; the sadness

of the time renders it fitting that the helmsman should guide the ship with few words spoken. Perhaps it is by his very reserve that General Lee has contributed, as much as by any other quality, to make the impression he has made on his fellow-citizens. He came before them at the beginning of the war by no means the American ideal of a great man. That personage was expected to appear with a hullabaloo; he was to descend in a shower of fireworks, and environed by a myriad of bursting lights and crackling explosions. For a quiet, undemonstrative gentleman to step upon the scenes was not at all to their liking; and therefore, in the beginning, General Lee was not popular."

"Here comes a man bred in the army. He had been reared a gentleman. He despised humbug. He loved order, and every thing and everybody in his place. He told the ladies at Culpepper Courthouse, in 1861, who came out to greet him, to 'go home.' In Richmond they said he had no manners; he attended to his business, and spoke little. They sent him to Western Virginia—a small theatre, when Beauregard was at Manassas and Johnston was at Winchester; he went, and made no comment. The campaign failed—they called him Turveydrop—he did not attempt to excuse himself. Soo we find him in a blaze of glory, the hero of the battles around Richmond. He is still silent. He marches to Manassas, and achieves another great victory. Not a word escapes him. He takes Winchester, is foiled at Sharpsburg for the want of men—defeats Burnside at Fredericksburg—Hooker at Chancellorsville—but he breaks not his silence. He has the terrible trial of Gettysburg—he only remarked, 'It was my fault'—and then in the present year he has conducted this greatest of all his campaigns—undoubtedly one of the finest in the war. Silent still. When will he speak? Has he nothing to say? What does he think of our affairs? Should he speak, how the country would hang upon every word that fell from him!"

THE SINKING OF THE PRIVATEER ALABAMA.

We must note here, as belonging to the period of Confederate successes we have narrated, an event of the war which considerably qualified the general exultation of the South.

While the general situation on land, especially in Virginia, was so advantageous for the Confederacy, and the grand events of the campaign of 1864 had so far been decided in its favor, there occurred an incident of disaster, which, though distant in point of space, and of but little real importance in the decision of the general fortune of the war, was yet the subject of keen and peculiar regret to the Confederates.

This incident was the loss of the famous privateer Alabama. She had eluded the Yankee naval vessels at the Cape of Good Hope and Straits of Sunda, and returning westward had proceeded to the French port of Cherbourg. Here Captain Semmes of the Alabama was strongly persuaded—probably by those who valued the *eclat* abroad of the Southern arms more than the substantial interests of the Confederacy, so unequally matched in the war, especially in point of naval power—to risk his vessel in a gratuitous fight with a Yankee steamer lying off the harbor—the Kearsarge. The only object of such a naval duel could be the desire of a certain glory on the part of Captain Semmes, for which he took the unwarrantable risk of sacrificing the only really formidable naval structure of the Confederates. It should have occurred to him that, even in the event of success, he would inflict no appreciable injury upon the enemy's naval power, and would secure nothing more than some of that idle glory which was already cheap with his countrymen.

The ships were about equal in match, the tonnage being about the same—the Alabama carrying one 7-inch Blakely rifled gun, one 8-inch smooth-bore pivot gun, and six 32-pounders, smooth-bore, in broadside ; the Kearsarge carrying four broadside 32-pounders, two 11-inch and one 28-pound rifle. On the morning of the 19th of June, the Alabama steamed out of the harbor of Cherbourg, for the purpose of engaging the Kearsarge, which had been lying off-and-on the port for several days previously. She came up with the latter at a distance of about seven miles from the shore. The vessels were about one mile from each other, when the Alabama opened with solid shot upon the enemy, to which he replied in a few minutes.

To prevent passing each other too speedily, and to maintain their respective broadsides bearing, it became necessary to fight in a circle, the two ships steaming around a common centre, and preserving a distance from each other of from a quarter to half a mile. The enemy's shot and shell began to tell upon the hull of the Alabama. Captain Semmes remarked that his shell, though apparently exploding against the sides of the Kearsarge, were doing her but little damage, and returned to solid shot firing, afterwards alternating with shot and shell.

In little more than an hour, the Alabama was ascertained to be in a sinking condition, the enemy's shell having exploded in her sides and between decks, opening large apertures, through which the water rushed with great rapidity. For some few minutes Captain Semmes had hopes of being able to reach the French coast, for which purpose he gave the ship all steam, and set such of the fore and aft sails as were available. The ship filled so rapidly, however, that before she had made much progress the fires were extinguished in the furnaces, and she was evidently on the point of sinking.

Captain Semmes hauled down his colors, when the Kearsarge was within four hundred yards of him. Yet the enemy fired upon the Alabama five times after her colors had been struck. "It is charitable to suppose," says Captain Semmes, " that a ship of war of a Christian nation could not have done this in tentionally."

As the Alabama was on the point of settling, every man, in obedience to a previous order which had been given the crew, jumped overboard and endeavored to save himself. There was no appearance of any boat coming from the enemy after the Alabama went down. Fortunately, however, the steam-yacht Deerhound, owned by a gentleman of Lancashire, England, Mr. John Lancaster, who was himself on board, steamed up in the midst of the drowning men, and rescued a number of both officers and men from the water, among them Captain Semmes himself.

The loss of the Alabama in killed and wounded was thirty. There was no life lost on the Kearsarge; and although she had received thirteen or fourteen shots in and about the hull, and sixteen or seventeen about the masts and rigging, she was not materially damaged. In his official report of the fight, Captain Semmes said: "At the end of the engagement, it was discovered by those of our officers who went alongside the enemy's ship with the wounded, that her midship section, on both sides, was thoroughly iron-coated; this having been done with chain constructed for the purpose, placed perpendicularly from the rail to the water's edge, the whole covered over by a thin outer planking, which gave no indication of the armor beneath. This planking had been ripped off in every direction by our shot and shell, the chain broken and indented in many places, and forced partly into the ship's side. She was most effectually guarded, however, in this section from penetration."

The loss of the Alabama was a most severe blow to the privateer service of the South. That service had already caused nearly a thousand Yankee vessels to be sold to foreign shipping merchants; and it was officially reported at Washington that 478,665 tons of American shipping were flying other flags. Such had been the terror inspired by Confederate privateers, of which the Alabama had been, by far, the most formidable. She alone had accomplished a work of destruction estimated at from eight to ten millions of dollars. It was reported that the news of her loss was received on the exchanges of New York and Boston with a joy far livelier than would have been conceived by these commercial patriots, if they had heard of a great victory over Lee's army in Virginia.

CHAPTER XVI.

PARALLEL and concurrent with Grant's summer campaign
in Virginia, was the more difficult but less deadly campaign
of Sherman in Georgia. Grant's *point d'appui* was on the
Rapidan, while Sherman's was at Chattanooga, in Tennessee.
The Alleghany Mountains separated these grand movements;
a thousand miles of distance intervened between them; communication between them was rare, and, to a certain extent,
impossible. There is no doubt that Sherman had the more
difficult task to accomplish. He had but a single line of railway to reach his objective point, Atlanta, and this traversed a
wild and mountainous country. Grant could change his base
at pleasure, or as circumstances required it; he had water
communication with the North, and transports within hailing
distance; he could run no danger from lack of subsistence or
munitions of war. Again, Sherman, passing through a broken
and intricate country, had to guard his flanks and rear, at
every step, from cavalry. Grant had only to put an army of
occupation in the Shenandoah Valley to close the single defile

between the great mountain ridges of Virginia, and thus securely protect his rear from even the possibility of danger.

It appears from the official report of General Sherman's operations, that he had estimated the force required to reach and capture Atlanta, at one hundred thousand men and two hundred and fifty pieces of artillery : he started with ninety-eight thousand seven hundred and ninety-seven men and two hundred and fifty-four guns. This force was divided as follows :—Army of the Cumberland, Major-General Thomas, sixty thousand seven hundred and seventy-three men, one hundred and thirty guns; Army of the Tennessee, Major-General McPherson, twenty-four thousand four hundred and sixty-five men, ninety-six guns ; Army of the Ohio, Major-General Schofield, thirteen thousand five hundred and fifty-nine men, twenty-eight guns. Sherman's intention was to make these proportions fifty thousand, thirty-five thousand, and fifteen thousand, but that wretched *fiasco* known as the Red River Expedition kept back some of McPherson's troops, and, besides ruining itself, did as much as possible towards impeding Sherman. It will be seen he was furnished within twelve hundred of the number of men he asked for.

Here again we have the repetition of the story of fearful odds against the Confederates. General Joseph E. Johnston, who had taken command of the Army of Tennessee, had held the Confederate lines in North Georgia, during the winter, with thirty odd thousand men. On the 1st of December, 1864, he enumerated the effective total of the infantry and artillery of the army, including two brigades belonging to the department of Mississippi, as 36,826. The effective total of the cavalry, including Roddy's command at Tuscumbia, was 5,613.

In the last weeks of February, 1865, General Johnston had proposed to the government at Richmond an offensive movement against the enemy, on the just ground that he was increasing the disproportion of numbers, and would take the Confederates at greater disadvantage than if they were to essay at once a forward movement and try issues with him. The proposition lingered in the War Department from February to May. General Bragg and President Davis had their own plan of offensive operations. General Johnston in vain telegraphed to Richmond: "I expressly accept taking the offensive; I only differ with you as to details." But "the details" dictated at Richmond were insisted upon; and when eventually, in the latter part of April, President Davis sent an officer to Georgia to explain his wishes to Johnston, the enemy had already prepared to make his long-meditated and formidable movement.

On the 1st of May, General Johnston reported the enemy ready to advance. The effective artillery and infantry of the Army of Tennessee amounted then to 40,900; the effective cavalry to about four thousand. With this force Johnston had to fight more than twice his numbers, and had no other prospect of compensation but in superior skill and strategy.

Sherman moved on Dalton in three columns; Thomas in front, Schofield from Cleveland on the northeast, while McPherson threw himself on the line of communication southwest at Resaca, fifteen miles south of Dalton. On the 7th of May Thomas occupied Tunnel Hill, ten miles northwest of Dalton, and took up a strong position at Buzzard's Roost. By the flank movement on Resaca, Johnston was forced to evacuate Dalton.

On the 14th the first important engagement of the campaign took place in Resaca valley. Two efforts were made to carry the breastworks of the Confederates, without success, when Johnston, in the afternoon, assumed the offensive, and drove the enemy some distance, with a loss which his own bulletins stated to be two thousand.

On the 15th there was desultory fighting, and on the 16th General Johnston took up, at leisure, his line of retrograde movement in the direction of the Etowah River, passing through Kingston and Cassville.

It was clear, in General Johnston's mind, that the great numerical superiority of the Yankee army made it expedient to risk battle only when position, or some blunder of the enemy, might give him counter-balancing advantages. He therefore determined to fall back slowly, until circumstances should put the chances of battle in his favor, keeping so near the Yankee army as to prevent its sending reinforcements to Grant, and hoping, by taking advantage of positions and opportunities, to reduce the odds against him by partial engagements. He also expected it to be materially reduced, before the end of June, by the expiration of the terms of service of many of the regiments which had not re-enlisted. In this way he fell back to Cassville in two marches.

Expecting to be attacked, Johnston had drawn up his troops in an excellent position on a bold ridge immediately in rear of Cassville, with an open valley before it. But there appears to have been some doubts among his officers as to the value of the position. Lieutenant-Generals Polk and Hood together expressed the opinion, very decidedly, that the Yankee artillery would drive them, the next day, from their positions, and urged General Johnston to abandon the ground immediately, and cross the Etowah. Lieutenant-General Hardee was confident that he could hold his position. Of this dilemma, General Johnston writes in his official report : " The other two officers, however, were so earnest and unwilling to depend on the ability of their corps to defend the ground, that I yielded, and the army crossed the Etowah on the 20th of May, *a step which I have regretted ever since.*"

ENGAGEMENT AT NEW HOPE CHURCH.

On the 25th the enemy was found to be intrenched near and east of Dallas. Hood's corps was placed with its centre near New Hope Church, and Polk's and Hardee's ordered between it and the Atlanta road, which Hardee's left was to cover. An hour before sunset Stewart's division, at New Hope Church, was fiercely attacked by Hooker's corps, which it repulsed after a hot engagement of two hours. Skirmishing was kept up on the 26th and 27th. At half past five, P. M., on the 27th, Howard's corps assailed Cleburne's division, and was driven back, about dark, with great slaughter. In these two actions the Confederates were not intrenched. Their loss in each was about four hundred and fifty in killed and wounded. On the 27th the enemy's dead, except those borne off, were counted six hundred, and a reasonable estimate of their entire loss may, therefore, be stated as certainly not less than three thousand

So far, the retrograde movement of Johnston was, in some respects, a success. It had been attended with at least two considerable victories—Resaca and New Hope; it had been executed deliberately, being scarcely ever under the immediate pressure of the enemy's advance; and it had now nearly approached the decisive line of the Chattahoochee, or whatever other line he, who was supposed to be the great strategist of the Confederacy, should select for the cover of Atlanta. The events of the campaign, so far, were recounted with characteristic modesty by General Johnston. On the 1st of June he telegraphed to Richmond of his army: "In partial engagements it has had great advantages, and the sum of all the combats amounts to a battle."

The two armies continued to manœuvre for position. Skirmishing was kept up until the 4th of June, the enemy gradually extending his intrenched line towards the railroad and Ackworth. On the morning of the 5th the army was formed with its left at Lost Mountain, its centre near Gilgath Church, and its right near the railroad. On the 7th, the right, covered by Noonday Creek, was extended across the Ackworth and Marietta road. The enemy approached under cover of successive lines of intrenchments. On the 19th a new line was taken by Johnston; Hood's corps with its right on the Marietta and Canton road, Loring's on the Kenesaw Mountain, and Hardee's with its left extending across the Lost Mountain and Marietta road. The enemy approached, as usual, under cover of intrenchment. In this position there was incessant fighting and skirmishing until July 3d, the enemy gradually extending his intrenched right towards Atlanta.

BATTLE OF KENESAW MOUNTAIN.

On the 27th of June, General Sherman directed an attack on Johnston's position at Kenesaw Mountain. This mountain was the apex of Johnston's lines. Both armies were in strong works, the opposite salients being so near, in some places, that skirmishers could not be thrown out. The assault of the enemy was made in three columns, about eight o'clock in the morning. It was repulsed on every part of the Confederate line. The assaults were most vigorous on Cheatham's and Cleburne's divisions of Hardee's corps, and French's and

Featherstone's of Loring's. Lieutenant-General Hardee reported that Cheatham's division lost in killed, wounded, and missing, one hundred and ninety-five. The enemy opposed to it, by the statement of staff-officers subsequently captured, lost two thousand. The loss of Cleburne's division was eleven, that of the enemy in his front, one thousand ; and Major-General Loring reported two hundred and thirty-six of his corps killed, wounded, and missing. The loss of the enemy, by their own estimates, was between twenty-five hundred and three thousand. Of this affair General Sherman wrote, with rare candor, or with peculiar recklessness, that it *was* a failure ; but that it demonstrated to General Johnston the enemy's courage—that it " would assault, and that boldly."

Sherman, on the failure of the Kenesaw assault, again resorted to manœuvring. McPherson's whole army was thrown rapidly to the Chattahoochee. On the 22d of July, Johnston finding the enemy's right nearer to Atlanta, by several miles, than our left, the army fell back, during the night, to Smyrna Church. On the 4th, Major-General Smith reported that he should be compelled to withdraw, on the morning of the 5th, to the line of intrenchments covering the railroad bridge and Turner's Ferry. The army was, therefore, ordered to retire at the same time to that line, to secure our bridges. The cavalry crossed the Chattahoochee—Wheeler observing it for some twenty miles above, and Jackson as far below.

Sherman was left master of the Chattahoochee, and Atlanta lay but eight miles distant. Peach-tree Creek, and the river below its mouth, was now taken by Johnston for his line of defence. A position on the high ground south of the creek was selected for the army, from which to attack the enemy while crossing. The engineer officers, with a large force of negroes, were set to work to strengthen the fortifications of Atlanta ; and the two armies confronted each other in what was unmistakably the crisis of the Georgia campaign.

We can easily state the just and historical merits of that question so much discussed in Confederate prints—the retreat of Johnston to Atlanta. Something may always be said on both sides of a question which has divided the public mind, and been a topic of a certain censure as well as of approbation.

It is true that, in some respects, Johnston's retreat to Atlanta was a sore disappointment to the Confederate public; for it had given up to the Yankees half of Georgia, abandoned one of the finest wheat districts of the Confederacy, almost ripe for harvest; and at Rome and on the Etowah River, had surrendered to the enemy iron-rolling mills, and government works of great value.

In other respects, however, the retreat had been a masterpiece of strategy, and a solid as well as a splendid success. The loss of our infantry and artillery, from the 5th of May, had been about ten thousand in killed and wounded, and four thousand seven hundred from all other causes. According to the opinions of our most experienced officers, daily reports of prisoners, and statements of Northern papers, the enemy's loss in action could not have been less than five times as great as ours.

The strategic advantages which Johnston had secured in his retreat were indisputable. "At Dalton," writes Johnston, "the great numerical superiority of the enemy made the chances of battle much against us; and, even if beaten, they had a safe refuge behind the fortified pass of Ringgold and in the fortress of Chattanooga. Our refuge, in case of defeat, was in Atlanta, one hundred miles off, with three rivers intervening. Therefore, victory for us could have been decisive, while defeat would have been utterly disastrous. Between Dalton and the Chattahoochee we could have given battle only by attacking the enemy intrenched, or so near intrenchments that the only result of success to us would have been his falling back into them; while defeat would have been our ruin. In the course pursued, our troops, always fighting under cover, had very trifling losses, compared with those they inflicted; so that the enemy's numerical superiority was reduced daily and rapidly, and we could reasonably have expected to cope with the Federal army on equal ground by the time the Chattahoochee was passed. Defeat on this side of the river would have been its destruction. We, if beaten, had a place of refuge in Atlanta, too strong to be assaulted, and too extensive to be invested."

It was clear, in the month of July, that a pause had been given to the parallel operations of the enemy in Virginia and Georgia; aimed, the one at Richmond, which the Yankees entitled the heart and brains of the Confederacy; and the other at Atlanta, the centre of important manufacturing en terprises, and the door to the great granary of the Gulf States. Both movements were for the time unmistakably in check; and the interlude of indecision afforded a curious commentary on the boastful confidence that had recorded the fall of Richmond and the capture of Atlanta as the expectations of each twenty-four hours.

There was reason, indeed, for the North to be depressed. The disappointment of the Yankees was with particular reference to the campaign of Grant in Virginia. The advance from the Rapidan, which we have followed to its recoil before Petersburg, had been made under conditions of success which had attended no other movement of the enemy. It was made after eight months' deliberate preparation. In the Congress at Washington it was stated that, in these eight months, the Government had actually raised seven hundred thousand men, an extent of preparation which indicated an intention to overwhelm and crush the Confederacy by a resistless combined attack. Nor was this all. One hundred thousand three months' men were accepted from Ohio and other States, for defensive service, in order that General Grant might avail himself of the whole force of trained soldiers. The result of the campaign, so far, did not justify the expectations on which it had been planned. The Yankee Government which, since the commencement of the war, had called for a grand total of twenty-three hundred thousand men, and had actually raised eighteen hundred thousand men, of an average term of service of three years, to crush the Confederacy, saw, in the fourth year of the war, the Confederacy erect and defiant, and Richmond shielded by an army which had so far set at naught the largest preparations and most tremendous exertions of the North.

There had been successes, too, in other parts of the Confederacy than Virginia and Georgia. While the movements we have just been relating were taking place in Georgia, an important event had taken place in the Southwest—the defeat of the Yankee expedition under Sturgis on its way from Memphis to operate in Sherman's rear. In this action, at Guntown (13th June), Sturgis lost most of his infantry and all of his artillery and trains, and the Confederates, under Forrest, achieved a victory that had an important influence on the campaign in Georgia. Forrest took two thousand prisoners, and killed and wounded an equal number.

This expedition, so severely punished, was one of peculiar atrocity. Its crimes were enough to sicken the ear. I flourished the title of the "Avengers of Fort Pillow." "Before the battle," says a correspondent, "fugitives from the counties through which Sturgis and his troops were advancing came into camp, detailing incidents which made men shudder, who are accustomed to scenes of violence and bloodshed. I cannot relate the stories of these poor frightened people. Rude unlettered men, who had fought at Shiloh, and in many subsequent battles, wept like children when they heard of the enormities to which their mothers, sisters, and wives had been subjected by the negro mercenaries of Sturgis."

Indeed, we may state here, that the enemy's summer campaign in Virginia and in the West was, more than any other, marked by the barbarities of the enemy. These barbarities had, by regular augmentation, become more atrocious as the war had progressed. In this year, they exceeded all that was already known of the brutality of our enraged enemy.

General Sherman illustrated the campaign in the West by a letter of instructions to General Burbridge, commanding in the Department of Kentucky, charging him to treat all partisans of the Confederates in that State as "*wild beasts*." It was the invariable and convenient practice of the Yankees to designate as "guerillas" whatever troops of the Confederates were particularly troublesome to them; and the opprobrious term was made, by General Sherman, to include the regularly commissioned soldiers of General Morgan's command, and whatever bodies of Confederate cavalry chose to roam over territory which the enemy disputed.*

---

* Burbridge was not slow to carry out the suggestions or instructions of his masters. The following is a copy of a section of one of his orders.

HEADQUARTERS DISTRICT KENTUCKY,
FIFTH DIVISION, TWENTY-THIRD ARMY CORPS,
Lexington, Kentucky, July 16, 1864.

Rebel sympathizers living within five miles of any scene of outrage committed by armed men, not recognized as public enemies by the rules and

Some expressions in the orders referred to were chara :ter istic of the Yankee, and indicated those notions of constitu tional law which had rapidly demoralized the North. General Sherman declared that he had already recommended to Gov ernor Bramlette of Kentucky, " at one dash to arrest every man in the country who was dangerous to it." " The fact is," said this military Solomon, " in our country personal liberty has been so well secured, that public safety is lost sight of in our laws and institutions; and the fact is, we are thrown back one hundred years in civilization, laws, and every thing else, and will go right straight to anarchy and the devil, if some body don't arrest our downward progress. We, the military, must do it, and we have right and law on our side. . . . . Under this law, everybody can be made to stay at home and mind his or her own business, and, if they won't do that, can be sent away." These sage remarks on American liberty were concluded with the recommendation that all males and females, in sympathy with so-called " guerillas," should be arrested and sent down the Mississippi to some foreign land, where they should be doomed to perpetual exile.

As Sherman advanced into the interior of Georgia he laid waste the country, fired the houses, and even did not hesitate at the infamous expedient of destroying the agricultural imple ments of all those who produced from the soil subsistence for man. He declared to the persecuted people that this time he would have their property, but, if the war continued, next year he would have their lives. Four hundred factory girls whom he captured in Georgia he bundled into army wagons,

---

usages of war, will be arrested and sent beyond the limits of the United States.

In accordance with instructions from the major-general commanding the military district of the Mississippi, so much of the property of rebel sympathiz ers as may be necessary to indemnify the Government or loyal citizens for losses incurred by the acts of such lawless men, will be seized and appropriated for this purpose.

Whenever an unarmed Union citizen is murdered, four guerillas will be selected from the prisoners in the hands of the military authorities, and pub licly shot to death in the most convenient place near the scene of outrage. By command of

Brevet Major-General S. G. BURBRIDGE.

J. B. DICKSON, Captain and A A. General.

and ordered them to be transported beyond the Ohio, where the poor girls were put adrift, far from home and friends, in a strange land.*

From Chattanooga to Marietta there was presented to the eye one vast scene of misery. The fugitives from ruined villages or deserted fields sought shelter in the mountains. Cities were sacked, towns burnt, populations decimated. All along the roads were great wheat-fields, and crops sufficient to feed all New England, which were to be lost for want of laborers. The country had been one of the most beautiful of the Confederacy. One looked upon the gentle undulations of the valleys, terminating in the windings of the rivers, and flanked by the majestic barriers of the mountains. This beautiful country had been trodden over by both armies. In every town the more public buildings and the more conspicuous residences had been devoured by fire, or riddled with shot and shell. Every house used as headquarters, or for Confederate commissary stores, or occupied by prominent citizens, had been singled out by the enemy for destruction. In some instances churches

---

* The following announcement appeared in the Louisville newspapers:

"ARRIVAL OF WOMEN AND CHILDREN FROM THE SOUTH.—The train which arrived from Nashville last evening brought up from the South two hundred and forty-nine women and children, who are sent here by order of General Sherman, to be transferred north of the Ohio River, there to remain during the war. We understand that there are now at Nashville fifteen hundred women and children, who are in a very destitute condition, and who are to be sent to this place to be sent North. A number of them were engaged in the manufactories at Sweet Water at the time that place was captured by our forces. These people are mostly in a destitute condition, having no means to provide for themselves a support. Why they should be sent here to be transferred North is more than we can understand."

It was also stated in these same papers that, when these women and children arrived at Louisville, they were detained there and advertised to be hired out as servants, to take the place of the large number of negroes who had been liberated by the military authorities and were now gathered in large camps throughout Kentucky, where they were fed and supported in idleness and viciousness at the expense of the loyal taxpayers. Thus, while these negro women were rioting and luxuriating in the Federal camps, on the bounty of the Government, the white women and children of the South were arrested at their homes, and sent off as prisoners to a distant country, to be sold in bondage, as the following advertisement fully attests:

"NOTICE.—Families residing in the city or the country, wishing seamstresses or servants, can be suited by applying at the refugee quarters on Broadway, between Ninth and Tenth. This is sanctioned by Captain Jones, provost-marshal."

had not escaped. They had been stripped for fire-wood or con verted into barracks and hospitals. Fences were demolished, and here and there a lordly mansion stood an unsightly ruin.

The vandalism of Hunter in Virginia drew upon him the censure of the few journals in the North which made any pretension to the decencies of humanity. At Lexington, he had burned the Virginia Military Institute with its valuable library, philosophical and chemical apparatus, relics and geological specimens; sacked Washington College, and burned the house of ex-Governor Letcher, giving his wife only ten minutes to save a few articles of clothing.

Such enormities were monstrous enough; they shocked the moral sentiment of the age; yet they did not affright the soul of the South. The outrages practised upon helpless women, more helpless old age, and hopeless poverty, assured the people of the Confederacy of the character of their enemies, and the designs of the war, and awakened resolution to oppose to the last extremity the mob of murderers and lawless miscreants who desecrated their soil and invaded their homes.

We turn from the dominant and controlling events of the campaign of 1864, in Virginia and Georgia, to other fields of the war, which were within, or close upon the period which our narrative so far has traversed.

There properly belonged to the campaign of the summer and early fall of 1864 three projects of the Confederate invasion of the territory held or disputed by the enemy. These were Early's invasion of Maryland and Pennsylvania, Morgan's invasion of Kentucky, and Price's invasion of Missouri. Their results were small; opportunities were badly used; in brief, the Confederate attempts of 1864 at invasion did not differ from the former weak experiments of the kind.

EARLY'S INVASION OF MARYLAND, ETC.

The Confederates had planned a series of offensive operations on a small scale, the object of which was to interrupt the main campaigns in the East and West. This line of operations began with Early's invasion of Maryland. About the same time the enemy was startled by the news of an invasion of Kentucky by a considerable body of Confederates, moving into that State through Pound Gap. But Early's movement was the superior one, and commands attention first.

After the engagement at Lynchburg, June 18, Hunter found no way of escape so convenient as through the Blue Ridge to Gauley. This left the way open for Early to move up the valley. He did so, accompanied by a cavalry force under Ransom, and reached the Baltimore and Ohio Railroad, July 3, at a point just above Harper's Ferry, threatening Martinsburg. Sigel, holding the latter place, fell back towards Sharpsburg. The Confederates immediately occupied Martinsburg, where they captured valuable stores. The same day a fight occurred at Leetown, south of the railroad, in which General Mulligan, covering Sigel's retreat, was finally forced back to Sharpsburg, where he joined Sigel, and another engagement occurred. The Yankee forces being overpowered, fell back to Maryland Heights. Max Weber, evacuating Harper's Ferry, joined Sigel. In the mean time, General E. B. Tyler, protecting the railroad from Baltimore to the Monocacy, prepared for resisting the Confederates and to reinforce Sigel. General Lew Wallace joined him on the afternoon of the 3d.

On Saturday, July 9, the Confederates disappeared from Greencastle, Hagerstown, and from other points threatened; but this was only for the purpose of concentration. The Yankee forces had evacuated Frederick the previous night, and fallen back to Monocacy Bridge.

BATTLE OF MONOCACY BRIDGE.

The bridge is four miles from Frederick City. The river runs due north and south. The railroad and national road cross the river at very nearly the same point. As our troops advanced towards the river from Frederick it became apparent that some forces of the enemy, supposed at the time to be cavalry, were holding the east bank. A couple of our batteries opened on them from the front, while our cavalry were ordered to go up the stream and cross over the bridge. At the same time a considerable force of our infantry moved down the stream, and crossing south of the bridge, formed in a piece of woods on the high ground. It was still believed that the enemy had nothing but cavalry on the ground, but our infantry being ordered forward, emerged into an open field and discovered the enemy's infantry drawn up in line of battle along the railroad at the further end of the field. The railroad being several feet lower than the field, the enemy had all the advantages of an intrenched position. Evans's brigade charged across this field under a heavy fire of musketry. When within fifty yards of the enemy's position, another body of the enemy emerged from the woods on our right and attacked the brigade in flank, and rendered its position critical; but other of our forces coming up, the enemy's flank movement was counteracted. A simultaneous charge was then made by our whole line, when the enemy broke and fled, leaving between a thousand and twelve hundred dead and wounded, and seven hundred prisoners in our hands. The enemy left the railroad and national pike and fled north in the direction of Gettysburg.

In this action, which lasted about two hours from the time of firing the first shot, we lost in killed and wounded between five and six hundred men and some valuable officers.

Our forces did not follow the enemy, but proceeded directly towards Washington and Baltimore, making rapid marches, but collecting cattle and horses along the route.

The Yankee capital was in imminent peril, and the whisper ran through the North that it was already lost or surely doomed. General Early might have taken it by assault. There were only a few regiments to man its defences, and the advance of the Confederates was waited hourly by a population thrown into pitiable consternation. But General Early did not seize the great opportunity of 1864. He passed the time in which he might have struck the decisive blow in weak hesitation; he reconnoitred the defences of Washington; he scattered his forces into expeditions to destroy telegraphs and intercept trains; but he could not make up his mind to attack the Yankee capital, and with that characteristic Confederate stupidity which never completed its victories, and was easily pleased with half-way successes, he was satisfied with the results of a raid, where, with more enterprise and persistence, he might have achieved the most decisive and brilliant success of the war—marched into Washington, and made his name as illustrious as that of Stonewall Jackson.

About the middle of July the Confederates began to disappear across the Potomac fords, carrying with them many of the fruits of their expedition. It was reported by General Early that he brought south of the Potomac five thousand horses and twenty-five hundred beef-cattle. Besides this, his cavalry and artillery were all supplied with new and valuable horses. He had also created a useful diversion, and compelled Grant to weaken his army materially before Petersburg. But it must be confessed that the results of his expedition fell below public expectation in the South, and that he was justly charged with not having made full use of his opportunities.

After crossing the Potomac, General Early had occasion to give another sharp lesson to the enemy. He turned back upon Crook, who was pursuing him with about 15,000 infantry and cavalry. The fight commenced between Bartonsville and Kernestown, about five miles from Winchester. Our forces ran the enemy to Bunker's Hill, twelve miles beyond Winchester, and thoroughly routed them. General Crook confessed to a loss of one thousand in killed and wounded. Our entire loss was sixty. After this General Early occupied Martinsburg, and a pause ensued in the campaign in the Valley nothing of any importance occurring for some weeks, except the raid of a few hundred Confederate cavalry to Chambersburg, Pennsylvania, who burned a considerable portion of the town.

MORGAN'S INVASION OF KENTUCKY.

General John Morgan's expedition into Kentucky was, on the whole, a failure. In the early part of June, with some 2,500 men, he entered Kentucky by Pound Gap, and by swift movements got possession of Paris, Georgetown, Cynthia, Williamstown, Mount Sterling, and other towns. A passenger train on the Louisville and Lexington Railroad, near Smithfield, was attacked, and two passenger cars and a baggage car burned. Other trains were attacked, and railroad communication was for some days interrupted. On the 9th of June General Burbridge, who followed Morgan from Pound Gap.

came up with him at Mount Sterling, and had an indecisive engagement. A portion of Morgan's command entered Lexington at two o'clock the next morning, burned the Kentucky Central Railroad depot, and left at ten o'clock, in the direction of Georgetown and Frankfort. Part of the town of Cynthia was also burned. Two Ohio regiments stationed there were captured. On the 12th June, General Burbridge fell upon Morgan's forces while at breakfast near Cynthia, and after an hour's hard fighting defeated him, killing three hundred, wounding nearly as many, and capturing nearly four hundred, besides recapturing nearly one hundred of the Ohio troops, and over one thousand horses.

PRICE'S INVASION OF MISSOURI.

It was late in September when offensive operations were essayed in the distant and obscure country west of the Mississippi. In that month, General Price moved into Missouri with a force estimated at from ten to twenty thousand men. A great excitement was produced, and it was thought that a raid was contemplated on St. Louis.

Price's main army moved against the village of Pilot Knob, 86 miles south of St. Louis, the terminus of the railroad, and the depot for supply of the lower outposts. Several desperate assaults were made on this strongly fortified position of the enemy. Under cover of the night, General Ewing, the Yankee in command, evacuated Pilot Knob, and effected a disastrous retreat to Rolla. In his official report he said : "The refugees, men, women, and children, white and black, who clung to the command, nearly sacrificed it by their panics. I had to throw out the available fighting force, infantry and cavalry, as advance and rear guards and flankers, leaving in the body of the column the affrighted non-combatants and two sections of artillery, not often brought into action on the retreat. Repeated and stubborn efforts were made to bring us to a stand, and could they have forced a halt of an hour they would have enveloped and taken us; but our halts, though frequent, were brief, and were only to unlimber the artillery, stagger the pursuers with a few rounds, and move on."

General Price stopped short of Rolla. For some cause—probably the demoralization of his army and their disappointment of active sympathy in the country they had penetrated—he seems to have abandoned at this stage the original designs of his expedition. He subsequently went into winter-quarters in the vicinity of Washington. He collected but few supplies, and his men were reported to be in worse plight than when they left Arkansas.

CHAPTER XVII.

Great revulsion in the public mind of the North in the summer of 1864.—A genera outcry for peace.—Spirit of Yankee newspapers.—The Niagara Falls "Commission."—The Jacques-Gilmore Affair.—Sorry figure of the Confederacy in these negotiations.—The question of peace negotiations in the Confederacy.—True method of peace.—Manifesto of the Confederate Congress.—Position of President Davis—His letter to Governor Vance, of North Carolina.—The CHICAGO CONVENTION, etc.—Speeches, etc.—The real programme of the Democratic party.—Why it broke down.—No virtue in public opinion in the North.—The true peace men of the North.—Their Convention at Cincinnati.—A reaffirmation of Jeffersonian Democracy.—A masterpiece of statesmanship.—The Presidential campaign of 1864.—The RIVAL ADMINISTRATIONS AT RICHMOND AND WASHINGTON.—A COMPARATIVE VIEW OF NORTHERN DESPOTISM.—The conscription and impressment laws of the Confederacy.—The offerings of Southern patriotism.—The Yankee record in the matter of slavery.—"Military necessity."—The Yankee record in the matter of civil liberty.—An outrage upon history.

GRANT's complete failure in the Virginia campaign, and Sherman's dead-lock at Atlanta—the first marked, by the most frightful slaughter—had produced an evident and great revulsion in the public mind of the North. The masses in that country appeared to have become at last thoroughly aroused to a true sense of their condition. On every side arose the demand for peace. Popular demonstrations had already taken place in several localities, showing that the people of the North were growing tired of the war, and demanded that it should be stopped. Yankee newspapers, that were at one time earnest advocates for a vigorous prosecution of the war, were now still more earnestly in favor of a vigorous prosecution of peace. They no longer spoke with bated breath and whispering humbleness. They said what they meant.*

---

* As a most interesting evidence of the extent of this disposition to peace in the Northern mind, we collate the following extracts from "the peace press," as well as from papers that had given a *quasi* support to the war:

From the New York Tribune.

We feel certain that two-thirds of the American people on either side of the dividing line anxiously, absorbingly, *desire peace*, and are ready to make all needful sacrifices to insure it. Then why shall it be long withheld? Let us

In the summer of 1864 there were certain movements look·ing to a special negotiation for peace, which drew no little ot the public attention.   These movements were fruitless—in some respects they were unworthy and absurd ; but they are interesting as indicating, at the time they took place, a general popular disposition to peace, proceeding from the Northern despondency on the one hand, and the consequent hopes of the South.

---

know, as soon as may be, the most that the rebel chiefs will do to secure peace ; let us know what is the "ultimatum" on our side. We have no sympathy with the shuddering dread that our Government may, by listening to propositions from the rebels, virtually acknowledge their independence. Etiquette is the disease of little minds, great souls are never troubled by it.

Washington Constitutional Union.

The cry for peace is rung into our ears from every section of the country—from all divisions and parties. Even the fanatics have cooled down, in measure, from their fury for blood, have lost the vampire instincts ; and, horrified at the tales of slaughter they read, and shocked at the sights of hospital suffering, and of the maimed and crippled crawling about our streets, they even wish the termination of strife which, unprocreative of benefit to either party, even to the *medius terminus*, the negro, is crushing the vital and social existence of both. Physical calamity constantly displayed before their vision, and high prices crushing out the means of comfortable subsistence, has at length softened the heart of the hardened abolitionist into a lurking yearning for the cessation of arms.

Dayton (Ohio) Daily Empire.

We can have no peace so long as the men are allowed to prescribe its terms. Let the people, in their sovereign might, command that this cruel war be ended, and all differences between the States be submitted to the arbitrament of a convention.

Troy Daily Press.

To-day, the people of the "loyal" and seceded States would be able to agree upon conditions of peace and stop the war. And it is the duty of the hour to hasten an opportunity for this, by shoving aside extreme men and placing in power those who believe that, in a government like ours, concession, conciliation and compromise, are better remedies for differences than eternal strife and war.

Chicago Times.

The necessity for peace upon honorable terms is too imperative to permit its sacrifice to a blind, selfish, or corrupt partnership. The alternatives now presented to the nation are peace with honor, and war with dishonor ; peace with preservation of life, and war with its extended and murderous conflicts ; peace with national and individual solvency, and war with national and individual bankruptcy.

From the World.

The new President, to be nominated at Chicago, and elected in November, must be a man ready and willing to meet any and every overture for peace, a

In the month of July the whole Northern public was aroused by a sudden statement in the newspapers, that Messrs. C. C. Clay and Jacob Thompson, Southern Commissioners to negotiate a peace, and who had associated with them George Saunders, and also obtained the intermediate services of Horace Greeley, were at Niagara Falls soliciting a safe conduct to Washington, and that "terms of peace were already passing over the wires."

There was the usual Yankee exaggeration in this news. Messrs. Clay and Thompson had sought a safe conduct to Washington, for an informal conference to ascertain if there was any possible common ground on which negotiations for peace might be initiated ; and they had been unmercifully snubbed by the authorities, after the usual Yankee fashion of treating all the humble and begging attempts of the Confederates to reach the back-door of Washington. Mr. Lincoln dispatched a reply, addressed " *To whom it may concern*," declaring that the Union, with the additional and positive condition of the abandonment of slavery, was the *sine qua non* of peace.

Almost contemporary with the Niagara Falls affair there was an incident in Richmond, which put in striking contrast the sturdy indifference of Mr. Lincoln, and the simplicity and pliancy of the Confederate authorities.

In the same month of July a letter was received from General Grant, asking permission of the Confederate authorities for Colonel Jacques, of the 73d Illinois infantry, and one J. R. Gilmore, to meet Colonel Ould, the Confederate Commissioner of Exchange, between the lines of the two armies. Ould brought the two Yankees to Richmond for the purpose of seeing President Davis. It appeared that they came with the knowledge and approval of President Lincoln, and under his

---

man who shall represent truly the dignity and power of the nation, and who will not be unwilling even to tender an armistice suggesting a National Convention of all the States.

From the New York News.

The peace Democracy will indorse a nomination that faithfully represents the sentiments herein stated. They are willing to trust to the good sense and patriotism of the people for the realization of a definite peace as the sequel of an armistice and National Convention.

pass; and, while they disclaimed the character of authorized commissioners, they professed to be directly acquainted with the views of the Washington authorities, and plainly hinted that their business was to pave the way for a meeting of formal commissioners authorized to negotiate for peace.

These two obscure Yankees were treated with silly distinction in Richmond. They were admitted to a personal inter view with President Davis, who " grasped the hand of one of them with effusion," and entertained them with a long disquisition on State Rights, Secession, etc. There was, of course, some Yankee dramatization in the interview. Jacques had arrived in Richmond attired in a large linen duster; but no sooner had he confronted the Confederate President than he threw off the garment, disclosing the military uniform and in · signia of a Yankee colonel.

It appears that these parties had not a single definite proposition to make, and that they sounded Mr. Davis thoroughly, and, easily approaching his vanity, induced him to make a very elaborate and rhetorical exposition of his views and designs. They carried a long story back to the Yankee newspapers, and made no little capital out of their visit to Richmond by "sensations" in the Northern pictorials and itinerant "lectures" at twenty-five cents a head.

The more intelligent and worthy portion of the Confederate public were greatly wounded in their pride by the behavior of their authorities on the peace question. Many of these persons had, since the very commencement of the war, insisted on the futility and impropriety of essaying to open any special negotiations with the enemy on peace. There were the many distinct avowals of the purpose of the war on our side, in the declarations and acts of the Government, invariably protesting our simple desire " to be let alone," which were already a clear and standing tender of peace. The issues could not be made more distinct or more urgent than in the official record. Why, they argued, should we go beyond it by attempts at kitchen conferences, which might not only be insolently rebuffed by the enemy, to the damage of our self-respect, but which, as our experiences had so far shown, were invariably misinterpreted, and not without plausibility, as signs of decadence and weakness in our military affairs. True, the proud and intelligent persons in the Coi federacy were as anxious for peace as those who were constantly professing their devotion to this end. But they considered that the honor and self-respect of their countrymen had been lowered by devious and unworthy attempts at negotiation. Having once announced the terms of peace sufficiently, they judged they would do right, while awaiting the overtures of the enemy, not to betray their anxiety, or open any unnecessary discussions on the subject. And there could be no doubt of the sufficiency of these announcements.

A few weeks before the Jacques-Gilmore " mission" the Confederate Congress had published a manifesto naming the terms of peace, sufficiently explaining to the enemy the demands of the Richmond Government, and certainly leaving no occasion for discussing the matter with Yankee intermeddlers, who might choose to visit the Confederate capital on the errands of curiosity, or perhaps in the office of spies. The principles, sentiments, and purposes by which these States had been actuated, were set forth in that paper with all the authority due to the solemn declaration of the legislative and executive departments of the Government, and with a clearness which left no room for comment or explanation. In a few sentences it was pointed out that all we asked was immunity from interference with our internal peace and prosperity, " and to be left in the undisturbed enjoyment of those inalienable rights of life, liberty, and the pursuit of happiness, which our common ancestors declared to be the equal heritage of all parties to the social compact. Let them forbear aggressions upon us, and the war is at an end. If there be questions which require adjustment by negotiation, we have ever been willing, and are still willing, to enter into communication with our adversaries, in a spirit of peace, of equity, and manly frankness."

President Davis himself had even more explicitly indicated the methods of peace, excluded special efforts at negotiation with the enemy, and taken a position to which his conduct a few months subsequently was absurdly and inexplicably opposite.

Governor Vance of North Carolina had written to him, referring to certain political discontent in that State, and proposing an effort at negotiation with the enemy, which would appease the malcontents, and, if unsuccessful, would strengthen and intensify the war feeling.

On the 8th of January, 1864, President Davis wrote a long letter in reply. Some passages of this letter are of sufficient interest to be reproduced by the side of the events of the summer of the same year. The President wrote:

"We have made three distinct efforts to communicate with the authorities at Washington, and have been invariably unsuccessful. Commissioners were sent before hostilities were begun, and the Washington Government refused to receive them or hear what they had to say. A second time I sent a military officer with a communication addressed by myself to President Lincoln. The letter was received by General Scott, who did not permit the officer to see Mr. Lincoln, but promised that an answer would be sent. No answer has ever been received. The third time, a few months ago, a gentleman was sent, whose position, character, and reputation were such as to insure his reception, if the enemy were not determined to receive no proposals whatever from the Government. Vice-President Stephens made a patriotic tender of his services, in the hope of being able to promote the cause of humanity; and although little belief was entertained of his success, I cheerfully yielded to his suggestion, that the experiment should be tried. The enemy refused to let him pass through their lines or to hold any conference with them. He was stopped before he reached Fortress Monroe, on his way to Washington. To attempt again (in the face of these repeated rejections of all conference with us) to send commissioners or agents to propose peace, is to invite insult and contumely, and to subject ourselves to indignity without the slightest chance of being listened to. . . .

"I cannot recall at this time one instance in which I have failed to announce that our only desire was peace, and the only terms which formed a *sine qua non* were precisely those that you suggested, namely, 'a demand only to be let alone.' But suppose it were practicable to obtain a conference through commissioners with the Government of President Lincoln, is it at this moment that we are to consider it desirable, or even at all admissible? Have we not just been apprized by that despot that we can only expect his gracious pardon by emancipating all our slaves, swearing allegiance and obedience to him and his proclamation, and becoming in point of fact the slaves of our own negroes?"

But the peace movements in the North, to which we have referred, were to take a more practical direction, in view of the approaching Presidential election in that country.

THE CHICAGO CONVENTION, ETC.

The Democratic National Convention met at Chicago on the 29th of August. The Convention was called to order by Mr. August Belmont, who said that " four years of misrule by a sectional, fanatical, and corrupt party had brought our country to the verge of ruin. The past and present are sufficient warnings of the disastrous consequences which would befall us if Mr. Lincoln's re-election should be made possible by our want of patriotism and unity."

Mr. Bigler, formerly Governor of Pennsylvania, and Senator in Congress, was chosen as temporary chairman. He said : " The termination of democratic rule in this country was the end of the peaceful relations between the States and the people. The men now in authority, through a feud which they have long maintained with violent and unwise men at the South, because of a blind fanaticism about an institution in some of the States, in relation to which they have no duties to perform and no responsibilities to bear, are utterly incapable of adopting the proper means to rescue our country from its present lamentable condition."

The Convention was permanently organized by appointing as chairman, Horatio Seymour, the Governor of New York. In his speech, upon assuming the chair, he inveighed bitterly against the Lincoln Administration and the party in power. " They were," he said, " animated by intolerance and fanaticism, and blinded by an ignorance of the spirit of our institutions, the character of our people, and the condition of our land. Step by step they have marched on to results from which at the onset they would have shrunk with horror ; and even now, when war has desolated our land, has laid its heavy burdens upon labor, and, when bankruptcy and ruin overhang us, they will not have the Union restored unless upon conditions unknown to the Constitution. They will not let the shedding of blood cease, even for a little time, to see if Christian charity, or the wisdom of statesmanship, may not work out a method to save our country. They will not even listen to a proposal for peace which does not offer what this Government has no right to ask. This Administration cannot now save the country if it would. It has placed obstacles in its pathway which it cannot overcome. It has hampered its own freedom of action by unconstitutionalities." "The failure of the policy of the Administration," he said, "was not due to any want of courage or devotion on the part of the soldiers: they had done all that arms could do; and had wise statesmanship secured the fruits of their victories, there would to-day have been peace in the land." "This Administration," he continued, "cannot save the Union. We can. We demand no conditions for the restoration of the Union. We are shackled with no hates, no prejudices, no passions. We wish for fraternal relations with the people of the South. We demand for them what we demand for ourselves, the full recognition of the rights of the States."

The platform of the Convention consisted of a series of six resolutions drawn up by a committee appointed for that purpose, consisting of one member from each State, chosen by the respective delegations. The two most important resolutions were as follows:

"*Resolved*, That this Convention does explicitly declare, as the sense of the American people, that after four years of failure to restore the Union by the experiment of war, during which, under the pretence of a military necessity, or war power higher than the Constitution, the Constitution itself has been disregarded in every part, and public liberty and private right alike trodden down, and the material prosperity of the country essentially impaired, justice, humanity, liberty, and the public welfare demand that immediate efforts be made for a cessation of hostilities, with a view to an ultimate convention of all the States, or other peaceable means, to the end that, at the earliest practicable moment, peace may be restored on the basis of the federal Union of the States."

"*Resolved*, That the aim and object of the Democratic party is to preserve the Federal Union and the rights of the States unimpaired, and they hereby declare that they consider the administrative usurpation of extraordinary and dangerous powers not granted by the Constitution, the subversion of the civil by military law in States not in insurrection, the arbitrary military arrest, imprisonment, trial, and sentence of American citizens in States where civil law exists in full force, the suppression of freedom of speech and of the press, the denial of the right of asylum, the open and avowed disregard of State rights, the employment of unusual test-oaths, and the interference with and denial of the right of the people to bear arms, as calculated to prevent a restoration o the Union, and the perpetuation of a government deriving its just powers frcn the consent of the governed."

The platform was adopted with but four dissenting votes.

On the 31st the Convention proceeded to ballot for candi dates. Governor Seymour, of New York, peremptorily refused to allow his name to be used. The vote at first stood one hundred and sixty-two for McClellan, and sixty-four for all others. Several delegations then changed their votes, and the result was two hundred and two and a half for George B. Mc-Clellan, and twenty-three and a half for Thomas H. Seymour. Delaware and Maryland voted for Seymour, who also received nearly half the votes of Ohio, Indiana, and Missouri. The remaining eighteen States voted unanimously for McClellan, whose nomination, on motion of Mr. Vallandigham, was made unanimous.

Despite the protestations of attachment to the Union by the Chicago Convention, there is but little doubt that the real programme of its operations had, for its final conclusion, the ac knowledgment of the independence of the Confederate States.

It was proposed, perhaps, to get to this conclusion by distinct and successive steps, so as not to alarm too much the Union sentiment of the country. The first step was to be the proposition of the "Union as it was," in a convention of the States; if that was voted down, then the proposition of a new principle of federation, limited to the foreign relations and to the revenue; if that was rejected, then the proposition of an Inter-Confederate Union, to preserve, as far as possible, by an extraordinary league, the American prestige; and, if all these prop ositions, intended as successive tests of the spirit of the South, were to fail, then, at last, the independence of the Confederate States, made the *sine qua non*, was to be conceded by the Democratic party of the North, as the last resort of pacification, and the one of two alternatives where their choice could no longer hesitate. In short, it appeared to be the design of the Democratic party to get the North on the naked issue of war and separation.

Why this programme broke down is explained almost in a

word. The military events which took place between the date
of the Chicago Convention and election-day put upon the war
a more encouraging aspect for the North, and with these
changes the Democratic party abandoned ground which they
took professedly on principle, but really on the mean consid
erations of expediency and time-serving. The fact was that
all party changes in the North, since the war, might be said
to be constantly accommodating themselves to the course of
military events ; so little was there of virtue or of principle in
the public opinion of the Yankee. After the Chicago Convention, the peace party moved inversely with the scale of military
success ; and, as that mounted in Northern opinion, it fell until,
as we shall see months later, it almost approached zero.

It was to be expected, by those acquainted with the true
springs of action in Yankee politics, that the changes in the
military situation, during the fall months of 1864, to the advantage of the North, would induce the Democratic party and
their candidate, McClellan, to swerve from the resolutions of
the Chicago Convention, and to adopt shifting and equivocal
grounds with reference to the war. This shameful departure
from the former professions and recorded principles of the so-
called Democratic party of the North was the occasion of the
secession of that portion of it which, declaring for peace on
principle and disdaining time-serving, attempted the organization of a peace party upon " State Rights Jeffersonian Democratic principles." A convention of the true " peace men"
was called at Cincinnati on the 18th of October. It nominated
no candidates ; its actual political influence had become very
small ; but it had the merit of placing on record one of the
most perspicuous and complete expositions of the American
system of government that had ever come from any modern
pen. As a reaffirmation of the old and true doctrine of that
once great organization in America known as the Democratic
party, applied to the conduct of the existing war, the platform
of the Cincinnati Convention has a noble and permanent interest ; it deserves to be studied, both as a declaration of statesmanship and as a piece of history. There was scarcely any
thing that could exceed in luminous, compact, and forcible
style the two following resolutions of this body :

" 1. *Resolved,* That the several States composing the United

States are not united on the principle of unlimited submission to their General Government, but that by a compact, under the style and title of a Constitution for the United States, and of amendments thereto, they constituted a General Government for special purposes—delegated to the Government certain definite powers, reserving each State to itself the residuary mass of right to their self-government; and that whenever the General Government assumes undelegated power, its acts are unauthoritative, void, and of no force; that to this compact each State acceded as a State, and as an integral party, its co-States forming, as to itself, the other party; that the Government created by this compact was not made the exclusive or final judge of the extent of the powers delegated to itself, since that would have made its discretion, and not the Constitution, the measure of its powers; but that, as in all other cases of compact among powers having no common judge, each party has an equal right to judge for itself, as well of infractions as of the mode and measure of redress.

"2. *Resolved*, That as Jefferson made the rugged issue of doctrine with Adams, so must we make it with the Federal Administration, if we would resist effectually the infinitely greater dangers which surround us. We do, consequently, declare THE WAR WHOLLY UNCONSTITUTIONAL, and on that ground we hold it should be stopped. If a majority of the copartnership States can retain a member by force, they may expel one by force, which has not yet been pretended by anybody. The Federal agency at Washington, backed up by a majority of the States in Congress, without right, in the vain attempt to subjugate the minority of the States, is destroying their liberty, and crushing the federal system to atoms by thus attacking the Constitution. The Administration, and that majority, are the real enemies of the Union, which cannot and ought not to exist after its conditions are destroyed. The Chicago platform, and General McClellan and his war-record letter, which he has laid over it, must all be repudiated by Democrats for the same reason. If we admit that the war is constitutional, we must not murmur at the monstrous abuses which attend it, for they all naturally grow out of the original atrocity.

"The evils of paper money, of a protective tariff, of the public debt; the military draft; the military governors; the arbitrary arrests; the provost-marshals; the fifteen bastiles; the drum-head courts-martial; the bayonet elections; the padlocked lips; the fettered press; the wholesale confiscation; the constructive treason; our immense armies and navies, are mere incidents of the war itself; and so are President Lincoln's futile proclamations of slave emancipation, and his general amnesties. Half truths and narrow issues have been the bane of Democracy for many years, and they have so contracted the minds and hearts of Democrats, that all sense of justice, and all knowledge of constitutional law which sat there so long enthroned, have departed, and left us an easy prey to the violence of President Lincoln's Administration, and to corrupt managers of our own party in State and national conventions."

We shall not undertake here to follow the course, or enumerate the details of the Presidential campaign of 1864. We may anticipate our narrative generally to say, that that campaign resulted in the signal triumph of fanaticism and violence in the North, and in the election of Abraham Lincoln by the vote of every Northern State except Delaware, Kentucky, and New Jersey.

THE RIVAL ADMINISTRATIONS AT RICHMOND AND WASHINGTON.—
A COMPARATIVE VIEW OF NORTHERN DESPOTISM.

While on political subjects in the war, it will not be amiss here to put in comparison the internal administrations of the rival governments at Washington and Richmond. We have, on other occasions, developed some points of this comparison. It is fruitful of many considerations; it is after all the most interesting inquiry in the war; and it comes up naturally and conveniently for another review at the date of the Northern election which approved Mr. Lincoln's policy, and bestowed upon him a second term of office.

There were many persons to be found in the North, who, admitting the rapid decline, since the commencement of the war, of their government to despotism, attempted a consolation by the assertion that a similar lapse of liberty had taken place in the Confederate States. This opinion obtained to a remarkable extent, even among those who were not unfriendly to the South, and certainly were not disposed to do her in-

ıustice. It is to be largely ascribed to the very prevalent
ignorance in the North, even among men otherwise well informed and intelligent, of the internal policy of the Confed
erate States, and of the true spirit of their peculiar legislation
with reference to the war. It was not only the Black Republican party that circulated the idea of an iron-handed tyranny
in the Confederate States; but that idea was admitted to a
large extent in the minds of those who were disposed to think
well of the Southern experiment, but were not proof against
the impressions derived from such peremptory laws as required
men to take up arms in mass, to devote certain property to the
government, and to hold themselves, generally, in subjection
to the necessities of the war. These measures wore the appearance of the machinery of despotism to them, simply because they did not understand their true nature; while they
added to their ignorance the mistake of viewing them from a
stand-point which put the North and the South in the same
circumstances.

It is quite true that the conscription and impressment laws
of the Confederacy were apparently harsh measures. Yet
there is something to be said of them beyond the justification
of necessity; and this is, that they were really nothing more
than the organized expressions of the *popular devotion* of the
South' in the war; intended only to give effect and uniformity
to it. They were not instances of violent legislation imposed
upon the people; they were merely the formulas of willing
and patriotic contributions of men and means to a war, in
which not only a nation fought for its very existence, but each
individual for the practical stake of his own fortune. It was
difficult to make Northern men understand this: that, while
they had a mortal terror of the draft and other demands of
the war, the people of the South were cheerfully willing to
take up arms, and to devote their substance to the government.
It is thus that the conscription and impressment laws, which,
in the North, would have been the essence of despotism, were
really in the South not edicts of violence, but mere conven-
tionalisms of the war, through which the patriotism of the
people acted with effect and regularity.

But, beyond these laws, even the *appearance* of despotism
stopped in the Southern Confederacy. We have only to com-

pare the established routine there with what was constantly observed in the North, to show how divergent, since the first gun was fired at Fort Sumter, had been the histories of the belligerents on all questions affecting political and civil liberty There were no military governors in the Confederacy; there was no martial law there; there was, properly called, no political police there—the police establishment being limited to a mere detective force to apprehend, in the communities in which they were placed, spies and emissaries of the enemy. At no time in the war had soldiers ever been placed at a polling-place in the Confederacy; at no time had newspapers ever been suppressed; and at no time had a single instance of arbitrary arrest, or of imprisonment without distinct charges and the opportunity to reply, occurred within the Confederate jurisdiction. These are facts which carry their own comment on the base reflection that in the war the South had declined, along with the North, in its civil administration, and had kept company with it on its road to despotism.

When we speak of the *despotism* at Washington, we do not design a figure or an exaggeration of rhetoric. We merely name a clearly defined species of human government, as we would any other fact in history. The Presidential election of 1864 gave occasion for a full review of the acts of the Washington authorities. We may sum up that review in some brief paragraphs, dividing it into two branches: First, Mr. Lincoln's unconstitutional course on the rights of the States on the slavery question; second, his course on the rights of his own people in all matters of civil liberty;—these two classes of outrage being a convenient division of his Administration, viewed both as to its intentions upon the South and its effects upon the North.

As to the slavery question, it is only necessary to state the record.

1. The convention which nominated Abraham Lincoln President of the United States in 1860, passed a resolution affirming " the maintenance inviolate of the rights of the States, and *especially the right of each State to order and control its own domestic institutions according to its own judgment exclusively.*"

2. Mr. Lincoln, in his inaugural of March, 1861, inserted this resolution at length, and declared that to him it would be

" a law," and added, "I now reiterate these sentiments ;" and
"in doing so, I only press upon the public attention the most
*conclusive evidence of which the case is susceptible, that the
property, peace, and security of no section are not to be in any-
wise endangered by the now in-coming administration.*" In the
same State paper he had before said, quoting approvingly from
one of his own speeches, " I have no purpose, directly or indirectly, to interfere with the institution of slavery in the States
where it now exists ;" and subjoined, "*I believe I have no lawful right to do so, and I have no inclination to do so.*"

3. In Secretary Seward's famous letter to the minister of the
United States, resident at Paris, designed as a diplomatic circular to the European courts, and written " by direction of the
President," occurs the following paragraph : " The condition
of slavery in the several States will remain just the same,
whether it (' the rebellion') succeeds or fails. The rights of the
States, and the condition of every human being in them, will
remain subject to exactly the same laws and forms of administration, whether the revolution shall succeed, or whether it shall
fail. Their constitutions, and laws, and customs, habits and
institutions, in either case, will remain the same. It is hardly
necessary to add, to this incontestable statement, the further
fact that the new President, as well as the citizens through
whose suffrages he has come into the administration, has
always repudiated all designs whatever, and wherever imputed
to him and them, of *disturbing the system of slavery as it is
existing under the Constitution and the laws.* The case, however, would not be fully presented were I to omit to say that
any such effort on his part would be *unconstitutional*, and all
his acts in that direction would be prevented by the judicial
authorities, even though they were assented to by Congress
and the people."

4. In his message to Congress of the 6th of March, 1862,
known as his emancipation message, after recommending to
that body that they should pass a resolution that the United
States ought to co-operate with the States by means of pecuniary aid in effecting the gradual abolishment of slavery, Mr.
Lincoln expressly disavowed, for the Government, any authority over the subject, except with State assent. His language
was, that his proposition " sets up no claim of a right, by Fed-

eral authority, to interfere with slavery within State limits, referring, as it does, the absolute control of the subject in each case to the State, and its people immediately interested.'

5. The act of Congress of the 6th of August, 1861, emanci pated only the slaves of " rebels" employed in the " rebellion,' and submitted the decision of such cases exclusively to the courts. Major-General Fremont, on the 30th of that month, being then in command in Missouri, by proclamation declared free all the slaves within the State. This, as soon as it came to Mr. Lincoln's knowledge, he disapproved, and declared it, in a formal order of 11th of September, to be void as far as it transcended the provisions of the act of Congress. And in a letter of Mr. Joseph Holt to President Lincoln, of the 22d of the month, that person, being alarmed for the effect of Fremont's order, stated that " the act of Congress was believed to embody the conservative policy of your administration." This statement Mr. Lincoln never denied.

6. On the 9th of May, 1862, Major-General Hunter, military commander of the department of the South, embracing Georgia, Florida, and South Carolina, by an order of that date, declared all slaves within such States free. On the 19th of the month, even before he was officially advised of the measure, Mr. Lincoln, by proclamation, declared the same " whether genuine or false," to be " altogether void." In neither of these instances was there the slightest intimation of a change of opinion by Mr. Lincoln, either on the question of policy or of power. As to both, he then entertained the same opinion that he had announced in his inaugural.

7. On the 22d of July, 1862, Mr. Crittenden proposed, in the House of Representatives at Washington, a resolution which, after stating that the war was " forced upon the country by the disunionists" of the Southern States, declared that it " is not waged, on our part, in any spirit of oppression, or for any purpose of conquest or subjugation, or purpose of overthrowing or interfering with the rights of the established institution of these States (the seceded), but to defend and maintain the supremacy of the Constitution and the rights of the several States unimpaired; and that as soon as these objects are accom plished the war ought to cease." In the House only two votes were cast against it, and in the Senate but one Republican

vote, and it was at once and without hesitation approved by the President. No pretence was here suggested that slavery was to be abolished, or that any of the rights of the States in regard to it were to be interfered with.

Yet, in the face of all this accumulation of precedents, we find *Emancipation* proclamations put forward under the claim of executive power—the first on the 22d of September, 1862, and the second on the first day of the succeeding year. In the last, all slaves in certain States or parts of States were declared free; it mattered not whether the territory or the slaves should fall within the military occupation of the United States or not.

But it has been said that the emancipation proclamation was a *military measure,* and to be justified as such from necessities outside of the Constitution. It is difficult to find patience to reply to such nonsense. The plea is the most absurd stuff that was ever put in the mouth of fool or knave, to brazen out against the good sense and conscience of the world his fraud and outrage. Absurd, because we know, and all the world knows, that it was at the dictation and under the influence of a purely political party that the emancipation proclamation was issued by Mr. Lincoln. Absurd, because we knew, and had had recent assurance from Mr. Lincoln himself, that he did not intend emancipation of the negro to end with the war, which it would do *ipso facto* if a mere military measure, but had made the abandonment or extirpation of slavery the preliminary condition for peace, and thus, therefore, a primary object of the war.

It was this same dogma of "military necessity," applied to the slavery question, that Mr. Lincoln had used to fasten upon the necks of the white citizens of the North a heavy yoke of intolerance. It was only necessary to look upon what was every day passing before the eyes.

There was seen this despotism in the unreasonable searches and seizures of persons and papers, in direct violation of the Constitution.

It was seen in arrests of obnoxious individuals, and their imprisonment without warrant or charges preferred, and in some instances cut off from all communication with family friends, or counsel.

It was seen in the suppression of newspapers, and wanton arrest of editors.

It was seen in the assumption, by the President, of the power to regulate the right of suffrage in the States, and establish minority and *aristocratic* governments under the pretext of guaranteeing *republican* governments.

These are not fancy sketches, or the exaggerations of a narrative written with passion. It was notorious that such things had occurred in Missouri, Indiana, West Virginia, Maryland, Delaware, and New York; and yet even to question their legality was deemed disloyal, and men who maintained their inherited freedom in doing so, were designated by scurrilous abuse, and threatened with the penalties of a despot's all-powerful displeasure.

To compare the falsehoods and crimes of the Washington record with that rigor of measures in the Confederacy, which was really nothing more than the logical incident and the proper expression of resolute patriotism, is an outrage upon history. The noble memorials of self-sacrificing patriotism are very different from the scarlet record of ruthless despotism.

CHAPTER XVIII.

The business of blockade-running.—Its risks.—Interesting statistics.—Value of the port of Mobile.—NAVAL FIGHT AND CAPTURE OF THE FORTS IN MOBILE BAY.—A frightful disparity of force.—Heroic fight of the ram Tennessee.—Absurd boasts of the Yankees.—Surrender of Fort Gaines.—Fall of Fort Morgan.—THE GEORGIA CAMPAIGN.—Its importance.—Johnston's situation at Atlanta.—His removal by President Davis.—A fatal error.—Lieutenant-General Hood.—THE BATTLES OF ATLANTA.—THE FALL OF "THE GATE CITY."—Reckless and desperate fighting—Yankee raid on the Macon road.—Hood's "magnificent advance."—Bombardment of Atlanta.—Hood's fatal mistake.—Sherman's new movement.—He "cuts the Confederates in two."—The Yankees in Atlanta.—Sherman's cruelties.—His depopulation of Atlanta.—Enormity of the order.—Sherman as a pacificator.—Governor Brown's letter.—Position of Vice-President Stephens.—Effects of the fall of Atlanta.—President Davis's Macon speech.—Its swollen tone.—CAPTURE OF THE CONFEDERATE PRIVATEER FLORIDA.—Its cowardice and outrage.—Yankee idea of glory.—THE DESTRUCTION OF THE CONFEDERATE RAM ALBEMARLE.—Yankee estimation of the exploit.—The North Carolina Sounds.—THE ST. ALBANS RAID.—Stories of the savage vengeance of the Confederates.—How much truth there was in them.

A LARGE capital in the Confederacy was engaged in running the blockade. The risks of this business were by no means so great as generally supposed; and it had made a steady and valuable contribution to the war. The London insurance offices had been in the habit of charging sixty per cent. premium for policies on vessels and goods running the blockade. This was a rate adopted at the beginning of the war, before any facts had been developed to establish the real average of risk. But persons engaged in the business soon found that the real risk was by no means commensurate with the nominal risk as established by the London offices, and they consequently ceased to insure; or, in other words, adopted the plan of being their own insurers. This is naturally the case when the true risk is much below the nominal risk. That such was the case in the blockade-running business was clear from the fact that those engaged in it no longer insured.

A correspondent of the London *Index* gave a list of vessels employed in running the blockade from the port of Nassau, between November, 1861, and March 10, 1864. The list com prised eighty-four vessels. Of these, thirty-seven had been captured, twenty-five had been lost or beached, one foundered at sea, one condemned, two converted into Confederate gunboats, and the rest were supposed to be still in the business or aid up. The total number of losses which can be ascribed to causes connected with blockade-running was sixty-two. The number of successful round trips made by these vessels was two hundred and fourteen. Thus the risk to the vessels on the round trip was twenty-nine per cent. The percentage on goods was not by any means so great. If the risks out and in had been equal, it would have been fourteen and a half per cent. each way. But the inward risk was much greater than the outward. We are perhaps justified in assuming, on the whole, that the real risk on goods imported into the Confederacy through the blockade was not higher than twenty per cent.

Mobile was one of the principal ports for the blockade-running trade. It was guarded at its entrance by two imposing fortifications; it was difficult to blockade; it was a nursery of the Confederate navy; and vessels were already being constructed there with a view of raising the blockade. It had been the steady purpose of the Yankees to get possession of Mobile Bay as soon as operations on the Mississippi would permit the detachment of a sufficient co-operating military force for the expedition.

NAVAL FIGHT AND CAPTURE OF THE FORTS IN MOBILE BAY.

In the early part of August, Admiral Farragut, who commanded the Yankee fleet off Mobile, secured the military co-operation of General Canby for attacking and investing the forts in the harbor of Mobile. On the morning of the 5th of August, the Yankee fleet, numbering fourteen steamers and four monitors, carrying in all more than two hundred guns, and manned by twenty-eight hundred men, made their *entrée* into Mobile Bay. The entire Confederate naval force that was to encounter this huge armada was composed of *one iron-clad and three wooden vessels.* Such was the frightful disparity of force in a fight which the Yankees afterwards claimed to take rank with the victories of Nelson!

In the early light of the morning the attacking fleet moved steadily up the main ship channel, when Fort Morgan opened upon them, and was replied to by a gun from the Brooklyn A moment later, and the Yankee iron-clad Tecumseh, struck by a torpedo, disappeared instantaneously beneath the waves carrying with her her commander, T. A. M. Craven, and nearly all her crew. The Yankee flag-ship Hartford now took the lead, and had scarcely passed the fort, when the Confederate ram Tennessee dashed out at her. The three Confederate gunboats, the Morgan, the Gaines, and the Selma, were ahead. After a desperate struggle between the fleets, the Gaines retired to Fort Morgan in a sinking condition; the Selma, cut off, surrendered; and the Morgan escaped to Fort Morgan.

Having passed the forts and dispersed the gunboats, Farragut ordered most of the vessels to anchor, when about nine o'clock he perceived the Confederate ram Tennessee standing up for the Hartford. He immediately ordered all the Yankee monitors, and such of his wooden ships as were adapted for the purpose, to attack the ram, not only with their guns, but bows on at full speed. And then began one of the most remarkable naval conflicts of the war. A single vessel was beset by a whole fleet. She was struck three times, and as the Hartford, the third vessel which struck her, rasped along her side, the Yankee poured a whole broadside of nine-inch solid shot within ten feet of her casement. The Chickasaw was pounding away at her stern; the Hartford and three others of the fleet were again heaving down upon her, determined upon her destruction; her smoke-stack had been shot away, her steering chains were gone, and she lay at the mercy of the enemy. It was not until resistance was hopeless that Admiral Buchanan, himself wounded on the Tennessee, surrendered the vessel, and ordered the white flag to be hoisted just as she was about being struck by the vessels converging upon her, and when she was already disabled, and her crew almost in a smothering condition.

Such was the naval fight in Mobile Bay, which the Yankees ranked among their most brilliant victories; exalting Farragut above Nelson; apostrophizing their hero after the modern New York fashion of big dinners, and having hired poets to recite to him in public "masterly ballads." The Confederates had a very different and very plain estimation of the affair Their loss in killed and wounded had been only twenty-two. That of the enemy was near three hundred, not including the one hundred and twenty-three who went down in the Tecumseh. The Richmond *Examiner* gave a list of the twenty-eight Yankee vessels engaged, having two hundred and twelve guns, with the four Confederates having twenty-two guns. It said: "It was a most unequal contest in which our gallant little navy was engaged; and we lost the battle, but our ensign went down in a blaze of glory."

But although our little fleet in the bay of Mobile had been destroyed or dispersed, the forts were still held, and the Yankee success was incomplete. The fall of these, however, was to follow unexpectedly to the South, and not without some circumstances of humiliation.

On the 6th of August, one of the Yankee iron-clads commenced shelling Fort Gaines. This was a powerful work; it was provisioned for six months, and had a garrison of 600 men. Colonel Anderson, in command, communicated with the enemy's fleet by flag of truce, without the sanction of General Page, who was in command at Fort Morgan. General Page inquired by signals what his purpose was, but received no answer. His attention was attracted by signal-guns. General Page repeatedly telegraphed, "Hold on to your fort." The same night he visited Fort Gaines, and found Anderson on board the Yankee fleet, arranging terms of capitulation. He left peremptory orders for Anderson, on his return, not to surrender the fort, and relieved him of his command. Fort Morgan signalled the next morning, but no answer was received, except the hoisting of the Yankee flag over the ramparts of Fort Gaines.

From this time onward, movements of the enemy were in progress for capturing Fort Morgan; and on the 22d of August, at day-dawn, a bombardment was opened from the shore batteries, the monitors and ships inside, and the vessels outside the bay. At 6 A. M. of the 23d, a white flag was displayed by the Confederates, and at 2 o'clock P. M. tne fort was surrendered.

Fort Powell had been already attacked on the night of the 5th, and blown up, the guns falling into the enemy's hands.

The capture of Forts Powell, Gaines, and Morgan, and the destruction of the Confederate fleet, gave the Yankees possession of the bay, and closed the port to all ingress or egress of blockade-runners. The city of Mobile was still in possession of the Confederates, and months were to elapse before the enemy were to make any demonstration upon it, and then only with the co-operation of a land force. The Yankee success, so far, although the occasion of a brief blaze of excitement in the North, was not of any great importance; and it had been dearly purchased.

THE GEORGIA CAMPAIGN.

We return to more important events—those of the Georgia campaign—which indeed were to put a new aspect on the war; to annihilate the peace party in the North; to give a new hope and impetus to the enemy; and to date the serious and rapid decline of the fortunes of the Confederacy.

When we last left off the story of this campaign, Johnston was holding Atlanta, and busied in strengthening its defences.* His position in Atlanta was not less secure than that of Lee in Petersburg; and judging prospective by past events, it was impossible to doubt that he would have held Sherman as well as Lee held Grant. He could at least have done that; and if he succeeded in destroying his land communications—very much more easy to reach than that of Grant over water—he might have forced the enemy into disastrous retreat on Tennessee.

At midsummer, therefore, the two campaigns, for which the enemy had surrendered the Trans-Mississippi and North Carolina, were both failures. That military success which would

---

* In an official report, General Johnston said: "The proofs that I intended to hold Atlanta are, the fact that under my orders the work of strengthening its defences was going on vigorously, the communication on the subject made by me to General Hood, and the fact that my family was in the town. That the public workshops were removed, and no large supplies deposited in the town, as alleged by General Bragg, were measures of common prudence, and no more indicated the intention to abandon the place than the sending the wagons of an army to the rear, on a day of battle, proves a foregone determination to abandon the field."

alone bring him money, and by which alone could the Lincoln government retain power, was not forthcoming, or even dimly visible in the future. Had the campaign of Georgia pursued its parallel with that of Virginia, McClellan or some other man capable of negotiation would have been elected, and perhaps an honorable peace could have been attained. If no peace, at least the invasion would have lost its venom with its hope— the enemy would be a bankrupt, his army impotent, and his people indisposed to further exactions.

These bright prospects were changed in a day. President Davis, moved not so much by popular clamor as by a persistent personal dislike of Johnston, who resented his catechising interference with his campaign, took occasion to remove from the command of what had become the most important army in the Confederacy a first-rate military man, who had never lost a battle or a regiment in his whole career; who was executing the masterpiece of his professional life with a perfection of design and detail which delighted his own troops and filled his adversary with involuntary admiration; who had done the wonderful thing of conducting an army in retreat over three hundred miles of intricate country, absolutely without any loss in material or prisoners. Johnston was removed, and Lieutenant-General Hood put in command of the army—President Davis declaring that if the people wanted "a fighting general" they should have such in this man, who was brave, headstrong, incompetent; who had the heart of a lion, but, unfortunately, with it a head of wood.

THE BATTLES OF ATLANTA.—THE FALL OF "THE GATE CITY."

The effective force which General Johnston transferred to General Hood was about forty-one thousand infantry and artillery, and ten thousand cavalry. It constituted one of the largest armies the Confederacy had ever put in a single field, and was only a little less numerous than that with which General Lee had fought the campaign of the Rapidan.

On the 20th of July, Hood attacked the enemy's right on Peach-tree Creek, near the Chattahoochee, gaining some temporary advantage, and capturing colors and prisoners.

GEN. HOOD.

It was one of the most reckless, massive, and headlong charges of the war. A little past three in the evening, and with the celerity of lightning, the bulk of Hood's army massed in enormous columns against Newton's division, came on without skirmishing, and with yells whose volume exceeded any battle-shout that had yet been heard. It was the aim of Hood to take advantage of a gap between Newton's division and another division of Palmer's corps, to strike the enemy at a vital point, and to destroy his forces on the right. The charge was gallantly led by Walker's and Bates' divisions of Hardee's corps. The column poured down an open but rocky series of fields towards Newton's left, evidently aiming at his bridges. At this point, however, the enemy succeeded, with admirable quickness, in massing their artillery, and pouring a terrible fire upon the Confederates. The Yankee gunners worked with frantic energy; the Confederate columns slackened pace, and began to waver and lose their careful arrangement; and in less than half an hour the attack was drawn off in good order, but having plainly and unquestionably failed to accomplish its object.

On the 22d of July, Hood's army shifted its position, forming on Peach-tree Creek, and Stewart's and Cheatham's corps formed line of battle around the city. Hardee's corps made a night march, and attacked the enemy's extreme left at one o'clock on the 22d, and drove him from his works, capturing sixteen pieces of artillery and five stands of colors. Cheatham attacked the enemy at four o'clock in the afternoon with a portion of his command, and drove the enemy, capturing six pieces of artillery. During the engagement we captured about two thousand prisoners.

After the battle of the 22d, Sherman's army was transferred from its position on the east side of Atlanta to the extreme right of Hood's army, on the west side, threatening the Macon road. He slowly and gradually drew his lines about Atlanta, feeling for the railroads which supplied Hood's army and made Atlanta a place of importance.

It remained to break the Macon road. For this purpose Stoneman was sent with five thousand cavalry, and McCook with four thousand men, to meet on the railroad near Lovejoy's and to tear it up, and also to attack and drive Wheeler. Stone man did not go to Lovejoy's. He tore up much of the railroad, and got down in front of Macon; and on his retreat was hemmed in by Iverson, and was himself captured, together with one thousand of his men and two guns, besides losing many in killed and wounded. McCook cut his way out, losing about five hundred men as prisoners. "On the whole," Sherman reported, "the cavalry raid is not deemed a success."

On the 28th of July, Hood made another grand attack on Sherman. Coming out of Atlanta by the Bell's Ferry road, he advanced in parallel lines directly against the Fifteenth Corps, expecting to catch that flank in air. Of this movement General Sherman said: "His advance was magnificent, but founded on an error that cost him sadly; for our men coolly and deliberately cut down his men, and, spite of the efforts of the rebel officers, his ranks broke and fled. But they were rallied again and again, as often as six times at some points; and a few of the rebel officers and men reached our lines of rail-piles only to be killed or hauled over as prisoners." The Yankee accounts claimed a loss on the Confederate side in this engagement of six thousand men. General Hood stated his loss at fifteen hundred killed and wounded. The excellent intrenchments of the Yankees and the skilful formation of their lines saved them from any considerable loss, and secured them the fortune of the day.

General Sherman now extended his lines southwestward towards East Point, in the hope of drawing the Confederates out, from the fear of having their communications severed; but Hood extended his fortified line accordingly, and refused to abandon his works. For several weeks Sherman continued the siege of Atlanta, bombarding it with but little effect. He had satisfied himself that to take Atlanta he must resort to new means, and had concluded to plant his armies away below on the Macon road, Hood's main line of supply. The grand movement was assigned for the 18th of August.

But at this time Hood made the fatal mistake. He sent off Wheeler and his entire cavalry to raid on Sherman's line of communications. "At last," wrote Sherman, "he made the mistake we had waited for so long, and sent his cavalry to our rear, far beyond the reach of recall."

Instantly the Yankee cavalry was on the Macon road. Sherman followed quickly with his principal army. On the 31st of August, Howard, on the right, had reached Jonesboro' Thomas, in the centre, was at Couch's; and Schofield, on the left, was near Rough and Ready.

The Confederate forces were at this time in a most singular position. They had been divided into two main armies, separated by an interval of twenty-two miles. One part of the army was intrenched at Atlanta, and the other was at Jonesboro', under General Hardee, and was also intrenched. The cause of this separation of the forces arose from the fact that Hood had found out, by Kilpatrick's raid, that it was necessary he should protect his communications at that point by a large force. Sherman's army was therefore between Hood's forces, and had literally divided the Confederates in two.

On the evening of the 30th of August, the enemy made a lodgment across Flint River, near Jonesboro'. The Confederates attacked them there on the evening of the 31st, with two corps, but failed to dislodge them. Of this event, General Hood telegraphed to Richmond: "This made it necessary to abandon Atlanta, which was done on the night of the 1st of September."

On the evening of the 1st of September, General Hardee's corps, in position at Jonesboro', was assaulted by a superior force of the enemy; and being outflanked, was compelled to withdraw during the night, with the loss of eight guns.

The sum of Hood's disasters was now complete. He had remained in Atlanta to find that he was outflanked, his line of supply cut off, and the Yankee troops between him and a large portion of his army. In order to save that portion of his command then with him, he determined to evacuate the fortified city; and on the night of September 1st he blew up his magazines, destroyed all his supplies that he could not remove, consisting of seven locomotives and eighty-one cars loaded with ammunition, small-arms, and stores, and left the place by the turnpike roads.

Sherman dispatched to Washington: "Atlanta is ours, and fairly won. Since the 5th of May we have been in one continued battle or skirmish, and need rest." The pause in military operations afforded him the opportunity of launching measures of the most extraordinary cruelty against the non combatant people of Atlanta. He ordered the entire depopulation of the city, and proceeded to drive from their homes thousands of helpless women and children. General Hood protested against the measure as " unprecedented, studied, and ungenerous cruelty." Sherman wrote diffuse replies to him and to the Mayor of Atlanta. This Yankee general wrote a sort of tangled English, interlarded with slang phrases, which the North accepted as a model of forcible and elegant style. He replied to Hood, " Talk thus *to the marines*, and not to me ;" and gave to the mayor this bit of military philosophy : " War is cruelty, and you *cannot refine it*." He continued : " You might as well appeal against the thunder-storm as against these terrible hardships of war. They are inevitable ; and the only way the people of Atlanta can hope once more to live in peace and quiet at home is to stop this war."

It appears that the Yankee general had shut his eyes to every element and law of civilization in war. He ordered into exile the whole population of a city, drove men, women, and children from their homes at the point of the bayonet, under the plea that it was to the interest of his Government, and on the claim that it was an act of " kindness to these families of Atlanta." Butler only banished from New Orleans the registered enemies of his Government, and acknowledged that he did it as a punishment. Sherman issued a sweeping edict covering all the inhabitants of a city, and added insult to the injury heaped upon the defenceless by assuming that he had done them a kindness.

Shortly after the fall of Atlanta, it was affirmed that many of the leading men of Georgia, including Governor Brown and Alexander H. Stephens, were in favor of that State withdrawing from the Confederacy and making a separate peace ; and that negotiations to that effect had been opened with General Sherman. The facts were these : A Mr. King had brought to Governor Brown a message to the effect that he would be pleased to confer with him and others upon the state of the country, with a view to a settlement of the difficulties, and would give him a pass through the Federal lines, going and returning, for that purpose. To this the governor replied, that he, as governor of a State, and General Sherman, as a com mander of an army in the field, had no authority to enter upon negotiations for peace. Georgia might perhaps be overrun, but could not be subjugated, and would never treat with a conqueror upon her soil. That while Georgia possessed the sovereign power to act separately, her faith had been pledged by implication to her Southern sisters, and she would not exercise this power without their consent and co-operation. She had entered into the contest knowing all the responsibilities which it involved, and would never withdraw from it with dishonor. "She will never," he says, "make separate terms with the enemy, which may free her territory from invasion and leave her confederates in the lurch. Whatever may be the opinion of her people as to the injustice done her by the Confederate Administration, she will triumph with her confederate sisters, or she will sink with them in common ruin. . . The independent expression of condemnation of the measures of the Administration is one thing, and disloyalty to our sacred cause is another and quite a different thing." "If Mr. Lincoln would stop the war, let him," said Governor Brown, "recognize the sovereignty of the States, and leave to each to determine for herself whether she will return to the old Union or remain in her present league."

About the same time Vice-President Stephens explained his own position in an elaborate letter, in which he declared that the only solution for present and prospective troubles was "the simple recognition of the fundamental principle and truth upon which all American constitutional liberty is founded, and upon the maintenance of which alone it can be preserved—that is, the sovereignty—the ultimate, absolute sovereignty—of the States." He concluded : "All questions of boundaries, confederacies, and union or unions would naturally and easily adjust themselves, according to the interests of parties and the exigencies of the times. Herein lies the true law of balance of the power and the harmony of States."

The fall of Atlanta was a serious blow to the Confederacy. "On that day," said the Richmond *Examiner*, "McClellan's nomination fell still-born, and an heir was born to the Abolition dynasty. On that day, peace waved those ' white wings,' and fled to the ends of the morning. On that day, calculations of the war's duration ceased to be the amusements even of the idle."

The catastrophe moved President Davis in Richmond. To-wards the close of September, he made a journey to Georgia. He delivered an elaborate and ill-tempered speech at Macon. He said that it would have gladdened his heart to have met his auditors in prosperity instead of adversity. Still, though misfortune had befallen the Confederates from Decatur to Jonesboro', the cause was not lost. Sooner or later Sherman must retreat, and then he would meet the fate that befell Napoleon in the retreat from Moscow. He knew the deep disgrace felt by Georgia at the army falling back from Dalton to the interior of the State; but he was not one who felt that Atlanta was lost when the army crossed the Chattahoochee, and he had put a man at the head of the army who would strike a manly blow for the city. It did not become him to revert to disaster. Hood's army must be replenished. He had been asked to send reinforcements from Virginia to Georgia, but the disparity in numbers was as great in Virginia as in Georgia. The army under Early had been sent to the valley of the Shenandoah, instead of to Georgia, because the enemy had penetrated to Lynchburg; and now, if Early was withdrawn, there was nothing to prevent the Federal troops from putting a complete cordon of men around Richmond. He had counselled with General Lee upon all these points; his mind had roamed over the whole field, and his conclusion was, that " if one-half of the men now absent from the field would return to duty, we can defeat the enemy. With that hope, I am now going to the front. I may not realize this hope, but I know that there are men there who have looked death too often in the face to despond now."

The swollen tone of the Confederate President was not without effect upon the public mind. Confidence was in a measure revived; and expectation stood on tiptoe for the results of that wonderful strategy which President Davis had counselled with Hood, and which he promised his Macon audience was to recover Atlanta, and bring Sherman to a grief unparalleled in the war. The President's vivid hint of such a campaign was the occasion of new hopes with some people of the Confederacy But they had forgotten of what ill omen had been his former visits to the Western army; how disaster had followed on his heels; and how his former plans of campaign in this department, attended with like vapors, had turned out to be the veriest clap-traps in military science. But the sequel of the Macon speech belongs to another period of time, and must be reserved for another chapter.

We turn here, at this period, to the narration of some naval and military incidents which belong to it, and which, although of no great importance in themselves, are of considerable interest, either on account of the principles they involved or the spirit they illustrated.

CAPTURE OF THE CONFEDERATE PRIVATEER FLORIDA.

The Florida had originally sailed from England under the name of Oreto, and under that name she was, on reaching Nassau, brought before the court through the efforts of the Yankee consul. The neutral authorities decided in favor of the vessel, which was permitted to proceed. Leaving Nassau she went to Green Bay, where she received on board her armament, ran into Mobile, changed her name to that of Florida, and had since carried on an effective war on Yankee commerce.

In February, 1864, availing herself of a dark night, she escaped from Brest, eluding the Kearsarge, which was off that port. In June, she visited the neutral port of St. Georges, Bermuda, and remained there nine days. Leaving St. Georges on the 27th of that month, she remained outside, but in sight, for three or four days, boarding all vessels that approached the island. On the 10th of July she captured the Electric Spark, near the coast, while several vessels were cruizing for her ; but she escaped, and was next heard from at Teneriffe, on the 4th of August. Subsequently she entered the bay of San Salvador, Brazil.

While the Florida was at her anchorage in this neutral port, and a portion of her crew, with her commander, were ashore, not dreaming of danger, Captain Napoleon Collins, of the Yankee steamer Wachusett, had conceived the extraordinary and outrageous design of stealing upon the Confederate vessel, and destroying or capturing her by a cowardly stratagem in a neutral port.

About three o'clock in the morning of the 7th of October the cables were slipped, and the Wachusett bore down upon the Confederate vessel under a full head of steam. So little expectation was there of such a proceeding, that one-half the officers and crew of the Florida, seventy in number, and including Captain Morris, were on shore. The Florida's officer on deck supposed the collision, which he saw to be imminent, to be merely accidental, and cried out: "You will run into us if you don't look out." The design of Captain Collins was to strike the Florida amidships, with full steam on, crushing her side, and send her at once to the bottom. The Wachusett, however, did not strike her adversary fairly, but hit her in the stern, carrying away the mizen-mast and main-yard. The Florida was not seriously injured by the collision; but the broken spar fell across the awning over her hatchway in such a manner as to prevent her crew from getting on deck from below. The recoil which followed the shock carried the Wachusett back several yards. In the confusion which ensued, several pistol shots were fired from both vessels, chiefly at random and entirely without effect. Two of the guns of the Wachusett were also discharged, but the shots did not strike the Florida.

Captain Collins, of the Wachusett, immediately called out: "Surrender, or I will blow you out of the water!" The lieutenant in charge of the Florida replied: "Under the circumstances, I surrender." Without the delay of an instant, dozens of Yankee sailors boarded the prize, and made fast a hawser, connecting her with their own vessel, and the Wachusett turned her course seaward, moving at the top of her speed, and towing the Florida in her wake.

The fleet of Brazilian vessels was so situated, that the two steamers were obliged to pass under the stern of one of the largest in order to penetrate their line. The Wachusett was challenged, but did not deign a word of reply, and the Florida, when hailed and commanded to halt a moment after, replied that a pause was impossible, as she was towed by the vessel in front. The Brazilians soon divined the state of affairs, and in another moment or two the heavy guns of the fort, under the muzzles of which the capture had been made, opened fire on the Wachusett as she disappeared in the darkness. Three shots were fired after her, all passing harmlessly far above her pennant and striking the water.

To those familiar with the Yankee disposition to misrepresent and boast, it will not appear strange that this stroke of Napoleon Collins' genius—a piece of cowardice and outrage for which Mr. Seward was afterwards compelled to apologize to the Brazilian government—should have been generally thought, in the North, very commendable and admirable. But what shall be said of this sentiment in a New York newspaper : " *Certainly no page of history can show a more daring achievement, or one executed with more brilliant rapidity or more complete success !*"

THE DESTRUCTION OF THE CONFEDERATE RAM ALBEMARLE.

A few weeks later, and another naval exploit of the Yankees was heralded to the public. This was the destruction of the formidable ram Albemarle, in the Roanoke River. With fourteen officers and men, Lieutenant Cushing, of the Yankee navy, on the night of the 27th October, ascended the Roanoke to Plymouth, in a torpedo boat, crept upon the ram at her wharf, and sunk her by the explosion of the torpedo.

The exploit was a most dastardly one—a rare exhibition of cowardice; for no sooner had the Yankees exploded the Albemarle than, instead of making fight, they cried out, " We surder, we surrender !" and while the vessel was sinking, called for quarter from those upon whom they had stolen under the cover of darkness.

The Confederates would have been justifiable in dispatching these men on the spot. The Yankees had, in more than one instance, executed in cold blood members of the torpedo corps of the Confederate States ; and when Butler ascended the James River, in May, 1864, the story was grimly told in the New York papers, that certain torpedo-men captured on that occasion " would never give any more trouble." But in the case of the Albemarle, the Confederates, with characteristic softness and simplicity of heart, took and treated as prisoners of war the dastardly creatures, whose enterprise had been of no more peril than that of the assassin who stabs in the back, and, as his victim turns to revenge himself, throws up his hands for mercy.

It is a peculiarity of the Yankee that the success of an ingenious device of cowardice is more highly extolled than any exhibition of real courage. No wonder, then, that the affair of the Albemarle was exploited as one of the sensations of the day; and that Lieutenant Cushing, the commander of the Yankee party, was dubbed "hero," and his physiognomy recorded on the first pages of the New York pictorials.

The destruction of the Albemarle removed the reliable defence of Plymouth. On the 31st of October the Yankees took possession of the place, capturing some prisoners and cannon, and re-establishing their supremacy in the sounds of North Carolina.

THE ST. ALBANS RAID.

In the month of October, a great and undue excitement was created in the North by an expedition of twenty-five Confederates from the Canadian frontier into the town of St. Albans, Vermont. The raid occurred on the 18th of October. The banks were robbed of over one hundred thousand dollars, and a citizen was shot; the raiders declaring that they "intended retaliation for Sherman's cruelties in Atlanta." They escaped across the frontier, but were arrested by the Canadian authorities. The raid was followed by great excitement, and in a few hours the whole frontier was under arms.

The apparent complicity of the Confederate authorities in the St. Albans raid furnished the Yankees with the occasion of connecting the Government at Richmond with all sorts of real and pretended schemes, concocted on the Canadian frontier, to execute savage justice upon the North. These stories are familiar to the world. It was declared on affidavit, on different occasions, that Confederate agents, on neutral territory, had plotted the burning of Northern cities, the conflagration of hotels, the destruction of railroad trains, the infection of the Northern people with pestilence, and all manner of savage and inhuman retribution.

The slight element of truth in these libels is easily indicated. No human creature is more ingenious and industrious in misrepresentation than the Yankee; and his unscrupulous and busy attempt to hand down the Confederates to history as a savage foe, is to be constantly met in the history of the war.

It is true that President Davis was a credulous man, and very accessible to the claims of foreign adventurers, to the propositions of "blowers," and the game of "confidence-men." It is quite possible that he may have given countenance to some of these plausible creatures, who afterwards exceeded their instructions; and having been designated for legitimate "secret service," assumed, on their own account, the part of highwaymen and incendiaries. But it is an incontestable fact in history, that the Confederates, so far from being savage avengers, were deficient in the policy and tame in the spirit of retaliation; that they moderated their warfare with an excess of chivalry and sentimentalism that was more than once laughed at by the enemy, or seriously censured by the more intelligent and just persons of the South; and that in their general temper in the war, and its well-attested facts of history, they give the conclusive and unmistakable contradiction to the multitudinous Yankee stories of "rebel barbarities" in the episodes of the war.

CHAPTER XIX.

THE events on the Richmond lines in the fall months of 1864
were not without importance.

THE FALL OF FORT HARRISON, ETC.

Early on the night of the 28th of September it was discovered that the enemy was crossing a force to the north side of
the James, at Deep Bottom, and in a few hours developed the
fact that he was crossing infantry, cavalry, and artillery in.
heavy columns. General Gregg, who was in command at that
point, after notifying General Ewell of the situation, placed
two brigades of Field's division in readiness to meet an attack.

At daybreak on the 29th, our pickets were driven in at several points, showing that a formidable advance was being made,
and that the force to oppose it was inadequate to cover all the
ground threatened. The best disposition possible, however,
was made of the small force present. The first determined assault was made near the Phillips House, on both sides of the
Four Mile Run. The Texas brigade was hastened in double-

quick to that point, and placed in position just in time to repel the attack. The enemy, in very heavy force, had reached the abattis, thirty or forty yards in front, but were there met by a most terrific and galling fire, which mowed them down with terrible slaughter. The white troops fled in great confusion, but, the entangled brush greatly impeding their speed, many of them fell under the fire of the well-aimed rifles of the Texans.

The negroes, who were driven up at the point of the bayonet, lay flat upon the ground, just in rear of the abattis, hoping thereby to shield themselves from the sad havoc in their ranks, but the Texans, mounting the works, shot them like sheep led to the shambles. The New York *Herald* said one hundred and ninety-four negroes were buried upon that spot. Counting the wounded at five times as great, which is a low estimate, at least twelve hundred killed and wounded cumbered the ground in front of that little brigade.

Beaten back at this point, the enemy immediately hurled another column of white troops against General Geary, near the Drill House, on New Market Heights, and met a like bloody repulse.

Beaten back with terrible slaughter from the heights of New Market, the Yankees determined to accomplish, by flank movements and overwhelming numbers, what their courage failed to do.

A heavy column moved up the river for the purpose of attacking the works on Chaffin's farm, while others moved up the Darbytown and New Market roads. A force of Confederates was hastened off in double-quick to reinforce Fort Harrison and adjacent works; but before they could reach them the enemy assaulted the fort, which, after a very feeble resistance on the part of the artillery and a portion of Colonel Maury's command, was abandoned to the enemy. This fort occupied a commanding position below Drury's Bluff, and constituted the main defence at that point.

In the mean time the force that moved up New Market road had massed in a ravine on Taylor's farm, northwest of Fort Gilmer, and were moving in two heavy columns upon it and the works to the left. Law's brigade of Field's division (under Colonel Bowls), which had just arrived, opened a destructive fire on the line advancing upon the works to the left and re-pulsed them. The whole force was then hurled, with great impetuosity, against Fort Gilmer.

The open plateau in front gave the Confederates, in and to the left of the fort, an opportunity to pour a galling and destructive fire into the enemy's front and flank for several hundred yards before they could reach the goal at which they aimed. The negroes, as usual, were in front, and rushed forward frantically, under dread of the bayonets at their backs, shooting but seldom, and wide of their mark. Their only object seemed to be to gain the ditch, and save themselves from slaughter. The white soldiers never reached the ditch. They were repulsed, and fell back in confusion.

The total sum of the day's labor was six battle-flags, two guidons, and about five hundred prisoners, besides at least seven hundred of the enemy killed, and three thousand five hundred wounded.

General Field arrived just prior to the assault upon Fort Gilmer, and, after a careful survey of the situation, favored an attack upon Fort Harrison that evening, before the enemy could strengthen the position. But his superior officers thought it best to defer it until the next day. The sequel shows that General Field was right. Twenty-four hours elapsed, during which time the enemy greatly improved and strengthened his position. The plan determined upon was to attack at two o'clock on the evening of the 30th. Generals Anderson's, Bratton's, and Law's brigades, of Field's division, were to make the assault in front, while Hoke attacked at the same time the side next to the Bluff. By means of a ravine the latter was enabled to form within two or three hundred yards of the fort, while Field was probably three times that distance. At the expiration of a certain time, after a given signal, the assault was to commence. As soon as General Field's line moved up, on a line opposite to General Hoke, he was to advance, and the attack was to be made simultaneous. In accordance with this arrangement, the assaulting columns were put in readiness, and the signal given. In order to cause no delay, and to make sure of getting all the men out of the trenches, a short while before the time expired, General Field ordered General Anderson to move his brigade in front of the works he then occupied, adjust his line, and make the men lie down until the other two brigades could form upon it. General Anderson failing to give his men the necessary instruction as to his object, as soon as they leaped the breastworks they rushed forward with a yell, and he was unable to control them. This necessitated rapid movement on the part of the other brigades. General Hoke, awaiting the expiration of the time, did not move forward as was designed, in concert with the brigades of Field's division, and thus the enemy was enabled to concentrate his fire upon both assaults.

The troops did not attack with their usual impetuosity. Law's brigade accomplished its object, in sweeping up the old works, retaking a redan to the left of the fort, and thus protecting our left flank. But the main attack failed. Hoke met a like repulse. Had General Field's plan to attack the evening before been adopted, in all human probability the fort would have been recaptured, and the enemy driven back across the river.

ENGAGEMENT ON THE CHARLES CITY ROAD.

On the morning of the 6th of October, the Yankee host forty thousand strong, lay encamped on the north side of James River, the main body in the neighborhood of Fort Harrison, ten miles southeast of Richmond, the Tenth (Birney's) army corps and Kautz's cavalry being five and a half miles nearer the city, and in position between the Darbytown and Charles City roads.

With the first early light, General Geary's brigade of cavalry and a considerable force of our infantry struck the enemy's right, resting on the Charles City road, at a point from four and a half to five miles from the city. The Yankees were completely surprised, and with little resistance fled into their intrenchments, a short distance in their rear. Here they were in strong force, and prepared for a desperate resistance; but our troops, following up their first blow with great impetuosity, carried the works and drove the Yankees out, capturing nine pieces of cannon, one hundred artillery horses, and several hundred prisoners.

General Geary, by this time, had Kautz on the run, and was driving him ahead of the infantry.

Our infantry continued to press the Tenth Corps back. Our troops then pressed forward towards a second line of the enemy's intrenchments, which were carried after a sharp contest, and the enemy routed and pursued some distance towards Fort Harrison, when our men were withdrawn from the pursuit to the enemy's line of intrenchments just taken.

The enemy, in the course of an hour or two, having been rapidly reinforced from the grand army at Fort Harrison, advanced with confidence to the recapture of their former position. They were, after a long and desperate fight, repulsed with great slaughter, and as night closed in we held all the ground we had taken.

In this fight the brave and chivalrous General Gregg, commanding the Texan brigade, fell at the head of his troops, pierced through the neck by a minie ball.

ENGAGEMENT ON THE WILLIAMSBURG AND BOYDTON ROADS— ANOTHER GRAND ATTEMPT ON RICHMOND.

On the 27th of October, General Grant moved against the Confederate right and left flank. An interval of a month had occurred since his capture of Fort Harrison, and the extension of his right to the Darbytown road. The armies of the James and the Potomac moved simultaneously.

It was soon ascertained that the Eighteenth Corps had made a detour around White Oak swamp, and was advancing in heavy columns up the Williamsburg and Nine Mile roads. The object of this movement was to find, and if possible turn, Lee's left flank. General Longstreet at once ordered General Field to take position on the Nine Mile road.

He moved the division with great celerity, and gained the Williamsburg road just in time to repel an assault and save the fort and guns immediately on the road.

On his arrival, he found that the enemy's heaviest force was massed upon that road, and that would be the point of main attack.

Two or three brigades of negroes had been sent up the Nine

Mile road, and had charged and carried the works, and captured one piece of artillery, just as the Hampton Legion, of Geary's cavalry, was going into position. But the Twenty-fourth Virginia cavalry coming up, they, in conjunction with the legion, charged and regained the works and artillery, and drove the negroes back with heavy slaughter.

Severe skirmishing and artillery duels were being waged on the Darbytown and Charles City roads; and one or two determined assaults had been made upon Hoke's line, but had been handsomely repulsed.

In the mean time, the enemy had planted two heavy field-batteries near the Williamsburg road, and were shelling our works most furiously. Their artillery was handled with great skill and precision. Our batteries did not respond, because they desired to hold their fire for the advance of the infantry. Their silence misled the enemy. Soon a line of battle debouched from the woods on the left of the Williamsburg road, evidently bent upon the capture of the fort. This time the negroes were in the rear, perhaps because the white soldiers, believing that the fort and its guns were but feebly manned, expected to make easy and quick work of it, and get all the glory. In this they were disastrously deceived. They had to advance through an open and level field for half a mile. The fort opened upon them with grape and canister; and when within five hundred yards, Anderson's, the Texas, and Bratton's brigades poured terrible volleys of minies from their Enfield rifles into their wavering ranks; and by the time they arrived within two hundred yards, the fire from the artillery and musketry had become so destructive that they broke in every direction, and were charged by our skirmishers. The result, in addition to one hundred dead and many wounded, was the capture of 500 prisoners.

On the Boydton plank-road the day had been no less decisive. The main attack of the enemy here was directed against the Southside Railroad. The enemy was encountered here by three brigades under General Mahone in front, and General Hampton in the rear. Mahone captured four hundred prisoners, three stand of colors, and six pieces of artillery. The latter could not be brought off, the enemy having possession of the bridge.

In the attack subsequently made by the enemy, General Mahone broke three lines of battle, and during the night the enemy retreated from the Boydton road, leaving his wounded and more than two hundred and fifty dead on the field.*

Thus failed, almost shamefully, Grant's ambitious movement of October. It had been easily repulsed at all points. There is no doubt that Grant had designed, at this season, an "On to Richmond," which was to electrify the North and carry for Lincoln the approaching Presidential election, only a few days distant. But he had utterly failed to respond to the "electoral necessity" at Washington; although it must be admitted that events, to which we shall presently refer, in other parts of Virginia, had amply supplied it, and adorned the Yankee arms with no mean success.

THE CAMPAIGN IN THE VALLEY OF VIRGINIA.

These Yankee successes were to occur in a quarter where they were least expected—in the Valley of Virginia, a district heretofore illuminated by brilliant Confederate victories, and associated with heroic names.

Early's army in the Valley, first designed to threaten Washington, and to do a not less important service in saving the harvests of the Shenandoah, had become, in other respects, a most necessary part of General Lee's combination to protect Richmond.

Of the four railroads which enter Richmond, two—the Fredericksburg and the York River railroads—had become of but little account; they drained a country already exhausted. But the Gordonsville road, connecting Richmond with the fertile

---

* In the series of engagements on the Richmond lines just narrated, Field's division had borne a conspicuous part, and deserves a distinct mention. A correspondent wrote: "For thirty days this division has stood at the gates of the capital against overwhelming odds; and, almost unaided, has beaten back, with sad havoc, five of Grant's grand 'Ons to Richmond.' It has lost, in killed, wounded, and missing, about twelve hundred men; and yet is stronger to-day than it was a month ago. It has killed more than one thousand of the enemy, wounded five times that number, captured over 1,200 prisoners, several hundred stands of arms, five guidons, and fifteen battle-flags."

Valley of the Shenandoah, was of great importance. It was a part of Early's mission to guard this communication, but a more important part of that mission was to cover the approach to Lynchburg. After the occupation of the Weldon road by Grant, the safety of Lynchburg became absolutely essential to the maintenance by Lee of any defensive position in Virginia. For Lynchburg was then the key to all the communications left to his army; and if once captured by the Yankee forces and made a military station, it could be held by a small army, and made the centre of a new system of operations on the west side of Richmond.

On the 8th of August, General Sheridan was placed in command of what was called the Middle Military Division, superseding General Hunter, his force consisting at that time of the Sixth, Eighth, and Nineteenth Corps, together with Crook's, Averill's, and Kelly's commands. On receiving his command, Sheridan established his headquarters at Harper's Ferry.

Concentrating his troops at once along the Potomac, in the immediate vicinity of the Shenandoah Valley, whither General Early, now in command of the Confederate forces, had withdrawn, Sheridan gradually advanced upon the important positions of Martinsburg, Williamsport, etc., garrisoning these as fast as they were relinquished, and establishing complete and prompt communications between his headquarters and the advanced posts. Early fell back gradually, for the purpose of luring Sheridan on. As Early retired, Sheridan took the opportunity of seizing and securing Winchester on the 12th of August, throwing out a cavalry detachment to Front Royal. This accomplished, he fell back in turn, abandoning Winchester, and awaiting at Harper's Ferry and its vicinity the concentration of his forces.

On the 18th of September, General Early, with comparatively a small force, was confronting Sheridan north of Winchester. Sheridan attacked him on Opequan Creek, and captured fifty men belonging to the Eighth South Carolina regiment, who were on picket. Immediately Sheridan telegraphed to Stanton, "I have captured one entire regiment, officers included."

BATTLE NEAR WINCHESTER.

On the morning of the 19th of September, the enemy advanced upon Winchester, near which place General Early met his attack. About daylight the enemy advanced, by the Berryville road, on Ramseur, who was posted at the Spout Spring, on the same road, some four miles east of Winchester. General Gordon was at Bunker Hill, twelve miles from Winchester, and ten miles from Martinsburg, on a reconnoissance. General Rhodes was at Hopewell Church, near Whitehall, to the left of the Martinsburg road, and about eight miles below Winchester. Gordon commenced moving back to the point of attack about daylight, and Rhodes moved in the same direction about seven o'clock. Wharton, meanwhile, remained on the extreme left, on the Martinsburg road, a short distance below Winchester. Between ten and eleven o'clock all of our troops were in position on the field, our line facing towards the east, the enemy's towards the west. The situation was as follows : Ramseur's troops stretched from Abraham Creek to the Berryville pike ; Rhodes had taken position between Ramseur and Gordon ; and Wharton, as above stated, held the left. The battle now raged heavily, and bore strongly towards our left. It was about half-past twelve when General Rhodes, while placing a battery in the gap between himself and Gordon, was struck in the head by a ball, and borne from the field. He was carried to Winchester, where he died in about half an hour after reaching the place.

In some battles there is a marked crisis, when the fortune of the day is visibly and instantly decided. As the enemy pressed forward in the attack, a brigade, in Grover's division of the Nineteenth Corps, was forced to retire ; another was thrown into confusion, and the entire left of the division subsequently gave way. A Confederate battery opened upon the flying troops. Their shells, descending among the broken columns of Grover, demoralized and shattered them still more. The entire infantry of the Confederates charged in turn, pouring in severe and rapid volleys towards the point of breakage.

" The moment," says a Yankee correspondent, " was a fearful

one. Such a sight rarely occurs more than once in any battle, as was presented on the open space between two pieces of woodland, into which the cheering enemy poured, in their eagerness. Their whole line, reckless of bullets, reckless even of the shells of our batteries, constantly advanced. Captain Steven's battery, posted immediately in their front, poured its fire unflinchingly into their columns to the last. The men of the battery kept it at work in the face of the foe, who advanced at least within two hundred yards of the muzzles of the guns. General Rickett's division, pressed heavily in flank, gradually broke, and commenced falling back. General Getty's division, on the left, partially fell back likewise. The day, had such a situation been suffered to continue fifteen minutes longer, would certainly have been lost to us."

The enemy ordered up his reserves in the rear of his broken centre. His columns were gradually reformed, and the battle raged with renewed fury.

The Yankees now continued to push their line around our left, and about four o'clock in the afternoon, their cavalry, on the extreme right, made a charge upon our cavalry, completely routing it. Up to this time the battle had been progressing very favorably; but the stampede of our cavalry enabled the enemy to pass on our flank and in our rear, and made it necessary for our infantry to fall back, which it did, reaching Winchester about sundown. The same evening our whole army retired to Newtown, and the next morning to Fisher's Hill. This position, pronounced by military men to be the strongest in the Valley, was eighteen miles from Winchester, and seventy-two from Staunton. It was overlooked, from the east, by the Massanutton Mountain, from which it was separated by the north branch of the Shenandoah River, while on the west it was protected by the North Mountain, and along its front base flowed a small branch called Cumberland Run.

The disaster of this defeat was painfully recognized by the Confederate public. In the fight, General Early lost three thousand men, from all causes, and three cannon. The misbehavior of our cavalry was an especial subject of mortification. It had undoubtedly lost the day. Though outnumbered four to one our troops had met the attack nobly, and actually beat Sheridan's infantry, and were driving them back at all points, when our cavalry, who were relied upon to protect our flanks, gave way on our right. The enemy's cavalry immediately assaulted the right of our victorious columns, and the fortunes of the day were changed, and a defeat of the Confederates ensued. Yet it was at least hoped that Early would be able to hold the immensely strong position of Fisher's Hill against all comers. and that there the tide of disaster would be stayed. But in this the Confederate public was to be infinitely disappointed.

THE BATTLE OF FISHER'S HILL.

On the 22d of September, Sheridan brought up his entire force to assault the strong position of the Confederates on Fisher's Hill. The works were too formidable to be carried by an attack in front alone, and therefore, while keeping up a feint of a front attack, the Eighth Corps was sent far to the right, and, sweeping about Early's left, flanked him, and attacked him in the rear, driving him out of his intrenchments while the Sixth Corps attacked at the same time in the centre front, and the Nineteenth Corps on the left. Confused and disorganized by attacks at so many different points, the Confederates broke at the centre, and fled, in disorganization, towards Woodstock. Artillery, horses, wagons, rifles, knapsacks, and canteens were abandoned, and strewn along the road. Several hundred prisoners and twelve pieces of artillery were captured. The pursuit was continued until the 25th, and did not conclude until Early had been driven below Port Republic.

This second most unexpected reverse of Early was the occasion of no little despondency in Richmond. The total of his losses in men and material was considerable; and although the story of the Yankees, that in one week ten thousand of his men had been put out of combat, was absurdly false, enough was known in Richmond of the extent of the disaster to occasion the most serious misgivings and alarm. The harvests of the Shenandoah Valley had been lost; the most productive districts of Virginia were opened to the waste of the enemy; and the second capture of Staunton, that was to ensue, was to be the signal of another alarm for the safety of Lynchburg.

While Sheridan made his headquarters at Port Republic, he sent his cavalry, under Torbert, forward to Staunton; which place they captured, and destroyed all the storehouses, machine-shops, and other buildings, owned or occupied by the Confederate government, and also the saddles, small-arms, hard-bread, and other military stores found in the place. They then proceeded to Waynesboro', also on the Virginia Central Railroad; tore up seven miles of the railroad track, destroyed the depot, the iron bridge over the Shenandoah, a government tannery, and other stores. General Sheridan also improved the time of holding possession of the Shenandoah Valley to destroy all the grain, hay and forage to be found there, excepting what was necessary for the subsistence of his own army. The whole valley being thus devastated, General Sheridan moved leisurely northward, and on the 6th of October made his headquarters at Woodstock. South of this point over two thousand barns filled with wheat and hay, and over seventy mills stocked with wheat and flour had been destroyed; and a vast herd of stock, and more than three thousand sheep had been reserved for the supply of the army. The Luray Valley, as well as the Little Fort Valley, were subjected to the same devastation. In the marauding expedition into the former valley, sixty-five hundred head of cattle, and five hundred horses were captured, and thirty-two large flouring mills, thirty distilleries, four blast-furnaces, and over fifty barns were destroyed.

The horror and crime of this devastation was remarkable even in Yankee warfare. They impoverished a whole population; they reduced women and children to beggary and starvation; they left the black monuments of Yankee atrocity all the way from the Blue Ridge to the North Mountain. It is remarkable that the worst of Yankee atrocities were always done in the intoxication of unexpected success, when no longer the fears of previous disasters held in check their cruel cowardice, and intimidated their native ferocity.

On the 9th of October, Sheridan had an affair with Rosser's cavalry, which had hung on his rear. One division of the Yankee cavalry charged along the Strasburg pike, while another, moving by a back road, took Rosser in flank. Sheridan claimed in this affair to have taken eleven pieces of artillery, and over three hundred prisoners. He wrote to the

War Department, at Washington, a dispatch in which profanity and slang marked his lively sense of victory. He had "finished 'the Savior of the Valley,'" and the worsted Confederates he had pursued "*on the jump*" for twenty-six miles.

THE BATTLE OF CEDAR CREEK.

The most important battle of the campaign in the Valley was yet to take place.

On the 18th of October, Early lay at Fisher's Hill with two corps of Sheridan's army in his front, on the north side of Cedar Creek. Another corps, the Sixth, was between Middletown and Newtown. Sheridan himself was at Winchester, and his cavalry a little withdrawn from the front. The two corps on Cedar Creek were heavily fortified on the left (looking towards Middletown) of the turnpike, but their works on the right of the road were complete.

This being the situation, Early determined to attack and, if possible, to surprise the force at Cedar Creek. Accordingly, at nightfall of the 18th, he marched out of his works at Fisher's Hill to the stone bridge which crosses the little stream at the foot of the hill. Here his army was divided, the larger column moving to the right of the turnpike, the lesser to the left—the object being simultaneous attack on both flanks of the enemy. In order to flank the enemy's works on the right of the road, it was necessary to move the larger column through a narrow pass in the mountains, where two men could not walk abreast. Thus, marching in single file, the whole night was consumed before the large column found itself in a proper position to make the attack. Seven miles of rugged country was to be marched along the mountain side, and down hills so steep that horses could hardly travel, the men holding by bushes, and moving in single rank. The Shenandoah had to be crossed twice, the last time in the face of the enemy's pickets. Canteens had been left at camp, and the men required to keep silent.

Everybody was up to time; every thing ready. Payne charged across the river, driving in the pickets at a gallop, and pressing in the direction of Sheridan's headquarters, and towards Middletown. The infantry was then rushed across, Gordon's division in front, next Ramseur's—Pegram's in reserve. Nothing was to be done but close up ranks, face to the front, and fight *rapidly*. The firing began at all points, Kershaw charging in front, and with great success.

The enemy was struck by a fatal and terrible surprise. The Eighth and Nineteenth Corps were entirely routed. Great numbers of the Yankees were slain in their camps. Eighteen pieces of artillery were captured, fifteen hundred prisoners, small arms without number, wagons and camps, every thing on the ground. Two-thirds of Sheridan's army was routed ; nothing was left to cover their disorderly retreat but the Sixth Corps and their cavalry, which had not as yet been brought into action. It was now ten in the morning. Had our victorious forces pressed on in hot and vigorous pursuit and struck the Sixth Corps, they would have involved the whole of Sheridan's army in complete rout, and achieved one of the most magnificent successes of the war.

But our troops stopped. There was no more rushing, no more charging. They had betaken themselves to plundering the enemy's camp ; demoralization was fast ensuing ; the fire and flush of their victorious charge was quenched ; the fighting was now at long range ; the infantry was pushed forward at a snail's pace ; there was no longer any ardor or enthusiasm.

For four or five hours there was comparative quiet ; the Confederates ranging the camps of the enemy for plunder, and taking no further notice of his forces in the distance, beyond some skirmishing and desultory firing.

The enemy, in the mean time, were not idle. Sheridan had slept at Winchester the previous night, but, hearing the cannonade in the morning, he took his horse and pushed on towards Strasburg at full gallop, arriving on the field at ten o'clock A. M., just as the army had taken up its position north of Middletown. On his way he had met the throng of wounded and stragglers. He immediately ordered a new line of battle : the Nineteenth Corps on the right, the Sixth in the centre, and the recovered Eighth Corps on the left. Custer's cavalry was on the extreme right, and Merritt's on the left. At three o'clock Sheridan assumed the offensive, and attacked with vigor.

Gordon's division, notwithstanding his efforts, soon broke. Kershaw's and Ramseur's divisions were fighting well, but soon followed the example of Gordon's division. Five or six guns in the rear were immediately driven back when the line broke, and placed on a high hill, where, with no aid from the infantry, who were flying in every direction, they kept the enemy at bay for an hour or more. Having exhausted their ammunition, they were compelled to withdraw.

By this time Wharton's and Pegram's men had caught the panic, and the field became covered with flying men. The artillery retired, firing slowly, and sustained only by Pegram's old brigade and Evans' brigade. After the creek was crossed, Pegram's and Evans' brigades participated in the demoralization—the road was filled with fugitives. The enemy's cavalry charged again in the rear of our train, and not a gun was fired in its defence. Many ordnance and medical stores, and twenty-three pieces of artillery, besides those taken by us in the morning, were captured.

It was a shameful rout. Our troops behaved as they never behaved before. Our loss in killed, wounded, and prisoners was, perhaps, not greater than three thousand; but the route of the retreat was strewn with abandoned wagons, ambulances, and small arms thrown away by the panic-stricken fugitives. Early had lost nearly all of his artillery. He had, in fact, received a stunning defeat from which his army never recovered.*

---

* The following address of General Early to his troops, on the occasion of this disaster, testifies to its causes, and is one of the most candid and memorable papers of the war :

HEADQUARTERS VALLEY DISTRICT, October 22, 1864.

Soldiers of the Army of the Valley :

I had hoped to have congratulated you on the splendid victory won by you on the morning of the 19th, at Belle Grove, on Cedar Creek, when you surprised and routed two corps of Sheridan's army, and drove back several miles the remaining corps, capturing eighteen pieces of artillery, one thousand five hundred prisoners, a number of colors, a large quantity of small arms, and many wagons and ambulances, with the entire camps of the two routed corps; but I have the mortification of announcing to you that, by your subsequent misconduct, all the benefits of that victory were lost, and a serious disaster incurred. Had you remained steadfast to your duty and your colors, the vic-

From this point the Valley campaign ceased to engage much of the public attention; and with the withdrawal of the bulk of the opposing forces to the Richmond lines, the interest in military events was again transferred to that quarter.

For six weeks after the battle of Cedar Creek, there were occasional skirmishes of greater or less severity between Tor-

---

tory would have been one of the most brilliant and decisive of the war; you would have gloriously retrieved the reverses at Winchester and Fisher's Hill, and entitled yourselves to the admiration and gratitude of your country. But many of you, including some commissioned officers, yielding to a disgraceful propensity for plunder, deserted your colors to appropriate to yourselves the abandoned property of the enemy; and, subsequently, those who had previously remained at their posts, seeing their ranks thinned by the absence of the plunderers, when the enemy, late in the afternoon, with his shattered columns, made but a feeble effort to retrieve the fortunes of the day, yielded to a needless panic, and fled the field in confusion, thereby converting a splendid victory into a disaster.

Had any respectable number of you listened to the appeals made to you, and made a stand, even at the last moment, the disaster would have been averted, and the substantial fruits of victory secured. But under the insane dread of being flanked, and a panic-stricken terror of the enemy's cavalry, you would listen to no appeal, threat, or order, and allowed a small body of cavalry to penetrate to our train, and carry off a number of pieces of artillery an wagons which your disorder left unprotected. You have thus obscured the glorious fame won in conjunction with the gallant men of the Army of Northern Virginia, who still remain proudly defiant in the trenches around Richmond and Petersburg. Before you can again claim them as comrades, you will have to erase from your escutcheons the blemishes which now obscure them. And this you can do if you will but be true to your former reputation, your country, and your homes. You who have fought at Manassas, Richmond, Sharpsburg, Fredericksburg, Chancellorsville, Gettysburg, and from the Wilderness to the banks of James River; and especially you who were with the immortal Jackson in all his triumphs are capable of better things.

Arouse yourselves, then, to a sense of your manhood, and appreciation of the sacred cause in which you are engaged! Yield to the mandates of discipline; resolve to stand by your colors in future at all hazards, and you can yet retrieve your reputation, and strike effective blows for your country and the cause. Let every man spurn from him the vile plunder gathered on the field of the 19th; and let no man, whatever his rank, whether combatant or noncombatant, dare exhibit his spoils of that day. They will be badges of his dishonor; the insignia of his disgrace. The officer who pauses in the career of victory to place a guard over a sutler's wagon, for his private use, is as bad as the soldier who halts to secure for himself the abandoned clothing or money of a flying foe; and they both soil the honor of the army, and the blood of their country for a paltry price. He who follows his colors into the ranks of the enemy in pursuit of victory, disdaining the miserable passion for gathering booty, comes out of the battle with his honor untarnished; and though bare

bert's cavalry, or some portion of it, and the Confederate cavalry officers Rosser and Lomax; but Early, though moving
uneasily up and down the Valley from Mount Jackson or New
Market to Fisher's Hill, carefully avoided any thing like a
general engagement, and in December sent a part of his forces
to strengthen General Lee.

SOUTHWESTERN VIRGINIA.

In Southwestern Virginia, during the period we have traversed and the early winter of 1864, there was a desultory campaign, to which we should briefly refer.

---

footed and ragged, is far more to be envied than he that is laden with rich
spoils gathered in the trail of his victorious comrades. There were some exceptions to the general misconduct on the afternoon of the 19th, but it would
be difficult to specify them all. Let those who did their duty be satisfied with
the consciousness of having done it, and mourn that their efforts were paralyzed by the misbehavior of others. Let them be consoled, to some extent, by
the reflection that the enemy has nothing to boast of on his part.

• The artillery and wagons taken were not won by his valor. His camps
were destroyed; his army terribly shattered and demoralized; his losses far
heavier than ours, even in proportion to the relative strength of the armies
his plans materially impeded; and he was unable to pursue by reason of his
crippled condition. Soldiers of the Army of the Valley, I do not speak to you
in anger; I wish to speak in kindness, though in sorrow. My purpose is to
show you the cause of our late misfortune, and point out the way to avoid
similar ones in future, and insure success to our arms. Success can only be
secured by the enforcement and observance of the most rigid discipline. Officers, whatever their rank, must not only give orders, but set the example of
obeying them, and the men must follow that example.

Fellow-soldiers, I am ready to lead you again in defence of our common
cause; and I appeal to you by the remembrance of the glorious career in
which you have formerly participated, by the woes of your bleeding country,
the ruined homes and devastated fields you see around you, the cries of anguish which come up from the widows and orphans of your dead comrades,
the horrors which await you and all that is yours in the future, if your country is subjugated, and your hopes of freedom for yourselves and your posterity,
to render a cheerful and willing obedience to the rules of discipline, and to
shoulder your musket again with the determination never more to turn your
backs upon the foe, but to do battle like men and soldiers until the last vestige
of the footsteps of our barbarous and cruel enemies is erased from the soil they
desecrate, and the independence of our country is firmly established. If you
will do this, and rely upon the protecting care of a just and merciful God, all
will be well; you will again be what you once were, and I will be proud to
lead you once more to battle.

J. A. EARLY, Lieutenant-General.

On the 2d of October, General Breckinridge, who had relieved Echols in Southwestern Virginia, encountered Burbridge, who was advancing on the salt-works at Saltville, Virginia, and on the banks of the Holtston River defeated him, giving him a severe lesson. In November, Breckinridge, having joined Vaughn in East Tennessee, defeated the Yankee General Gillem, at Morristown, taking four hundred prisoners; and on the 18th of the month, engaged and defeated the enemy again at Strawberry Plains.

On the 20th of December, the salt-works at Saltville were captured by the Yankees, who in the early part of the month had been raiding on the Tennessee road. Our forces there were attacked by the whole force of Burbridge, numbering about five thousand. The fight was kept up all the evening, mainly with artillery, our forces being commanded by Colonel Preston, and numbering, it is said, not more than three hundred and fifty. When night fell they still held their own; but, under cover of the darkness, the Yankees succeeded in reaching Fort Breckinridge, one of the main defences of the place, in overpowering numbers, and captured it. Colonel Preston, deeming it impractible to hold the works longer, then ordered the evacuation. The works were fired the next morning. The Yankees did not remain long, and left for East Tennessee. At Abingdon, they destroyed two entire blocks of buildings.

CHAPTER XX.

Mr. Lincoln's extraordinary, triumph.—Reassembling of the Richmond Congress.—
President Davis' review of the situation.—A memorable boast.—New demands of
the Confederate conscription.—Military resources of the North and South compared.—Plethoric wealth of the North.—" Twenty against one."—Two advantages
the South had in the war.—Its conditions of success.—The value of *endurance* on
the part of the South.—The Hood-Sherman Campaign.—Speeches at headquarters.
—Hood commences his march.—Capture of Dalton.—Sherman follows as far as
Gaylesville.—He turns back.—Georgia and South Carolina " at his mercy."—An
extraordinary campaign.— Hood and Sherman marching away from each other.—
Hood crosses into Tennessee.—The Yankee retreat to Franklin.—The Battle of
Franklin.—Great loss in Confederate officers.—The enemy retreats to Nashville.—
Battle of Nashville.—The giving way of Bates' division.—A shameful stampede.
—Hood's losses.—The whole scheme of Confederate defence west of the Alle-
ghanies broken down.—The errors of Hood's campaign.

WE have already stated that the military successes of the
two or three preceding months secured the re-election of President Lincoln on the 8th of November. His re-election was
singularly triumphant. General McClellan received only the
electoral vote of Delaware (3), Kentucky (11), and New Jersey
(7), 21 in all. Mr. Lincoln received that of the remaining 22
States, 213 in all. Mr. Lincoln had the vote of all the States
which he received in 1860, with the exception of the half vote
of New Jersey, which was cast for him in consequence of a
division in the opposition party. Besides these, he received
the 7 electoral votes of Maryland, which in 1860 were cast for
Mr. Breckinridge; the 11 votes of Missouri, cast for Douglas;
and the 11 votes of the new States of Kansas, West Virginia,
and Nevada. In the States which voted at this election, there
was in 1860 a popular majority of about 100,000 against Mr.
Lincoln; the popular majority in his favor now was about
3)0,000.

A few days before this election, the Confederate Congress
had reassembled in Richmond. The message of President
Davis opened with an ingenious review of the campaign of
1864. " At the beginning of the year," he said, "Texas was partially in the possession of the enemy; now no Federal soldiers

were in the State, except as prisoners. In Northwestern Louisiana, a large Federal army and fleet had been defeated, and had only escaped with a loss of one-third of its numbers, and a large part of its munitions and vessels. Arkansas had been nearly recovered; and the Confederate forces had penetrated into Missouri. On the east of the Mississippi, in spite of some reverses, the Confederates had been on the whole successful; Northern and Western Mississippi, Northern Alabama, and Western Tennessee were in their possession. On the seacoast, the successes of the Federals had been confined to the capture of the outer defences of Mobile Bay. Their armies had been defeated in different parts of Virginia; and after a series of defeats around Richmond, they were still engaged in the effort, commenced four months before, to capture Petersburg. The army of Sherman, though it had captured Atlanta, had gained no real advantage beyond the possession of a few fortified points which could be held only by large garrisons, and were menaced with recapture."

President Davis concluded his review with a memorable boast. "The Confederacy," he declared, " *had no vital points*. If Richmond, and Wilmington, and Charleston, and Savannah, and Mobile were all captured, the Confederacy would remain as defiant as ever, and no peace would be made which did not recognize its independence."

The Confederate President, while professing to see no cause for despondency in the military situation, took occasion to recommend the repeal of all laws granting exemption from military service. He said that " no position or pursuit should relieve any one who is able to do active duty from the enrolment in the army," unless he could be more useful in another sphere, and this could not be the case with entire classes. The military authorities should have the power to exempt individuals only, whose services may be more valuable in than out of the army. In regard to the question of the employment of slaves in the army, Mr. Davis recommended that slaves to the number of 40,000 should be " acquired" by the general government, who should be employed not merely as ordinary laborers, cooks, and teamsters, but as engineer and pioneer laborers. He recommended that these slaves should be liberated on their discharge, after faithful service, rather than that

they should be manumitted at once, or retained in servitude
He was opposed, under present circumstances, to arming the
slaves; but he added: "The subject is to be viewed solely in
the light of policy and our social economy. Should the alternative ever be presented of subjugation or of the employment
of the slave as a soldier, there seems to be no reason to doubt
what then should be our decision."

We have, at different periods in the history of the war, instituted a comparison between the material resources of the
belligerents. They were terribly unequal at this period. Mr.
Lincoln, in his message to Congress, referred to a fact which
could not be denied: that the steady expansion of population, improvement, and governmental institutions over the
new and unoccupied portion of the North had scarcely been
checked, much less impeded or destroyed by the war. New
and immense resources had been recently developed by the
enemy; and it seemed, indeed, that providential circumstances
had come to his aid in the war. The discovery and development of petroleum had added immensely to the national wealth,
and it was calculated that in a few years it would become an
article of export to the extent of one hundred and fifty millions
of dollars. Mineral resources, almost fabulous, had been
brought to light. What once seemed a barren and uninhabitable waste, between the Atlantic States and those which had
grown up on the Pacific Ocean, had proved a new El Dorado.
It was estimated that the products of the mines of gold, silver,
and cinnabar in that region had, in the past year, exceeded one
hundred millions of dollars. It was discovered that a vast
belt of some one or two hundred miles in width and eight or
nine hundred in length, embracing portions of Idaho, Nevada,
acd Arizona, was rich in silver ore. The North had become suddenly plethoric with wealth; and for men and material for the purposes of war, it had the whole world to draw
upon.

A Yankee newspaper said: "We have now over twenty-six
millions of people within the Union lines, against less than five
millions (over one-half negro slaves) within the lines of Davis.
All things considered, the actual, positive available strength
of Lincoln against Davis is more than twenty against one.
The war, then, should be, at the furthest, brought to an end

within six months, and with becoming energy on the part of the administration it might be finished in three."

But there was one element which the newspaper did not take into its calculation; and which, despite the almost appalling disparity of resources between the belligerents, insured, *on certain conditions*, the final success of the South. It was the vast extent of territory which the North proposed to subjugate, and which never yet, in the history of wars, was brought to such a fate, on the single condition that its people remained firm in their resolution and purpose. Against the inequality of resources between the North and the South, we may put these considerations, in which the latter had immense advantages: that the South was fighting on the defensive, and had, therefore, no need of positive victories; that she only sought a negative conclusion, and might win by endurance; and that her territory was so extensive that it would take several millions of men to garrison it, as long as its people were firmly disposed to dispute the authority of the invaders.

With reflecting persons in the North, the real question touching the war had come to be the measure of Southern endurance; and this virtue had obtained a new and vital value in the stages through which the war was now passing. It was fashionable for Yankees to laugh at Confederate expectations of political revolutions or financial rupture in the North; they concluded that the time was past when the Confederates could expect to win their independence by a grand military *coup* or force of military successes. All these calculations were lightly or insolently regarded by Northern men. Their real anxiety was, the measure of endurance on the part of the South. The great curiosity of Northern politicians was as to the real spirit of the South, and the questions of thinking men among them invariably went to the point of the probable term of Southern endurance. This quality had assumed a new value in Northern eyes. It had become morally certain that by force of it alone the South would obtain her independence. Such was the silent but general concession of the Northern mind. There was but one condition to assure the independence of the South: that the spirit of the people and the army would not break by some unworthy impatience, or not be deliberately broken down by insane persistence in folly on the part of Davis and his clique of toadies and encouragers.

There were two parties in the North, perhaps equally intelligent, and each claiming to draw their opinions from Southern sources of information, which differed as to the real spirit o. the South: one claiming that it was resolute, and even in the last necessity desperate; the other contending that it was fast being broken by reverses, and would end in submission. One found this question in every circle in the North. Reliable information upon it was far more valuable to the Washington Government than maps of all the fortifications in the Confederate States. To convince the North of the spirit of the Southern people was more important than half-a-dozen victories; for it was to convince them of the hopelessness of war, and to put before their eyes the immediate necessity of conscription.

President Davis said rightly that the Confederacy " had no vital points ;" but the declaration implied *the condition that the spirit of the people, despite of temporary disasters, was to remain erect and unbroken.* And a period of the war was now approaching when precisely that condition was to be tested, and the spirit of the people of the Confederacy was to be tried, as it had never before been, by the fire and sword of the invader. To the events of this remarkable period we must now draw the attention of the reader.

THE HOOD-SHERMAN CAMPAIGN.

The public did not have long to wait for the development of that curious strategy which President Davis had planned with Hood for the compensation of the loss of Atlanta. Indeed, no secret was made of its general movement and designs.

On the 18th of September, President Davis arrived at General Hood's headquarters, and the following day reviewed the whole army. In the evening, the President addressed the soldiers in hopeful and encouraging tones. Turning to Cheatham's division of Tennesseeans, he said : " Be of good cheer, for within a short while your faces will be turned homeward, and your feet pressing Tennessee soil."

General Hood was enthusiastically called for. He said:

" Soldiers, it is not my province to make speeches : I was not born for such work; that I leave to other men. Within a few days I expect to give the command ' Forward !' and I believe you are, like myself, willing to go forward, even if we live on parched corn and beef. I am ready to give the command ' Forward !' this very night. Good-night."

On the 29th of September, Hood began his march, getting well in the rear of Sherman, and next day encamping near the old battle-ground of New Hope Church. His first movement attracted but little attention. The incautious language of President Davis first led the enemy to suppose that this movement was preliminary to something more extensive, and General Sherman's suspicions also were apparently aroused by it; for we find him about this time sending his spare forces to the rear, under General Thomas, and distributing strong detachments, under Newton, Corse, and Schofield, at different points immediately in the rear of Atlanta. He also ordered frequent reconnoissances of the enemy in his position near Newnan. The Yankee cavalry reported, on September 27, further movements of Hood towards the Chattahoochee. On October 1, Generals Fuller and Ransom made a reconnoissance towards Newnan, and discovered that the Confederates had crossed the Chattahoochee River on September 29 and 30, and had concentrated in the vicinity of Powder Springs, Ga. On the 3d of October, General Sherman, with the bulk of his army, moved in pursuit, vowing his intention to destroy Hood.

On the 5th of October, when Hood's advance assaulted Allatoona, Sherman was on Kenesaw Mountain, signalling to the garrison at Allatoona, over the heads of the Confederates, to hold out until he relieved them. Hood moved westward, and crossing the Etowah and Oostananla rivers by forced marches, attacked Dalton on the 12th, which was surrendered.

After obstructing Snake Creek Gap as much as possible, in order to delay Sherman, who continued to press him, Hood moved west, passing through the gap of Pigeon Mountain, and entered Lafayette on the 15th of October. He had now advanced as far north as it was thought possible to do without fighting, and a battle appeared to be imminent in the vicinity of the old battle-field of Chickamauga. But Hood, after holding the gaps of Pigeon Mountain as long as possible, suddenly

moved south from Lafayette to Gadsden, Alabama, closely followed as far as Gaylesville by General Sherman. This movement was looked upon as a retreat, and as the end of the great
raid of which Hood and Davis had promised and boasted so
much. But it soon became apparent that Hood was not yet
at the end of his strategy, and that the campaign was only
about to begin in earnest.

On October 23, Hood moved from Gadsden, through Look
out Mountain, towards Gunter's Landing and Decatur, on the
Tennessee River, near the last of which places he formed a
junction with a portion of General Dick Taylor's army, which
had meantime quietly moved up the Mobile and Ohio Railroad to Corinth, and thence to Tuscumbia, the new base of
supplies. He thus placed himself far in General Sherman's
rear before that officer could take steps to transfer his army to
the new front of the Confederates on the Tennessee. Hood's
advance had probably reached the Tennessee before Sherman
positively knew that he had abandoned Gadsden. Undoubtedly it was much to his surprise when, on October 25, he tried
the gap and found it abandoned by Hood. The position was
certainly startling. He dared not follow, thus abandoning his
line of supplies to venture in a mountainous country, through
which a large army had just passed. It was impossible to
transfer his entire army to Hood's front in time to meet him
and thus hold his communications intact. The position demanded resolution and action.

General Sherman seems here to have comprehended Hood's
designs. On the junction of Taylor's army with him, he rea-
soned that the two would strike a blow for the recovery of
Middle Tennessee; and, if successful, then for East Tennessee
also. But he calculated that Tennessee would be safe in charge
of General Thomas, to whom he could assign a force sufficient
to grapple with Hood, Taylor, or Beauregard; while for himself he had projected another campaign. Turning eastward,
then, from Gaylesville, he announced to his army that he
should follow Hood no longer, but let him go north as far as
he pleased. "If he will go to the river," he said, "I will give
him his rations." Giving his instructions to General Thomas,
and dividing his army so as to spare him a part of the Army
of the Cumberland and the Army of the Ohio, he moved

southeast towards Atlanta by the 1st of November, causing the railroad track to be removed from Atlanta to Chattanooga, and sent to the latter city. On the 4th of November, he began his preparations for his new movement; and the same day telegraphed his intentions to Washington, in the following words: "Hood has crossed the Tennessee. Thomas will take care of him and Nashville, while Schofield will not let him into Chattanooga or Knoxville. Georgia and South Carolina are at my mercy—and I shall strike. Do not be anxious about me. I am all right." The campaign he had projected was neither more nor less than this: with the four corps, and the cavalry force still under his immediate command, an army of not far from sixty thousand infantry and artillery, and about five thousand cavalry, he purposed, cutting loose from all bases, and constituting a strictly movable column, with thirty or forty days' rations, and his train reduced to the smallest possible dimensions, to move southeastward, through the heart of the country, upon Savannah; and thence, should circumstances favor, northward through South Carolina and North Carolina, to compel the surrender or evacuation of Richmond.

And now commenced one of the most extraordinary campaigns of any war—presenting the singular spectacle of two great antagonistic chieftains *both* at once acting on the offensive, day after day marching away from each other, and moving diametrically apart.

On the 20th of November, General Hood commenced to move his army from Northern Alabama to Tennessee. His line of march from Florence followed two parallel roads to the chief town of Wayne County, in Tennessee—Waynesboro'. Simultaneously with this advance, the Yankees evacuated or surrendered Decatur and Huntsville. The Fourth Army Corps, under General Stanley, two divisions of the Twenty-third Corps, under General Schofield, and an aggregation of fort-garrisons from the surrounding country, under General Richard W. Johnson, concentrated at Pulaski. Hood, immediately after his arrival at Waynesboro', changed front to the northwest; and, while marching directly upon Columbia, threatened, with Forrest's cavalry, to cut off the Yankee retreat from Pulaski. That position, about to be flanked, was at once abandoned. Schofield, with the force that had been concentrated there, retreated on the 23d ; and, while his cavalry were being pressed in upon his rear by those of Hood, attempted, by a forced march, to reach Columbia. Forrest had, however, fallen upon the Yankee base, and, having forced them back rapidly, had advanced within four miles of Columbia. Schofield's infantry had, however, come up in time to save the place from capture, and to hold back the Confederates until the works covering the place had been made impassable by a *chevaux de frize* of Yankee bayonets.

Hood's infantry marched on. On the 25th, they had commenced a movement for flanking Columbia on the eastward, in conjunction with an attempt of Forrest to cut that place off from railroad communication with Nashville. Under heavy skirmishing and cannonading, Forrest succeeded in extending his flank to Duck River, and in throwing a large force of his cavalry to the opposite bank. The Confederate infantry, filing at the same time around the place on the east, the state of affairs became critical, and compelled Schofield to fall back hurriedly, with a loss of stores, on the night of the 26th.

The retreat to Franklin was one of constant fighting. Skirmishing of the very heaviest and deadliest character was maintained all the way. Forrest hung like a raging tiger upon the rear, and occasionally pressing Wilson back, brought face to face the retreating and the pursuing infantry. On the 29th, General Cox, commanding Schofield's rear, was brought to bay at Spring Hill, midway between Columbia and Franklin, and, after a struggle to delay the advance, retreated successfully to the main body at Franklin.

The Confederates pressed on, Forrest leading, Stewart next, and Cheatham following. Lee was still in the rear, but coming up. The enemy were closely pushed, retreated rapidly, and left evidences of their haste on every side ; wagons half burned or with wheels cut, and animals, weltering in their own fresh blood, were strewn along the road. After travelling in this manner for about seven miles, Stewart sent word to the rear that he had brought the Yankees to bay, and they were two miles in his front, in line of battle, occupying a ridge of hills.

By the time a disposition of our forces was made for an assault, the Yankee columns broke into marching order, and moved on as before. A short distance ahead the Yankees again made a stand. The Confederates prepared, as before, to attack. No sooner were the preparations complete, however, than the Yankees resumed their march, and thus gained time for their wagon trains and artillery. On reaching the last bridge on which the enemy had halted, Hood saw before him the town of Franklin, and in front of it three strong lines of battle, in three heavy series of breastworks.

THE BATTLE OF FRANKLIN.

It was late in the evening of the 30th of November, when the Confederate army approached Franklin. General Hood resolved to attack at once. Had he waited till the next morning, a new and formidable line of works would have confronted him, and the second and inner line would have been so greatly strengthened, that it would have been madness to have attacked. General Hood knew that Thomas would endeavor to hold the old line of Nashville, Murfreesboro', and Franklin; and he felt that if he could fight the battle of Nashville at Franklin, and be successful, that Nashville would fall, Tennessee be given up, and the war transferred to the Ohio.

Stewart and Forrest made a detour to the right, and by five o'clock had struck the enemy a stunning blow on his left flank. Cheatham now moved up, and joining his right, as near as practicable, to Stewart's left, the battle was joined, and waged with fierceness on both sides.

Thousands of our soldiers were standing once more on their own native soil, and some in sight of their own homes; and they fought with every incentive in their hearts that can urge manhood to noble deeds. The enthusiasm of the troops was glorious; the country a vast, unbroken plain, as level as a table; and the sight of those long dark lines, fringed with fire and smoke, with twenty thousand rifles mingling their sharp notes with the deeper thunders of the artillery, was well calculated to inspire the heroism which impelled our army on to victory. Major-generals, brigadiers, and colonels rode in front of their commands, waving hats, and urging on the troops. Men fell wounded and dead—great rents were torn—but, with the steadiness of veterans, the gaps were filled by the living and the column moved on.

The first line of breastworks was swept clean. Our loss had been great. General Pat. Cleburne, the " Stonewall Jackson' of the West, fell, shot through the head with four balls, and died on the ramparts. General Gist, previously wounded in the leg, had refused to leave the field, limping along on foot, cheering his men, and finally received a ball through the breast, killing him instantly. Brown, Manigault, Johnson, Strahl, and scores of field and staff officers, who had ex· posed themselves at the head of their troops, were either killed or wounded. Still our men faltered not. Dashing on, they reached the second line. The Yankees were stubborn. On the right they had charged Bates' division, and gained a momentary advantage ; but recovering, that gallant officer was again at the front, and, with his brave Tennesseeans, doing splendid service.

For a time the Yankees held their breastworks, and the fighting was hand to hand between those in the ditch on the outside, and those behind the intrenchments. But the struggle was not long, and again the foe was flying across the field. It was night, however, and the difficulties of continuing the battle so great, that at two o'clock A. M., save the occasional spattering of musketry, the grand chorus of battle was at an end. The next morning it was discovered that the Yankees had evacuated the position, and were in full retreat to Nashville. It was likewise discovered that Thomas had been largely reinforced, and thus enabled to make the stubborn resistance which had not been anticipated by General Hood.

Just before the battle of Franklin had been joined, Hood had ridden along the lines of his army, telling his men that the Yankee lines were weak, and that once broken, the army would be driven out of Tennessee. He had been extravagant in his promises. The Yankee General Thomas lay at Nashville with his main force.

Hood now advanced upon Nashville, and laid siege to it on the 2d of December, closely investing it for a fortnight.

THE BATTLE OF NASHVILLE.

While Hood was intrenching before Nashville, Thomas wa preparing for an assault on the Confederate position. Rein forcements were received from several sources, until by the 12th the Yankee ranks were swelled to an extent which warranted Thomas to advance to the attack whenever his arrangements were completed. A consultation of the Yankee commanders was held on the 12th, and it was determined to attack the Confederate lines on the following day. This plan was frustrated by Hood, who fell back to a stronger position, two miles south of that held by him on the 12th. Another council was held on the 14th, and all things being in readiness, it was agreed to make the attack next morning.

On the morning of the 15th of October, the enemy attacked both flanks of Hood's army. They were repulsed on the right with heavy loss; but towards evening they drove in the Confederate infantry outposts on the left flank.

The next day the enemy made a general attack on Hood's entire line. The battle raged furiously from dawn till dark. Thomas' overwhelming numbers enabled him to throw heavy columns against Hood's left and centre. All the enemy's assaults were repulsed until about half-past three o'clock in the afternoon. When it was supposed by General Hood that he had in his grasp a splendid victory, a stampede suddenly took place in one of his divisions, and the day was lost in a moment.

Bates' division was to the left of the Confederate centre. It had repulsed the enemy in the morning. He advanced again late in the evening, and was repulsed again from the other points of the line fronting Bates' division, but rushed over this point, and by sheer force of numbers beat down and run over, killing, wounding, and capturing, in the ditches, nearly every man holding them. Support had been asked for by General Bates and General Walthall, as is understood; both of them were within forty yards of this point all the day. Instead of getting support at this, the only salient point in the whole Confederate line, one brigade was taken from the right and another from the left of this point, to save the extreme left or the line. When this was done, so confident was General Bates of the coming disaster, that he ordered his artillery back on the Franklin pike, which was then its only exit.

The break in Bates' division was the signal for a general panic in Hood's army. The moment a small break was made in his lines, the whole of two corps unaccountably and instantly fled from their ditches, most of them without firing a gun. It was a disgraceful retreat. Fifty pieces of artillery and nearly all of Hood's ordnance wagons were left to the enemy. Our loss in killed and wounded was disgracefully small; and it was only through want of vigor in Thomas' pursuit that Hood's shattered and demoralized army effected its retreat.

He finally made his escape across the Tennessee River with the remnant of his army, having lost from various causes more than ten thousand men, half of his generals, and nearly all of his artillery. Such was the disastrous issue of the Tennessee campaign, which put out of existence, as it were, the splendid army that Johnston had given up at Atlanta, and terminated forever the whole scheme of Confederate defence west of the Alleghanies.

General Hood recrossed the Tennessee at Florence, General Forrest covering his retreat, and was at Tupelo on the 6th of January, 1865, where, on the 23d, he took leave of the army in the following order:

"HEADQUARTERS ARMY OF THE TENNESSEE,
TUPELO, Miss., Jan. 23, 1865.

"SOLDIERS—At my request, I have this day been relieved from the command of the army. In taking leave of you, accept my thanks for the patience with which you have endured your hardships during the recent campaign. I am alone responsible for its conception, and strove hard to do my duty in its execution. I urge upon you the importance of giving your entire support to the distinguished soldier who now assumes command, and shall look with deep interest on all your future operations, and rejoice at your success.

"J. B. HOOD."

The complete and disastrous failure of General Hood was freely acknowledged in the Confederacy; and the glaring errors in his campaign did not escape the savage criticisms of the Richmond newspapers. It was said, with obvious justice, that his greatest mistake had been at Nashville. He had sat down before that city for a fortnight, and proceeded to invest it on the south. Had he struck boldly across the Cumberland, and settled himself on the Yankee communications, he would have forced Thomas to evacuate Nashville and fall back towards Kentucky. But he adopted another plan, and paid the penalty of his error in defeat and heavy loss.

While at one end of the line of the Tennessee-Georgia campaign the Confederates had thus come to grief, at the other end, stretching towards the sea, there were other more important disasters and occasions of peculiar trial, such as the spirit of the Confederacy had never before experienced. The effect of Sherman's march to the sea on the *morale* of the Confederacy dates the first chapter of its subjugation.

CHAPTER XXI.

Sherman's march from the mountains to the sea.—Yankee boasts.—Easy nature of Sherman's enterprise.—"Grand" mistake of the Confederates.—The burning of Atlanta.—Five thousand houses in ruins.—Sherman's route to Milledgeville.—Second stage of the march to Millen.—Last stage of the march.—Wheeler's cavalry. —THE FALL OF SAVANNAH.—Capture of Fort McAllister.—Probable surprise of Hardee.—The Confederates evacuate Savannah.—Sherman's *Christmas-gift* to Mr. Lincoln.—The true value of Sherman's exploit.—His own estimation of it.—Despondency in the South.—Depletion of the Confederate armies.—THE EXCHANGE OF PRISONERS, etc.—Bad faith of the Yankees.—Their misrepresentations.—The question of recaptured slaves.—A Yankee calculation.—The Washington Government responsible for the sufferings of Yankee prisoners.—How capital was made out of their sufferings.—A game with "sick" prisoners.—How "rebel barbarities" were manufactured.—Noble conduct of General Grant.—Its commentary on the Washington cabinet.—His "victory" over that body.

THERE was scarcely a Yankee newspaper that did not find more or less frequent occupation in extolling the genius of the march which Sherman had undertaken from the mountains of Georgia to the sea, and placing it above the achievements of Hannibal, Napoleon, and Marlborough. But the simple fact was, that the Davis-Hood strategy was a grand mistake, and Sherman's advantage of it proportionally grand. By this strategy Georgia was uncovered, and Sherman had plain marching to the sea. There was no considerable force to oppose him. The whole plan, which had originated in the brain of President Davis, to compensate for the enemy's offensive movement in Georgia by penetrating Tennessee was outrageously foolish, from the simple consideration that the two invasions were necessarily unequal: for that into the enemy's country could not seriously affect his superabundant resources, while that into the Southern interior went right into the heart of the Confederacy; and having once passed the frontiers, on which the South had necessarily thrown out all its resources in men, was destined to realize General Grant's assertion, that the Confederacy was merely a shell.

Before undertaking his great campaign towards Savannah,

Sherman ordered the destruction of most of the inhabitable part of Atlanta. He destroyed, in all, nearly five thousand houses here, and left behind him a picture of ruin and desolation, such as is seldom to be found in the ravages of war.*

On the 15th day of November, Sherman began his march to the sea. He moved forward in two columns, General Howard commanding the right and General Slocum the left, while his cavalry covered his flanks. General Howard's column moved through East Point, Rough-and-Ready, Griffin, Jonesboro',

---

* An agent of Governor Brown, of Georgia, made the following official report of the extent of the destruction done by the enemy in Atlanta: " The property of the State was destroyed by fire, yet a vast deal of valuable material remains in the ruins. Three-fourths of the bricks are good, and will be suitable for rebuilding if placed under shelter before freezing weather. There is a quantity of brass in the journals of burned cars, and in the ruins of the various machinery of the extensive railroad shops; also, a valuable amount of copper from the guttering of the State depot, the flue pipes of destroyed engines, stop cocks of machinery, etc., etc.

The car-wheels that were uninjured by fire were rendered useless by breaking the flanges. In short, every species of machinery that was not destroyed by fire, was most ingeniously broken and made worthless in its original form —the large steam-boilers, the switches, the frogs, etc. Nothing has escaped. The fire-engines, except Tallulah No. 3, were sent North. Tallulah has been overhauled, and a new fire-company organized. Nos. 1 and 2 fire-engine houses were saved. All the city pumps were destroyed, except one on Marrietta-street. The car-sheds, the depots, machine shops, foundries, rolling mills, merchant mills, arsenal, laboratory, armory, etc., were all burned.

In the angle between Hunter-street, commencing at the City Hall, running east, and McDonough-street, running south, all houses were destroyed. The jail and calaboose were burned. All business houses, except those on Alabama-street, commencing with the Gate City Hotel, running east to Lloyd-street, were burned. All the hotels, except the Gate City, were burned. By referring to my map you will find about four hundred houses standing. The scale of the map is four hundred feet to one inch. Taking the car-shed for the centre, describe a circle, the diameter of which is twelve inches, and you will perceive that the circle contains about three hundred squares. Then, at a low estimate, allow three houses to every four hundred feet; and we will have thirty-six hundred houses in the circle. Subtract the number of houses indicated on the map as standing, and you will see by this estimate the enemy have destroyed thirty-two hundred houses. Refer to the exterior of the circle, and you will discover that it is more than half a mile to the city limits in every direction, which was thickly populated, say nothing of the houses beyond, and you will see that the enemy have destroyed from four to five thousand houses. Two-thirds of the shade-trees in the park and city, and of the timber in the suburbs have been destroyed. The suburbs present to the eye one vast, naked, ruined, deserted camp."

McDonough, Forsythe, Hillsboro', Monticello, and bridging the Ocmulgee entered Milledgeville on the 20th of November. Here General Sherman made his headquarters for a few days, while Howard moved on through Saur.dersville, Griswold, towards Louisville, the point of rendezvous, with the left wing. That wing, under the command of General Slocum, had meantime passed through Decatur, Covington, Social Circle, Madison; made a feint of an attack upon Macon; passed through Buckhead and Queensboro', and, dividing one detachment, moved towards Augusta, and the other to Eatonton and Sparta. The second stage of Sherman's march may be taken as from Milledgeville to Millen. The distance was about seventy-five miles, and the time occupied in the march eight days, from November 24th to December 2d.

The Yankee troops left Milledgeville admirably clothed and equipped. Each man had eighty rounds of ammunition: while their wagons contained fixed material without stint. Rations for forty days. had been prepared, and they suffered for nothing. The Yankee cavalry, with the left wing, on crossing the Oconee, had visited Sparta, which is on a line between Warrenton and Milledgeville, about equi-distant from both. On the evening of the 24th, General Slocum's advance encamped at Devereux, seven miles west of Sparta, and the cavalry scoured the whole country, one of the most fertile and thickly settled in the whole State, and vast quantities of forage and provisions, many horses, and mules were obtained, and much cotton burned. For several days the Yankees raided through the entire country between the two railroads in the vicinity last described. Abundance of food and forage was secured, and every thing was destroyed which could be useful to the enemy. The march was leisurely—Sherman evidently finding himself master of the situation. He did not start directly for the seaboard until he had all the provisions he desired.

Sherman was now ready to enter upon the third and last stage of his march. Behind him the Georgia Central Railroad lay destroyed for more than a hundred miles, and the Georgia road for full sixty. The railroad-bridge over the Oconee and the Ogeechee, on the Georgia Central, had been destroyed, and also those over Brier Creek and Buckhead Creek, on the

THE LAST YEAR.   429

Waynesboro' Branch connecting Augusta with Millen. Incalculable damage had been done. It only remained to move down to the Atlantic, and crown the campaign in the capture of Savannah.

From Millen, then, on the 2d of December, the Yankee army swung southerly down on the final stage of its journey to Savannah, in half a dozen columns, moving over as many different roads for the sake of convenience and speed. The Confederate forces, massed at Augusta, were left hopelessly in Sherman's rear. The army was protected on either flank by a large river, and cavalry formed the vanguard and rear-guard. Its mission, as a curtain for the concealment of infantry operations, had now been accomplished. The country traversed was covered with pine forests, cut up by numerous creeks, and intersected by wide stretches of swamps; and further on the coastwise, swamps and the low rice-fields became the prevalent character of the region.

So far General Sherman's march had been almost without opposition. It had had one or two small conflicts with Wheeler's cavalry ; and some few militiamen and conscripts, hastily assembled and badly organized, were easily brushed from his path. Ten miles from Savannah, where his left wing struck the Charleston Railroad, he encountered Confederate skirmishers posted in a swamp near by, which indicated the presence of the Confederate forces under Hardee for the first time.

THE FALL OF SAVANNAH.

On the 10th of December, Sherman lay in line of battle, confronting the outer works of Savannah, about five miles distant from the city. It was easy for him to see that his first task was to open communication with the fleet.

That part of the coast of Georgia, at the mouth of the Savannah, is of that amphibious character which marks so much of the Southern coast in general—the ravelled and unfinished ends of nature's web, where sea and land join. The ocean breaks in between Great Wassaw and Ossabaw Islands, forming Ossabaw Sound, and into this estuary flow the Great and Little Ogeechee and the Vernon rivers. The land, or rather the marsh on each side of the Ogeechee, was almost *à fleur d'eau*, certainly hardly rising a foot above the level of the river, while at times it is entirely submerged. For miles and miles on every hand there was nothing to be seen but these low and level islands and islets, covered with reeds and rank grasses, save where a lustier vegetation had pushed up in occasional clumps of trees called " hummocks."

About six miles from the mouth of Ossabaw Sound, near where the Savannah, Albany, and Gulf Railroad crosses the Ogeechee, the river jets out into a promontory named Point Genesis, covered by one of these hummocks of more than ordinary size. Behind this, hidden from the river, lay Fort McAllister, an earthwork of considerable strength, erected by the Confederates early in the war. Its batteries completely commanded the river.

On the 12th of December, Hazen's division of the Fifteenth Corps was selected for the important work of carrying Fort McAllister. At half-past four o'clock of the 13th, the division went forward to the assault, another division supporting it, over an open space of more than five hundred yards. The Yankees rushed on at the double-quick. The fort was approached and stormed from all sides. Resistance was useless, as by a singular improvidence the fort was garrisoned by not more than two or three hundred Confederates; and there is no doubt that General Hardee had been surprised by the quickness and decision of the enemy.

Sherman himself had ordered the assault, and witnessed the execution of the order from the top of a house not far distant; and as soon as he saw the men on the parapets, he exclaimed to his staff, " The fort is ours! Order me a boat—I am going down to the fleet."

The possession of Fort McAllister opened Ossabaw Sound, effected communication with Dahlgren's fleet, and made the capture of Savannah, where Hardee had allowed himself to be shut up with fifteen thousand men, but a question of time. In fact Sherman had now invested the city on all but the eastern side. His right held King's Bridge, far in the rear of Savannah, and controlled the Ogeechee, whence his lines stretched across the Savannah River, his left being about three miles above the city. He had cut off all the railroad supplies of

Savannah. On the south, he had struck the Savannah, Albany, and Gulf Railroad, which formerly had transported large supplies of cattle and provisions from Florida to Savannah. The railroads from Augusta and Macon were thoroughly broken. Foster's batteries had gotten within shelling distance of the Charleston Railroad, and prevented the passage o. trains. It only remained to move regularly upon the city by systematic approaches. It could not hope for outside succor of any kind; Sherman's prompt seizure of Fort McAllister having prevented reinforcements down the Charleston road, and cut off General G. W. Smith, who, with several thousand Confederates, was on the other side of the Ogeechee.

From the 10th to the 16th of December heavy artillery firing and skirmishing went on all along the lines, but no regular engagement occurred. On the 16th, Sherman formally demanded the surrender of the city from its commander, Hardee, who declined next day to accede to the demand. Sherman instantly hurried more heavy siege-guns upon his lines, and on the 20th was prepared to bombard the city and assault its works. But Hardee had already taken the alarm. Finding that only the eastern exit was open to him, and that on that Sherman was already cannonading, and soon might capture it by assault, Hardee resolved to evacuate Savannah. On the afternoon of the 20th, his iron-clads and batteries opened a tremendous fire, lasting into the night, and, under cover of the demonstration, the Confederate general crossed his fifteen thousand men and his large force of negro laborers upon a pontoon bridge, laid below his rear batteries, to the South Carolina side, and marched them off towards Charleston on the Union causeway. The night was exceedingly favorable for such a movement, it being very dark, with a west wind blowing. Next morning, at break of day, the pickets of Geary's division crept forward, advanced still farther, and went over the works; and Geary himself, marching into Savannah, received, on the morning of the 21st December, 1864, its formal surrender at the hands of its mayor. The troops were gone. The navy-yard, two iron-clads, many smaller vessels, and a vast amount of ammunition, ordnance stores, and supplies had been destroyed before the evacuation, but all the rest of the uninjured city fell into the hands of the Yankees.

Sherman sent a characteristic dispatch to Washington. He wrote to President Lincoln: "I beg to present you, *as a Christmas gift*, the city of Savannah, with one hundred and fifty heavy guns and plenty of ammunition, and also about twenty-five thousand bales of cotton."

And so ended Sherman's famous march to the sea—an exploit which Yankee newspapers declared had not been excelled since William of Normandy crossed the English Channel and burned his boats on the shore; and since Hernando Cortez plunged into Mexico, on the most astounding of expeditions, and stranded his ships at Vera Cruz. But Sherman himself had a much juster and more modest estimation of his exploit. On receiving the congratulations of the President and also of his personal friends, on account of his success, and seeing himself greatly praised in the public journals at home and abroad, he wrote: "I am now a great favorite because I have been successful; but if Thomas had not whipped Hood at Nashville, six hundred miles away, my plans would have failed, and I would have been denounced the world over." In his special congratulatory orders, he said: "The armies serving in Georgia and Tennessee, as well as the local garrisons of Decatur, Bridgeport, Chattanooga, and Murfreesboro', are alike entitled to the common honor, and each regiment may inscribe on its colors at pleasure the words 'Savannah' or 'Nashville.'"

The fall of Savannah was the occasion, whether duly or not, of great despondency in the South. The single disaster was not very considerable; but the march through Georgia that had led to it had afforded a painful exhibition of the decay of the spirit of the Confederates, and the moral effect of this exhibition was far worse than any disaster the South had ever yet suffered in the field. It suggested a general review of the situation of the Confederacy; the people commenced to calculate the cost and sacrifices of the war, and to estimate the terrible depletion that had taken place in the armies of the Confederacy during the campaign of 1864.

That depletion had ensued from various causes. The Yankees had encouraged desertion to an extent never known before, and they had managed to keep in captivity nearly every prisoner they had taken west of the Mississippi since the battle of Gettysburg. The history of Yankee *finesse* in this matter deserves a distinct place in the records of the war, and may properly be reviewed here at the close of the year 1864.

THE EXCHANGE OF PRISONERS, ETC.

It may be truly and emphatically said that on no subject had the enemy shown such bad faith as on that of the exchange of prisoners. During the year 1864, the Confederate authorities had, at different times, put forth every exertion to obtain an exchange of prisoners; but such exertion to this end was met by some new pretence of the Yankees, who had resolved to avoid a general exchange, and to coin a certain advantage out of the sufferings of their own men in Southern prisons.

The Confederate authorities had at first insisted upon the release of all prisoners, the excess to be on parole. The enemy refused to comply with this plain requirement of the cartel, and demanded, when a delivery of prisoners was made, an equal number in return. Seeing a persistent purpose on the part of the Yankee Government to violate its agreement, our authorities, moved by the sufferings of the brave men who were so unjustly held in the Northern prisons, determined to abate their just demands. On the 10th of August, 1864 Colonel Ould, the Confederate commissioner, offered to exchange the prisoners respectively held by the two belligerents, officer for officer and man for man. Although this offer was substantially what had often been proposed by the Yankee authorities, and would have left in their hands whatever excess of prisoners they might have had, yet it was not accepted.

Another pretence put forth by the Yankees for declining a general exchange of prisoners was, that the Confederates had refused to include in the cartel negro soldiers. This was a misrepresentation. The extent of the claim of the Confederates on this point was simply that they would not return to the enemy *recaptured slaves;* for to do this the Confederate Government would stultify itself, ignore the law of its social system, and be a party to an outrage on the rights of property in its own citizens.

But this proper position of the Confederate authorities involved the disposition of only a few hundred persons; and it is not reasonable to suppose that a punctilious care for them really stood in the way of the duties of humanity to forty or fifty thousand white captives. This professed care for two or three hundred black slaves, which was made to weigh down all considerations of humanity in behalf of thousands of white men pining in prison, was plainly nothing more than a pretence, a new ground of frivolous excuse, to refuse a general exchange. In November, Colonel Ould wrote to the Confederate secretary of war:

"My own firm conviction is, that even if we were to agree to the unjust demands of the enemy in this respect, we would not secure a general exchange.   *   *   *   I think it very doubtful whether they would agree to a general exchange, even if we consented to treat recaptured slaves as prisoners of war, and delivered those whose term of service had not expired. I am satisfied their course is the result of a conviction forced upon them by the events of the war, that a Confederate soldier is more valuable than a Federal. The miseries of tens of thousands of their own people are as nothing when weighed against a calculation."

Here was the true secret of the game which the North played on the subject of exchange. Men were scarce in th South; the Confederate soldier was superior in prowess to the Yankee; and thus the Government at Washington was convinced that any exchange, man for man, would be to its disadvantage, and deliberately adopted the remorseless and inhuman policy of enforcing the captivity, with all its attendant sufferings, of the prisoners on both sides during the war. This policy of the Yankees exhibited to the unhappy victims from their army an amount of ingratitude that was to the last degree monstrous. General Sherman had not hesitated to avow, with utter disregard of the claims of his captive soldiers on his consideration and protection, that as the terms of service of many had expired, they were not to be regarded as subjects of general exchange.

But the Washington Government was not satisfied, for considerations of certain advantage, to consign its soldiers to the extraordinary sufferings of imprisonment incident to the scant supplies in the South, which indeed it was daily endeavoring to diminish by blockade and devastation. It went a step further. It paraded these very sufferings, for which it was responsible, which indeed its own malignity had produced, to raise a clamor about the cruelty of the Confederates, and thus engage the sympathies of the world.

It is almost impossible to sound the depths of Yankee cruelty in this subject of exchange.

At one time, in the fall of 1864, the Yankees refused to exchange any prisoners but those who were *sick;* and then to accuse the inhumanity of the Confederates, the poor, wasted victims of prison diseases were paraded through the country, and had their photographs taken for pictorials, as fair specimens of the results of life in Confederate prisons. The calculation that could have prompted such an exhibition appears indeed to partake of an ingenuity of beings other than man.*

---

* The following *exposé* was made in a Richmond paper. It refers to an exchange of sick prisoners made in the fall of 1864:

"The mortality among our unfortunate prisoners sent by sea to Savannah to be exchanged was very remarkable. We have published a list of one hundred and seventeen who died on the passage to Savannah; also a list of thirty-two who died within a few days after being landed. Distressing as is this mortality, the Confederate newspapers have not been so inconsiderate as to impute it to a wrong cause. Revolting at the shocking inhumanity which limits exchanges to the sick, the feeble, and the dying, we have received home our brethren, emaciated as they are with long-protracted disease, and we have wondered, not that so many died, but tha tso many, travelling in such a condition, should live.

"We have sent to the truce-boat a similar class of the Federal prisoners in our hands; it is for these only that the Yankees have bargained. When the poor creatures reach them, worn and wasted by sickness, and evidencing, in their appearance, that they should be in the hospitals instead of travelling, in place of the sense of shame which the Yankee authorities and people should feel at the consequences of their inhuman policy, with such audacious hypocrisy as a Yankee only can manifest, they seize the occasion to calumniate the Confederates, a reluctant party to a commerce worse than 'the middle passage,' and only better than protracted imprisonment. They pretend to consider the returned men as samples of those who have been left behind; they charge their weakness and emaciation to starvation, and not to sickness; they clamor like so many howling dervishes; and with an effrontery that the world beside cannot equal, they extract self-glorification out of their own crime, and heap reproaches on us who are its victims!

"We know that their treatment of our prisoners is horrible enough. But, much as we execrate such conduct, and the people who can practise it, we respect ourselves too much to slander them. We do not pretend that the sick men who are sent home to us are samples of the rest. We are not so false as to represent their emaciation as due to starvation and not to disease. Multi-

In connection with the history of the prisons of the war, there is something of tribute to be paid to the conduct of General Grant. This high officer, however profuse of the lives of his men in battle, had certainly an unaffected sympathy and interest for the imprisoned soldier. It was through his offices that, in the later months of 1864, an agreement, first proposed by General Lee, was concluded, to the effect that, without releasing either Government from the obligation of affording due provision to its captives, each should have the right of furnishing to its own prisoners, in the possession of the other, under the direction of officers among them, to be paroled for the purpose, such additional supplies of necessary articles as it might deem expedient to send. It is, indeed, indicative of the remorseless policy of the Yankee Government that such concessions to the claims of humanity should have been made sooner by the stern soldier in the field than by their statesmen in the cabinet.

We may add here, in advance of the order of our narrative, that General Grant, having been subsequently empowered with the duties of exchanging prisoners, and put in a position to overrule the behests of such men as Stanton and Butler, did himself immortal honor in instantly authorizing a general exchange, and breaking by a stroke of the pen all the tissues of falsehood and cunning in which this matter had been so long entangled. This act has done more for his reputation in just and humane history than any victory of his in the field. But the benefit of it came too late for the South, and only a few thousand Confederate prisoners reached home in time to witness the catastrophe of the spring of 1865.

---

tudes of the poor sufferers die, as we have seen, on their way to our lines. Many die before we can take them to our arms. Many die before we can get them into our hospitals; and many there languish and die without a sight of the home for which they risked the travel. In all our distress at this mortality, we are candid enough to recognize the cause, and to tell the truth amid our resentments. Not so the Yankees."

CHAPTER XXII.

WILMINGTON had long been a thorn in the enemy's side. Mr. Welles, the Yankee secretary of the navy, had declared, in his last official report, that Wilmington, owing to the peculiarity of its situation, could not be absolutely closed to blockade-runners, without the co-operation of the army; for the forts which protected it were in such shoal water that the heavily armed ships could not get at them. Fifty fast Yankee steamers had been unable to close this port.

FIRST EXPEDITION AGAINST FORT FISHER.

At the close of the summer of 1864, an expedition had been planned against Fort Fisher, according to Mr. Welles' suggestion of the co-operation of a land force. It was delayed, for various reasons, until the winter. Vice-Admiral Farragut was selected by the Yankee Government to take charge of the naval force, but was unable to assume that duty on account of ill ⱬealth. Rear-Admiral Porter was then transferred from the command of the Mississippi squadron to the command of the North-Atlantic blockading squadron. The most powerful fleet ever known in American history was assembled at Hampton Roads, under command of Admiral Porter. The land force consisted of six thousand five hundred infantry, two batteries of artillery, and a few cavalry. On the 13th and 14th of December the expedition started, General Butler with the army transports proceeding to a place twenty-five miles off New Inlet. Admiral Porter, with his fleet, proceeded to Beaufort to complete taking on his ammunition and supplies, including some powder for a vessel proposed to be exploded before Fort Fisher, and some ammunition for the monitors, which were towed light from Fortress Monroe to Beaufort.

Wilmington was then but feebly garrisoned. A number of Confederate troops there had been sent to increase the forces opposed to Sherman in his march across the State of Georgia. General Butler had supposed that he would find an easy conquest there; and, in fact, he had foisted himself upon the expedition to get what he supposed would be a cheap glory, for the command of it had been given to General Weitzel, and Butler had insisted upon accompanying him, for the reason that the scene of operations was within his department, and the troops from his command.

A novel feature was introduced into the expedition against Fort Fisher, viz., a vessel loaded with a large quantity of powder to be exploded as near the fort as possible. The idea appears to have originated with General Butler, in consequence of reading of the terrible effects of the explosion of a large quantity of gunpowder at Erith, England, some time before. He suggested it to the departments at Washington, and they submitted it to their engineer and ordnance officers for examination and report. Those officers, while not anticipating any very wonderful results from this new experiment, still deemed it of such importance as to recommend its trial.

On Friday, 23d of December, Admiral Porter gave orders that the powder vessel be sent in as near Fort Fisher as possible, and exploded that night at one o'clock. Information of what he proposed to do was sent to General Butler at Beaufort, but did not reach him until Saturday morning, when he immediately started for Fort Fisher, ordering the transports to follow as rapidly as possible. The powder-boat was exploded a little before two o'clock on Saturday morning, and the Yankee navy commenced their bombardment about noon of that day.

The explosion of the powder-boat was a ridiculous failure, and attracted such little attention in the fort that General Whiting, who was in command there, supposed it to be nothing more than the bursting of one of the enemy's guns. The bombardment of the fort continued for two days. It was probably the heaviest which had ever occurred in the annals of naval warfare. The huge frigates of Porter's fleet led the way; then the grim ugly Ironsides; then the monitors and the great line of smaller vessels, stretching away out, almost as far as the eye could reach. From every vessel could be seen the white curl of smoke, and high up in the air hundreds of smoky rings were formed from the explosion of guns. Thick flew the shell; loud sounded the thunder of artillery; lurid were the flashes of great guns as they vomited forth their missiles of death and destruction. Nobly stood the Confederates to their guns. From Shephard's battery to the mound, they stood unquailing and defiant, loading and firing coolly and calmly; the gunners sighting their guns as if they were practising at a target.

After the arrival of General Butler a conference was had with Admiral Porter as to operations next day. It was arranged that General Weitzel should land with some two or three thousand troops, and reconnoitre the fort with the view of assaulting it.

The expectation of the garrison that they would have a night-fight was not realized. The night was spent in watching and in repairing the slight damage sustained by the fight. As the morning dawned, the fleet could be discerned in the distance getting ready to renew the attack; but it was not expected that operations would commence before high tide, which would be about half-past twelve o'clock. However, every man was at his post, ready, at any moment, to again engage the fleet. About ten o'clock the fleet commenced moving in—their extreme right resting near Gatlin's battery, about six miles up the beach, and their left extending down to the fort. The Ironsides led the attack, the frigates resting on her right and left, and the monitors to the right of the frigates. There were counted fifty-two vessels in all—one Ironsides three or four monitors, four frigates, and forty-seven other vessels. They steamed in very slowly, two of the frigates going round to the sea front of the fort, and the iron-clads and monitors lying abreast of the centre front. The Ironsides and monitors came up within a mile; the rest of the fleet remained out about one and a-half miles. At half-past ten A. M. the first gun was fired by the Ironsides, followed by the rest of the fleet —firing very slowly and deliberately for the while. The fort reserved its fire, thinking that the wooden fleet would be tempted to come in closer range. Finding, however, that they would not come closer, it opened, also firing very slowly.

About noon the fleet commenced firing with great rapidity. The dull, heavy, thumping sounds of the enemy's guns, as they were fired, could be heard first, and then the whistling, shrieking sound of the shells as they came whizzing and buzzing through the air. Their explosion and the myriad fragments that went rattling by, thick almost as hail, were terrible to listen to. The air was hot with fire; the earth shook; there was no interval of quiet; all was noise—crash, bang, and crash all the time.

A shell whistled close to General Whiting. It buried itself, exploding, and covering him all over with the wet sand. He did not even move, not even take his pipe from his mouth, and only remarked coolly, "Well, it spattered me."

While the bombardment was at its height, it was discovered that the enemy had succeeded in landing a force at Anderson and Holland batteries, and that their line of skirmishers were advancing on the fort. All was excitement now. The infantry man the parapets, and the sharp crack of the rifle is heard instead of the heavy booming of guns. The lull was of short duration—the most terrific bombardment now commenced; the fleet had seen their land forces, and they opened with greater fury than ever to keep the Confederates from engaging the skirmishers.

But there was to be no battle on land. Weitzel had reported to Butler that it was not advisable to attack; and that commander had very promptly desisted from the enterprise.

His troops (more than two thousand had been landed) were ordered back to the transports; and his whole force, consisting of sixty-five hundred men, was summarily withdrawn from the expedition, and with such singular celerity that the next day they were on the way back to Fortress Monroe.

As night came on the fire of the fleet fell off. The fort had made a gallant and complete defence; and the success of the Confederates could no longer be disputed. The enemy's attack the first day lasted five hours; on the second day, seven hours; firing altogether over twenty thousand shots from fifty odd vessels.

The Confederates responded with six hundred and sixty-two shots the first day, and six hundred the second. Their loss was only three killed and fifty-five wounded.

The ground in front and rear of the fort was covered with shells, and was torn in deep pits. But the damage to the works was not considerable. Two guns in the fort burst, two were dismounted by the Confederates, and two by the enemy's fire; but the fort was unhurt.

The failure of the expedition against Fort Fisher, the out post of the defences of Wilmington, was the occasion of some sharp recrimination between Admiral Porter and General Butler. It is very certain that the latter officer, who had boasted that he would eat his Christmas dinner at Wilmington, was generally considered to have retired from the scene of action in disgrace, and that a few days thereafter he was made to pay the penalty of his failure by an order from Washington, removing him from the Army of the James, and sending him to his home in Massachusetts.*

---

* General Grant testified as follows before a committee of the Yankee Congress, appointed to inquire into Butler's conduct:

Question—The expectation was to surprise the fort?

Answer—Yes, sir; and my instructions were very clear, and if they effected a landing there above Fort Fisher, that in itself was to be considered a success; and if the fort did not fall immediately upon their landing, then they were to intrench themselves, and remain there and co-operate with the navy until the fort did fall. In my instructions I provided for a bold dash for the capture of Wilmington, in case Fort Fisher did fall immediately upon the landing of the troops. If it did not fall, then they were to intrench, enter upon a siege of the place, and remain there until it did fall. And the capture of Wilmington would thus become a matter for future consideration. General Butler came away from Fort Fisher in violation of the instructions which I gave him.

SECOND EXPEDITION AGAINST FORT FISHER.—FALL OF WILMINGTON

Neither General Grant nor the Washington authorities were
satisfied with Butler's conclusion that Fort Fisher was impreg
nable. The naval force remained in the vicinity during some
very stormy weather, while a second military force was organized under command of General Terry. This force consisted
of some eight thousand five hundred men, with siege guns and
intrenching tools. On the 13th of January, the troops were
landed on the beach above Fort Fisher, and proceeded to
throw up intrenchments.

The enemy landed, under cover of his fleet, near Battery
Gatlin, about nine miles from Fort Fisher. While he was
landing, General Hoke appeared and drew up in line parallel,
to watch his movements, and intercept them when possible to
do so. It was not possible to prevent the landing, owing to
the situation of the point chosen. The enemy landed on the
banks, just above the neck of the sound, thus interposing a
small surface of water between them and an attacking force;
or compelling such force to circle around the lower extreme of
the sound—either of which movements would have to be done
under the fire of the whole fleet.

When General Hoke found this to be the situation, he established a line facing the sea, and threw out cavalry on his
right flank, towards Battery Anderson, which was down the
beach towards Fort Fisher, about four miles. The intervening
country here was broken; and the low places were grown up
with thick bushes, and were marshy. The purpose of the
cavalry was to observe the movements, and give the signal of
the first advance of the enemy towards establishing a line
across the neck of land to the river, it being the order and
purpose of General Bragg to have General Hoke attack him as
soon as he advanced. During the night, however, the enemy,
passing between the cavalry, and threading their way through
the thick, marshy undergrowth, made their way to the river,
and next morning General Hoke found an intrenched line on
his right flank, extending across the peninsula, from the sea
to, or near to the river. He succeeded, however, in maintaining his base at Sugarloaf, immediately changed his line, and

informed General Bragg of the situation. Then General Bragg gave the order to charge the enemy in their works. In the mean time, General Hoke had made a close reconnoissance, under the fire of the enemy, and discovered the strength of their force and position. On receiving the order to charge he communicated the result of his observations, and asked General Bragg to reconnoitre in person, which he did; and both of these officers concurred that it was not proper to assault the lines. It was then determined to re-enforce the fort. By this time the enemy, four thousand strong, were secure behind their works; and the fleet proceeded to bombard Fort Fisher, which was done uninterruptedly until Sunday, the 15th of January, about six o'clock in the evening.

At this time the column of assault, numbering about four thousand, moved from the enemy's lines, and as they advanced, they were plainly visible from Fort Fisher. But the beleaguered garrison was kept close confined within the bomb-proofs by the concentrated and continued fire of seven hundred guns pouring torrents of shell and missiles on every spot. On the land side of Fort Fisher the Confederates had seventeen guns—sufficient, could they have been used, to make it impossible that any force could have advanced under their fire. But, as the line of assailants got nearer to the fort, the whole fleet concentrated the fire, in richochet shot, on the land side, and speedily dismounted every gun; and this unintermittent *feu d'enfer* was kept up until the enemy's line was within sixty yards of the works. Then it ceased, and with a rush and yell the charge was made. Captain Braddy commanded the company guarding the sally-port. On him the hope of the garrison hung to keep the assailants out until the men and officers, who had been packed in the bomb-proofs for fifty-six hours, could get out and make ready. This officer and his command, it is said, surrendered, and the enemy entered the open gate. The Confederates were benumbed and exhausted, and the thing was the work of a moment. They were obliged to fall back in order to rally. Colonel Lamb brought his men into line near headquarters, General Whiting being present, encouraging and cheering on the troops and creating enthusiasm by his ardent heroism. Under these inspiring influences the men were brought to the charge. The numbers were against them in the proportion of four thousand, aided by two thousand marines, to two thousand, but they forced the enemy back to the mound, and a hand-to-hand fight, of unmitigated desperation and fury, ensued, continuing from seven to about ten o'clock, when bravery, endurance, and devotion failed to overcome numbers. The Confederates were overpowered, and the work of assault was accomplished; but not until the enemy had paid dearly for his prize. He had not lost a man until he entered the fort.

Thus fell Fort Fisher after a heroic defence. About midnight, General Whiting surrendered himself and his men to General Terry as prisoners of war, numbering over eighteen hundred, the remainder of his force being killed or wounded. The enemy confessed a loss of seven or eight hundred in killed and wounded. General Whiting received three wounds in the thigh, and thus wounded was fated to languish and die in a Yankee prison.

The fall of Fort Fisher did not clear the way to Wilmington. Yet it was decisive of the fate of that city. On the 19th of February, Fort Anderson, higher up the river, was evacuated under a heavy fire from Porter's fleet, with a co-operating Yankee force eight thousand strong, which Schofield had moved up from Smithville. The troops were pushed for Wilmington, while at the same time Porter's vessels passed the obstructions and steamed up the river. Wilmington was occupied without resistance. The eight or ten thousand Confederate troops there, under the command of General Bragg, had been withdrawn towards what was now the dominant theatre of the war in the interior of the Carolinas.

The capture of Wilmington, indeed, had been an arranged parallel of Sherman's grand expedition through the Carolinas; it was intended to open still another base of operations towards Richmond; and it proved, in fact, a great element of success in that extraordinary march that carried the Yankee banners from Savannah to Goldsboro'. To that movement attention must now be directed in the logical order of our narrative.

SHERMAN'S SIXTY DAYS IN THE CAROLINAS.

About the 16th of January, hardly a month from his entry into Savannah, Sherman had reviewed and reorganized his command, but only partially refitted it, owing to delays in forwarding the necessary supplies. Appreciating the value of time, he hurried forward his preparations, and dispatching Howard's wing by water to Beaufort, from whence it penetrated up the Pocotaligo, deceived the Confederates into the belief that this force was the advance of his army moving upon Charleston. The interval between the embarkation of Howard at Savannah and his arrival in front of the Branchville and Charleston Railroad was well employed by Sherman, who marched Slocum's wing towards Augusta, Davis' corps on the Georgia side, and William's on the Carolina side of the Savannah River, to Sister's Ferry.

The laborious duty of the campaign commenced with the crossing of the Savannah River. The Confederate forces to oppose Sherman were scattered all the way from Augusta to Charleston; the design being to guard all the approaches to the railway that connected Charleston with the interior. This want of concentration was the secret of Sherman's success.

Early in February, Sherman struck the railroad between Branchville and Charleston, compelled the Confederates to evacuate Branchville on the 11th of February, and broke up the South Carolina Railroad for sixty or seventy miles, thus preventing any reinforcements from the west. The left wing, by rapid marches of eighteen miles per day, had made a détour far to the left, within thirty miles of Augusta, gained a lodgment upon the road, and severed communications. Here was a dangerous position for the Confederates; Sherman's whole force of cavalry, militia, and veterans at Branchville, and Augusta open to capture by a sudden swoop of Kilpatrick's cavalry. That city, with its arsenals, laboratories, machine-shops, rolling stock, and cotton, was too valuable to be neglected; and Cheatham's corps of Hood's army, was marched night and day to its relief, arriving there in time to find that Sherman had turned the cold shoulder upon Augusta, and by a dexterous movement thrown his left wing between Hill and the main force in his front.

Continuing his march north, Sherman entered Orangeburg on the 16th of February; and General Beauregard, who, owing to the extraordinary dispersion of the Confederate plan of defence, had certainly not more than ten thousand men at Columbia, was already preparing to evacuate the capital of South Carolina.

THE FALL OF CHARLESTON.

In the mean time, the movement of Sherman had already been decisive of the fate of Charleston. General Hardee finding himself flanked at Charleston, and appreciating the instant necessity of effecting a junction with Beauregard and Cheatham, and concentrating all available forces in Sherman's path, resolved to evacuate this city, so famous in the war and so long coveted by the Yankees. But he was resolved to leave as little as possible for the enemy's rapacity.

At an early hour of the morning, before the retirement of General Hardee's troops, every building, warehouse, or shed, stored with cotton, was fired by a guard detailed for the purpose. The engines were brought out, but with the small force at the disposal of the fire department, very little else could be done than to keep the surrounding buildings from igniting. On the western side of the city the conflagration raged with great fury.

The horrors of the conflagration were heightened by a terrible catastrophe. It appears some boys had discovered a quantity of powder at the depot of the Northwestern Railroad, and amused themselves by flinging handfuls of it upon the masses of burning cotton in the streets. It was not long before the powder running from their hands formed a train upon the ground leading from the fire to the main supplies of powder in the depot. The result is easily conjectured. A spark ignited the powder in the train, there was a leaping, running fire along the ground, and then an explosion which shook the city to its very foundation from one end to the other. The build ing was. in a second, a whirling mass of ruins, in a tremendou.

volume of flame and smoke. About two hundred lives were lost by the explosion, and not less than one hundred and fifty bodies were found charred in that fiery furnace.

From the depot the fire spread rapidly, and communicating with the adjoining buildings, threatened destruction to that part of the town. Four squares, embracing the area bounded by Chapel, Alexander, Charlotte, and Washington-streets, were consumed before the conflagration was subdued.

The destruction of public property in Charleston had been as complete as General Hardee could make it. He burned the cotton warehouses, arsenals, quartermaster's stores, railroad bridges, two iron-clads, and some vessels in the ship-yard.

Among the captured property were two hundred pieces of artillery, spiked and temporarily disabled, as they could not be brought off.

The Yankees occupied Charleston on the 18th of February. A scarred city, blackened by fire, with evidences of destruction and ruin wrought by the enemy at almost every step, had at last come into their possession; but not until a heroic defence running through nearly four years, and at last only by the stratagem of a march many miles away from it. The appearance of the city was eloquent of the sacrifice and heroism of its people. A Yankee correspondent who had joined in the triumphal entry into Charleston thus described the scene before his eyes : " Not a building for blocks here that is exempt from the marks of shot and shell. All have suffered more or less. Here is a fine brown-stone bank building, vacant and deserted, with great gaping holes in the sides and roof, through which the sun shines and the rain pours, windows and sashes blown out by exploding shell within, plastering knocked down, counters torn up, floors crushed in, and fragments of mosaic pavement, broken and crushed, lying around on the floor, mingled with bits of statuary, stained glass, and broken parts of chandeliers. Ruin within and without, and its neighbor in no better plight. The churches, St. Michael's and St. Philip's, have not escaped the storms of our projectiles. Their roofs are perforated, their walls wounded, their pillars demolished, and within the pews filled with plastering. From Bay-street, studded with batteries, to Calhoun-street, our shells have carried destruction and desolation, and often death with them."

CAPTURE AND BURNING OF COLUMBIA.

While the Yankees were making a triumphal entry into the burning city of Charleston, a scene yet more terrible and dramatic was taking place in the capital of South Carolina. General Beauregard had evacuated Columbia in haste. Sherman entered it on the 18th of February. A white flag displayed from the steeple of the City Hall announced the surrender of the town. With bands playing, drum-corps beating, flags flying, and their men in step, the Yankee army marched down Main-street to the Capitol square.

No sooner had the enemy entered Columbia than a wild and savage scene of pillage commenced. Stragglers, " bummers," pontoon men, and the riffraff of the army were to be met in every street and almost every house. If they wanted a pair of boots they took them from one's feet. Watches were in constant demand—in several instances being snatched from the persons of ladies. Ear and finger-rings were taken by force, and, in isolated cases, the dresses of ladies were torn from their bodies by villains who expected to find jewels or plate concealed. Search for silver and provisions was made in every conceivable place. Ramrods were used as probes to indicate where boxes were buried; and gardens, outhouses, cellars, garrets, chimneys, and nooks, never thought of by anybody but a thief in search of plunder, were turned, so to speak, inside out. Rev. Mr. Shand, the Episcopalian clergyman, while conveying a trunk containing the communion service of silver from the church to the South Carolina College, was accosted by a Yankee and a negro, who compelled him, under threat of death, to give it up.

The conflagration which destroyed the city commenced about dusk. The fire started near the rear of the jail. A high wind prevailed, and in a short time the flames were in full and unconquerable progress, spreading rapidly in three directions—up and down Main-street and eastwardly. From ten until three o'clock in the morning the scene was appalling. The sky was one broad sheet of flame, above which, amid the lurid smoke, drifted in eddying circles a myriad of sparks. These falling scattered the conflagration on every side. The monotone of the roaring, leaping, hissing tongues of flame, as they careered on their wild course, alone filled hearts with dismay. The air was like that of a furnace. Many of the streets were impassable. Frightened men, women, and children ran in all directions, some only to flee again from the fresh attacks of the destroying element. Property thrown out of houses was either burned or stolen. Many of the Federal soldiers, maddened by liquor, dashed through the city with lighted torches to inflame the dwellings yet untouched. Morning revealed to some extent the broad sweep of destruction. Four thousand or more citizens were houseless and homeless. From the State-house to Cotton Town, and an average of two or three squares on each side of Main-street, nothing but blackened ruins remained. Every vestige of the once busy street was gone.

After having completed, as far as possible, the destruction of Columbia, Sherman continued his march northward. The Seventeenth and Twentieth corps moved in two columns upon Winnsboro', thirty miles north, on the Columbia and Charlotte Railroad; the Seventeenth destroying the railroad, and twisting the rails so that they could not be used again. From Winnsboro', where they found many of the refugees from Charleston and Columbia, General Sherman sent Kilpatrick's cavalry still northward towards Chesterville, to keep up the delusion that he was moving on Charlotte, but Sherman himself with his main army moved directly eastward, crossing the Catawba or Wateree nearly east of Winnsboro', and moving his left wing directly towards Cheraw, while the right threatened Florence.

After leaving Columbia, the rapidly increasing mass of refugees, black and white, who followed the army, were organized into an emigrant train, and put under the charge of the officers and men who had escaped from the Confederate prisons at Salisbury and elsewhere on the route. Under the direction of their escort they foraged for themselves, and being supplied liberally with horses and mules, wagons and other vehicles, of which large numbers were taken along the route, they moved on with very little expense or trouble to the army. This organization, known as that of "Sherman's bummers," often mixed up with the regular troops of the army, carried devastation, ruin, and horror along the march. It was said, indeed, that Sherman's march through the Carolinas was tracked by a column of smoke, and that stragglers never found any difficulty in rejoining the command, when this ghastly evidence of its march stood constantly in the sky.

At Winnsboro', private dwellings were entered ruthlessly all kind of necessaries and luxuries of life were stolen, and, in some cases, helpless women were cursed and threatened to be shot if they did not deliver up keys of apartments. This town was also fired. Charred ruins met the eye, where once the busy feet of men passed in the daily pursuits of life. Wedding-rings and mementos of deceased husbands or parents were stolen as ruthlessly as gold coin would have been; watches and jewelry were cut from the persons of ladies, and, in some instances, their shoes removed on the pretence of searching for rings.

Leaving this town, the enemy took their line of march on the State road leading to Blackstocks. On the route their road could be easily distinguished by tall chimneys standing solitary and alone, and blackened embers, as it were, laying at their feet. Every fine residence, all corn-cribs, smoke-houses, cotton-gins—all that could give comfort to man—were committed to the flames; dead animals—horses, mules, cows, calves, and hogs—slain by the enemy, were scattered along the road. The railroad track from Winnsboro' to about four hundred yards on the other side of Blackstocks was in one mass of ruins. Horses and mules that were hid in dense forests were found and taken. Corn, fodder, and shucks that the enemy could not use were burned; gentlemen were robbed of what funds they had about their person; watches were jerked from the pockets of both 'male and female; in truth every indignity and every insult that could be offered to citizens was perpetrated.*

---

* The following are extracts from some private letters giving some account of Sherman's pillagers in the Carolinas:

"My Dear ——: Sherman has gone, and terrible has been the storm that has swept over us with his coming and going. They deliberately shot two of our citizens—murdered them in cold blood—one of them a Mr. Murphy, a wounded soldier, Confederate States Army. They hung up three others and one lady, merely letting them down just in time to save life, in order to make them tell where their valuables were concealed. There was no place, no chamber, trunk, drawer, desk, garret, closet, or cellar that was private to their unholy

On the 3d of March Sherman occupied Cheraw. The feint upon Charlotte was intended to uncover Fayetteville to Sherman and Goldsboro' to Schofield, who, with a large and victorious army, was sweeping up from the coast with reinforce-

---

eyes. Their rude hands spared nothing but our lives, and those they would have taken but they knew that therein they would only accomplish the death of a few helpless women and children—they would not in the least degree break or bend the spirit of our people. Squad after squad unceasingly came and went and tramped through the halls and rooms of our house day and night during the entire stay of the army.

"At our house they killed every chicken, goose, turkey, cow, calf, and every living thing, even to our pet dog. They carried off our wagons, carriages, and horses, and broke up our buggy, wheelbarrow, garden implements, axes, hatchets, hammers, saws, etc., and burned the fences. Our smoke-houses and pantry—that a few days ago were well stored with bacon, lard, flour, dried fruit, meal, pickles, preserves, etc.—now contain nothing whatever, except a few pounds of meal and flour, and five pounds of bacon. They took from old men, women, and children alike, every garment of wearing apparel save what we had on, not even sparing the napkins of infants! Blankets, sheets, quilts, etc., such as did not suit them to take away, they tore to pieces before our eyes. After destroying every thing we had, and taking from us every morsel of food (save the pittance I have mentioned), one of these barbarians had to add insult to injury by asking me 'what you (I) would live upon now?' I replied, 'Upon patriotism; I will exist upon the love of my country as long as life will last, and then I will die as firm in that love as the everlasting hills.'"

A lady residing in South Carolina, who was in the enemy's lines for five days, writes her experience to a friend in Augusta as follows:

. . . "Pauline came rushing up to me saying the Yankees had come, A hasty glance from the window confirmed her words, and we instantly retreated to aunt's room. This being on the first floor, was speedily filled with armed men. At first I very politely unlocked several trunks, assuring them that they only contained ladies' apparel, but as the number increased we gladly retreated to the sitting-room, where the whole family soon collected. There we remained from twelve to six o'clock, while this band of one hundred and fifty men ransacked every nook and corner; breaking open trunks and boxes, singing, whistling, swearing. Many passed through the room in which we were. At first none addressed us. At last one young villain came in, fastened the door, demanded our watches, and using the most profane language and terrible threats, ordered us to confess where our gold and silver was buried; laid his hands on Pauline's shoulder and mine, while we obediently emptied our pockets. They then marched Dr. —— into the entry, stripped the poor old gentleman to the waist, robbing him of the one thousand dollars he had succeeded in bringing from his own house, which meanwhile has been laid in ashes—so he is homeless. We have lost in silver, china, and glass. All our blankets, quilts, bowls, and all the pillow-cases were used as bags to remove provisions. Great destruction in clothing, dresses torn up, etc. Hardly a handkerchief in the house."

ments for Sherman, establishing a line of supplies as he moved.

On the afternoon and night of the 6th of March, the Yankee army crossed the Great Pedee River in safety, and swept for ward the next day—the main army, in four columns, moving on Laurel Hill and Montpelier, North Carolina, and the cavalry, under Kilpatrick, guarding the extreme left, and approaching Rockingham, North Carolina, where they came in contact with Butler's division of Wade Hampton's cavalry, with which they had some desultory skirmishing. A long and heavy rain delayed somewhat the Yankee approach to Fayette-ville, but that place was reached on the 11th of March.

Some more severe and important fighting than Sherman had yet experienced since he and Johnston parted at Atlanta was now to take place; the latter general having been put in com-mand of the Confederate forces in the Carolinas.

On the 10th of March General Wade Hampton approached before daylight Kilpatrick's headquarters, at Monroe's planta-tion, and administered to him a severe lesson, taking guns and prisoners.

At Fayetteville Sherman communicated with Schofield at Wilmington. He had fixed upon the vicinity of Goldsboro' as the place where he would form a junction with Schofield, and the 22d of March as the time—before leaving Savannah— and having brought his army thus far in time, he was dis-posed to move slowly to allow Schofield time to reach the rendezvous.

On the 16th of March General Hardee, with about half a corps (Rhett's and Elliot's brigades), was intrenched between Black Creek and Cape Fear River, at no great distance from the confluence of these streams. This small detachment of Confederate force was attacked here by two corps of Sherman's veterans, under Slocum, together with Kilpatrick's cavalry. The Confederates held their ground with the most determined valor. Three different charges of the enemy were repulsed. At last, to prevent being flanked, General Hardee had to fall back with the loss of two guns. This engagement took place at Averysboro', on the Cape Fear River, about half-way between Raleigh and Fayetteville. The loss of the enemy was out of all proportion to our own. General Johnston tele-

GEN. WADE HAMPTON.

graphed to Richmond that the total Confederate loss was four hundred and fifty ; that of the Yankees *thirty-three hundred.*

THE BATTLE OF BENTONVILLE.

On the 19th of March a yet more important engagement was to occur. It was Johnston's purpose to cripple Sherman, if possible, before he could effect a junction with Schofield; and, accordingly, he brought what troops he had in hand by a forced march into position at Bentonville, intending to fling them upon Sherman's left wing, commanded by Slocum.

About nine o'clock in the morning the fight commenced. On the right, Bate's and Cleburne's division charged and carried two lines of breastworks, driving the enemy two miles. Hill, commanding Lee's corps, and Loring, commanding Stewart's corps, did similarly on the left. The Confederates fought gallantly. Three guns were taken from the enemy, and his whole line pushed back.

A mile in rear the enemy rallied upon fresh troops, but was forced back slowly, until six o'clock P. M., when, receiving more troops, he apparently assumed the offensive, which movement was resisted without difficulty until dark.

During the night the enemy threw up heavy intrenchments, and the next morning General Johnston did not think it advisable to renew the attack. The engagement had been a very severe one. The total loss of the Confederates was about twenty-five hundred. Although they had achieved a success, Johnston appears to have been well convinced that he had not force sufficient to cope with Sherman and resist his junction with Schofield. On the night of the 20th the enemy abandoned their works and moved towards Goldsboro'. General Johnston then withdrew towards Raleigh.

In the mean time, Schofield, from Newbern, had entered and occupied Goldsboro', and Terry, from Wilmington, had secured Cox's bridge crossing, and laid a pontoon bridge across the Neuse River. Sherman was thus in the position he had planned more than two months ago in Savannah; he had brought up every part of the combination in perfect order; and so far had achieved a success at once brilliant and com-

plete.   On the 22d of March he published in Goldsboro' a con
gratulatory address to his troops.   He said : "After a march
of the most extraordinary character, nearly five hundred miles
over swamps and rivers deemed impassable to others, at th
most inclement season of the year, and drawing our chief sup
plies from a poor and wasted country, we reach our destination
in good health and condition."

We must leave Sherman at Goldsboro'—the proper termination of his campaign in the Carolinas.   The position was
critical enough for the Confederates.   Between Sherman's
army, augmented by the corps of Schofield and Terry, and the
army of Grant, the Confederacy was in danger of being
crushed.   The two armies were separated by only one hundred and fifty miles, and a railroad, which could be rapidly
put in order, connected them.   No sooner had Sherman disposed his army in camp at Goldsboro' than he hastened to
City Point, Virginia, for an interview with General Grant and
President Lincoln.   The results of that conference were soon
to be known to the Confederacy, and meant any thing else
than that "peace negotiation" into which some lively imagi-
nations in Richmond construed this collection of distinguished
persons.

CHAPTER XXIII.

The date of distrust in the Southern mind.—Observation of General Lee.—A peculiar moral condition of the Confederacy.—Want of confidence in President Davis' administration.—Impatience of the prolongation of the war.—Davis' unpopularity. —Weak attempts in Congress at a counter-revolution.—General Lee made commander-in chief.—The title a nominal one.—The Virginia delegation and the President.—Mr. Seddon's resignation.—President Davis' defiance to Congress.—The Davis-Johnston imbroglio.—Senator Wigfall's speeches.—Johnston's restoration. —President Davis' opinion of homœopathy.—Sullen and indifferent disposition of the Southern people.—How they might have accomplished their independence.— Review of the military situation.—Analysis of the peace feeling in the North.— How it was likely to be developed by a long war.—The Union not the enemy's *sine qua non*.—Two contingencies that limited the war.—The worthless title of Yankee invasion.—"Cob-web" occupation of the Confederacy.—*Note:* an address in the Richmond newspapers.—The two fatal facts in the condition of the Confederacy.— THE FORTRESS MONROE COMMISSION.—How it was brought about.—The Yankee ultimatum.—Official narrative of the Confederate commissioners.—A new attempt to rally the spirit of the South.—The meeting at the African church in Richmond. —President Davis' boasts.—His noble allusion to history.—How the cause of the Confederacy was in danger.—PROPOSITION TO ARM THE SLAVES OF THE SOUTH,— Indicative of a desperate condition of the public mind.—General Lee's opinion.— The slaveholding interest.—Its selfishness and insolence.—A weak conclusion of the matter.—"Catching at straws" in the Confederate Congress.—Character of this body.

IN the winter of 1864–5, intelligent minds in the Confederacy became, for the first time, impressed with the idea that its victory and independence were no longer certain conclusions, and conceived a painful distrust as to the issues of the war.

General Lee, a man who used few words, and had the faculty of going directly to the point of a discussion, and putting sagacious judgments in plain phrases, once said of the conduct of the people of the Confederacy in the war, that "they were only half in earnest." But this remark, unlike most of Lee's judgments, was only half true. No one can doubt that the Confederates had been thoroughly and terribly in earnest in the first periods of the war; and if, in its later periods, they appeared to lack earnestness, the truth was they did not lack it so much as they did confidence in their rulers, and a disposition to continue the war under an administration, whose squanderings and make-shifts turned all the sacrifices of the people to naught. In the later periods of the terrible conflict through which the Confederacy had passed, its moral condition was peculiar. All confidence in the administration at Richmond was gone; the people were heart-broken; they had been cheated too often by the highly colored prophesies of President Davis, and those boastful predictions, which are unfailing characteristics of the weak mind; they saw that their sacrifices were squandered, and their most patriotic efforts misapplied; they were so far demoralized by want of confidence in their authorities, and, in some instances, by positive antipathy to them, that it may be said that in the last periods of the war, a majority of the people of the Confederacy actually deprecated any single success, and did not desire a victory to their arms which might give a new occasion of prolongation of the war—for having already taken it for granted as hopeless, they prayed in their hearts that it would be closed at the earliest moment. They did not desire the delay of any mere fluctuations of fortune, which they were sure was to be adverse at the last. "If failure was to ensue, then the sooner the better." Such was the phrase of the vulgar judgment which everywhere in the Confederacy assailed the ears of nobler and more resolute men.

Whatever share the maladministration at Richmond may have had in producing this public demoralization, it is not to be excused entirely on this account. It involved with it much that was shameful, for which the people had themselves to blame, and to charge to the account of their own disposition to let the war lapse to its final conclusions of defeat and ruin.

For months Mr. Davis had been a President, with nothing at his back but a clique of office-holders. The people had become thoroughly estranged from him. If all did not speak of him in terms of derision or hate, there were but few who named him without expressions of distrust. But although the country was thus thoroughly dissatisfied with Mr. Davis' administration, there was not nerve enough in it, not courage enough among its public men, to overthrow his rule, or put it under a severe and effective check.

In the first months of 1865 there were introduced in Congress some partial but remarkable measures to correct the administration. They indicated public sentiment; but they failed and utterly broke down in their execution, and left Davis the defiant and angry master of the field.

The first of these was an act of the Confederate Congress making General Lee commander-in-chief of the armies. The intention of this law was never executed. Lee was unwilling to accept practically its trust; he was unwilling, too, to break a personal friendship with the President; and so he remained in immediate command of the Army of Northern Virginia, and Davis continued in the practical control of the armies at large, without any diminution of his power or insolence.

In January, 1865, the Virginia delegation in the House of Representatives, headed by Mr. Bocock, the speaker of the House, addressed to the President an earnest, but most respectful paper, expressing their want of confidence in the capacity and services of his cabinet, the members of which for four years had been mere figure-heads in Richmond. Mr. Davis resented the address as impertinent. Mr. Seddon, the secretary of war, a citizen of Virginia, recognizing the censure as coming from Virginians, and, therefore, as peculiarly applicable to himself, and conscious of the excessive unpopularity he had incurred in the administration of his office—an ugly little circumstance of which had recently come to light, namely, that while he had been impressing the grain of the Virginia farmers at nominal prices, he had sold his own crop of wheat to the Government at forty dollars a bushel—insisted upon resigning, and thus appeasing the public indignation against himself. Mr. Davis opposed this action of his secretary, sought to dissuade him from it; and when Mr. Seddon did resign, the President went out of his way to declare in a letter, published in the newspapers, that the event of this resignation would in no manner change the policy or course of his administration, and thus, in words not to be mistaken, threw down his defiance to Congress and the country.

Another point which Congress made with the President was the restoration of General Joseph E. Johnston to command. For weeks in the Confederate Senate, Mr. Wigfall, of Texas—a course, heavy man, of large brain, who, under an unsentimental exterior, possessed more of the courage and fire of the orator than any other man in the South—dealt his sledge-hammer blows on the President, who, he declared, not satisfied with persecuting Johnston, was trying to make him the scapegoat for his own sins. The debate in the Johnston-Davis imbroglio was a memorable one in the dreary annals of the Confederate Congress. The fierce impatience of Mr. Wigfall more than once caused him to launch into philippics against the President, which most of the Richmond newspapers did not dare to report. The President was denounced without mercy. "He was," said Mr. Wigfall, summing up on one occasion his points of indictment, "an amalgam of malice and mediocrity."

The President did restore Johnston; but under circumstances which made it no concession to the public. To an intimate friend he remarked with grim humor, that "if the people wanted to try homœopathic treatment—*similia similibus curantur*—he would give them another dose of Johnston." He restored this commander, as he well knew, to the conduct of a campaign that was already lost; he put him in command of a broken and disorganized force that Sherman had already swept before him through two States into the forests of North Carolina; and Johnston was right when some weeks before he wrote to a private friend that he was quite sure that if the authorities at Richmond restored him to command, they were resolved not to act towards him in good faith and with proper support, but to put him in circumstances where defeat was inevitable, and thus confirm to the populace the military judgment of President Davis.

The people of the Confederacy, towards the final periods of the war, may be said to have looked with folded arms upon the sins of its Government, and to have regarded its general tendency to disaster and ruin with a sullen disposition to let matters take their own course, or with weak and blank despair. These sins were not only the fruit of Mr. Davis' violent and imperious animosities; they covered the whole conduct of his administration, and involved as much the want of capacity as that of official candor and personal impartiality. Everywhere the military establishment was falling to decay, and although the Confederacy was still full of fighting men and war material, there was nothing but the dregs of its resources at the practical command of the Government.

The most remarkable fact in the later days of the Confed

eracy was, that while the country was really capable of fighting the war indefinitely, and accomplishing its independence, if by nothing more, yet surely by the virtue of endurance, it had in active employment but the smallest portion of its resources, and was loitering on the brink of destruction at a time when victory, *with proper efforts*, was never more surely in its grasp.

To understand this great and melancholy fact in the history of the war—that the Confederates, with an abler government and a more resolute spirit, might have accomplished their independence—we have only to review, with candor, the situation as it existed in the opening of the memorable year of 1865.

In the summer of 1864 everywhere the thought of the North was peace; not so much in the newspapers, whose office, especially with the Yankees, was rather to disguise public sentiment than to express or apply it; but in every circle of conversation, and every quarter where men dared to unmask their minds and to substitute their true convictions for the stereotypes of affectation, there was to be found a real desire for peace, which had almost ripened into a popular demand, ready to define its terms and resolved to insist upon its concession. The Chicago Convention meant peace; this and that man, least suspected of generosity to the Confederacy or of deference to truth, privately confessed the war to be a failure; even Republicans of Mr. Lincoln's school, seizing upon certain amiable expressions in the Confederate Congress of the summer of 1864, wanted to know if they might not mean some accommodation of the question of the war, and replied to them with those affectations of generosity with which the dexterous cowardice of the Yankee is always ready to cover his sense of defeat.

This disposition of the public mind in the North was easily accounted for, when it was closely observed. It was clearly not the fruit of any decisive disasters to the Northern arms in the summer campaign of 1864. But that campaign had been negative. Atlanta had not fallen. All the engagements in Northern Georgia had not amounted, as Johnston said, to the sum of more than one battle, and it was yet doubtful on which side to strike the average of success. Richmond was erect and defiant; and Lee's army had given new and conspicuous proofs of fortitude at Cold Harbour and Petersburg. Nowhere, then, could the enemy find any prospect of the speedy termination of the war; and though he had searched every link of the armor of the Confederacy he had been unable to plant anywhere a serious wound. It was simply because the enemy's campaign was negative; simply in prospect of a prolongation of the war that, in midsummer of 1864, the Yankee public halted in its opinions and seriously meditated a proposition of peace.

The great lesson which the South was to learn of public opinion in the North was this: that the prospect of a long war was quite as sure to obtain the success and independence of the Confederacy, as the positive victories of her arms. It might not have been so in the first periods of the war, when the resolution of the enemy was fresh and patient, and the Union was then really the apple of his eye. But it was when patience had been worn threadbare by promises—when expectation had stood on tip-toe until it had ached; when the sentiment of Union had lost all its original inspiration; when "the Union as it was" had become more and more impossible to the hopes of the intelligent, and the attempt to realize it had fallen from the resolution of a sovereign necessity to a mere preference of alternatives—that we find the enemy quite as likely to be defeated by the prospect of a prolonged war, as by the dint of positive disaster, and, in fact, meditating more anxiously the question of Southern endurance, than the immediate fortunes of any military campaign.

It was a great mistake to suppose that in these later years of the war, the North was fighting for the Union as the *sine qua non*, the indispensable thing. That was the clack of Yankee newspapers and the drone of demagogues. But the facts were to the contrary. It was to be admitted that the North, in the development of her resources in the war, and the discovery contemporary with it of an almost fabulous wealth in her oil regions and mines, and new fields of enterprise opened along the entire slope of the Rocky Mountains, had obtained a confidence which had assured her, among other things, that, even apart from the South, she had in herself the elements of a great national existence. It was this swollen wealth—some of it the windfalls of a mysterious Providence—which had appeased much of that avarice which formed so large a share in the Northern desire for the Union. Again, as the war had progressed, it had become more and more obvious to countless intelligent persons in the North, that it had wasted what was most desirable in the Union; destroyed its *esprit;* left nothing to be recovered but its shadow, and that along with such paltry recovery of a mere name, were to be taken the consequences of such despotic government as would be necessary to hold two hostilized countries under a common rule. It was thus that the sentiment of the Union had lost much of its power in the North. The first fervors of the war were scarcely now to be discovered among a people who had chosen to carry on hostilities by the mercenary hands of foreigners and negroes, and had devised a system of substitution—a vicarious warfare —to an extent that was absolutely without parallel in the history of any modern nation.

All persons in the North, with the exception of some hundreds, professed that they preferred the Union; it was a universal desire spoken everywhere; but spoken only as a preference and desire, and no longer as a passion that insisted upon an object which it considered death and ruin to dispense with. Of all who declared for the Union, but few were ready to testify sincerely that they were for it at all hazards and consequences. Whatever might be the convenient language or the fulsome protestation of public opinion in the North, two things were certain.

First, that the North would not insist upon the Union in plain prospect of a war indefinitely prolonged.

And second, that the North would never fight the war beyond that moderate point of success on the part of the South, where she would be disposed to accommodate the enemy with certain treaty favors which might stand in lieu of the old Union, and where she would not be quite confident enough in her position to insist upon a severe independence.

It was thus that the war, on the part of the North, was limited by contingencies, which were very far short of decisive results one way or the other, and which might transpire even without any very signal successes of the Confederate arms.

What had been said of the peace movement in the North

in the summer of 1864, before the fall of Atlanta, has its application to the times of which we are now writing. That movement was simply the result of a conviction, not that the South was about to accomplish a positive triumph, but that she was able to endure the war much longer than had been expected, and yet had not reached that point of confidence where she would not be likely to make valuable concessions to the North for the early and graceful acknowledgment of her independence. That acknowledgment the North was then on the eve of making under certain disguises, it is true, of party convenience, but none the less certainly because it sought decent excuse for the act. The Democratic party was then well nigh a unit on the subject of peace. " Burn my letter," wrote a distinguished politician of New England to a Confederate then in New York; " but when you get to Richmond, hasten to President Davis, and tell him the Chicago Convention means peace, and nothing but peace." It was the military events which followed that interrupted this resolution, and showed how little there was of principle or of virtuous intention in Yankee parties; and with the fall of Atlanta, Savannah, Wilmington, and Charleston, and Sherman's campaign of magnificent distances, the Northern mind had again become inflamed with the fervor of new hopes, and clamored for unconditional war, when it thought that it was in the last stages of success.

Yet in face of this clamor it was plain enough that if the Confederates could ever regain substantially nothing more than the *status quo* of seven months ago; if they could ever present to the North the same prospect of a long war as they did then, and put before them the weary task of overcoming the fortitude of a brave people, they would have peace and independence in their grasp. It was a vulgar mistake that to accomplish our success in this war we had to retrieve all of the past and recover by arms all the separate pieces of our territory. It was to be remembered that we were fighting on the defensive, and had only to convince the enemy that we were able to protect the vital points of our country to compel him to a peace in which all was surrendered that he had overrun, and all the country that he held by the worthless title of invasion, would fall from him as by the law of gravitation.

It may be said briefly that if the Confederates could only regain the situation of the last summer, or even if they would only give a proof to the enemy that they were not at the extremity of their resources, or at the last limits of resolution—that they were able and determined to fight the war indefinitely—they had then accomplished the important and vital conditions of peace. Nor was the first impossible—to recover substantially, in all important respects, the losses of the past few months, and even add to the *status quo* of last summer new elements of advantage for us. To defeat Sherman at any stage short of Richmond would be to reopen and recover all the country he had overrun. If the enemy was left in possession of the seaports, these had but little value to us as ports of entry, and were but picket-posts in our system of defences. Sherman's campaign clearly came to naught if he could not reach Grant—nothing left of it but the brilliant zig-zag of a raid vanishing as heat lightning in the skies. The consequences of Sherman's misadventure would be obvious enough. Grant's army, without the looked-for aid from the Carolinas, was by no means certain of the capture of Richmond. It was true that Grant was within a few miles of the Confederate capital, when the same time last year he was on the Rapidan. But that was a fool's measure of danger, for in each case we had the same army shielding Richmond, and whether that shield was broken ten or one hundred miles away was of no importance to the interest it covered.

There was nothing really desperate in the military situation of the Confederacy, unless to fools and cowards who drew lines on paper to show how the Yankees were at this place and at that place, and thought that this cob-web occupation of the country, where the enemy had no garrisons and no footholds, indicated the extent of Yankee conquest and gave the true measure of the remnant of the Confederacy! And yet this was too much the popular fashion of the time in estimating the military situation. Men were drawing for themselves pictures of despair out of what were, to those who thought profoundly and bravely, no more important than the passages of the hour. It is not to be disguised that the condition of the Confederacy was demoralized in the extreme, and that it was difficult to reorganize, as the patriots of 1861, men who were now exclaim ing everywhere their despair, and counselling embassies of submission.*

Briefly, if the fatal facts in the condition of the Confede-

---

* In March, 1865, the author printed an address in the Richmond newspapers, of which the following was the concluding portion. The occasion and spirit of this address are significant enough of what was taking place in Richmond at that time :

"I am determined to express the truth, no matter how painful to myself or unwelcome to others. In the first period of this war who was not proud of the Confederacy and its heroic figure in history! Yet now it is to be confessed that a large portion of our people have fallen below the standards of history, and hold no honorable comparison with other nations that have fought and struggled for independence. It is easy for the tongue of the demagogue to trip with flattery on the theme of the war ; but when we come to the counsels of the intelligent the truth must be told. We are no longer responding to the lessons and aspirations of history. You speak of the scarcity of subsistence. But Prussia, in her wars, drained her supplies until black bread was the only thing eat in the king's palace ; and yet, under Frederick, she won not only her independence, but a position among the five great powers of Europe. You speak of the scarcity of men. Yet with a force not greater than that with which we have only to hold an invaded country and maintain the defensive, Napoleon fought his splendid career, and completed a circle of victories that touched the boundaries of Europe.

" It is enough to sicken the heart with shame and vexation that now, when, of all times, it is most important to convince the enemy of our resolution— now, when such a course, for peculiar reasons, will insure our success—there are men who not only whine on the streets about making terms with the enemy, but intrude their cowardice into the official places of the Government, and, sheltered by secret sessions and confidential conversations, roll the word ' reconstruction ' under the tongue. Shame upon the Congress that closed its doors that it might better consult of dishonorable things! Shame upon those leaders who should encourage the people, and yet have broken down their confidence by private conversations ; and who, while putting in newspapers some cheap words of patriotism, yet in the same breath express their despair by a suspicious cant about trusting in Providence, and go off to talk submission with their intimates in a corner! Shame upon those of the people who have now no other feeling in the war than an exasperated selfishness ! who are ready to sink, if they can carry down in their hands some little trash of *property !* who will give their sons to the army, but not their precious negro slaves! who are for hurrying off embassies to the enemy to know at what price of dishonor they may purchase some paltry remnants of their possessions ! Do these men ever think of the retributions of history ?

" When Cato the Younger was pursued to Utica by the victorious arms of Cæsar, Plutarch relates of him on this occasion certain conversations and sentiments which singularly apply to our own condition in a besieged city, and may almost be taken as repeated in the streets of Richmond :

" ' One of the Council,' writes Plutarch, ' observed the expediency of a decree for enfranchising the slaves, and many commended the motion. Cato,

racy at the time of which we write, are to be summed up, they are simply these:

1. A want of confidence in the administration of Mr. Davis

---

however, said: 'He would not do that, because it was neither just nor lawful; but such as their masters would voluntarily discharge, he would receive, provided they were of proper age to bear arms.' This many promised to do; and Cato withdrew, after having ordered lists to be made out of all that should offer.

. . . All of the patrician order with great readiness enfranchised and armed their slaves; but as for the three hundred, who dealt in traffic and loans of money at high interest, and whose slaves were a considerable part of their fortune, the impression which Cato's speech had made upon them did not last long. As some bodies readily receive heat, and as easily grow cold again when the fire is removed, so the sight of Cato warmed and liberalized these traders; but when they came to consider the matter among themselves, the dread of Cæsar soon put to flight their reverence for Cato and for virtue. For thus they talked: 'What are we, and what is the man whose orders we refuse to receive? Is it not Cæsar, into whose hands the whole power of the Roman empire is fallen? And surely none of us is a Scipio, a Pompey, or a Cato. Shall we, at a time when their fears make all men entertain sentiments beneath their dignity—shall we, in Utica, fight for the liberty of Rome with a man against whom Cato and Pompey the Great durst not make a stand in Italy? Shall we enfranchise our slaves to oppose Cæsar, who have no more liberty ourselves than that conqueror is pleased to leave us? Ah! wretches that we are! Let us at last know ourselves, and send deputies to intercede with him for mercy.' . . . . They told Cato that they had resolved to send deputies to Cæsar to intercede first and principally for him. If that request should not be granted, they would have no obligation to him for any favor to themselves, but as long as they had breath would fight for Cato. Cato made his acknowledgments for their regard, and advised them to send immediately to intercede for themselves. 'For me,' said he, 'intercede not. It is for the conquered to turn suppliants, and for those who have done an injury to beg pardon. For my part, I have been unconquered through life, and superior in the things I wished to be; for in justice and honor I am Cæsar's superior.''

"The arguments of the traders and time servers in Utica are not unknown in Richmond. But shall we not also find in this city something of the aspirations of Cato—a determination, even if we are overcome by force, to be unconquered in spirit, and, in any and all events, to remain superior to the enemy—in honor.

"I do not speak to you, my countrymen, idle sentimentalism. I firmly believe that the great commonwealth of Virginia, and this city, which has a peculiar title to whatever there is of good and illustrious report in this war, have been recently, and are yet in some measure on the verge of questions which involve an interest immeasurably greater than has yet been disclosed in this contest—that of their historical and immortal honor.

"I know—I have had opportunities of informing myself—that there are influences at work to place the State of Virginia, in certain contingencies, in

—sucn as was never before exhibited between a people and its rulers in a time of revolution.

---

communication with the public enemy, for terms of peace, which cannot be otherwise than coupled with the condition of her submission to the Federal authority. The extent of this conspiracy against the honor of Virginia has been screened by secret sessions, and been covered up by half-mouthed suggestions, and the *ifs* and *ands* of men who are not yet ready to disclose their corruption, and to spit from their lips the rottenness in their hearts. I know the fashionable arguments of these men. 'If there is to be a wreck,' say they, why not save what we can from it?' 'Honor,' they say, 'is a mere rhetorical laurel;' 'General Lee talks like a school-girl when he speaks of preferring to die on the battle-field to getting the best terms of submission he can;' 'let us be done with this sentimental rubbish, and look to the care of our substantial interests.'

"My friends, this is not rubbish. The glory of history is indifferent to events; it is simply honor. The name of Virginia in this war is historically and absolutely more important to us than any other element of the contest; and the coarse time-server who would sell an immortal title of honor as a trifling sentimentalism, and who has constantly in his mouth the phrase of 'substantial interests,' is the inglorious wretch who laughs at history and grovels in the calculations of the brute.

"Those who have lived entirely in the South since the commencement of this war have little idea of the measure of honor which Virginia has obtained in it, and the consideration she has secured in the eyes of the world. One away from home, finds even in intercourse with our enemies, that the name of Virginian is an ornament to him, and that the story of this her heroic capital—the record of Richmond—is universally accepted in two hemispheres as the most illustrious episode of the war. Honor such as this is not a piece of rhetoric or a figure of speech; it is something to be cherished under all circumstances, and to be preserved in all events.

"It is scarcely necessary to say that I regard subjugation but as the vapor of our fears. But if remote possibilities are to be regarded, I have simply to say, that in all events and extremities, all chances and catastrophes, I am for Virginia going down to history, proudly and starkly, with the title of a subjugated people—a title not inseparable from true glory, and which has often claimed the admiration of the world—rather than as a people who ever submitted, and bartered their honor for the mercy of an enemy—in our case a mercy whose *pittance* would be as a mess of pottage weighed against an immortal patrimony!

"The issue I would put before you is: No submission; no State negotiations with the enemy; no conventions for such objects, however proper for others. Let Virginia stand or fall by the fortunes of the Confederate arms, with her spotless honor in her hands.

"If Virginia accepts the virtuous and noble alternative, she saves, in all events, her honor, and by the resolution which it implies, may hope to secure a positive and glorious victory; and I, among the humblest of her citizens, will be proud to associate myself with a fate which, if not happy, at least can

2. And as main consequence of that want of confidence, when all measures to repair it had failed, a general breaking down of the public virtue, and the debasement of a people who, having lost hope in the existing order—rather the exist ing disorder—and having no heart for a new experiment, or thinking it too late, descend to the condition of time-servers, and those who tamely and infamously submit to fortune.

THE FORTRESS MONROE COMMISSION.

But another and last appeal was to be made to the resolution of the South.

In January, 1865, Mr. Francis P. Blair, of Maryland, made several visits to Richmond, which were the occasion of much speculation and curiosity in the public mind. He had gone to Richmond with Mr. Lincoln's pass; but the objects of his mission were not committed to paper. However, they were soon developed. On his return to Washington, Mr. Blair showed Mr. Lincoln a letter which President Davis had written, stating that Mr. Blair was at liberty to say to Mr. Lincoln that Mr. Davis was now, as he always had been, willing to send commissioners, if assured they would be received, or to receive any that should be sent; that he was not disposed to find obstacles in forms. He would send commissioners to confer with the Northern President with a view to the restoration of peace between the two countries, if he could be assured they would be received.

Mr. Lincoln, therefore, on the 18th day of January, ad dressed a note to Mr. Blair, in which, after acknowledging that he had read the note of Mr. Davis, he said that he was, and always should be, willing to receive any agent that Mr. Davis, or any other influential person now actually resisting the authority of the Government, might send to confer in-

never be ignoble. But, if she chooses to submit, and make terms for Yankee clemency, the satisfaction will at least remain to me of not sharing in the dishonor of my native State, and of going to other parts of the world, where I may say: 'I, too, was a Virginian, but not of those who sold the jewels of her history for the baubles and cheats of her conquerors.' "

formally with him, with a view to the restoration of peace to the people of "our common country."

In consequence of this notification President Davis requested Vice-President Stephens, Senator Hunter, and Judge John A. Campbell, to proceed through the lines to hold a conference with Mr. Lincoln, or such persons as he might depute to represent him. The following report, made by the Confederate commissioners, gives the official narrative of the affair:

RICHMOND, February 6th.

To the President of the Confederate States:

SIR—Under your letter of appointment of commissioners, of the 8th, we proceeded to seek an informal conference with Abraham Lincoln, President of the United States, upon the subject mentioned in the letter. A conference was granted, and took place on the 30th, on board the steamer anchored in Hampton Roads, where we met President Lincoln and Hon. Mr. Seward, secretary of State of the United States. It continued for several hours, and was both full and explicit. We learned from them that the message of President Lincoln to the Congress of the United States, in December last, explains clearly his sentiments as to the terms, conditions, and mode of proceeding by which peace can be secured to the people; and we were not informed that they would be modified or altered to obtain that end. We understood from him that no terms or proposals of any treaty or agreements looking to an ultimate settlement would be entertained or made by him with the authorities of the Confederate States, because that would be recognition of their existence as a separate power, which, under no circumstances, would be done; and for like reasons, that no such terms would be entertained by him from the States separately; that no extended truce or armistice, as at present advised, would be granted or allowed, without the satisfaction or assurance in advance, of the complete restoration of the authority of the constitution and laws of the United States over all places within the States of the Confederacy; that whatever consequence may follow from the re-establishment of that authority, it must be accepted; but all individuals subject to the pains and penalties under the laws of the United States, might rely upon a very liberal use of the power confided to him to remit those pains and penalties if peace be restored. During the conference, the proposed amendments to the constitution of the United States, adopted by Congress on the 31st, was brought to our notice. These amendments provide that neither slavery nor involuntary servitude, except for crime, should exist within the United States or any place within its jurisdiction, and Congress should have power to enforce the amendment by appropriate legislation. Of all the correspondence that preceded the conference herein mentioned, and leading to the same, you have heretofore been informed.

Very respectfully, your obedient servants.

A. H. STEPHENS,
R. M. T. HUNTER,
J. A. CAMPBELL.

Of the conference Mr. Seward testified that "the Richmond

P'Neill. N.D.

ALEX. H. STEPHENS.

From a Photograph taken from life.

party approached the discussion rather indirectly, and at no time did they make categorical demands, or tender formal stipulations or absolute refusals; nevertheless, during the conference, which lasted four hours, the several points at issue between the Government and the insurgents were distinctly raised and discussed fully, intelligently, and in an amicable spirit. What the insurgent party seemed chiefly to favor was a postponement of the question of separation upon which the war was waged, and a mutual direction of the efforts of the Government, as well as those of the insurgents, to some extraneous policy or scheme for a season, during which passions might be expected to subside, and the armies be reduced, and trade and intercourse between the people of both sections be resumed."

The proposition which looked to an armistice or truce was distinctly answered by Mr. Lincoln, who stated that he would agree to no cessation or suspension of hostilities unless on the basis of the disbandment of the Confederate forces. There were no notes of the conference. There was no attendance of clerks or secretaries; and nothing was written or read. But the result of the whole conversation, which was earnest and free, may be summarily stated to have shown that the enemy refused to enter into negotiations with the Confederate States, or any of them separately, or give to their people any other terms or guarantees than those which Congress might grant; or to permit the Southern people to have a vote on any other basis than unconditional submission to their rule, coupled with the acceptance of the recent legislation at Washington, including an amendment to the Constitution for the emancipation of all negro slaves.

The failure of the Fortress Monroe commission was made the occasion in the South of a new attempt to rally the spirit of its people, and to infuse into the war a new element of desperate passion. The people were told that the result of the conference at Fortress Monroe showed plainly enough that every avenue to peace was closed, except such as might be carved out by the sword. It was calculated ingeniously enough that the party in the South which had so long clamored for negotiations with Washington would now abandon its visions of reconciliation and generosity, and give in their adhesion to a renewed and even desperate prosecution of the war.

These expectations were not realized. The attempt to raise the drooping spirits of the South, and to introduce, as some of the public men in Richmond fondly imagined, a new era of resolution and devotion in the war, shamefully failed. The Fortress Monroe affair produced in the Confederacy a feeble flare of excitement which was soon extinguished. A mass-meeting was called at the African church in Richmond, that the people might renew their testimony of devotion to the Confederacy. The meeting was held at high noon; all business in the city of Richmond was suspended, as if to give extraordinary solemnity to the occasion; fiery addresses were made, and tokens of enthusiasm were said in the newspapers to have been abundant. But speeches and hurrahs are cheap things. The public mind of the South made but a sickly response to what was undoubtedly, in all its circumstances, one of the most powerful appeals ever calculated to stir the heart and nerve the resolution of a people fighting for liberty; and in its relapse into the abject and timid counsels of the submissionists, exhibited a want of spirit which, it must be confessed, must ever make a painful and humiliating page in the history of the Confederacy.

Mr. Davis also spoke at the African church. He did not omit the occasion of exhorting the people. But he unfortunately fell into that style of boastful prediction and bombastic speech which was characteristic of all his public addresses; which was evidence of his weak mind; and which furnished the grave ground of accusation against him that in his public declarations he never dealt with the people in a proper spirit of candor. He declared that the military affairs of the Confederacy were in excellent condition; he hinted at great victories which were about to be accomplished; he boasted that "Sherman's march through Georgia would be his last;" he completed his rhetorical flourish with the strange prediction that before the summer solstice fell upon the country it would be the Yankees who would be asking for terms of peace and the grace of conferences in which the Confederates might make known their demands.

But in this unfortunate address of the President there was one just and remarkable sentiment. He referred to the judgment of history upon Kossuth, who had been so weak as to abandon the cause of Hungary with an army of *thirty thousand* men in the field ; and spoke of the disgrace of surrender, if the Confederates should abandon their cause with an army on our side and actually in the field more numerous than those which had made the most brilliant pages in European history ; an army more numerous than that with which Napoleon achieved his reputation ; an army standing among its homesteads ; an army in which each individual man was superior in every martial quality to each individual man in the ranks of the invader, and reared with ideas of independence, and in the habits of command !

It was very clear that the Confederacy was very far from the historical necessity of subjugation. But it was at any time near the catastrophe of a panic. If the cause was to be lost, it was to be so by weak despair ; by the cowardice of suicide ; by the distress of weak minds.

PROPOSITION TO ARM THE SLAVES OF THE SOUTH.

A measure indicative of the desperate condition of the Southern mind was that to extend the conscription to the slaves. A proposition to arm the negroes of the South, and use them as soldiers in the Confederate Army, had been debated in the Richmond press as early as the fall of 1864. It was favored by General Lee, but variously received by the general public. There were many persons who argued that the negro might be effectively used in this new department of service ; that military experience had shown that a soldier could be made of any thing that had arms and legs ; that the United States had formerly recruited its regular army from the dregs of humanity ; that the experience of the North with the negro had shown him to be a serviceable soldier ; and that the South could offer him superior inducements to good service, by making him a freeman in his own home, and could give him officers who could better understand his nature, and better prompt his good qualities, than his Yankee military taskmasters. These views were encouraged by General Lee. Indeed, this distinguished officer made no secret of his opinion, that the military service of the slave should be secured on the basis of general emancipation; arguing, with no little ingenuity, that the institution of slavery had been so shaken by the invasions and raids of the enemy, which had penetrated every portion of the country, that its practical value had become but a small consideration in view of the insecure tenure of the property; that it might, eventually, be broken up if the war continued; and that, by a decree of emancipation, the South might make a virtue of necessity, remove a cause of estrangement, however unjust, between it and the Christian world, and possibly neutralize that large party in the North, whose sympathy and interest in the war were mainly employed with the negro.

The question divided the country. The slaveholding interest, in its usual narrow spirit—in its old character of a greedy, vulgar, insolent aristocracy—took the alarm, and in Congress and in the newspapers, proclaimed that the use of negroes as soldiers was the entering wedge of Abolition; that it would stultify the whole cause of the Confederacy; that it would give up what they falsely imagined to be the leading object of the war—the protection of the interests of less than a quarter of a million of people who owned slaves in the South. The Charleston Mercury declared that if the slaves were armed, South Carolina could no longer have any interest in prosecuting the war.

But beyond the opposition of the slaveholders and the cotton aristocrats, there were many intelligent men in the South who seriously doubted both the capacity and fidelity of the negro as a Confederate soldier. General Lee and many of his distinguished officers were not among these.

A majority of the Confederate Army were probably in favor of the experiment of negro soldiers; and many who doubted their efficiency at the front were persuaded that they might be made useful in other parts of the military field. General Ewell, who commanded in the Department of Henrico, declared that the employment of the negroes in the trenches, around Richmond, would relieve fifteen thousand white soldiers, who might be used on the enemy's front, and thus make an important accession to our forces actually in the field.

The action of the Confederate Congress with reference to the military employment of the negro was characteristic of that body. The subject was debated threadbare, discussed and dissected in open and secret session; but no practical action could be obtained on the matter, but what was too late in respect of time, and absurdly small with reference to the measure of the necessities by which legislation on the subject had been invoked.

Congress took no action on the subject until at the heel of its session. A bill was passed on the 7th of March authorizing the President to ask and accept from the owners of negro slaves as many able-bodied negroes as he might deem expedient, to perform military service in any capacity he might direct, and providing that nothing in the act should be construed to alter the existing relation between master and slaves.

The entire results of this ridiculously small and visionary legislation, which proposed to obtain negro soldiers from such volunteers as their masters might patriotically dedicate to the Confederate service, and was ominously silent on the subject of their freedom, were two fancy companies raised in the city of Richmond, who were allowed to give balls at the Libby, and to parade in Capitol Square, and were scarcely intended to be more than decoys to obtain sable recruits. But they served not even this purpose. The measure passed by Congress may be taken, indeed, as an indication of that vague desperation in the Confederacy which caught at straws, and had not nerve enough to make a practical and persistent effort at safety.

The Congress of the Confederate States was a weak, spasmodic body. There was no organization of opinion in it; no leaders; plenty of idle debate, capricious measures, weak recrimination, and but little of the sense and order of legislative assemblies. It went in and out of secret session almost every twenty-four hours; it was fruitful of propositions without results; and it finally adjourned on the 18th of March, after a session of four months, in which it had failed to enact any effective measure to recruit the army, to improve the finances, to mobilize the subsistence of the country, or, in fact, to serve one single important interest in the Confederacy.

CHAPTER XXV.

The last address and appeal of the Confederate Congress.—The war in a geographical point of view.—THE CONFEDERATE CONGRESS AND PRESIDENT DAVIS.—THE EXECUTIVE DEPARTMENTS.—A sharp recrimination.—A committee of the Senate reply to President Davis.—Maladministration in the War Department.—Two-thirds of the Confederate Army absentees.—Lee loses nearly half his army by desertions.—The other half threatened with starvation.—Ample supply of food in the country.—The fault in the Commissary Department.—Commissary Northrop a "pepper-doctor" as the favorite of Davis.—Analysis of President Davis' character for firmness. —How Northrop starved Richmond.—HISTORY OF THE CONFEDERATE COMMISSARIAT.—Secret testimony in Congress.—President Davis' refusal to trade cotton for meat.—Persistent delusion about "king cotton."—Venality of the enemy.—Davis takes no advantage of it.—Record of the rations in Lee's army.—Startling statistics.—Attempts to get meat from Europe.—General Lee's army without meat.— His telegram to President Davis.—The necessities of the Commissary Department summed up in secret session of Congress.—But little done to meet them.—How the cause of the Confederacy would have failed without a catastrophe of arms.—The military narrative resumed.—MILITARY EVENTS IN VIRGINIA IN THE WINTER OF 1864-5.—SHERIDAN'S RAID.—Thirteen counties traversed.—Amount of destruction accomplished by the enemy.—THE RICHMOND LINES.—HATCHER'S RUN.—Extension of Grant's line.—BATTLE OF HARES HILL.—Gallantry of Gordon's command.— Vigor and brilliancy of the fighting of the Confederates.—No decisive results.

ON the occasion of what was to be its final adjournment, Congress published an address to the people of the Confederate States. It was more prolix than other documents of this sort But it contained one just and admirable reflection, to which we have already referred in the pages of the preceding chapter.

It said: "The extent of our territory, the food-producing capacity of our soil, the amount and character of our population, are elements of strength which, carefully husbanded and wisely employed, are amply sufficient to insure our final triumph. The passage of hostile armies through our country, though productive of cruel suffering to our people, and great pecuniary loss, gives the enemy no permanent advantage or foothold. To subjugate a country, its civil government must be suppressed by a continuing military force, or supplanted by another, to which the inhabitants yield a voluntary or forced obedience. The passage of hostile armies through our territory cannot produce this result. Permanent garrisons would have to be stationed at a sufficient number of points to strangle all civil government before it could be pretended, even by the United States Government itself, that its authority was extended over these States. How many garrisons would it require? How many hundred thousand soldiers would suffice to suppress the civil government of all the States of the Confederacy, and to establish over them, even in name and form, the authority of the United States? *In a geographical point of view, therefore, it may be asserted that the conquest of these Confederate States is impracticable.*"

THE CONFEDERATE CONGRESS AND PRESIDENT DAVIS.—THE EXECUTIVE DEPARTMENTS.

The last Confederate Congress concluded with a sharp recrimination between it and President Davis as to the responsibility for the low state to which the public defence had lapsed. The President had charged, in a public message, that the measures of Congress for recruiting the army were insufficient, and that it had generally neglected to supply the urgent need of men and supplies for the army.

A committee of the Senate made an elaborate reply to this accusation. It declared that all the measures recommended by the President, to promote the efficiency of the army, had been adopted, except the entire repeal of class exemption; and that some measures not suggested by him—such as the creation of general-in-chief—were originated and passed by Congress, with a view to the restoration of public confidence and the energetic administration of military affairs.

The committee retorted upon the executive the charge that by a system of details, in which corruption and favor were dominant, the Conscription Law had been robbed of its legitimate fruits, and the army enfeebled. They said that in remarkable contrast to the number of persons relieved from military service by the exemptions enacted by Congress, the report of the Conscript Bureau exhibited the fact, that east of the Mississippi River, twenty-two thousand and thirty-five men

had been *detailed* by executive authority. It was, they de
clared, in consequence of this abuse of the power of detail,
that Congress had passed an act revoking all details, and lim-
iting the exercise of that power in the future.

We shall not go at large into the merits of this recrimination between the Confederate Congress and the executive.
Each, undoubtedly, had its share of responsibility for the
general improvidence and mismanagement that had fatally
involved the fortunes of the Confederacy. But the mal-admin-
istration in the War Department was even greater than Congress chose to indicate. From that department the confession
had repeatedly gone forth, that two-thirds of our army were
absentees; and yet nothing was done to enforce discipline or
to punish desertions, and the *morale* of the Confederate Army
was left entirely to the regulation of loose patriotic sentiment
among those who composed it. No more forcible commentary
can be made on the feeble execution of the military laws of
the Confederacy, and the omission of the most ordinary discipline in the army, than to state the simple and indisputable
fact that in the winter of 1864-5 Lee lost *nearly half his army*
by desertions alone.

And that half was frequently in a condition bordering on
starvation. There was really no lack of supplies in the country. It is needless to go into details, or to adduce statistics in
proof of this. It is obvious to every well-informed mind.
Although the occupation by the enemy, and his ruthless policy
of destroying the harvests, granaries, and agricultural implements of the people, wherever he moved, had, undoubtedly,
diminished the amount of cereals in the South, still, in view of
the fact that in every State of the Confederacy without exception, its agricultural labor had been devoted almost exclusively
to the raising of breadstuffs (while before the war it was mainly
devoted to the production of cotton, tobacco, and other exports), it was impossible to doubt that there was ample supply
of food in the country.

The fault was in the Commissary Department at Richmond;
where a man flagrantly incompetent, appointed to the most
important post in the country, on no other ground of selection
than that many years ago he had been the college chum of the
President, seemed busy for almost four years in bearing down

all common sense and advice, practising the most ridiculous quackeries, and stifling the very life of the Confederacy.

It is a remarkable fact in history that many famous men who have prided themselves on their firmness and resolution in public affairs, and indeed have displayed these qualities to the generality of mankind, have yet been discovered to be under the dominion of the most paltry influences—in many instances governed by women, court-jesters, and the smallest of favorites. Such an apparent contradiction of character was to be found in President Davis. He could brace his mind and set his face against Congressmen and counsellors generally. But he was absurdly uxorious; he was surrounded by adventurers and "confidence-men;" and some old West Point or Washington acquaintance might readily obtain his ear and favor when they were denied to the first men of the Confederacy.

Commissary Northrop, whose profession Mr. Foote declared in Congress had been that of a "pepper doctor," was one of the small favorites of President Davis. This old man was an extraordinary combination of ignorance and obstinacy; and it was remarked of him that such was his perversity, that whenever advice or suggestion was offered to him, he instantly and invariably took the precisely opposite course.

Richmond was now almost destitute of supplies, through the mismanagement and conceit of this man. His latest fancy had been to prohibit to the general public the importation of any supplies whatever into the Confederate capital. The farmer could not bring a bushel of corn or a pound of meat into Richmond without running the gauntlet of impressment agents. Permits to get flour into Richmond were valued at high figures, and obtained only through special favors. The consequences of Mr. Northrop's folly were, that large stocks of supplies were kept at home in different parts of the interior of Virginia; that they were thus exposed to Yankee devastation, and, in time, became an easy prey of the enemy's raids. It was through such mismanagement that the rich harvests of the Shenandoah were lost to the Confederacy. There had been ample time to have gathered into Richmond at least a large portion of these rich and accessible supplies. Numerous persons had gone to Commissary Northrop with the proposition to bring into Richmond grain and flour from the Valley and were willing to make the condition that any part of their stocks would be given up to the Government, whenever there was any occasion for it to encroach upon the private storehouses of Richmond. But Mr. Northrop closed the door to all such applications, and the commission houses and provision stores of Richmond were left almost empty; while the law of supply and demand was sending prices up far beyond the reach of the general customer.

HISTORY OF THE CONFEDERATE COMMISSARIAT.

In the last Congress of the Confederate States, a secret commission was appointed to investigate the affairs of the Commissary Department. There was thus obtained within closed doors a mass of testimony which covered the whole history of the commissariat, and contains, indeed, subjects of the greatest interest in the war. This testimony was never permitted to see the light in the Confederacy; probably because it so deeply involved President Davis and his associates in the charge of maladministration.

It appeared before the secret commission that as early as the second year of the war, the meat supplies of the Confederacy were discovered to be largely deficient. This became evident enough on the successive captures of Forts Donelson and Henry. The subsequent campaign lost us Kentucky and much of Tennessee, and left us comparatively bare of meat.

At this time a number of propositions were made to the Richmond authorities, by responsible parties, to exchange through the enemy's lines meat for cotton. One man, whose ability to meet his engagements was never questioned, offered to deliver thirty thousand hogsheads of bacon through the lines in exchange for cotton. It was urged that there was enough cotton to feed and clothe our army, in a section tributary to Memphis—which city was then, and had been for some time previous, in the secure possession of the enemy; that such cotton must otherwise probably be destroyed, to prevent its falling into the hands of the enemy; but that the owners as a general rule, though willing to let the Government have their crops, were averse, if not stubbornly opposed, to having them destroyed.

Against every proposition to get meat through the inland military lines, President Davis set his face as flint. He had got an idea into his head that the enemy's finances were about to collapse, and that if a little cotton might be kept from them they would be unable to pay the January interest of 1863. It appears, indeed, to have been impossible for him and his associates to rid themselves of their early conceit of the power of cotton; and it was this wretched delusion in hoarding this inert wealth of the South, that did more than any thing else to wreck the finances of the Confederacy, and eventually to reduce the rations of its armies to one-quarter of a pound of meat a day per man.

The venality of the enemy afforded full opportunity to the Richmond authorities to use the Mississippi from Memphis to New Orleans, until all their needed supplies should be obtained. But no advantage was ever taken of this ample and obvious opportunity. The arguments used against trade in cotton through the lines were:

First—That the Federal finances were in such a condition that if they could not obtain cotton, upon which to draw bills wherewith to pay their then accruing interest, their credit would explode, and the war would speedily cease from the bankrupting of our assailants. Hence they wanted cotton.

Second—That they did not want cotton, but only sought, under cover of a contract for supply, to find out the channels of navigable streams, to ascertain the location and condition of certain defences, and otherwise to spy out the land.

Third—That the trade on the part of the Government would demoralize the people among whom it might be conducted.

Fourth—That to trade through New Orleans, and let cotton clear from that port, " would make Europe think we had caved, who thereupon would decline to recognize us, or to intervene."

The reader will recognize for himself the little value of these arguments—some of them childish—by the side of the great necessity of feeding the armies of the South.

The record of the narrow escapes of Lee's army alone from starvation, is sufficient commentary upon the management at Richmond. In consequence of the refusal to be allowed to purchase on the Mississippi, the army, especially in Virginia was put upon short rations. First, they were reduced to one-half pound of meat per day,—which, if it could have been kept up at that, would have been sufficient; then to one-third of a pound—though this allowance was not agreed to or adhered to by several of the generals commanding; and then to one-quarter of a pound. Upon this last allowance the Army of Northern Virginia wintered in 1864–5.

On the 18th of October, 1864, a memorandum was communicated to President Davis, showing that there were on hand in the Confederate States 4,105,048 rations of fresh meat, and 3,426,519 rations of bacon and pork, which would subsist three hundred thousand men twenty-five days. The authorities were now compelled to subsist, independent of the armies of the Confederacy, many thousand prisoners of war who were collected in different camps throughout the country.

In 1863 a feeble and badly organized attempt had been made to get meat from Europe through the blockade. Much of it was allowed to remain at Nassau and Bermuda until it spoiled. Contracts for supplies, payable in cotton in our Atlantic ports, were made with several parties; but in no instance with success. Either the amount involved was too small, to tempt the venality of those who could control or purchase an evasion of the blockade; or the engagement to deliver meat alone, was found to be too small an inducement to those engaged in blockade-running.

In the winter of 1864 the subsistence of the Confederate armies appeared to be in the last stages of exhaustion. Major Ruffin, assistant-commissary-general, testifies before a secret committee of Congress:

"On the 5th of December I brought the condition of things to the attention of the Secretary of War, coupling it with a statement of subsistence on hand, which showed nine days' rations on hand for General Lee's army; and, quoting his letter to the commissary-general, that day received, stating that his men were deserting on account of short rations, I urged prompt action; but none was taken. On the 14th of December, nine days afterwards, General Lee telegraphed Mr. Davis that his army was without meat."

In January, 1865, the following points were presented in secret session of Congress:

First—That there was not meat enough in the Southern Confederacy for the armies it had in the field.

Second—That there was not in Virginia either meat or bread enough for the armies within her limits.

Third—That the bread supply from other places depended absolutely upon the keeping open the railroad connections of the South.

Fourth—That the meat must be obtained from abroad through a seaport, and by a different system from that which has heretofore prevailed.

Fifth—That the bread could not be had by impressment, but must be paid for in market rates.

Sixth—That the payment must be made in cash, which, so far, had not been furnished; and, if possible, in a better medium than treasury scrip.

Seventh—That the transportation was not adequate, from whatever cause, to meet the necessary demands of the service.

Eighth—That the supply of fresh meat to General Lee's army was precarious; and if the army fell back from Richmond and Petersburg, there was every probability that it would cease altogether.

Nothing was done by the Confederate Government commensurate with the necessities indicated above—nothing, in fact, done to meet them beyond a visionary scheme, enacted in the last days of Congress, to raise three millions in specie to purchase supplies from those producers of the Confederacy who were no longer willing to take scrip for their commodities. But few persons outside of official circles in the Confederacy were acquainted with the true state of affairs; so hedged in with secrecy was the weak and recluse government of Mr. Davis. To the well-informed and intelligent the appalling fact was manifest—*that the whole system of Confederate defence was bound to break down by sheer mismanagement in the commissariat, even without a catastrophe of arms.*

Before we reach the final and sudden catastrophe that was to befall the arms of the Confederacy, there is a slight space in our military narrative which we have to cover by a brief relation of the events of the war in Virginia in the winter of

1864–5. This record is a very slender one. But it is the preface, in point of time at least, to those great events which, in
April, 1865, were to bring the war to a singular.y abrupt close,
and with a precipitation heretofore but little known in the
history of great contests.

MILITARY EVENTS IN VIRGINIA IN THE WINTER OF 1864–5— SHERIDAN'S RAID.

Our last reference to the campaign in the Valley of Virginia was, when the forces there had been much reduced and
the scale of operations had become inconsiderable ; the bulk
of Early's troops having been withdrawn to General Lee's
lines. Sheridan, too, had sent most of his infantry to Grant.
In December, the Sixth Corps was returned to the Army of
the Potomac ; and the Army of the Shenandoah for nearly two
months acted principally as an army of observation.

Towards the last of February, 1865, Sheridan began to "ride"
again up the Valley of the Shenandoah, leaving Hancock in
command of his department at Winchester. On reaching
Waynesboro' a battle occurred between Early and Custer's
divisions, which resulted in the rout of the Confederates.
Sheridan captured about thirteen hundred prisoners—nearly
all of Early's little command ; which indeed fell an easy prey
to the magnificent Yankee cavalry. Early himself escaped
with difficulty, some of his staff-officers and his personal baggage being captured.

Charlottesville was surrendered the next day. From this
point, on the 6th of March, Sheridan moved in two columns
southward towards the James. One division, under General
Deven, took a directly southern route to Scottsville, destroying
all mills, merchandise, and bridges on the line of march, and
along the Rivanna River to Columbia. The other division
proceeded down on the railroad to Lynchburg, destroying it
as far as Amherst—a distance of over forty miles. From
Scottsville, Deven's division proceeded westward along the
banks of the James, destroying every lock on the canal as far
as Dugaldsville, twenty miles from Lynchburg. Not being
able to cross the James on account of the high water, Sheridan

moved around the north side of Richmond, and, crossing at Deep Bottom, joined General Meade's army south of Petersburg.

The destruction accomplished by this raid was serious enough. The country through which it passed was devastated, and a Yankee correspondent, who accompanied the expedition, boasted that two million dollars worth of provisions and war material were destroyed in a single day. The damage to the Kanawha and James River Canal was almost irreparable; as to the railroads between Waynesboro' and Charlottesville, Charlottesville and Amherst Court-house, and Louisa Court-house, and the South Anna, and between Chesterfield Station and the Chickahominy River, every bridge, nearly every culvert, and scores of miles of the rail itself, had been completely destroyed; and in thirteen counties traversed by the expedition, mills of various kinds, tobacco warehouses, manufactured and leaf tobacco, and various other descriptions of private property were pillaged or destroyed.

THE RICHMOND LINES—HATCHER'S RUN.

On the lines around Richmond and Petersburg, during the winter of 1864–5, there were no very important events. Two very considerable engagements were fought on them in this time; but they were wholly indecisive and strangely barren of results commensurate with the scale of fighting. Pegram's division, of Lee's army, whilst reconnoitring on the morning of the 6th of February, was attacked by cavalry and infantry in heavy force. The enemy's cavalry at one time broke through one of his brigades, but the men fought them all the while. Capturing some in rear of our lines, driving the others off, the division was pressed slowly back, occupying a very long line, but fighting obstinately, under the direction of its gallant commander.

Evans, commanding Gordon's division, arrived, and was formed on the left. The two divisions now charged, and drove the enemy back. They were finally overpowered, and driven back a short distance; but reforming, charged again and again.

The battle raged fiercely for hours over a space of ground not more than five hundred yards in width. Every effort of the Yankees to break through the Confederate lines was repulsed. Mahone's division came up and reported late in the afternoon, and was formed between the other two, when the three divisions made a most spirited advance and drove the enemy in the greatest disorder from the field to his fortifications on Hatcher's Run. The pursuit was continued until after dark. General Pegram fell in the last charge, just before Mahone's division came up.

The enemy kept his position on Hatcher's Run, which prolonged his line, but did not advance it in the direction of Petersburg. The advantage of this extension was even questionable; and after this important movement quiet was resumed on the Richmond lines, unbroken by any remarkable incident for several weeks.

BATTLE OF HARE'S HILL.

At daylight, on the 25th of March, General Lee suddenly attacked Grant's lines south of the Appomattox. The attack was immediately directed by General Gordon on the enemy's works at Hare's Hill. But there is no doubt that General Lee's plan was more extensive; that his design was to follow up the first success by the capture of the neighboring works, and then making the line a part of his own, to command Grant's military railroad. If his success should be all that he hoped, he might even venture to cut Grant's entire left from its base at City Point and from the army north of the James.

About four o'clock in the morning, every thing being in readiness, the corps of sharpshooters, about two hundred and fifty strong, left our works, and, with empty guns, advanced stealthily but rapidly upon the enemy's positions. They fell like a thunder-clap upon the Yankees, behind the first line of works they struck, clubbing such as they found awake with their muskets, taking a good many prisoners, and capturing several hundred yards of breastworks. Not a musket was fired, and not a man injured on our side. Meantime the several brigades massed, both to support and assist them, came up, and the formidable force on Hare's Hill, with a considerable portion of the heavy line of works adjoining and connecting with it, were charged and captured, additional prisoners and numerous mortars and guns falling into our hands. Unfortunately some of the Yankees, who had escaped in the darkness, fled and aroused the men in the rear line of works; and the alarm was quickly spread throughout the reserve camps behind, so that a formidable force was soon alert. By the time our troops had formed into line on either side of the captured fort the enemy was thoroughly aroused, and was prepared for further offensive operations on our side; otherwise the advance of our troops would have been irresistible and successful beyond anticipation. As it was, they came into a position subject to an enfilading fire on either side, and confronted by heavy forts and breastworks. The Yankees were not slow to take advantage of the opportunity thus afforded them, and they quickly massed artillery in the neighboring forts and infantry in our front. They made several fierce assaults upon our columns in heavy lines, which were repulsed with great coolness and vigor; and in which, it is believed, the enemy sustained much loss. Finding it impossible to dislodge the Confederates by their infantry attacks, the enemy opened upon them with their artillery. A battery on the river, and Fort Steadman on the right, both so situated as thoroughly to command and enfilade the captured fort and works, belched forth their terrible discharges of shell, grape, and canister into our ranks, and rendered the position almost untenable. Further advance by our troops, in the face of the terrible obstacles that presented themselves, was deemed impracticable, and General Gordon gave the command to retire.

The success of the day was incomplete, and of but little value, although Gordon had shown the greatest gallantry, and the Confederates had fought with a vigor and brilliancy that reminded one of Lee's old campaigns. They had swept the enemy's lines for a distance of four or five hundred yards to the right and left, and two efforts made to recover the captured works had been handsomely repulsed. It was only when it was found that the inclosed works in rear, commanding the enemy's main line, could only be taken at a great sacrifice, that our troops were withdrawn to their original position.

Gordon captured nine pieces of artillery, eight mortars and between five and six hundred prisoners, amongst them one brigadier-general and a number of officers of lower grade. It being impracticable to bring off the captured guns, owing to the nature of the ground, they were disabled and left.

CHAPTER XXIV.

THE BATTLES AROUND PETERSBURG.—The movement of Sheridan's cavalry.—The Five Forks.—General Lee's counter-movement.—Repulse of Sheridan.—Re-enforced by Grant.—The Confederates flanked at the Five Forks.—The situation in front of Petersburg.—Lee's lines broken in three places.—Capture of Fort Mahone by the enemy.—General Lee loses his entire line of defence, and the Southside Railroad. —THE EVACUATION OF RICHMOND.—Great surprise in the Confederate capital.—The news in the churches.—Dr. Hoge's address.—Consternation and uproar in the streets.—The city on fire.—A reckless military order.—Scenes of horror.—Mobs of plunderers.—The scene at the commissary depot.—Weitzel's entry into Richmond. —Suffering of the people.—Scene on Capitol Square.--Devastations of the fire.— The burnt district.—Weitzel's and Shepley's general orders.—Yankee rejoicings over the fall of Richmond.—Bell-ringings, hymns, and dancing in the streets of New York.—A grand illumination in Washington.—Yankee mottoes.—A memorable speech.

GRANT was quick in retaliating for General Lee's attempt on his lines, which, as we have seen, drove the enemy at Hare's Hill, but did not hold the ground it traversed, or accomplish any decisive results.

THE BATTLES AROUND PETERSBURG.

On the 29th of March, Grant began a heavy movement towards the Southside Railroad. The cavalry command, consisting of General Crook's division and Sheridan's cavalry, moved out on the Jerusalem plankroad, about three and a half miles from Hancock Station, where they took the country road leading across the Weldon Railroad at Ream's Station, and into the Vaughn road one mile from the Dinwiddie Courthouse, General Crook's division going in advance. They reached Dinwiddie Court-house about four o'clock in the evening.

In the mean time the Fifth and Second corps of infantry had been moving in a parallel line on the Vaughn road. General Grant's headquarters on the night of the 29th were cn the Boydtown Plankroad, in the neighborhood of Gravelly Run.

The next day heavy rains impeded operations ; but the force of the enemy pressed on towards the Five Forks, the extreme right of Lee's line on the Southside Railroad.

General Lee had not been idle in meeting this movement. On the 31st of March, the enemy found on his front, prepared to contest the prize of the railroad, Pickett's division of infantry, and General Fitzhugh Lee's and General William H. Lee's divisions of cavalry. In the afternoon of the day, the Confederates made a determined and gallant charge upon the whole cavalry line of the Yankees, forced it back, and drove the enemy to a point within two miles of Dinwiddie Courthouse.

But the news of Sheridan's repulse had no sooner reached General Grant, than the Fifth Corps was moved rapidly to his relief. The re-enforcement arrived in time to retrieve the fortunes of the enemy. The next day, April 1st, the combined forces of Yankee cavalry and Warren's infantry advanced against the Confederates. Overpowered by numbers, the Confederates retreated to the Five Forks, where they were flanked by a part of the Fifth Corps, which had moved down the White Oak road. It was here that several thousand prisoners were taken.

On the night of Saturday, April 1st, the prospect was a most discouraging one for General Lee. Grant had held all his lines in front of Petersburg, had manœuvred troops far to his left, had turned Lee's right, and was now evidently prepared to strike a blow upon the thin lines in front of Petersburg.

By daylight, on Sunday, April 2d, these lines were assaulted in three different places by as many different Yankee corps. They were pierced in every place. The Sixth Corps went through first, at a point about opposite the western extremity of Petersburg; the Twenty-fourth, a little way further west ; and the Ninth Corps further east, near to the Jerusalem plankroad, capturing Fort Mahone, one of the largest forts in the Petersburg defences. The Confederates made a desperate struggle for Fort Mahone, which was protracted through the day, but

without success. At dark the position of the contending parties was the same as during the day.

The Yankees had congratulated themselves that, by the success of the Sixth Corps, they had cut Lee's army in two—cutting off the troops that were not in Petersburg. As that place
was supposed to be the Confederate point of manœuvre—as it
was supposed that troops could not cross the Appomattox except through the city—their capture was taken as certain by
the enemy, since they were hemmed in between Sheridan, the
Sixth Corps, and the river. But in this they were mistaken.
The Confederates easily forded the river; and the close of the
day found Lee's army brought together within the inner line
of the Petersburg defences.*

---

* Among the Confederate killed was the brave General A. P. Hill, whose
name had been illustriously connected with the Army of Northern Virginia
all during the war. He had desired to obtain a nearer view of a portion of the
Yankee line during the attack of the 2d of April, and leaving his staff behind
in a place of safety, rode forward, accompanied by a single orderly, and soon
came upon a squad of Yankees, who had advanced along ravines far beyond
their lines. He immediately ordered them to surrender, which they were on
the point of doing, under the supposition that a column of troops were at hi
heels. They soon discovered he was nearly unattended, and shot him through
the heart.

General Hill was a native of Culpepper County, Virginia, and descended
from an ancient family, famous in the political annals of that portion of the
commonwealth; although he himself had had nothing to do with civil or political life. He appeared to be about thirty-six or thirty-seven years of age,
and was a soldier by profession. He was graduated at West Point, entered the
army, and served in the Mexican war, and made arms not only his profession,
but an enthusiastic study, to which he was prompted by the natural tastes and
disposition of his mind.

General Hill was, undoubtedly, a commander of remarkable talents and
qualities. He had risen rapidly in the war by the force of personal merit. At
the famous field of Manassas he was colonel of the Thirteenth Virginia regiment, in General Johnston's army, which, it will be recollected, arrived on the
field in time to secure and complete the great victory of that memorable day.
At the battle of Williamsburg he had risen to the rank of brigadier-general;
and in that fight he exhibited an extraordinary spirit and energy, which were
recognized by all who observed his behavior on that field, and drew the eyes
of the public upon him.

General Hill made his greatest reputation by his conspicuous part in the
seven days' battles around Richmond, in the summer of 1862. Having then
been made major-general, he occupied, with his division, the extreme left of our
position in the neighborhood of Meadow Bridge. He was put in command of
one of the largest divisions of the Army of Richmond, his division being com

But the disasters which had already ocurred were, in General Lee's opinion, irretrievable. In killed and wounded his loss had been small—two thousand would probably cover it in the entire series of engagements ; but he had lost an entire line of defence around Petersburg, and with it the Southside Railroad, so important to Richmond as an avenue of supply

THE EVACUATION OF RICHMOND.

The morning of Sunday, the 2d of April, broke calmly and pleasantly over the city of Richmond. The usual crowds were collected at the Post-office and the War Department, asking for news, discussing common-places, and idling away the irk some hours of the Sabbath in Richmond. There was not a breath of excitement in the general community. It is a re- markable circumstance that, outside of official circles, not half a dozen persons in Richmond knew, on that Sunday morning, of the three days' fighting that had taken place around Peters- burg, and at the distance of only a few hours' ride from the capital. For months past, the Government had been reticent of all military news whatever; the newspapers had been warned not to publish any military matters, but what should be dictated to them from the War Department ; and the public was left to imagine pretty much what it pleased concerning the progress of the war. Indeed, the idea current in the streets on this Sunday morning was rather pleasant and reassuring than

---

posed of the brigades of Anderson, Branch, Pender, Gregg, Field, and perhaps some others. He rapidly brought his division to perfection in organization. It was made his duty to cross at Meadow Bridge, and make the first attack upon McClellan's forces. He performed this duty alone, without waiting for other movements ; and, unassisted by a portion of his command (for Generals Branch and Gregg did not come up until late in the evening), he sustained a terrible conflict with the enemy, encouraging his troops by examples of per- sonal audacity, which kept him constantly exposed to the enemy's fire. That position of the enemy being gained, the division of General Hill followed his subsequent movements, being placed first in the line of our advance, and bearing the brunt of the action to Frazier's farm, where occurred the memor- able engagement in which the command of General Hill, composed of his own division and one division of General Longstreet's two, fought the whole Yan- kee force, and achieved a success which broke the spirit of the enemy, and completed the circuit of our famous victories around Richmond in 1862.

otherwise; for there was a general impression that Johnston was moving to Lee's lines, and that the combined force was to take the offensive against the enemy. Beyond this general anticipation, the Richmond public had on the day referred to not the slightest inkling of the situation. The news which a few hours later was to overwhelm them, of the reverse of Lee and the forced evacuation of Richmond, was to burst upon them like a thunderclap from clear skies.

The first breath of the report was obtained in the churches. While President Davis was seated in his pew in St. Paul's church, the services were interrupted by a messenger handing him a dispatch. It was from General Lee; it stated that his lines had been broken in three places, and that preparations should be made to evacuate Richmond by eight o'clock the ensu ing night, in the event that he should be unable to re-establish his lines. The President left the church with a measured, but nervous step. It was the constrained calmness of despair. No one but himself knew the exact contents of the dispatch; but an uneasy whisper ran through the congregation, and, as they were hastily dismissed, the rumor was caught up in the streets that Richmond was to be evacuated, and was soon carried to the ends of the city.

In another of the churches, the news was more plainly told. Dr. Hoge, the beloved pastor of the Presbyterian church, than whom there was no brighter Christian or nobler patriot within the limits of Richmond, had, at the conclusion of his sermon, given out a beautiful hymn to be sung by his congregation. Before they raised their voices, he told them, with his own voice broken with emotion, that he had sad news to communicate; that our army had "met with a reverse;" that without being exactly apprised of the extent and nature of the reverse, he was convinced that it was probable that they might never again meet in that house of God; and then he spoke to those who had so long known and loved him a tender farewell, in such beautiful and plaintive words that there was not a dry eye among all those dismayed faces which hung upon his words.

Men, women, and children rushed from the churches, passing from lip to lip news of the impending fall of Richmond And yet it was difficult to believe it. To look up to the calm, beautiful sky of the spring day unassailed by one single noise of battle, to watch the streets unvexed by artillery or troops, stretching away into the quiet hazy atmosphere, and believe that the capital of the Confederacy, so peaceful, so apparently secure, was in a few hours to be the prey of the enemy, and to be wrapped in the infernal horrors of a conflagration!

It was late in the afternoon when the signs of evacuation became apparent to the incredulous. Wagons on the streets were being hastily loaded at the departments with boxes, trunks, etc., and driven to the Danville depot. Those who had determined to evacuate with the fugitive Government looked on with amazement; then, convinced of the fact, rushed to follow the Government's example. Vehicles suddenly rose to a premium value that was astounding; and ten, fifteen, and even a hundred dollars in gold or federal currency was offered for a conveyance. Suddenly, as if by magic, the streets became filled with men, walking as though for a wager, and behind them excited negroes with trunks, bundles, and luggage of every description. All over the city it was the same—wagons, trunks, bandboxes, and their owners, a mass of hurrying fugitives, filling the streets. The banks were all open, and depositors were as busy as bees removing their specie deposits; and the directors were equally active in getting off their bullion. Hundreds of thousands of dollars of paper money was destroyed, both State and Confederate. Night came, and with it came confusion worse confounded. There was no sleep for human eyes in Richmond that night.

The city council had met in the evening, and resolved to destroy all the liquor in the city, to avoid the disorder consequent on the temptation to drink at such a time. About the hour of midnight the work commenced, under the direction of committees of citizens in all the wards. Hundreds of barrels of liquor were rolled into the street and the heads knocked in. The gutters ran with a liquor freshet, and the fumes filled and impregnated the air. Fine cases of bottled liquors were tossed into the street from third story windows, and wrecked into a thousand pieces. As the work progressed, some straggling soldiers, retreating through the city, managed to get hold of a quantity of the liquor. From that moment law and order ceased to exist. Many of the stores were pillaged, and the sidewalks were encumbered with broken glass, where the thieves had smashed the windows in their reckless haste to get their hands on the plunder within. The air was filled with the wild cries of distress, or the yells of roving pillagers.

But a more terrible element was to appear upon the scene. An order had been issued from General Ewell's headquarters to fire the four principal tobacco warehouses of the city—namely, the public warehouse, situated at the head of the basin, near the Petersburg Railroad depot; Shockoe warehouse, situated near the centre of the city, side by side with the Gallego flour-mills; Mayo's warehouse, and Dibrell's warehouse, on Cary-street, a square below the Libby prison.

Late in the night, Mayor Mayo had dispatched, by a committee of citizens, a remonstrance against this reckless military order, which plainly put in jeopardy the whole business portion of Richmond. It was not heeded. Nothing was left for the citizens but to submit to the destruction of their property. The warehouses were fired. The rams in the James River were blown up. The Richmond, Virginia, and another one, were all blown to the four winds of heaven. The Patrick Henry, a receiving ship, was scuttled. Such shipping, very little in amount, as was lying at the Richmond wharves, was also fired, save the flag-of-truce steamer Allison.

The bridges leading out of the city—namely, the Danville Railroad bridge, the Petersburg Railroad bridge, Mayo's bridge, leading to Manchester and the opposite side of the James, were also fired, and were soon wrapped in flames.

Morning broke upon a scene such as those who witnessed 't can never forget. The roar of an immense conflagration sounded in the ears; tongues of flame leaped from street to street; and in this baleful glare were to be seen, as of demons, the figures of busy plunderers, moving, pushing, rioting, through the black smoke and into the open street, bearing away every conceivable sort of plunder.

The scene at the commissary depot, at the head of the dock, beggared description. Hundreds of government wagons were loaded with bacon, flour, and whiskey, and driven off in hot haste to join the retreating army. Thronged about the depot were hundreds of men, women, and children, black and white provided with capacious bags, baskets, tubs, buckets, tin pans and aprons; cursing, pushing, and crowding, awaiting the throwing open of the doors, and the order for each to help himself.

About sunrise the doors were opened to the populace, and a rush, that almost seemed to carry the building off its foundation, was made, and hundreds of thousands of pounds of bacon, flour, etc., were soon swept away by a clamorous crowd.

In the mean time, let us see what was passing on the Yankee lines. When General Ord withdrew to the lines investing Petersburg, he carried with him exactly one-half of his army. On the north side, occupying his entire line, he left Weitzel, with Kautz's division of the Twenty-fourth Corps, and Ashborne's and Thomas' divisions of the Twenty-fifth Corps.

While the fighting was in progress around Petersburg Weitzel's entire line was perfectly quiet, not a shot anywhere. His command had orders to make as great a show as possible. At night he set all his bands to work upon national airs, and the night was filled with melodious strains.

Towards midnight this musical entertainment ceased, and a silence, complete and absolute, brooded over the contending lines. At this hour, the enemy's camps were startled into life again, by explosions heard in Richmond.

To Weitzel's brain the full meaning of the event came home at once, and he did not need the confirmatory lurid light he saw hanging over the Confederate capital to tell him that the hour had come. His orders were to push on, whenever satisfied of his ability to enter the city.

Day had no sooner broke than Weitzel dispatched Major A. H. Stevens, of the Fourth Massachusetts cavalry, and Major E. E. Graves, of his staff, with forty cavalry, to investigate the condition of affairs. The troops rode steadily into Richmond. On a trot they proceeded to the Capitol, and creeping to its summit, planted the stars and stripes. The symbols of the United States thus hoisted by the halyards, consisted of two guidons from companies E and H of the Fourth Massachusetts cavalry, of which Stevens was one of the field-officers. The colors of the enemy fluttered in the early morning light over the Capitol of the Confederacy.

As the day advanced, Weitzel's troops poured through the

streets of the city. Long lines of negro cavalry swept by the Exchange Hotel, brandishing their swords and uttering savage shouts. These shouts, the roar of devouring flames, the endless processions of plunderers passing from street to street, tugging away the prizes they had drawn from the hellish circle of the fire, made up an indescribable horror. Here were the garish Yankee troops sweeping up towards the Capitol Square, with music and wild cheers; everywhere, almost, the pandemonium of fire and pillage; and in the midst of all the wild agony, the fugitive distress of women and children rushing towards the open square for a breath of pure air, all that was now left them in heaven's great hollowness. And even that was not to be obtained there. The air, even in the square of the Capitol, was almost choking; and one traversed it blinded by cinders and struggling for breath. Beneath the trees, on the sward, were piles of furniture, dragged from the ruins of burning homes; and on carpets, stretched on the slopes of the hill, were family groups, making all sorts of uncouth arrangements to protect their little ones, and to patch up, with broken tables and bureaus, some sort of home in the open air.

In the afternoon, the fire had burned itself out. It had consumed the very heart of the city. A surveyor could scarcely have designated more exactly the business portion of the city, than did the boundaries of the fire. Commencing at the Shockoe warehouse, the fire radiated front and rear, and on two wings, burning down to, but not destroying, the store No. 77 Main-street, south side, half way between Fourteenth and Fifteenth streets, and back to the river, through Cary and all the intermediate streets. Westward, on Main, the fire was stayed at Ninth-street, sweeping back to the river. On the north side of Main the flames were stayed between Thirteenth and Fourteenth streets. From this point the flames raged on the north side of Main up to Eighth-street, and back to Bank-street.

Among some of the most prominent buildings destroyed were, the Bank of Richmond, Traders' Bank, Bank of the Commonwealth, Bank of Virginia, Farmers' Bank, all the banking houses, the American Hotel, the Columbian Hotel, the Enquirer building on Twelfth-street, the Dispatch office and job rooms, corner of Thirteenth and Main-streets; all that block of buildings known as Belvin's Block; the Examiner office,

engine, and machinery rooms ; the Confederate Post-office Department building ; the State Courthouse, a fine old building
situated on Capitol Square at its Franklin-street entrance ; the
Mechanics' Institute, vacated by the Confederate War Depart
ment, and all the buildings on that square up to Eighth-stree
and back to Main-street ; the Confederate arsenal and laboratory, Seventh-street.

The streets were crowded with furniture and every description of wares, dashed down to be trampled in the mud or
burned up where it lay. All the government storehouses
were thrown open, and what could not be gotten off by the
Government was left to the people.

Next to the river the destruction of property was fearfully
complete. The Danville and Petersburg Railroad depots, and
the buildings and shedding attached, for the distance of half
a mile from the north side of Main-street to the river, and between Eighth and Fifteenth streets, embracing upwards of
twenty blocks, presented one waste of smoking ruins, blackened walls, and solitary chimneys.

On the occupation of Richmond, General Weitzel established
his headquarters in the State Capitol, in the hall lately occu
pied by the Virginia House of Delegates, and instituted meas
ures to restore order. He immediately issued the following
order :

HEADQUARTERS DETACHMENT ARMY OF THE JAMES,
Richmond, Va., April 3, 1865.

Major-General Godfrey Weitzel, commanding detachment of the Army of
the James, announces the occupation of the city of Richmond by the Armies of
the United States, under command of Lieutenant-General Grant. The people
of Richmond are assured that we come to restore to them the blessings of peace,
prosperity, and freedom, under the flag of the Union.

The citizens of Richmond are requested to remain, for the present, quietly
within their houses, and to avoid all public assemblages or meetings in the
public streets. An efficient provost-guard will immediately re-establish order
and tranquillity within the city.

Martial law is, for the present, proclaimed.

Brigadier-General George F. Shepley, United States Volunteers, is hereby
appointed military governor of Richmond.

Lieutenant-Colonel Fred. L. Manning, provost-marshal-general, Army of
the James, will act as provost-marshal of Richmond. Commanders of detach
ments doing guard-duty in the city will report to him for instructions.

By command of

MAJOR-GENERAL WEITZEL.

D. D WHEELER, Assistant Adjutant-General.

Brigadier-General G. F. Shepley, having been announced as military governor of Richmond, issued the following order:

HEADQUARTERS MILITARY GOVERNOR OF RICHMOND
Richmond, Va., April 3, 1865.

I. The armies of the rebellion having abandoned their effort to enslave the people of Virginia, have endeavored to destroy by fire the capital which they could not longer occupy by their arms. Lieutenant-Colonel Manning, provost-marshal-general of the Army of the James and provost-marshal of Richmond, will immediately send a sufficient detachment of the provost-guard to arrest, if possible, the progress of the flames. The fire department of the city of Richmond, and all the citizens interested in the preservation of their beautiful city, will immediately report to him for duty, and render every possible assistance in staying the progress of the conflagration. The first duty of the Armies of the Union will be to save the city doomed to destruction by the armies of the rebellion.

II. No person will leave the city of Richmond, without a pass from the office of the provost-marshal.

III. Any citizen, soldier, or any person whatever, who shall hereafter plunder, destroy, or remove any public or private property of any description whatever, will be arrested and summarily punished.

IV. The soldiers of the command will abstain from any offensive or insulting words or gestures towards the citizens.

V. No treasonable or offensive expressions, insulting to the flag, the cause, or the Armies of the Union, will hereafter be allowed.

VI. For an exposition of their rights, duties, and privileges, the citizens of Richmond are respectfully referred to the proclamations of the President of the United States in relation to the existing rebellion.

VII. All persons having in their possession, or under their control, any property whatever of the so-called Confederate States, or of any officer thereof, or the records or archives of any public officer whatever, will immediately report the same to Colonel Manning, provost-marshal.

In conclusion, the citizens of Richmond are assured that, with the restoration of the flag of the Union, they may expect the restoration of that peace, prosperity, and happiness which they enjoyed under the Union, of which that flag is the glorious symbol.

G. F. SHEPLEY, Brigadier-General U. S. V.,
and Military Governor of Richmond.

While the scenes of terror and destruction we have narrated were taking place in Richmond, the North was celebrating, with those fervors and shows known only to the Yankee, the fall of the Confederate capital. In New York and in Washington were the most swollen exhibitions of the popular triumph.

In the former city there was an unlimited display of flags; bells were rung; impromptu meetings were gotten up, and wild and enthusiastic congratulations were exchanged on the streets. The New York Herald said : "People fairly danced in the excess of enthusiasm. To state that they howled would sound harsh and flat, but it would nevertheless be the simple truth. Huzzaing and cheering were heard, as never they were heard before. Singing also formed part of the popula. mode of letting off the exuberant feelings of the masses. Down in Wall-street, a chorus, which Maretzek could never hope to rival, almost made the ancient piles of stone and brick tremble in sympathy."

The rage for flags was immense. Half an hour after the receipt of the news of the capture of the Confederate capital, there was, says a New York paper, not a single large flag of a national character in the whole city left unpurchased. Every housekeeper showed his loyalty and satisfaction, by exhibiting the stars and stripes from some portion of his establishment. The railway cars and horses were decorated with miniature flags. Carts, stages, and wagons, all over the city, displayed the same symbol of loyalty ; and every spot, where a piece of bunting could properly be fastened, was so decorated.

At noon, the bells of Trinity and St. Paul churches were rung. The chimes of Trinity resounded melodiously through the air, above the din of rumbling stages and heavy vehicles of every description. The example of these two churches was speedily followed by almost every church in the city ; and for half an hour or more the ringing was heard from Trinity to Harlem—a distance of six miles.

A large meeting of leading merchants, and other prominent citizens, was held at the custom-house, to make arrangements for a suitable celebration of the great victory. A number of speeches were made on the occasion. At the conclusion of one of the speeches, some persons present, with a grand chorus, began the hymn, to the tune of "Old Hundred," generally known in churches as the Doxology :

> "Praise God, from whom all blessings flow ;
> Praise Him, all creatures here below ;
> Praise Him above, ye heavenly host ;
> Praise Father, Son, and Holy Ghost."

The whole crowd joined in. The chimes of Trinity came in

at the proper time with good effect, and, as the voices of over twenty thousand singers subsided, the echoes of the chimes from the towers of Trinity came floating on the breeze, and repeating in musical accord—

" Praise Him, all creatures here below." *

---

* From the appearance of the New York papers one would suppose that the general excitement, produced by the capture of Richmond, had culminated in the commercial metropolis of the North.

The Tribune occupied one-half of its first page with an enormous spread eagle, and the eighth page with a map of Richmond. The editor, while congratulating his readers on the fall of Richmond, could not avoid saying, that "it might have been ours long ago." An Irish drinking song, prepared for the occasion, and beginning, " Bad luck to the man who is sober to-night," was published on the inside, and proposed a good health to every official who had been connected with the military department of the Government, not excepting " Shtanton."

The World's columns were chiefly occupied with a brilliant and lengthy account of the battles, but the displayed heads of the news were jubilant and expressive; and the editor declared, that " the taking of Richmond was a greater event, and more fully justified exuberant rejoicing, than any previous achievement in the history of the war."

The New York Herald declared, that the taking of Richmond was " one o the grandest triumphs that had crowned human efforts for centuries."

The following specimen of Yankee poetry on the occasion was published in a New York paper:

RICHMOND IS OURS!

Richmond is ours! Richmond is ours!
    Hark! to the jubilant chorus!
Up, through the lips that no longer repress it,
Up, from the Heart of the People! God bless it!
        Swelling with loyal emotion,
        Leapeth our joy, like an ocean!—
Richmond is ours! Richmond is ours!
Babylon falls, and her temples and towers
        Crumble to ashes before us!

Glory to Grant! Glory to Grant!
    Hark! to the shout of our Nation!
Up, from the Irish heart, up from the German—
Glory to Sheridan! Glory to Sherman!
        Up, from all peoples uniting—
        Freedom's high loyalty plighting—
Glory to all! Glory to all!—
Heroes who combat, and martyrs who fall!
        Lift we our joyous ovation!

The people of Washington vied with those of New York in demonstrations of joy over the fall of Richmond and Petersburg. In accordance with the recommendation of the Secretary of State, the Executive Mansion, the Capitol, and all the departments and other public buildings, and the City Hall, were at night illuminated, and each in a blaze of light was exhibited in its beautiful proportions. The National flag was a prominent adornment, and appropriate mottoes were conspicuously displayed. Pennsylvania Avenue and the principal streets were thronged with pedestrians. Bonfires were kindled in various parts of the city, and rockets ignited. Washington was, in short, ablaze with lights. The residences of the heads of the departments, and other officers of the Government, were also adorned and illuminated.

The Capitol made a splendid appearance. It was the centre of attraction, and from basement to dome was a blaze of light. Over the main entrance, fronting on Pennsylvania Avenue, was a large transparency, on which was inscribed, "This is the Lord's doing, and it is marvellous in our eyes."

Over the main entrance to the War Department was the motto, "The Union must and shall be preserved," and underneath an eagle, the word, "Richmond."

Over the main entrance to the Patent Office building was an immense gas-jet, displaying the word, "Union." Over the

---

Fling out the Flag! Flash out the Flag!
Up from each turret and steeple!
Up from the cottage, and over the mansion,
Fling out the symbol of Freedom's expansion!
Victory crowneth endeavor!
Liberty seals us forever!
Up from each valley, and out from each crag,
Fling out the Flag! Flash out the Flag!
Borne on the breath of the People!

Richmond is ours! Richmond is ours!
Hark! how the welkin is riven!
Hark! to the joy that our Nation convulses,
Timing all hearts to the cannon's loud pulses;
Voices of heroes ascending,
Voices of martyred ones blending:
Mingling like watchwords on Liberty's towers,
"Richmond is ours! Richmond is ours!"
Freedom rejoiceth in Heaven!

lower entrance of the Treasury building, on Fifteenth-street, was a huge transparency representing a ten-dollar Treasury note, over which was the motto, " U. S. greenbacks and U. S Grant—Grant gives the greenbacks a metallic ring."

Over the front entrance of the State Department was displayed the motto, " At home, union is order, and order is strength; abroad, union is strength, and strength is peace." Over the Fifteenth-street entrance was the following motto, " Peace and good-will to all nations; but no entangling alliances, and no foreign intervention."

Thousands of persons of both sexes attended a public meeting at the southern portico of the Patent Office, where the word " Union" was largely prominent in flaming gas-jets. Speeches were delivered by a number of persons, among them Vice-President Johnson. He made a long and intensely Union speech, in the course of which he said he could live down all the slanders which had been uttered against him. He was particularly severe on " the rebels," at the head of whom he placed Jefferson Davis, and he asked, what should be done with him. The response from many voices was, " Hang him! hang him!" To this he agreed, and applause succeeded his remark that Davis ought to be hanged twenty times higher than Haman.

The following are passages from Vice-President Johnson's speech:

" At the time that the traitors in the Senate of the United States plotted against the Government, and entered into a conspiracy more foul, more execrable, and more odious than that of Catiline against the Romans, I happened to be a member of that body. I was then and there called upon to know what I would do with such traitors, and I want to repeat my reply here. I said, if we had an Andrew Jackson, he would hang them as high as Haman. Humble as I am, when you ask me what I would do, my reply is, I would arrest them; I would try them; I would convict them; and I would hang them. I say this: ' The halter to intelligent, influential traitors.' But to the honest boy, to the deluded man, who has been deceived into the rebel ranks, I would extend leniency; I would say, return to your allegiance, renew your support to the Government, and become a good citizen; but the leaders I would hang. . . . . It is not my intention to make any imprudent remarks or allusions, but the hour will come when those nations that exhibited towards us such insolence and improper interference in the midst of our adversity, and, as they supposed, of our weakness, will learn that this is a Government of the people, possessing power enough to make itself felt and respected."

The passages of this speech, quoted above, as we must pre sume correctly, from the columns of a New York paper, ob tained a most important significance in view of the tragical death of Mr. Lincoln, on the 14th day of April, and the succes- sion of Mr. Johnson to the office of President of the United States, and that of dictator of the programme of subjugation consequent upon the war. But these events lie beyond the period and purpose of our narrative of the war, and we make only this brief and passing reference to them.

CHAPTER XXVI.

What the Confederates anticipated on the fall of Richmond.—Two opinions.—Prophetic words of the Richmond Examiner.—Disintegration of Lee's army.—The line of his retreat.—Grant's pursuit.—Sheridan captures prisoners, guns, and wagons.—Sheridan's dispatch.—Change in the movements of both armies.—The situation at Appomattox Court-house.—How Lee was surrounded.—SURRENDER OF THE ARMY OF NORTHERN VIRGINIA.—A frightful demoralization of the army.—More than two-thirds of the men deserted.—Pickett's division.—Reasons to suppose that General Lee had predetermined a surrender on moving from Richmond and Petersburg.—Straggling of his soldiers.—Official correspondence concerning the surrender.—Interview between General Lee and General Grant at McLean's house.—How General Lee looked.—Grant's generous conduct.—Scenes between the lines of the two armies.--An informal conference of officers.—How the news of surrender was received in the Yankee army.—How received at Washington.--Secretary Stanton's dispatch.—President Lincoln's speech.--" Dixie" in Washington.—General Lee's farewell address to his army.—His return to Richmond.--Effect of Lee's surrender. -General Johnston's department.—MOVEMENTS IN THE SOUTHWEST.--FALL OF MOBILE.—Wilson's cavalry expedition through Alabama and Georgia.—SURRENDER OF JOHNSTON'S ARMY.--Sherman's "basis of negotiations" repudiated at Washington.—The policy of the Northern Government unmasked.—Sherman's reply.--SURRENDER OF TAYLOR'S ARMY.—SURRENDER OF KIRBY'S SMITH'S ARMY.—" War meetings" in Texas.—\\ ant of public resolution.—The last act of the war.—A sudden peace, and what it implied.

FOR a long time there had been two opinions in the Confederacy, as to the effect the fall of Richmond would have upon the war. Many intelligent persons considered that Richmond was not a vital point in the Confederacy; and now that it had been evacuated, there were not a few persons who still indulged the hope of the supremacy of the Southern arms and the dream of independence. There were found sanguine persons in Richmond the day after the evacuation, who pleased themselves with the imagination that that event was only about to date a new era in the Confederate defence; that the Government would re-establish itself, perhaps, in Georgia, and with advantages and under auspices it had never had before; that it might reopen Georgia and the Carolinas, and thus place itself nearer its resources of subsistence, and have the control of a territory practically much larger than that in the Richmond jurisdiction. But these hopeful and ingenious persons wholly failed to take into account the moral effect of the loss of the Confederate capital, and to calculate the easy transition in such circumstances from despondency to despair.

Several weeks before the catastrophe the Richmond Examiner had used the following almost prophetic language ' " The evacuation of Richmond would be the loss of all respect and authority towards the Confederate Government, the disintegration of the army, and the abandonment of the scheme of an independent Southern Confederation. Each contestant in the war has made Richmond the central object of all its plans and all its exertions. It has become the symbol of the Confederacy. Its loss would be material ruin to the cause, and, in a moral point of view, absolutely destructive, crushing the heart and extinguishing the last hope of the country. Our armies would lose the incentive inspired by a great and worthy object of defence. Our military policy would be totally at sea ; we should be without a hope or an object ; without civil or military organization ; without a treasury or a commissariat ; without the means of keeping alive a wholesome and active public sentiment ; without any of the appliances for supporting a cause depending upon a popular faith and enthusiasm ; without the emblems or the semblance of nationality."

These sad but intelligent anticipations were now to be vividly realized. The disintegration of Lee's army commenced with its withdrawal from the Richmond and Petersburg lines.

In his last telegram to Richmond from Petersburg, Sunday evening, the 2d of April, General Lee stated that some time during the night he would fall back behind the Appomattox— that is, to the north bank of that stream, to prevent being flanked. The Appomattox rises in Appomattox County, eighty miles west of Petersburg, flows northeast to Matoax Station, on the Danville Railroad, twenty-seven miles from Richmond, and thence southeast to City Point. When Lee sent his telegram above alluded to, his troops were holding a semicircular line south of the river, and including Petersburg ; his left resting on the Appomattox, his right on the Southside Railroad, some fifteen miles west of the town. The Yankee armies were pressing his whole line, Sheridan being on his extreme right. During Sunday night he got across the Appomattox, and com menced to push up the north bank of that stream. The Yankee forces were hurried up the Southside Railroad to Burkesville Junction to cut him off. Sheridan made direct pursuit, with the double object of harassing the rear of the retreating columns, and cutting off such troops as were retreating from Richmond and attempting to join Lee.

Grant was possessed of the interior or shorter lines to Burkesville. He might thus hope to cut off Lee's retreat from Danville or from Lynchburg. Indeed, there appeared but one way for Lee to escape—namely, a tremendous run up the bank of the Appomattox, to reach the Southside Railroad at Farmville, destroying the bridges in his rear. Even this chance Sheridan was sanguine of cutting off.

On the 5th of April, Sheridan made an important capture of prisoners, guns, and wagons. It appears that Lee's army was moving as rapidly west as his limited transportation and the demoralized condition of his troops would permit, on the road between Amelia Court-house and Jetersville. The Yankee cavalry having gained possession of the Danville Railroad some time previous, were not long in discovering his whereabouts. Sheridan immediately sent Davies' brigade around on his left flank; and although they were repulsed and driven back upon the infantry, it was not until they had taken several hundred prisoners, five guns, and a number of wagons.

On the evening of the 5th of April, a portion of the advance of Grant's army was at Burkesville Station (the junction of the Southside and Danville railroads). Sheridan, with the main body of his cavalry, at three P. M. of that day, was at Jetersville, on the Danville road, a station forty-three miles from Richmond. Lee, at the same date, with the remnants of his army, was at Amelia Court-house, a point thirty-six miles from Richmond, and seven miles north of Sheridan's advance.

In this situation Sheridan telegraphed to Grant: "I feel confident of capturing the entire Army of Northern Virginia, if we exert ourselves. I see no escape for Lee."

On the 6th, at daylight, General Meade, with the Second, Fifth, and Sixth corps, was at Burkesville Station, Lee being near Amelia Court-house; the Yankee forces were south and west of him. Sheridan's advance was at Jetersville; and, as it moved towards Amelia Court-house, its left stretched well ou towards Painesville, a point about ten miles northwest of Amelia Court-house, and directly on the line of Lee's retreat towards the Appomattox.

It seemed as if Sheridan's position at Jetersville, with his left across the line of Lee's westward march to the Appomattox, would compel Lee to stand still. Hence the enemy's movement towards the Appomattox was given up, and the men were faced about and moved northeast, towards Amelia Court-house, expecting to fight Lee there. Lee, however, was already on his way from the court-house towards the river; and when this became known, the direction of the enemy's movement was changed once more.

On the evening of the 6th, two divisions of the Sixth Army Corps came up with Lee's retreating columns at the intersection of the Burkesville Station road with the road upon which they were moving. Some desultory fighting ensued. Sheridan telegraphed: " If the thing is pressed, I think Lee will surrender." He claimed already to have captured Generals Ewell, Kershaw, Button, Corse, De Bare, and Custis Lee, several thousand prisoners, fourteen pieces of artillery, with caissons, and a large number of wagons.

The position into which the remnant of Lee's army had now been forced was one from which it was impossible to extricate it without a battle, which it was no longer capable of fighting. His army lay massed a short distance west of Appomattox Court-house; his last avenue of escape towards Danville, on the southwest, was gone; he was completely hemmed in. Meade was in his rear on the east, and on his right flank north of Appomattox Court-house; Sheridan had headed him off completely, by getting between him and Lynchburg; General Ord was on the south of the court-house, near the railroad; the Yankee troops were in the most enthusiastic spirits, and what remained of the Army of Northern Virginia was plainly doomed.

SURRENDER OF THE ARMY OF NORTHERN VIRGINIA.

The line of Lee's retreat afforded ample evidence of the excessive, frightful demoralization of his army. It was strewn with arms and accoutrements, with abandoned caissons, with knapsacks, blankets, and clothing—in short, with whatever could be most readily cast away in flight. The whole intervening country was tracked by deserters returning in squads to their homes; and who, anticipating a surrender of the army, were anxious to avoid what they supposed would be the conditions of such an event. The extent of this desertion was without precedent. Lee's whole army had almost ran through his fingers. He had had on the lines he had abandoned between twenty-seven and twenty-eight thousand men; at Appomattox Court-house he had scarcely ten thousand men for a battle, and actually surrendered less than eight thousand.* On the Petersburg lines Pickett's division had been roughly estimated at eight thousand men. It surrendered only forty-five muskets. Such were the moral effects of the fall of Richmond, and such the necessities which brought with it the terrible consequence of the surrender of what had been by far the most formidable army the Confederates had ever had in the field.

There can be no doubt in history that General Lee, in taking his army away from Richmond and Petersburg, had decided, in his own mind, upon the hopelessness of the war, and had predetermined its surrender. The most striking proof of this is, that on his retreat there was no order published against straggling—a thing unprecedented in all deliberate and strategic retreats—and nothing whatever done to maintain discipline. The men were not animated by the style of general orders usual on such occasions. They straggled and deserted almost at will. An idea ran through the Virginia troops that with the abandonment of Richmond the war was hopeless, and that they would be justified in refusing to fight outside the limits of their State. Nothing was done to check the notorious

---

* The looseness of historical statement in the North with reference to the war is very remarkable. We must expect exaggeration and brag in Yankee newspapers; but in the magazine, pamphlet, report, and those deliberate forms of literature, which stand between the daily paper and the bound volume, some effort at accuracy of statement is to be expected. Yet we see in the columns of a popular Northern magazine that Lee surrendered at Appomattox Court house *fifty thousand men!* And this absurd statement is quite as likely to go into Yankee history as any other absurd piece of statistics about the extent and glory of Yankee conquests.

circulation of this notion in the army. The Virginia troops scattered off to their homes at almost every mile of the route. We have seen that Pickett was left with only a handful or men. Some of the brigade commanders had not hesitated to advise their men that the war was virtually over, and that they had better go home and " make crops."

But there are other proofs, besides the omission of the measures against straggling usual on retreats, that General Lee had prevised a surrender of his army. He carried off from Petersburg and Richmond all the transportation of his army, sufficient, perhaps, for one hundred thousand men, certainly largely in excess of the actual needs of the retreat. The ex cessive number of Virginia troops who were permitted to drop out of the ranks and return to their homes, shows very well that there was no firm purpose to carry the war out of the limits of that State. Prisoners taken on the retreat invariably reported that the army was soon to be halted for a surrender ; and General Custis Lee, when captured by the enemy, is alleged to have made the same revelation of his father's designs.

While the pursuit of Lee's army by Grant's overwhelming forces was still in progress, the following correspondence ensued between the two commanders :

I.

APRIL 7, 1865.

GENERAL R. E. LEE, *Commanding C. S. A.:*

GENERAL—The result of the last week must convince you of the hopelessness of further resistance on the part of the Army of Northern Virginia in this struggle. I feel that it is so, and regard it as my duty to shift from myself the responsibility of any further effusion of blood, by asking of you the surrender of that portion of the Confederate Southern army, known as the Army of Northern Virginia.

Very respectfully,

Your obedient servant,

U. S. GRANT,

Lieut.-Gen. commanding Armies of the United States

II.

APRIL 7, 1865.

GENERAL—I have received your note of this day. Though not entirely of the opinion you express of the hopelessness of further resistance on the part of the Army of Northern Virginia, I reciprocate your desire to avoid useless effusion of blood, and therefore, before considering your proposition, ask the terms you will offer on condition of its surrender.

R. E. LEE, General.

To LIEUTENANT-GENERAL U. S. GRANT,
  Commanding Armies of the United States.

III.

APRIL 8, 1865.

To GENERAL R. E. LEE, *Commanding C. S. A.:*

GENERAL—Your note of last evening, in reply to mine of the same date, asking the conditions on which I will accept the surrender of the Army of Northern Virginia is just received.

In reply, I would say, that peace being my first desire, there is but one condition that I insist upon, viz.:

That the men surrendered shall be disqualified for taking up arms again against the Government of the United States until properly exchanged.

I will meet you, or designate officers to meet any officers you may name for the same purpose, at any point agreeable to you, for the purpose of arranging definitely the terms upon which the surrender of the Army of Northern Virginia will be received.

  Very respectfully,
    Your obedient servant,
      U. S. GRANT, Lieutenant-General,
        Commanding Armies of the United States.

IV.

APRIL 8, 1865.

GENERAL—I received, at a late hour, your note of to-day in answer to mine of yesterday.

I did not intend to propose the surrender of the Army of Northern Virginia, but to ask the terms of your proposition

To be frank, I do not think the emergency has arisen to ca.l for the surrender.

But as the restoration of peace should be the sole object of all, I desire to know whether your proposals would tend to that end.

I cannot, therefore, meet you with a view to surrender the Army of Northern Virginia ; but so far as your proposition may affect the Confederate States forces under my command and tend to the restoration of peace, I should be pleased to meet you at ten A. M. to-morrow, on the old stage-road to Richmond, between the picket-lines of the two armies.

Very respectfully,
Your obedient servant,
R. E. LEE, General C. S. A

To LIEUTENANT-GENERAL GRANT,
    Commanding Armies of the United States.

v.

APRIL 9, 1865.

GENERAL R. E. LEE, *Commanding C. S. A.:*

GENERAL—Your note of yesterday is received. As I have no authority to treat on the subject of peace, the meeting pro posed for ten A. M. to-day could lead to no good. I will state, however, General, that I am equally anxious for peace with yourself; and the whole North entertain the same feeling. The terms upon which peace can be had are well understood. By the South laying down their arms they will hasten that most desirable event, save thousands of human lives, and hundreds of millions of property not yet destroyed.

Sincerely hoping that all our difficulties may be settled without the loss of another life, I subscribe myself,

Very respectfully,
Your obedient servant,
U. S. GRANT,
Lieutenant-General United States Army

VI.

APRIL 9, 1865.

GENERAL—I received your note of this morning on the picket-line, whither I had come to meet you and ascertain definitely what terms were embraced in your proposition of yesterday with reference to the surrender of this army.

I now request an interview in accordance with the offer contained in your letter of yesterday for that purpose.

Very respectfully,
Your obedient servant,
R. E. LEE, General.

To LIEUTENANT-GENERAL GRANT,
Commanding Armies of the United States.

VII.

APRIL 9, 1865.

GENERAL R. E. LEE, *Commanding C. S. A.:*

Your note of this date is but this moment, 11.50 A. M., received.

In consequence of my having passed from the Richmond and Lynchburg road to the Farmville and Lynchburg road, I am, at this writing, about four miles west of Walter's Church, and will push forward to the front for the purpose of meeting you.

Notice sent to me on this road where you wish the interview to take place, will meet me.

Very respectfully, your obedient servant,
U. S. GRANT, Lieutenant-General.

VIII.

APPOMATTOX COURT-HOUSE, April 9, 1865

GENERAL R. E. LEE, *Commanding C. S. A.:*

In accordance with the substance of my letter to you of the 8th inst., I propose to receive the surrender of the Army of Northern Virginia on the following terms, to wit:

Rolls of all the officers and men to be made in duplicate, one copy to be given to an officer designated by me, the other to be retained by such officers as you may designate.

The officers to give their individual parole not to take arms against the Government of the United States until properly exchanged; and each company or regimental commander to sign a like parole for the men of their commands.

The arms, artillery, and public property to be parked and stacked, and turned over to the officers appointed by me to receive them.

This will not embrace the side-arms of the officers, nor their private horses or baggage.

This done, each officer and man will be allowed to return to their homes, not to be disturbed by United States authority so long as they observe their parole and the laws in force where they may reside.

Very respectfully,

U. S. GRANT, Lieutenant-General.

IX.

HEADQUARTERS ARMY OF NORTHERN VIRGINIA, April 9, 1865.

LIEUT.-GENERAL U. S. GRANT, *Commanding U. S. A.:*

GENERAL—I have received your letter of this date, containing the terms of surrender of the Army of Northern Virginia, as proposed by you. As they are substantially the same as those expressed in your letter of the 8th inst., they are accepted. I will proceed to designate the proper officers to carry the stipulations into effect.

Very respectfully, your obedient servant,

R. E. LEE, General.

Thus in two days time, and by means of nine short letters, was accomplished the decisive event of the war, and what in fact was to prove its complete conclusion.

General Lee and General Grant had met at the house of Mr. Wilmer McLean. The interview was very simple, and unattended by any ceremony. General Lee was attended only by Colonel Marshal, one of his aids, while with Grant there were several of his staff-officers; and a number of Yankee generals entered the room during the interview. The two commanders greeted each other with courtesy, and without idle words or dramatic flourishes proceeded at once and simply to business.

General Lee immediately alluded to the conditions of the surrender, characterized them as lenient, and said he would leave the details to General Grant's own discretion. General Grant stated the terms of the parole; that the arms should be stacked, the artillery parked, and the supplies and munitions turned over to him, the officers retaining their side-arms,

horses, and personal effects. General Lee promptly assented
to the conditions, and the agreement of surrender was engrossed
and signed by General Lee at half-past three o'clock in the
afternoon.

A Yankee correspondent thus described the appearance of
General Lee in this memorable interview: "General Lee
looked very much jaded and worn, but, nevertheless, presented
the same magnificent *physique* for which he has always been
noted. He was neatly dressed in gray cloth, without em-
broidery or any insignia of rank, except three stars worn on
the turned portion of his coat-collar. His cheeks were very
much bronzed by exposure, but still shone ruddy underneath
it all. He is growing quite bald, and wears one of the side
locks of his hair thrown across the upper portion of his forehead, which is as white and fair as a woman's. He stands
fully six feet one inch in height, and weighs something over
two hundred pounds, without being burdened with a pound of
superfluous flesh. During the whole interview he was retired
and dignified to a degree bordering on taciturnity, but was
free from all exhibition of temper or mortification. His demeanor was that of a thoroughly possessed gentleman who
had a very disagreeable duty to perform, but was determined
to get through it as well and as soon as he could."

It is to be fairly and cheerfully admitted that General
Grant's conduct, with respect to all the circumstances of the
surrender, exhibited some extraordinary traits of magnanimity.
He had not dramatized the affair. He had conducted it
with as much simplicity as possible, avoided "sensation," and
spared every thing that might wound the feelings or imply
the humiliation of a vanquished foe. Such conduct was
noble. Before the surrender, General Grant had expressed to
his own officers his intention not to require the same formalities as are required in a surrender between the forces of
two foreign nations or belligerent powers, and to exact no
conditions for the mere purpose of humiliation.

While the interview with reference to the surrender was
taking place between the commanders, a strange scene was
transpiring between the lines of the two armies, and occupied
the period of the armistice. An informal conference and
mingling of officers of both armies gave to the streets of the

village of Appomattox Court-house a strange appearance. On the Yankee side were Generals Ord, Sheridan, Crook, Gibbon, Griffin, Merritt, Ayres, Bartlett, Chamberlain, Forsyth, and Michie. On the Confederate side were Generals Longstreet, Gordon, Heth, Wilcox, and others. The conference lasted some hour and a half. None but general officers were allowed to pass through the skirmish line. There were mutual introductions and shaking of hands ; and soon was passed about some whiskey, and mutual healths were drank. Gradually the area of the conference widened. The parties filled the streets, and before this singular conference closed, some were seated on the steps, and others, for lack of more comfortable accommodations, chatted cosily, seated on a contiguous fence.

Between the skirmish lines of the two armies there was a great suspense, for it was felt that great interests were at stake between them. Skirmish line confronted skirmish line, lines of battle confronted lines of battle, cannon confronted cannon. Eager hopes hung on the interview between the opposing great commanders of the two armies. Peace might follow this interview. It might end in resumption of hostilities, in fiercest battle, in terrible carnage. The two armies were plainly visible to one another. The Confederates skirted a strip of wood in rear of the town. Through the vistas of the streets might be seen their wagon-trains. The minutes passed but slowly. The approach of every horseman attracted an eager look. Two o'clock had been appointed by Grant for the resumption of hostilities. It arrived, and the Yankee skirmish line commenced to advance. The Confederate pickets were in plain sight, and stationary. A moment more, and the crack of the rifle would indicate the resumption of carnage. But a clatter of hoofs is heard, and a flag of truce appears upon the scene, with an order from General Grant that hostilities should cease until further orders.

After the interview at McLean's house, General Lee returned to his own camp, about half a mile distant, where his leading officers were assembled awaiting his return. He announced the result, and the terms. They then approached him in order of rank, shook hands, expressing satisfaction at his course and their regret at parting, all shedding tears on the occasion. The fact of surrender and the terms were then announced to the troops and when General Lee appeared among them he was loudly cheered.

At four o'clock it was announced in Grant's army that the surrender had been consummated, and the articles signed. And now the enthusiasm which had been restrained by uncertainty broke loose. The various brigade commanders announced the joyful news to their commands, and cheers of the wildest description followed. The men threw their hats high in the air, leaped, ran, jumped, threw themselves into each other's arms, and seemed mad with joy.

But this scene of joy was but slight in comparison with what was taking place in distant parts of the North, where the news of the surrender had been carried by the telegraph. Secretary Stanton, in Washington, immediately telegraphed an order to the headquarters of every army and department, and to every fort and arsenal in the United States, to fire a salute of two hundred guns in celebration of the event. To Grant he dispatched: "Thanks be to Almighty God for the great victory with which He has this day crowned you and the gallant armies under your command. The thanks of this department, and of the Government, and of the people of the United States —their reverence and honor have been deserved—will be rendered to you and the brave and gallant officers and soldiers of your army for all time."

The clerks of the departments, in Washington, went in procession to the President's house, and entertained him with the "Star Spangled Banner" and "Old Hundred." A crowd of several thousands were soon assembled in front of the executive mansion. They shouted for Mr. Lincoln. The President testified his participation in the joy by calling for the once popular *secession* song of "Dixie." He said: "I have always thought that 'Dixie' was one of the best songs I ever heard. Our adversaries over the way, I know, have attempted to appropriate it; but I insist that on yesterday we fairly captured it. I referred the question to the attorney-general, and he gave it as his legal opinion that it is now our property. (Laughter and loud applause.) I now ask the band to give us a good turn upon it."

The day after the surrender General Lee bid farewell to his army in the following simple address, so characteristic of his plain and manly style of writing:

GENERAL ORDER NO. 9.

HEADQUARTERS ARMY NORTHERN VIRGINIA,
April 10, 1865.

After four years of arduous service, marked by unsurpassed courage and fortitude, the Army of Northern Virginia has been compelled to yield to overwhelming numbers and resources.

I need not tell the survivors of so many hard-fought battles, who have remained steadfast to the last, that I have consented to this result from no distrust of them; but feeling that valor and devotion could accomplish nothing that could compensate for the loss that would have attended the continuation of the contest, I have determined to avoid the useless sacrifice of those whose past services have endeared them to their countrymen.

By the terms of agreement, officers and men can return to their homes and remain there until exchanged.

You will take with you the satisfaction that proceeds from the consciousness of duty faithfully performed; and I earnestly pray that a merciful God will extend to you his blessing and protection.

With an unceasing admiration of your constancy and devotion to your country, and a grateful remembrance of your kind and generous consideration of myself, I bid you an affectionate farewell.

R. E. LEE, General.

A few days after the surrender, General Lee, attended by five members of his staff, rode into Richmond over the pontoon bridge at the foot of Seventeenth-street, and thence up Main street to his residence on Franklin-street between Seventh and Eighth streets.

Passing rapidly through the city he was recognized by but few citizens, who raised their hats, a compliment which was in every case returned; but on nearing his residence, the fact of his presence having spread quickly, a great crowd rushed to see him, and set up a loud cheering, to which he replied by simply raising his hat. As he descended from his horse, a large number of persons pressed forward and shook hands with him. In a few moments the General made his way into his house, the crowd dispersed, and thus quietly passed from the theatre of action and public observation the great and famous commander of the Army of Northern Virginia.

The surrender of General Lee drew after it important and rapid consequences, and, in effect, terminated the war.

It left Johnston with no alternative but surrender. On the 26th of April, by the official returns of the Army of Tennessee,

the number of infantry and artillery, present and absent, was
seventy thousand five hundred and ten; the total present,
eighteen thousand five hundred and seventy-eight; the effective fighting force, fourteen thousand one hundred and
seventy-nine. The effective total of the cavalry was only a
a little over five thousand. These statistics afford a startling
exhibition of the demoralization of the Confederates, and or
the amount of that offence in our armies mildly called "absenteeism;" but for which, in military language, there could
be no name but desertion.

The limits of Johnston's command included North and South
Carolina, Georgia, and Florida. In the distant districts of his
department the situation was even more deplorable and desperate than in the vicinity of Raleigh. In South Carolina the
Confederates had only a division of cavalry, less than one
thousand, and in Florida they were as weak.

In General Dick Taylor's department there had been disastrous events. Mobile had fallen, and there were no means of
opposing the formidable Yankee army under General Canby.

MOVEMENTS IN THE SOUTHWEST.—FALL OF MOBILE, ETC.

The operations against this city had been renewed late in
March, when two corps of Canby's army invested the Spanish
Fort, one of the principal defences on the east side of the bay.
The design of this renewal of operations against Mobile was to
give the crowning stroke to the system of Confederate defence
in the Southwest. After Hood's defeat before Nashville, General Thomas indicated to the Washington authorities that he
would not, on account of the state of the roads and for other
reasons, be able to enter immediately upon another campaign.
But he offered to co-operate with General Canby by sending
to the latter one-half of his infantry force, and almost all his
cavalry, the former under the command of General A. J.
Smith, the latter under General Wilson.

In addition to these movements, another column of Yankee
troops under Steele had left Pensacola, Florida, on the 20th of
March, arrived in front of Mobile, and opened communication
with General Canby's force. On his march General Steele had

considerable skirmishing, but met with no serious opposition His command arrived on the 22d of April, having cut the Mobile and Montgomery Railroad near Pollard.

On the 8th of April, an extraordinary force was brought to bear upon Spanish Fort. Twenty-two Parrott guns were got within half a mile of the work, while other powerful batteries were still nearer. Two gunboats joined in the tremendous cannonade. The result was, that the fort surrendered a little after midnight. Fort Alexandria followed, and the guns of these two were turned against Forts Tracy and Huger, in the harbor, at the mouth of the Blakely and Appalachee rivers. But these had already been abandoned. The monitors then went busily to work removing torpedoes, and ran up to within shelling distance of the city. On the 12th of April the city of Mobile was occupied by the Yankee forces, General Maury, the Confederate commander, having evacuated the city with the bulk of his army.

In the mean time Wilson's movements were completing the plan of subjugation in the Southwest. His cavalry force had moved almost unresisted through the Southwest, captured Selma, in Alabama, were already in the vicinity of Macon Georgia, and might easily calculate upon the capture of every place of importance west of Augusta.

Selma was occupied by the Yankee forces on the 2d of April. The first resistance met by the enemy's forces was at Monticello, where, after a short engagement, they continued to advance. On the 1st of April, Forrest, Lyon, and Chalmers having formed a junction, the first named took command, and the Confederates again made a stand, and were driven back with loss. They then retreated to Selma, where an obstinate defence was prepared for. On the next day, the 2d of April, Wilson moved to the attack of the place, and after about an hour of severe fighting, the fortifications were carried by assault, and his troops entered the town, capturing over two thousand prisoners, one hundred cannon, large numbers of horses and mules, and immense quantities of supplies, ammunition, etc. Besides these, there fell into the enemy's possession millions of dollars worth of cotton, a large arsenal, naval iron-works and other manufactories, all of which were destroyed.

M ntgomery, the first Confederate capital, was peaceably surrendered on the 12th. Columbus, Georgia, was captured on the 16th. Macon was approached on the 21st. Here Wil son was met by a flag of truce from Howell Cobb, announcing an armistice between Sherman and Johnston.

The survey of the situation south of Virginia leads to the conclusion that to carry on the war east of the Mississippi the Confederacy had to depend on Johnston's army alone. The enemy could have brought against it twelve or fifteen times its number in the armies of Generals Grant, Sherman, and Canby. With such odds against us, without the means of procuring ammunition or repairing arms, without money or credit to provide food, it was thought by Johnston impossible to continue the war with any reasonable hope of success.

SURRENDER OF JOHNSTON'S ARMY.

This conclusion the Confederate commander announced to the governors of the States within his department by telegraph as follows :

"The disaster in Virginia, the capture by the enemy of all our workshops for the preparation of ammunition and repairing of arms, the impossibility or recruiting our little army, opposed to more than ten times its number, or supplying it except by robbing our own citizens, destroyed all hope of successful war. I have, therefore, made a military convention with Major-General Sherman to terminate hostilities in North and South Carolina, Georgia, and Florida. I made this convention to spare the blood of this gallant little army, to prevent further suffering of our people by the devastation and ruin inevitable from the marches of invading armies, and to avoid the crime of waging a hopeless war."

Johnston had at first made an attempt to obtain terms to give security to citizens as well as to his own soldiers. The first result of his negotiations with Sherman was a basis of agreement, which that Yankee commander declared in a circular address was to secure instant peace in all parts of the country, and would involve the surrender of every battalion of Confederates within the limits of the United States. The following is a copy of the important paper signed by the com manders of the two armies :

MEMORANDUM, OR BASIS OF AGREEMENT, made this eighteenth day of April A. D., 1865, near Durham Station, in the State of North Carolina, by and between General Joseph E. Johnston, commanding Confederate Army, and Major-General W. T. Sherman, commanding Army of the United States, in North Carolina, both being present:

1. The contending armies now in the field to maintain the *status quo*, until notice is given by the commanding general of any one to its opponent, and reasonable time, say forty-eight hours, allowed.

2. The Confederate armies now in existence to be disbanded, and conducted to their several state capitals, therein to deposit their arms and public property in the state arsenal, and each officer and man to execute and file an agreement to cease from acts of war, and to abide the action of both State and Federal authorities. The number of arms and munitions of war to be reported to the chief of ordnance at Washington City, subject to the future action of the Congress of the United States, and in the mean time to be used solely to maintain peace and order within the borders of the States respectively.

3. The recognition by the Executive of the United States of the several State governments, on their officers and legislatures taking the oath prescribed by the constitution of the United States ; and where conflicting State governments have resulted from the war, the legitimacy of all shall be submitted to the Supreme Court of the United States.

4. The re-establishment of all federal courts in the several States, with powers as defined by the constitution and laws of Congress.

5. The people and inhabitants of all these States to be guaranteed, so far as the Executive can, their political rights and franchises, as well as their rights of person and property, as defined by the constitution of the United States and of the States respectively.

6. The executive authority of the Government of the United States not to disturb any of the people by reason of the late war, so long as they live in peace and quiet and abstain from acts of armed hostility, and obey the laws in existence at the place of their residence.

7. In general terms, the war to cease—a general amnesty, so far as the Executive of the United States can command, on the condition of the disbandment of the Confederate armies, distribution of the arms, and the resumption of peaceable pursuits by the officers and men hitherto composing said armies.

Not being duly empowered by our respective principals to fulfil these terms, we individually and officially pledge ourselves to promptly obtain an answer thereto, and to carry out the above programme.

> W. T. SHERMAN, Major-General,
>> Commanding Army U. S. in N. C.
> J. E. JOHNSTON, General,
>> Commanding C. S. A. in N. C.

Sherman's vivid vision of restoring " peace to the banks of the Rio Grande" did not take at Washington. The announcement there of the nature and terms of his conference with Johnston was the signal for the outpouring of such censure and denunciation as required all his military reputation to withstand. In fact, Sherman had committed the unpardonable offence of attempting to substitute for the idea of subjugation that of a restored Union ; and it was easy enough now to see that the profession of the latter purpose had all along been nothing more than the mask of the real designs of the Washington Government, which would be content with nothing short of the abolition of slavery in the South, the extinction of the State governments, or their reduction to provisional establishments, and the programme of a general confiscation of property. The President rejected Sherman's terms; the department disallowed them, and General Grant, although a warm personal friend of Sherman, disapproved them.

It was fiercely argued by the Washington authorities that the terms proposed by Sherman would bring the war to naught; that if the State governments were re-established in the South, they might re-enact slavery, and set up a power in defiance of the General Government; and that it was the madness of generosity to abolish the confiscation laws, and relieve "rebels" from all pains and penalties for their crimes.

General Sherman replied to the censures uttered or instigated at Washington, by including in the official report of his campaign an elaborate justification of his course in entering upon the convention with Johnston which was disavowed by the Government. The substance of his defence was, that General Johnston wished, in addition to the terms granted to General Lee, some general concessions that would enable him to control his followers until they could be got back to the neighborhood of their homes, thereby saving North Carolina from the devastation which would result from turning the men loose and unprovided for, and by the pursuit of these scattered bodies through the State. All of Sherman's generals were in favor of his granting, as far as lay in his power, such concessions. At the next meeting Sherman stated that Johnston satisfied him that he had power to disband all the Confederate armies, as well as those under his own immediate command. What the Confederate commander especially dreaded was, that the States would be dismembered and deprived of any political existence, and that the absolute disarming of his men would leave the South powerless and exposed to the depredations of assassins and robbers. " In any case," concluded Sherman,

" the memorandum was a mere basis for reference to the President, to enable him, if he chose, at one blow to dissipate the power of the Confederacy, which had threatened the national safety for years. It admitted of modification, alteration, and change. It had no appearance of an ultimatum, and by no false reasoning can it be construed into a usurpation of powers on my part."

The dissatisfaction at Washington with Sherman's conduct was so extreme, that Grant was ordered to proceed at once to North Carolina, to take control of Sherman's army, and to force Johnston to an immediate and unconditional surrender. In this instance, Grant again showed that magnanimity which seems to have been largely developed in the hours of his triumph, and in the last scenes of the war—at a time, indeed, when the true character of the popular hero is most surely tested. In the most fortunate period of the life of any living man in America, Grant was not intoxicated by vanity or conceit. He was incapable of an attempt upon the reputation of a rival. He went to North Carolina, but he kept the operations in the hands of Sherman. He insisted upon giving him the honor of concluding the final negotiations with Johnston and receiving his surrender. It was concluded on the same terms as had been conceded to General Lee.

SURRENDER OF TAYLOR'S ARMY.

On the 4th of May, General Dick Taylor surrendered to General Canby all " the forces, munitions of war, etc., in the Department of Alabama, Mississippi, and East Louisiana." The negotiations for this surrender took place at Citronville, Alabama. The terms were essentially the same as those accorded to Johnston: officers and men to be paroled until duly exchanged or otherwise released by the United States; officers to give their individual paroles; commanders of regiments and companies to sign paroles for their men; arms and munitions to be given up to the United States; officers and men to be allowed to return to their homes, and not to be molested so long as they kept their paroles, and obeyed the laws where they reside, but persons resident in Northern States not to return without permission; officers to be allowed to retain their side arms, private horses, and baggage; horses, the private property of enlisted men, not to be taken from them, but they to be allowed to retain them for private purposes only. This surrender virtually involved that of the Confederate vessels blockaded in the Tombigbee River.

SURRENDER OF KIRBY SMITH'S ARMY.

In the first days of May, 1865, all the Confederate forces east of the Mississippi River had been surrendered. But west of that stream, in Western Louisiana and Texas, there remained a considerable force of Confederates, under command of General E. Kirby Smith. There was yet a prospect that the war might be continued there for some indefinite period. The country was ill adapted for the advance of an invading army. The fortune of the Confederate arms in the Trans-Mississippi had been superior, in the average of successes, to that east or the river; because there our forces, not tied down to any particular cities or forts, or any particular line of defence—which indeed had been the cardinal error in the general system of the Confederate warfare—had fought as opportunity occurred, and generally on ground of their own selection.

When the news of Lee's surrender first reached Kirby Smith, he issued, from his headquarters at Shreveport, a stirring general order to his troops. He reminded them that they had the means of long resisting invasion; he declared that they had hopes of succor from abroad; he promised them that if they protracted the struggle, they would surely receive the aid of nations who already deeply sympathized with them. He said :

"The great resources of the department, its vast extent, the numbers, discipline, and the efficiency of the army, will secure to our country terms that a proud people can with honor accept, and may, under the providence of God, be the means of checking the triumph of our enemy, and securing the final success of our cause."

War meetings were held in different parts of Texas. At Houston, General Magruder addressed the citizens ; he declared that he was not at all discouraged by the position of affairs; and he ended by protesting that he had rather be a " Camanche Indian" than bow the knee to the Yankees. In Washington County, the citizens submitted to the military authorities a proposition that every white male over the age of thirteen years should be called into the army; that every male slave should be brought in with his master; and that every white female should be provided with arms. Resolutions and plans of this sort were rife for some weeks in Texas.

But these were but spasmodic expressions of the public mind in the first moments of disappointment and rage; they lacked resolution and steadiness. When Kirby Smith published his address at Shreveport, the extent of the disasters east of the Mississippi River was not fully known. When it was fully known, a demoralization, which it was impossible to check, quickly ensued in Smith's army, and involved most of the people of Texas. His force was daily wasting away by desertions, and it had received but few accessions from across the Mississippi. On the 23d of May, he sent officers to General Canby, at Baton Rouge, to negotiate terms of surrender. These were agreed upon on the 26th of May, and were such as had been conceded to the other Confederate forces.*

With this act there passed from the great stage of the war the last armed Confederate. The last action of the war had been a skirmish near Brazos, in Texas. Peace now reigned from the Potomac to Rio Grande.

Contrary to the plausible expectations of those who supposed that if the war went adverse to the South, it would drag out its last terms in irregular fighting in mountain warfare, and such desultory contests, complete and profound peace fell

---

* On the 1st of June, General Brown, commanding the Yankee forces, occupied and garrisoned Brownsville. On the 2d of June, Generals Kirby Smith and Magruder met, in the harbor of Galveston, General A. J. Smith, representing Major-General Canby, and General Kirby Smith then and there signed the terms of surrender previously agreed on at New Orleans. On the 5th of June, full and formal possession of Galveston was delivered up to the Yankee forces, and the flag of the Union raised. On the 8th of June, Admiral Thatcher went ashore, and was received by the Confederate naval and military authorities, who requested a part of the United States naval force to remain there for their protection. General Sheridan was subsequently assigned to command in Texas, and the blockade of Galveston raised.

upon the Confederacy as the calm after the hurricane. "Surrender" was the word, as the news of Lee's disaster travelled from point to point, from camp to camp, in the Confederacy. The quick succession of these surrenders—the suddenness and completeness of the catastrophe—show plainly enough that there was a widely spread rottenness in the affairs of the Confederacy, and that its cause went down in a general demoralization of the arm" and people.

APPENDIX.

APPENDIX No. I.

AMERICAN IDEAS: THE KEYS TO THE HISTORY OF THE WAR.

I.

Political Iconoclasm in America.—The two idols of "the Constitution" and "the Union."—Extravagant praises of the Constitution.—Its true value.—It contained a noble principle and glaring defects.—Character of the founders of the Constitution. —Hamilton.—Franklin.—His cookery-book philosophy.—His absurdities in the Convention.—The call for the Convention that formed the Constitution.—Three parties in the Convention.—The idea of a "national" government.—Conflict between the small and large States.—The result of this, the distinguishing feature of the Constitution.—That feature an accident, and not an *a priori* discovery.—Enumeration of defects in the Constitution.—The weakness and ignorance of its framers. —Its one conspicuous virtue and original principle.—Combination of State-rights with a common authority.—How involved in the construction of the Senate.—How made more precise in the Amendments.—Particulars in which the element of *the States* was recognized.—A new rule of construction applied to the American Union. —The necessity which originated it.—The Constitution of the United States not a political revolution.—The creature of the States.—True interpretation of its moral grandeur.—The bond of the Union a voluntary one.—No mission apart from the States.—Why coercion of the States was not necessary.—How the Union stood for an American nationality.—Its power to reach *individuals*.—The Union, in practice, rather a rough companionship than a national identity.—Right of secession.—Not necessary to discuss it.—The development of the Union a North and South, and not disintegrated States.—Profound invention of Calhoun of South Carolina.—How it was a Union measure, and not " Nullification."

An effect of great civil commotions in the history of a people is to liberate reason, and to give to intelligence the opportunity to assert itself against the traditions and political idolatries of the past. Such a period is essentially one of political iconoclasm—the breaking of idols which we find we have heretofore unduly cherished, and with it the recovery from the delusions of an unworthy and traditional worship. When there is little in the present to interest men, and their lives are passed in an established routine, it is natural for them to exaggerate and to adorn the past. But when the present has its own historical convulsion, it is then that men find new standards with which to judge the past, and a period in which rightly to estimate it,—destroying or dwarfing, it is true, much that before claimed their admiration or enchained their worship; but, on the other hand, ofttimes exalting what before had had an obscure and degraded place in popular estimation. It is in such periods that the native historian of his country finds the justest time for determining the correct value of the past, and distinguishing between what were its mere idols, and what should have been its true aspirations.

It is thus, from the stand-point of the recent great war in America, that one may justly contemplate the true value of its past history, measure correctly its great men of a former period, and master the delusions of an old political idolatry. The world knows how before this war the people of North America had, for nearly three-quarters of a century, worshipped, as its two political idols, the Federal constitution and the Union of States formed under it. Looking back at these from the present period in American history, which has freed us from the restraints of mere sentiment and tradition, he who thus makes the calm and intelligent retrospect is astonished to find what extravagance and delusion were in the minds of these worshippers, and what acts of devotion were made to what were ofttimes but gilded images of clay.

For two generations of men, the almost miraculous wisdom of the Federal constitution of America has been preached and exclaimed, until it was thought to be political blasphemy to impugn it. Its praises were hymned by poets. The public orator was listened to with impatience who had not some exaggerated tribute to pay to the sacred virtues of what Daniel Webster called the consti-*tew*-tion, and the almost angelic excellence of "the forefathers" who had framed it. It was seriously asserted, that in this instrument had been combined the political wisdom of all ages, and that it was the epitome of the human science of government. The insolent heights to which this extravagance arose were astounding. The world's last hopes of good government were said to be contained in these dozen pages of printed matter.

Unhappily for such hopes, or for such boasts, we are now at a period when we may estimate the right value of this wonderful constitution, and take the severe judgment of history upon it. We may now dare to state that judgment briefly: it is, that never did a political instrument contain, from the necessity of its circumstances, a nobler principle, or present the folly and ignorance of men in more glaring defects, than did the Federal constitution of the United States.

It is no longer required, by the political fashion of the times, for an American to say, that the men who formed this constitution were either intellectual giants or wonderful scholars. Beyond a few names—such as Randolph and Patrick Henry, "the forest-born Demosthenes," of Virginia, Pinckney and Luther Martin, of Maryland, Hamilton, of New York, and Franklin, of Pennsylvania—the Convention which formed this instrument may be described as a company of very plain men, but little instructed in political science, who, in their debates, showed sometimes the crudities and chimeras of ignorant reform, and exhibited more frequently a loose ransacking of history for precedents and lessons, such as rather might have been expected in a club of college sophomores than in a council of statesmen.

The two last names mentioned on the list of distinction in the Convention—Hamilton and Franklin—may be taken as examples of the American exaggeration of their public men, which, indeed, more peculiarly belonged to the people of the Northern States—that division of the American people which after-events have classified as *Yankees*. Hamilton, who had a school of his own in the Convention, was readily exalted as an idol by the party which he so early begot in the history of his country. The man who was honored by pageants and processions in the streets of New York, at the close of the Convention, must be declared, by the just and unimpassioned historian, to have been superficial as a statesman, and defective as a scholar. He had, indeed, neither the intuition of genius, nor the power of analysis. He was a man of little mind. But he had studied a peculiar style in writing, which Washington was weak enough to take for a model, and, it is said, sometimes appropriated. There was no point or sharp edges in the style either of Alexander Hamilton or George Washington. Both wrote and spoke in those long sentences in which common places are pompously dressed up, and in which the sense is so overlaid with qualifications that it is almost impossible to probe it. But Washington made no pretensions to literature and scholarship, while Hamilton had no titles to fame other than these. And in these it must be confessed that he had scarcely any other merit than that of a smooth constructer of words, a character which with the vulgar often passes for both orator and statesman.

Benjamin Franklin was thoroughly a representative Yankee, the first clear-cut type we recognize in history of that materialism, coarse selfishness, pelf, low cunning, and commercial smartness, which passes with the contemporary Yankee as the truest philosophy and highest aim of life. It is alike curious and amusing to examine the grounds of estimation in the minds of his countrymen, which conferred the high-sounding title of *philosopher* on an old gentleman in blue stockings, who, in France, was the butt of the Parisian wits, and who left a legacy of wisdom to posterity in the "*Maxims of Poor Richard.*" How many modern Yankees have been educated in the school of the "Maxims" of Franklin it would be difficult to over-esti mate. If a gross and materialistic value of things is to pass as "philosophy;" if the hard maxims of selfishness, and the parings of penuriousness, such as "Poor Richard" dins to American youth, do really contain the true lessons and meaning of life, then we may declare, in the phrases of Yankee admiration, that Benjamin Franklin was a philosopher and a sage, who eclipsed all other lights in the world, and "whipped the universe." But really, after all, may we not doubt the value of this cookery-book philosophy of smart things; think it doubtful whether the mighty problem of how pence make pounds, be the largest or best part of human wisdom; and conclude that Benjamin Franklin, though not the greatest celebrity America has ever produced, was neither worse nor better than a representative Yankee.

We are almost inclined to laugh at the part which this queer figure acted in the Convention which formed the constitution of the United States. No member had more clap-traps in the way of political inventions. His ignorance of political science and of popular motives was alike profound; and we find him proposing to govern the country after a fashion scarcely less beautiful and less practicable than the Republic of Plato and the Arcadia of Sydney. He thought that magistrates might serve the public from patriarchal affection or for the honor of titles. He quoted in the Convention a maxim that sounds curiously enough to American ears : that "in all cases of public service, the less profit, the greater honor." He was in favor of the nonsense of a plural executive. He insisted in the Convention on the practicability of "finding three or four men in all the United States with public spirit enough to bear sitting in peaceful council, for perhaps an equal term, merely to preside over our civil concerns, and see that our laws were duly executed." Such was the political sagacity of this person, who, it must be confessed, made what reputation he had rather in the handbooks of Yankee economy than in monuments of statesmanship.

But we shall find a better key to the real value of the constitution in a summary review of its debates, than in a portraiture, however interesting, of the men who composed it. The Convention of delegates assembled from the different States at Philadelphia, on the second Monday in May, 1787, had met on a blind errand. They had been called by Congress, "for the sole and express purpose of *revising* the Articles of Confederation, and reporting to Congress and the several legislatures such *alterations* and provisions therein, as shall, when agreed to in Congress and confirmed by the States, render the Federal constitution adequate to the exigencies of government and the preservation of the Union."

This singularly confused language, in the call of the Convention, naturally gave rise to differences of opinion. One party in the Convention—representing what was known as the New Jersey proposition—took the ground that its power was limited to a mere revision and amendment of the existing Articles of Confederation : that it was, therefore, necessary to take the present federal system as the basis of action, to proceed upon terms of the federal equality of the States ; in short, to remedy the defects of the existing government, not to supplant it. Hamilton and his party were for a new and violent system of reform. They were said to favor the establishment of a monarchy. The extent to which this was true is, that they were in

favcr of the annihilation of the State governments and the perma
nent tenure of public offices.   A third party in the Conventioi
avoided both extremes, insisted upon a change of the federa
principle, and proposed a "national" government, in the sense
of a supreme power with respect to certain objects commor
between the States, and committed to it, and which would
have some kind of direct compulsory action upon *individuals*
The word "national" was used only in this limited sense.   The
great defect of the existing Confederation was, that it had no
power to reach individuals, and thus enforce its decrees.   The
proposed Union, or "national" government, was to be a league
of States, but with power to reach individuals; and yet these
only in certain severely defined respects, and through powers
expressly delegated by the States.   In the nature of things, this
power could not act upon the States collectively; that is, not
in the usual and peaceful mode in which governments are conducted.   All that was claimed for it, and all that could be
claimed for it, was to reach individuals in those specifications
of authority that the States should make to it.

The plan of this party was no sooner developed in the Convention than it met the furious opposition of the smaller
States.   It was declared by Luther Martin, that those who
advocated it " wished to establish such a system as could give
their own States undue power and influence in the government
over the other States."   Both Mr. Randolph, of Virginia, and
Mr. Pinckney, of Maryland, who had brought before the
Convention drafts of the plan referred to, agreed that the
members of the Senate should be elected by the House of
Representatives; thus, in effect, giving to the larger States
power to construct the Senate as they chose.   Mr. Randolph
had given additional offence to the smaller States.   He proposed that, instead of an equal vote by States, " the right of
suffrage in the National Legislature ought to be proportioned
to the quotas of contribution, or to the number of free inhabitants."

There was thus excited in the Convention a jealousy between
the larger and smaller States; the former insisting upon a
preponderating influence in both houses of the National
Legislature, and the latter insisting on an equality of representation in each house.   This jealous controversy is tracked

through the debates of the Convention. It proceeded to a degree of warmth and anger in which the Convention was on the point of dissolution. When the vote was taken, five States were for an equality of representation and five against it. At this critical period, a conference committee was appointed. It resulted in a compromise; the opponents of an unequal representation agreeing to yield their objections to it in the lower House, provided its advocates would pledge themselves to support an equal representation in the Senate: and on this basis of agreement was reared the constitution of the United States of America.

The reader must observe here, that the great distinguishing feature of this constitution, the peculiar virtue of the American system—namely, the mixed representation of *the people* and *the States*—was purely the result of a jealousy between the larger and the smaller States, the fruit of an accident. It contained the true virtue of a political instrument, which, as we shall see, was otherwise full of faults and glaring with defects. It was that in which it was original. But it was not an *a priori* discovery. It was not the result of the wisdom of our ancestors. History abounds in instances where accidental or empirical settlements have afterwards been discovered to contain great elements of wisdom and virtue; and it has been natural and pleasing for succeeding generations to account these rather as the result of human reason and prescience, than as the product of blind circumstances. But we are forced to confess, that in that great political novelty of the American system—in which the world was to see, for the first time combined and harmonized, the principle of geographical sovereignties with that of a confederate unity, which, for certain purposes, was to stand for national identity—the " wisdom" of our forefathers had no part, but acted unconsciously under the pressure of circumstances, or the direction of divine Providence.

This statement is not pleasant to American vanity. But it is due to the truth of history. It is highly probable that the framers of the constitution did not fully comprehend the importance of the principles of the combination of State sovereignty with that of the simple republic on which they had stumbled. If they had, it might be supposed that they would have defined with a much severer accuracy the political relations of the States and the General Government; for it has been for the want of such accuracy that room has been found, at least for disputation, and the creation of two political parties, which have run through the whole of American history.

And here it is we must turn from the consideration of that principle in the constitution which was its distinctive feature and its saving virtue, to view briefly the enormous defects and omissions of an instrument that has shared so much of the undue admiration of mankind.

It is impossible to resist the thought, that the framers of the constitution were so much occupied with the controversy of jealousy between the large and the small States that they overlooked many great and obvious questions of government, which have since been fearfully developed in the political history of America. Beyond the results and compromises of that jealousy, the debates and the work of the Convention show one of the most wonderful blanks that has, perhaps, ever occurred in the political inventions of civilized mankind. They left behind them a list of imperfections in political prescience, a want of provision for the exigencies of their country, such as has seldom been known in the history of mankind.

A system of negro servitude existed in some of the States. It was an object of no solicitude in the Convention. The only references in the constitution to it are to be found in a provision in relation to the rendition of fugitives "held to service or labor," and in a mixed and empirical rule of popular representation. However these provisions may imply the true status of slavery, how much is it to be regretted that the Convention did not make (what might have been made so easily) an explicit declaration on the subject, that would have put it beyond the possibility of dispute, and removed it from even the plausibilities of party controversy!

For many years the very obvious question of the power of the General Government to make "internal improvements" has agitated the councils of America; and yet there is no text in the constitution to regulate a matter which should have stared its authors in the face, but what may be derived, by the most forced and distant construction, from the powers of Congress " to regulate commerce," and to " declare war," and " raise and support armies."

For a longer period, and with a fierceness once almost fatal to the Union, has figured in the politics of America, " the tariff question," a contest between a party for revenue and a party for protective prohibitions. Both parties have fought over that vague platitude of the constitution, the power of Congress " to regulate commerce ;" and in the want of a more distinct language on a subject of such vast concern, there has been engendered a controversy which has progressed from the threshold of the history of the Union up to the period of its dissolution.

With the territorial possessions of America, even at the date of the Convention, and with all that the future promised in the expansion of a system that yet scarcely occupied more than the water-slopes of a continent, it might be supposed that the men who formed the constitution would have prepared a full and explicit article for the government of the territories. That vast and intricate subject—the power of the General Government over the territories, the true nature of these establishments, the status and political privileges of their inhabitants—is absolutely dismissed with this bald provision in the constitution of the United States :

"New States may be admitted by Congress into this Union."—ART. iv., SEC. 3.

But however flagrant these omissions of the constitution, and however through them sprung up much that was serious and deplorable in party controversy, we must lose neither sight nor appreciation of the one conspicuous and character-istic virtue of this instrument. That was the combination of State rights with an authority which should administer the common concerns of the States. This principle was involved in the construction of the Senate. It was again more fully and perfectly developed in the amendments of the constitu-tion ; these amendments having a peculiarity and significance as parts of the instrument, since they were, in a certain sense, conditions precedent made by the States to their ratification of it. They provide :

"The enumeration in the constitution, of certain rights, shall not be construed to deny or disparage others retained by the people.

"The powers not delegated to the United States by the constitution, nor prohibited by it to the States, are reserved to the States respectively, or to the people." *

It may be said, that whereas the element of the States was recognized in the construction of the Senate, that element was precisely adjusted and admeasured in the amendments which we have just quoted. In the debates in the legislatures of the different States on the ratification of the constitution, it was never doubted that their original existence was already recognized in it; not only in the text of the instrument, but in the composition *by States* of the convention that framed it, and in the ratification *by States* which was necessary to promulgate it, and give it force and existence. The design of the amendments referred to, was simply to adjust in more precise language a vital and important element in the new system, and to declare formally what sense the States had of it, and with what understanding they approved it.

---

* These amendments, which were the fruit of the legislative wisdom of the States, not of that of the Convention, and were designed to give a full development and a proper accuracy to what was certainly ill-performed work in it, will be found embodied in the official declarations of at least six of the States, coupled with their ratification of the constitution.

MASSACHUSETTS.—"That it be explicitly declared, that all powers not expressly delegated by the aforesaid constitution, are reserved to the several States, to be by them exercised."

NEW HAMPSHIRE.—"That it be explicitly declared, that all powers not expressly and particularly delegated by the aforesaid constitution, are reserved to the several States, to be by them exercised."

SOUTH CAROLINA.—"This convention doth also declare, that no section or paragraph of the said constitution warrants a construction that the States do not retain every power not expressly relinquished by them, and vested in the General Government of the Union."

VIRGINIA.—"We, the delegates of the people of Virginia, etc., do, in the name and in behalf of the people of Virginia, declare and make known that the powers granted under the constitution, being derived from the people of the United States, may be resumed by them, whensoever the same shall be perverted to their injury or oppression, and that every power not granted thereby remains with them, and at their will; that, therefore, no right, of any denomination, can be cancelled, abridged, restrained, or modified, by the Con-

But even if these official texts are—as a party in America has long contended—insufficient to establish the political element of the States, and to measure it as the depository of sovereignty by the rule of reserved rights, we are left a rule of construction as to the true nature of the American Union, which is completely out of the reach of any ingenious torture of language, and far above any art of quibble on words.*

---

gress, by the Senate, or House of Representatives, acting in any capacity, by the President, or any department or officer of the United States, except in those instances in which power is given by the constitution for those purposes; and that, among other essential rights, the liberty of conscience, and of the press, cannot be cancelled, abridged, restrained, or modified, by any authority of the United States."

NEW YORK.—" That the powers of government may be resumed by the people whensoever it shall become necessary to their happiness; that every power, jurisdiction, and right, which is not by the said constitution clearly delegated to the Congress of the United States, or the departments of the Government thereof, remains to the people of the several States, or to their respective State governments, to whom they may have granted the same; and that those clauses in the said constitution, which declare that Congress shall not have or exercise certain powers, do not imply that Congress is entitled to any powers not given by the said constitution; but such clauses are to be construed either as exceptions to certain specified powers, or as inserted merely for greater caution."

RHODE ISLAND.—" That those clauses in the constitution which declare that Congress shall not have or exercise certain powers, do not imply that Congress is entitled to any powers not given by the said constitution; but such clauses are to be construed as exceptions to certain specified powers, or as inserted merely for greater caution."

* It is curious to notice to what lengths of verbal torture that party in America that denied the sovereignty of the States, and represented the Union as a popular consolidated government, have gone.

Thus it has been fashionable to quote in the school of consolidation a decla-ration in the letter of George Washington, president of the Convention, sub-mitting the constitution to the States for their ratification, in which he says:

" It is obviously impracticable in the Federal Government of these States to secure ALL the rights of independent sovereignty to each, and yet provide for the interest and safety of all."—*Eliot's Debates*, Vol. I., p. 17.

Yet the word " ALL," which we have capitalized for emphasis, and which a hasty reader might lose in the context, is directly opposed to the theory of consolidation, and directly implies the residuum of sovereignty in the States.

Again, the word " United States" has been used as a popular argument for a consolidated government. Yet we find in the history of America that the same words designated all the former associations of the colonies and of the States; that the first assembly of delegates to take into consideration the grievances that led to the revolt from the British crown were known as the

That rule is found in the historical circumstances and exigen cies in which the constitution of the United States was formed. It is decisive. For surely there is no juster measure of a grant of political powers than the necessity which originated it, if that necessity be at once intelligible and precise.

Such was the necessity which originated the constitution of the United States. It was a necessity for purely economical purposes. It could not have been intended as a revolution in the sense of a proclamation of new civil polity; for the civil institutions of the States, as derived from the common law of England, were already perfect and satisfactory, and have remained without material change for nearly a century. The constitution of the United States was thus not a political revolution. It was a convenience of the States, growing out of their wants of a system by which they might have a common agent and a uniform code on concerns common between themselves. Is it too much to conclude, therefore, that the new Union had no mission apart from the States; that it was the government of the States; that, in short, it could not have been intended to destroy the very bodies which invoked it as a benefactor to each as well as to all?

It is in this sense that the moral grandeur of the American Union is interpreted: in this sense that its great political virtue was contained. There was put before the eye of man-

---

Congress of delegates of the *United States;* that the Declaration of Independence emanated from "the representatives of the *United States of America,*" and that the style of the subsequent confederation was declared in its first article to be, "The United States of America." So, if the words "United States" are at all to be considered, their natural force and their precedent use are alike in direct opposition to the dogma of consolidation.

Of a similar style of puerile argument for this dogma is this: Whereas, the preamble of the constitution recites, "We, the people of the United States," the people are, therefore, represented as one corporation. Daniel Webster, who was always ready to catch at sophomorial crudities, actually descended to an argument so absurd. The explanation of this phraseology is simple to the last degree. The names of the contracting States were first inserted in the preamble of the constitution. They were suppressed because it was still uncertain what States would adopt it; and as it was impossible to know which might be the first nine States of the Union—that number being necessary to establish the constitution as between themselves—it was agreed to use the corporate style we have quoted in the preamble, that it might include those only who adhered to it.

kind, not a consolidated nationality; not a simple republic, with an anomalous and indefinable appendage of "States," which were not provinces, or cantons, or territories, and yet subordinate; not some undefined and misshapen political mongrel; but a spectacle such as it had never seen—an association of coequal and sovereign States, with a common authority, the subjects of which were yet sufficient enough to give it the effect of an American and national identity; "a republic of republics;" a government which derived its entire life from the good-will, the mutual interests, and the unconstrained devotion of the States which at once originated and composed it.

It may be said that the admission of the sovereignty of the States breaks at once the bond of their association. Yet, this can be said only in a low and narrow sense. The wants and hopes of men operate with the same effect in political bodies as in the social community. Men will scarcely withdraw from a society in which they are alike happy and fortunate. Nor was it to be supposed that any of the American States would be so mad as to withdraw from a Union through which they were to be profited and to ascend, as long as it fulfilled its designs of affording them protection against foreign powers, commercial interchanges, justice and welcome among themselves, the charms and benefits of social intercourse; or that after these, its essential designs might have, within the exigencies of history or the possibilities of human depravity, ceased to be fulfilled, any State could be held in it without violating quite as well the spirit of republican institutions, and the obligations of public morals, as the written text of a compact.

Such undoubtedly were the designs and the law of the American Union. It was a compact which covered only the interests which it specified; yet quite large enough to stand as an American nationality for all practical purposes. It had no dynastic element; it had no mission separate from the States; it had no independent authority over *individuals*, except within the scope of the powers delegated to it by the States. The States retained the power to control their own soil, their own domestic institutions, and their own morals. In respect to the powers which they *prohibited* to the General Government, they retained, *of necessity*, the right of exclusive judgment. That Government was not a mere league; it did have the power to reach *individuals* within the scope of powers delegated by the States; and as to *these* powers, its own courts —the Federal judiciary—were made the exclusive judge. In this sense—only in this sense—it had the qualities of a government; but a government founded exclusively on the good of the States, resting in their consent, and to which the law of force was as foreign in respect of its maintenance, as it had been in respect of its ordination.

The Union was beautiful in theory. It might have been beautiful in practice. If it did prove in the history of America rather a rough companionship, scarcely ever a national identity in the common concerns intrusted to it, such was not the result of inherent defects, but of that party abuse and usurpation, in which have been wrecked so many of the political fabrics of mankind.

The right of secession, whether involved or not by the principle of State sovereignty, was not necessarily the weak point of the Union. We shall see hereafter that the development of this Union was two hostile sections—a political North and a political South—and not disintegration of States; that the Union was sacrificed, not to the dogma of secession, but to the overruling event of a sectional rupture. In view of, and in connection with, these events, it will be wholly unnecessary to discuss "the right of secession."

Forty years after the ordination of the constitution of the United States, we shall see how there sprung up the profound invention of the greatest political scholar of America—John C. Calhoun, of South Carolina—to avoid this very issue of secession; how it was designed to erect over the Union a council of States, and to submit it to their august guardianship; how it represented the true and sublime theory of the association of the States; and how, avoiding the issue of secession, it proposed a measure that would have perpetuated the Union, carried the constitution of the United States to the highest point of development, perfected the American system, introduced into it the principle of adaptability to all circumstances, and given it that elasticity which is the first virtue of wise governments, and the best element of their endurance. We shall see how this scheme of the South Carolina statesmen

—emphatically *a Union measure*—was rejected by the Northern States under a shallow clamor and the coarsest and most ignorant of all party libels in America—" Nullification ;" and how this rejection left no other resource to dissatisfied States than what Mr. Calhoun of all men most deplored, and most sought to avoid—disunion. These assertions may already sound strange to those who have got their political history of America from Northern sources. But we must not anticipate too much here what is undoubtedly the most interesting period in American history, between the dates of Union and Disunion —the era of Calhoun.

* * * * * * * *

II.

What the American colonies contended for.—Burke's idea.—The first American C ɪ
gress.—Its demands.—How the question of independence was developed.—Virginia the first to move for independence.—The Declaration of Independence.—The
Articles of Confederation.—Diverse character and circumstances of the colonies.—
The gentry of Virginia and the Carolinas.—Early type of the *Yankee.*—Difference
of races.—Its value in historical inquiries.—Commercial spirit of New England
in the revolution.—The nature and the value of "the Confederation."—John Adams' idea —" Perpetual Union."—The Confederation a makeshift of the war.—
"State-rights" in the treaty of 1788.—How the revolution succeeded.—Its illustration of the value of endurance.—Liberty invariably the fruit of rebellion.—The
two conditions of all history.

IN their dissatisfaction with the British government, the
American colonies did not at first propose the experiment of
independence. They only claimed equality with Englishmen
at home in respect of rights; contending that the ancient and
existing charters of Englishmen—the guaranties of Magna
Charta, and the later muniments acquired under the Stuarts
—were theirs by birthright; and resenting the idea that they
were an inferior class of British subjects, to be governed as
Charles I. proposed, and as even that luminary of the law—
Blackstone—with curious obtuseness justified, as the denizens
of a *conquered* country.

No man in England better understood the temper of the
colonists, or better divined the future as containing the question of peace and war between Great Britain and America,
than did Edmund Burke. This illustrious man, who was not
only a superb artist of words, but an orator in action, defended
the cause of the colonies with a happiness of expression, and a
measure of zeal, that have since confirmed to the world his reputation as the most acute and eloquent of English statesmen.
"Freedom," said he, "and not servitude, is the cure of anarchy." He declared in the House of Commons a plan of
pacification alike simple, generous, and effective. "My idea,"
he said, "without considering whether we yield as matter of
right, or grant as matter of favor, is, to admit the people of
our colonies into an interest in our constitution."

The pacific counsels did not prevail. The "day-star of the English constitution," as Burke termed it—*alba stella*—was not decreed to arise over the troubled waters and shed its influence of peace. The colonists were left to contest as best they might their claim of equality with other subjects of the British crown.

They did nothing more than this on the very threshold of the revolution. In 1774, the first American Congress of delegates met at Philadelphia. On the 14th of October it made a declaration and adopted resolutions relative to the rights and grievances of the colonies. It was unanimously resolved, "that the respective colonies are entitled to the common law of England, and more especially to the great and inestimable privilege of being tried by their peers of the vicinage, according to the course of that law;" "that they were entitled to the benefit of such statutes as existed at the time of their colonization, and which they have, by experience, respectively found to be applicable to their several and local circumstances;" and that their ancestors, at the time of their immigration, were " entitled to all the rights, liberties, and immunities of free and natural-born subjects within the realms of England."

But with actual hostilities came the full development of the question, the opportunity to compromise which had been lost. It was the assertion of *independence*. Such was the reply of the colonies, provoked by the insolence of power that had too long disdained all means of peace, but what it supposed the easy compulsion of three millions of people by the arms of an empire, upon which it was boasted the sun never set.

To Virginia belongs the honor of the first motion for independence. In Congress, on the 7th of June, 1776, the delegates from Virginia moved, in obedience to instructions from their constituents, that the Congress should declare that " these United Colonies are, and of right ought to be, free and independent States; that they are absolved from all allegiance to the British crown; that all political connection between them and the State of Great Britain is, and ought to be, totally dissolved; and that measures should be immediately taken for procuring the assistance of foreign powers, and a confederation formed to bind the colonies more closely together."

The proposition aroused a deep anxiety, and was received

with no little opposition. Other colonies had not kept pace with the spirit of Virginia. The middle colonies—Maryland, Delaware, Pennsylvania, the Jerseys, and New York—were no ripe for the dissolution of the British connection. Their dele gates declared that it would be improper for Congress to take such a capital step until the voice of the people *drove* them into it.

The final decision was postponed to the 1st of July. It was taken on the original motion made by the delegates of Virginia; but the ultimate question was postponed for a day, in order to obtain unanimity; and on the *second* of July twelve colonies gave their voice for it,—New York withdrawing from the question for instructions, but subsequently adhering to the others through the decision of her convention. But the hesitation of Congress was not yet entirely over. The motion of Virginia has been triumphantly carried; but it remained to pass upon the text of the "declaration" of independence. "The pusillanimous idea," said Thomas Jefferson, the author of this famous paper, "that we had friends in England worth keeping terms with, still haunted the minds of many." But the declaration was at last and substantially agreed to on the evening of the *fourth* of July, and subscribed by the autographs of the members present; and thus from this paper which introduced as it were the august ceremony of personal pledges, rather than from the official act of Congress on the motion of Virginia, concluded on the *second* of July, dates the natal day of American Independence.

The natural companion of the act of independence—" the Unanimous Declaration of the Thirteen United States of America"—was the confederation of the States, to enable them to conduct the war with a common and effective purpose. It had been proposed on the motion of Virginia. Eight days after the declaration of independence, articles of confederation were reported. It was an obvious necessity of the war. The average population of the colonies was less than two hundred and thirty thousand inhabitants; and it would have been absurd for any one of them to attempt to measure arms singly with the British power, and for each to conduct the war on its own responsibility.

It was fortunate indeed that a common military necessity had supplied what scarcely any thing else could have supplied—a political bond between colonies suddenly erected into sovereign States. There had been no similarity of natural circumstances to unite the colonies. They had been planted at different times, from 1606 to 1732, and by different stocks or population. Differences of government, the sharpest antagonism of religious faith, the natural difficulties of intercourse, and the obstructions of trade between them, as the effect of the navigation laws, which hindered the development of their marine, had not only separated the colonies, but drawn through them lines of exasperated division.

The New England colonies were settled by a people very different from those who laid the foundations of empire in Virginia and the Carolinas. In those latter countries the notions of chivalry were early planted by the Cavaliers; and in Virginia especially, the British gentry founded many families whose names have become illustrious in American history.* With such a stock of ancestors in the South the

---

* Dr. Randall, in his Life of Jefferson (Vol. I., pp. 3, 4, and 5), has drawn a strong and graphic picture of the early lowland aristocracy of Virginia, which we reproduce here for its historical interest, especially with reference to its contrast to the Puritan stock of population in America:

"In the early settlement of Virginia, the inhabitants found the river-bottoms of the tide-water region more fertile than the intervening sandy ridges; and the rivers themselves for a long period furnished the only convenient means for transporting heavy products to or from the seaboard. The population, therefore, clung to their banks, each new wave of foreign emigration, or younger and spreading generation of the inhabitants, advancing higher towards their sources. Lands were obtained on easy conditions from the government and otherwise; and provident individuals secured vast estates. This was particularly the case on James River, where the most enterprising and wealthy of the earlier emigrants established themselves. Some of these, men of particular mark and energy, acquired possessions vying in extent with those of the proudest nobles of their native land. These were perpetuated in their families by entails, the laws regulating which were ultimately rendered more stringent in Virginia than in England itself. As their lands rose gradually in value, the great lowland proprietors began to vie with English nobles in wealth as well as in territory. Many of them lived in baronial splendor. Their abodes, it is true, were comparatively mean, as the country did not yet furnish permanent building materials, except at vast cost, nor did it furnish architects to make use of them; but their tables were loaded with plate and with the luxuries of the old and new world; numerous slaves, and white persons whose times they owned for a term of years, served them in every capacity which use, luxury, or ostentation could dictate; and when they travelled in state, their cumbrous and richly appointed coaches were dragged by

Roundhead regicide of the New England settlements had but little sympathy, and few points of agreement. The religion o₁ the Puritan settler; his fierce and relentless persecution, even to the extremity of death, of those who dissented from *dissent;* his hypocritical and canting selfishness, with which he robbed the Indians of their lands for " the Lord's people," and sold some of them into West Indian slavery ; his pious formulas of selfish aggrandizement, were a detestable barrier between him and the Episcopalian of Virginia and the Carolinas ; and a diversity prominent in religion naturally ran through the manners, morals, and politics of the two early stocks of population in America.

---

six horses, driven by three postillions. But usually the mistress of the household, with her children and maids, appropriated this vehicle. The Virginia gentleman of that day, with much of the feeling of earlier feudal times, when the spur was the badge of knighthood, esteemed the saddle the most manly, if not the only manly way of making use of the noblest of brutes. He accordingly performed all his ordinary journeys on horseback. When he went forth with his whole household, the cavalcade consisted of the mounted white males of his family, the coach-and-six lumbering through the sands, and a retinue of mounted body-servants, grooms with spare led horses, etc., in the rear.

" In their general tone of character, the lowland aristocracy of Virginia resembled the cultivated landed gentry of the mother country. Numbers o₁ them were highly educated and accomplished by foreign study and travel ; and nearly all, or certainly much the largest portion, obtained an excellent education at William and Mary College, after its establishment, or respectable acquirements in the classical schools kept in nearly every parish by the learned clergy of the established Church. As a class, they were intelligent, polished in manner, high-toned, and hospitable—and sturdy in their loyalty and in their adherence to the national Church. Their winters were often spent in the gayeties and festivities of the provincial capital ; their summers, when not connected with the public service, principally in supervising their immense estates, in visiting each other, and in such amusements as country life afforded. Among the latter the chase held a prominent place. Born almost to the saddle and to the use of firearms, they were keen hunters ; and when the chase was over they sat round groaning boards, and drank confusion to Spaniard and Frenchman abroad, and to Roundhead and Prelatist at home. When the lurking and predatory Indian became the object of purt, no strength of the red-man could withstand, no speed of his elude this y and gallantly mounted cavalry. The social gulf which separated this from the common class of colonists became about as deep and wide, and as difficult to overleap in marriage and other social arrangements, as that which divided the gentry and peasantry of England. Such were the Carters, the Carys, the Burwells, the Byrds, the Fairfaxes, the Harrisons, the Lees, the Randolphs, and many other families of early Virginia."

It is certainly not a mere speculation which has thought to discover in the history of the New England settlements some of the elements of the character of the modern *Yankee*. We must, however, take care not to push the speculation too far. It has been often an over-refinement in the treatment of history to trace up the character of nations to differences in race and blood; forgetting how much of that character is due to those developments of events and interests which have taken place between the first beginnings of a people and the period of historical retrospect. We are not disposed to risk the analysis of the modern Yankee character on those elements of race and blood which were involved in the early settlement of America. We shall see, in the progress of this inquiry, how much of this character was due to subsequent development and education in the crooked paths of their political history, and what a large and various addition of meanness was thus made to the nature and habit of the original New England colonist.

But in that early type of the colonist we certainly do discover some traits, more or less imperfect, of the Yankee of a later period. We would only warn the reader from expecting to discover too much here, reminding him that the character of a people, although undoubtedly deriving some elements from its ancestry, takes, as does the individual life, additions and modifications from the school of events and influences; that, in short, the geometrical accuracy of ethnology is an imperfect and sophistical guide to the truth of history.

Modern events have most largely produced the Yankee of our day. Yet in the sniffling Puritan, with his stock of pious excuses for every ferocious scheme of selfishness, and in the Massachusetts "trader," with his early code of *commercial* politics, which, in fact, he carried into the revolution of 1776, we find no slight likeness to the present generation of their Northern descendants. It is not overstating the case to say, that the New England colonies went into the revolution rather resenting the restraints upon their commerce than animated by the pure love of liberty. Their commercial casuistry had long defied the laws and authority of the mother country. Sir William Berkeley, the Governor of Virginia, when remonstrating, in 1671, against the Navigation Act cutting off all trade with foreign countries, made it the subject of particular complaint that, while the Virginians were "most obedient to all laws, the New England men break through, and men trade to any place that their interest leads them." He had already discovered two different rules of public morals in the beginnings of American history.

It is no wonder that the confederation, despite the plain military necessity which demanded it, was an achievement of no little difficulty, and a bond of very partial and imperfect effect. It was debated for nearly five years. It was not consummated until the 1st of March, 1781. It lasted nominally about eight years, but, practically, not more than two. It was distinctly founded on the sovereignty of the States; was ratified by the State legislatures, and gave Congress the power of determining questions only by the vote of the States. True, it was something more than a military alliance. It was intended to unite the resources of the States, and to establish a foundation for public credit for the purposes of the war. It was intended for nothing more. In the circular letter of Congress, urging the reluctant States to accede to the confederation, they were urged " to conclude the glorious compact, which, by uniting the wealth, strength, and councils of the whole, might bid defiance to external violence and internal dissensions, whilst it secured the public credit at home and abroad."

The compact had been ostentatiously styled in its title a " perpetual Union," and Mr. John Adams, of Massachusetts, had really desired to incorporate into it the features of a consolidated government. These, however, were the fancies of ignorance, and the dreams of extravagance. The confederation, indeed, even as an association to give a common direction to, and create a common fund for, the war, was very imperfect and lamentably loose. It had no power to reach *individuals*, and to enforce the common will of the States. It could only apportion the quota to be paid by each State, but had no way of compelling the payment. It could make commercial treaties with foreign States, but, unless the legislatures of the States chose to adopt such commercial regulations in their ports as might be necessary, the treaties might be utterly inoperative. Such an anomaly, such a weak pretence of a common government, could scarcely be expected to last beyond the war, of which it was the makeshift. At the peace, it naturally went

t) pieces. "Each State," says Madison, "yielding to the voice of immediate interest or convenience, withdrew its support from the confederation, till the frail and tottering edifice was ready to fall upon our heads and crush us beneath its ruins." The "perpetual Union" was practically terminated by the uninterrupted free will of the States which composed it.

The treaty of 1783, which crowned the success of the American revolution, contained the only description which had ever been made, on the part of Great Britain, of the nature of the new power which was recognized in recognizing American independence. What was recognized, was the independence severally of the thirteen States formerly colonies. And it is especially to be remarked that these States were recognized severally, and not jointly, in the treaty.

The revolution was thus crowned with success. But it is doubtful whether there was any merit in obtaining it other than *endurance*. The American armies were generally unsuccessful; the American troops—however American vanity may proclaim the contrary—fought no better than the British veterans. George Washington was not a military genius. The diplomacy of the revolution was neither a monument of wisdom nor of letters.* The result of the war was the triumph of the endurance of a people resolved to be free, over the less determined wishes and interests of those who desired merely an ad dition of empire.

The war of the American States added another illustration to a curious fact in all history. This fact is, that no system of liberty ever yet emanated from the generosity or wisdom of human rulers; it has invariably been the fruit of rebellion— the result of a contest between the natural tendency of power to centralize and exaggerate its authority, and the opposition of its subjects, naturally intermittent, in its checks on usurpation.

---

* It is true that the American States, in their war with Great Britain, made connections and some advantageous arrangements in Europe; but these were natural results, rather than skilful achievements. The diplomacy of the revolution was a botch. In the beginning of the revolution the foreign correspondence was intrusted to a committee. The confederation included a department of foreign affairs; but the secretary had no power to perform any thing but the specific acts authorized by Congress, which, at that time, was at once the executive and the legislative power.

We embrace here the two conditions of history : the tendency of all political power, and the disposition of its subjects. So true are these of man, everywhere, that they have passed into two general declarations, which have the force of maxims. The first is, that "tyranny, when possible, is always certain." The second is found in the text of the American Declaration of Independence: " All experience hath shown that mankind are more disposed to suffer, while evils are sufferable, than to right themselves by abolishing the forms to which they are accustomed."

*   *   *   *   *   *   *   *

III.

The times of Thomas Jefferson.—Manners and appearance of the man.—His Democracy.—Its application to the relations of the States and Federal Government.—Origin of the Republican or Democratic party.—The idea of consolidation.—New York, and the New England States.—Early political preaching in New England.—The Alien and Sedition laws.—How the latter infringed the rights of the States.—The Kentucky Resolutions.—A fact not in the record.—Mr. Jefferson on " nullification."—Why the Kentucky Resolutions were modified.—The Virginia Resolutions.—The replies of the New England States, and of New York.—Jefferson's triumph.—A new era at Washington.

It has been fashionable for two generations to entitle Thomas Jefferson, of Virginia, the father of the Democratic party of America. Unlike most of the party phrases of tradition, this is strictly true.

The name of Jefferson fills a large space in American history; it is identified with an important and enraged political crisis; it is connected with much of party controversy; and for more than sixty years his name has been, on the one hand, adorned with titles of popular adulation, and on the other, coupled with the very same terms which Hamilton, his contemporary enemy, and the best representative of Federalist rancor, applied to him—" an atheist in religion, and a fanatic in politics."

Thomas' Jefferson was a remarkable man. He was thoroughly a Virginian; and he was by nature a Democrat. Born of a moderate family in Chesterfield County, he carried, through all the honors and illustrious passages of his life, the plain, unostentatious, and kindly manners of a Virginia farmer. His sandy hair, and strong features, and large bones, were Virginian. His dress had always the quaintness of a countryman; he wore under-waistcoats and woollen tippets; and his manners, unaffected as his dress, invited all classes of persons to approach him.

We have said that Thomas Jefferson was a Democrat by nature. His official residence in France, as minister to that court from 1784 to 1789, is reported to have been the occasion

of contracting peculiar views on the subject of popular rights
It, no doubt, added something to them; but he had contracted
his king-phobia in the Revolution, in his own country, and
before there was such a thing as a Democrat in France. His
hatred of monarchy was expressed in such intense words, as
could only have come from ideas identified with the constitution of the mind. There was a savage sincerity in all he ever
said or wrote of monarchies. The people who lived under
them, he divided into two classes,—"wolves and sheep."
Among the lessons which he recommended to those of his
countrymen, who were, in 1787, debating the idea of a new
constitution, were "never to call on foreign powers to settle
their differences; to guard against hereditary magistrates; to
prevent their citizens from becoming so established in wealth
and power, as to be thought worthy of alliance, by marriage,
with the nieces, sisters, etc., of kings; and, in short, to besiege
the throne of Heaven with eternal prayers, to extirpate from
creation that class of human lions, tigers, and mammoths, called
kings." There is an unpleasant excess in these views. But
we may certainly pardon something to the rhetorical fervor of
strong convictions.

When Jefferson returned to America, the name of Democrat
was not popular there. His most careful biographer, Dr.
Randall says: "In 1786, and for some period later, there
were few, if any, prominent Americans who avowed themselves in favor of a broadly Democratic system. In the
Federal Convention of 1787 (which framed our constitution),
not a man could be found who advocated such systems, or was
willing to be suspected of, at heart, favoring them. There
were gentlemen in that Convention who avowed themselves
monarchists in theory; but not one could be found who would
take the name of Democrat! Jefferson was the first, and for
a long time the only very prominent American we know of,
who was willing persistently to avow that Democracy constituted the essence of his system, or the rule of construction
which he would apply to the mixed forms of the State and
Federal Governments."

It is in its application to the relations subsisting between
the State and Federal authority that we find the technical
meaning of that broad nomenclature—the Democratic party

of America. The application of the general principle of Democracy—the doctrine of popular rights—to this relation was obvious. Mr. Jefferson was, to the end of his life, persuaded that there was a monarchical party, more or less disguised, in America. It is probable that he fought nothing more than a shadow in this, and mistook a fondness of the Federalists for the traditions and fashions of the ante-revolutionary period—a depraved appetite for social ceremonies in New York and Philadelphia—as a desire for the substance as well as the trappings of monarchy.

But Jefferson had a real substance to fight in the *consolidation* school of politics, which was early established in New York, and in the New England States. It is true that the propositions of this school bordered on the monarchical idea; but it is extravagant to say that they fully implied it. They suggested no change in the republican forms of the General Government. But the idea of the Federalists was to accumulate power in that Government at the expense of the States; to impair these original political institutions of America; and to strike down, in the States, that principle of local sovereignty which had been interposed between the general authority and people, and which, in fact, from the days of the Saxon Octarchy to those of the American Union, may be taken as constituting the most important bulwark of popular liberty.

The idea of consolidation had obtained early popularity and rapid growth in the Northern States. Mr. Jefferson found his most powerful enemies in the compact masses of Federalists in New England. It was during his party contests with Mr. Adams' administration, and his subsequent campaign for the presidency, that we may find the development of the peculiar spirit of hierocracy in New England—a disposition of the clergy to control in secular affairs—and date that era of *political preaching*, which has had so much to do with Yankee politics, and the party education of Northern mobs. Mr. Jefferson was never pelted from the hustings and ward-rooms with viler abuse, than from the pulpits of New England. Rev. Cotton Mather Smith, of Shena, declared that he had been guilty of "fraud and robbery;" and with that usual decent and Christian weapon of New England—an attack on private life—deluged him with vituperations from the pulpit and pronounced stern maranatha on the man. Aι other New England divine made an elaborate parallel between the distinguished Virginian and the wicked Rehoboam, printed his " sermon," and distributed it through the land. This Puritanical rancor mingled largely in the party conflicts of Mr. Jefferson's time; but probably disturbed him less than any other element of enmity. He had a greater contempt for religious fanaticism than for any other form of error ; he was inclined to jest on it ; he was never disposed to appease attacks on his private character; he was satisfied to trust himself to the tests of reason, and to do his work faithfully and patiently for history. That work was the foundation of the Republican party, known long after him as the Democratic, or State-rights party of America.

The administration of John Adams was distinguished by two important assaults on the liberties of the country—one of them involving an obvious infringement of the principle of State sovereignty. These were the Alien and the Sedition laws. The first, passed Congress on the 22d day of June, 1798, authorized the President to deport at pleasure, aliens whom he might judge " dangerous to the peace and safety of the United States." The second, passed the 14th of July, 1798, abridged the freedom of the press, by an odious bill of penalties, and assumed to punish, by fine and imprisonment, " false, scandalous, and malicious writings" against the Government. It did more than aim a blow at civil liberty : it conveyed an attack against the structure of the Government, and the vital principle of the Federal compact. It was inferred, from the existence of State laws on the subject, that Congress had a similar power of legislation ; that its authority might thus be deduced from implication ; violating the cardinal principle of the Democratic or Republican school, that the State sovereignties were only diminished by the powers specifically enumerated, and that the Federal agency had no power whatever to intrude upon the reserved ground. It is easily seen that the extent of the pretension was to endow Congress with a power of legislation in all cases whatsoever, to strip the States of their sovereignty, and to despoil them of all the rights they had reserved to themselves.

Against this tremendous pretension, Jefferson raised the

stai.dard of party revolt. The leading republicans in Congress formed a plan of action, which was, "to retire from that field, and take a stand in the State legislatures" against Federalist enterprises on the constitution. The co-operation of Kentucky with Virginia was assured. Mr. Jefferson was consulted, and from his pen emanated the famous Kentucky Resolutions, which were passed almost unanimously by the Legislature of that State, in November, 1798, and which have since constituted the most august text of the principles of American Democracy, and for two generations have been the exacting standard of party authority.

The first of these resolutions was in the nature of a general declaration of principles, while others of the series practically applied to the Alien and Sedition laws and other excesses of the Federalists. It is sufficient to quote it:

"*Resolved*, That the several States composing the United States of America, are not united on the principle of unlimited submission to their General Government; but that by compact, under the style and title of a constitution of the United States, and of amendments thereto, they constituted a General Government for special purposes, delegated to that Government certain definite powers, reserving, each State to itself, the residuary mass of right to their own self-government; and, that whensoever the General Government assumes undelegated powers, its acts are unauthoritative, void, and of no force; that to this compact each State acceded as a State, and is an integral party; that this Government, created by this compact, was not made the exclusive or final judge of the extent of the powers delegated to itself; since that would have made its discretion, and not the constitution, the measure of its powers ; but, that as in all other cases of compact among parties having no common judge, each party has an equal right to judge for itself, as well of infractions as of the mode and measure of redress."

But there was something behind this record which is not to be omitted from history. Mr. Jefferson, in the original draft of the resolutions, as it came from his hand, had proposed *the remedy* for an assumption by Congress of powers not delegated to it. He was too logical to state conclusions delicately. He declared the right of *nullification*. In the ninth of the series of resolutions, he wrote: "That in cases of an abuse of the delegated powers, the members of the General Government being chosen by the people, a change by the people would be the constitutional remedy; but, where powers are assumed which have not been delegated, a nullification of the act is the rightful remedy ; that every State has a natural right in cases not within the compact (*casus non fœderis*), to nullify, of their own authority, all assumptions of power by others within their limits ; that, without this right, they would be under the dominion, absolute and unlimited, of whosoever might exercise this right of judgment over them ; that, nevertheless, this commonwealth, from motives of regard and respect for its co-states, has wished to communicate with them on the subject."

It remained for another generation of American people to consider the "rightful remedy" of nullification, and for the masterly mind of Mr. Calhoun to develop Mr. Jefferson's idea expressed above ; to modify it, as Mr. Jefferson himself, in another period of his life, did modify it to *a call of convention of States;* and to draw out of this first crude suggestion of a remedy the most finished and conservative plan that was ever devised in the politics of America, to exorcise the spirit of sectionalism, and to save an imperilled Union.

But the peril of 1798 was not important enough to force a discussion of the remedy which Mr. Jefferson had indicated. He was satisfied to declare the right of it. It was supposed that the repeal of the Alien and Sedition laws might be effected without invoking extraordinary remedies ; and that it was best to accomplish it without unnecessary ferment, and through the forms of polite remonstrance. Mr. Jefferson thought so. He wrote to a friend : " For the present, I shall be for resolving the Alien and Sedition laws to be against the constitution, and merely void, and for addressing the other States to obtain similar declarations ; and I would not do any thing at this moment which should commit us further, but reserve ourselves to shape our future measures, or no measures, by the events which may happen."

It was in a similar conviction, and probably with the concurrence of Mr. Jefferson, that the Kentucky Legislature modified the eighth resolution, so as to omit any allusion to ulterior remedies, simply requiring their representatives to use their best endeavors for the repeal in Congress of the obnoxious legislation referred to. The governor was requested to transmit the resolutions to the other States, and solicit their concurrence in procuring the desired repeal.

Virginia followed the action of Kentucky. In December, 1798, her legislature passed a series of resolutions responsive to those of Kentucky. They were drafted by Mr. Madison. They referred to the spirit of the Federal Government " to enlarge its powers by forced constructions of the constitutional charter," and " so to consolidate the States by degrees into one sovereignty." They peremptorily declared that they viewed " the powers of the Federal Government, as resulting from the compact, to which the States are parties, as limited by the plain sense and intention of the instrument constituting that compact, as no further valid than they are authorized by the grants enumerated in that compact; and that in case of a deliberate, palpable, and dangerous exercise of other powers, not granted by the said compact, the States, who are parties thereto, have the right, and are in duty bound, to interpose for arresting the progress of the evil, and for maintaining within their respective limits, the authorities, rights, and liberties appertaining to them."

The resolutions of Virginia and Kentucky were communicated to the other States for council and co-operation. They drew upon them a unanimous burst of Federalist denunciation from all of the New England States. The replies of these States, and that of New York, reveal the extent of the early establishment of the consolidation school in the North, and discover those principles from which have flowed the more modern political principles of the Yankee.

Each of the New England States, confounding judicial cases with political questions, declared that the State legislatures had no power to supervise the acts of the General Government (which, it is scarcely necessary to say, parenthetically, was to nullify the political influence of the States); that the construction of such laws as the Alien and Sedition acts was exclusively vested in the judicial courts of the United States. Yet each of these States went out of the way to affirm, speculatively, the constitutionality and expediency of these acts. Massachusetts declared, that in no circumstances had the State legislatures " the right to denounce the administration of that government to which the people themselves, by a solemn compact, had exclusively committed their national concerns." The State of Rhode Island and Providence Plantation declared, that the resolutions of Virginia were " very unwarrantable," and " hazarded an interruption of the peace of the States by civil discord." Connecticut " explicitly disavowed" the principles contained in these resolutions. New Hampshire thought the State legislatures were not the proper tribunals to pass upon the laws of the General Government. Vermont "highly disapproved" of the Virginia resolutions, and thought them " unconstitutional in their nature, and dangerous in their tendency." New York, then united to New England by the tie of Federalism, and long kept in that bad alliance by the influence of Hamilton, exceeded even the intolerance of her Puritan associates. Her legislature declared that they observed with anxiety and regret " the inflammatory and pernicious sentiments, and doctrines which are contained in the resolutions of Virginia and Kentucky."

On the issues involved in the Virginia and Kentucky resolutions, Mr. Jefferson achieved a decisive triumph, and by his election to the presidency in 1800 put the Federalist party almost out of existence. After that event, it may be said to have degenerated into a mere local faction. Mr. Jefferson launched the country into a career of Democratic simplicity, and real substantial prosperity, that ran through many years.

He abolished all the stately ceremonials which had grown up in Washington's administration. He discontinued the levees at the Executive Mansion ; he dispensed with the pageant of opening Congress ; he threw the doors of that assembly open, for the first time, to newspaper reporters, and broke down, as far as possible, every barrier of ceremony and exclusiveness between the Government and the people. The simplicity of his inauguration into office made people stare. An English spectator thus describes his appearance on the occasion : " His dress was of plain cloth, and he rode on horseback to the Capitol, without a single guard, or even servant, in his train ; dismounted without assistance, and hitched the bridle of his horse to the palisades."

But Mr. Jefferson marked the administration of his high office with changes much more important than outward tokens of Democratic simplicity. He instituted a rule of rigid economy in every department of the Government. By economy alone, he reduced the public debt twelve millions of dollars.

By the purchase of Louisiana and treaties with the Indians,
he doubled the area of the United States. The second census
of the United States presented an increase of exports from
nineteen to ninety-four millions of dollars. The country was
on the high and plain road to prosperity.

*   *   *   *   *   *   *   *

IV.

THE peaceful and fortunate career on which Mr. Jefferson's administration launched the country was to meet with a singular interruption. That interruption was the sectional agitation which finally broke the bonds of the Union and plunged North and South into one of the fiercest wars of modern times. The occasion of that conflict was what the Yankees called—by one of their convenient libels in political nomenclature—*slavery ;* but what was in fact nothing more than a system of negro servitude in the South; well guarded by laws, which protected the negro laborer in the rights of humanity; moderated by Christian sentiments which provided for his welfare; and, altogether, one of the mildest and most beneficent systems of servitude in the world.

It is not our purpose here to enter upon a moral defence of slavery in the South (using, as we would remind the reader, that opprobrious term, wherever it occurs in these pages, under a constant protest, and simply because it has become the familiar word in the party controversies of America to describe the peculiar institution of labor in the South). Our object in these pages is simply with the political complications of slavery. But as a problem in morals there are but two principles which decide it ; and these we may briefly turn our pen to announce, candidly believing them to be the summary of the entire ethics of negro servitude in the South:

1. The white being the superior race, and the black the inferior, subordination, with or without law, must be the status of the African in the mixed society of whites and blacks.

2. It thus becomes the interest of both races, especially of the inferior race, that this status should be fixed and protected by law; and it was simply the declaration and definition of this principle that went by the name of negro slavery in the South.

Slavery (without that moderation of legislative checks and Christian sentiments which were the constant employment of the South) had been planted in America by the direct and persistent action of the British government. It was the common law of the thirteen colonies before their separation from England. The mother country established negro slavery in the colonies. It maintained and protected the institution. It originated and carried on the slave trade. It forbade the colonies permission either to emancipate or export their slaves. It prohibited them from inaugurating any legislation in diminution or discouragement of the institution. Even after the Continental Congress had been assembled, and the battle of Lexington had been fought, the earl of Dartmouth, British Secretary of State, in answer to a remonstrance from the agent of the colonies on the subject of the slave trade, replied: " We cannot allow the colonies to check or discourage in any degree a traffic so beneficial to the nation."

In the constitution of the United States, the slavery question had been singularly accommodated. Two clauses covered it. The first guaranteed to the South its property—it provided for the return of slaves recognized as the property of their Southern masters. Another clause, in the interest of the North, prevented a disturbance of the representative system by an importation of slaves, and provided that the South should not increase her negro population (five of which in the basis of representation were made equal to three white men) by importation after the lapse of twenty years.

The political history of the slavery question in the early periods of the American Union is scarcely more than an enumeration of dates or of measures which were taken as matters of course. The action of the first Congress, in relation to slavery in the territories, was simply to acquiesce in a government for the Northwest territory, based upon a *pre-existing* anti-slavery ordinance—the ordinance of 1784–87. The Fugitive Slave Act of 1793 was passed without opposition and without a division in the Senate; and in the House, by a vote of forty-eight to seven. The slave trade was declared piracy. Petitions upon the slavery question were at first referred to a committee; and afterwards were rejected, and in one instance returned to the petitioner. Louisiana and Florida, both slaveholding countries, were added to our territories without agitation in Congress. Kentucky, Tennessee, Mississippi, and Alabama were admitted into the Union, bringing the institution of slavery with them, without a murmur of opposition.

It is to be remarked, however, that that jealousy of Southern domination which was the characteristic and controlling element of the Northern mind, and which afterwards became singularly associated with the slavery discussion, may be dated with the acquisition of Louisiana. The famous Hartford Convention, held in 1814, aimed two remarkable blows at the power of the South. It proposed to strike down the slave representation in Congress, and to have the representation conformed to the number of free persons in the Union; and as a further restriction upon the power of the South—the extension of our territory being then in that direction—it proposed an amendment to the constitution, to the effect that no new States should be admitted into the Union without the concurrence of two-thirds of both Houses of Congress.

But the slavery question was as yet only incidental to this sectional rivalry, and was scarcely yet developed into a distinct and independent controversy. There was some general discussion as to the policy of the extension of slavery into the new territories; and some political union, without, however, any distinct lines of party organization, had already been occasioned in the North by a proposition to extend the ordinance of 1787 west of the Mississippi River. It is a remarkable circumstance, in connection with these early discussions of the "Free-Soil" school, that Mr. Jefferson, notwithstanding his connection with the ordinance of 1787, was in favor of the free and unlimited extension of slavery over the new soil acquired by the United States. And he maintained this view on a very singular and ingenious ground: it was that " the diffusion of the slaves over a greater surface would make them individually happier, and proportionably facilitate the accomplishment of their emancipation, by dividing the burden on a greater number of coadjutors."

It may be said generally—notwithstanding the episode of the Hartford Convention—which fell into early disrepute—that there was nothing in the precedents of the Government to betoken that wild and violent controversy nursed in the selfish mind of the North, which, in 1820, was to break through the bonds of secret jealousy and array the country into two sectional parties struggling for supremacy, on opposite convictions, or perhaps on opposite pretences, with regard to the slavery question.

The Missouri legislation—by which the institution of slavery was bounded by a line of latitude—naturally divided the United States into geographical parties, and tore the country in twain. It created for the first time a distinct political North and a distinct political South. It is to be taken as the proper initial point of that war of sections which raged in America for forty years, and at last culminated in an appeal to arms. The discussion of the Missouri matter awoke the anti-slavery sentiment of the country that had for some years past been almost completely dormant. It was the occasion of a call of a convention of abolitionists at Philadelphia. It fired the passions of the populace, and to the serious statesmen of the country gave unbounded alarm. " From the battle of Bunker's Hill to the treaty of Paris we never had so ominous a question," said Mr. Jefferson. To a friend he wrote : " This momentous question, like a fire-bell in the night, awakened and filled me with terror." After the passage of what was called " a compromise " in Congress, he wrote : " The question sleeps for the present, but is not dead." " A geographical line, coinciding with a marked principle, moral and political, once conceived and held up to the angry passions of men will not be obliterated ; and every new irritation will make it deeper and deeper." The Sage of Monticello spoke prophetically, and in one of his letters put on record this remarkable declaration :

" I regret that I am now to die in the belief that the useless sacrifice of themselves, by the generation of 1776, to acquire self-government and happiness to their country, is to be thrown away by the unwise and unworthy passions of their sons ; and that my only consolation is to be, I live not to weep over it. If they would but dispassionately weigh the blessings they will throw away, against an abstract principle more likely to be affected by union than by scission, they would pause before they would perpetrate this act of suicide on themselves, and of treason against the hopes of the world."

Mr. Jefferson was right in designating the Missouri Restriction as the preliminary trace of disunion. Thereafter, the slavery question was developed as a well-defined controversy ; and for forty years the most ingenious attempts to appease it, and to erase the geographical line, which was drawn in 1820, were worse than ineffectual.

But it is to be remarked that the true causes of sectional animosity between the North and the South were beyond the slavery question, although unavoidably and indissolubly connected with it. If we are to analyze that animosity, we shall discover that its deep-lying causes were certain radical antipathies, which discovered slavery as the most prominent ground of distinction between the two sections, and seized upon it as the readiest point of controversy. We must not fall into the common error of taking occasions for original agents, and confounding as one a number of causes, attached to each other, or even grown out of each other, and yet logically distinct. The war between North and South was essentially a war between two great political schools, and what is more, between two distinct civilizations. Yet in both regards, the slavery question was bound up in the conflict, being, in the first place, an inevitable issue between the States-rights and consolidation schools ; and, in the second place, itself being the most prominent cause of the distinction between the civilizations, or social autonomies of North and South.

It is thus that the slavery question, although subordinate—although, so to speak, a smaller question than those with which it was associated—pervaded al' of American politics, and played the conspicuous part in the dissolution of the Union. The two great political tendencies in America—that of consolidation and that of State-rights—naturally joined issue on slavery; for the first school, recognizing the authority at Washington as a national one, could easily presume it responsible for what was denounced as "the plague-spot of the country," and deplored as a tarnish of the American name. Again, as the North envied the peculiar intellectual civilization of the South, its higher sentimentalism, and its superior refinements of scholarship and manners, it would naturally find the leading cause of these things in the peculiar institution of slavery, and concentrate upon it all the unscrupulous rage of jealousy, and that singularly bitter hate, which is inseparable from a sense of inferiority.

Free labor founded in the North a material civilization, a pestilent system of public schools, and that insolent democracy which went by the phrase, "D—n you, I am as good as you." That, and "commercial" politics, made the North prosperous; a showy, glittering mass of all the national elements of civilization, by the side of the apparently scanty, but refined, South. Northern men were apt to sneer at the uncultivated aspects of the South; to point to the slight nets of internal improvements that stretched over tracts of wild timber and swamps; to laugh at the plain architecture in the cities of the South; and to talk, with great self-complacency, of "the want of enterprise" in the slaveholding States. Yet after all, the Yankee trader had a sneaking, irrepressible consciousness that the Southern planter, in his homespun garb, was infinitely his superior as a gentleman; that he could not compete with him in courage, in the sentiment of honor, in the refinements of manners, or in any of the solid and meritorious accomplishments of manhood. The sleek business men of New York, Boston, and Philadelphia might be very impressive in their exteriors, but they never had any manners; they were not even accustomed to the words, "Sir" and "gentleman," in their conversation; they might talk a learned jargon about stocks and markets, but beyond that, in matters of history and literature, many of these well-dressed men were as ignorant as the draymen at their door.

Despite the plainness of the South, and the absence there of

the shows and gauds of material prosperity, and the insepar
able companion of such prosperity in a *moneyed* aristocracy,
there was recognizable, in this slaveholding country, a noble
and singularly pure type of civilization. Slavery introduced
elements of order and conservatism in the society of the
South; and yet, after all, there was no truer democracy in the
world than there: the lower white classes recognizing, it is
true, certain distinctions in social intercourse; but outside of
these, having a manly sense of equality, and claiming, from
the more prosperous orders of society, a consideration and
measure of respect that the poor man in the North, where
society was made up of browbeating on the one hand, and an
insolent assertion of equality on the other, in vain contended
for. Slavery trained the white race of the South in habits of
command; and though, sometimes, these may have degenerated
into cruelty and insolence, yet they were generally the occasions
of the revival of the spirit of chivalry in the nineteenth
century; of the growth of many noble and generous virtues;
and of a knightly polish of manners, that the shopkeeping
aristocracy of the North, being unable to emulate, was satisfied to ape in its hotels and caravansaries. Slavery relieved
the better classes in the South from many of the demands of
physical and manual labor; but although in some instances
idle or dissolute lives may have been the consequence of this,
yet it afforded opportunity for extraordinary intellectual culture in the South, elevated the standards of scholarship and
mental cultivation there, and furnishes some explanation of
the extraordinary phenomenon in American history, that the
statesmanship of the country was peculiarly, and almost exclusively, the production of the slaveholding States.

The vulgar North envied the South, even down to the small
hands and feet of its people. For the better civilization and
higher refinement of slaveholders, the North retaliated that
the South was dull and unenterprising, and had to import all
of its luxuries, and many of its comforts from Yankee shops.
This was true; but it proved nothing, or it might prove more
than the Yankee argument might desire, for with Northern
luxuries there came into the South Northern vices. It was said,
with a coarse wit, but with not a little meaning, that there were
" three things" for which the South would always be depend

ent upon the North, and never could produce for herself; they were "ice, play-actors, and prostitutes." There is a certain exaggeration in every *bon mot;* but the witticism is a good one, as it gives an indication of that coarse, vulgar measure of superiority which the North applied to itself to compensate for its defects in refinement, and in the nobler attributes of national life by the side of the South.

With reference to the singular point of contrast between the North and the South in the exhibitions of statesmanship and political scholarship, we discover the most remarkable feature of American history. Slavery appears, indeed, to have been the school of American statesmanship, for it is from its domains there came by far the most considerable contribution to the political literature of the country. The smallness of Yankee contribution in this respect has been a subject of remark by every impartial historian of America; and there are but few candid persons who will deny that the quality of Yankee statesmanship was always intensely sophomorical. It may have been that slavery afforded to the statesmen of the South certain fields of observation, and applied certain influences of conservatism that qualified them for their peculiar studies; but it is unquestionably true, that to them we must look for the monuments of political literature in America. It has been acutely remarked by a Yankee writer, in the anonymous pages of a magazine, that the public men of the North were generally actuated by an ambition to make a show on what they imagined the theatre of *national* life; that they neglected the obscure theatres, but noble schools, of *State* politics; and that to this shallow, ostentatious ambition is to be attributed much of the Yankee distaste for the severity and exclusiveness of the States-rights school.

*   *   *   *   *   *   *   *

V.

Contrast between the North and South in material progress.—The times of Andrew
Jackson.—The tariff controversy.—Calhoun and Webster as representative men.
—The latter a sophomore in American politics.—Mr. Webster's private correspondence and poetry.—His superficial accomplishments.—"Nullification," another
libel of political nomenclature.—A true explanation and analysis of Mr. Calhoun's
scheme to save and perpetuate the Union.—Jefferson Davis' defence of Calhoun.
New England's regard for the Union.—The veneration of the Union peculiarly a
Southern sentiment.—Mr. Calhoun's Fort Hill speech.—The ignorance or hypocrisy of Webster and his party.—How the South was driven to "disunion."

THE inequality between the North and the South, with
respect to material progress, was perhaps never more marked
than at the time of the memorable administration of Andrew
Jackson. Referring to this period, a Northern biographer of
President Jackson writes in the following style of Yankee
conceit:

"The North was rushing on like a Western high-pressur
steamboat, with resin in the furnace and a man on the safety
valve. All through Western New York, Ohio, Indiana, and
Illinois, the primeval wilderness was vanishing like a mist,
and towns were springing into existence with a rapidity that
rendered necessary a new map every month, and spoiled the
gazetteers as fast as they were printed. The City of New York
began already to feel itself the London of the New World, and
to calculate how many years must elapse before it would be
the London of the World.

"The South, meanwhile, was depressed and anxious. Cotton
was down; tobacco was down; corn, wheat, and pork were
down. For several years the chief products of the South had
either been inclining downward, or else had risen in price too
slowly to make up for the (alleged) increased price of the commodities which the South was compelled to buy. Few new
towns changed the Southern map. Charleston languished, or
seemed to languish—certainly did not keep pace with New

York, Boston, and Philadelphia. No Cincinnati of the South became the world's talk by the startling rapidity of its growth. No Southern river exhibited at every bend and coyne of vantage a rising village. No Southern mind, distracted with the impossibility of devising suitable names for a thousand new places per annum, fell back in despair upon the map of the Old World, and selected at random any convenient name that presented itself, bestowing upon clusters of log huts such titles as Utica, Rome, Palermo, Naples, Russia, Egypt, Madrid, Paris, Elba, and Berlin. No Southern commissioner, compelled to find names for a hundred streets at once, had seized upon the letters of the alphabet and the figures of arithmetic, and called the avenues A, B, C, and D, and instead of naming his cross streets, numbered them."

The Yankee writer attributes this inequality of conditions to the influence of negro slavery in the South. But it has another interpretation. The tariff measures, which were closely associated with the slavery question—being the *commercial* application of that doctrine of the power of numerical majorities, taught in the consolidation schools, which had attained its *moral and sentimental* development in the war upon slavery— had been used by the North as the stepping-stones to prosperity, and the most profitable expedients of sectional aggrandizement. In 1831 the public debt of the United States was near extinction; and it was calculated that, with the tariff then in force, there would be, in three years thereafter, a surplus in the treasury. The South demanded the repeal of a measure which was no longer necessary for the purposes of public revenue; which had been used to promote the manufacturing and commercial interests of the North; and which, taxing her for the benefit of the Yankees, had restricted and embarrassed her resources, and put upon her the badge of inferiority.

The tariff controversy of 1831–2 introduced on the political stage two of the most remarkable men in America, who more than any others. are to be regarded as the representative men of the North and the South, and the clear-cut anti-types of consolidation and State-rights. They were John C. Calhoun, of South Carolina, and Daniel Webster, of Massachusetts. The issue between these men was the broadest and most compre-

hensive ever made in the political history of the country, involving not only the slavery and tariff questions, but going to
the very roots of the constitution, and embracing the whole
American system of politics.

Mr. Calhoun was a splendid type of the accomplished scholar
of the South, and a consummate champion of State-rights.
He was the opposite of the shallow and rhetorical Massachusetts man in every respect.   He was an ascetic in his private habits and tastes ; he was a devotee of " the midnight
lamp ;" he was the most exact logician that ever figured in
political life ; he had no *ad captandum* arguments for the
vulgar ; his phrases were almost syllogisms, and his language
as clear-cut as the diamond.

If Daniel Webster, of Massachusetts, can be described by a
phrase, he may be briefly designated as a representative of the
smattering of New England education and the rhapsody of
" spread-eagleism." This may offend the taste of his worshippers ; but of that we are careless, as long as we do not
offend the truth of history.   To the end of his days, Mr. Webster was nothing more than a ready-spoken sophomore in
politics—a man who adorned common-places with silken ora-
tions—who had an unrivalled " Fourth-of-July" style of public
speaking—but who never invented or discovered any thing in
politics, and who defended his doctrines much more with frothy
sentiments than with sound arguments.   There is nothing so
injurious to posthumous reputation as the publication of " private correspondence," where the great man is discovered in
undress ; and the officious friends of Mr. Webster, who published two octavo volumes of his letters, after his death, have
exhibited the intellectual hero of Massachusetts as a vapid,
sophomorical, shallow statesman, who could not afford to wear
his literary court-dress—a tinsel one at that—but on state
occasions.   Mr. Webster had the weakness of putting scraps of
law Latin in his correspondence; and it is doubtful whether his
attainments in the dead languages extended beyond this cheap
collection from his professional glossary.   In his early days he
affected a taste for poetry, and wrote tawdry and conceited
verses to his friends.   In one instance—as a specimen of his
muse, some years after his admission to the bar—we are given
this bit of the Yankee pastoral ·

"Nor health alone—be four more blessings thine !—
CASH, and the Fair One, Friendship, and the Nine."

But it is scarcely just to estimate Mr. Webster's mind from his experiments in Latin or in verse, or from any other of hi notoriously weak efforts at scholarship. In his political life— his so-called " statesmanship"—he was an excellent represent- ative of the shallowness and fluency of the New England mind. He had the Yankee tact of showing his little learning to the greatest advantage. In vulgar estimation, he could overwhelm the most logical opponent by the beauty of a peroration. He had an abundance of catch-phrases and bril- liant illustrations; his manner was pompous, slow, and sage; his figure, in social life, was that of a good liver—a well-fed and well-drunken Sir Oracle. In short, he was a man who might easily be imposed upon the vulgar as a proficient in eloquence and a pundit in politics. A mind like Mr. Web- ster's readily seized upon the crude plausibilities of the con- solidation school of politics, and was admirably suited to employ, to the best advantage, its superficial though captious arguments.

In connection with the tariff dispute, Mr. Calhoun devel- oped his so-called scheme of "Nullification." This masterly scheme of politics was misrepresented by a Yankee word, so adept were the Northern people in conveying libels in the party nomenclature they imposed upon the world. Mr. Cal- houn's proposition was in no sense *nullification*. Strange as it may sound to those who have got American history from the narrow and sophistical pages of Yankee books, it was emphati- cally a *Union-saving measure*; devised in deference to the Union sentiment of the country; and better calculated, in reality, to maintain the bonds of confederation between the States than any thing ever planned or suggested by the American mind.

A loose impression has gained in the world, that our State institutions were schools of provincialism; that they were a partial and incomplete expression of the nationality of America; and that their logical tendency was to the disrup- tion of the confederate bond. Mr. Calhoun was not the first to conceive, although more than any other he expressed logi- cally and clearly, that the rights of the States were the only solid foundation of the Union; and that, so far from being an tagonistic to it, they constituted its security, realized its perfection, and gave to it all the moral beauty with which : appealed to the affections of the people. It was in this sense that the great South Carolina statesman, so frequently calumniated as "nullifier," agitator, etc., was indeed the real and devoted friend of the American Union. He maintained the rights of the States—the sacred distribution of powers between them and the General Government—as the life of the Union, and its bond of attachment in the hearts of the people. And in this he was right. The State institutions of America, properly regarded, were not discordant; nor were they unfortunate elements in our political life. They gave certain occasions to the divisions of industry; they were instruments of material prosperity; they were schools of pride and emulation; above all, they were the true guardians of the Union, keeping it from degenerating into that vile and short-lived government in which power is consolidated in a mere numerical majority.

Mr. Calhoun's so-called doctrine of Nullification is one of the highest proofs ever given by any American statesman of attachment to the Union. The assertion is not made for paradoxical effect. It is clear enough in history, read in the severe type of facts, without the falsehoods and epithets of that Yankee literature which has so long defamed us, distorted our public men, and misrepresented us, even to ourselves.

The so-called and miscalled doctrine of Nullification marked one of the most critical periods in the controversies of America, and constitutes one of the most curious studies for its philosophic historian. Mr. Calhoun was unwilling to offend the popular idolatry of the Union; he sought a remedy for existing evils short of disunion, and the consequence was what was called, by an ingenious slander, or a contemptible stupidity, Nullification. His doctrine was, in fact, an accommodation of two sentiments: that of Yankee injustice, and that of reverence of the Union. He proposed to save the Union by the simple and august means of an appeal to the sovereign States that composed it. He proposed that should the General Government and a State come into conflict, the power should be invoked that called the General Government into existence and gave it all of its authority. "In such a case," said Mr. Calhoun, "the States themselves may be appealed to, three-fourths of which, in fact, form a power whose decrees are the constitution itself, and whose voice can silence all discontent. The utmost extent, then, of the power is, that a State acting in its sovereign capacity, as one of the parties to the constitutional compact, may compel the Government created by that compact to submit a question touching its infraction to the parties who created it." He proposed a peculiar, conservative, and noble tribunal for the controversies that agitated the country and threatened the Union. He was not willing that vital controversies between the sovereign States and the General Government should be submitted to the Supreme Court, which properly excluded political questions, and comprehended those only where there were parties amenable to the process of the court. This was the length and breadth of Nullification. It was intended to reconcile impatience of Yankee injustice, and that sentimental attachment to the Union which colors so much of American politics; it resisted the suggestion of revolution; it clung to the idolatry of the Union, and marked that passage in American history in which there was a combat between reason and that idolatry, and in which that idolatry made a marked conquest.

The doctrine, then, of Mr. Calhoun was this: he proposed only to constitute a conservative and constitutional barrier to Yankee aggression; and, so far from destroying the Union, proposed to erect over it the permanent and august guard or a tribunal of those sovereign powers which had created it. It was this splendid, but hopeless vision of the South Carolina statesmen, which the North slandered with the catch-word of Nullification; which Northern orators made the text of indignation; on which Mr. Webster piped his schoolboy rhetoric; and on which the more modern schools of New England have exhausted the lettered resources of their learned blacksmiths and senatorial shoemakers.

The suggestion of the real safety of the Union, first made by Jefferson,* and reproduced by Calhoun, the North slandered

---

* At a late period of his life Mr. Jefferson wrote: "With respect to our State and Federal governments, I do not think their relations are correctly

as nullification, insulted as heresy, and branded as treason. "It was," said Jefferson Davis, on occasion of his taking leave of the United States Senate in 1861, "because of his deep-seated attachment to the Union, his determination to find some remedy for existing ills, short of a severance of the ties which bound South Carolina to the other States, that Mr. Calhoun advocated the doctrine of Nullification, which he proclaimed to be peaceful, to be within the limits of State power; not to disturb the Union, but only to be the means of bringing the agent before the tribunal of the States for their judgment." Mr. Davis, on that occasion, publicly confessed that the South was about to resort to another class of remedies than that proposed by the great South Carolinian—Secession—and, vindicating the name of Calhoun, suggested that, as the door had been closed to his great and efficient proposition to save the Union, there was no longer any hope for the South but in violent measures.

Daniel Webster had no complicated or nice theory about the American Union. In his eyes, the Government at Washington was nothing more than a central organization of numbers, with scarcely any feature of originality to distinguish it from other rude democracies of the world. "It had," he said, "created direct relations between itself and individuals;" and "no State authority had power to dissolve these relations." He scouted the whole doctrine of State-rights. He spoke as the mouth-piece of manufacturing interests in the North; apostrophized "the glorious Union;" declared its benefits and gains, and easily led the whole North to worship the Union, in the base spirit of commercial idolatry, as a pretty machinery to secure tariffs nd bounties, and to aggrandize a section.

Mr. Calhoun and his school worshipped the American Union in a very different sense from the Yankee material-

---

understood by foreigners. They suppose the former subordinate to the latter. This is not the case. They are co-ordinate departments of one simple and integral whole. But, you may ask, if the two departments should claim each the same subject of power, where is the umpire to decide between them? In cases of little urgency or importance, the prudence of both parties will keep them aloof from the questionable ground; but, if it can neither be avoided nor compromised, a convention of the States must be called to ascribe the doubtful power to that department which they may think best."

ists. The *moral veneration* of the Union was peculiarly a sentiment of the South. The political ideas of the North, as represented by Mr. Webster and his school, excluded that of any peculiar moral character about the Union; the doctrine of State-rights was rejected by them for the prevalent notion that America was a single democracy; thus, the Union to them was nothing more than a geographical name, entitled to no peculiar claims upon the affections of the people. It was different with the South. The doctrine of State-rights gave to the Union its moral dignity; this doctrine was the only really possible source of sentimental attachment to the Union; and this doctrine was the received opinion of the Southern people, and the most marked peculiarity of their politics. The South venerated the Union, because she discovered in it a sublime moral principle; because she regarded it as a peculiar association, in which sovereign States were held by high considerations of good faith; by the exchanges of equity and comity; by the noble attractions of social order; by the enthused sympathies of a common destiny of power, honor, and renown.

In his famous Fort Hill speech, delivered in 1831, Mr. Calhoun said:

"I yield to none, I trust, in a deep and sincere attachment to our political institutions and the Union of these States. I never breathed an opposite sentiment; but, on the contrary, I have ever considered them the great instruments of preserving our liberty, and promoting the happiness of ourselves and of our posterity; and next to these I have ever held them most dear. Nearly half of my life has passed in the service of the Union, and whatever public reputation I have acquired is indissolubly identified with it. With these strong feelings of attachment, I have examined with the utmost care the bearing of the doctrine in question; and so far from anarchical or revolutionary, I solemnly believe it to be the only solid foundation of our system, and of the Union itself; and that the opposite doctrine, which denies to the States the right of protecting their reserved powers, and which would vest in the General Government (it matters not through what department) the right of determining exclusively and finally the powers delegated to it, is incompatible with the sovereignty of the

States and of the Constitution itself, considered as the basis
of a Federal Union. * * * To realize the perfection of
this Union, we must view the General Government and the
States as a whole, each in its proper sphere sovereign and
independent; each perfectly adapted to their respective
objects; the States acting separately, representing and protecting the local and peculiar interests; acting jointly, through
the General Government, with the weight respectively assigned
to each by the constitution, representing and protecting the
interests of the whole, and thus perfecting, by an admirable
but simple arrangement, the great principle of representation
and responsibility, without which no government can be free
or just.   To preserve this sacred distribution as originally
settled, by coercing each to move in its prescribed orb, is the
great and difficult problem, on the solution of which the duration of our constitution, of our Union, and in all probability,
our liberty depends. * * * I must think the fear of weakening the Government too much in this case to be in a great
measure unfounded, or at least, that the danger is much less
from that than the opposite side.   I do not deny that a power
of so high a nature," [that of demanding the judgment of a
convention of States on questions disputed with the General
Government,] "may be abused by a State; but when I reflect
that the States unanimously called the General Government
into existence, with all of its powers, which they freely surrendered on their part, under the conviction that their common
peace, safety, and prosperity required it; that they are bound
together by a common origin, and the recollection of common
suffering and common triumph in the great and splendid
achievement of their independence; and the strongest feelings of our nature, and among the love of national power and
distinction, are on the side of the Union; it does seem to me
that the fear which would strip the States of their sovereignty,
and degrade them, in fact, to mere dependent corporations,
lest they should abuse a right indispensable to the peaceable
protection of those interests, which they reserved under their
own peculiar guardianship, when they created the General
Government, is unnatural and unreasonable."

Such were the just views and noble sentiments of the man
whom Webster and his party hounded as a traitor, and who

has gone down to history in Yankee books in the utterly false character of a Disunionist.

The failure of Mr. Calhoun's scheme to bind up the right of the States with the interests and glory of the Union, was to the consolidation school a new and decisive era of power State-rights fell into a loose disrepute from which they never recovered; the sectional controversy between North and South went on with increased force; and influences were combining to force the South at last to abandon all conservative expedients and to accept the conclusion of Disunion. That conclusion remained as the only possible protection against that Northern party which founded the school of consolidation only to use the Government at Washington as the organ of numerical majorities and the engine of sectional oppression.

* * * * * * * *

VI.

A Fourth of July sentiment in 1851.—Slavery not the Cause of Disunion.—The war of 1861.—What it has decided.—The incense of weak minds to the Yankee.—Last sentiment of President Davis.

On the Fourth of July, 1851, the foundation was laid for an addition to the Capitol at Washington. Under the corner-stone of the addition, Daniel Webster deposited a paper, in his own handwriting, containing the following sentence: "If therefore, it shall be hereafter the will of God that this structure shall fall from its base, that its foundations be upturned, and the deposit beneath this stone brought to the eyes of men, be it then known that on this day the Union of the United States of America stands firm—that their constitution still exists unimpaired, and with all its original usefulness and glory, growing every day stronger and stronger in the affections of the great body of the American people, and attracting more and more the admiration of the world."

But ten years after this glowing tribute to the permanency of American institutions, the Union was rent in twain, and the States which composed it were ranged in one of the most immense and violent wars of modern times. On the Fourth of July, 1861, a remnant of Congress met at Washington, to raise armies and means for a war upon the Southern States, which having realized the constitution as a farce, and the Union as the penalty of association of the oppressed with the oppressors, were prepared to take their political destinies in their own hands.

The disruption of the Union, in 1861, was by no means the direct or the logical consequence of the slavery discussion. The dispute on that subject had at last narrowed down to a solitary point—whether it was competent for the Congress of the United States, directly or indirectly, to exclude slavery from the territories of the Union; and to this proposition the Supreme Court of the United States had given a negative answer.

The terrible war which ensued on Disunion must be taken as the result of a profound and long-continued conflict between the political and social systems of North and South, with which slavery had a conspicuous connection, but was not indeed an independent controversy; a conflict on which was ranged on one side the party that professed the doctrines or consolidation and numerical majorities; that represented the material civilization of America; that had the commerce and the manufactures, the ships, the workshops, the war-material of the country—on the other side, the party that maintained the doctrinés of State-rights, studied government as a system of checks and balances, and cultivated the highest schools of statesmanship in America; that represented a civilization scanty in shows and luxuries, but infinitely superior in the moral and sentimental elements; that devoted itself to agriculture, and had nothing but its fields and brave men to oppose to a people that whitened every sea with their commerce, and by the power of their wealth and under the license of "legitimacy," put the whole world under tribute for troops and munitions.

It is said that in this war the material civilization of the North has conquered; that the principle of consolidation is supremely triumphant, and that hereafter, under the captivating title of an Imperial Republic, it is to found, without dispute, a new and permanent order of things in America.

The latter part of the proposition we dispute. The principle of State-rights, which for three generations has been harbored in the American mind, cannot be destroyed by an act of war. The just opinions of men are immortal; suppressed or terrified at times, they reassert themselves on opportunity; punished in one instance, although they may never resort again to the fatal experiment, they discover new resources of contest, and find new modes of expression and activity.

Since the close of the war, a newspaper published by Virginians in Virginia has thus attempted to state the issues it decided:

"We accept the verdict; we renounce our theory of the Federal compact; we abandon our ideas of State sovereignty; we abjure our faith in the right of secession. Henceforth, in our conception, the Federal Government is supreme."

The declaration is gratuitous; it is not even demanded by the enemy; it is the passing and ephemeral incense of weak minds to the Yankee. We shall find in another instance a truer indication of the future of the South, and a better expression of what remains of its spirit. When Jefferson Davis, the President of the Confederate States, was seeking safety in flight, a fellow traveller remarked to him that the cause of the Confederates was lost. He replied:

"*It appears so. But the principle for which we contended is bound to reassert itself, though it may be at another time and in another form.*"

*   *   *   *   *   *   *   *

CONSTITUTION

OF THE

CONFEDERATE STATES OF AMERICA.

WE, the people of the Confederate States, each State acting in its sovereign and independent character, in order to form a permanent federal government, establish justice, insure domestic tranquillity, and secure the blessings of liberty to ourselves and our posterity—invoking the favor and guidance of Almighty God—do ordain and establish this Constitution for the Confederate States of America.

ARTICLE I.

SECTION 1.

All legislative powers herein delegated shall be vested in a Congress of the Confederate States, which shall consist of a Senate and House of Representatives.

SECTION 2.

1. The House of Representatives shall be composed of members chosen every second year by the people of the several States; and the electors in each State shall be citizens of the Confederate States, and have the qualifications requisite for electors of the most numerous branch of the State Legislature; but no person of foreign birth, not a citizen of the Confederate States, shall be allowed to vote for any officer, civil or political, State or Federal.

2. No person shall be a Representative who shall not have attained the age of twenty-five years, and be a citizen of the Confederate States, and who shall not, when elected, be an inhabitant of that State in which he shall be chosen.

3. Representatives and direct taxes shall be apportioned among the several States which may be included within this Confederacy, according to their respective numbers, which shall be determined by adding to the whole number of free persons, including those bound to service for a term of years, and excluding Indians not taxed, three-fifths of all slaves. The actual enumeration shall be made within three years after the first meeting of the Congress of the Confederate States, and within every subsequent term of ten years, in such manner as they shall by law direct. · The number of Representatives shall not exceed one for every fifty thousand; but each State shall have at least one Representative; and until such enumeration shall be made, the State of South Carolina shall be entitled to choose six; the State of Georgia ten; the State of Alabama nine; the State of Florida two; the State of Mississippi seven; the State of Louisiana six; and the State of Texas six.

4. When vacancies happen in the representation from any State, the Executive authority thereof shall issue writs of election to fill such vacancies.

5. The House of Representatives shall choose their Speaker and other officers; and shall have the sole power of impeachment; except that any judicial or other federal officer resident and acting solely within the limits of any State, may be impeached by a vote of two-thirds of both branches of the Legislature thereof.

SECTION 3.

1. The Senate of the Confederate States shall be composed of two Senators from each State, chosen for six years by the Legislature thereof, at the regular session next immediately preceding the commencement of the term of service; and each Senator shall have one vote.

2. Immediately after they shall be assembled, in consequence of the first election, they shall be divided as equally as may be into three classes. The seats of the Senators of the first class shall be vacated at the expiration of the second year; of the second class, at the expiration of the fourth year; and of the third class, at the expiration of the sixth year; so that one-third may be chosen every second year; and if vacancies happen, by resignation or otherwise, during the recess of the Legislature of any State, the Executive thereof may make temporary appointments until the next meeting of the Legislature, which shall then fill such vacancies.

3. No person shall be a Senator who shall not have attained the age of thirty years, and be a citizen of the Confederate States; and

who shall not, when elected, be an inhabitant of the State for which he shall be chosen.

4. The Vice-president of the Confederate States shall be President of the Senate, but shall have no vote unless they be equally divided.

5. The Senate shall choose their other officers, and also a President pro tempore, in the absence of the Vice-president, or when he shall exercise the office of President of the Confederate States.

6. The Senate shall have the sole power to try all impeachments. When sitting for that purpose they shall be on oath or affirmation. When the President of the Confederate States is tried, the Chief-justice shall preside; and no person shall be convicted without the concurrence of two-thirds of the members present.

7. Judgment in cases of impeachment shall not extend further than removal from office, and disqualification to hold and enjoy any office of honor, trust, or profit under the Confederate States; but the party convicted shall, nevertheless, be liable and subject to indictment, trial, judgment, and punishment, according to law.

Section 4.

1. The times, places, and manner of holding elections for Senators and Representatives, shall be prescribed in each State by the Legislature thereof, subject to the provisions of this Constitution; but the Congress may, at any time, by law, make or alter such regulations, except as to the times and places of choosing Senators.

2. The Congress shall assemble at least once in every year; and such meeting shall be on the first Monday in December, unless they shall, by law, appoint a different day.

Section 5.

1. Each House shall be the judge of the elections, returns, and qualifications of its own members, and a majority of each shall constitute a quorum to do business; but a smaller number may adjourn from day to day, and may be authorized to compel the attendance of absent members, in such manner and under such penalties as each House may provide.

2. Each House may determine the rules of its proceedings, punish its members for disorderly behavior, and, with the concurrence of two-thirds of the whole number, expel a member.

3. Each House shall keep a journal of its proceedings, and, from time to time, publish the same, excepting such parts as may in its judgment require secrecy, and the ayes and nays of the members of

either House, on any question, shall, at the desire of one-fifth of those present, be entered on the journal.

4. Neither House, during the session of Congress, shall, without the consent of the other, adjourn for more than three days, nor to any other place than that in which the two Houses shall be sitting.

Section 6.

1. The Senators and Representatives shall receive a compensation for their services, to be ascertained by law, and paid out of the Treasury of the Confederate States. They shall, in all cases except treason and breach of the peace, be privileged from arrest during their attendance at the session of their respective Houses, and in going to and returning from the same; and for any speech or debate in either House, they shall not be questioned in any other place.

2. No Senator or Representative shall, during the time for which he was elected, be appointed to any civil office under the authority of the Confederate States, which shall have been created, or the emoluments whereof shall have been increased during such time; and no person holding any office under the Confederate States shall be a member of either House during his continuance in office. But Congress may, by law, grant to the principal officer in each of the Executive Departments a seat upon the floor of either House, with the privilege of discussing any measure appertaining to his department.

Section 7.

1. All bills for raising revenue shall originate in the House of Representatives; but the Senate may propose or concur with amendments as on other bills.

2. Every bill which shall have passed both Houses, shall, before it becomes a law, be presented to the President of the Confederate States; if he approve, he shall sign it; but if not, he shall return it with his objections to that House in which it shall have originated, who shall enter the objections at large on their journal, and proceed to reconsider it. If, after such reconsideration, two-thirds of that House shall agree to pass the bill, it shall be sent, together with the objections, to the other House, by which it shall likewise be reconsidered, and if approved by two-thirds of that House, it shall become a law. But in all such cases, the votes of both Houses shall be determined by yeas and nays, and the names of the persons voting for and against the bill shall be entered on the journal of each House respectively. If any bill shall not be returned by the President within ten days (Sundays excepted) after it shall have been pre

sented to him, the same shall be a law in like manner as if he had signed it, unless the Congress, by their adjournment, prevent its return; in which case it shall not be a law. The President may approve any appropriation and disapprove any other appropriation in the same bill. In such case he shall, in signing the bill, designate the appropriations disapproved; and shall return a copy of such appropriations, with his objections, to the House in which the bill shall have originated; and the same proceedings shall then be had as in case of other bills disapproved by the President.

3. Every order, resolution, or vote, to which the concurrence of both Houses may be necessary (except on questions of adjournment) shall be presented to the President of the Confederate States; and before the same shall take effect shall be approved by him; or being disapproved by him, may be repassed by two-thirds of both Houses, according to the rules and limitations prescribed in case of a bill.

SECTION 8.

The Congress shall have power—

1. To lay and collect taxes, duties, imposts, and excises, for revenue necessary to pay the debts, provide for the common defence, and carry on the Government of the Confederate States; but no bounties shall be granted from the Treasury; nor shall any duties or taxes on importations from foreign nations be laid to promote or foster any branch of industry; and all duties, imposts, and excises shall be uniform throughout the Confederate States.

2. To borrow money on the credit of the Confederate States.

3. To regulate commerce with foreign nations, and among the several States, and with the Indian tribes; but neither this, nor any other clause contained in the Constitution, shall be construed to delegate the power to Congress to appropriate money for any internal improvement intended to facilitate commerce; except for the purpose of furnishing lights, beacons, and buoys, and other aids to navigation upon the coasts, and the improvement of harbors, and the removing of obstructions in river navigation, in all which cases such duties shall be laid on the navigation facilitated thereby as may be necessary to pay the costs and expenses thereof.

4. To establish uniform laws of naturalization, and uniform laws on the subject of bankruptcies throughout the Confederate States, but no law of Congress shall discharge any debt contracted before the passage of the same.

5. To coin money, regulate the value thereof, and of foreign coin, and fix the standard of weights and measures.

6. To provide for the punishment of counterfeiting the securities and current coin of the Confederate States.

7. To establish post-offices and post-routes; but the expenses of the Post-office Department, after the first day of March, in the year of our Lord eighteen hundred and sixty-three, shall be paid out of its own revenues.

8. To promote the progress of science and useful arts, by securing, for limited times, to authors and inventors, the exclusive right to their respective writings and discoveries.

9. To constitute tribunals inferior to the Supreme Court.

10. To define and punish piracies and felonies committed on the high seas, and offences against the law of nations.

11. To declare war, grant letters of marque and reprisal, and make rules concerning captures on land and water.

12. To raise and support armies; but no appropriation of money to that use shall be for a longer term than two years.

13. To provide and maintain a navy.

14. To make rules for the government and regulation of the land and naval forces.

15. To provide for calling forth the militia to execute the laws of the Confederate States, suppress insurrections, and repel invasions.

16. To provide for organizing, arming, and disciplining the militia, and for governing such part of them as may be employed in the service of the Confederate States, reserving to the States respectively the appointment of the officers, and the authority of training the militia according to the discipline prescribed by Congress.

17. To exercise exclusive legislation, in all cases whatsoever, over such district (not exceeding ten miles square) as may, by cession of one or more States, and the acceptance of Congress, become the seat of the Government of the Confederate States; and to exercise like authority over all places purchased by the consent of the legislature of the State in which the same shall be, for the erection of forts, magazines, arsenals, dock-yards, and other needful buildings, and

18. To make all laws which shall be necessary and proper for carrying into execution the foregoing powers, and all other powers vested, by this Constitution, in the Government of the Confederate States, or in any department or officer thereof.

Section. 9

1. The importation of negroes of the African race, from any foreign country, other than the slaveholding States or Territories of

tne United States of America, is hereby forbidden, and Congress is required to pass such laws as shall effectually prevent the same.

2. Congress shall also have power to prohibit the introduction oi slaves from any State not a member of, or Territory not belonging to, this Confederacy.

3. The privilege of the writ of habeas corpus shall not be suspended, unless when, in cases of rebellion or invasion, the public safety may require it.

4. No bill of attainder, or ex post facto law, or law denying or impairing the right of property in negro slaves, shall be passed.

5. No capitation or other direct tax shall be laid, unless in proportion to the census or enumeration hereinbefore directed to be ⅃ken.

6. No tax or duty shall be laid on articles exported from any State, except by a vote of two-thirds of both Houses.

7. No preference shall be given, by any regulation of commerce or revenue, to the ports of one State over those of another.

8. No money shall be drawn from the Treasury but in consequence of appropriations made by law ; and a regular statement and account of the receipts and expenditures of all public money shall be published from time to time.

9. Congress shall appropriate no money from the treasury except by a vote of two-thirds of both Houses, taken by yeas and nays, unless it be asked and estimated for by some one of the heads of departments, and submitted to Congress by the President ; or for the purpose of paying its own expenses and contingencies ; or for the payment of claims against the Confederate States, the justice of which shall have been judicially declared by a tribunal for the investigation of claims against the government, which it is hereby made the duty of Congress to establish.

10. All bills appropriating money shall specify in federal currency the exact amount of each appropriation, and the purposes for which it is made ; and Congress shall grant no extra compensation to any public contractor, officer, agent, or servant, after such contract shall have been made or such service rendered.

11. No title of nobility shall be granted by the Confederate States; and no person holding any office of profit or trust under them shall, without the consent of the Congress, accept of any present, emolument, office, or title of any kind whatever, from any king, prince, or foreign state.

12. Congress shall make no law respecting an establishment oi ɪeligion, or prohibiting the free exercise thereof; or abridging the

freedom of speech or of the press; or the right of the people peaceably to assemble and petition the Government for a redress of grievances.

13. A well-regulated militia being necessary to the security of a free State, the right of the people to keep and bear arms shall not be infringed.

14. No soldier shall, in time of peace, be quartered in any house without the consent of the owner; nor in time of war, but in a manner prescribed by law.

15. The right of the people to be secure in their persons, houses, papers, and effects against unreasonable searches and seizures, shall not be violated; and no warrant shall issue but upon probable cause, supported by oath or affirmation, and particularly describing the place to be searched, and the person or things to be seized.

16. No person shall be held to answer for a capital or otherwise infamous crime, unless on a presentment or indictment of a grand jury, except in cases arising in the land or naval forces, or in the militia, when in actual service, in time of war, or public danger; nor shall any person be subject for the same offence to be twice put in jeopardy of life or limb; nor be compelled in any criminal case to be a witness against himself; nor be deprived of life, liberty, or property, without due process of law; nor shall private property be taken for public use without just compensation.

17. In all criminal prosecutions the accused shall enjoy the right to a speedy and public trial, by an impartial jury of the State and district wherein the crime shall have been committed, which district shall have been previously ascertained by law, and to be informed of the nature and cause of the accusation; to be confronted with the witnesses against him; to have compulsory process for obtaining witnesses in his favor; and to have the assistance of counsel for his defence.

18. In suits at common law, where the value in controversy shall exceed twenty dollars, the right of trial by jury shall be preserved; and no fact so tried by a jury shall be otherwise re-examined in any court of the Confederacy than according to the rules of the common law.

19. Excessive bail shall not be required, nor excessive fines imposed, nor cruel or unusual punishments inflicted.

20. Every law, or resolution having the force of law, shall relate to but one subject, and that shall be expressed in the title.

SECTION 10.

1 No State shall enter into any treaty, alliance, or confederation grant letters of marque and reprisal; coin money; make any thing but gold and silver coin a tender in payment of debts; pass any bill of attainder, or ex post facto law, or law impairing the obligation of contracts; or grant any title of nobility.

2. No State shall, without the consent of Congress, lay any imposts or duties on imports or exports, except what may be absolutely necessary for executing its inspection laws; and the net produce of all duties and imposts laid by any State on imports or exports, shall be for the use of the Treasury of the Confederate States; and all such laws shall be subject to the revision and control of Congress.

3. No State shall, without the consent of Congress, lay any duty of tonnage, except on sea-going vessels, for the improvement of its rivers and harbors navigated by the said vessels; but such duties shall not conflict with any treaties of the Confederate States with foreign nations; and any surplus of revenue thus derived, shall, after making such improvement, be paid into the common treasury; nor shall any State keep troops or ships of war in time of peace, enter into any agreement or compact with another State, or with a foreign power, or engage in war, unless actually invaded, or in such imminent danger as will not admit of delay. But when any river divides or flows through two or more States, they may enter into compacts with each other to improve the navigation thereof.

ARTICLE II.

SECTION 1.

1. The Executive power shall be vested in a President of the Confederate States of America. He and the Vice-president shall hold their offices for the term of six years; but the President shall not be re-eligible. The President and Vice-president shall be elected as follows:

2. Each State shall appoint, in such manner as the Legislature thereof may direct, a number of electors equal to the whole number of Senators and Representatives to which the State may be entitled in Congress; but no Senator or Representative, or person holding an office of trust or profit under the Confederate States, shall be appointed an elector.

3. The electors shall meet in their respective States and vote by ballot for President and Vice-president, one of whom, at least, shall

not be an inhabitant of the same State with themselves; they shall name in their ballots the person voted for as President, and in distinct ballots the person voted for as Vice-president, and they shall make distinct lists of all persons voted for as President, and of all persons voted for as Vice-president, and of the number of votes for each; which list they shall sign, and certify, and transmit, sealed, to the Government of the Confederate States, directed to the President of the Senate. The President of the Senate shall, in the presence of the Senate and House of Representatives, open all the certificates, and the votes shall then be counted; the person having the greatest number of votes for President shall be the President, if such number be a majority of the whole number of electors appointed; and if no person have such majority, then, from the persons having the highest numbers, not exceeding three, on the list of those voted for as President, the House of Representatives shall choose immediately, by ballot, the President. But, in choosing the President, the votes shall be taken by States, the representation from each State having one vote; a quorum for this purpose shall consist of a member or members from two-thirds of the States, and a majority of all the States shall be necessary to a choice. And if the House of Representatives shall not choose a President, whenever the right of choice shall devolve upon them, before the fourth day of March next following, then the Vice-president shall act as President, as in case of the death or other constitutional disability of the President.

4. The person having the greatest number of votes as Vice-president shall be the Vice-president, if such number be a majority of the whole number of electors appointed; and if no person have a majority, then, from the two highest numbers on the list, the Senate shall choose the Vice-president; a quorum for the purpose shall consist of two-thirds of the whole number of Senators, and a majority of the whole number shall be necessary for a choice.

5. But no person constitutionally ineligible to the office of President shall be eligible to that of Vice-president of the Confederate States.

6. The Congress may determine the time of choosing the electors, and the day on which they shall give their votes; which day shall be the same throughout the Confederate States.

7. No person except a natural born citizen of the Confederate States, or a citizen thereof at the time of the adoption of this Constitution, or a citizen thereof born in the United States prior to the 20th December, 1860, shall be eligible to the office of President

neither shall any person be eligible to that office who shall not have attained the age of thirty-five years, and been fourteen years a resident within the limits of the Confederate States, as they may exist at the time of his election.

8. In case of the removal of the President from office, or of his death, resignation, or inability to discharge the powers and duties of the said office, the same shall devolve on the Vice-president; and the Congress may, by law, provide for the case of the removal, death, resignation, or inability, both of the President and Vice-president, declaring what officer shall then act as President, and such officer shall act accordingly until the disability be removed, or a President shall be elected.

9. The President shall, at stated times, receive for his services a compensation, which shall neither be increased nor diminished during the period for which he shall have been elected; and he shall not receive within that period any other emolument from the Confederate States, or any of them.

10. Before he enters on the execution of the duties of his office, he shall take the following oath or affirmation:

"I do solemnly swear (or affirm) that I will faithfully execute the office of President of the Confederate States, and will, to the best of my ability, preserve, protect, and defend the Constitution thereof."

SECTION 2.

1. The President shall be commander-in-chief of the army and navy of the Confederate States, and of the militia of the several States, when called into the actual service of the Confederate States; he may require the opinion, in writing, of the principal officer in each of the Executive Departments, upon any subject relating to the duties of their respecting offices; and he shall have power to grant reprieves and pardons for offences against the Confederate States, except in cases of impeachment.

2. He shall have power, by and with the advice and consent of the Senate, to make treaties, provided two-thirds of the Senators present concur; and he shall nominate, and, by and with the advice and consent of the Senate, shall appoint ambassadors, other public ministers, and consuls, judges of the Supreme Court, and all other officers of the Confederate States, whose appointments are not herein otherwise provided for, and which shall be established by law; but the Congress may by law vest the appointment of such inferior officers, as they think proper, in the President alone, in the courts of law, or in the heads of departments.

3. The principal officer in each of the Executive Departments, and all persons connected with the diplomatic service, may be removed from office at the pleasure of the President. All other civil officers of the Executive Department may be removed at any time by the President, or other appointing power, when their services are unnecessary, or for dishonesty, incapacity, inefficiency, misconduct, or neglect of duty; and when so removed, the removal shall be reported to the Senate, together with the reasons therefor.

4. The President shall have power to fill all vacancies that may happen during the recess of the Senate, by granting commissions which shall expire at the end of their next session; but no person rejected by the Senate shall be reappointed to the same office during their ensuing recess.

Section 3.

The President shall, from time to time, give to the Congress information of the state of the Confederacy, and recommend to their consideration such measures as he shall judge necessary and expedient; he may, on extraordinary occasions, convene both Houses, or either of them; and, in case of disagreement between them, with respect to the time of adjournment, he may adjourn them to such time as he shall think proper; he shall receive ambassadors and other public ministers; he shall take care that the laws be faithfully executed, and shall commission all the officers of the Confederate States.

Section 4.

The President, Vice-president, and all civil officers of the Confederate States, shall be removed from office on impeachment for, and conviction of, treason, bribery, or other high crimes and misdemeanors.

ARTICLE III.

Section 1.

The judicial power of the Confederate States shall be vested in one Superior Court, and in such inferior courts as the Congress may from time to time ordain and establish. The judges, both of the Supreme and inferior courts, shall hold their offices during good behavior, and shall, at stated times, receive for their services a compensation, which shall not be diminished during their continuance in office.

Section 2.

1. The judicial power shall extend to all cases arising under this Constitution, the laws of the Confederate States, and treaties made or which shall be made under their authority; to all cases affecting ambassadors, other public ministers, and consuls; to all cases of admirality and maritime jurisdiction; to controversies to which the Confederate States shall be a party; to controversies between two or more States; between a State and citizens of another State, where the State is plaintiff; between citizens claiming lands under grants of different States, and between a State or the citizens thereof, and foreign States, citizens, or subjects; but no State shall be sued by a citizen or subject of any foreign State.

2. In all cases affecting ambassadors, other public ministers, and consuls, and those in which a State shall be a party, the Supreme Court shall have original jurisdiction. In all the other cases before mentioned, the Supreme Court shall have appellate jurisdiction, both as to law and fact, with such exceptions and under such regulations as the Congress shall make.

3. The trial of all crimes, except in cases of impeachment, shall be by jury, and such trial shall be held in the State where the said crimes shall have been committed; but when not committed within any State, the trial shall be at such place or places as the Congress may by law have directed.

Section 3.

1. Treason against the Confederate States shall consist only in levying war against them, or in adhering to their enemies, giving them aid and comfort. No person shall be convicted of treason unless on the testimony of two witnesses to the same overt act, or on confession in open court.

2. The Congress shall have power to declare the punishment of treason, but no attainder of treason shall work corruption of blood, or forfeiture, except during the life of the person attainted.

ARTICLE IV.

Section 1.

Full faith and credit shall be given in each State to the public acts, records, and judicial proceedings of every other State. And the Congress may, by general laws, prescribe the manner in which such acts, records, and proceedings shall be proved, and the effect thereof

Section 2.

1. The citizens of each State shall be entitled to all the privileges and immunities of citizens of the several States, and shall have the right of transit and sojourn in any State of this confederacy, with their slaves and other property; and the right of property in said slaves shall not be thereby impaired.

2. A person charged in any State with treason, felony, or other crime against the laws of such State, who shall flee from justice, and be found in another State, shall, on demand of the Executive authority of the State from which he fled, be delivered up to be removed to the State having jurisdiction of the crime.

3. No slave or other person held to service or labor in any State or Territory of the Confederate States, under the laws thereof, escaping or unlawfully carried into another, shall, in consequence of any law or regulation therein, be discharged from such service or labor; but shall be delivered up on claim of the party to whom such slave belongs, or to whom such service or labor may be due.

Section 3.

1. Other States may be admitted into this Confederacy by a vote of two-thirds of the whole House of Representatives, and two-thirds of the Senate, the Senate voting by States; but no new State shall be formed or erected within the jurisdiction of any other State; nor any State be formed by the junction of two or more States, or parts of States, without the consent of the Legislatures of the States concerned as well as of the Congress.

2. The Congress shall have power to dispose of and make all needful rules and regulations concerning the property of the Confederate States, including the lands thereof.

3. The Confederate States may acquire new territory; and Congress shall have power to legislate and provide governments for the inhabitants of all territory belonging to the Confederate States, lying without the limits of the several States, and may permit them, at such times, and in such manner as it may by law provide, to form States to be admitted into the Confederacy. In all such territory, the institution of negro slavery, as it now exists in the Confederate States, shall be recognized and protected by Congress and by the territorial government; and the inhabitants of the several Confederate States and Territories shall have the right to take to such territory any slaves lawfully held by them in any of the States or Territories of the Confederate States.

4. The Confederate States shall guarantee to every State that now is or hereafter may become a member of this Confederacy, a republican form of government, and shall protect each of them against invasion; and on application of the Legislature (or of the Executive when the Legislature is not in session,) against domestic violence.

ARTICLE V

Section 1.

Upon the demand of any three States, legally assembled in their several Conventions, the Congress shall summon a Convention of all the States, to take into consideration such amendments to the Constitution as the said States shall concur in suggesting at the time when the said demand is made; and should any of the proposed amendments to the Constitution be agreed on by the said Convention—voting by States—and the same be ratified by the Legislatures of two-thirds of the several States, or by Conventions in two-thirds thereof—as the one or the other mode of ratification may be proposed by the general Convention—they shall thenceforward form a part of this Constitution. But no State shall, without its consent be deprived of its equal representation in the Senate.

ARTICLE VI.

Section 1.

1. The Government established by this Constitution is the successor of the Provisional Government of the Confederate States of America, and all the laws passed by the latter shall continue in force until the same shall be repealed or modified; and all the officers appointed by the same shall remain in office until their successors are appointed and qualified, or the offices abolished.

2. All debts contracted and engagements entered into before the adoption of this Constitution, shall be as valid against the Confederate States under this Constitution as under the Provisional Government.

3. This Constitution, and the laws of the Confederate States made in pursuance thereof, and all treaties made, or which shall be made under the authority of the Confederate States, shall be the supreme law of the land, and the judges in every State shall be bound thereby, any thing in the Constitution or laws of any State to the contrary notwithstanding.

4. The Senators and Representatives before mentioned, and the members of the several State Legislatures, and all executive and judicial officers, both of the Confederate States and of the several States, shall be bound, by oath or affirmation, to support this Constitution ; but no religious test shall ever be required as a qualification to any office of public trust under the Confederate States.

5. The enumeration, in the Constitution, of certain rights, shall not be construed to deny or disparage others retained by the people of the several States.

6. The powers not delegated to the Confederate States by the Constitution, nor prohibited by it to the States, are reserved to the States respectively, or to the people thereof.

ARTICLE VII.

SECTION 1.

1. The ratification of the Conventions of five States shall be sufficient for the establishment of this Constitution between the States so ratifying the same.

When five States shall have ratified this Constitution in the manner before specified, the Congress, under the provisional Constitution, shall prescribe the time for holding the election of President and Vice-president, and for the meeting of the electoral college, and for counting the votes and inaugurating the President. They shall also prescribe the time for holding the first election of members of Congress under this Constitution, and the time for assembling the same. Until the assembling of such Congress, the Congress under the provisional Constitution shall continue to exercise the legislative powers granted them; not extending beyond the time limited by the Constitution of the Provisional Government.

Adopted unanimously, March 11, 1861,

AT MONTGOMERY, ALABAMA.

ERRATA.

THE attention of the author was directed to some particulars of his work, which required some correction or explanation, at the time when it was passing through the press. It was then too late to modify the passages referred to, unless in the form of a postscript or appendix. The author congratulates himself that he has found *real* occasion for so few corrections or explanations.

Page 42.—The date of Anderson's evacuation of Fort Moultrie should be the 26th of December instead of the 20th; the error occurred through a mistake of the digit 6 for 0 in the rough notes of the author.

Page 183.—In noticing the expedition of our cavalry to Guyandotte, we should have associated with this bold enterprise the name of Col. Clarkson who originated it and was intrusted with its execution by Gen. Floyd. The services of Col. Clarkson on this and other enterprises, and his intrepidity on some of the most critical occasions in the western Virginia campaign, deserve mention, and we regret that we can give it no further within the limits of this postscript, than to supply the omission of credit justly due him in connection with the famous expedition of our cavalry to the Ohio.

Page 253.—The circumstances in which Governor Harris left Nashville were imperfectly known at the time; and there is no doubt but that some injustice was done to one of the most ardent and courageous patriots of the South, in attributing his conduct on this occasion to panic or embarrassment. The circumstances in which he acted have been ascertained from unquestionable sources of testimony, and may be briefly narrated here: On the morning of Sunday, the 16th of February, at ten minutes after 4 o'clock, a messenger arrived at Gen. Johnston's head-quarters at Edgefield, opposite Nashville, with a dispatch announcing the fall of Donelson. Orders were at once issued to push the army forward across the river as soon as possible. The city papers or extras of that morning published dispatches announcing a "glorious victory." The city was wild with joy. About the time the people were assembling at the churches, it was announced by later extras that "Donelson had fallen." The revulsion was great. Governor Harris, however, had been informed of the fact early in the morning, and had proceeded to Gen. Johnston's head-quarters to advise with him as to the best course to adopt under the altered circumstances. The action of the State authorities would, of course, be greatly influenced by the course Gen. Johnston intended to adopt with the army. The general told the governor that Nashville was utterly indefensible, that the army would pass right through the city; that any attempt to defend it with the means at his command would result in disaster to the army and the destruction of the city; that the first and highest duty of the governor was to the public trusts in his hands, and he thought, to discharge them properly, he should at once remove the archives and public records to some safer place, and call the Legislature together elsewhere than a Nashville. Governor Harris did all this quietly, energetically, and patriotically. Just as soon as he had deposited these papers, he returned to Nashville The confusion at Nashville did not reach its height until a humane attemp was made to distribute among the poor a portion of the public stores which could not be removed. The lowest passions seemed to have been aroused in a large mass of men and women, and the city appeared as if it was in the hands of a mob. The military authority, however (Gen. Floyd having been put in command by Gen. Johnston), asserted its supremacy, and comparative order was restored. During these excitements it became publicly known, for the first time, that Governor Harris was out of the city, but few really knowing that he had quietly gone away in the discharge of a public duty. His absence was wholly misunderstood, and, of course, misrepresented. There is no doubt but that, in the course of these misrepresentations in the newspapers, injustice was done to a man who illustrated his devotion to the South by distinguished courage on the battle-field, and who, from the moment that he first rebuffed the Washington government in his famous defiance to Lincoln's call for troops, down to recent periods in the history of the revolution, had given the most constant and honorable proofs of his attachment to the liberties and fortunes of the South.